# CODES &
## CHEATS

### VOL. 2 2012

**Prima Games**
An Imprint of Random House, Inc.
3000 Lava Ridge Court, Suite 100
Roseville, CA 95661
www.primagames.com

The Prima Games logo is a registered trademark of Random House, Inc., registered in the United States and other countries. Primagames.com is a registered trademark of Random House, Inc., registered in the United States.

**Code Compiler:** Michael Knight
**Product Manager:** JJ Zingale
**Layout:** David Sanborn, Melissa Jeneé Smith, Jamie Knight Bryson, Rick Wong

All products and characters mentioned in this book are trademarks of their respective companies.

Please be advised that the ESRB Ratings icons, "EC," "E," "E10+," "T," "M," "AO," and "RP" are trademarks owned by the Entertainment Software Association, and may only be used with their permission and authority. For information regarding whether a product has been rated by the ESRB, please visit www.esrb.org. For permission to use the Rating icons, please contact marketing at esrb.org.

**Important:**
Prima Games has made every effort to determine that the information contained in this book is accurate. However, the publisher makes no warranty, either expressed or implied, as to the accuracy, effectiveness, or completeness of the material in this book; nor does the publisher assume liability for damages, either incidental or consequential, that may result from using the information in this book. The publisher cannot provide any additional information or support regarding gameplay, hints and strategies, or problems with hardware or software. Such questions should be directed to the support numbers provided by the game and/or device manufacturers as set forth in their documentation. Some game tricks require precise timing and may require repeated attempts before the desired result is achieved.

Australian warranty statement:

This product comes with guarantees that cannot be excluded under the Australian Consumer Law. You are entitled to a replacement or refund for a major failure and for compensation for any other reasonably foreseeable loss or damage. You are also entitled to have the goods repaired or replaced if the goods fail to be of acceptable quality and the failure does not amount to a major failure.

This product comes with a 1 year warranty from date of purchase. Defects in the product must have appeared within 1-year, from date of purchase in order to claim the warranty.

All warranty claims must be facilitat[...] in accordance with the retailer's returns policies and pri[...] [...]uct to the retailer of purchase - are the [...]

AU wholesale distributor: Bluemou[...]
Victoria, 3141. (+613 9646 4011)

Email: support@bluemouth.com.a[...]

**ISBN: 978-0-307-89434-2**   **ISBN: 978-0-307-894[...]**

Printed in the United States of America

# NEW CODES!...

Akai Katana Shin (XBOX 360) ......................19

Armored Core V (PlayStation 3) ......................23

Armored Core V (XBOX 360) ......................24

Army Corps of Hell (PlayStation Vita) ......................26

Asphalt: Injection (PlayStation Vita) ......................27

Asura's Wrath (PlayStation 3) ......................28

Asura's Wrath (XBOX 360) ......................29

Atelier Meruru: The Apprentice
of Arland (PlayStation 3) ......................29

Battleship (PlayStation 3) ......................30

Battleship (XBOX 360) ......................31

Ben 10: Galactic Racing (PlayStation Vita) ......................32

Binary Domain (PlayStation 3) ......................36

Binary Domain (XBOX 360) ......................37

Birds of Steel (PlayStation 3) ......................34

Birds of Steel (XBOX 360) ......................37

Blades of Time (PlayStation 3) ......................39

Blades of Time (XBOX 360) ......................40

BlazBlue: Continuum Shift
Extend (PlayStation Vita) ......................40

Brave: The Video Game (PlayStation 3) ......................42

Brave: The Video Game (XBOX 360) ......................43

Disgaea 3: Absence of
Detention (PlayStation Vita) ......................47

Dragon's Dogma (PlayStation 3) ......................49

Dragon's Dogma (XBOX 360) ......................51

Dungeon Hunter: Alliance (PlayStation Vita) ......................52

Dynasty Warriors Next (PlayStation Vita) ......................53

F1 2011 (PlayStation Vita) ......................55

FIFA Soccer (PlayStation Vita) ......................56

FIFA Street (PlayStation 3) ......................57

FIFA Street (XBOX 360) ......................58

Game of Thrones (PlayStation 3) ......................59

Game of Thrones (XBOX 360) ......................61

Grand Slam Tennis 2 (PlayStation 3) ......................62

Grand Slam Tennis 2 (XBOX 360) ......................64

Gravity Rush (PlayStation Vita) ......................65

Hot Shots Golf: World
Invitational (PlayStation Vita) ......................66

Hyperdimension Neptunia mk2
(PlayStation 3) ......................67

Ice Age: Continental Drift -
Arctic Games (PlayStation 3) ......................68

Ice Age: Continental Drift -
Arctic Games (XBOX 360) ......................69

Inversion (PlayStation 3) ......................70

Inversion (XBOX 360) ......................72

Kidou Senshi Gundam Seed: Battle Destiny
(PlayStation Vita) ......................73

Kinect Rush: A Disney-Pixar
Adventure (XBOX 360) ......................74

Kinect Star Wars (XBOX 360) ......................76

Kingdom Hearts 3D: Dream
Drop Distance (3DS) ......................78

Kingdoms of Amalur: Reckoning
(PlayStation 3) ......................79

Kingdoms of Amalur: Reckoning
(XBOX 360) ......................80

LEGO Batman 2: DC Super
Heroes (PlayStation 3) ......................81

LEGO Batman 2: DC Super
Heroes (PlayStation Vita) ......................82

LEGO Batman 2: DC Super Heroes
(XBOX 360) ......................83

LEGO Harry Potter: Years 5-7
(PlayStation Vita) ......................84

Little Deviants (PlayStation Vita) ......................85

Lollipop Chainsaw (PlayStation 3) ......................87

Lollipop Chainsaw (XBOX 360)......................88

Lumines: Electronic Symphony
(PlayStation Vita) ......................................90

Madagascar 3: The Video Game
(PlayStation Vita) ......................................90

Mahjong Fight Club: Shinsei
Zenkoku Taisen Han (PlayStation Vita)..........91

Major League Baseball 2K12
(PlayStation 3) ..........................................92

Major League Baseball 2K12
(XBOX 360)................................................94

Mass Effect 3 (PlayStation 3)......................95

Mass Effect 3 (XBOX 360) ..........................97

Max Payne 3 (PlayStation 3)........................98

Max Payne 3 (XBOX 360) ............................99

Men in Black: Alien Crisis (PlayStation 3) ....100

Men in Black: Alien Crisis (XBOX 360) ........102

Metal Gear Solid 2:
Sons of Liberty (PlayStation Vita) ................103

Metal Gear Solid 3:
Snake Eater (PlayStation Vita)......................106

Michael Jackson The
Experience HD (PlayStation Vita) ..................110

MLB 12: The Show (PlayStation 3)................111

MLB 12: The Show (PlayStation Vita)............113

ModNation Racers: Road Trip
(PlayStation Vita) ......................................115

Mortal Kombat (PlayStation Vita) ................116

Naruto Shippuden: Ultimate Ninja Storm
Generations (PlayStation 3)........................117

Naruto Shippuden: Ultimate Ninja Storm
Generations (XBOX 360)..............................118

NCAA Football 13 (PlayStation 3)................120

NCAA Football 13 (XBOX 360) ....................121

NeverDead (PlayStation 3)..........................122

NeverDead (XBOX 360) ..............................123

Ninja Gaiden 3 (PlayStation 3)....................124

Ninja Gaiden 3 (XBOX 360) ........................125

Ninja Gaiden Sigma Plus
(PlayStation Vita) ......................................126

Persona 4 Arena (PlayStation 3)..................128

Persona 4 Arena (XBOX 360) ......................129

Phantom Breaker (XBOX 360) ....................131

Phineas and Ferb: Across the 2nd
Dimension (PlayStation Vita) ......................132

Pikmin 2 (Wii) ..........................................133

Prototype 2 (PlayStation 3)........................134

Prototype 2 (XBOX 360) ............................135

Rayman Origins (PlayStation Vita) ..............136

Reality Fighters (PlayStation Vita) ..............137

Resident Evil: Operation
Raccoon City (PlayStation 3) ......................138

Resident Evil: Operation
Raccoon City (XBOX 360)............................140

Resident Evil: Revelations (3DS)..................141

Resistance: Burning Skies
(PlayStation Vita) ......................................142

Ridge Racer (PlayStation Vita) ....................142

Ridge Racer Unbounded (PlayStation 3)........144

Ridge Racer Unbounded (XBOX 360) ............145

Risen 2: Dark Waters (PlayStation 3) ..........147

Risen 2: Dark Waters (XBOX 360) ..............147

Shinobido 2: Revenge of Zen
(PlayStation Vita) ......................................149

Silent Hill: Downpour (PlayStation 3)..........150

Silent Hill: Downpour (XBOX 360) ..............151

Sniper Elite V2 (PlayStation 3) ..................152

Sniper Elite V2 (XBOX 360)........................153

SoulCalibur V (PlayStation 3) ....................154

SoulCalibur V (XBOX 360) ............................156

Spec Ops: The Line (PlayStation 3) ................158

Spec Ops: The Line (XBOX 360) ....................159

SSX (PlayStation 3) .....................................160

SSX (XBOX 360) ..........................................162

Steel Battalion: Heavy Armor
(XBOX 360) ................................................163

Street Fighter X Tekken (PlayStation 3) ..........164

Street Fighter X Tekken (XBOX 360) ..............166

Super Monkey Ball: Banana
Splitz (PlayStation Vita) ..............................167

Supremacy MMA: Unrestricted
(PlayStation Vita) ........................................168

Syndicate (PlayStation 3) .............................169

Syndicate (XBOX 360) ..................................171

Tales of Graces f (PlayStation 3) ...................172

Tales of the Abyss (3DS) .............................174

Test Drive: Ferrari Racing Legends
(PlayStation 3) ............................................174

Test Drive: Ferrari Racing Legends
(XBOX 360) ................................................175

The Amazing Spider-Man (3DS) ...................23

The Amazing Spider-Man (PlayStation 3) .........20

The Amazing Spider-Man (XBOX 360) ...........22

Theatrhythm Final Fantasy (3DS) .................176

The Darkness II (PlayStation 3) .......................44

The Darkness II (XBOX 360) ...........................45

The Witcher 2: Assassins of Kings
(XBOX 360) ................................................196

Tiger Woods PGA Tour 13 (PlayStation 3) ......179

Tiger Woods PGA Tour 13 (XBOX 360) ..........180

Tom Clancy's Ghost Recon:
Future Soldier (PlayStation 3) ........................181

Tom Clancy's Ghost Recon:
Future Soldier (XBOX 360) ............................183

Touch My Katamari (PlayStation Vita) ............185

Twisted Metal (PlayStation 3) .......................185

UEFA Euro 2012 (PlayStation 3) ....................186

UEFA Euro 2012 (XBOX 360) .........................187

UFC Undisputed 3 (PlayStation 3) ..................187

UFC Undisputed 3 (XBOX 360) ......................188

Ultimate Marvel vs. Capcom 3 (PlayStation Vita) .
190

Uncharted: Golden Abyss
(PlayStation Vita) ........................................191

Unit 13 (PlayStation Vita) .............................192

Virtua Tennis 4: World Tour Edition
(PlayStation Vita) ........................................193

Wipeout 2048 (PlayStation Vita) ....................194

Yakuza: Dead Souls (PlayStation 3) ................197

# ALL CODES...

50 Cent: Blood on the Sand (PlayStation 3) ...199

300: March to Glory (PSP) ...........................199

1942: Joint Strike (XBOX 360) ....................199

A Boy and His Blob (Wii) ............................199

Ace Combat: Assault Horizon
(PlayStation 3) ...........................................199

ActRaiser (Wii) ..........................................201

Adventure Island (Wii) ..............................202

Adventures of Lolo 2 (Wii) .........................203

Adventures of Lolo (Wii) ............................202

After Burner Climax (PlayStation 3) ............204

Age of Empires: Mythologies (DS) ..............205

AiRace (NDS) .............................................206

Air Conflicts: Secret Wars (XBOX 360) ........205

Air Zonk (Wii) ...........................................206

Akai Katana Shin (XBOX 360) .......................19

Alan Wake (XBOX 360) ...............................206

Alex Kidd in the Enchanted Castle (Wii) ......206

Alex Rider: Stormbreaker (DS) ....................207

Alice in Wonderland (DS) ...........................207

Alice: Madness Returns (XBOX 360) ............207

Alien Crush (Wii) .......................................208

Alien Vs. Predator (XBOX 360) ....................208

Alone In the Dark: Inferno (PlayStation 3) ......208

Altered Beast (Wii) ....................................208

Amped 3 (XBOX 360) ..................................208

Armored Core V (PlayStation 3) ...................23

Armored Core V (XBOX 360) .........................24

Army Corps of Hell (PlayStation Vita) ...........26

Army of Two (PlayStation 3) ........................210

Art of Fighting (Wii) ...................................210

Ar tonelico Qoga: Knell of Ar Ciel
(PlayStation 3) ...........................................209

Asphalt: Injection (PlayStation Vita) .............27

Assassin's Creed: Brotherhood (XBOX 360) ...210

Assassin's Creed: Revelations (XBOX 360) ..211

Asura's Wrath (PlayStation 3) .......................28

Asura's Wrath (XBOX 360) ............................29

Atelier Meruru: The Apprentice of Arland
(PlayStation 3) .............................................29

Atelier Totori: The Adventurer of Arland
(PlayStation 3) ...........................................213

Band Hero (XBOX 360) ...............................215

Banjo-Kazooie: Nuts & Bolts (XBOX 360) ...215

Bases Loaded (Wii) ....................................215

Batman: Arkham Asylum (PlayStation 3) ......216

Batman: Arkham City (PlayStation 3) ..........216

Battle City (Wii) .........................................217

Battlefield 3 (XBOX 360) .............................217

Battlefield: Bad Company (XBOX 360) ..........219

Battleship (PlayStation 3) .............................30

Battleship (XBOX 360) ..................................31

Battlestations: Midway (XBOX 360) ............219

Bayonetta (XBOX 360) ................................219

Bejeweled 2 Deluxe (XBOX 360) .................219

Ben 10: Galactic Racing (PlayStation Vita) ........32

Binary Domain (PlayStation 3) ......................36

Binary Domain (XBOX 360) ...........................37

Bionicle Heroes (Wii) ..................................220

Birds of Steel (PlayStation 3) ........................34

Birds of Steel (XBOX 360) .............................37

Blackwater (XBOX 360) ...............................220

Blades of Time (PlayStation 3) .......................39

# ►CONTENTS

Blades of Time (XBOX 360) ............................40

BlazBlue: Calamity Trigger (XBOX 360) ........221

BlazBlue: Continuum Shift Extend
(PlayStation Vita) ............................................40

BlazBlue: Continuum Shift II (3DS) ............221

BlazBlue: Continuum Shift (XBOX 360) ........221

Blazing Angels 2: Secret Missions of WWII
(PlayStation 3) ..............................................225

Blazing Angels: Squadrons of WWII
(PlayStation 3) ..............................................225

Blitz: Overtime (PSP) ................................225

Blitz: The League (XBOX 360) ....................225

Bloody Wolf (Wii) ....................................226

Bodycount (XBOX 360) ..............................226

Bolt (PlayStation 3) ..................................227

Brave: The Video Game (PlayStation 3) ............42

Brave: The Video Game (XBOX 360) ................43

Bulletstorm (PlayStation 3) (XBOX 360) ........227

Bully Scholarship Edition (Wii) ..................228

Burnout Paradise (PlayStation 3) ................228

Bust-A-Move Bash! (Wii) ..........................228

Cabela's Survival: Shadows of Katmai
(PlayStation 3) ..............................................229

Call of Duty 2 (XBOX 360) ........................237

Call of Duty 3 (Wii) ..................................237

Call of Duty 3 (XBOX 360) ........................237

Call of Duty 4: Modern Warfare
(PlayStation 3) ..............................................239

Call of Duty 4: Modern Warfare
(XBOX 360) ..................................................237

Call of Duty: Black Ops
(PlayStation 3) (XBOX 360) ..........................230

Call of Duty: Black Ops (Wii) ....................230

Call of Duty: Modern Warfare 2
(XBOX 360) ..................................................232

Call of Duty: Modern Warfare 3
(XBOX 360) ..................................................234

Call of Duty: World at War (XBOX 360) ........236

Call of Juarez: Bound in Blood
(PlayStation 3) ..............................................241

Call of Juarez: The Cartel (PlayStation 3) ......241

Capcom Classic Collection Remixed (PSP) ...243

Cars 2: The Video Game (XBOX 360) ............243

Cars (Wii) ................................................243

Cars (XBOX 360) ......................................243

Castlevania: Order of Ecclesia (DS) ............243

Castlevania: Symphony of the Night
(XBOX 360) ..................................................244

Castlevania: the Adventure Rebirth (Wii) ....244

Catherine (PlayStation 3) ..........................244

Chew-Man-Fu (Wii) ..................................246

Children of Eden (PlayStation 3) ................246

China Warrior (Wii) ..................................248

Chrono Trigger (DS) ..................................248

Cloning Clyde (XBOX 360) ........................249

Comix Zone (Wii) ....................................249

Conduit 2 (Wii) ........................................250

Contra (XBOX 360) ....................................250

Crash: Mind Over Mutant (Wii) ..................250

Crash: Mind Over Mutant (XBOX 360) ........250

Cratermaze (Wii) ......................................250

Crescent Pale Mist (PlayStation 3) ..............250

Cybernator (Wii) ......................................252

Dance Central 2 (XBOX 360) ......................253

Dante's Inferno (PlayStation 3) ..................254

Darksiders (PlayStation 3) ..........................256

Darksiders (XBOX 360) ..............................256

Dark Souls (PlayStation 3) ..........................254

Dead Island (XBOX 360) ............................256

Dead Moon (Wii) ......................................258

Dead or Alive: Dimensions (3DS) ................258

Dead Rising 2: Case 0 (XBOX 360).............259

Dead Rising 2: Off the Record
(PlayStation 3) .................................262

Dead Rising 2: Off the Record
(XBOX 360) .....................................260

Dead Rising 2 (PlayStation 3) .........259

Dead Rising (XBOX 360) ...................258

Dead Space 2 (XBOX 360)...........................264

Dead Space (PlayStation 3) ............................264

Dead Space (XBOX 360) .............................264

Death Jr. II: Root of Evil (PSP)....................266

Despicable Me: Minion Mayhem (DS)........266

Despicable Me (PSP)....................................266

Deus Ex: Human Revolution (XBOX 360)......267

Devil May Cry 4 (XBOX 360) ......................268

Devil's Crush (Wii).......................................269

Dirt 2 (XBOX 360, PlayStation 3) ..................269

Dirt 3 (XBOX 360, PlayStation 3) ......................270

Disgaea 3: Absence of Detention
(PlayStation Vita) .................................47

Disgaea 3: Absence of Justice
(PlayStation 3) .................................271

Disgaea: Afternoon of Darkness (PSP) ........272

Disney's Chicken Little: Ace in Action
(Wii)...........................................273

Disney's Kim Possible Kimmunicator (DS)...274

Disney Universe (XBOX 360) .....................275

Dissidia 012: Duodecim Final Fantasy
(PSP)...........................................276

Double Dungeons (Wii)................................276

Dragon Age II (PlayStation 3) ......................276

Dragon Age: Origins (XBOX 360)..................276

Dragon Ball Z: Ultimate Tenkaichi
(PlayStation 3) .................................276

Dragon Quest IX: Sentinels of the Starry Skies
(PlayStation 3) .................................278

Dragon Quest Monsters: Joker 2 (DS) ........278

Dragon's Curse (Wii)...................................279

Dragon's Dogma (PlayStation 3)......................49

Dragon's Dogma (XBOX 360) ........................51

Dragon Spirit (Wii) .....................................279

Dreamcast Collection (XBOX 360) ................280

Driver: Parallel Lines (Wii) ..........................281

Driver: San Francisco (XBOX 360) ...............281

Dungeon Explorer (Wii)...............................283

Dungeon Hunter: Alliance (PlayStation Vita) .....52

Dynasty Warriors 6 (XBOX 360) ..................284

Dynasty Warriors 7 (PlayStation 3)................285

Dynasty Warriors 7 (XBOX 360) ..................285

Dynasty Warriors: Gundam 3 (XBOX 360)......286

Dynasty Warriors Next (PlayStation Vita) .........53

EA Sports NBA Jam (XBOX 360)..................287

Ecco: The Tides of Time (Wii)......................287

Elements of Destruction (DS) ......................289

El Shaddai: Ascension of the Metatron
(XBOX 360) .....................................289

Eragon (XBOX 360) .....................................291

Escape from Bug Island (Wii).......................291

ESWAT: City Under Siege (Wii)....................291

Exit (PSP) ...................................................291

F1 2011 (PlayStation 3) ..............................292

F1 2011 (PlayStation Vita) .............................55

F.3.A.R. (XBOX 360).....................................293

Fable III (XBOX 360) ...................................295

Fable II (XBOX 360) ....................................294

Fallout 3 (XBOX 360) ..................................295

Fallout: New Vegas (PS3)............................296

Fallout: New Vegas (XBOX 360)...................296

Far Cry 2 (PlayStation 3) .............................297

Far Cry Instincts Predator (XBOX 360)..........297

Far Cry Vengeance (Wii) ..............................298

# ▶ CONTENTS

Fatal Fury (Wii) ..............................298

FIFA Soccer 12 (PlayStation 3) .....................298

FIFA Soccer (PlayStation Vita) ........................56

FIFA Street 3 (XBOX 360, PlayStation 3) ...........299

FIFA Street (PlayStation 3) .......................57

FIFA Street (XBOX 360) ..........................58

FIFA World Cup South Africa - 2010 (Wii) ...............................300

FIFA World Cup South Africa - 2010 (XBOX 360) ..............................299

Fight Night Champion (PlayStation 3) ............300

Fight Night Round 4 (XBOX 360) .................301

Final Fantasy Crystal Chronicles: The Crystal Bearers (Wii) ...............................301

Final Fantasy Fables: Chocobo's Dungeon (Wii) ...............................301

Final Fantasy IV: Complete Collection (PSP) ...............................302

Final Fantasy XIII (XBOX 360, PlayStation 3) ....302

Final Fight: Double Impact (PlayStation 3) ....302

Final Fight: Double Impact (XBOX 360) .........303

Final Soldier (Wii) ..............................303

FlatOut: Head On (PSP) .......................303

Flock (PlayStation 3 , XBOX 360) .................303

Folklore (PlayStation 3) ...........................303

Forza Motorsport 4 (XBOX 360) ...................303

Frogger (XBOX 360) ...........................305

Frontlines: Fuel of War (PlayStation 3) ...........305

Full Auto 2: Battlelines (PlayStation 3) ...........305

Full Auto 2: Battlelines (PSP) ...................305

Gain Groun (Wii) ..............................306

Galaga '90 (Wii) ..............................306

Game of Thrones (PlayStation 3) ...................59

Game of Thrones (XBOX 360) .......................61

Gauntlet (XBOX 360) ...........................306

Gears of War 2 (XBOX 360) .....................306

Gears of War 3 (XBOX 360) .......................307

Gears of War (XBOX 360) .......................306

Genpei Toumaden (Wii) ..........................310

Ghostbusters the Videogame (PlayStation 3, XBOX 360) ......................310

Ghouls 'n Ghosts (Wii) ..........................310

G.I. Joe: The Rise of Cobra (XBOX 360) ........306

God of War: Ghost of Sparta (PSP) ...........312

God of War III (PlayStation 3) ...................311

Godzilla: Unleashed (Wii) .......................312

Golden Axe 2 (Wii) ..............................313

Golden Axe (Wii) ..............................312

GoldenEye 007: Reloaded (XBOX 360) ........313

Gradius 2 (Wii) ..............................315

Gradius 3 (Wii) ..............................315

Gradius Collection (PSP) .......................316

Gradius (Wii) ..............................314

Grand Slam Tennis 2 (PlayStation 3) ................62

Grand Slam Tennis 2 (XBOX 360) .....................64

Grand Theft Auto 4 (PlayStation 3, XBOX 360) ......................316

Grand Theft Auto 4: The Ballad of Gay Tony (XBOX 360) ...............................317

Grand Theft Auto: Chinatown Wars (DS) ......318

Grand Theft Auto: Chinatown Wars (PSP) ....318

Grand Theft Auto: Liberty City Stories (PSP) 318

Grand Theft Auto: Vice City Stories (PSP) ....319

Gran Turismo 5 (PlayStation 3) ......................320

Gravity Rush (PlayStation Vita) ........................65

Guitar Hero 3: Legends of Rock (XBOX 360) 320

Guitar Hero 5 (Wii) ..............................322

Guitar Hero 5 (XBOX 360, PlayStation 3) .........321

Guitar Hero: Aerosmith (XBOX 360, PlayStation 3) ......................322

Guitar Hero: Metallica (Wii) ......................323

Guitar Hero: Metallica
(XBOX 360, PlayStation 3) ................................ 323

Guitar Hero: Van Halen (XBOX 360) ............... 324

Guitar Hero: Warriors of Rock (Wii) ............ 324

Guitar Hero: Warriors of Rock
(XBOX 360, PlayStation 3) ................................ 324

Gunstar Heroes (Wii) ................................... 326

Half-Life 2: The Orange Box (PlayStation 3) ... 327

Half-Life 2: The Orange Box (XBOX 360) ..... 327

Halo 3: ODST (XBOX 360) ............................ 330

Halo 3 (XBOX 360) ...................................... 327

Halo: Reach (XBOX 360) .............................. 331

Halo Wars (XBOX 360) ................................. 331

Harry Potter and the Deathly Hallows, Part 1
(XBOX 360) ................................................... 333

Harry Potter and the Deathly Hallows, Part 2
(XBOX 360) ................................................... 333

Harry Potter and the Half Blood Prince
(XBOX 360) ................................................... 334

Harvest Moon: The Tale of Two Towns
(DS) ............................................................. 334

Hot Shots Golf: World Invitational
(PlayStation Vita) .......................................... 66

Hulk Hogan's Main Event (XBOX 360) .......... 336

Hyperdimension Neptunia mk2
(PlayStation 3) .............................................. 67

Ice Age 2: The Meltdown (Wii) .................... 337

Ice Age: Continental Drift – Arctic Games
(PlayStation 3) .............................................. 68

Ice Age: Continental Drift – Arctic Games
(XBOX 360) ................................................... 69

Image Fight (Wii) ........................................ 337

Indiana Jones and the Staff of Kings
(Wii) ............................................................. 337

inFamous 2 (PlayStation 3) .......................... 338

Infinite Space (DS) ...................................... 339

Inversion (PlayStation 3) .............................. 70

Inversion (XBOX 360) ................................... 72

JASF: Jane's Advanced Strike Fighters
(XBOX 360) ................................................... 340

Jonah Lomu Rugby Challenge
(XBOX 360) ................................................... 341

Juiced 2: Hot Import Nights
(XBOX 360) ................................................... 341

Jurassic: The Hunted (XBOX 360) ................. 342

Just Cause 2 (XBOX 360) ............................. 342

Just Dance 3 (XBOX 360) ............................ 342

Karaoke Revolution
(XBOX 360, PlayStation 3) ............................. 344

Kidou Senshi Gundam Seed: Battle Destiny
(PlayStation Vita) .......................................... 73

Killzone 3 (PlayStation 3) ............................ 344

Kinect: Disneyland Adventures
(XBOX 360) ................................................... 273

Kinect Rush: A Disney-Pixar Adventure
(XBOX 360) ................................................... 74

Kinect Sports Season Two (XBOX 360) ........ 346

Kinect Star Wars (XBOX 360) ...................... 76

Kingdom Hearts 3D: Dream Drop Distance
(3DS) ........................................................... 78

Kingdom Hearts: Birth by Sleep (PSP) ....... 348

Kingdoms of Amalur: Reckoning
(PlayStation 3) .............................................. 79

Kingdoms of Amalur: Reckoning
(XBOX 360) ................................................... 80

Knights in the Nightmare (DS) .................... 348

Kung Fu Panda (Wii) ................................... 348

Kung Fu Panda
(XBOX 360, PlayStation 3) ............................. 348

Lair (PlayStation 3) ..................................... 349

Left 4 Dead (XBOX 360) .............................. 349

LEGO Batman 2: DC Super Heroes
(PlayStation 3) .............................................. 81

LEGO Batman 2: DC Super Heroes (PlayStation
Vita) ............................................................ 82

LEGO Batman 2: DC Super Heroes
(XBOX 360) ................................................... 83

# ► CONTENTS

LEGO Batman (DS) ..............................351

LEGO Batman (PSP) .............................352

LEGO Batman (Wii) .............................351

LEGO Batman (XBOX 360), (PlayStation 3).......349

Lego Harry Potter: Years 1-4 (DS)..............355

Lego Harry Potter: Years 1-4
(XBOX 360), (PlayStation 3), (Wii) .............353

LEGO Harry Potter: Years 5-7
(PlayStation 3) ...............................355

LEGO Harry Potter: Years 5-7
(PlayStation Vita) .............................84

LEGO Harry Potter: Years 5-7
(Wii) .........................................358

LEGO Harry Potter: Years 5-7
(XBOX 360).....................................357

LEGO Indiana Jones 2: The Adventure Continues
(XBOX 360), (Wii) .............................363

LEGO Indiana Jones:
The Original Adventures .......................359

LEGO Indiana Jones: The Original Adventures
(DS) ..........................................361

LEGO Indiana Jones: The Original Adventures
(PSP) .........................................361

LEGO Pirates of the Caribbean
(DS), (PSP), (3DS).............................364

LEGO Pirates of the Caribbean (XBOX 360),
(PlayStation 3), (Wii) ........................364

LEGO Rock Band (DS) ...........................365

LEGO Star Wars III: The Clone Wars
(PlayStation 3, (XBOX 360).....................368

LEGO Star Wars III: The Clone Wars
(Wii) .........................................369

LEGO Star Wars II: The Original Trilogy
(DS) ..........................................367

LEGO Star Wars II: The Original Trilogy
(PSP)..........................................367

LEGO Star Wars II: The Original Trilogy
(XBOX 360).....................................366

LEGO Star Wars: The Complete Saga
(XBOX 360).....................................365

LIMBO (XBOX 360)...............................369

Little Big Planet 2 (PlayStation 3)............371

Little Big Planet (PlayStation 3)..............369

Little Deviants (PlayStation Vita) .............85

Littlest Pet Shop: Jungle (DS).................371

Lode Runner (Wii) ............................371

Lollipop Chainsaw (PlayStation 3)...............87

Lollipop Chainsaw (XBOX 360) ..................88

Lord of Arcana (PSP) ..........................371

Lost Planet 2 (PlayStation 3)..................374

Lost Planet 2 (XBOX 360).......................373

Lost Planet: Extreme Condition
(XBOX 360).....................................375

Lumines: Electronic Symphony
(PlayStation Vita) ............................90

Madagascar 3: The Video Game
(PlayStation Vita) ............................90

Madden NFL 10 (Wii)............................376

Madden NFL 12 (XBOX 360) ......................376

Magician's Quest: Mysterious Times (DS) ...380

Magic: The Gathering—Duels of the
Planeswalkers (XBOX 360) ......................377

Mahjong Fight Club: Shinsei Zenkoku Taisen
Han (PlayStation Vita)........................91

Major League Baseball 2K8 (XBOX 360)......381

Major League Baseball 2K11
(PlayStation 3) ...............................381

Major League Baseball 2K12
(PlayStation 3) ...............................92

Major League Baseball 2K12 (XBOX 360)......94

Man vs. Wild (XBOX 360) .......................382

Marvel: Ultimate Alliance 2 (PlayStation 3) ...384

Marvel: Ultimate Alliance 2 (Wii) .............385

Marvel: Ultimate Alliance 2 (XBOX 360) .......383

Mass Effect 2 (PlayStation 3).................387

Mass Effect 2 (XBOX 360).......................387

Mass Effect 3 (PlayStation 3) ..........................95

Mass Effect 3 (XBOX 360)...............................97

Mass Effect (XBOX 360)................................386

Max Payne 3 (PlayStation 3) .........................98

Max Payne 3 (XBOX 360) ..............................99

Medal of Honor: Airborne (XBOX 360) ...........387

MediEvil Resurrection (PSP)..........................388

Mega Man 10 (Wii) .....................................388

Mega Man (Wii) ..........................................388

Men in Black: Alien Crisis (PlayStation 3) ......100

Men in Black: Alien Crisis (XBOX 360) ..........102

Mercenaries 2: World in Flames
(XBOX 360)................................................388

Metal Gear Acid 2 (PSP) ..............................389

Metal Gear Acid (PSP) .................................388

Metal Gear Solid 2: Sons of Liberty
(PlayStation Vita) .......................................103

Metal Gear Solid 3: Snake Eater
(PlayStation Vita) .......................................106

Metal Gear Solid 4: Guns of the Patriots
(PlayStation 3) ...........................................390

Metal Marines (Wii)....................................394

Michael Jackson The Experience (DS)...........394

Michael Jackson The Experience HD
(PlayStation Vita) .......................................110

Michael Jackson The Experience
(XBOX 360)................................................394

Military Madness (Wii)................................396

Milon's Secret Castle (Wii)..........................397

MLB 11: The Show (PlayStation 3) ................397

MLB 12: The Show (PlayStation 3) ................111

MLB 12: The Show (PlayStation Vita) ............113

ModNation Racers: Road Trip
(PlayStation Vita) .......................................115

Monster Tale (DS) ......................................398

Mortal Kombat (PlayStation 3) .....................398

Mortal Kombat (PlayStation Vita) .................116

Mortal Kombat vs. DC Universe
(PlayStation 3)...........................................401

Mortal Kombat vs. DC Universe
(XBOX 360)................................................401

Mortal Kombat (XBOX 360).........................400

MotionSports Adrenaline (PlayStation 3) .......401

MotoGP 10/11 (XBOX 360) ..........................403

MotorStorm: Apocalypse (PlayStation 3)........404

Motorstorm (PlayStation 3) ..........................404

MVP Baseball (PSP)....................................405

MX Vs. ATV Refle (XBOX 360)......................406

MX vs. ATV Unleashed (PlayStation 2)..........406

MX Vs. ATV Untamed (Wii)..........................406

MX Vs. ATV Untamed
(XBOX 360), (PlayStation 3), (PlayStation 2) ......406

MySims Agents (Wii)...................................407

MySims Kingdom (Wii) ...............................408

MySims Party (Wii).....................................408

MySims Racing (Wii) ..................................408

MySims (Wii) .............................................406

Namco Museum Essentials (PlayStation 3) ...409

Naruto: Clash of Ninja Revolution (Wii).......410

Naruto Shippuden: Shinobi Rumble (DS) .....410

Naruto Shippuden: Ultimate Ninja Impact
(PSP).........................................................411

Naruto Shippuden: Ultimate Ninja Storm
Generations (PlayStation 3).........................117

Naruto Shippuden: Ultimate Ninja Storm
Generations (XBOX 360) .............................118

NASCAR 09 (XBOX 360)..............................411

NASCAR 2011: The Game (PlayStation 3).....411

NASCAR Kart Racing (Wii)...........................412

NASCAR Unleashed (XBOX 360)...................412

Naughty Bear (XBOX 360)............................413

NBA 2K10 (PlayStation 3)............................414

NBA 2K10 (Wii)..........................................414

# ▸ CONTENTS

NBA 2K10 (XBOX 360) ............................414

NBA 2K11 (PlayStation 3) ..........................415

NBA 2K11 (PSP) .....................................415

NBA 2K11 (XBOX 360) ............................415

NBA 2K12 (PlayStation 3) ..........................415

NBA 09: The Inside (PlayStation 3) ...............413

NBA Ballers: Rebound (PSP) ......................417

NBA Jam (XBOX 360) ..............................418

NBA Live 10 (PlayStation 3) .......................418

NBA Live 10 (PSP) ...................................419

NBA Live 10 (XBOX 360) ..........................418

NBA Live 10 (XBOX 360, PlayStation 3) .........418

NCAA Football 10 (XBOX 360) ..................420

NCAA Football 12 (PlayStation 3) ................420

NCAA Football 13 (PlayStation 3) ................120

NCAA Football 13 (XBOX 360) ...................121

NCIS (XBOX 360) ....................................421

N+ (DS) ...............................................409

Need for Speed: Most Wanted
(XBOX 360) ..........................................422

Need for Speed: ProStreet
(PlayStation 3, XBOX 360) .......................422

Need for Speed: ProStreet (Wii) .................422

Need for Speed: The Run (PlayStation 3) ........423

Need for Speed: Undercover
(XBOX 360, PlayStation 3) ........................424

Neutopia II (Wii) ....................................424

NeverDead (PlayStation 3) .........................122

NeverDead (XBOX 360) ............................123

New Adventure Island (Wii) .......................424

NHL 2K6 (XBOX 360) ..............................426

NHL 2K9 (XBOX 360), (PlayStation 3) ...........426

NHL 2K10 (XBOX 360), (Wii) ......................426

NHL 10 (XBOX 360), (PlayStation 3) .............424

NHL 12 (PlayStation 3) .............................424

Ninja Gaiden 3 (PlayStation 3) ....................124

Ninja Gaiden 3 (XBOX 360) .......................125

Ninja Gaiden II (XBOX 360) .......................426

Ninja Gaiden Sigma Plus (PlayStation Vita) ....126

Ninja Gaiden (Wii) ..................................426

No More Heroes 2: Desperate Struggle
(Wii) ..................................................427

N+ (PSP) .............................................409

Okamiden (DS) .......................................428

Onslaught (Wii) ......................................428

Open Season (Wii) ..................................428

Operation Flashpoint: Dragon Rising
(XBOX 360) ..........................................429

Operation Flashpoint: Red River
(XBOX 360) ..........................................429

Opoona (Wii) .........................................430

Ordyne (Wii) .........................................430

Pac-Man World 3 (PSP) ............................431

Patapon 2 (PSP) .....................................431

Patapon 3 (PSP) .....................................431

Persona 4 Arena (PlayStation 3) ..................128

Persona 4 Arena (XBOX 360) .....................129

Phantom Breaker (XBOX 360) ....................131

Phineas and Ferb: Across the 2nd Dimension
(PlayStation Vita) ...................................132

Pikmin 2 (Wii) .......................................133

Pinball Hall of Fame (PSP) .........................431

Pirates of the Caribbean: At World's End
(DS) ...................................................432

Pirates PlundArrr (Wii) .............................432

PixelJunk Eden (PlayStation 3) ....................432

Plants vs. Zombies (XBOX 360) ..................432

Pokémon Black (DS) ................................432

Pokémon HeartGold (DS) ..........................433

Pokémon Rumble Blast (3DS) ................... 433

Pokémon SoulSilver (DS) ...................... 434

Pokemon White (DS) .......................... 434

Portal 2 (XBOX 360) .......................... 435

Portal: Still Alive (XBOX 360) ............... 435

PowerUp Heroes (XBOX 360) .................... 436

Prince of Persia: Classic (XBOX 360) ......... 437

Pro Evolution Soccer 09 (XBOX 360) ........... 437

Pro Evolution Soccer 2010 (PlayStation 3) .... 438

Pro Evolution Soccer 2010 (XBOX 360) ......... 437

Pro Evolution Soccer 2012 (PlayStation 3) .... 438

Professor Layton and the Diabolical Box
(DS) ......................................... 439

Prototype 2 (PlayStation 3) .................. 134

Prototype 2 (XBOX 360) ....................... 135

Prototype (PlayStation 3) .................... 440

Prototype (XBOX 360) ......................... 439

Pro Wrestling (Wii) .......................... 439

Pulseman (Wii) ............................... 440

Puss in Boots (XBOX 360) ..................... 440

Puyo Pop Fever (DS) .......................... 441

Quake 4 (XBOX 360) ........................... 441

Quantum Redshift (XBOX) ...................... 441

Rage (XBOX 360) .............................. 442

Ragnarok DS (DS) ............................. 443

Raiden Fighters Jet (XBOX 360) ............... 443

Rampage: Total Destruction (Wii) ............. 444

Raving Rabbids: Alive & Kicking
(XBOX 360) ................................... 444

Rayman Origins (PlayStation Vita) ............ 136

Rayman Origins (XBOX 360) .................... 445

Reality Fighters (PlayStation Vita) .......... 137

Red Dead Redemption (PS3) .................... 446

Red Dead Redemption (XBOX 360) ............... 447

Red Faction: Armageddon (XBOX 360) ........... 447

Red Faction: Guerrilla (PlayStation 3) ....... 449

Red Faction: Guerrilla (XBOX 360) ............ 449

Red Steel 2 (Wii) ............................ 449

Resident Evil 5: Lost in Nightmares
(XBOX 360) ................................... 449

Resident Evil 5 (PlayStation 3) .............. 449

Resident Evil: Operation Raccoon City
(PlayStation 3) .............................. 138

Resident Evil: Operation Raccoon City
(XBOX 360) ................................... 140

Resident Evil: Revelations (3DS) ............. 141

Resident Evil: The Mercenaries 3D
(3DS) ........................................ 449

Resistance 2 (PlayStation 3) ................. 451

Resistance 3 (PlayStation 3) ................. 452

Resistance: Burning Skies
(PlayStation Vita) ........................... 142

Ridge Racer 3D (3DS) ......................... 454

Ridge Racer (PlayStation Vita) ............... 142

Ridge Racer Unbounded (PlayStation 3) ........ 144

Ridge Racer Unbounded (XBOX 360) ............. 145

Risen 2: Dark Waters (PlayStation 3) ......... 147

Risen 2: Dark Waters (XBOX 360) .............. 147

Risen (XBOX 360) ............................. 454

Ristar (Wii) ................................. 454

River City Ransom (Wii) ...................... 455

Rock Band 2 (XBOX 360) ....................... 455

Rock Band 3 (PS3) ............................ 456

Rock Band 3 (Wii) ............................ 456

Rock Band 3 (XBOX 360) ....................... 456

Rock Band (Wii) .............................. 455

Rock Band (XBOX 360) ......................... 455

Rocksmith (XBOX 360) ......................... 457

Rockstar Games Presents Table Tennis
(Wii) ........................................ 458

R-Type 2 (Wii) ............................... 442

# ► CONTENTS

R-Type 3 (Wii) ..................................442

R-Type (Wii) ....................................442

Rugby World Cup 2011 (PlayStation 3) .........459

Rune Factory 2: A Fantasy Harvest Moon
(DS) ..........................................460

Rune Factory: Tides of Destiny
(PlayStation 3) ...............................460

Rush 'n Attack (XBOX 360) ....................461

Saints Row: The Third (PlayStation 3) ........464

Saints Row: The Third (XBOX 360) .............468

Saints Row (XBOX 360, PlayStation 3) .........462

Samurai Warriors: Katana (Wii) ...............471

Schizoid (XBOX 360) ..........................471

Scott Pilgrim Vs. the World
(PlayStation 3)) .............................472

Scrap MetaL (XBOX 360) .......................472

Scribblenauts (DS) ...........................472

Section 8 (XBOX 360) .........................474

Shadow Land (Wii) ............................474

Shadows of the Damned (XBOX 360) .............475

Shift 2 Unleashed: Need for Speed
(XBOX 360) ...................................476

Shining Force (Wii) ..........................477

Shinobido 2: Revenge of Zen
(PlayStation Vita) ...........................149

Silent Hill: Downpour (PlayStation 3) ........150

Silent Hill: Downpour (XBOX 360) .............151

Silent Hill: Shattered Memories (Wii) ........478

SimCity DS (DS) ..............................478

Skate 2 (PlayStation 3) ......................481

Skate 2 (XBOX 360) ...........................480

Skate 3 (PlayStation 3) ......................481

Skate 3 (XBOX 360) ...........................481

Small Arms (XBOX 360) ........................481

Smash T (XBOX 360) ...........................481

Sniper Elite V2 (PlayStation 3) ..............152

Sniper Elite V2 (XBOX 360) ...................153

Snoopy Flying Ace (XBOX 360) .................481

SOCOM 4: U.S. Navy SEALS
(PlayStation 3) ..............................482

Soldier Blade (Wii) ..........................483

Soldner-X 2: Final Prototype
(PlayStation 3) ..............................483

Solomon's Key (Wii) ..........................483

Sonic 3D Blast (Wii) .........................483

Sonic Generations (PlayStation 3) ............486

Sonic Generations (XBOX 360) .................484

Sonic Rush Adventure (DS) ....................489

Sonic Spinball (Wii) .........................489

Sonic the Hedgehog 2 (Wii) ...................490

Sonic the Hedgehog 2 (XBOX 360) ..............490

Sonic the Hedgehog 3 (Wii) ...................492

Sonic the Hedgehog 4: Episode I
(PlayStation 3) ..............................493

Sonic the Hedgehog 4: Episode I
(XBOX 360) ...................................493

Sonic the Hedgehog (PlayStation 3) ...........489

Sonic the Hedgehog (Wii) .....................490

Soulcalibur IV (XBOX 360) ....................493

SoulCalibur V (PlayStation 3) ................154

SoulCalibur V (XBOX 360) .....................156

Space Marine (XBOX 360) ......................496

Spec Ops: The Line (PlayStation 3) ...........158

Spec Ops: The Line (XBOX 360) ................159

Speed Racer (Wii) ............................497

Spider-Man 2 (PSP) ...........................500

Spider-Man 3 (Wii) ...........................500

Spider-Man: Edge of Time (Wii) ...............500

Spider-Man: Edge of Time (XBOX 360) ..........498

Spider-Man: Friend or Foe (Wii) ..............500

Spider-Man: Friend or Foe (XBOX 360) ........500

Splatterhouse (PS3) ..............................501

Splatterhouse (Wii) ..............................500

Splatterhouse (XBOX 360) ......................501

'Splosion Man (XBOX 360) ......................462

SpongeBob SquarePants: Creature from the
Krusty Krab (Wii) ................................501

Spyborgs (Wii) ....................................502

SSX Blur (Wii) ....................................502

SSX (PlayStation 3) ..............................160

SSX (XBOX 360) ..................................162

Star Ocean: The Last Hope International
(PlayStation 3) ....................................502

Star Soldier (Wii) ................................502

Star Trek: Legacy (XBOX 360) ..................502

Star Wars Battlefront II (PSP) ..................502

Star Wars: The Clone Wars—Republic Heroes
(Wii) ................................................502

Star Wars: The Clone Wars—Republic Heroes
(XBOX 360) ........................................502

Star Wars: The Force Unleashed (DS) ........506

Star Wars: The Force Unleashed II (Wii) .....507

Star Wars: The Force Unleashed II
(XBOX 360) ........................................507

Star Wars: The Force Unleashed (PSP) ........506

Star Wars: The Force Unleashed (Wii) ........505

Star Wars: The Force UnleasheD
(XBOX 360), (PlayStation 3) ....................504

Steel Battalion: Heavy Armor (XBOX 360) ....163

Stranglehold (PlayStation 3) ....................508

Street Fighter 4 (PlayStation 3) ................510

Street Fighter 4 (XBOX 360) ....................508

Street Fighter X Tekken (PlayStation 3) ........164

Street Fighter X Tekken (XBOX 360) ............166

Streets of Rage 2 (Wii) ..........................511

Streets of Rage 3 (Wii) ..........................511

Streets of Rage (Wii) ............................511

Super Castlevania IV (Wii) ......................512

Super Contra (XBOX 360) ......................514

Super C (Wii) ......................................512

Super Ghouls 'N Ghosts (Wii) ..................514

Superman Returns (XBOX 360) ................519

Super Monkey Ball: Banana Splitz
(PlayStation Vita) ................................167

Super Scribblenauts (DS) ........................514

Super Star Soldier (Wii) ..........................515

Super Street Fighter IV: 3D Edition
(3DS) ................................................517

Super Street Fighter IV
(XBOX 360), (PlayStation 3) ....................516

Super Thunder Blade (Wii) ......................518

Supremacy MMA: Unrestricted
(PlayStation Vita) ................................168

Surf's Up (PlayStation 3) ........................519

Surf's Up (Wii) ....................................519

Sword of Vermilion (Wii) ........................520

Syndicate (PlayStation 3) ........................169

Syndicate (XBOX 360) ............................171

Tales of Graces f (PlayStation 3) ................172

Tales of the Abyss (3DS) ........................174

Tatsunoko Vs. Capcom: Ultimate All Stars
(Wii) ................................................521

Teenage Mutant Ninja Turtles 2:
The Arcade Game (Wii) ..........................521

Teenage Mutant Ninja Turtles (PSP) ..........521

Teenage Mutant Ninja Turtles (Wii) ............521

Tekken 6 (XBOX 360) ............................522

Test Drive: Ferrari Racing Legends
(PlayStation 3) ....................................174

Test Drive: Ferrari Racing Legends
(XBOX 360) ........................................175

The 3rd Birthday (PSP) ..........................523

The Adventures of Tintin: The Game
(PlayStation 3) .................................................524

The Amazing Spider-Man (3DS) ...................23

The Amazing Spider-Man (PlayStation 3) .........20

The Amazing Spider-Man (XBOX 360)..............22

Theatrhythm Final Fantasy (3DS).................176

The Beatles: Rock Band (Wii).......................457

The Beatles: Rock Band (XBOX 360) ............456

The Chronicles of Narnia: The Lion, The Witch,
and The Wardrobe (DS)..............................248

The Conduit (Wii) ........................................249

The Cursed Crusade (PlayStation 3) ..............251

The Darkness II (PlayStation 3).......................44

The Darkness II (XBOX 360) ...........................45

The Darkness (PlayStation 3)........................256

The Darkness (XBOX 360) .............................256

The Elder Scrolls V: Skyrim (XBOX 360).......525

The Godfather: Blackhand Edition (Wii)........311

The Godfather: The Don's Edition
(PlayStation 3) .............................................311

The Godfather (XBOX 360) ............................311

The Gunstringer (XBOX 360).........................325

The House of the Dead: Overkill (Wii)..........336

The King of Fighters XIII (PlayStation 3) .......526

The King of Fighters XIII (XBOX 360) ............528

The Lord of the Rings: War in the North
(XBOX 360)....................................................372

The Sims 2 (DS)............................................479

The Sims 2: Pets (Wii).................................480

The Sims 3 (DS) ...........................................480

The Witcher 2: Assassins of Kings
(XBOX 360) ...................................................196

Thrillville (PSP) ...........................................530

Tiger Woods PGA Tour '10 (PlayStation 3) .....530

Tiger Woods PGA Tour '10 (XBOX 360) ........530

Tiger Woods PGA Tour 12: The Masters
(XBOX 360)....................................................530

Tiger Woods PGA Tour 13 (PlayStation 3)......179

Tiger Woods PGA Tour 13 (XBOX 360) ..........180

Time Crisis 2 (PlayStation 2) ..........................532

TMNT (Wii) ..................................................532

TMNT (XBOX 360).........................................532

ToeJam and Earl in Panic on Funkotron
(Wii) .............................................................533

ToeJam and Earl (Wii) .................................532

Tomb Raider: Legends (PSP).........................536

Tomb Raider Legends (XBOX 360)..................536

Tomb Raider: Underworld (PlayStation 3).......536

Tomb Raider: Underworld (XBOX 360) ...........536

Tom Clancy's EndWar (PlayStation 3) ............533

Tom Clancy's EndWar (XBOX 360)..................533

Tom Clancy's Ghost Recon: Future Soldier
(PlayStation 3) ..............................................181

Tom Clancy's Ghost Recon: Future Soldier
(XBOX 360) ...................................................183

Tom Clancy's HAWX (PlayStation 3)...............534

Tom Clancy's HAWX (XBOX 360) ..................534

Tom Clancy's Rainbow Six Vegas 2
(PlayStation 3) ..............................................535

Tom Clancy's Rainbow Six Vegas 2
(XBOX 360) ...................................................534

Tom Clancy's Splinter Cell: Chaos Theory
(DS) ..............................................................535

Tom Clancy's Splinter Cell: Essentials
(PSP)..............................................................536

Tony Hawk's American Wasteland
(XBOX 360)....................................................537

Tony Hawk's Downhill Jam (Wii)................537

Tony Hawk's Project 8 (PlayStation 3)............538

Tony Hawk's Project 8 (XBOX 360) .............538

Tony Hawk's Proving Ground (DS) ..............540

# CONTENTS

Tony Hawk's Proving Ground (PlayStation 3) .................... 539

Tony Hawk's Proving Ground (Wii) ..... 540

Tony Hawk's Underground 2 Remix (PSP) ..... 541

Toshinden (Wii) ..................... 541

Touch My Katamari (PlayStation Vita) ........... 185

Touch the Dead (DS) ..................... 542

Tower of Druaga (Wii) ..................... 542

Toy Soldiers (XBOX 360) ..................... 542

Transformers: Revenge of the Fallen (PlayStation 3) ..................... 543

Transformers: Revenge of the Fallen (XBOX 360) ..................... 542

Transformers: The Game (Wii) ..................... 544

Transformers: The Game (XBOX 360) ........... 543

Trinity Universe (Wii) ..................... 544

Tron Evolution: Battle Grids (Wii) ..................... 545

Tron Evolution (PSP) ..................... 545

Tropico 4 (XBOX 360) ..................... 545

Twisted Metal Head On (PSP) ..................... 546

Twisted Metal (PlayStation 3) ..................... 185

Two Worlds II (PlayStation 3) ..................... 547

Two Worlds II (XBOX 360) ..................... 546

UEFA Euro 2012 (PlayStation 3) ..................... 186

UEFA Euro 2012 (XBOX 360) ..................... 187

UFC 2009 Undisputed (XBOX 360, PlayStation 3) ..................... 549

UFC Personal Trainer: The Ultimate Fitness System (XBOX 360) ..................... 549

UFC Undisputed 3 (PlayStation 3) ..................... 187

UFC Undisputed 3 (XBOX 360) ..................... 188

Ultimate Marvel vs. Capcom 3 (PlayStation 3) ..................... 550

Ultimate Marvel vs. Capcom 3 (PlayStation Vita) ..................... 190

Ultimate Marvel vs. Capcom 3 (XBOX 360) ..................... 552

Ultimate Mortal Kombat 3 (XBOX 360) ..................... 553

Uncharted 2: Among Thieves (PlayStation 3) ..................... 555

Uncharted 3: Drake's Deception (PlayStation 3) ..................... 556

Uncharted: Drake's Fortune (PlayStation 3) ..................... 554

Uncharted: Golden Abyss (PlayStation Vita) ..................... 191

Unit 13 (PlayStation Vita) ..................... 192

Valkyria Chronicles: Behind her Blue Flame DLC (PlayStation 3) ..................... 559

Valkyria Chronicles (PlayStation 3) ..................... 559

Vandal Hearts: Flames of Judgment (PlayStation 3) ..................... 559

Vanquish (XBOX 360) ..................... 560

Vectorman (Wii) ..................... 560

Virtua Fighter 2 (Wii) ..................... 560

Virtua Fighter 5 (PlayStation 3) ..................... 561

Virtua Tennis 3 (XBOX 360) ..................... 561

Virtua Tennis 4: World Tour Edition (PlayStation Vita) ..................... 193

Virtua Tennis World Tour (PSP) ..................... 561

Viva Piñata (XBOX 360) ..................... 561

WALL-E (PSP) ..................... 562

WALL-E (Wii) ..................... 562

WALL-E (XBOX 360) ..................... 562

Wanted: Weapons of Fate (PlayStation 3) ..... 563

Wanted: Weapons of Fate (XBOX 360) ........ 563

Water Warfare (Wii) ..................... 563

Wet (XBOX 360) ..................... 564

Where the Wild Things Are (XBOX 360) ...... 564

White Knight Chronicles II (PlayStation 3) ..................... 564

# ►CONTENTS

Wipeout 2048 (PlayStation Vita) ....................194

Wipeout in the Zone (XBOX 360) ..................566

Wolfenstein (XBOX 360) ...........................567

Wonder Boy in Monster World (Wii) ...........567

World Series of Poker: Tournament of
Champions (Wii) ......................................567

WRC: FIA World Rally Championship
(PSP) ....................................................567

Wrecking Crew (Wii) ................................567

WWE '12 (Wii) ........................................571

WWE '12 (XBOX 360) ..............................567

WWE All Stars (PlayStation 3) ..................573

WWE All Stars (Wii) .................................574

WWE All Stars (XBOX 360) ........................573

WWE Smackdown Vs. Raw 2010
(PlayStation 3) .........................................576

WWE Smackdown Vs. Raw 2010
(PSP) .....................................................578

WWE Smackdown Vs. Raw 2010
(XBOX 360) ..............................................574

WWE SmackDown vs. Raw 2011
(Wii) ......................................................578

WWE SmackDown vs. Raw 2011
(XBOX360) ..............................................578

X-Blades (PlayStation 3) ...........................580

X-Blades (XBOX 360) ...............................580

(XBOX 360), (PlayStation 3), (Wii), ............359

X-Men: Destiny (PlayStation 3) ..................580

X-Men: Destiny (XBOX 360) .......................581

X-Men Legends 2: Rise of Apocalypse
(PSP) ....................................................583

X-Men Legends (PlayStation 3) ..................583

X-Men Origins: Wolverine (PlayStation 3) .....584

X-Men Origins: Wolverine (XBOX 360) .......584

Yakuza 4 (PlayStation 3) ..........................585

Yakuza: Dead Souls (PlayStation 3) ...........197

You Don't Know Jack (XBOX 360) ...............585

Yu-Gi-Oh! 5D's World Championship 2010
Reverse of Arcadia (DS) ...........................585

Yu-Gi-Oh! 5D's World Championship 2011:
Over the Nexus (DS) ................................588

Zombie Apocalypse (PlayStation 3) .............592

Zombie Apocalypse (XBOX 360) .................592

Zombie Panic in Wonderland (Wii) ............592

## AKAI KATANA SHIN (XBOX 360)

### ACHIEVEMENTS

| UNLOCKABLE | HOW TO UNLOCK |
|---|---|
| #^&@%&! (5) | Got hit by a bullet in Phantom form, and then died from another bullet immediately afterward. |
| 100 Million and Counting (10) | Earned 100,000,000 points (Origin Mode). |
| 128 Hits! (5) | Earned 128 hits (Origin Mode). |
| 200 Million and Counting (15) | Earned 200,000,000 points (Origin Mode). |
| 256 Hits! (10) | Earned 256 hits (Origin Mode). |
| 400 Million and Counting (10) | Earned 400,000,000 points (Slash Mode). |
| 600 Million and Counting (15) | Earned 600,000,000 points (Slash Mode). |
| 800 Million and Counting (20) | Earned 800,000,000 points (Slash Mode). |
| Absorption Power (5) | Absorb items into your ship. |
| Armored Helicopter (25) | Defeated the helicopter mid-boss in Stage 5. |
| Attack Ships on Fire (5) | Sunk the Fujibara attack ship. |
| Ayame & Ran of the 10 Suns (45) | Defeated Ayame & Ran. |
| Back Against the Wall (30) | While in Phantom form, filled up the screen with more than 800 bullets. |
| Big Catch (5) | Rotated 72 guiding energy items (large) around your ship. |
| Breaching Submarine (20) | Defeated the Arakashi submarine in Stage 4. |
| Bullet-proof (30) | Reflected more than 1000 bullets while in Phantom form. |
| Decay and Dissolution (10) | Lost more than 20 score items that were rotating around your ship during a game. |
| Destroying the Limit (20) | Earned 3000 hits (Slash Mode). |
| Emperor Bashou of the 10 Suns (50) | Defeated Emperor Bashou. |
| Energy Gauge MAX (5) | Filled up your energy gauge. |
| Heavy Attack Helicopter (35) | Brought down the Himeshikara heavy attack helicopter. |
| Hiiragi of the 10 Suns (10) | Defeated the 1st stage boss, Hiiragi. |
| Katana of Justice (30) | Hit a boss with 16 steel orbs. |
| Katana of Truth (40) | Hit a boss with 16 katanas. |
| Learning Type 1 (30) | Cleared the game with the Type 1 ship. |
| Learning Type 2 (30) | Cleared the game with the Type 2 ship. |
| Learning Type 3 (30) | Cleared the game with the Type 3 ship. |
| M76 Heavy Tank (10) | Defeated the Goura heavy tank in Stage 2. |
| Malice Speed Destruction (20) | Destroyed a mid-boss within 2 seconds. |
| Marigold (30) | Cleared the game using Type 1 without continuing. |
| Nazuna of the 10 Suns (30) | Defeated the 5th stage boss, Nazuna. |
| Opening Salvo (5) | Started up the game for the first time. |
| Orchid (30) | Cleared the game using Type 2 without continuing. |

**CODES & CHEATS**

| Sakura (30) | Cleared the game using Type 3 without continuing. |
| --- | --- |
| Shakunage of the 10 Suns (20) | Defeated the 3rd stage boss, Shakunage. |
| Shumeigiku of the 10 Suns (15) | Defeated the 2nd stage boss, Shumeigiku. |
| Summoning (5) | Summoned your Phantom. |
| Tank Bombardment (15) | Defeated the Gaimon tank in Stage 3. |
| The Gold Ring (5) | Rotated over 200 score items (large) around your ship while playing as the Phantom. |
| The Hidden Form (15) | Equipped a total of 16 katanas and 16 steel orbs on your Phantom. |
| The Phantom (15) | Caused a boss to change forms, or destroyed it while playing as the Phantom. |
| The Sharpened Blade (20) | Earned 300,000,000 points (Origin Mode). |
| War Fiend Hiiragi (25) | Defeated the 4th stage boss, War Fiend Hiiragi. |

## THE AMAZING SPIDER-MAN (PlayStation 3)

### TROPHY

| UNLOCKABLE | HOW TO UNLOCK |
| --- | --- |
| A Dash of Spider (Bronze) | Complete all XTreme Race challenges |
| All Tied Up (Silver) | Defeat 100 enemies by performing Stealth Takedowns |
| Amazing Spider-Man (Bronze) | Unlock all concept art |
| Apparent Defeat (Bronze) | Defeat Iguana |
| Beating the Odds (Bronze) | Clear the second fight against the Hunter robots |
| Big Apple, Big Worm (Silver) | Defeat the S-02 |
| Call Interrupted (Bronze) | Destroy a Seeker before it can call a Hunter |
| Car Hopper (Bronze) | Clear all car chases |
| Clean Victory (Silver) | Defeat a Hunter without using your Web-Shooters |
| Corporate (Bronze) | Collect all Oscorp Manuals |
| Deeply Sorry (Bronze) | Defeat Nattie |
| Does everything a spider can! (Platinum) | Unlock all Trophies |
| Down for the Count (Bronze) | Defeat Rhino in the sewers |
| Friendly Neighbor (Bronze) | Save a hostage caught in a petty crime |
| FYI I'm Spider-Man (Bronze) | Perform 25 Signature Moves |
| Gladiator (Bronze) | Complete all Oscorp Secret Research Labs |
| Haymaker (Bronze) | Perform a Web-Rush punch |
| Heavyweight Champion (Gold) | Defeat 1000 enemies |
| I'm on a Roll! (Silver) | Achieve a combo streak of 42 |
| Jinxed (Bronze) | Defeat Felicia |
| Journalist (Bronze) | Collect all audio evidence |
| Keep It Together (Bronze) | Immobilize 6 enemies simultaneously with web |
| Librarian (Bronze) | Collect all magazines |
| Lightweight Champion (Bronze) | Defeat 100 enemies |
| Middleweight Champion (Silver) | Defeat 500 enemies |
| Negotiator (Bronze) | Resolve all police deadlocks |
| On the Fly (Bronze) | Collect all 700 Spider-Man Comic Pages |

| | |
|---|---|
| Peace of Mind (Bronze) | Return all escapees to the police |
| Pest Control (Bronze) | Defeat Scorpion in the city |
| Peter Parker (Bronze) | Complete the game on human difficulty |
| Sanitized (Bronze) | Rescue all infected civilians |
| Siege Averted (Silver) | Defeat the S-01 |
| Sky Captain (Bronze) | Chain 10 Web-Rushes in the city |
| Smell You Later (Bronze) | Defeat Vermin |
| Speed Bump Ahead (Bronze) | Defeat Rhino in the city |
| Spider-Man (Gold) | Complete the game on super hero difficulty |
| Stick to the Plan (Bronze) Stealth Takedowns | Defeat 50 enemies by performing |
| Switched Off (Silver) | Rescue Alistaire Smythe |
| Tail? You Lose (Bronze) | Defeat Scorpion in quarantine |
| Tech Savvy (Bronze) | Collect all hidden Tech Pieces |
| The Camera Loves You (Bronze) | Complete all XTreme Video challenges |
| The Sky Is the Limit (Silver) | Defeat the S-01 without touching the ground |
| Tomorrow Is Saved (Silver) | Defeat the S-03 |
| Ultimate Spider-Man (Bronze) | Acquire all upgrades |
| Vigilante (Silver) | Complete the game on hero difficulty |
| Welcome Back, Friend (Silver) | Defeat Lizard |
| Who's the Prey? (Bronze) | Clear the first fight against the Hunter robots |

## UNLOCKABLE

| UNLOCKABLE | HOW TO UNLOCK |
|---|---|
| 1st Black Cat | 125 pages of comics collected |
| 1st Gwen Stacy | 350 pages of comics collected |
| 1st Iguana | 250 pages of comics collected |
| 1st Lizard | 15 pages of comics collected |
| 1st Rhino | 50 pages of comics collected |
| 1st Scorpion | 80 pages of comics collected |
| 1st Smythe | 500 pages of comics collected |
| 1st Spider-Man | 5 pages of comics collected |
| Modern Lizard | 30 pages of comics collected |
| Vs. Vermin | 175 pages of comics collected |
| Big Time Suit | In Times Square behind the red bleachers, on the glass. |
| Classic Black Suit | Under the Gazebo in the narrow park, left of the main Oscorp Building downtown. |
| Classic Spider-man Costume | Unlocks with the activation of the Rhino Challenge DLC |
| Cross Species Spider-Man | Complete the game on any setting |
| Future Foundation Suit | Behind the gas station store in a small alley. One block right of north bridge |
| Negative Zone Suit | On top of Beenox building, second building inward from Brooklyn Bridge. |
| New Black Suit | Complete the game 100% |
| Scarlet Spider (2012) Costume | You need the camera to unlock this costume. Go to Central Park and from the fountain move north away from it until you see a bridge. |

## THE AMAZING SPIDER-MAN (XBOX 360)

### ACHIEVEMENT

| UNLOCKABLE | HOW TO UNLOCK |
| --- | --- |
| A Dash of Spider (15) | Completed all XTreme Race challenges |
| All Tied Up (15) | Defeated 100 enemies by performing Stealth Takedowns |
| Amazing Spider-Man (20) | Unlocked all concept art |
| Apparent Defeat (20) | Defeated Iguana |
| Beating the Odds (30) | Cleared the second fight against the Hunter robots |
| Big Apple, Big Worm (30) | Defeated the S-02 |
| Call Interrupted (15) | Destroyed a Seeker before it could call a Hunter |
| Car Hopper (15) | Cleared all car chases |
| Clean Victory (20) | Defeated a Hunter without using your Web-Shooters |
| Corporate (15) | Collected all Oscorp Manuals |
| Deeply Sorry (20) | Defeated Nattie |
| Down for the Count (20) | Defeated Rhino in the sewers |
| Friendly Neighbor (15) | Saved a hostage caught in a petty crime |
| FYI I'm Spider-Man (10) | Performed 25 Signature Moves |
| Gladiator (15) | Completed all Oscorp Secret Research Labs |
| Haymaker (10) | Performed a Web-Rush punch |
| Heavyweight Champion (30) | Defeated 1000 enemies |
| I'm on a Roll! (15) | Achieved a combo streak of 42 |
| Jinxed (20) | Defeated Felicia |
| Journalist (15) | Collected all audio evidence |
| Keep It Together (15) | Immobilized 6 enemies simultaneously with web |
| Librarian (15) | Collected all magazines |
| Lightweight Champion (15) | Defeated 100 enemies |
| Middleweight Champion (20) | Defeated 500 enemies |
| Negotiator (15) | Resolved all police deadlocks |
| On the Fly (25) | Collected all 700 Spider-Man Comic Pages |
| Peace of Mind (15) | Returned all escapees to the police |
| Pest Control (20) | Defeated Scorpion in the city |
| Peter Parker (25) | Completed the game on human difficulty |
| Sanitized (15) | Rescued all infected civilians |
| Siege Averted (30) | Defeated the S-01 |
| Sky Captain (15) | Chained 10 Web-Rushes in the city |
| Smell You Later (20) | Defeated Vermin |
| Speed Bump Ahead (20) | Defeated Rhino in the city |
| Spider-Man (100) | Completed the game on super hero difficulty |
| Stick to the Plan (15) | Defeated 50 enemies by performing Stealth Takedowns |
| Switched Off (25) | Rescued Alistaire Smythe |
| Tail? You Lose (20) | Defeated Scorpion in quarantine |
| Tech Savvy (15) | Collected all hidden Tech Pieces |
| The Camera Loves You (15) | Completed all XTreme Video challenges |
| The Sky Is the Limit (20) | Defeated the S-01 without touching the ground |
| Tomorrow Is Saved (30) | Defeated the S-03 |

| Ultimate Spider-Man (20) | Acquired all upgrades |
| Vigilante (50) | Completed the game on hero difficulty |
| Welcome Back, Friend (30) | Defeated Lizard |
| Who's the Prey? (30) | Cleared the first fight against the Hunter robots |

### UNLOCKABLE

| UNLOCKABLE | HOW TO UNLOCK |
| --- | --- |
| Cross Species Spiderman | Beat on any difficulty. |

## THE AMAZING SPIDER-MAN (3DS)

### ACHIEVEMENT

| UNLOCKABLE | HOW TO UNLOCK |
| --- | --- |
| Classic Suit | Complete all petty crimes. |

## ARMORED CORE V (PlayStation 3)

### TROPHY

| UNLOCKABLE | HOW TO UNLOCK |
| --- | --- |
| A Job Well Done (Bronze) | Awarded for successfully completing a job as a mercenary. |
| AC Wrecker (Bronze) | Awarded for winning a battle against an AC. Any type of mission counts. |
| Accomplish Territory Mission (Bronze) | Awarded for claiming victory on a Territory Mission. |
| Air Master (Bronze) | Awarded for destroying Raijin. |
| Assembler (Bronze) | Awarded for assembling an AC in a workshop. |
| Big Bird (Platinum) | Awarded for getting all trophies. |
| Blackbird (Bronze) | Awarded for destroying Exusia. |
| Charge Master (Bronze) | Awarded for destroying an enemy with a boost charge. Any type of enemy counts. |
| Color Customizer (Bronze) | Awarded for setting an AC's coloring in a workshop. |
| Communicator (Bronze) | Awarded for editing a message from the team member list. |
| Complete Custom Part (Bronze) | Awarded for continuing to use an arm unit to maximize its performance. |
| Complete Order Missions (Bronze) | Awarded for completing all Order Missions. |
| Complete Story Missions (Silver) | Awarded for completing all Story Missions. |
| Conquest Mission Sortie (Bronze) | Awarded for going on a Conquest Mission. |
| Conquest Mission Victory (Bronze) | Awarded for claiming victory on a Conquest Mission. |
| Customize Territory (Bronze) | Awarded for acquiring territory and placing gun batteries. |
| Earth Master (Bronze) | Awarded for destroying Type D No. 5. |
| Emblem Designer (Bronze) | Awarded for editing an emblem in a workshop. |
| Emblem Master (Bronze) | Awarded for getting all emblems and emblem pieces by buying them at the shop and/or destroying ACs. (Excludes downloadable emblems.) |
| Giant Killing (Bronze) | Awarded for destroying LLL. |
| Mercenary (Bronze) | Awarded for accepting and going on a job as a mercenary. |

NEW!

A
B
C
D
E
F
G
H
I
J
K
L
M
N
O
P
Q
R
S
T
U
V
W
X
Y
Z

| | |
|---|---|
| Migrant (Bronze) | Awarded for raising your money to 10 million Au or more. |
| MoH (Bronze) | Awarded for wiping out MoH. |
| Operator (Bronze) | Awarded for leading your team to victory on a Conquest Mission or Territory Mission. |
| Order Mission (Bronze) | Awarded for completing at least one Order Mission. |
| Overlord (Bronze) | Awarded for holding ten different territories at the same time. |
| Perfect Mission (Bronze) | Awarded for completing emergency Territory/Conquest Mission w/four or more members, all surviving. |
| Rookie (Bronze) | Awarded for joining a team. |
| Ruler (Gold) | Awarded for holding one territory in all areas at the same time. |
| Sea Master (Bronze) | Awarded for destroying St Elmo. |
| Story 00 (Bronze) | Awarded for completing Story Mission 00. |
| Story 01 (Bronze) | Awarded for completing Story Mission 01. |
| Story 02 (Bronze) | Awarded for completing Story Mission 02. |
| Story 03 (Bronze) | Awarded for completing Story Mission 03. |
| Story 04 (Bronze) | Awarded for completing Story Mission 04. |
| Story 05 (Bronze) | Awarded for completing Story Mission 05. |
| Story 06 (Bronze) | Awarded for completing Story Mission 06. |
| Story 07 (Bronze) | Awarded for completing Story Mission 07. |
| Story 08 (Bronze) | Awarded for completing Story Mission 08. |
| Story 09 (Bronze) | Awarded for completing Story Mission 09. |
| Story Master (Gold) | Awarded for completing all Story Missions with Rank S. |
| Subquest Master (Gold) | Awarded for completing all Story Mission and Order Mission subquests. |
| Subquests 30% (Bronze) | Awarded for completing 30% of all Story Mission and Order Mission subquests. |
| Subquests 50% (Bronze) | Awarded for completing 50% of all Story Mission and Order Mission subquests. |
| Team Level 10 (Bronze) | Awarded for raising the team level of your team to 10 or higher. |
| Team Level 50 (Silver) | Awarded for raising the team level of your team to 50 or higher. |
| Team Sortie (Bronze) | Awarded for going on a Conquest Mission or Territory Mission with four or more team members. |
| Territorial Claim (Silver) | Awarded for claiming victory and taking territory on a Conquest Mission. |
| Territory Mission Sortie (Bronze) | Awarded for going on a Territory Mission. |
| Territory Mission Victory (Silver) | Awarded for claiming victory on a Territory Mission in an emergency state. |
| Zodiac (Silver) | Awarded for destroying all Zodiac members. |

## ARMORED CORE V (XBOX 360)

### ACHIEVEMENT

| UNLOCKABLE | HOW TO UNLOCK |
|---|---|
| A Job Well Done (10) | Awarded for successfully completing a job as a mercenary. |

| | |
|---|---|
| **AC Wrecker (15)** | Awarded for winning a battle against an AC. Any type of mission counts. |
| **Accomplish Territory Mission (10)** | Awarded for claiming victory on a Territory Mission. |
| **Air Master (30)** | Awarded for destroying Raijin. |
| **Assembler (5)** | Awarded for assembling an AC in a workshop. |
| **Blackbird (30)** | Awarded for destroying Exusia. |
| **Charge Master (5)** | Awarded for destroying an enemy with a boost charge. Any type of enemy counts. |
| **Color Customizer (5)** | Awarded for setting an AC's coloring in a workshop. |
| **Communicator (5)** | Awarded for editing a message from the team member list. |
| **Complete Custom Part (15)** | Awarded for continuing to use an arm unit to maximize its performance. |
| **Complete Order Missions (40)** | Awarded for completing all Order Missions. |
| **Complete Story Missions (50)** | Awarded for completing all Story Missions. |
| **Conquest Mission Sortie (5)** | Awarded for going on a Conquest Mission. |
| **Conquest Mission Victory (30)** | Awarded for claiming victory on a Conquest Mission. |
| **Customize Territory (10)** | Awarded for acquiring territory and placing gun batteries. |
| **Earth Master (30)** | Awarded for destroying Type D No. 5. |
| **Emblem Designer (5)** | Awarded for editing an emblem in a workshop. |
| **Emblem Master (30)** | Awarded for getting all emblems and emblem pieces by buying them at the shop and/or destroying ACs. (Excludes downloadable emblems.) |
| **Giant Killing (30)** | Awarded for destroying LLL. |
| **Mercenary (5)** | Awarded for accepting and going on a job as a mercenary. |
| **Migrant (20)** | Awarded for raising your money to 10 million Au or more. |
| **MoH (30)** | Awarded for wiping out MoH. |
| **Operator (15)** | Awarded for leading your team to victory on a Conquest Mission or Territory Mission. |
| **Order Mission (10)** | Awarded for completing at least one Order Mission. |
| **Overlord (30)** | Awarded for holding ten different territories at the same time. |
| **Perfect Mission (30)** | Awarded for completing emergency Territory/ Conquest Mission w/four or more members, all surviving. |
| **Rookie (5)** | Awarded for joining a team. |
| **Ruler (50)** | Awarded for holding one territory in all areas at the same time. |
| **Sea Master (30)** | Awarded for destroying St Elmo. |
| **Story 00 (10)** | Awarded for completing Story Mission 00. |
| **Story 01 (10)** | Awarded for completing Story Mission 01. |
| **Story 02 (10)** | Awarded for completing Story Mission 02. |
| **Story 03 (10)** | Awarded for completing Story Mission 03. |

NEW!

A B C D E F G H I J K L M N O P Q R S T U V W X Y Z

| | |
|---|---|
| **Story 04 (10)** | Awarded for completing Story Mission 04. |
| **Story 05 (10)** | Awarded for completing Story Mission 05. |
| **Story 06 (10)** | Awarded for completing Story Mission 06. |
| **Story 07 (10)** | Awarded for completing Story Mission 07. |
| **Story 08 (10)** | Awarded for completing Story Mission 08. |
| **Story 09 (10)** | Awarded for completing Story Mission 09. |
| **Story Master (50)** | Awarded for completing all Story Missions with Rank S. |
| **Subquest Master (50)** | Awarded for completing all Story Mission and Order Mission subquests. |
| **Subquests 30% (20)** | Awarded for completing 30% of all Story Mission and Order Mission subquests. |
| **Subquests 50% (20)** | Awarded for completing 50% of all Story Mission and Order Mission subquests. |
| **Team Level 10 (15)** | Awarded for raising the team level of your team to 10 or higher. |
| **Team Level 50 (40)** | Awarded for raising the team level of your team to 50 or higher. |
| **Team Sortie (15)** | Awarded for going on a Conquest Mission or Territory Mission with four or more team members. |
| **Territorial Claim (30)** | Awarded for claiming victory and taking territory on a Conquest Mission. |
| **Territory Mission Sortie (5)** | Awarded for going on a Territory Mission. |
| **Territory Mission Victory (30)** | Awarded for claiming victory on a Territory Mission in an emergency state. |
| **Zodiac (40)** | Awarded for destroying all Zodiac members. |

## ARMY CORPS OF HELL   (PlayStation Vita)

### TROPHY

| UNLOCKABLE | HOW TO UNLOCK |
|---|---|
| **Alchemist of Hell (Gold)** | Alchemized all possible weapons, armor, and items. |
| **Bastion of Bloodshed (Silver)** | Completely filled the Demonic Compendium. |
| **Champion of Courage (Bronze)** | Alchemized equipment for spearmen. |
| **Cleanser of Hell (Gold)** | Crushed 3,000 foes. |
| **Demon God's Bane (Silver)** | Defeated all bosses. |
| **Eternal Reaper (Silver)** | Crushed 1,000 foes. |
| **Grim Trailer (Silver)** | Achieved an overall platinum rating ten or more times. |
| **Hell's Magi (Bronze)** | Cleared a stage between 11 and 20 with magi only. |
| **Hell's Serenader (Bronze)** | Achieved the maximum rating (excellent) in one of the musical instrument mini-games. |
| **Hell's Soldiers (Bronze)** | Cleared a stage between 11 and 20 with soldiers only. |
| **Hell's Spearmen (Bronze)** | Cleared a stage between 11 and 20 with spearmen only. |
| **Infamy of Hell (Bronze)** | Cleared a stage between 11 and 20 with an overall platinum rating. |
| **Infamy of Purgatory (Silver)** | Cleared a Purgatory stage (21-30) with an overall platinum rating. |
| **Infamy of Tartarus (Gold)** | Cleared a Tartarus stage (31-40) with an overall platinum rating. |

| | |
|---|---|
| Lord of Hell (Bronze) | Cleared up to stage 20. |
| Lord of Purgatory (Silver) | Cleared all Purgatory stages (21-30). |
| Lord of Tartarus (Gold) | Cleared all Tartarus stages (31-40). |
| Overlord of the Underworld (Platinum) | Obtained all trophies. |
| Pinnacle of Gore (Gold) | Exceeded 66,666 jewels in your possession. |
| Purgatory's Magi (Silver) | Cleared a Purgatory stage (21-30) with magi only. |
| Purgatory's Soldiers (Silver) | Cleared a Purgatory stage (21-30) with soldiers only. |
| Purgatory's Spearmen (Silver) | Cleared a Purgatory stage (21-30) with spearmen only. |
| Resurrection Inceptor (Bronze) | Cleared the first stage. |
| Ringleader of the Wretched (Bronze) | Alchemized first equipment for magi. |
| Sage of Antiquity (Bronze) | Alchemized first equipment for soldiers. |
| Sage of Spears (Silver) | Alchemized all weapons and armor for spearmen. |
| Sage of Staffs (Silver) | Alchemized all weaons and armor for magi. |
| Sage of Swords (Silver) | Alchemized all weapons and armor for soldiers. |
| Sage of the Abyss (Bronze) | Alchemized all consumable items. |
| Sin's Slaughterer (Bronze) | Crushed 100 foes. |

## CODES

| NAME | CODE |
|---|---|
| Gouls Attack! | G75i8K8a |
| GxSxD | GUK218Jh |
| KING'S-EVIL | KB2p3tAs |
| KNIGHTS OF ROUND | K77w3P5a |
| Rachel Mother Goose | RJ53z42i |
| Rebel-Survive | S4R29dlu (l is a capitol "i") |
| United | U541337k |

## ASPHALT: INJECTION  (PlayStation Vita)

### TROPHY

| UNLOCKABLE | HOW TO UNLOCK |
|---|---|
| 1, 2, 3 (Bronze) | Perform 3 knockdowns in 10 seconds |
| Accomplished (Gold) | Finish every race in Career Mode |
| Air Time (Bronze) | Hit at least 1 jump in each lap in a single race |
| Around the world (Gold) | Earn over 1000 drift points in a single drift |
| Asphalt Domination (Platinum) | Collect all Asphalt trophies |
| Berserk (Silver) | Perform 5 knockdowns in 20 seconds |
| Blowout (Bronze) | Finish each lap in first place in a single race |
| Bouncing Bucket (Bronze) | Jump 1000m in a single race |
| Brute (Bronze) | Knock down 10 opponents in a race |
| CARnage! (Silver) | Knock down 15 opponents in a race |
| Catapulting Clunker (Silver) | Jump 1500m in a single race |
| Collection Master (Bronze) | Collect more than half of the purple cash items in a Collector race |
| Contender (Silver) | Win 10 multiplayer races |
| Drift to the beat (Bronze) | Earn over 500 drift points in a Beat 'em All race |
| Drift Warrior (Gold) | Knock down an opponent while drifting |

A
B
C
D
E
F
G
H
I
J
K
L
M
N
O
P
Q
R
S
T
U
V
W
X
Y
Z

| | |
|---|---|
| Drifter (Bronze) | Earn over 2000 drift points in a single race |
| First First! (Bronze) | Finish in 1st place! |
| Get Away From Me! (Bronze) | Complete a Normal Race without touching an opponent |
| Harasser (Bronze) | Perform at least 3 knockdowns on the same opponent |
| Legend (Gold) | Win 100 multiplayer races |
| Lickety Split (Bronze) | Collect 25 Nitro power-ups in a single race |
| Perfectionist (Silver) | Obtain the maximum amount of stars for all events in a league |
| Persistant (Bronze) | Complete 50 races |
| Photo finish (Silver) | Finish 1st in a MP race less than 1s ahead of the 2nd-place finisher |
| Safety First (Bronze) | Complete a Normal Race without crashing once |
| Shakedown (Gold) | Knock down each opponent at least once in a single race |
| Show-off (Bronze) | Cross the finish line while drifting |
| Spotless (Bronze) | Complete a Normal Race without touching a wall |
| Survivor (Bronze) | Win an Under Pressure race without crashing once |
| Three in a Row! (Bronze) | Finish in 1st place 3 times in a row! |
| Tire-Greater (Silver) | Earn over 3000 drift points in a single race |
| Too Good (Bronze) | Win a race without using Nitro |
| Velocius (Silver) | Collect 35 Nitro power-ups in a single race |
| Veteran (Silver) | Complete 100 multiplayer races |

## ASURA'S WRATH (PlayStation 3)

### TROPHY

| UNLOCKABLE | HOW TO UNLOCK |
|---|---|
| Platinum (Platinum) | Obtain all trophies. |
| A Cry of Anger (Bronze) | Activate Burst 50 times. |
| A Roar of Fury (Bronze) | Activate Burst 100 times. |
| Hit'Em Hard (Bronze) | Defeat 100 enemies with a special attack. |
| Hit'Em Harder (Bronze) | Defeat 300 enemies with a special attack. |
| Can't Touch This (Bronze) | Perform 50 counterattacks. |
| Can't Touch That (Bronze) | Perform 100 counterattacks. |
| They Don't Stand a Chance (Bronze) | Defeat 50 enemies while in Unlimited Mode. |
| Unstoppable Force (Bronze) | Defeat 100 enemies while in Unlimited Mode. |
| Taking Out the Trash (Bronze) | Defeat 300 enemies with heavy attacks and/or lock-on fire. |
| Quick on the Draw (Bronze) | Achieve 70 EXCELLENT synchronic impact rankings. |
| Lightning Reflexes (Bronze) | Achieve 150 EXCELLENT synchronic impact rankings. |
| Be the Fist (Bronze) | Achieve an overall synchronic rate average of 80% on any difficulty. |
| Pain Is Universal (Bronze) | Accumulate a total of 10000 of damage. |
| Too Legit to Quit (Bronze) | Continue the game after falling in battle. |
| Look Ma, No Eyes! (Silver) | Complete the game with the Blind Master gauge equipped. |
| Who Needs Health? (Gold) | Complete the game with the Mortal gauge equipped. |
| Ka-ching! (Silver) | Accumulate a total of 120000 Battle points. |

| View of the Valley (Bronze) | Continue to stare at the hot spring attendant's assets. |
| Like a Fish (Bronze) | Consume more alcohol than you should. |
| Sometimes I Feel Like... (Bronze) | Find all the peeping Doji at the hot spring. |
| Shut Up, Wyzen! (Bronze) | Interrupt Wyzen's monologue. |
| Shut Up, Kalrow! (Bronze) | Interrupt Kalrow's monologue. |
| Shut Up, Augus! (Bronze) | Interrupt Augus' monologue. |

## ASURA'S WRATH (XBOX 360)

### ACHIEVEMENT

| UNLOCKABLE | HOW TO UNLOCK |
|---|---|
| A Cry of Anger (15) | Activate Burst a certain number of times. |
| A Roar of Fury (20) | Activate Burst a certain number of times. |
| Hit'Em Hard (15) | Defeat a certain number of enemies with a special attack. |
| Hit'Em Harder (20) | Defeat a certain number of enemies with a special attack. |
| Can't Touch This (15) | Perform a certain number of counterattacks. |
| Can't Touch That (20) | Perform a certain number of counterattacks. |
| They Don't Stand a Chance (15) | Defeat a certain number of enemies while in Unlimited Mode. |
| Unstoppable Force (20) | Defeat a certain number of enemies while in Unlimited Mode. |
| Taking Out the Trash (15) | Defeat a certain number of enemies with heavy attacks, lock-on fire, or both. |
| Quick on the Draw (15) | Achieve a certain number of EXCELLENT synchronic impact rankings. |
| Lightning Reflexes (20) | Achieve a certain number of EXCELLENT synchronic impact rankings. |
| Be the Fist (20) | Achieve a certain percentage for your overall synchronic rate average. |
| Pain Is Universal (15) | Prove that you can take a beating. |
| Too Legit to Quit (15) | If at first you don't succeed... |
| Look Ma, No Eyes! (30) | Complete all episodes with a certain gauge equipped. |
| Who Needs Health? (90) | Complete all episodes with a certain gauge equipped. |
| Ka-ching! (30) | Accumulate a certain number of battle points. |
| View of the Valley (15) | When visiting the hot spring , look at the hostess' chest. |
| Like a Fish (15) | Knock back a few bottles. |
| Sometimes I Feel Like... (15) | Find all the peeping toms at the hot spring. |
| Shut Up, Wyzen! (15) | Interrupt the fat one's monologue. |
| Shut Up, Kalrow! (15) | Interrupt the old one's monologue. |
| Shut Up, Augus! (15) | Interrupt your former master's monologue. |

## ATELIER MERURU: THE APPRENTICE OF ARLAND (PlayStation 3)

### TROPHY

| UNLOCKABLE | HOW TO UNLOCK |
|---|---|
| A Rich Nation (Silver) | Make Arls rich, developing it into an agricultural powerhouse. |
| Admission Ceremony (Bronze) | Reach the initial goal and help Arls merge with Arland. |
| Alchemist! (Gold) | Become an alchemist of Arland and open Atelier Meruru. |

**CODES & CHEATS**

| | |
|---|---|
| All Trophies Earned (Platinum) | Obtain all trophies. |
| Atelier Totori (Current) (Bronze) | Hear the stories of Miss Totori and her friends. |
| Boy's Bath (Silver) | Transform Arls into a grand vacation paradise. |
| Brothers Together (Bronze) | Witness Lias bask in the glow of Rufus's approval. |
| Castle Life (Silver) | Return to your boring life in the castle. |
| Certain Sisters (Bronze) | Take a peek at Filly and Esty's intimate sisterhood. |
| Changing the Past (Bronze) | Bring closure to the tragedy of Arls. |
| Closer to God (Bronze) | Stare into the abyss and win out against the evil goddess. |
| Drunkard Legend EX (Bronze) | Suffer the indignity of a drunk's advances at the tavern. |
| End of the Duel (Bronze) | Encounter a master-pupil showdown between Sterk and Gino. |
| Finally, As Planned (Silver) | Make friends with the forever-14 Rorolina Frixell. |
| Friendship, Love (Bronze) | Help Totori and Mimi get along. |
| Girl's Bath (Bronze) | Visit the hot spring with a group of all girls. |
| God of the Forest (Bronze) | Put the energetic spirit of the tree into an eternal slumber. |
| How Do I Look...? (Bronze) | Force Keina to wear some princessly clothes. |
| Look into the Past (Bronze) | Glimpse Gio lost in thought at the fort. |
| Masked Man Reappears (Bronze) | Run into Arland's manly masked crusader. |
| Meruru Statue Complete! (Gold) | Construct a statue of Meruru to mark your achievements. |
| Miss Popular (Gold) | Gain popularity with everyone. |
| Now, Go Bravely (Silver) | Arm Arls to the teeth and take command of it all. |
| Ominous Box (Bronze) | Battle the coffin-bound monster in the mine and emerge victorious. |
| One from the Sky (Bronze) | Ascend to the ancient city and cast down the ruler of the sky. |
| One Normal Day (Bronze) | Let Keina help you change at the workshop. |
| Pie Shop Opens (Bronze) | Construct a Pie Shop and visit with Rorona. |
| Presence of the Flame (Bronze) | Subdue the Volcano Incarnate. |
| Resemblance (Bronze) | Find Rufus and Sterk getting along at the tavern. |
| Rorona Introduction (Bronze) | Watch as a legendary alchemist and her troupe visit the workshop. |
| Secret Tea Party (Bronze) | Stumble upon Rufus's solitary tea time. |
| Stars Never Change (Bronze) | Gaze at a starry night sky with Keina and reminisce about the past. |
| Strongest Princess (Gold) | Become a hero and the land's strongest princess. |
| Topsy-Turvy (Gold) | Take Arls's population to the limit and turn it into a superpower. |
| Waterside Encounter (Bronze) | Discover Hanna as she bathes. |
| Witch's Tea Party (Gold) | Master alchemy and together become feared as the Four Witches. |

## BATTLESHIP (PlayStation 3)

### TROPHY

| UNLOCKABLE | HOW TO UNLOCK |
|---|---|
| A Global Force (Platinum) | Collect all Trophies. |
| Arleigh Burke (Silver) | Destroy 20 enemy ships with the USS John Quincy Adams. |

| Bombs away! (Bronze) | Downed 5 enemies with one support call. |
|---|---|
| Brought a Knife to a Gun Fight? (Bronze) | Downed a Thug with the pistol. |
| Down But Not Out! (Bronze) | Recover 5 ships. |
| E.O.D. (Bronze) | Disarm or plant 20 charges. |
| Earth's Hero (Gold) | Complete the game on any Difficulty. |
| Escort (Silver) | Complete "Retaliation" on any Difficulty. |
| Extra Credit (Bronze) | Downed 3 or more enemies with one shot from the Railgun. |
| Fire in the Hole! (Bronze) | Down 40 enemies with Grenades. |
| Fish In A Barrel (Silver) | Down 40 enemies that are stunned by the LRAD. |
| High Velocity (Silver) | Down 40 enemies with the Alien Railgun. |
| Incoming! (Bronze) | Used your first support call. |
| Infestation (Bronze) | Complete "Overrun" on any Difficulty. |
| Iowa (Silver) | Destroy 20 enemy ships with the USS Missouri. |
| Lawnmower (Silver) | Down 40 enemies with the KRAW. |
| Locked and Loaded (Bronze) | Fully outfit a ship with the maximum number of Wild cards available. |
| Los Angeles (Silver) | Destroy 20 enemy ships with the USS Laredo. |
| Mighty Mo (Bronze) | Complete "The Big Guns" on any Difficulty. |
| Naval Mastery (Bronze) | Occupied all support positions in "Overrun". |
| Navy Cross (Gold) | Complete the game on Admiral Difficulty. |
| Navy Distinguished Service (Gold) | Complete the game on Captain Difficulty or higher. |
| No Man Left Behind (Silver) | Complete "They're Back!" on any Difficulty. |
| Officer of the Deck (Bronze) | Defeated 40 enemy vessels in Ship Control gameplay. |
| Oliver Hazard Perry (Silver) | Destroy 10 enemy ships with the USS Chesapeake. |
| PEGS! (Bronze) | Found all 28 hidden pegs. |
| Quick Draw (Silver) | Down 40 enemies with the Pistol. |
| Rain of Fire (Gold) | Down 200 enemies with artillery support calls. |
| Sharp Shooter (Silver) | Down 40 enemies with the Carbine. |
| The Bigger They Are... (Silver) | Complete "End Game" on any Difficulty. |
| The Dome (Bronze) | Complete "Construction" on any Difficulty. |
| Ticonderoga (Silver) | Destroy 20 enemy ships with the USS Yukon. |
| Up Close and Personal (Silver) | Down 40 enemies with the Shotgun. |
| Welcome to the Islands (Bronze) | Complete "The Arrival" on any Difficulty. |

## BATTLESHIP (XBOX 360)

### ACHIEVEMENT

| UNLOCKABLE | HOW TO UNLOCK |
|---|---|
| Arleigh Burke (30) | Destroyed 20 enemy ships with the USS John Quincy Adams. |
| Bombs away! (15) | Downed 5 enemies with one support call. |
| Brought a Knife to a Gun Fight? (10) | Downed a Thug with the pistol. |

| | |
|---|---|
| **Down But Not Out! (15)** | Recovered 5 ships. |
| **E.O.D. (15)** | Disarmed or planted 20 charges. |
| **Earth's Hero (60)** | Completed the game on any Difficulty. |
| **Escort (40)** | Completed "Retaliation" on any Difficulty. |
| **Extra Credit (15)** | Downed 3 or more enemies with one shot from the Railgun. |
| **Fire in the Hole! (15)** | Downed 40 enemies with Grenades. |
| **Fish In A Barrel (30)** | Downed 40 enemies that are stunned by the LRAD. |
| **High Velocity (30)** | Downed 40 enemies with the Alien Railgun. |
| **Incoming! (10)** | Used your first support call. |
| **Infestation (30)** | Completed "Overrun" on any Difficulty. |
| **Iowa (30)** | Destroyed 20 enemy ships with the USS Missouri. |
| **Lawnmower (30)** | Downed 40 enemies with the KRAW. |
| **Locked and Loaded (20)** | Fully outfitted a ship with the maximum number of Wild cards available. |
| **Los Angeles (30)** | Destroyed 20 enemy ships with the USS Laredo. |
| **Mighty Mo (30)** | Completed "The Big Guns" on any Difficulty. |
| **Navy Cross (100)** | Completed the game on Admiral Difficulty. |
| **Navy Distinguished Service (60)** | Completed the game on Captain Difficulty or higher. |
| **No Man Left Behind (40)** | Completed "They're Back!" on any Difficulty. |
| **Officer of the Deck (20)** | Defeated 40 enemy vessels in Ship Control gameplay. |
| **Oliver Hazard Perry (30)** | Destroyed 10 enemy ships with the USS Chesapeake. |
| **PEGS! (15)** | Found all 28 hidden pegs. |
| **Quick Draw (30)** | Downed 40 enemies with the Pistol. |
| **Rain of Fire (50)** | Downed 200 enemies with artillery support calls. |
| **Sharp Shooter (30)** | Downed 40 enemies with the Carbine. |
| **The Bigger They Are... (40)** | Completed "End Game" on any Difficulty. |
| **The Dome (30)** | Completed "Construction" on any Difficulty. |
| **Ticonderoga (30)** | Destroyed 20 enemy ships with the USS Yukon. |
| **Up Close and Personal (30)** | Downed 40 enemies with the Shotgun. |
| **Welcome to the Islands (30)** | Completed "The Arrival" on any Difficulty. |

## BEN 10: GALACTIC RACING (PlayStation Vita)

### TROPHY

| UNLOCKABLE | HOW TO UNLOCK |
|---|---|
| **Absolutely Smashing (Bronze)** | Successfully bump an opponent by landing on him in Single Player mode. |
| **Air Show (Bronze)** | Take out an opponent with a power-up while the opponent is airborne in Single Player mode. |
| **Alien Force (Bronze)** | Successfully bump 50 karts in Single Player mode. |
| **Beat the Clock (Bronze)** | Escape elimination in an Ultimate Elimination showdown with less than 10 seconds on the clock in Single Player mode. |
| **Beginner's Luck Complete (Bronze)** | Complete the Beginner's Luck circuit in third place or higher in Single Player mode. |

| | |
|---|---|
| **Big Air (Bronze)** | Complete a jump with an air time of 3 seconds in a race in Single Player mode. |
| **Boom! Winning! (Silver)** | Successfully hit every opponent in a race at least once with any Power-Up in Single Player mode. |
| **Bumper Karts (Bronze)** | Successfully bump 25 karts in Single Player mode. |
| **Close Call (Bronze)** | Win a race by less than a second in Single Player mode. |
| **Codon Infusion (Gold)** | Unlock all characters in the game. |
| **Counter Measure (Bronze)** | Destroy an incoming attack by firing an attack of your own in Single Player mode. |
| **Double Trouble (Bronze)** | Complete 10 2X stunt combos while racing in Single Player mode. |
| **Driverus Primus (Bronze)** | Beat the Track Best time in a Time Trial on any Primus track. |
| **Freezeway Jungle Complete (Bronze)** | Complete the Freezeway Jungle circuit in third place or higher in Single Player mode. |
| **Galactic Racing Champion (Silver)** | Win a trophy on every circuit in Single Player mode. |
| **Get My Drift? (Bronze)** | Execute a 500-meter drift in a race in Single Player mode. |
| **Give 'Em the Slip (Bronze)** | Pass an opponent while drifting in Single Player mode. |
| **Got Skillz (Bronze)** | Beat the Track Best time in a Time Trial on any track by 10 seconds or more. |
| **Ice Water Expanse Complete (Bronze)** | Complete the Ice Water Expanse circuit in third place or higher in Single Player mode. |
| **Infinity Circuit Complete (Bronze)** | Complete the Infinity Circuit in third place or higher in Single Player mode. |
| **Kart Collector (Silver)** | Unlock all karts in the game. |
| **Kineceleration (Bronze)** | Execute a continuous boost of 8 seconds or more in a race in Single Player mode. |
| **Leapfrog (Bronze)** | Pass an opponent by jumping over/past them in Single Player mode. |
| **Missed Me! (Bronze)** | Finish a race in first, second, or third place without being affected by an enemy attack in Single Player mode. |
| **Not Even a Scratch (Bronze)** | Block/avoid 100 attacks using your Defensive Power in Single Player mode. |
| **Nothin' But Maximum Skill (Silver)** | Win a race on any Advanced track without using an Omni-Node or Offensive Power in Single Player mode. |
| **Nothin' But More Skill (Bronze)** | Win a race on any Intermediate track without using an Omni-Node or Offensive Power in Single Player mode. |
| **Nothin' But Skill (Bronze)** | Win a race on any Basic track without using an Omni-Node or Offensive Power in Single Player mode. |
| **Null Prime Complete (Bronze)** | Complete the Null Prime circuit in third place or higher in Single Player mode. |
| **Omni-Node Master (Silver)** | Pick up 8 different Omni-Node types in each of 10 different races in Single Player mode. |
| **Omni-Trickster (Silver)** | Complete 10 4X stunt combos while racing in Single Player mode. |
| **On the Right Track (Silver)** | Unlock all grand prix tracks. |
| **Outta My Way!!!!! (Silver)** | Successfully bump 100 karts in Single Player mode. |

NEW!

A
B
C
D
E
F
G
H
I
J
K
L
M
N
O
P
Q
R
S
T
U
V
W
X
Y
Z

| Prime Drifter (Bronze) | Execute a 750-meter drift in a race in Single Player mode. |
| Primus Dominus Complete (Bronze) | Complete the Primus Dominus circuit in third place or higher in Single Player mode. |
| Shattered (Bronze) | Destroy 10 Shard Mines using the EMP power-up in Single Player mode. |
| Showdowns Galore (Silver) | Unlock all arena tracks. |
| Snow Drifter (Bronze) | Beat the Track Best time in a Time Trial on any Kylmyys track. |
| Tag! I'm It! (Bronze) | Win 10 individual Omni-Tag showdowns in Single Player mode. |
| Tag! We're It! (Bronze) | Win 10 Team Omni-Tag showdowns in Single Player mode. |
| Trash Truckin' (Bronze) | Beat the Track Best time in a Time Trial on any Vulpin track. |
| Triple Threat (Bronze) | Complete 10 3X stunt combos while racing in Single Player mode. |
| Ultimate Alienator (Bronze) | Win 10 Ultimate Alienation showdowns in Single Player mode. |
| Ultimate Racer! (Platinum) | Earn all trophies in the game. |
| Ultimate Trophy Room (Gold) | Win a first place trophy on every circuit in Single Player mode. |
| Unstoppable! (Bronze) | Win a race by tumbling or spinning over the finish line in Single Player mode. |
| Volcano Void Complete (Bronze) | Complete the Volcano Void circuit in third place or higher in Single Player mode. |
| Warp Driver (Bronze) | Beat the Track Best time in a Time Trial on any Null Void track. |
| Wave Runner (Bronze) | Beat the Track Best time in a Time Trial on any Piscciss track. |
| Way Bigger Air (Bronze) | Complete a jump with an air time of 4 seconds or more in a race in Single Player mode. |
| Wet Wasteland Complete (Bronze) | Complete the Wet Wasteland circuit in third place or higher in Single Player mode. |

## BIRDS OF STEEL (PlayStation 3)

### TROPHY

| UNLOCKABLE | HOW TO UNLOCK |
| --- | --- |
| Bird of Steel (Platinum) | Earn all available Trophies for Birds of Steel. |
| Blitz Attack (Bronze) | Destroy 6 enemy bombers before they reach the Wake in the mission "Japanese Raid". |
| Bombshell (Bronze) | Damage destroyer with machine gun fire in the mission "Invasion of Tulagi". |
| Brave Spirit (Silver) | Win a battle against superior forces in Versus mode. |
| Choose Your Favorite (Bronze) | Fly in one of each country's planes. |
| Combat Pilot (Bronze) | Earn the fifth rank. |
| Coral Sea (Bronze) | Complete the American chapter "Battle of the Coral Sea". |
| Defender (Bronze) | Destroy 3 enemy bombers in each wave on Realistic difficulty in the "First Carrier Fleet" mission. |
| Eagle-Eyed (Bronze) | Find the TF-17 carrier fleet in the "Counterattack" mission. |
| Fast and Furious (Bronze) | Complete the first objective in less than 5 minutes in the "Tulagi Landing" mission. |

| | |
|---|---|
| **First Wave (Bronze)** | Destroy all vehicles on Wheeler Field in the mission "First Wave". |
| **Formation Keeper (Bronze)** | Stay near the flight leader all the way to the enemy fleet in the "American Strike" mission. |
| **From The Far East (Gold)** | Complete the Japanese Historical campaign. |
| **Good Start (Silver)** | Receive 5 medals. |
| **Guadalcanal (Bronze)** | Complete the Japanese chapter "Guadalcanal Campaign". |
| **Half-Way (Silver)** | Earn the tenth rank. |
| **Hedgehopper (Bronze)** | Destroy 5 light targets on Midway Island on Simulator difficulty in the "Midway Atoll" mission. |
| **It Was Easy (Bronze)** | Land on an aircraft carrier. |
| **Killer (Bronze)** | Kill 15 enemy infantry units in the "Battle for Henderson Field" mission. |
| **Kuban (Bronze)** | Complete any mission in the Single Missions chapter "Battle for the Kuban". |
| **Leader (Silver)** | Win a battle in Versus mode as the leader. |
| **Make a Flight (Bronze)** | Complete any mission in CO-OP mode. |
| **Malta (Bronze)** | Complete any mission in the Single Missions chapter "Siege of Malta". |
| **Midway Atoll (Bronze)** | Complete the Japanese chapter "Battle of Midway". |
| **New Decal (Bronze)** | Earn any decal for your plane. |
| **New Guinea (Bronze)** | Complete any mission in the Single Missions chapter "New Guinea Campaign". |
| **New Record (Silver)** | Destroy 100 planes. |
| **New Skin (Bronze)** | Earn any skin for your plane. |
| **New Weapon (Silver)** | Destroy 100 ground units. |
| **Not a Victim (Bronze)** | Destroy two hostile fighters with the rear gunner in the mission "To Scratch One Flat-top". |
| **One of a Few (Bronze)** | Land on the Zuikaku at the end of the "Battle of South Pacific" mission on Realistic difficulty. |
| **Pearl Harbor (Bronze)** | Complete the Japanese chapter "Attack on Pearl Harbor". |
| **Preparing (Bronze)** | Complete the Pre-War chapter. |
| **Return to Oahu (Bronze)** | Make "Touch and Go" on Ford Island in the mission "Return to Oahu". |
| **Rookie (Bronze)** | Earn the second rank. |
| **Ruhr (Bronze)** | Complete any mission in the Single Missions chapter "Battle of Ruhr". |
| **Second Breath (Bronze)** | Rearm on the airfield between attacks on hostile ships in the mission "American Counterattack". |
| **Second Wave (Bronze)** | Bomb two different targets by one loadout in the mission "Second Wave". |
| **Sentinel (Bronze)** | Don't let enemy fighters destroy any bomber of your group in the mission "Attack on Lexington". |
| **Sharp Shooter (Bronze)** | Destroy 5 enemy planes on Realistic difficulty in the "Battle of the Eastern Solomons" mission. |
| **Survivor (Bronze)** | Land your damaged aircraft on the airfield in the mission "The Two Against Thirty-Nine". |
| **Take-Off (Bronze)** | Take off. |

A B C D E F G H I J K L M N O P Q R S T U V W X Y Z

| | |
|---|---|
| The Australian (Silver) | Fly in each Australian plane. |
| The Italian (Silver) | Fly in each Italian plane. |
| To The Far East (Gold) | Complete the American Historical campaign. |
| Total Annihilation (Bronze) | Destroy at least 20 enemy bombers in the "Battle of the Santa Cruz" mission. |
| Untouchable (Bronze) | Don't die in the mission "Shokaku Defense". |
| Wake Island (Bronze) | Complete the American chapter "Battle of Wake Island". |
| Way of the Sun (Bronze) | Complete the 1st secondary mission objective in the "Fate of Hiryu" mission. |
| Winner (Bronze) | Complete any Dynamic campaign. |
| You Will Be Ace (Bronze) | Destroy 4 planes in Versus mode. |

## BINARY DOMAIN (PlayStation 3)

### TROPHY

| UNLOCKABLE | HOW TO UNLOCK |
|---|---|
| A Friend Indeed (Bronze) | Purchase nanomachines for a teammate. |
| All Members (Bronze) | Add each teammate to the party at least once. |
| Assault Shooter Killer (Bronze) | Destroy 100 Assault Shooters in Campaign. |
| Battlemaster (Bronze) | Win an online vs. match with all rule sets. |
| Challenge Master (Gold) | Clear all online mode challenges. |
| Craftsman (Bronze) | Fully upgrade one weapon category. |
| Data Collector (Bronze) | Collect 20 SECURITY-COM in Campaign. |
| Data Retrieval Complete (Silver) | Collect all SECURITY-COM in Campaign. |
| First Victory (Bronze) | Win an online vs. match with any rule set. |
| Hacker (Bronze) | Destroy all enemies with the mobile gun battery. |
| Headshot Master (Bronze) | Get 50 headshot bonuses in Campaign. |
| Jackpot (Bronze) | Hit the jackpot on a vending machine. |
| Jumper (Bronze) | Get onto the Grand Lancer's head. |
| Lifesaver (Bronze) | Use first-aid kits to revive teammates 10 times. |
| Multi-Kill Master (Bronze) | Get 50 multi-kill bonuses in Campaign. |
| One-Shot Master (Bronze) | Get 50 one-shot bonuses in Campaign. |
| Platinum Trophy (Platinum) | Earn all other trophies in the game. |
| Resistance Hero (Bronze) | Clear all stages in INVASION mode. |
| Rust Crew (Silver) | Clear all chapters on SURVIVOR Mode. |
| Shop Master (Bronze) | Access all shopping terminals. |
| Skill Master (Silver) | Get all nanomachines within 1 playthrough in Campaign. |
| Smash Master (Bronze) | Get 50 smash bonuses in Campaign. |
| Spend 10,000 credits at vending machines | Spend 10,000 credits at vending machines. |
| Spider Killer (Bronze) | Destroy all of the Spider's legs. |
| Still Alive (Bronze) | Clear a stage in INVASION mode. |
| Tactician (Bronze) | Get enemies to kill each other 50 times. |
| Transport Takedown (Bronze) | Destroy the Iron Whale's four engines. |
| Veteran Soldier (Silver) | Reach online level 50. |
| Weapon Crafter (Bronze) | Upgrade a weapon. |

## BINARY DOMAIN (XBOX 360)

### ACHIEVEMENT

| UNLOCKABLE | HOW TO UNLOCK |
|---|---|
| A Friend Indeed (15) | Purchase nanomachines for a teammate. |
| All Members (20) | Add each teammate to the party at least once. |
| Assault Shooter Killer (15) | Destroy 100 Assault Shooters in Campaign. |
| Battlemaster (30) | Win an Xbox LIVE vs. match with all rule sets. |
| Challenge Master (50) | Clear all Xbox LIVE mode challenges. |
| Completion (5) | Earn all other achievements in the game. |
| Craftsman (30) | Fully upgrade one weapon category. |
| Data Collector (30) | Collect 20 SECURITY-COM in Campaign. |
| Data Retrieval Complete (30) | Collect all SECURITY-COM in Campaign. |
| First Victory (15) | Win an online vs. match with any rule set. |
| Hacker (15) | Destroy all enemies with the mobile gun battery. |
| Headshot Master (20) | Get 50 headshot bonuses in Campaign. |
| Jackpot (15) | Hit the jackpot on a vending machine. |
| Jumper (10) | Get onto the Grand Lancer's head. |
| Lifesaver (10) | Use first-aid kits to revive teammates 10 times. |
| Multi-Kill Master (20) | Get 50 multi-kill bonuses in Campaign. |
| One-Shot Master (20) | Get 50 one-shot bonuses in Campaign. |
| Resistance Hero (30) | Clear all stages in INVASION mode. |
| Rust Crew (30) | Clear all chapters on SURVIVOR Mode. |
| Shop Master (15) | Access all shopping terminals. |
| Skill Master (30) | Get all nanomachines within 1 playthrough in Campaign. |
| Smash Master (20) | Get 50 smash bonuses in Campaign. |
| Spendthrift (15) | Spend 10,000 credits at vending machines. |
| Spider Killer (15) | Destroy all of the Spider's legs. |
| Still Alive (15) | Clear a stage in INVASION mode. |
| Tactician (15) | Get enemies to kill each other 50 times. |
| Transport Takedown (15) | Destroy the Iron Whale's four engines. |
| Veteran Soldier (30) | Reach Xbox LIVE level 50. |
| Weapon Crafter (15) | Upgrade a weapon. |

## BIRDS OF STEEL (XBOX 360)

### ACHIEVEMENT

| UNLOCKABLE | HOW TO UNLOCK |
|---|---|
| Blitz Attack (10) | Destroy 6 enemy bombers before they reach the Wake in the mission "Japanese Raid". |
| Bombshell (10) | Damage destroyer with machine gun fire in the mission "Invasion of Tulagi". |
| Brave Spirit (30) | Win a battle against superior forces in Versus mode. |
| Choose Your Favorite (30) | Fly in one of each country's planes. |
| Combat Pilot (40) | Earn the fifth rank |
| Defender (10) | Destroy 3 enemy bombers in each wave on Realistic difficulty in the "First Carrier Fleet" mission. |
| Eagle-Eyed (10) | Find the TF-17 carrier fleet in the "Counterattack" mission. |
| Fast and Furious (10) | Complete the first objective in less than 5 minutes in the "Tulagi Landing" mission. |

A B C D E F G H I J K L M N O P Q R S T U V W X Y Z

| | |
|---|---|
| **First Wave (10)** | Destroy all vehicles on Wheeler Field in the mission "First Wave". |
| **Formation Keeper (10)** | Stay near the flight leader all the way to the enemy fleet in the "American Strike" mission. |
| **From The Far East (50)** | Complete the Japanese Historical campaign. |
| **Good Start (40)** | Receive 5 medals |
| **Guadalcanal (20)** | Complete the Japanese chapter "Guadalcanal Campaign". |
| **Half-Way (20)** | Earn the tenth rank |
| **Hedgehopper (10)** | Destroy 5 light targets on Midway Island on Simulator difficulty in the "Midway Atoll" mission. |
| **It Was Easy (20)** | Land on an aircraft carrier. |
| **Killer (10)** | Kill 15 enemy infantry units in the "Battle for Henderson Field" mission. |
| **Kuban (20)** | Complete any mission in the Single Missions chapter "Battle for the Kuban". |
| **Leader (30)** | Win a battle in Versus mode as the leader. |
| **Make a Flight (30)** | Complete any mission in CO-OP mode |
| **Malta (20)** | Complete any mission in the Single Missions chapter "Siege of Malta". |
| **Midway Atoll (20)** | Complete the Japanese chapter "Battle of Midway". |
| **New Decal (30)** | Earn any decal for your plane |
| **New Guinea (20)** | Complete any mission in the Single Missions chapter "New Guinea Campaign". |
| **New Record (50)** | Destroy 100 planes |
| **New Skin (30)** | Earn any skin for your plane |
| **New Weapon (50)** | Destroy 100 ground units |
| **Not a Victim (10)** | Destroy two hostile fighters with the rear gunner in the mission "To Scratch One Flat-top". |
| **One of a Few (10)** | Land on the Zuikaku at the end of the "Battle of South Pacific" mission on Realistic difficulty. |
| **Pearl Harbor (20)** | Complete the Japanese chapter "Attack on Pearl Harbor". |
| **Preparing (20)** | Complete the Pre-War chapter. |
| **Return to Oahu (10)** | Make "Touch and Go" on Ford Island in the mission "Return to Oahu". |
| **Rookie (10)** | Earn the second rank |
| **Ruhr (20)** | Complete any mission in the Single Missions chapter "Battle of Ruhr". |
| **Second Breath (10)** | Rearm on the airfield between attacks on hostile ships in the mission "American Counterattack". |
| **Second Wave (10)** | Bomb two different targets by one loadout in the mission "Second Wave". |
| **Sentinel (10)** | Don't let enemy fighters destroy any bomber of your group in the mission "Attack on Lexington". |
| **Sharp Shooter (10)** | Destroy 5 enemy planes on Realistic difficulty in the "Battle of the Eastern Solomons" mission. |
| **Survivor (10)** | Land your damaged aircraft on the airfield in the mission "The Two Against Thirty-Nine". |
| **The Australian (20)** | Fly in each Australian plane. |
| **The Coral Sea (20)** | Complete the American chapter "Battle of the Coral Sea". |
| **The Italian (20)** | Fly in each Italian plane. |
| **To The Far East (50)** | Complete the American Historical campaign. |

| | |
|---|---|
| **Total Annihilation (10)** | Destroy at least 20 enemy bombers in the "Battle of the Santa Cruz" mission. |
| **Untouchable (10)** | Don't die in the mission "Shokaku Defense". |
| **Wake Island (20)** | Complete the American chapter "Battle of Wake Island". |
| **Way of the Sun (10)** | Complete the 1st secondary mission objective in the "Fate of Hiryu" mission. |
| **Winner (20)** | Complete any Dynamic campaign |
| **You Will Be Ace (10)** | You Will Be Ace |

## BLADES OF TIME (PlayStation 3)

### TROPHY

| UNLOCKABLE | HOW TO UNLOCK |
|---|---|
| **Angry (Bronze)** | Kill 100 enemies during your Time Rewind Berserk buff. |
| **Annihilation Kill (Silver)** | Kill 10 enemies at the same time. |
| **Big Corpse (Gold)** | Defeat Giant Worm. |
| **Brutal Kill (Bronze)** | Kill 5 enemies at the same time. |
| **Brutal Lands (Gold)** | Kill the Vicar of Chaos. |
| **Clear the Jungle (Silver)** | Kill the Shaman Boss. |
| **Collector (Silver)** | Find all the notes. |
| **Coral Dash (Bronze)** | Get the ability to dash to the corals. |
| **Curious (Bronze)** | Find half the notes. |
| **Double Attack (Bronze)** | Kill 25 heavy enemies using the Time Rewind double attack. |
| **Dragon (Bronze)** | Ayumi receives her Dragon form. |
| **Enemy Dash (Bronze)** | Get the ability to dash to enemies. |
| **Experienced (Bronze)** | Play 5 Outbreak matches. |
| **Famous Hunter (Bronze)** | Kill 1000 enemies in total. |
| **Faster Than You! (Bronze)** | Use Counterattack 100 times. |
| **Free to go! (Silver)** | Kill the Gateguard. |
| **Gather Chi (Bronze)** | Get the ability to gather Chi. |
| **Grasshopper (Bronze)** | Use Dash 30 times without touching the ground. |
| **Hard Times Are Over (Gold)** | Finish the game on the Hard difficulty level. |
| **I'm Rich (Bronze)** | Find all the chests in story mode on the Normal difficulty level. |
| **Keeper Is Dead (Gold)** | Finish the game on any difficulty level. |
| **Old Temple (Bronze)** | Reach the Sanctuary. |
| **Order Spell (Bronze)** | Survive Chaos event. |
| **Out of My Way (Bronze)** | Kill an enemy player in an Outbreak match. |
| **Outbreak Hero (Silver)** | Kill each Outbreak boss at least once. |
| **Platinum (Platinum)** | Awarded for successfully collecting all trophies. |
| **Rain of Bullets (Bronze)** | Shoot off Magic Armor from 50 enemies using Time Rewind clones. |
| **Ready To Fight (Bronze)** | Find all types of equipment. |
| **Rifle (Bronze)** | Find the rifle. |
| **Sky Islands (Gold)** | Leave the Sky Islands. |
| **Time Rewind (Bronze)** | Get the ability to rewind time. |
| **Too Hot For You (Bronze)** | Kill Brutal Maul without being frozen by his shockwave. |
| **Treasure Hunter (Silver)** | Find all the chests in story mode on the Hard difficulty level. |

| Unstoppable (Bronze) | Win any Outbreak match. |
|---|---|
| World of Order (Silver) | Defeat Skyguard Commander. |
| Your Fire Is Nothing (Bronze) | Kill the Shaman Boss without taking damage from his massive fire spell. |

## BLADES OF TIME (XBOX 360)

### ACHIEVEMENT

| UNLOCKABLE | HOW TO UNLOCK |
|---|---|
| Angry (15) | Kill 100 enemies during your Time Rewind Berserk buff. |
| Annihilation Kill (30) | Kill 10 enemies at once. |
| Brutal Kill (15) | Kill 5 enemies at once. |
| Collector (30) | Find all notes. |
| Curious (15) | Find half of the notes. |
| Double Attack (15) | Kill 25 heavy enemies using the Time Rewind double attack. |
| Experienced (10) | Play 5 Outbreak matches. |
| Famous Hunter (15) | Kill 1000 enemies in total. |
| Faster Than You! (15) | Use Counterattack 100 times. |
| Grasshopper (15) | Use Dash 30 times without touching the ground. |
| I'm Rich (15) | Find all the chests in story mode on the Normal difficulty level. |
| Out of My Way (15) | Kill an enemy player in Outbreak match. |
| Outbreak Hero (30) | Kill each Outbreak boss at least once. |
| Rain of Bullets (15) | Shoot off Magic Armor from 50 enemies using Time Rewind clones. |
| Ready To Fight (15) | Find all types of equipment. |
| Too Hot For You (15) | Kill Brutal Maul without being frozen by his shockwave. |
| Treasure Hunter (30) | Find all the chests in story mode on the Hard difficulty level. |
| Unstoppable (15) | Win any Outbreak match. |

## BLAZBLUE: CONTINUUM SHIFT EXTEND (PlayStation Vita)

### TROPHY

| UNLOCKABLE | HOW TO UNLOCK |
|---|---|
| *Wheeze*...Just Getting Started (Bronze) | Increased all character stats to 50 in [Abyss] mode. |
| A Spectacle (Bronze) | Landed Carl's Vivace, Cantabile, and Allegreto during a combo. |
| Aaaaaand I'm Spent (Bronze) | Used up the Ignis gauge while fighting as Relius. |
| About Half Way (Bronze) | Defeated the boss at level 500 of the [Abyss]. |
| Abyssmal Shopaholic (Gold) | Acquired all the items from the shop in [Abyss] mode. |
| Artwork?! Gimmie! (Bronze) | Unlocked 50% of the items in the [Gallery]. |
| Better Safe Than Sorry (Bronze) | Dished out significantly more damage than the opponent's remaining HP. |
| Breaking in the New Guys (Bronze) | Finished Makoto's, Valkenhayn's, Platinum and Relius's scenarios in [Story] mode. |
| Domestic Battery (Bronze) | Using Relius, fight a battle without depleting the Ignis gauge. |
| Don't Give A Kaka (Silver) | Sucessfully executed jumping D, jumping ?+D and jumping ?+D in the middle of a combo. |

| | |
|---|---|
| **Eye of the Tiger (Bronze)** | Trained for more than 30 minutes, non-stop. |
| **Fangs for the Memories! (Bronze)** | Used Hazama's Rising, Falling and Devouring Fangs during a battle. |
| **Feels Like the First Time (Bronze)** | Won your first team [Player Match]. |
| **Fight for Survival (Bronze)** | Using Tsubaki, executed all of the 'D' versions of her special attacks in a single combo. |
| **Finger on the Button (Bronze)** | Defeated an opponent while using the Stylish Layout. |
| **Gallery Guru (Gold)** | Unlocked everything there is to see in the [Gallery]. |
| **Get Off My Lawn! (Bronze)** | Performed a 30+ hit combo using Valkenhayn. |
| **Getting Down to Abyss-ness (Silver)** | Defeated the boss at level 999 of the [Abyss]. |
| **I can't Stop Winning (Bronze)** | Won three [Ranked Matches]. |
| **I See What You Did There (Bronze)** | Played back replay data over 10 times in [Replay Theater]. |
| **Ice Ice Ice Baby (Bronze)** | Used all three of Jin's special attacks that freeze opponents in a single combo. |
| **Insecticide (Bronze)** | Summoned and used all of Arakune's bugs during a single combo. |
| **Just Getting Used To It (Silver)** | Raised any character's PSR to over 200 in a [Ranked Match] |
| **Just How I...*wheeze*...Planned (Bronze)** | Using Bang, had Fu-Rin-Ka-Zan activated for more than 30 seconds of the battle. |
| **Just the Beginning (Bronze)** | Defeated the boss level at level 100 of the [Abyss]. |
| **Kaka-kaze (Bronze)** | Have been blown up by the chibi-kakas in [Unlimited Mars] mode. |
| **Level 20 (Bronze)** | Reached level 20. |
| **Like a Boss (Bronze)** | Fought 100 matches in [Ranked Match]. |
| **Lunatic (Bronze)** | Equipped all of Luna's weapons during one round. |
| **Mars Need Winnin' (Bronze)** | Attempted [Unlimited Mars] mode over 10 times. |
| **Mastered the Basics (Bronze)** | Cleared over 50 missions in [Challenge] mode. |
| **Mastered the...Master? (Silver)** | Cleared over 100 missions in [Challenge] mode. |
| **Mind on my Money (Bronze)** | Accumulated over 100,000P$. |
| **Murakumo...AWAKEN! (Silver)** | Defeated the secret boss in [Arcade] mode. |
| **Nooooo...el! (Bronze)** | Finished off an opponent with Noel's Nemesis Stabilizer. |
| **Oh—NOW I Get It...! (Bronze)** | Finished the Calamity Trigger scenario in [Story] mode. |
| **Over 9000?! (Silver)** | Dealt over 10,000 damage to an opponent in a single combo. |
| **Plays Well With Others (Bronze)** | Fought ten team [Player Matches]. |
| **Power of the Azure (Bronze)** | Performed a 90+ hit combo using Ragna. |
| **Sharp Shooter (Silver)** | Hit the opponent with all of Litchi's Great Whell attacks. |

| | |
|---|---|
| Shocking... Positively Shocking (Bronze) | Using Rachel, shocked your opponent more than 15 times during a single combo. |
| Squirrel Power! (Bronze) | Executed Makoto's super, Particle Flare, with only Level 3 punches. |
| Tager? Don't Even Know Her! (Bronze) | Turned the tide and won a battle using Genesic Emerald Tager Buster. |
| That Will Suffice (Bronze) | Finished the [Tutorial] mode. |
| The Beginning of the End (Silver) | Finished [Score Attack] mode. |
| There's No 'I' In Team (Bronze) | Won a team elimination match without even fighting. |
| Threat Level... Escalated (Silver) | During the course of one combo, placed all four of Mu's Stein's Gunners. |
| Time to Hit the Arcades (Bronze) | Finished [Arcade] mode. |
| To Be Continued—! (Silver) | Witnessed the true ending in [Story] mode. |
| Un...believable (Platinum) | Mastered BlazBlue Continuum Shift – Extend. |
| You've Been... Terminated (Bronze) | With Lambda, summoned every type of sword during a single round. |

## BRAVE: THE VIDEO GAME (PlayStation 3)

### TROPHY

| UNLOCKABLE | HOW TO UNLOCK |
|---|---|
| Affluent (Bronze) | Accumulate a total of 5000 currency. |
| All bunched up (Bronze) | As Merida, defeat 5 enemies with a single charged shot. |
| Ante up (Bronze) | Purchase an upgrade. |
| Bowlicious (Silver) | Collect all bows. |
| Bowsome (Bronze) | Collect a bow. |
| Breezy (Bronze) | Defeat 100 enemies using the Wind charm. |
| Brilliant (Bronze) | Solve all triplet puzzles. |
| Carpet runner (Bronze) | Collect a tapestry piece. |
| Charge it up (Bronze) | Defeat 100 enemies using charged shot. |
| Clothes horse (Silver) | Collect all outfits. |
| Cooling off (Bronze) | Defeat 100 enemies using the Ice charm. |
| Digging in the dirt (Bronze) | Find the earth charm. |
| Dirty work (Bronze) | Cleanse the ring of stones. |
| Domination (Silver) | Defeat 250 enemies using power attack. |
| Earthquake (Silver) | Defeat 250 enemies using the Earth charm. |
| Everyone knows it's windy (Bronze) | Find the wind charm. |
| Full of power (Bronze) | Purchase 15 upgrades. |
| Gaelic hero (Gold) | Defeat the game on Brave difficulty, without changing it. |
| Get out of my way (Bronze) | As Elinor, charge 5 enemies with a single charge attack. |
| Gotta snag 'em all (Silver) | Purchase all upgrades. |
| Great scot (Gold) | Defeat Mor'du. |
| Heating up (Bronze) | Defeat 100 enemies using the Fire charm. |
| Hurricane (Silver) | Defeat 250 enemies using the Wind charm. |
| Ice cold (Silver) | Defeat 250 enemies using the Ice charm. |
| Ice to see you (Bronze) | Find the ice charm. |

| Impressive (Bronze) | As Merida, defeat 15 enemies in a row without taking damage. |
|---|---|
| Minimum wage (Bronze) | Accumulate a total of 1000 currency. |
| Mopping up (Bronze) | Defeat the harpy guardian. |
| Mum's the word (Bronze) | Defeat 100 enemies as Queen Elinor. |
| My fair lassie (Bronze) | Collect an outfit. |
| On Fire (Silver) | Defeat 250 enemies using the Fire charm. |
| Platinum (Platinum) | Earn all other Trophies. |
| Power hungry (Bronze) | Defeat 100 enemies using power attack. |
| Ranged only (Bronze) | Complete a level without using your sword. |
| Super bow (Silver) | Defeat 250 enemies using charged shot. |
| Swordful (Bronze) | Collect a sword. |
| Swordtacular (Silver) | Collect all swords. |
| Taking out the trash (Bronze) | Defeat the rock golem guardian. |
| Throw rug (Bronze) | Complete a tapestry. |
| Toasty (Bronze) | Find the fire charm. |
| Tremble (Bronze) | Defeat 100 enemies using the Earth charm. |
| Triple H's (Bronze) | Solve a triplet puzzle. |
| Untouchable (Silver) | As Merida, defeat 30 enemies in a row without taking damage. |
| Wall to wall carpeting (Silver) | Complete all tapestries. |
| Wealthy (Silver) | Accumulate a total of 15 000 currency. |

## BRAVE: THE VIDEO GAME (XBOX 360)

### ACHIEVEMENT

| UNLOCKABLE | HOW TO UNLOCK |
|---|---|
| Affluent (25) | Accumulate a total of 5000 currency. |
| All bunched up (25) | As Merida, defeat 5 enemies with a single charged shot. |
| Ante up (10) | Purchase an upgrade. |
| Bowlicious (25) | Collect all bows. |
| Bowsome (5) | Collect a bow. |
| Breezy (15) | Defeat 100 enemies using the wind charm. |
| Brilliant (25) | Solve all triplet puzzles. |
| Carpet runner (5) | Collect a tapestry piece. |
| Charge it up (15) | Defeat 100 enemies using charged shot. |
| Clothes horse (25) | Collect all outfits. |
| Cooling off (15) | Defeat 100 enemies using the ice charm. |
| Digging in the dirt (5) | Find the earth charm. |
| Dirty work (5) | Cleanse the ring of stones. |
| Domination (25) | Defeat 250 enemies using power attack. |
| Earthquake (25) | Defeat 250 enemies using the earth charm. |
| Everyone knows it's windy (20) | Find the wind charm. |
| Full of power (25) | Purchase 15 upgrades. |
| Gaelic hero (100) | Defeat the game on Brave difficulty, without changing it. |
| Get out of my way (25) | As Elinor, charge 5 enemies with a single charge attack. |
| Gotta snag 'em all (40) | Purchase all upgrades. |
| Great scot (50) | Defeat Mor'du. |
| Heating up (15) | Defeat 100 enemies using the fire charm. |

A
B
C
D
E
F
G
H
I
J
K
L
M
N
O
P
Q
R
S
T
U
V
W
X
Y
Z

| | |
|---|---|
| Hurricane (25) | Defeat 250 enemies using the wind charm. |
| Ice cold (25) | Defeat 250 enemies using the ice charm. |
| Ice to see you (15) | Find the ice charm. |
| Impressive (20) | As Merida, defeat 15 enemies in a row without taking damage. |
| Minimum wage (15) | Accumulate a total of 1000 currency. |
| Mopping up (35) | Defeat the harpy guardian. |
| Mum's the word (15) | Defeat 100 enemies as Queen Elinor. |
| My fair lassie (10) | Collect an outfit. |
| On Fire (25) | Defeat 250 enemies using the fire charm. |
| Power hungry (15) | Defeat 100 enemies using power attack. |
| Ranged only (25) | Complete a level without using your sword. |
| Super bow (25) | Defeat 250 enemies using charged shot. |
| Swordful (5) | Collect a sword. |
| Swordtacular (25) | Collect all swords. |
| Taking out the trash (20) | Defeat the rock golem guardian. |
| Throw rug (20) | Complete a tapestry. |
| Toasty (10) | Find the fire charm. |
| Tremble (15) | Defeat 100 enemies using the earth charm. |
| Triple H's (10) | Solve a triplet puzzle. |
| Untouchable (40) | As Merida, defeat 30 enemies in a row without taking damage. |
| Wall to wall carpeting (40) | Complete all tapestries. |
| Wealthy (40) | Accumulate a total of 15000 currency. |

## THE DARKNESS II  (PlayStation 3)

### TROPHY

| UNLOCKABLE | HOW TO UNLOCK |
|---|---|
| 2 guys 1 Pole (Bronze) | Kill 2 enemies with one javelin |
| Allies in Strange Places (Bronze) | Escape the asylum with help from the inside |
| At Home in the Dark (Gold) | Finish all chapters in New Game+ on any difficulty |
| Back in the Saddle (Bronze) | Rescue Jackie from the Iron Maiden |
| Bonnie & Clyde wannabes (Bronze) | Kill Jean-Luc Lambert and Amelie Dubois |
| Burned His Mansion (Bronze) | Kill Luigi Palladino |
| Carnie Kid (Bronze) | Earn a score of over 1000 in each of the carnival games |
| Cheque Please! (Bronze) | Survive the hit |
| Conquered the Darkness (Platinum) | Unlock all trophies |
| Coward (Bronze) | Kill Cedro Valdez |
| Cut and Run (Bronze) | Kill 50 enemies with the Demon Arm Slash attack |
| Dark Akimbo (Bronze) | Kill 100 enemies while dual wielding 2 different guns as Jackie |
| Dark Ninjutsu (Bronze) | Complete a mission as Inugami |
| Date Night (Bronze) | Protect Jenny |
| Decisions, Decisions (Bronze) | Refuse to cooperate with Victor in the Interrogation |
| Don of Darkness (Gold) | Finish the game on Don difficulty |
| Embraced the Darkness (Bronze) | In Vendettas, acquire all the talents for one character |

| Escape the Brotherhood (Bronze) | Survive the interrogation |
|---|---|
| Executioner (Bronze) | Kill 50 enemies with Executions while playing as Jackie |
| Free the Mind (Silver) | Finish the game on any difficulty |
| Hell Hath No Fury... (Bronze) | Complete a mission as Shoshanna |
| I'm Just Getting Started (Bronze) | Find and interrogate Swifty |
| Impish Delight (Bronze) | Kill 15 enemies while playing as the Darkling |
| It's 12pm Somewhere! (Bronze) | Complete a mission as Jimmy |
| Jackie's Got Talent (Bronze) | Purchase a Talent in the single player campaign |
| Karma's a Bitch (Bronze) | Kill a shielded enemy with his own shield |
| Mmmm Essence! (Bronze) | Pick up 5 Relics in the single player campaign |
| One Flew Over... (Bronze) | Return to reality...? |
| One Man Army (Bronze) | Kill 25 enemies while being dragged from the restaurant, without dying or restarting checkpoint |
| Ready for the Big Leagues (Bronze) | Kill 50 enemies with thrown objects |
| Relic Hunter (Silver) | Find all 29 Relics in the single player campaign |
| Romantic (Bronze) | Real guys know how to dance |
| Should Have Called 555-2368... (Silver) | Survive the battle against the Hell Beast |
| Skeet Shoot (Bronze) | Throw an enemy into the air and kill him with gunfire before he lands |
| Step into Hell... (Bronze) | Defeat Victor |
| Storm the Mansion (Bronze) | Take back your mansion |
| Suck it Up (Bronze) | Kill 50 enemies with Black Hole while playing as Jackie |
| Sweet Revenge (Bronze) | Avenge your Aunt Sarah |
| Talent Show (Silver) | Max out all of Jackie's Talent Trees |
| Technical difficulties (Bronze) | Kill the NewsWatch 6 team of Tom Dawson, Bud Langley and Sara Stephens |
| That's Why I'm the Boss (Bronze) | Impress Dolfo in two different ways |
| The Bird is the Word (Bronze) | Avoid being run over in the parking garage |
| The Brotherhood Crumbles (Gold) | Complete Vendettas Campaign |
| The Old Gibber (Bronze) | Kill 100 enemies with Gun Channeling while playing as Jackie |
| The Swarm King (Bronze) | Kill 50 enemies who are swarmed while playing as Jackie |
| This Kid's Got Potential (Bronze) | Max out 1 of Jackie's Talent Trees |
| Truly Talented (Bronze) | Max out 3 of Jackie's Talent Trees |
| Versatile Killer (Bronze) | Kill enemies in 5 different ways within 30 seconds |
| Voodoo is More Than Dolls (Bronze) | Complete a mission as JP |
| Whipping Boy (Bronze) | Kill Frank Marshall |
| You've Made My Hit List (Silver) | Complete 6 Hit List exclusive missions |

## THE DARKNESS II    (XBOX 360)

### ACHIEVEMENT

| UNLOCKABLE | HOW TO UNLOCK |
|---|---|
| 2 Guys 1 Pole (25) | Kill 2 enemies with one javelin |
| Allies in Strange Places (20) | Escape the asylum with help from the inside |

|  |  |
|---|---|
| At Home in the Dark (50) | Finish all chapters in New Game+ on any difficulty |
| Back in the Saddle (20) | Rescue Jackie from the Iron Maiden |
| Bonnie & Clyde Wannabes (20) | Kill Jean-Luc Lambert and Amelie Dubois |
| Burned His Mansion (20) | Kill Luigi Palladino |
| Carnie Kid (20) | Earn a score of over 1000 in each of the carnival games |
| Cheque Please! (10) | Survive the hit |
| Coward (20) | Kill Cedro Valdez |
| Cut and Run (10) | Kill 50 enemies with the Demon Arm Slash attack |
| Dark Akimbo (10) | Kill 100 enemies while dual wielding 2 different guns while playing as Jackie |
| Dark Ninjutsu (10) | Complete a mission as Inugami |
| Date Night (25) | Protect Jenny |
| Decisions, Decisions (5) | Refuse to cooperate with Victor in the Interrogation |
| Don of Darkness (100) | Finish the game on Don difficulty |
| Embraced the Darkness (25) | In Vendettas, acquire all the talents for one character |
| Escape the Brotherhood (25) | Survive the interrogation |
| Executioner (10) | Kill 50 enemies with Executions while playing as Jackie |
| Free the Mind (25) | Finish the game on any difficulty |
| Hell Hath No Fury... (10) | Complete a mission as Shoshanna |
| I'm Just Getting Started (25) | Find and interrogate Swifty |
| Impish Delight (10) | Kill 15 enemies while playing as the Darkling |
| It's 12pm Somewhere! (10) | Complete a mission as Jimmy |
| Jackie's Got Talent (5) | Purchase a Talent in the single player campaign |
| Karma's a Bitch (10) | Kill a shielded enemy with his own shield |
| Mmmm Essence! (10) | Pick up 5 Relics in the single player campaign |
| One Flew Over... (20) | Return to reality...? |
| One Man Army (10) | Kill 25 enemies while being dragged from the restaurant, without dying or restarting checkpoint |
| Ready for the Big Leagues (10) | Kill 50 enemies with thrown objects |
| Relic Hunter (50) | Find all 29 Relics in the single player campaign |
| Romantic (5) | Real guys know how to dance |
| Should Have Called 555-2368... (10) | Survive the battle against the Hell Beast |
| Skeet Shoot (10) | Throw an enemy into the air and kill him with gunfire before he lands |
| Step into Hell... (25) | Defeat Victor |
| Storm the Mansion (25) | Take back your mansion |
| Suck It Up (10) | Kill 50 enemies with Black Hole while playing as Jackie |
| Sweet Revenge (25) | Avenge your Aunt Sarah |
| Talent Show (50) | Max out all of Jackie's Talent Trees |
| Technical Difficulties (20) | Kill the NewsWatch 6 team of Tom Dawson, Bud Langley and Sara Stephens |
| That's Why I'm the Boss (15) | Impress Dolfo in two different ways |
| The Bird is the Word (5) | Avoid being run over in the parking garage |

| | |
|---|---|
| **The Brotherhood Crumbles (50)** | Complete Vendettas Campaign |
| **The Old Gibber (10)** | Kill 100 enemies with Gun Channeling while playing as Jackie |
| **The Swarm King (10)** | Kill 50 enemies who are swarmed while playing as Jackie |
| **This Kid's Got Potential (10)** | Max out 1 of Jackie's Talent Trees |
| **Truly Talented (25)** | Max out 3 of Jackie's Talent Trees |
| **Versatile Killer (20)** | Kill enemies in 5 different ways within 30 seconds |
| **Voodoo is More Than Dolls (10)** | Complete a mission as JP |
| **Whipping Boy (20)** | Kill Frank Marshall |
| **You've Made My Hit List (25)** | Complete 6 Hit List exclusive missions |

## DISGAEA 3: ABSENCE OF DETENTION (PlayStation Vita)

### TROPHY

| UNLOCKABLE | HOW TO UNLOCK |
|---|---|
| **10 Piece Combo Meal (Bronze)** | Destroy your enemies with evil teamwork! |
| **A Single Step (Bronze)** | Welcome to Disgaea 3: Absence of Detention! We welcome new and returning players alike! Enjoy! |
| **All-Pro Receiver (Bronze)** | Let's cross this continent! |
| **Arcarnageologist (Gold)** | Reaching the 100th floor...in Carnage! |
| **As the World Turns (Bronze)** | If it spins, it's only natural to want to spin it. |
| **BGM Lover (Bronze)** | How 'bout buying some music for a change? |
| **Call Me Nacho Cinco! (Bronze)** | We're going to outer space, baby! |
| **Ch.1 Netherworld Honor Student Complete (Bronze)** | I am indeed the No.1 Honor Student! |
| **Ch.2 Mao's Heart Complete (Bronze)** | I was supposed to pour salt and pepper on it, instead of hot sauce! |
| **Ch.3 The Freshmen Leader! Complete (Bronze)** | Boss! Boss! Boss! |
| **Ch.4 Almaz the Hero Complete (Bronze)** | Babuu. |
| **Ch.5 Grand War Complete (Bronze)** | Hot Hot Sensitive Tongue Slash! Kiiiiiaaaaahhhhh! |
| **Ch.6 The Reckoning Complete (Bronze)** | Hmhmhm. |
| **Ch.7 An Eye for an Eye Complete (Bronze)** | Gimme an autograph later! |
| **Combo No. 255 (Bronze)** | I won't stop hitting until you stop getting up. |
| **Commando King (Bronze)** | Now you're the Class World King! |
| **Cross Fists as Friends (Bronze)** | It's a story about a friendship born through fisticuffs. |
| **Demon King: Have It Your Way (Bronze)** | Force your will on them, like the demon your are! |
| **Eryngi Baal Slayer (Bronze)** | I'm not going to get my "a" back? |
| **Finale Complete (Bronze)** | I will...become the Overlord! |
| **Finger Flicking Good (Bronze)** | Mooove! My fingers are on fire!!! |
| **First Setback (Bronze)** | That was just a warm. Now I'm ready to go! |
| **Giga Damage! (Bronze)** | More training! You can do more! |
| **Gotcha! (Bronze)** | Yay! You got a new ally! |
| **Hardcore Gamer! (Bronze)** | Thanks for playing! But we suggest you take a break. |

| | |
|---|---|
| Hop, Step, Jump (Bronze) | Isn't jumping sooo much fun? |
| I Got Gummed... (Bronze) | Why me...? |
| I Had an Axeldent! (Bronze) | Axel never stops working! Even in the Item World! |
| It's Da Bomb! (Bronze) | Playing with bombs in Homeroom? You're quite an honor student. |
| Item Spelunker (Bronze) | Congratulations on reaching the 100th floor! You're on the right track to become a hardcore player! |
| IWCA Flyweight Champion (Bronze) | You are the Item World Champ! |
| Kneel Before Cat God! (Bronze) | *blush* Oh, you can stand, meow. |
| Magichangician (Bronze) | Transform! Yeah! |
| Majin Academy Complete (Bronze) | I shall take over this Academy! |
| Master of the Chain (Bronze) | Do massive chains! Use your brain to the max! |
| Mega Damage! (Bronze) | You gotta train! For starters, a million damage! |
| Omni Bonus! (Bronze) | It's only natural for a demon to take everything. |
| PE Teacher Destroyer (Silver) | It's always been a dream to defeat a PE teacher... |
| Platinum Trophy (Platinum) | Congratulations on getting all the trophies! |
| Playing Favorites (Bronze) | Aren't you happy to be surrounded by your favorite characters? |
| Puzzle Master (Bronze) | Erase everything! Train that brain! |
| Raspberyl Version Complete (Bronze) | You all graduate, today! |
| Reverse Pirates! Everything is Mine! (Gold) | Reverse Pirates, yeah! Nothing is left in our wake... |
| Reverse Pirates! I Shall Take Your Innocents! (Silver) | Reverse Pirates, yeah! We're taking all the Innocents with us! |
| Reverse Pirates! Your Treasure is Mine! (Bronze) | Reverse Pirates, yeah! All that treasure's just for me! |
| Shopping Spree (Bronze) | As a proud demon, I'll buy everything at the store! |
| Shut Up Already! (Bronze) | I'll never stop talking! |
| Super Honor Student (Bronze) | The HQ at this school is truly amazing. |
| Survival Class: Passed (Bronze) | You truly are the Survival Master! |
| Tera Damage! (Silver) | Even more training! Good job! |
| The Shamshank Redemon (Bronze) | I'm just testing your loyalty. |
| The Towertastic Ten (Bronze) | This is the epitome of a tower! |
| Treasure Hunter (Bronze) | Don't your legs feel stronger from all that jumping? |
| Trophy Shopper (Bronze) | I've been waiting for you in this Mystery Room! |
| Almaz's Ending | Win stage 8-4 with Almaz alone and the battle after |
| Death Institute, Majin Academy Ending | Clear Death Institute, Majin Academy Side Story |
| Human World Ending | Kill more then 99 allies and clear two alt. stages by stage 7-6 |
| Laharl's Ending | Go to homeroom and propose "Watch a New Ending" and clear the stage |
| Mao's Ambition Ending | Clear stage 1-9 on 2nd or higher cycle before stage 4-4 |

| | |
|---|---|
| Normal Ending | Don't meet any other ending's requirement |
| Raspberyl Version Ending | Clear Raspberyl Version Side Story |
| Raspberyl's Ending 1 | Lose against Raspberyl on stage 1-5 |
| Raspberyl's Ending 2 | Lose against Raspberyl on stage 2-1 |
| Super Hero Ending | Use Mao at Lv 500 or higher to defeat final boss |
| Aramis | Clear Class World Command Attack with less than 145 commands |
| Asagi | Beat extra map 4 |
| Axel | Beat extra map 6 |
| Laharl, Etna, and Flonne | Beat extra map 7 |
| Marona | Beat extra map 5 |
| Master Big Star | Beat extra map 1 |
| Pleinair | In Survival, get 7 Level Spheres and wish for the Mascot Character |
| Prism Red | Beat extra map 3 |
| Salvatore | Beat extra map 2 |
| Super hero Aurum | Finish 3rd Period of 'Raspberyl version' |

### UNLOCKABLE

| UNLOCKABLE | HOW TO UNLOCK |
|---|---|
| Archer | Have a level 15 Valkyrie and Cleric |
| Armored Knight | Have a level 15 Warrior and Martial Artist |
| Beast Master | Have a level 15 Valkyrie and Fight Mistress |
| Berserker | Have a level 40 Armored Knight and Beast Master |
| Celestial Host | Beat the Item World Command Attack on any difficulty in under 145 commands |
| Cheerleader | Have a level 25 Wiseman and Cleric |
| Dragon | Defeat a Dragon in Item World or Class World |
| Factory Desco | Unlock Desco, pass the, "Create a Final Boss?" bill as Mao |
| Felynn | Defeat a Felynn in Item World or Class World |
| Female Samurai | Have a level 35 Valkyrie and Archer |
| Gunner | Have a level 15 Magician and Thief |
| Gunslinger | Have a level 15 Witch and Thief |
| Kunoichi | Have a level 30 Fight Mistress and Witch |
| Magic Knight | Have a level 25 Warrior/Valkyrie and Magician/Witch |
| Majin | Get the Normal or Good ending |
| Masked Hero | Have a level 45 Thief and Gunner/Gunslinger |
| Ninja | Have a level 30 Martial Artist and Magician |
| Ranger | Have a level 15 Warrior and Clergy |
| Samurai | Have a level 35 Warrior and Ranger |
| Shaman | Have a level 25 Wiseman and Magician/Witch |
| Wiseman | Having a level 20 Martial Artist/Fight Mistress and Male/Female Cleric |

## DRAGON'S DOGMA (PlayStation 3)

### TROPHY

| UNLOCKABLE | HOW TO UNLOCK |
|---|---|
| A New Ally (Bronze) | Summoned your own pawn. |
| A Queen's Regalia (Bronze) | Dressed a male party member in women's clothing. |

A
B
C
D
E
F
G
H
I
J
K
L
M
N
O
P
Q
R
S
T
U
V
W
X
Y
Z

| | |
|---|---|
| **Affinity and Beyond (Bronze)** | Raised a person's affinity to the maximum. |
| **Closure (Gold)** | Put an end to all things. |
| **Come Courting (Bronze)** | Attended an audience with the duke. |
| **Destiny (Bronze)** | Accepted the Godsbane blade. |
| **Dragon Forged (Silver)** | Strengthened equipment in wyrmfire. |
| **Eye Contact (Bronze)** | Defeated an evil eye. |
| **Foreign Recruit (Bronze)** | Enlisted a pawn to your party from beyond the rift. |
| **Freedom (Bronze)** | Escaped the yoke of eternity. |
| **Getting a Head (Bronze)** | Earned the approval of the Enlistment Corps. |
| **Headshunter (Bronze)** | Defeated a hydra or archydra. |
| **Human Resources (Bronze)** | Changed your vocation. |
| **Inhuman Resources (Bronze)** | Changed your main pawn's vocation. |
| **Into Dripstone Cave (Bronze)** | Entered the azure caverns. |
| **Into Soulflayer Canyon (Bronze)** | Entered the Soulflayer Canyon. |
| **Into the Ancient Quarry (Bronze)** | Entered the ancient quarry. |
| **Into the Frontier Caverns (Bronze)** | Entered the southwestern caves. |
| **Into the Manse (Bronze)** | Entered the duke's manse. |
| **It Begins (Bronze)** | Completed the prologue. |
| **Local Recruit (Bronze)** | Directly enlisted a pawn to your party. |
| **Mercy (Bronze)** | Dealt the blow of deliverance. |
| **Onward (Bronze)** | Departed from Cassardis. |
| **Peace (Bronze)** | Took refuge in an illusion. |
| **Rough Landing (Bronze)** | Completed the urgent mission. |
| **Serpents' Bane (Bronze)** | Defeated a drake, wyrm, and wyvern. |
| **Servitude (Bronze)** | Soar unto a new world. |
| **Solitude (Bronze)** | Obtained the almighty power of sovereignty. |
| **The Captain (Bronze)** | Enlisted a large number of pawns. |
| **The Coin Collector (Silver)** | Earned a total of 10,000,000G. |
| **The Courier (Bronze)** | Entered Gran Soren. |
| **The Craftsman (Bronze)** | Combined two materials to make an item. |
| **The Escort (Bronze)** | Acted as a reliable travel companion. |
| **The Ever-Turning Wheel (Gold)** | Completed the adventure a second time. |
| **The Explorer (Silver)** | Visited 150 locations. |
| **The Hero (Silver)** | Completed all pre-planned, non-notice board quests. |
| **The Knave (Bronze)** | Obtained a forgery. |
| **The Laborer (Bronze)** | Completed 50 notice board quests. |
| **The Message (Bronze)** | Received the duke's commendation. |
| **The Messiah (Gold)** | Defeated the Ur-Dragon. |
| **The Patron (Bronze)** | Helped Madeleine open her shop. |
| **The Philanthropist (Bronze)** | Gave 50 presents. |
| **The Savior (Bronze)** | Used a Wakestone to restore the dead to life. |
| **The Specialist (Silver)** | Learned all the skills of a single vocation. |
| **The Tourist (Bronze)** | Visited 50 locations. |
| **The True Arisen (Platinum)** | Collected all other Dragon's Dogma trophies. |
| **The Vagabond (Bronze)** | Visited 100 locations. |
| **The Veteran (Bronze)** | Defeated 3,000 enemies. |
| **Treacherous (Bronze)** | Peered into the very depths of the world. |

| Well Equipped (Bronze) | Obtained 350 pieces total of weapons and armor. |
| --- | --- |
| Writ Large (Bronze) | Received a writ from the castle. |

## DRAGON'S DOGMA (XBOX 360)

### ACHIEVEMENT

| UNLOCKABLE | HOW TO UNLOCK |
| --- | --- |
| A New Ally (10) | Summoned your own pawn. |
| A Queen's Regalia (20) | Dressed a male party member in women's clothing. |
| Affinity and Beyond (10) | Raised a person's affinity to the maximum. |
| Closure (40) | Put an end to all things. |
| Come Courting (15) | Attended an audience with the duke. |
| Destiny (25) | Accepted the Godsbane blade. |
| Dragon Forged (30) | Strengthened equipment in wyrmfire. |
| Eye Contact (30) | Defeated an evil eye. |
| Foreign Recruit (5) | Enlisted a pawn to your party from beyond the rift. |
| Freedom (10) | Escaped the yoke of eternity. |
| Getting a Head (15) | Earned the approval of the Enlistment Corps. |
| Headshunter (30) | Defeated a hydra or archydra. |
| Human Resources (20) | Changed your vocation. |
| Inhuman Resources (20) | Changed your main pawn's vocation. |
| Into Dripstone Cave (10) | Entered the azure caverns. |
| Into Soulflayer Canyon (15) | Entered the Soulflayer Canyon. |
| Into the Ancient Quarry (10) | Entered the ancient quarry. |
| Into the Frontier Caverns (15) | Entered the southwestern caves. |
| Into the Manse (20) | Entered the duke's manse. |
| It Begins (5) | Completed the prologue. |
| Local Recruit (5) | Directly enlisted a pawn to your party. |
| Mercy (30) | Dealt the blow of deliverance. |
| Onward (5) | Departed from Cassardis. |
| Peace (20) | Took refuge in an illusion. |
| Rough Landing (10) | Completed the urgent mission. |
| Serpents' Bane (40) | Defeated a drake, wyrm, and wyvern. |
| Servitude (20) | Soar unto a new world. |
| Solitude (20) | Obtained the almighty power of sovereignty. |
| The Artisan (10) | Combined two materials to make an item. |
| The Captain (15) | Enlisted a large number of pawns. |
| The Coin Collector (30) | Earned a total of 10,000,000G. |
| The Courier (10) | Entered Gran Soren. |
| The Escort (10) | Acted as a reliable travel companion. |
| The Ever-Turning Wheel (50) | Completed the adventure a second time. |
| The Explorer (35) | Visited 150 locations. |
| The Hero (40) | Completed all pre-planned, non-notice board quests. |
| The Knave (15) | Obtained a forgery. |
| The Laborer (20) | Completed 50 notice board quests. |
| The Message (15) | Received the duke's commendation. |
| The Messiah (50) | Defeated the Ur-Dragon. |
| The Patron (15) | Helped Madeleine open her shop. |

| | |
|---|---|
| The Philanthropist (15) | Gave 50 presents. |
| The Savior (10) | Used a Wakestone to restore the dead to life. |
| The Specialist (40) | Learned all the skills of a single vocation. |
| The Tourist (10) | Visited 50 locations. |
| The Vagabond (20) | Visited 100 locations. |
| The Veteran (35) | Defeated 3,000 enemies. |
| Treacherous (10) | Peered into the very depths of the world. |
| Well Equipped (30) | Obtained 350 pieces total of weapons and armor. |
| Writ Large (10) | Received a writ from the castle. |

## DUNGEON HUNTER: ALLIANCE  (PlayStation Vita)

### TROPHY

| UNLOCKABLE | HOW TO UNLOCK |
|---|---|
| Along Came a Spider... (Bronze) | Defeat Seba the Man-Eater in a single or multiplayer game. |
| Ashes To Ashes (Bronze) | Defeat the Warlord in a single or multiplayer game. |
| Assassin (Bronze) | Defeat 300 monsters using only daggers. |
| Avenge the Fallen (Bronze) | Defeat Jeremo in a single or multiplayer game. |
| Battle of the Elements (Bronze) | Defeat all five Generals in a single or multiplayer game. |
| Berserker (Bronze) | Defeat 300 monsters using only axes (1H or 2H). |
| Big Spender (Bronze) | Purchase at least one item from every merchant. |
| Blademaster (Bronze) | Defeat 300 monsters using only swords (1H or 2H) |
| Bloodlust (Bronze) | Defeat 10,000 monsters with one character. |
| Boss Goblin Go Boom (Bronze) | Defeat the Goblin King in a single or multiplayer game. |
| Bottoms Up (Bronze) | Drink 200 potions with one character. |
| Broken Wings (Bronze) | Defeat the Cloud Beast in a single or multiplayer game. |
| Champion of Gothicus (Platinum) | Earn all trophies in the game. |
| Chatterbox (Bronze) | Initiate a conversation with every NPC in the game. |
| Courage And Grace (Bronze) | Complete the game as a rogue. |
| Crystal Scavenger (Bronze) | Use the fairies to uncover 10 crystals buried underground. |
| Dead Dog (Bronze) | Defeat the Big Bad Wolf in a single or multiplayer game. |
| Dragon Lancer (Bronze) | Defeat 300 monsters using only polearms. |
| Dungeon Explorer (Bronze) | Reach level 50 with one character. |
| Dungeon Master (Bronze) | Reach level 75 with one character. |
| Dungeon Raider (Bronze) | Reach level 10 with one character. |
| Dungeon Seeker (Bronze) | Reach level 25 with one character. |
| Dungeon Trainee (Bronze) | Reach level 2 with one character. |
| Dust To Dust (Bronze) | Defeat the Stone Devil in a single or multiplayer game. |
| Eagle Eye (Bronze) | Defeat 300 monsters using only crossbows. |
| Eternal Punishment (Bronze) | Defeat Gilgrath Zire in a single or multiplayer game. |
| Executioner (Bronze) | Defeat a monster with a single blow. |
| Failure Is Not an Option (Bronze) | Defeat the Corrupted Captain in a single or multiplayer game. |
| Gladiator (Bronze) | Defeat 300 monsters using only maces. |

| Good Night, Sweet Prince (Bronze) | Defeat the Bandit Prince in a single or multiplayer game. |
|---|---|
| Grand Magus (Bronze) | Defeat 500 monsters using Fairy Spells. |
| Guardian Angel (Bronze) | Resurrect 20 teammates in a multiplayer game. |
| He Slimed Me (Bronze) | Defeat the Depth Beast in a single or multiplayer game. |
| Hero Of The People (Bronze) | Complete all quests in Hero difficulty. |
| Hunter (Bronze) | Defeat 300 monsters using only bows. |
| Killer Instinct (Gold) | Defeat the Dark Fairy in a single or multiplayer game without taking damage. |
| Little Women (Silver) | Control the fairies to damage 200 enemies. |
| Long Live The King (Silver) | Complete the game with all 3 character classes. |
| Looking For Loot (Bronze) | Open 30 treasure chests with one character. |
| Night Stalker (Bronze) | Defeat 300 monsters by wielding two daggers at the same time. |
| Panzer Hand (Bronze) | Defeat 2,000 monsters using only 2H weapons. |
| Playing with fire (Bronze) | Defeat the Forge Monster in a single or multiplayer game. |
| Power And Wisdom (Bronze) | Complete the game as a mage. |
| Pure Skill (Silver) | Defeat a boss using only skills, no basic attacks. |
| Rest In Peace (Bronze) | Defeat Lord Plenko in a single or multiplayer game. |
| Rise from Your Grave (Bronze) | Defeat Reldin in a single or multiplayer game. |
| Shake It! (Bronze) | Recover from Stun, Fear, or Confuse 25 times by shaking the PS Vita system. |
| Shalandriel's Chosen (Bronze) | Defeat Shalandriel the Eternal Keeper in a single or multiplayer game. |
| Sorcerer (Bronze) | Defeat 300 monsters using only orbs. |
| Strength And Honor (Bronze) | Complete the game as a warrior. |
| The Darkness Defeated (Bronze) | Defeat the Dark Queen in a single or multiplayer game. |
| The Legend Can Be Told (Silver) | Complete the game on Legend difficulty. |
| To Catch a Killer (Bronze) | Defeat the Darklin Assassin in a single or multiplayer game. |
| United We Stand (Gold) | Complete the game in a 4-player multiplayer game on any difficulty level. |
| Warlock (Bronze) | Defeat 300 monsters using only staffs. |
| Warmancer (Silver) | Use every skill in the game once. |

## DYNASTY WARRIORS NEXT  (PlayStation Vita)

### TROPHY

| UNLOCKABLE | HOW TO UNLOCK |
|---|---|
| A Land United (Bronze) | Cleared the stage, 'A Land United.' |
| A Man of Virtue (Bronze) | Cleared the stage, 'A Man of Virtue.' |
| Ambition Personified (Silver) | Cleared the Conquest Mode a total of 50 times. |
| An Endless Quest (Bronze) | Cleared the stage, 'An Endless Quest.' |
| An Everlasting Love (Bronze) | Formed a marriage pact with another officer. |
| Anti-Dong Zhou Coalition (Bronze) | Cleared the stage, 'Anti-Dong Zhou Coalition.' |
| Armor Collector (Bronze) | Obtained all of the available armor. |
| Army of One (Bronze) | Defeated 1,000 enemies in one battle. |
| Battle of Chibi (Bronze) | Clear the stage, 'Battle of Chibi.' |
| Benevolent Ruler (Bronze) | Achieved the best possible Governance Rating. |

| | |
|---|---|
| **Card Collector (Gold)** | Obtained all of the available Officer Cards. |
| **Character Collector (Bronze)** | Created 10 Edit Characters. |
| **Coalition Leader (Bronze)** | Completed all of the battles within the Coalition Mode. |
| **Combo Master (Bronze)** | Completed a 500 hit combo. |
| **Conqueror of Jiangdong (Bronze)** | Cleared the stage, 'Conqueror of Jiangdong.' |
| **End of the Road (Bronze)** | Completed a five forces map in Conquest Mode. |
| **Equipment Collector (Bronze)** | Obtained all of the available growth items. |
| **Eyes in the Back of Your Head (Silver)** | Successfully completed all of the Sudden Encounters with the best possible rating. |
| **Family Ties (Gold)** | Formed a sworn oath with all of the officers. |
| **Friends to the End (Bronze)** | Formed a sworn oath with another officer. |
| **Great Emperor (Silver)** | Cleared all of the stages in the game. |
| **Jack of All Trades (Bronze)** | Completed Steeplechase, Bastion, Marksman and Calligrapher within the Gala Mode. |
| **Malevolent Ruler (Bronze)** | Achieved the worst possible Governance Rating. |
| **Master Matchmaker (Gold)** | Formed a marriage pact with all of the officers. |
| **Master of the Kingdom (Bronze)** | Earned 100,000 Exp. |
| **Master of the Land (Silver)** | Earned 1,000,000 Exp. |
| **Master of the Realm (Bronze)** | Earned 500,000 Exp. |
| **Movie Collector (Bronze)** | Viewed all of the movies in the game. |
| **New Recruit (Bronze)** | Created a save data file. |
| **Orb Collector (Bronze)** | Obtained all of the available orbs. |
| **Quiet Ambition (Bronze)** | Cleared the stage, 'Quiet Ambition.' |
| **Say Cheese (Bronze)** | Took a picture using the Musou Snapshot feature of the Gala Mode. |
| **Seasoned Veteran (Bronze)** | Successfully completed all of the Sudden Encounters. |
| **The Goal is Within Sight (Bronze)** | Completed a four forces map in Conquest Mode. |
| **The God of War (Silver)** | Defeated more than 100,000 enemies. |
| **The Great Creator (Silver)** | Obtained all of the available Edit Character parts. |
| **The Journey Begins (Bronze)** | Completed a two forces map in Conquest Mode. |
| **The Kingdom in Three (Bronze)** | Cleared the stage, 'The Kingdom in Three.' |
| **The Path of Ambition (Bronze)** | Cleared the Conquest Mode a total of 5 times. |
| **The Plot Thickens (Bronze)** | Completed a three forces map in Conquest Mode. |
| **The Struggle for Power (Bronze)** | Cleared the stage, 'The Struggle for Power.' |
| **The Three Visits (Bronze)** | Cleared the stage, 'The Three Visits.' |
| **The Tiger's Advance (Bronze)** | Cleared the stage, 'The Tiger's Advance.' |
| **True Warrior of the Three Kingdoms (Platinum)** | Obtained all trophies. |
| **Unrivaled Warrior (Bronze)** | Defeated 3,000 enemies in one battle. |
| **Untouchable (Bronze)** | Completed a battle in either Campaign Mode, or Conquest Mode without taking any damage. |
| **Weapons Collector (Silver)** | Obtained all of the available weapons. |
| **Yellow Turban Rebellion (Bronze)** | Cleared the stage, 'Yellow Turban Rebellion.' |
| **You Can Pursue Lu Bu (Bronze)** | Defeated Lu Bu in the Campaign Mode. |

### UNLOCKABLE

| UNLOCKABLE | HOW TO UNLOCK |
|---|---|
| **Chaos Difficulty** | Reach Rank 19 |

| | |
|---|---|
| **Ancient Remedy** | Campaign Mode - Conquer "Changsha" in "A Land United" - Hard mode or higher |
| **Art of War** | Campaign Mode - Conquer "BeiPing" in "The Tiger's Advance" - Medium mode or higher |
| **Bai Hu's Jewel** | Coalition Mode - "Blitz" Kill all 6 enemy general with 4 mins time left |
| **Bear Mount** | Campaign Mode - Conquer "Changan" in "Anti-Dong Zhuo Coalition" - Chaos mode |
| **Charge Bracer** | Coalition Mode - "Sentinel" protect all 7 bases, clear game with 6 mins time left |
| **Dragon Greaves** | Campaign Mode - Conquer "Hefei" in "Conqueror of Jiangdong" - Hard mode or higher |
| **Elephant Mount** | Campaign Mode - Conquer "Nanzhong" in "A Man of Virtue" - Medium mode or higher |
| **Hex Mark Saddle** | Gala Mode - Complete Steeplechase under 1'30 |
| **Jade Earrings** | Campaign Mode - Conquer "Jiaozhi" in "The Three Visits" - Easy mode or higher |
| **Master of Musou** | Campaign Mode - Conquer "Jiaozhi" in "Quiet Ambition" - Easy mode or higher |
| **Meat Bun Pouch** | Campaign Mode - Complete "Yellow Turban Rebellion" - Easy mode or higher |
| **Obsidian Remedy** | Campaign Mode - Conquer "Xiangyang" in "Battle of Chibi" - Easy mode or higher |
| **Power Rune** | Coalition Mode - Complete "Sudden Death" with the time left more than 24'30s, kill 1500 |
| **Red Hare Saddle** | Campaign Mode - Complete "The Endless Quest" Hard mode or chaos mode |
| **Shadow Runner Saddle** | Campaign Mode - Conquer "Luoyang" in "The Struggle for Power" - Chaos mode |
| **Stimulant Remedy** | Coalition Mode - "Marauder" Take all bases (without lose any base to enemy again), kill all enemy general with 25 mins time left |
| **Survival Guide** | Campaign Mode - Conquer "Xiangyang" in "The Three Visits" - Chaos mode |
| **Hex Mare** | Complete Steeplechase in Gala Mode |
| **Musou Armor** | Complete Marksman in Gala Mode |
| **Way of Musou** | Complete Calligraphy in Gala Mode under 2 minutes |
| **Wind Scroll** | Complete Bastion in Gala Mode |

## F1 2011 (PlayStation Vita)

### TROPHY

| UNLOCKABLE | HOW TO UNLOCK |
|---|---|
| **April shower (bronze)** | Win a race in the wet |
| **Banger racing (silver)** | Repair damage to your car in the pits and go on to win the race |
| **Challenger (bronze)** | Complete a challenge with a c rank or above |
| **Champion (gold)** | Beat sebastian vettel in the challenge mode head to head race |
| **Clean sweep (silver)** | Win every grand prix |
| **Complete (platinum)** | Congratulations on completing f1 2011 |
| **Driving legend (gold)** | Beat the real world lap record on any circuit |
| **Endurance (bronze)** | Complete a 100% distance race |
| **Flying lap (bronze)** | Achieve your first time trial medal |
| **Get noticed (bronze)** | Achieve the fastest lap in a grand prix |
| **Go the distance (silver)** | Drive 1000 miles (1610km) |

| Grade a performance (bronze) | Earn an a rank in challenge mode |
|---|---|
| Grand prix win (bronze) | Win your first grand prix |
| High roller (silver) | Win the monte carlo grand prix with vehicle damage enabled |
| Leader of the pack (silver) | Achieve pole on every circuit |
| Learning to fly (silver) | Post a flying lap to win a time trial medal with all driving aids disabled |
| Legendary charge! (gold) | Win a race starting from 24th on the grid |
| Made the cut (bronze) | Reach q3 in qualifying |
| Manual master (bronze) | Finish a race using only manual gears |
| Must dash! (gold) | Earn 14 pole positions in a single season |
| Pole position (bronze) | Achieve pole position |
| Prancer (silver) | Complete a lap of monza with an average speed greater than 150mph (241 km/h) |
| Shoe maker (gold) | Earn 149 championship points in a single season |
| Speed demon (bronze) | Drive faster than 230mph (370km/h) |
| Stirling performance (silver) | Lap every car in a race in wet conditions |
| The greatest of all time (silver) | Win eight world championships |
| Timed to perfection (gold) | Achieve all gold time trial trophies |
| Toe to toe (bronze) | Win a head to head challenge |
| Tuned to perfection (bronze) | Take pole position in qualifying with a tuned vehicle |
| Unassisted (bronze) | Finish a race with all driving aids turned off |
| Unplugged (silver) | Win a race with all driving aids disabled |

## FIFA SOCCER   (PlayStation Vita)

### TROPHY

| UNLOCKABLE | HOW TO UNLOCK |
|---|---|
| Aerial Threat (Bronze) | Score a header in a match with a player with the Aerial Threat Speciality |
| Against the Odds (Bronze) | Win a Head to Head Ranked Match using a weaker team |
| All My Own Work (Bronze) | Win a Match with Manual Controls |
| Around the World (Silver) | Play a match with a team from every league |
| Back of the Net (Bronze) | Score 5 goals in the Arena |
| Control the Open Space (Bronze) | Make a successful lob pass using the touchscreen in a match |
| Crosser (Bronze) | Create a goal with a cross with a player with the Crosser Speciality |
| Distance Shooter (Bronze) | Score from outside the box with a player with the Distance Shooter Speciality |
| Established Keeper (Silver) | Play a season as a goalkeeper in Career Mode |
| Experimental (Bronze) | Play 5 consecutive Head to Head Ranked Matches with different teams |
| FIFA for Life (Gold) | Spend 50 hours on the pitch |
| Folklore (Silver) | Become a Legend as a player in Career Mode |
| Good Form (Silver) | Play 5 consecutive Head to Head Ranked Matches without losing |
| Good Week! (Bronze) | Get yourself selected in the Team of the Week in Career Mode |
| Great Month (Bronze) | Win the Manager of the Month award in Career Mode |
| Home and Away (Silver) | Play and win every Stadium |
| Home Maker (Bronze) | Change the Home Stadium of any team |

| | |
|---|---|
| Hundred and Counting (Gold) | Play 100 Head to Head Ranked Matches |
| In for the Win (Bronze) | Take a Head to Head Ranked Match to extra time with a weaker team |
| In the game (Bronze) | Create a Virtual Pro |
| It's in the Blood (Silver) | Go from being a Player to the Manager (or Player Manager) in Career Mode |
| Mastermind (Bronze) | Have a substitute score a goal in Career Mode |
| Nimble Fingers (Bronze) | Score a touchscreen or rear touch pad goal from a touchscreen pass |
| Once in a Lifetime (Silver) | Score as the Goalkeeper in any match |
| Pass Master (Silver) | Make 100 successful passes using the touchscreen |
| Perfect Keeping (Bronze) | Play as the Goalkeeper in a Kick-Off match and finish with 100% Saving Accuracy |
| Pinpoint Accuracy (Bronze) | Score a goal using the screen (touchscreen) shot, or a rear touch pad shot |
| Playmaker (Bronze) | Create a goal with a player with the Playmaker Speciality |
| Poacher (Bronze) | Score from inside the box with a player with the Poacher Speciality |
| Pressure is On (Bronze) | Score a penalty kick using a touch shot |
| Rising Talent (Silver) | Complete 100 Accomplishments with your Virtual Pro |
| Safe Hands (Bronze) | Play any match as the Goalkeeper with no assistance |
| Sharp Shooter (Silver) | Score 50 goals using a touch shot |
| Soccer Legend (Platinum) | Unlock all other trophies (excluding additional content trophies) |
| Thread the Needle (Bronze) | Make a successful through pass using the touchscreen |
| Training Time (Bronze) | Work on your skills in any Arena Practice Mode |
| Virtual Legend (Gold) | Play 100 matches with your Virtual Pro |
| Warming the Gloves (Bronze) | Make 10 saves in the Arena |
| Woodwork and In! (Bronze) | Score off the post or cross bar in a match |
| You Pointing at Me? (Bronze) | Make a successful direct pass using the touchscreen |

## FIFA STREET (PlayStation 3)

### TROPHY

| UNLOCKABLE | HOW TO UNLOCK |
|---|---|
| 5 Tool Player (Gold) | Upgrade 5 attributes on a created player to maximum |
| Are we there yet? (Bronze) | Reach the World Tour map screen for the first time |
| Attributed Success (Silver) | Upgrade one of your created players attributes to Max |
| Career Milestone (Silver) | Score 100 goals with your created player in any game modes |
| Challenge the pros (Bronze) | Win a street challenge against an authentic club team in stage 4 of world tour |
| European Champion (Silver) | Win stage 3 of World Tour |
| Friendly Publicity (Bronze) | Watch a video posted by one of your Friends |
| Geometry was good for something (Bronze) | Score a goal by deflecting the ball off a wall |
| Globetrotter (Gold) | In any game mode win a match/event in every venue |

NEW!

A
B
C
D
E
F
G
H
I
J
K
L
M
N
O
P
Q
R
S
T
U
V
W
X
Y
Z

| | |
|---|---|
| Got any Nutmeg? (Bronze) | Panna your first Opponent |
| It's Tricky (Silver) | Unlock 10 tricks on a created player |
| Local Heroes (Bronze) | Win the final national tournament with at least 8 created players on your team |
| Making new Friends (Bronze) | Add a new Friend using the Friend Recommendation feature |
| Mighty Heroes (Silver) | Have a team with at least 8 created players that are level 50 or higher |
| Mister Entertainment (Silver) | Earn 100,000 Style Points with your created player in any game mode |
| Moving on up (Silver) | In a street season obtain promotion to the next division |
| National Street Champion (Silver) | Win stage 2 of World Tour |
| New Champion (Bronze) | Win a World Tour Tournament for the first time |
| Online Cup Champion (Silver) | Win any Online Cup |
| Online Dominance (Gold) | Win all 9 online cups |
| Online-Enthusiast (Bronze) | Win a game of 5 a side, 6 a side and Futsal online |
| Regional Street Champion (Bronze) | Win stage 1 of World Tour |
| Rush Keepers! (Silver) | Score a goal while controlling your Goal Keeper |
| Shopping Spree (Bronze) | Wear an Unlocked item in any game mode |
| Sightseer (Silver) | In any game mode win a match/event in 50% of the venues |
| Street Legend (Silver) | Defeat Messi in a street challenge game |
| Time to Celebrate (Bronze) | Unlock a created player celebration and perform it in game |
| Total Street Domination (Platinum) | Collect all FIFA Street Trophies |
| Ultimate Humiliation (Bronze) | Score a goal with a Panna |
| Very Entertaining (Silver) | Earn at least 1500 Style Points without losing possession |
| Video Proof (Bronze) | Upload a saved video |
| Watching Film (Bronze) | Watch a gameplay tutorial video |
| Who brought the snacks? (Bronze) | Win a tournament with a local Co-Op player |
| World Grand Champion (Gold) | Win stage 4 of World Tour |
| World Tour Around the World (Silver) | Win any World Tour tournament Online |

## FIFA STREET (XBOX 360)

### ACHIEVEMENT

| UNLOCKABLE | HOW TO UNLOCK |
|---|---|
| 5 Tool Player (50) | Upgrade 5 attributes on a created player to maximum as the lead profile |
| Are we there yet? (10) | Reach the World Tour map screen for the first time as the lead profile |
| Attributed Success (25) | Upgrade one of your created players attributes to Max as the lead profile |
| Career Milestone (25) | Score 100 goals with your created player in any game modes as the lead profile |
| Challenge the pros (20) | Win a street challenge against an authentic club team in stage 4 of world tour as the lead profile |
| European Champion (50) | Win stage 3 of World Tour as the lead profile |
| Friendly Publicity (15) | Watch a video posted by one of your Friends as the lead profile |

| Geometry was good for something (20) | Score a goal by deflecting the ball off a wall |
|---|---|
| Globetrotter (95) | In any game mode win a match/event in every venue as the lead profile |
| Got any Nutmeg? (15) | Panna your first Opponent |
| It's Tricky (20) | Unlock 10 tricks on a created player as the lead profile |
| Local Heroes (25) | Win the final national tournament with at least 8 created players on your team as the lead profile |
| Making new friends (15) | Add a new Friend using the Friend Recommendation feature as the lead profile |
| Mighty Heroes (40) | Have a team with at least 8 created players that are level 50 or higher as the lead profile |
| Mister Entertainment (25) | Earn 100,000 Style Points with your created player in any game mode as the lead profile |
| Moving on up (25) | In a street season obtain promotion to the next division as the lead profile |
| National Street Champion (25) | Win stage 2 of World Tour as the lead profile |
| New Champion (15) | Win a World Tour Tournament for the first time as the lead profile |
| Online Cup Champion (25) | Win any Online Cup as the lead profile |
| Online Dominance (100) | Win all 9 online cups as the lead profile |
| Online Enthusiast (20) | Win a game of 5 a side, 6 a side and Futsal online as the lead profile |
| Regional Street Champion (20) | Win stage 1 of World Tour as the lead profile |
| Rush Keepers! (25) | Score a goal while controlling your Goal Keeper |
| Shopping Spree (10) | Wear an Unlocked item in any game mode as the lead profile |
| Sightseer (25) | In any game mode win a match/event in 50% of the venues as the lead profile |
| Street Legend (20) | Defeat Messi in a street challenge game as the lead profile |
| Time to Celebrate (15) | Unlock a created player celebration and perform it in game as the lead profile |
| Ultimate Humiliation (15) | Score a goal with a Panna |
| Very Entertaining (25) | Earn at least 1500 Style Points without losing possession |
| Video Proof (20) | Upload a saved video as the lead profile |
| Watching Film (20) | Watch a gameplay tutorial video as the lead profile |
| Who brought the snacks? (15) | Win a tournament with a local Co-Op player as the lead profile |
| World Grand Champion (100) | Win stage 4 of World Tour as the lead profile |
| World Tour Around the World (30) | Win any World Tour tournament Online as the lead profile |

## GAME OF THRONES  (PlayStation 3)

### TROPHY

| UNLOCKABLE | HOW TO UNLOCK |
|---|---|
| 'Tis but a scratch! (Bronze) | Chapter 9: suffer all the physical abuse during the torture sequence |
| Am I not merciful? (Bronze) | Chapter 8: save Orys from the City Watch |
| As high as honor (Bronze) | Finish chapter 12 |
| Bloodhound (Bronze) | Chapter 7: find all the corrupt brothers of the Night's Watch |

| | |
|---|---|
| **Clever dog (Bronze)** | Gain all the skills linked to the dog with Mors |
| **Collector (Silver)** | Seize the three objects of value from the Collector with Alester |
| **Come try me (Bronze)** | Finish chapter 11 |
| **Dark wings, dark words (Bronze)** | Finish chapter 3 |
| **Dead men sing no songs (Bronze)** | Finish chapter 6 |
| **Desecration (Bronze)** | Chapter 8: find the key in Alester's father's tomb |
| **Devout follower (Silver)** | Find all the statues of the Seven |
| **Disciplinarian (Bronze)** | Chapter 1: confront the four recruits during the training session with Mors |
| **End of the line (Bronze)** | Chapter 6: don't lose pursuit of the bastard |
| **Endless watch (Silver)** | Send 10 recruits to the Wall with Mors |
| **Family is hope... (Bronze)** | Finish chapter 2 |
| **Family, duty, honor (Bronze)** | Finish chapter 8 |
| **Fetch! (Silver)** | Use Mors' dog's sense of smell to find 5 secret objects |
| **Fire and blood (Bronze)** | Finish chapter 10 |
| **Golden touch (Silver)** | Acquire 1 golden dragon |
| **Great teamwork (Silver)** | Finish the game without a single ally (except Mors and Alester) being KO'd |
| **Growing strong (Bronze)** | Finish chapter 13 |
| **Hear me roar (Bronze)** | Finish chapter 4 |
| **Here we stand (Bronze)** | Finish chapter 7 |
| **Know your place (Bronze)** | Chapter 2: protect the nobility with Alester |
| **Lesser of two evils (Bronze)** | Chapter 14: come to the aid of the Reapers |
| **Man of the people (Bronze)** | Chapter 2: protect the people with Alester |
| **Man's best friend (Bronze)** | Kill 10 enemies with Mors' dog in skinchanger mode |
| **Master of light and flame (Bronze)** | Master of light and flame |
| **Master-at-arms (Bronze)** | Learn all skills within a character's stance tree |
| **Merciless (Bronze)** | Mete out 5 deathblows |
| **My darkest hour (Bronze)** | Chapter 15: execute the judgement passed down on the Westfords |
| **Once more unto the breach (Silver)** | Chapter 7: attack the camp without killing the sentries at the start |
| **Pimp (Silver)** | Convince Bethany to return to Chataya's brothel with Alester |
| **Platinum trophy (Platinum)** | Earn all the trophies in Game of Thrones |
| **Proud to be faithful (Bronze)** | Finish chapter 5 |
| **Quiet as a shadow (Silver)** | Chapter 13: reach Jeyne's room without ever being seen |
| **R'hllor sees all (Silver)** | Find 10 secrets with the vision of R'hllor |
| **Red priest of R'hllor (Bronze)** | Finish Alester's story |
| **Swift and deadly (Silver)** | Chapter 11: bring an end to the trial by combat in under 2 minutes |
| **Sworn brother (Bronze)** | Finish Mors' Story |
| **The butcher comes to dinner (Silver)** | Chapter 9: kill 6 of Lord Harlton's soldiers during the fight at dinner |

| The Greatest (Silver) | Emerge triumphant in the final arena combat |
|---|---|
| The night is dark... (Bronze) | Finish chapter 15 |
| The true face of the Spider (Bronze) | Lose the final battle |
| Thorough (Gold) | Complete all the secondary objectives of the story |
| True warrior (Bronze) | Kill 400 enemies |
| Unbowed, unbent, unbroken (Bronze) | Finish chapter 9 |
| Unrivaled strategist (Silver) | Chapter 12: take back Riverspring with a total victory |
| Valar morghulis (Bronze) | Finish chapter 14 |
| Warlord (Silver) | Reach the maximum level |
| Winter is coming (Bronze) | Finish chapter 1 |

## GAME OF THRONES (XBOX 360)

### ACHIEVEMENT

| UNLOCKABLE | HOW TO UNLOCK |
|---|---|
| 'Tis but a scratch ! (20) | Chapter 9: suffer all the physical abuse during the torture sequence |
| Am I not merciful? (15) | Chapter 8: save Orys from the City Watch |
| As high as honor (10) | Finish chapter 12 |
| Bloodhound (25) | Chapter 7: find all the corrupt brothers of the Night's Watch |
| Clever dog (30) | Gain all the skills linked to the dog with Mors |
| Collector (30) | Seize the three objects of value from the Collector with Alester |
| Come try me (10) | Finish chapter 11 |
| Dark wings, dark words (10) | Finish chapter 3 |
| Dead men sing no songs (10) | Finish chapter 6 |
| Desecration (15) | Chapter 8: find the key in Alester's father's tomb |
| Devout follower (30) | Find all the statues of the Seven |
| Disciplinarian (10) | Chapter 1: confront the four recruits during the training session with Mors |
| End of the line (20) | Chapter 6: don't lose pursuit of the bastard |
| Endless watch (30) | Send 10 recruits to the Wall with Mors |
| Family is hope... (10) | Finish chapter 2 |
| Family, duty, honor (10) | Finish chapter 8 |
| Fetch! (30) | Use Mors' dog's sense of smell to find 5 secret objects |
| Fire and blood (10) | Finish chapter 10 |
| Golden touch (30) | Acquire 1 golden dragon |
| Great teamwork (30) | Finish the game without a single ally (except Mors and Alester) being KO'd |
| Growing strong (10) | Finish chapter 13 |
| Hear me roar (10) | Finish chapter 4 |
| Here we stand (10) | Finish chapter 7 |
| Know your place (15) | Chapter 2: protect the nobility with Alester |
| Lesser of two evils (15) | Chapter 14: come to the aid of the Reapers |
| Man of the people (15) | Chapter 2: protect the people with Alester |
| Man's best friend (20) | Kill 10 enemies with Mors' dog in skinchanger mode |
| Master of light and flame (30) | Gain all the skills linked to R'hllor's fire with Alester |

| | |
|---|---|
| Master-at-arms (25) | Learn all skills within a character's stance tree |
| Merciless (20) | Mete out 5 deathblows |
| My darkest hour (10) | Chapter 15: execute the judgement passed down on the Westfords |
| Once more unto the breach (35) | Chapter 7: attack the camp without killing the sentries at the start |
| Pimp (30) | Convince Bethany to return to Chataya's brothel with Alester |
| Proud to be faithful (10) | Finish chapter 5 |
| Quiet as a shadow (35) | Chapter 13: reach Jeyne's room without ever being seen |
| R'hllor sees all (30) | Find 10 secrets with the vision of R'hllor |
| Red priest of R'hllor (10) | Finish Alester's story |
| Swift and deadly (35) | Chapter 11: bring an end to the trial by combat in under 2 minutes |
| Sworn brother (10) | Finish Mors' Story |
| The butcher comes to dinner (35) | Chapter 9: kill 6 of Lord Harlton's soldiers during the fight at dinner |
| The Greatest (30) | Emerge triumphant in the final arena combat |
| The night is dark... (10) | Finish chapter 15 |
| The true face of the Spider (10) | Lose the final battle |
| Thorough (40) | Complete all the secondary objectives of the story |
| True warrior (20) | Kill 400 enemies |
| Unbowed, unbent, unbroken (10) | Finish chapter 9 |
| Unrivaled strategist (35) | Chapter 12: take back Riverspring with a total victory |
| Valar morghulis (10) | Finish chapter 14 |
| Warlord (30) | Reach the maximum level |
| Winter is coming (10) | Finish chapter 1 |

## GRAND SLAM TENNIS 2 (PlayStation 3)

### TROPHY

| UNLOCKABLE | HOW TO UNLOCK |
|---|---|
| Australian Open Title (Bronze) | Career - Win the Australian Open |
| Beat Borg at the French Open (Bronze) | Career - Defeat Bjorn Borg at the French Open |
| Beat Evert at US Open (Bronze) | Career - Defeat Chris Evert in the US Open |
| Beat Federer at Australian Open (Bronze) | Career - Defeat Roger Federer at the Australian Open |
| Beat Henin at the French Open (Bronze) | Career - Defeat Justine Henin at the French Open |
| Beat McEnroe at US Open (Bronze) | Career - Defeat John McEnroe in the US Open |
| Beat Navratilova at Wimbledon (Bronze) | Career - Defeat Martina Navratilova at Wimbledon |
| Beat Sampras at Wimbledon (Bronze) | Career - Defeat Pete Sampras at Wimbledon |
| Beat Serena at Australian Open (Bronze) | Career - Defeat Serena Williams at the Australian Open |
| Best of 1980's (Silver) | ESPN Grand Slam Classics - Beat all 80's Matches |
| Best of 1990's (Bronze) | ESPN Grand Slam Classics - Beat all 90's Matches |

| | |
|---|---|
| Best of 2000 (Bronze) | ESPN Grand Slam Classics - Beat all 2000's Matches |
| Best of All Time (Bronze) | ESPN Grand Slam Classics - Beat all All-Time Matches |
| Boom Boom (Bronze) | Any Game Mode - Hit four aces in a row |
| Break Back (Bronze) | Any Game Mode - Break service immediately after being broken |
| Broke (Bronze) | Any Game Mode - Win a match without being broken |
| Calendar Year Grand Slam (Gold) | Career - Win all four Grand Slam tournaments consecutively in the same calendar year |
| Career Grand Slam (Silver) | Career - Win all four Grand Slam tournaments |
| Clean Break (Bronze) | Any Game Mode - Break Service |
| Collector (Gold) | Career - Earn all racquets and shoes in Tennis Store |
| EA SPORTS™ GRAND SLAM TENNIS 2 Platinum Trophy (Platinum) | Collected all other EA SPORTS™ GRAND SLAM TENNIS 2 trophies |
| Flushing Meadows Big Show (Bronze) | Career - Play Arthur Ashe Stadium at US Open |
| French Open Title (Bronze) | Career - Win the French Open |
| Friendly Competition (Bronze) | Online - Win a ranked doubles online match against a Friend |
| History Buff (Silver) | ESPN Grand Slam Classics - Beat all Fantasy Matches |
| Melbourne Park Big Show (Bronze) | Career - Play Rod Laver Arena at Australian Open |
| Never Broken (Bronze) | Career - Win a tournament without being broken |
| No Set Lost (Bronze) | Career - Win a tournament without losing a set |
| Non-Calendar Year Grand Slam (Silver) | Career - Win all four Grand Slam tournaments consecutively, but not in the same calendar year |
| Pair of Aces (Bronze) | Any Game Mode - Hit 2 aces in a row |
| Popular (Bronze) | Share A Pro - Download a Tennis Player |
| Rocket (Bronze) | Any Game Mode - Hit a 209 KMH (130 MPH) serve |
| Roland Garros Big Show (Bronze) | Career - Play Court Philippe Chatrier at French Open |
| School Master (Silver) | Training - Complete all Tennis School Lessons |
| Sharer (Bronze) | Share A Pro - Upload a Tennis Player |
| Silver Set (Bronze) | Any Game Mode - Win a set without losing a game |
| Small Grand Slam (Silver) | Career - Win three of the four Grand Slam tournaments in the same year |
| Streak (Silver) | Online - Win 10 matches in a row |
| The Legend (Gold) | Career - Finish ranked #1 |
| Tie Break Win (Bronze) | Any Game Mode - Win a tiebreak |
| US Open Title (Bronze) | Career - Win the US Open |

NEW!

A
B
C
D
E
F
G
H
I
J
K
L
M
N
O
P
Q
R
S
T
U
V
W
X
Y
Z

| Wimbledon Big Show (Bronze) | Career - Play Centre Court at Wimbledon |
| Wimbledon Title (Bronze) | Career - Win Wimbledon |

## GRAND SLAM TENNIS 2 (XBOX 360)

### ACHIEVEMENT

| UNLOCKABLE | HOW TO UNLOCK |
|---|---|
| Australian Open Title (20) | Career - Win the Australian Open |
| Beat Borg at the French Open (20) | Career - Defeat Bjorn Borg at the French Open |
| Beat Evert at US Open (20) | Career - Defeat Chris Evert in the US Open |
| Beat Federer at Australian Open (20) | Career - Defeat Roger Federer at the Australian Open |
| Beat Henin at the French Open (20) | Career - Defeat Justine Henin at the French Open |
| Beat McEnroe at US Open (20) | Career - Defeat John McEnroe in the US Open |
| Beat Navratilova at Wimbledon (20) | Career - Defeat Martina Navratilova at Wimbledon |
| Beat Sampras at Wimbledon (20) | Career - Defeat Pete Sampras at Wimbledon |
| Beat Serena at Australian Open (20) | Career - Defeat Serena Williams at the Australian Open |
| Best of 1980's (20) | ESPN Grand Slam Classics - Beat all 80's Matches |
| Best of 1990's (20) | ESPN Grand Slam Classics - Beat all 90's Matches |
| Best of 2000 (20) | ESPN Grand Slam Classics - Beat all 2000's Matches |
| Best of All Time (20) | ESPN Grand Slam Classics - Beat all All-Time Matches |
| Boom Boom (20) | Any Game Mode - Hit four aces in a row |
| Break Back (20) | Any Game Mode - Break service immediately after being broken |
| Broke (20) | Any Game Mode - Win a match without being broken |
| Calendar Year Grand Slam (50) | Career - Win all four Grand Slam tournaments consecutively in the same calendar year |
| Career Grand Slam (35) | Career - Win all four Grand Slam tournaments |
| Clean Break (20) | Any Game Mode - Break Service |
| Collector (50) | Career - Earn all racquets and shoes in Tennis Store |
| Flushing Meadows Big Show (20) | Career - Play Arthur Ashe Stadium at US Open |
| French Open Title (20) | Career - Win the French Open |
| Friendly Competition (20) | Xbox LIVE - Win a ranked doubles Xbox LIVE match against a Friend |
| History Buff (30) | ESPN Grand Slam Classics - Beat all Fantasy matches |
| Melbourne Park Big Show (20) | Career - Play Rod Laver Arena at Australian Open |
| Never Broken (20) | Career - Win a tournament without being broken |
| No Set Lost (20) | Career - Win a tournament without losing a set |

| | |
|---|---|
| **Non-Calendar Year Grand Slam (35)** | Career - Win all four Grand Slam tournaments consecutively, but not in the same calendar year |
| **Pair of Aces (20)** | Any Game Mode - Hit 2 aces in a row |
| **Popular (20)** | Share A Pro - Download a Tennis Player |
| **Rocket (20)** | Any Game Mode - Hit a 209 KMH (130 MPH) serve |
| **Roland Garros Big Show (20)** | Career - Play Court Philippe Chatrier at French Open |
| **School Master (35)** | Training - Complete all Tennis School Lessons |
| **Sharer (20)** | Share A Pro - Upload a Tennis Player |
| **Silver Set (20)** | Any Game Mode - Win a set without losing a game |
| **Small Grand Slam (35)** | Career - Win three of the four Grand Slam tournaments in the same year |
| **Streak (20)** | Xbox LIVE - Win 10 matches in a row |
| **The Legend (50)** | Career - Finish ranked #1 |
| **Tie Break Win (20)** | Any Game Mode - Win a tiebreak |
| **US Open Title (20)** | Career - Win the US Open |
| **Wimbledon Big Show (20)** | Career - Play Centre Court at Wimbledon |
| **Wimbledon Title (20)** | Career - Win Wimbledon |

## GRAVITY RUSH (PlayStation Vita)

### TROPHY

| UNLOCKABLE | HOW TO UNLOCK |
|---|---|
| **A Hundred and One Nights (Bronze)** | Completed episode 8 |
| **A Meeting with Destiny (Bronze)** | Completed episode 5 |
| **Adreaux On Call (Bronze)** | Completed episode 18 |
| **All That Glitters (Gold)** | Gold-medaled EVERY challenge. |
| **An Unguarded Moment (Bronze)** | Completed episode 20 |
| **Ancient Game Hunter (Silver)** | Defeated the rare Nevi in Rift Planes: The Ruins. |
| **Burning Game Hunter (Silver)** | Defeated the rare Nevi in Rift Planes: The Inferno. |
| **Children of the Past (Bronze)** | Completed episode 16 |
| **Curiosity Killed the Cat (Bronze)** | Completed episode 10 |
| **Fading Light (Bronze)** | Completed episode 17 |
| **Falling to Pieces (Bronze)** | Completed episode 19 |
| **Frequent Flyer (Silver)** | Landed 10 gravity kicks without landing or taking damage. |
| **From Oblivion (Bronze)** | Completed episode 1 |
| **Gem Aficionado (Gold)** | Collected a total of 40,000 precious gems. |
| **Gem Collector (Silver)** | Collected a total of 20,000 precious gems. |
| **Going Underground (Silver)** | Discovered every manhole. |
| **Gold Medalist (Bronze)** | Gold-medaled a challenge. |
| **Gravitational Anomaly (Silver)** | Defeated 8 enemies with one special attack. |
| **Home Sweet Home (Bronze)** | Completed episode 3 |
| **Illusory Game Hunter (Silver)** | Defeated the rare Nevi in Rift Planes: The Mirage. |
| **It's all Relative (Platinum)** | Collected every trophy. Congratulations! |
| **Kids Just Don't Understand (Bronze)** | Completed episode 13 |
| **Learner's Permit (Bronze)** | Mastered the fundamentals of gravity. |
| **Letting Old Ghosts Die (Bronze)** | Completed episode 9 |

| | |
|---|---|
| Look Out Below (Bronze) | Completed episode 12 |
| Lost in Time and Space (Silver) | Heard the mysterious couple's complete story. |
| Lost Kat (Bronze) | Awakened in Auldnoir. |
| Memories of Another World (Bronze) | Completed episode 15 |
| New Challenger (Bronze) | Cleared a challenge. |
| No Rest for the Virtuous (Gold) | Completed episode 21 |
| Pitching Machine (Silver) | Hurled 10 objects into enemies without missing or taking damage. |
| Shadows Over the City (Bronze) | Completed episode 2 |
| Silver Lining (Silver) | Earned a silver or better in every challenge. |
| The Hekseville Phantom (Bronze) | Completed episode 4 |
| The Lost City (Bronze) | Completed episode 6 |
| The Lost Tribe (Bronze) | Completed episode 14 |
| Thick Skin (Bronze) | Completed episode 11 |
| Too Many Secrets (Bronze) | Completed episode 7 |
| Top Cat (Gold) | Raised Kat's reputation to 'Top Cat.' |
| True Challenger (Bronze) | Cleared EVERY challenge. |

## HOT SHOTS GOLF: WORLD INVITATIONAL (PlayStation Vita)

### TROPHY

| UNLOCKABLE | HOW TO UNLOCK |
|---|---|
| A True Hot Shots Golfer (Bronze) | Win VS Grace on Pro Rank. |
| Absolute Class (Bronze) | Purchase a Lv3 club or ball. |
| All our thanks to Everybody's Golfers! (Platinum) | Get every trophy. |
| Art Fancier (Bronze) | Purchase every piece of concept art. |
| Audiophile (Bronze) | Purchase every Music track. |
| Chaser of the Flame (Silver) | Perform a homing shot in an official round. |
| Chewing Up Challenges (Bronze) | Win VS Stuart on Bronze Rank. |
| Courses Complete! (Bronze) | Gain membership to every course. |
| Daily Participant (Bronze) | Enter a Daily Int'l Tournament and complete the round. |
| Fancy Dresser (Bronze) | Purchase a costume. |
| Fear the Receptionist! (Bronze) | Gain access to Amy as a playable character. |
| Gear Collector (Bronze) | Purchase every type of ball and club. |
| Gear Master (Silver) | Purchase Lv3 versions of every ball with levels. |
| Go for the Ace! (Silver) | Score an hole-in-one in an official round. |
| Greased Lightning (Silver) | Perform a rising shot in an official round. |
| I Love Everybody! (Gold) | Raise all characters' loyalty to max. |
| It's a Miracle! (Silver) | Score an albatross in an official round. |
| Journey's End...? (Silver) | Win VS Pandora on Gold Rank. |
| King of Kings (Gold) | Collect every crown in Challenge Mode. |
| Lobby Character Part Collector (Bronze) | Collect over 50% of the normal parts. |
| Lobby Character Part Lover (Silver) | Collect over 50% of the special parts. |
| Lobby Character Part Maniac (Gold) | Collect over 50% of the deluxe parts. |
| My First Birdie (Bronze) | Score a birdie in an official round. |
| My First Chip-In (Bronze) | Perform a chip-in in an official round. |
| Overwhelming Power (Bronze) | Hit a drive over 350 yards in an official round. |
| Perfect Spiral (Silver) | Perform a spiral shot in an official round. |

| | |
|---|---|
| Putting Pro (Bronze) | Sink a putt over 15m long in an official round. |
| Rockin' Score (Bronze) | Score an eagle in an official round. |
| Shot Type Selector (Bronze) | Use every shot type in an official round. |
| So Long, Amateur League (Bronze) | Win VS Pancho on Amateur Rank. |
| SOLD OUT (Gold) | Purchase every item in the shop. |
| Starry Night (Silver) | Collect every star in Challenge Mode. |
| The Challenge Begins (Bronze) | Win VS Isabelle on Beginner Rank. |
| The Climax! (Bronze) | Win VS Max on Silver Rank. |
| The Real Ending! (Gold) | Win VS Izzak on Platinum Rank. |
| True Dedication (Bronze) | Raise one character's loyalty to max. |
| Watery Wonder (Bronze) | Skip the ball across water three or more times in a row in an official round. |

## HYPERDIMENSION NEPTUNIA MK2 (PlayStation 3)

### TROPHY

| UNLOCKABLE | HOW TO UNLOCK |
|---|---|
| 5pb. chan (Bronze) | 5bp chan joined your party. |
| Battle Master (Bronze) | Fought over 500 battles. |
| Blanc (Bronze) | Blanc joined your party. |
| Brave the Hard (Bronze) | Beat Brave the Hard. |
| Candidates of Lastation Goddess (Bronze) | Encountered with Uni. |
| Candidates of Luwian Goddess (Bronze) | Encountered with Rom and Ram. |
| Chain original combo (Bronze) | Chained your original combo. |
| Chain the combo (Bronze) | Chained 80+ original combo. |
| Counter Stop (Silver) | All characters reached level 99. |
| Create Items (Bronze) | Created items. |
| Delphinus (Gold) | Beat Delphinus. |
| Goddess-ize (Bronze) | Watched the event 'Trapped Goddess' |
| Grave of the industry (Bronze) | Watched the event 'Grave of the industry' |
| GUST chan (Bronze) | GUST chan joined your party. |
| Hard-bitten (Bronze) | Fought over 100 battles. |
| Hot Spring (Bronze) | Watched the event 'Hot Spring' |
| Judge the Hard (Bronze) | Beat Judge the Hard. |
| Lastation Ending (Silver) | Watched the 'Lastation' Ending. |
| Leanbox Ending (Silver) | Watched the 'Leanbox' Ending. |
| Let's play games (Bronze) | Watched the event 'Let's play games' |
| Live Stage (Bronze) | Watched the event 'Live Stage' |
| Lowee Ending (Silver) | Watched the 'Lowee' Ending. |
| Magic Sword (Bronze) | Obtained the Magic sword. |
| Magic the Hard (Bronze) | Beat Magic the Hard. |
| Makers Ending (Silver) | Watched the 'Makers' Ending. |
| Maximum Power (Bronze) | Dealt maximum 100000+ damage. |
| Nepgear Start (Bronze) | Started the game. |
| Nepgear Version Up (Bronze) | Nepgear upgraded. |
| Neptune (Bronze) | Neptune joined your party. |
| Nippon Ichi chan (Bronze) | Nippon Ichi chan joined your party. |
| Noire (Bronze) | Noire joined your party. |
| Normal Ending (Silver) | Watched the Normal Ending. |

A
B
C
D
E
F
G
H
I
J
K
L
M
N
O
P
Q
R
S
T
U
V
W
X
Y
Z

| | |
|---|---|
| PeroPero (Bronze) | Watched the event 'PeroPero' |
| Planeptune Ending (Silver) | Watched the 'Planeptune' Ending. |
| Rehabilitation (Bronze) | Fought your first battle. |
| Release Planeptune (Bronze) | Released Planeputune. |
| Rescue the Goddess (Bronze) | Watched the event 'Rescue the Goddess' |
| Rom and Ram Version Up (Bronze) | Rom and Ram upgraded |
| Ruling Ending (Gold) | Watched the 'Ruling' Ending. |
| The fateful encounter (Bronze) | Watched the event 'Encounter with Histoire' |
| Trapped Goddess (Bronze) | Watched the event 'Trapped Goddess' |
| Trick the Hard (Bronze) | Beat Trick the Hard. |
| True Ending (Gold) | Watched the True Ending. |
| Ultimate Neptune Mk2 Master (Platinum) | Acquired all trophies. |
| Uni Version Up (Bronze) | Uni upgraded |
| Uranus (Bronze) | Encountered with Uranus. |
| Vert (Bronze) | Vert joined your party. |

## ICE AGE: CONTINENTAL DRIFT - ARCTIC GAMES  (PlayStation 3)

### TROPHY

| UNLOCKABLE | HOW TO UNLOCK |
|---|---|
| Acorn Nut (Bronze) | Collect every Acorn in Glacier Hopping. |
| Bob Smasher (Bronze) | Finish a Bob-Smashing race in Story Mode. |
| Bring home the Gold (Gold) | Get a Gold Acorn on every single game event. |
| Bullseye (Bronze) | Place all your shells on the target in one round of Shell Slide. |
| Cliffhanger (Bronze) | Collect all acorns and reach the goal in under 1:00 minute in Ice Smash. |
| Coconut Slinger (Bronze) | Finish a Coconut Slingshot game in Story Mode. |
| Come on, fraidy cat! (Bronze) | Fall into the water 15 times with either Diego or Shira. |
| Dream come true (Bronze) | Find the hidden Acorn in the Scrat Cannon event. |
| Drifting like a sir (Bronze) | Pass through every gate in a single Mountain Drift race. |
| Further down the road (Bronze) | Reach the end of the level bouncing 20 times or less in Scrat Cannon. |
| Glacier Hopper (Bronze) | Finish a Glacier Hopping race in Story Mode. |
| Golden Breaker (Bronze) | Obtain a Gold Acorn time in Ice Smash (Free Play only). |
| Golden Flyer (Bronze) | Obtain a Gold Acorn score in Scrat Cannon (Free Play only). |
| Golden Glider (Bronze) | Obtain a Gold Acorn score in Shell Slide (Free Play only). |
| Golden Hopper (Bronze) | Obtain a Gold Acorn time in Glacier Hopping (Free Play only). |
| Golden Jumper (Bronze) | Obtain a Gold Acorn score in Style Jump (Free Play only). |
| Golden Plumber (Bronze) | Obtain a Gold Acorn score in Prehistoric Plumber (Free Play only). |
| Golden Skier (Bronze) | Obtain a Gold Acorn time in Mountain Drift (Free Play only). |
| Golden Slider (Bronze) | Obtain a Gold Acorn time in Slip Slide (Free Play only). |

| | |
|---|---|
| **Golden Slingshooter (Bronze)** | Obtain a Gold Acorn score in Coconut Slingshot (Free Play only). |
| **Golden Smasher (Bronze)** | Obtain a Gold Acorn score in Bob-Smashing (Free Play only). |
| **Herd Hero (Gold)** | Finish the Story mode while playing on the Herd's side. |
| **Herd Migration (Silver)** | Slide down 1000 miles of ice or snow. |
| **Ice Breaker (Bronze)** | Finish a Ice Smash game in Story Mode. |
| **Learn to Fly (Silver)** | Fly 500 miles over land or sea. |
| **Master Bullseye (Silver)** | Place a shell in the exact center of the target, without steering it or hitting any other shell. |
| **Mountain Drifter (Bronze)** | Finish a Mountain Drift race in Story Mode. |
| **None left standing (Bronze)** | Break every wall of your team without breaking any wall of the opposing team in a Bob-Smashing race. |
| **Oak Forest (Silver)** | Collect 1000 acorns. |
| **Pirate Captain (Gold)** | Finish the Story mode while playing on the Crew's side. |
| **Platinum Acorn (Platinum)** | Obtain every other trophy in the game. |
| **Scrat Cannoneer (Bronze)** | Finish a Scrat Cannon game in Story Mode. |
| **Scrat Plumber (Bronze)** | Finish a Prehistoric Plumber game in Story Mode. |
| **Sharp Shooter (Silver)** | Destroy all targets in Coconut Slingshot. |
| **Shell Slider (Bronze)** | Finish a Shell Slide game in Story Mode. |
| **Slip Slider (Bronze)** | Finish a Slip Slide race in Story Mode. |
| **Speedster (Bronze)** | Finish a Slip Slide race without hitting any snow patches. |
| **Strike the Pose (Bronze)** | Successfully complete 8 tricks in a single Style Jump game. |
| **Style Jumper (Bronze)** | Finish a Style Jump game in Story Mode. |
| **That treasure is mine! (Silver)** | Win a Tournament against a friend. |
| **The most beautiful story ever (Gold)** | Finish Story mode without losing a single game event. |

## ICE AGE: CONTINENTAL DRIFT - ARCTIC GAMES (XBOX 360)

### ACHIEVEMENT

| UNLOCKABLE | HOW TO UNLOCK |
|---|---|
| **Acorn Nut (15)** | Collected every Acorn in Glacier Hopping. |
| **Bob-Smasher (20)** | Finished a Bob-Smashing race in Story Mode. |
| **Bring home the Gold (75)** | Got a Gold Acorn on every single game event. |
| **Bullseye (15)** | Placed all your shells on the target in one round of Shell Slide. |
| **Cliffhanger (15)** | Collected all acorns and reached the goal in under 1:00 minute in Ice Smash. |
| **Coconut Slinger (20)** | Finished a Coconut Slingshot game in Story Mode. |
| **Come on, fraidy cat! (10)** | Fell into the water 15 times with either Diego or Shira. |
| **Dream comes true (20)** | Found the hidden Acorn in the Scrat Cannon event. |
| **Drifting like a sir (15)** | Passed through every gate in a single Mountain Drift race. |
| **Further down the road (15)** | Reached the end of the level bouncing 20 times or less in Scrat Cannon. |
| **Glacier Hopper (20)** | Finished a Glacier Hopping race in Story Mode. |
| **Golden Breaker (20)** | Obtained a Gold Acorn time in Ice Smash (Free Play only). |
| **Golden Flyer (20)** | Obtained a Gold Acorn score in Scrat Cannon (Free Play only). |

| | |
|---|---|
| Golden Glider (20) | Obtained a Gold Acorn score in Shell Slide (Free Play only). |
| Golden Hopper (20) | Obtained a Gold Acorn time in Glacier Hopping (Free Play only). |
| Golden Jumper (20) | Obtained a Gold Acorn score in Style Jump (Free Play only). |
| Golden Plumber (20) | Obtained a Gold Acorn score in Prehistoric Plumber (Free Play only). |
| Golden Skier (20) | Obtained a Gold Acorn time in Mountain Drift (Free Play only). |
| Golden Slider (20) | Obtained a Gold Acorn time in Slip Slide (Free Play only). |
| Golden Slingshooter (20) | Obtained a Gold Acorn score in Coconut Slingshot (Free Play only). |
| Golden Smasher (20) | Obtained a Gold Acorn score in Bob-Smashing (Free Play only). |
| Herd Hero (50) | Finished the Story Mode while playing on the Herd's side. |
| Herd Migration (40) | Slid down 1000 miles of ice or snow. |
| Ice Breaker (20) | Finished an Ice Smash game in Story Mode. |
| Learn to Fly (30) | Flew 500 miles over land or sea. |
| Master Bullseye (30) | Placed a shell in the exact center of the target, without steering it or hitting any other shells. |
| Mountain Drifter (20) | Finished a Mountain Drift race in Story Mode. |
| None left standing (15) | Broke every wall of your team without breaking any wall of the opposing team in a Bob-Smashing race. |
| Oak Forest (40) | Collected 1000 acorns. |
| Pirate Cap'n (50) | Finished the Story Mode while playing on the Crew's side. |
| Scrat Cannoneer (20) | Finished a Scrat Cannon game in Story Mode. |
| Scrat Plumber (20) | Finished a Prehistoric Plumber game in Story Mode. |
| Sharp Shooter (30) | Destroyed all targets in Coconut Slingshot. |
| Shell Slider (20) | Finished a Shell Slide game in Story Mode. |
| Slip Slider (20) | Finished a Slip Slide race in Story Mode. |
| Speedster (15) | Finished a Slip Slide race without hitting any snow patches. |
| Strike the Pose (15) | Successfully struck 8 poses in a single Style Jump game. |
| Style Jumper (20) | Finished a Style Jump game in Story Mode. |
| That treasure is mine! (30) | Won a Tournament against a friend. |
| The most beautiful story ever (75) | Finished Story Mode without losing a single game event. |

## INVERSION (PlayStation 3)

### TROPHY

| UNLOCKABLE | HOW TO UNLOCK |
|---|---|
| Ah Gross! (Bronze) | Use the Gravlink to throw a corpse at your friend (Co-op mode) |
| All Up In Them Guts (Bronze) | Use a Shotgun to gib 25 Lutadore enemies (Any Difficulty) |
| Brotastic! (Bronze) | Revive a friend online (Co-op mode) |
| Burn it Down (Bronze) | Set 25 Lutadore enemies on fire with the Lavagun (Any Difficulty) |
| Chapter Eight (Bronze) | Complete the final checkpoint in Into the Depths on Normal or High Difficulty |

| | |
|---|---|
| **Chapter Eleven (Bronze)** | Complete the final checkpoint in Red Sky on Normal or High Difficulty |
| **Chapter Five (Bronze)** | Complete the final checkpoint in Street Fight on Normal or High Difficulty |
| **Chapter Four (Bronze)** | Complete the final checkpoint in Road Home on Normal or High Difficulty |
| **Chapter Nine (Bronze)** | Complete the final checkpoint in Enlightenment on Normal or High Difficulty |
| **Chapter One (Bronze)** | Complete the final checkpoint in Vanguard Down on Normal or High Difficulty |
| **Chapter Seven (Bronze)** | Complete the final checkpoint in Edge of the World on Normal or High Difficulty |
| **Chapter Six (Bronze)** | Complete the final checkpoint in Road to Hell on Normal or High Difficulty |
| **Chapter Ten (Bronze)** | Complete the final checkpoint in Reveal on Normal or High Difficulty |
| **Chapter Thirteen (Bronze)** | Complete the final checkpoint in Reversion on Normal or High Difficulty |
| **Chapter Three (Bronze)** | Complete the final checkpoint in Breakout on Normal or High Difficulty |
| **Chapter Twelve (Bronze)** | Complete the final checkpoint in Deja Vanguard on Normal or High Difficulty |
| **Chapter Two (Bronze)** | Complete the final checkpoint in Caged on Normal or High Difficulty |
| **Dude Bro! (Bronze)** | Complete a Campaign level with a Friend (Any Difficulty) |
| **Easy Going (Bronze)** | Finish the Campaign on Low Gravity Difficulty |
| **Enforcer (Bronze)** | Reach Gold Grav Major Rank |
| **Feats Don't Fail Me Now (Gold)** | Complete All Multiplayer Basic Challenges |
| **Fivesome (Silver)** | Use the Gravlink to kill 5 Lutadores with one object (Campaign) |
| **Gold Star (Bronze)** | Get 1st Place in a Deathmatch game (Matchmaking) |
| **Grand Master Gravity (Platinum)** | Unlock all trophies |
| **Grappler (Silver)** | Take the Gravlink from the Lutadores |
| **Gravlink Gangsta (Silver)** | Use the Gravlink to throw 50 Lutadore Enemies (Campaign) |
| **Gravlink Hustler (Silver)** | Use the Gravlink to throw 30 Lutadore Enemies (Campaign) |
| **Gravlink Thug (Bronze)** | Use the Gravlink to throw 15 Lutadore Enemies (Campaign) |
| **Half Sack (Bronze)** | Reach Silver Grav Sergeant Rank |
| **High G Amateur (Bronze)** | Perform 10 Finishing Moves using High Grav Powers (Campaign) |
| **High G Champ (Silver)** | Perform 50 Finishing Moves using High Grav Powers (Campaign) |
| **I'm About to Blow (Silver)** | Kill 100 Lutadore Enemies with explosives in the Campaign (Grenades, Rockets, Barrels) |
| **I'm Designer (Bronze)** | Change your multiplayer character's appearance |
| **Kicking Weightless Ass (Silver)** | Escape from a Lurker's grasp 5 times during single player |
| **Low G Amateur (Bronze)** | Perform 10 Finishing Moves using Low Grav Powers (Campaign) |
| **Low G Champ (Silver)** | Perform 50 Finishing Moves using Low Grav Powers (Campaign) |
| **Man of Mayhem (Bronze)** | Reach Diamond Grav Commander Rank |

| | |
|---|---|
| **Master Blaster (Silver)** | Complete All Multiplayer Weapon Challenges |
| **Meatheads (Bronze)** | Finish the Campaign with a Friend (Any Difficulty) |
| **Meet Your Master (Bronze)** | Defeat The Prophet Kiltehr (Any Difficulty) |
| **Normal Guy (Silver)** | Finish the Campaign on Normal Gravity Difficulty |
| **Rock Hard (Gold)** | Finish the Campaign on High Gravity Difficulty |
| **Soldier (Bronze)** | Reach Bronze Grav Captain Rank |
| **Spot me Bro! (Bronze)** | Have a friend boost you over a ledge (Co-op mode) |
| **Teamster (Bronze)** | Be a part of a winning team in Team Deathmatch (Matchmaking) |
| **That's Assault Brotha! (Bronze)** | Be a part of a winning team in Assault Mode (Matchmaking) |
| **The Collector (Bronze)** | Defeat The Slave Driver (Any Difficulty) |
| **The Great Destroyer (Bronze)** | Defeat The Brute (Any Difficulty) |
| **The Tin Man (Bronze)** | Defeat The Butcher (Any Difficulty) |
| **Threesome (Bronze)** | Use the Gravlink to kill 3 Lutadores with one object (Campaign) |
| **William Tell Routine (Bronze)** | Shoot off 100 Lutadore Helmets (Any Difficulty) |

## INVERSION (XBOX 360)

### ACHIEVEMENT

| UNLOCKABLE | HOW TO UNLOCK |
|---|---|
| **Ah Gross! (5)** | Use the Gravlink to throw a corpse at your friend (Co-op mode) |
| **All Up In Them Guts (25)** | Use a Shotgun to gib 25 Lutadore enemies (Any Difficulty) |
| **Brotastic! (5)** | Revive a friend online (Co-op mode) |
| **Burn it Down (25)** | Set 25 Lutadore enemies on fire with the Lavagun (Any Difficulty) |
| **Chapter Eight (10)** | Complete the final checkpoint in Into the Depths on Normal or High Difficulty |
| **Chapter Eleven (10)** | Complete the final checkpoint in Red Sky on Normal or High Difficulty |
| **Chapter Five (10)** | Complete the final checkpoint in Street Fight on Normal or High Difficulty |
| **Chapter Four (10)** | Complete the final checkpoint in Road Home on Normal or High Difficulty |
| **Chapter Nine (10)** | Complete the final checkpoint in Enlightenment on Normal or High Difficulty |
| **Chapter One (10)** | Complete the final checkpoint in Vanguard Down on Normal or High Difficulty |
| **Chapter Seven (10)** | Complete the final checkpoint in Edge of the World on Normal or High Difficulty |
| **Chapter Six (10)** | Complete the final checkpoint in Road to Hell on Normal or High Difficulty |
| **Chapter Ten (10)** | Complete the final checkpoint in Reveal on Normal or High Difficulty |
| **Chapter Thirteen (10)** | Complete the final checkpoint in Reversion on Normal or High Difficulty |
| **Chapter Three (10)** | Complete the final checkpoint in Breakout on Normal or High Difficulty |
| **Chapter Twelve (10)** | Complete the final checkpoint in Deja Vanguard on Normal or High Difficulty |
| **Chapter Two (10)** | Complete the final checkpoint in Caged on Normal |

| | or High Difficulty |
|---|---|
| Dude Bro! (5) | Complete a Campaign level with a Friend (Any Difficulty) |
| Easy Going (25) | Finish the Campaign on Low Gravity Difficulty |
| Enforcer (25) | Reach Gold Grav Major Rank |
| Feats Don't Fail Me Now (50) | Complete All Multiplayer Basic Challenges |
| Fivesome (50) | Use the Gravlink to kill 5 Lutadores with one object (Campaign) |
| Gold Star (10) | Get 1st Place in a Deathmatch game (Matchmaking) |
| Grappler (25) | Take the Gravlink from the Lutadores |
| Gravlink Gangsta (25) | Use the Gravlink to throw 50 Lutadore Enemies (Campaign) |
| Gravlink Hustler (15) | Use the Gravlink to throw 30 Lutadore Enemies (Campaign) |
| Gravlink Thug (10) | Use the Gravlink to throw 15 Lutadore Enemies (Campaign) |
| Half Sack (5) | Reach Silver Grav Sergeant Rank |
| High G Amateur (15) | Perform 10 Finishing Moves using High Grav Powers (Campaign) |
| High G Champ (25) | Perform 50 Finishing Moves using High Grav Powers (Campaign) |
| I'm About to Blow (25) | Kill 100 Lutadore Enemies with explosives in the Campaign (Grenades, Rockets, Barrels) |
| I'm Designer (5) | Change your multiplayer character's appearance |
| Kicking Weightless Ass (10) | Escape from a Lurker's grasp 5 times during single player |
| Low G Amateur (15) | Perform 10 Finishing Moves using Low Grav Powers (Campaign) |
| Low G Champ (25) | Perform 50 Finishing Moves using Low Grav Powers (Campaign) |
| Man of Mayhem (50) | Reach Diamond Grav Commander Rank |
| Master Blaster (50) | Complete All Multiplayer Weapon Challenges |
| Meatheads (50) | Finish the Campaign with a Friend (Any Difficulty) |
| Meet Your Master (15) | Defeat The Prophet Kiltehr (Any Difficulty) |
| Normal Guy (50) | Finish the Campaign on Normal Gravity Difficulty |
| Rock Hard (75) | Finish the Campaign on High Gravity Difficulty |
| Soldier (15) | Reach Bronze Grav Captain Rank |
| Spot me Bro! (5) | Have a friend boost you over a ledge (Co-op mode) |
| Teamster (15) | Be a part of a winning team in Team Deathmatch (Matchmaking) |
| That's Assault Brotha! (15) | Be a part of a winning team in Assault Mode (Matchmaking) |
| The Collector (10) | Defeat The Slave Driver (Any Difficulty) |
| The Great Destroyer (10) | Defeat The Brute (Any Difficulty) |
| The Tin Man (10) | Defeat The Butcher (Any Difficulty) |
| Threesome (25) | Use the Gravlink to kill 3 Lutadores with one object (Campaign) |
| William Tell Routine (50) | Shoot off 100 Lutadore Helmets (Any Difficulty) |

## KIDOU SENSHI GUNDAM SEED: BATTLE DESTINY (PlayStation Vita)

### TROPHY

| UNLOCKABLE | HOW TO UNLOCK |
|---|---|
| 100 Kills (Bronze) | Shoot down a total of 100 enemy mobile suits. |

**CODES & CHEATS**

| 1000 Kills (Silver) | Shoot down a total of 1000 enemy mobile suits. |
|---|---|
| 150 Kills (Bronze) | Shoot down a total of 150 enemy mobile suits. |
| 1500 Kills (Silver) | Shoot down a total of 1500 enemy mobile suits. |
| 200 Kills (Bronze) | Shoot down a total of 200 enemy mobile suits. |
| 2000 Kills (Silver) | Shoot down a total of 2000 enemy mobile suits. |
| 3000 Kills (Silver) | Shoot down a total of 3000 enemy mobile suits. |
| 400 Kills (Bronze) | Shoot down a total of 400 enemy mobile suits. |
| 50 Kills (Bronze) | Shoot down a total of 50 enemy mobile suits. |
| 500 Kills (Silver) | Shoot down a total of 500 enemy mobile suits. |
| 700 Kills (Silver) | Shoot down a total of 700 enemy mobile suits. |
| Ace Pilot (Bronze) | Clear 20 missions in story mode with an A-Rank. |
| Battle Mania (Silver) | Win 100 times in VS mode. |
| Captain (Bronze) | Clear 20 missions in story mode. |
| Destiny Clear (Bronze) | Clear the final CE 73 story mission. |
| Elite Earth Alliance Pilot (Silver) | Clear all of the CE 71 and CE 73 story missions as an Earth Alliance pilot. |
| Elite Pilot (Bronze) | Clear a story mode mision with an S-Rank. |
| Elite ZAFT Pilot (Silver) | Clear the CE 71 and CE 73 story missions as a ZAFT pilot. |
| Ensign (Bronze) | Clear 5 missions in story mode. |
| Excellent Pilot (Silver) | Clear all of the Hyper Boss Battle extra missions. |
| Great Pilot (Bronze) | Clear 10 missions in story mode with an S-Rank. |
| Gundam Seed Freak (Gold) | Clear story mode with all three factions. |
| Killing-King (Silver) | Shoot down 5000 enemy mobile suits. |
| Lacus-sama Banzai! (Silver) | Clear all of the CE 71 and CE 73 story missions as an Archangel pilot. |
| Legendary Pilot (Silver) | Clear 25 missions in story mode with an S-Rank. |
| Lieutenant (Bronze) | Clear 10 missions in story mode. |
| MS Collector (Silver) | Obtain 80 mobile suits. |
| Pilot Collector (Silver) | Collect all 30 pilots. |
| Recruit (Bronze) | Clear 1 mission in story mode. |
| Seed Clear (Bronze) | Clear the final CE 71 story mission. |
| Skill Collector (Silver) | Collect all 40 skills. |
| Super Ace Pilot (Gold) | Clear the CE 73 story missions, "Another" and, "Battle Destiny." |
| Trophy Complete (Platinum) | Obtain all other trophies in the game. |
| Ultimate Pilot (Gold) | Clear all story missions. |
| Veteran Pilot (Silver) | Clear 30 missions in story mode with an A-Rank. |

## KINECT RUSH: A DISNEY-PIXAR ADVENTURE (XBOX 360)

### ACHIEVEMENT

| UNLOCKABLE | HOW TO UNLOCK |
|---|---|
| A Friend Indeed (30) | Open all buddy areas in the game, alone or with a friend. |
| A New Me! (10) | Complete your first scanning. |
| A New You! (20) | Unlock your first playable character, alone or with a friend. |
| Absolute Perfection! (30) | Win your first platinum medal, alone or with a friend. |
| All Around the World (30) | Unlock all of the episodes in the game, alone |

| | or with a friend. |
|---|---|
| Better the Second Time Around (25) | Unlock all secondary goals in a world, alone or with a friend. |
| Bronze Away! (10) | Win your first bronze medal, alone or with a friend. |
| Can I Cook or What? (20) | Complete the Ratatouille world, alone or with a friend. |
| Checkered Flag (20) | Complete the Cars world, alone or with a friend. |
| Compliments to the Chef (15) | Play the entire Ratatouille world as Remy, alone or with a friend. |
| Fast Learner (20) | Complete your first episode, alone or with a friend. |
| Friends Forever (30) | Unlock all buddy characters, alone or with a friend. |
| Golden! (25) | Win your first gold medal, alone or with a friend. |
| Hat Trick (30) | Win three gold medals in a row, alone or with a friend. |
| I Am Speed (15) | Play the entire Cars world as Lightning McQueen, alone or with a friend. |
| I Can See in the Dark (20) | Find all night vision areas in the "Omnidroid Bash" episode, alone or with a friend. |
| Just Like Old Times (15) | Play the entire Incredibles world as Mr. Incredible, alone or with a friend. |
| Linear Thinking (15) | Jump from zipline to zipline 10 times in the "Free the Birds!" episode, alone or with a friend. |
| Loyal to the End (15) | Open all buddy areas in all UP episodes, alone or with a friend. |
| Say It with Rockets (20) | Open all boxes with rockets in the "Daycare Dash" episode, alone or with a friend. |
| Second Helping (15) | Unlock your first secondary goal, alone or with a friend. |
| Second to None (30) | Unlock all secondary goals in the game, alone or with a friend. |
| See What I Did! (15) | Share an award with KinectShare. |
| See? I Can Do Anything! (20) | Share 10 KinectShare awards. |
| Senior Wilderness Explorer (15) | Play the entire UP world as RU.S.S.ell, alone or with a friend. |
| Showtime! (20) | Unlock your first special ability, alone or with a friend. |
| Silverado! (20) | Win your first silver medal, alone or with a friend. |
| Simply Super (20) | Complete the Incredibles world, alone or with a friend. |
| Spirit of Adventure (20) | Complete the UP world, alone or with a friend. |
| Stay 'Til the Lights Come Up (10) | Watch the credits without skipping. |
| Steady Drivin' (15) | Complete the entire "Fancy Drivin'" episode without hitting any obstacles. |
| Super Poise (25) | Slide through the entire "Save Metroville" episode without falling. |
| Super Teamwork (15) | Open all buddy areas in all of the Incredibles episodes, alone or with a friend. |
| The Gang's All Here (30) | Unlock all playable characters, alone or with a friend. |

| The Grand Canyoneer (20) | Survive the entire "Canyon Expedition" episode without falling. |
| Throw It All Away (15) | Throw 20 tennis balls in the "Floodgates" episode, alone or with a friend. |
| To Infinity ... and Beyond! (15) | Play the entire Toy Story world as Buzz Lightyear, alone or with a friend. |
| Top of the Charts (20) | See the leaderboards for an episode, alone or with a friend. |
| Toys Stick Together (20) | Open all buddy areas in all Toy Story episodes, alone or with a friend. |
| Traffic Jam (15) | Reach all areas using glide and missiles in all Cars episodes, alone or with a friend. |
| True Adventurer (20) | Complete your first world, alone or with a friend. |
| We Belong Together (15) | Unlock your first buddy, alone or with a friend. |
| We Don't Need Roads (20) | Perform a 100-meter glide in the "Bomb Squad" episode. |
| We'll Always Have Paris (10) | Open all buddy areas in all Ratatouille episodes, alone or with a friend. |
| Whip It Good (20) | Open all areas with the whip in the "House Chase" episode, alone or with a friend. |
| Work/Play Balance (15) | Complete the entire "Daycare Dash" episode without falling. |
| You ... Are ... a ...TOY! (20) | Complete the Toy Story world, alone or with a friend. |
| You Can Do It All (30) | Unlock all special abilities, alone or with a friend. |
| You Will Believe a Rat Can Fly (20) | Perform an 8-second glide in the "Rooftop Run" episode in one try. |
| You're Not the Boss of Me (40) | Defeat all bosses, alone or with a friend. |

## KINECT STAR WARS (XBOX 360)

### ACHIEVEMENT

| UNLOCKABLE | HOW TO UNLOCK |
|---|---|
| Angry World Traveller (10) | Played any map at level 5 or higher in Rancor Rampage, alone or with a friend. |
| Arch-Rivals! (10) | Raced with Sebulba's Podracer, alone or with a friend. |
| Bantha Poodoo (10) | Crossed the finish line last in a race, alone or with a friend. |
| Ben-Hur, Done That (10) | Completed the Podracing Destiny as a Rookie, alone or with a friend. |
| Boonta Clause (30) | Completed the Podracing Destiny as a Veteran, alone or with a friend. |
| Catch-22 (20) | Completed 2 two-player races. |
| Crowd Control (20) | Knocked down 15 people or droids in one attack, alone or with a friend. |
| Decapitalized (20) | Destroyed the Subjugator-class Capital ship, alone or with a friend. |
| Don't Get Cocky (40) | Completed all four Space Combat missions without restarting, alone or with a friend. |
| Down with the Royals (10) | Destroyed every statue in Theed in Rancor Rampage in 1 session, alone or with a friend. |
| Duels Mode Unlocked (10) | Completed the Jedi Adventures Duels tutorial, alone or with a friend. |

| | |
|---|---|
| **Felucia In a Flash (25)** | Completed all Felucia missions in a single session, alone or with a friend. |
| **Fighter Ace (20)** | Destroyed 5 TIE fighters in 1 mode in Rancor Rampage, alone or with a friend. |
| **Going Somewhere, Solo? (50)** | Completed "I'm Han Solo" without losing a multiplier, alone or with a friend. |
| **Hot Potato (10)** | Made a creature or droid jump to an enemy vehicle in Podracing, alone or with a friend. |
| **I Just Wanna Dance (10)** | Completed your first song in co-op mode. |
| **I'm Invincible! (30)** | Completed Mos Espa wihout losing a life in Rancor Rampage, alone or with a friend. |
| **It's a Trap! (20)** | Completed Providence Mission 1 without your ship being destroyed, alone or with a friend. |
| **Mastering the Juyo Form (20)** | Completed any Duel in less than 3 minutes, alone or with a friend. |
| **Now Face the Chosen One (15)** | Defeated Ror with a Jedi Knight rating, alone or with a friend. |
| **Now this is Podracing! (10)** | Won a race for the first time in the Podracing Destiny, alone or with a friend. |
| **One Buffed Dude (30)** | Played any map at level 10 in Rancor Rampage, alone or with a friend. |
| **One Up, Two Down (10)** | In Rancor Rampage, leveled a Felucian Heavy Missile Platform in 1 throw, alone or with a friend. |
| **Only a Master of Evil (25)** | Completed the Vader Duel with a Jedi Master rating, alone or with a friend. |
| **Rebel Commando (10)** | Knocked out the shield of the Imperial garrison in Mos Eisley, alone or with a friend. |
| **Savior of Coruscant (50)** | Completed the Jedi Adventures: Dark Side Rising campaign, alone or with a friend. |
| **Sky Walker (20)** | Completed the Podracing Destiny as a Professional, alone or with a friend. |
| **Sleemo! (40)** | Destroyed 3 enemy Podracers in a single race, alone or with a friend. |
| **Sorry About the Mess (15)** | Defeated 13 enemy speeders in the Kashyyyk forest speederbike level, alone or with a friend. |
| **Teras Kasi (10)** | Defeated an enemy by kicking them off a ledge, alone or with a friend. |
| **The Chosen One (30)** | Scored at least 500,000 points on any song on the Death Star, alone or with a friend. |
| **The Force That Binds (20)** | Completed a co-op Jedi Adventures ground combat mission with neither player being knocked out. |
| **The Only Human Who Can Do It (15)** | Placed first in 3 Podraces in a row in a single session, alone or with a friend. |
| **The Real Force in the Galaxy (20)** | Played the Coloi Rancor, alone or with a friend. |
| **The Shield Is Down! (15)** | Disabled the Commerce Guild fortress shield, alone or with a friend. |
| **This Party's Over (40)** | Earned 5 stars playing "Celebration" on extended difficulty, alone or with a friend. |
| **To the Rescue (15)** | Reached the Jedi training camp on Kashyyyk, alone or with a friend. |
| **Tusken Raider Revenge (20)** | Destroyed all Podracers in Mos Espa in Rancor Rampage, alone or with a friend. |

NEW!

A
B
C
D
E
F
G
H
I
J
K
L
M
N
O
P
Q
R
S
T
U
V
W
X
Y
Z

| | |
|---|---|
| Two-For-One Discount (10) | Defeated at least two droids with a single use of Force powers, alone or with a friend. |
| Unlimited Power! (10) | Used a fully upgraded powerup in Podracing at least once, alone or with a friend. |
| Untouchable (30) | Completed any Duel without taking a single hit, alone or with a friend. |
| Very Very Angry (10) | Played Rancor Rampage Fury in co-op mode. |
| We Got Company! (20) | Earned 5 stars each on a song while playing with another person in co-op mode. |
| Well, Wookiee There! (10) | Destroyed 10 Trandoshan slave ships while escaping from Kashyyyk, alone or with a friend. |
| Who's Keeping Score? (25) | Completed all Providence missions in a single session, alone or with a friend. |
| Witness the Power (10) | Used all special attacks in 1 mode in Rancor Rampage, alone or with a friend. |
| Wookiee Life Debt (40) | Completed all Kashyyyk missions in a single session, alone or with a friend. |
| Wookiee Wingman (15) | Teamed up with a friend to complete a speeder bike chase in 2-player co-op mode. |
| You May Fire When Ready (20) | Destroyed all shield arrays in a single pass on Felucia Mission 5, alone or with a friend. |
| You Must Have Jedi Reflexes (15) | Won all Destiny races in one sitting, with racing line & drive assist off, alone or with a friend. |

## KINGDOM HEARTS 3D: DREAM DROP DISTANCE   (3DS)

### TROPHY

| UNLOCKABLE | HOW TO UNLOCK |
|---|---|
| Badge of Pride | Finish the story on Proud Mode |
| Critical Praise | Finish the story on Critical Mode |
| Daring Diver | Score more than 7,500,000 points in Dive Mode |
| Dream Pleaser | Max out every Spirit's Affinity Level |
| Frequent Friend | Place at least 30 Link Portals |
| In the Clear | Finish the story |
| In the Munny | Amass 5,000 munny |
| Keyslinger | Take out 2,500 Dream Eaters |
| King of Rush | Take first place in every Flick Rush cup |
| Memento Maniac | Save at least 20 photos while bonding with Spirits |
| Motion Slickness | Defeat 1,000 enemies while in Flowmotion |
| Portal Champ | Complete every Special Portal and Secret Portal |
| Pro Linker | Link with your Spirits at least 50 times |
| Reality Shifter | Defeat 50 enemies using Reality Shift |
| Spirit Guide | Obtain at least one of every Spirit |
| Stat Builder | Max out every stat-boosting ability |
| Stop Drop Roller | Rack up 2,000 Drop Points |
| Treasure Seeker | Find every last treasure |

### UNLOCKABLE

| UNLOCKABLE | HOW TO UNLOCK |
|---|---|
| Critical Mode | Finish the game on any difficulty |
| Secret Message in Glossary | Get all the glowing letters to spell "Secret Message Unlocked" to get an extra item in your glossary. |

## TROPHY

| UNLOCKABLE | HOW TO UNLOCK |
| --- | --- |
| A Life of Crime (Bronze) | Got caught committing a crime 25 times. |
| A Wink and a Smile (Bronze) | You have succeeded at 50 Persuasion attempts. |
| And Then There Were None (Bronze) | Killed 500 enemies with abilities. |
| Big Spender (Bronze) | Spent 200,000 gold. |
| Blades of Glory (Bronze) | Acquired 10 Unique weapons (Special Delivery weapons excluded). |
| Bookworm (Bronze) | Read 50 books. |
| Breaking and Entering (Bronze) | Picked 50 locks. |
| Bull in a China Shop (Bronze) | Smashed 1,000 objects. |
| Cartographer (Bronze) | Discovered 100 locations. |
| Cleaning Up the Streets (Bronze) | Killed 50 bandits. |
| Crime Doesn't Pay (Bronze) | Spent over 10,000 gold in crime bribes. |
| Destiny Defiant (Silver) | You have defeated Tirnoch, and defied destiny. |
| Destiny Dominated (Gold) | You have won the game on Hard difficulty. |
| Diamond in the Rough (Bronze) | Crafted a Pristine Shard. |
| Elixir of Fate (Bronze) | Made a potion with the Essence of Fate. |
| Five Finger Discount (Bronze) | Stole and fenced an item. |
| Foiled Again! (Bronze) | Parried 100 times. |
| Good as New (Bronze) | Repaired a piece of equipment. |
| Green Thumb (Bronze) | Harvested 10 of each type of reagent. |
| Hero of Mel Senshir (Gold) | You have defeated the great Balor. |
| House of Ballads (Silver) | Completed the House of Ballads storyline quests. |
| House of Sorrows (Silver) | Completed the House of Sorrows storyline quests. |
| It Didn't Explode! (Bronze) | Made a stable potion by experimenting. |
| It is Your Destiny (Bronze) | Unlocked a top tier destiny. |
| Jack of All Trades (Bronze) | Unlocked a Jack of All Trades destiny. |
| Jailbreak (Bronze) | You broke out of jail. |
| Juggler (Silver) | Landed 5 consecutive hits on a launched enemy. |
| Loremaster (Bronze) | Found all Lorestones. |
| Master of the Forge (Bronze) | Crafted an item that uses all 5 forge component slots. |
| Niskaru Slayer (Bronze) | Killed 25 Niskaru. |
| No Destiny, All Determination (Bronze) | You have met High King Titarion, and have been confronted with the true scope of your powers. |
| Open Sesame (Bronze) | Dispelled 50 wards. |
| Out of Your League (Bronze) | Killed an enemy 4 levels higher than you. |
| Perfectionist (Platinum) | Awarded all trophies. |
| Reborn (Bronze) | You were reborn from the Well of Souls, and have escaped Allestar Tower. |
| Reckoning Rampage (Bronze) | Killed 5 enemies with a single Fateshift. |
| Riposte! (Bronze) | Landed 25 special attacks out of Parry. |

A
B
C
D
E
F
G
H
I
J
K
L
M
N
O
P
Q
R
S
T
U
V
W
X
Y
Z

| | |
|---|---|
| Romancing the Gem (Bronze) | Crafted an Epic Gem. |
| Scholia Arcana (Silver) | Completed the Scholia Arcana storyline quests. |
| Shock and Awe (Bronze) | Killed 100 enemies with abilities. |
| Shop Class (Bronze) | Crafted a piece of equipment with Blacksmithing. |
| Some of This, Some of That (Bronze) | Unlocked a two-class hybrid destiny. |
| Streaker (Bronze) | You spoke to someone while not wearing clothes. |
| The Great Detective (Bronze) | Detected 25 hidden things. |
| They Never Saw it Coming (Bronze) | Backstabbed 20 enemies. |
| Trapper (Bronze) | Killed 25 enemies with traps. |
| Travelers (Silver) | Completed the Travelers storyline quests. |
| Turning the Tide (Silver) | A ruse has baited Octienne into betraying the necromantic nature of his experiments. |
| Warsworn (Silver) | Completed the Warsworn storyline quests. |
| Where's My Wallet? (Bronze) | Pickpocketed 20 times. |
| Would You Like Fries with that? (Bronze) | Landed 100 complete attack chains. |

## KINGDOMS OF AMALUR: RECKONING (XBOX 360)

### ACHIEVEMENT

| UNLOCKABLE | HOW TO UNLOCK |
|---|---|
| A Life of Crime (15) | Get caught committing a crime 25 times. |
| A Wink and a Smile (15) | Succeed at 50 Persuasion attempts. |
| And Then There Were None (20) | Kill 500 enemies with abilities. |
| Big Spender (15) | Spend 200,000 gold. |
| Blades of Glory (15) | Acquire 10 Unique weapons (Special Delivery weapons excluded). |
| Bookworm (15) | Read 50 books. |
| Breaking and Entering (15) | Pick 50 locks. |
| Bull in a China Shop (15) | Smash 1,000 objects. |
| Cartographer (20) | Discover 100 locations. |
| Cleaning Up the Streets (20) | Kill 50 bandits. |
| Complete the Travelers storyline quests | Complete the Travelers storyline quests. |
| Crime Doesn't Pay (10) | Spend over 10,000 gold in crime bribes. |
| Destiny Defiant (75) | You have defeated Tirnoch, and defied destiny. |
| Destiny Dominated (100) | You have won the game on Hard difficulty. |
| Diamond in the Rough (10) | Craft a Pristine Shard. |
| Elixir of Fate (20) | Make a potion with the Essence of Fate. |
| Five Finger Discount (10) | Steal and fence an item. |
| Foiled Again! (15) | Parry 100 times. |
| Good as New (10) | Repair a piece of equipment. |
| Green Thumb (15) | Harvest 10 of each type of reagent. |
| Hero of Mel Senshir (75) | You have defeated the great Balor. |
| House of Ballads (20) | Complete the House of Ballads storyline quests. |
| House of Sorrows (20) | Complete the House of Sorrows storyline quests. |

| | |
|---|---|
| It Didn't Explode! (10) | Make a stable potion by experimenting. |
| It is Your Destiny (50) | Unlock a top tier destiny. |
| Jack of All Trades (10) | Unlock a Jack of All Trades destiny. |
| Jailbreak (10) | Break out of jail. |
| Juggler (20) | Land 5 consecutive hits on a launched enemy. |
| Loremaster (20) | Discover all Lorestones. |
| Master of the Forge (20) | Romancing the Gem (15) |
| Niskaru Slayer (20) | Kill 25 Niskaru. |
| No Destiny, All Determination (15) | You have met High King Titarion, and have been confronted with the true scope of your powers. |
| Open Sesame (15) | Dispel 50 wards. |
| Out of Your League (20) | Kill an enemy 4 levels higher than you. |
| Pickpocket 20 times. | Pickpocket 20 times. |
| Reborn (10) | You were reborn from the Well of Souls, and have escaped Allestar Tower. |
| Reckoning Rampage (20) | Kill 5 enemies with a single Fateshift. |
| Riposte! (10) | Land 25 special attacks out of Parry. |
| Romancing the Gem (15) | Craft an Epic Gem. |
| Scholia Arcana (20) | Complete the Scholia Arcana storyline quests. |
| Shock and Awe (15) | Kill 100 enemies with abilities. |
| Shop Class (10) | Craft a piece of equipment with Blacksmithing. |
| Some of This, Some of That (10) | Unlock a two-class hybrid destiny. |
| Streaker (10) | You spoke to someone while not wearing clothes. |
| The Great Detective (10) | Detect 25 hidden things. |
| They Never Saw it Coming (10) | Backstab 20 enemies. |
| Trapper (15) | Kill 25 enemies with traps. |
| Turning the Tide (20) | A ruse has baited Octienne into betraying the necromantic nature of his experiments. |
| Warsworn (20) | Complete the Warsworn storyline quests. |
| Would You Like Fries with that? (15) | Land 100 complete attack chains. |

## LEGO BATMAN 2: DC SUPER HEROES (PlayStation 3)

### TROPHY

| UNLOCKABLE | HOW TO UNLOCK |
|---|---|
| Arkham Asylum Antics (Bronze) | Complete story level 3 |
| Asylum Assignment (Bronze) | Complete story level 4 |
| Chemical Crisis (Bronze) | Complete story level 5 |
| Chemical Signature (Bronze) | Complete story level 6 |
| City Slicker (Gold) | Collect all the gold bricks (Single Player Only) |
| Combo Hero (Bronze) | Do a finishing move |
| Complete Hero (Platinum) | Collected all of the Trophies |
| Core Instability (Bronze) | Complete story level 13 |
| Destination Metropolis (Bronze) | Complete story level 8 |
| Down to Earth (Bronze) | Complete story level 10 |
| Dynamic Duo (Bronze) | Play a level in co-op |

NEW!

A
B
C
D
E
F
G
H
I
J
K
L
M
N
O
P
Q
R
S
T
U
V
W
X
Y
Z

| | |
|---|---|
| **Extra! Extra! (Bronze)** | Collect all the red bricks (Single Player Only) |
| **Girl Power (Silver)** | Unlock all female heroes and villains. (Single Player Only) |
| **Gorilla Thriller (Bronze)** | Climb to the top of Wayne tower while riding a Gorilla and playing as a female character. |
| **Green Lantern's Light (Bronze)** | Defeat Sinestro as Green Lantern |
| **Halfway Through (Silver)** | Get 50% (Single Player Only) |
| **Harboring a Criminal (Bronze)** | Complete story level 2 |
| **Heroes Unite (Bronze)** | Complete story level 15 |
| **Inferior Machines (Bronze)** | With Brainiac, defeat any LexBot |
| **It's A Bird... It's A Plane... (Bronze)** | Fly with Superman |
| **Justice League (Silver)** | Unlock all Justice League characters (Single Player Only) |
| **Kal-El Last Son of Krypton (Bronze)** | Defeat Zod as Superman |
| **Minikit Hero (Gold)** | Use all the Minikit vehicles |
| **My Hero (Silver)** | Rescue all Citizens in Peril (Single Player Only) |
| **Research and Development (Bronze)** | Complete story level 9 |
| **Subway Hero (Bronze)** | Use the Gotham City Metro |
| **Super Hero (Silver)** | Get Super Hero in all levels (Single Player Only) |
| **Super-Villain (Silver)** | Unlock all the Bosses (Single Player Only) |
| **Team Building (Gold)** | Unlock all characters (Single Player Only) |
| **Test Hero (Silver)** | Test a custom character |
| **The End (Gold)** | Get 100% (Single Player Only) |
| **The House of Luthor (Silver)** | Obtain more than 10,100,000,000 Studs (Single Player Only) |
| **The Next President (Bronze)** | Complete story level 12 |
| **Theatrical Pursuits (Bronze)** | Complete story level 1 |
| **Tower Defiance (Bronze)** | Complete story level 14 |
| **Toy Gotham (Bronze)** | Complete the Bonus level |
| **Underground Retreat (Bronze)** | Complete story level 11 |
| **Unwelcome Guests (Bronze)** | Complete story level 7 |

## LEGO BATMAN 2: DC SUPER HEROES (PlayStation Vita)

### TROPHY

| UNLOCKABLE | HOW TO UNLOCK |
|---|---|
| **A Winning Formula (Bronze)** | Complete ACE Chemicals. |
| **A-maze-ing Chase (Bronze)** | Complete Arkham Estate. |
| **All Change! (Silver)** | Swap characters using Super Freeplay. |
| **Bad Influence (Gold)** | Collect all the Villain characters. |
| **Bane of my Life (Bronze)** | Take down Batman with Bane. (Single Player Only) |
| **Batter Up! (Silver)** | Using the Batman glide ability, spend 5 seconds or more in the air. |
| **Behind Enemy Lines (Bronze)** | Complete Attack on LexCorp. |
| **Brick by Brick (Silver)** | Collect all the Red Bricks. |
| **Call Shotgun (Silver)** | Stun an enemy using Commissioner Gordon's trusty weapon and finish them. (Single Player Only) |

| | |
|---|---|
| **Complete Hero (Platinum)** | Collect all trophies. |
| **Deconstructive Criticism (Bronze)** | Complete The Batcave. |
| **Dishonourably Discharged! (Bronze)** | Complete Arkham Asylum. |
| **Double-crossed! (Bronze)** | Complete Brawl at City Hall. |
| **Flying Lessons (Bronze)** | Complete Assault the VTOL. |
| **Frequent Flyer (Bronze)** | Complete Robot Sky Battle. |
| **Happy Daze (Gold)** | Stun 100 enemies. |
| **Hero in Train-ing (Bronze)** | Complete Gotham Metro. |
| **Hostile Takeover (Bronze)** | Complete Wayne Industries. |
| **Justice is Served (Gold)** | Win gold in every arena in Justice League Mode. |
| **Justice League, Assemble! (Bronze)** | Complete The Final Battle. |
| **MVP (Gold)** | Complete every arena in Justice League Mode. |
| **Open Mic Knight (Bronze)** | Complete Gotham Theatre. |
| **Road to Ruin (Bronze)** | Complete Juggernaut Chase. |
| **Siamese Bat (Silver)** | As Catwoman, use the Stealth Takedown ability to attack Batman. (Single Player Only) |
| **Sound Advice (Silver)** | Collect all the Sound Bite tokens. |
| **Starter Pack (Silver)** | Unlock all the Ability packs for the Character Customiser. |
| **Super Friends (Gold)** | Collect all the Hero characters. |
| **Taking the Plunge (Silver)** | Help an enemy off a ledge in Wayne Industries. |
| **The Big Brick Theory (Bronze)** | Create your first character in the Character Customiser. |
| **The Joke's on you! (Bronze)** | Complete The Joker Getaway. |
| **True Hero (Silver)** | Achieve a True Hero stud total. |
| **Unbreakable (Gold)** | Finish a level without losing all your hearts. |

### CODE

| UNLOCKABLE | HOW TO UNLOCK |
|---|---|
| **Clown Goon** | 9ZZZBP |
| **Lexbot** | W49CSJ |
| **Mime Goon** | ZQA8MK |
| **Regenerate Hearts** | ZXEX5D |
| **Riddler Goon** | Q285LK |
| **Studs X2** | 74EZUT |
| **Two-Face Goon** | 95KPYJ |

## LEGO BATMAN 2: DC SUPER HEROES (XBOX 360)

### ACHIEVEMENT

| UNLOCKABLE | HOW TO UNLOCK |
|---|---|
| **Arkham Asylum Antics (25)** | Complete story level 3 |
| **Asylum Assignment (25)** | Complete story level 4 |
| **Chemical Crisis (25)** | Complete story level 5 |
| **Chemical Signature (25)** | Complete story level 6 |
| **City Slicker (35)** | Collect all the gold bricks (Single Player Only) |
| **Combo Hero (20)** | Do a finishing move |
| **Core Instability (25)** | Complete story level 13 |
| **Destination Metropolis (25)** | Complete story level 8 |
| **Down to Earth (25)** | Complete story level 10 |

**CODES & CHEATS**

| Dynamic Duo (20) | Play a level in co-op |
| --- | --- |
| Extra! Extra! (20) | Collect all the red bricks (Single Player Only) |
| Girl Power (20) | Unlock all female heroes and villains. (Single Player Only) |
| Gorilla Thriller (20) | Climb to the top of Wayne tower while riding a Gorilla and playing as a female character. |
| Green Lantern's Light (20) | Defeat Sinestro as Green Lantern |
| Halfway Through (50) | Get 50% (Single Player Only) |
| Harboring a Criminal (25) | Complete story level 2 |
| Heroes Unite (25) | Complete story level 15 |
| Inferior Machines (20) | With Brainiac, defeat any LexBot |
| It's A Bird... It's A Plane... (20) | Fly with Superman |
| Justice League (20) | Unlock all Justice League characters (Single Player Only) |
| Kal-El Last Son of Krypton (20) | Defeat Zod as Superman |
| Minikit Hero (20) | Use all the Minikit vehicles |
| My Hero (50) | Rescue all Citizens in Peril (Single Player Only) |
| Research and Development (25) | Complete story level 9 |
| Subway Hero (20) | Use the Gotham City Metro |
| Super Hero (50) | Get Super Hero in all levels (Single Player Only) |
| Super-Villain (20) | Unlock all the Bosses (Single Player Only) |
| Team Building (50) | Unlock all characters (Single Player Only) |
| Test Hero (20) | Test a custom character |
| The End (70) | Get 100% (Single Player Only) |
| The House of Luthor (20) | Obtain more than 10,100,000,000 Studs (Single Player Only) |
| The Next President (25) | Complete story level 12 |
| Theatrical Pursuits (25) | Complete story level 1 |
| Tower Defiance (25) | Complete story level 14 |
| Toy Gotham (20) | Complete the Bonus level |
| Underground Retreat (25) | Complete story level 11 |
| Unwelcome Guests (25) | Complete story level 7 |

## LEGO HARRY POTTER: YEARS 5-7 (PlayStation Vita)

### TROPHY

| UNLOCKABLE | HOW TO UNLOCK |
| --- | --- |
| A Siriusly Cold Dish (Bronze) | As Sirius, defeat Bellatrix in the Duelling Club |
| All Finished! (Platinum) | Acquire all trophies. |
| Beat the Parents (Bronze) | As a custom character, defeat Lily and James Potter in the Duelling club. |
| Bellatrix Beaten (Silver) | As Molly Weasley, defeat Bellatrix without taking damage in the Final Battle. |
| Blind as a Basilisk (Bronze) | Blind an enemy creature. |
| Bonus Category Duelling Champion (Silver) | Defeat all duellers in the Bonus Duelling category. |
| Bricked! (Silver) | Collect all the Red Bricks. |
| Complete Collection (Silver) | Collect all the characters. |
| Creature Confusion (Bronze) | Force any enemy creature to attack another. |
| Death Eater Category Duelling Champion (Bronze) | Defeat all duellers in the Death Eater Duelling category. |
| Deathly Hallows - Part 1 Trophy (Silver) | Complete Deathly Hallows - Part 1. |

| | |
|---|---|
| **Deathly Hallows - Part 2 Trophy (Silver)** | Complete Deathly Hallows - Part 2. |
| **Draco's Disco (Silver)** | As Draco Malfoy, cast Tarantallegra at another character. |
| **Dumbledore's Army Category Duelling Champion (Bronze)** | Defeat all duellers in the Dumbledore's Army Duelling category. |
| **Falling to Pieces (Bronze)** | Fail to put together puzzle pieces after six attempts |
| **Half-Blood Prince Trophy (Silver)** | Complete Half-Blood Prince. |
| **Hogwarts Category Duelling Champion (Bronze)** | Defeat all duellers in the Hogwarts Duelling category. |
| **I said, bow! (Silver)** | As Voldemort, defeat Harry Potter in Duelling Club. |
| **Infer Inferi are Inferior (Silver)** | Cause the Inferi to destroy each other in the cave. |
| **Kitted Out (Silver)** | Collect all Minikits. |
| **Know Your Enemy (Bronze)** | Defeat one of each enemy. |
| **Kreacher Confusion (Bronze)** | Cast Confundo on Kreacher in Grimmauld Place |
| **Master Dueller (Gold)** | Defeat all duellers in each category. |
| **Ministry of Magic Category Duelling Champion (Bronze)** | Defeat all duellers in the Ministry of Magic Duelling category. |
| **Niceties Must be Observed (Gold)** | Defeat Voldemort without taking any damage. |
| **Open Category Duelling Champion (Bronze)** | Defeat all duellers in the Open Duelling category. |
| **Order of the Phoenix Trophy (Silver)** | Complete Order of the Phoenix. |
| **Phoenix Category Duelling Champion (Bronze)** | Defeat all duellers in the Order of the Phoenix Duelling category. |
| **Playtime (Silver)** | Enjoy all the fun in the playground |
| **Put me down! (Bronze)** | Cast Levicorpus on an enemy. |
| **Richer by the Galleon (Bronze)** | Bank 10,000,000 studs. |
| **Shield Charm Master (Bronze)** | Take no damage when duelling in Duelling Club. |
| **Student Category Duelling Champion (Bronze)** | Defeat all duellers in the Student Duelling category. |
| **Suits You! (Bronze)** | As Voldemort in a suit, defeat Arthur Weasley in a suit in the Duelling Club. |
| **The Best Offense is a Strong Defense (Silver)** | Use only Protego during a duel in the Duelling Club. |
| **The End (Gold)** | Complete 100% of the game. |
| **The Enemy Within (Bronze)** | As a Death Eater, cast at anyone in the Hogwarts hub. |
| **This is Knuts! (Bronze)** | Bank 100,000,000 studs. |
| **Too True (Silver)** | Achieve a single True Wizard Stud Total |
| **Trans-figure-ation (Bronze)** | Create your own character in the character customiser. |
| **Well Done Draco (Bronze)** | As Draco, defeat Dumbledore in the Duelling Club. |

## LITTLE DEVIANTS (PlayStation Vita)

### TROPHY

| UNLOCKABLE | HOW TO UNLOCK |
|---|---|
| **A Head for Heights (Bronze)** | Complete Stage 1 of Risky Inclination with at least 30 seconds remaining. |
| **Air Miles And Miles (Bronze)** | Fly 1,000,000m. |
| **Blackrust Refinery (Bronze)** | Unlock Blackrust Refinery region. |

| | |
|---|---|
| **Blink and you'll miss it (Bronze)** | Pick up the Star from the secret chamber in Risky Rambler. |
| **Bomb 'Em, Man (Bronze)** | Destroy 2 or more Dead 'Uns with one fire attack in Corridor Calamity. |
| **Cat-alouged (Silver)** | All Moggers collected. |
| **Cave Brave (Bronze)** | Collect at least 120 pickups in a single game of Risky Trails. |
| **Chillrock Gorge (Bronze)** | Unlock Chillrock Gorge region. |
| **Cold As Ice (Bronze)** | Smash 5 frozen Botz or more in a game of Corridor Complications. |
| **Competent Deviant (Silver)** | Win at least a silver spaceship on all games. |
| **Crate Breaker (Bronze)** | Break open a crate in under half a second in Rolling Shores. |
| **Day None Patch (Bronze)** | Complete Hot Air Hero without patching the ballon once. |
| **Dead 'Un Masher (Bronze)** | Splat 6 or more Dead 'Uns with one shot in Rotten Rumble. |
| **Deviant Storm (Bronze)** | Boost over the finishing line in Street Speeder. |
| **Devilish Deviant (Gold)** | Win a gold spaceship on all games. |
| **Dipped into Deviants (Bronze)** | Win your first bronze spaceship. |
| **Exhibitionist (Silver)** | All gallery items unlocked. |
| **Fint the Time (Silver)** | Collect 1,000 Clocks. |
| **Full Controller (Bronze)** | Complete Rolling Pastures with full health at the end of the game. |
| **Fun Deviant (Bronze)** | Win at least a bronze spaceship on all games. |
| **Grave Digger (Silver)** | Destroy 500 Dead 'Uns. |
| **Heavy Metal (Bronze)** | Destroy 20 Botz in Destructor Constructor. |
| **Honor Upheld (Bronze)** | Defeat a challenge from a PlayStation Network friend. |
| **I didn't wipe (Bronze)** | Complete Botz Blast without wiping any green goo from the screen. |
| **Jump Around (Bronze)** | Jump on one platform 5 times in Bouncer Trouncer. |
| **Just made it! (Bronze)** | Finish Stage 4 of Depth Avenger with at least 10 seconds remaining. |
| **Kyle says, "Don't touch..." (Bronze)** | Score 35,000 points in Shack Shover without hitting a Whoman or a Deviant. |
| **Laaaaaaaaaaaaaa! (Bronze)** | Hold a note in Smashing Tune for at least 5 seconds. |
| **Long Way Roller (Bronze)** | Roll 500,000m. |
| **Meow! (Bronze)** | Collect your first Mogger. |
| **Metroburg (Bronze)** | Unlock Metroburg region. |
| **Mmm, hardware (Bronze)** | Use each of the PlayStation Vita system's input devices that are featured in Little Deviants. |
| **No-Electro Hero (Bronze)** | Complete Corridor Caper without using any EMP pickups. |
| **Over-boinged (Silver)** | Bounce a Deviant 1,500 times. |
| **Perfect 12 (Bronze)** | In City Shover hit all 12 Number-Botz in sequence. |
| **Scored! (Bronze)** | Post a score to the online leaderboard. |
| **Sharpshooter (Bronze)** | Destroy 10 Botz without missing a shot in a game of Botz Invasion. |
| **Smooth Mover (Bronze)** | Complete Depth Charge without hitting any walls. |

| | |
|---|---|
| **Star Barred (Bronze)** | Complete Aqua Speeder without picking up more than 20 Stars. |
| **Starry Eyed (Silver)** | Collect 5,000 Stars. |
| **Stay on target! (Bronze)** | Boost 5 times in a row without crashing in Death Speeder. |
| **Storm Chaser (Bronze)** | Hit at least 10 different wind vortices in Depth Dive and still complete the game. |
| **Stream Saver (Bronze)** | Complete Neutron Nudger without any Botz damaging the energy sphere. |
| **Surfcrest Bay (Bronze)** | Unlock Surfcrest Bay region. |
| **Taste of Victory (Bronze)** | Win your first gold spaceship. |
| **Teacher's Pet (Bronze)** | Input 3 consecutive codes correctly in Cannon Codes. |
| **Terminated (Silver)** | Destroy 2,500 Botz. |
| **The Mighty Boost (Bronze)** | Boost through all the rings in any single stage of Cloud Rush. |
| **The right way is the wrong way (Bronze)** | Complete Manic Melter by only twisting the platform clockwise. |
| **They mostly come at night, mostly (Bronze)** | Play Rolling Horror between 00:00 and 01:00. |
| **Throwdown (Bronze)** | Challenge a PlayStation Network friend. |
| **Timeless (Bronze)** | Score at least 28,000 points in Chalet Shover without using any Clock pickups. |
| **Trophyumphant (Platinum)** | Unlock all other trophies. |
| **Twisty Root Groove (Bronze)** | Unlock Twisty Root Grove region. |
| **Watch the Birdy (Bronze)** | Collect 3 bird pickups in a single game of Tower of Boing. |

## LOLLIPOP CHAINSAW (PlayStation 3)

### TROPHY

| UNLOCKABLE | HOW TO UNLOCK |
|---|---|
| **Accidental Vandalism (Bronze)** | Destroyed 300 objects in the game. |
| **Aced Auto-shop Class (Bronze)** | Clear all the Kill Car QTE's in a row. |
| **Advanced Zombie Hunter (Silver)** | Clear Stage 3, surpassing Dad's score. |
| **Always On The Phone (Bronze)** | Collected all telephone messages. |
| **Beginner Zombie Hunter (Silver)** | Clear Stage 1, surpassing Dad's score. |
| **Cheerleader Overboard! (Bronze)** | Succeed in QTE at edge of Vikke's ship. |
| **Congratulations! Happy Birthday! (Gold)** | Watched the happy ending. |
| **Critical UFO Finish (Bronze)** | Funk Josey in the last 10 seconds. |
| **Dirty Hippy (Bronze)** | Defeated Mariska. |
| **Disco's Dead (Bronze)** | Defeated Josey. |
| **Elephant Tamer (Bronze)** | Counter Lewis' attack 10 times. |
| **Endorsed by Cordelia (Bronze)** | Get 30 headshots. |
| **Excellent Zombie Hunter (Silver)** | Clear Stage 5, surpassing Dad's score. |
| **Fingered (Bronze)** | Cut off 20 fingers during Killabilly's fight! |
| **Go, Medal Racer, Go! (Bronze)** | Picked up all zombie medals on the rooftop with Chainsaw Dash. |
| **Groovy Hunter (Bronze)** | Kill 500 zombies. |
| **Gunn Struck (Bronze)** | Struck by lightning 10 times. |
| **Horrid Birthday (Bronze)** | Watched the bad ending. |
| **I Came, I Saw, I Kicked Its Ass (Bronze)** | Defeated Killabilly. |
| **I Swear! I Did It By Mistake! (Bronze)** | Peeped under Juliet's skirt once. |

A B C D E F G H I J K L M N O P Q R S T U V W X Y Z

| | |
|---|---|
| **Intermediate Zombie Hunter (Silver)** | Clear Stage 2, surpassing Dad's score. |
| **International Zombie Hunter (Bronze)** | Registered in world leaderboards for all stages. |
| **JULIET51 (Bronze)** | 51 successful dropkicks. |
| **Leapfrog girl (Bronze)** | Leapfrogged 10 times in a row. |
| **Legendary harvester (Bronze)** | Harvested all crops in the 1st field with the combine in Stage 3. |
| **Legendary Zombie Hunter (Platinum)** | 100% Complete! Thank you for playing! |
| **Life Guard (Bronze)** | Rescued all classmates in Prologue. |
| **Little Sisters Are The Worst! (Bronze)** | Do not get hit by Rosalind's wrecking ball. |
| **Lollipop Addict (Silver)** | Collected all lollipop wrappers. |
| **Love Nick (Bronze)** | Kissed Nick 100 times. |
| **Master Sushi Chef (Silver)** | Collected all combos. |
| **Master Zombie Hunter (Silver)** | Clear Stage 6, surpassing Dad's score. |
| **Millionaire Hunter (Silver)** | Pick up 10,000 zombie medals. |
| **n00b Zombie Hunter (Silver)** | Clear Prologue, surpassing Dad's score. |
| **No Fear Of Heights (Bronze)** | Beat the Gondola game without shooting. |
| **OMG, Music Is Soooo Coooool (Silver)** | Collected all BGM. |
| **Perfect Body (Silver)** | Completely level up Juliet. |
| **Rich Hunter (Bronze)** | Pick up 1,000 zombie medals. |
| **Rock'n Roll Isn't Here Anymore (Bronze)** | Defeated Lewis LEGEND. |
| **San Romero Knights Savior (Silver)** | Rescued All Classmates. |
| **Sparkle Hunting Master (Bronze)** | Succeed in 7 zombie Sparkle Hunting. |
| **Super Shopper (Bronze)** | Spend 10,000 medals at Chop2Shop. Zom. |
| **Super Zombie Hunter (Silver)** | Clear Stage 4, surpassing Dad's score. |
| **Third Eye (Bronze)** | Dodge all balloon attacks in Mariska battle. |
| **Unclean and Uncool (Bronze)** | Defeated Hazmat in Prologue. |
| **Viking Metal Rules! (Bronze)** | Defeated Vikke. |
| **Watch Out For The Balls (Bronze)** | Dodge & Counter Zed's Electric Balls 15 times. |
| **Zed's Dead, Baby, Zed's Dead (Bronze)** | Defeated Zed. |
| **Zombie Fancier (Silver)** | Completed the zombie album. |
| **Zombie Hunter Apprentice (Bronze)** | Buy a combo at Chop2Shop.Zom and use it. |
| **Zombie Slayer?! (Silver)** | Kill 3,000 zombies. |

## LOLLIPOP CHAINSAW (XBOX 360)

### ACHIEVEMENT

| UNLOCKABLE | HOW TO UNLOCK |
|---|---|
| **Accidental Vandalism (15)** | Destroyed 300 objects in the game. |
| **Aced Auto-shop Class (15)** | Clear all the Kill Car QTE's in a row. |
| **Advanced Zombie Hunter (30)** | Clear Stage 3, surpassing Dad's score. |
| **Always On The Phone (30)** | Collected all telephone messages. |
| **Beginner Zombie Hunter (30)** | Clear Stage 1, surpassing Dad's score. |
| **Cheerleader Overboard! (10)** | Succeed in QTE at edge of Vikke's ship. |
| **Congratulations! Happy Birthday! (100)** | Watched the happy ending. |
| **Critical UFO Finish (10)** | Funk Josey in the last 10 seconds. |
| **Dirty Hippy (15)** | Defeated Mariska. |

**NEW!**

| | |
|---|---|
| **Disco's Dead (15)** | Defeated Josey. |
| **Elephant Tamer (10)** | Counter Lewis' attack 10 times. |
| **Endorsed by Cordelia (10)** | Get 30 headshots. |
| **Excellent Zombie Hunter (30)** | Clear Stage 5, surpassing Dad's score. |
| **Fingered (10)** | Cut off 20 fingers during Killabilly's fight! |
| **Go, Medal Racer, Go! (15)** | Picked up all zombie medals on the rooftop with Chainsaw Dash. |
| **Groovy Hunter (10)** | Kill 500 zombies. |
| **Gunn Struck (10)** | Struck by lightning 10 times. |
| **Horrid Birthday (15)** | Watched the bad ending. |
| **I Came, I Saw, I Kicked Its Ass (15)** | Defeated Killabilly. |
| **I Swear! I Did It By Mistake! (10)** | Peeped under Juliet's skirt once. |
| **Intermediate Zombie Hunter (30)** | Clear Stage 2, surpassing Dad's score. |
| **International Zombie Hunter (15)** | Registered in world leaderboards for all stages. |
| **JULIET51 (15)** | 51 successful dropkicks. |
| **Leapfrog Girl (10)** | Leapfrogged 10 times in a row. |
| **Legendary harvester (15)** | Harvested all crops in the 1st field with the combine in Stage 3. |
| **Life Guard (15)** | Rescued all classmates in Prologue. |
| **Little Sisters Are The Worst! (15)** | Do not get hit by Rosalind's wrecking ball. |
| **Lollipop Addict (30)** | Collected all lollipop wrappers. |
| **Love Nick (15)** | Kissed Nick 100 times. |
| **Master Sushi Chef (30)** | Collected all combos. |
| **Master Zombie Hunter (30)** | Clear Stage 6, surpassing Dad's score. |
| **Millionaire Hunter (30)** | Pick up 10,000 zombie medals. |
| **n00b Zombie Hunter (30)** | Clear Prologue, surpassing Dad's score. |
| **No Fear Of Heights (15)** | Beat the Gondola game without shooting. |
| **OMG, Music Is Soooo Coooool (30)** | Collected all BGM. |
| **Perfect Body (30)** | Completely level up Juliet. |
| **Rich Hunter (10)** | Pick up 1,000 zombie medals. |
| **Rock'n Roll Isn't Here Anymore (15)** | Defeated Lewis LEGEND. |
| **San Romero Knights Savior (30)** | Rescued All Classmates. |
| **Sparkle Hunting Master (10)** | Succeed in 7 zombie Sparkle Hunting. |
| **Super Shopper (15)** | Spend 10,000 medals at Chop2Shop.Zom. |
| **Super Zombie Hunter (30)** | Clear Stage 4, surpassing Dad's score. |
| **Third Eye (10)** | Dodge all balloon attacks in Mariska battle. |
| **Unclean and Uncool (15)** | Defeated Hazmat in Prologue. |
| **Viking Metal Rules! (15)** | Defeated Vikke. |
| **Watch Out For The Balls (10)** | Dodge & Counter Zed's Electric Balls 15 times. |
| **Zed's Dead, Baby, Zed's Dead (15)** | Defeated Zed. |
| **Zombie Fancier (30)** | Completed the zombie album. |
| **Zombie Hunter Apprentice (5)** | Buy a combo at Chop2Shop.Zom and use it. |
| **Zombie Slayer?! (30)** | Kill 3,000 zombies. |

A
B
C
D
E
F
G
H
I
J
K
L
M
N
O
P
Q
R
S
T
U
V
W
X
Y
Z

## LUMINES: ELECTRONIC SYMPHONY  (PlayStation Vita)

### TROPHY

| UNLOCKABLE | HOW TO UNLOCK |
|---|---|
| A Perfect Storm (Bronze) | Use a Chain Block to connect at least 25 blocks. |
| A True Pioneer (Bronze) | Clear 10 Skins in Voyage Mode. |
| Avatar Addicts (Bronze) | Use Avatar Abilities 200 times. |
| Black Belt (Silver) | Unlock Master Zone 5. |
| Journey's End (Silver) | Clear all Skins in Voyage Mode. |
| Lucky 5 (Bronze) | Create 5 Squares with 1 Shuffle Block. |
| New Recruit (Bronze) | Get a total score of 50,000. |
| Prodigy (Bronze) | Achieve a BONUSx3. |
| Thank You (Bronze) | Watch through the entire Credits sequence. |
| The DJ Is In The House (Bronze) | Create, save and then clear 12 Playlists. |
| Time Stands Still (Silver) | Erase 30 Squares in Stopwatch Mode – 30 Seconds. |
| True Believer (Bronze) | Play for over 3 hours within 24 hours. |
| Winner Takes It All (Gold) | Unlock all Skins and all Avatars. |

## MADAGASCAR 3: THE VIDEO GAME  (PlayStation Vita)

### TROPHY

| UNLOCKABLE | HOW TO UNLOCK |
|---|---|
| 3 Rings of Fun! (Bronze) | Get 5 Stars in any Flaming Rings Act |
| A Proper Send-Off! (Bronze) | Get 5 Stars in any Trapeze Act |
| A Rare Sight! (Silver) | Find all 195 Thermometers For Melman |
| A Real Blast! (Silver) | Find all 195 Cannonball Balloons for Marty |
| A Sure Hit! (Bronze) | Get 5 Stars in any Cannonball Act |
| All Aboard for Adventure! (Silver) | Finish Italian Countryside Tutorials |
| Arrivederci, Rome! (Bronze) | Finish Rome Circus |
| Au Revoir, Dubois! (Bronze) | Defeat Chantal Dubois |
| Au Revoir, Paris! (Bronze) | Finish Paris Circus |
| Aye Aye, Skipper! (Bronze) | Finish A Mission for Skipper |
| Back to the Big Apple (Bronze) | Get the Gang to New York |
| Belisima! (Bronze) | Complete the Leaning Tower Publicity Stunt |
| Biggest Star Under the Big Top! (Silver) | Get 5 Stars in each Circus Act |
| Boss of the Toss! (Bronze) | Get 5 Stars in any Snack Toss |
| Ciao, Pisa! (Bronze) | Finish Pisa Circus |
| Circus Beauty! (Silver) | Find all 195 Flowers for Gloria |
| Colossal! (Bronze) | Complete the Colosseum Publicity Stunt |
| Everything! (Platinum) | Earn every Trophy in the game |
| Farewell, London! (Bronze) | Finish London Circus |
| For King Julien (Silver) | Complete All King Julien's Tasks |
| High Wire Highness! (Bronze) | Get 5 Stars in any High Wire Act |
| International Superstar (Gold) | Get 5 Stars on All City Events |
| King of the Circus (Bronze) | Finish New York Circus |
| Lemur Located: London (Bronze) | Find Mort in London |
| Lemur Located: Paris (Bronze) | Find Mort in Paris |
| Lemur Located: Pisa (Bronze) | Find Mort in Pisa |
| Lemur Located: Rome (Bronze) | Find Mort in Rome |
| Lon-Done! (Bronze) | Finish London City Events |

| | |
|---|---|
| **London Circus Superstar (Silver)** | Get 5 Stars in all London Circus Acts |
| **London City Superstar (Silver)** | Complete all London City events with 5 Stars |
| **Mort is Everywhere! (Bronze)** | Find Mort in all Cities |
| **New York Circus Superstar! (Silver)** | Get 5 Stars in all New York Circus Acts |
| **Paris Circus Superstar (Silver)** | Get 5 Stars in all Paris Circus Acts |
| **Paris City Superstar (Silver)** | Complete all Paris City events with 5 Stars |
| **Penguin Problem Solved! (Silver)** | Get all the Items Skipper Needs |
| **Pisa Cake! (Bronze)** | Finish Pisa City Events |
| **Pisa Circus Superstar (Silver)** | Get 5 Stars in all Pisa Circus Acts |
| **Pisa City Superstar (Silver)** | Complete all Pisa City events with 5 Stars |
| **Roman Circus Superstar (Bronze)** | Get 5 Stars in all Rome Circus Acts |
| **Roman City Superstar (Bronze)** | Complete all Rome City events with 5 Stars |
| **Running Things in Rome! (Bronze)** | Finish Rome City Events |
| **Scrapwood Surplus! (Bronze)** | Find All the Scrap Wood Skipper Needs |
| **The Circus is Coming to Town (Bronze)** | Complete All Poster Races |
| **The Ultimate Showman! (Silver)** | Find all 195 Stars for Alex |
| **The Whole Frenchilada! (Bronze)** | Finish Paris City Events |
| **Ticket to Adventure! (Bronze)** | Get 5 Stars in any Ticket Sales |
| **Towering Bridge Star! (Bronze)** | Complete the Tower Bridge Publicity Stunt |
| **What an Eye Full! (Bronze)** | Complete the Eiffel Tower Publicity Stunt |
| **Wild About the Circus! (Bronze)** | Free All Captured Compadres |
| **Yes, Your Highness! (Bronze)** | Finish A Mission for King Julien |
| **You Went Bananas! (Bronze)** | Get 5 Stars in any Banana Race |

## MAHJONG FIGHT CLUB: SHINSEI ZENKOKU TAISEN HAN (PlayStation Vita)

### TROPHY

| UNLOCKABLE | HOW TO UNLOCK |
|---|---|
| **100 Dora Breakthrough (bronze)** | Use a total of 100 dora bonus tiles |
| **100 National Matches Breakthrough (silver)** | Complete 100 online matches (of 2 rounds each) |
| **200 Dora Breakthrough (silver)** | Use a total of 200 dora bonus tiles |
| **200 National Matches Breakthrough (gold)** | Complete 200 online matches (of 2 rounds each) |
| **50 National Matches Breakthrough (bronze)** | Complete 50 online matches (of 2 rounds each) |
| **50,000 pts (hidden bronze)** | Finish with a score of 50,000+ points |
| **70,000 pts (hidden silver)** | Finish with a score of 70,000+ points |
| **Baiman (bronze)** | Win with a baiman hand (8-10 han) |
| **Buttobashi (hidden bronze)** | Bust other players a total of ten times |
| **Buttobashi Double (hidden bronze)** | Bust two players at the same time |
| **Consecutive Tops (hidden bronze)** | Come first in five consecutive matches |
| **Dora 4 (bronze)** | Win with four dora bonus tiles |
| **Dora 5 (hidden bronze)** | Win with five dora bonus tiles |
| **Dora 6 (hidden bronze)** | Win with six dora bonus tiles |
| **Dora 7 (hidden silver)** | Win with seven dora bonus tiles |
| **Dora 8+ (hidden silver)** | Win with eight or more dora bonus tiles |
| **GII Winner (silver)** | Achieve GII |
| **GIII Winner (bronze)** | Achieve GIII |
| **Haneman (bronze)** | Win with a haneman hand (6-7 han) |

| Inverted Ron (hidden bronze) | Use the "inverted ron" function to win a hand by ron |
| Inverted Tsumo (hidden bronze) | Use the "inverted ron" function to win a hand by tsumo |
| Kouryuu Level 10 (hidden silver) | Achieve Golden Dragon level 10 |
| Kouryuu Level 20 (hidden gold) | Achieve Golden Dragon level 20 |
| Kouryuu Summons (hidden silver) | Enter the Golden Dragon ranks |
| Mangan (bronze) | Win with a mangan hand (5 han / 4 han with 40+ fu / 3 han with 70+ fu) |
| Master Summons (silver) | Achieve Master rank |
| Reverse Touch (hidden bronze) | Use the "reverse touch" function |
| Sanbaiman (silver) | Win with a sanbaiman hand (11-12 han) |
| Shijin Index 800 (hidden bronze) | Achieve a rating of 800+ over your past 50 matches |
| Shijin Index 900 (hidden silver) | Achieve a rating of 900+ over your past 50 matches |
| Swift Attack (hidden bronze) | Win a hand within six turns |
| Thunder 100 (gold) | Win 100 hands at any limit (mangan etc) |
| Thunder 30 (bronze) | Win 30 hands at any limit (mangan etc) |
| Trophies Complete (platinum) | Collect all other trophies |
| Yakuman (gold) | Win with a yakuman hand (top limit) |

## MAJOR LEAGUE BASEBALL 2K12 (PlayStation 3)

### TROPHY

| UNLOCKABLE | HOW TO UNLOCK |
| --- | --- |
| 2-Peat (Silver) | Win Back to Back World Series in My Player Mode. |
| A Job Well Done (Silver) | Win 100+ games in a season in My Player Mode. |
| A Pitcher's Best Friend (Bronze) | Turn a double play in a non-simulated game. |
| A Virtue (Silver) | Face 10 pitches as the batter in a non-simulated game. |
| Almost There (Bronze) | Hit 37 triples with your user profile. |
| As Good as a Hit (Silver) | Walk 233 times with your user profile. |
| Back to the Cage (Bronze) | Get a Golden Sombrero (strikeout 4 times in 1 game) in My Player Mode. |
| Chicks Dig It (Bronze) | Hit 74 home runs with your user profile. |
| Count it (Bronze) | Complete and win a ranked match. |
| Domination (Bronze) | Save 63 games with your user profile. |
| Don't Call it a Comeback (Bronze) | Win after being down by 4 after the 6th inning in a non-simulated game. |
| Down But Not Out (Bronze) | Get a hit with 2 strikes in a non-simulated game. |
| Dual Threat (Bronze) | Steal a base with a pitcher in a non-simulated game. |
| Fanning the Flames (Bronze) | Strike out 514 batters with your user profile. |
| Grab Some Pine (Bronze) | Get a strikeout to end the inning in a non-simulated game. |
| He Taketh Away (Bronze) | Rob a Home Run by climbing the wall in a non-simulated game. |
| Home, Sweet Home (Bronze) | Score 193 runs with your user profile. |
| I Came, I Saw... (Bronze) | Hit a Walk-off Home Run in a non-simulated game. |

| | |
|---|---|
| King of the Hill (Bronze) | Get to the top of the Best of the Best ladder in Home Run Derby Mode. |
| Mr. Consistency (Silver) | Get a hit in all 9 innings in a non-simulated game. |
| My Fellow Man (Bronze) | Complete and win an online league game. |
| My Main Squeeze (Bronze) | Bunt the man home in a non-simulated game. |
| No Hole too Deep (Bronze) | Battle Back: Down 0-2, get walked in a non-simulated game. |
| One Man Show (Gold) | Throw a No-Hitter in a 9 inning, non-simulated game. |
| Payback (Bronze) | Hit a home run off a former team in My Player Mode. |
| Production (Bronze) | Drive in 192 RBI with your user profile. |
| Productivity (Bronze) | Get 263 hits with your user profile. |
| Remember Me (Bronze) | Break a record in Franchise Mode. (play at least 20 games) |
| Set the Table (Bronze) | Hit 68 doubles with your user profile. |
| State Farm: The Road to Victory (Bronze) | Get 3 consecutive batters on base in a non-simulated game. |
| Stooges (Bronze) | Strikeout all three hitters in the inning in a non-simulated game. |
| Take That (Bronze) | Get an RBI after getting brushed back off the plate in a non-simulated game. |
| The Call (Bronze) | Get called up to the Majors in My Player Mode. |
| The Champs (Silver) | Win a World Series in Franchise Mode. (play at least 20 games) |
| The Goal (Bronze) | Accomplish a Team Season Goal in My Player Mode. |
| The Hall (Silver) | Make the Hall of Fame in My Player Mode. |
| The Road to Greatness (Bronze) | Complete and win 3 ranked matches in a row. |
| The Spice of Life (Bronze) | Play 10 ranked matches using 10 different teams. |
| The Star (Silver) | Make the All-Star team in My Player Mode. |
| The Start of Something Special (Bronze) | Lead off an inning by hitting a triple in a non-simulated game. |
| The Team to Beat (Bronze) | Beat the St. Louis Cardinals in a completed online match. |
| The Top (Silver) | Become the #1 ranked player in your My Player organization. |
| This is Why I'm Here (Bronze) | Be successful in a major league clutch moment in My Player Mode. |
| Throw First and Aim Later (Bronze) | Miss your throw to first base with 2 outs in a non-simulated game. |
| To the Rescue (Bronze) | Get a save with the tying run on base in a non-simulated game. |
| Upset Alert (Bronze) | Use the Houston Astros in a completed ranked match. |
| Walk Off (Platinum) | Unlock all Trophies |
| What's Your Ring Size? (Gold) | Win a World Series in My Player Mode. |
| You Make Your Own Destiny (Bronze) | Steal 139 bases with your user profile. |

| You're Special (Bronze) | Win a Season award in Franchise Mode. (play at least 20 games) |
| Your Day (Bronze) | Win player of the game in an MLB game in My Player Mode. |

## MAJOR LEAGUE BASEBALL 2K12 (XBOX 360)

### ACHIEVEMENT

| UNLOCKABLE | HOW TO UNLOCK |
|---|---|
| 2-Peat (25) | Win Back to Back World Series in My Player Mode. |
| A Job Well Done (25) | Win 100+ games in a season in My Player Mode. |
| A Pitcher's Best Friend (10) | Turn a double play in a non-simulated game. |
| A Virtue (20) | Face 10 pitches as the batter in a non-simulated game. |
| Almost There (10) | Hit 37 triples with your user profile. |
| As Good as a Hit (40) | Walk 233 times with your user profile. |
| Back to the Cage (10) | Get a Golden Sombrero (strikeout 4 times in 1 game) in My Player Mode. |
| Chicks Dig It (10) | Hit 74 home runs with your user profile. |
| Count it (10) | Complete and win a ranked match. |
| Domination (20) | Save 63 games with your user profile. |
| Don't Call it a Comeback (10) | Win after being down by 4 after the 6th inning in a non-simulated game. |
| Down But Not Out (5) | Get a hit with 2 strikes in a non-simulated game. |
| Dual Threat (20) | Steal base with pitcher in a non-simulated game. |
| Fanning the Flames (10) | Strike out 514 batters with your user profile. |
| Grab Some Pine (5) | Get a strikeout to end the inning in a non-simulated game. |
| He Taketh Away (20) | Rob a Home Run in a non-simulated game. |
| Home, Sweet Home (10) | Score 193 runs with your user profile. |
| I Came, I Saw... (20) | Hit a Walk-off Home Run in a non-simulated game. |
| King of the Hill (20) | Get to the top of the Best of the Best ladder in Home Run Derby Mode. |
| Mr. Consistency (20) | Get a hit in all 9 innings in a non-simulated game. |
| My Fellow Man (10) | Complete and win an online league game. |
| My Main Squeeze (15) | Bunt the man home in a non-simulated game. |
| No Hole too Deep (10) | Battle Back: Down 0-2, get walked in a non-simulated game. |
| One Man Show (80) | Throw a No-Hitter in a 9 inning, non-simulated game. |
| Payback (15) | Hit a home run off a former team in My Player Mode. |
| Production (20) | Drive in 192 RBI with your user profile. |
| Productivity (20) | Get 263 hits with your user profile. |
| Remember Me (20) | Break a record in Franchise Mode. (play at least 20 games) |
| Set the Table (15) | Hit 68 doubles with your user profile. |
| State Farm: The Road to Victory (20) | Get 3 consecutive batters on base in a non-simulated game. |

| | |
|---|---|
| Stooges (10) | Strikeout all three hitters in the inning in a non-simulated game. |
| Take That (15) | Get an RBI after getting brushed back off the plate in a non-simulated game. |
| The Call (20) | Get called up to the Majors in My Player Mode. |
| The Champs (20) | Win a World Series in Franchise Mode. (play at least 20 games) |
| The Goal (10) | Accomplish a Team Season Goal in My Player Mode. |
| The Hall (75) | Make the Hall of Fame in My Player Mode. |
| The Road to Greatness (20) | Complete and win 3 ranked matches in a row. |
| The Spice of Life (10) | Play 10 ranked matches using 10 different teams. |
| The Star (40) | Make the All-Star team in My Player Mode. |
| The Start of Something Special (10) | Lead off an inning by hitting a triple in a non-simulated game. |
| The Team to Beat (15) | Beat the St. Louis Cardinals in a completed online match. |
| The Top (30) | Become the #1 ranked player in your My Player organization. |
| This is Why I'm Here (15) | Be successful in a major league clutch moment in My Player Mode. |
| Throw First and Aim Later (10) | Miss your throw to first base with 2 outs in a non-simulated game. |
| To the Rescue (10) | Get a save with the tying run on base in a non-simulated game. |
| Upset Alert (10) | Use the Houston Astros in a completed ranked match. |
| What's Your Ring Size? (80) | Win a World Series in My Player Mode. |
| You Make Your Own Destiny (20) | Steal 139 bases with your user profile. |
| You're Special (20) | Win a Season award in Franchise Mode. (play at least 20 games) |
| Your Day (15) | Win player of the game in an MLB game in My Player Mode. |

## MASS EFFECT 3 (PlayStation 3)

### TROPHY

| UNLOCKABLE | HOW TO UNLOCK |
|---|---|
| A Personal Touch (Bronze) | Modify a weapon. |
| Almost There (Bronze) | Reach level 15 in multiplayer or level 50 in single-player. |
| Always Prepared (Bronze) | Obtain two non-customizable suits of armor. |
| Arbiter (Bronze) | Win a political stand-off. |
| Battle-Scarred (Bronze) | Promote a multiplayer character to the Galaxy at War or import an ME3 character. |
| Bringer of War (Bronze) | Chase down an assassin. |
| Bruiser (Bronze) | Kill 100 enemies with melee attacks. |
| Combined Arms (Silver) | Perform any combination of 50 biotic combos or tech bursts. |
| Defender (Bronze) | Attain the highest level of readiness in each theater of war. |
| Driven (Bronze) | Return to active duty. |
| Enlisted (Bronze) | Start a character in multiplayer or customize a character in single-player. |
| Executioner (Bronze) | Defeat an old adversary. |

**CODES & CHEATS**

| | |
|---|---|
| Explorer (Bronze) | Complete three multiplayer matches or five N7 missions. |
| Eye of the Hurricane (Bronze) | Kill a brute while it's charging you. |
| Fact Finder (Bronze) | Discover an enemy's monstrous origin. |
| Focused (Bronze) | Evolve any of your powers to rank 6. |
| Giant Killer (Bronze) | Defeat a Harvester. |
| Gunsmith (Silver) | Upgrade any weapon to level 10. |
| Hard Target (Bronze) | Call down an orbital strike. |
| Hijacker (Bronze) | Hijack an Atlas mech. |
| Insanity (Gold) | Finish the game on Insanity without changing difficulty after leaving Earth. |
| Last Witness (Bronze) | Extract ancient technology. |
| Legend (Silver) | Mission accomplished. |
| Liberator (Bronze) | Stop a Cerberus kidnapping. |
| Long Service Medal (Silver) | Complete Mass Effect 3 twice, or once with a Mass Effect 2 import. |
| Lost and Found (Bronze) | Dispatch 10 probes to retrieve people or resources in Reaper territory. |
| Mail Slot (Bronze) | Kill 10 guardians with headshots from the front while their shields are raised. |
| Master and Commander (Silver) | Deliver most of the Galaxy at War assets to the final conflict. |
| Mobilizer (Bronze) | Bring a veteran officer aboard. |
| N7 Elite (Platinum) | Acquire all trophies. |
| Overload Specialist (Bronze) | Overload the shields of 100 enemies. |
| Paramour (Bronze) | Establish or rekindle a romantic relationship. |
| Party Crasher (Bronze) | Sabotage a dreadnought. |
| Pathfinder (Bronze) | Explore a lost city. |
| Patriot (Bronze) | Make the final assault. |
| Peak Condition (Bronze) | Reach level 20 in multiplayer or level 60 in single-player. |
| Problem Solver (Bronze) | Evacuate a scientific facility. |
| Pyromaniac (Bronze) | Set 100 enemies on fire with powers. |
| Recruit (Bronze) | Kill 250 enemies. |
| Saboteur (Bronze) | Disable a group of fighter squadrons. |
| Shopaholic (Bronze) | Visit a store in the single-player campaign. |
| Sky High (Bronze) | Lift 100 enemies off the ground with powers. |
| Soldier (Bronze) | Kill 1,000 enemies. |
| Tour of Duty (Bronze) | Finish all multiplayer maps or all N7 missions in single-player. |
| Tourist (Bronze) | Complete one multiplayer match or two N7 missions. |
| Tunnel Rat (Bronze) | Survive the swarm. |
| Untouchable (Bronze) | Escape a Reaper in the galaxy map. |
| Unwavering (Gold) | Finish all multiplayer maps on Gold or all single-player missions on Insanity. |
| Veteran (Silver) | Kill 5,000 enemies. |
| Well Connected (Bronze) | Send a warning across the galaxy. |
| World Shaker (Bronze) | Destroy an Atlas dropped from orbit. |

### ACHIEVEMENT

| UNLOCKABLE | HOW TO UNLOCK |
| --- | --- |
| A Personal Touch (10) | Modify a weapon. |
| Almost There (15) | Reach level 15 in multiplayer or level 50 in single-player. |
| Always Prepared (10) | Obtain two non-customizable suits of armor. |
| Arbiter (25) | Win a political stand-off. |
| Battle Scarred (25) | Promote a multiplayer character to the Galaxy at War or import an ME3 character. |
| Bringer of War (10) | Chase down an assassin. |
| Bruiser (10) | Kill 100 enemies with melee attacks. |
| Combined Arms (25) | Perform any combination of 50 biotic combos or tech bursts. |
| Defender (25) | Attain the highest level of readiness in each theater of war. |
| Driven (5) | Return to active duty. |
| Enlisted (5) | Start a character in multiplayer or customize a character in single-player. |
| Executioner (25) | Defeat an old adversary. |
| Explorer (15) | Complete three multiplayer matches or five N7 missions. |
| Eye of the Hurricane (10) | Kill a brute while it's charging you. |
| Fact Finder (15) | Discover an enemy's monstrous origin. |
| Focused (25) | Evolve any of your powers to rank 6. |
| Giant Killer (10) | Defeat a harvester. |
| Gunsmith (25) | Upgrade any weapon to level 10. |
| Hard Target (15) | Call down an orbital strike. |
| Hijacker (10) | Hijack an Atlas mech. |
| Insanity (75) | Finish the game on Insanity without changing difficulty after leaving Earth. |
| Last Witness (25) | Extract ancient technology. |
| Legend (50) | Mission accomplished. |
| Liberator (15) | Stop a Cerberus kidnapping. |
| Long Service Medal (50) | Complete Mass Effect 3 twice, or once with a Mass Effect 2 import. |
| Lost and Found (25) | Dispatch 10 probes to retrieve people or resources in Reaper territory. |
| Mail Slot (10) | Kill 10 guardians with headshots from the front while their shields are raised. |
| Master and Commander (50) | Deliver most of the Galaxy at War assets to the final conflict. |
| Mobilizer (15) | Bring a veteran officer aboard. |
| Overload Specialist (15) | Overload the shields of 100 enemies. |
| Paramour (25) | Establish or rekindle a romantic relationship. |
| Party Crasher (15) | Sabotage a dreadnought. |
| Pathfinder (15) | Explore a lost city. |
| Patriot (25) | Make the final assault. |
| Peak Condition (25) | Reach level 20 in multiplayer or level 60 in single-player. |
| Problem Solver (15) | Evacuate a scientific facility. |
| Pyromaniac (15) | Set 100 enemies on fire with powers. |

A
B
C
D
E
F
G
H
I
J
K
L
M
N
O
P
Q
R
S
T
U
V
W
X
Y
Z

| Recruit (10) | Kill 250 enemies. |
|---|---|
| Saboteur (15) | Disable a group of fighter squadrons. |
| Shopaholic (10) | Visit a store in the single-player campaign. |
| Sky High (15) | Lift 100 enemies off the ground with powers. |
| Soldier (15) | Kill 1,000 enemies. |
| Tour of Duty (20) | Finish all multiplayer maps or all N7 missions in single-player. |
| Tourist (5) | Complete one multiplayer match or two N7 missions. |
| Tunnel Rat (15) | Survive the swarm. |
| Untouchable (10) | Escape a Reaper in the galaxy map. |
| Unwavering (50) | Finish all multiplayer maps on Gold or all single-player missions on Insanity. |
| Veteran (25) | Kill 5,000 enemies. |
| Well Connected (15) | Send a warning across the galaxy. |
| World Shaker (15) | Destroy an Atlas dropped from orbit. |

### UNLOCKABLE

| UNLOCKABLE | HOW TO UNLOCK |
|---|---|
| N7 Helmet Avatar Award | Return to Active Duty. |
| Omniblade Avatar Award | Kill 25 Enemies with Melee Attacks. |

## MAX PAYNE 3 (PlayStation 3)

### TROPHY

| UNLOCKABLE | HOW TO UNLOCK |
|---|---|
| A Few Hundred Bullets Back (Bronze) | Use Every Weapon In The Game |
| A License To Kill (Silver) | Collect All Golden Guns |
| A New York Minute (Gold) | Finish In A New York Minute |
| All Of The Above (Gold) | Finish All Single Player Grinds |
| Along For The Ride (Bronze) | Trigger A Bullet Cam On The Zipline [FREE AIM] |
| Amidst The Wreckage (Bronze) | Destroy All The Models In The Boardroom |
| An Echo Of The Past (Bronze) | Find All Clues |
| Colder Than The Devil's Heart (Bronze) | Kill 30 Enemies In 2 Minutes |
| Dearest Of All My Friends (Bronze) | Kill Someone On Your Friends List |
| Deathmatch Challenge (Bronze) | Winner In Any Public Deathmatch |
| Feel The Payne (Bronze) | Story Complete [MEDIUM] |
| Full Monty (Bronze) | Complete One Of Each Game Mode Including All Gang Wars |
| Grave Robber (Bronze) | Looted A Body |
| It Was Chaos And Luck (Bronze) | Get 6 Kills While Riding The Push Cart [FREE AIM] |
| It's Fear That Gives Men Wings (Bronze) | 10 Bullet Time Kills In A Row |
| Man Of Many Faces (Bronze) | Unlock All Faction Characters |
| Man Of Many Weapons (Bronze) | Unlock All Weapons |
| Max Payne Invitational (Bronze) | Invite someone to play through the in-game contact list |
| Maximum Payne (Gold) | Story Complete [OLD SCHOOL] |
| One Bullet At A Time (Bronze) | 300 Headshots |
| Out The Window (Bronze) | Get 6 Kills While Diving Through The VIP Window [FREE AIM] |
| Part I Complete (Bronze) | Complete Part I Of The Story |

| | |
|---|---|
| Part II Complete (Bronze) | Complete Part II Of The Story |
| Part III Complete (Bronze) | Complete Part III Of The Story |
| Past The Point Of No Return (Bronze) | Take 100 Painkillers |
| Payne Bringer (Silver) | Kill 100 Other Players |
| Payne In The Ass (Bronze) | Story Complete [HARDCORE] |
| Platinum Trophy (Platinum) | Unlock All Max Payne 3 Trophies |
| Serious Payne (Silver) | Story Complete [HARD] |
| So Much For Being Subtle (Bronze) | Get 9 Kills While Being Pulled By A Chain [FREE AIM] |
| Something Wicked This Way Comes (Bronze) | Get 7 Kills While Jumping From The Rickety Boat [FREE AIM] |
| Sometimes You Get Lucky (Bronze) | Get A Headshot During The Rooftop Tremors |
| Sweep (Bronze) | Flawless Team Gang Wars Victory |
| That Old Familiar Feeling (Bronze) | Clear The Hallway Of Lasers |
| The Fear Of Losing It (Bronze) | Survive A Level Without Painkillers |
| The Gambler (Bronze) | Won A Wager |
| The One Eyed Man Is King (Bronze) | Cover Passos With Perfect Aim |
| The Only Choice Given (Bronze) | Get 8 Kills While Dangling From A Chain [FREE AIM] |
| The Road-Kill Behind Me (Bronze) | Total Everything On The Runway |
| The Shadows Rushed Me (Silver) | Unlock And Complete New York Minute Hardcore |
| Training Complete (Silver) | Achieve Level Rank 50 |
| Trouble Had Come To Me (Bronze) | Clear Everyone On The Bus Ride |
| With Practiced Bravado (Bronze) | 100 Kills During Shootdodge |
| You Might Hurt Someone With That (Bronze) | Shoot 10 Airborne Grenades |
| You Play, You Pay, You Bastard (Bronze) | 100 Kills With Melee |
| You Push A Man Too Far (Bronze) | Don't Shoot The Dis-Armed Man |
| You Sure Know How To Pick A Place (Bronze) | Discover All Tourist Locations |

## MAX PAYNE 3 (XBOX 360)

### ACHIEVEMENT

| UNLOCKABLE | HOW TO UNLOCK |
|---|---|
| A Few Hundred Bullets Back (20) | Use Every Weapon In The Game |
| A License To Kill (40) | Collect All Golden Guns |
| A New York Minute (100) | Finish In A New York Minute |
| All Of The Above (100) | Finish All Single Player Grinds |
| Along For The Ride (10) | Trigger A Bullet Cam On The Zipline [FREE AIM] |
| Amidst The Wreckage (5) | Destroy All The Models In The Boardroom |
| An Echo Of The Past (35) | Find All Clues |
| Colder Than The Devil's Heart (15) | Kill 30 Enemies In 2 Minutes |
| Dearest Of All My Friends (10) | Kill Someone On Your Friends List |
| Deathmatch Challenge (20) | Winner In Any Public Deathmatch |
| Feel The Payne (30) | Story Complete [MEDIUM] |
| Full Monty (10) | Complete One Of Each Game Mode Including All Gang Wars |
| Grave Robber (5) | Looted A Body |
| It Was Chaos And Luck (10) | Get 6 Kills While Riding The Push Cart [FREE AIM] |
| It's Fear That Gives Men Wings (20) | 10 Bullet Time Kills In A Row |

A B C D E F G H I J K L M N O P Q R S T U V W X Y Z

| Man Of Many Faces (25) | Unlock All Faction Characters |
|---|---|
| Man Of Many Weapons (25) | Unlock All Weapons |
| Max Payne Invitational (5) | Invite someone to play through the in-game contact list |
| Maximum Payne (80) | Story Complete [OLD SCHOOL] |
| One Bullet At A Time (20) | 300 Headshots |
| Out The Window (10) | Get 6 Kills While Diving Through The VIP Window [FREE AIM] |
| Part I Complete (20) | Complete Part I Of The Story |
| Part II Complete (20) | Complete Part II Of The Story |
| Part III Complete (20) | Complete Part III Of The Story |
| Past The Point Of No Return (10) | Take 100 Painkillers |
| Payne Bringer (30) | Kill 100 Other Players |
| Payne In The Ass (20) | Story Complete [HARDCORE] |
| Serious Payne (50) | Story Complete [HARD] |
| So Much For Being Subtle (10) | Get 9 Kills While Being Pulled By A Chain [FREE AIM] |
| Something Wicked This Way Comes (10) | Get 7 Kills While Jumping From The Rickety Boat [FREE AIM] |
| Sometimes You Get Lucky (5) | Get A Headshot During The Rooftop Tremors |
| Sure Know How To Pick A Place (10) | Discover All Tourist Locations |
| Sweep (10) | Flawless Team Gang Wars Victory |
| That Old Familiar Feeling (10) | Clear The Hallway Of Lasers |
| The Fear Of Losing It (20) | Survive A Level Without Painkillers |
| The Gambler (15) | Won A Wager |
| The One Eyed Man Is King (10) | Cover Passos With Perfect Aim |
| The Only Choice Given (10) | Get 8 Kills While Dangling From A Chain [FREE AIM] |
| The Road-Kill Behind Me (10) | Total Everything On The Runway |
| The Shadows Rushed Me (10) | Unlock And Complete New York Minute Hardcore |
| Training Complete (25) | Achieve Level Rank 50 |
| Trouble Had Come To Me (15) | Clear Everyone On The Bus Ride |
| With Practiced Bravado (20) | 100 Kills During Shootdodge. |
| You Might Hurt Someone With That (20) | Shoot 10 Airborne Grenades |
| You Play, You Pay, You Bastard (20) | 100 Kills With Melee |
| You Push A Man Too Far (5) | Don't Shoot The Dis-Armed Man |

## MEN IN BLACK: ALIEN CRISIS (PlayStation 3)

### TROPHY

| UNLOCKABLE | HOW TO UNLOCK |
|---|---|
| 100 Enemies - Adorian Crossbow (Bronze) | Defeat 100 enemies with the Adorian Crossbow |
| 200 Enemies - The BANGer (Bronze) | Defeat 200 enemies with the BANGer |
| 250 Enemies - Tribarrel (Bronze) | Defeat 250 enemies with the Tribarrel |
| 350 Enemies - Tribarrel (Silver) | Defeat 350 enemies with the Tribarrel |
| 50 Enemies - Std. Issue 1995 (Bronze) | Defeat 50 enemies with the Std. Issue 1995 |

| | |
|---|---|
| **60 Enemies - Noisy Cricket (Bronze)** | Defeat 60 enemies with the Noisy Cricket |
| **Assert Fail (Silver)** | Defeat Khnemu in Story Mode |
| **Brute Force (Bronze)** | Achieve a 25x multiplier in a Story Mode |
| **Conqueror (Bronze)** | Achieve at least 300,000 points in one V.R. Mission |
| **Demolition Expert (Silver)** | Defeat 20 enemies with the Rocket Launcher while flying the car |
| **Dodge and Weave (Bronze)** | Dodge the mines placed by Nethera in Story Mode |
| **Duelist (Bronze)** | Complete all the Competitive maps in V.R. Missions |
| **Enjoy the Ride (Bronze)** | Start playing in Story Mode |
| **Flying Car? Where? (Bronze)** | Don't be detected while flying the car |
| **Group Off (Bronze)** | Destroy 3 enemy platforms in Story Mode |
| **Hide'n'Seek (Bronze)** | Scan 2 hidden aliens in Story Mode |
| **High Score (Bronze)** | Successfully finish the Virtual Reality training program in Story Mode |
| **High Standards (Gold)** | Defeat Nethera and save Catyana |
| **HOT Streak (Gold)** | Defeat 900 enemies |
| **Juggernaut (Bronze)** | Use the Refracto Shield to reflect 100 enemy projectiles |
| **Junior Agent (Silver)** | Complete Story Mode as an Agent |
| **Keep it Slow (Silver)** | Defeat 30 enemies while they're under the effect of Cerebro Accelerator |
| **Kicking and Screaming (Bronze)** | Escape Serleena's drag attack |
| **MIB Veteran (Platinum)** | Unlock all trophies in game |
| **Own the Road (Bronze)** | Defeat 70 bikers in Story Mode |
| **Party Crasher (Bronze)** | Crash Chauncey's party in Story Mode |
| **Pest Control (Silver)** | Defeat 700 enemies |
| **Road Hog (Bronze)** | Defeat 40 bikers in Story Mode |
| **Save the Universe (Gold)** | Complete all the missions in Story Mode |
| **Senior Agent (Gold)** | Complete Story Mode as an Elite Agent |
| **Shattered Expectations (Bronze)** | Freeze 30 enemies with the Icer |
| **Smile for the Camera! (Bronze)** | Neuralize 7 humans in Story Mode |
| **Superior Fighter (Bronze)** | Achieve at least 150,000 points in one V.R. Mission |
| **Superstar (Bronze)** | Achieve at least 200,000 points in one V.R. Mission |
| **The Gatherer (Gold)** | Gather 50 upgrade points |
| **The Spice of Life (Bronze)** | Defeat enemies using 10 different combos |
| **This Won't Take Long (Bronze)** | Defeat Nakkadan Elite Guard in Story Mode |
| **Ugly on the Inside (Bronze)** | Defeat Adorian Elite Guard in Story Mode |
| **What Goes Up... (Silver)** | Use the Anti-Gravity grenade on 30 enemies |

A
B
C
D
E
F
G
H
I
J
K
L
M
N
O
P
Q
R
S
T
U
V
W
X
Y
Z

## MEN IN BLACK: ALIEN CRISIS (XBOX 360)

### ACHIEVEMENT

| UNLOCKABLE | HOW TO UNLOCK |
|---|---|
| 100 Enemies - Adorian Crossbow (30) | Defeated 100 enemies with the Adorian Crossbow (P1) |
| 200 Enemies - The BANGer (30) | Defeated 200 enemies with the BANGer (P1) |
| 250 Enemies - Tribarrel (30) | Defeated 250 enemies with the Tribarrel (P1) |
| 350 Enemies - Tribarrel (30) | Defeated 350 enemies with the Tribarrel (P1) |
| 50 Enemies - Std. Issue 1995 (30) | Defeated 50 enemies with the Std. Issue 1995 (P1) |
| 60 Enemies - Noisy Cricket (30) | Defeated 60 enemies with the Noisy Cricket (P1) |
| Assert Fail (20) | Defeated Khnemu in Story Mode |
| Brute Force (20) | Achieved a 25x multiplier in Story Mode |
| Conqueror (25) | Achieved at least 300,000 points in one V.R. Mission (P1) |
| Demolition Expert (30) | Defeated 20 enemies with the Rocket Launcher while flying the car |
| Dodge and Weave (20) | Dodged the mines placed by Nethera in Story Mode |
| Duelist (30) | Completed all the Competitive maps in V.R. Missions (P1) |
| Enjoy the Ride (20) | Started playing in Story Mode |
| Flying Car? Where? (20) | Didn't get detected while flying the car |
| Group Off (20) | Destroyed 3 enemy platforms in Story Mode |
| Hide'n'Seek (10) | Scanned 2 hidden aliens in Story Mode |
| High Score (20) | Successfully finished the Virtual Reality training program in Story Mode |
| High Standards (30) | Defeated Nethera and saved Catyana |
| HOT Streak (30) | Defeated 900 enemies (P1) |
| Juggernaut (20) | Used the Refracto Shield to reflect 100 enemy projectiles (P1) |
| Junior Agent (50) | Completed Story Mode as an Agent |
| Keep it Slow (20) | Defeated 30 enemies while they were under the effect of the Cerebro Accelerator (P1) |
| Kicking and Screaming (20) | Escaped Serleena's drag attack |
| Own the Road (20) | Defeated 70 Bikers in Story Mode |
| Party Crasher (20) | Crashed Chauncey's party in Story Mode |
| Pest Control (30) | Defeated 700 enemies (P1) |
| Road Hog (20) | Defeated 40 bikers in Story Mode |
| Save the Universe (50) | Completed all the missions in Story Mode |
| Senior Agent (60) | Completed Story Mode as an Elite Agent |
| Shattered Expectations (30) | Froze 30 enemies with the Icer (P1) |
| Smile for the Camera! (20) | Neuralized 7 humans in Story Mode |
| Superior Fighter (25) | Achieved at least 150,000 points in one V.R. Mission (P1) |
| Superstar (30) | Achieved at least 200,000 points in one V.R. Mission (P1) |
| The Gatherer (30) | Gathered 50 upgrade points |

| The Spice of Life (20) | Defeated enemies using 10 different combos (P1) |
|---|---|
| This Won't Take Long (20) | Defeated the Nakkadan Elite Guard in Story Mode |
| Ugly on the Inside (20) | Defeated the Adorian Elite Guard in Story Mode |
| What Goes Up… (20) | Used the Anti-Gravity grenade on 30 enemies (P1) |

## METAL GEAR SOLID 2: SONS OF LIBERTY (PlayStation Vita)

### TROPHY

| UNLOCKABLE | HOW TO UNLOCK |
|---|---|
| A Cut Above (Gold) | Beat the Tanker and Plant chapters on any difficulty |
| Animal Control (Bronze) | Collect a dog tag |
| Another Snake Bites the Dust (Bronze) | Defeat Solidus Snake |
| Beagle (Bronze) | Get the brown wig |
| Bohemian Candidate (Bronze) | Meet President James Johnson |
| Bomb Squad (Bronze) | Learn how to defuse C4 bombs from Peter Stillman |
| Bye Bye Big Brother (Bronze) | Destroy 15 cameras |
| Complete Stealth (Gold) | Clear the game without entering alert mode (not including events where alert mode is mandatory) |
| Don't Taze Me, Bro (Bronze) | Tranquilize 100 enemies |
| Down in Smoke (Bronze) | Disorient an enemy with a cloud of smoke from a fire extinguisher |
| Extremely Solid (Platinum) | Collect all trophies |
| Great Dane (Gold) | Collect all dog tags in the Plant chapter to obtain the Blue Wig |
| Hurt Locker (Bronze) | Put an enemy in a locker |
| I Think You Need a Hug, E (Bronze) | Find Emma Emmerich |
| In It To Win It (Silver) | Place first in 50 different VR/Alternative Missions |
| Johnny on the Spot (Bronze) | Hear Johnny's bowel noises in two locations |
| Kissing Booth (Bronze) | Kiss a poster in a locker |
| Lights Out (Bronze) | Defeat Olga Gurlukovich |
| Love Hurts (Bronze) | Watch Rose kill Raiden on a rooftop |
| Moving Day (Silver) | Collect all boxes |
| No Boss of Mine (Silver) | Complete Boss Survival |
| No Ray, José (Bronze) | Defeat Metal Gear RAY |
| No-Fly Zone (Bronze) | Destroy the AV-88 Harrier II |
| Nothing Personal (Bronze) | Break the neck of 30 enemies |
| Party's Over (Bronze) | Defeat Fatman |
| Photo Finish (Bronze) | Acquire the digital camera |
| Piece of Cake (Bronze) | Complete a VR or Alternative mission |
| Poodle (Bronze) | Get the Tanker stealth suit |
| Rent Money (Bronze) | Beat 30 enemies unconscious |
| Sexting (Bronze) | Send Otacon a picture of the marine with no pants |
| Sharing Is Caring (Bronze) | Befriend Olga Gurlukovich |
| Shiba Inu (Bronze) | Get the Plant stealth suit |

| | |
|---|---|
| **Silence is Golden (Bronze)** | Shoot 10 enemy radios |
| **Snake Beater (Bronze)** | Get caught by Otacon stimulating yourself |
| **Spaghetti Cinema (Bronze)** | Meet Revolver |
| **St. Bernard (Bronze)** | Get the orange wig |
| **Steamed (Bronze)** | Kill 5 enemies with pipe steam |
| **Steel Grip (Bronze)** | Attain grip level 3 |
| **Tell Me a Tale (Silver)** | Complete all Snake Tales |
| **Thanks, Ames (Bronze)** | Learn the location of the president |
| **To Catch a Predator (Bronze)** | Lure a guard with a girlie magazine |
| **Vamp Eyer (Bronze)** | Catch a glimpse of Vamp standing in the streets of New York during the end cinematic |
| **Vampire Slayer (Bronze)** | Defeat Vamp |
| **Virtually Impossible (Gold)** | Complete alL VR and Alternative missions |
| **Who Ya Gonna Call? (Silver)** | Take a clear photograph of the ghost image in Hold No. 2 |
| **Yorkie (Bronze)** | Get the bandana |

### UNLOCKABLE

| UNLOCKABLE | HOW TO UNLOCK |
|---|---|
| **Bandana (gives you infinite ammo)** | Beat the game. Select Tanker. Get over 30 dog tags. |
| **Blue Wig (gives you infinite 02)** | Collect all the dog tags. |
| **Brown Wig (unlimited ammo for Raiden)** | Beat normal mode with more than 100 dog tags |
| **Orange Wig (infinite grip)** | Beat the game with 150 dog tags. |
| **Shaver** | Grip yourself over behind the caged fence when you start with Raiden. |
| **Stealth Camo** | Beat the game. Select "Tanker". Get more than 60 dog tags. |
| **Stealth Camo #2** | Beat the game with 120 dog tags. |
| **Ranking: Bat - Normal Difficulty** | Tanker: 1 alert, Plant: 2 alerts, Tanker-Plant: 3 alerts |
| **Ranking: Big Boss - Extreme Difficulty (Tanker-Plant)** | Radar off, under 3hr clear, Damage: under 10.5, Shots Fired: under 700, under 3 alerts, 0 kills, 0 continues, 0 rations, 0-8 saves, no special items |
| **Ranking: Capybara - Normal Difficulty** | Tanker: 5+ hours, Plant: 25+ Hours, Tanker-Plant: 30+ Hours |

| UNLOCKABLE | HOW TO UNLOCK |
|---|---|
| Tanker-Plant: 100 + saves | |
| **Ranking: Chicken - Very Easy/ Easy Difficulty** | Radar: off, 250+ alerts, 250+ kills, 60+ continues, 31+ rations used, 100+ saves |
| **Ranking: Cow - All Difficulty Levels** | Tanker: 50+ Alerts, Plant: 200+ alerts, Tanker-Plant: 250+ alerts |
| **Ranking: Deer - Normal Difficulty** | Tanker: 25+ saves, Plant: 75+ saves, Tanker-Plant: 100 + saves |
| **Ranking: Doberman - Hard Difficulty (Tanker-Plant)** | Under 3hr clear, under 3 alerts, 0 kills, 0 escapes, 0 continues, 0-3 rations, no special items |
| **Ranking: Doberman - Normal Difficulty (Tanker-Plant)** | Radar off, under 3hr clear, Damage: under 10.5, Shots Fired: under 700, under 3 alerts, 0 kills, 0 continues, 0 rations, 0-8 saves, no special items |
| **Ranking: Eagle - Extreme Difficulty** | Tanker: 18 minutes or less, Plant: 2hrs 45 min or less, Tanker-Plant: 3hrs or less |

| | |
|---|---|
| **Ranking: Elephant - Normal Difficulty** | 31 Rations used |
| **Ranking: Falcon - Normal Difficulty** | Tanker: 18 minutes or less, Plant: 2hrs 45 min or less, Tanker-Plant: 3hrs or less |
| **Ranking: Flying Fox - Hard Difficulty** | Tanker: 1 alert, Plant: 2 alerts, Tanker-Plant: 3 alerts |
| **Ranking: Flying Squirrel - Very Easy/ Easy Difficulty** | Tanker: 1 alert, Plant: 2 alerts, Tanker-Plant: 3 alerts |
| **Ranking: Fox - Extreme Difficulty (Tanker-Plant)** | Under 3hr clear, under 3 alerts, 0 kills, 0 escapes, 0 continues, 0-3 rations, no special items |
| **Ranking: Fox - Hard Difficulty (Tanker-Plant)** | Radar off, under 3hr clear, Damage: under 10.5, Shots Fired: under 700, under 3 alerts, 0 kills, 0 continues, 0 rations, 0-8 saves, no special items |
| **Ranking: Gazelle - All Difficulty Levels** | Tanker: 50+ Clearing Escapes, Plant: 100+ clearing escapes, Tanker-Plant: 150+ Clearing Escapes |
| **Ranking: Giant Panda - Extreme Difficulty** | Tanker: 5+ hours, Plant: 25+ Hours, Tanker-Plant: 30+ Hours |
| **Ranking: Hawk - Hard Difficulty** | Tanker: 18 minutes or less, Plant: 2hrs 45 min or less, Tanker-Plant: 3hrs or less |
| **Ranking: Hippopotamus - Extreme Difficulty** | Tanker: 25+ saves, Plant: 75+ saves, Tanker-Plant: 100 + saves |
| **Ranking: Hound - Easy Difficulty (Tanker-Plant)** | Radar off, under 3hr clear, Damage: under 10.5, Shots Fired: under 700, under 3 alerts, 0 kills, 0 continues, 0 rations, 0-8 saves, no special items |
| **Ranking: Hound - Normal Difficulty (Tanker-Plant)** | Under 3hr clear, under 3 alerts, 0 kills, 0 escapes, 0 continues, 0-3 rations, no special items |
| **Ranking: Jaws - Hard Difficulty** | Tanker: 50+ Enemies killed, Plant: 200+ Enemies killed, Tanker-Plant: 250+ Enemies killed |
| **Ranking: Koala - Very Easy/Easy Difficulty** | Tanker: 5+ hours, Plant: 25+ Hours, Tanker-Plant: 30+ Hours |
| **Ranking: Mammoth - Hard Difficulty** | 31 Rations used |
| **Ranking: Mouse - Normal Difficulty** | Radar: off, 250+ alerts, 250+ kills, 60+ continues, 31+ rations used, 100+ saves |
| **Ranking: Night Owl - Extreme Difficulty** | Tanker: 1 alert, Plant: 2 alerts, Tanker-Plant: 3 alerts |
| **Ranking: Orca - Extreme Difficulty** | Tanker: 50+ Enemies killed, Plant: 200+ Enemies killed, Tanker-Plant: 250+ Enemies killed |
| **Ranking: Ostrich - Extreme Difficulty** | Radar: off, 250+ alerts, 250+ kills, 60+ continues, 31+ rations used, 100+ saves |
| **Ranking: Pig - Very Easy/Easy Difficulty** | 31 Rations used |
| **Ranking: Pigeon - All Difficulty Levels** | No Enemies Killed |
| **Ranking: Piranha - Very Easy/ Easy Difficulty** | Tanker: 50+ Enemies killed, Plant: 200+ Enemies killed, Tanker-Plant: 250+ Enemies killed |
| **Ranking: Rabbit - Hard Difficulty** | Radar: off, 250+ alerts, 250+ kills, 60+ continues, 31+ rations used, 100+ saves |
| **Ranking: Sea Louce - All Difficulty Levels** | Beat the game with a Sea Louce in your inventory |
| **Ranking: Shark - Normal Difficulty** | Tanker: 50+ Enemies killed, Plant: 200+ Enemies killed, Tanker-Plant: 250+ Enemies killed |
| **Ranking: Sloth - Hard Difficulty** | Tanker: 5+ hours, Plant: 25+ Hours, Tanker-Plant: 30+ Hours |

NEW!

A
B
C
D
E
F
G
H
I
J
K
L
M
N
O
P
Q
R
S
T
U
V
W
X
Y
Z

| Ranking: Swallow - Very Easy/ Easy Difficulty | Tanker: 18 minutes or less, Plant: 2hrs 45 min or less, 3hrs or less |
| --- | --- |
| Ranking: Whale - Extreme Difficulty | 31 Rations used |
| Ranking: Zebra - Hard Difficulty | Tanker: 25+ saves, Plant: 75+ saves, Tanker-Plant: 100 + saves |
| Grip Gauge Level 2 | Do 100 Pull-ups |
| Grip Gauge Level 3 | Do 100 Pull-ups after unlocking Grip Gauge Level 2 |

## METAL GEAR SOLID 3: SNAKE EATER (PlayStation Vita)

### TROPHY

| UNLOCKABLE | HOW TO UNLOCK |
| --- | --- |
| A Bird in the Hand... (Bronze) | Collect every type of bird |
| A Good Man Is Hard to Find (Bronze) | Achieve a camouflage index of 100% |
| Beekeeper (Bronze) | Use bees to harass an enemy |
| Believe It or Not (Silver) | Catch a Tsuchinoko (mythical serpent) |
| Can I Keep It? (Bronze) | Capture any animal alive |
| Charmer (Bronze) | Collect every type of snake |
| Close Shave (Bronze) | CQC Slit an enemy's throat |
| Don't Touch The Sides (Bronze) | Use a knife to remove a bullet |
| Everything Is in Season (Bronze) | Collect every type of fruit |
| Fashionista (Silver) | Find every type of camouflage |
| Fungus Among Us (Bronze) | Collect every type of mushroom |
| Grounded (Bronze) | Defeat Volgin in a fist fight |
| Houston, We HAD a Problem (Bronze) | Defeat The Fury |
| I Can Totally See You (Bronze) | Achieve a camouflage index of +90% |
| If It Bleeds, We Can Kill It (Bronze) | Defeat The Fear |
| It Ain't Easy Being Green (Gold) | Find all 64 Kerotans |
| Just Because (Bronze) | Blow up a munitions shed with TNT |
| Just What the Doctor Ordered (Bronze) | Collect every type of medicinal plant |
| King of the Jungle (Gold) | Obtain the title of MARKHOR |
| Like a Boss (Gold) | Finish the game on any difficulty |
| Mama Said (Bronze) | CQC Slam a guard and knock him out |
| Mostly Dead (Bronze) | Use the Fake Death Pill |
| Only Skin Deep (Silver) | Find every type of face paint |
| Pain Relief (Bronze) | Defeat The Pain |
| PEACE WALKER (Gold) | Finish the game without killing anyone |
| Prince Charming (Bronze) | Shoot a kerotan for the first time |
| Problem Solved, Series Over (Bronze) | Create the Ocelot Time Paradox |
| Ralph Called (Bronze) | Make Snake throw up |
| River of Pain (Bronze) | Defeat The Sorrow |
| Serenity Now (Bronze) | Call one Healing Radio frequency |
| Shagadelic (Bronze) | Defeat Shagohod |
| Snake Bit (Bronze) | Poison a guard |
| Snake Eaten (Platinum) | Collect all trophies |
| Snake Eater (Bronze) | Eat a snake of any type |
| Snake Eyes (Bronze) | See all of the first-person views that are not indicated by the R button icon |
| Tall Tale (Bronze) | Collect every type of fish |
| Tell Me Where the Bomb Is (Bronze) | CQC Interrogate an enemy |

| The Cat's out of the Bag (Bronze) | Catch a glimpse of Ocelot, who's seen behind the president when he tries to shake Snake's hand |
| --- | --- |
| The Early End (Silver) | Kill The End before the boss battle |
| The End (Bronze) | Defeat The End |
| The Patriot (Bronze) | Defeat The Boss |
| Them's Good Eatin' (Bronze) | Collect every type of frog |
| Tune-In Tokyo (Bronze) | Call every Healing Radio frequency |
| You Snooze, You Lose (Silver) | Sneak up on The End and hold him up |
| Young Gun (Bronze) | Submit Ocelot |

## UNLOCKABLE

| UNLOCKABLE | HOW TO UNLOCK |
| --- | --- |
| Animals | Beat Ocelot |
| Cold War | Beat Volgen |
| Fire | Beat The Fury |
| Hornet Stripe | Beat The Pain |
| Moss | Hold up The End |
| Snake | Beat The Boss |
| Spider | Beat The Fear |
| DPM Camouflage | Beat Special Duel Mode |
| Green Face Paint | Beat Normal Duel Mode |
| "Box" Conversation | Equip a Box and call Sigint. (Very Funny) |
| "Chocolate Chip" Conversation | Wear "Choco Chip" Camo and call Sigint |
| "Glowcap" Conversation | Eat a Glowcap and Call Para-Medic |
| "Granin" Conversation | Call Sigint after speakng to Granin |
| "Patriot" Conversation | Call Sigint with the Patriot equiped |
| "Pretty" Convo | Call Para-Medic after catching a Green Tree Python |
| "Tsuchinoko" Conversation | Catch a Tsuchinoko and Call Para-Medic |
| Funny Conversation | Wear "Naked" Camo and call Sigint |
| Raiden conversation | Call Major Zero after obtaining the Officer camo, with the mask and Officer camo equipped |
| Sigint's nightmare conversation | Call Sigint after waking up from nightmare (the nightmare appears when you load a save file while in the prison cell) |
| Banana Camouflage | Get the highest record time in every stage of Snake vs. Monkey |
| Colt Single Action Army | Choose the gun on the right during the final duel. |
| Extreme Difficulty Mode | Complete the game once |
| Intro movie on title screen | Complete Virtuous Mission |
| Mechanic Uniform | In Second Locker on Far Right in Groznjy Grad (Near the locker where you put Major Raikov at) |
| Mosin Nagant | Defeat The End/MK22 only |
| Moss Camo | Defeat The End by sneaking up behind him during battle and pointing a gun at him. He will lay on the ground. Point the gun at his head three times, aiming elsewhere when he speaks. |
| Patriot | Complete the game once |
| Snake vs. Monkey levels 4 and 5 | Complete the game once |

| | |
|---|---|
| Sneaking Suit | In Locker you put Major Raikov in (Second time you go to Groznjy Grad) |
| Stealth Camouflage | Find and shoot all 64 Kerotan frogs that are scatter through out the whole game. |
| Stealth Camouflage (alternate method) | Beat the game with no alerts |
| Tuxedo Camouflage | Complete the game once |
| Camo Chocolate Chip | Bolshaya Past South. |
| Camo Ga-Ko | Chyornyj Prud, underwater in northeast. |
| Camo Grenade | Download it to your memory card. |
| Camo Mummy | Download it to your memory card. |
| Camo Rain Drop | Dremuchij North, under the rope bridge on the far side. |
| Camo Santa | Download it to your memory card. |
| Camo Snow | Peschera Cave, on the right branch before the Pain. |
| Camo Splitter | Bolshaya Past South. |
| Camo Valentine | Download it to your memory card. (JP and EU versions) |
| Camo Water | Bolshaya Past Base. |
| Facepaint Desert | Ponizovje Warehouse. |
| Facepaint Kabuki | Tikhogornyj, at the bottom of the pool before the waterfall. |
| Facepaint Oyama | Graniny Gorky Lab, Exterior. In the air duct. |
| Facepaint Snow | Bolshaya Past Base, In the fox hole on the left side of the middle building |
| Facepaint Water | After talking to Granin and fighting The Fear, go all the way back to the beginning of Ponizovje South. |
| Facepaint Zombie | Rassvet during snake eater mission. Behind the building. |
| Fly Camouflage | In the third bathroom stall on the second floor of the building where Granin is (it's locked so break the door down). |
| Infinity Face Paint | Beat the game with the Foxhound Rank |
| Infinity Face Paint (alternate method) | Catch a live Tsuchinoko before torture scene. After you get your weapons, go back and capture it again just outside. Finish the game with it alive. |
| Monkey Mask | Complete every level in Snake vs. Monkeys |
| Spirit camouflage | Last all the way through Sorrow's river |
| Uniform Maintenance | Groznyj Grad Weapons Lab: East Wing in locker. Same time as the Sneaking Suit. |
| Uniform Officer | Steal it from Raikov. |
| Uniform Scientist | Given to you by Eva. |
| Uniform Sneaking Suit | Groznyj Grad Weapons Lab: East Wing. In the locker with the red stripe. |
| Peep Show Movie. | Collect all the Movies in Demo Theatre. |
| Alligator - Any Difficulty | 81-249 Alerts, 41 or more Continues, 101-299 Kills |
| Bat - Normal Ranking | No Alerts |
| Capybara - Normal Ranking | Play Time over 30 hours |
| Cat - Easy and Very Easy Ranking | Save over 100 times |
| Centipede - Any Difficulty | 1-20 Alerts, 41 or more continues, 1-100 kills |

| | |
|---|---|
| **Chicken - Easy and Very Easy Difficulties** | Alert Mode over 300 times, Kill over 300 people, Eat more than 31 Meals, Play Time over 30 hours, Continue over 60 times, Save over 100 times |
| **Cow - Special Ranking** | Alert Mode raised over 300 times |
| **Crocodile - Any Difficulty** | 81-249 Alerts, 0-40 Continues, 101-299 Kills |
| **Deer - Normal Ranking** | Save over 100 times |
| **Doberman - Extreme Ranking** | No Special Item used, 1 Alert, 0 Kills, Under 3 Life Meds, Under 5:15 play time, 0 continues |
| **Doberman - Hard Ranking** | No Special Item used, 0 Alerts, 0 Kills, 0 Life Meds, Under 5:00 play time, under 50 saves, 0 continues |
| **Doberman - Normal Ranking** | No Special Item used, 0 Alerts, Under 10 Life Bars of Damage, 0 Kills, 0 Life Meds, Under 5:00 play time, under 25 saves, 0 continues |
| **Eagle - Extreme Ranking** | Play Time under 5:00 |
| **Elephant - Normal Ranking** | Over 31 Meals Eaten |
| **Falcon - Normal Ranking** | Play Time under 5:00 |
| **Flying Fox - Hard Ranking** | No Alerts |
| **Flying Squirrel - Easy and Very Easy Ranking** | No Alerts |
| **Fox - Extreme Ranking** | No Special Item used, 0 Alerts, 0 Kills, 0 Life Meds, Under 5:00 play time, under 50 saves, 0 continues |
| **Fox - Hard Ranking** | No Special Item used, 0 Alerts, Under 10 Life Bars of Damage, 0 Kills, 0 Life Meds, Under 5:00 play time, under 25 saves, 0 continues |
| **Foxhound - Extreme Ranking** | No Special Item used, 0 Alerts, Under 10 Life Bars of Damage, 0 Kills, 0 Life Meds, Under 5:00 play time, under 25 saves, 0 continues |
| **Giant Panda - Extreme Ranking** | Play Time over 30 hours |
| **Hawk - Hard Ranking** | Play Time under 5:00 |
| **Hippopotamus - Extreme Ranking** | Save over 100 times |
| **Hound - Easy Ranking** | No Special Item used, 0 Alerts, Under 10 Life Bars of Damage, 0 Kills, 0 Life Meds, Under 5:00 play time, under 25 saves, 0 continues |
| **Hound - Extreme Ranking** | No Special Item used, 2 Alerts, 0 Kills, Under 5:00 play time, under 25 saves, 0 continues |
| **Hound - Hard Ranking** | No Special Item used, 1 Alert, 0 Kills, Under 3 Life Meds, Under 5:15 play time, 0 continues |
| **Hound - Normal Ranking** | No Special Item used, 0 Alerts, 0 Kills, 0 Life Meds, Under 5:00 play time, under 50 saves, 0 continues |
| **Hyena - Any Difficulty** | 51-80 Alerts, 41 or more Continues, 101-299 Kills |
| **Iguana - Any Difficulty** | 81-249 Alerts, 0-40 Continues, 1-100 Kills |
| **Jackal - Any Difficulty** | 51-80 Alerts, 0-40 Continues, 1-100 Kills |
| **Jaguar - Any Difficulty** | 21-50 Alerts, 0-40 Continues, 1-100 Kills |
| **Kerotan - Special Ranking** | Shoot all 64 Kerotan Frogs |
| **Koala - Easy and Very Easy Ranking** | Play Time over 30 hours |

| | |
|---|---|
| Komodo Dragon - Any Difficulty | 81-249 Alerts, 41 or more Continues, 1-100 Kills |
| Leech - Special Ranking | Clear the Game with Leech attached |
| Leopard - Any Difficulty | 21-50 Alerts, 41 or more Continues, 1-100 Kills |
| Mammoth - Hard Ranking | Kill over 300 Humans |
| Markhor - Special Ranking | Every Plant and Animal Captured, Cure Supply Plant, and non animal-plant item (RC Mate, Noodles, etc.) |
| Mongoose - Any Difficulty | 51-80 Alerts, 41 or more Continues, 1-100 Kills |
| Mouse - Normal Difficulty | Alert Mode over 300 times, Kill over 300 people, Eat more than 31 Meals, Play Time over 30 hours, Continue over 60 times, Save over 100 times |
| Night Owl - Extreme Ranking | No Alerts |
| Orca - Extreme Ranking | Kill 250 or more Humans |
| Ostrich - Extreme Difficulty | Alert Mode over 300 times, Kill over 300 people, Eat more than 31 Meals, Play Time over 30 hours, Continue over 60 times, Save over 100 times |
| Panther - Any Difficulty | 21-50 Alerts, 0-40 Continues, 101-299 Kills |
| Pig - Easy and Very Easy Ranking | Over 31 Meals Eaten |
| Pigeon - Special Ranking | No Kills |
| Piranha - Easy and Very Easy Ranking | Kill over 300 Humans |
| Puma - Any Difficulty | 21-50 Alerts, 41 or more Continues, 101-299 Kills |
| Rabbit - Hard Difficulty | Alert Mode over 300 times, Kill over 300 people, Eat more than 31 Meals, Play Time over 30 hours, Continue over 60 times, Save over 100 times |
| Scorpion - Any Difficulty | 1-20 Alerts, 0-40 continues, 1-100 kills |
| Shark - Normal Ranking | Kill over 300 Humans |
| Sloth - Hard Ranking | Play Time over 30 hours |
| Spider - Any Difficulty | 1-20 Alerts, 41 or more continues, 101-299 kills |
| Swallow - Easy and Very Easy Ranking | Play Time under 5:00 |
| Tarantula - Any Difficulty | 1-20 Alerts, 0-40 continues, 101-299 kills |
| Tasmanian Devil - Any Difficulty | 51-80 Alerts, 0-40 Continues, 101-299 Kills |
| Tsuchinoko - Special Ranking | Clear game with living Tsuchinoko captured |
| Whale - Extreme Ranking | Kill over 300 Humans |
| Zebra - Hard Ranking | Save over 100 times |

## MICHAEL JACKSON THE EXPERIENCE HD (PlayStation Vita)

### TROPHY

| UNLOCKABLE | HOW TO UNLOCK |
|---|---|
| A Glove for Any Occasion! (Gold) | Unlock all the Gloves in the game. |
| A Smooth Criminal... (Silver) | Hold a Max Combo Level for 90 seconds on Smooth Criminal (Medium difficulty) |
| Feelin' Good! (Silver) | Complete 150 Perfect moves on The Way You Make Me Feel (Medium difficulty) |
| Figure Collector (Gold) | Unlock all the Michael Jackson Figures in the game |
| Freeway Dancer! (Bronze) | Complete Speed Demon 6 times |

| | |
|---|---|
| Going Hollywood... (Gold) | Perform 50 Perfect moves in a row on Hollywood Tonight (Expert difficulty) |
| Legendary (Gold) | Become Legend (Level 20) |
| Not Alone (Bronze) | Unlock, equip and dance with the alternate costume on Leave Me Alone |
| Out on the Dance floor (Bronze) | Draw only lines and spins during Freestyle on Blood on The Dance Floor |
| Papparazzi! (Bronze) | Score at least 80,000 on Billie Jean |
| Perfect Expert (Gold) | Perform 30 Perfect moves in a row on Thriller (Expert difficulty) |
| Remember the Sequence! (Silver) | Perform the secret freestyle sequence on Remember The Time |
| Rock The Night Away! (Silver) | Don't miss a single move on Rock With You (Medium difficulty) |
| Still Not Enough! (Bronze) | Win 3 multiplayer Battles on Don't Stop 'Til You Get Enough |
| Supernatural! (Silver) | Perform 250 Perfect moves on Ghosts |
| The Negiotiator (Gold) | Score 145,000 Points on Beat It |
| The Setlist (Bronze) | Complete every song once |
| The Spectator (Bronze) | Watch any song in the "On demand Performance" Mode |
| The Tour Begins... (Bronze) | Become a Trainee (Level 2) |
| The Tour Continues... (Silver) | Become a Dance Fanatic (Level 10) |
| Thriller Tonight! (Bronze) | Get a B grade or better on Thriller (Medium difficulty) |
| Top of the World! (Silver) | Get the highest score in the leaderboard on Black or White |
| Unbreakable (Platinum) | Obtain all the trophies in Michael Jackson The Experience HD |
| Wardrobe! (Silver) | Unlock, equip and dance with an alternate costume for the first time |
| Who's Bad? (Silver) | Get an A grade on Bad (Medium difficulty) |
| Zombie Dance (Bronze) | Perform the special Thriller move during Freestyle |

### UNLOCKABLE

| UNLOCKABLE | HOW TO UNLOCK |
|---|---|
| Black Armguard | Draw 50 Perfect Shapes in a Row on Hollywood Tonight on Expert Difficulty |
| Emerald Glove | Draw 45 Perfect Shapes in a Row on Smooth Criminal |
| Golden Glove | Reach the top position on the leaderboard for "Leave Me Alone" |
| Red Ruby Glove | Wear the Alternate Outfit on Ghosts. |
| Star Sapphire Glove | Score 145,000 Points on Beat It |

## MLB 12: THE SHOW (PlayStation 3)

### TROPHY

| UNLOCKABLE | HOW TO UNLOCK |
|---|---|
| "RESPECT THE GAME!" (Bronze) | In any game mode, enter a game with a mismatching uniform. |
| A Year in the Life (Silver) | Play through one season (5 games) in Diamond Dynasty mode. |
| Back, Back, Back, Back, Back... (Bronze) | Hit a home run of 490ft or more in Home Run Derby. |
| Boom Goes the Dynamite (Bronze) | In any game mode, hit a home run with your first batter of the game. |

| | |
|---|---|
| **Collector (Gold)** | In Diamond Dynasty mode, acquire one of every card type. (Bronze, Silver, Gold, Platinum, MLB) |
| **Congratulations! (Platinum)** | You got all of the MLB 12 The Show Trophies! |
| **Contact Killer (Silver)** | In any mode excluding RttS, play an entire 9 inning game without striking out. Must be done in a full, uninterrupted, 9 inning game against a CPU control |
| **Cruzball (Bronze)** | Playing as the pitcher in any game mode, intentionally walk a batter, then turn a double play. Must be done against a CPU controlled team. |
| **Deep Dish (Bronze)** | Hit a home run into the Bullpen Sports Grill in rightfield at U.S. Cellular Field. (CWS) |
| **Don't Phase Me Bro (Silver)** | In any game mode, hit a home run off a 100+ MPH pitch. Must be done against a CPU controlled team. |
| **Don't Try That Again (Bronze)** | On defense, throw a runner out at 3B or home plate from the outfield. Must be done against a CPU controlled team. |
| **Early Exit (Silver)** | In any game mode, knock out the opponent's starting pitcher before the end of the 3rd inning. Must be done against a CPU controlled team. |
| **Everyone's a Winner (Gold)** | Win a game with every MLB team. Must be done in full, uninterrupted, 9-inning games. |
| **Fish off a Barrel (Bronze)** | Hit the aquarium behind home plate at Marlins Park. (MIA) |
| **Free Baseball (Bronze)** | In any game mode, win a game in extra innings. |
| **Go Chasin' Waterfalls (Bronze)** | Hit a home run into a waterfall at Kauffman Stadium. (KC) |
| **In The Bag! (Bronze)** | As the batter, hit 1st, 2nd, or 3rd base with the ball. Trophy is not achievable in Home Run Derby or Challenge of the Week. |
| **King Slayer (Gold)** | In Exhib. Mode, beat team that's ranked 1st overall in team select screen w/Pitching & Batting dif.set Legend. Be done in full, uninterrupted, 9 inning game |
| **Loud and Clear (Bronze)** | Hit a home run into the speaker in center field at Dodger Stadium. (LAD) |
| **Masterpiece (Bronze)** | Create a Diamond Dynasty team and custom logo including at least 20 layers. |
| **Meatball Buffet (Silver)** | Bat around in an inning. Must be comple. on All-Star or higher Batting diff. Must be done in a full, uninterrupted, 9 inning game against a CPU control |
| **Million Dollar Arm (Gold)** | In any game mode, throw a perfect game against a CPU contolled team. Must be done in a full, uninterrupted, 9 inning game. |
| **Plowman (Bronze)** | As a baserunner, plow the catcher. Must be done against a CPU controlled team. |
| **Pulsating (Bronze)** | With the pitching difficulty set to All-Star or higher, use Pulse Pitching to strike out the side. Must be done against a CPU controlled team. |
| **Quality Start (Silver)** | Throw more than 70% first pitch strikes in a complete game victory. Must be done in a full, uninterrupted, 9 inning game against a CPU controlled team |

| | |
|---|---|
| **Run Benjie, Run! (Bronze)** | Steal a base with a player whose primary position is Catcher. Must be done against a CPU controlled team. |
| **Slinging in the Rain (Silver)** | Play a full game in the rain without making an error. |
| **Sombrero Dealer (Bronze)** | In any mode, strike out the same player four times in a game. Must be done against a CPU controlled team. |
| **Squeezeball (Silver)** | In any game mode, win the game with an RBI bunt. Must be done in a full, uninterrupted, 9 inning game against a CPU controlled team. |
| **Texas Two-Step (Bronze)** | Hit a home run onto Greene's Hill in CF at Rangers Ballpark In Arlington. (TEX) |
| **The Old Fashioned Way (Bronze)** | In any mode, earn a save by having your reliever pitch last 3 innings of a win. Must be done in full, uninterrupted, 9 inning game against a CPU control |
| **Vulture a Win (Bronze)** | In any mode, blow a save and get the win with the same pitcher. Must be done in a full, uninterrupted, 9 inning game against a CPU controlled team. |
| **Winning (Gold)** | Hit 10 consecutive home runs in Home Run Derby. |
| **You Blew It (Bronze)** | In any mode, blow your opponents save opportunity. Must be done against a CPU controlled team. |
| **Zone Plus Analog Blast (Bronze)** | With hitting difficulty set to All-Star or harder, hit a home run using Zone Plus Analog controls. This trophy is not unlockable in Home Run Derby modes |

## MLB 12: THE SHOW    (PlayStation Vita)

### TROPHY

| UNLOCKABLE | HOW TO UNLOCK |
|---|---|
| **'RESPECT THE GAME!' (Bronze)** | In any game mode, enter a game with a mismatching uniform. |
| **Back, Back, Back, Back, Back... (Bronze)** | Hit a home run of 490ft or more in Home Run Derby. |
| **Congratulations (Platinum)** | You got all of the MLB 12 The Show Trophies! |
| **Contact Killer (Silver)** | In any mode, excluding RttS, play an entire 9 inning game w/o striking out. Must be done in full, uninterrupted, 9 inning game against a CPU controlled team. |
| **Cruzball (Bronze)** | Playing as the pitcher in any game mode, intentionally walk a batter, then turn a double play. Must be done against a CPU controlled team. |
| **Deep Dish (Bronze)** | Hit a home run into the Bullpen Sports Grill in rightfield at U.S. Cellular Field. (CWS) |
| **Don't Phase Me Bro (Silver)** | In any game mode, hit a home run off a 100+ MPH pitch. Must be done against a CPU controlled team. |
| **Don't Try That Again (Bronze)** | On defense, throw a runner out at 3B or home plate from the outfield. Must be done against a CPU controlled team. |
| **Early Exit (Silver)** | In any game mode, knock out the opponent's starting pitcher before the end of the 3rd inning. Must be done against a CPU controlled team. |
| **Fish off a Barrel (Bronze)** | Hit the aquarium behind home plate at Marlins Park. (MIA) |
| **For the Greater Good (Silver)** | In any game mode, get a broken bat base hit. |

| | |
|---|---|
| **Go Chasin' Waterfalls (Bronze)** | Hit a home run into a waterfall at Kauffman Stadium. (KC) |
| **In The Bag! (Bronze)** | As the batter, hit 1st, 2nd, or 3rd base with the ball. Trophy is not achievable in Home Run Derby. |
| **King Slayer (Gold)** | In Exhib Mode, beat team ranked 1st overall in team select screen w/Pitching&Batting difficulties to Legend. Must be done in full, uninterrupted, 9 inning |
| **Loud and Clear (Bronze)** | Hit a home run into the speaker in center field at Dodger Stadium. (LAD) |
| **Meatbull Buffet (Silver)** | Bat around in inning. Must be completed on All-Star or higher Batting difficulty. Must be done in full, uninterrupted, 9 inning game against CPU control |
| **Million Dollar Man (Gold)** | In any game mode, throw a perfect game against a CPU controlled team. Must be done in a full, uninterrupted, 9 inning game. |
| **Mr. 300 (Silver)** | Reach 300 XP in online play. |
| **On The Beach (Bronze)** | Hit a home run into the sand area in Petco Park. (SD) |
| **Plowman (Bronze)** | As a baserunner, plow the catcher. Must be done against a CPU controlled team. |
| **Pulsating (Bronze)** | With the pitching difficulty set to All-Star or higher, use Pulse Pitching to strike out the side. Must be done against a CPU controlled team. |
| **Quality Start (Silver)** | Throw > 70% 1st pitch strikes in complete game victory. Must be done in full, uninterrupted, 9 inning game against CPU controlled team. |
| **Rally Killer (Silver)** | In any game mode, hit into 2 double plays in a game with the same player. Must be done against a CPU controlled team. |
| **Run Benjie, Run! (Bronze)** | Steal a base with a player whose primary position is Catcher. Must be done against a CPU controlled team. |
| **Solid D (Silver)** | Using Pure Analog Throwing, w/throwing difficulty to All-Star or higher, complete 9 inning game w/o error. Must be done against CPU controlled team. |
| **Sombrero Dealer (Bronze)** | In any mode, strike out the same player four times in a game. Must be done against a CPU controlled team. |
| **Sooo Close! (Gold)** | Lose your shot at a perfect game or no hitter in the 9th inning. Must be done against a CPU controlled team. |
| **Squeezeball (Bronze)** | In any game mode, win the game with an RBI bunt. Must be done in a full, uninterrupted, 9 inning game against the CPU controlled team. |
| **Take Out Your Rival (Bronze)** | In any mode, hit the opposing pitcher with a pitch. |
| **Texas Two-Step (Bronze)** | Hit a home run onto Greene's Hill in CF at Rangers Ballpark In Arlington. (TEX) |
| **The Old Fashioned Way (Bronze)** | In any mode, earn save by having your reliever pitch last 3 innings of a win. Must be done in full, uninterrupted, 9 inning game against CPU controlled |
| **Vulture a Win (Bronze)** | In any mode, blow save & get win w/ same pitcher Must be done in full, uninterrupted, 9 inning game against the CPU controlled team. |
| **Winning (Gold)** | Hit 10 consecutive home runs in Home Run Derby(TM). |

| | |
|---|---|
| **You Blew It (Bronze)** | In any mode, blow your opponents save opportunity. Must be done against a CPU controlled team. |
| **You're the Man! (Gold)** | Reach 500 XP in online play. |
| **Zone Plus Analog Blast (Bronze)** | W/ hitting difficulty set to All-Star or harder, hit home run using Zone Plus Analog controls. This trophy isn't unlockable in Home Run Derby modes. |

## MODNATION RACERS: ROAD TRIP (PlayStation Vita)

### TROPHY

| UNLOCKABLE | HOW TO UNLOCK |
|---|---|
| **Aggro Racer (Bronze)** | Sideswipe 75 opponents |
| **Anonymous (Bronze)** | Play an Ad Hoc race |
| **Beat Down (Bronze)** | Win your first Ad Hoc action race on a particular published track |
| **Bonus Tour Winner (Silver)** | Get 1st place overall in the Bonus Tour |
| **Bonus! (Silver)** | Complete all 5 Tours and pass the Career Stat thresholds |
| **Bruiser (Bronze)** | Get a total of 200 takedowns |
| **Busting Ghosts (Bronze)** | Beat one ghost in Time Trial |
| **Cashing In (Bronze)** | Cash in an Item Pod 50 times |
| **Dominator (Gold)** | Come 1st in every race in the career |
| **Dresser (Bronze)** | Create a Mod in Mod Studio |
| **Drifting Superstar (Bronze)** | Earn 100,000 drift points in one drift |
| **Fast Learner (Bronze)** | Complete all the race tutorials |
| **Fill 'Er Up (Bronze)** | Fill your boost meter |
| **Headspinner (Bronze)** | Do a 1080 spin and land successfully |
| **Hoarder (Silver)** | Collect all the tokens in the single player career |
| **Join the Team (Silver)** | Beat all 30 developer best lap times in career |
| **Knockin' Boost (Bronze)** | Drive over 100 boost pads |
| **Level of Merit (Silver)** | Complete all the career challenges |
| **Mechanic (Bronze)** | Create a kart in Kart Studio |
| **ModNation Legend (Platinum)** | Earn all the ModNation Racers: Road Trip trophies to unlock this platinum trophy |
| **ModNation Superstar (Gold)** | Achieve level rank 28 |
| **Offering Opinions (Bronze)** | Rate 10 tracks, 10 Mods, and 10 karts |
| **Pacifist (Bronze)** | Win an action race in Career without firing any weapons |
| **Pioneer Racer (Bronze)** | Post the first Time Trial time on a published track |
| **Post Cards for Everyone (Bronze)** | Create a Post Card |
| **Remixer (Bronze)** | Remix a Mod, a kart, and a track |
| **Say Cheese! (Bronze)** | Use photo mode in a race or studio |
| **Sculptor (Bronze)** | Create a track in Track Studio |
| **Sharing Karts (Bronze)** | Publish a kart and have at least 10 people download it |
| **Sharing Mods (Bronze)** | Publish a Mod and have at least 10 people download it |
| **Sharing Splines (Bronze)** | Publish a track and have at least 10 people download it |
| **Shields Up! (Bronze)** | Successfully defend yourself with your shield 20 times |

| Shopping Spree (Bronze) | Enter the Shop |
| Slow and Steady (Bronze) | Win an action race in Career without using any boost or boost pads of any type |
| Star Creator (Gold) | Earn at least 50,000 Create XP |
| Startline Booster (Bronze) | Successfully boost off the line 20 times |
| Taster Session (Bronze) | Try all the game modes in Single Player Race |
| The Drifter (Bronze) | Drift 1,000 times in total |
| Third Eye (Bronze) | Hit 5 opponents with mines in a Career Race |
| Time Stamp (Bronze) | Post your time while in a time trial |
| Top of the Ladder (Silver) | Place first on a time trial leaderboard |
| Tour 1 Winner (Bronze) | Get 1st place overall in Tour 1 |
| Tour 2 Winner (Bronze) | Get 1st place overall in Tour 2 |
| Tour 3 Winner (Bronze) | Get 1st place overall in Tour 3 |
| Tour 4 Winner (Bronze) | Get 1st place overall in Tour 4 |
| Tour 5 Winner (Silver) | Get 1st place overall in Tour 5 |
| Trigger Happy (Bronze) | Use all the weapons in the game |

## MORTAL KOMBAT (PlayStation Vita)

### TROPHY

| UNLOCKABLE | HOW TO UNLOCK |
| --- | --- |
| A For Effort (Bronze) | Complete Tutorial Mode |
| Arcade Champion (Silver) | Complete Arcade Ladder with All Fighters |
| Back In Time... (Silver) | Complete Story Mode 100% |
| Balancing Act (Bronze) | Complete all Test Your Balance mini-game challenges |
| Best...Alternate...Ever! (Bronze) | Unlock Mileena's 3rd Alternate Costume |
| Block This! (Bronze) | Perform a 10-hit combo with any fighter |
| Brotherhood of Shadow (Bronze) | Discover and fight Hidden Kombatant 4 in Arcade Ladder |
| Complet-ality (Bronze) | Perform 1 of each type of "-ality" |
| Cyber Challenger (Bronze) | Complete 100 Versus Matches |
| Dim Mak! (Bronze) | Complete all Test Your Strike mini-game challenges |
| Don't Jump! (Bronze) | Win A Ranked Online Match without jumping |
| e-X-cellent! (Bronze) | Successfully land every playable fighter's X-Ray |
| Fatality! (Bronze) | Perform a Fatality! |
| Finish Him? (Bronze) | Perform any fighter's hidden finishing move |
| Finish What You Start! (Bronze) | Perform a Fatality with all playable fighters |
| Halfway There! (Bronze) | Complete Story Mode 50% |
| Hide and Seek (Bronze) | Discover and fight Hidden Kombatant 2 in Arcade Ladder |
| Humiliation (Bronze) | Get a Flawless Victory in a Versus Match |
| I "Might" Be the Strongest (Bronze) | Complete all Test Your Might mini-game challenges |
| Ladder Master (Bronze) | Complete Arcade Ladder on max difficulty without using a continue |
| License to Kill (Bronze) | Complete Fatality Trainer |
| Luck Be A Lady (Bronze) | Get all MK Dragons in Test Your Luck |
| My Kung Fu Is Strong (Silver) | Gain Mastery of 1 Fighter |
| My Kung Fu Is Stronger (Gold) | Gain Mastery of All Fighters |

| | |
|---|---|
| Outstanding! (Silver) | Win 10 Ranked Online Matches in a row |
| Pit Master (Bronze) | Discover and fight Hidden Kombatant 3 in Arcade Ladder |
| Platinum Trophy (Platinum) | You've unlocked all Trophies! |
| Robots Rule! (Bronze) | Win Arcade Tag Ladder with robot Sektor and Cyrax |
| Slice of Life (Bronze) | Swipe your way through a set of all-new mini-game challenges |
| Tag, You're It! (Bronze) | Perform and land a Tag Combo |
| The Fall Guy! (Bronze) | Discover all the deathtraps in Test Your Balance |
| The Grappler (Bronze) | Perform every fighter's forward and backwards throws |
| The Krypt Keeper (Silver) | Unlock 100% of the Krypt |
| There Will Be Blood! (Bronze) | Spill 10000 pints of blood |
| These Aren't My Glasses! (Bronze) | Complete all Test Your Sight mini-game challenges |
| Three's Company (Silver) | Unlock Kenshi, Skarlet, and Rain Alternate Costumes |
| Throws Are For Champs (Bronze) | Perform 8 throws in an Online Ranked Match |
| Touch and Go (Bronze) | Perform 1 "-ality" using the PlayStation®Vita system touchscree |
| Tough Guy! (Bronze) | Win a Versus Match |
| Tower Apprentice (Bronze) | Complete 25 Tower missions |
| Tower Champion (Silver) | Complete 100 bonus tower missions |
| Tower God (Gold) | Complete all 150 bonus tower missions |
| Tower Master (Silver) | Complete all Tower missions |
| Tower Recruit (Bronze) | Complete 50 bonus tower missions |
| Ultimate Humiliation (Silver) | Perform every fighter's hidden finishing move |
| Undertaker (Bronze) | Unlock 50% of the Krypt |
| Wavenet... (Silver) | Win 100 total Versus Matches |
| What Does This Button Do?? (Bronze) | Complete Arcade Ladder without blocking (allowed to continue) |
| Where's The Arcade? (Bronze) | Complete Arcade Ladder with Any Fighter |
| You Found Me! (Bronze) | Discover and fight Hidden Kombatant 1 in Arcade Ladder |
| You've Got Style! (Bronze) | Unlock all Alternate Costumes |

## NARUTO SHIPPUDEN: ULTIMATE NINJA STORM GENERATIONS (PlayStation 3)

### TROPHY

| UNLOCKABLE | HOW TO UNLOCK |
|---|---|
| 10 Down (Silver) | You've defeated 10 opponents in Ultimate Survival. |
| Advanced Survivor! (Bronze) | You've completed all of Advanced Survival. |
| Akatsuki Tournament Champ! (Bronze) | You've completed the Akatsuki Tournament. |
| Beginner Survivor! (Bronze) | You've completed all of Beginner Survival. |
| Boy's Life Tournament Champ! (Bronze) | You've completed the Boy's Life Tournament. |
| First Ninja Tool Edit! (Bronze) | You've edited a ninja tool set for the first time. |

A B C D E F G H I J K L M N O P Q R S T U V W X Y Z

| First S Rank! (Bronze) | You've earned your first S Rank in a battle. |
| First Shopping! (Bronze) | You've done your first shopping. |
| Five Kage Tournament Champ! (Bronze) | You've completed the Five Kage Tournament. |
| I'm the greatest ninja! (Platinum) | You've acquired all trophies. |
| Image Master (Bronze) | Images collected: 80% |
| Intermediate Survivor! (Bronze) | You've completed all of Intermediate Survival. |
| Introductory Stage Survivor! (Bronze) | You've completed all of Introductory Survival. |
| Leaf Chunin Tournament Champ! (Bronze) | You've completed the Leaf Chunin Tournament. |
| Leaf Genin Tournament Champ! (Bronze) | You've completed all Leaf Genin Tournament battles. |
| Leaf Higher-Up Tournament Champ! (Bronze) | You've completed the Leaf Higher-Up Tournament. |
| New Team Seven Tournament Champ! (Bronze) | You've completed the New Team Seven Tournament. |
| Ninja Info Card Collector (Bronze) | Ninja Info Card images collected: 50% |
| Ninja Tool Master (Bronze) | Ninja Tools collected: 80% |
| Peerless Ninja Tournament Champ! (Bronze) | You've completed the Peerless Ninja Tournament. |
| Sand Genin Tournament Champ! (Bronze) | You've completed the Sand Genin Tournament. |
| Shippuden Tournament Champ! (Bronze) | You've completed the Shippuden Tournament. |
| Substitution Jutsu Master (Bronze) | Substitution Jutsu collected: 80% |
| Tale of Naruto Uzumaki complete (Bronze) | Completed Tale of Naruto Uzumaki. |
| Tale of Sasuke Uchiha complete (Bronze) | Completed Tale of Sasuke Uchiha. |
| Tale of Young Naruto complete (Bronze) | Completed Tale of Young Naruto. |
| Team Seven Tournament Champ! (Bronze) | You've completed the Team Seven Tournament. |
| Ultimate Jutsu Movie Master (Bronze) | Ultimate Jutsu scenes collected: 80% |
| Ultimate Ninja Tournament Champ! (Bronze) | You've completed the Ultimate Ninja Tournament. |
| Wealthy Ninja (Silver) | You've earned a total of 1,000,000 Ryo. |

## NARUTO SHIPPUDEN: ULTIMATE NINJA STORM GENERATIONS (XBOX 360)

### ACHIEVEMENT

| UNLOCKABLE | HOW TO UNLOCK |
| --- | --- |
| 10 Down (30) | You've defeated 10 opponents in Ultimate Survival. |
| Advanced Survivor! (15) | You've completed all of Advanced Survival. |
| Akatsuki Tournament Champ! (15) | You've completed the Akatsuki Tournament. |
| Alias Master (100) | Titles collected: 80% |
| Beginner Survivor! (15) | You've completed all of Beginner Survival. |
| Boy's Life Tournament Champ! (15) | You've completed the Boy's Life Tournament. |

| | |
|---|---|
| **Card Collection Master (100)** | Ninja Info Card images collected: 80% |
| **First Ninja Tool Edit! (5)** | You've edited a ninja tool set for the first time. |
| **First S Rank! (5)** | You've earned your first S Rank in a battle. |
| **First Shopping! (5)** | You've done your first shopping. |
| **Five Kage Summit (5)** | All Kage at the Five Kage Summit can now be used. |
| **Five Kage Tournament Champ! (15)** | You've completed the Five Kage Tournament. |
| **Game Master! (30)** | You've played for a total of over 30 hours. |
| **Gimme a hand! (5)** | You can now use all support characters. |
| **I'm the greatest ninja! (0)** | You've unlocked all achievements. |
| **Image Master (15)** | Images collected: 80% |
| **Intermediate Survivor! (15)** | You've completed all of Intermediate Survival. |
| **Introductory Stage Survivor! (15)** | You've completed all of Introductory Survival. |
| **Leaf Chunin Tournament Champ! (15)** | You've completed the Leaf Chunin Tournament. |
| **Leaf Genin Tournament Champ! (15)** | You've completed all Leaf Genin Tournament battles. |
| **Leaf Higher-Up Tournament Champ! (15)** | You've completed the Leaf Higher-Up Tournament. |
| **Master Survivor! (30)** | You've completed all of Survival Mode. |
| **New Team Seven Tournament Champ! (15)** | You've completed the New Team Seven Tournament. |
| **Ninja Info Card Collector (5)** | Ninja Info Card images collected: 50% |
| **Ninja Lover! (50)** | You've used all leader characters. |
| **Ninja Tool Master (15)** | Ninja Tools collected: 80% |
| **Past Hokages (5)** | You can now use all past Hokages. |
| **Peerless Ninja Tournament Champ! (15)** | You've completed the Peerless Ninja Tournament. |
| **Sand Genin Tournament Champ! (15)** | You've completed the Sand Genin Tournament. |
| **Shippuden (15)** | You can use all the characters from Shippuden. |
| **Shippuden Tournament Champ! (15)** | You've completed the Shippuden Tournament. |
| **Substitution Jutsu Master (15)** | Substitution Jutsu collected: 80% |
| **Tale of Gaara complete (15)** | Completed Tale of Gaara. |
| **Tale of Itachi Uchiha complete (15)** | Completed Tale of Itachi Uchiha. |
| **Tale of Jiraiya complete (15)** | Completed Tale of Jiraiya. |
| **Tale of Kakashi Hatake complete (15)** | Completed Tale of Kakashi Hatake. |
| **Tale of Killer Bee complete (15)** | Completed Tale of Killer Bee. |
| **Tale of Madara Uchiha complete (15)** | Completed Tale of Madara Uchiha. |
| **Tale of Minato Namikaze complete (15)** | Completed Tale of Minato Namikaze. |
| **Tale of Naruto Uzumaki complete (15)** | Completed Tale of Naruto Uzumaki. |
| **Tale of Sasuke Uchiha complete (15)** | Completed Tale of Sasuke Uchiha. |
| **Tale of Young Naruto complete (15)** | Completed Tale of Young Naruto. |
| **Tale of Zabuza and Haku complete (15)** | Completed Tale of Zabuza Momochi and Haku. |

NEW!

A
B
C
D
E
F
G
H
I
J
K
L
M
N
O
P
Q
R
S
T
U
V
W
X
Y
Z

**CODES & CHEATS**

| Team Seven Tournament Champ! (15) | You've completed the Team Seven Tournament. |
| Tournament Champ! (30) | You've completed all Challenge Tournaments. |
| Ultimate Jutsu Movie Master (15) | Ultimate Jutsu scenes collected: 80% |
| Ultimate Ninja Gathering (50) | You can now use all characters. |
| Ultimate Ninja Tournament Champ! (15) | You've completed the Ultimate Ninja Tournament. |
| Wealthy Ninja (50) | You've earned a total of 1,000,000 Ryo. |
| Younger Version (15) | You can use all the characters of the Young Version. |

## NCAA FOOTBALL 13   (PlayStation 3)

### TROPHY

| UNLOCKABLE | HOW TO UNLOCK |
| --- | --- |
| And the Winner Is... (Bronze) | Win the Heisman Memorial Trophy® in single team Dynasty Mode, Road to Glory Mode, or Heisman Challenge Mode. |
| Best Class Ever (Bronze) | Have the #1 ranked recruiting class in a season in single team Dynasty Mode. |
| Don't Run Home to Mamma (Bronze) | In Dynasty, convince a homesick player to stay at your school instead of transferring. |
| Dream Job (Silver) | Become the head coach of your alma mater in Dynasty (Coach Contracts on). |
| Dual Threat Coach (Gold) | Win the BCS Championship & have the #1 recruiting class in a single season as head coach in Dynasty. |
| Earn My Trust (Silver) | Reach the max coach trust in Road to Glory Mode. |
| Future Star (Bronze) | Become a 5-star prospect in Road to Glory Mode. |
| Go Ahead, Ask me Anything (Bronze) | Earn a minimum of 75 recruiting points on a Prospect Choice topic. |
| Go for Broke (Bronze) | Complete a pass for 50 or more yards (excludes Co-Op). |
| Heisman Performance (Platinum) | Congratulations for unlocking all trophies in NCAA® Football 13! |
| High School Champ (Bronze) Game in any state. | Play and win the High School Championship |
| Highlight of the Year (Bronze) | Upload a photo or video to EASports.com. |
| Hometown Hero (Gold) | Lead your alma mater to a National Championship as a head coach in Dynasty (Coach Contracts on). |
| I am Andre Ware (Silver) | Win the Heisman with Andre Ware. |
| I am Barry Sanders (Silver) | Win the Heisman with Barry Sanders. |
| I am Carson Palmer (Silver) | Win the Heisman with Carson Palmer. |
| I am Charlie Ward (Silver) | Win the Heisman with Charlie Ward. |
| I am Desmond Howard (Silver) | Win the Heisman with Desmond Howard. |
| I am Doug Flutie (Silver) | Win the Heisman with Doug Flutie. |
| I am Eddie George (Silver) | Win the Heisman with Eddie George. |
| I am Herschel Walker (Silver) | Win the Heisman with Herschel Walker. |
| I am Marcus Allen (Silver) | Win the Heisman with Marcus Allen. |
| I am RG III (Silver) | Win the Heisman with Robert Griffin III. |
| Keep 'em Honest (Bronze) | Gain 200 rushing yards and 200 passing yards in the same game (excludes Co-Op and Road to Glory). |

| | |
|---|---|
| Let's Do it Again (Silver) | As a head coach in Dynasty, sign an extension to stay at the same school (Coach Contracts on). |
| Living Legend (Gold) | Reach a coach prestige of A+ with a created coach in Dynasty (Coach Contracts on). |
| Look at the Game Tape! (Bronze) | Unlock 5 attributes on a single scouting session. |
| My Two Cents (Bronze) | In Online Dynasty, write a comment on a Dynasty Wire story. |
| No Regrets (Bronze) | Convince a player to stay for their senior year using only one promise to get their degree. |
| Pick Up 20 (Bronze) | Break off a 20 yard run (excludes Co-Op). |
| Put Your Helmet On (Bronze) | Become a starter in Road to Glory Mode. |
| Read and React (Bronze) | Intercept a pass while using Reaction Time. |
| Take What's Mine (Silver) | Win a position battle in Road To Glory Mode. |
| Tire Fire Offense (Silver) | Win a game without scoring an offensive touchdown and gaining less than 200 yards (excludes Co-Op). |
| Unstoppable (Bronze) | Win a game by 35+ points on Heisman difficulty (excludes Co-Op). |
| Up the Gut for the Score (Bronze) | Score a touchdown handing off to the fullback on a triple option play (excludes Co-Op). |
| Welcome to the Club (Silver) | Win the National Championship in year 1 of Dynasty with either UMASS, UTSA, or Texas State. |

## NCAA FOOTBALL 13 (XBOX 360)

### ACHIEVEMENT

| UNLOCKABLE | HOW TO UNLOCK |
|---|---|
| And the Winner Is… (15) | Win the Heisman Memorial Trophy® in single team Dynasty, Road to Glory, or Heisman Challenge Mode. |
| Best Class Ever (15) | Have the #1 ranked recruiting class in a season in single team Dynasty Mode. |
| Don't Run Home to Mamma (20) | In Dynasty, convince a homesick player to stay at your school instead of transferring. |
| Dream Job (35) | Become the head coach of your alma mater in Dynasty (Coach Contracts on). |
| Dual Threat Coach (160) | Win the BCS Championship & have the #1 recruiting class in a single season as head coach in Dynasty. |
| Earn My Trust (25) | Reach the max coach trust in Road to Glory Mode. |
| Future Star (15) | Become a 5-star prospect in Road to Glory Mode. |
| Go Ahead, Ask me Anything (15) | Earn a minimum of 75 recruiting points on a Prospect Choice topic. |
| Go for Broke (20) | Complete a pass for 50 or more yards (excludes Co-Op). |
| High School Champ (15) | Play and win the High School Championship Game in any state. |
| Highlight of the Year (10) | Upload a photo or video to EASports.com. |
| Hometown Hero (50) | Lead your alma mater to a National Championship as a head coach in Dynasty (Coach Contracts on). |
| I am Andre Ware (30) | Win the Heisman with Andre Ware. |
| I am Barry Sanders (30) | Win the Heisman with Barry Sanders. |
| I am Carson Palmer (30) | Win the Heisman with Carson Palmer. |

A
B
C
D
E
F
G
H
I
J
K
L
M
N
O
P
Q
R
S
T
U
V
W
X
Y
Z

| | |
|---|---|
| I am Charlie Ward (30) | Win the Heisman with Charlie Ward. |
| I am Desmond Howard (30) | Win the Heisman with Desmond Howard. |
| I am Doug Flutie (30) | Win the Heisman with Doug Flutie. |
| I am Eddie George (30) | Win the Heisman with Eddie George. |
| I am Herschel Walker (30) | Win the Heisman with Herschel Walker. |
| I am Marcus Allen (30) | Win the Heisman with Marcus Allen. |
| I am RG III (30) | Win the Heisman with Robert Griffin III. |
| Keep 'em Honest (15) | Gain 200 rushing yards and 200 passing yards in the same game (excludes Co-Op and Road to Glory). |
| Let's Do It Again (20) | As a head coach in Dynasty, sign an extension to stay at the same school (Coach Contracts on). |
| Living Legend (50) | Reach a coach prestige of A+ with a created coach in Dynasty (Coach Contracts on). |
| Look at the Game Tape! (20) | Unlock 5 attributes on a single scouting session. |
| My Two Cents (10) | In Online Dynasty, write a comment on a Dynasty Wire story. |
| No Regrets (20) | Convince a player to stay for their senior year using only one promise to get their degree. |
| Pick Up 20 (20) | Break off a 20 yard run (excludes Co-Op). |
| Put Your Helmet On (15) | Become a starter in Road to Glory Mode. |
| Read and React (20) | Intercept a pass while using Reaction Time. |
| Take What's Mine (20) | Win a position battle in Road To Glory Mode. |
| Tire Fire Offense (30) | Win a game without scoring an offensive touchdown and gaining less than 200 yards (excludes Co-Op). |
| Unstoppable (15) | Win a game by 35+ points on Heisman difficulty (excludes Co-Op). |
| Up the Gut for the Score (10) | Score a touchdown handing off to the fullback on a triple option play (excludes Co-Op). |
| Welcome to the Club (40) | Win the National Championship in year 1 of Dynasty with either UMASS, UTSA, or Texas State. |

## NEVERDEAD (PlayStation 3)

### TROPHY

| UNLOCKABLE | HOW TO UNLOCK |
|---|---|
| A pain in the ass! (Bronze) | Defeat the Sword Pig. |
| Antiquarian (Bronze) | Destroy less than 25% of the museum exhibits. |
| Big Spender (Gold) | Purchase all abilities. |
| Boulder Dodge (Bronze) | Dodge the boulders. |
| BryceBQ (Bronze) | Kill an enemy with Fire. |
| Completist (Bronze) | Unlock all Prestige Badges. |
| Criminal Damages (Silver) | Destroy $1,000,000 worth of objects. |
| Curiosity Killed the Cat (Bronze) | Explore all of Arcadia's Apartment. |
| De-Cyphered (Bronze) | Take a trip down memory lane... |
| Don't Stop, Look or Listen (Bronze) | Dodge the traffic on the bridge. |
| Easter Bunny (Bronze) | Win an Egg Hunt challenge. |
| Endangered Species (Silver) | Kill 8 panda bears. |
| Evacuation Plan (Bronze) | Get all the civilians to the chopper. |
| Ever Dead (Silver) | Complete the game on easy difficulty. |
| Explosive Personality (Bronze) | Blow up 35 enemies in the Asylum using barrels. |

| | |
|---|---|
| Eye for an eye (Bronze) | Defeat Astaroth, King of Hell. |
| Four-to-one Odds (Bronze) | Defeat Quad Jaw. |
| Frail Friend (Bronze) | Win a Fragile Alliance challenge. |
| Funky Dunker (Bronze) | Put head through all basketball hoops. |
| Group Hug (Silver) | Kill 5 enemies with a single limb explosion. |
| Hop, Skip and Jump (Bronze) | Hop, roll and jump... |
| I'll bite your legs off! (Platinum) | Get all trophies. |
| Insurance Fraud (Bronze) | Destroy $100,000 worth of objects. |
| Let There be Light (Bronze) | Light all the sewer barrels. |
| Level Up (Silver) | Purchase 50% of the abilities. |
| Mind the gap (Bronze) | Lure Panda Bear in front of a train. |
| Never Dead (Gold) | Complete the game on hardcore difficulty. |
| Onslaughter (Bronze) | Complete an Arena Onslaught Challenge. |
| Out of the Frying Pan (Bronze) | Lure Panda Bear into lava. |
| Premature Evacuation (Bronze) | You win some, you lose some... |
| Rarely Dead (Silver) | Complete the game on normal difficulty. |
| Runner (Bronze) | Complete an Onslaught Challenge. |
| Sangria, on ice (Bronze) | Defeat Sangria, Duke of Hell. |
| Saviour (Bronze) | Complete a Search and Rescue challenge. |
| Serve and Protect (Bronze) | Save Nikki. |
| Shock and Awe (Bronze) | Kill an enemy with Electricity. |
| Swiss Army Bryce (Bronze) | Kill an enemy with every weapon. |
| The Great Collector (Gold) | Find all Major Collectibles. |
| There can be only one! (Bronze) | Defeat your nemesis. |
| Tower'n Inferno (Bronze) | Take down the water tower. |
| Tumble Dried (Bronze) | Get caught up in the whirlwind. |
| Womb with a view (Bronze) | Defeat Sullivan. |
| You and whose army? (Silver) | Shoot 50 enemies with dismembered limbs. |

## NEVERDEAD (XBOX 360)

### ACHIEVEMENT

| UNLOCKABLE | HOW TO UNLOCK |
|---|---|
| A pain in the ass! (20) | Defeat the Sword Pig. |
| Antiquarian (25) | Destroy less than 25% of the museum exhibits. |
| Big Spender (50) | Purchase all abilities. |
| Boulder Dodge (20) | Dodge the boulders. |
| BryceBQ (20) | Kill an enemy with Fire. |
| Completist (50) | Unlock all Prestige Badges. |
| Criminal Damages (25) | Destroy $1,000,000 of objects |
| Curiosity Killed the Cat (20) | Explore all of Arcadia's Apartment. |
| De-Cyphered (20) | Take a trip down memory lane. |
| Don't Stop, Look or Listen (20) | Dodge the traffic on the bridge. |
| Easter Bunny (20) | Win an Egg Hunt challenge. |
| Endangered Species (20) | Kill 8 panda bears. |
| Evacuation Plan (20) | Get all the civilians to the chopper. |
| Ever Dead (40) | Complete the game on easy difficulty. |
| Explosive Personality (20) | Blow up 35 enemies in the Asylum using barrels. |
| Eye for an eye (20) | Defeat Astaroth, King of Hell. |
| Four-to-one Odds (20) | Defeat Quad Jaw. |

| | |
|---|---|
| Frail Friend (20) | Win a Fragile Alliance challenge. |
| Funky Dunk (30) | Put head through all basketball hoops. |
| Group Hug (20) | Kill 5 enemies with a single arm explosion |
| Hop, Skip and Jump (10) | Hop, roll and jump... |
| Insurance Fraud (10) | Destroy $100,000 worth of objects. |
| Let There be Light (20) | Light all the sewer barrels. |
| Level Up (25) | Purchase 50% of the abilities. |
| Mind the gap (20) | Lure Panda Bear in front of a train. |
| Never Dead (50) | Complete the game on hardcore difficulty. |
| Onslaughter (20) | Complete an Arena Onslaught Challenge. |
| Out of the Frying Pan (20) | Lure Panda Bear into lava. |
| Premature Evacuation (5) | You win some, you lose some... |
| Rarely Dead (45) | Complete the game on normal difficulty. |
| Runner (20) | Complete an Onslaught Challenge. |
| Sangria, on ice (20) | Defeat Sangria, Duke of Hell. |
| Saviour (20) | Complete a Search and Rescue challenge. |
| Serve and Protect (20) | Save Nikki. |
| Shock and Awe (20) | Kill an enemy with Electricity. |
| Swiss Army Bryce (20) | Kill an enemy with every weapon. |
| The Great Collector (50) | Find all Major Collectibles. |
| There can be only one! (20) | Defeat your nemesis. |
| Tower'n Inferno (20) | Take down the water tower. |
| Tumble Dried (20) | Get caught up in the whirlwind. |
| Womb with a view (20) | Defeat Sullivan |
| You and whose army? (25) | Shoot 50 enemies with dismembered arms. |
| Unlock Assault Bowguns | Beat the game on any difficulty |

## NINJA GAIDEN 3 (PlayStation 3)

### TROPHY

| UNLOCKABLE | HOW TO UNLOCK |
|---|---|
| Abysmal Creations (Bronze) | Escape from the Chimera Disposal Facility. |
| Advent of the Goddess (Bronze) | Finish Day 7. |
| Ahab (Bronze) | Attack the Black Narwhal. |
| An Honorable Death (Bronze) | Perform harakiri. |
| Antediluvian Slumber (Bronze) | Finish Day 3. |
| Atonement (Bronze) | One more death to make amends. |
| Beyond the Flames (Bronze) | Make it through the fire. |
| Brothers (Bronze) | The sibling rivalry comes to an end. |
| Bumpy Ride (Bronze) | Finish Day 2. |
| Evil Twin (Bronze) | Defeat the Epigonos. |
| Falcon Dive (Bronze) | Learn the Falcon Dive. |
| Flying Bird Flip (Bronze) | Learn the Flying Bird Flip. |
| Guardian of the Village (Bronze) | Play the Hidden Village stage 10 times. |
| Hayabusa Style Grand Master (Bronze) | Reach level 50. |
| Hero (Silver) | Clear the game on Hero. |
| I Got Your Back (Bronze) | Play a Co-op Ninja Trial with a partner. |
| Inferno (Bronze) | Learn Ninpo. |
| Initiate (Bronze) | Clear 10 Acolyte Trials. |

| Initiation (Bronze) | Play a Clan Battle. |
| Izuna Drop (Bronze) | Learn the Izuna Drop. |
| Kunai Climb (Bronze) | Learn the Kunai Climb. |
| Lone Ninja (Silver) | Clear 10 Solo Ninja Trials. |
| Master Ninja (Gold) | Clear the game on Master Ninja. |
| Master of the Katana (Bronze) | Raise the katana to level 10. |
| Master of the Secret Arts (Platinum) | Obtain all trophies. |
| Mentor (Silver) | Clear the game on Hard. |
| Mind the Gap (Bronze) | Escape from the monorail. |
| Observer (Bronze) | Play the Watchtower stage 10 times. |
| One Against the World (Bronze) | Win a battle royale match. |
| Overlord (Silver) | Clear 5 Master Ninja Trials. |
| Prestige (Bronze) | Clear 5 Leader Trials. |
| Rope Crossing (Bronze) | Learn how to cross a rope. |
| Shady (Bronze) | Perform a betrayal. |
| Shinobi (Silver) | Clear the game on Normal. |
| Sliding (Bronze) | Learn how to slide. |
| Sneaky (Bronze) | Perform a ghost kill. |
| Snowman (Bronze) | Play the Snowfield stage 10 times. |
| Steel on Bone (Bronze) | Cut down 100 enemies with Steel on Bone attacks. |
| Steel on Steel (Bronze) | Destroy the Steel Spider. |
| Teamwork (Bronze) | Win 10 team battles. |
| The Acolyte (Bronze) | Successfully clear the Sanji event in Hayabusa Village. |
| The Great Escape (Bronze) | Finish Day 4. |
| The Grip of Murder (Bronze) | Finish Day 1. |
| The Karma of a Shinobi (Bronze) | Finish Day 5. |
| The Spice of Life (Bronze) | Get 10 customization parts. |
| Ultimate Ninja (Gold) | Clear 3 Ultimate Ninja Trials. |
| Ultimate Technique (Bronze) | Learn the Ultimate Technique. |
| Veteran (Bronze) | Clear 10 Mentor Trials. |
| Waiting (Bronze) | Finish Day 6. |
| Walking Dictionary (Silver) | Get 100 kanji. |
| Wall Run (Bronze) | Learn the Wall Run. |

## NINJA GAIDEN 3 (XBOX 360)

### ACHIEVEMENT

| UNLOCKABLE | HOW TO UNLOCK |
| --- | --- |
| Abysmal Creations (15) | Escaped from the Chimera Disposal Facility. |
| Advent of the Goddess (15) | Finish Day 7. |
| Ahab (15) | Land on the Black Narwhal. |
| An Honorable Death (10) | Perform harakiri. |
| Antediluvian Slumber (15) | Finish Day 3. |
| Atonement (15) | Defeated Theodore. |
| Beyond the Flames (15) | Made it through the fire. |
| Brothers (15) | Defeated Cliff. |
| Bumpy Ride (10) | Finish Day 2. |
| Evil Twin (15) | Defeated the Epigonos. |
| Falcon Dive (10) | Learn the Falcon Dive. |

| Flying Bird Flip (10) | Learn the Flying Bird Flip. |
|---|---|
| Guardian of the Village (10) | Play the Hidden Village stage 10 times. |
| Hayabusa Style Grand Master (15) | Reached level 50. |
| Hero (50) | Cleared the game on Hero. |
| I Got Your Back (10) | Play a Co-op Ninja Trial with a partner. |
| Inferno (10) | Learned Ninpo. |
| Initiate (10) | Cleared 10 Acolyte Trials. |
| Initiation (10) | Play a Clan Battle. |
| Izuna Drop (10) | Learn the Izuna Drop. |
| Kunai Climb (10) | Learn the Kunai Climb. |
| Lone Ninja (50) | Cleared 10 Solo Ninja Trials. |
| Master Ninja (100) | Cleared the game on Master Ninja. |
| Master of the Katana (15) | Raised the katana to level 10. |
| Mentor (60) | Cleared the game on Hard. |
| Mind the Gap (10) | Escaped from the monorail. |
| Observer (10) | Play the Watchtower stage 10 times. |
| One Against the World (10) | Win a battle royale match. |
| Overlord (50) | Cleared 5 Master Ninja Trials. |
| Prestige (10) | Cleared 5 Leader Trials. |
| Rope Crossing (10) | Learn how to cross a rope. |
| Shady (10) | Perform a betrayal. |
| Shinobi (50) | Cleared the game on Normal. |
| Sliding (10) | Learn how to slide. |
| Sneaky (10) | Perform a ghost kill. |
| Snowman (10) | Play the Snowfield stage 10 times. |
| Steel on Bone (10) | Cut down 100 enemies with Steel on Bone attacks. |
| Steel on Steel (10) | Destroyed the Steel Spider. |
| Teamwork (10) | Win 10 team battles. |
| The Acolyte (15) | Successfully responded to Sanji's ambush. |
| The Great Escape (15) | Finish Day 4. |
| The Grip of Murder (10) | Finish Day 1. |
| The Karma of a Shinobi (15) | Finish Day 5. |
| The Spice of Life (10) | Get 10 customization parts. |
| Ultimate Ninja (100) | Cleared 3 Ultimate Ninja Trials. |
| Ultimate Technique (10) | Learn the Ultimate Technique. |
| Veteran (10) | Cleared 10 Mentor Trials. |
| Waiting (15) | Finish Day 6. |
| Walking Dictionary (50) | Get 100 kanji. |
| Wall Run (10) | Learn the Wall Run. |

## NINJA GAIDEN SIGMA PLUS (PlayStation Vita)

### TROPHY

| UNLOCKABLE | HOW TO UNLOCK |
|---|---|
| Cleared 10 Trials | Clear Secrets of Fighting, Military Destruction, Descent of the Fiends, and Captivating Goddesses (Bronze) |
| Cleared 14 Trials | Clear Desperation, Fateful Confrontation, Battlefield of the Abyss, and Giants of the Underworld (Bronze) |

| | |
|---|---|
| **Cleared 2 Trials (Bronze)** | Clear all Ninja Tutorials and Path to the Ultimate Ninja. |
| **Cleared 6 Trials(Bronze)** | Clear Unrivalef Meeting, Nightmarish Phantasms, Abysmal Lair, and Secrets of shooting |
| **Cleared all Trials. (Bronze)** | Clear Unearthed Challenge and Eternal Legend |
| **Cleared Hard** | Finish all chapters of the game on Hard (Bronze) |
| **Cleared Master Ninja** | Finish all chapters of the game on Master Ninja (Gold) |
| **Cleared Tairon Under Alert** | Completed Chapter 10 (Bronze) |
| **Cleared The Caverns** | Completed Chapter 15 (Bronze) |
| **Cleared The Fiend Hunter** | Completed Chapter 5 (Bronze) |
| **Cleared The Way of the Ninja (Bronze)** | Completed Chapter 1. |
| **Cleared Very Hard** | Finish all chapters of the game on Very Hard (Bronze) |
| **Coin Aficionado(Silver)** | clear 50 missions in ninja trials |
| **Coin Collector** | Get coins in all Ninja Trials (Silver) |
| **Coin Master** | Get platinum coins in all Ninja Trials (Gold) |
| **Dabilahro Master (Bronze)** | Defeat 1000 enemies with the Dabilahro. |
| **Dragon Sword Master (Bronze)** | Defeat 1000 enemies with the Dragon Sword. |
| **Dual Kitana Master (Bronze)** | Defeat 1000 enemies with the Dual Kitana. |
| **Feat of Ultimate Destruction (Bronze)** | Use the strongest Ultimate Technique on 100 enemies. |
| **Fire Wheels Master (Bronze)** | Use Fire Wheels successfully 100 times. |
| **First Clear(Bronze)** | Finish all chapters of the game. |
| **Guillotine Throw Master (Bronze)** | Use the Guillotine Throw on 100 enemies. |
| **Heroes Never Give Up** | Activate Hero Mode 100 times (Bronze) |
| **Ice Storm Master (Bronze)** | Use Ice Storm successfully 100 times. |
| **Inazuma Master (Bronze)** | Use Inazuma successfully 100 times. |
| **Inferno Master (Bronze)** | Use Inferno successfully 100 times. |
| **Izuna Drop Master (Bronze)** | Use the Izuna Dro on 100 enemies. |
| **Just Put Me on(Bronze)** | Hold/keep up to 99,999 Yellow Essence |
| **Kitetsu Master (Bronze)** | Defeat 1000 enemies with the Kitetsu. |
| **Lead Scarab Hunter(Bronze)** | find 10 scarabs. |
| **Legendary Scarab Hunter(Silver)** | Find all scarabs. |
| **Lunar Staff Master (Bronze)** | Defeat 1000 enemies with the Lunar Staff. |
| **Master Scarab Hunter(Bronze)** | find 30 scarabs. |
| **Ninja Carnage** | Kill every enemy in an Ambush (Bronze) |
| **Ninja Massacre** | Kill every enemy in all Ambushes (Silver) |
| **Ninja Slaughter** | Kill every enemy in 6 Ambushes (Bronze) |
| **Over 10,000,000 Karma(Bronze)** | In ninja trials get this score. best way to get this trophy is playing mission 2 of Unrivaled Meeting |
| **Over 50,000,000 Karma** | Get 50,000,000 Karma (Silver) |
| **Projectile Weapons (Bronze)** | Defeat 100 enemies with projectile weapons. |
| **Rachel Master** | Defeat 500 enemies with Rachel (Bronze) |
| **Rookie Scarab Hunter(Bronze)** | find 1 scarab. |
| **Sorcery Master** | Use Ice Storm successfully 100 times. (Bronze) |
| **Thanks for Finding Me!(Bronze)** | Find all the Team Ninja logos in story mode. |
| **Thanks for playing! -from) Team NINJA (Gold** | Get Master on all chapters on Master Ninja. |

NEW!

A
B
C
D
E
F
G
H
I
J
K
L
M
N
O
P
Q
R
S
T
U
V
W
X
Y
Z

| The Journey to Master Ninja (Bronze) | Get Master Ninja on all chapters. |
|---|---|
| The Long Journey to Master Ninja (Bronze) | Get Master Ninja on all chapters on Hard. |
| The Really Long Journey to Master Ninja (Bronze) | Get Master Ninja on all chapters on Very Hard. |
| True Ultimate Ninja (Platinum) | Collect all trophies. |
| Vigoorian Flail Master (Bronze) | Defeat 1000 enemies with the Vigoorian Flail. |
| War Hammer Master (Bronze) | Defeat 1000 enemies with the War Hammer (Hayabusa). |
| Wooden Sword/Unlabored Flawlessness Master (Bronze) | Defeat 1000 enemies with the Wooden Sword/Unlabored Flawlessness. |

### UNLOCKABLE

| UNLOCKABLE | HOW TO UNLOCK |
|---|---|
| Master Ninja | Clear the game on Very Hard |
| Ninja Dog | Die 3 times while playing on Normal |
| Very Hard | Clear the game on Hard |
| Biker (Rachel) | Clear the game on Hard |
| Doppelganger (Ryu) | Clear the game on Normal |
| Formal Attire (Rachel) | Clear the game on Normal |
| Legendary Ninja (Ryu) | Clear the game on Normal |
| The Grip of Murder (Ryu) | Clear the game on Very Hard difficulty setting. |

## PERSONA 4 ARENA   (PlayStation 3)

### TROPHY

| UNLOCKABLE | HOW TO UNLOCK |
|---|---|
| Action! (Bronze) | You performed 100 Furious Actions in Arcade Mode or online. |
| All-Out Attack to the MAX! (Bronze) | You finished an All-Out Attack with a Fatal Counter in Arcade Mode or online. |
| Amazing, Sensei! (Bronze) | You've earned your first online victory! You've bear-ly scratched the surface. |
| BAM! (Bronze) | You used every character's Instant Kill move in Arcade Mode or online! |
| Belt Collector (Gold) | You completed Arcade Mode with all characters. |
| Black Belt (Silver) | You have reached Grade C in Ranked Matches. |
| C'est Magnifique! (Gold) | You completed Score Attack Mode with all characters. |
| Calm Down. (Bronze) | You suffered a Persona Break in Arcade Mode or online. It happens to everybody... |
| Champion! (Bronze) | You completed Arcade Mode with one character. |
| Combo Crazy (Gold) | You have completed all the Challenges! Funky Student would be proud. |
| Combo Master (Silver) | You have completed 300 Challenges. |
| Die for Me! (Bronze) | You performed 30 Fatal Counters in Arcade Mode or online. |
| Halfway There (Bronze) | You completed Stage 6 in Score Attack. |
| I am Thou... (Platinum) | You have mastered P4A. |
| I Learned a Few Moves (Bronze) | You have completed 150 Challenges. |
| I Mastered that One (Silver) | You have completed all of one character's Challenges! |
| Meat Dimension (Bronze) | You defeated an opponent in Arcade Mode or online before he Awakened! Now, that's a real challenge! |

| | |
|---|---|
| Null Physical (Bronze) | You performed 50 Instant Blocks in Arcade Mode or online. |
| One More! (Bronze) | You performed 20 One More Bursts in Arcade Mode or online. |
| Per...so......na...! (Bronze) | Have you burned your dread? Or reached out to the truth? |
| Perfect! (Bronze) | You had a perfect victory in Arcade Mode or online. |
| Persona Breaker (Bronze) | You created 10 Persona Breaks in Arcade Mode or online. |
| Replay Reviewer (Bronze) | You watched a Replay in the Theater. Are you as good as you remember? |
| School's Out (Bronze) | You've aced all the tests. |
| Serious Gamer (Silver) | You have reached Level 30 by playing online matches! |
| Speak with Your Fists! (Bronze) | You've battled against every character in online matches. You're a grizzly'd warrior now! |
| Stylish! (Bronze) | You performed 100 Auto Combos in Arcade Mode or online. |
| The Angel (Bronze) | Aigis' Story chapter has been told. |
| The Beast (Bronze) | Teddie's Story chapter has been told. |
| The Boxer (Bronze) | Akihiko's Story chapter has been told. |
| The Captain (Bronze) | Yosuke's Story chapter has been told. |
| The Carnivore (Bronze) | Chie's Story chapter has been told. |
| The Detective (Bronze) | Naoto's Story chapter has been told. |
| The Emperor (Bronze) | Kanji's Story chapter has been told. |
| The Kingpin (Bronze) | Yu's Story chapter has been told. |
| The Queen (Bronze) | Mitsuru's Story chapter has been told. |
| The Unconquerable (Bronze) | Yukiko's Story chapter has been told. |
| They Call Me... (Bronze) | You've created a Title for your online matches. |
| Time for the All-Out Attack! (Bronze) | You performed 100 All-Out Attacks in Arcade Mode or online. |
| Trained in Seclusion (Bronze) | You spent 30 minutes in Training in one sitting. Now take it to the streets! |
| Tres Bien! (Bronze) | You completed Score Attack Mode with one character. |
| Veteran (Bronze) | You have completed 100 online matches, win or lose. No bear puns here. Congrats. |
| Victory Cry (Bronze) | You won 30 Rounds in Arcade Mode or Online by using SP Skills or Awakened SP Skills. |
| Wild (Bronze) | You have used all the characters in Arcade Mode or Online. Variety is good for you! |
| You know the Midnight Channel? (Bronze) | Tuned In |
| You Should Leave Him Be... (Bronze) | You were afflicted with every ailment in Arcade Mode or online. Not even Mr. Edogawa can help you. |

## PERSONA 4 ARENA (XBOX 360)

### ACHIEVEMENT

| UNLOCKABLE | HOW TO UNLOCK |
|---|---|
| Action! (10) | You performed 100 Furious Actions in Arcade Mode or online. |
| All-Out Attack to the MAX! (10) | You finished an All-Out Attack with a Fatal Counter in Arcade Mode or online. |

A B C D E F G H I J K L M N O P Q R S T U V W X Y Z

| | |
|---|---|
| **Amazing, Sensei! (20)** | You've earned your first online victory! You've bear-ly scratched the surface. |
| **BAM! (30)** | You used every character's Instant Kill move in Arcade Mode or online! |
| **Belt Collector (80)** | You completed Arcade Mode with all characters. |
| **Black Belt (40)** | You have reached Grade C in Ranked Matches. |
| **C'est Magnifique! (80)** | You completed Score Attack Mode with all characters. |
| **Calm Down. (10)** | You suffered a Persona Break in Arcade Mode or online. It happens to everybody... |
| **Champion! (10)** | You completed Arcade Mode with one character. |
| **Combo Crazy (80)** | You have completed all the Challenges! Funky Student would be proud. |
| **Combo Master (40)** | You have completed 300 Challenges. |
| **Die for Me! (10)** | You performed 30 Fatal Counters in Arcade Mode or online. |
| **Halfway There (20)** | You completed Stage 6 in Score Attack. |
| **I Learned a Few Moves (20)** | You have completed 150 Challenges. |
| **I Mastered that One (40)** | You have completed all of one character's Challenges! |
| **Meat Dimension (20)** | You defeated an opponent in Arcade Mode or online before he Awakened! Now, that's a real challenge! |
| **Null Physical (20)** | You performed 50 Instant Blocks in Arcade Mode or online. |
| **One More! (10)** | You performed 20 One More Bursts in Arcade Mode or online. |
| **Per...so......na...! (10)** | Have you burned your dread? Or reached out to the truth? |
| **Perfect! (10)** | You had a perfect victory in Arcade Mode or online. |
| **Persona Breaker (10)** | You created 10 Persona Breaks in Arcade Mode or online. |
| **Replay Reviewer (10)** | You watched a Replay in the Theater. Are you as good as you remember? |
| **School's Out (10)** | You've aced all the tests. |
| **Serious Gamer (40)** | You have reached Level 30 by playing online matches! |
| **Speak with Your Fists! (30)** | You've battled against every character in online matches. You're a grizzly'd warrior now! |
| **Stylish! (10)** | You performed 100 Auto Combos in Arcade Mode or online. |
| **The Angel (10)** | Aigis' Story chapter has been told. |
| **The Beast (10)** | Teddie's Story chapter has been told. |
| **The Boxer (10)** | Akihiko's Story chapter has been told. |
| **The Captain (10)** | Yosuke's Story chapter has been told. |
| **The Carnivore (10)** | Chie's Story chapter has been told. |
| **The Detective (10)** | Naoto's Story chapter has been told. |
| **The Emperor (10)** | Kanji's Story chapter has been told. |
| **The Kingpin (10)** | Yu's Story chapter has been told. |
| **The Queen (10)** | Mitsuru's Story chapter has been told. |
| **The Unconquerable (10)** | Yukiko's Story chapter has been told. |
| **They Call Me... (10)** | You've created a Title for your online matches. |
| **Time for the All-Out Attack! (10)** | You performed 100 All-Out Attacks in Arcade Mode or online. |

| Trained in Seclusion (10) | You spent 30 minutes in Training in one sitting. Now take it to the streets! |
| --- | --- |
| Tres Bien! (30) one character. | You completed Score Attack Mode with one character. |
| u003e You Should Leave Him Be... (10) | You were afflicted with every ailment in Arcade Mode or online. Not even Mr. Edogawa can help you. |
| Veteran (30) | You have completed 100 online matches, win or lose. No bear puns here. Congrats. |
| Victory Cry (20) | You won 30 Rounds in Arcade Mode or Online by using SP Skills or Awakened SP Skills. |
| Wild (10) | You have used all the characters in Arcade Mode or Online. Variety is good for you! |
| You know the Midnight Channel? (10) | Tuned In |

## PHANTOM BREAKER (XBOX 360)

### ACHIEVEMENT

| UNLOCKABLE | HOW TO UNLOCK |
| --- | --- |
| Aerial Combat! (25) | Landed a total of 25 hits during clock-up with overdrive in one round. |
| All I've got (20) | Unlocked by using a Critical-Burst. |
| Break free! (15) | Perform at least 30 successful counter-attacks in one round [Story, Arcade, and Online matches only] |
| Brick wall defense! (10) | Blocked a total of 15 hits during clock-up with overdrive in one round. |
| Clocked-in power?! (10) | Executed a total of 40 hits during clock-up with overdrive in one round. |
| Cocoa (30) | Story Mode: Viewed the ending for Cocoa. |
| Count your sins! (10) | Fin has arrived! |
| Counter master (30) | Broke through a total of 3,000 counter-attacks. |
| Didn't even need it (5) | In burst gauge MAX mode, chose weak attack to win. |
| Don't stop me now! (25) | Unlocked after fighting 50 ranked matches. |
| Escape artist (25) | Broke through slip shift a total of 250 times. |
| Flash! (5) | Use Overdrive mode while the fight style is set to Quick [Story, Arcade, and Online matches only] |
| Going slightly mad! (10) | Use a Counter-Burst. [Story, Arcade, and Online matches only] |
| I won't be caught (10) | Succeeded in escaping a throw. |
| I'll kill your illusions (10) | Rimi has arrived! |
| I'll open your head (10) | Kurisu has arrived! |
| I'm not your damn maid. (20) | Unlocked Kurisu. |
| Itsuki (30) | Story Mode: Viewed the ending for Itsuki. |
| Keep blocking (15) | Used protection 15 times in one round. |
| Keep escaping (15) | Used slip shift 15 times in one round. |
| Keep yourself alive! (15) | Unlocked after winning ranked matches twice in a row. |
| Locked up! (15) | Unlocked by using a deadly technique for the deadly technique cancel enforcement. |
| M (30) | Story Mode: Viewed the ending for M. |
| Mei (30) | Story Mode: Viewed the ending for Mei. |
| Mikoto (35) | Story Mode: Viewed the ending for Mikoto. |
| Nailed it! (15) | Successfully executed a throw combo. |

| | |
|---|---|
| **Now I have to use it (15)** | Unlocked by using an ultra deadly technique. |
| **Now I'm here! (5)** | Unlocked after winning a ranked match for the first time. |
| **Phantom breaker maniacs (10)** | Saving Phantom Breaker demo version data, or cancelling all performance records. |
| **Phantom Breaking (50)** | Broke through a total of 500 blocks. |
| **Quit dreaming! (20)** | Unlocked Rimi. |
| **Ren (30)** | Story Mode: Viewed the ending for Ren. |
| **Revival (20)** | Unlocked by launching Imagine Mode in one round. |
| **Ria (30)** | Story Mode: Viewed the ending for Ria. |
| **Rock you! (5)** | Use Overdrive mode while the fight style is set to Hard. [Story, Arcade, and Online matches only] |
| **Rushing headlong! (15)** | Unlocked after fighting 25 ranked matches. |
| **Save me! (10)** | Unlocked when emergency is used.[Story, Arcade, and Online matches only] |
| **Schroedinger's Cat! (20)** | Unlocked Fin. |
| **Textbook fighter (5)** | Read all of the game reference. |
| **The neverending one (20)** | Unlocked Infinity. |
| **Think you just captured me?! (15)** | Succeeded in escaping a just throw. |
| **To be continued...? (30)** | Story Mode: Viewed the ending for Fin. |
| **Tokiya (30)** | Story Mode: Viewed the ending for Tokiya. |
| **Uke artist (25)** | Broke through protection a total of 250 times. |
| **Under pressure? (10)** | Unlocked when guard break is applied [Story, Arcade, and Online matches only] |
| **Waka (30)** | Story Mode: Viewed the ending for Waka. |
| **Wasn't expecting an uppercut... (15)** | Unlocked by using a cross Counter-Burst. |
| **Yodame Cantabile (60)** | Achieve an attack damage of 65,536 points. |
| **You are the champion! (30)** | Unlocked when arcade mode is completed on any difficulty. |
| **Yuzuha (30)** | Story Mode: Viewed the ending for Yuzuha. |

## PHINEAS AND FERB: ACROSS THE 2ND DIMENSION (PlayStation Vita)

### TROPHY

| UNLOCKABLE | HOW TO UNLOCK |
|---|---|
| **Agh, Bees! (Bronze)** | Run through the bee path in under 38 seconds. |
| **Balloon Gold (Silver)** | Collect all of the gold tokens in the balloon dimension. |
| **Barging Through (Bronze)** | Ride the entire balloon barge without falling once. |
| **Charging Goozim (Bronze)** | Make the Goozim charge into all the gnome village wreckage. |
| **Chiptastic (Silver)** | Collect every upgrade,effect,and mod chip in the game. |
| **Commander Counselor (Bronze)** | Defeat 3 Dooftron Commanders in the level. (The giant buildings.) |
| **Cruiser Destroyer (Bronze)** | Don't let any cruisers get away. (Shoot them all down.) |
| **Cruising through Crushers (Bronze)** | Get through all the crushers without getting hit. |
| **Dimensional Gold Claim (Gold)** | Collect all of the gold tokens across all the dimensions. |
| **Evil Doof's Gold (Silver)** | Collect all of the gold tokens assaulting Evil Doof's HQ. |
| **Evil Vanquisher (Bronze)** | Beat all the levels in the game. |
| **Fantasy Gold (Silver)** | Collect all of the gold tokens in the gnome dimension. |

| | |
|---|---|
| Figure Madman (Gold) | Collect Every Figure in the game. |
| First Gadget (Bronze) | Collect all the parts and construct your first gadget. |
| Gelatin Freedom-Fighter (Bronze) | Beat all the gelatin dimension levels. |
| Gelatin Gold (Silver) | Collect all of the gold tokens in the gelatin dimension. |
| Gelatin Revolution (Bronze) | Defeat the Gelatin Monster in under 180 seconds. |
| Gnome Toppler (Bronze) | Complete all the gnome dimension levels. |
| Grand Slam (Silver) | Use only the Baseball Launcher to defeat the Doof-Robot. |
| I'm A-levelin' Mah Gadgets! (Bronze) | Get each and every gadget up to maximum level. |
| Just Bouncy (Bronze) | Climb up the gelatin mountain but never bounce more than once on the same bouncy pad. |
| Laser Tracer (Silver) | Avoid 4 quad-laser attacks in a row. |
| Let's Play Dress-Up (Gold) | Unlock all 17 additional skins |
| Lifetime Accomplishment Award (Platinum) | Collect every trophy in the game. |
| Modtacular (Bronze) | Collect all the mod chips in the game. |
| Old Timey Winds (Silver) | Go across the windy canyon without falling down once. |
| Padfoot (Bronze) | Don't trip any turret shots by stepping on the laser sensors. |
| Platform Walker (Bronze) | Stay on the moving platforms for at least 60 seconds. (Don't touch solid ground.) |
| Quick and Timely Champion (Bronze) | Don't miss any button prompts during the giant robot fight. |
| Robot Rioter (Bronze) | Complete all the robot factory levels. |
| Robotic Gold (Silver) | Collect all of the gold tokens in the robot factory. |
| Rush to the Sewers (Bronze) | Get from the treehouse all the way into the sewers as quickly as possible. |
| That Old Timey Life (Bronze) | Complete all the old timey dimension levels. |
| The Full Cast (Silver) | Unlock every single playable character (Baljeet, Isabella, Pinky, Peter). |
| There's Gold in Them Thar Hills (Silver) | Collect all of the gold tokens in the old timey dimension. |
| Ticket Stockpiler (Silver) | Have 500 tickets in your posession at once. |
| Up, Up and Away... (Bronze) | Complete all the balloon dimension levels. |
| Version 2.0 (Silver) | Install half of the upgrade chips in the game. |
| Weekend at the Arcade (Bronze) | Earn 2000 tickets in the course of the game. |
| What the Boulder's Cooking (Silver) | Defeat 3 enemies with boulders. |

## PIKMIN 2 (Wii)

### UNLOCKABLE

| UNLOCKABLE | HOW TO UNLOCK |
|---|---|
| Challenge Mode | Defeat the Beady Long Legs at the bottom of the Spider Citadle, and bring the key to the recon drone thing. |
| Cinemas and Credits | Collect 10,000 pocos |
| Gold Ship | Collect 10,000 pokos |
| Louie's Cooking Notes | Rescue Louie from Titan Dweevil at Dream Den |
| Louie's Dark Secret movie | Complete all 30 Challenge Mode Arenas obtaining pink flowers (ie no Pikmin deaths). |
| Sales Pitch | Collect all items in any series |
| Shacho | Collect 10,000 pocos to save Hokotate Intergalactic Delivery, then choose to continue. |

A
B
C
D
E
F
G
H
I
J
K
L
M
N
O
P
Q
R
S
T
U
V
W
X
Y
Z

| Treasure Completion Movie | Collect all the pieces and rescue Looie. |
| Awakening Wood Level | Collect the sphere map in Emergence Cave. |
| Perplexing Pool Level | Collect the exploration map in the Awakening Wood. |
| Wistful Wild Level | Repay the 10,000 pokos of your company's debt. |

## PROTOTYPE 2 (PlayStation 3)

### TROPHY

| UNLOCKABLE | HOW TO UNLOCK |
|---|---|
| //BLACKNET Hacker (Silver) | Complete all //BLACKNET dossiers. |
| All Growed Up (Silver) | Fully upgrade Heller. |
| All Together Now (Bronze) | 10 or more kills with a single Black Hole attack. |
| Anger Management (Silver) | Destroy 5 vehicles using a Finisher. |
| Arcade Action (Bronze) | Karate kick a helicopter. |
| Back Atcha! (Bronze) | Deflect 5 missiles at enemies using Shield Block. |
| Cannonball! (Bronze) | 20 or more kills with a single Hammerfist dive attack. |
| Compulsive Eater (Bronze) | 5 consumes in 10 seconds or less. |
| Do the Evolution (Bronze) | Acquire 5 Mutations. |
| Eating Your Way to the Top (Silver) | Acquire 30 upgrades through Consumes. |
| Finally Full (Gold) | Acquire all 46 upgrades through Consumes. |
| Follow Your Nose (Silver) | Find all BlackBoxes. |
| Hard to Please (Silver) | Acquire a Mutation in each of the 5 categories. |
| Hijack Be Nimble (Bronze) | Stealth hijack 5 tanks or APCs. |
| I Caught a Big One! (Bronze) | Mount a helicopter using Whipfist. |
| I Want Some More (Bronze) | Complete RESURRECTION. |
| Icarus (Bronze) | Reach the highest point in the world. |
| It's an Epidemic (Bronze) | Complete MEET YOUR MAKER. |
| Just a Flesh Wound (Bronze) | Dismember a Brawler. |
| Lair to Rest (Bronze) | Destroy a single Lair. |
| Master Prototype (Silver) | Complete the game on HARD difficulty. |
| Murder your Maker? (Gold) | Complete the game. |
| One by One (Bronze) | Stealth Consume 50 Blackwatch troopers. |
| Over-Equipped (Bronze) | Weaponize 10 vehicles. |
| Platinum Trophy (Platinum) | Unlock all Trophies. |
| Project Closed (Bronze) | Complete a //BLACKNET operation. |
| Religious Experience (Bronze) | Meet Father Guerra. |
| Road Rage (Silver) | Destroy 10 Blackwatch tanks, APCs or helicopters using a single hijacked tank or APC. |
| Sic 'em! (Bronze) | Destroy 5 helicopters using Pack Leader. |
| So Above It All (Silver) | Spend at least 25 consecutive seconds in the air (helicopters don't count). |
| Something to Live For (Silver) | Complete FALL FROM GRACE. |
| Spindler's Search (Silver) | Destroy all Lairs. |
| Strike, You're Out. (Bronze) | Destroy a Strike Team in 15 seconds or less. |
| The Best Offense (Bronze) | Counter enemy attacks 20 times using Shield. |

| The Floor is Lava (Bronze) | Travel a half mile using only Wall Run, Glide, Jump and Air Dash. |
| --- | --- |
| The Mad Scientist (Silver) | Complete NATURAL SELECTION. |
| This is a Knife (Bronze) | Acquire a Prototype Power. |
| Two for the Price of One (Bronze) | Simultaneously kill 2 Brawlers using a single Devastator. |
| Up to No Good (Silver) | Defeat all Field Ops teams. |
| Vitamin B-rains (Bronze) | Acquire 10 upgrades through Consumes. |
| Wanted Man (Bronze) | Trigger 50 alerts. |
| What a Bitch (Silver) | Complete LABOR OF LOVE. |
| Who Watches the Watchers? (Silver) | Consume 10 //BLACKNET targets. |
| You're the Bomb (Bronze) | 10 or more kills using a single Bio-Bomb. |

### UNLOCKABLE

| UNLOCKABLE | HOW TO UNLOCK |
| --- | --- |
| New Game + | Complete the game on any difficulty |
| Insane Mode | Complete the game on any difficulty |

## PROTOTYPE 2 (XBOX 360)

### ACHIEVEMENT

| UNLOCKABLE | HOW TO UNLOCK |
| --- | --- |
| //BLACKNET Hacker (40) | Completed all //BLACKNET dossiers. |
| All Growed Up (50) | Fully upgraded Heller. |
| All Together Now (20) | 10 or more kills with a single Black Hole attack. |
| Anger Management (20) | Destroyed 5 vehicles using a Finisher. |
| Arcade Action (10) | Karate kicked a helicopter. |
| Back Atcha! (20) | Deflected 5 missiles at enemies using Shield Block. |
| Cannonball! (10) | 20 or more kills with a single Hammerfist dive attack. |
| Compulsive Eater (10) | 5 consumes in 10 seconds or less. |
| Do the Evolution (20) | Acquired 5 Mutations. |
| Eating Your Way to the Top (30) | Acquired 30 upgrades through Consumes. |
| Finally Full (50) | Acquired all 46 upgrades through Consumes. |
| Follow Your Nose (30) | Found all BlackBoxes. |
| Hard to Please (20) | Acquired a Mutation in each of the 5 categories. |
| Hijack Be Nimble (15) | Stealth hijacked 5 tanks or APCs. |
| I Caught a Big One! (10) | Mounted a helicopter using Whipfist. |
| I Want Some More (10) | Complete RESURRECTION. |
| Icarus (15) | Reached the highest point in the world. |
| It's an Epidemic (10) | Complete MEET YOUR MAKER. |
| Just a Flesh Wound (10) | Dismembered a Brawler. |
| Lair to Rest (15) | Destroyed a single Lair. |
| Master Prototype (50) | Completed the game on HARD difficulty. |
| Murder your Maker? (100) | Complete the game. |
| One by One (20) | Stealth Consumed 50 Blackwatch troopers. |
| Over-Equipped (20) | Weaponized 10 vehicles. |
| Project Closed (20) | Completed a //BLACKNET mission. |
| Religious Experience (10) | Meet Father Guerra. |

A
B
C
D
E
F
G
H
I
J
K
L
M
N
O
P
Q
R
S
T
U
V
W
X
Y
Z

| Road Rage (20) | Destroyed 10 Blackwatch tanks, APCs or helicopters using a single hijacked tank or APC. |
| Sic 'em! (20) | Destroyed 5 helicopters using Pack Leader. |
| So Above It All (20) | Spend at least 25 consecutive seconds in the air (helicopters don't count). |
| Something to Live For (30) | Complete FALL FROM GRACE. |
| Spindler's Search (40) | Destroyed all Lairs. |
| Strike, You're Out. (10) | Destroyed a Strike Team in 15 seconds or less. |
| The Best Offense (20) | Countered enemy attacks 20 times using Shield. |
| The Floor is Lava (15) | Traveled a half mile using only Wall Run, Glide, Jump and Air Dash. |
| The Mad Scientist (30) | Complete NATURAL SELECTION. |
| This is a Knife (20) | First Prototype Power aquired. |
| Two for the Price of One (20) | Simultaneously killed 2 Brawlers using a single Devastator. |
| Up to No Good (30) | Defeated all Field Ops teams. |
| Vitamin B-rains (10) | Acquired 10 upgrades through Consumes. |
| Wanted Man (20) | Triggered 50 alerts. |
| What a Bitch (30) | Complete LABOR OF LOVE. |
| Who Watches the Watchers? (20) | Consumed 10 //BLACKNET targets. |
| You're the Bomb (10) | 10 or more kills using a single Bio-Bomb. |

### UNLOCKABLE

| UNLOCKABLE | HOW TO UNLOCK |
| --- | --- |
| Avatar Award: Alex Mercer Outfit | With RADNET activated, access the Events Screen for unlock details. |
| Avatar Award: Heller Hoodie | With RADNET activated, access the Events Screen for unlock details. |
| Avatar Award: James Heller Outfit | With RADNET activated, access the Events Screen for unlock details. |
| Avatar Award: Shield | With RADNET activated, access the Events Screen for unlock details. |
| Avatar Award: T-Shirt | With RADNET activated, access the Events Screen for unlock details. |

## RAYMAN ORIGINS (PlayStation Vita)

### TROPHY

| UNLOCKABLE | HOW TO UNLOCK |
| --- | --- |
| B Side! (Bronze) | Played an Unlocked Character in any map. |
| Back At You! (Bronze) | You Bubblized a Hunter with his own live missile! |
| Beautiful Beats! (Bronze) | Holly Luya, the Music Nymph is Free! |
| Betilla's Back! (Bronze) | Head Nymph Betilla is Free! |
| Blue Baron! (Silver) | Beat the Giant Eel within 60 Seconds in 'Aim for the Eel.' |
| Boing! Boing! Boing! (Bronze) | Bounce-Bubblized 11 Enemies without landing in 'Polar Pursuit!' |
| Bubble Wrap Maniac! (Bronze) | Popped 100 Item Bubbles with tap |
| Clear Sighted (Bronze) | You found 30 Relics |
| Crush Combo! (Bronze) | Simultaneously crushed 4 enemies. |
| Crusher! (Bronze) | Crushed 50 Enemies. |
| Dr. Lividstone, I presume? (Gold) | You found ALL hidden cages. |
| Eagle Eyed (Silver) | You found all Relics. |

| | |
|---|---|
| Electoon Friend (Bronze) | Completed 10 Medallions. |
| Electoon Hero (Silver) | Completed 25 Medallions. |
| Electoon Legend (Gold) | Completed ALL Medallions. |
| Explorer (Silver) | You found 25 hidden cages. |
| Feed the Fairy! (Bronze) | Edith Up, the Gourmet Fairy is Free! |
| Fisher King! (Bronze) | Swam a Marathon! |
| Full Mouth (Silver) | Earned 5 Skull Teeth. |
| Grim Reaper (Bronze) | Popped 50 Enemy Bubbles with tap |
| Hover Happy! (Bronze) | One hour of flight time! |
| Hyperspeed! (Bronze) | Sprinted for an Entire Level! |
| I'm Back! (Bronze) | Replayed any completed map. |
| Kung Fu Combo! (Bronze) | Perform a swipe-to-air Kick Combo! |
| Merm-Aid! (Bronze) | Annetta Fish, the Ocean Nymph is Free! |
| Milk Tooth (Bronze) | Earned 1 Skull Tooth. |
| Nitro! (Gold) | Earned ALL speed trophies! |
| No Panic! (Bronze) | Saved ALL Darktooned Wizards in 'Port 'O Panic'. |
| Nothing Lasts Forever... (Gold) | Ding, Dong, the Livid Boss is Dead! |
| Nymphs Rock! (Bronze) | Helena Handbasket, the Mountain Nymph is Free! |
| Painless! (Bronze) | Completed a level without taking a hit! |
| Scout (Bronze) | You found 10 hidden cages. |
| Speedy! (Bronze) | Earned 5 speed trophies. |
| Sprinter! (Bronze) | Sprinted a Marathon! |
| Survivor (Bronze) | Survived a Piranha Pond without a scratch! |
| Sweet Dreams! (Platinum) | Won ALL trophies in the game! SICK! |
| The Bubblizer! (Bronze) | Chain-Bubblized 4 Enemies. |
| The Jaw (Gold) | Earned ALL Skull Teeth. |
| Turbo! (Silver) | Earned 15 speed trophies! |
| Vacuum Snack! (Bronze) | Inhaled 50 things on Moskito-back. |

## REALITY FIGHTERS (PlayStation Vita)

### TROPHY

| UNLOCKABLE | HOW TO UNLOCK |
|---|---|
| Advanced Survival (Silver) | Win 20 combats in survivor mode in a single run |
| Against the Clock (Bronze) | Reach Bronze score in all Time Attack Challenges |
| Ballerina Master (Bronze) | Perform all the moves for the Ballerina fight style in a single fight |
| Basic Survival (Bronze) | Win 10 combats in survivor mode in a single run |
| Beat Reality Fighters (Platinum) | Get all Gold, Silver and Bronze trophies |
| Boxing Master (Bronze) | Perform all the moves for the Boxing fight style in a single fight |
| Break Dance Master (Bronze) | Perform all the moves for the Break Dance fight style in a single fight |
| Capoeira Master (Bronze) | Perform all the moves for the Capoeira fight style in a single fight |
| Cowboy Master (Bronze) | Perform all the moves for the Cowboy fight style in a single fight |
| Disco Master (Bronze) | Perform all the moves for the Disco fight style in a single fight |
| Extreme Survival (Gold) | Win 30 combats in survivor mode in a single run |
| Karate Master (Bronze) | Perform all the moves for the Karate fight style in a single fight |

NEW!

A
B
C
D
E
F
G
H
I
J
K
L
M
N
O
P
Q
R
S
T
U
V
W
X
Y
Z

| | |
|---|---|
| Kung Fu Master (Bronze) | Perform all the moves for the Kung Fu fight style in a single fight |
| Love Challenge IV (Gold) | Discover the Disco Inferno and the Dancing Dino costumes |
| Lovely Challenge I (Silver) | Discover the Space Cowboy and the Fisher King costumes |
| Lovely Challenge II (Silver) | Discover the Lord of the Gnomes and the Handyman costumes |
| Lovely Challenge III (Gold) | Discover the Rocket Rocker and the Thumbling Stone costumes |
| Master of Time (Gold) | Achieve Gold score in all Time Attack challenges |
| Muay Thai Master (Bronze) | Perform all the moves for the Muay Thai fight style in a single fight |
| Perfect combat (Bronze) | Defeat an enemy receiving no damage at all |
| Rodeo Drive (Gold) | Buy all clothing, weapons and fight styles |
| Rush hour (Silver) | Beat five different friends in Infrastructure in less than one hour |
| Samurai Master (Bronze) | Perform all the moves for the Samurai fight style in a single fight |
| Sorcerer Master (Bronze) | Perform all the moves for the Sorcerer fight style in a single fight |
| Super Hero Master (Bronze) | Perform all the moves for the Super Hero fight style in a single fight |
| Super Heroine Master (Bronze) | Perform all the moves for the Super Heroine fight style in a single fight |
| The New Sensei (Gold) | Complete the story mode |
| Time Warrior (Silver) | Reach silver score in all Time Attack challenges |
| Wrestling Master (Bronze) | Perform all the moves for the Wrestling fight style in a single fight |
| Zombie Master (Bronze) | Perform all the moves for the Zombie fight style in a single fight |

## RESIDENT EVIL: OPERATION RACCOON CITY (PlayStation 3)

### TROPHY

| UNLOCKABLE | HOW TO UNLOCK |
|---|---|
| A Gun by Any Other Name (Bronze) | Kill an enemy with each weapon type including special weapons. |
| A Hero Spared! (Bronze) | Attempt "The Rescue" and survive. |
| Baker's Dozen (Bronze) | Kill 13 zombified teammates. |
| Betrayal (Bronze) | Complete the fifth mission of the U.S.S. campaign. |
| Bloody Good Time (Bronze) | Kill 5 enemies with Blood Frenzy in a single campaign game or multiplayer match. |
| By Trail Of Dead (Bronze) | Kill 50 opponents in Versus. (lifetime) |
| Chaos Averted (Bronze) | Kill an infected teammate with a headshot before they become a zombie in any mode. |
| Choices Aplenty (Bronze) | Purchase 15 weapons. |
| Clingy (Bronze) | 13 Parasite Zombies killed (lifetime) |
| Corrupted (Bronze) | Complete the second mission of the U.S.S. campaign. |
| Danger, High Voltage! (Bronze) | Complete the third mission of the U.S.S. campaign. |
| Died Trying (Bronze) | Attempt "The Rescue" and fail |
| Down Boy (Bronze) | Kill 13 zombie dogs (lifetime) |

| | |
|---|---|
| **Down in the Labs (Bronze)** | Complete the sixth mission of the U.S.S. campaign. |
| **Epic Standards (Silver)** | Upgrade all abilities for all characters to its maximum level. |
| **Fallen Idols (Silver)** | In Heroes mode, eliminate 4 Heroes in one game. |
| **Feelin' Stronger Every Day (Bronze)** | Fully upgrade an ability. |
| **Great Success (Gold)** | Gain S+ on all U.S.S. missions on Veteran or Professional difficulty |
| **Green Thumb (Bronze)** | Heal with 101 Green Herbs (lifetime) |
| **Hat Trick (Bronze)** | 3 Tyrants Killed (lifetime) |
| **Like a Bee (Silver)** | Kill 10 enemy players in one multiplayer game with CQC. |
| **Like a Butterfly (Bronze)** | Kill 100 zombies with CQC (lifetime) |
| **Look What I Can Do (Bronze)** | Purchase all abilities for one character class. |
| **Mr. Death (Platinum)** | Get all Trophies. |
| **No Sample For You (Bronze)** | Force 25 enemies to drop G-Virus Samples in Biohazard (lifetime). |
| **Now That's G (Bronze)** | Collect 3 G-Virus Samples in one match. |
| **On A Roll (Bronze)** | Achieve a 5 kill streak in a Versus match. |
| **One Trick Pony (Bronze)** | Purchase an ability. |
| **Only Hurts For A While (Bronze)** | Infected 13 times (lifetime) |
| **Organic Shield (Silver)** | Kill 5 enemies while using a zombie as a shield. |
| **Outbreak Survivalist (Silver)** | Complete all U.S.S. missions on Veteran. |
| **Quite The Collection (Silver)** | Purchase all available weapons. |
| **Raccoon City Cleanser (Gold)** | Complete all U.S.S. missions on Professional. |
| **Raccoon City Mascot (Bronze)** | Collect all 7 Raccoons |
| **Ready To Dominate (Bronze)** | Fully upgrade all abilities for one character class. |
| **Revival (Silver)** | Revive 31 teammates (lifetime) |
| **Rogue's Gallery (Bronze)** | Complete the fourth mission of the U.S.S. campaign. |
| **Sampler (Bronze)** | Play at least one match in every game mode type. |
| **Skill... Or Luck? (Silver)** | Achieve a 10 kill streak in a Versus match. |
| **So Hot Right Now (Bronze)** | Kill 103 enemies with incendiary rounds (lifetime) |
| **So Many Choices (Silver)** | Purchase all abilities for all character classes. |
| **Stop Squirming (Bronze)** | 17 Hunters Killed (lifetime) |
| **Success (Silver)** | Complete all U.S.S. missions with an S Rank. |
| **Supreme Survivors (Bronze)** | In Survivors mode, have all 4 players on your team Survive the game. |
| **The Loyalists (Bronze)** | Follow orders and defeat all liabilities. |
| **These Will Do (Bronze)** | Purchase 5 weapons. |
| **This Place Crawls (Bronze)** | 31 Parasites killed (lifetime) |
| **Tongue Tied (Bronze)** | Free teammate from Licker grapple. |
| **Up Close and Personal (Bronze)** | Kill 5 players in one multiplayer game with CQC Kills. |

| Witness (Bronze) | Witness the beginning of the Raccoon City outbreak. |
| You Love to Hate My 98 (Silver) | Complete 98 versus games |

## RESIDENT EVIL: OPERATION RACCOON CITY (XBOX 360)

### ACHIEVEMENT

| UNLOCKABLE | HOW TO UNLOCK |
| --- | --- |
| A Gun by Any Other Name (15) | Kill an enemy with each weapon type including special weapons. |
| A Hero Spared! (15) | Attempt "The Rescue" and survive. |
| Baker's Dozen (30) | Kill 13 zombified teammates. |
| Betrayal (20) | Complete the fifth mission of the U.S.S. campaign. |
| Bloody Good Time (20) | Kill 5 enemies by causing Blood Frenzy in a single campaign game or multiplayer match. |
| By Trail Of Dead (10) | 50 Versus opponents killed (lifetime) |
| Chaos Averted (5) | Kill an infected teammate with a headshot before they become a zombie in any mode. |
| Choices Aplenty (15) | Purchase 15 weapons. |
| Clingy (10) | 13 Parasite Zombies killed (lifetime) |
| Corrupted (20) | Complete the second mission of the U.S.S. campaign. |
| Danger, High Voltage! (20) | Complete the third mission of the U.S.S. campaign. |
| Died Trying (15) | Attempt "The Rescue" and fail |
| Down Boy (15) | Kill 13 zombie dogs (lifetime) |
| Down in the Labs (20) | Complete the sixth mission of the U.S.S. campaign. |
| Epic Standards (40) | Upgrade all abilities for all characters to its maximum level. |
| Fallen Idols (30) | In Heroes mode, eliminate 4 Heroes in one game. |
| Feelin' Stronger Every Day (15) | Fully upgrade an ability. |
| Great Success (45) | Gain S+ on all U.S.S. mission on Professional/ Veteran difficulty |
| Green Thumb (25) | Heal with 101 Green Herbs (lifetime) |
| Hat Trick (15) | 3 Tyrants Killed (lifetime) |
| Like a Bee (20) | Kill 10 enemy players in one Versus game with CQC. |
| Like a Butterfly (15) | Kill 100 zombies with CQC (lifetime) |
| Look What I Can Do (20) | Purchase all abilities for one character class. |
| No Sample For You (30) | Force 25 enemies to drop G-Virus Samples in Biohazard (lifetime). |
| Now That's G (15) | Collect 3 G-Virus Samples in one Biohazard match. |
| On A Roll (15) | Achieve a 5 kill streak in a Versus match. |
| One Trick Pony (10) | Purchase an ability. |
| Only Hurts For A While (10) | Infected 13 times (lifetime) |
| Organic Shield (20) | Kill 5 enemies consecutively while using a zombie as a shield. |
| Outbreak Survivalist (25) | Complete all U.S.S. missions on Veteran. |
| Quite The Collection (30) | Purchase all available weapons. |
| Raccoon City Cleanser (35) | Complete all U.S.S. missions on Professional. |
| Raccoon City Mascot (15) | Collect all 7 Raccoons. |
| Ready To Dominate (20) | Fully upgrade all abilities for one character class. |

| | |
|---|---|
| Revival (20) | Revive 31 team mates (lifetime) |
| Rogue's Gallery (20) | Complete the fourth mission of the U.S.S. campaign. |
| Sampler (20) | Play at least one match in every Versus game type |
| Skill... Or Luck? (25) | Achieve a 10 kill streak in a Versus match. |
| So Hot Right Now (15) | Kill 103 enemies with incendiary rounds (lifetime) |
| So Many Choices (30) | Purchase all abilities for all character classes. |
| Stop Squirming (10) | 17 Hunters Killed (lifetime) |
| Success (30) | Complete all U.S.S. missions with an S Rank. |
| Supreme Survivors (20) | In Survivors mode, have all 4 players on your team Survive the game. |
| The Loyalists (15) | Stop Squirming (10) |
| These Will Do (10) | Purchase 5 weapons. |
| This Place Crawls (15) | 31 Parasites killed (lifetime) |
| Tongue Tied (10) | Kill a Licker that is grappling a Teammate. |
| Up Close and Personal (10) | Kill 5 players in one multiplayer game with CQC Kills. |
| Witness (20) | Witness the beginning of the Raccoon City outbreak. |
| You Love to Hate my 98 (50) | Complete 98 Versus games |

## RESIDENT EVIL: REVELATIONS (3DS)

### *UNLOCKABLE*

| UNLOCKABLE | HOW TO UNLOCK |
|---|---|
| Chris, outfit 1 (Snow) | Clear episode 1-3 in the main game |
| Chris, outfit 2 (Ship) | Reach player level 30 |
| Jessica, outfit 1 (Snow) | Reach player level 10 |
| Jessica, outfit 2 (Ship) | Clear every stage on Trench difficulty |
| Jessica, outfit 3 (Terragrigia) | Reach player level 40 |
| Jill, outfit 1 (Ship) | Clear episode 1-3 in the main game |
| Jill, outfit 2 (Beach) | Reach player level 5 |
| Keith, outfit 1 (Snow) | Clear episode 4-6 in the main game |
| Keith, outfit 2 (HQ) | Clear 50 missions |
| Morgan | Find the real exit on stage 21 |
| Norman | Obtain all rare weapons |
| O'Brian | Clear every stage on Abyss difficulty |
| Parker, outfit 1 (Ship) | Clear episode 1-3 in the main game |
| Parker, outfit 2 (Beach) | Reach player level 20 |
| Parker, outfit 3 (Terragrigia) | Obtain one rare weapon |
| Quint, outfit 1 (Snow) | Clear 100 missions |
| Quint, outfit 2 (HQ) | Reach player level 50 |
| Raymond | Clear every stage on Chasm difficulty |
| Trench Difficulty | Complete all Raid Mode stages on Chasm Difficulty |
| Abyss Difficulty | Complete all Raid Mode stages on Trench Difficulty |
| Raid Mode Bonus Stage 21 | Clear the game |
| Raid Mode Stages 1-7 | Clear Episodes 1-3 |
| Raid Mode Stages 13-17 | Clear Episodes 7-9 |
| Raid Mode Stages 18-20 | Clear episodes 10-12 |
| Raid Mode Stages 8-12 | Clear Episodes 4-6 |
| Hell Difficulty | Complete the game once on normal |

| Hydra Shotgun | Complete the game on Normal difficulty or higher |
| Infinite Rocket Launcher | Complete the Game on Hell difficulty |
| New Game+ | Complete the game once on any difficulty. |

## RESISTANCE: BURNING SKIES (PlayStation Vita)

### TROPHY

| UNLOCKABLE | HOW TO UNLOCK |
|---|---|
| Axed (Silver) | Kill 50 Chimera with Riley's axe in the Single Player Campaign |
| Boom (Silver) | Kill 100 Chimera with headshots in the Single Player Campaign |
| Combine (Silver) | Upgrade both slots of a weapon in the Single Player Campaign |
| Conversion Tower (Bronze) | Successfully complete level 6 |
| Customize (Gold) | Upgrade all weapons in the Single Player Campaign |
| Dangerous (Bronze) | Kill 250 Chimera in the Single Player Campaign |
| Deadly (Silver) | Kill 500 Chimera in the Single Player Campaign |
| Ellis Island (Bronze) | Successfully complete level 4 |
| Executed (Silver) | Kill an Executioner |
| G-man (Gold) | Kill Gorrell |
| George Washington Bridge (Bronze) | Successfully complete level 3 |
| Giant (Gold) | Kill any combination of 18 Impalers or Executioners |
| Impaled (Silver) | Kill an Impaler |
| Incite (Gold) | Complete one round of multiplayer |
| Indiscriminate (Bronze) | Kill an enemy with every weapon in the Single Player Campaign |
| Inhuman (Gold) | Kill the Leviathan |
| Lethal (Gold) | Kill 1000 Chimera in the Single Player Campaign |
| Military Ocean Terminal (Bronze) | Successfully complete level 2 |
| Overheat (Silver) | Kill 50 Chimera by detonating their heatstacks in the Single Player Campaign |
| Platinum (Platinum) | Earn all trophies |
| Protection Camp (Bronze) | Successfully complete level 5 |
| Staten Island (Bronze) | Successfully complete level 1 |
| Unnatural (Gold) | Kill the Abomination |
| Upgrade (Bronze) | Upgrade a weapon in the Single Player Campaign |
| Variety (Bronze) | Use the secondary fire of each weapon in the Single Player Campaign |

## RIDGE RACER (PlayStation Vita)

### TROPHY

| UNLOCKABLE | HOW TO UNLOCK |
|---|---|
| Accomplished (Silver) | Your Skill Grade has increased to Level 10. You can proudly claim to have earned a rank among the top ridge racers of the world. |
| Been Around the Block (Bronze) | You raced at least once in every race mode. |
| Capable (Bronze) | Your Skill Grade has increased to Level 2. Your rivals will be equally tougher. Make it a worthwile victory. |
| Claim to Fame VIP (Silver) | You've been selected as today's Spotlight VIP for your team. |
| Divinity (Silver) | You beat the legendary Angel Car in all races. |

| | |
|---|---|
| **Dynamic and Dangerous (Bronze)** | You placed first in a race with the most Dynamic drift settings. |
| **Ectoplasmed (Bronze)** | You submitted your race to Ghost Battle. Now they're out to get you! |
| **Electronic Warfare (Bronze)** | You obtained Hacker Kit and Data Jammer for hi-tech electronic tactics. |
| **Exorcist (Silver)** | You beat the legendary Devil Car in all races. |
| **Filthy VIP (Silver)** | You ranked high in Credit Ranking and earned the title of VIP. |
| **Free Agent (Gold)** | You obtained over 30,000 CR, meaning you can transfer to a new team after watching Team Vision. |
| **Friend or Foe? (Bronze)** | You raced with a Friend in an Online Battle. |
| **Generous at Heart (Bronze)** | You uploaded 100 Victory Points to your team through Team Vision. |
| **Ghost Contender (Bronze)** | You beat a Ghost that is higher than 10 G. |
| **Ghost Hunter (Bronze)** | You beat over 50 races in Ghost Battle. |
| **Gift from Beyond (Bronze)** | You received the Devil's Gift and now Ridge Racer and Reiko took on a whole new look... |
| **Journeyman (Bronze)** | You raced on all 3 courses– Southbay Docks, Highland Cliffs, and Harborline 765 (including R courses). So which did you like best? |
| **Machine Junkie (Bronze)** | You raced at least once with each of the 5 machines (BISARGENTO, RAUNA, FIERA, EO, SYNCi). So which driving style and design did you like best? |
| **Mad Mechanic (Bronze)** | You reached the first branch-off point in the Machine Upgrade Map. Every great invention has its roots in risk. |
| **Mild and Menacing (Bronze)** | You placed first in a race with the most Mild drift settings. |
| **Nitrous Master (Silver)** | You obtained all types of Nitrous kits on the Machine Upgrade Map. Learn to take advantage of each one's unique properties. |
| **Nitrous-Free (Bronze)** | You placed first without using any Nitrous. |
| **Parting Gift (Bronze)** | You regifted the Devil's Gift to another racer on PlayStationNetwork. |
| **Platinum Ridge Racer (Platinum)** | You earned all the trophies in RIDGE RACER. |
| **Practice Makes Perfect (Bronze)** | You raced in over 50 Spot Races. That same commitment will pay off in the World Races, too. |
| **Prodigy (Bronze)** | Your team sponsor acknowledges your steady efforts, and has upgraded your machine's specs to the next level. Keep up the good work. |
| **Rocketeer (Bronze)** | You successfully pulled off a rocket start. |
| **Single Lap Spirit (Bronze)** | You raced more than 200 laps in Lap Time Attack. |
| **Skillful (Bronze)** | Your Skill level has increased to level 5. You're making your way to being a top ridge racer! |
| **Socialite (Bronze)** | You raced in over 50 Face-to-Face Battles. |
| **Solid Foundation (Bronze)** | You've maxed-out your machine's basic specs. All that's left is letting your choice of upgrade kits and driving technique determine the winner. |
| **Speed Demon (Bronze)** | You reached the maximum speed with a maxed-up machine, and added a maximum nitrous. |
| **Steal the Spotlight (Bronze)** | You raced against a VIP racer in an Online Battle. |
| **Stellar (Gold)** | Your Skill Grade has increased to Level 16. You can now claim the title of "ultimate racer." |
| **Stop and Smell the Roses (Bronze)** | You stopped by that special spot on the Harborline 765 course. |
| **Switching Sides (Silver)** | You transferred teams. |

| | |
|---|---|
| Tech Tree Climber (Gold) | You completed the Machine Upgrade Map. |
| Technician (Bronze) | You mastered the paddle shift in a race. |
| Tinkerer (Bronze) | You took the first momentous step toward developing an upgrade kit on the Machine Upgrade Map. |
| Top Dog VIP (Silver) | You ranked high in Score Ranking and earned the title of VIP. |
| Triple Lap Trickster (Bronze) | You raced in Total Time Attack over 50 times. |
| Triple Threat (Bronze) | You equipped an upgrade kit from Groups A through C for the first time. |
| Welcome to Circlite Racing! (Bronze) | You signed with Circlite Racing. |
| Welcome to Squaris GP! (Bronze) | You signed with Squaris GP. |
| Welcome to Trianchor Alliance! (Bronze) | You signed with Trianchor Alliance. |
| Welcome to Xealot Motorspot! (Bronze) | You signed with Xealot Motorsport. |
| Wind Whipper (Bronze) | You obtained Super Slipstream and Zero Slipstream for controlling the effects of slipstreaming. |
| World Racer (Bronze) | You raced in over 50 Online Battles. |

## RIDGE RACER UNBOUNDED (PlayStation 3)

### TROPHY

| UNLOCKABLE | HOW TO UNLOCK |
|---|---|
| Award Collector (Bronze) | Get all Race Awards. |
| Award Hogger (Silver) | Receive 20 awards in one race. |
| Best In The World (Gold) | Win all 5 events in any 8 player City Domination match. |
| Bombardment (Bronze) | Frag a total of 10 racers while airborne. |
| Boost Scrooge (Bronze) | Finish 1st in any 8 player multiplayer race without using boost. |
| Can't Touch This (Bronze) | Finish 1st in 10 Domination Races without crashing or getting fragged. |
| Challenger (Bronze) | Dominate 10 challenge events. |
| Champion (Bronze) | Finish 1st in 20 Domination Races. |
| City Creator (Bronze) | Publish a city with 5 events. |
| City Demolisher (Bronze) | Destroy 10 city targets in one race. |
| City-Wide Destruction (Bronze) | Destroy 100 City Targets. |
| Creative Destruction (Silver) | Destroy 25 targets in one event. |
| Dealing with Rage Issues (Silver) | Destroy all targets and frag 5 racers in one race. |
| Domination Incarnate (Silver) | Dominate all districts in Shatter Bay. |
| Drift Master (Bronze) | Get three domination stars from all Shatter Bay Drift Attacks. |
| Drift to Win (Bronze) | Finish 1st with 2,000 m/yd of total Drifting in any 8 player Domination Race. |
| Fanboy's Revenge (Bronze) | Win an 8 player multiplayer race with the Crinale. |
| Flashing Fury (Bronze) | Frag a total of 200 police cars in Frag Attack events. |
| Frag Capacitor (Bronze) | Frag 10 racers in one race. |
| Frag Master (Bronze) | Get three domination stars from all Shatter Bay Frag Attacks. |
| Fragging Ball (Silver) | Multiplayer. Frag 10 cars in one 8 player Domination Race. |

| Garage Hoarder (Bronze) | Unlock all cars. |
|---|---|
| Getting Creative (Bronze) | Create a track that uses Advanced Editor. |
| GG HF (Bronze) | Complete the Shatter Bay career. |
| High Flyer (Bronze) | Get 10,000 m/yd of total Airtime. |
| Homage (Bronze) | Unlock the Nakamura Racer '70. |
| I Just Want to Sing! (Bronze) | Finish 1st in 20 Domination Races with 0 frags. |
| I Know You! (Bronze) | Frag same racer three times in one multiplayer race. |
| Interceptor (Bronze) | Frag a racer just before the finish line. |
| Learning The Ropes (Bronze) | Complete Domination Race tutorial. |
| Litterbug (Bronze) | Cause $10,000 worth of collateral damage in one race. |
| Mechanic's Nightmare (Bronze) | Get your own car destroyed 100 times. |
| Model Citizen (Silver) | Finish in top three without causing any collateral damage. |
| My City (Bronze) | Publish a city. |
| Not Easy Being Mean (Bronze) | Frag 20 cars in one race. |
| Nothing but Wreck (Bronze) | Frag 200 racers in total. |
| Platinum Trophy (Platinum) | You've earned all Trophies |
| Public Enemy (Bronze) | Cause $100,000 worth of collateral damage in total. |
| Pure Racing Blood (Bronze) | Finish 1st in any 8 player multiplayer race without fragging anyone. |
| Race Dominator (Bronze) | Finish 1st in 50 Domination Races. |
| Race Master (Gold) | Finish 1st in every Shatter Bay Domination Race. |
| Shattered Bay (Silver) | Destroy one of every City Target in the game. |
| Sideslammer (Bronze) | Frag any racer a total of 10 times while drifting. |
| Super Drifter (Bronze) | Get 50,000 m/yd of total Drifting. |
| Tail Chaser (Bronze) | Get 35,000 m/yd of total Chasing. |
| Time Lord (Silver) | Get three domination stars in all Time Attack events. |
| Ultimate Dominator (Bronze) | Reach rank 30. |
| Unbeatable (Bronze) | Finish 1st in 50 multiplayer races. |
| Unbounded Gang Member (Bronze) | Reach rank 10. |
| Winning! (Bronze) | Finish 1st in 150 Domination Races. |
| World Domination (Bronze) | Dominate 50 challenge events. |

## RIDGE RACER UNBOUNDED (XBOX 360)

### ACHIEVEMENT

| UNLOCKABLE | HOW TO UNLOCK |
|---|---|
| Award Collector (15) | Get all Race Awards. |
| Award Hogger (25) | Receive 20 awards in one race. |
| Best In The World (100) | Win all 5 events in any 8 player City Domination match. |
| Bombardment (15) | Frag a total of 10 racers while airborne. |
| Boost Scrooge (15) | Finish 1st in any 8 player multiplayer race without using boost. |
| Can't Touch This (15) | Finish 1st in 10 Domination Races without crashing or getting fragged. |
| Challenger (15) | Dominate 10 challenge events. |

A
B
C
D
E
F
G
H
I
J
K
L
M
N
O
P
Q
R
S
T
U
V
W
X
Y
Z

| Champion (15) | Finish 1st in 20 Domination Races. |
|---|---|
| City Creator (15) | Publish a city with 5 events. |
| City Demolisher (15) | Destroy 10 city targets in one race. |
| City-Wide Destruction (15) | Destroy 100 City Targets. |
| Creative Destruction (25) | Destroy 25 targets in one event. |
| Dealing with Rage Issues (25) | Destroy all targets and frag 5 racers in one race. |
| Domination Incarnate (25) | Dominate all districts in Shatter Bay. |
| Drift Master (15) | Get three domination stars from all Shatter Bay Drift Attacks. |
| Drift to Win (15) | Finish 1st with 2,000 m/yd of total Drifting in any 8 player Domination Race. |
| Fanboy's Revenge (15) | Win an 8 player multiplayer race with the Crinale. |
| Flashing Fury (15) | Frag a total of 200 police cars in Frag Attack events. |
| Frag Capacitor (15) | Frag 10 racers in one race. |
| Frag Master (15) | Get three domination stars from all Shatter Bay Frag Attacks. |
| Fragging Ball (25) | Frag 10 cars in one 8 player Domination Race. |
| Garage Hoarder (15) | Unlock all cars. |
| Getting Creative (15) | Create a track that uses Advanced Editor. |
| GG HF (15) | Complete the Shatter Bay career. |
| High Flyer (15) | Get 10,000 m/yd of total Airtime. |
| Homage (15) | Unlock the Nakamura Racer '70. |
| I Just Want to Sing! (15) | Finish 1st in 20 Domination Races with 0 frags. |
| I Know You! (15) | Frag the same racer three times in one multiplayer race. |
| Interceptor (15) | Frag a racer just before the finish line. |
| Learning The Ropes (15) | Complete Domination Race tutorial. |
| Litterbug (15) | Cause $10,000 worth of collateral damage in one race. |
| Mechanic's Nightmare (15) | Get your own car destroyed 100 times. |
| Model Citizen (25) | Finish in top three without causing any collateral damage. |
| My City (15) | Publish a city. |
| Not Easy Being Mean (15) | Frag 20 cars in one race. |
| Nothing but Wreck (15) | Frag 200 racers in total. |
| Public Enemy (15) | Cause $100,000 worth of collateral damage in total. |
| Pure Racing Blood (15) | Finish 1st in any 8 player multiplayer race without fragging anyone. |
| Race Dominator (15) | Finish 1st in 50 Domination Races. |
| Race Master (100) | Finish 1st in every Shatter Bay Domination Race. |
| Shattered Bay (25) | Destroy one of every City Target in the game. |
| Sideslammer (15) | Frag any racer a total of 10 times while drifting. |
| Super Drifter (15) | Get 50,000 m/yd of total Drifting. |
| Tail Chaser (15) | Get 35,000 m/yd of total Chasing. |
| Time Lord (25) | Get three domination stars in all Time Attack events. |
| Ultimate Dominator (15) | Reach rank 30. |
| Unbeatable (15) | Finish 1st in 50 multiplayer races. |
| Unbounded Gang Member (15) | Reach rank 10. |
| Winning! (15) | Finish 1st in 150 Domination Races. |
| World Domination (15) | Dominate 50 challenge events. |

## RISEN 2: DARK WATERS (PlayStation 3)

### TROPHY

| UNLOCKABLE | HOW TO UNLOCK |
|---|---|
| 100% (Platinum) | Earn all Risen 2 trophies to unlock the platinum trophy |
| All-Rounder (Silver) | Learned each skill once |
| Bane of the Beasts (Silver) | Killed 500 monsters |
| Beginner (Bronze) | Killed 10 monsters |
| Big Game Hunter (Silver) | Killed 2000 monsters |
| Birdbrain (Bronze) | Used parrot 5 times |
| Blademaster (Bronze) | Learned everything about blades |
| Captain (Silver) | 'A New Ship' completed |
| Cash Cow (Silver) | Acquired 100,000 gold |
| Cheese Knife (Bronze) | 'The Cunning Captain' completed |
| Crab Catcher (Bronze) | Killed 10 giant crabs |
| Crack Shot (Bronze) | Hit 10 times in one game in the shooting mini-game |
| Deep Sea Fisherman (Bronze) | Killed 50 sea monsters |
| Digger (Bronze) | Dug up 50 treasures |
| Drunkard (Bronze) | Won drinking duel mini-game 10 times |
| Friend of the Gnomes (Bronze) | 'The Gnome Eater' completed |
| Gunslinger (Bronze) | Learned everything about firearms |
| Harpooner (Bronze) | 'The Titan Weapon' completed |
| Just a little tipple... (Bronze) | Drank first rum |
| Kleptomaniac (Bronze) | Picked 100 locks |
| Knight in Shining Armour (Bronze) | 'Rescue Patty!' completed |
| Legendary Hero (Bronze) | Collected 20 legendary items |
| Liberator (Bronze) | 'Free Hawkins' completed |
| Made of Money (Silver) | Acquired 300,000 gold |
| Mr Industrious (Gold) | Completed 250 quests |
| Necromancer (Bronze) | 'The Split Soul' completed |
| Pet Cemetery (Bronze) | Killed 20 ambient animals |
| Protector (Bronze) | Won duel against Severin |
| Provisions Master (Bronze) | 'Ship's Equipment' completed |
| Rogue (Bronze) | Learned everything about cunning |
| Skinflint (Bronze) | Acquired 1000 gold |
| Storyteller (Bronze) | Collected 10 legendary items |
| The Hand of God (Bronze) | 'The Greedy Captain' completed |
| The Right Hand (Bronze) | 'Chaka Datu's Legacy' completed |
| Tour Guide (Bronze) | At least 5 crew members on the ship |
| Treasure Hunter (Bronze) | Found first treasure in the game |
| Tub Captain (Bronze) | 'Build a Raft' completed |
| Voodoo Pirate (Bronze) | 'The Ancestors' Blessing' completed |
| Voodoo Wizard (Bronze) | Learned everything about voodoo |

## RISEN 2: DARK WATERS (XBOX 360)

### ACHIEVEMENT

| UNLOCKABLE | HOW TO UNLOCK |
|---|---|
| All-Rounder (30) | Learned each skill once |
| Artefact Hunter (20) | 'Steelbeard's Artefact' completed |

NEW!

A
B
C
D
E
F
G
H
I
J
K
L
M
N
O
P
Q
R
S
T
U
V
W
X
Y
Z

**CODES & CHEATS**

| | |
|---|---|
| Bane of the Beasts (30) | Killed 500 monsters |
| Beginner (10) | Killed 10 monsters |
| Big Game Hunter (50) | Killed 2000 monsters |
| Birdbrain (10) | Used parrot 5 times |
| Blademaster (20) | Learned everything about blades |
| Bookworm (20) | 'Following Garcia's Trail' completed |
| Captain (30) | 'A New Ship' completed |
| Cash Cow (30) | Acquired 100,000 gold |
| Cheese Knife (20) | 'The Cunning Captain' completed |
| Crab Catcher (10) | Killed 10 giant crabs |
| Crack Shot (10) | Hit 10 times in one game in the shooting mini-game |
| Deep Sea Fisherman (10) | Killed 50 sea monsters |
| Detective (20) | 'Garcia's Masquerade Uncovered' completed |
| Digger (10) | Dug up 50 treasures |
| Drunkard (10) | Won drinking duel mini-game 10 times |
| Friend of the Gnomes (20) | 'The Gnome Eater' completed |
| Ghost Pirate (20) | 'The Journey to the Underworld' completed |
| Gunslinger (20) | Learned everything about firearms |
| Harpooner (20) | 'The Titan Weapon' completed |
| He Really Exists! (20) | 'Find Steelbeard' completed |
| Just a little tipple... (10) | Drank first rum |
| Kleptomaniac (10) | Picked 100 locks |
| Knight in Shining Armour (10) | 'Rescue Patty!' completed |
| Legendary Hero (20) | Collected 20 legendary items |
| Liberator (10) | 'Free Hawkins' completed |
| Lord of the Tentacle (50) | 'Defeat the Kraken' completed |
| Made of Money (50) | Acquired 300,000 gold |
| Monkey Dance (10) | Used monkey 20 times |
| Mr Industrious (50) | Completed 250 quests |
| Necromancer (20) | 'The Split Soul' completed |
| Pet Cemetery (10) | Killed 20 ambient animals |
| Pirate (20) | 'Become a Pirate' completed |
| Pirate with Muskets (20) | 'Four Muskets against Crow' completed |
| Protector (10) | Won duel against Severin |
| Provisions Master (20) | 'Ship's Equipment' completed |
| Rogue (20) | Learned everything about cunning |
| Seafarer (10) | Travelled by ship 20 times |
| Skinflint (10) | Acquired 1000 gold |
| Storyteller (10) | Collected 10 legendary items |
| The Curse Is Broken! (50) | 'Kill Mara' completed |
| The Hand of God (20) | 'The Greedy Captain' completed |
| The Right Hand (20) | 'Chaka Datu's Legacy' completed |
| Tough Bastard (20) | Learned everything about toughness |
| Tour Guide (10) | At least 5 crew members on the ship |
| Treasure Hunter (10) | Found first treasure in the game |
| Tub Captain (20) | 'Build a Raft' completed |
| Voodoo Pirate (20) | 'The Ancestors' Blessing' completed |
| Voodoo Wizard (20) | Learned everything about voodoo |

### TROPHY

| UNLOCKABLE | HOW TO UNLOCK |
|---|---|
| Alchemical Aspirations (Bronze) | Use alchemy to create an original ninja tool. |
| Alchemical Genius (Silver) | Create the symbol of an Alchemical Genius. |
| Apprentice Ninja (Bronze) | Beat the game on Easy Difficulty. |
| Assassin's Pedigree (Silver) | Perform all the special Chimatsuri Sappo successfully. |
| Bandit Buster (Bronze) | Leave no bandit alive. |
| Chimatsuri Sappo (Bronze) | Perform a Chimatsuri Sappo successfully. |
| Counter Puncher (Bronze) | Perform a Mikiri successfully. |
| Covert Ninja (Bronze) | A true ninja always goes unseen. |
| Cutie Kaede (Bronze) | Kaede is so cute! I wish I could play as her... |
| Familiar Faces (Bronze) | You met some familiar ninja from bygone days. |
| First Class Ninja (Silver) | Beat the game on Hard difficulty. |
| Flying the Night Skies (Bronze) | Use the Fukurou to fly. |
| Full-fledged Ninja (Bronze) | Beat the game on Normal difficulty. |
| Gaga for Greens (Silver) | Collect every type of weed. |
| Gears and Springs (Bronze) | I love wind-up toys!! |
| Gecko Hunter (Silver) | Collect every type of gecko. |
| Grapple Hook King (Bronze) | Throw that grapple hook!! |
| Hard Worker (Bronze) | Complete all the tutorials. |
| Headhunter (Bronze) | Perform a Zankoku successfully. |
| Ichijo's Peace (Bronze) | View Ichijo's ending event. |
| Jack-of-All-Trades (Silver) | Versatility is part of being a ninja. |
| Kazama is Never Satisfied (Bronze) | View Kazama's ending event. |
| Kihan's New Journey (Bronze) | View Kihan's ending event. |
| Killing Spree (Bronze) | Kill 2 enemies with a single Zankoku. |
| King of the Beasts (Silver) | Encounter a bear like none other. |
| Legendary Ninja (Gold) | Beat the game on Deadly difficulty. |
| Mikiri Maestro (Bronze) | Find fortune in peril. |
| Moneymaker (Silver) | A true ninja also knows how to save. |
| Mushroom Village (Silver) | Collect every type of mushroom. |
| Ninja Hunter (Silver) | Every ninja must die. |
| Ninja Initiation (Bronze) | Level up for the first time. |
| Ninja Tool Craftsman (Bronze) | Become a connoisseur of alchemical ninja tools. |
| Obsession (Bronze) | Finish Chapter 3. |
| One Flower (Bronze) | View the "One Flower" ending. |
| Onigami (Silver) | Become a master of using Chimatsuri Sappo. |
| Person of Power (Bronze) | You gave it your all to wipe the enemy out. |
| Recovery Elixir Popper (Bronze) | Coming back from the brink of death is part of being a ninja. |
| Reflections (Bronze) | View the "Reflections" ending. |
| Reunion (Bronze) | Finish Chapter 2. |
| Saint (Silver) | A ninja loves all without bias. |
| Salmon, Salmon, and More Salmon (Bronze) | You really like salmon, don't you? |
| Scattered Petals, Burning Petals (Bronze) | Finish Chapter 1. |
| Shinobido Mastery (Platinum) | Acquire every trophy. |

NEW!

A
B
C
D
E
F
G
H
I
J
K
L
M
N
O
P
Q
R
S
T
U
V
W
X
Y
Z

| Shuriken Sharpshooter (Bronze) | Prove the strength of the shuriken. |
|---|---|
| Sticky Fingers (Bronze) | Did you steal something? |
| The First Step (Bronze) | Complete the first mission successfully. |
| The Only One I Love (Bronze) | Finish Chapter 4. |
| The Silencer (Bronze) | Silence every witness to your deeds. |
| The Zankoku One (Bronze) | Become a master of using Zankoku. |
| Two Flowers (Bronze) | View the "Two Flowers" ending. |
| Uzumbi Artisan (Bronze) | It's their fault for stepping on it. |

## SILENT HILL: DOWNPOUR  (PlayStation 3)

### TROPHY

| UNLOCKABLE | HOW TO UNLOCK |
|---|---|
| Art Appreciation (Bronze) | Completed "The Art Collector" side quest. |
| Ashes, Ashes (Bronze) | Collected 3 pages of the rhyme book. |
| Birdman (Bronze) | Completed the "Bird Cage" side quest. |
| Broken Cycle (Bronze) | Defeated The Bogeyman. |
| Calling All Cars (Bronze) | Completed the "All Points Bulletin" side quest. |
| Capital Punishment (Gold) | Completed the game on the hard game difficulty setting, any ending. |
| Cutting Room Floor (Bronze) | Completed the "Cinéma Vérité" side quest. |
| Dust to Dust (Bronze) | Completed the "Ashes to Ashes" side quest. |
| Ending A (Silver) | Achieved "Forgiveness" ending. |
| Ending B (Silver) | Achieved "Truth & Justice" ending. |
| Ending C (Silver) | Achieved "Full Circle" ending. |
| Ending D (Silver) | Achieved "Execution" ending. |
| Ending E (Silver) | Achieved "Surprise!" ending. |
| Fight or Flight? (Silver) | Escaped from 20 monsters. |
| Found a Friend! (Bronze) | Met DJ Ricks in the Radio Station. |
| Going off the Rails (Bronze) | Escaped from Devil's Pit. |
| Good Behavior (Silver) | Completed the game on any difficulty without killing any monsters. |
| Gun Control (Bronze) | Killed 25 monsters with the Pistol or Shotgun. |
| Hypochondriac (Bronze) | Used 20 First Aid Kits. |
| Lockdown (Silver) | Killed or incapacitated 10 Prisoner Minions. |
| Long Walk, Short Pier (Bronze) | Completed the "Ribbons" side quest. |
| Neighborhood Watch (Bronze) | Completed the "Stolen Goods" side quest. |
| No Turning Back (Bronze) | Reached Overlook Penitentiary. |
| Now You're Cooking... (Bronze) | Survived the Diner Otherworld. |
| Out of the Frying Pan (Bronze) | Rode the Sky Tram to Devil's Pit. |
| Piñata Party (Silver) | Killed or incapacitated 10 Weeping Bats. |
| Puzzle Master (Gold) | Completed the game on the hard puzzle difficulty setting, any ending. |
| Rain Maker (Platinum) | Collected all trophies. |
| Shadow Boxer (Silver) | Killed or incapacitated 10 Dolls. |
| Silence is Golden (Silver) | Killed or incapacitated 10 Screamers. |
| Silent Alarm (Bronze) | Completed "The Bank" side quest. |
| Silent Hill Historic Society (Silver) | Completed Murphy's Journal with all Mysteries. |
| Silent Hill Tour Guide (Gold) | Completed all side quests. |

| | |
|---|---|
| **Spot the Difference (Bronze)** | Completed the "Mirror, Mirror" side quest. |
| **Stay of Execution (Silver)** | Incapacitated 20 monsters without killing them. |
| **Telltale Heart (Bronze)** | Completed the "Dead Man's Hand" side quest. |
| **The Bigger They Are... (Silver)** | Killed or incapacitated 10 Prisoner Juggernauts. |
| **Turn Back Time (Bronze)** | Completed "The Gramophone" side quest. |
| **Useless Trinkets (Bronze)** | Completed the "Digging up the Past" side quest. |
| **What's Your Sign? (Bronze)** | Completed the "Shadow Play" side quest. |
| **Whatever Doesn't Kill You... (Bronze)** | Escaped the Radio Station Otherworld. |
| **Will Work For Food (Bronze)** | Completed the "Homeless" side quest. |

## UNLOCKABLE

| UNLOCKABLE | HOW TO UNLOCK |
|---|---|
| **Unlock Nail Gun and Double Axe** | When you reach a green locker type in 171678 to unlock. |

## SILENT HILL: DOWNPOUR (XBOX 360)

### ACHIEVEMENT

| UNLOCKABLE | HOW TO UNLOCK |
|---|---|
| **Art Appreciation (5)** | Completed "The Art Collector" side quest. |
| **Ashes, Ashes (10)** | Collected 3 pages of the rhyme book. |
| **Birdman (5)** | Completed the "Bird Cage" side quest. |
| **Broken Cycle (10)** | Defeated The Bogeyman. |
| **Calling All Cars (5)** | Completed the "All Points Bulletin" side quest. |
| **Capital Punishment (100)** | Completed the game on the hard game difficulty setting, any ending. |
| **Cutting Room Floor (5)** | Completed the "Cinéma Vérité" side quest. |
| **Dust to Dust (5)** | Completed the "Ashes to Ashes" side quest. |
| **Ending A (50)** | Achieved "Forgiveness" ending. |
| **Ending B (50)** | Achieved "Truth & Justice" ending. |
| **Ending C (50)** | Achieved "Full Circle" ending. |
| **Ending D (50)** | Achieved "Execution" ending. |
| **Ending E (70)** | Achieved "Surprise!" ending. |
| **Fight or Flight? (20)** | Escaped from 20 monsters. |
| **Found a Friend! (10)** | Met DJ Ricks in the Radio Station. |
| **Going off the Rails (10)** | Escaped from Devil's Pit. |
| **Good Behavior (50)** | Completed the game on any difficulty without killing any monsters. |
| **Gun Control (25)** | Killed 25 monsters with the Pistol or Shotgun. |
| **Hypochondriac (10)** | Used 20 First Aid Kits. |
| **Lockdown (20)** | Killed or incapacitated 10 Prisoner Minions. |
| **Long Walk, Short Pier (5)** | Completed the "Ribbons" side quest. |
| **Neighborhood Watch (5)** | Completed the "Stolen Goods" side quest. |
| **No Turning Back (10)** | Reached Overlook Penitentiary. |
| **Now You're Cooking... (10)** | Survived the Diner Otherworld. |
| **Out of the Frying Pan (10)** | Rode the Sky Tram to Devil's Pit. |
| **Piñata Party (20)** | Killed or incapacitated 10 Weeping Bats. |
| **Puzzle Master (100)** | Completed the game on the hard puzzle difficulty setting, any ending. |

| | |
|---|---|
| **Shadow Boxer (20)** | Killed or incapacitated 10 Dolls. |
| **Silence is Golden (20)** | Killed or incapacitated 10 Screamers. |
| **Silent Alarm (5)** | Completed "The Bank" side quest. |
| **Silent Hill Historic Society (50)** | Completed Murphy's Journal with all Mysteries. |
| **Silent Hill Tour Guide (100)** | Completed all side quests. |
| **Spot the Difference (5)** | Completed the "Mirror, Mirror" side quest. |
| **Stay of Execution (25)** | Incapacitated 20 monsters without killing them. |
| **Telltale Heart (5)** | Completed the "Dead Man's Hand" side quest. |
| **The Bigger They Are... (20)** | Killed or incapacitated 10 Prisoner Juggernauts. |
| **Turn Back Time (5)** | Completed "The Gramophone" side quest. |
| **Useless Trinkets (5)** | Completed the "Digging up the Past" side quest. |
| **What's Your Sign? (5)** | Completed the "Shadow Play" side quest. |
| **Whatever Doesn't Kill You... (10)** | Escaped the Radio Station Otherworld. |
| **Will Work For Food (5)** | Completed the "Homeless" side quest. |

## SNIPER ELITE V2 (PlayStation 3)

### TROPHY

| UNLOCKABLE | HOW TO UNLOCK |
|---|---|
| **Apprentice Sniper (Bronze)** | Destroy the V2 Facility and escape to safety |
| **Bedpan Commando (Bronze)** | Resuscitate your partner in coop 10 times |
| **Bomb Happy (Bronze)** | Survive 10 Games of bombing run |
| **Can Do! (Silver)** | Complete all co-op Overwatch Missions |
| **Cooking Off (Bronze)** | Snipe a grenade on an enemy's webbing from 100m |
| **Deadeye (Bronze)** | Snipe an enemy through his eye |
| **Detonator (Silver)** | Career total of 50 shots on explosives |
| **Double Dose (Bronze)** | Snipe 2 people with one shot |
| **Ear Plugs (Bronze)** | Snipe an enemy while your rifle fire is masked by a loud sound |
| **Expert Sniper (Bronze)** | Eliminate Müller |
| **Feared Sniper (Bronze)** | Destroy the V2 rocket |
| **Fish Tank (Bronze)** | Send the tank into the river by blowing up the bridge |
| **Front and Center (Bronze)** | Get a scoped headshot over 150m |
| **Fuel Tank (Bronze)** | Destroy a tank by sniping the fuel supply |
| **Get Off the ground (Bronze)** | Kill everyone in the convoy from ground level, except for Kreidl |
| **Go the Distance (Silver)** | Get a cumulative sniped kill distance of a marathon |
| **Gold Rush (Silver)** | Find and retrieve all the stolen gold bars |
| **Gung Ho (Silver)** | Snipe 100 moving targets |
| **Head Honcho (Silver)** | Get 100 sniped headshots |
| **Hide and Hope (Silver)** | Complete a level without being shot a single time |
| **High and Mighty (Bronze)** | Wipe out the Elite Russian Sniper Team from the rooftops |
| **Iron Lung (Silver)** | Hold your breath for a cumulative time of half an hour |
| **Journeyman Sniper (Bronze)** | Hold off the Russian advance |

| | |
|---|---|
| Jungle Juice (Gold) | Find and snipe all the hidden bottles throughout the game |
| Kilroy was Here (Bronze) | Make it through the tower to the winch room without being spotted |
| Legendary Sniper (Silver) | Prevent Wolff from escaping |
| Make Every Bullet Count (Silver) | Complete a level with 100% accuracy, using only rifles |
| Master Sniper (Bronze) | Uncover Wolff's plan |
| Mousetrap Fuse (Bronze) | Use a trip mine to kill an enemy who is trying to assault your position |
| Novice Sniper (Bronze) | Stop the convoy |
| Pass the Buck (Silver) | Get a sniped ricochet headshot |
| Platinum Trophy (Platinum) | Win all other trophies to take your place as the world's greatest sniper |
| Potato Masher (Silver) | Kill 100 enemies with explosives |
| Pro Sniper (Bronze) | Collect intel from the church and make it out alive |
| Silent but deadly (Bronze) | Covertly kill 25 unaware enemies |
| Skilled Sniper (Bronze) | Stop the execution |
| Sniper Elite (Gold) | Complete all missions on highest difficulty |
| Target Eliminated! (Silver) | As a sniper in Overwatch, snipe 50 enemies tagged by your partner |
| Target Spotted! (Silver) | As a spotter in Overwatch, tag 50 enemies |
| Trainee Sniper (Bronze) | Escape the German assault |
| Veteran Sniper (Bronze) | Discover the location of the V2 launch site |
| World Record (Silver) | Get 506 cumulative sniper kills |

## SNIPER ELITE V2 (XBOX 360)

### ACHIEVEMENT

| UNLOCKABLE | HOW TO UNLOCK |
|---|---|
| Apprentice Sniper (20) | Destroy the V2 Facility and escape to safety |
| Bedpan Commando (20) | Resuscitate your partner in coop 10 times |
| Bomb Happy (20) | Survive 10 Games of bombing run |
| Can Do! (20) | Complete all co-op Overwatch Missions |
| Cooking Off (20) | Snipe a grenade on an enemy's webbing from 100m |
| Deadeye (10) | Snipe an enemy through his eye |
| Detonator (20) | Career total of 50 shots on explosives |
| Double Dose (20) | Snipe 2 people with one shot |
| Ear Plugs (10) | Snipe an enemy while your rifle fire is masked by a loud sound |
| Expert Sniper (20) | Eliminate Müller |
| Feared Sniper (20) | Destroy the V2 rocket |
| Fish Tank (15) | Send the tank into the river by blowing up the bridge |
| Front and Center (10) | Get a scoped headshot over 150m |
| Fuel Tank (10) | Destroy a tank by sniping the fuel supply |
| Get Off the ground (15) | Kill everyone in the convoy from ground level, except for Kreidl |
| Go the Distance (20) | Get a cumulative sniped kill distance of a marathon |
| Gold Rush (50) | Find and retrieve all the stolen gold bars |
| Gung Ho (20) | Snipe 100 moving targets |
| Head Honcho (20) | Get 100 sniped headshots |
| Hide and Hope (50) | Complete a level without being shot a single time |

NEW!

A
B
C
D
E
F
G
H
I
J
K
L
M
N
O
P
Q
R
S
T
U
V
W
X
Y
Z

| | |
|---|---|
| **High and Mighty (15)** | Wipe out the Elite Russian Sniper Team from the rooftops |
| **Iron Lung (20)** | Hold your breath for a cumulative time of half an hour |
| **Journeyman Sniper (20)** | Hold off the Russian advance |
| **Jungle Juice (50)** | Find and snipe all the hidden bottles throughout the game |
| **Kilroy was Here (15)** | Make it through the tower to the winch room without being spotted |
| **Legendary Sniper (65)** | Prevent Wolff from escaping |
| **Make Every Bullet Count (25)** | Complete a level with 100% accuracy, using only rifles |
| **Master Sniper (20)** | Uncover Wolff's plan |
| **Mousetrap Fuse (10)** | Use a trip mine to kill an enemy who is trying to assault your position |
| **Novice Sniper (20)** | Stop the convoy |
| **Pass the Buck (30)** | Get a sniped ricochet headshot |
| **Potato Masher (20)** | Kill 100 enemies with explosives |
| **Pro Sniper (20)** | Collect intel from the church and make it out alive |
| **Silent but deadly (10)** | Covertly kill 25 unaware enemies |
| **Skilled Sniper (20)** | Stop the execution |
| **Sniper Elite (100)** | Complete all missions on highest difficulty |
| **Target Eliminated! (30)** | As a sniper in Overwatch, snipe 50 enemies tagged by your partner |
| **Target Spotted! (30)** | As a spotter in Overwatch, tag 50 enemies |
| **Trainee Sniper (20)** | Escape the German assault |
| **Veteran Sniper (20)** | Discover the location of the V2 launch site |
| **World Record (30)** | Get 506 cumulative sniper kills |

## SOULCALIBUR V  (PlayStation 3)

### TROPHY

| UNLOCKABLE | HOW TO UNLOCK |
|---|---|
| **A Soul Coalesces (Bronze)** | Edited a player license. |
| **Adored by Heaven (Bronze)** | Performed 20 grapple breaks. |
| **Alluring Kaleidoscope (Bronze)** | Landed brave edge 100 times. |
| **Awakened to Violence (Bronze)** | Reached E4 rank in ranked match. |
| **Beginning of Destiny (Bronze)** | Registered 3 rivals. |
| **Black Sword of Death (Bronze)** | K.O. with critical edge 30 times. |
| **Carry Out Your Beliefs (Bronze)** | Won 5 times in one style on PlayStationNetwork. |
| **Colorful Illusion (Bronze)** | Creation: took a thumbnail by manually setting a decoration frame and background. |
| **Conqueror of the Arena (Gold)** | Won 50 times on PlayStationNetwork. |
| **Courageous Warrior (Silver)** | Won 20 times on PlayStationNetwork. |
| **Fancy of a Mad King (Bronze)** | Guard bursted 30 times. |
| **Fetal Soul (Bronze)** | Player level reached 5. |
| **First Step of a Legend (Silver)** | Reached D1 rank in ranked match. |
| **Footprints of Soldiers (Bronze)** | Defeated 100 male characters. |
| **Gale Forces (Bronze)** | K.O. the opponent 25 times with an attack after a quick move. |
| **Give in to Temptation (Bronze)** | Defeated 100 female characters. |
| **Hands of the Abyss (Bronze)** | Won by ring out 50 times. |

| | |
|---|---|
| **Hero Carved in History (Silver)** | Fought 100 times on PlayStationNetwork. |
| **History Repeats (Bronze)** | Battled in SOULCALIBUR V for the first time (excluding training and VS battle). |
| **Home is Faraway (Gold)** | Story: cleared final episode. |
| **Like a Flowing Stream (Bronze)** | Successfully performed a just guard 5 times. |
| **Lively Pub (Bronze)** | Changed the BGM in options. |
| **Mask Another's Memory (Bronze)** | Arcade: cleared a ranking route with a record better than your rival. |
| **Mercenary of War (Bronze)** | Fought 30 times on PlayStationNetwork. |
| **Momentary Pleasure (Bronze)** | Successfully performed an impact 100 times. |
| **Never Ending Effort (Bronze)** | Landed an attack 20,000 times. |
| **No-hitter (Silver)** | Ranked Match: won 10 times with Ezio. |
| **Notes on Rivals (Bronze)** | Play backed another player's replay. |
| **Parrier of Swords (Bronze)** | Perfect won 50 times. |
| **Passionate Artist (Bronze)** | Creation: created a character with full-on coordination (used everything except for height). |
| **Path to Glory (Bronze)** | Quick Battle: defeated 50 warriors. |
| **Perfect Trainee (Bronze)** | Arcade: cleared Asia route. |
| **Proof of a Fighter (Bronze)** | Won consecutive matches on PlayStationNetwork. |
| **Purge of the Holy (Bronze)** | Story: cleared episode 1. |
| **Pursuit of Obsession (Bronze)** | Quick Battle: defeated Harada TEKKEN. |
| **Reason to Fight For (Bronze)** | Reached E1 rank in ranked match. |
| **Resurrection of Order (Silver)** | Story: cleared episode 16. |
| **Road to the Duel (Bronze)** | Quick Battle: defeated 150 warriors. |
| **Shields Come Together (Bronze)** | Story: cleared episode 8. |
| **Sings Own Praise (Bronze)** | Uploaded a replay of your win. |
| **Skills for Duels (Silver)** | Legendary Souls: won with brave edge. |
| **Soul Fulfilled (Silver)** | Player level reached maximum. |
| **Stalwart Barbarian (Bronze)** | Performed a wall hit 50 times. |
| **Strategist of War (Silver)** | Fought 75 times on PlayStationNetwork. |
| **Sudden Temptation (Silver)** | Quick Battle: defeated all warriors. |
| **Synchronize DNA (Bronze)** | Used Ezio in a player match. |
| **Throbbing Soul (Bronze)** | Player level reached 50. |
| **Unwritten History (Platinum)** | Obtained all trophies. |
| **Usurped True Name (Bronze)** | Quick Battle: won against 10 players with titles and used the obtained title on the player license. |
| **War Veteran (Silver)** | Arcade: cleared any route with difficulty set on hard. |
| **Wind of Battle (Bronze)** | Reached over 87,600 m in total movement distance in battle. |

## UNLOCKABLE

| UNLOCKABLE | HOW TO UNLOCK |
|---|---|
| Algol | Defeat him in either Legendary Souls / Quick Battle (As Teramos) / Arcade Mode. Or, reach Player Level 31. |
| Alpha Patroklos | Complete Episode 12 in Story Mode or reach Player Level 15. |
| Edge Master | Complete Episode 16 in Story Mode or reach Player Level 19. |
| Elysium | Beat Story Mode or reach Player Level 27. |

A
B
C
D
E
F
G
H
I
J
K
L
M
N
O
P
Q
R
S
T
U
V
W
X
Y
Z

| | |
|---|---|
| Kilik | Beat Him In Either Legendary Souls or Arcade Mode, or reach Player Level 9. |
| Pyrrha Omega | Complete Episode 19 in Story Mode or reach Player Level 23. |
| Soul Of Devil Jin Fighting Style | Reach Player Level 5 |
| Ancient Citadel: Peacetime | Finish Episode 4 in Story mode or Player level 7 |
| Astral Chaos: Pathway | Player level 25 |
| Conqueror's Coliseum: Underground Fight | Player level 13 |
| Denever Castle: Eye of Chaos | Unlock Omega Pyrrha |
| Denever Castle:Assualt | Finish Episode 18 in Story mode or Player level 18 |
| Last Rites on the Battleground | Finish Episode 18 in Story mode or Player 40 |
| Penitentiary of Destiny | Unlock Kilik |
| Tower of Glory: Most Holy Dichotomy | Unlock Angol |
| Tower of Glory: Spiral of Good and Evil | Unlock Edgemaster |
| Unknown Forest: Dark Night | Finish Episode 7 in Story mode or Player level 21 |
| Utopia of the Blessed | Unlock Elysium |

## SOULCALIBUR V (XBOX 360)

### ACHIEVEMENT

| UNLOCKABLE | HOW TO UNLOCK |
|---|---|
| A Soul Coalesces (5) | Edit a player license. |
| Adored by Heaven (10) | Perform 20 grapple breaks. |
| Alluring Kaleidoscope (10) | Land a brave edge 100 times. |
| Awakened to Violence (10) | Reach E4 rank in ranked match. |
| Beginning of Destiny (5) | Register 3 rivals. |
| Black Sword of Death (10) | K.O. with critical edge 30 times. |
| Carry Out Your Beliefs (10) | Win 5 times in one style on Xbox LIVE. |
| Colorful Illusion (10) | Creation: take a thumbnail by manually setting a decoration frame and background. |
| Conqueror of the Arena (100) | Win 50 times on Xbox LIVE. |
| Courageous Warrior (25) | Win 20 times on Xbox LIVE. |
| Fancy of a Mad King (15) | Guard burst 30 times. |
| Fetal Soul (5) | Player level reaches 5. |
| First Step of a Legend (30) | Reach D1 rank in ranked match. |
| Footprints of Soldiers (10) | Defeat 100 male characters. |
| Gale Forces (20) | K.O. the opponent 25 times with an attack after a quick move. |
| Give in to Temptation (10) | Defeat 100 female characters. |
| Hands of the Abyss (10) | Win by ring out 50 times. |
| Hero Carved in History (50) | Fight 100 times on Xbox LIVE. |
| History Repeats (5) | Battle in SOULCALIBUR V for the first time (excluding training and VS battle). |
| Home is Faraway (80) | Story: clear final episode. |
| Like a Flowing Stream (10) | Successfully perform a just guard 5 times. |
| Lively Pub (5) | Change the BGM in options. |
| Mask Another's Memory (20) | Arcade: clear a leaderboard route with a record better than your rival. |
| Mercenary of War (20) | Fight 30 times on Xbox LIVE. |

| | |
|---|---|
| **Momentary Pleasure (15)** | Successfully perform an impact 100 times. |
| **Never Ending Effort (10)** | Land an attack 20,000 times. |
| **No-hitter (30)** | Ranked Match: win 10 times with Ezio. |
| **Notes on Rivals (5)** | Play back another player's replay. |
| **Parrier of Swords (20)** | Perfect win 50 times. |
| **Passionate Artist (20)** | Creation: create a character with full-on coordination (used everything except for height). |
| **Path to Glory (10)** | Quick Battle: defeat 50 warriors. |
| **Perfect Trainee (20)** | Arcade: clear Asia route. |
| **Proof of a Fighter (15)** | Win consecutive matches on Xbox LIVE. |
| **Purge of the Holy (10)** | Story: clear episode 1. |
| **Pursuit of Obsession (15)** | Quick Battle: defeat Harada TEKKEN. |
| **Reason to Fight For (20)** | Reach E1 rank in ranked match. |
| **Resurrection of Order (30)** | Story: clear episode 16. |
| **Road to the Duel (20)** | Quick Battle: defeat 150 warriors. |
| **Shields Come Together (20)** | Story: clear episode 8. |
| **Sings Own Praise (10)** | Upload a replay of your win. |
| **Skills for Duels (50)** | Legendary Souls: win with brave edge. |
| **Soul Fulfilled (30)** | Player level reaches maximum. |
| **Stalwart Barbarian (10)** | Perform a wall hit 50 times. |
| **Strategist of War (25)** | Fight 75 times on Xbox LIVE. |
| **Sudden Temptation (40)** | Quick Battle: defeat all warriors. |
| **Synchronize DNA (5)** | Use Ezio in a player match. |
| **Throbbing Soul (15)** | Player level reaches 50. |
| **Usurped True Name (20)** | Quick Battle: win against 10 players with titles and use the obtained title on the player license. |
| **War Veteran (40)** | Arcade: clear any route with difficulty set on hard. |
| **Wind of Battle (10)** | Reach over 87,600 m in total movement distance in battle. |

## UNLOCKABLE

| UNLOCKABLE | HOW TO UNLOCK |
|---|---|
| "The Master" | Reach Player Level 25 |
| Algol | Defeat in Arcade or Legendary Souls Mode |
| Alpha Patroklos | Clear Story Mode |
| Arcarde Route: "Extra" | Reach Player Level 17 |
| Astral Chaos: Pathway | Fight against Alpha Patroklos in Quick Battle |
| Devil Jin Style | Reach player level 5 |
| Edge Master | Clear Story Mode |
| Elysium | Clear Story Mode |
| Kilik | Defeat in Arcade or Legendary Souls Mode |
| Pyrrha Omega | Clear Story Mode |
| Stage: Denever Castle: Eye of Chaos | Defeat Pyrrha Omega in Story Mode |
| Stage: Penitentiary of Destiny | Defeat Kilik in Legendary Souls Mode or Arcade Mode |
| Stage: Tower of Glory: Most Holy Dichotomy | Defeat Algol Fear in Legendary Souls Mode or Arcade Mode |
| Stage: Tower of Glory: Spiral of Good & Evil | Defeat Edge Master in Legendary Souls Mode or Arcade Mode |

A
B
C
D
E
F
G
H
I
J
K
L
M
N
O
P
Q
R
S
T
U
V
W
X
Y
Z

| Stage: Utopia of the Blessed | Defeat Elyssia in Story Mode |
|---|---|
| Weapon set 8 (Joke Weapons)" | Reach player Level 53 |

## SPEC OPS: THE LINE (PlayStation 3)

### TROPHY

| UNLOCKABLE | HOW TO UNLOCK |
|---|---|
| A Bridge Too Far (Bronze) | The end of the line. |
| A Farewell To Arms (Bronze) | You are relieved. |
| A Line, Crossed (Bronze) | Choose vengeance. |
| A Line, Held (Bronze) | Choose restraint. |
| A Man of Action (Bronze) | Play it loose. |
| A Man of Patience (Bronze) | Play it smart. |
| Adapt and Overcome (Bronze) | Blow up 10 explosive objects, killing at least one enemy each time. (campaign only) |
| Aim High (Bronze) | Kill 250 enemies with headshots. (campaign only) |
| Airspace Control (Bronze) | Kill 10 enemies while they use zip lines or are rappelling. (campaign only) |
| All You Can Be (Bronze) | Complete any chapter with 60%+ accuracy without dying or reloading a checkpoint. |
| Applied Force (Bronze) | Hit 10 enemies with your melee attack. (campaign only) |
| Army of One (Bronze) | Kill 3 enemies with a single grenade. (campaign only) |
| Battle Management (Bronze) | Kill 50 enemies using only the Attack Command. (campaign only) |
| Blind Luck (Bronze) | Kill 5 enemies using blind fire. (campaign only) |
| Boot (Bronze) | Complete game on "Walk on the Beach" difficulty. |
| Close Combat Carnage (Bronze) | Kill 4 enemies with a shotgun in 10 seconds or less. (campaign only) |
| Damn Close (Bronze) | Kill an Edged Weapon Expert while he is up to 5 meters away. (campaign only) |
| Damned if You Do (Bronze) | Follow your orders. |
| Damned if You Don't (Bronze) | Buck the chain of command. |
| Deer Hunter (Bronze) | Kill an oryx. (campaign only) |
| Desert Storm (Bronze) | Engineer an exit strategy. |
| Friendly Fire (Bronze) | Show mercy. |
| Good Training (Bronze) | Sprint into cover 10 times while under fire. (campaign only) |
| In Your Face (Bronze) | Kick an enemy by vaulting over a cover. (campaign only) |
| Intel Operative (Gold) | Recover all Intel Items. |
| Legion of Merit (Platinum) | Unlock all Trophies. |
| Marksman - Grenade (Bronze) | Kill 50 enemies with grenades. (campaign only) |
| Marksman - Heavy Arms (Bronze) | Kill 150 enemies with any heavy weapon. (campaign only) |
| Marksman - Rifle (Bronze) | Kill 350 enemies with any rifle. (campaign only) |
| Marksman - Shotgun (Bronze) | Kill 75 enemies with any shotgun. (campaign only) |
| Marksman - Small Arms (Bronze) | Kill 100 enemies with any pistol or SMG. (campaign only) |
| Marksman - Sniper (Bronze) | Kill 50 enemies with any sniper rifle. (campaign only) |

| | |
|---|---|
| **MFWIC (Gold)** | Complete game on "FUBAR" difficulty. |
| **Preventive Diplomacy (Bronze)** | Kill an enemy just as they are throwing a grenade. (campaign only) |
| **Recon (Silver)** | Recover 12 Intel Items. |
| **Sierra Hotel (Silver)** | Complete three chapters in a row without being killed or reloading a checkpoint. |
| **Situational Awareness (Bronze)** | Stun an enemy by dumping sand on their head. (campaign only) |
| **Spotter (Bronze)** | Recover one Intel Item. |
| **The Devil's Disciple (Gold)** | Complete game on "Suicide Mission" difficulty. |
| **The Great Escape (Bronze)** | Get out of here! |
| **The Horror (Bronze)** | Face the horrors of war. |
| **The Human Factor (Bronze)** | Kill an enemy by tagging him with a sticky grenade. (campaign only) |
| **The Lost Battalion (Bronze)** | We have contact. |
| **The Road Back (Silver)** | Live and let live. |
| **The Road To Glory (Silver)** | Live and let die. |
| **They Live (Bronze)** | What's lost is found. |
| **Three Kings (Bronze)** | Stand united. |
| **Too Late The Hero (Bronze)** | Carry on, soldier. |
| **Treacherous Ground (Bronze)** | Look out below. |
| **Unfriendly Fire (Bronze)** | Save a bullet. |
| **We Were Soldiers (Silver)** | Complete game on "Combat Op" difficulty. |

## SPEC OPS: THE LINE (XBOX 360)

### *ACHIEVEMENT*

| UNLOCKABLE | HOW TO UNLOCK |
|---|---|
| **A Bridge Too Far (10)** | The end of the line. |
| **A Farewell To Arms (30)** | You are relieved. |
| **A Line, Crossed (10)** | Choose vengeance. |
| **A Line, Held (10)** | Choose restraint. |
| **A Man of Action (10)** | Play it loose. |
| **A Man of Patience (10)** | Playing it smart. |
| **Adapt and Overcome (20)** | Blow up 10 explosive objects, killing at least one enemy each time. (campaign only) |
| **Aim High (20)** | Kill 250 enemies with headshots. (campaign only) |
| **Airspace Control (20)** | Kill 10 enemies while they use zip lines or are rappelling. (campaign only) |
| **All You Can Be (20)** | Complete any chapter with 60%+ accuracy without dying or reloading a checkpoint. |
| **Applied Force (20)** | Hit 10 enemies with your melee attack. (campaign only) |
| **Army of One (20)** | Kill 3 enemies with a single grenade. (campaign only) |
| **Battle Management (20)** | Kill 50 enemies using only the Attack Command. (campaign only) |
| **Blind Luck (20)** | Kill 5 enemies using blind fire. (campaign only) |
| **Boot (15)** | Complete game on "Walk on the Beach" difficulty. |
| **Close Combat Carnage (20)** | Kill 4 enemies with a shotgun in 10 seconds or less. (campaign only) |
| **Damn Close (20)** | Kill an Edged Weapon Expert while he is up to 5 meters away. (campaign only) |

A B C D E F G H I J K L M N O P Q R S T U V W X Y Z

| | |
|---|---|
| **Damned if You Do (10)** | Follow your orders. |
| **Damned if You Don't (10)** | Buck the chain of command. |
| **Deer Hunter (20)** | Kill an oryx. (campaign only) |
| **Desert Storm (10)** | Engineer an exit strategy. |
| **Friendly Fire (10)** | Show mercy. |
| **Good Training (20)** | Sprint into cover 10 times while under fire. (campaign only) |
| **In Your Face (20)** | Kick an enemy by vaulting over a cover. (campaign only) |
| **Intel Operative (50)** | Recover all Intel Items. |
| **Marksman - Grenade (25)** | Kill 50 enemies with grenades. (campaign only) |
| **Marksman - Heavy Arms (25)** | Kill 150 enemies with any heavy weapon. (campaign only) |
| **Marksman - Rifle (25)** | Kill 350 enemies with any rifle. (campaign only) |
| **Marksman - Shotgun (25)** | Kill 75 enemies with any shotgun. (campaign only) |
| **Marksman - Small Arms (25)** | Kill 100 enemies with any pistol or SMG. (campaign only) |
| **Marksman - Sniper (25)** | Kill 50 enemies with any sniper rifle. (campaign only) |
| **MFWIC (50)** | Complete game on "FUBAR" difficulty. |
| **Preventive Diplomacy (20)** | Kill an enemy just as they are throwing a grenade. (campaign only) |
| **Recon (25)** | Recover 12 Intel Items. |
| **Sierra Hotel (50)** | Complete three chapters in a row without being killed or reloading a checkpoint. |
| **Situational Awareness (20)** | Stun an enemy by dumping sand on their head. (campaign only) |
| **Spotter (10)** | Recover one Intel Item. |
| **The Devil's Disciple (30)** | Complete game on "Suicide Mission" difficulty. |
| **The Great Escape (10)** | Get out of here! |
| **The Horror (10)** | Face the horrors of war. |
| **The Human Factor (20)** | Kill an enemy by tagging him with a sticky grenade. (campaign only) |
| **The Lost Battalion (10)** | We have contact. |
| **The Road Back (30)** | Live and let live. |
| **The Road To Glory (30)** | Live and let die. |
| **They Live (10)** | What's lost is found. |
| **Three Kings (10)** | Stand united. |
| **Too Late The Hero (30)** | Carry on, soldier. |
| **Treacherous Ground (10)** | Look out below. |
| **Unfriendly Fire (10)** | Save a bullet. |
| **We Were Soldiers (20)** | Complete game on "Combat Op" difficulty. |

## SSX   (PlayStation 3)

### TROPHY

| UNLOCKABLE | HOW TO UNLOCK |
|---|---|
| **Around The World (Bronze)** | Ride with all three Pilots with each member of Team SSX |
| **Buried Alive (Silver)** | Survive Avalanche Deadly Descent without equipping armor (in World Tour) |
| **Caution Low Visibility (Silver)** | Survive Whiteout Deadly Descent without equipping pulse goggles (in World Tour) |

| | |
|---|---|
| **Do You See What I See (Silver)** | Survive Darkness Deadly Descent without equipping a headlamp or pulse goggles (in World Tour) |
| **Gear Pack (Silver)** | Collect all Gear Badges |
| **Gear Up! (Bronze)** | Make your first Gear Purchase |
| **Grindage (Bronze)** | Grind your first rail (not achievable in Tutorial) |
| **Heart Of Gold (Silver)** | Earn your 1st Gold in a Survive Event (in Explore) |
| **I Ain't Afraid of Snow Ghost (Silver)** | Beat a Friend's Rival Ghost in every Range (in Explore) |
| **I Am A Ghost (Bronze)** | Upload your first personal ghost |
| **I Need A Boost (Bronze)** | Make your first Mod Purchase |
| **I'm Alive! (Bronze)** | Rewind out of Death for the First Time (not achievable in Tutorial) |
| **I'm Flying! (Bronze)** | Deploy your wingsuit for the first time (not achievable in Tutorial) |
| **Ice To See You (Silver)** | Survive Ice Deadly Descent without equipping ice axes (in World Tour) |
| **It's Cold Out Here (Silver)** | Survive Cold Deadly Descent without equipping a solar panel (in World Tour) |
| **Leave No One Behind (Bronze)** | Earn a Bronze in a Survive Event with every member of Team SSX (in Explore) |
| **Pass The Baton (Bronze)** | Earn a Bronze in a Race Event with every member of Team SSX (in Explore) |
| **Pass The Board Wax (Bronze)** | Make your first Board Purchase |
| **Peak-A-Boo (Bronze)** | Participate in a Global Event in every Peak |
| **Playing Favorites (Silver)** | Reach level 10 with any character |
| **Rocky Road (Silver)** | Survive Rock Deadly Descent without equipping armor (in World Tour) |
| **Survival Guide (Silver)** | Collect all Survive Badges |
| **Tag Team (Bronze)** | Earn a Bronze in a Trick Event with every member of Team SSX (in Explore) |
| **Team SSX (Bronze)** | Unlock every member of Team SSX through World Tour (or purchase in Explore or Global Events) |
| **That Was Easy (Bronze)** | Unlock all Game Modes |
| **The Apple Theory (Silver)** | Survive Gravity Deadly Descent without equipping a wingsuit (in World Tour) |
| **The Finish Line (Silver)** | Collect all Race Badges |
| **The Gold Miner (Gold)** | Collect all Explore Badges |
| **The Gold Spender (Gold)** | Collect all Global Events Badges |
| **The Gold Standard (Silver)** | Earn your 1st Gold in a Race Event (in Explore) |
| **The Golden Campaign (Gold)** | Collect all World Tour Badges |
| **The Golden Trick IT (Silver)** | Earn your 1st Gold in a Trick Event (in Explore) |
| **The SSX Standard (Platinum)** | Earn All Trophies |
| **The Tricker (Silver)** | Collect all Tricky Badges |
| **Tree Hugger (Silver)** | Survive Trees Deadly Descent without equipping armor (in World Tour) |
| **Uberlesscious (Silver)** | Earn a Bronze Medal on a Trick Event in Explore without landing any Super Übers |
| **Who Needs Boost (Silver)** | Earn a Bronze Medal on a Race Event in Explore without using any boost |

## SSX (XBOX 360)

### ACHIEVEMENT

| UNLOCKABLE | HOW TO UNLOCK |
|---|---|
| Around The World (10) | Ride with all three Pilots with each member of Team SSX |
| Buried Alive (25) | Survive Avalanche Deadly Descent without equipping armor (in World Tour) |
| Caution Low Visibility (25) | Survive Whiteout Deadly Descent without equipping pulse goggles (in World Tour) |
| Do You See What I See (25) | Survive Darkness Deadly Descent without equipping a headlamp or pulse goggles (in World Tour) |
| Gear Up! (5) | Make your first Gear Purchase |
| Grindage (5) | Grind your first rail (not achievable in Tutorial) |
| Heart Of Gold (10) | Earn your 1st Gold in a Survive Event (in Explore) |
| I Ain't Afraid of Snow Ghost (10) | Beat a Friend's Rival Ghost in every Range (in Explore) |
| I Am A Ghost (5) | Upload your first personal ghost |
| I Need A Boost (5) | Make your first Mod Purchase |
| I'm Alive! (5) | Rewind out of Death for the First Time (not achievable in Tutorial) |
| I'm Flying! (5) | Deploy your wingsuit for the first time (not achievable in Tutorial) |
| Ice To See You (25) | Survive Ice Deadly Descent without equipping ice axes (in World Tour) |
| It's Cold Out Here (25) | Survive Cold Deadly Descent without equipping a solar panel (in World Tour) |
| Leave No One Behind (10) | Earn a Bronze in a Survive Event with every member of Team SSX (in Explore) |
| Pass The Baton (10) | Earn a Bronze in a Race Event with every member of Team SSX (in Explore) |
| Pass The Board Wax (5) | Make your first Board Purchase |
| Peak-A-Boo (10) | Participate in a Global Event in every Peak |
| Playing Favorites (25) | Reach level 10 with any character |
| Rocky Road (25) | Survive Rock Deadly Descent without equipping armor (in World Tour) |
| Tag Team (10) | Earn a Bronze in a Trick Event with every member of Team SSX (in Explore) |
| Team SSX (10) | Unlock every member of Team SSX through World Tour (or purchase in Explore or Global Events) |
| That Was Easy (5) | Unlock all Game Modes |
| The Apple Theory (25) | Survive Gravity Deadly Descent without equipping a wingsuit (in World Tour) |
| The Bronze Badger (10) | Collect all Bronze Tricky Badges |
| The Bronze Campaign (10) | Collect all Bronze World Tour Badges |
| The Bronze Finish (10) | Collect all Bronze Race Badges |
| The Bronze Miner (10) | Collect all Bronze Explore Badges |
| The Bronze Spender (10) | Collect all Bronze Global Events Badges |
| The Bronze Survival Guide (10) | Collect all Bronze Survive Badges |
| The Gold Finish (50) | Collect all Gold Race Badges |
| The Gold Miner (50) | Collect all Gold Explore Badges |
| The Gold Spender (50) | Collect all Gold Global Events Badges |

| | |
|---|---|
| **The Gold Standard (10)** | Earn your 1st Gold in a Race Event (in Explore) |
| **The Golden Campaign (50)** | Collect all Gold World Tour Badges |
| **The Golden Survival Guide (50)** | Collect all Gold Survive Badges |
| **The Golden Trick It (10)** | Earn your 1st Gold in a Trick Event (in Explore) |
| **The Golden Tricker (50)** | Collect all Gold Tricky Badges |
| **The Silver Boarder (25)** | Collect all Silver Tricky Badges |
| **The Silver Campaign (25)** | Collect all Silver World Tour Badges |
| **The Silver Finish (25)** | Collect all Silver Race Badges |
| **The Silver Miner (25)** | Collect all Silver Explore Badges |
| **The Silver Spender (25)** | Collect all Silver Global Events Badges |
| **The Silver Survival Guide (25)** | Collect all Silver Survive Badges |
| **This Gear Is Bronze (10)** | Collect all Bronze Gear Badges |
| **This Gear Is Golden (50)** | Collect all Gold Gear Badges |
| **This Gear Is Silver (25)** | Collect all Silver Gear Badges |
| **Tree Hugger (25)** | Survive Trees Deadly Descent without equipping armor (in World Tour) |
| **Who Needs Boost (20)** | Earn a Bronze Medal on a Race Event in Explore without using any boost |
| **Überlesscious (20)** | Earn a Bronze Medal on a Trick Event in Explore without landing any Super Übers |

## STEEL BATTALION: HEAVY ARMOR (XBOX 360)

### ACHIEVEMENT

| UNLOCKABLE | HOW TO UNLOCK |
|---|---|
| **Acrophiliac (30)** | Complete "King of the Hill" and leave no Uncles to talk about it. |
| **Air Superiority (10)** | Complete the November 2082 campaign. |
| **Angel of War (50)** | Guide Bravo 1 through the entire war without sustaining a single casualty. |
| **Auspicious June (30)** | Guide Bravo 1 through the June 2082 campaign without sustaining a single casualty. |
| **Bad Nephew (10)** | Take down your first enemy combatant. |
| **Bombs Away (15)** | Give the signal to a friendly bomber. |
| **Bridge Blowout (30)** | Complete "Bridge Blowout" and leave no Uncles to talk about it. |
| **Brother in Arms (15)** | Survive the war with an inseparable friend. |
| **By the Dawn's Early Light (10)** | Complete the April 2084 campaign. |
| **Choices, Choices (20)** | Obtain 11 pieces of equipment for your vertical tank. |
| **Corporal Punishment? (15)** | Teach your subcom a valuable lesson. |
| **CQC (10)** | Take out an enemy soldier in close quarters. |
| **Dark Destrier (20)** | Destroy 100 enemy vertical tanks. |
| **Davy Jones (20)** | Send 3 armed freighters to the bottom of the sea. |
| **Evidence Eraser (30)** | Complete "Crash Site" and leave no Uncles to talk about it. |
| **Family Portrait (40)** | After the war, complete Bravo 1's platoon photo by reversing the fate of its fallen members. |
| **Fortunate July (30)** | Guide Bravo 1 through the July 2083 campaign without sustaining a single casualty. |
| **Four by Four (20)** | Create a platoon with three other players and complete a mission without any player casualties. |
| **Gatecrasher (10)** | Complete the January 2084 campaign. |
| **Gift to the Future (15)** | Save the most precious of lives. |

NEW!

A
B
C
D
E
F
G
H
I
J
K
L
M
N
O
P
Q
R
S
T
U
V
W
X
Y
Z

**CODES & CHEATS**

| | |
|---|---|
| Golden January (30) | Guide Bravo 1 through the January 2084 campaign without sustaining a single casualty. |
| Happy November (30) | Guide Bravo 1 through the November 2082 campaign without sustaining a single casualty. |
| Home Veet Home (40) | Obtain 21 pieces of equipment for your vertical tank. |
| Iron Coffin (10) | Prevent being gunned down by closing the armored shutter. |
| Jewel of the Nihil (15) | Find a valuable vacuum tube in the middle of nowhere. |
| Joyful October (30) | Guide Bravo 1 through the October 2083 campaign without sustaining a single casualty. |
| Lemmings to Lemonade (30) | Complete "Lemmings" and leave no Uncles to talk about it. |
| Lights Out, Berlin (30) | Complete "Berlin After Dark" and leave no Uncles to talk about it. |
| Lucky August (30) | Guide Bravo 1 through the August 2082 campaign without sustaining a single casualty. |
| Metal of Honor (20) | Destroy an HVT (heavy vertical tank). |
| Multitasker (10) | Double up as a loader. |
| New Toy (10) | Obtain your first piece of vertical tank equipment. |
| Octa-gone (10) | Knock out 8 enemy soldiers with a single HEAT round. |
| Officer and a Gentleman (15) | Give a generous share of food to your mechanic. |
| One-way Ticket (10) | Complete the October 2083 campaign. |
| Perfect April (30) | Guide Bravo 1 through the April 2084 campaign without sustaining a single casualty. |
| Pirouette (15) | Perform a pivot turn in high-speed mode to take out an enemy behind you. |
| Port Authority (10) | Complete the August 2082 campaign. |
| Reach for the Sky! (20) | Knock an enemy bomber out of the skies. |
| Repatriation (10) | Complete the June 2082 campaign. |
| Sign of Life (15) | Celebrate a victory with your loader. |
| Surgeon General (10) | Successfully purge the cockpit of smoke. |
| The Graduate (10) | Complete basic training. |
| Uncle Slam (20) | Take down 1000 enemy soldiers. |
| Urban Warrior (30) | Complete "Urban Warfare" and leave no Uncles to talk about it. |
| Watch and Learn (10) | Create a platoon with another player and complete a successful mission. |
| Waterside Wipeout (30) | Complete "Waterside Warehouse" and leave no Uncles to talk about it. |
| What a Shot! (20) | Hit an enemy using rear ammo. |
| With You in Spirit (10) | Join another player's platoon and fall in battle while the commanding unit fights on. |
| World Traveler (10) | Complete the July 2083 campaign |

## STREET FIGHTER X TEKKEN (PlayStation 3)

### TROPHY

| UNLOCKABLE | HOW TO UNLOCK |
|---|---|
| A Glimmering Light (Bronze) | Activate your Assist Gems 100 times. |
| A Perfect Victory! (Bronze) | Win a round without getting hit 100 times. |
| A Splendid Conclusion (Bronze) | Finish a round with a Super Art 300 times. |
| A Very Special Gift (Bronze) | Connect with 500 Special Moves. |

| | |
|---|---|
| **After The Dust Has Settled (Bronze)** | Clear Arcade mode on Medium difficulty or higher. |
| **An Unknown Power (Bronze)** | Activate Pandora 500 times. |
| **Any Time, Any Place! (Bronze)** | Use Arcade Fight Request 30 times. |
| **Anything Goes (Bronze)** | Activate Cross Assault 500 times. |
| **Blink Of An Eye (Bronze)** | Connect with 500 EX Special Moves. |
| **Doused In My Color! (Bronze)** | Customize a character's color. |
| **Evangelist Of The "X" (Bronze)** | Have your replay downloaded 20 times in My Channel's Broadcast Mode. |
| **Forge Your Own Path (Bronze)** | Win 10 matches online. |
| **Fruits of Labor (Bronze)** | Go into Training mode 10 times. |
| **Head Of The Dojo (Bronze)** | Create 10 lobbies in Endless Battle. |
| **Here's My Shoutout (Bronze)** | Customize your player comment. |
| **It's Just For Research! (Bronze)** | Access the Store. |
| **Just The Beginning (Bronze)** | Clear one trial in Trial mode. |
| **Learn The Fundamentals (Bronze)** | Win 5 matches online. |
| **Let's Heat Things Up! (Bronze)** | Activate your Boost Gems 100 times. |
| **Love Is Blind (Bronze)** | Use a character in battle over 300 times. |
| **Maelstrom Of Combos (Bronze)** | Connect with 100 Quick Combos. |
| **Maturity Through Discipline (Bronze)** | Clear all of the lessons in the Tutorial. |
| **Mission Specialist (Silver)** | Clear all of the missions in Mission mode. |
| **My Big First Step (Bronze)** | Clear one lesson in the Tutorial. |
| **Observer (Bronze)** | View 50 replays in the Replay Channel. |
| **One Down! (Bronze)** | Win in a Ranked Match. |
| **Power Consumes All (Bronze)** | Finish a round with Pandora 300 times. |
| **Proof Of Your Victory (Gold)** | Get to C rank for the first time in Ranked Match. |
| **Sturm und Drang (Bronze)** | Finish a round with Cross Assault 300 times. |
| **The Battle Never Ends (Bronze)** | Win a match in Endless Battle. |
| **The Cross Revolution (Bronze)** | Finish a round with a Cross Art 300 times. |
| **The Crossroads of Tragedy (Bronze)** | Fight 100 matches online. |
| **The Endless Road (Gold)** | Fight 500 matches online. |
| **The Excellence of Execution (Bronze)** | Clear 300 trials in Trial mode. |
| **The First Mission (Bronze)** | Clear one mission in Mission mode. |
| **The Harsh Road (Silver)** | Fight 300 matches online. |
| **The Root Of Chaos (Silver)** | Defeat all of the bosses in Arcade mode on the hardest difficulty. |
| **The Stones Guide Me (Bronze)** | Customize a Gem Unit. |
| **The Trump Card (Bronze)** | Connect with 500 Super Arts. |
| **The Warrior's Road (Bronze)** | Fight 50 matches online. |
| **This Is How I Roll (Bronze)** | Customize your player Title. |
| **Time For Some Fireworks! (Bronze)** | Connect with 500 Launchers. |
| **Title Idol (Silver)** | Obtain 300 Titles. |
| **To The Victor... (Silver)** | Raise your battle class rank for the first time in Ranked Match. |
| **Trail Of Ruined Dreams (Bronze)** | Defeat 5 rival teams in Arcade mode on Medium difficulty or higher. |
| **Transcend All You Know (Silver)** | Win 50 matches online. |
| **Trial Expert (Bronze)** | Clear ten trials in Trial mode. |
| **Two Minds, Fighting As One (Bronze)** | Connect with 500 Cross Arts. |

A
B
C
D
E
F
G
H
I
J
K
L
M
N
O
P
Q
R
S
T
U
V
W
X
Y
Z

| Your Legend Will Never Die (Gold) | Win 100 matches online. |
| Zenith (Platinum) | Unlock all Trophies. |

## STREET FIGHTER X TEKKEN (XBOX 360)

### ACHIEVEMENT

| UNLOCKABLE | HOW TO UNLOCK |
|---|---|
| A Glimmering Light (10) | Activate your Assist Gems 100 times. |
| A Perfect Victory! (50) | Win a round without getting hit 100 times. |
| A Splendid Conclusion (30) | Finish a round with a Super Art 300 times. |
| A Very Special Gift (10) | Connect with 500 Special Moves. |
| After The Dust Has Settled (10) | Clear Arcade mode on Medium difficulty or higher. |
| An Unknown Power (10) | Activate Pandora 500 times. |
| Any Time, Any Place! (10) | Use Arcade Fight Request 30 times. |
| Anything Goes (10) | Activate Cross Assault 500 times. |
| Blink Of An Eye (10) | Connect with 500 EX Special Moves. |
| Doused In My Color! (10) | Customize a character's color. |
| Evangelist Of The "X" (30) | Have your replay downloaded 20 times in My Channel's Broadcast Mode. |
| Forge Your Own Path (20) | Win 10 matches over Xbox LIVE. |
| Fruits of Labor (10) | Go into Training mode 10 times. |
| Head Of The Dojo (20) | Create 10 lobbies in Endless Battle. |
| Here's My Shoutout (10) | Customize your player comment. |
| It's Just For Research! (10) | Access the Store. |
| Just The Beginning (10) | Clear one trial in Trial mode. |
| Learn The Fundamentals (10) | Win 5 matches over Xbox LIVE. |
| Let's Heat Things Up! (10) | Activate your Boost Gems 100 times. |
| Love Is Blind (30) | Use a character in battle over 300 times. |
| Maelstrom Of Combos (10) | Connect with 100 Quick Combos. |
| Maturity Through Discipline (10) | Clear all of the lessons in the Tutorial. |
| Mission Specialist (30) | Clear all of the missions in Mission mode. |
| My Big First Step (10) | Clear one lesson in the Tutorial. |
| Observer (30) | View 50 replays in the Replay Channel. |
| One Down! (10) | Win in a Ranked Match. |
| Power Consumes All (30) | Finish a round with Pandora 300 times. |
| Proof Of Your Victory (50) | Get to C rank for the first time in Ranked Match. |
| Sturm und Drang (30) | Finish a round with Cross Assault 300 times. |
| The Battle Never Ends (10) | Win a match in Endless Battle. |
| The Cross Revolution (30) | Finish a round with a Cross Art 300 times. |
| The Crossroads of Tragedy (20) | Fight 100 matches over Xbox LIVE. |
| The Endless Road (50) | Fight 500 matches over Xbox LIVE. |
| The Excellence of Execution (30) | Clear 300 trials in Trial mode. |
| The First Mission (10) | Clear one mission in Mission mode. |
| The Harsh Road (30) | Fight 300 matches over Xbox LIVE. |
| The Root Of Chaos (30) | Defeat all of the bosses in Arcade mode on the hardest difficulty. |
| The Stones Guide Me (10) | Customize a Gem Unit. |
| The Trump Card (10) | Connect with 500 Super Arts. |
| The Warrior's Road (10) | Fight 50 matches over Xbox LIVE. |

| | |
|---|---|
| **This Is How I Roll (10)** | Customize your player Title. |
| **Time For Some Fireworks! (10)** | Connect with 500 Launchers. |
| **Title Idol (50)** | Obtain 300 Titles. |
| **To The Victor... (30)** | Raise your battle class rank for the first time in Ranked Match. |
| **Trail Of Ruined Dreams (20)** | Defeat 5 rival teams in Arcade mode on Medium difficulty or higher. |
| **Transcend All You Know (30)** | Win 50 matches over Xbox LIVE. |
| **Trial Expert (20)** | Clear ten trials in Trial mode. |
| **Two Minds, Fighting As One (10)** | Connect with 500 Cross Arts. |
| **Your Legend Will Never Die (50)** | Win 100 matches over Xbox LIVE. |
| **Zenith (0)** | Unlock all Achievements. |

## SUPER MONKEY BALL: BANANA SPLITZ (PlayStation Vita)

### TROPHY

| UNLOCKABLE | HOW TO UNLOCK |
|---|---|
| **100UP (Bronze)** | You got 100 extra monkeys in Monkey Ball! |
| **Advanced Course World 1 Clear (Bronze)** | Cleared Monkey Ball Advanced Course World 1! |
| **Advanced Course World 2 Clear (Bronze)** | Cleared Monkey Ball Advanced Course World 2! |
| **Advanced Course World 3 Clear (Bronze)** | Cleared Monkey Ball Advanced Course World 3! |
| **Advanced Course World 4 Clear (Bronze)** | Cleared Monkey Ball Advanced Course World 4! |
| **Advanced Course World 5 Clear (Silver)** | Cleared Monkey Ball Advanced Course World 5! |
| **Banana Bandit (Bronze)** | You stole 15 bananas in Monkey Rodeo! |
| **Banana Boycott (Bronze)** | You cleared a Monkey Ball stage without collecting any bananas! |
| **Banana Master (Gold)** | Collected all bananas in all Monkey Ball stages! |
| **Banana Sheriff (Bronze)** | You got 30 bananas in Monkey Rodeo! |
| **Banana Splitz (Platinum)** | You earned all other trophies! |
| **Beginner Course World 1 Clear (Bronze)** | Cleared Monkey Ball Beginner Course World 1! |
| **Bingo! (Bronze)** | You got a bingo in Monkey Bingo! |
| **Bingo! Bingo! (Bronze)** | You got two bingos in a single game of Monkey Bingo! |
| **Bumper Boss (Bronze)** | You crashed into a 100 bumpers! |
| **Countdown Competitor (Bronze)** | You cleared 10 Monkey Ball stages in the last 10 seconds! |
| **Edit Anniversary (Bronze)** | You created 100 edit stages! |
| **Editor-in-Chief (Bronze)** | You've saved as many edited stages as possible! |
| **Excellent Point (Bronze)** | You landed a 500-point location in Monkey Target! |
| **Falling Monkey (Bronze)** | You fell off 100 times in Monkey Ball! |
| **Funky Baby Monkey (Bronze)** | You played Monkey Ball with Baby 250 times! |
| **Go Go GonGon (Bronze)** | You played Monkey Ball with GonGon 250 times! |
| **Goal Anniversary (Bronze)** | Cleared 100 Monkey Ball stages! |
| **Good Hustle (Bronze)** | You dropped two balls in one shot in Battle Billiards! |
| **Hard Shaker (Bronze)** | You shook a lot in Edit Mode! |
| **Hide-and-Seek Monkey (Silver)** | Passed through all Monkey Ball warp goals! |

| | | |
|---|---|---|
| **Hustle King (Bronze)** | | You sunk one monkey ball from each team in a match of Battle Billiards! |
| **I Love AiAi (Bronze)** | | You played Monkey Ball with AiAi 250 times! |
| **I My MeeMee (Bronze)** | | You played Monkey Ball with MeeMee 250 times! |
| **Just-in-Time Monkey (Bronze)** | | Reached the goal in a Monkey Ball stage with 0 seconds left! |
| **Magic Touch (Bronze)** | | You got 50 correct in one round of Number Ball! |
| **Monkey Express (Bronze)** | | You ran at top speed for 5 seconds in Monkey Ball! |
| **Monkey Master (Silver)** | | Cleared Monkey Ball Master Course! |
| **Motion Simian (Gold)** | | Clear all Monkey Ball stages in Beginner,Normal and Advanced using motion sensor controls! |
| **Mountain Climber (Bronze)** | | You uploaded a high score! |
| **My Monkey and Me (Bronze)** | | Both characters reached the goal simultaneously in Love Maze! |
| **Never Give Up (Bronze)** | | You retried 10 times in Monkey Ball! |
| **Normal Course World 1 Clear (Bronze)** | | Cleared Monkey Ball Normal Course World 1! |
| **Normal Course World 2 Clear (Bronze)** | | Cleared Monkey Ball Normal Course World 2! |
| **Normal Course World 3 Clear (Silver)** | | Cleared Monkey Ball Normal Course World 3! |
| **Perfect Primate (Bronze)** | | You got to ten in a row in Number Ball without any mistakes! |
| **Photographer (Bronze)** | | You retook pictures in Edit Mode 5 times! |
| **Picture Perfect (Bronze)** | | You got 10 pixies to appear in one shot in Pixie Hunt! |
| **Pixie Hunter (Bronze)** | | You got a chain of 10 or more in Pixie Hunt! |
| **Pro Irregubowler (Bronze)** | | You got a turkey in an abnormal lane in Monkey Bowling! |
| **Pro Monkey Bowler (Bronze)** | | You got a turkey in a regular lane in Monkey Bowling! |
| **Super Monkey Master (Gold)** | | Cleared all Monkey Ball stages with no continues! |
| **Supersonic Monkey (Silver)** | | You cleared 10 stages in 10 seconds or less in Monkey Ball! |
| **Target Master (Bronze)** | | You got 1000 points in a single round of Monkey Target! |
| **Through Thick and Thin (Bronze)** | | You got a synchronization rating of 200% in Love Maze! |
| **Travelogue (Bronze)** | | You saved 10 instances of Monkey Ball replay data! |

## SUPREMACY MMA: UNRESTRICTED  (PlayStation Vita)

### TROPHY

| UNLOCKABLE | HOW TO UNLOCK |
|---|---|
| **Adrenaline Rush (Silver)** | Complete 50 challenges |
| **Apply Yourself (Bronze)** | Complete 10 challenges. |
| **Blood. Sweat. Fear. (Gold)** | Complete 90 challenges. |
| **Contender (Silver)** | Win 5 ranked matches. |
| **Diversity (Bronze)** | Attain Level 5 with all fighters. |
| **Domination (Silver)** | Complete 80 challenges. |
| **Double or Nothing (Gold)** | Win 10 Revenge matches. |
| **Every Fighter has a Story (Gold)** | Complete all fighter stories. |

| | |
|---|---|
| Future Champ (Gold) | Win 10 ranked matches. |
| Getting the Hang of This (Bronze) | Attain Level 5 with any fighter. |
| I Let You Win (Bronze) | Win 1 Final Fight match. |
| In the Zone (Bronze) | Complete 30 challenges |
| Keep'em Coming (Bronze) | Complete 20 challenges. |
| Last Laugh (Silver) | Win 5 Final Fight matches. |
| Legend (Gold) | Complete 100 challenges. |
| Master (Gold) | Attain Level 15 with any fighter. |
| Multitalented (Silver) | Attain Level 10 with all fighters. |
| Rampage (Silver) | Complete 70 challenges. |
| Relentless (Bronze) | Complete 40 challenges. |
| Rematch! (Bronze) | Win 1 Revenge match. |
| Rookie (Bronze) | Win 1 ranked match. |
| Run It Back (Silver) | Win 5 Revenge matches. |
| Sandbagger (Gold) | Win 10 Final Fight matches. |
| Supremacy (Platinum) | Obtain all Trophies. |
| Unstoppable (Silver) | Complete 60 challenges |

## SYNDICATE (PlayStation 3)

### TROPHY

| UNLOCKABLE | HOW TO UNLOCK |
|---|---|
| Platinum (Platinum) | Obtain all trophies. |
| Syndicated (Bronze) | Complete the game on any difficulty (given at the end of Datacore). |
| Business Is War (Gold) | Complete all chapters which track difficulty, on hard difficulty. |
| All Aboard (Bronze) | Complete chapters 2, 3, 4 and 5 on normal or hard difficulty. |
| Campaign: EuroCorp (Bronze) | Complete chapters 7 and 8 on normal or hard difficulty. |
| Campaign: La Ballena (Bronze) | Complete chapters 10 and 11 on normal or hard difficulty. |
| Campaign: Downzone (Bronze) | Complete chapters 12, 13, 14 and 15 on normal or hard difficulty. |
| Welcome to EuroCorp (Bronze) | Complete Wakeup Call. |
| See No Evil (Gold) | Defeat Kris without making him visible using EMP or DART Overlay, on normal or hard difficulty. |
| Revival Meeting (Bronze) | Defeat the final boss without allowing any agent to be revived, on normal or hard difficulty. |
| Missile Command (Bronze) | Breach an entire barrage of five missiles in the Ramon boss fight, on normal or hard difficulty. |
| Top Marks (Bronze) | Achieve a perfect result in all the Tutorial challenges. |
| Golden Handshake (Bronze) | Achieve CEO ranking on any level. |
| Little Black Box (Bronze) | Find all business cards (unlock all the business card infobank entries). |
| Wetware Integrity Policy (Bronze) | Don't kill any EuroCorp civilians with the minigun in chapter 8. |
| Gaggle of Guidance (Bronze) | Use the Swarm's multi-target lock-on firing mode to kill 3 UAV drones with one volley. |

NEW!

A
B
C
D
E
F
G
H
I
J
K
L
M
N
O
P
Q
R
S
T
U
V
W
X
Y
Z

| | |
|---|---|
| **Augmented Reality (Bronze)** | Kill 3 specters in chapter 14 without using EMP effects on them, on normal or hard difficulty. |
| **Cover Lover (Bronze)** | Make it past the conveyor belt without taking any damage from the turret. |
| **Make Them Watch (Gold)** | Kill Agent Crane before you kill his two sidekicks, on normal or hard difficulty. |
| **Ambassador of Peace (Bronze)** | Kill enemy soldiers of two different syndicates fast enough to receive a rampage energy bonus. |
| **Mastermind (Bronze)** | Unlock the Datacore in the minimum number of breaches. |
| **Linked In (Bronze)** | Obtain a health bonus from network connect links from your upgrade choices (single player only). |
| **With Friends Like These (Bronze)** | Kill an enemy from the explosion of a reactive armor unit. |
| **Deny Everything (Bronze)** | Find all propaganda tags (unlock all propaganda tag infobank entries). |
| **Every Bullet Counts (Bronze)** | Defeat Tatsuo without restocking your ammunition from the UAVs, on normal or hard difficulty. |
| **Shocking (Bronze)** | Kill 3 or more enemies from the electricity discharge of a dying electro armor unit. |
| **Greed is Good (Bronze)** | Achieve CEO ranking on all combat levels on hard difficulty. |
| **Shield Breaker (Bronze)** | Successfully sprint tackle 25 riot shield units. |
| **Initiation Complete (Bronze)** | Complete all Co-Op maps on any difficulty. |
| **High Value Asset (Bronze)** | Complete all Co-Op maps on expert difficulty. |
| **Initial Public Offering (Bronze)** | Be a member of a Syndicate consisting of at least 4 people. |
| **Hostile Takeover (Bronze)** | Defeat an enemy agent squad. |
| **Mace Ace (Bronze)** | Save a team member that is stunned by an electron mace. |
| **Super Soldier (Bronze)** | Complete a mission without going down. |
| **Highly Adaptable (Bronze)** | Kill 4 enemies in 4 different ways within 1 minute. |
| **Field Surgeon (Bronze)** | Heal 3 team members for at least 50% of their health within 1 minute. |
| **Oh no you don't! (Bronze)** | Complete 10 Contracts against members of your syndicate. |
| **High Flyer (Bronze)** | Score a 2,000 points combo. |
| **Employee of the Month (Bronze)** | Complete a mission after earning a team savior score. |
| **In The Name of Science (Bronze)** | Finish your first research. |
| **Application Manager (Bronze)** | Do 10,000 points of damage to enemies and heal or block 10,000 points of damage on team members using applications. |
| **Middle Management (Bronze)** | 50% completion (level, research and challenges). |
| **CEO (Gold)** | 100% completion (level, research and challenges). |
| **The Professional (Bronze)** | Kill 50 enemies with all the weapons in the game. |
| **Hurt Locker (Bronze)** | Breach 873 grenades. |

| | |
|---|---|
| **Warpath (Bronze)** | Get the rampage bonus up to 5 sequential kills. |
| **Make It Snappy (Bronze)** | Kill 50 enemies with melee executions. |
| **Nowhere To Hide (Bronze)** | Use a penetration weapon to kill 500 enemies through cover, while in DART Overlay. |
| **Half-Millionaire (Bronze)** | Collect 500,000 energy. |
| **Hacker (Bronze)** | Use breach abilities 300 times. |
| **Rampageous (Bronze)** | Do 250 rampage kills/kill streaks. |

## SYNDICATE (XBOX 360)

### ACHIEVEMENT

| UNLOCKABLE | HOW TO UNLOCK |
|---|---|
| **Syndicated (20)** | Complete the game on any difficulty (given at the end of Datacore). |
| **Business Is War (50)** | Complete all chapters which track difficulty, on hard difficulty. |
| **All Aboard (20)** | Complete chapters 2, 3, 4 and 5 on normal or hard difficulty. |
| **Campaign: EuroCorp (20)** | Complete chapters 7 and 8 on normal or hard difficulty. |
| **Campaign: La Ballena (20)** | Complete chapters 10 and 11 on normal or hard difficulty. |
| **Campaign: Downzone (20)** | Complete chapters 12, 13, 14 and 15 on normal or hard difficulty. |
| **Welcome to EuroCorp (5)** | Complete Wakeup Call. |
| **See No Evil (30)** | Defeat Kris without making him visible using EMP or DART Overlay, on normal or hard difficulty. |
| **Revival Meeting (30)** | Defeat the final boss without allowing any agent to be revived, on normal or hard difficulty. |
| **Missile Command (30)** | Breach an entire barrage of five missiles in the Ramon boss fight, on normal or hard difficulty. |
| **Top Marks (15)** | Achieve a perfect result in all the Tutorial challenges. |
| **Golden Handshake (5)** | Achieve CEO ranking on any level. |
| **Little Black Box (30)** | Find all business cards (unlock all the business card infobank entries). |
| **Wetware Integrity Policy (20)** | Don't kill any EuroCorp civilians with the minigun in chapter 8. |
| **Gaggle of Guidance (5)** | Use the Swarm's multi-target lock-on firing mode to kill 3 UAV drones with one volley. |
| **Augmented Reality (15)** | Kill 3 specters in chapter 14 without using EMP effects on them, on normal or hard difficulty. |
| **Cover Lover (10)** | Make it past the conveyor belt without taking any damage from the turret. |
| **Make Them Watch (30)** | Kill Agent Crane before you kill his two sidekicks, on normal or hard difficulty. |
| **Ambassador of Peace (15)** | Kill enemy soldiers of two different syndicates fast enough to receive a rampage energy bonus. |
| **Mastermind (5)** | Unlock the Datacore in the minimum number of breaches. |
| **Linked In (5)** | Obtain a health bonus from network connect links from your upgrade choices (single player only). |
| **With Friends Like These (15)** | Kill an enemy from the explosion of a reactive armor unit. |
| **Deny Everything (30)** | Find all propaganda tags (unlock all propaganda tag infobank entries). |

| | |
|---|---|
| Every Bullet Counts (30) | Defeat Tatsuo without restocking your ammunition from the UAVs, on normal or hard difficulty. |
| Shocking (10) | Kill 3 or more enemies from the electricity discharge of a dying electro armor unit. |
| Greed is Good (35) | Achieve CEO ranking on all combat levels on hard difficulty. |
| Shield Breaker (10) | Successfully sprint tackle 25 riot shield units. |
| Initiation Complete (10) | Complete all Co-Op maps on any difficulty. |
| High Value Asset (25) | Complete all Co-Op maps on expert difficulty. |
| Initial Public Offering (10) | Be a member of a Syndicate consisting of at least 4 people. |
| Hostile Takeover (10) | Defeat an enemy agent squad. |
| Mace Ace (5) | Save a team member that is stunned by an electron mace. |
| Super Soldier (10) | Complete a mission without going down. |
| Highly Adaptable (10) | Kill 4 enemies in 4 different ways within 1 minute. |
| Field Surgeon (10) | Heal 3 team members for at least 50% of their health within 1 minute. |
| Oh no you don't! (10) | Complete 10 Contracts against members of your syndicate. |
| High Flyer (15) | Score a 2,000 points combo. |
| Employee of the Month (10) | Complete a mission after earning a team savior score. |
| In The Name of Science (5) | Finish your first research. |
| Application Manager (20) | Do 10,000 points of damage to enemies and heal or block 10,000 points of damage on team members using applications. |
| Middle Management (50) | 50% completion (level, research and challenges). |
| CEO (100) | 100% completion (level, research and challenges). |
| The Professional (20) | Kill 50 enemies with all the weapons in the game. |
| Hurt Locker (30) | Breach 873 grenades. |
| Warpath (5) | Get the rampage bonus up to 5 sequential kills. |
| Make It Snappy (10) | Kill 50 enemies with melee executions. |
| Nowhere To Hide (30) | Use a penetration weapon to kill 500 enemies through cover, while in DART Overlay. |
| Half-Millionaire (30) | Collect 500,000 energy. |
| Hacker (30) | Use breach abilities 300 times. |
| Rampageous (15) | Do 250 rampage kills/kill streaks. |

## TALES OF GRACES F (PlayStation 3)

### TROPHY

| UNLOCKABLE | HOW TO UNLOCK |
|---|---|
| A Gentlemanly Triumph (Silver) | Defeated a true Gentleman. Good show! |
| A Pact Fulfilled (Gold) | Completed Chapter 8. |
| A Throne Reclaimed (Bronze) | Completed Chapter 3. |
| Appellatrix (50 titles) (Bronze) | Acquired 50 different titles for Pascal. |
| Bryce in 60 Seconds (Bronze) | Defeated that jerk with the claw in a minute or less. |
| Captain Ephinea (100 titles) (Bronze) | Acquired 100 different titles for Malik. |
| Captain First Class (50 titles) (Bronze) | Acquired 50 different titles for Malik. |
| Childhood's End (Bronze) | Completed Chapter 1. |

| | |
|---|---|
| **Dispaters in 60 Seconds (Bronze)** | Defeated the monsters Richard sicced on you in a minute or less. |
| **Emboldened (50 titles) (Bronze)** | Acquired 50 different titles for Hubert. |
| **Empowered (100 titles) (Bronze)** | Acquired 100 different titles for Hubert. |
| **Entitled (20 titles) (Bronze)** | Acquired 20 different titles for Hubert. |
| **Epithetologist (100 titles) (Bronze)** | Acquired 100 different titles for Pascal. |
| **First Flower (20 Titles) (Bronze)** | Acquired 20 different titles for Sophie. |
| **Flower Power (100 Titles) (Bronze)** | Acquired 100 different titles for Sophie. |
| **Fodra Queen in 60 Seconds (Silver)** | Defeated the Fodra Queen in a minute or less. |
| **Full Flower (50 Titles) (Bronze)** | Acquired 50 different titles for Sophie. |
| **Gagonged! (Silver)** | Defeated the Rockgagong. |
| **Game Clear: Chaos (Bronze)** | Completed the game on the Chaos difficulty setting. |
| **Game Clear: Evil (Bronze)** | Completed the game on the Evil difficulty setting. |
| **Game Clear: Hard (Bronze)** | Completed the game on the Hard difficulty setting. |
| **Game Clear: Moderate (Bronze)** | Completed the game on the Moderate difficulty setting. |
| **Kurt in 60 Seconds (Bronze)** | Ended your fateful battle with Kurt in a minute or less. |
| **Lambda Angelus in 60 Seconds (Gold)** | Defeated Lambda in the final battle in a minute or less. |
| **Lambda in 60 Seconds (Silver)** | Defeated the materialized Lambda in a minute or less. |
| **Lineage & Legacies (Silver)** | Completed Chapter 9. Next up: the Zhonecage! The what? Look to the skits for a hint! |
| **Lionhearted (100 titles) (Bronze)** | Acquired 100 different titles for Cheria. |
| **Mixer Maxed (Silver)** | Maxed out your Eleth Mixer by boosting its eleth capacity to 9999. |
| **One with Oblivion (Silver)** | Defeated Lambda Theos. Impressive! |
| **Openhearted (20 titles) (Bronze)** | Acquired 20 different titles for Cheria. |
| **Polycarpus in 60 Seconds (Silver)** | Defeated the guardian of the ruins in a minute or less. |
| **Queen Slime in 60 Seconds (Bronze)** | Defeated the ruler of all oozes in a minute or less. |
| **Richard in 60 Seconds (Bronze)** | Defeated the friend who betrayed you in a minute or less. |
| **Richard the Radiant (20 Titles) (Bronze)** | Acquired 20 different titles for Richard. |
| **Richard the Redeemed (80 Titles) (Bronze)** | Acquired 80 different titles for Richard. |
| **Richard the Righteous (50 Titles) (Bronze)** | Acquired 50 different titles for Richard. |
| **Sobriquetian (20 titles) (Bronze)** | Acquired 20 different titles for Pascal. |
| **Terma-nated (Silver)** | Defeated Solomus and the Terma Ten. |
| **The Fallen Eden (Bronze)** | Completed Chapter 7. |
| **The Infiltration of Fendel (Bronze)** | Completed Chapter 5. |
| **The Lord of Lhant (Bronze)** | Completed Chapter 2. |
| **The Other Side of the Sky (Bronze)** | Completed Chapter 6. |

| The Sands of Strahta (Bronze) | Completed Chapter 4. |
| Title Fighter (20 Titles) (Bronze) | Acquired 20 different titles for Asbel. |
| Title Holder (50 Titles) (Bronze) | Acquired 50 different titles for Asbel. |
| Title Master (100 Titles) (Bronze) | Acquired 100 different titles for Asbel. |
| Training Captain (20 titles) (Bronze) | Acquired 20 different titles for Malik. |
| True Grace (Platinum) | Acquired all trophies. Amazing! |
| Who Were Those Guys, Again? (Silver) | Defeated Veigue, Reala, and Amber. |
| Wholehearted (50 titles) (Bronze) | Acquired 50 different titles for Cheria. |

## TALES OF THE ABYSS (3DS)

### UNLOCKABLE

| UNLOCKABLE | HOW TO UNLOCK |
|---|---|
| Game Record | Available at the title screen after beating the game |
| Grade Shop | Save a clear file after beating the game, and you will be able to start your new game+ file with the grade shop with your cleared file. |
| Sound Test | Available at the title screen after beating the game |
| Unknown Mode | Beat the game once |
| Very Hard Mode | Beat the game once |
| The Abyss Replica Facility | This is a secret dungeon that can only be unlocked while playing a second playthrough. To gain access, you need to have saved Shiba and completed the Ortion Cavern(East) side quest. Go to Sheridan and talk to the two men in the northwest part of town, then Shiba, and you will at last be taken to the dungeon. |
| Secret Shop(Brillante) | Complete the Collector's Book |

## TEST DRIVE: FERRARI RACING LEGENDS (PlayStation 3)

### TROPHY

| UNLOCKABLE | HOW TO UNLOCK |
|---|---|
| 40th Anniversary (Bronze) | Complete this Silver Era Mission. |
| 430 Redline (Bronze) | Complete this Modern Era Mission. |
| 50th Anniversary (Bronze) | Complete this Modern Era Mission. |
| 512 Pro Championship (Bronze) | Complete this Silver Era Mission. |
| A Good Foundation (Bronze) | Complete this Golden Era Mission. |
| All Time Great (Gold) | Complete all the Eras. |
| Celebration Tour (Bronze) | Complete this Golden Era Mission. |
| Challenge Stradale (Bronze) | Complete this Modern Era Mission. |
| Champ's Day 68 (Bronze) | Complete this Golden Era Mission. |
| Champs Day 84 (Bronze) | Complete this Silver Era Mission. |
| Competizione (Bronze) | Complete this Silver Era Mission. |
| Dino Challenge (Bronze) | Complete this Golden Era Mission. |
| Driver For Hire (Bronze) | Complete this Silver Era Mission. |
| Drivers Training 101 (Bronze) | Complete this Golden Era Mission. |
| F355 Pro-Trofeo (Bronze) | Complete this Modern Era Mission. |
| F50 GT Supercup (Bronze) | Complete this Modern Era Mission. |
| Foot in the door (Bronze) | Complete this Golden Era Mission. |
| Freelance Driver, Chapter 1 (Bronze) | Complete this Modern Era Mission. |
| Freelance Driver, Chapter 2 (Bronze) | Complete this Modern Era Mission. |
| Freelance Driver, Chapter 3 (Bronze) | Complete this Modern Era Mission. |
| FXX Invitationals (Bronze) | Complete this Modern Era Mission. |

| | |
|---|---|
| Game Complete (Platinum) | All Trophies unlocked |
| GTO Pro Challenge (Bronze) | Complete this Silver Era Mission. |
| Mid Life Master (Silver) | Complete the Silver Era. |
| Modern Ferrari World (Bronze) | Complete this Modern Era Mission. |
| Modern Miracle (Silver) | Complete the Modern Era. |
| Old Timer (Silver) | Complete the Golden Era. |
| Prototype (Bronze) | Complete this Modern Era Mission. |
| Prototype Sports Cup (Bronze) | Complete this Modern Era Mission. |
| Quattrovalvole Cup (Bronze) | Complete this Silver Era Mission. |
| Ranked Ace (Gold) | Reach the rank of Ace. |
| Ranked Amateur (Bronze) | Reach the rank of Amateur. |
| Ranked Champ (Gold) | Reach the rank of Champ. |
| Ranked Legend (Gold) | Reach the rank of Legend. |
| Ranked Pro (Silver) | Reach the rank of Pro. |
| Ranked Semi-Pro (Silver) | Reach the rank of Semi-Pro. |
| Scuderia Spec (Bronze) | Complete this Modern Era Mission. |
| Season 74 (Bronze) | Complete this Silver Era Mission. |
| Season 79 (Bronze) | Complete this Silver Era Mission. |
| Season 90 (Bronze) | Complete this Silver Era Mission. |
| Seasonal Changes (Bronze) | Complete this Golden Era Mission. |
| The 250 Challenge (Bronze) | Complete this Golden Era Mission. |
| The Big League (Bronze) | Complete this Golden Era Mission. |
| The Enzo Tribute (Bronze) | Complete this Modern Era Mission. |
| The Nordschleife (Bronze) | Complete this Modern Era Mission. |
| The Rookies (Bronze) | Complete this Golden Era Mission. |

## TEST DRIVE: FERRARI RACING LEGENDS (XBOX 360)

### ACHIEVEMENT

| UNLOCKABLE | HOW TO UNLOCK |
|---|---|
| 40th Anniversary (10) | Complete this Silver Era Mission. |
| 430 Redline (10) | Complete this Modern Era Mission. |
| 50th Anniversary (10) | Complete this Modern Era Mission. |
| 512 Pro Championship (10) | Complete this Silver Era Mission. |
| A Good Foundation (10) | Complete this Golden Era Mission. |
| All Time Great (100) | Complete all the Eras. |
| Celebration Tour (10) | Complete this Golden Era Mission. |
| Challenge Stradale (10) | Complete this Modern Era Mission. |
| Champ's Day 68 (10) | Complete this Golden Era Mission. |
| Champ's Day 84 (10) | Complete this Silver Era Mission. |
| Competizione (10) | Complete this Silver Era Mission. |
| Dino Challenge (10) | Complete this Golden Era Mission. |
| Driver For Hire (10) | Complete this Silver Era Mission. |
| Drivers Training 101 (10) | Complete this Golden Era Mission. |
| F355 Pro-Trofeo (10) | Complete this Modern Era Mission. |
| F50 GT Supercup (10) | Complete this Modern Era Mission. |
| Foot In The Door (10) | Complete this Golden Era Mission. |
| Freelance Driver, Chapter 1 (10) | Complete this Modern Era Mission. |
| Freelance Driver, Chapter 2 (10) | Complete this Modern Era Mission. |
| Freelance Driver, Chapter 3 (10) | Complete this Modern Era Mission. |

NEW!

A
B
C
D
E
F
G
H
I
J
K
L
M
N
O
P
Q
R
S
T
U
V
W
X
Y
Z

| | |
|---|---|
| XX Invitationals (10) | Complete this Modern Era Mission. |
| GTO Pro Challenge (10) | Complete this Silver Era Mission. |
| Mid Life Master (60) | Complete the Silver Era. |
| Modern Ferrari World (10) | Complete this Modern Era Mission. |
| Modern Miracle (60) | Complete the Modern Era. |
| Old Timer (60) | Complete the Golden Era. |
| Prototype (10) | Complete this Modern Era Mission. |
| Prototype Sports Cup (10) | Complete this Modern Era Mission. |
| Quattrovalvole Cup (10) | Complete this Silver Era Mission. |
| Ranked Ace (80) | Reach the rank of Ace. |
| Ranked Amateur (20) | Reach the rank of Amateur. |
| Ranked Champ (70) | Reach the rank of Champ. |
| Ranked Legend (100) | Reach the rank of Legend. |
| Ranked Pro (60) | Reach the rank of Pro. |
| Ranked Semi-Pro (40) | Reach the rank of Semi-Pro |
| Scuderia Spec (10) | Complete this Modern Era Mission. |
| Season 74 (10) | Complete this Silver Era Mission. |
| Season 79 (10) | Complete this Silver Era Mission. |
| Season 90 (10) | Complete this Silver Era Mission. |
| Seasonal Changes (10) | Complete this Golden Era Mission. |
| The 250 Challenge (10) | Complete this Golden Era Mission. |
| The Big League (10) | Complete this Golden Era Mission. |
| The Enzo Tribute (10) | Complete this Modern Era Mission. |
| The Nordschleife (10) | Complete this Modern Era Mission. |
| The Rookies (10) | Complete this Golden Era Mission. |

## THEATRHYTHM FINAL FANTASY (3DS)

### UNLOCKABLE

| UNLOCKABLE | HOW TO UNLOCK |
|---|---|
| Aerith (FFVII) | Gather 8 Pink Crystal Fragments |
| Ashe (FFXII) | Gather 8 Crimson Crystal Fragments |
| Cid (FFIII) | Gather 8 Yellow Crystal Fragments |
| Cosmos (Dissidia) | Gather 8 Rainbow Crystal Fragments |
| Faris (FFV) | Gather 8 Red Crystal Fragments |
| Kain (FFIV) | Gather 8 Navy Blue Crystal Fragments |
| Locke (FFVI) | Gather 8 Blue Crystal Fragments |
| Minwu (FFII) | Gather 8 Silver Crystal Fragments |
| Princess Sarah (FFI) | Gather 8 Gold Crystal Fragments |
| Prish (FFXI) | Gather 8 Purple Crystal Fragments |
| Rydia (FFIV) | Gather 8 Emerald Crystal Fragments |
| Seifer (FFVIII) | Gather 8 Grey Crystal Fragments |
| Sephiroth (FFVII) | Gather 8 Black Crystal Fragments |
| Snow (FFXIII) | Gather 8 White Crystal Fragments |
| Vivi (FFIX) | Gather 8 Orange Crystal Fragments |
| Yuuna (FFX) | Gather 8 Sapphire Crystal Fragments |

### PASSWORD

| UNLOCKABLE | HOW TO UNLOCK |
|---|---|
| 01 Warrior of Light | Warrior of Light |
| 01 Warrior of Light | Class Change |

| | |
|---|---|
| 02 Firion | Wild Rose |
| 04 Cecil | Dark Knight |
| 06 Terra | Magitek Armor |
| 06 Terra | Flowered tights |
| 07 Cloud | Lifestream |
| 08 Squall | Lionheart |
| 09 Zidane | Zidane Tribal |
| 09 Zidane | Tantalus |
| 09 Zidane | Beloved Dagger |
| 10 Tidus | Jecht Shot |
| 13 Lightning | Serah's sister |
| 14 Princess Sarah | Cornelia |
| 15 Minwu | White Mage |
| 16 Cid | The Enterprise |
| 18 Faris | Princess of Tycoon |
| 20 Aerith | Cetra |
| 21 Seifer | Disciplinary Committee |
| 22 Vivi | Master Vivi |
| 22 Vivi | Black Mage |
| 23 Yuna | Y.R.P. |
| 23 Yuna | Eternal Calm |
| 24 Prishe | Feed me |
| 25 Ashe | Amalia? |
| 26 Snow | Do-rag |
| 26 Snow | Sis! |
| 27 Kain | Cecil's best friend |
| 27 Kain | Son of Richard |
| 28 Sephiroth | Masamune |
| 28 Sephiroth | One-winged angel |
| 28 Sephiroth | Black Materia |
| 29 Cosmos | Goddess of Harmony |
| 30 Chocobo | Gysahl Greens |
| 30 Chocobo | Fat Chocobo |
| 31 Moogle | Red pompom |
| 31 Moogle | Bat wings |
| 32 Shiva | Ice Queen |
| 32 Shiva | Diamond Dust |
| 32 Shiva | Heavenly Strike |
| 33 Ramuh | Judgment Bolt |
| 34 Ifrit | Hellfire |
| 35 Odin | Zantetsuken |
| 36 Bahamut | Mega Flare |
| 36 Bahamut | Rat tail |
| 37 Goblin | Goblin Punch |
| 40 Malboro | Bad Breath |
| 42 Black Knight | Yoichi Bow |
| 42 Black Knight | Sun Blade |
| 44 Hein | Barrier Shift |

A
B
C
D
E
F
G
H
I
J
K
L
M
N
O
P
Q
R
S
T
U
V
W
X
Y
Z

| 45 Ahriman | Good at magic |
|---|---|
| 46 Xande | Libra! |
| 50 Barbariccia | Maelstrom |
| 53 Tonberry | Everyone's Grudge |
| 53 Tonberry | Knife and lantern |
| 54 Gilgamesh | Big Bridge |
| 54 Gilgamesh | Bartz's rival |
| 55 Enikdu | White Wind |
| 56 Omega | Wave Cannon |
| 57 Shinryu | Ragnarok |
| 57 Shinryu | Tidal Wave |
| 58 Cactuar | 1000 Needles |
| 58 Cactuar | 10000 Needles |
| 58 Cactuar | Gigantuar |
| 59 Hill Gigas | Magnitude 8 |
| 60 Ultros | Mr. Typhon |
| 62 Kefka | I just can't believe it! |
| 62 Kefka | Heartless Angel |
| 63 Ultima Weapon | Shadow Flare |
| 64 Jenova Synthesis | Countdown to Ultima |
| 64 Jenova Synthesis | Mother |
| 65 Safer Sephiroth | Pale Horse |
| 65 Safer Sephiroth | Super Nova |
| 66 Esthar Soldier | Shotgun |
| 66 Esthar Soldier | Terminator |
| 67 Gesper | Degenerator |
| 68 Pupu | Elixir please! |
| 68 Pupu | UFO? |
| 69 Black Waltz No. 3 | Triple time |
| 71 Anima | Pain |
| 74 Shadow Lord | Implosion |
| 74 Shadow Lord | Xarcabard |
| 74 Shadow Lord | The Crystal War |
| 76 Mandragoras | Sochen Cave Palace |
| 77 Judge | Gabranth |
| 77 Judge | Judge Magister |
| 78 Psicom Enforcer | The Hanging Edge |
| 79 Manasvin Warmech | Targeting |
| 79 Manasvin Warmech | Crystal Rain |
| 80 Adamantoise | Trapezohedron |
| 80 Adamantoise | Earth Shaker |
| 80 Adamantoise | Platinum Ingot |
| 81 Chaos | God of Discord |
| 81 Chaos | Demonsdance |

### UNLOCKABLE

| UNLOCKABLE | HOW TO UNLOCK |
|---|---|
| Hard Mode Series Setlists | clear that Series' three songs in the Challenge section on hard difficulty |

## TIGER WOODS PGA TOUR 13 (PlayStation 3)

### TROPHY

| UNLOCKABLE | HOW TO UNLOCK |
|---|---|
| Amateur Years (Bronze) | Complete the Amateur Years in Tiger Legacy Challenge |
| Can you give me a Boost? (Bronze) | Play an 18 hole round with Boost Pins equipped |
| Check out my Custom Settings (Bronze) | Complete an 18 hole round using a Custom Difficulty |
| Dig Deep (Silver) | Land within 1 yard of the flagstick from a bunker |
| Don't quit your day job (Bronze) | Win the Masters as an amateur |
| Early Years (Bronze) | Complete the Early Years in Tiger Legacy Challenge |
| From the Ladies Tees (Bronze) | Complete an 18 hole round using the Red Tees |
| Going Green with a Hybrid (Bronze) | Land on the green from over 175 yards away using a Hybrid |
| He's going the distance (Bronze) | Hit a drive over 400 yards |
| I Finally Belong! (Bronze) | Create or Join a Country Club in Game |
| I Need a Commitment (Bronze) | Earn a Four Day loyalty Bonus |
| I Own this Place (Silver) | Defend your title in any Major |
| Internal Conflict (Silver) | Compete with a teammate in a head-to-head match launched from the Clubhouse lobby |
| It's a Start (Bronze) | Master 1 course |
| It's all in the Hips (Bronze) | Sink a 40ft putt |
| Junior Years (Bronze) | Complete the Junior Years in Tiger Legacy Challenge |
| King of the Hill (Bronze) | Become #1 in the EA SPORTS Golf Rankings |
| Like a Boss (Gold) | Master 16 Courses |
| Like a Homing Pigeon (Bronze) | From the Fairway, land within 1 yard of the flagstick from 150 yards out |
| Like a Metronome (Bronze) | Complete 10 perfect Tempo Swings with TOUR Pro Difficulty or better |
| Live from your couch (Bronze) | Play in a Live Tournament |
| Members Only (Bronze) | Play in a Country Club Tournament |
| Never leave home without it (Bronze) | Earn PGA TOUR card |
| No Handouts Please (Bronze) | Actually get a hole in 1 in the 1982 First Hole in One event in Tiger Legacy Challenge |
| Now we're talking (Bronze) | Master 8 courses |
| One Small Step for Mankind (Bronze) | Win the Green Jacket in Career Mode |
| Play Date (Bronze) | Play a Four Player online match with all players using toddlers |
| Present Day (Silver) | Complete the Present Day in Tiger Legacy Challenge |
| Pro Gamer (Platinum) | Congratulations for unlocking all trophies in Tiger Woods PGA TOUR® 13! |
| Pro Years (Bronze) | Complete the Pro Years in Tiger Legacy Challenge |
| Putt from the rough (Bronze) | Make a putt from the rough |
| Rookie Years (Bronze) | Complete the Rookie Years in Tiger Legacy Challenge |

A
B
C
D
E
F
G
H
I
J
K
L
M
N
O
P
Q
R
S
T
U
V
W
X
Y
Z

| Shouting at Amen Corner (Silver) | Complete Amen Corner (Augusta 11,12,13) with a birdie or better on each in a single round |
| --- | --- |
| Small Tiger, Big Bite (Bronze) | Complete an 18 hole online head-to-head match with toddler Tiger |
| So Much Easier than Putting (Silver) | Make a hole in one |
| That was GIRrrreat! (Bronze) | Complete an 18 hole round with a 100 percent GIR. GIR = Green in Regulation |
| The Future (Bronze) | Complete the Future in Tiger Legacy Challenge |
| Tiger Slam (Bronze) | Complete the Tiger Slam in Tiger Legacy Challenge |
| Tigers have FIR (Bronze) | Complete an 18 hole round with a 100 percent FIR. FIR = Fairway in Regulation |
| Toddler Years (Bronze) | Complete Toddler Years in Tiger Legacy Challenge |
| Top 10 Hits (Bronze) | Break the top 10 in EA SPORTS Golf Rankings |
| Top 50 Countdown (Bronze) | Break the top 50 in EA SPORTS Golf Rankings |
| Unstoppable! (Bronze) | Win the Green Jacket for a Record 7 times in Career Mode |
| When do we get paid? (Bronze) | Compete in an amateur championship |

## TIGER WOODS PGA TOUR 13   (XBOX 360)

### ACHIEVEMENT

| UNLOCKABLE | HOW TO UNLOCK |
| --- | --- |
| Amateur Years (15) | Complete the Amateur Years in Tiger Legacy Challenge |
| Can you give me a Boost? (15) | Play an 18 hole round with Boost Pins equipped |
| Check out my Custom Settings (15) | Complete an 18 hole round using a Custom Difficulty |
| Child's Play (15) | Complete an 18 hole round with toddler Ricky |
| Dig Deep (15) | Land within 1 yard of the flagstick from a bunker |
| Don't quit your day job (15) | Win the Masters as an amateur |
| Early Years (15) | Complete the Early Years in Tiger Legacy Challenge |
| From the Ladies Tees (15) | Complete an 18 hole round using the Red Tees |
| Going Green with a Hybrid (30) | Land on the green from over 175 yards away using a Hybrid |
| He's going the distance (30) | Hit a drive over 400 yards |
| I Finally Belong! (15) | Create or Join a Country Club in Game |
| I Need a Commitment (15) | Earn a Four Day loyalty Bonus |
| I Own this Place (25) | Defend your title in any Major |
| Internal Conflict (15) | Compete with a teammate in a head-to-head match launched from the Clubhouse lobby |
| It's a Start (15) | Master 1 Course |
| It's all in the Hips (15) | Sink a 40ft putt |
| Junior Years (15) | Complete the Junior Years in Tiger Legacy Challenge |
| King of the Hill (50) | Become #1 in the EA SPORTS Golf Rankings |
| Like a Boss (60) | Master 16 Courses |

| | |
|---|---|
| Like a Homing Pigeon (15) | From the Fairway, land within 1 yard of the flagstick from 150 yards out |
| Like a Metronome (15) | Complete 10 perfect Tempo Swings with TOUR Pro Difficulty or better |
| Live from your couch (25) | Play in a Live Tournament |
| Members Only (15) | Play in a Country Club Tournament |
| Never leave home without it (15) | Earn PGA TOUR card |
| No Handouts Please (10) | Actually get a hole in 1 in the 1982 First Hole in One event in Tiger Legacy Challenge |
| Now we're talking (30) | Master 8 Courses |
| One Small Step for Mankind (35) | Win the Green Jacket in Career Mode |
| Play Date (15) | Play a Four Player online match with all players using toddlers |
| Present Day (30) | Complete the Present Day in Tiger Legacy Challenge |
| Pro Years (20) | Complete the Pro Years in Tiger Legacy Challenge |
| Putt from the rough (15) | Make a putt from the rough |
| Rookie Years (15) | Complete the Rookie Years in Tiger Legacy Challenge |
| Shouting at Amen Corner (10) | Complete Amen Corner (Augusta 11,12,13) with a birdie or better on each in a single round. |
| Small Tiger, Big Bite (15) | Complete an 18 hole online head-to-head match with toddler Tiger |
| So Much Easier than Putting (30) | Make a hole in one |
| Swing and a miss (10) | Whiff the ball |
| That was Easy (30) | Beat the course record of 63 at the Masters (In Career Mode) |
| That was GIRrrreat! (15) | Complete an 18 hole round with a 100 percent GIR. GIR = Green in Regulation |
| The Future (30) | Complete the Future in Tiger Legacy Challenge |
| Tiger Slam (20) | Complete the Tiger Slam in Tiger Legacy Challenge |
| Tigers have FIR (30) | Complete an 18 hole round with a 100 percent FIR. FIR = Fairway in Regulation |
| Toddler Years (15) | Complete Toddler Years in Tiger Legacy Challenge |
| Top 10 Hits (30) | Break the top 10 in EA SPORTS Golf Rankings |
| Top 50 Countdown (15) | Break the top 50 in EA SPORTS Golf Rankings |
| Unstoppable! (75) | Win the Green Jacket for a Record 7 times in Career Mode |
| When do we get paid? (15) | Compete in an amateur championship |

## TOM CLANCY'S GHOST RECON: FUTURE SOLDIER (PlayStation 3)

### TROPHY

| UNLOCKABLE | HOW TO UNLOCK |
|---|---|
| ...I Can Do Better (Bronze) | Complete 20 Daily Friend Challenges in Quick Matches |
| ...Must Come Down (Bronze) | Destroy the plane with the weapons system on board while it is in flight |
| Actionable Intel (Bronze) | Complete 10 Coordinated Kills in Quick Matches |
| Advanced Warfighter (Silver) | Complete the campaign in Veteran |

**CODES & CHEATS**

| | |
|---|---|
| **Anything You Can Do... (Bronze)** | Complete a Daily Friend Challenge through all return fire volleys in Quick Matches |
| **Armorer (Silver)** | Spend 25 attachment credits with each role |
| **Backup (Bronze)** | Assist a teammate 5 times who is taking fire, suppressed, or has called for help in Quick Matches |
| **Battle Buddies (Bronze)** | Complete the campaign in Co-op |
| **Blood Brother (Bronze)** | Rescue the Georgian Spec Ops |
| **Breathing Room (Bronze)** artillery | Destroy the second piece of enemy |
| **Call, Answered (Silver)** | Earn all Tour of Duty Trophies |
| **Conflict Domination (Bronze)** | Be part of a squad match where your team wins by a margin of 5 points or more |
| **Coordinated Assault (Bronze)** | Use the Coordination System to reach an objective in a Quick Match |
| **Counter-Intelligence (Bronze)** | Interrupt enemy data hacks on teammates 5 times by killing or stunning them in Quick Matches |
| **Cross Trained (Bronze)** | Reach Level 10 on one Rifleman, one Scout, and one Engineer character |
| **Decoy Domination (Bronze)** | Be part of 5 squad matches where your team completes the true objective first |
| **Doing Work (Bronze)** | Kill 1000 enemies while in Guerrilla mode |
| **EOD (Bronze)** | Destroy the Russian weapons transfer station |
| **Field Tested (Bronze)** | Play 5 MP matches of each game type in Quick Matches |
| **Fuel for the Fire (Bronze)** | Secure the drilling ships and complete the mission |
| **Future Soldier (Gold)** | Complete the campaign in Elite |
| **Good Effect on Target (Bronze)** | Kill more than 5 enemies with an airstrike |
| **Good Enough for Government Work (Bronze)** | Have a Ghost Skill of 80% for all missions |
| **High Speed, Low Drag (Gold)** | Reach Level 50 on any character |
| **High-Value Target (Bronze)** | Kill 5 High-Value Targets in Quick Matches |
| **Just a Box (Bronze)** | While in Guerrilla mode, complete an infiltration sequence without being detected |
| **Just Another Day at the Office (Silver)** | Complete the campaign |
| **Kitted Out (Bronze)** | Spend attachment credits to customize 1 weapon at all external attachment points |
| **Loose Thread (Bronze)** | Secure Gabriel Paez |
| **Master Tactician (Silver)** | Complete 100% of the tactical challenges |
| **Mod Pro (Silver)** | Spend 50 Attachment points to add attachments to various guns |
| **Mod Rookie (Bronze)** | Spend an attachment credit to add an attachment to any gun |
| **No Loose Ends (Bronze)** | Eliminate the leader of the Raven's Rock faction |
| **Platinum Trophy (Platinum)** | Platinum Trophy |
| **Precious Cargo (Bronze)** | Secure the VIP and transfer him to the exfiltration team |
| **Qualified (Bronze)** | Have a Ghost Skill of 90% for a single mission |
| **Quality Beats Quantity (Silver)** | Defeat all 50 enemy waves on Guerilla mode (any difficulty, any map) |

| Recon Specialist (Bronze) | Complete 5 Intel Assists in Quick Matches |
|---|---|
| Relieved of Command (Bronze) | Kill the general commanding the Moscow defenses |
| Saboteur Domination (Bronze) | Be part of a squad match where your team takes the objective into the enemy base in under 2 minutes |
| Siege Domination (Bronze) | Be part of a squad match where your team captures the objective in under 2 minutes |
| Source Control (Bronze) | Secure the VIPs and transfer them to the exfiltration team |
| Special Election (Bronze) | Rescue Russian President Volodin from the prison camp |
| Tactician (Bronze) | Complete 50% of the tactical challenges |
| Total Domination (Bronze) | Earn all of the Domination Trophies |
| Tour of Duty: Arctic (Bronze) | Win 3 Quick Matches of any game type on each: Buried, Milled, and Alpha maps |
| Tour of Duty: Nigeria (Bronze) | Win 3 Quick Matches of any game type on each: Depleted, Abandoned, Blinded, and Collapsed maps |
| Tour of Duty: North Sea (Bronze) | Win 3 Quick Matches of any game type on each: Harbored, Hijacked, and Rigged maps |
| True Ghost (Bronze) | Get 10 consecutive kills in one Quick Match without dying |
| Tuned Up (Bronze) | Spend attachment credits to customize all the internal parts of one weapon |
| What Goes Up... (Bronze) | Shoot down the cargo plane |

## TOM CLANCY'S GHOST RECON: FUTURE SOLDIER (XBOX 360)

### ACHIEVEMENT

| UNLOCKABLE | HOW TO UNLOCK |
|---|---|
| ...I Can Do Better (5) | Complete 20 Daily Friend Challenges |
| ...Must Come Down. (20) | Destroy the plane with the weapons system on board while it is in flight |
| Actionable Intel (10) | Complete 10 Coordinated Kills |
| Advanced Warfighter (40) | Complete the campaign in Veteran |
| Anything You Can Do... (20) | Complete a Daily Friend Challenge through all return fire volleys |
| Armorer (35) | Spend 25 Attachment Credits with each role |
| Backup (5) | Complete 5 Savior Kills in Quick Matches |
| Battle Buddies (30) | Complete the campaign in Co-op |
| Blood Brother (20) | Rescue the Georgian Spec Ops |
| Breathing Room (20) | Destroy the second piece of enemy artillery |
| Call, Answered (35) | Complete all Tours of Duty |
| Conflict Domination (10) | Be part of a squad match where your team wins by a margin of 500 points or more |
| Coordinated Assault (5) | Use the Coordination System to reach an objective |
| Counter-Intelligence (10) | Interrupt an enemy's attempt to data hack a teammate 5 times, by killing or stunning the enemy |
| Cross-trained (10) | Reach Level 10 on one Rifleman, one Scout, and one Engineer character |

NEW!

A
B
C
D
E
F
G
H
I
J
K
L
M
N
O
P
Q
R
S
T
U
V
W
X
Y
Z

| | |
|---|---|
| Decoy Domination (10) | In squad matches your team completes the key objective first, five times. |
| Doing Work (10) | Kill 1000 enemies while in Guerrilla mode |
| EOD (20) | Destroy the Russian weapons transfer station |
| Field Tested (5) | Play 5 MP matches of each game type |
| Fuel for the Fire (20) | Secure the drilling ships and complete the mission |
| Future Soldier (50) | Complete the campaign in Elite |
| Good Effect on Target (10) | In Guerrilla mode, kill more than 5 enemies with an airstrike |
| Good Enough for Government Work (10) | Achieve a Ghost skill rating above 80% for all missions |
| High Speed, Low Drag (50) | Reach Level 50 on any character |
| High-Value Target (5) | Kill a member of the dev team, or kill someone who has |
| Just a Box (10) | While in Guerrilla mode, complete an infiltration sequence without being detected |
| Just Another Day at the Office (30) | Complete the campaign for the first time |
| Kitted Out (25) | Customize 1 weapon with an external attachment at every attachment point |
| Loose Thread (20) | Secure Gabriel Paez |
| Master Tactician (25) | Complete 100% of the Tactical challenges |
| Mod Pro (40) | Spend 50 Attachment Credits to add attachments to various guns |
| Mod Rookie (5) | Add an attachment to any gun |
| No Loose Ends (20) | Eliminate the leader of the Raven's Rock faction |
| Precious Cargo (20) | Secure the VIP and transfer him to the exfiltration team |
| Qualified (25) | Achieve a Ghost skill rating of above 90% on one mission |
| Quality Beats Quantity (30) | Defeat all 50 enemy waves on Guerrilla mode (any difficulty, any map) |
| Recon Specialist (25) | Complete 5 Intel Assists in Quick Matches |
| Relieved of Command (20) | Kill the general commanding the Moscow defenses |
| Saboteur Domination (10) | Be part of a squad match where your team takes the bomb into the enemy base in under 2 minutes |
| Siege Domination (10) | Be part of a squad match where your team captures the objective in under 2 minutes |
| Source Control (20) | Secure the VIP and transfer them to the exfiltration team |
| Special Election (20) | Rescue Russian President Volodin from the prison camp |
| Tactician (10) | Complete 50% of the Tactical challenges |
| Total Domination (40) | Complete all of the Domination achievements |

| | |
|---|---|
| Tour of Duty: Arctic (25) | Win 3 MP matches of any game type on each: Underground, Mill, and Alpha maps |
| Tour of Duty: Nigeria (25) | Win 3 MP of any game type on each: Pipeline, Market, Sand Storm, and Overpass maps |
| Tour of Duty: North Sea (25) | Win 3 MP matches of any game type on each: Harbor, Cargo, and Rig maps |
| True Ghost (10) | Get 10 consecutive kills in one Quick Match without dying |
| Tuned Up (25) | Customize all the internal parts of one weapon |
| What Goes Up... (20) | Shoot down the cargo plane |

## TOUCH MY KATAMARI    (PlayStation Vita)

### TROPHY

| UNLOCKABLE | HOW TO UNLOCK |
|---|---|
| Congratulations! (Bronze) | Completed all Requests. |
| Connoisseur (Silver) | Collected all objects within the Curio Collection. |
| Fanatic (Gold) | Obtained the ultimate fashion item. |
| Hoarder (Silver) | Collected all Presents. |
| Katamari Aficionado (Bronze) | Collected all songs. |
| Katamari Fan Damacy (Bronze) | Obtained a Fan Damacy for the first time. |
| Katamari Noob (Bronze) | Completed "Make It Big: Playtime". |
| Long Live Katamari! (Bronze) | Unlocked Eternal and Katamari Drive modes for all Requests. |
| Sweet Talker (Silver) | Used 3 Candy Tickets at the same time. |
| The King of Style (Silver) | Collected all of the King's fashion items. |
| We Love Cousins (Bronze) | Rolled up all Cousins. |

## TWISTED METAL    (PlayStation 3)

### TROPHY

| UNLOCKABLE | HOW TO UNLOCK |
|---|---|
| ...and I thank you for playing Twisted Metal. (Bronze) | Complete the Story mode on any difficulty |
| 60 to 0 (Bronze) | Kill a player with full health in one shot. |
| A la Mode (Silver) | Win 10 Ranked games in each game type. |
| All sales are final (Bronze) | Win at least 1 Ranked Online game per day for 30 straight days |
| Am I not merciful? (Bronze) | Kill 100 flaming gunners and/or drivers in campaign mode. |
| Another Level (Silver) | Win 10 Ranked games in each map. Map size does not matter. |
| Any car will do (Gold) | Earn 50 Kills with Each Vehicle in Online Ranked Games |
| Because I care (Bronze) | Complete a campaign game without hitting a single pedestrian. |
| Birth Control (Bronze) | Defeat the semi before a single enemy is spawned in Juggernaut DM - Watkyn's Harbor. |
| Blah, Blah, Blah, Gimme the trophy (Bronze) | Play and finish the "Live Training" tutorial mode |
| Calypso (Bronze) | Achieve the Highest Online Rank |
| Cookie Party (Bronze) | Kill 3 enemies in a single game using drop mines. |

| | |
|---|---|
| **Fire in the sky (Bronze)** | Shoot down an enemy missile 1 time in a ranked game of NUKE. |
| **Grace Under Fire (Bronze)** | Beat Metro Square Electric Cage on HARD MODE with 5 SECONDS LEFT in your GRACE PERIOD meter. Cooperative Story is allowed. |
| **Grimm's Dark Trip Back (Bronze)** | Complete the Grimm story on any difficulty. |
| **He's not heavy (Bronze)** | As Talon, pick up teammate (ranked, unranked, split screen, campaign co-op). |
| **I am Sweet Tooth (Platinum)** | All Trophies |
| **I h8 poachers (Bronze)** | Finish a ranked game with the most damage done and fewest kills overall |
| **In your Face (Bronze)** | Hit a statue with a Nuke. |
| **Make up your mind (Bronze)** | Use the garage 25 times. |
| **Medic! (Bronze)** | Heal a teammate. |
| **Old School (Bronze)** | Play a 2,3,4 player split screen local game |
| **Point, Shoot, Kill (Gold)** | Kill 100 enemies with every missile during Ranked games. |
| **Racing? In a Twisted Metal game?! (Silver)** | Don't miss any gates and win the battle in Race #2, one player only. |
| **Remote Nuke (Silver)** | Kill 3 players with a single remote bomb. |
| **Right Place, Right Time (Bronze)** | Kill a player less than 5 seconds after you respawn, in an online game |
| **So much anger... (Bronze)** | Discover the secret of Sophie Kane |
| **Tantric Twisted (Gold)** | Reach 50 cars killed by yourself in Endurance mode |
| **That. Just. Happened. (Bronze)** | Kill yourself with a freeze cheap shot in ranked DM or LMS, or in any unranked or offline play |
| **The most dangerous game (Bronze)** | Be The Hunted/Stay the Hunted- in ranked, unranked, or split screen local-HUNTED GAME MODE for at least 4 minutes. |
| **The One That Got Away (Bronze)** | Complete the Sweet Tooth story on any difficulty. |
| **TMA (Gold)** | Complete Story mode without dying or switching cars in the garage. |
| **Tradin' Paint (Bronze)** | Ram 5 players to death in a single online game. |
| **Truly Twisted (Silver)** | Complete the Story mode on Twisted Difficulty |
| **Twisted Gold (Gold)** | Earn a gold medal in every campaign event and boss fight on Twisted difficulty |
| **Twofer (Bronze)** | Kill two enemies with a single rat rocket. |
| **Up, Up and Away (Bronze)** | Launch a Nuke |
| **Watch Me Shine! (Bronze)** | Complete the Doll Face story on any difficulty. |
| **We buy gold! (Bronze)** | Earn a gold medal on every campaign event in any difficulty mode including co-op. |
| **You think this game made itself? (Bronze)** | Watch the credits, start to finish |

## UEFA EURO 2012   (PlayStation 3)

### TROPHY

| UNLOCKABLE | HOW TO UNLOCK |
|---|---|
| **Collector (Silver)** | Collect all mosaic pieces in Expedition |
| **Creating History Together (Bronze)** | Win UEFA EURO 2012 with more than 1 user playing for the same team in all 6 matches |

| Expeditionary Nature (Silver) | Defeat all 53 nations in Expedition |
|---|---|
| Glory Moment (Bronze) | Win Online UEFA EURO 2012 |
| Make It Possible (Bronze) | Succeed in a Challenge |
| My Euro (Silver) | Win a match in each UEFA EURO 2012 game mode |
| National Pride (Bronze) | Win an Expedition match with all starting 11 from the same nation |
| On All Fronts (Bronze) | Defeat one team from each group in Expedition |
| One Down (Bronze) | Defeat all possible teams from a group in Expedition |
| We Are The Champions (Bronze) | Win UEFA EURO 2012 |

## UEFA EURO 2012 (XBOX 360)

### ACHIEVEMENT

| UNLOCKABLE | HOW TO UNLOCK |
|---|---|
| Collector (50) | Collect all mosaic pieces in Expedition |
| Creating History Together (30) | Win UEFA EURO 2012 with more than 1 user playing for the same team in all 6 matches |
| Expeditionary Nature (40) | Defeat all 53 nations in Expedition |
| Glory Moment (30) | Win Online UEFA EURO 2012 |
| Make It Possible (10) | Succeed in a Challenge |
| My Euro (40) | Win a match in each UEFA EURO 2012 game mode |
| National Pride (10) | Win an Expedition match with all starting 11 from the same nation |
| On All Fronts (10) | Defeat one team from each group in Expedition |
| One Down (10) | Defeat all teams from a group in Expedition |
| We Are The Champions (20) | Win UEFA EURO 2012 |

## UFC UNDISPUTED 3 (PlayStation 3)

### TROPHY

| UNLOCKABLE | HOW TO UNLOCK |
|---|---|
| A Quarter Down, Three to Go (Silver) | Clear 25% or more of all game modes. |
| Artiste (Bronze) | Create a Logo and apply it to a CAF as a Tattoo. |
| Bragging Rights (Bronze) | Create a Highlight Reel. |
| Breaking your Best Toys (Silver) | Win against a CAF that obtained Career Hall of Fame in Exhibition on Expert Difficulty or higher. |
| Breaking your Toys (Bronze) | Win a match against the COM on Experienced Difficulty while using a CAF in Exhibition Mode. |
| Brute Force (Bronze) | Submission Slam or Stomp Escape the COM in Exhibition on Advanced Difficulty or Higher |
| Chopping 'em Down (Bronze) | Get the TKO win by damaging the opponent's legs. |
| Determined Champion (Silver) | Clear Title Mode without any interruption. |
| Dual Division Champion (Silver) | Use 1 fighter in Career Mode to win the UFC championship in 2 weight divisions. |
| Even Rocky Had a Montage (Silver) | Create a Highlight Reel with 10 or more different fighters. |

| | |
|---|---|
| **Everyone's a Critic (Bronze)** | Rate contents created by other players in Content Sharing. |
| **Exhibition Excellence (Bronze)** | Win 5 ranked Online matches in a row. |
| **Extracurricular (Bronze)** | Join an Online camp. |
| **Fight Camp Frenzy (Silver)** | Win 10 consecutive Fight Camp Exhibition matches. |
| **Finish the Fight (Gold)** | After a KO or TKO, land 4 finishing blows and win the match. |
| **First of Many! (Bronze)** | Win a ranked Online match for the first time. |
| **Getting A Leg Up (Silver)** | Defeat a COM on Advanced or higher in Exhibition or Tournament Mode with each Leg Submission. |
| **GOOOAAL!!! (Silver)** | KO the opponent with a soccer kick. |
| **Hall of famer (Silver)** | Enter the Hall of Fame with a fighter in Career Mode. |
| **History is Best Both Ways (Silver)** | Obtain a 100% completion score with both fighters in a fight in Ultimate Fights Mode. |
| **Making it Rain (Bronze)** | 10,000 or more shop points accumulated. |
| **Online Amateur (Bronze)** | Play 10 or more Online matches. |
| **Online Journeyman (Silver)** | Play 500 or more ranked Online matches. |
| **Platinum (Platinum)** | Obtain all trophies |
| **Pound for Pound (Silver)** | Win in each division in Exhibition with Advanced Difficulty or higher. |
| **Practice Makes Perfect (Bronze)** | Play an Online Fight Camp Sparring match. |
| **Prepared to Win! (Bronze)** | Play through each Training Game with a fighter in Career Mode. |
| **PRIDE of a champion (Bronze)** | Win 25 fights consecutively in Title Defense Mode. |
| **Prime Time Fighting (Bronze)** | Play and complete a 6, 7 or 8 card event in Event Mode. |
| **Prolific Champion (Gold)** | Use 1 fighter in Career Mode and win the WFA Championship, UFC Championship, and PRIDE Grand Prix. |
| **Punching is Hard Work (Bronze)** | Win a match on Ultimate in Exhibition or Tournament Mode with the Simulation Energy Settings. |
| **Puppeteer (Bronze)** | Create a CAF and modify the face with CREATE A FIGHTER. |
| **Storied Career (Bronze)** | Complete Career Mode with a CAF or Roster Fighter. |
| **Training Expertise (Silver)** | Obtain a 4-star score in a Training Game with a fighter in Career Mode. |
| **Triple Threatening (Silver)** | Obtain any level 3 move for 1 fighter in Career Mode. |
| **Willingness (Bronze)** | Select a guided tutorial |

## UFC UNDISPUTED 3 (XBOX 360)

### ACHIEVEMENT

| UNLOCKABLE | HOW TO UNLOCK |
|---|---|
| A Quarter Down, Three to Go (50) | Clear 25% or more of all game modes. |
| All About the Show (10) | Watch a PRIDE entrance in Exhibition once without skipping. |

**NEW!**

| | |
|---|---|
| **Bragging Rights (5)** | Create a Highlight Reel. |
| **Breaking your Best Toys (30)** | Win against a CAF that obtained Career Hall of Fame in Exhibition on Expert Difficulty or higher. |
| **Breaking your Toys (10)** | Win a match against the COM on Experienced Difficulty while using a CAF in Exhibition Mode. |
| **Brute Force (15)** | Submission Slam or Stomp Escape the COM in Exhibition on Advanced Difficulty or Higher |
| **Chopping 'em Down (5)** | Get the TKO win by damaging the opponent's legs. |
| **Determined Champion (30)** | Clear Title Mode without any interruption. |
| **Dual Division Champion (30)** | Use 1 fighter in Career Mode to win the UFC championship in 2 weight divisions. |
| **Even Rocky Had a Montage (50)** | Create a Highlight Reel with 10 or more different fighters. |
| **Everyone's a Critic (5)** | Rate contents created by other players in Content Sharing. |
| **Exhibition Excellence (30)** | Win 5 ranked Xbox LIVE matches in a row. |
| **Extracurricular (10)** | Join an Xbox LIVE Fight Camp. |
| **Fight Camp Frenzy (35)** | Win 10 consecutive Fight Camp Exhibition matches. |
| **Finish the Fight (100)** | After a KO or TKO, land 4 finishing blows and win the match. |
| **First of Many! (10)** | Win a ranked Xbox LIVE match for the first time. |
| **Getting A Leg Up (45)** | Defeat a COM on Advanced or higher in Exhibition or Tournament Mode with each Leg Submission. |
| **GOOOAAL!!! (15)** | KO the opponent with a soccer kick. |
| **Hall of famer (30)** | Enter the Hall of Fame with a fighter in Career Mode. |
| **History is Best Both Ways (30)** | Obtain a 100% completion score with both fighters in a fight in Ultimate Fights Mode. |
| **Making it Rain (15)** | 10,000 or more shop points accumulated. |
| **Online Amateur (10)** | Play 10 or more ranked Xbox LIVE matches. |
| **Online Journeyman (30)** | Play 500 or more ranked Xbox LIVE matches. |
| **Pound for Pound (50)** | Win in each division in Exhibition with Advanced Difficulty or higher. |
| **Practice Makes Perfect (5)** | Play an Xbox LIVE Fight Camp Sparring match. |
| **Prepared to Win! (10)** | Play through each Training Game with a fighter in Career Mode. |
| **PRIDE of a champion (20)** | Win 25 fights consecutively in Title Defense Mode. |
| **Prime Time Fighting (15)** | Play and complete a 6, 7 or 8 card event in Event Mode. |
| **Prolific Champion (100)** | Use 1 fighter in Career Mode and win the WFA Championship, UFC Championship, and PRIDE Grand Prix. |
| **Punching is Hard Work (5)** | Win a match on Ultimate in Exhibition or Tournament Mode with the Simulation Energy Settings. |
| **Puppeteer (5)** | Create a CAF and modify the face with CREATE A FIGHTER. |
| **Storied Career (15)** | Complete Career Mode with a CAF or Roster Fighter. |

A
B
C
D
E
F
G
H
I
J
K
L
M
N
O
P
Q
R
S
T
U
V
W
X
Y
Z

**CODES & CHEATS**

| | |
|---|---|
| **Training Expertise (50)** | Obtain a 4-star score in a Training Game with a fighter in Career Mode. |
| **Triple Threatening (30)** | Obtain any level 3 move for 1 fighter in Career Mode. |
| **Willingness (5)** | Select a guided tutorial |

## ULTIMATE MARVEL VS. CAPCOM 3 (PlayStation Vita)

### TROPHY

| UNLOCKABLE | HOW TO UNLOCK |
|---|---|
| **A Friend in Need (Bronze)** | Perform 100 Crossover Assists. (Arcade/Online only) |
| **A Warrior Born (Bronze)** | Earn 5,000 Player Points (PP). |
| **Above Average Joe (Bronze)** | Land a Viewtiful Combo. (Arcade/online only) |
| **Advancing Guardian (Bronze)** | Perform 100 Advancing Guards. (Arcade/Online only) |
| **Assemble! (Bronze)** | Participate in an 8 player Lobby online. |
| **Big Bang Theory (Bronze)** | Perform 30 Hyper Combo Finishes. (Arcade/online only) |
| **Brave New World (Bronze)** | Participate in any mode online. |
| **Comic Collector (Gold)** | Unlock all items in the Gallery. |
| **Crazy Good (Bronze)** | Surpass the rank of Fighter. |
| **Defender (Bronze)** | Block 100 times. (Arcade/Online only) |
| **Devil with a Blue Coat (Bronze)** | Earn 30,000 Player Points (PP). |
| **Divine Brawler (Silver)** | Earn 100,000 Player Points (PP). |
| **Dominator (Silver)** | Collect 100 titles. |
| **Dreaded Opponent (Bronze)** | Participate in 200 matches online. |
| **Fighting Machine (Silver)** | Win 100 battles in Ranked Match. |
| **First Strike (Bronze)** | Land 50 First Attacks. (Arcade/Online only) |
| **Forged From Steel (Silver)** | Participate in 300 matches online. |
| **Full Roster (Silver)** | Battle against all characters online. |
| **Gravity? Please... (Bronze)** | Land 50 Team Aerial Combos. (Arcade/Online only) |
| **Hard Corps (Bronze)** | Perform 30 Crossover Combination Finishes. (Arcade/online only) |
| **Hellbent (Bronze)** | Participate in 100 matches online. |
| **High-Score Hero (Silver)** | Earn 500,000 points in Arcade mode. |
| **Hotshot (Bronze)** | Win 10 battles in Ranked Match. |
| **Incredible (Bronze)** | Win without calling your partners or switching out in an online match. |
| **Master of Tasks (Silver)** | Clear 480 missions in Mission mode. |
| **Mega Buster (Bronze)** | Use 1,000 Hyper Combo Gauge bars. (Arcade/online only) |
| **Mega Good (Silver)** | Surpass the 6th rank of any class. |
| **Mighty Teamwork (Bronze)** | Land 30 Team Aerial Counters. (Arcade/Online only) |
| **Missions? Possible. (Bronze)** | Clear 120 missions in Mission mode. |
| **Mutant Master (Bronze)** | Land an Uncanny Combo. (Arcade/online only) |
| **Need a Healing Factor (Bronze)** | Win without blocking in an online match. |
| **Noble Effort (Bronze)** | Get a 5-game win streak in Ranked Match. |
| **Passport to Beatdown Country (Bronze)** | Fight in all of the stages. |
| **Perfect X-ample (Bronze)** | Use X-Factor 50 times. (Arcade/Online only) |

| | |
|---|---|
| Quick Change-Up (Bronze) | Perform 50 Crossover Counters. (Arcade/Online only) |
| Rivals Welcome (Silver) | Play in Online Mode for over 30 hours. |
| Savage Playing (Bronze) | Perform 50 Snap Backs. (Arcade/Online only) |
| Saving My Quarters (Bronze) | Beat Arcade mode without using any continues. |
| Seductive Embrace (Bronze) | Play in Online Mode for over 5 hours. |
| Slam Master (Bronze) | Win 50 battles in Ranked Match. |
| The Best There Is (Bronze) | Beat Arcade mode on the hardest difficulty. |
| The Points Do Matter (Bronze) | Earn 400,000 points in Arcade mode. |
| The Ultimate (Platinum) | Obtain all Trophies. |
| Training in Isolation (Silver) | Play in Offline Mode for over 30 hours. |
| Training Montage (Bronze) | Play in Offline Mode for over 5 hours. |
| Up To The Challenge (Silver) | Clear 240 missions in Mission mode. |
| Waiting for the Trade (Gold) | View all endings in Arcade mode. |

## UNCHARTED: GOLDEN ABYSS  (PlayStation Vita)

### TROPHY

| UNLOCKABLE | HOW TO UNLOCK |
|---|---|
| 100 Headshots (Bronze) | Defeat 100 enemies with headshots. |
| 200 Kills: GAU - 19 (Bronze) | Defeat 200 enemies with the GAU - 19. |
| 250 Headshots (Silver) | Defeat 250 enemies with headshots. |
| 30 Kills: Desert - 5 (Bronze) | Defeat 30 enemies with the Desert - 5. |
| 30 Kills: Mk - NDI (Bronze) | Defeat 30 enemies with the Mk - NDI. |
| 30 Kills: Moss - 12 (Bronze) | Defeat 30 enemies with the Moss - 12. |
| 30 Kills: RPG - 7 (Bronze) | Defeat 30 enemies with the RPG - 7. |
| 30 Kills: Wes - 44 (Bronze) | Defeat 30 enemies with the Wes - 44. |
| 50 Kills: 92FS - 9mm (Bronze) | Defeat 50 enemies with the 92FS - 9mm. |
| 50 Kills: Dragon Sniper (Bronze) | Defeat 50 enemies with the Dragon Sniper. |
| 50 Kills: GP32 - BND. (Bronze) | Defeat 50 enemies with the GP32 - BND. |
| 50 Kills: M79 (Bronze) | Defeat 50 enemies with the M79. |
| 50 Kills: Micro - 9mm (Bronze) | Defeat 50 enemies with the Micro - 9mm. |
| 70 Kills: FAL (Bronze) | Defeat 70 enemies with the FAL. |
| 70 Kills: M4 (Bronze) | Defeat 70 enemies with the M4. |
| 70 Kills: SAS - 12 (Bronze) | Defeat 70 enemies with the SAS - 12. |
| Bare-knuckle Slugger (Silver) | Defeat 50 enemies with hand-to-hand combat. |
| Bounty: Arcana (Bronze) | Complete the bounty set. |
| Bounty: Cádiz (Bronze) | Complete the bounty set. |
| Bounty: Gemstones (Bronze) | Complete the bounty set. |
| Bounty: Pieces of Silver (Bronze) | Complete the bounty set. |
| Charted! - Crushing (Gold) | Finish the game in Crushing Mode. |
| Charted! - Easy (Bronze) | Finish the game in Easy Mode. |
| Charted! - Hard (Gold) | Finish the game in Hard Mode. |
| Charted! - Normal (Silver) | Finish the game in Normal Mode. |
| Hangman (Bronze) | Defeat 20 enemies with gunfire by aiming while hanging. |
| Master Ninja (Silver) | Defeat 50 enemies with stealth attacks. |
| Odessa Mining Company (Bronze) | Complete the Mystery. |
| Paparazzo (Bronze) | Complete all photographs. |
| Platinum (Platinum) | Collect all other 55 Trophies for this Trophy. |

| | |
|---|---|
| **Poisoned Powder (Bronze)** | Complete the Mystery. |
| **Proof of Life (Bronze)** | Complete the Mystery. |
| **Puzzle Master (Bronze)** | Complete all puzzles. |
| **Relic Finder (Bronze)** | Find the strange relic. |
| **Rub One Out (Bronze)** | Complete all rubbings. |
| **Ruffle My Feathers (Bronze)** | Force José Parrot to squawk out 8 unique quips. |
| **Run-and-Gunner (Bronze)** | Defeat 20 enemies by shooting from the hip (without aiming). |
| **Secrets of the Kuna (Bronze)** | Complete the Mystery. |
| **Steel Fist Expert (Silver)** | Defeat 10 enemies in a row with a single punch, after softening them up with gunfire. |
| **Steel Fist Master (Bronze)** | Defeat 20 enemies with a single punch, after softening them up with gunfire. |
| **Survivor (Bronze)** | Defeat 75 Enemies in a row without dying. |
| **The Circle of Heaven (Bronze)** | Complete the Mystery. |
| **The Collector (Bronze)** | Collect first treasure or mystery. |
| **The Conquistadors (Bronze)** | Complete the Mystery. |
| **The Friar's Pilgrimage (Bronze)** | Complete the Mystery. |
| **The Lost Civilization (Bronze)** | Complete the Mystery. |
| **The Revolution (Bronze)** | Complete the Mystery. |
| **The Ring of Earth (Bronze)** | Complete the Mystery. |
| **The Sete Cidades (Bronze)** | Complete the Mystery. |
| **Touch My Rear (Bronze)** | Use the rear touch pad to climb a rope or chain. |
| **Trail of Vincent Perez (Bronze)** | Complete the Mystery. |
| **Treasure: Jade Carvings (Bronze)** | Complete the treasure set. |
| **Treasure: Minor Deities (Bronze)** | Complete the treasure set. |
| **Treasure: The Menagerie (Bronze)** | Complete the treasure set. |
| **Treasure: Turquoise Glyphs (Bronze)** | Complete the treasure set. |

## UNIT 13 (PlayStation Vita)

### TROPHY

| UNLOCKABLE | HOW TO UNLOCK |
|---|---|
| **13 Squared (Bronze)** | Eliminate 169 enemies over the course of your career. |
| **13-Star General (Platinum)** | Obtain all Bronze, Silver, and Gold trophies in Unit 13. |
| **Action Hero (Silver)** | Complete all Direct Action operations. |
| **Adapt and Overcome (Bronze)** | Complete a Daily Challenge operation. |
| **Anti-Venom (Silver)** | Eliminate VIPER. |
| **Badass and Bulletproof (Bronze)** | Eliminate 13 enemies without taking damage. |
| **Blast from the Past (Bronze)** | Find an homage to what has come before... |
| **Brainstorm (Bronze)** | Score 13 headshots in a single operation. |
| **By Strength and Guile (Bronze)** | Reach level 10 with RINGO. |
| **Ch13f Op3r471v3 (Silver)** | Complete all Elite operations. |
| **Cloud Nine (Gold)** | Eliminate all High Value Targets. |
| **Crowd Control Jr. (Bronze)** | Eliminate 2 enemies with a single grenade. |
| **De Oppresso Liber (Bronze)** | Reach level 10 with ANIMAL. |
| **Dead Winger (Silver)** | Eliminate PHOENIX. |
| **Doublecrossed (Silver)** | Eliminate GRIFTER. |
| **Extra Credit(S) (Bronze)** | Watch the credits. |

| | |
|---|---|
| Facit Omnia Voluntas (Bronze) | Reach level 10 with ZEUS. |
| Fangdango (Silver) | Eliminate VAMPIRE. |
| Fat Chance (Silver) | Eliminate BIG SLICK. |
| Finish Him! (Silver) | Eliminate SCORPION. |
| Friendly Rivalry (Bronze) | Get a higher mission score than someone on your friends list. |
| Honneur et Fidélité (Bronze) | Reach level 10 with CHUCKLES. |
| It Pays to be a Winner (Bronze) | Reach level 10 with PYTHON. |
| L337 $0LD13R (Bronze) | Complete an Elite operation. |
| Lamplighter (Bronze) | Complete a Covert operation. |
| Last Laugh (Silver) | Eliminate HYENA. |
| Less Me, More We (Bronze) | Complete an operation in co-op. |
| Life of the Party (Bronze) | Show your enemy that you get down with the best of 'em. |
| Lucky 13 (Silver) | Achieve a 5-star rating in 13 operations. |
| Master Ninja (Silver) | Complete all Covert operations. |
| New Recruit (Bronze) | Complete the Unit 13 Training Course. |
| One Shot, One Kill (Bronze) | Reach level 10 with ALABAMA. |
| Sine Labore Nihil (Gold) | Max out all operatives. |
| Snakechaser (Bronze) | Complete a Direct Action operation. |
| Speed Demon (Bronze) | Complete a Deadline operation. |
| Sworded Out (Silver) | Eliminate SCIMITAR. |
| Time Killer (Silver) | Complete all Deadline operations. |
| Trick Shot (Bronze) | Eliminate an enemy by setting off a mine. |
| Twin Foiled (Bronze) | Eliminate 2 enemies with a single melee attack. |
| Two For One (Bronze) | Eliminate 2 enemies with a single bullet. |
| Unstoppable (Silver) | Achieve the highest score multiplier. |
| Variety is the Spice of Life (Silver) | Complete 13 different Dynamic missions. |
| Witchiker (Silver) | Eliminate WIZARD. |
| World Peace in 36 Easy Steps (Silver) | Complete all Covert, Deadline, Direct Action, and Elite operations. |

## VIRTUA TENNIS 4: WORLD TOUR EDITION   (PlayStation Vita)

### TROPHY

| UNLOCKABLE | HOW TO UNLOCK |
|---|---|
| Accomplished (Silver) | Become: Accomplished |
| Arcade Beginner (Bronze) | Clear a stage in Arcade Mode |
| Balloon Popper (Bronze) | Pop 30 balloons in Practice Mode |
| Best Stroker (Bronze) | Win 100 points with ground strokes |
| Big Hitter (Silver) | Hit 250 MAX Serves |
| Bomb Fiend (Bronze) | Detonate 20 bombs in the opponent's court in Bomb Match |
| Breakthrough (Bronze) | Win 10 games as the receiving player |
| Classic Photographer (Bronze) | Take a classic photo with VT CAM |
| Doubles Beginner (Bronze) | Clear a stage in Arcade Mode Doubles |
| Doubles Grand Slammer (Bronze) | Clear Doubles Mode |
| Emergency Stop (Bronze) | Stop the ships 10 times in Rock the Boat |
| Endless Rally! (Bronze) | Sustain a rally for 30 shots |
| Exhibitionist (Bronze) | Play 10 Exhibition Matches |
| Famous (Bronze) | Become: Famous |

NEW!

A
B
C
D
E
F
G
H
I
J
K
L
M
N
O
P
Q
R
S
T
U
V
W
X
Y
Z

| | |
|---|---|
| **First Online Victory (Bronze)** | Win a match online |
| **Full Swing! (Bronze)** | Hit 50 MAX power shots |
| **Future Champion (Bronze)** | Win the final tournament of the Tour Break |
| **Grand Slammer (Bronze)** | Clear Singles Mode |
| **Great King (Silver)** | Defeat the King in Arcade Mode Singles |
| **Great Sniper (Bronze)** | Achieve a 5x Combo in Clay Shooting |
| **Hat Tricker (Bronze)** | Score 3 goals in a row in Ace Striker |
| **In Your Face Tennis! (Bronze)** | Win 5 VR matches |
| **International Traveler (Bronze)** | Play an online visitor 10 times |
| **Jack of all Trades (Gold)** | Take lessons for all play styles |
| **Look Alike (Bronze)** | Create a player by taking a picture |
| **Loving It! (Bronze)** | Win 10 Love games |
| **Marathon Runner (Bronze)** | Run 42km (26mi) |
| **Moneybags (Bronze)** | Collect 1000 coins in Coin Match |
| **Mother Hen (Bronze)** | Deliver at least 10 chicks simultaneously to their mother in Egg Collector |
| **Online Debut (Bronze)** | Play online with a customised character |
| **Online Master (Gold)** | Reach Rank A |
| **Online Streak (Bronze)** | Win three consecutive matches online |
| **Poker Face (Silver)** | Get 10 royal straight flushes in Royal Poker |
| **Power Smash! (Silver)** | Hit 250 smashes |
| **Pro-Tennis Fan (Bronze)** | Play using all the real tennis players |
| **Regular Customer (Bronze)** | Stop at the Management Office 30 times |
| **Screen Sharer (Bronze)** | Play a Touch VS game |
| **Shopeholic (Bronze)** | Purchase 50 types of items in the Kit Catalouge |
| **Super Player (Silver)** | Hit 100 super shots |
| **Swing Machine (Bronze)** | Swing 5000 times |
| **Tennis God (Platinum)** | Collect every trophy |
| **Ticket to the SPT Finals (Gold)** | Make it to the playoffs |
| **Top Condition (Silver)** | Reach a Condition level of 20 |
| **Turkey Bowler (Bronze)** | Get a turkey in Pin Crusher |
| **Tycoon (Bronze)** | Earn 1,000,000 in total prize money |
| **Volley Master (Bronze)** | Win 100 points with volleys |
| **Wall Whiz (Bronze)** | Hit a wall 5 times with the ball in one Wall Match |
| **Wind Master (Bronze)** | Pop 3 balloons in one Wind Match |
| **World Tour Cleared! (Bronze)** | Clear the game |

## WIPEOUT 2048  (PlayStation Vita)

### TROPHY

| UNLOCKABLE | HOW TO UNLOCK |
|---|---|
| **1 Down, 19 To Go (Bronze)** | Complete your first Online Multiplayer Level |
| **2048 Champion (Bronze)** | Complete the 2048 season |
| **2048 Elite 1 (Bronze)** | Get an ELITE PASS on the C Class Time Trial on Capital Reach in 2048 |
| **2048 Elite 2 (Bronze)** | Get an ELITE PASS on Empire Climb Zone Mode in 2048 |
| **2048 Elite 3 (Bronze)** | Get an ELITE PASS on the C Class Combat Event on Metro Park in 2048 |
| **2048 Speed Pads (Silver)** | Hit a total of 2048 Speed Pads |
| **2049 Champion (Bronze)** | Complete the 2049 season |

| | |
|---|---|
| 2049 Elite 1 (Bronze) | Get an ELITE PASS on the B Class Race on Unity Square 2049 |
| 2049 Elite 2 (Bronze) | Get an ELITE PASS on the A Class Time Trial on Metro Park in 2049 |
| 2049 Elite 3 (Bronze) | Get an ELITE PASS on Downtown Zone Mode in 2049 |
| 2050 Champion (Bronze) | Complete the 2050 season |
| 2050 Elite 1 (Bronze) | Get an ELITE PASS on Queens Mall Zone Mode in 2050 |
| 2050 Elite 2 (Bronze) | Get an ELITE PASS on the A Class Race on Empire Climb in 2050 |
| 50 Kills (Bronze) | Destroy 50 ships in Online Multiplayer |
| 50 MP Events (Silver) | Finish 50 Online Multiplayer events |
| Beat Zico (Gold) | Altima, C Class, Speed Lap, Pir-hana Speed – beat 52.00 seconds |
| Completist (Silver) | Complete all events in the Single Player Campaign |
| Elite Completist (Gold) | ELITE PASS every event in the Single Player Campaign |
| Halfway There (Silver) | Complete 10 Online Multiplayer Levels |
| Mach 1.5 (Gold) | Reach Zone 65 in any Zone Event |
| Multiplayer Begins (Bronze) | Finish an Online Multiplayer event |
| Multiplayer Completist (Gold) | Complete all nodes in the Online Multiplayer Campaign |
| Multiplayer Finished (Gold) | Finish the Online Multiplayer Campaign |
| Perfect Pir-hana (Silver) | Get a Perfect Lap in the Pir-hana Prototype, in the A Class, Unity Square, Speed Lap |
| Prototype (Silver) | ELITE PASS all Prototype Ship Challenges |
| Rank 25 (Silver) | Reach Rank 25 |
| Rank 50 (Gold) | Reach Rank 50 |
| Speed Thrills (Silver) | ELITE PASS any A+ Class Challenge |
| The Unlucky 7 (Silver) | Destroy 7 opposition ships in any Race in the Single Player Campaign |
| This is WipEout! (Platinum) | Obtain every Trophy in WipEout 2048 |
| AG-Systems: Agility | Successfully complete the 2048 Ship unlock event |
| AG-Systems: Fighter | Reach Rank 7 |
| AG-Systems: Prototype | Successfully complete the Prototype challenge unlocked at Rank 26. |
| Auricom: Agility | Reach Rank 9 |
| Auricom: Fighter | Reach Rank 46 |
| Auricom: Prototype | Successfully complete the Prototype challenge unlocked at Rank 20. |
| Auricom: Speed | Reach Rank 41 |
| Feisar: Agility | Reach Rank 13 |
| Feisar: Prototype | Successfully complete the Prototype challenge unlocked at Rank 10. |
| Pir-Hana: Agility | Reach Rank 17 |
| Pir-Hana: Fighter | Reach Rank 35 |
| Pir-Hana: Prototype | Successfully complete the Prototype challenge unlocked at Rank 50. |
| Pir-Hana: Speed | Successfully complete the 2050 ship unlock event |

A
B
C
D
E
F
G
H
I
J
K
L
M
N
O
P
Q
R
S
T
U
V
W
X
Y
Z

| Quirex: Fighter | Successfully complete the 2049 ship unlock event |
| Quirex: Prototype | Successfully complete the Prototype challenge unlocked at Rank 30. |
| Quirex: Speed | Reach Rank 24 |

# THE WITCHER 2: ASSASSINS OF KINGS (XBOX 360)

## ACHIEVEMENT

| UNLOCKABLE | HOW TO UNLOCK |
|---|---|
| Alea Iacta Est (10) | Complete Chapter 2. |
| Apprentice (10) | Use alchemy to brew five potions or oils. |
| Artful Dodger (30) | Cut off a tentacle using the kayran trap. |
| Avenger (30) | Finish the game by killing Letho. |
| Backbone (20) | Craft a suit of armor from elements of the kayran's carapace. |
| Being Witcher George (20) | Kill the dragon. |
| Black Ops (20) | Sneak through the lower camp without raising the alarm. |
| Craftsman (10) | Hire a craftsman to create an item. |
| Dragonheart (20) | Spare or save Saskia. |
| Eagle Eye (10) | Hit Count Etcheverry using the ballista. |
| Fat Man (15) | Kill the draug. |
| Focus (30) | Perform three successful ripostes in a row. |
| Friend of Trolls (15) | Spare all trolls in the game. |
| Gambler (15) | Win an arm wrestling match, a dice poker game and a fist fight. |
| Gladiator (15) | Defeat all opponents in the Kaedweni arena. |
| Guru (50) | Achieve character level 35. |
| Heartbreaker (10) | Seduce Ves. |
| Intimidator (15) | Intimidate someone. |
| Journeyman (10) | Achieve character level 10. |
| Kayranslayer (10) | Kill the kayran. |
| Kingmaker (15) | Help Roche rescue Anais from the Kaedweni camp. |
| Last Man Standing (15) | Survive your 30th fight in the Arena |
| Librarian (30) | Find all additional information about the insane asylum's history. |
| Madman (100) | Finish the game while playing at the Dark difficulty level. |
| Man of the Shadows (15) | Successfully sneak through Loredo's garden and find the component of the kayran trap. |
| Master Alchemist (10) | Acquire the Mutant ability. |
| Master of Magic (10) | Acquire the Sense of Magic ability. |
| Miser (10) | Collect 10000 orens. |
| Mutant! (30) | Enhance abilities using mutagens at least five times. |
| Necromancer (50) | Relive all of Auckes's memories in Dethmold's vision. |
| Old Friends (30) | Finish the game by sparing Letho. |
| Once Ain't Enough (15) | Complete Chapter 3. |
| Perfectionist (15) | Kill 10 foes in a row without losing any Vitality. |
| Pest Control (20) | Finish all quests involing the destruction of monster nests. |
| Poker! (30) | Roll five-of-a-kind at dice poker. |

| | |
|---|---|
| **Reasons of State (15)** | Stop Roche from killing Henselt. |
| **Ricochet (10)** | Kill a foe by deflecting his own arrow at him. |
| **Sensitive Guy (10)** | Save Sîle from dying in the unstable portal. |
| **Spellbreaker (15)** | Help Iorveth find the dagger needed to free Saskia from the spell that holds her. |
| **Swordmaster (10)** | Acquire the Combat Acumen ability. |
| **The Butcher of Blaviken (30)** | Kill 500 foes. |
| **The Fugitive (5)** | Complete the Prologue. |
| **Threesome (15)** | Kill three foes at once by performing a group finisher. |
| **To Aedirn! (5)** | Complete Chapter 1. |
| **To Be Continued... (50)** | Finish the game at any difficulty level. |
| **Torn Asunder! (15)** | Kill more than one opponent using a single exploding bomb. |
| **Tourist (10)** | Tour the camp with Zyvik. |
| **Tried-and-True (10)** | Survive your 5th fight in the Arena |
| **Trollslayer (30)** | Kill all the trolls in the game. |
| **Witch Hunter (10)** | Leave Sîle to die in the unstable portal. |

## YAKUZA: DEAD SOULS (PlayStation 3)

### TROPHY

| UNLOCKABLE | HOW TO UNLOCK |
|---|---|
| **A Weapon Freak is Born (Bronze)** | Create at least one weapon from each category. |
| **Akiyama Trophy (Silver)** | Land 100 head shots with Akiyama. |
| **All Units, Report! (Bronze)** | Train at Gary's Boot Camp with all four protagonists. |
| **Amon's Vanquisher (Gold)** | Defeat Amon. |
| **Brainiac (Bronze)** | Win at mahjong and shogi once each. |
| **Casino Master (Bronze)** | Play each casino game once. |
| **Getting Some Action (Bronze)** | Fight zombies together with a hostess. |
| **Goda Trophy (Silver)** | Destroy 100 wield-able objects with Goda. |
| **Golden Brown (Bronze)** | Defeat 50 zombies with fire. |
| **Hasegawa's Right Hand (Bronze)** | Cumulative point total from Hasegawa's directives hit 5,000. |
| **Heavily Armed Bank (Bronze)** | Amass over 10 million yen. |
| **Indoor Sportsman (Bronze)** | Go batting, bowling, and play table tennis three times each. |
| **Kamurocho Spelunker (Bronze)** | Initiate the Kamurocho Subterranea mission. |
| **Kiryu Trophy (Silver)** | Defeat 100 mutant variants with Kiryu. |
| **Life of the Party (Bronze)** | Play every song at karaoke. |
| **Lounge Lizard (Bronze)** | Play darts and pool five times each. |
| **Majima Trophy (Silver)** | Defeat 100 enemies using Heat Sniping with Majima. |
| **Mission Complete! (Bronze)** | Clear a directive from Hasegawa. |
| **My Eyes! (Bronze)** | Daze 50 zombies with stun grenades. |
| **My First Mod (Bronze)** | Mod one weapon or piece of armor. |
| **Nice Try (Bronze)** | Shoot down an enemy projectile with a Heat Snipe. |
| **Official Sponsor (Bronze)** | Fully upgrade Kamiyama's truck. |
| **Oh, the Humanity! (Bronze)** | Successfully Heat Snipe a gas tanker. |

| | |
|---|---|
| **Old-School (Bronze)** | Defeat 10 zombies using wield-able objects. |
| **Outdoorsman (Bronze)** | Go golfing and fishing once each. |
| **Pachinko Wizard (Bronze)** | Obtain the "trophy" prize at the Volcano Prize Exchange counter. |
| **Part I Complete (Bronze)** | Complete the four chapters of Part I. |
| **Part II Complete (Bronze)** | Complete the four chapters of Part II. |
| **Part III Complete (Bronze)** | Complete the four chapters of Part III. |
| **Part IV Complete (Bronze)** | Complete the four chapters of Part IV. |
| **Platinum Trophy (Platinum)** | Earn all other trophies in the game. |
| **Pro Gambler (Bronze)** | Play each Japanese gambling game once. |
| **Recycler (Bronze)** | Collect 100 items in battle. |
| **Road Rage (Bronze)** | Run over 10 zombies with a forklift or bulldozer. |
| **Savior of Kamurocho (Gold)** | Complete Dead Souls Mode. |
| **Social Butterfly (Bronze)** | Have all 14 partner characters available. |
| **Start of Something Good (Bronze)** | Befriend your first Perfect Partner character. |
| **Steamed Vegetable (Bronze)** | Kill a Hermit with fire while it is still armored. |
| **Substory 20 (Bronze)** | Finish 20 substories. |
| **Substory 4 (Bronze)** | Finish 4 substories. |
| **Substory 40 (Bronze)** | Finish 40 substories. |
| **Thanks for Playing! (Gold)** | Complete the Final Chapter. |
| **The True Ending (Silver)** | Complete Extra Hard Mode. |
| **Underground Kings (Silver)** | Clear 50 floors in the Endless Subterranea. |
| **Unsurpassed Power (Silver)** | Reach the maximum character level. |
| **Vigilante Gourmet (Bronze)** | Order from every restaurant at least once. |
| **Welcome to SEGA (Bronze)** | Play each game in Club SEGA. |
| **Zombie Collector (Bronze)** | Defeat each type of mutant variant. |
| **Zombie Hunter (Bronze)** | Defeat 100 zombies. |

## 1942: JOINT STRIKE (XBOX 360)

### SECRET PLANE

Beat the game on Wing King Difficulty setting, then select Shinden in the Plane Selection screen by pressing "Y." This enables you to use a black and red version of the Shinden with maxed out power.

## 300: MARCH TO GLORY (PSP)

Enter this code while the game is paused.

| UNLOCKABLE | CODE |
| --- | --- |
| 25,000 Kleos | ⇩, ⇨, ⇩, ⇦, ⇧, ⇦ |

## 50 CENT: BLOOD ON THE SAND (PlayStation 3)

### UNLOCKABLES

Accessed through the Unlockables menu.

| UNLOCKABLE | HOW TO UNLOCK |
| --- | --- |
| Infinite Ammo | Earn 52 medals/badges in Story mode. |
| Infinite Grenades | Earn 56 medals/badges in Story mode. |

## A BOY AND HIS BLOB (Wii)

### UNLOCKABLES

| UNLOCKABLE | HOW TO UNLOCK |
| --- | --- |
| Bonus Content | Complete a Challenge Level to unlock bonus content that is accessible from the hideout. |
| Challenge Levels | Find all three treasure chests in a regular level to unlock a Challenge Level that is accessible from the hideout. |

## ACE COMBAT: ASSAULT HORIZON (PlayStation 3)

### TROPHY

| UNLOCKABLE | HOW TO UNLOCK |
| --- | --- |
| Ace of Aces (Silver) | Obtained an A rank for every mission (free mission). |
| Aerial Sniper (Bronze) | Used DFM to destroy 10 airborne enemies in competitive online. |
| All Rounder (Silver) | Obtained all MVPs. |
| Bail Out (Bronze) | Ejected from a damaged aircraft. |
| Berserker (Bronze) | Destroyed the air defense system, opening the way for allied pilots. |
| Bomber Master (Bronze) | Defeated a large number of enemies while flying a bomber. |
| Calamity (Bronze) | Used Trinity to wipe out the enemy (free mission). |
| Category 5 (Bronze) | Pursued the enemy and shot down Major Illich. |
| Chain Master (Silver) | Took down 5 hostiles in a row with an assault chain. |
| Checking In (Bronze) | Flew through the big hotel's gates. |
| Critical Hit (Silver) | Took down a hostile fighter with a charged homing missile. |
| Defender of World Heritage (Bronze) | Prevented enemy from using Trinity to destroy Derbent. |

A B C D E F G H I J K L M N O P Q R S T U V W X Y Z

**CODES & CHEATS**

| UNLOCKABLE | HOW TO UNLOCK |
|---|---|
| Diverse Strikes (Bronze) | Defeated hostiles with all 3 of the gunship's weapons. |
| Eagle Eye (Bronze) | Successfully focused on 3 targets. |
| Emergency (Bronze) | Attempted an emergency landing in a damaged aircraft. |
| Fearsome Guardian (Bronze) | Protected your allies using the gunship, and led a successful attack on the base. |
| Fire Hazard (Bronze) | Removed enemy presence from the oil field and the base. |
| Formation Attack (Silver) | Joined the same DFM with two others and shot down a hostile (mission co-op). |
| Friendly Fire (Bronze) | Alleviated the attack on Miami and helped Guts bail out. |
| Ground Pounder (Bronze) | Used ASM to destroy 30 ground enemies in competitive online. |
| Guardian (Bronze) | Protected Washington D.C. from the threat of Trinity, and returned alive. |
| Gun Master (Bronze) | Took out a large number of hostiles as the door gunner. |
| Guns Guns Guns (Bronze) | Destroyed 5 hostile vehicles from the air as the door gunner. |
| Hard Strike (Bronze) | Wiped out hostile ground forces with ASM. |
| Hot Pit (Bronze) | Successfully took off to protect allies amid heavy hostile fire. |
| Interceptor (Bronze) | Used an attack helicopter and destroyed 10 missiles or bombs in competitive online. |
| Life Saver (Bronze) | Rescued Major Illich from enemy captivity. |
| Limbo (Bronze) | Flew beneath a falling chimney. |
| Machine Gun Faithful (Bronze) | Destroyed an enemy aircraft using only the standard machine gun while piloting an aircraft. |
| Nice Assist (Bronze) | Used DFM support or ASM support to join a flight member. |
| Nice Kill (Silver) | Shot down a large number of hostile players in competitive online. |
| Nice Save (Bronze) | Saved an ally being targeted by hostile players in DFM in competitive online. |
| Nick of Time (Bronze) | Destroyed the ICBMs. |
| One Million Tons of Scrap Prime Metal (Bronze) | Sank the enemy fleet and saved the Russian Minister. |
| Patriot (Bronze) | Protected Moscow from destruction, freeing it from enemy control. |
| Pursuit Master (Bronze) | Successfully pursued 3 enemies with counter maneuvers. |
| Shot Master (Bronze) | Took down 5 hostiles with a direct shot. |
| Sierra Hotel (Platinum) | Obtained all Trophies. |
| Smooth Flight (Silver) | Managed to get Sova 1 to land safely. |
| Speed Demon (Bronze) | Destroyed all radar missile defense systems in a short period of time. |
| Stay On Target (Bronze) | Obtained and destroyed 10 enemies in a helicopter. |
| Steel Hunter (Bronze) | Eliminated enemy threat from the Suez Canal. |
| Successive Kill (Bronze) | Took down 3 hostiles in a row with an assault chain. |
| Switch Master (Silver) | Successfully switched from defense to offense 10 times with counter maneuvers. |

| | |
|---|---|
| The Collector (Bronze) | Piloted all aircraft in the game. |
| Total Annihilation (Bronze) | Disintegrated enemy bombers in mid-air, keeping damage to the city to a minimum. |
| Veteran Pilot (Silver) | Sortied for 50 hours in competitive online or mission co-op. |
| Warwolf 1 (Gold) | Cleared all missions. |
| Warwolf Squadron (Gold) | Cleared all levels in mission co-op. |
| Welcome to Mission Co-Op (Bronze) | Cleared 1 level in mission co-op. |
| World Tour (Silver) | Played on all maps in competitive online. |

## UNLOCKABLE

| UNLOCKABLE | HOW TO UNLOCK |
|---|---|
| Unlock Call Sign - Antares | Obtain a toal of 1,000,000 points |
| Unlock Call Sign - Aquila | Receive "Survivor" bonus in Mutiplayer |
| Unlock Call Sign - Burner | Win 20 times in Capital Conquest |
| Unlock Call Sign - Cougar | Shoot down 100 enemy players in Competitive Multiplayer |
| Unlock Call Sign - Dragon | Win 10 times in Capital Conquest |
| Unlock Call Sign - Falco | Receive "Ace Stiker" bonus in Mutiplayer |
| Unlock Call Sign - Galm | Receive "Ace Pilot" bonus 5 times in Mutiplayer |
| Unlock Call Sign - Garuda | Complete the Campaign Mode |
| Unlock Call Sign - Gryphus | Receive "Hero" bonus 5 times in Mutiplayer |
| Unlock Call Sign - Mobius | Receive "Hero" bonus in Multiplayer |
| Unlock Call Sign - Mohawk | Earn 100,000 points |
| Unlock Call Sign - Phoenix | Rank first place in Deathmatch |
| Unlock Call Sign - Racer | Perform DFM support 50 times in Multiplayer |
| Unlock Call Sign - Renegade | Earn 300,000 points |
| Unlock Call Sign - Scarface | Receive "Ace Pilot" bonus in Mutiplayer |
| Unlock Call Sign - Strigon | Receive "Survivor" bonus 5 times in Mutiplayer |
| Unlock Call Sign - Sweeper | Destroy 50 enemies with helicopter in Multiplayer |
| Unlock Call Sign - Viking | Earn 20,000 points |
| Unlock Call Sign - Wardog | Receive "Ace Striker" bonus 5 times in Mutiplayer |
| Unlock Call Sign - Wildcat | Shoot down 50 enemy players in Multiplayer |
| Unlock Color 2 for all aircraft | Complete the Campaign Mode |
| Unlock F-15E Strike Eagle | Complete the Campaign Mode |
| Unlock Mi-24 (HIND) | Complete the Campaign Mode |
| Unlock PAK-FA | Complete the Campaign Mode |

## ACTRAISER (Wii)

### HIDDEN EXTRA LIVES

Do the following to find four hidden extra lives in the game's towns.

| TOWN | ACTION |
|---|---|
| Fillmore | When you get the Compass, use it here. |
| Bloodpool | Make it rain over the big lake. |
| Kasandora | Cause an earthquake after uncovering the pyramid. |
| Northwall | Strike the town's shrine with a lightning bolt. |

### PROFESSIONAL MODE

| UNLOCKABLE | HOW TO UNLOCK |
|---|---|
| Professional Mode | First, beat the game. Then on the title screen, highlight "New Game" and press ⬆ or SELECT. |

## ADVENTURE ISLAND (Wii)

### PASSWORDS

| PASSWORD | EFFECT |
|---|---|
| 3WSURYXZY763TE | Advanced items/abilities |
| RMAYTJEOPHALUP | Disable sounds |
| NODEGOS0000000 | Start the game as Hu man |
| 3YHURYW7Y7LL8C | Start the game as Hawk man |
| 3YHURYW7Y7LRBW | Start the game as Lizard man |
| 3YHURYW7Y7LN84 | Start the game as Piranha man |
| 3YHURYW7Y7LK88 | Start the game as Tiger man |

## ADVENTURES OF LOLO (Wii)

### LEVEL PASSWORDS

| PASSWORD | EFFECT |
|---|---|
| BCBT | Level 1-2 |
| BDBR | Level 1-3 |
| BGBQ | Level 1-4 |
| BHBP | Level 1-5 |
| BJBM | Level 2-1 |
| BKBL | Level 2-2 |
| BLBK | Level 2-3 |
| BMBJ | Level 2-4 |
| BPBH | Level 2-5 |
| BQBG | Level 3-1 |
| BRBD | Level 3-2 |
| BTBC | Level 3-3 |
| BVBB | Level 3-4 |
| BYZZ | Level 3-5 |
| BZZY | Level 4-1 |
| CBZV | Level 4-2 |
| CCZT | Level 4-3 |
| CDZR | Level 4-4 |
| CGZQ | Level 4-5 |
| CHZP | Level 5-1 |
| CJZM | Level 5-2 |
| CKZL | Level 5-3 |
| CLZK | Level 5-4 |
| CMZJ | Level 5-5 |
| CPZH | Level 6-1 |
| CQZG | Level 6-2 |
| CRZD | Level 6-3 |
| CTZC | Level 6-4 |
| CVZB | Level 6-5 |
| CYYZ | Level 7-1 |
| CZYY | Level 7-2 |
| DBYV | Level 7-3 |
| DCYT | Level 7-4 |
| DDYR | Level 7-5 |
| DGYQ | Level 8-1 |
| DHYP | Level 8-2 |
| DJYM | Level 8-3 |
| DKYL | Level 8-4 |
| DLYK | Level 8-5 |

| Password | Level |
|---|---|
| DMYJ | Level 9-1 |
| DPYH | Level 9-2 |
| DQYG | Level 9-3 |
| DRYD | Level 9-4 |
| DTYC | Level 9-5 |
| DVYB | Level 10-1 |
| DYVZ | Level 10-2 |
| DZVY | Level 10-3 |
| GBVV | Level 10-4 |
| GCVT | Level 10-5 |

### LEVEL SKIP

| UNLOCKABLE | HOW TO UNLOCK |
|---|---|
| Level Skip | This only works if you have a password that starts with A, B, C, or D and if the second letter in the password appears earlier in the alphabet than the fourth letter. If so, switch the second and fourth letters in the password. Use the new password to start at a level one higher than the original. |

## ADVENTURES OF LOLO 2   (Wii)

### NEW DIFFICULTY LEVELS

| PASSWORD | EFFECT |
|---|---|
| PPHP | Floor 01, Room 1 |
| PHPK | Floor 01, Room 2 |
| PQPD | Floor 01, Room 3 |
| PVPT | Floor 01, Room 4 |
| PRPJ | Floor 01, Room 5 |
| PZPC | Floor 02, Room 1 |
| PGPG | Floor 02, Room 2 |
| PCPZ | Floor 02, Room 3 |
| PLPY | Floor 02, Room 4 |
| PBPM | Floor 02, Room 5 |
| PYPL | Floor 03, Room 1 |
| PMPB | Floor 03, Room 2 |
| PJPR | Floor 03, Room 3 |
| PTPV | Floor 03, Room 4 |
| PDPQ | Floor 03, Room 5 |
| PKPH | Floor 04, Room 1 |
| HPPP | Floor 04, Room 2 |
| HHKK | Floor 04, Room 3 |
| HQKD | Floor 04, Room 4 |
| HVKT | Floor 04, Room 5 |
| HRKJ | Floor 05, Room 1 |
| HBKM | Floor 05, Room 2 |
| HLKY | Floor 05, Room 3 |
| HCKZ | Floor 05, Room 4 |
| HGKG | Floor 05, Room 5 |
| HZKC | Floor 06, Room 1 |
| HYKL | Floor 06, Room 2 |
| HMKB | Floor 06, Room 3 |
| HJKR | Floor 06, Room 4 |
| HTKV | Floor 06, Room 5 |

| HDKQ | Floor 07, Room 1 |
|------|------------------|
| HKKH | Floor 07, Room 2 |
| QPKP | Floor 07, Room 3 |
| QHDK | Floor 07, Room 4 |
| QQDD | Floor 07, Room 5 |
| QVDT | Floor 08, Room 1 |
| QRDJ | Floor 08, Room 2 |
| QBDM | Floor 08, Room 3 |
| QLDY | Floor 08, Room 4 |
| QCDZ | Floor 08, Room 5 |
| QGDG | Floor 09, Room 1 |
| QZDC | Floor 09, Room 2 |
| QYDL | Floor 09, Room 3 |
| QMDB | Floor 09, Room 4 |
| QJDR | Floor 09, Room 5 |
| QTDV | Floor 10, Room 1 |
| QDDQ | Floor 10, Room 2 |
| QKDH | Floor 10, Room 3 |
| VPDP | Floor 10, Room 4 |
| VHTK | Floor 10, Room 5 |
| VQTD | Last Level |

## AFTER BURNER CLIMAX (PlayStation 3)

### UNLOCKABLE

| UNLOCKABLE | HOW TO UNLOCK |
|------------|---------------|
| Clouds of Twilight | Finish stage 9A or 9B with at least 4 stars. |
| Golden Valley | Finish stage 5 with at least 4 stars. |
| After Burner Helmet | Complete your Medal Collection. |
| After Burner Logo T-Shirt (females) | Unlock all Ex Options. |
| After Burner Logo T-Shirt (males) | Unlock all Ex Options. |

### EX OPTIONS

Meet the following conditions during Arcade Mode to unlock these special settings in EX Options. They can only be used in Arcade Mode.

| UNLOCKABLE | HOW TO UNLOCK |
|------------|---------------|
| Aircraft Count: 1 | Play a Secret Stage five times. |
| Aircraft Count: 5 | Play a Secret Stage one time. |
| Aircraft Count: 9 | Play a Secret Stage three times. |
| Aircraft Speed: Fast | Play three different branched stages (A/B). |
| Aircraft Speed: Slow | Play all eight branched stages (A/B). |
| Armor: 1% | Get a down rate of over 70% 20 times. |
| Armor: Half Damage | Get a down rate of over 70% 10 times. |
| Armor: No Damage | Get a down rate of over 70% 50 times. |
| Auto-Missiles: On | Reach ending A. |
| Climax Gauge Recovery: Fast | Activate Climax Mode 50 times. |
| Climax Gauge Recovery: Free | Activate Climax Mode 200 times. |
| Climax Gauge Recovery: Slow | Activate Climax Mode 100 times. |
| Combo Window: Free | Get a combo totaling 3,000. |
| Combo Window: Long | Get a combo totaling 1,000. |
| Credits: 5 | Get a Game Over one time. |

| Credits: 7 | Get a Game Over three times. |
|---|---|
| Credits: 9 | Get a Game Over five times. |
| Credits: Free | Get a Game Over 10 times. |
| Display: No Info | Get a score of over 2,000,000 points in one game. |
| Display: No Smoke (All) | Get a score of over 1,000,000 points in one game. |
| Display: No Smoke (Explosions) | Get a score of over 800,000 points in one game. |
| Display: No Smoke (Missiles) | Get a score of over 600,000 points in one game. |
| Enemy Attack: 1 Level Down | Shoot down 1,000 enemies. |
| Enemy Attack: 2 Levels Down | Shoot down 3,000 enemies. |
| Enemy Attack: 3 Levels Down | Shoot down 5,000 enemies. |
| Enemy Attack: No Attack | Shoot down 10,000 enemies. |
| Gun Power: Down | Shoot down 200 enemies with the gun. |
| Gun Power: Up | Shoot down 50 enemies with the gun. |
| Lock-On: Auto | Reaching the ending 10 times. |
| Lock-On: Large Cursor | Reaching the ending one time. |
| Lock-On: No Cursor | Reaching the ending five times. |
| Missile Recovery: Free | Fire 5,000 missiles. |
| Missile Recovery: Off | Fire 2,000 missiles. |
| Secret Mission: Always | Play Emergency Orders 20 times. |

## AGE OF EMPIRES: MYTHOLOGIES (DS)

### UNLOCKABLES

| UNLOCKABLE | HOW TO UNLOCK |
|---|---|
| Ladon the Lamia | Beat the Greek campaign. |
| Setekh | Beat the Egyptian campaign. |

## AIR CONFLICTS: SECRET WARS (XBOX 360)

### ACHIEVEMENT

| UNLOCKABLE | HOW TO UNLOCK |
|---|---|
| Ace-of-Aces (40) | Kill 100 players in multiplayer |
| All missions (60) | All missions completed |
| Bird Collector (50) | Unlock all planes in single player campaign |
| Blue Max (30) | Kill 5 players in multiplayer without dying |
| Bomber Ace (40) | Destroy 100 ground units in Campaign Game |
| Bullseye (20) | Long range Rocket Kill in Multiplayer |
| Cracking Good Show (50) | Place first in Deathmatch with at least 6 players |
| Fall Blau (40) | Complete Chapter II |
| Fighter Ace (40) | Shoot down 100 aircraft in Campaign Game |
| Good Show (30) | Place in top half in Deathmatch with at least 6 players |
| Great War Officer (40) | Win 5 multiplayer matches with any Great War Team |
| Liberation of Balkans (50) | Complete Chapter VII |
| Lucky Shot (50) | Enemy aircraft shot down in single player with rocket at great range |
| Luftwaffe Officer (40) | Win 5 multiplayer matches with Luftwaffe team |
| Operation Belt (40) | Complete Chapter IV |
| Operation Black (40) | Complete Chapter III |
| Operation Overlord (40) | Complete Chapter V |
| RAF Officer (40) | Win 5 multiplayer matches with RAF team |

| Red Air Force Officer (40) | Win 5 multiplayer matches with Red Air Force team |
| Red Baron (50) | Kill 10 players in multiplayer without dying |
| Rocket Sniper (50) | Extra long range Rocket Kill in Multiplayer |
| Siege of Tobruk (40) | Complete Chapter I |
| Slovak Uprising (50) | Complete Chapter VI |
| Tally Ho! (30) | Play 50 multiplayer matches |

## ALAN WAKE (X8OX 360)

### UNLOCKABLES

| UNLOCKABLE | HOW TO UNLOCK |
| --- | --- |
| Jacket and Scarf (female) | Play the Limited Collector's Edition Bonus Disc. |
| Jacket and Scarf (male) | Play the Limited Collector's Edition Bonus Disc. |
| Nightmare Mode | Successfully complete the game. |

## AIRACE (NDS)

### CLASS AND AIRCRAFT UNLOCKABLES

Compete in the Championship mode of the game to unlock the following classes and aircraft.

| UNLOCKABLE | HOW TO UNLOCK |
| --- | --- |
| Class II—Delta 21 (Vought F4U Corsair) | Complete Class I, Race V |
| Class II—Fatboy (Brewster F2A Buffalo) | Complete Class I, Race V |
| Class II—Sky Warrior (Supermarine Spitfire) | Complete Class I, Race V |
| Class III—Guardian (Mikoyan-Gurevich MiG-17 Fresco) | Complete Class II, Race VI |
| Class III—Interceptor (Messerschmitt Me-262) | Complete Class II, Race VI |
| Class III—Razor (Yakovlev Yak-17 Feather) | Complete Class II, Race VI |

### COURSES

| UNLOCKABLE | HOW TO UNLOCK |
| --- | --- |
| Amazon River (Backward) | Complete Class I, Race III |
| City Streets | Complete Class I, Race I |
| City Streets (Backward) | Complete Class III, Race I |
| Great Canyon | Complete Class II, Race I |
| Great Canyon (Backward) | Complete Class II, Race VI |
| Hangars | Complete Class I, Race V |
| Hangars (Backward) | Complete Class III, Race II |
| Land of the Ice | Complete Class I, Race II |
| Land of the Ice (Backward) | Complete Class II, Race II |
| Storm Drains (Backward) | Complete Class I, Race IV |

## AIR ZONK (Wii)

### CODES

| UNLOCKABLE | HOW TO UNLOCK |
| --- | --- |
| Expert Mode | On the Configuration screen, hold ⬆ and press SELECT |
| Sound Test | Hold ① and ② and SELECT as you turn on the game |

## ALEX KIDD IN THE ENCHANTED CASTLE (Wii)

### SKIP BOSS SEQUENCES

| UNLOCKABLE | HOW TO UNLOCK |
| --- | --- |
| Skip Boss Sequences | Wait until the conversation with the boss has ended. After that, Press START to get to the Options screen, then press START again and you should skip the sequence. |

## ALEX RIDER: STORMBREAKER (DS)

Enter the password screen from the main menu and input the following.

| PASSWORD | EFFECT |
| --- | --- |
| JESSICA PARKER | Allows you to purchase black belt |
| 6943059 | Allows you to purchase disk 6 after completing game |
| VICTORIA PARR | Allows you to purchase M16 badge |
| RENATO CELANI | Allows you to purchase the fugu |
| SARYL HIRSCH | Allows you to purchase the sunglasses |
| 9785711 | Allows you to select level HARD |
| 4298359 | Everything at shop is at half price! |
| 9603717 | Gallery is added to Secret mode |
| 5204025 | Get 10,000 spy points |
| 6894098 | Outfit change is added to Secret mode |

## ALICE IN WONDERLAND (DS)

### DGAMER HONORS + DGAMER AVATAR UNLOCKABLES

Before you begin the game, set up a DGamer profile and create an avatar in off-line mode. Go back to the game once you're done creating your avatar. As you play through the game, you'll unlock "Honors" and gain Alice-themed costumes and gear for your DGamer avatar by completing certain tasks during the game.

| UNLOCKABLE | HOW TO UNLOCK |
| --- | --- |
| Alice Dress/Alice Armor | Gain all pieces of the Magic Armor. |
| Caterpillar Outfit | Have Absolem join your team. |
| Cheshire Outfit | Have the Cheshire Cat join your team. |
| Dormouse Coat | Enter "3676" at Password screen. |
| Hatter Outfit | Have the Hatter Join your team. |
| Living Oraculum | Unlock every chapter. |
| Puzzle Master | Find every map piece/explore all map locations. |
| Red Guard Outfit | Defeat one of the tougher, armed Red Guards for the first time. |
| Rushed Rabbit | Defeat 50 enemies using McTwisp's Slow Down Ability. |
| Savior of Underland | Beat the Jabberwocky! |
| Stayne Eyepatch | Defeat Stayne Twice. |
| Stayne Mantle | Defeat Stayne Once. |
| Vorpal Sword | Find the Vorpal Sword. |
| Weird, Wise, Malicious | Gain the remaining three characters in your party. |
| White Rabbit Jacket | Complete Chapter One. |

## ALICE: MADNESS RETURNS (XBOX 360)

### UNLOCKABLE

Dresses are unlocked after completing each chapter.

| UNLOCKABLE | HOW TO UNLOCK |
| --- | --- |
| Classic (Regain health when shrunk) | Complete Infernal Train (Chapter 6) |
| Misstitched (Shrink Sense duration is doubled) | Complete The Dollhouse (Chapter 5) |
| Royal Suit (Health limited to 4 Roses total) | Complete Queensland (Chapter 4) |
| Silk Maiden (Enemies drop twice as many Teeth) | Complete Oriental Grove (Chapter 3) |
| Siren (Enemies drop twice as many Roses) | Complete Deluded Depths (Chapter 2) |
| Steamdress (Breakables drop more Teeth and Roses) | Complete Hatter's Domain (Chapter 1) |
| New Game + | Complete the game on any difficulty level. |

## ALIEN CRUSH (Wii)

### BONUS

| UNLOCKABLE | HOW TO UNLOCK |
|---|---|
| 1 Million Points + Bonus Ball | Get to the bonus round with skulls and green aliens. Kill everything except for one skull. Keep going until a pterodactyl appears. Hit the pterodactyl with the ball to get a million points and a bonus ball once the stage is cleared. |

## ALIEN VS. PREDATOR (XBOX 360)

### SKINS

Reach the indicated rank to unlock each skin.

| UNLOCKABLE | HOW TO UNLOCK |
|---|---|
| Claw (Predator) | Obtain Rank 03. |
| Connor (Marine) | Obtain Rank 05. |
| Gibson (Marine) | Obtain Rank 02. |
| Hunter (Predator) | Obtain Rank 16. |
| Johnson (Marine) | Obtain Rank 22. |
| Moss (Marine) | Obtain Rank 13. |
| Nethead (Alien) | Obtain Rank 34. |
| Praetorian (Alien) | Obtain Rank 19. |
| Ridged (Alien) | Obtain Rank 10. |
| Rookie (Marine) | Obtain Rank 28. |
| Spartan (Predator) | Obtain Rank 31. |
| Stalker (Predator) | Obtain Rank 07. |
| Warrior Dome (Alien) | Obtain Rank 04. |
| Wolf (Predator) | Obtain Rank 25. |

## ALONE IN THE DARK: INFERNO (PlayStation 3)

### CODES

Enter the following code (combination of Action Buttons and D-Pad) in the game, when in third-person view and without anything in the hands. Entering the same code again will disable the Infinite Ammo Cheat.

| EFFECT | CODE |
|---|---|
| Infinite Ammo Enabled | ▲,●,⇩,■,↑,→,↓,←,▲,■,×,●,↑,←,↓,→ |

## ALTERED BEAST (Wii)

### CODES

Enter these on the title screen.

| UNLOCKABLE | HOW TO UNLOCK |
|---|---|
| Beast Select | Hold Ⓐ+Ⓑ+Ⓒ+✛ and then press START |
| Character Kicks Credits | When the credits are being displayed on the screen after you have beaten the game, you can control your character to kick away the credited names |
| Continue from Last Stage Played | Hold Ⓐ and press SELECT after a Game Over |
| Level Select | Press Ⓑ and START |
| Sound Test | Hold Ⓐ+Ⓒ+✛ and then press START |

## AMPED 3 (XBOX 360)

At the Main menu, go into Options, then into the Cheats menu to enter this code.

| UNLOCKABLE | CODE |
|---|---|
| All Sleds | ⑉, Ⓧ, ⑉, ♀, ⬥, ⓁⒷ, ⑉, ⑉, Ⓨ, Ⓧ |

## TROPHIES

| UNLOCKABLE | HOW TO UNLOCK |
| --- | --- |
| Bronze - Bad Ending | Fail to defeat MYU before Song Completes. |
| Bronze - Battle Enthusiast | Fight and win 100 battles. |
| Bronze - Battle Lover | Fight and win 200 battles. |
| Bronze - Battle Maniac | Fight and win 300 battles. |
| Bronze - Chained Finnel | Finnel Cosmosphere L5 Event. |
| Bronze - Coward | Run from battle 100 times. |
| Bronze - Destroyer | Empty the Encounter Bar 25 times. |
| Bronze - Finnel Friendship | 30% of Finnel's Cosmosphere Completed. |
| Bronze - Finnel Love Love | 60% of Finnel's Cosmosphere Completed. |
| Bronze - Finnel Love Love 1 | Phase 2 Finnel route Event. |
| Bronze - Finnel Love Love 2 | Phase 3 Finnel route Event. Must have MAXED Hearts! |
| Bronze - Finnel Normal End | View Finnel's Normal Ending. |
| Bronze - Finnel's Master | 100% of Finnel's Cosmosphere Completed. |
| Bronze - Frightened | Tilia Binary Field Game L3 Event. |
| Bronze - Frustration | Collect Max DP for any one of the girls. |
| Bronze - Game to a certain extent | Clock over 100 hours of game time. |
| Bronze - Hot Springs Panic! | Phase 2 Event. |
| Bronze - Longing for | Tilia Binary Field Game L2 and L3 Event. |
| Bronze - Older Sister Sakiya | Saki Cosmosphere L9 Event. |
| Bronze - On Stage! | Saki Cosmosphere L4 Event. |
| Bronze - Phase 1 Clear | Complete Phase 1 of the story. |
| Bronze - Phase 2 Clear | Complete Phase 2 of the story. |
| Bronze - Pregnant!? | Saki Cosmosphere L8 Event, Auto if Saki is chosen girl (3 hearts) or accept her love. |
| Bronze - Reunion with the children | Phase 2 Event. |
| Bronze - Saki Friendship | 30% of Saki's Cosmosphere Completed. |
| Bronze - Saki Love Love | 60% of Saki's Cosmosphere Completed. |
| Bronze - Saki Love Love 1 | Phase 2 Saki route Event. |
| Bronze - Saki Love Love 2 | Phase 3 Saki route Event. Must have MAXED Hearts! |
| Bronze - Saki Normal End | View Saki's Normal Ending. |
| Bronze - Saki Strips! | Saki Cosmosphere L3 or L4 Event. |
| Bronze - Saki's Groom | 100% of Saki's Cosmosphere Completed. |
| Bronze - Salapator's Wedding | Phase 1 Event. |
| Bronze - Saving often is necessary don't you think? | Save the game 100 times. |
| Bronze - Singing to create a new world | Finnel Cosmosphere L9 Event. |
| Bronze - Soma Uninstall | Phase 2 Event. |
| Bronze - Soma VS Soma | Finnel Cosmosphere L7 Event. |
| Bronze - Synthesis Beginner | Synthesize 10 unique items |
| Bronze - Synthesis Expert | Synthesize 60 unique items |
| Bronze - Synthesis Intermediate | Synthesize 30 unique items |

A
B
C
D
E
F
G
H
I
J
K
L
M
N
O
P
Q
R
S
T
U
V
W
X
Y
Z

| Bronze - The Long Missing Heart | Saki Cosmosphere L6 Event. |
|---|---|
| Bronze - Tilia Friendship | 30% of Tilia's Binary Field Game Completed. |
| Bronze - Tilia Normal End | View Tilia's Normal Ending. |
| Bronze - Tilia's Husband | 100% of Tilia's Binary Field Game Completed. |
| Bronze - Tillia Love Love 1 | Tilia Phase 3 Event & Accepted her love. |
| Bronze - Tlia Love Love | 60% of Tilia's Binary Field Game Completed. |
| Bronze - Treasure Hunter | Found and Opened all Treasure Chests. |
| Bronze - Truth | Tilia Binary Field Game L3 Event. |
| Bronze - Wailing | Finnel Cosmosphere L8 Event. |
| Bronze - Wealthy | Obtain Maximum Gold. |
| Bronze - Yurishica's Great Advance!! | Finnel Cosmosphere L3 Optional Event. |
| Gold - Purge Festival | In battle, purge heroine 3 levels, and all 3 members have used their super wazas. |
| Platinum - Ar tonelico thank you once again and next time | Collect all other Trophies |
| Silver - Breeder | Get to LV99 for all party members. |
| Silver - Cocona End | View Cocona's Ending. |
| Silver - Finnel True End | View Finnel's True Ending |
| Silver - Oyaki Master | Press Select during Cosmosphere dialouge 100 times. |
| Silver - Saki True End | View Saki's True Ending. |
| Silver - Tilia True End | View Tilia's True Ending. |
| Silver - What's wrong with being a pervert!? | Purge heroine 3 levels at once. (On red beat, with animation) |

### SECRETS

Once you are able to access the Cosmosphere, dive into it. Inside the cosmosphere, Hold L2 and press the triangle button to access the debug menu. In this menu you are able to open flag events, change character levels and parameters, even add money and create clear game files.

## ARMY OF TWO  (PlayStation 3)

### CODES

During gameplay press the following:

| EFFECT | CODE |
|---|---|
| Unlimited Life and Ammo | ▲, ▲, ✕, ✕, L2, R2, R1, R2, ●, ■ |

## ART OF FIGHTING  (Wii)

### CHARACTER UNLOCKABLES

| UNLOCKABLE | HOW TO UNLOCK |
|---|---|
| Mr. Big | Get to Mr. Big in 1-player mode and lose the match. Restart the game and Mr. Big will now be unlocked in 2-player mode. |
| Mr. Karate | Get to Mr. Karate in 1-player mode and lose the match. Restart the game and Mr. Karate will now be unlocked in 2-player mode. |

## ASSASSIN'S CREED: BROTHERHOOD  (XBOX 360)

### CAPES

| UNLOCKABLE | HOW TO UNLOCK |
|---|---|
| Auditore Cape | Rebuild Rome |
| Borgia Cape | Collect all Borgia Flags |

| Medici Cape | You need to get to Level 30 on the "Assassin's Creed: Project Legacy" Facebook game |
| Venetian Cape | You need to get to Level 30 on the "Assassin's Creed: Project Legacy" Facebook game |

## COSTUMES

| UNLOCKABLE | HOW TO UNLOCK |
| --- | --- |
| Raiden's Costume | Complete all of the tasks in the Animus 2.0 training mode |

## MEMORY EXTRAS

When you complete a memory sequence, you will be awarded with a cheat that you can activate when you are replaying a completed memory.

| UNLOCKABLE | HOW TO UNLOCK |
| --- | --- |
| Buns of Steel | 100% sync on Sequence 2 |
| Desmond Everywhere | 100% sync on Sequence 8 |
| Killing Spree | 100% sync on Sequence 3 |
| Ride the Unicorn | 100% sync on Sequence 1 |
| Sisterhood | 100% sync on Sequence 4 |
| Ultimate Guild | 100% sync on Sequence 5 |
| Unlimited Assassin Signals | 100% sync on Sequence 6 |

## GUILD REWARDS

By leveling up with the guilds, you can obtain certain items for Ezio to use. They will appear in Ezio's hideout.

| UNLOCKABLE | HOW TO UNLOCK |
| --- | --- |
| Assassin's Guild Crest | Complete all Assassins Guild challenges. |
| Bartolomeo's Axe | Get each guild to Level 3 |
| Courtesans Guild Crest | Get each guild to Level 2 |
| La Volpe's Bite | Get each guild to Level 3 |
| Maria's Dagger | Get each guild to Level 3 |
| Mercenaries Guild Crest | Get each guild to Level 2 |
| Sword of Altair | Complete all Assassins Guild challenges |
| Thieves Guild Crest | Get each guild to Level 2 |

## UPLAY UNLOCKABLES

| UNLOCKABLE | HOW TO UNLOCK |
| --- | --- |
| Altair armor skin for Ezio | Obtain 20 Uplay points and use them via Uplay account |
| Altair skin | Obtain 20 Uplay points and use them via Uplay account |
| Assassin's Creed Brotherhood Theme | Gain 10 Uplay points and spend them |
| Florentine Noble in-game skin | Gain 20 Uplay points and spend them |
| Hellequin (multiplayer character) | Obtain 40 Uplay points |
| Upgrade hidden pistol ammo capacity | Gain 30 Uplay points and spend them |

## ASSASSIN'S CREED: REVELATIONS (XBOX 360)

### UNLOCKABLE

The following are unlocked as you collect Animus Data Fragments in the game.

| UNLOCKABLE | HOW TO UNLOCK |
| --- | --- |
| "Capped" Achievement | Collect 100 Fragments |
| Animus Data Fragments appear on Map | Collect 50 Fragments |
| Desmond Memory Sequence 1 | Collect 5 Fragments |
| Desmond Memory Sequence 2 | Collect 10 Fragments |

| Desmond Memory Sequence 3 | Collect 15 Fragments |
|---|---|
| Desmond Memory Sequence 4 | Collect 20 Fragments |
| Desmond Memory Sequence 5 | Collect 30 Fragments |
| Ishak Pasha's Memoir Pages available to buy at Book Shop | Collect 25 Fragments |

## UNLOCKABLE

Complete the following to unlock these.

| UNLOCKABLE | HOW TO UNLOCK |
|---|---|
| Altaïr's Sword | Complete the Set 3 Assassin Challenges |
| Broadsword | Complete the Set 3 Mercenary Challenges |
| Buns of Steel | Complete Sequence 2 with 100% sync |
| Calling All Assassins | Complete Sequence 5 with 100% sync |
| Desmon Miles skin | Complete the Desmond memory gates |
| Hired Mercenaries stop beggars | Complete the Set 2 Mercenary Challenges |
| Hired Romanies poison guards | Complete the Set 2 Romani Challenges |
| Hired Thieves pickpocket akçe | Complete the Set 2 Thief Challenges |
| Infinite Ammunition | Complete Sequence 7 with 100% sync |
| Ishak Pasha's Armor | Collect all 10 Memoir Pages |
| Killing Spree | Complete Sequence 3 with 100% sync |
| Ottoman Mace | Complete the Set 3 Thief Challenges |
| Permanent Secrecy | Complete Sequence 6 with 100% sync |
| Romani Stiletto | Complete the Set 3 Romani Challenges |
| The Old Eagle Outfit | Complete Sequence 8 with 100% sync |
| Ultimate Guild | Complete Sequence 4 with 100% sync |

## ACHIEVEMENT

| UNLOCKABLE | HOW TO UNLOCK |
|---|---|
| A Friend Indeed (20) | Complete all Faction Creed Challenges from a single faction. |
| Achiever (10) | Complete a Challenge (Multiplayer). |
| Almost Flying (20) | Parachute directly from the top of the Galata Tower to the golden horn. |
| Are You Desmond Miles? (20) | Complete Desmond Sequence 5. |
| Armchair General (20) | Control all cities (except Rhodes) simultaneously in the Mediterranian Defense game. |
| Best Served Cold (20) | Complete DNA Sequence 1. |
| Bully (20) | Find and beat up Duccio. |
| Capped (20) | Collect all animus data fragments. |
| Craft Maniac (20) | Craft 30 bombs. |
| Escape To New York (20) | Complete Desmond Sequence 3. |
| Explorer (20) | Finish a session of each game mode (Multiplayer). |
| Fast Fingers (20) | Loot 50 dead guards with thief looting. |
| Fond Memories (20) | Achieve 100% Synchronization in all Sequences. |
| Holy Wisdom (20) | Complete the Hagia Sofia challenge level. |
| I can see you (20) | Kill 5 guards while under the cover of a smoke screen bomb. |
| Iron Curtain (20) | Perform a perfect den defense without using the cannon. |
| Istanbul and Constantinople (20) | Complete DNA Sequence 2. |
| Lightning Strikes (20) | Kill 5 guards in 5 seconds using only your hidden blades. |

| | |
|---|---|
| Looking Good (10) | Customize a PERSONA (Multiplayer). |
| Make the Headlines (30) | Obtain 12 different Accolades (Multiplayer). |
| Mastering the Art (30) | Earn the INCOGNITO bonus (Multiplayer). |
| Monster's Dance (20) | Have a guard incapacitate 3 civilians while he's poisoned. |
| Mosh Pit (20) | Have 10 guards poisoned at the same time. |
| Mouse Trap (20) | Kill 5 guards with a scaffold after they have been stunned by caltrops. |
| My Protégé (20) | Have one trainee reach the rank of Master Assassin. |
| Old Boss, New Boss (20) | Complete DNA Sequence 7. |
| Overkiller (20) | Assassinate 50 guards with the hidden blade. |
| Priorities (20) | Complete DNA Sequence 8. |
| Pyromaniac (20) | Complete all Bomb Missions. |
| Revelations (50) | Complete DNA Sequence 9. |
| Sage (20) | Collect all available books. |
| Seal the Deal (20) | Complete DNA Sequence 3. |
| Show-Off (20) | Parachute onto a zipline. |
| Silent But Deadly (20) | Kill three guards simultaneously with only throwing knives. |
| Spider Assassin (20) | Climb Hagia Sofia, from the ground to the pinnacle, in under 25 seconds. |
| Successes and Failures (20) | Complete DNA Sequence 6. |
| Tactician (30) | Score at least 2500 points in a session (Multiplayer). |
| Tax Evasion (10) | Get your money back from a Templar tax collector. |
| The Early Years (20) | Complete Desmond Sequence 1. |
| The Mentor (20) | Have seven trainees reach the rank of Master Assassin. |
| The Plot Thickens (20) | Complete DNA Sequence 5. |
| The Prince (20) | Complete DNA Sequence 4. |
| The Reluctant Assassin (20) | Complete Desmond Sequence 2. |
| The Rotten Apple (20) | Complete Desmond Sequence 4. |
| The Way I Like It (20) | Edit your TEMPLAR PROFILE to change your title, emblem, and patron (Multiplayer). |
| There Is No I in Team (20) | Win a session of a team mode (Multiplayer). |
| Tools of the Templar (10) | Purchase your first ABILITY in the Abstergo Store (Multiplayer). |
| True Templar (20) | Reach level 20 (Multiplayer). |
| Worth A Thousand Words (20) | Collect all of Ishak Pasha's memoir pages. |

## ATELIER TOTORI: THE ADVENTURER OF ARLAND (PlayStation 3)

### TROPHY

| UNLOCKABLE | HOW TO UNLOCK |
|---|---|
| A New Journey (Silver) | See Marc's Ending. |
| Adventurer BFFs (Silver) | See Mimi's Ending. |
| Alchemy Restaurant (Gold) | With limitless funding, Totori opens a restaurant. |
| Ambushed (Silver) | View the event where Melvia and Ceci are cornered. |
| Arise, McVellion! (Silver) | View the event where McVellion activates. |
| Aristocratic Love (Silver) | View the event where Mimi tries to cheer Totori up. |

| | |
|---|---|
| **Bad End (Bronze)** | Watched the bad ending. |
| **Catch of the Day (Bronze)** | Haul in a 'fishy fishy' from Alanya. |
| **Chivalrous Defender (Silver)** | View the event where Gino learns his strongest skill. |
| **Cuteness Swarm! (Bronze)** | See the event detailing Chim's birth. |
| **Fishing Festival (Gold)** | Hold the swimsuit contest. |
| **Haunted Doll? (Silver)** | Learn the truth about Pamela. |
| **Indecisive Knight (Silver)** | See Sterk's Ending. |
| **Legendary 'Fish' (Silver)** | Learned the true nature of the 'Guardian.' |
| **Legendary Drunkard (Silver)** | Went with Tiffani and Filly to have a drink. |
| **Like the Flash (Bronze)** | Get rescued on your way to Arland. |
| **Monstrous Power (Bronze)** | View Melvia's introduction. |
| **Normal End (Silver)** | Watched the normal ending. |
| **Promises (Silver)** | See Melvia's Ending. |
| **Receive All Other Trophies (Platinum)** | Received All Other Trophies. |
| **Shouting Match (Bronze)** | Witness Cordelia and some other girl arguing. |
| **Still a Child (Silver)** | View the event where Ceci embraces Totori. |
| **The Hardest Workers (Silver)** | See Chim's Ending. |
| **Tragic Discovery (Gold)** | Learn the final whereabouts of Totori's mother. |
| **True End (Gold)** | Watched the true ending. |
| **Two Masters (Silver)** | See Gino's Ending. |
| **Unlikely Party (Silver)** | Reminisce with Rorona and her friends at Iksel's restaurant. |
| **Usual Scenery (Bronze)** | Watched the opening event. |
| **Who's the Teacher? (Silver)** | See Rorona's Ending. |

## BAND HERO (XBOX 360)

### CODES

Select "Input Cheats" under the Options menu. G = Green, R = Red, Y = Yellow, B = Blue.

| EFFECT | CODE |
|---|---|
| Air Instruments | B,Y,B,R,R,Y,G,Y |
| All HO/POs | R,G,B,G,B,G,R,G |
| Always Slide | Y,G,Y,Y,Y,R,B,R |
| Auto Kick | Y,G,Y,B,B,R,B,R |
| Electrika Steel Unlocked | B,B,R,Y,R,Y,B,B |
| Focus Mode | Y,Y,G,G,R,R,B,B |
| HUD-Free Mode | G,R,G,R,Y,B,G,R |
| Invisible Characters | G,R,Y,G,Y,B,Y,G |
| Most Characters Unlocked | B,Y,G,Y,R,G,R,Y |
| Performance Mode | Y,Y,B,G,B,R,R,R |

### BONUS CHARACTERS

Complete the mission on Tour to unlock the listed characters.

| UNLOCKABLE | HOW TO UNLOCK |
|---|---|
| Adam Levine | Successfully complete the Maroon 5 "She Will Be Loved" gig. |
| Adrian Young | Successfully complete the No Doubt "Don't Speak" gig. |
| Frankenrocker | Successfully complete the Diamond Bonus Challenge for the Fall Out Boy "Sugar, We're Goin' Down" gig. |
| Gwen Stefani | Successfully complete the No Doubt "Don't Speak" gig. |
| Shadow Character | Successfully complete the Gold Bonus Challenge for the David Bowie "Let's Dance" gig. |
| Taylor Swift | Successfully complete the Taylor Swift "Love Story" gig. |
| Tom Dumont | Successfully complete the No Doubt "Don't Speak" gig. |
| Tony Kanal | Successfully complete the No Doubt "Don't Speak" gig. |

## BANJO-KAZOOIE: NUTS & BOLTS (XBOX 360)

### UNLOCKABLES

After beating the game, L.O.G. will give you a Banjo Head Vehicle. The Banjo Head Vehicle can be loaded from the L.O.G's choice option.

## BASES LOADED (Wii)

### PASSWORDS

| PASSWORD | EFFECT |
|---|---|
| LFBDJHE | Boston, one game away from the World Series |
| PFACNHK | DC, one game away from the World Series |
| CHXAACC | Game 162 |
| LNADJPD | Hawaii, one game away from the World Series |
| CBIDNEP | Jersey, last game of the World Series |
| LFADNHH | Jersey, one game away from the World Series |
| PNCBNHD | Kansas, one game away from the World Series |
| PFBCNPD | LA, one game away from the World Series |

| PFCANHK | Miami, one game away from the World Series |
| PFDAJHH | New York, one game away from the World Series |
| LNDAJPD | Omaha, one game away from the World Series |
| JAELECO | Password for Pennant, must have selected "Pennant" option from menu |
| LFDBJHE | Philly, one game away from the World Series |
| Select Pennant Mode and Enter JALECO as Password | Skip to the last team |
| LNCBJPD | Texas, one game away from the World Series |
| LNBCJPD | Utah, one game away from the World Series |

### OTHER ACTIONS

| ACTION | HOW TO ENACT |
| --- | --- |
| Don't Get Ejected During a Fight | Continually press Ⓑ during the fight |
| Hitter Charges the Mound and Gets Ejected | After the 3rd inning, bean the 3rd or 4th hitter in the lineup |

## BATMAN: ARKHAM ASYLUM (PlayStation 3)

### UNLOCKABLES

| UNLOCKABLE | HOW TO UNLOCK |
| --- | --- |
| Armored-suit Batman | Complete the game. Can only be used in Challenge Mode. |

## BATMAN: ARKHAM CITY (PlayStation 3)

### TROPHY

| UNLOCKABLE | HOW TO UNLOCK |
| --- | --- |
| 50x Combon (Bronze) | Complete a combo of 50 moves (any play mode, any character) |
| Acid Bath (Bronze) | Save the damsel, but is she in distress? |
| Aggravated Assault (Bronze) | Stop all assaults in Arkham City |
| AR Knight (Silver) | Complete all augmented reality training exercises |
| Bargaining Chip (Bronze) | Reunite the separated couple |
| Brainteaser (Silver) | Rescue the fifth hostage from Riddler |
| Broken Toys (Silver) | Destroy it all |
| Bronze Revenge (Bronze) | Obtain 24 medals on the original Arkham City ranked maps (as Batman) |
| Campaign Bronze (Bronze) | Obtain 36 medals on the original Arkham City campaigns (as Batman) |
| Campaign Gold (Silver) | Obtain all 108 medals on the original Arkham City campaigns (as Batman) |
| Campaign Silver (Bronze) | Obtain 72 medals on the original Arkham City campaigns (as Batman) |
| Catch (Bronze) | Find someone to play remote Batarang catch with |
| Chimney Sweep (Bronze) | There is only one way in |
| Communication Breakdown (Bronze) | Clear the airwaves |
| Contract Terminated (Silver) | Stop the contract operative |
| Conundrum (Bronze) | Rescue the first hostage from Riddler |
| Dial Z For Murder (Silver) | Stop the phone booth killer |
| Distress Flare (Bronze) | Answer the call for help |
| Exit Stage Right (Silver) | All the world is a stage |
| Flawless Freeflow Fighter 2.0 (Bronze) | Complete one combat challenge without taking damage (any character) |

| | |
|---|---|
| **Forensic Expert (Bronze)** | Collect enough evidence to locate the gun for hire |
| **Freefall (Bronze)** | Don't look down |
| **Fully Loaded (Bronze)** | Collect all of Batman's gadgets and upgrades |
| **Gadget Attack (Bronze)** | Use 5 different Quickfire gadgets in one fight (any play mode) |
| **Genius (Silver)** | Rescue all the hostages from Riddler |
| **Ghost Train (Silver)** | Fight for survival |
| **Gladiator (Bronze)** | Last man standing |
| **Gold Revenge (Silver)** | Obtain all 72 medals on the original Arkham City ranked maps (as Batman) |
| **Gotham Base Jumper (Bronze)** | Jump off the tallest building in Arkham City and glide for 1 minute without touching the ground. |
| **Hide And Seek (Silver)** | A deadly game of hide and seek |
| **I'm Batman (Bronze)** | Become the Bat |
| **Intellectual (Bronze)** | Rescue the fourth hostage from Riddler |
| **IQ Test (Bronze)** | Solve the first riddle |
| **Lost And Found (Bronze)** | Uncover the secret of Arkham City |
| **Mastermind (Bronze)** | Rescue the second hostage from Riddler |
| **Mystery Stalker (Bronze)** | Reveal the mystery watcher |
| **One-Armed Bandit (Bronze)** | Hammer the point home |
| **Pay Your Respects (Bronze)** | A moment of remembrance |
| **Perfect Freeflow 2.0 (Bronze)** | Perform a perfect combo including all of Batman's combat moves (any play mode) |
| **Perfect Knight - Day 2 (Gold)** | Complete every challenge in Arkham City - Main Story, Side Missions, Upgrades, Collectables, New Game Plus and Riddlers Revenge (as Batman) |
| **Platinum (Platinum)** | Congratulations! |
| **Puzzler (Bronze)** | Rescue the third hostage from Riddler |
| **Ring Ring (Bronze)** | Answer a ringing phone |
| **Sandstorm (Silver)** | We are legion |
| **Savior (Bronze)** | Save the medical volunteers |
| **Serial Killer (Silver)** | Track down the serial killer |
| **Silver Revenge (Bronze)** | Obtain 48 medals on the original Arkham City ranked maps (as Batman) |
| **Stop the Clock (Bronze)** | Time is running out |
| **Storyteller (Bronze)** | Have 12 murderous dates with Calendar Man |
| **Twice Nightly (Silver)** | Complete New Game Plus |
| **Wrecking Ball (Silver)** | Stop the unstoppable |

## BATTLE CITY (Wii)

### STAGE SELECT

| UNLOCKABLE | HOW TO UNLOCK |
|---|---|
| Stage Select | When you start the game and see the screen with "Stage 1," press Ⓐ and Ⓑ to choose any stage you want. |

## BATTLEFIELD 3 (XBOX 360)

### ACHIEVEMENT

| UNLOCKABLE | HOW TO UNLOCK |
|---|---|
| 1st Loser (30) | Finish as 2nd MVP in a ranked match |
| Army of Darkness (30) | Shoot out the 4 lights with 4 bullets in Night Shift |
| Army of Two (50) | Complete all co-op missions on Hard |

| | |
|---|---|
| **Between a rock and a hard place (15)** | Beat Solomon, flawlessly, in The Great Destroyer |
| **Bullseye (20)** | Reach and save the hostages without alerting any enemies in Drop 'em Like Liquid |
| **Butterfly (25)** | Take down the jet in one attempt in Rock And A Hard Place |
| **Car Lover (20)** | Complete the mission without losing a humvee in Operation Exodus |
| **Colonel (50)** | Achieve rank 45 |
| **Decorated (50)** | Obtain one of each ribbon in the game |
| **FlashForward (10)** | Completed Semper Fidelis |
| **In the nick of time (20)** | Disarm the bomb in under 20 seconds in The Eleventh Hour |
| **Infantry Efficiency (30)** | Obtain all 4 weapon efficiency ribbons |
| **Involuntary Euthanasia (25)** | Kill the 2 soldiers before the building falls on them in Uprising |
| **It's better than nothing! (30)** | Finish as 3rd MVP in a ranked match |
| **Lock 'n' Load (30)** | Unlock all unique co-op weapons |
| **M.I.A (20)** | Obtain your first enemy Dog Tag |
| **Most Valuable Player (30)** | Finish as MVP in a ranked match |
| **Ninjas (20)** | Reach the VIP without setting off the alarm in Exfiltration |
| **No Escape (30)** | Captured Kaffarov |
| **Not on my watch (25)** | Protect Chaffin from the soldiers in the street in Operation Swordbreaker |
| **Ooh-rah! (30)** | Complete the campaign story |
| **Practice makes perfect (15)** | Headshot each of the targets in the gun range in Kaffarov |
| **Push On (20)** | Reach the garage without going into man-down state in Hit and Run |
| **Roadkill (20)** | Kick the car to kill the soldiers in Uprising |
| **Scrap Metal (25)** | Destroy 6 enemy tanks before reaching the fort in Thunder Run |
| **Semper Fidelis (50)** | Complete the campaign story on Hard |
| **Shock Troop (15)** | Survived the quake |
| **Support Efficiency (30)** | Obtain all 4 support efficiency ribbons |
| **The Professional (30)** | Complete the street chase in Comrades in under 2 minutes 30 seconds without dying |
| **This is the end (20)** | Failed to prevent the attack |
| **Two-rah! (30)** | Complete all co-op missions |
| **Twofor (15)** | Take down 2 enemies with 1 bullet in Night Shift |
| **Untouchable (20)** | Complete the mission without using the fire extinguisher in Fire From The Sky |
| **Vehicle Warfare (30)** | Obtain all 3 vehicle warfare ribbons |
| **Wanted: Dead or Alive (20)** | Captured Al Bashir |
| **What the hell *are* you? (20)** | Take a russian Dog Tag in the forest ambush in Rock And A Hard Place |
| **Where are the other two? (20)** | Found the nuke |
| **You can be my wingman anytime (30)** | Complete Going Hunting in a perfect run |

## BATTLEFIELD: BAD COMPANY (XBOX 360)

### FIND ALL FIVE WEAPONS

| UNLOCKABLE | HOW TO UNLOCK |
|---|---|
| Assault Rifle | Register your old *Battlefield* games at *http://www.veteran.battlefield.com/*. |
| Light Machine Gun | Sign up for the newsletter at *http://www.findallfive.com/*. |
| Semi-Automatic Shotgun | After playing an Online game, login and check your stats at *http://www.findallfive.com/*. |
| Sniper Rifle | Pre-order the game from a participating retailer before June 23rd, 2008. |
| Uzi | Play the "Battlefield: Bad Company Demo" and get to rank 4. (2,300 EXP required to reach rank 4.) |

## BATTLESTATIONS: MIDWAY (XBOX 360)

Enter this code at the mission select screen.

| UNLOCKABLE | CODE |
|---|---|
| Unlock All Levels | Hold ⓡⓑ, ■, ↑, ↖ and push ↘ |

## BAYONETTA (XBOX 360)

### EXTRA COSTUMES

To unlock the extra costumes, you have to beat all chapters on Normal first. Load your Clear Data, go to "Gates of Hell," and then go to "Rodin's Treasure" menu. You'll see a Super Mirror there, which costs 100,000 Halos. Purchase this, and you'll unlock the rest of the costumes (Couture Bullets). To change costumes, press R1 at the Chapter Start screen, go to "Costume Change," and then choose your costume there.

| UNLOCKABLE | HOW TO UNLOCK |
|---|---|
| d'Arc (Jeanne-like costume) | Purchase "Couture Bullet (d'Arc)" at Gates of Hell for 100.000 Halos. |
| Nun | Purchase "Couture Bullet (Nun)" at Gates of Hell for 100,000 Halos. |
| Old | Purchase "Couture Bullet (Old) at Gates of Hell for 100,000 Halos. |
| P.E. Uniform: Types A, B & C are available | Purchase "Couture Bullet (P.E. Uniform)" at Gates of Hell for 100,000 Halos. |
| Queen | Purchase "Couture Bullet (Queen)" at Gates of Hell for 100,000 Halos. |
| Umbra | Purchase "Couture Bullet (Umbra)" at Gates of Hell for 100,000 Halos. |
| Umbran Komachi (Kimono): Type A, B & C are available | Purchase "Super Mirror" at Gates of Hell for 100,000 Halos. |
| Various: Type A (Bikini), B (Bikini) & C (Cheerleader) are available | Purchase "Couture Bullet (Various)" at Gates of Hell for 100,000 Halos. |

## BEJEWELED 2 DELUXE (XBOX 360)

### MODE UNLOCKABLES

| UNLOCKABLE | HOW TO UNLOCK |
|---|---|
| Remove Background Grid | Hold ⓛⓑ ⓛⓣ ⓡⓑ ⓡⓣ then press ❸ |
| Change Jewel Types | Hold ⓛⓑ ⓛⓣ ⓡⓑ ⓡⓣ then press Ⓐ |
| Unlock Cognito Mode | Finish all the puzzles in Puzzle mode. It is okay to look at hints constantly to solve all the puzzles. Cognito mode is basically Puzzle mode with no hints. |
| Finity Mode | Complete 280 levels of Endless mode |
| Hyper Mode | Complete 8 levels of Action mode |
| Twilight Mode | Complete 17 levels of Classic mode |

| Original Mode | Go into Play Game when you first load up the game. Select the Classic, Action, Endless, and Puzzle mode buttons (in that order) at the menu screen repeatedly (so you're basically maneuvering the cursor across the screen clockwise). After several rounds, a window will come up saying "Please Wait," and Original mode will load up. |

## BIONICLE HEROES (Wii)

### SECRET CHARACTER

| UNLOCKABLE | HOW TO UNLOCK |
| --- | --- |
| Vezon | Complete the game once |

## BLACKWATER (XBOX 360)

### ACHIEVEMENT

| UNLOCKABLE | HOW TO UNLOCK |
| --- | --- |
| After Party (5) | Complete all competition maps with 8 players |
| Alamo Compound (5) | Complete Mission 2 |
| Best in Town (60) | Kill all 6 Foreign Fighters on each difficulty |
| Blackwater Operator (60) | Reach experience level 56 |
| Bravo! (20) | Get over 100% accuracy in a combat arena |
| Brought to You By... (5) | Watch the credits from begining to end |
| Cut the Chatter (10) | Find 5 Death Radios |
| Don't Cross This Line (10) | Kill 25 melee attackers before they strike |
| Elite Club (5) | Get Veteran time in a combat arena |
| Figure It Out (10) | Find 5 Limbano Lions |
| Foot First (5) | Complete 100 kick quick-time events |
| Going Pro (10) | Get Pro time in a combat arena |
| Grenade! (20) | Get 200 grenade kills |
| Hat-Trick (5) | Kill 3 enemies with one grenade |
| Here, Hold This... (10) | Get 50 grenade kills |
| Jumping Jack (5) | Complete 100 jump quick-time events |
| Just Normal (40) | Complete all missions on Normal |
| Lion's Den (20) | Find all Limbano Lions |
| No Mercenaries (10) | Kill 5 Foreign Fighters |
| No Score in Sight (5) | Get less than 2,000 points in a combat arena |
| Nothing Thrown (5) | Complete a combat arena without using grenades |
| Nothing's Too Hard (60) | Complete all missions on Hard |
| Off the Air (20) | Find all Death Radios |
| Over Easy (20) | Complete all missions on Easy |
| Overwatch (60) | Fully upgrade Eddi |
| Party Time (5) | Complete a competition map with 8 players |
| Plan B (5) | Get 5 kills with the pistol |
| Propaganda (10) | Find 5 Graffiti |
| Quick Draw (20) | Get 200 kills with the pistol |
| Recon Expert (20) | Discover 50% of the paths in all combat arenas |
| Recon Master (60) | Discover ALL of the paths in the game |
| Recon Recruit (10) | Discover all paths in a combat arena |
| Recruit (5) | Complete the training map |
| Rescue Dila (10) | Complete Mission 5 |
| Riding Shotgun (60) | Fully upgrade Smash |

| Sir, You Forgot Your Hat (20) | Get 200 headshots |
| --- | --- |
| Spray and Pray (40) | Fully upgrade Devon |
| Stop This Madness (20) | Find all Graffiti |
| The Bridge (5) | Complete Mission 3 |
| The Exiled Leader (5) | Complete Mission 4 |
| The Long Way Back (20) | Complete Mission 6 |
| The Red Barrel (5) | Blow up 50 red barrels |
| The Right Person (60) | Fully upgrade Baird |
| This Ain't Your Daddy's Shotgun! (20) | Kill 6 enemies with the shotgun without reloading |
| Tight-Aim (10) | Get 50 headshots |
| Tired Yet? (60) | Complete 1,000 quick-time events |
| Welcome to Harri (5) | Complete Mission 1 |
| What Time? Can't Tell. (40) | Get at least 7,000 points in a combat arena |

## BLAZBLUE: CALAMITY TRIGGER (XBOX 360)

### UNLOCKABLES

| UNLOCKABLE | HOW TO UNLOCK |
| --- | --- |
| True Ending | Individually clear each character's Story Mode. |
| Unlimited Hakumen | Beat Hakumen's Arcade Mode. |
| Unlimited Rachel | Beat Rachel's Arcade Mode. |
| Unlimited Ragna | Beat Ragna's Arcade Mode. |
| Unlimited v-13 | Beat v-13's Arcade Mode. |

### ASTRAL HEAT

Ragna starts with his Astral Heat (finisher), but every other character needs to unlock theirs. Beat their Arcade Mode and they'll get their own.

## BLAZBLUE: CONTINUUM SHIFT (XBOX 360)

### UNLOCKABLES

| UNLOCKABLE | HOW TO UNLOCK |
| --- | --- |
| Mu-12 | Achieve every character's Clear ending in Story Mode, and complete the True Ending. This also unlocks her stage and theme song for use in various game modes. |
| True Ending | Beat Ragna's Story, Jin's Story, Noel's Story, Rachel's Story, Tsubaki's Story, Hakumen's Story, and Hazama's story to unlock the True Ending. |
| Unlimited Characters | To unlock the Unlimited version of a character you must clear Score Attack Mode with that character. |

## BLAZBLUE: CONTINUUM SHIFT II (3DS)

### UNLOCKABLE

| UNLOCKABLE | HOW TO UNLOCK |
| --- | --- |
| Arcade Mode Credits | Beat Arcade Mode |
| Console Credits | Complete the True Ending in Story Mode |
| Extra Story 1: Military Academy | Reach Noel's canon ending in Story Mode. |
| Extra Story 2: Sector Seven | Reach Tager's bad ending in Story Mode. |

### UNLOCKABLE

| UNLOCKABLE | HOW TO UNLOCK |
| --- | --- |
| Illustration Contest Fighting Spirit Award #10: Ianka | Reach Profile Level 6. |
| Illustration Contest Fighting Spirit Award #11: Siting Zeng | Reach Profile Level 6. |
| Illustration Contest Fighting Spirit Award #12: Minari | Reach Profile Level 6. |
| Illustration Contest Fighting Spirit Award #13: Wanda | Reach Profile Level 6. |
| Illustration Contest Fighting Spirit Award #1: AME | Reach Profile Level 6. |

| | |
|---|---|
| Illustration Contest Fighting Spirit Award #2: Eiji | Reach Profile Level 6. |
| Illustration Contest Fighting Spirit Award #3: GANCO | Reach Profile Level 6. |
| Illustration Contest Fighting Spirit Award #4: Kodama Hibiki | Reach Profile Level 6. |
| Illustration Contest Fighting Spirit Award #5: Shirahira Kousuke | Reach Profile Level 6. |
| Illustration Contest Fighting Spirit Award #6: Shirai | Reach Profile Level 6. |
| Illustration Contest Fighting Spirit Award #7: Chigimita | Reach Profile Level 6. |
| Illustration Contest Fighting Spirit Award #8: Byakuren | Reach Profile Level 6. |
| Illustration Contest Fighting Spirit Award #9: Fujimachi | Reach Profile Level 6. |
| Illustration Contest Grand Winner | Reach Profile Level 10. |
| Illustration Contest Honorable Mention #1 | Reach Profile Level 7. |
| Illustration Contest Honorable Mention #2 | Reach Profile Level 7. |
| Illustration Contest Honorable Mention #3 | Reach Profile Level 7. |
| Illustration Contest Runner-Up #1 | Reach Profile Level 9. |
| Illustration Contest Runner-Up #2 | Reach Profile Level 9. |
| Special CG #03 | Reach Profile Level 6. |
| Special CG #09 | Reach Profile Level 6. |
| Special CG #12 | Reach Profile Level 9. |
| Special CG #13 | Reach Profile Level 6. |
| Special CG #15 | Reach Profile Level 10. |
| Special CG #17 | Reach Profile Level 6. |
| Special CG #18 | Reach Profile Level 6. |
| Special CG #19 | Reach Profile Level 6. |
| Special CG #21 | Reach Profile Level 7. |
| Special CG #23 | Reach Profile Level 6. |
| Special CG #24 | Reach Profile Level 7. |
| Special CG #25 | Reach Profile Level 8. |
| Special CG #26 | Reach Profile Level 6. |
| Special CG #27 | Reach Profile Level 6. |
| Special CG #28 | Reach Profile Level 6. |
| Special CG #29 | Reach Profile Level 10. |
| Special CG #30 | Reach Profile Level 10. |
| Special CG #31 | Reach Profile Level 6. |
| Special CG #35 | Reach Profile Level 8. |
| Special CG #36 | Reach Profile Level 7. |
| Special CG #37 | Reach Profile Level 9. |
| Special CG #38 | Reach Profile Level 9. |
| Special CG #40 | Reach Profile Level 11. |
| Special CG #41 | Reach Profile Level 9. |
| Special CG #42 | Reach Profile Level 14. |
| Special CG #43 | Reach Profile Level 15. |
| Special CG #44 | Reach Profile Level 11. |
| Special CG #45 | Reach Profile Level 17. |
| Special CG #46 | Reach Profile Level 6. |
| Special CG #47 | Reach Profile Level 7. |
| Special CG #48 | Reach Profile Level 9. |
| Special CG #50 | Reach Profile Level 6. |
| Special CG #51 | Reach Profile Level 6. |

| | |
|---|---|
| Special CG #52 | Reach Profile Level 6. |
| Special CG #53 | Reach Profile Level 7. |
| Special CG #54 | Reach Profile Level 9. |
| Special CG #55 | Reach Profile Level 10. |
| Special CG #56 | Reach Profile Level 11. |
| Special CG #57 | Reach Profile Level 14. |
| Special CG #58 | Reach Profile Level 16. |
| Special CG #59 | Reach Profile Level 17. |
| Special CG #60 | Reach Profile Level 19. |
| Special CG #61 | Reach Profile Level 6. |
| Special CG #62 | Reach Profile Level 6. |
| Special CG #63 | Reach Profile Level 6. |
| Special CG #64 | Reach Profile Level 6. |
| Special CG #65 | Reach Profile Level 6. |
| Special CG #66 | Reach Profile Level 6. |
| Special CG #67 | Reach Profile Level 6. |
| Special CG #68 | Reach Profile Level 8. |
| Special CG #69 | Reach Profile Level 8. |
| Special CG #70 | Reach Profile Level 8. |
| Special CG #71 | Reach Profile Level 8. |
| Special CG #72 | Reach Profile Level 8. |
| Special CG #73 | Reach Profile Level 8. |
| Special CG #74 | Reach Profile Level 8. |
| Special CG #75 | Reach Profile Level 8. |
| Special CG #76 | Reach Profile Level 11. |
| Special CG #77 | Reach Profile Level 11. |
| Special CG #78 | Reach Profile Level 11. |
| Special CG #79 | Reach Profile Level 11. |
| Special CG #80 | Reach Profile Level 11. |
| Special CG #81 | Reach Profile Level 11. |
| Special CG #82 | Reach Profile Level 12. |
| Special CG #83 | Reach Profile Level 12. |
| Special CG #84 | Reach Profile Level 12. |
| Special CG #85 | Reach Profile Level 12. |
| Special CG #86 | Reach Profile Level 13. |
| Special CG #87 | Reach Profile Level 13. |
| Special CG #88 | Reach Profile Level 13. |
| Special CG #89 | Reach Profile Level 13. |
| Special CG #90 | Reach Profile Level 13. |
| System Voice BBCS Default | Reach Profile Level 15. |
| System Voice Kakihara Tetsuya A | Reach Profile Level 15. |
| System Voice Kakihara Tetsuya B | Reach Profile Level 15. |
| System Voice Saito Chiwa | Reach Profile Level 15. |
| System Voice Sawashiro Miyuki A | Reach Profile Level 15. |
| System Voice Sawashiro Miyuki B | Reach Profile Level 15. |
| Arakune Motion Storyboard | Reach Profile Level 16. |
| Arcade Version of the BlazBlue Continuum Shift II Poster Illustration | Reach Profile Level 20. |
| Back Cover Illustration of the BlazBlue Official Comic 1 | Reach Profile Level 20. |

| | |
|---|---|
| Back Cover Illustration of the BlazBlue Official Comic 2 | Reach Profile Level 20. |
| Bang Motion Storyboard | Reach Profile Level 16. |
| Bascule Image Board | Reach Profile Level 17. |
| BlazBlue Continuum Shift II Illustration Package | Reach Profile Level 20. |
| Carl Motion Storyboard | Reach Profile Level 16. |
| Cover Illustration of the BlazBlue Official Comic 1 | Reach Profile Level 20. |
| Cover Illustration of the BlazBlue Official Comic 2 | Reach Profile Level 20. |
| Cover Illustration of the BlazBlue – Phase 0 Novel | Reach Profile Level 20. |
| Hakumen Motion Storyboard | Reach Profile Level 16. |
| Hazama 3D Model | Reach Profile Level 18. |
| Hazama Motion Storyboard | Reach Profile Level 17. |
| Heritage Museum Image Board | Reach Profile Level 17. |
| Jin Motion Storyboard | Reach Profile Level 15. |
| Lambda Motion Storyboard | Reach Profile Level 16. |
| Litchi Motion Storyboard | Reach Profile Level 16. |
| Makoto 3D Model | Reach Profile Level 18. |
| Makoto Motion Storyboard | Reach Profile Level 19. |
| Mu Motion Storyboard | Reach Profile Level 17. |
| Noel Motion Storyboard | Reach Profile Level 15. |
| Nu 3D Model | Reach Profile Level 18. |
| Platinum 3D Model | Reach Profile Level 18. |
| Platinum Motion Storyboard | Reach Profile Level 19. |
| Rachel Motion Storyboard | Reach Profile Level 16. |
| Ragna Motion Storyboard. | Reach Profile Level 15. |
| Score Attack Mode Illustration | Reach Profile Level 20. |
| Tager Motion Storyboard | Reach Profile Level 16. |
| Taokaka Motion Storyboard | Reach Profile Level 16. |
| Tsubaki 3D Model | Reach Profile Level 18. |
| Tsubaki Motion Storyboard | Reach Profile Level 17. |
| Valkenhayn 3D Model | Reach Profile Level 18. |
| Valkenhayn Motion Storyboard | Reach Profile Level 19. |

## UNLOCKABLE

Each character has a special Unlimited version that has unique moves and abilities. To unlock them, you must gain enough points to level up your profile, and then acquire them in the Gallery.

| UNLOCKABLE | HOW TO UNLOCK |
|---|---|
| Unlimited Arakune | Reach Profile Level 7. |
| Unlimited Bang | Reach Profile Level 6. |
| Unlimited Carl | Reach Profile Level 6. |
| Unlimited Hakumen | Reach Profile Level 8. |
| Unlimited Hazama | Reach Profile Level 8. |
| Unlimited Jin | Reach Profile Level 7. |
| Unlimited Lambda | Reach Profile Level 6. |
| Unlimited Litchi | Reach Profile Level 7. |
| Unlimited Makoto | Reach Profile Level 6. |
| Unlimited Mu | Reach Profile Level 8. |
| Unlimited Noel | Reach Profile Level 7. |
| Unlimited Platinum | Reach Profile Level 6. |
| Unlimited Rachel | Reach Profile Level 7. |

| Unlimited Ragna | Reach Profile Level 8. |
| Unlimited Tager | Reach Profile Level 6. |
| Unlimited Taokaka | Reach Profile Level 6. |
| Unlimited Tsubaki | Reach Profile Level 6. |
| Unlimited Valkenhayn | Reach Profile Level 7. |

## BLAZING ANGELS 2: SECRET MISSIONS OF WWII (PlayStation 3)

### CODES

Enter the code for unlocking the planes and missions in the main menu, and enter the other two codes while paused when on a mission.

| EFFECT | CODE |
|--------|------|
| Damage Increased/Normal | Hold [L2] and press [L1], [L1], [R1]. Release [L2], hold [R2] and press [R1], [R1], [L1]. |
| God Mode Active/Inactive | Hold [L2] and press ■, ▲, ▲, ■. Release [L2], hold [R2] and press ▲, ■, ■, ▲. |
| Unlock All Planes and Missions | Hold both [R2], [L2] then press ■, [L1], [R1], ▲, ▲, [R1], [L1], ■. |

## BLAZING ANGELS: SQUADRONS OF WWII (PlayStation 3)

Enter these codes while the game is paused.

| UNLOCKABLE | CODE |
|-----------|------|
| Increase Damage of Weapons | Hold [L2] and quickly press [L1], [L1], [R1]; release [L2], then hold [R2] and quickly press [R1], [R1], [L1] |
| Invincibility | Hold [L2] and press ■, ▲, ▲, ■; release [L2], then hold [R2] and quickly press ▲, ■, ■, ▲ |

Enter this code at the Title menu while holding [L2]+[R2]

| UNLOCKABLE | CODE |
|-----------|------|
| All Campaign Missions and Planes | ■, [L1], [R1], ▲, ▲, [R1], [L1], ■ |

## BLITZ: OVERTIME (PSP)

### PASSWORD

In the main menu in the "extras" option, input these codes to unlock the following.

| PASSWORD | EFFECT |
|----------|--------|
| ONFIRE | Ball trails always on. Only affects Quick Play mode. |
| BOUNCY | Beach Ball. Only affects Quick Play mode. |
| PIPPED | Double unleash icons. Only affects Quick Play mode. |
| CHAMPS | In Campaign mode, highlight a team but do not select it. Stay on the menu and press ■, ■, ▲; Triangle to instantly win against the selected team. |
| NOTTIRED | Stamina disabled. Only affects Quick Play mode. |
| CLASHY | Super Clash mode. Only affects Quick Play mode. |
| BIGDOGS | Super Unleash Clash mode. Only affects Quick Play mode. |
| CHUWAY | Two player co-op mode. |

## BLITZ: THE LEAGUE (XBOX 360)

Enter these passwords in the Code menu under Extras.

| UNLOCKABLE | PASSWORD |
|-----------|----------|
| Ball Trail Always On | ONFIRE |
| Beach Ball | BOUNCY |
| Double Unleash Icons | PIPPED |
| Stamina Off | NOTTIRED |
| Two Player Co-op | CHUWAY |

| Unlimited Clash Icons | CLASHY |
|---|---|
| Unlimited Unleash | BIGDOGS |

## BLOODY WOLF (Wii)

### CODES

| UNLOCKABLE | HOW TO UNLOCK |
|---|---|
| 10 Flash Bombs | When your strength is at "1," climb a barricade and press ⬆+⬅+RUN+② |
| 10 Super Grenades | When your strength is at "1," climb a barricade and press ⬆+⬅+RUN+② |
| 50 Bazooka Rounds | When your strength is at "2," climb a fence and press ⬅+①+② |
| 50 Flame Thrower Charges | Hold ⬆+①+② and press RUN when parachuting at the start of level 2 or level 5 |
| 50 Shotgun Rounds | When your strength is at "2," climb a fence and press ⬅+①+② |
| Fast Mode | At the title screen, press ⬆, ⬇, ⬅, ⬅, ①, ①, ② SELECT, RUN |
| Hover Mode (in game, press jump to hover) | At the title screen, press ⬆, ⬇, ⬅, ⬆, ②, ②, ①, SELECT, RUN |
| Sound Test | At the title screen, press ⬆, then hold ①+②+SELECT |

### LEVEL SELECT CODES

Press ②, ①, ①, ②, ①, ②, ②, ① at the title screen. Then press the following for the appropriate level.

| CODE | EFFECT |
|---|---|
| Up | Level 1 |
| Up/Right | Level 2 |
| Right | Level 3 |
| Down/Right | Level 4 |
| Down | Level 5 |
| Down/Left | Level 6 |
| Left | Level 7 |
| Up/Left | Level 8 |

## BODYCOUNT (XBOX 360)

### ACHIEVEMENT

| UNLOCKABLE | HOW TO UNLOCK |
|---|---|
| 2nd place equals death! (15) | Won a Deathmatch |
| A very bad feeling (20) | Survived K-8 Nemesis Widowmaker encounter |
| Bad medicine (20) | Medic Population Diminished |
| Beat the street (10) | Survived the Street siege |
| Boombastic (5) | Killed 10 enemies with explosives |
| Bullet dodger (30) | Single player challenge complete on normal |
| Bullet Repellent (50) | OSB Adrenaline upgraded |
| Bullet with their name on it (5) | Killed 10 enemies with the last round in your weapon |
| Distance warfare (20) | Achieved Sniper Distance Kill |
| Don't call a doctor (10) | Survived the Militarised Compound siege |
| Easy-peasy (20) | Single player challenge complete on easy |
| Finger on the pulse (50) | OSB Pulse Wave upgraded |
| Hitman (5) | Killed 10 enemies with a headshot |
| Hot potato (5) | Killed 10 enemies with grenades |
| Kept at bay (10) | Survived the Pirate Bay siege |

| Killed 'em all (50) | Won 10 Deathmatches of any type |
|---|---|
| Kilo-killer (50) | 1000 online kills |
| Last breath death (5) | Killed 10 enemies while health is low |
| Leg frag (5) | Killed 10 enemies with mines |
| Lighting their fire (50) | OSB Explosive bullets upgraded |
| Military intelligence (10) | Highest value intel collected following multiple skillkills |
| Multiboom-doom (10) | Killed 3 enemies at once with a single grenade |
| Network weapon (50) | Skillkill x10 |
| Never say 'Die' (50) | Achieved 100 co-op kills within a siege |
| Nowhere to hide (5) | killed 10 enemies through cover |
| Online can of whoop-ass (30) | Achieved 50 co-op kills within a siege |
| Out of the darkness (10) | Survived the Mine siege |
| Planes and flames (50) | OSB Airstrike upgraded |
| Rain of fire (30) | Killed 5 enemies at once with a single Airstrike |
| Robert Ford style (5) | Killed 10 enemies from behind |
| Sleep when I'm dead (50) | Defeated K-8 Nemesis Widowmaker |
| Stealing is wrong, kids! (20) | Scavenger Population Diminished |
| Team Bodycount®! (15) | Won a Team Deathmatch |
| The Professional (50) | Skillkill x25 |
| Under their nose (5) | 10 surprise kills executed |
| Up close and personal (5) | Killed 10 enemies using melee |
| Warmonger (45) | Single player challenge complete on hard |
| Welcome to Africa - Tutorial (15) | Induction Completed |
| Wind of change (50) | Achieved all objectives in Africa |
| Wishing this was Vegas (30) | Achieved all objectives in Asia |
| You FTW (30) | Broke down the enemy's door |

## BOLT    (PlayStation 3)

### CODES

Enter the "Extras" menu, then select "Cheats." Enter one of the following codes to unlock the corresponding cheat option. To toggle a cheat on or off, pause gameplay and enter the "Cheats" menu.

| EFFECT | CODE |
|---|---|
| Unlimited Invulnerability | ↓, ↓, ↑, ← |
| Unlimited Laser Eyes | ←, ←, ↓, → |
| Unlimited Stealth Camo | ←, ↓, ↓, ↓ |
| Unlimited Enhanced Vision | ←, ↑, ↑, ↓ |
| Unlimited Gas Mines | →, ←, ←, ↑, ↓, → |
| Unlimited SuperBark | →, ←, ←, ↑, ↓, ↑ |
| Level Select | →, ↑, ←, →, ↑, → |
| All Mini Games | →, ↑, →, → |
| Unlimited Ground Pound | →, ↑, →, ↑, ←, ↓ |

## BULLETSTORM    (PlayStation 3) (XBOX 360)

### UNLOCKABLE

You can unlock the Emerald-colored Leash by beating the Bulletstorm demo then playing the full game. The Leash behaves exactly the same as the Blue Leash, it's just a different color.

| UNLOCKABLE | HOW TO UNLOCK |
|---|---|
| Emerald-colored Leash | Beat the Bulletstorm demo. |

## BULLY SCHOLARSHIP EDITION (Wii)

### UNLOCKABLES

| UNLOCKABLE | HOW TO UNLOCK |
|---|---|
| Black Ninja Suit | Take a picture of all the students of Bullworth. |
| BMX Helmet | Complete all bike races. |

| UNLOCKABLE | HOW TO UNLOCK |
|---|---|
| Crash Helmet | Win the first set of Go-Kart races. |
| Double Carnival Tickets | Collect all G & G cards. |
| Fireman's Hat | Pull the fire alarm 15 times to unlock the fireman's hat. |
| Mo-Ped | Buy from carnival for 75 tickets. |
| Pumpkin Head | Smash all pumpkins either on Halloween or in basement. |
| Robber Mask | Break into 15 people's lockers without getting caught. |
| Rubber Band Ball | Collect all rubber bands. |

## BURNOUT PARADISE (PlayStation 3)

### UNLOCKABLE CARS

Acquire an A level license, then insert these codes in the in-game Cheats menu.

| UNLOCKABLE | HOW TO UNLOCK |
|---|---|
| Best Buy Car | Type BESTBUY |
| Circuit City Car | Type CIRCUITCITY |
| Game Stop Car | Type GAMESTOP |
| Wal-Mart Car | Type WALMART |

### OTHER UNLOCKABLE CARS

Insert this code in the in-game Cheats menu under the "sponsor codes" section.

| UNLOCKABLE | HOW TO UNLOCK |
|---|---|
| Steel Wheels Car | Type: U84D 3Y8K FY8Y 58N6 |

### LICENSES

To unlock licenses, win the corresponding number of events in the game.

| UNLOCKABLE | HOW TO UNLOCK |
|---|---|
| A | 26 events |
| B | 16 events |
| C | 7 events |
| D | 2 events |
| Burnout Paradise | 45 events |
| Elite | 110 events |

### PAINT COLORS

| UNLOCKABLE | HOW TO UNLOCK |
|---|---|
| Gold Paint | Earn the elite license |
| Platinum Paint | Earn the elite license and achieve 100 percent completion. |

## BUST-A-MOVE BASH! (Wii)

### MORE STAGES

| UNLOCKABLE | HOW TO UNLOCK |
|---|---|
| 250 More Stages | After completing the first 250 stages in Puzzle mode, return to the Select screen and press Ⓐ with the cursor hovering over Stage Select. The area should be mostly orange now instead of blue, and only the first stage will be available. This is how you access stages 251-500. |

## CABELA'S SURVIVAL: SHADOWS OF KATMAI (PlayStation 3)

### TROPHY

| UNLOCKABLE | HOW TO UNLOCK |
| --- | --- |
| A Good Explorer (Bronze) | Finished the Story Mode on Easy difficulty setting |
| Cat Dominator (Silver) | Hunted four cougars in Story Mode |
| Down Bear, Down! (Silver) | Hunted three bears in Story Mode |
| Focus Master (Silver) | Hunted 20 animals using Focus Shot in Story Mode |
| Focus Novice (Bronze) | Hunted 10 animals using Focus Shot in Story Mode |
| Getting Down (Silver) | Landed the plane without hitting any obstacles |
| Getting The Hang Of It (Bronze) | Hunted two animals in latching situations in Story Mode |
| Gold All The Way (Gold) | Obtained gold medals in all of the Quick Draw Shooting Galleries |
| Hangman (Silver) | Hunted 20 targets while hanging in Story Mode |
| Hunt 10 With Semi Auto Rifle | Hunted 10 animals with the semi auto rifle in Story (Silver) Mode |
| Hunt 20 With Handgun (Bronze) | Hunted 20 animals with the handgun in Story Mode |
| Hunt 20 With Shotgun (Bronze) | Hunted 20 animals with the shotgun in Story Mode |
| Hunt 30 With Bolt (Bronze) | Hunted 30 animals with the bolt-action rifle in Story Mode |
| Hunting For Gold (Gold) | Obtained gold medals in all of the Trek Shooting Galleries |
| Keep Them Off (Bronze) | Successfully repelled 10 animals using melee attacks in Story Mode |
| Latch Master (Gold) | Hunted four animals in latching situations in Story Mode |
| Latch Proficient (Silver) | Hunted three animals in latching situations in Story Mode |
| Latch Them Down (Silver) | Hunted five animals in latching situations in Shooting Galleries |
| Master of Survival (Platinum) | Unlocked all Trophies |
| Novice Challenger (Bronze) | Won five challenges in Shooting Galleries |
| Practiced Challenger (Silver) | Won 10 challenges in Shooting Galleries |
| Pro Challenger (Gold) | Won 15 challenges in Shooting Galleries |
| Pro Hunter (Silver) | Finish three hunts in Story Mode |
| Shooting Galleries Expert (Gold) | Obtained gold medals in all of the Survival Shooting Galleries |
| Survivor (Silver) | Hunted 30 animals in a row without dying in Story Mode |
| The Pro Adventurer (Silver) | Finished Story Mode on the Medium difficulty setting |
| The Story's Taking Shape (Silver) | Gathered 15 collectable elements in Story Mode |
| The True Adventurer (Gold) | Finished Story Mode on the Hard difficulty setting |

**CALL OF DUTY: BLACK OPS (Wii)**

### CODES

You have to use the classic controller for this to work. At the Main menu, look down at your hands and press "ZL" and "ZR" a couple of times to break free from the chair. Walk around behind the chair you were in, and you will see a computer. Press and hold the button it says to access the computer. Now you can use the computer like the other systems, but the codes don't work the same way.

| EFFECT | CODE |
| --- | --- |
| A text-based game that you can plug a USB keyboard into your Wii to play | ZORK |
| Get a list of commands; it works like an old UNIX or DOS system | HELP |
| Unlock all the missions in the Mission Select screen in Campaign mode (no Zombie maps) | 3ARC UNLOCK |
| Unlocks all the intel in the game | 3ARC INTEL |

### TERMINAL CODES

Access the Central Intelligence Agency Data System and type the case-sensitive command "login." When you are prompted to log in with an account, enter the following usernames and passwords. Access their documents with the "dir" command or e-mail with the "mail" command.

| EFFECT | CODE |
| --- | --- |
| Adrienne Smith | Username: asmith; password: roxy |
| Bruce Harris | Username: bharris; password: goskins |
| D. King | Username: dking; password: mfk |
| Frank Woods | Username: fwoods; password: philly |
| Grigori "Greg" Weaver | Username: gweaver; password: gedeon |
| J. Turner | Username: Jturner; password: condor75 |
| Jason Hudson | Username: jhudson; password: bryant1950 |
| John F. Kennedy | Username: jfkennedy; password: lancer |
| John McCone | Username: jmccone; password: berkley22 |
| Vannevar Bush | Username: vbush; password: manhattan |

**CALL OF DUTY: BLACK OPS (PlayStation 3) (XBOX 360)**

### CIA DATA SYSTEM ACCOUNTS

When using the computer to access the CIA Data system, you can use the following login IDs and passwords. After logging into an account, you may then browse each user's unique files using the DIR command or read messages with the MAIL command.

| EFFECT | CODE |
| --- | --- |
| The user account of Alex Mason, already logged in when you first use the terminal | Username: amason; password: PASSWORD |
| The user account of Bruce Harris | Username: bharris; password: GOSKINS |
| The user account of D. King | Username: dking; password: MFK |
| The user account of Dr. Adrienne Smith | Username: asmith; password: ROXY |
| The user account of Dr. Vannevar Bush | Username: vbush; password: MANHATTAN |
| The user account of Frank Woods | Username: fwoods; password: PHILLY |
| The user account of Grigori "Greg" Weaver | Username: gweaver; password: GEDEON |
| The user account of J. Turner | Username: jturner; password: CONDOR75 |
| The user account of Jason Hudson | Username: jhudson; password: BRYANT1950 |
| The user account of John McCone, director of Central Intelligence, 1961–1965 | Username: jmccone; password: BERKLEY22 |

| | |
|---|---|
| The user account of Joseph Bowman | Username: jbowman; password: UWD |
| The user account of President John Fitzgerald Kennedy | Username: jfkennedy; password: LANCER |
| The user account of President Lyndon Baines Johnson | Username: lbjohnson; password: LADYBIRD |
| The user account of President Richard Nixon | Username: rnixon; password CHECKERS |
| The user account of Richard Helms, director of the CIA from 1966 to 1973 | Username: rhelms; password: LEROSEY |
| The user account of Richard Kain | Username: rkain; password: SUNWU |
| The user account of Ryan Jackson | Username: rjackson; password: SAINTBRIDGET |
| The user account of T. Walker | Username: twalker; password: RADIO (zero, not "O") |
| The user account of Terrance Brooks | Username: tbrooks; password: LAUREN |
| The user account of William Raborn, director of Central Intelligence from 1965–1966 | Username: wraborn; password: BROMLOW |

## TERMINAL CODES

On the Main menu, and press the L2 and R2 buttons repeatedly. After about five times for each button, you'll break free of your interrogation chair. When you get up, walk around behind you to a computer. When you access it, enter the following using the onscreen keyboard.

| EFFECT | CODE |
|---|---|
| Activates Dead Ops Arcade | DOA |
| Displays a list of system commands in the terminal and Pentagon user e-mail access | HELP |
| FI FIE FOE | FOOBAR |
| Get to root of directory and see all codes | cd .. [Enter] cd .. [Enter] cd bin [Enter] ls [Enter] |
| Gives a list of audio files and pictures that you can open with the CAT command (e.g., CAT NoteX.txt) | DIR |
| Gives a list of login names for use with the RLOGIN function (but they require a password) | WHO |
| It will list all of your audio files and pictures | CAT |
| To List a directory (same as DIR but for LINUX) | LS |
| To view a file in a directory using the TYPE command "NAMEOFFILE.EXTENSION" | TYPE |
| Unlocks all Intel in the game for viewing | 3ARC INTEL |
| Unlocks Dead Ops Arcade and Presidential Zombie Mode | 3ARC UNLOCK |
| Unlocks Zork I: The Great Underground Adventure (a text adventure game from 1980) for play in Black Ops | ZORK |
| Virtual Therapist Software | ALICIA |

## EASTER EGGS

### Nuketown Mannequin Secret

On the multiplayer map Nuketown, if you blow the heads off of all the mannequins in a short amount of time, the song "Sympathy for the Devil" by the Rolling Stones will play in the background.

### Play the song "Don't Back Down" by Eminem in Five zombie maps

There are three red phones throughout the pentagon that ring and flash. The first is located where you first start after opening a set of doors in the corner. The second is on the catwalk circling the room after leaving the first elevator. The third is in one of the rooms after leaving the second elevator on the floor the power is on. Just listen for a cell phone ring and follow it to the red rotary phone. Look at them and hold X till the ringing stops and you hear a busy signal. Once you get the third phone, the music starts.

A B C D E F G H I J K L M N O P Q R S T U V W X Y Z

## CALL OF DUTY: MODERN WARFARE 2   (XBOX 360)

### EXTRA CUSTOM CLASS SLOT

| UNLOCKABLE | HOW TO UNLOCK |
| --- | --- |
| Extra Custom Class Slot | Obtain level 70 in multiplayer and enter Prestige Mode to unlock a sixth custom class slot. |

### KILLSTREAK REWARDS

You can unlock the Killstreaks by receiving the amount designated before dying.

| UNLOCKABLE | HOW TO UNLOCK |
| --- | --- |
| AC130 Gunship (be the gunner of the AC130) | 11 Kills |
| Attack Helicopter | 07 Kills |
| Care Package (drops ammo/Killstreaks) | 04 Kills |
| Chopper Gunner (be the gunner of the Helicopter) | 11 Kills |
| Counter UAV (jams enemy radars) | 04 Kills |
| Emergency Airdrop (4 ammo/Killstreak drops) | 08 Kills |
| EMP (disables electronics) | 15 Kills |
| Harrier Strike (choose bomb location and defending Harrier) | 07 Kills |
| Nuclear Strike (kills everyone on map) | 25 Kills |
| Pave Low (Armored Helicopter) | 09 Kills |
| Precision Airstrike (drop airstrike) | 06 Kills |
| Predator (guided missiles) | 05 Kills |
| Sentry Gun (deployable gun) | 05 Kills |
| UAV (shows enemy location) | 03 Kills |

### PROFESSIONAL PERKS

With each perk you unlock you can upgrade it by completing various requirements.

| UNLOCKABLE | HOW TO UNLOCK |
| --- | --- |
| Bling Pro (two primary weapon attachments + two secondary weapon attachments) | Get 200 Kills with a weapon with two attachments. |
| Cold-Blooded Pro (undetectable by UAV, air support, sentries, and thermal imaging + no red crosshair or name when you are targeted) | Destroy 40 enemy Killstreak Rewards with Cold-Blooded Perk. |
| Commando Pro (increased Melee Distance + no falling damage) | Get 20 Melee Kills using Commando Perk. |
| Danger Close Pro (increased explosive weapon damage + extra air support damage) | Get 100 Kills with explosives while using Danger Close Perk. |
| Hardline Pro (Killstreak Rewards require 1 less Kill + Deathstreak Rewards require 1 less death) | Get 40 Killstreaks (two or more in a row without dying) with Hardline Perk. |
| Last Stand Pro (pull out your pistol before dying + use equipment in last stand) | Get 20 Kills while in last stand. |
| Lightweight Pro (move faster + quick aim after sprinting) | Run 30 miles with Lightweight Perk. |
| Marathon Pro (unlimited sprint + climb obstacles faster) | Run 26 miles with Marathon Perk. |
| Ninja Pro (invisible to heartbeat sensors + your footsteps are silent) | Get 50 close-range Kills using Ninja Perk. |
| One Man Army Pro (swap classes at any time + swap classes faster) | Get 120 Kills using One Man Army. |
| Scavenger Pro (resupply from dead enemies + extra mags) | Resupply 100 times with Scavenger Perk. |

| | |
|---|---|
| Scrambler Pro (jam enemy radar near you + delay enemy claymore explosions) | Get 50 close-range Kills using Scrambler Perk. |
| Sitrep Pro (detect enemy explosives and tactical insertions + louder enemy footsteps) | Destroy 120 detected explosives or tactical insertions with Sitrep Perk. |
| Sleight of Hand Pro (faster reloading + faster aiming) | Get 120 kills with Sleight of Hand Perk. |
| Steady Aim Pro (increased hip fire accuracy + longer hold breath duration) | Get 80 hip fire Kills using Steady Aim. |
| Stopping Power Pro (extra bullet damage + extra damage to enemy vehicles) | Get 300 Kills with Stopping Power Perk. |

## MODERN WARFARE 2 MUSEUM

The Museum can be selected from the Mission Select screen once you've completed the game.

| UNLOCKABLE | HOW TO UNLOCK |
|---|---|
| An evening with Infinity Ward: Modern Warfare 2 Gallery Exhibit | Complete the campaign. |

## MULTIPLAYER WEAPONS AND EQUIPMENT

Reach the level indicated to unlock the weapon and/or piece of equipment.

| UNLOCKABLE | HOW TO UNLOCK |
|---|---|
| .44 Magnum (Pistol) | Level 26 |
| AA-12 (Shotgun) | Level 12 |
| ACR (Assault Rifle) | Level 48 |
| AK-47 (Assault Rifle) | Level 70 |
| AT4-HS (Grenade Launcher) | Level 01 |
| AUG HBAR (LMG) | Level 32 |
| Barret .50 Cal (Sniper) | Level 04 |
| Blast Shield | Level 19 |
| C4 | Level 43 |
| Claymore | Level 31 |
| Desert Eagle (Pistol) | Level 62 |
| F2000 (Assault Rifle) | Level 60 |
| FAL (Assault Rifle) | Level 28 |
| FAMAS (Assault Rifle) | Level 01 |
| Frag Grenade | Level 01 |
| Glock 18 (Secondary) | Level 22 |
| Intervention (Sniper Rifle) | Level 01 |
| Javelin (Grenade Launcher) | Level 50 |
| L86 LSW (LMG) | Level 01 |
| M1014 (Shotgun) | Level 54 |
| M16A4 (Assault Rifle) | Level 40 |
| M21 EBR (Sniper Rifle) | Level 56 |
| M240 (LMG) | Level 52 |
| M4A1 (Rifle) | Level 04 |
| M9 (Pistol) | Level 46 |
| M93 Raffica (Secondary) | Level 38 |
| MG4 (LMG) | Level 16 |
| Mini Uzi (SMG) | Level 44 |
| MP5K (SMG) | Level 04 |

NEW!

A
B
C
D
E
F
G
H
I
J
K
L
M
N
O
P
Q
R
S
T
U
V
W
X
Y
Z

| P90 (SMG) | Level 24 |
| --- | --- |
| PP-2000 (Secondary) | Level 01 |
| Ranger (Shotgun) | Level 42 |
| RPD (SMG) | Level 04 |
| RPG-7 (Grenade Launcher) | Level 65 |
| SCAR-H (Assault Rifle) | Level 08 |
| Semtex Grenade | Level 01 |
| SPAS-12 (Shotgun) | Level 01 |
| Stinger (Grenade Launcher) | Level 30 |
| Striker (Shotgun) | Level 34 |
| Tactical Insertion | Level 11 |
| TAR-21 (Assault Rifle) | Level 20 |
| Throwing Knife | Level 07 |
| Thumper (Grenade Launcher) | Level 14 |
| TMP (Secondary) | Level 58 |
| UMP .45 (SMG) | Level 01 |
| USP .45 (Pistol) | Level 01 |
| Vector (SMG) | Level 12 |
| WA2000 (Sniper) | Level 36 |
| Winchester 1887 (Shotgun) | Level 67 |

## CALL OF DUTY: MODERN WARFARE 3 (XBOX 360)

### ACHIEVEMENT

| UNLOCKABLE | HOW TO UNLOCK |
| --- | --- |
| 50/50 (20) | Complete a Special Ops Mission Mode game with the same number of kills as your partner. |
| Arms Dealer (20) | Buy all items from the Survival Weapon Armory. |
| Back in the Fight (5) | Start the Single Player Campaign on any difficulty. |
| Back Seat Driver (10) | Track down Volk. Complete "Bag and Drag" on any difficulty. |
| Bad First Date (10) | Find the girl. Complete "Scorched Earth" on any difficulty. |
| Birdie (20) | Kill 2 enemy helicopters without getting hit in a Special Ops Survival game. |
| Brag Rags (10) | Earn 1 star in Special Ops Mission Mode. |
| Carpe Diem (10) | Escape the mountain safe house. Complete "Persona Non Grata" on any difficulty. |
| City of Lights (25) | Complete "Bag and Drag" and "Iron Lady" on Veteran difficulty. |
| Danger Close (20) | Take down a chopper with an AC-130 smoke grenade in "Bag and Drag." |
| Danger Zone (20) | Buy all items from the Survival Air Support Armory. |
| Defense Spending (20) | Buy all items from the Survival Equipment Armory. |
| Diamond in the Rough (10) | Rescue the Russian President. Complete "Down the Rabbit Hole" on any difficulty. |
| Flight Attendant (20) | Kill all 5 enemies during the zero-g sequence in "Turbulence." |
| For Whom the Shell Tolls (20) | Destroy all targets during the mortar sequence with only 4 shells in "Back on the Grid." |
| Frequent Flyer (10) | Defend the Russian President. Complete "Turbulence" on any difficulty. |

| | |
|---|---|
| Get Rich or Die Trying (25) | Have $50,000 current balance in a Special Ops Survival game. |
| I Live (10) | Survive 1 wave in a Special Ops Survival game. |
| Informant (20) | Collect 22 Intel Items. |
| Jack the Ripper (20) | Melee 5 enemies in a row in Single Player or Special Ops. |
| Kill Box (20) | Kill 20 enemies with the Chopper Gunner in a single run in "Return to Sender." |
| Ménage à Trois (20) | Destroy 3 tanks with a single 105mm shot in "Iron Lady." |
| Nein (20) | Kill 9 enemies with A-10 strafing runs in "Scorched Earth." |
| No Assistance Required (20) | Complete a Special Ops Mission Mode game on Hardened or Veteran with no player getting downed. |
| One Way Ticket (10) | Make it to Westminster. Complete "Mind the Gap" on any difficulty. |
| Out of the Frying Pan… (25) | Complete "Persona Non Grata", "Turbulence", and "Back on the Grid" on Veteran difficulty. |
| Overachiever (40) | Earn 48 stars in Special Ops Mission Mode. |
| Payback (25) | Complete "Mind the Gap", "Goalpost", and "Return to Sender" on Veteran difficulty. |
| Requiem (10) | Escape the city. Complete "Blood Brothers" on any difficulty. |
| Sandstorm! (10) | Assault the shipping company. Complete "Return to Sender" on any difficulty. |
| Scout Leader (35) | Collect 46 Intel Items. |
| Serrated Edge (15) | Finish a Juggernaut with a knife in Special Ops. |
| Storm the Castle (10) | Discover Makarov's next move. Complete "Stronghold" on any difficulty. |
| Strike! (20) | Kill 5 enemies with a single grenade in Single Player or Special Ops. |
| Survivor (20) | Reach Wave 10 in each mission of Special Ops Survival mode. |
| Tactician (20) | Earn 1 star in each mission of Special Ops Mission Mode. |
| The Best of the Best (100) | Complete the campaign on Hardened or Veteran difficulty. |
| The Big Apple (25) | Complete "Black Tuesday" and "Hunter Killer" on Veteran difficulty. |
| The Darkest Hour (25) | Complete "Eye of the Storm", "Blood Brothers", and "Stronghold" on Veteran difficulty. |
| This Is My Boomstick (20) | Kill 30 enemies with the XM25 in "Black Tuesday." |
| This is the End (25) | Complete "Scorched Earth", "Down the Rabbit Hole", and "Dust to Dust" on Veteran difficulty. |
| Too Big to Fail (10) | Destroy the Jamming Tower. Complete "Black Tuesday" on any difficulty. |
| Unstoppable (40) | Reach Wave 15 in each mission of Special Ops Survival mode. |
| Up to No Good (10) | Infiltrate the village. Complete "Back on the Grid" on any difficulty. |
| Vive la Révolution! (10) | Reach the church. Complete "Eye of the Storm" on any difficulty. |
| We'll Always Have Paris (10) | Escape Paris with Volk. Complete "Iron Lady" on any difficulty. |

| Welcome to WW3 (10) | Save the US Vice President. Complete "Goalpost" on any difficulty. |
| Wet Work (10) | Take back New York Harbor. Complete "Hunter Killer" on any difficulty. |
| What Goes Up… (20) | Destroy all the choppers with only the UGV's grenade launcher in "Persona Non Grata." |
| Who Dares Wins (40) | Complete the campaign on any difficulty. |

## CALL OF DUTY: WORLD AT WAR    (XBOX 360)

### MODES

| UNLOCKABLE | HOW TO UNLOCK |
| --- | --- |
| Veteran mode | Reach Level 32 to unlock Veteran mode. |
| Zombie mode | Successfully complete Campaign mode to unlock Zombie mode, which is a four-player co-op mode against endless waves of Nazi zombies. |

### MULTIPLAYER UNLOCKABLES

Reach a certain rank on online multiplayer to achieve each unlockable.

| UNLOCKABLE | HOW TO UNLOCK |
| --- | --- |
| .357 Magnum | Reach Level 49 |
| Arisaka | Reach Level 4 |
| BAR | Reach Level 4 |
| Browning M1919 | Reach Level 61 |
| Clan Tag | Reach Level 11 |
| Colt M1911 | Reach Level 3 |
| Custom Class Slot 10 | Reach Prestige Level 10 |
| Custom Class Slot 6 | Reach Prestige Level 1 |
| Custom Class Slot 7 | Reach Prestige Level 2 |
| Custom Class Slot 8 | Reach Prestige Level 4 |
| Custom Class Slot 9 | Reach Prestige Level 7 |
| Double-Barreled Shotgun | Reach Level 29 |
| DP-28 | Reach Rank 13 |
| FG-42 | Reach Rank 45 |
| Gewehr 47 | Reach Rank 6 |
| Kar98K | Reach Rank 41 |
| M1 Garand | Reach Rank 17 |
| M1A1 Carbine | Reach Rank 65 |
| M2 Flamethrower | Reach Rank 65 |
| MG-42 | Reach Rank 33 |
| Mosin-Nagant | Reach Rank 21 |
| MP-40 | Reach Rank 10 |
| Nambu | Reach Rank 1 |
| PPSh 41 | Reach Rank 53 |
| PTRS 41 | Reach Rank 57 |
| Springfield | Reach Rank 3 |
| STG-44 | Reach Rank 37 |
| SVT-40 | Reach Rank 1 |
| Thompson | Reach Rank 1 |
| Tokarev TT38 | Reach Rank 21 |
| Trench Gun | Reach Rank 2 |
| Type-100 | Reach Rank 25 |

| Type-99 | Reach Rank 1 |
| Walther P38 | Reach Rank 2 |

## MULTIPLAYER PERK UNLOCKABLES

Reach a certain rank on online multiplayer to achieve each unlockable perk.

| UNLOCKABLE | HOW TO UNLOCK |
| --- | --- |
| Bandolier | Reach Level 40 |
| Bouncing Betty x 2 | Reach Level 24 |
| Camouflage | Reach Level 12 |
| Coaxial Machine Gun (vehicle) | Reach Level 40 |
| Dead Silence | Reach Level 52 |
| Double Tap | Reach Level 36 |
| Fireproof | Reach Level 48 |
| Iron Lungs | Reach Level 60 |
| Juggernaut | Reach Level 4 |
| Leadfoot (vehicle) | Reach Level 28 |
| M2 Flamethrower | Reach Level 65 |
| Martydom | Reach Level 20 |
| Ordinance Training (vehicle) | Reach Level 12 |
| Overkill | Reach Level 56 |
| Primary Grenades x 2 | Reach Level 44 |
| Reconnaissance | Reach Level 64 |
| Second Chance | Reach Level 9 |
| Shades | Reach Level 32 |
| Sleight of Hand | Reach Level 28 |
| Toss Back | Reach Level 6 |

## CALL OF DUTY 2 (XBOX 360)

Enter this code on the Mission Select screen.

| UNLOCKABLE | CODE |
| --- | --- |
| Unlock all levels | Hold both the left and right bumpers, then quickly input ○, ○, ○, ○, ♥, ♥ |

## CALL OF DUTY 3 (XBOX 360)

Enter this code at the Chapter Select screen.

| UNLOCKABLE | CODE |
| --- | --- |
| Unlock All Levels and Pictures | Hold ⊗ then press ○, ○, ○, ○, ✗, ✗ |

## CALL OF DUTY 3 (Wii)

Enter this code in the Chapter Select screen.

| UNLOCKABLE | CODE |
| --- | --- |
| Unlock All Levels | Hold ⊕ and press ⬆, ⬆, ⬆, ⬆, ②, ② |
| Unlock All Extras | At the Chapter Select screen, hold ⊕, and press ⬆, ⬆, ⬆, ⬆, ②, ② |

## CALL OF DUTY 4: MODERN WARFARE (XBOX 360)

### ARCADE AND CHEAT OPTIONS

These unlock automatically for completing *Call of Duty 4: Modern Warfare* on any difficulty level. During gameplay, find the Cheat menu in the Options menu.

| UNLOCKABLE | HOW TO UNLOCK |
| --- | --- |
| Arcade Mode | Complete game on any difficulty |
| Cheat Menu | Complete game on any difficulty |

## CHEATS

Unlock cheats by collecting enemy intel (intelligence), which look like laptop computers that are hidden throughout the campaign. Note: Using cheats disables Achievements.

### UNLOCKABLE CHEATS

| UNLOCKABLE | HOW TO UNLOCK |
|---|---|
| A Bad Year: When you kill enemies, they explode into tires! | Collect 15 pieces of enemy intel. |
| Cluster Bombs: After one of your frag grenades explodes, four more explode in a cross-shaped pattern. | Collect 10 pieces of enemy intel. |
| CoD Noir: Turns all gameplay into black and white. | Collect 2 pieces of enemy intel. |
| Infinite Ammo: Weapons have unlimited ammo. Doesn't work with Perk 1 abilities such as C4 and Claymores. | Collect 30 pieces of enemy intel. |
| Photo-Negative: Inverses all of the game's colors. | Collect 4 pieces of enemy intel. |
| Ragtime Warfare: Gameplay goes black and white, dust and scratches fill the screen, it plays at 2x speed, and the music becomes piano music. | Collect 8 pieces of enemy intel. |
| Slow-Mo Ability: Use the melee button to change the game to slow-mo and play at half-speed. | Collect 20 pieces of enemy intel. |
| Super Contrast: Dramatically increases the game's contrast, making the darks much darker and the lights much lighter. | Collect 6 pieces of enemy intel. |

Golden weapons are a special camo (or skin) that you unlock when you fully complete all the challenges under the weapon subtype in the barracks (SMG, LMG, etc.). Access them by choosing the camo of the respective weapon. The effect is purely cosmetic and does not enhance the ability of the weapon in any way.

### GOLDEN WEAPONS

| UNLOCKABLE | HOW TO UNLOCK |
|---|---|
| Golden AK-47 | Complete all Assault Rifle challenges. |
| Golden Desert Eagle | Get to Level 55. |
| Golden Dragunov | Complete all Sniper challenges. |
| Golden M1014 | Complete all Shotgun challenges. |
| Golden M60 | Complete all LMG challenges. |
| Golden Mini-Uzi | Complete all SMG challenges. |

### MULTIPLAYER UNLOCKABLES

| UNLOCKABLE | UNLOCKED AT RANK: |
|---|---|
| AK-74U Submachine Gun | 28 |
| Bandolier Perk Class 1 | 32 |
| Barret Sniper Rifle | 49 |
| Bomb Squad Perk Class 1 | 13 |
| \Boot Camp Challenges 1 | 08 |
| Boot Camp Challenges 2 | 14 |
| Boot Camp Challenges 3 | 17 |
| Clan Tag | 11 |
| Claymore Perk Class 1 | 23 |
| Commander Prestige Mode | 55 |
| Create a Class | 03 |
| Dead Silence Perk Class 3 | 44 |
| Demolitions Class Weapon Class | 01 |

| | |
|---|---|
| Desert Eagle Pistol | 43 |
| Double Tab Perk Class 2 | 29 |
| Dragunov Sniper Rifle | 22 |
| Eavesdrop Perk Class 3 | 35 |
| Elite Challenges | 51 |
| Elite Challenges 2 | 53 |
| Elite Challenges 3 | 54 |
| Frag x 3 Perk Class 1 | 41 |
| G3 Assault Rifle | 25 |
| G36C Assault Rifle | 37 |
| Golden Desert Eagle | 55 |
| Gun Challenges | 04 |
| Humiliation Challenges | 42 |
| Humiliation Challenges 2 | 45 |
| Humiliation Challenges 3 | 47 |
| Humiliation Challenges 4 | 48 |
| Humiliation Challenges 5 | 50 |
| Iron Lungs Perk Class 3 | 26 |
| Killer Challenges | 30 |
| Killer Challenges 2 | 33 |
| Killer Challenges 3 | 36 |
| Killer Challenges 4 | 39 |
| Last Stand Perk Class 3 | 07 |
| M1014 Shotgun | 31 |
| M14 Assault Rifle | 46 |
| M1911 Pistol | 15 |
| M4 Carbine Assault Rifle | 09 |
| M40 Sniper Rifle | 06 |
| M60E4 Light Machine Gun | 18 |
| Martyrdom Perk Class 2 | 16 |
| Mini Uzi Submachine Gun | 12 |
| MP44 Assault Rifle | 52 |
| New Playlists | 05 |
| Operations Challenges | 20 |
| Operations Challenges | 21 |
| Operations Challenges 2 | 24 |
| Operations Challenges 3 | 27 |
| Overkill Perk Class 2 | 38 |
| P90 Submachine Gun | 40 |
| \R700 Sniper Rifle | 34 |
| Sleight of Hand Perk Class 2 | 19 |
| Sniper Class Weapon Class | 02 |
| UAV Jammer Perk Class 2 | 10 |

## CALL OF DUTY 4: MODERN WARFARE (PlayStation 3)

Enter this code in the Chapter Select screen.

| UNLOCKABLE | CODE |
|---|---|
| Unlock All Levels | Hold SELECT and press ⇦, ⇨, ⇦, ⇦, ■, ■ |

## Arcade and Cheat Options

These unlock automatically for completing *Call of Duty 4: Modern Warfare* on any difficulty level. During gameplay, find the Cheat menu in the Options menu.

| UNLOCKABLE | HOW TO UNLOCK |
|---|---|
| Arcade Mode | Complete game on any difficulty |
| Cheat Menu | Complete game on any difficulty |

### EASTER EGG (HIDDEN MISSION)

Beat the game on any difficulty and let the credits run all the way through. When they finish, you'll start another mission. This mission takes place on a plane that resembles Air Force One, wherein you must fight your way through a horde of baddies, save the V.I.P., and escape the plane in less than two minutes.

### CHEATS

Unlock cheats by collecting enemy intel (intelligence), which look like laptop computers that are hidden throughout the campaign. Note: Using cheats disables Achievements.

### UNLOCKABLE CHEATS

| UNLOCKABLE | HOW TO UNLOCK |
|---|---|
| A Bad Year: When you kill enemies, they explode into tires! | Collect 15 pieces of enemy intel. |
| Cluster Bombs: After one of your frag grenades explodes, four more explode in a cross-shaped pattern. | Collect 10 pieces of enemy intel. |
| CoD Noir: Turns all gameplay into black and white. | Collect 2 pieces of enemy intel. |
| Infinite Ammo: Weapons have unlimited ammo. Doesn't work with Perk 1 abilities such as C4 and Claymores. | Collect 30 pieces of enemy intel. |
| Photo-Negative: Inverses all of the game's colors. | Collect 4 pieces of enemy intel. |
| Ragtime Warfare: Gameplay goes black and white, dust and scratches fill the screen, it plays at 2x speed, and the music becomes piano music. | Collect 8 pieces of enemy intel. |
| Slow-Mo Ability: Use the melee button to change the game to slow-mo and play at half-speed. | Collect 20 pieces of enemy intel. |
| Super Contrast: Dramatically increases the game's contrast, making the darks much darker and the lights much lighter. | Collect 6 pieces of enemy intel. |

Golden weapons are a special camo (or skin) that you unlock when you fully complete all the challenges under the weapon subtype in the barracks (SMG, LMG, etc.). Access them by choosing the camo of the respective weapon. The effect is purely cosmetic and does not enhance the ability of the weapon in any way.

### GOLDEN WEAPONS

| UNLOCKABLE | HOW TO UNLOCK |
|---|---|
| Golden AK-47 | Complete all Assault Rifle challenges. |
| Golden Desert Eagle | Get to Level 55. |
| Golden Dragunov | Complete all Sniper challenges. |
| Golden M1014 | Complete all Shotgun challenges. |
| Golden M60 | Complete all LMG challenges. |
| Golden Mini-Uzi | Complete all SMG challenges. |

### MULTIPLAYER UNLOCKABLES

| UNLOCKABLE | UNLOCKED AT RANK |
|---|---|
| Assault Rifle (G3) | Rank 25 |
| Assault Rifle (G36C) | Rank 37 |
| Assault Rifle (M14) | Rank 46 |
| Assault Rifle (M4) | Rank 10 |

| Assault Rifle (MP44) | Rank 52 |
| LMG (M60E4) | Rank 19 |
| Pistol (Desert Eagle) | Rank 43 |
| Pistol (Golden Desert Eagle) | Rank 55 |
| Pistol (M1911) | Rank 16 |
| Shotgun (M1014) | Rank 31 |
| SMG (AK-74U) | Rank 28 |
| SMG (Mini Uzi) | Rank 13 |
| SMG (P90) | Rank 40 |
| Sniper Rifle (Barret) | Rank 49 |
| Sniper Rifle (Dragunov) | Rank 22 |
| Sniper Rifle (M40) | Rank 04 |
| Sniper Rifle (R700) | Rank 34 |

## CALL OF JUAREZ: BOUND IN BLOOD (PlayStation 3)

### CODES

From the Main menu go into Exclusive content and enter code.

| EFFECT | CODE |
|---|---|
| Bonus Cash to be able to buy better weapons earlier in the game. | 735S653J |

## CALL OF JUAREZ: THE CARTEL (PlayStation 3)

### TROPHY

| UNLOCKABLE | HOW TO UNLOCK |
|---|---|
| Ace of Spades (Platinum) | Collect all other trophies. |
| Alamo! (Bronze) | Enter 10 rooms using Team Entry. |
| Alba Varden (Bronze) | Witness ship destruction on the Docks level. |
| Armorer (Bronze) | Unlock at least 10 new weapons in the campaign mode. |
| Bad guy (Bronze) | Kill at least 40 enemies during Gang Bang mission. |
| Been there, done that (Silver) | Play at least one full round on all maps in competitive mode. |
| Berserker (Bronze) | Kill at least 3 enemies in a row while being severely wounded. |
| Brain Surgery (Silver) | Kill 50 enemies with headshots. |
| Bullet dodger (Bronze) | During highway chase on Disco level successfully avoid all rockets. |
| Chain reaction (Bronze) | Kill at least 20 enemies by exploding nearby vehicles. |
| Clean shot (Silver) | Complete the campaign mode without killing any civilian. |
| DEA, keep your hands up! (Silver) | Complete the game playing as Eddie Guerra. |
| Deadly Ballet (Bronze) | In a three-player co-op game, make sure everyone scores at least one kill during Team Entry. |
| Dental Plan (Bronze) | Kill at least 10 enemies with a weapon melee attack. |
| Did you see that? (Bronze) | Destroy 5 helicopters. (Campaign) |
| Dirty cop (Bronze) | Successfully pick up 15 secret items. |
| Do you feel lucky, punk? (Gold) | Complete the campaign mode on hard difficulty. |
| Don't miss the train (Bronze) | Successfully manage to pass the train on Juan Chase level. |

| Drive-by (Bronze) | While riding in a car, shoot 50 enemies. |
| Driving lessons (Bronze) | Kill at least 10 enemies by ramming them with a vehicle. |
| Eh...what's up, doc? (Bronze) | In cooperative mode, revive wounded players 5 times. |
| F.R.A.G.S (Bronze) | Kill 10 enemies using grenades. |
| FBI! Don't move! (Silver) | Complete the game playing as Kim Evans. |
| Good Cop, Bad Cop, & The Ugly (Gold) | Complete the campaign mode playing all 3 different characters. |
| Guns. Lots of guns. (Bronze) | Use 10 different weapons to kill enemies. |
| Gunslinger (Bronze) | Kill 20 enemies using dual-wielded firearms. |
| Heat (Bronze) | Destroy 20 cars. |
| High Noon (Bronze) | Kill at least 3 enemies between 12.00-12.05 local time. |
| Highway Patrol (Bronze) | Drive any type of a vehicle for more than 20 miles total. |
| Interagency Task Force (Bronze) | Play through one entire mission with two other live players. |
| Ladder Goat (Bronze) | Find Ladder Goat movie on the Fort level. |
| Level 21 (Silver) | Unlock all weapons in the campaign mode. |
| Little Bighorn (Bronze) | Win at least one game in competitive mode. |
| Magpie (Bronze) | Collect at least 75% of secret items on any level, without being caught. |
| Move! Moving! (Bronze) | Kill 30 enemies by using the Team Cover technique. |
| Nail'd It! (Bronze) | Finish the downhill car chase on Plantation level without damaging the car too much. |
| None of their business. (Bronze) | Successfully finish two Secret Agendas. |
| Peeper (Bronze) | On the Disco level, watch dancers for at least 30 seconds. |
| Police Academy (Bronze) | Finish the first chapter. |
| Police, everybody down! (Silver) | Complete the game playing as Ben McCall. |
| Protect and serve (Bronze) | Don't kill any of the civilians on the marketplace during Juan's chase. |
| Raining Bullets (Bronze) | Shoot over 1000 bullets during the Ghost Town level. |
| Rio Bravo (Silver) | Kill 10 enemies using revolvers. |
| Rubber Duck (Bronze) | Successfully drive off the highway on Convoy level. |
| SloMo (Bronze) | Kill at least 4 enemies during a single Concentration Mode. |
| Spy vs. Spy (Bronze) | In cooperative mode, prevent 10 attempts of picking up secret items. |
| Texas Ranger (Bronze) | Disable 20 enemies with your bare fists. |
| The Border Crossed Us! (Bronze) | Cross U.S.–Mexican border. |
| Time is on my side (Silver) | Kill 50 enemies while having Concentration Mode active. |
| Tomb Raider (Silver) | Go through cemetary in less than 3 minutes. |
| Wild West (Bronze) | Enter the Ghost Town. |

## CAPCOM CLASSIC COLLECTION REMIXED  (PSP)

Enter this code at the Press Start screen.

| UNLOCKABLE | CODE |
|---|---|
| Arts, Tips, and Sound Tests for Every Game | Press ⇦, ⇨ on D-pad, ⇦, ⇨ on Analog stick, ■, ●, ⇧, ⇩ |

## CARS  (XBOX 360)

### PASSWORDS

| PASSWORD | EFFECT |
|---|---|
| CONC3PT | All art concept |
| WATCHIT | All movies |
| R4MONE | All paint jobs |
| IMSPEED | Super fast start |
| VROOOOM | Unlimited boost |
| YAYCARS | Unlock all cars |
| MATTL66 | Unlock all races |
| IF900HP | Unlock everything in the game |

## CARS  (Wii)

Input codes in the password section under the Options menu.

| UNLOCKABLE | CODE |
|---|---|
| All Cars | YAYCARS |
| All Concept Art | CONC3PT |
| All Movies | WATCHIT |
| All Paint Jobs | R4MONE |
| All Races | MATTL66 |
| All Tracks and Mini-games | IF900HP |
| Mater's Speedy Circuit and Mater's Countdown Clean Up | TRGTEXC |
| Super Fast Start | IMSPEED |
| Unlimited Boost | VROOOOM |

## CARS 2: THE VIDEO GAME  (XBOX 360)

### UNLOCKABLE

Enter these codes at the Cheat menu to unlock features

| UNLOCKABLE | HOW TO UNLOCK |
|---|---|
| Unlock all modes and all tracks | 959595 |
| Unlock lazers | 123456 |
| Cars 2: The Video Game | Wii |

### UNLOCKABLE

Enter these codes at the Cheat menu to unlock features

| UNLOCKABLE | HOW TO UNLOCK |
|---|---|
| Unlock all modes and all tracks | 959595 |
| Unlock lazers | 123456 |

## CASTLEVANIA: ORDER OF ECCLESIA  (DS)

### UNLOCKABLES

| UNLOCKABLE | HOW TO UNLOCK |
|---|---|
| Boss Medals | During a boss fight, do not get hit once. After the fight, a treasure chest will appear from the ground to present you with the medal. |
| New Game+ | After finishing the game, go to your file and press right to access the clear sign and start a new game. |
| Albus Mode | Complete the game after saving all villagers. |

| Boss Rush Mode | Complete the game after saving all villagers. |
| Hard Difficulty | Beat the game once. |
| Hard Mode Level 255 | Complete Hard Mode Level 1 OR connect to Castlevania: Judgment |
| Sound Mode | Complete the game after saving all villagers. |

## CASTLEVANIA: SYMPHONY OF THE NIGHT (XBOX 360)

### PLAY AS OTHER CHARACTERS AND EXTRAS

You must complete the game as Alucard with 180% or more and have a "CLEAR" Save.

| PASSWORD | EFFECT |
|---|---|
| Enter AXEARMOR as your name | Alucard with Axelord armor |
| Enter RICHTER as your name | Play as Richter Belmont |
| Enter X-X!V"Q as your name | Alucard with lower stats and MAX Luck |

## CASTLEVANIA: THE ADVENTURE REBIRTH (Wii)

### LEVEL SELECT

At the title screen, select "Game Start" and hold right on the D-pad for a few seconds. You'll be able to select and play any levels you have previously reached on the same difficulty.

## CATHERINE (PlayStation 3)

### TROPHY

| UNLOCKABLE | HOW TO UNLOCK |
|---|---|
| 3-Star Man (Bronze) Normal or Hard | Unlock Menhir by earning 3 Gold Prizes on |
| 5-Star Man (Bronze) on Normal or Hard | Unlock the Obelisk by earning 5 Gold Prizes |
| A God is Born! (Gold) | Conquer the final stage of Babel |
| A Life Without Regrets… (Bronze) | View the true Freedom ending |
| A Mystery Within a Puzzle (Bronze) | Uncover the truth behind Rapunzel |
| A New Look (Bronze) | Help Todd out of his trouble |
| Altar Conquered! (Bronze) | Complete Stage 1 of Babel |
| Babel's Calling (Bronze) Normal or Hard | Unlock the Altar by earning 1 Gold Prize on |
| Beer Baron (Bronze) | Listen to all the beer factoids |
| Bomberlamb (Bronze) | Hit 15 blocks with a single explosion (Golden Playhouse) |
| Cheers To You! (Platinum) | Unlock all other Trophies! |
| Cocktail Connoisseur (Bronze) | Listen to all the cocktail trivia |
| Crossing the Courtyard (Bronze) | Conquer Stage 5 |
| Dreams Come True (Gold) | View all of the endings |
| Everyday Hero (Silver) | Help everyone out of their predicaments |
| Have an Ice Day (Bronze) | Slide an Ice Block 5 or more blocks (Golden Playhouse) |
| Hit the Road, Vincent (Bronze) | View the bad Cheater ending |
| I Can Fly! (Silver) | Jump on a Spring Block 3 times in a row (Golden Playhouse) |
| Just Like Old Times (Bronze) | View the normal Lover ending |
| Legendary Prince (Silver) | Hear Rapunzel's sad song |
| Let My Sheep Go (Bronze) | Conquer Stage 3 |
| Lord of the Night (Bronze) | View the true Cheater ending |
| Love is Patient, Love is Kind (Bronze) | Resolve Daniel's dilemma |
| Making Legends (Bronze) | Conquer Stage 8 |

| | |
|---|---|
| **Menhir Conquered! (Bronze)** | Complete Stage 2 of Babel |
| **Mother Inferior (Bronze)** | Help Archie work through his quandary |
| **Nighty Night (Bronze)** | View the bad Lover ending |
| **No One Expects the... (Bronze)** | Conquer Stage 4 |
| **Obelisk Conquered! (Bronze)** | Complete Stage 3 of Babel |
| **One Last Case (Bronze)** | Help Morgan clean up his mess |
| **Past a Heap of Puzzles (Bronze)** | Beat Stage 64 of Rapunzel |
| **Path to the Altar (Bronze)** | Conquer Stage 7 |
| **Play It Again, Vince... (Bronze)** | Use the jukebox to change the music |
| **Push It to the Limit! (Bronze)** | Push 5 blocks at once (Golden Playhouse) |
| **Read All About It! (Bronze)** | Get Justin out of his jam |
| **Sake Sensei (Bronze)** | Listen to all the sake sound bites |
| **Sleepless Nights (Bronze)** | View the normal Cheater ending |
| **Starting a New Life (Bronze)** | View the true Lover ending |
| **Take Your Time (Silver)** | Move a Dark Block 10 times in a row (Golden Playhouse) |
| **Taking on the Gods (Silver)** | Unlock Axis Mundi by earning all Gold Prizes on Normal or Hard |
| **Text Junkie (Bronze)** | Reply to at least 20 text messages by the end of the final day |
| **The Golden Child (Gold)** | Earn Gold Prizes on all Hard difficulty stages |
| **The Great Escape (Bronze)** | Conquer Stage 2 |
| **The Nightmares Have Just Begun (Bronze)** | Conquer Stage 1 |
| **True Freedom! (Silver)** | Conquer Stage 9 |
| **Welcome to the Colosseum (Bronze)** | Unlock the Colosseum mode |
| **What Time is It? (Bronze)** | Conquer Stage 6 |
| **Whatever, Buddy (Bronze)** | View the normal Freedom ending |
| **Whisky Wiseman (Bronze)** | Listen to all the whisky minutiae |
| **You Don't Have To Go Home... (Bronze)** | Stay in the bar until all the other customers leave |

### CODE

At the Rapunzel arcade game title screen, enter the code. Enter the code again to disable it.

| EFFECT | CODE |
|---|---|
| **Unlocks new Rapunzel stages** | ↑,↓,↓,↑,↑,↑,↓,↓,↓,↓,→ |

### CODE

At the Title screen where you can select game modes, activate a new mode.

| UNLOCKABLE | HOW TO UNLOCK |
|---|---|
| **Very Easy Mode** | Highlight Golden Playhouse and hold Select until the screen flashes whilte |

### UNLOCKABLE

Earn Gold Prizes in the Golden Playhouse to unlock randomized stages in Babel Mode

| UNLOCKABLE | HOW TO UNLOCK |
|---|---|
| **Altar** | Earn one Gold Prize from the Golden Playhouse on Normal difficulty or higher. |
| **Axismundi** | Earn nine Gold Prizes from the Golden Playhouse on Normal difficulty or higher. |
| **Menhir** | Earn three Gold Prizes from the Golden Playhouse on Normal difficulty or higher. |

| Obelisk | Earn five Gold Prizes from the Golden Playhouse on Normal difficulty or higher. |
|---|---|

### UNLOCKABLE

Unlock a new mode by beating the game.

| UNLOCKABLE | HOW TO UNLOCK |
|---|---|
| Colosseum Mode | Beat the game once. |

### SECRET

| UNLOCKABLE | HOW TO UNLOCK |
|---|---|
| Skip a Stage | If you clear all the stages in a chapter in Normal or higher difficulty level with a gold trophy on each stage, you get a gold trophy for the chapter. When you replay the chapter, press Start to skip any stage, including the Boss. |

## CHEW-MAN-FU    (Wii)

### CODES

| UNLOCKABLE | HOW TO UNLOCK |
|---|---|
| Golden Balls | At the title screen, hold ①+SELECT and press ⬅+➡ |

### PASSWORDS

| PASSWORD | EFFECT |
|---|---|
| 573300 | Area 1, Round 1 (2nd Playthrough) |
| 344710 | Area 1, Round 1 (3rd Playthrough) |
| 274510 | Area 1, Round 1 (4th Playthrough) |
| 321310 | Area 1, Round 1 (5th Playthrough) |
| 536300 | Area 1, Round 1 (6th Playthrough) |
| 301710 | Area 1, Round 1 (7th Playthrough) |
| 231510 | Area 1, Round 1 (8th Playthrough) |
| 256310 | Area 1, Round 1 (9th Playthrough) |
| 441300 | Area 1, Round 1 (10th Playthrough) |
| 677261 | Area 5, Round 50 |
| 075653 | Fight enemy opponents only |

## CHILDREN OF EDEN    (PlayStation 3)

### TROPHY

| UNLOCKABLE | HOW TO UNLOCK |
|---|---|
| Absolutely Fabulous (Bronze) | Cleared all the Archives on Normal Difficulty and achieved 100% purification. |
| Automaton (Bronze) | Achieved a 4 Star Clear Rank. |
| Collector (Bronze) | 25% of Extra bonuses unlocked. |
| Constellation Overdrive (Bronze) | Obtained more than 800,000 points in the Passion Archive on Normal Difficulty. |
| Crackerjack (Bronze) | Cleared the Evolution Archive on Normal Difficulty and achieved 100% purification. |
| Dabbler (Bronze) | 10% of Extra bonuses unlocked. |
| Endless Passion (Bronze) | Obtained all items in the Passion Archive. |
| Evolution Pack Rat (Bronze) | Obtained all items in the Evolution Archive. |
| Eye Of The Beholder (Bronze) | Obtained all items in the Beauty Archive. |
| Feel The Beat (Bronze) | Achieved a Perfect Octa-Lock. |
| Field Of Dreams (Bronze) | Cleared the Beauty Archive on Normal Difficulty Mode. |
| Figure Eight (Bronze) | Purified an enemy using Octa-Lock. |
| Fireworks From Heaven (Silver) | Obtained more than 800,000 points in the Beauty Archive on Hard Difficulty. |

| | |
|---|---|
| **Flawless Beauty (Bronze)** | Obtained more than 800,000 points in the Beauty Archive on Normal Difficulty. |
| **Genius Play (Bronze)** | Cleared the Matrix Archive on Normal Difficulty and achieved 100% purification. |
| **Giver Of Life (Bronze) Mode.** | Cleared the Journey Archive on Normal Difficulty |
| **Gunslinger (Silver)** | Obtained more than 800,000 points in the Journey Archive on Hard Difficulty. |
| **Hierophant (Silver)** | Achieved a Gold Star Clear Rank. |
| **Hope Springs Eternal (Silver)** | Cleared the Hope Archive. |
| **Hot Shot (Bronze)** | Achieved a total of 100 Perfect Octa-Locks. |
| **If The Spirit Moves You (Bronze)** | Cleared the Passion Archive on Normal Difficulty Mode. |
| **Impeccable Virtue (Bronze)** | Obtained more than 800,000 points in the Journey Archive on Normal Difficulty. |
| **Luminous (Bronze)** | Cleared the Passion Archive on Normal Difficulty and achieved 100% purification. |
| **Magnificent Aura (Bronze)** | Obtained more than 800,000 points in the Evolution Archive on Normal Difficulty. |
| **Maniac Play (Bronze)** | 75% of Extra bonuses unlocked. |
| **Master of Eden (Gold)** | Cleared all Archives on Normal and Hard Difficulty Mode with a Gold Star Clear Rank. |
| **Matrix Archivist (Bronze)** | Cleared the Matrix Archive on Hard Difficulty Mode. |
| **Matrix Completionist (Bronze)** | Obtained all items in the Matrix Archive. |
| **Phoenix Rising (Bronze)** | Cleared the Evolution Archive on Normal Difficulty Mode. |
| **Pulse-Pounding (Bronze)** | Obtained more than 800,000 points in the Matrix Archive on Normal Difficulty. |
| **Radiant Avalon (Bronze)** | Cleared the Journey Archive on Normal Difficulty and achieved 100% purification. |
| **Savant (Bronze)** | Achieved a 5 Star Clear Rank. |
| **Shimmering Brightness (Bronze)** | Cleared the Beauty Archive on Hard Difficulty Mode |
| **SRSBZNS (Bronze)** | 50% of Extra bonuses unlocked. |
| **Super Collider (Silver)** | 100% of Extra bonuses unlocked. |
| **The Calculator (Silver)** | Obtained more than 800,000 points in the Evolution Archive on Hard Difficulty. |
| **The Cleaner (Bronze)** | All enemy types purified. |
| **The Great Evolution Round-Up (Bronze)** | Cleared the Evolution Archive on Hard Difficulty Mode. |
| **The Journey's End (Bronze)** | Cleared the Journey Archive on Hard Difficulty Mode. |
| **The Purest Shining Light (Platinum)** | Unlocked all Trophies. |
| **The Skills That Pay The Bills (Bronze)** | Achieved 10 consecutive Perfect Octa-Locks. |
| **The Thinker (Bronze)** | Cleared the Beauty Archive on Normal Difficulty and achieved 100% purification. |
| **The Wireframe Web Expands (Bronze)** | Cleared the Matrix Archive on Normal Difficulty. Mode |
| **Time Becomes A Loop (Silver)** | Obtained more than 800,000 points in the Matrix Archive on Hard Difficulty. |
| **Total Eclipse Of The Heart (Silver)** | Cleared all the Archives on Hard Difficulty and achieved 100% purification. |

| Total Enlightenment (Bronze) | Euphoria used. |
|---|---|
| Ultimate Compiler (Gold) | Collected all Reward Items in Lumi's Garden. |
| Unforgettable Fire (Bronze) | Cleared the Passion Archive on Hard Difficulty Mode. |
| Wanderer (Bronze) | Obtained all items in the Journey Archive. |
| You Sure Showed Them (Silver) | Obtained more than 800,000 points in the Passion Archive on Hard Difficulty. |

## CHINA WARRIOR (Wii)

### CODES

| UNLOCKABLE | HOW TO UNLOCK |
|---|---|
| Enable Invincibility and Level Select | Press RUN+SELECT to reset the game, keep the buttons held, then release RUN and press ✛ when the title screen is displayed. Release Select and press ✛, ✛, ✛, ✛, ✛, ✛, ✛, ✛, ✛, ✛, ✛, ✛. |
| Level Skip | Hold ✛ then SELECT+①+② to skip the first level. For the other levels, hold ✛ instead of ✛. |
| Continue (up to three times) from the Start of the Las Level Played | Hold ①+②+✛ and press RUN, RUN when the phrase "The End" appears after gameplay is over. Alternately, hold ①+2+✛ and press RUN at the title screen after game play is over. |

## THE CHRONICLES OF NARNIA: THE LION, THE WITCH, AND THE WARDROBE (DS)

Enter these codes at the Main menu.

| UNLOCKABLE | CODE |
|---|---|
| Acquire Armor | Ⓐ, Ⓧ, Ⓨ, Ⓑ, ↑, ↑, ↑, ↓ |
| All Blessings | ←, ↑, Ⓐ, Ⓑ, →, ↓, Ⓧ, Ⓨ |
| All Skills at Maximum | Ⓐ, ←, →, Ⓑ, ↑, ↑, Ⓧ, Ⓧ |
| Extra Money | ↑, Ⓧ, ↑, Ⓧ, ↓, Ⓑ, ↓, Ⓑ |
| Invincibility | Ⓐ, Ⓨ, Ⓧ, Ⓑ, ↑, ↑, ↓, ↓ |
| Maximum Attributes | ←, Ⓑ, ↑, Ⓨ, ↓, Ⓧ, →, Ⓐ |
| Restore Health | ←, →, ↑, ↓, Ⓐ, Ⓐ, Ⓐ, Ⓐ |
| Stronger Attacks | Ⓐ, ↑, Ⓑ, ↓, Ⓧ, Ⓧ, Ⓨ, Ⓨ |

## CHRONO TRIGGER (DS)

### UNLOCKABLE ENDINGS

| UNLOCKABLE | HOW TO UNLOCK |
|---|---|
| Ending 1 "Beyond Time" | Defeat Lavos after reviving Crono at Death Peak. |
| Ending 10 "Dino Age" | Defeat Lavos after facing Magus, but before facing Azala. |
| Ending 11 "What the Prophet Seeks" | Defeat Lavos after facing Azala, but before Schala opens the sealed door. |
| Ending 12 "Memory lane" | Defeat Lavos after Schala opens the sealed door, but before restoring the light to the pendant. |
| Ending 13 "Dream's Epilogue" | Defeat the Dream Devourer beyond Time's Eclipse |
| Ending 2 "Reunion" | Defeat Lavos while Crono is dead. |
| Ending 3 "The Dream Project" | Defeat Lavos in the Ocean Palace or immediately upon starting a new game. |
| Ending 4 "The successor of Guardia" | Defeat Lavos after saving Leene and Marle, but before visiting the End of Time. |
| Ending 5 "Good Night" | Defeat Lavos after visiting the End of Time, but before returning to the Middle Ages. |
| Ending 6 "The Legendary Hero" | Defeat Lavos after arriving in the Middle Ages, but before obtaining the Hero's Badge. |

| Ending 7 "The Unknown Past" | Defeat Lavos after obtaining the Hero's Badge, but before the Gate key is stolen. |
| Ending 8 "People of the times" | Defeat Lavos after regaining the gate key, but before giving the Masamune to Frog. |
| Ending 9 "The Oath" | Defeat Lavos after giving the Masamune to Frog but before fighting Magus. |

### ITEM DUPLICATION

Once you reach the Arena of Ages, send your monster out to train until it returns back with an item. When it returns, you will see the monster's status window showing the item it brought back. Without closing this window, press the A button to select the option "Train Monster." Then press the A button a second time and you will now be on the Consumables item screen. Press the B button once to return back to the original screen. This will duplicate the item that the monster brought back (though you will not see any evidence of this until you look in your own inventory). You can continue to do this to get 99 of that item. This is a great way to stock up on magic, speed, or strength capsules.

## CLONING CLYDE (XBOX 360)

### UNLOCK MUTANT CLYDE

| UNLOCKABLE | HOW TO UNLOCK |
| --- | --- |
| Mutant Clyde | Beat all levels under par time |

## COMIX ZONE (Wii)

### UNLOCKABLES

| UNLOCKABLE | HOW TO UNLOCK |
| --- | --- |
| Fart | In some areas, press ⬇. |
| Sega Plug | At any time during the main game, press START to pause. After a few seconds, Sketch will yell, "Sega!" |
| Stage Select | Go to the Jukebox mode and place the red checker on the following numbers in order, pressing ⬇ at each one: 14, 15, 18, 5, 13, 1, 3, 18, 15, 6. Now, highlight a number from 1 to 6 and press ⬇ to warp to the corresponding stage. |
| Unlimited Health | Go to Jukebox in the Options menu and push ⬇ on these numbers: 3, 12, 17, 2, 2, 10, 2, 7, 7, 11. You hear Sketch say "oh yeah." |
| View Credits | At the Options mode, press Ⓐ+Ⓑ+Ⓒ. |
| Paper Airplane | During gameplay press and hold the Punch button. After a second or so Sketch will tear a piece of paper from the background and make a paper airplane out of it. The plane will travel to the edge of the panel and circle back around. The plane does massive damage to all enemies, objects, and Sketch himself, so be careful. You lose a considerable amount of health when creating the plane. |

## THE CONDUIT (Wii)

### CODES

Enter the code from the cheats menu

| EFFECT | CODE |
| --- | --- |
| Custom ASE unlocked | NewASE11 |
| Secret Agent skin unlocked | SuitMP13 |
| Unlock Drone for Single-player | Drone4SP |

### UNLOCKABLES

These cheats can be unlocked after gaining achievements. Enable the cheats in the Cheats Menu, under Extras.

| UNLOCKABLE | HOW TO UNLOCK |
| --- | --- |
| Fiery Death: Enemies Die As If They Had Been Killed By A Charged Shot | Complete the "Secret Master" achievement. |

| Fully Stocked: Infinite Ammo | Complete the "Annihilator Award" achievement. |
| Stopping Power: One Shot Kill | Complete the "Campaign Award" achievement. |

## CONDUIT 2 (Wii)

### CODE

In the Extras option, go to Promotional Codes and type the following codes in.

| EFFECT | CODE |
| --- | --- |
| Unlock Eye of Ra ASE. | EYEOFRA |
| Unlock Golden Destroyer armor. (Online only.) | 14KARMOR |

## CONTRA (XBOX 360)

### CODES

| CODE | EFFECT |
| --- | --- |
| Up, Up, Down, Down, Left, Right, Left, Right, B, A | Start game with 30 lives. Your score is not eligible for the High Score Leader Board. |

## CRASH: MIND OVER MUTANT (XBOX 360)

### CODES

While playing story mode, pause the game. Hold guard and press the following buttons on the D-pad very quickly! To deactivate a cheat, enter its code again.

| EFFECT | CODE |
| --- | --- |
| Crash freeze any enemy he touches | Down, Down, Down, Up |
| Crash turns into a shadow | Left, Right, Left, Right |
| Enemies leave behind x4 damage (Boxing glove) | Up, Up, Up, Right |
| Enemies leave behind Wumpa fruit | Right, Right, Right, Up |
| Make different parts of Crash bigger | Left, Left, Left, Down |

## CRASH: MIND OVER MUTANT (Wii)

### CODES

While playing Story Mode, pause the game. Hold guard and press the following buttons on the D-pad very quickly! To deactivate a cheat, enter its code again.

| EFFECT | CODE |
| --- | --- |
| Crash freezes any enemy he touches | Right, Right, Right, Right |
| Crash turns into a shadow | Left, Left, Left, Left |
| Enemies leave behind x4 damage (Boxing glove) | Up, Up, Up, Down |
| Enemies leave behind Wumpa fruit | Down, Down, Down, Up |
| Make different parts of Crash bigger | Down, Down, Down, Down |

## CRATERMAZE (Wii)

### PASSWORDS

| PASSWORD | EFFECT |
| --- | --- |
| Unlock All Normal Levels | Press RUN on the title screen and select Password. Enter this password, then use ① and ② to select a level before pressing RUN. Blue/Left, Blue/Left, Blue/Right, Red/Front |
| Expert Level Select | Blue/Back, Blue/Back, Red/Right, Blue/Forward |

## CRESCENT PALE MIST (PlayStation 3)

### UNLOCKABLES

| UNLOCKABLE | HOW TO UNLOCK |
| --- | --- |
| Boss Only mode | Obtain the Mysterious Button from the enemy D'Artagnan on stage 5 (Normal mode and up only) |

| Fear difficulty | Obtain the terror medallion from one of the three black star enemies on stage 4 (Hard mode only); then beat the game on Hard mode |
|---|---|
| Music Room | Locate the music room key on stage 6 (Normal mode and up only) |
| Planeriel difficulty | Obtain the nightmare medallion from the nightmare of legend enemy on stage 3 (Fear mode only); then beat the game on Fear mode |

## THE CURSED CRUSADE (PlayStation 3)

### TROPHY

| UNLOCKABLE | HOW TO UNLOCK |
|---|---|
| ...And My Axe! (Bronze) | Master the Axe and Shield technique! |
| A Change of Perspective (Bronze) | Clear 'The Capitolium' in any difficulty setting. |
| A Templar Rides into a Forest... (Bronze) | Clear 'Forest Roads' in any difficulty setting. |
| Axes of Evil (Bronze) | Master the Double Axe technique! |
| Blunt Trauma (Bronze) | Master the Double Mace technique! |
| Classic Cleric (Bronze) | the Mace and Shield technique! |
| Cross the Crosses (Silver) | Find all the Blood Crucifixes! |
| Cursed and Loving It (Silver) | Enhance your character's Templar's Curse to its maximum! |
| Cutsman (Bronze) | Master the Sword and Axe technique! |
| Deflect 30 attacks with the Deflection Counter! | Deflect 30 attacks with the Deflection Counter! |
| Demon Slayer (Bronze) | Clear 'Hagia Sophia Basilica' in any difficulty setting. |
| End of the Chain (Bronze) | Perform a 100 hit combo. |
| Evasive Maneuvers (Silver) | Dodge 30 Guard Breaks! |
| Gold Before Glory (Gold) | Find all the coffers! |
| Greek Poetry in Motion (Bronze) | Master the Spear and Shield technique! |
| Hatchet Man (Bronze) | Master the One-Handed Axe! |
| Here's Your Trophy! (Bronze) | Find the ninth Blood Crucifix! |
| Innocent Blood (Bronze) | Defend Constantinople's civilians! |
| Knight in Shining Armor (Bronze) | Master the Sword and Shield technique! |
| Live by the Sword (Bronze) | Master the One-Handed Sword! |
| Mace Effect (Bronze) | Master the One-Handed Mace! |
| Maelstrom of Fire (Bronze) | Acquire the power Fire Maelstrom! |
| Make the Voices Stop (Bronze) | Clear 'The Fall of Zara' in any difficulty setting. |
| Master of War (Gold) | Master all the martial techniques! |
| Offense is the Best Defense (Bronze) | Master the Sword and Mace technique! |
| One-Man Army (Gold) | Enhance all of your character's statistics to their maximum! |
| Overcompensating (Bronze) | Master the Two-Handed Sword! |
| Playing the Tortuga (Silver) | Enhance your character's Armor Mastery to its maximum! |
| Roar of Flames (Bronze) | Acquire the power Roaring Flames! |
| Saint Longinus (Bronze) | Master the Spear! |

| | |
|---|---|
| **Slow and Steady (Silver)** | Clear 'The Road to the Peninsula' without losing any of the soldiers pushing the ballista. |
| **Strong as a Spanish Cow (Silver)** | Enhance your character's Strength to its maximum! |
| **Symphony of Hell (Platinum)** | Get all the trophies of The Cursed Crusade! |
| **That Man's On Fire (Bronze)** | Acquire the power Purifying Fire! |
| **The Cursed Crusader (Bronze)** | Clear the game on any difficulty setting. |
| **The Cursed Templar (Gold)** | Clear the game on the 'Nightmare' difficulty setting. |
| **Timber! (Bronze)** | Master the Two-Handed Axe! |
| **Unconventional Assault (Bronze)** | Master the Axe and Mace technique! |
| **Unstoppable (Bronze)** | Perform a 50 hit combo. |
| **Was That Supposed Hurt? (Silver)** | Enhance your character's Constitution to its to maximum! |
| **We Are the Champions, My Friend (Bronze)** | Win the Tournament of Ecry. |
| **Weapons of Mass Purification (Silver)** | Enhance your character's Weapon Mastery to its maximum! |
| **What's Better Than One Sword? (Bronze)** | Master the Double Sword technique! |

## CYBERNATOR (Wii)

### CODES

| UNLOCKABLE | HOW TO UNLOCK |
|---|---|
| Extra Continues | At the title screen, hold ✛+✛+✛ and then press START. |
| Napalm Gun | Complete the first level without shooting anything except the boss, then complete level 2 without dying. |
| Secret Bad Ending | Go through the first level, and do not destroy the boss. Finish the rest of the game to see the failed ending. |

## DANCE CENTRAL 2 (XBOX 360)

### ACHIEVEMENT

| UNLOCKABLE | HOW TO UNLOCK |
|---|---|
| All Over the Place (20) | Nail moves in each column on the screen in a Free-4-All. |
| All That Glitters (10) | Master The Glitterati's routines on Easy skill level. |
| Biggest Winner (20) | Burn your first 100 calories in Fitness mode. |
| Bit of a Lu$h (10) | Master Lu$h Crew's routines on Easy skill level. |
| Bragging Rights (20) | Earn more than 100,000 points in a Free-4-All. |
| Certified Double Platinum (25) | Get a solo score of at least 2,000,000 points on a song. |
| Chump to Champ (20) | Go from 2nd place to 1st in a Free-4-All. |
| Dance Hall Legend (40) | Earn 5 stars on every song in the game. |
| Dance Machine (10) | Defeated Dr. Tan's army of robots on Easy skill level. |
| Def to the World (10) | Master Hi-Def's routines on Easy skill level. |
| Eclectic Taste (20) | Gold Digger (20) |
| Endless-ish Setlist (15) | Complete a playlist that is 15 minutes in length or longer. |
| Finishing Touch (20) | Earn a Flawless Finish on a song. |
| Fitness Fanatic (15) | Complete an entire Fitness Playlist. |
| Flash in the Pan (15) | Master Flash4wrd's routines on Medium skill level. |
| For the Record (15) | Get a perfect score on a move after using Video Record in Break It Down mode. |
| Forward Motion (10) | Master Flash4wrd's routines on Easy skill level. |
| Friend of Flash4wrd (20) | Master Flash4wrd's routines on Hard skill level. |
| Friend of Hi-Def (20) | Master Hi-Def's routines on Hard skill level. |
| Friend of Lu$h Crew (20) | Master Lu$h Crew's routines on Hard skill level. |
| Friend of Riptide (20) | Master Riptide's routines on Hard skill level. |
| Full Dance Card (30) | Dance with every original crew member in the game. |
| Get the Picture (15) | Upload a Photo to Kinect Share. |
| Getting Ripped (10) | Master Riptide's routines on Easy skill level. |
| Gold Digger (20) | Earn Gold Stars on a song. |
| Hard Act to Follow (20) | Earn 3 stars on any song on Hard skill level. |
| Hi and Mighty (15) | Master Hi-Def's routines on Medium skill level. |
| In It to Twin It (15) | Master The Glitterati's routines on Medium skill level. |
| Latest Model (30) | Have your picture taken 1000 times. |
| Lu$h Fund (15) | Master Lu$h Crew's routines on Medium skill level. |
| Minion Potential (25) | Defeated Dr. Tan's army of robots on Medium skill level. |
| Nailed It! (15) | Skip to the next move by nailing a move the first time you see it in Break It Down. |

| Patience Is a Virtue (10) | Listen to the entire background theme of the game in one sitting. |
|---|---|
| Perfect Pair (30) | Earn 5 stars on a co-op performance. |
| Photo Bomb! (20) | Perform a Freestyle section with 3 or more people. |
| Provad Your Point (20) | Win 3 Dance Battles in a row. |
| Recapable (20) | Get a perfect score on a Recap in Break It Down mode. |
| Shop and Lock (30) | Unlock the alternate outfits for the 10 crew members. |
| Slow Profile (15) | Get a perfect score on a move after using Slo-Mo in Break It Down mode. |
| Solo and Steady (20) | Earn 5 stars on a solo performance. |
| Star Quality (25) | Earn over 100 stars. |
| Survival of the Fittest (20) | Log 5 total hours in Fitness mode. |
| Targeted Practice (15) | Customize your Break It Down session by using the "Focus on Select Moves" feature. |
| Teacher's Pet (25) | Earn 5 stars on a song in Perform It immediately after completing it in Break It Down. |
| The Doctor Will See You Now (50) | Defeated Dr. Tan's army of robots on Hard skill level. |
| Thrash and Burn (40) | Burn 3500 calories in Fitness mode. |
| Turn the Tide (15) | Master Riptide's routines on Medium skill level. |
| Vanquisher (20) | Win 20 Dance Battles. |
| Working It Out (20) | Survival of the Fittest (20) |
| Worthy Adversary (20) | Master The Glitterati's routines on Hard skill level. |

### UNLOCKABLE

| UNLOCKABLE | HOW TO UNLOCK |
|---|---|
| Bring It Tee | Play every song in the game in Perform It mode. |
| Neon Tee | Get a solo score of at least 2,000,000 points on a song. |
| Ribbon Tee | Earn Gold Stars on a song. |

## DANTE'S INFERNO (PlayStation 3)

### UNLOCKABLES

| UNLOCKABLE | HOW TO UNLOCK |
|---|---|
| Making the Baby Feature | Beat the game on any difficulty. |
| Dante's Crusader Costume | Complete the game and start a new game (or Resurrection Mode game); you'll be prompted to choose the costume before the game begins. |
| Gates of Hell Survival Mode | Complete the game and it will be selectable from the Main menu. |
| New Game Plus (Resurrection Mode) | Complete the game. |
| Infernal Difficulty | Beat the game on any other difficulty. |

## DARK SOULS (PlayStation 3)

### TROPHY

| UNLOCKABLE | HOW TO UNLOCK |
|---|---|
| Art of Abysswalking (Bronze) | Acquire the Art of Abysswalking. |
| Bond of a Pyromancer (Silver) | Acquire all pyromancies. |
| Chaos Weapon (Bronze) | Acquire best wpn through chaos reinfrc. |
| Covenant: Blade of the Darkmoon (Silver) | Discover Blade of the Darkmoon covenant. |
| Covenant: Chaos Servant (Silver) | Discover Chaos Servant covenant. |

| | |
|---|---|
| Covenant: Darkwraith (Silver) | Discover Darkwraith covenant. |
| Covenant: Forest Hunter (Silver) | Discover Forest Hunter covenant. |
| Covenant: Gravelord Servant (Silver) | Discover Gravelord Servant covenant. |
| Covenant: Path of the Dragon (Silver) | Discover Path of the Dragon covenant. |
| Covenant: Princess's Guard (Silver) | Discover Princess's Guard covenant. |
| Covenant: Warrior of Sunlight (Silver) | Discover Warrior of Sunlight covenant. |
| Covenant: Way of White (Bronze) | Discover Way of White covenant. |
| Crystal Weapon (Bronze) | Acquire best wpn through crystal reinfrc. |
| Dark Lord (Gold) | Reach 'The Dark Lord' ending. |
| Defeat Bed of Chaos (Silver) | Defeat the Soul Lord Bed of Chaos. |
| Defeat Crossbreed Priscilla (Silver) | Defeat Crossbreed Priscilla, the Lifehunter. |
| Defeat Gravelord Nito (Silver) | Defeat the Soul Lord Gravelord Nito. |
| Defeat Seath the Scaleless (Silver) | Defeat Seath the Scaleless, inheritors of souls. |
| Defeat the Dark Sun Gwyndolin (Silver) | Defeat Dark Sun Gwyndolin, the Darkmoon God. |
| Defeat the Four Kings (Silver) | Defeat the Four Kings, inheritors of souls. |
| Divine Weapon (Bronze) | Acquire best wpn through divine reinfrc. |
| Enchanted Weapon (Bronze) | Acquire best wpn through enchanted reinfrc. |
| Enkindle (Bronze) | Light bonfire flame. |
| Estus Flask (Bronze) | Acquire Estes Flask. |
| Fire Weapon (Bronze) | Acquire best wpn through fire reinfrc. |
| Knight's Honor (Silver) | Acquire all rare weapons. |
| Lightning Weapons (Bronze) | Acquire best wpn through lightning reinfrc. |
| Lordvessel (Silver) | Acquire the Lordvessel. |
| Magic Weapon (Bronze) | Acquire best wpn through magic reinfrc. |
| Occult Weapon (Bronze) | Acquire best wpn through occult reinfrc. |
| Prayer of a Maiden (Silver) | Acquire all miracles. |
| Raw Weapon (Bronze) | Acquire best wpn through raw reinfrc. |
| Reach Anor Londo (Silver) | Arrive in Anor Londo. |
| Reach Lordran (Bronze) | Arrive in Lordran. |
| Ring the bell (Quelaag's Domain) (Bronze) | Ring Bell of Awakening in Quelaag's domain. |
| Ring the Bell (Undead Church) (Bronze) | Ring Bell of Awakening at Undead Church. |
| Rite of Kindling (Bronze) | Acquire the Rite of Kindling. |
| Strongest Weapon (Bronze) | Acquire best wpn through standard reinfrc. |
| The Dark Soul (Platinum) | All trophies obtained. Congratulations! |
| To Link the Fire (Gold) | Reach 'To Link the Fire' ending. |
| Wisdom of a Sage (Silver) | Acquire all sorceries. |

## THE DARKNESS (XBOX 360)

### SPECIAL DARKLINGS

At any in-game phone, enter the number and you will unlock a special Darkling

| PASSWORD | EFFECT |
|---|---|
| 555-GAME | Unlocks Special 2K Darkling |
| 555-5664 | Unlocks the European Retailer (Golfer) Special Darkling |

## THE DARKNESS (PlayStation 3)

### PHONE NUMBERS

Go to any phone and enter the 18 phone numbers, in no specific order, to unlock Keeper of Secrets accomplishment. Find these phone numbers throughout the game on posters, graffiti, etc. Out of the 25, you only need 18 to unlock the accomplishment.

| PHONE NUMBER | COUNT |
|---|---|
| 555-6118 | 1/18 |
| 555-9723 | 2/18 |
| 555-1847 | 3/18 |
| 555-5289 | 4/18 |
| 555-6667 | 5/18 |
| 555-6205 | 6/18 |
| 555-4569 | 7/18 |
| 555-7658 | 8/18 |
| 555-9985 | 9/18 |
| 555-1233 | 10/18 |
| 555-1037 | 11/18 |
| 555-3947 | 12/18 |
| 555-1206 | 13/18 |
| 555-9562 | 14/18 |
| 555-9528 | 15/18 |
| 555-7934 | 16/18 |
| 555-3285 | 17/18 |
| 555-7892 | 18/18 |

## DARKSIDERS (XBOX 360)

### CODES

Enter the Pause Screen during gameplay and select "Options." Under Game Options select "Enter Code" from the menu.

| EFFECT | CODE |
|---|---|
| "The Harvester" Scythe | The Hollow Lord |

## DARKSIDERS (PlayStation 3)

### CODES

Enter the Pause Screen during gameplay and select "Options." Under Game Options select "Enter Code" from the menu.

| EFFECT | CODE |
|---|---|
| "The Harvester" Scythe | The Hollow Lord |

## DEAD ISLAND (XBOX 360)

### ACHIEVEMENT

| UNLOCKABLE | HOW TO UNLOCK |
|---|---|
| 10 heads are better than 1 (15) | Kill 10 zombies in a row with headshots. |
| A taste of everything (25) | Kill a zombie with 10 different melee weapons. |
| A very special day (30) | Kill 250 zombies with modified weapons. |

| | |
|---|---|
| Ah! Spoiled meat! (10) | Kill a Butcher using an axe. |
| Banoi Redemption (30) | Complete act IV. |
| Busy, busy, busy (60) | Finish 75 quests cumulatively. |
| Can't touch this (20) | Use a hammer to kill a series of 15 zombies without taking damage. |
| Cardio (10) | Travel a distance of 20 kilometers on foot. |
| Catch! (10) | Kill an Infected with a grenade blast. |
| Dedicated student (25) | Reach level 25. |
| Everybody lies (20) | Use a large medkit to heal an injury of 5% or less. |
| First! (15) | Kill a Suicider with a grenade. |
| Gesundheit! (10) | Heal yourself with a medkit 100 times. |
| Going steady (25) | Complete 25 quests while playing with at least one co-op partner. |
| Gotta find'em all (20) | Find 60 collectibles. |
| Guns don't kill but they help (25) | Kill 250 zombies using firearms. |
| Hack & slash (25) | Kill 250 zombies using edged melee weapons. |
| Hell in paradise (30) | Complete act I. |
| How many days exactly? (10) | Play Dead Island at least 28 days after starting it for the first time. |
| Humanitarian (15) | Kill 50 human enemies. |
| I want one of those (30) | Customize 25 weapons. |
| Karma-geddon (15) | Kill 50 zombies using a vehicle. |
| King of the jungle (30) | Complete act III. |
| Knock, knock (15) | Breach a locked door with the first blow. |
| Learning the ropes (10) | Reach level 10. |
| Light my fire (20) | Set 10 zombies on fire simultaneously. |
| Ménage à trois (25) | Complete 5 quests with 3 co-op partners. |
| Nearly there (25) | Find 120 collectibles. |
| Need a hand? (10) | Join another player's game. |
| No raccoons in here (30) | Complete act II. |
| Oh, no you don't (10) | Kill a Ram using tackle skill. |
| One is all I need (20) | Kill 5 Infected in a row with a single blow. |
| Originality (10) | Play in a co-op team of 4 different playable characters. |
| People Person (10) | Play with 10 different co-op partners for at least 15 minutes each. |
| Rageman (25) | Kill 100 enemies with Fury attacks. |
| Right 4 Life (30) | Complete act I with 4 different characters. |
| Road Trip (10) | Drive a total distance of 10 kilometers. |
| Rootin' Tootin' Lootin' (30) | Loot 5 Exceptional Weapons. |
| Savior (20) | Save 5 people besieged by zombies. |
| School of hard knocks (30) | Reach level 50. |
| Steam Punk (30) | Create weapons to rival the gods of fire or thunder. |
| Swing them sticks (25) | Kill 150 enemies using Analog Fighting controls. |
| Tae Kwon Leap (25) | Kill 25 zombies with your bare fists. |
| There and back again (30) | Explore the entire island. |
| Tis but a flesh wound! (10) | Sever 100 limbs. |
| To put it bluntly (25) | Kill 250 zombies using blunt melee weapons. |

| Together in the light (10) | Complete 5 quests in a single co-op game with the same partners. |
| Warranty Void if Used (10) | Create a customized weapon. |

## DEAD MOON (Wii)

### UNLOCKABLE

| UNLOCKABLE | HOW TO UNLOCK |
| --- | --- |
| Option Screen | Hold the following: ✛+①+② and press SELECT |

## DEAD OR ALIVE: DIMENSIONS (3DS)

### CODES

When selecting a character, hold the following for costume variants, then select with Ⓐ.

| EFFECT | CODE |
| --- | --- |
| Kasumi Alpha: Braid | ⬅+Ⓧ |
| Kasumi Alpha: High Ponytail | ➡+Ⓧ |
| Kasumi Alpha: Low Ponytail | ⬅+⬅+Ⓧ |
| Kasumi: Braided hair | ⬅+Ⓧ |
| Kasumi: High Ponytail | ➡+Ⓧ |
| Kasumi: Low Ponytail | ⬅+⬅+Ⓧ |
| La Mariposa: No Mask | ⬅+Ⓧ |
| Lei Fang: Side Braids | ⬅+Ⓧ |
| Lei Fang: Short Ponytail | ➡+Ⓧ |
| Random Select: Shiden Costume 1 | ⬅+Ⓧ |
| Random Select: Shiden Costume 2 | ➡+Ⓧ |
| Random Select: Shiden Costume 3 | ⬅+⬅+Ⓧ |

### UNLOCKABLE

| UNLOCKABLE | HOW TO UNLOCK |
| --- | --- |
| Character Menu Voice | Play and win one round of survival mode |
| Geo-Thermal Plant(Metroid Stage) | Finish all of Arcade mode |

## DEAD RISING (XBOX 360)

### ENDING REQUIREMENTS

These are the requirements needed in 72 hour mode to unlock different endings, with A the best and F the worst.

| UNLOCKABLE | HOW TO UNLOCK |
| --- | --- |
| Ending A | Solve all cases, talk to Isabella at 10 am, and return to the heliport at 12 pm on the 22nd |
| Ending B | Don't solve all cases and be at the heliport on time |
| Ending C | Solve all cases but do not talk to Isabella at 10 am on the last day |
| Ending D | Be a prisoner of the special forces at 12 pm on the 22nd |
| Ending E | Don't be at the heliport and don't solve all cases |
| Ending F | Fail to collect all of Carlito's bombs on act 7-2 |

### UNLOCK WEAPON: MOLOTOV COCKTAIL

| UNLOCKABLE | HOW TO UNLOCK |
| --- | --- |
| Molotov Cocktail (infinite supply) | Use fire extinguisher to save Paul, then bring him to the security room. |

### UNLOCKABLES

A handful of the Achievements have Unlockable content that becomes available once they've been activated. These, rewards, which include special costumes and items, can be found inside Shopping Bags behind the air duct in the Security Room after you've finished the game.

| UNLOCKABLE | HOW TO UNLOCK |
|---|---|
| Ammo Belt | Perfect Gunner |
| Arthur's Boxers | 7 Day Survivor |
| Cop Hat | Saint |
| Hockey Mask | PP Collector |
| Laser Sword | 5 Day Survivor |
| Mall Employee Uniform | Transmissionary |
| Mega Man Boots | Unbreakable |
| Mega Man Tights | Punisher |
| Prisoner Garb | Carjacker |
| Pro Wrestling Boots | Item Smasher |
| Pro Wrestling Briefs | Karate Champ |
| Real Mega Buster | Zombie Genocide |
| Special Forces Boots | Legendary Soldier |
| Special Forces Uniform | Hella Copter |
| White Hat | Census Taker |

### UNLOCKABLE MODES

| UNLOCKABLE | HOW TO UNLOCK |
|---|---|
| Infinity Mode | Complete Overtime mode |
| Overtime Mode | Complete all missions in 72 mode, talk to Isabella at 10am, and return to the helipad by noon on the 22nd |

## DEAD RISING 2 (PlayStation 3)

### SUIT OF ARMOR

To get the suit of armor from Ghouls 'n Ghosts, you must gather all 4 pieces. When you wear all 4 pieces at once, your health is doubled, and just like in Ghouls 'n Ghosts, as you take damage, the armor chips away, leaving you in nothing but your underwear.

| UNLOCKABLE | HOW TO UNLOCK |
|---|---|
| Full Beard | In the back of the store "Moe's Migitations" in Royal Flush Plaza. |
| Knight Armor | Complete the game with the "S" ending. |
| Knight Boots | Buy at the pawnshop in the Platinum Strip. |
| Knight Helmet | Eliminate Jack in Strip Poker in the "Ante Up" side mission. |

### CLOTHING

| UNLOCKABLE | HOW TO UNLOCK |
|---|---|
| Champion's Jacket | Win a TIR episode (be the overall top player by the end). |
| Convicts | Kill 10 psychopaths. |
| Hockey Mask | Use every melee weapon on zombies. |
| Tattered Clothes | Kill 1,000 zombies using hand-to-hand combat. |
| TIR Helmet | Earn $1,000,000 in TIR Online. |
| TIR Outfit | Earn $5,000,000 in TIR Online. |
| Willemette Mall Costume | Rescue 50 survivors. |

## DEAD RISING 2: CASE 0 (XBOX 360)

### UNLOCKABLES

| UNLOCKABLE | HOW TO UNLOCK |
|---|---|
| Easy $1,500 | In the casino, there is a slot machine with a cow on it. Put in $100 to gamble and you will always win the first 5 times. |
| Ending A | Save all survivors, give Katey Zombrex, collect all bike parts, and leave. |
| Ending B | Collect all bike parts, give Katey Zombrex, then leave. |
| Ending C | Get caught by the military, away from Katey. |

| Ending D | Get caught by military on your bike. |
|---|---|
| Ending E | Forget to give Katey Zombrex. |
| Ending F (alt) | Forget to give Katey zombrex while near her. |

## DEAD RISING 2: OFF THE RECORD (XBOX 360)

### ACHIEVEMENT

| UNLOCKABLE | HOW TO UNLOCK |
|---|---|
| Adult Content (20) | Take an extremely erotic picture. |
| Alpha Vs. Omega (20) | Have Denyce attack and damage Sgt Boykin. |
| Award Winning Photography (20) | Photograph 75 PP stickers. |
| Best of Friends (20) | Defeat 5 psychopaths in co-op. |
| BFF (20) | Use the Snapshot skill move on a zombie. |
| Camera Crazy (20) | Take a picture of a psychopath. |
| Card Archive (20) | Collect 50 combo cards. |
| Card Collection (20) | Collect 20 combo cards. |
| Challenge Addict (20) | Get at least a bronze medal on 10 different single player challenges. |
| Challenge Domination (20) | Get a gold medal on all single player challenges. |
| Cramped Quarters (20) | Get 8 survivors into a vehicle. |
| Dominoes (20) | Use the Jump Kick to knock down 100 zombies. |
| Drugged Up (20) | Take a dose of Zombrex. |
| Elite Killer (20) | Kill 1337 zombies. |
| Even More Help From My Friends (20) | Get a gold medal on all co-op challenges. |
| Frank West: Cross Dresser (20) | Dress up completely in women's clothing. |
| Full Camera (20) | Fill your camera's memory. |
| Hands of Doom (20) | Unlock all skill moves. |
| Help From My Friends (20) | Get at least a bronze medal on 10 different co-op challenges. |
| I Got a Medal! (20) | Get a medal on a challenge in Sandbox Mode. |
| Luggage Code (20) | Kill 12,345 zombies. |
| Maintaining The City (20) | Visit 10 different maintenance rooms. |
| Making Memories (20) | Take a picture of your co-op partner during co-op play. |
| Mixed Messages (20) | Take a picture with elements of horror, brutality, outtake and erotica in a single shot. |
| More Help From My Friends (20) | Get at least a bronze medal on all co-op. challenges |
| New Hotness (20) | Build one of the combo weapons new to Dead Rising 2: Off The Record. |
| No Zombies In The Vents (20) | Unlock the secret shortcut. |
| Out With the Old (20) | Defeat the motorcycle-riding psychopath. |
| Party Time (20) | Get a survivor drunk. |
| Photo Album (20) | Photo Album (20) |
| Photo Album (20) | Photograph 25 PP stickers. |
| Photo Journalist (20) | Get back in the game by gaining lots of PP from pictures. |
| Photo School (20) | Take a high PP value picture. |
| Powered Up (20) | Restore power to the Yucatan Casino. |
| Prestigious PP (20) | Get over 2,000 PP from a single zombie kill. |

| | |
|---|---|
| **Prom Night (20)** | Kill 69 zombies. |
| **Puking Rally (20)** | Have a zombie slip in a puddle of vomit. |
| **Purewal Memorial Cup (20)** | Don't consume any meat, dairy or alcohol until the military arrives. |
| **Raw Emotion (20)** | Take a photo of a survivor in a very dramatic situation. |
| **Safety Check: Failed (20)** | Use the amusement park rides to kill 10 zombies at once. |
| **Save the Girl (20)** | Rescue a damsel in distress from the Twin Terrors. |
| **Save the Girl... Again (20)** | Save the damsel in distress a second time. |
| **Save the Girl... Yet Again (20)** | Save a damsel in distress for the third and final time. |
| **Six Digits?!? (20)** | Kill 100,000 zombies. |
| **Team Player (20)** | Avert a mutiny. |
| **Technological Terror (20)** | Destroy a "harvester". |
| **The Challenge Experience (20)** | Get at least a bronze medal on all single player challenges. |
| **Tiger Tamer (20)** | Have Snowflake attack and damage a psychopath. |
| **True Colors (20)** | Defeat the mastermind of the Fortune City incident. |
| **We Have a Winner! (20)** | Play a carney game and win |

## UNLOCKABLE

| UNLOCKABLE | HOW TO UNLOCK |
|---|---|
| **Dealer Outfit** | Find it in the managers office where you save Lenny Mooney in the Yucatan Casino |
| **Ninja Boots** | Found in The Mans Sport in Uranus Zone |
| **Ninja Hood** Plaza | Find it in the secret sniper spot in Royal Flush |
| **Ninja Outfit** | Get the achievement "Elite Killer" which is to kill 1337 zombies. |
| **Protoman Blaster and Shield** | Finish the game with an S Ending (Beat Overtime) |
| **Protoman Helmet** | Save Jack in the "Welcome to the Family" case, then beat him in strip poker in the "Ante Up" case. |
| **ProtoMan Suit** | Get Bronze or better on all challenges in Sandbox Mode. |
| **Psycho Boots** | Early in the game, once you get Rebecca to the security room, the boots are inside |
| **Psycho Mask** | It is in the wedding chapel where you fight Randy |
| **Psychopath Hair** | Wait the midnight Time Share movie in Paradise Platinum Screens |
| **Soldier Face Paint** | Find it in Shanks in Palisades Mall |
| **Soldier Goggles** | Buy them in the Silver Strip pawn shop for $2,000,000 |
| **Sports Fan Clothes** | On a rack on the first floor of KokoNutz in Palisades Mall |
| **Sports Fan Face Paint** | Find it on the awning at Americana Casino |
| **Sports Fan Helmet** | Hidden in the back room of Hot Excitorama |
| **Tattered Clothes** | Get the achievement "Party Time" which is to get a survivor drunk |
| **Willamette Mall Uniform** | Visit 10 Maintenance rooms (this also unlocks the Maintaining the City achievement) |

## DEAD RISING 2: OFF THE RECORD (PlayStation 3)

### TROPHY

| UNLOCKABLE | HOW TO UNLOCK |
|---|---|
| Adult Content (Bronze) | Take an extremely erotic picture. |
| Alpha Vs. Omega (Gold) | Have Denyce attack and damage Sgt Boykin. |
| Award Winning Photography (Gold) | Photograph 75 PP stickers. |
| Best of Friends (Bronze) | Defeat 5 psychopaths in co-op. |
| BFF (Bronze) | Use the Snapshot skill move on a zombie. |
| Camera Crazy (Bronze) | Take a picture of a psychopath. |
| Card Archive (Bronze) | Collect 50 combo cards. |
| Card Collection (Bronze) | Collect 20 combo cards. |
| Challenge Addict (Bronze) | Get at least a bronze medal on 10 different single player challenges. |
| Challenge Domination (Silver) | Get a gold medal on all single player challenges. |
| Cramped Quarters (Bronze) | Get 8 survivors into a vehicle. |
| Dominoes (Bronze) | Use the Jump Kick to knock down 100 zombies. |
| DR2:OTR Trophy Master (Platinum) | Acquire all the trophies in Dead Rising 2: Off The Record. |
| Drugged Up (Bronze) | Take a dose of Zombrex. |
| Elite Killer (Bronze) | Kill 1337 zombies. [Host Only] |
| Even More Help From My Friends (Silver) | Get a gold medal on all co-op challenges. |
| Frank West: Cross Dresser (Bronze) | Dress up completely in women's clothing. |
| Full Camera (Bronze) | Fill your camera's memory. |
| Hands of Doom (Bronze) | Unlock all skill moves. |
| Help From My Friends (Bronze) | Get at least a bronze medal on 10 different co-op challenges. |
| I Got a Medal! (Bronze) | Get a medal on a challenge in Sandbox Mode. |
| Luggage Code (Bronze) | Kill 12,345 zombies. [Host Only] |
| Maintaining the City (Bronze) | Visit 10 different maintenance rooms. |
| Making Memories (Bronze) | Take a picture of your co-op partner during co-op play. |
| Mixed Messages (Bronze) | Take a picture with elements of horror, brutality, outtake and erotica in a single shot. |
| More Help From My Friends (Bronze) | Get at least a bronze medal on all co-op. challenges |
| New Hotness (Bronze) | Build one of the combo weapons new to Dead Rising 2: Off The Record. |
| Nice Shot (Bronze) | Photograph a PP sticker. |
| No Zombies in the Vents (Bronze) | Unlock the secret shortcut. |
| Out With the Old (Bronze) | Defeat the motorcycle-riding psychopath. [Story Mode Only] |
| Party Time (Bronze) | Get a survivor drunk. |
| Photo Album (Silver) | Photograph 25 PP stickers. |
| Photo Journalist (Bronze) | Get back in the game by gaining lots of PP from pictures. |
| Photo School (Bronze) | Take a high PP value picture. |
| Powered Up (Bronze) | Restore power to the Yucatan Casino. |
| Prestigious PP (Bronze) | Get over 2,000 PP from a single zombie kill. |

| | |
|---|---|
| **Prom Night (Bronze)** | Kill 69 zombies. [Host Only] |
| **Puking Rally (Bronze)** | Have a zombie slip in a puddle of vomit. |
| **Purewal Memorial Cup (Bronze)** | Don't consume any meat, dairy or alcohol until the military arrives. |
| **Raw Emotion (Bronze)** | Take a photo of a survivor in a very dramatic situation. |
| **Safety Check: Failed (Bronze)** | Use the amusement park rides to kill 10 zombies at once. |
| **Save the Girl (Bronze)** | Rescue a damsel in distress from the Twin Terrors. |
| **Save the Girl... Again (Bronze)** | Save the damsel in distress a second time. |
| **Save the Girl... Yet Again (Bronze)** | Save a damsel in distress for the third and final time |
| **Six Digits?!? (Gold)** | Kill 100,000 zombies. [Host Only] |
| **Team Player (Bronze)** | Avert a mutiny. |
| **Technological Terror (Bronze)** | Destroy a 'harvester'. |
| **The Challenge Experience (Bronze)** | Get at least a bronze medal on all single player challenges. |
| **Tiger Tamer (Bronze)** | Have Snowflake attack and damage a psychopath. |
| **True Colors (Bronze)** | Defeat the mastermind of the Fortune City incident. |
| **We Have a Winner! (Bronze)** | Play a carney game and win. |

## UNLOCKABLE

| UNLOCKABLE | HOW TO UNLOCK |
|---|---|
| **Chuck Greene Outfit** | Have an Existing Dead Rising 2 Save File when loading up a game of Dead Rising 2: Off the Record |
| **Ninja Boots** | Located in the Mans Sport in Uranus Zone |
| **Ninja Clothes** | Unlocked by killing 1337 Zombies |
| **Ninja Hood** | Located in a hidden room along the ninja path in the Royal Flush. |
| **Ninja Mask** | Located on a mannequin near the Shoal Nightclub |
| **Protoman Arm Cannon / Shield** | Unlocked by completing "Save the girl yet again" Achievement / Trophy |
| **Protoman Armor** | Unlocked after getting "The Challenge Experience" Achievement / Trophy (Get at least a bronze medal in all single player sandbox challenges) |
| **Protoman Boots** | Located in the Ultimate Playhouse in the Palisades Mall |
| **Protoman Helmet** | Unlocked after beating Jack in Ante Up or Defeat him in Sandbox mode |
| **Psycho Boots** | Located in the Arena Security Room by a locker to the right of the door. |
| **Psycho Clothes** | Unlocked after beating Carl in the psycho fight "Mail Order Zombrex" |
| **Psycho Hair** | Unlocked after watching the Time Share movie at the Theater on the Platinum Strip running from 12am-2am (Also nets you 10,000PP) |
| **Psycho Mask** | Located on a pew in the Swept Away Wedding Chapel |
| **Soldier Boots** | Located in a box in a vacant store to the right of the Ultimate Playhouse at South Plaza's West End |

| Soldier Clothes | Complete The "Save the Girl... Again" Achievement / Trophy or kill 1337 Zombies |
|---|---|
| Soldier Facepaint | Located in Shanks in the Palisades Mall |
| Soldier Goggles | Purchase in the Platinum Strip Pawn Shop |
| Sports Fan Cleats | Located in SporTrance in the Royal Flush Plaza |
| Sports Fan Clothes | Located in Kokonutz Sports Town in the Palisades Mall |
| Sports Fan Facepaint | Located at the end of the Ninja Path in the Americana Casino |
| Sports Fan Helmet | Hidden in the back room of Hot Excitorama on the Silver Strip |
| Tattered Clothing | Unlocked after unlocking the "Party Time" Achievement / Trophy (Get a Survivor Drunk) |
| Willamet Security Outfit | Unlock the "Maintaining The City" Achievement / Trophy (Visit 10 Different Maintenance Rooms) |

## DEAD SPACE (XBOX 360)

### CODES

Press Start, then insert the following codes. You will hear a chime if you've done it correctly.

| EFFECT | CODE |
|---|---|
| 1,000 credits (one time only per playthrough) | ⊗,⊗,⊗,▽,⊗ |
| 10,000 credits (one time only per playthrough) | ⊗,⊗,▽,▽,▽,⊗,⊗,▽ |
| 2 Nodes (one time only per playthrough) | ▽,⊗,⊗,⊗,▽ |
| 2,000 credits (one time only per playthrough) | ⊗,⊗,⊗,▽,▽ |
| 5 Nodes (one time only per playthrough) | ▽,⊗,▽,⊗,⊗,▽,⊗,⊗,▽,⊗,⊗,▽ |
| 5,000 credits (one time only per playthrough) | ⊗,⊗,⊗,▽,⊗,▽ |
| Refill Your Oxygen | ⊗,⊗,▽,▽,▽ |
| Refill Your Stasis and Kinesis Energy | ▽,⊗,▽,▽,⊗,▽ |

## DEAD SPACE (PlayStation 3)

### Codes

Press Start, then insert the following codes. You will hear a chime if you've done it correctly.

| EFFECT | CODE |
|---|---|
| 1,000 Credits (one time only) | ■,■,■,▲,■ |
| 2,000 Credits (one time only) | ■,■,■,▲,▲ |
| 5,000 Credits (one time only) | ■,■,■,▲,■,▲ |
| 10,000 Credits (one time only) | ■,▲,▲,▲,■,■,▲ |
| Adds 2 Power Nodes (one time only) | ▲,■,■,■,▲ |
| Adds 5 Power Nodes (one time only) | ▲,■,▲,■,■,▲,■,▲,■,▲,■,▲ |
| Refill Your Oxygen | ■,■,▲,▲,▲ |
| Refill Your Stasis and Kinesis Energy | ▲,■,▲,▲,■,▲ |

## DEAD SPACE 2 (XBOX 360)

### UNLOCKABLE

Unlock these Necromorph upgrades as you play through a career online.

| UNLOCKABLE | HOW TO UNLOCK |
|---|---|
| Lurker Execution Attack Damage Increase | Reach Level 27 |
| Lurker Health Increase | Reach Level 43 |
| Lurker Melee Damage Increase | Reach Level 15 |
| Lurker Range Damage Increase | Reach Level 03 |
| Pack Execution Attack Damage Increase | Reach Level 18 |

| | |
|---|---|
| Pack Gets Out of Stasis Faster | Reach Level 48 |
| Pack Health Increase | Reach Level 31 |
| Pack Melee Damage Increase | Reach Level 06 |
| Puker Execution Attack Damage Increase | Reach Level 24 |
| Puker Health Increase | Reach Level 58 |
| Puker Melee Damage Increase | Reach Level 39 |
| Puker Ranged Damage Increase | Reach Level 12 |
| Spitter Execution Damage Increase | Reach Level 09 |
| Spitter Health Increase | Reach Level 53 |
| Spitter Melee Damage Increase | Reach Level 21 |
| Spitter Ranged Damage Increase | Reach Level 35 |

## UNLOCKABLE

Unlock these Human upgrades as you play through a career online.

| UNLOCKABLE | HOW TO UNLOCK |
|---|---|
| Force Gun | Reach Level 11 |
| Increased Damage (Seeker Rifle) | Reach Level 50 |
| Increased Magazine Size (Force Gun) | Reach Level 29 |
| Increased Magazine Size (Javelin Gun) | Reach Level 44 |
| Increased Magazine Size (Line Gun) | Reach Level 25 |
| Increased Magazine Size (Plasma Cutter) | Reach Level 14 |
| Increased Magazine Size (Seeker Rifle) | Reach Level 33 |
| Increased Weapon Damage (Force Gun) | Reach Level 46 |
| Increased Weapon Damage (Javelin Gun) | Reach Level 57 |
| Increased Weapon Damage (Line Gun) | Reach Level 42 |
| Increased Weapon Damage (Plasma Cutter) | Reach Level 34 |
| Javelin Gun | Reach Level 28 |
| Line Gun | Reach Level 07 |
| Pulse Rifle Magazine Size Increase | Reach Level 19 |
| Pulse Rifle Weapon Damage Increase | Reach Level 38 |
| Rivet Gun Magazine Size Increase | Reach Level 40 |
| Rivet Gun Weapon Damage Increase | Reach Level 54 |
| Seeker Rifle | Reach Level 17 |

## UNLOCKABLE

Unlock the following skins by completing the following requirements

| UNLOCKABLE | HOW TO UNLOCK |
|---|---|
| Solid Army Green Suit | Unlocked by reaching level 04 |
| Solid Black Suit | Unlocked by reaching level 14 |
| Solid Olive Suit | Unlocked by reaching level 16 |
| Solid Red Suit | Unlocked by reaching level 08 |
| Solid Viral Blue Suit | Unlocked by killing another player with this suit equipped |
| Solid Viral White Suit | Unlocked by killing another player with this suit equipped |
| Tiger Camo Army Green Suit | Unlocked by reaching level 45 |
| Tiger Camo Blue Suit | Unlocked by reaching level 41 |
| Tiger Camo Military Suit | Unlocked by reaching level 52 |
| Tiger Camo Red Suit | Unlocked by reaching level 49 |
| Tiger Camo Viral White | Unlocked by killing another player with this suit equipped |
| Urban Camo Army Green Suit | Unlocked by reaching level 23 |

| Urban Camo Blue Suit | Unlocked by reaching level 20 |
|---|---|
| Urban Camo Military Suit | Unlocked by reaching level 32 |
| Urban Camo Olive Suit | Unlocked by reaching level 36 |
| Urban Camo Red Suit | Unlocked by reaching level 26 |
| Urban Camo Viral Black | Unlocked by killing another player with this suit equipped |
| Urban Camo Viral Yellow | Unlocked by killing another player with this suit equipped |
| Visceral Games Suit | Unlocked by reaching level 59 |
| War-Torn Suit | Unlocked by reaching level 56 |
| Zealot Suit | Comes with collectors edition of the game |

## UNLOCKABLE

| UNLOCKABLE | HOW TO UNLOCK |
|---|---|
| Hardcore Mode | Beat the game on any difficulty |
| New Game+ | Beat the game on any difficulty |

## UNLOCKABLE

| UNLOCKABLE | HOW TO UNLOCK |
|---|---|
| Arctic Security Suit | Beat the game on Zealot difficulty to unlock at Store |
| Dead Space 1 Plasma Cutter | Have a Dead Space 1 Save File |
| Elite Advanced Suit | Find Schematic in New Game + in Chapter 11. When the yellow lift reaches the top, turn around and find it on the ledge between elevator and wall |
| Elite Engineer Suit | Find Schematicd in New Game + during Chapter 2. It is just before the first short outer space section. |
| Elite Riot Suit | Available at store during New Game + |
| Elite Security Suit | Find Schematic in New Game + in Chapter 9. After you exit the tram, search over the railing. |
| Elite Vintage Suit | Find Schematic in New Game + in Chapter 6. It is in the area where you fight the tank before the end of the chapter. |
| Hacker Suit | Have "Dead Space: Ignition" save file to unlock at Store |
| Soldier Suit | Beat the game on Hardcore Mode to unlock at Store |

## DEATH JR. II: ROOT OF EVIL    (PSP)

Enter these codes while the game is paused.

| UNLOCKABLE | CODE |
|---|---|
| All Weapon Upgrades | Hold L2 and press ⇧, ⇧, ⇩, ⇩, ⇦, ⇨, ⇦, ⇨, ✕, ● |
| Invincibility | Hold L2 and press ⇧, ⇧, ⇩, ⇩, ⇦, ⇨, ⇦, ⇨, ■, ▲ |
| Refill Ammunition | Hold L2 and press ▲, ▲, ✕, ✕, ■, ●, ■, ●, ⇩, ⇨ |
| Unlimited Ammunition | Hold L2 and press ▲, ▲, ✕, ✕, ■, ●, ■, ●, ⇩, ⇩ |

## DESPICABLE ME    (PSP)

### CODES

Input the codes in the Bonus menu while in Gru's Lab.

| EFFECT | CODE |
|---|---|
| Unlocks the Minionettes Costume Set | ●, ●, ■, ▲, ✕ |
| Unlocks the Taffy Web Gun | ⇧⇧✕, ●, ■, ✕, ▲ |
| Unlocks the Village Folk Costume Set | ▲, ✕, ✕, ●, ✕ |

## DESPICABLE ME: MINION MAYHEM    (DS)

### CODES

At the Mode Select screen, press Select to bring up the code entry window and enter the following:

| EFFECT | CODE |
|---|---|
| Unlock Despicable Gru Level | B, A, Down, Down, Y |
| Unlock Minion Mania | L, A, B, B, Y, Up |
| Unlock Minion Mania EX | L, A, B, B, Y, Down |
| Unlock the Girls' Room level | B, L, A, B, B, Y |
| World Level Unlock | B, Up, Down, Down, Y |

## DEUS EX: HUMAN REVOLUTION  (XBOX 360)

### ACHIEVEMENT

| UNLOCKABLE | HOW TO UNLOCK |
|---|---|
| Acquaintances Forgotten (10) | Follow Pritchard's lead to uncover the truth. |
| Balls (5) | Seems you like playing with balls, eh? |
| Bar Tab (10) | Help the Hive Bartender settle a tab. |
| Cloak & Daggers (10) | Deal with the man in the shadows. |
| Consciousness is Over-rated (15) | Knock out 100 enemies in a single playthrough. |
| Corporate Warfare (10) | Protect a client's interests by performing a less-than-hostile takeover. |
| Darker Shades (15) | You convinced a fast-talking bartender to let you see Tong Si Hung. |
| Deus Ex Machina (50) | Experience all the different endings that Deus Ex: Human Revolution has to offer. |
| Doctorate (50) | Read all 29 unique XP books within a single playthrough. |
| First Hack (5) | Perform your first Hack successfully. |
| First Takedown (5) | Perform your first Takedown. Civilians don't count, so be nice. |
| Foxiest of the Hounds (100) | Complete Deus Ex: Human Revolution without setting off any alarms. |
| Ghost (15) | You made it through an entire hostile area without so much as a squeak. |
| Good Soul (15) | Against all odds, you saved Faridah Malik's life. |
| Guardian Angel (10) | You paid poor Jaya's debt in full. How very... humane... of you. |
| Gun Nut (20) | Fully upgrade one of your weapons. |
| Hangar 18 (10) | You found and read the secret message. Now you know too much... |
| Hax0r1! (15) | Successfully hack 50 devices within the same playthrough. |
| Kevorkian Complex (10) | You granted a dying man his final request. |
| Ladies Man (10) | You convinced Mengyao to spill the beans on the mysterious Hyron Project. |
| Legend (100) | Complete Deus Ex: Human Revolution at its hardest setting without ever changing the difficulty. |
| Lesser Evil (10) | Deal with Mr. Carella's indiscretion. |
| Lucky Guess (10) | Next time, Jacob better use a more complex code to arm his bombs. |
| Motherly Ties (10) | Put a grieving mother's doubts to rest. |
| Old School Gamer (10) | You found all the hidden story items in Megan's office. Point and Click much? |
| Opportunist (15) | Perform 50 takedowns within the same playthrough. (Civilians don't count.) |

| | |
|---|---|
| Pacifist (100) | Complete Deus Ex: Human Revolution without anyone dying by your hand. (Boss fights don't count.) |
| Rotten Business (10) | Help a lady in the oldest of professions clean house. |
| Sentimental Value (10) | You kept Megan's bracelet for yourself. Apparently, letting go really is the hardest part. |
| Shanghai Justice (10) | It may take some sleuthing, but justice must be served. |
| Smash the State (10) | Help Officer Nicholas take out the trash. |
| Super Sleuth (10) | You really nailed your case against Lee Hong. |
| Talion A.D. (10) | Descend into the bowels of an urban jungle and confront a warrior-priest. |
| The Bull (25) | You defeated Lawrence Barrett, elite member of a secret mercenary hit squad. |
| The D Project (15) | You watched the entire credit list and saw the surprise at the end. |
| The Desk Job (15) | You convinced Wayne Haas to let you into the morgue. |
| The End (25) | You defeated Zhao Yun Ru and destroyed the Hyron Project. |
| The Fall (10) | You sent Diamond Chan on the trip of a lifetime. |
| The Final Countdown (15) | You showed millionaire Hugh Darrow that his logic was flawed. |
| The Last Straw (15) | You talked Doctor Isaias Sandoval out of suicide. |
| The Mantis (25) | You defeated Yelena Fedorova, elite member of a secret mercenary hit squad. |
| The Snake (25) | You defeated Jaron Namir, Leader of Belltower's Elite Special Operations Unit. |
| The Take (10) | Greedy bastard. You accepted O'Malley's blood money and let him go. |
| The Throwdown (15) | You convinced the smooth-talking politician Bill Taggart to tell the truth in public. |
| Transhumanist (5) | Fully upgrade your first augmentation of choice. |
| Trooper (50) | Complete Deus Ex: Human Revolution. |
| Unforeseen Consequence (15) | You convinced Zeke Sanders to let his hostage go. |
| Up the Ante! (15) | Upgrade your first weapon of choice. |
| Yes Boss (15) | You had an argument with your boss, David Sarif, and won. |

## DEVIL MAY CRY 4  (XBOX 360)

### UNLOCKABLES

| UNLOCKABLE | HOW TO UNLOCK |
|---|---|
| Bloody Palace Survival Mode | Complete the game on Devil Hunter difficulty or Human difficulty. |
| Bonus Art and Character Art | Complete the game on Devil Hunter difficulty or Human difficulty. |
| Gallery | Complete the game on Devil Hunter difficulty or Human difficulty. |
| History of Devil May Cry | Complete the game on Devil Hunter difficulty or Human difficulty. |
| Son of Sparda Difficulty | Complete the game on Devil Hunter difficulty. |

## DEVIL'S CRUSH (Wii)

### UNLOCKABLE

| UNLOCKABLE | HOW TO UNLOCK |
|---|---|
| Sound Mode | Press ⬇, ⬇, ⬇ after pausing |
| Sound Test | Press RUN, SELECT during gameplay to display the High Score screen, then press ⬇, ⬇, ⬇, ⬇, ① |

### PASSWORDS

| PASSWORD | EFFECT |
|---|---|
| EFGHIJKLMB | 924,000,000 points and 73 balls |
| AAAAAAAAAAAAAAAAB | A 2-player game with unlimited balls |
| THECRUSHEL | Beat the game—launch the ball and once you hit something, the game ends |
| DAVIDWHITE | Beat the game—launch the ball and once you hit something, the game ends |
| FFFFFFFEEE | Beat the game—launch the ball and once you hit something, the game ends |
| NAXATSOFTI | Infinite balls, 206,633,300 points |
| AAAAAAHAAA | Infinite balls, 734,003,200 points |
| DEVILSATAN | Infinite balls, 955,719,100 points |
| THEDEVILSI | Over 145,000,000 points and 70 balls |
| ONECRUSHME | Over 594,000,000 points and 27 balls |
| AAAAAAAAAAAAAAABCE | 2-player mode—gives player 1 unlimited balls and player 2 32 balls |
| PPPPPPPPPA | Unlimited balls |
| CKDEIPDBFM | 25 balls and a score of 300,138,400 |
| OJFJGDEJPD | 34 balls and a score of 404,330,300 |
| PNBIJOKJNF | 38 balls and a score of 533,501,000 |
| CGIAGPECGK | 42 balls and a score of 610,523,600 |
| OEHALCBGPF | 45 balls and a score of 710,529,000 |
| OLGGGEAPOF | 52 balls and a score of 804,379,700 |
| CBEOBLJGHA | 62 balls and a score of 900,057,102 |
| PFFMGHGOLK | 65 balls and a score of 999,927,400 |
| NLJBCFHGPO | 65 balls and a score of 999,999,000 |
| KGCMMCMLBN | 65 balls and a score of 999,999,600 |
| OMGANLOIJA | 67 balls and a score of 976,769,800 |

## DIRT 2 (XBOX 360, PlayStation 3)

### UNLOCKABLES

Beat the races below to unlock the cars.

| UNLOCKABLE | HOW TO UNLOCK |
|---|---|
| Colin McRae R4 (X-G Version) | 1st in X-Games Europe |
| Dallenbach Special | 1st in Trailblazer World Tour |
| Ford Escort MKII | 1st in ALL X-Games Events |
| Ford RS200 Evolution | 1st in Rally Cross World Tour |
| MG Metro 6R4 | 1st in ALL X-Games Events |
| Mitsubishi Lancer Evolution X (X-G Version) | 1st in X-Games Asia |
| Mitsubishi Pajero Dakar | 1st in Raid World Tour |
| Subaru Impreza WRX STi | 1st in Colin McRae Challenge |
| Subaru Impreza WRX STi (X-G Version) | 1st in X-Games America |
| Toyota Stadium Truck | 1st in Landrush World Tour |

## DIRT 3 (XBOX 360, PlayStation 3)

### ACHIEVEMENT

| UNLOCKABLE | HOW TO UNLOCK |
| --- | --- |
| Air Miles (15) | You have won a race in every location |
| Assistance is Futile (20) | You won a race without the use of any Driver Assists |
| Battered Battersea (50) | You completed 100% of the Battersea Compound Missions |
| Burnt Rubber (30) | You completed 75% of the Battersea Compound Missions |
| California Dreams (20) | You earned yourself a podium finish at the X Games Tournament |
| Call me Ace! (15) | You have completed a sensational performance in a Gymkhana Championship event |
| Can't Touch This! (10) | You have survived a round of Outbreak without being infected (Pro Tour & Jam Session) |
| Cheeze It! (10) | You evaded the cats, won the game and earned the fans |
| Cool Running (10) | You have beaten the bobsleigh in the DC Bobsleigh Challenge |
| Crash Proof (10) | You used a flashback to take you to victory after facing defeat. |
| DC Challenger (30) | You have completed all of the DC Challenges |
| DC Gold (10) | You earned all gold medals in the DC Challenges |
| DC Silver (10) | You earned all silver medals in the DC Challenges |
| Donut Addict (20) | You completed 50% of the Battersea Compound Missions |
| Driven (20) | You have won DiRT Tour races using vehicles from every discipline |
| Driving School (10) | You completed all of the Gymkhana tutorials |
| Eat my DiRT! (50) | You have unlocked Driver Rep level 30 |
| Flag Stealer (10) | You stole the flag from the opposing team 5 times in a game of Transporter (Pro Tour) |
| From DiRT to Glory (50) | You have achieved first place finishes in all DiRT Tour Events |
| Gym-Carnage (20) | You scored 500,000 points in a Gymkhana Event |
| Gymkhana Aficionado (30) | You completed all Gymkhana Championships in the DiRT Tour |
| Honorable Driver (10) | You competed via Xbox LIVE and earned a 'Cautious' rating |
| Hooning Around (10) | You completed 25% of the Battersea Compound Missions |
| Into the DiRT (10) | You have completed your first DiRT Tour race |
| Join the Party (20) | You won a game in every party mode |
| Kick Off the Training Wheels! (20) | You have achieved a podium finish in the Gymkhana Academy |
| King of the Road (10) | You have won an Xbox LIVE race in hardcore mode |
| No-bot Wars (20) | You smashed every robot in a Smash Attack DC Challenge |
| Pace Setter (15) | You have completed time trials using cars from each class of Rally |
| Perfect Sprint (20) | You gave a flawless performance in a Gymkhana Sprint DC Challenge |
| Platinum Performance (20) | You earned all platinum medals in the DC Challenges |
| Rally Evolution (10) | You have experienced key vehicles from Rally history and triumphed |

| | |
|---|---|
| **Reputation Boost (10)** | You have completed 5 bonus Race Objectives |
| **Rising Talent (10)** | You have unlocked Driver Rep level 10 |
| **Road Trip (10)** | You shared the experience of the Battersea Compound with your friends |
| **Self Preservation Society (10)** | You won a race using the Mini Cooper without receiving any damage |
| **Shake and Bake (30)** | You have unlocked Driver Rep level 20 |
| **Showcase Drifter (20)** | You have drifted past 25,000 points in a Drift Showcase DC Challenge |
| **Steer Hunter (10)** | You have completed a game of Invasion without any negative points (Pro Tour) |
| **Sub Zero Hero (20)** | You earned yourself a podium finish Winter X Games Tournament |
| **Super Star (30)** | You earned yourself enough fans to be considered a 'Superstar' |
| **SuperSeries Champion (100)** | You won the DC SuperSeries Championship |
| **Taking the Trophy (20)** | You have won 10 Xbox LIVE games |
| **Teacher's Pet (20)** | You earned a platinum medal in each one of the Gymkhana tutorials |
| **The Extra Mile (20)** | You have completed 25 bonus Race Objectives |
| **The Professional (10)** | You completed your first Xbox LIVE Pro Tour Race |
| **The Real Thing (10)** | You have experienced the thrill of Rally first hand and beat your competitors |
| **The Road Ahead (15)** | You have completed 25 Xbox LIVE games |
| **Today's Forecast is... Victory! (20)** | You have earned victories in all weather conditions |
| **World Renowned (20)** | You have achieved first place finishes and passed the DC Challenge in a World Tour event |

### UNLOCKABLE

| UNLOCKABLE | HOW TO UNLOCK |
|---|---|
| Racing Gloves | Reach Fan Level 24 |
| Racing Shoes | Reach Fan Level 12 |
| Racing Suit | Complete Season 1 |
| Rally Helmet | Complete Season 2 |

## DISGAEA 3: ABSENCE OF JUSTICE   (PlayStation 3)

### UNLOCKABLE CLASSES

| UNLOCKABLE | HOW TO UNLOCK |
|---|---|
| Archer (Female) | Level 15 Female Fighter and Level 15 Female Healer |
| Archer (Male) | Level 15 Male Fighter and Level 15 Male Healer |
| Berserker | Heavy Knight and Monster Tamer Level 40 |
| Cheerleader (Idol) | Geo Master and Healer Level 25 |
| Geo Master | Fist Fighter and Healer Level 20 |
| Gunner Female | Female Thief and Mage Level 15 |
| Gunner Male | Thief and Male Mage Level 15 |
| Heavy Knight | Male Fighter and Fist Fighter Level 15 |
| Magic Knight | Fighter and Mage Level 25 |
| Majin | Clear second play through tutorial |
| Masked Hero | Thief and Gunner Level 45 |
| Monster Tamer | Female Fighter and Fist Fighter Level 15 |
| Ninja (Female) | Level 30 Female Monk and Level 30 Female Magician |
| Ninja (Male) | Level 30 Male Monk and Level 30 Male Magician |

| Samurai (Female) | Level 35 Female Fighter and Level 35 Female Archer |
| Samurai (Male) | Level 35 Male Fighter and Level 35 Male Archer |
| Shaman | Geo Master and Mage Level 25 |

## UNLOCKABLE CAMEO CHARACTERS

| UNLOCKABLE | HOW TO UNLOCK |
| --- | --- |
| Asagi | Beat extra map 4 |
| Axel | Beat extra map 6 |
| Laharl, Etna, and Flonne | Beat extra map 7 |
| Marona | Beat extra map 5 |
| Master Big Star | Beat extra map 1 |
| Prism Red | Beat extra map 3 |
| Salvatore | Beat extra map 2 |

## UNLOCKABLE ENDINGS

| UNLOCKABLE | HOW TO UNLOCK |
| --- | --- |
| Almaz's Ending | Win stage 8-4 with Almaz alone and the battle after |
| Human World Ending | Kill more then 99 allies and clear two alt. stages by stage 7-6 |
| Laharl's Ending | Go to homeroom and propose "Watch a New Ending" and clear the stage |
| Mao's Ambition Ending | Clear stage 1-9 on 2nd or higher cycle before stage 4-4 |
| Normal Ending | Don't meet any other ending's requirement |
| Raspberyl's Ending 1 | Lose against Raspberyl on stage 1-5 |
| Raspberyl's Ending 2 | Lose against Raspberyl on stage 2-1 |
| Super Hero Ending | Use Mao at Level 500 or higher to defeat final boss |

## UNLOCKABLE DIFFICULTIES

| UNLOCKABLE | HOW TO UNLOCK |
| --- | --- |
| Samurai Mode | Complete the game at least once. |
| Tourny Mode | Complete the game on Samurai Difficulty. |

## DISGAEA: AFTERNOON OF DARKNESS    (PSP)

### ETNA MODE

*Disgaea* contains a hidden mode called Etna mode. Normally you have to get this mode by going through the game and reading Etna's diary every chapter, but you can unlock it instantly by entering the following code during the title screen, with the pointer on "New Game." If you're successful, you'll hear Etna's voice.

| EFFECT | CODE |
| --- | --- |
| Unlock Etna Mode (US) | ▲, ■, ●, ▲, ■, ●, ✕ |

### EXTRA CLASSES

| UNLOCKABLE | HOW TO UNLOCK |
| --- | --- |
| Angel | Female Cleric, Knight, and Archer all at level 100 or higher. |
| Archer | Level 3 or higher in Bow Weapon Mastery. |
| EDF Soldier | Level 30 or higher Gun Weapon Mastery. |
| Galaxy Mage | Level a Prism Mage to Level 50. |
| Galaxy Skull | Level a Prism Skull to Level 50. |
| Knight | Female Warrior and Female Mage each at level 10 or higher. |
| Majin | Male Warrior, Brawler, Ninja, Rogue, and Scout all at level 200 or higher. |
| Ninja | Male Fighter and Male Warrior with a total level of 10 or higher. |
| Prism Mage | Level a Star Mage to Level 35. |
| Prism Skull | Level a Star Skull to Level 35. |

| Rogue | Both Fighter and Warrior, Males or Females, each at level 5 or higher. |
|---|---|
| Ronin | Female Warrior and Female Fighter with a total level of 10 or higher. |
| Scout | Two Fighters/Warriors, Males or Females, each at level 5 or higher. |
| Star Mage | Get one Fire, Ice, and Wind Mage and level all three of them to level 5. |
| Star Skull | Get one Fire, Ice, and Wind Skull and level all three of them to level 5. |

## DISNEY'S CHICKEN LITTLE: ACE IN ACTION    (Wii)

Input the codes under Cheat option.

| UNLOCKABLE | CODE |
|---|---|
| All Levels Available | ⇦, ⇦, ⇦, ⇦, ⇦ |
| All Weapons Available | ⇦, ⇦, ⇦, ⇦ |
| Unlimited Shield Available | ⇦, ⇦, ⇦, ⇦, ⇦ |

## KINECT: DISNEYLAND ADVENTURES    (XBOX 360)

### ACHIEVEMENT

| UNLOCKABLE | HOW TO UNLOCK |
|---|---|
| Adventureland Explorer (15) | Complete 50% of Adventureland |
| Bargain Hunter (15) | Buy an item from each shop in the park |
| Bookworm (30) | Complete all of the photo albums and autograph books |
| Critter Country Explorer (15) | Complete 50% of Critter Country |
| Disneyland Adventurer (20) | Find 21 Secrets in the Haunted Mansion, Jungle Cruise and Winnie the Pooh attractions |
| Disneyland Mountaineer (20) | Win the gold pin badge on the Matterhorn, Big Thunder Mountain, Space Mountain and Splash Mountain |
| Dressed to Impress (10) | Buy a costume from the shop and wear it |
| Eye Spy (15) | Collected 50% of the Spyglass Secrets |
| Fantasyland Explorer (15) | Complete 50% of Fantasyland |
| Five for Five (25) | High five all of the Fab Five |
| Frontierland Explorer (15) | Complete 50% of Frontierland |
| Fully Equipped (50) | Acquired all of the magic items |
| Happiest Place on Earth (50) | Complete all of the adventures in the park |
| Happy Unbirthday (25) | Completed 21 tasks around the park |
| Hidden Mickey Investigator (15) | Find and photograph half of the Hidden Mickeys |
| Hidden Mickey Sleuth (30) | Find and photograph all of the Hidden Mickeys |
| Hip Hip Pooh-Ray! (25) | Helped Winnie the Pooh and his friends in the Hundred-Acre Wood |
| I Feel Like Dancing (20) | Get 10 perfect poses in "it's a small world", Princess Faire and Alice in Wonderland attractions |
| It Was This Big! (15) | Collected 50% of the Fishing Rod Secrets |
| M-I-C-K-E-Y (10) | Find and photograph a Hidden Mickey |
| Main Street, U.S.A. Explorer (15) | Complete 50% of Main Street, U.S.A. |
| Mickey's Toontown Explorer (15) | Complete 50% of Mickey's Toontown |
| Mine Mine Mine Mine (25) | Win the silver pin badge on all attractions |
| Mouseketeer (30) | Completed all of the adventures with the Fab Five |

| | |
|---|---|
| Music Maestro Please (15) | Get a perfect performance from all of the musical acts in the park |
| New Orleans Square Explorer (15) | Complete 50% of New Orleans Square |
| Not as Mean as They Look (25) | Hug all of the villain characters |
| Not Today, Zurg! (15) | Collected 50% of the Blaster Secrets |
| Pirate's Life for Me (20) | Win the swordfights in Peter Pan's Flight and Pirates of the Caribbean without being hit |
| Pixar Perfect (25) | Win the platinum badges on Buzz Lightyear's Astro Blasters and Finding Nemo Submarine Voyage |
| Pleased to Meet You! (25) | Use all of the gestures on the same character |
| Portal Master (60) | Win the platinum pin badge on all attractions |
| Roaring Success (15) | Collected 50% of the Megaphone Secrets |
| Say Cheese! (15) | Take a photo of a character and another player |
| Shutterbug (10) | Take your first photograph. |
| Sign of the Times (10) | Complete an autograph album. |
| Sorcerer's Apprentice (15) | Collected 50% of the Wand Secrets |
| Soundsational! (20) | Get 5 stars in any parade |
| Spectacular! (20) | Get 5 stars in any fireworks display |
| Steamboat Willie (10) | Complete your first task. |
| The Bare Necessities (15) | Win the bronze pin badge on all attractions |
| The Golden Ticket (5) | Complete the tutorial |
| The Wetter the Better (15) | Collected 50% of the Water Squirter Secrets |
| There's Gold in Them There Hills (35) | Win the gold pin badge on all attractions |
| To Infinity, and Beyond! (25) | Completed all of the missions for Star Command and Buzz Lightyear |
| Tomorrowland Explorer (15) | Complete 50% of Tomorrowland |
| What a Swell Pal (15) | Complete an attraction chapter with 2 players |
| You Must Be This Tall (15) | Ride all of the classic rides |
| You Will Go to the Ball (25) | Dance with all of the princesses |

### UNLOCKABLE

| UNLOCKABLE | HOW TO UNLOCK |
|---|---|
| Sorcerer Mickey Mouse Hat | Earn the Happiest Place on Earth Achievement. |

## DISNEY'S KIM POSSIBLE KIMMUNICATOR  (DS)

Enter these codes while playing—do not pause. You must hold down
Ⓛ+Ⓡ to enter these codes.

| UNLOCKABLE | CODE |
|---|---|
| 9,999 parts | Ⓨ, Ⓨ, Ⓧ, Ⓑ, Ⓐ, Ⓨ |
| 99 lives | Ⓐ, Ⓐ, Ⓐ, Ⓨ, Ⓧ, Ⓨ, Ⓑ, Ⓐ |
| Don't lose lives | Ⓨ, Ⓨ, Ⓨ, Ⓧ |
| Extra Life | Ⓐ, Ⓐ, Ⓐ, Ⓨ, Ⓧ, Ⓨ |
| Full Health | Ⓐ, Ⓐ, Ⓐ, Ⓨ |
| Invincibility | Ⓨ, Ⓨ, Ⓨ, Ⓧ, Ⓐ, Ⓑ |
| Unlock all gadgets | Ⓨ, Ⓨ, Ⓧ, Ⓑ, Ⓐ, Ⓨ, Ⓨ, Ⓐ |
| Unlock all missions | Ⓧ, Ⓨ, Ⓧ, Ⓐ, Ⓧ, Ⓑ |
| Unlock all outfits | Ⓑ, Ⓐ, Ⓧ, Ⓨ, Ⓐ, Ⓑ |

## ACHIEVEMENT

| UNLOCKABLE | HOW TO UNLOCK |
| --- | --- |
| All Together Now! (15) | Complete a level with 4 players. |
| Along for the Ride (15) | Complete a level in multiplayer. |
| Anti-Virus! (30) | Defeat 500 enemies. |
| Bad Dog! (15) | Defeat the Bulldog. |
| Bad Hair Day (15) | Defeat 5 enemies using a single Medusa power-up. |
| Boxing Clever (15) | Defeat 5 enemies using a single Power Punch power-up. |
| Challenge Addict (15) | Play 50 Challenges. |
| Champion of the Universe (90) | Get a Gold Grade for all worlds. |
| Collector (15) | Collect all of the World Collectables within one level. |
| Compulsive Collector (90) | Collect all of the World Collectables in the game. |
| Dizzy! (15) | Defeat Roto. |
| Dressed for Success! (30) | Purchase all of the costumes. |
| For The Win! (30) | Win 50 Challenges. |
| Four Star Costume! (15) | Fully upgrade a costume. |
| Freeze! (15) | Defeat 5 enemies using a single Snowman power-up. |
| Giddy Up! (15) | Defeat an enemy whilst riding an animal. |
| Gold Hoarder (15) | Store 1,000 coins in the bank. |
| Hero of the Sands (15) | Complete the Aladdin world. |
| It Means No Worries! (15) | Complete the Lion King world. |
| Keep 'Em Coming! (15) | Defeat 100 enemies. |
| Old School (10) | Complete a level without using help arrows. |
| Playing to Win! (15) | Defeat 5 players in a single level. |
| Rapid Fire (15) | Defeat 5 enemies using a single Shooter power-up. |
| Returning to Earth (15) | Complete the WALL-E world. |
| Richer than a McDuck! (30) | Store 10,000 coins in the bank. |
| Saviour of the Universe! (90) | Complete all of the worlds. |
| Scary Feet! (15) | Complete the Monsters, Inc. world. |
| Serious Collector (15) | Collect all of the World Collectables within a location. |
| Suit Up! (15) | Purchase a costume. |
| Swash Buckler (15) | Complete the Pirates of the Caribbean world. |
| Tag! You're it! (15) | Transfer a curse to another player. |
| The Bigger They Are... (15) | Defeat the Brute. |
| Time for a Diet! (15) | Defeat the Spawner. |
| Time for Tea! (15) | Complete the Alice world. |
| To Infinity... and Beyond! (15) | Defeat another player by throwing them. |
| Ultimate Cosmic Power! (90) | Fully upgrade all of the costumes in the game. |
| Unstoppable! (15) | Complete a level without respawning. |
| World Beater (30) | Get a Gold Grade for a world. |
| World of Hurt! (30) | Fully upgrade all of a world's costumes. |
| World Set Complete! (30) | Collect all of the World Collectables within a world. |

NEW!

A
B
C
D
E
F
G
H
I
J
K
L
M
N
O
P
Q
R
S
T
U
V
W
X
Y
Z

## DISSIDIA 012: DUODECIM FINAL FANTASY (PSP)

### UNLOCKABLE

Complete the following conditions and then purchase them from the PP Catalog.

| UNLOCKABLE | HOW TO UNLOCK |
|---|---|
| Play as Desperado Chaos | Complete Main Scenario 000. |
| Play as Gilgamesh | Complete Report 08 (6) with Bartz. |
| Play as Prishe | Complete Report 08 (2) with Shantotto. |

## DOUBLE DUNGEONS (Wii)

### PASSWORDS

At the Password screen, carefully enter the following passwords.

| PASSWORD | EFFECT |
|---|---|
| cHR0EScxgoAq or iky7ihOfeBGe | In front of the last boss door |
| 2R3KD4RG0J9D3YT0664LJ | Beginning of Level 22 |
| YNzYSMChriGlgLV-ih0dfCGe | End of Level 22 |
| Enter either Player01 or Player 02 as a password, with the remaining spaces filled inwith either +'s or -'s | Get 65,535 HP |
| Enter any working password for player 1, then enter KKKKKKKKKKKKKKKKKKKKKKKKKKK as a password for player 2 | Player 2 invincibility |

## DRAGON AGE: ORIGINS (XBOX 360)

### EARLY LEVELING EXPLOIT

In Ostargar, there is a mission called Tainted Blood. Collect the three Vials of Darkspawn Blood but do not collect the Grey Warden Treaties. Return to camp, talk to Duncan, and select the option, "We have the blood, but not the scrolls." You will get the experience for the mission. Then go back and repeat this process until you are the level you want, or have reached the Level 25 max.

## DRAGON AGE II (PlayStation 3)

### UNLOCKABLES

If you have a save of Dragon Age Origins on your hard drive with the Blood Dragon Armor unlocked, it automatically transfers to Dragon Age 2 as well.

### UNLOCKABLES

To unlock the armor set, you have to create an EA account first and then link it with your PSN ID. Play Dead Space 2, go the main menu and log into your account. Once you have done that, Dragon Age 2. You can find the set in your special delivery chest at your house.

## DRAGON BALL Z: ULTIMATE TENKAICHI (PlayStation 3)

### TROPHY

| UNLOCKABLE | HOW TO UNLOCK |
|---|---|
| All 7 Are Here! (Bronze) | Do a Chase Battle in Story Mode for the first time |
| Battle Rookie (Bronze) | Fight in an Online Battle 1 time |
| Battle Veteran (Bronze) | Fight in an Online Battle 30 times |
| Becoming Fashion Aware (Bronze) | Obtain a Hero costume for the first time |
| Beginning of a Fantastic Tale (Bronze) | Win 1 Event Battle in Story Mode |
| Cell Games Champion (Bronze) | Win the Cell Games. |
| Cell Games True Champion (Silver) | Champion of Cell Games on Hard Difficulty. |

| | |
|---|---|
| Counter Hero (Bronze) | Perform Defense Reaction-Intercept 100 times total in real battle. |
| Defense Learner (Bronze) | Perform Defense Reaction-Guard 10 times total in real battle. |
| Defense Professional (Bronze) | Perform Defense Reaction-Guard 100 times total in real battle. |
| Don't Forget the Basics (Bronze) | Complete Tutorial until the end. |
| Evasion Fiend (Bronze) | Perform Defense Reaction-Evade 100 times total in real battle. |
| Evasion Learner (Bronze) | Perform Defense Reaction-Evade 10 times total in real battle. |
| Expert (Bronze) | Successfully perform Clashes 20 times total in real battle. |
| Fight Seeker (Bronze) | Win 50 times in a 1P vs. 'Very Strong' CPU battle. |
| Goodbye, Dragon World (Silver) | Clear Story Mode for the first time |
| Great Air Battle! (Bronze) | Do a Sky Chase in Story Mode for the first time |
| Growing in Power (Bronze) | Obtain 500 Hero AP |
| How Do I Look? (Bronze) | Obtain a Hero hairstyle for the first time |
| I Changed the World! (Gold) | Clear Hero Mode for the first time |
| I See Right Through You! real (Bronze) | Successfully perform Clashes 100 times total in battle. |
| I Still Want To Fight (Bronze) | Win 5 times in 1P vs. CPU battle. |
| I Want to Fight Someone Strong! (Bronze) | Win 30 times in 1P vs. CPU battle. |
| I'm Going to Change the World! (Bronze) | Win 1 Event Battle in Hero Mode |
| Interception Learner (Bronze) | Perform Defense Reaction-Intercept 10 times total in real battle. |
| Limit Breaker (Silver) | Obtain 20000 Hero AP |
| Master of Moves (Bronze) | Perform 50 Ultimate Attacks total in real battle. |
| Master! Please Teach Me! (Bronze) | Obtain a Hero Master for the first time |
| Monster on a Full Moon (Bronze) | Clear a Giant Boss Battle in Story Mode for the first time |
| Moves On Parade (Bronze) | Perform 50 Super Attacks total in real battle. |
| OVER 9000!!!! (Platinum) | Obtain all the trophies. |
| Point Getter (Bronze) | Obtain 1000 Hero AP |
| Regular Battle Customer (Bronze) | Fight in an Online Battle 10 times |
| Skill Master (Silver) | Collect 20 Skills |
| Super Attack Collector (Silver) | Collect 30 Super Attacks |
| Tapping into Latent Power (Bronze) | Collect 10 Skills |
| The Actors are All in Play! (Silver) | Unlock all characters and forms. |
| The Martial Artist's Path (Bronze) | Obtain a Hero Fight Style for the first time |
| Title Holder (Bronze) | Collect 5 or more titles. |
| Title King (Silver) | Collect 30 or more titles. |
| Training All Over Again (Bronze) | Do Training for the first time. |

| W. Tournament True Champion (Silver) | Champion of World Tournament on Hard Difficulty. |
|---|---|
| Which One Shall I Choose? (Bronze) | Collect 10 Super Attacks |
| World Domination! (Bronze) | Fight on all maps. |
| World Tournament Champion (Bronze) | Win the World Tournament. |
| Your Real Training Starts Here (Bronze) | Clear Hero Mode training for the first time |

### UNLOCKABLE

| UNLOCKABLE | HOW TO UNLOCK |
|---|---|
| Bardock | Clear the Bardock vs Frieza fight in Story Mode |
| Raditz | Defeat Raditz with Goku & Piccolo in Story Mode |
| Trunks | Beat Goku in Story Mode as Trunks at the start of the Android Saga |

## DRAGON QUEST IX: SENTINELS OF THE STARRY SKIES (PlayStation 3)

### ITEM DUPLICATION THROUGH AD-HOC

First, connect your DQIX to someone else. Give them any items you can, then shut your game off WITHOUT leaving their world. Since you never saved after leaving their world, you'll still have the items you traded, and so will they!

### MINI MEDAL REWARDS

While playing the game, you will find numerous items called Mini Medals. In the town of Dourbridge, you can give these to a pirate king who lives there, and he will give you rare items in exchange. After you've given him 80 Mini Medals, he will sell you rare items. But you must use Mini Medals to buy them instead of Gold. Three Medals: Prayer Ring; 5 Medals: Elfin Elixir; 8 Medals: Saint's Ashes; 10 Medals: Reset Stone; 15 Medals: Orihalcum; 20 Medals: Pixie Boots.

| UNLOCKABLE | HOW TO UNLOCK |
|---|---|
| Bunny Suit | Reward for giving 13 Mini Medals to Cap'n Max Meddlin |
| Dragon Robe | Reward for giving 80 Mini Medals to Cap'n Max Meddlin |
| Jolly Roger Jumper | Reward for giving 18 Mini Medals to Cap'n Max Meddlin |
| Mercury Bandanna | Reward for giving 8 Mini Medals to Cap'n Max Meddlin |
| Meteorite Bracer | Reward for giving 50 Mini Medals to Cap'n Max Meddlin |
| Miracle Sword | Reward for giving 32 Mini Medals to Cap'n Max Meddlin |
| Rusty Helmet | Reward for giving 62 Mini Medals to Cap'n Max Meddlin |
| Sacred Armor | Reward for giving 40 Mini Medals to Cap'n Max Meddlin |
| Thief's Key | Reward for giving 4 Mini Medals to Cap'n Max Meddlin |
| Transparent Tights | Reward for giving 25 Mini Medals to Cap'n Max Meddlin |

### SECRET SHOP IN DOURBRIDGE

If you go around to the back of the village shop in Dourbridge, there is a hidden door. Enter it (requires the Ultimate Key), and then you see a flight of stairs. Go down the stairs, and you can get into a secret shop with rare items.

## DRAGON QUEST MONSTERS: JOKER 2 (DS)

### UNLOCKABLE

| UNLOCKABLE | HOW TO UNLOCK |
|---|---|
| Drakularge | have owned 100 different monsters |
| Grandpa Slime | have owned 200 different monsters |
| Great Argon Lizard | have owned 50 different monsters |
| Metal King Slime | have owned 150 different monsters |
| Free Argogreat | Get 50 different owned monsters in the monster library |

### *UNLOCKABLE*

In Dragon Quest VI you must activate Dreamsharing. In Dragon Quest IX you must activate Tag Mode.

| UNLOCKABLE | HOW TO UNLOCK |
|---|---|
| **Malevolamp** | Tag Dragon Quest VI |
| **Mottle Slime** | Tag Dragon Quest VI |
| **Noble Gasbagon** | Tag Dragon Quest VI |
| **Overkilling Machine** | Tag Dragon Quest VI |
| **Shogum** | Tag Dragon Quest IX |
| **Slime Stack** | Tag Dragon Quest IX |
| **Teeny Sanguini** | Tag Dragon Quest IX |

## DRAGON SPIRIT (Wii)

### *CODES*

| UNLOCKABLE | HOW TO UNLOCK |
|---|---|
| 100 Continues | Press ⬆, ⬇, SELECT, ⬆, ②, ⬇, ①, ⬅, SELECT, ⬇, ①, ②, ① at the title screen |
| Arcade Mode Screen | Hold Select and press RUN 57 times to reset the game for a narrow screen |
| Sound Test | ⬆, ⬆, ⬇, ⬇, SELECT, ⬆ at the title screen |
| Two Continues | Hold ① and press ② at the title screen |

## DRAGON'S CURSE (Wii)

### *UNLOCKABLE*

| UNLOCKABLE | HOW TO UNLOCK |
|---|---|
| Full Life | After dying, use a potion while holding ② |

### *PASSWORDS*

| PASSWORD | EFFECT |
|---|---|
| 3YHURYW7Y7LL8C | Start game at beginning with Max. Gold (983,040)/All Equipment/Full Health (8 Hearts)/Max. Stones (99)/All Items/Hawk-Man Status |
| 3YHURYW7Y7LPBS | Start game at beginning with Max. Gold (983,040)/All Equipment/Full Health (8 Hearts)/Max. Stones (99)/All Items/Hu-Man Status |
| 3YHURYW7Y7LRBW | Start game at beginning with Max. Gold (983,040)/All Equipment/Full Health (8 Hearts)/Max. Stones (99)/All Items/Lizard-Man Status |
| 3YHURYW7Y7LM80 | Start game at beginning with Max. Gold (983,040)/All Equipment/Full Health (8 Hearts)/Max. Stones (99)/All Items/Mouse-Man Status |
| 3YHURYW7Y7LN84 | Start game at beginning with Max. Gold (983,040)/All Equipment/Full Health (8 Hearts)/Max. Stones (99)/All Items/Piranha-Man Status |
| 3YHURYW7Y7LK88 | Start game at beginning with Max. Gold (983,040)/All Equipment/Full Health (8 Hearts)/Max. Stones (99)/All Items/Tiger-Man Status |
| W0CV5ATVKYR1SV | Start with all the necessary transformations and items to enter the final dungeon |
| MODE FOR 0000 000 | Be Hu Man at Start (JP ONLY) |
| PLAY THE ONGA KUN | Disable door noise (JP ONLY) |
| NODEGOSO0000000 | Start as Be Hu Man |
| 3WSURYXZY763TE | Start with advanced abilities and items |
| RMAYTJEOPHALUP | Take away the noises from doors |
| 3ZHURYNZY726VH | Start as Hu-Man with 8 hearts, all equipment, all transformations unlocked, and only the final dungeon to beat |

## DREAMCAST COLLECTION (XBOX 360)

### CODE

Enter during cutscenes or during non-gameplay segments. This disables all achievements, avatar awards and leaderboards

| EFFECT | CODE |
| --- | --- |
| All of Ulala's commands are done automatically | Hold (LT) + (RT) then press B, B, ↑, ←, A, ←, A, ←, A |

### UNLOCKABLE

Complete the following task

| UNLOCKABLE | HOW TO UNLOCK |
| --- | --- |
| Crazy Bike | Beat all the Crazy Box challenges. |

### CODE

Enter the code. You should hear the word "Fish" if you do it correctly.

| EFFECT | CODE |
| --- | --- |
| Infinite Time | A, B, Y, X, Y, A, B, ←, →, Y, X, A, B, A, Y, X, Y (on pause screen) |

### UNLOCKABLE

Complete the following tasks.

| UNLOCKABLE | HOW TO UNLOCK |
| --- | --- |
| Alternate clothing and boat colors | Reach the final tournament in original mode. |
| Bonus Falls Level (Arcade Mode) | Finish the last 2 tournaments in Consumer Mode |
| Bonus Palace Level (Arcade Mode) | Finish the first 2 tournaments in Consumer Mode |
| Extra Practice Levels | Complete the game once in Arcade Mode |
| Sonic Lure | Complete all 5 tournaments in Consumer Mode |

### SECRETS

While choosing your lure, press Up or Down to get a different color.

### SECRETS

When at the Area Select screen in Arcade Mode, press A + B simultaneously to control the female character.

### UNLOCKABLE

Beat the rest of the four courses. Note: Don't delete your your chao data or else you will have to do them again.

### UNLOCKABLE

Complete the tasks to unlock these

| UNLOCKABLE | HOW TO UNLOCK |
| --- | --- |
| Amy | Talk to her in the Casino as Sonic after finishing Sky Chase. |
| Big | Defeat Chaos 6 as Sonic. |
| E-102 Gamma | Defeat Gamma after finishing Sky Deck as Sonic or Tails. An alternate way to unlock him is to finish Twinkle Park as Amy and watch the FMAs after it. |
| Knuckles | Defeat him after finishing Ice cap as Sonic or Tails. |
| Miles Tails Prower | Finish the C mission of Emerald Coast action stage as Sonic. |
| Super Sonic | Finish the game as Sonic, Tails, Knuckles, Amy, Big and E-102 Gamma. Super Sonic will be avaliable only in Adventure Mode. |
| Super Sonic | Complete the game with every character |
| Ancient Light (Sonic) | On top of a rock on Angel Island |
| Booster (E-102) | In the Weapon's Armory on the Egg Carrier |

| | |
|---|---|
| Crystal Ring (Sonic) | Walk up the steps in the hotel, press the two buttons and use light speed dash |
| Fighting Gloves (Knuckles) | On a ledge over Big's house |
| Jet Anklet (Tails) | In a hole in the ceiling in the sewer behind Twinkle Park |
| Laser Blaster (E-102) | In the Restricted room on the Egg Carrier after it crashes |
| Life Belt (Big) | In the entrance to Icecap |
| Light Speed Shoes (Sonic) | Find it in the sewer (not the one behind Twinkle Park) |
| Long Hammer (Amy) | Beat your own high score on Hedgehog Hammer after the Egg Carrier crashes |
| Long Rod (Big) | Under the bed at Big's hut |
| Lure Upgrade 1 (Big) | In the sewer behind Twinkle Park |
| Lure Upgrade 2 (Big) | Under an sheet of ice in IceCap |
| Lure Upgrade 3 (Big) | In a cave in the forest |
| Lure Upgrade 4 (Big) | In one of the jail cells on the Egg Carrier |
| Rhythm Badge (Tails) | In the flashback with Tikal |
| Shovel Claw (Knuckles) | In the tunnel inside the tunnel where you find the cart to the Mystic Ruins Chao Garden |
| Warrior Feather (Amy) | Beat Eggman's high-score on Hedgehog Hammer |
| Easter Egg | Press X immediately before entering the snowboarding portion of the game to get a blue snowboard or B for a yellow snowboard. |
| Easter Egg | While playing with Sonic in Casinopolis, go to the pinball game with the NiGHTS motif. Hit the three little purple point givers in order to open up an entrance at the top of the board. Then make your way through the secret entrance. You'll now be in another NiGHTS motif pinball game. Whenever you fail to catch Sonic with the bumpers, don't worry about losing a ball. Instead, Sonic will be transported through a world very familiar to the NiGHTS level Splash Garden. |

## DRIVER: PARALLEL LINES (Wii)

### PASSWORD

| PASSWORD | EFFECT |
|---|---|
| steelman | Invincibility |

## DRIVER: SAN FRANCISCO (XBOX 360)

### ACHIEVEMENT

| UNLOCKABLE | HOW TO UNLOCK |
|---|---|
| Active! (5) | Complete an Activity |
| Against the Odds (20) | Complete Chapter 3 |
| Air Rage (15) | Spin out 10 Vehicles with Impulse (Public) |
| Another Perspective (40) | Complete Chapter 6 |
| Are You Insured? (5) | Buy your first Vehicle |
| Back on the Road (10) | Complete Chapter 1 |
| Car Nut (15) | Buy 50 Vehicles |
| Carry the Team (15) | Score 10 times in Capture the Flag (Public) |
| Connoisseur (15) | Swap or Spawn into 20 Unique Vehicles (Public) |
| Cops & Robbers (30) | Complete 30 Freedrive Cop Chases |
| Cut! Print It! (15) | Unlock 6 Movie Challenges |
| Deep Cover (30) | Complete Chapter 5 |
| Drivers Ed. (10) | Complete the Prologue |

NEW!

A

B

C

**D**

E

F

G

H

I

J

K

L

M

N

O

P

Q

R

S

T

U

V

W

X

Y

Z

| | |
|---|---|
| **Due for a Service (30)** | Drive over 1000 miles (~1610 km) (Story/Online) |
| **End of the Road (50)** | Complete the Story |
| **Eyes on the City (20)** | Complete Chapter 2 |
| **Fan Service (10)** | Complete the 'Blast from the Past' Challenge |
| **First Time Buyer (5)** | Buy your first Garage |
| **Getting Away With It (15)** | Reach 25 drop-off locations in Takedown (Public) |
| **Hey Big Spender! (30)** | Spend 5,000,000 WP |
| **Hyperactive! (15)** | Complete 25 Activities |
| **I'm On Fire! (15)** | Stay in both trails for 30s in Trailblazer (Public) |
| **Initiate (15)** | Reach Multiplayer Level 5 (Public) |
| **Keys to the City (15)** | Buy all of the Garages in the City |
| **Lights, Camera, Action! (5)** | Unlock a Movie Challenge |
| **Lombard Streak (10)** | Drive down Lombard Street, no collisions, over 20mph (Story) |
| **Master (75)** | Reach Multiplayer Level 38 (Public) |
| **Master Driver (30)** | Complete all 80 Dares |
| **Now You See Me... (30)** | Complete Chapter 4 |
| **Pass the Torch (15)** | Carry the Torch for 20s, 25 times in Relay Race (Public) |
| **Petrolhead (30)** | Buy all of the Vehicles from the Garage |
| **Picking Up the Pace (15)** | Place in the top 3 in Sprint GP 10 times (Public) |
| **Professional Racer (15)** | Place in the top 3 in Classic Race 10 times (Public) |
| **Radioactive! (30)** | Complete 50 Activities |
| **Ramped Up! (10)** | Complete a Getaway Activity in a Car Transporter |
| **Relentless Assault (15)** | Successfully attack the base 10 times in Blitz (Public) |
| **Round and Round You Go (15)** | Place in the top 3 in Shift Race 10 times (Public) |
| **Shift Happens (30)** | Shift 1000 Times (Story/Online) |
| **Show Off! (5)** | Perform a 250m Drift or Jump (Story/Online) |
| **Stay With the Pack (15)** | Score 1000 gates in Checkpoint/Team Rush (Online) |
| **Survivor (50)** | Complete Chapter 8 |
| **Tag, You're It! (15)** | Keep the Tag for 10s, 50 times in Tag (Public) |
| **That's a Wrap! (30)** | Unlock all 13 Movie Challenges |
| **The Challenger (5)** | Beat the Target Time/Score on any Challenge |
| **The Truth (40)** | Complete Chapter 7 |
| **This Can't Be Real (5)** | Complete the Shift Tutorial |
| **Tricked Out (15)** | Buy all of the Upgrades from the Garage |
| **Veteran (30)** | Reach Multiplayer Level 20 (Public) |
| **We Dare You... (5)** | Complete a Dare |
| **We Double Dare You... (15)** | Complete 40 Dares |

### UNLOCKABLE

For every 10 Movie Tokens, you unlock a movie scene in the Garage.

| UNLOCKABLE | HOW TO UNLOCK |
|---|---|
| **Blues Brothers, 1974 Dodge Monaco** | Collect 50 Movie Tokens |
| **Bullitt, 1968 Ford Mustang GT Fastback** | Collect 30 Movie Tokens |
| **Cannonball Run, 1978 Lamborghini Countach LP400S** | Collect 60 Movie Tokens |

| | |
|---|---|
| **Dukes of Hazard, 1969 Dodge Charger R/T** | Collect 70 Movie Tokens |
| **Gone In 60 Seconds, 1973 Ford Mustang Mach I** | Collect 10 Movie Tokens |
| **Redline, 2011 McLaren MP4-12C** | Collect 100 Movie Tokens |
| **Smokey & The Bandit, 1977 Pontiac TransAm Firebird** | Collect 110 Movie Tokens |
| **Starsky & Hutch, 1974 Dodge Monaco Cop** | Collect 20 Movie Tokens |
| **Test Drive, 1987 RUF CT-R Yellow Bird** | Collect 120 Movie Tokens |
| **The Driver, 1965 Chevrolet S-10** | Collect 90 Movie Tokens |
| **The French Connection, 1971 Pontiac LeMans** | Collect 40 Movie Tokens |
| **The Italian Job, 1972 Lamborghini Miura** | Collect All Movie Tokens |
| **Vanishing Point, 1970 Dodge Challenger R/T** | Collect 80 Movie Tokens |

## UNLOCKABLE

Perform these actions to unlock vehicles for purchase in the Garage.

| UNLOCKABLE | HOW TO UNLOCK |
|---|---|
| **1970 Dodge Challenger R/T** | Complete the story mode. |
| **1970 Oldsmobile Cutlass 4-4-2** | Complete Sprint Activity 2 |
| **1970 Pontiac GTO The Judge** | Complete Sprint Activity 4 |
| **1971 Pontiac LeMans** | Complete Sprint Activity 7 |
| **1974 Ford Gran Torino** | Purchase the first garage |
| **1983 DeLorean DMC-12** | Complete Sprint Activity 1 |
| **1999 Ford Crown Victoria** | Purchase the first garage. |
| **2006 Chevrolet Impala** | Purchase the Downtown garage |
| **2007 Lamborghini Murcielago LP640** | Purchase the Lighthouse Bay Garage |
| **2010 Cadillac DTS** | Purchase the first garage |
| **2011 Camion Firefighter 505** | Complete Firefighter Activity 1 |
| **2011 Camion Firefighter A.E.R.V.** | Complete all Firefigher Activities |

## DUNGEON EXPLORER (Wii)

### PASSWORDS

| PASSWORD | EFFECT |
|---|---|
| **CHECK NAMEA** | Change names |
| **ADGDP-CJLPG** | Final Dungeon is open |
| **DEBDE DEBDA then press RUN+①** | Invincibility |
| **JBBNJ HDCOG** | Play as Princess Aki |
| **IMGAJ MDPAI** | Play as the Hermit |
| **HOMING AAAA** | Precision guided weapons (smart weapons) |

### LEVEL SELECT

Enable the "Invincibility" code. Enter one of the following 15 bushes in front of Axis castle to jump to the corresponding location. (Bush 1 is on the left end, bush 15 is on the right end.)

| BUSH | LOCATION |
|---|---|
| 1 | Natas |
| 2 | Balamous Tower |
| 3 | Rotterroad (path to Judas) |

NEW!

A
B
C
D
E
F
G
H
I
J
K
L
M
N
O
P
Q
R
S
T
U
V
W
X
Y
Z

| 4 | Mistose Dungeon |
|---|---|
| 5 | Ratonix Dungeon |
| 6 | Reraport Maze |
| 7 | Rally Maze |
| 8 | Bullbeast |
| 9 | Melba Village |
| 10 | After Gutworm |
| 11 | Nostalgia Dungeon |
| 12 | Water Castle |
| 13 | Road to Cherry Tower |
| 14 | Stonefield |
| 15 | Karma Castle |

## UNLOCKABLES

| UNLOCKABLE | HOW TO UNLOCK |
|---|---|
| Secret Ending | Input the Invincibility code so you can pass through objects. When you take the ORA stone back to the King and he leaves, pass through the blockade to his throne, which initiates the secret ending. |
| Use the Harmit (Hermit) the hard way | To use the Harmit (*sic*), level a Bard until you have at least 50 HP. (Go into the second house to the west of Axis Castle.) |

## DYNASTY WARRIORS 6 (XBOX 360)

### CHARACTERS

| UNLOCKABLE | HOW TO UNLOCK |
|---|---|
| Cao Cao | Clear Musou mode with three Wei characters. |
| Cao Pi | Defeat Cao Pi within five minutes on Wu side of He Fei. |
| Cao Ren | Succeed in Battle Objective 2 on the Lu Bu side of Fan Castle. |
| Diao Chan | Clear Musou mode with one character from each Kingdom. |
| Dong Zhuo | Clear Musou mode with Lu Bu. |
| Gan Ning | Clear Musou mode with one Wu character. |
| Guan Ping | Succeed in two battle objectives on the Shu side of Fan Castle and finish battle with Guan Ping alive. |
| Huang Gai | Succeed in Battle Objective 3 on the Wu side of The Battle of Chi Bi. |
| Huang Zhong | Succeed in one battle objective on the Wei side of Ding Jun Mountain. |
| Ling Tong | Succeed in Battle Objective 1 on the Wei side of the Battle of Shi Ting. |
| Liu Bei | Clear Musou mode with three Shu characters. |
| Lu Bu | Clear Musou mode with Liu Bei, Cao Cao, and Sun Jian. |
| Lu Meng | Succeed in two battle objectives on the Wei side of He Fei. |
| Ma Chao | Succeed in two battle objectives on the Wei side of Han Zhong Attack Defense Battle. |
| Pang Tong | Succeed in three battle objectives at Cheng Du battle and finish battle with Pang Tong alive. |
| Sun Ce | Succeed in Battle Objective 1 on the Sun Jian side of the Battle of Xia Pi. |
| Sun Jian | Clear Musou mode with three Wu characters. |
| Sun Quan | Succeed in Battle Objective 1 on the Lu Bu side of the Battle of Chi Bi. |
| Taishi Ci | Defeat him in the Battle for Wu Territory. |
| Wei Yan | Succeed in two battle objectives on the Shu side of WuZhang Plains and finish battle with Wei Yan alive. |
| Xiahou Yuan | Succeed in one battle objective on the Shu side of Ding Jun Mountain. |
| Xiao Quio | Succeed in Battle Objective 3 on the Wu side of the Battle of Shi Ting. |

| Xu Chu | He Fei, Wu side, personally kill Cao Ren and Xu Chu. |
| Xu Huang | Succeed in two battle objectives on the Wei/Wu side of Fan Castle. |
| Yuan Shao | As Wei, complete all three targets and capture Wu Chao before completing the stage. |
| Yue Ying | Succeed in Battle Objective 1 on the Wei side of the Battle of Wu Zhang Plains. |
| Zhang Jiao | Beat stage while completing all three targets in the Yellow Turban Rebellion. Playable in only Free mode and Challenge mode. |
| Zhang Liao | Clear Musou mode with one Wei character. |
| Zhen Ji | Succeed in Battle Objective 1 on the Lu Bu side of the Xu Du Invasion. |
| Zheng He | Succeed in two battle objectives on the Shu side of Han Zhong Attack Defense Battle. |
| Zhou Tai | Succeed in three battle objectives on the Shu side of Yi Ling. |
| Zhuge Liang | Clear Musou mode with one Shu character. |

### DIFFICULTIES

| UNLOCKABLE | HOW TO UNLOCK |
| --- | --- |
| Chaos Difficulty | Clear Musou mode with one character from Wu, Shu, Wei, and Other. |
| Hell Difficulty | Beat Wei, Wu, Shu, and Other Musou mode. |
| Master Difficulty | Beat any Musou mode on Easy or Normal. |
| Very Hard Difficulty | Clear Musou mode with any one character. |

## DYNASTY WARRIORS 7 (PlayStation 3)

### UNLOCKABLE

To unlock characters that are not available after the completion of Story Mode, complete the Legendary Battles hex for that character in Conquest Mode. After you complete all the Legendary Battles for that character he or she will become unlocked.

### UNLOCKABLE

Complete the following tasks

| UNLOCKABLE | HOW TO UNLOCK |
| --- | --- |
| Qilin Blade | Completed all Tresure Battles in Conquest Mode. |
| Silver Stallion | Unlocked 7 capital cities in Conquest Mode. |

### UNLOCKABLE

Complete the following tasks to unlock guardian animals

| UNLOCKABLE | HOW TO UNLOCK |
| --- | --- |
| Hex Mark | Complete Champions of Chaos on Conquest Mode. |
| Red Hare | Complete Battle for Supremacy. |
| Shadow Runner | Complete Wolves of Chaos on Conquest Mode. |

## DYNASTY WARRIORS 7 (XBOX 360)

### UNLOCKABLE

To unlock characters that are not available after the completion of Story Mode, complete the Legendary Battles hex for that character in Conquest Mode. After you complete all the Legendary Battles for that character he or she will become unlocked.

### UNLOCKABLE

Complete the following tasks to unlock guardian animals

| UNLOCKABLE | HOW TO UNLOCK |
| --- | --- |
| Red Hare | Complete Battle for Supremacy. |
| Shadow Runner | Beat Wolves of Chaos |

## DYNASTY WARRIORS: GUNDAM 3     (XBOX 360)

### ACHIEVEMENT

| UNLOCKABLE | HOW TO UNLOCK |
|---|---|
| Ascent of Angels (20) | Clear all "Mobile Suit V Gundam" history missions |
| Avenger (20) | Shoot down more than 100 enemies online |
| Bounty Hunter (20) | Obtain more than 10,000 G |
| Celestial Being (20) | Clear all "Mobile Suit Gundam 00" history missions |
| Character Collector (20) | Complete the character gallery |
| Chosen Future (20) | Clear all "Mobile Suit Gundam Seed Destiny" history missions |
| Cross of Zeon (20) | Exceed 100 plays |
| Demon of the Lab (30) | Reach tech level 10 in the Mobile Suit lab |
| Fierce Avenger (30) | Shoot down more than 1,000 enemies online |
| Golden Autumn (20) | Clear all "Mobile Suit ∀ Gundam" history missions |
| Instructor from Hell (30) | Raise any one character's pilot level to 50 |
| Last One Standing (20) | Clear all "Mobile Suit Gundam Wing" history missions |
| Last Shooting (20) | Clear all "Mobile Suit Gundam" history missions |
| Leader of Humanity (20) | Completely finish either of the story missions "Those Who Understand" or "Those Who Fight." |
| Legendary Master Ace (30) | Shoot down 100,000 enemies |
| Licensed to Ride (30) | Obtain all licenses |
| Master Ace (20) | Shoot down 10,000 enemies |
| Mobile Suit Collector (20) | Complete the Mobile Suit gallery |
| Mobile Suit Gatherer (60) | Unlock all playable Mobile Suits |
| Movie Collector (20) | Complete the movie gallery |
| Nebula Medal (30) | Exceed 200 plays |
| Online Play 100 (30) | Play online more than 100 times |
| Online Play 20 (20) | Play online more than 20 times |
| Over the Rainbow (20) | Clear all "Mobile Suit Gundam Unicorn" history missions |
| Pilot Gatherer (60) | Unlock all playable characters |
| Purebred Innovator (60) | Friendship level of all characters reaches level 5 |
| Revolutionary (30) | Clear all story missions |
| Sound Collector (20) | Complete the BGM gallery |
| Space Pirate (20) | Clear all "Mobile Suit Gundam F91" history missions |
| Space Soarer (20) | Clear all "Mobile Suit Z Gundam" history missions |
| Starbow (20) | Clear all "Mobile Suit Gundam: Char's Counterattack" history missions |
| Stardust Memory (20) | Clear all "Mobile Suit Gundam 0083" history missions |
| Tales of Dark History (30) | Clear all history missions |
| The Moon in the Sky (20) | Clear all "After War Gundam X" history missions |
| To the Future! (20) | Clear all "Mobile Fighter G Gundam" history missions |
| True Gundam Dynasty Warrior (70) | Clear all missions |
| Warrior Again (20) | Clear all "Mobile Suit ZZ Gundam" history missions |

## EA SPORTS NBA JAM  (XBOX 360)

### UNLOCKABLES

| UNLOCKABLE | HOW TO UNLOCK |
| --- | --- |
| Team Adidas | When entering initials, enter ADI for player 1 and DAS for player 2. This unlocks Team Adidas, which includes Dwight Howard, Derick Rose, and Josh Smith. |
| Team Jordan | When entering initials, enter JOR for player 1 and DAN for player 2. This unlocks Team Jordan, which includes Dwayne Wade, Chris Paul, and Carmelo Anthony. |
| Team Sprite | When entering initials, enter SPR for player 1 and ITE for player 2. This unlocks Team Sprite, which includes Yellow and Green Lebron James. |
| J. Cole and 9th Wonder | Enter the following codes at the Start screen. A sound will confirm correct code entry. Select "Play Now" mode, then press Start at the Team Selection screen to have the corresponding character appear. Press Up, Left, Down, Right, Up, Left, Down, Right, A, B. |
| Beastie Boys | Enter the following codes at the Start screen. A sound will confirm correct code entry. Select "Play Now" mode, then press Start at the Team Selection screen to have the corresponding character appear. Press Up(2), Down(2), Left, Right, Left, Right, B, A. |
| Democrats | Enter the following codes at the Start screen. A sound will confirm correct code entry. Select "Play Now" mode, then press Start at the Team Selection screen to have the corresponding character appear. Press Left(13), A. |
| Michelle Beadle and Colin Cowherd from Sportsnation | In EA Sports NBA Jam for the Wii, you can unlock Colin Cowherd and Michelle Beadle. On the Enter Initials screen, type ESP for player 1 and NSN for player 2. Go to the Select Team screen and you should hear a noise confirming you've unlocked them, and you'll see them in the teams list. |
| NBA Mascots | On the Enter Initials screen, type MAS for player 1 and COT for player 2. Go to the Select Team screen; you should hear a noise confirming you've unlocked them, and you'll see them in the teams list. |
| Republicans | Enter the following codes at the Start screen. A sound will confirm correct code entry. Select "Play Now" mode, then press Start at the Team Selection screen to have the corresponding character appear. Press Right(13), A. |
| Tim Kitzrow (announcer) and Mark Turmell (developer) | On the Enter Initials screen, type MJT for player 1. Go to the Select Team screen and you should hear a noise confirming you've unlocked them, and you'll see them in the teams list. |

## ECCO: THE TIDES OF TIME  (Wii)

### UNLOCKABLES

| UNLOCKABLE | HOW TO UNLOCK |
| --- | --- |
| Debug Menu | Pause while Ecco is facing you. Once Ecco is facing you, press Ⓐ, Ⓑ, Ⓒ, Ⓑ, Ⓒ, Ⓐ, Ⓒ, Ⓐ, Ⓑ If you entered the code correctly, a menu will pop up with all sorts of options such as a sound test, level select, tempo, etc. This code can be entered as many times as you'd like, as long as the game is paused while Ecco is facing you. |
| Hard Mode | In the starting area, break the two shells above you, and then swim through the tunnel to start the game in Hard mode. |

## PASSWORDS

| LEVEL | PASSWORD |
| --- | --- |
| Crystal Springs | UEPMCVEB |
| Fault Zone | OZUNSKZA |
| Two Tides | KDKINTYA |
| Skyway | SZXHCLDB |
| Sky Tides | OZWIDLDB |
| Tube of Medusa | QSJRYHZA |
| Skylands | MULXRXEB |
| Fin to Feather | YCPAWEXA |
| Eagle's Bay | YCJPDNDB |
| Asterite's Cave | AOJRDZWA |
| Four Islands | UOYURFDB |
| Sea of Darkness | UQZWIIAB |
| Vents of Medusa | MMVSOPBB |
| Gateway | KDCGTAHB |
| Big Water | QQCQRDRA |
| Deep Ridge | UXQWJIZD |
| Hungry Ones | WBQHMIUE |
| Secret Cave | CHGTEYZE |
| Gravitorbox | UIXBGWXE |
| Globe Holder | SBFPWWJE |
| Dark Sea | MXURVMLA |
| Vortex Queen | OKIMTBPA |
| Home Bay | CSNCMRUA |
| Epilogue | CEWSXKPA |
| Fish City | SGTDYSPA |
| City of Forever | WSSXZKVA |

## PASSWORDS FOR HARD MODE   * = New level found only in Hard mode

| LEVEL | PASSWORD |
| --- | --- |
| Crystal Springs | WPHSAAFB |
| Fault Zone | CRNPTFZA |
| Two Tides | QUKGZZYA |
| Skyway | MCMBPJDB |
| Sky Tides | OZMRKIDB |
| Tube of Medusa | ODFADPYA |
| Aqua Tubeway* | KNHRKJYA |
| Skylands | WXRDJYEB |
| Fin to Feather | UQTFBRXA |
| Eagle's Bay | QSNVMMDB |
| Asterite's Cave | EGAQRVXA |
| Maze of Stone* | EUTQQQWA |
| Four Islands | CZVQNHCB |
| Sea of Darkness | WFMYIDAB |
| Vents of Medusa | SHWZZNBB |
| Gateway | QKLLFPHB |
| Moray Abyss | YCFSBRAB |
| The Eye | AGNEXBTE |
| Big Water | YCBXONIA |

| | |
|---|---|
| Deep Ridge | UPODMUQD |
| The Hungry Ones | YOHVUVLE |
| Secret Cave | SPKHHKISE |
| Lunar Bay | WTHXKISE |
| Black Clouds | USKIKDOE |
| GraviatorBox | WNQWZMME |
| Globe Holder | MIPGDOME |
| New Machine* | GOSTCXJA |
| Vortex Queen | OOSFBXAA |
| Home Bay | QNSGAPGA |
| Epilogue | AXBGKHBA |
| Fish City | WKGETHCA |
| City of Forever | WQHFTZHA |
| "Secret" Password | AVQJTCBA |

### UNLOCKABLE

| UNLOCKABLE | HOW TO UNLOCK |
|---|---|
| Unlimited Air and Health | Turn Ecco left or right and pause the game while Ecco is facing the screen. Press Ⓐ, Ⓐ, ⬇, Ⓐ, Ⓒ, Ⓐ, ⬇, Ⓐ, Ⓐ, ⬇, Ⓐ and then unpause. You will now never die from lack of air or injuries. |

## ELEMENTS OF DESTRUCTION (DS)

### CODES

Pause the game and hold the following four buttons simultaneously.

| UNLOCKABLE | HOW TO UNLOCK |
|---|---|
| Unlimited Energy | Ⓨ, Ⓛ, ⬇, +SELECT |
| Unlimited Time | Ⓧ, Ⓡ, ⬇, +SELECT |

### ALL LEVELS

Hold down the following buttons during the first cutscene to unlock all levels for the current profile.

| UNLOCKABLE | HOW TO UNLOCK |
|---|---|
| Unlock All Levels | Ⓑ, Ⓛ, +SELECT |

## EL SHADDAI: ASCENSION OF THE METATRON (XBOX 360)

### ACHIEVEMENT

| UNLOCKABLE | HOW TO UNLOCK |
|---|---|
| A Reliable Friend (15) | Raise your boost level to 10. |
| A Warm Welcome (15) | Finish Chapter 07. |
| Adept (30) | Earn a G rank in every chapter at the EASY difficulty level. |
| An Unfriendly Greeting (15) | Finish Chapter 03. |
| Angels (15) | Finish all chapters at the EASY difficulty level. |
| Arch Master (15) | Defeat 300 enemies with Arch. |
| Aren't You Happy, Too? (15) | Finish Chapter 08. |
| Battle for Honor (15) | Register for the Score Leaderboard. |
| Benevolent Missionary (15) | Defeat more than 500 enemies. |
| Benevolent Savior (30) | Defeat more than 1000 enemies. |
| Conqueror (90) | Earn a G rank in every chapter at the HARD difficulty level. |
| Counterstrike Artist (30) | Execute 100 Perfect Guards. |
| Dominions (30) | Finish all chapters at the HARD difficulty level. |
| Escape From The Darkness (15) | Finish the Darkness stage. |

# CODES & CHEATS

| | |
|---|---|
| Finish Chapter 02. (15) | Welcome to the Tower |
| Gale Master (15) | Defeat 300 enemies with Gale. |
| Good Listener (15) | Obtain all of the Freemen's Notes. |
| Hunter-Gatherer (15) | Take 100 weapons from enemies. |
| I Will Mourn You (30) | Obtain all entries in the Prophecies of Ishtar. |
| I'll take the best you have. (15) | Take every weapons from all of the enemies and finish Chapter 10. |
| I'm Not Afraid of Watcher 1 (15) | Defeat Nether Sariel without executing a recover. |
| I'm Not Afraid of Watcher 2 (15) | Defeat Nether Ezekiel without executing a recover. |
| I'm Not Afraid of Watcher 3 (15) | Defeat Nether Azazel without executing a recover. |
| I'm Not Afraid of Watcher 4 (15) | Defeat Dark Armaros without executing a recover. |
| Indomitable Soul (15) | Execute 50 recovers. |
| Journey's End (15) | Finish Chapter 01. |
| Living Miracle (30) | Finish all chapters without a single Game Over. |
| Lord of the Metatron (0) | Earn all of the Achievements. |
| Martial Arts Master (15) | Defeat 100 enemies with bare hands |
| My Acrobatic Friend (30) | Finish Chapter 08 without dying. |
| My Beautiful Children... (15) | Finish Chapter 10. |
| Nephilim Party (15) | Finish Chapter 04. |
| No Problem (30) | Finish any chapter without collecting any armor-recovery items. |
| Out of Control (15) | Break 500 destroyable objects. |
| Principalities (15) | Finish all chapters at the NORMAL difficulty level. |
| Pushing the Limit (15) | Launch an Overboost. |
| Quite a Find (10) | Collect the Eyes of Truth. |
| Rest in Peace (15) | Defeat 50 of Souls of the Beloved |
| Seraphim (90) | Finish all chapters at the EXTRA difficulty level. |
| Show No Mercy (15) | Execute 100 Guard Breaks. |
| The armor okay? If not, I could... (15) | Finish Chapter 10 without taking any weapons from enemies. |
| The Journey Begins (15) | Finish Chapter 00. |
| The Last Job (15) | Finish Chapter 11. |
| The name is too long (15) | Have your weapon destroyed. |
| Time In The Spotlight (15) | Defeat 50 enemies during Armaros show. |
| Unnatural Evolution (15) | Finish Chapter 06. |
| Veil Master (15) | Defeat 300 enemies with Veil. |
| Visitor from Beyond Time (15) | Finish Chapter 05. |
| Welcome Back, Enoch (15) | Finish Chapter 09. |
| What's Yours Is Mine (15) | Acquire all the Pearls from the servant beasts. |

## UNLOCKABLE

After clearing the game, choose "New Game" and you will be able to choose new outfits that you have unlocked. They can be unlocked at any difficulty level.

| UNLOCKABLE | HOW TO UNLOCK |
|---|---|
| Dark Enoch - Enoch, transformed into a warrior of darkness by the Dark World | Achieve rank "A" (Adamantly) or higher on Chapter 8 |
| Old Armor A - Armor Enoch wears when he first asaults the Watchers (Blue) | Clear the game |

| Old Armor B - Armor Enoch wears when he first assaults the Watchers (Brown) | Clear the game |
| Rider - The riding outfit the motorcycle stage in the futuristic city | Achieve rank "A" (Adamantly) or higher on **from** Chapter 6 |
| Special - A special outfit worn by Enoch. You take no damage with this outfit on | Collect all Ishtar Bone Fragments from the Dark World portals |

## ERAGON (XBOX 360)

### *UNLIMITED FURY MODE*

Pause the game while in a level.

| UNLOCKABLE | HOW TO UNLOCK |
|---|---|
| Unlimited Fury Mode | Hold ❶ + ⓛⓣ + ❶ + ⓡⓣ and press ❽ ❾ ❾ ❾ (Note: This makes magic cooldown go much faster.) |

## ESCAPE FROM BUG ISLAND (Wii)

### *UNLOCKABLE*

| UNLOCKABLE | HOW TO UNLOCK |
|---|---|
| Samurai Sword and Death Scythe in Inventory | If you clear the game with either an "A" or "S" ranking, the next time you start the game, both the Samurai Sword and Death Scythe will be in your inventory. |

## ESWAT: CITY UNDER SIEGE (Wii)

### *UNLOCKABLES*

| UNLOCKABLE | HOW TO UNLOCK |
|---|---|
| Level Select | Start a game, and the Hero and Mission screen appears. Now hold down Ⓐ+Ⓑ+Ⓒ and press ⬅, ⬆, ⬆, ⬆. Select the level by pressing ⬅/⬇. Then during the ending sequence, press and hold Ⓐ+Ⓐ+Ⓒ+⬆+⬅. Keep holding these and press START until the Sound Test screen appears. |

## EXIT (PSP)

In order to use these codes, you must complete the first situation level.

| UNLOCKABLE | CODE |
|---|---|
| Unlocks Situation 8 | Ⓛ, Ⓡ, ⬅, ➡, ■, ●, ✕, ▲ |
| Unlocks Situation 9 | ▲, ⬇, ●, ⬅, ✕, ⬆, ■, ➡ |
| Unlocks Situation 10 | ➡, ⬇, ⬆, ⬅, ●, ✕, Ⓡ, Ⓛ |

## F1 2011 (PlayStation 3)

### TROPHY

| UNLOCKABLE | HOW TO UNLOCK |
|---|---|
| 10 Online (Bronze) | You have won 10 Online Races |
| 35 Online (Bronze) | You have won 35 Online Races |
| Blue Flag (Bronze) | You lapped at least 6 other cars during a Race in any game mode |
| Car Control (Bronze) | You won a Race without any Driver Assists enabled in any game mode |
| Co-op Drivers' World Champion (Silver) | You won the Drivers' World Championship in a Co-op season |
| Complete (Platinum) | Congratulations. You've completed F1 2011™ |
| Completionist (Bronze) | You have set a time in all of the Time Attack scenarios |
| Constructors' World Champion (Gold) | You have won the Constructors' World Championship in Career |
| Do it Yourself (Bronze) | You won a Race in any mode using manual gears |
| Down to the Wire (Silver) Race and won | You took the lead on the final lap of a 20%+ distance |
| Drivers' World Champion (Gold) | You have won the Drivers' World Championship in Career |
| Drivers' World Champion (Hard) (Gold) | You have won the Drivers' World Championship in Career on Hard or Expert Difficulty |
| Glancing Blow (Bronze) | With Damage on Full you made contact with the wall at Monaco and won the Race |
| Have You Considered DiRT3? (Bronze) | You performed a drift of 10 metres or more |
| Impeccable Performance (Silver) | You won a Race after Qualifying in Pole Position in any game mode |
| Is Jenson going to pass or not? (Bronze) | You won the Turkish Grand Prix driving as Lewis Hamilton |
| It's the Driver not the Car (Bronze) | You have won the Drivers' World Championship with two different teams in Career or Co-op |
| Just the Beginning (Silver) | You have taken your first Career victory |
| Keep Your Friends Close (Bronze) | You have completed a full Co-op season |
| Keeping it Clean (Bronze) | You completed an Online Race without making contact with an opponent's car |
| Lightning Fast (Bronze) | You set the fastest penalty-free lap of the Race in any game mode |
| On the Bounce (Gold) | You have beaten Alberto Ascari's record of 9 successive Career victories |
| On the Podium (Silver) | You have finished a Career Race in the top three |
| Opportunist (Bronze) | You have performed a Pit-stop during a Safety Car period |
| Pole Position (Silver) | You have taken the first Pole Position of your Career |
| Precision Driving (Silver) | You completed a Race without colliding with another car or object |

| | |
|---|---|
| **Push the Button (Bronze)** | You cleanly overtook an opponent while KERS was activated |
| **Robot-Like Consistency (Silver)** | You have completed 5 successive laps within a quarter of a second of each other |
| **Season Opener (Bronze)** | You have completed your first Career Race |
| **Senna-esque (Bronze)** | You took the lead on lap 1, in heavy rain, after starting in 5th or lower |
| **Slap on the Wrist (Bronze)** | You were awarded a Drive-through Penalty and still went on to win the Race |
| **Slingshot (Bronze)** | You have spent a total of 10 minutes slipstreaming your opponents in any game mode |
| **Solid Performance (Silver)** | You scored points at every round of a Career or Co-op season |
| **Sublime Talent (Bronze)** | You set the fastest lap in every session of a Long Race Weekend in any mode |
| **Teamwork (Silver)** | You won the Constructors' World Championship in a Co-op Championship |
| **Test Driver (Bronze)** | You've covered at least 500 Practice miles / 805 kilometres in your Career |
| **They're on Which Buttons? (Bronze)** | You won a Race without activating KERS or the DRS once |
| **Trophy Collector (Silver)** | You have won a Race at each of the 19 circuits in any game mode |
| **Winging It (Bronze)** | You cleanly overtook an opponent while the DRS was activated |

## F.3.A.R. (XBOX 360)

### ACHIEVEMENT

| UNLOCKABLE | HOW TO UNLOCK |
|---|---|
| **A Precursor (5)** | In the Poker Room of Prison, kill all 3 enemies with headshots before slo-mo ends |
| **Almost Halfway (10)** | Attain Rank 10 |
| **Art Collector (15)** | Pin 100 total enemies with The Penetrator or Leaper knives |
| **Big Brother's Helper (15)** | As Fettel, suspend 100 enemies that Point Man kills |
| **Cannibal Run (15)** | Attain a total of 95,000 score on Interval 03 |
| **Completionist (50)** | Complete every challenge at least once |
| **Crossing Over (15)** | Attain a total of 70,000 score on Interval 06 |
| **Dead Blind (10)** | Spend an entire round of Contractions in deep fog without going into Last Stand |
| **Doll Collector (20)** | Find the Alma Doll on every Mission |
| **Dream Score (10)** | Attain a total of 50,000 score on Interval 08 |
| **Earl of Pain (10)** | Kill 1000 enemies by any method in any game mode |
| **Extremist (20)** | Complete any campaign level on INSANE without reloading checkpoints or going into Last Stand |
| **Footy Foul (10)** | Kill 2 enemies with 1 Slide Kick during Slow Mo |
| **Get To The Chopper (10)** | Complete Interval 02 |
| **God Among Men (25)** | Kill 250 total enemies during Slow Mo |
| **Handle with Care (20)** | Return 30 crates in one game of Contractions |
| **Hanging 20 (20)** | Complete wave 20 in Contractions |
| **Head Crab Removal (10)** | 20 kills with a crowbar |
| **Homecoming King (25)** | Complete Interval 08 |
| **House Arrest (15)** | Attain a total of 105,000 score on Interval 04 |
| **I F.E.A.R. Nothing! (15)** | Finish a wave of Contractions on INSANE without anyone going into Last Stand |

| I'm not a Doctor, I'm a Medic! (10) | Perform 50 revives in any game mode |
| Indecisive (10) | Possess 20 different enemies in one round of Soul King |
| Insider Trading (15) | Possess every type of possessable enemy |
| Little Brother's Helper (15) | As Point Man, kill 100 enemies suspended by Fettel |
| Magna Slum Laude (15) | Attain a total of 85,000 score on Interval 02 |
| Man Mode (100) | Finish the Campaign on INSANE difficulty |
| Mission… accomplished? (50) | Finish the Campaign on any difficulty (all Intervals complete) |
| Monarch (20) | Win 20 rounds of Soul King |
| No can defense! (20) | Kill 100 enemies with Jump Kick or Slide Kick |
| Pain, In Bulk (15) | Complete Interval 03 |
| Point Authority (15) | Attain a total of 110,000 score on Interval 07 |
| Point Taken (15) | Attain a total of 110,000 score on Interval 05 |
| Prison Impossible (10) | Complete Interval 01 |
| Score Monger (30) | Complete 30 challenges in one Interval |
| Soul Gatherer (15) | Attain a total of 6,000 Souls in one round of Soul King |
| Soul Hoarder (20) King match | Attain a total of 25,000 Souls across all rounds of a Soul |
| Spiritually Attuned (20) | Make 100 Psychic Links (Share or Steal) |
| State-of-the-art. Bang, ) bang! (20 | Kill 10 enemies in a row with Sniper Rifle headshots |
| Supreme Challenger (25) | Complete 500 total challenges between all categories |
| Terminal Victory (25) | Complete Interval 07 |
| That's a lot of Zeros (50) | Attain a total of 250,000 points through challenges |
| Through the Haystack (20) | Complete Interval 05 |
| Town Hall Beating (15) | Complete Interval 04 |
| Trouble Cross (20) | Complete Interval 06 |
| Unstoppable! (15) | Win all 5 rounds of a 5-round Soul King match |
| Up The River (15) | Attain a total of 95,000 score on Interval 01 |
| We'll Try Again Tomorrow! (15) | Survive 3 waves in Contractions in a row without anyone bringing back a crate |
| Yo, Adrian! (15) | Find something worth punching! |
| You've got the Touch! (25) | Attain Rank 21 |

### UNLOCKABLE

In order to unlock the Insane difficulty level, you must first beat the game on any difficulty level.

| UNLOCKABLE | HOW TO UNLOCK |
|---|---|
| Insane difficulty level | Beat the game. (Any Difficulty) |

## FABLE II  (XBOX 360)

### EASTER EGG

In the side quest "Treasure Island of Doom," the Lionhead Studios Lion can be found when you get to the treasure island. Look at the island in the middle of the lake and you'll see it is in the shape of the Studio's Lionhead logo.

### INFINITE EXPERIENCE

Once you have access to Bowerstone Market, walk to Town Square. There is a potion shopkeeper on the left side. Walk around the right side of the buildings there and down an alley to find a house known as Monster Manor. Sleep there to gain its benefit (+1 star of Physique) Once you gain this benefit, go to your abilities list, select physique, and hit Y to unlearn it. The bonus star from the house does not disappear, but the experience is given to you anyway. Repeat this process as many times as you like, the more stars you have in physique the more exp you get each time. This experience is general experience and can be applied to any skills.

## INFINITE EXPERIENCE II

Wait until your character is at least somewhat leveled up. Plug in a second controller and begin a co-op game without using a second profile. Using the second controller, go to your henchman's abilities and discard all of them, returning the experience to the pool. Then quit out of the co-op game. You should find that all the "leftover" experience has been transferred to your hero. Repeat as often as you like. Note: Your co-op henchman will have the same abilities that you do, so the stronger the hero, the more abilities there are to sell off and thus more experience.

## FABLE III (XBOX 360)

### AVATAR AWARDS

| UNLOCKABLE | HOW TO UNLOCK |
|---|---|
| Crown | Become the ruler of Albion |
| Royal Boots | Win the support of the Dwellers |
| Royal Shirt | Win the support of the Bowerstone |
| Royal Trousers | Win the support of the Swift Brigade |

### DUPLICATION (PRE-PATCH)

This glitch allows you to duplicate gold or anything else. With a second controller, join your game. Then use player 1 to "gift" player 2 whatever you want to duplicate, then have player 2 leave player 1's sanctuary. Have player 2 go into his sanctuary and find the gift. Now have him reject the gift to send it back to player 1. Immediately have player 2 leave his sanctuary, then immediately drop him from the game. Now player 1 has a rejected gift in his sanctuary and player 2 will not be saved, meaning when you reload him, he will also have a gift the game didn't save as being rejected. You can dupe up to 100,000 gold at a time using this.

### LIONHEAD STUDIO EASTER EGG

Swim out into the ocean in the Driftwood area. Once you hit the border, tilt your camera to look down into the water. There should be a Lionhead Studios logo on the sea floor.

### PORTAL EASTER EGG

When going to capture Nigel Ferret (during the Hideout mission of bowerstone) you will come across a room with a silver key. At the far end of the room there is a path around the boxes to the other jail cell. The cell contains a hobbe worshiping the companion cube from Portal and there is of course some cake.

## FALLOUT 3 (XBOX 360)

### INFINITE XP

You can gain infinite XP if your Speech skill is high enough (approximately level 30). Go Big Town, north of Vault 101. Speak with a girl named Bittercup. She'll tell you about her dating exploits. After speaking with her, go into the house marked "Common House" and speak to a man named Pappy. There should be a speech skill dialogue option that says "You came here with Bittercup, right?" You get XP every time you click it. Continue to do this as long as you like to gain free XP.

### EARLY DETECTION

When heading into seemingly hostile territory, try hitting the VATS button over and over again as you make your character turn around, searching all angles. Doing so will alert you to any enemies you may not yet see by zooming in on them in VATS mode. You won't be able to do damage to your foes from such a distance, but it's a good way to spot foes before they spot you so you know what you're getting yourself into.

### SANDMAN GLITCH (PRE-PATCH)

This a glitch for getting infinite experience. Steps: Reach Level 10 with a sneak skill of 60 and get the Mr. Sandman perk. Go to Andale (south central part of the map). Wait until around 1 A.M. and go into the Smith house while they are sleeping. Go upstairs and into the kid's bedroom. Use sandman on him (crouch and select him and use the first option). Repeat the last steps. Increase difficulty for more XP.

## FALLOUT: NEW VEGAS (XBOX 360)

### INFINITE XP GLITCH

With a Speech skill at 50 or higher, you can persuade Old Ben to offer his escort services to the local bar and gain 61 XP if you succeed in the speech challenge. Then follow him back to the bar and wait until he sits down, speak to him again, and redo the speech challenge for as much XP as you like! Old Ben is usually sitting by a fire close to the King's headquarters in Freeside.

### INFINITE CAPS GLITCH

First, you must go to the town of Primm. Complete the "My Kind of Town" quest for them by getting a sheriff for the town. After you get them a sheriff, or the NCR's troops, you have to wait 3 to 7 in-game days, and the Vikki and Vance Casino will open again in Primm. Go there, and exchange some caps for some of the casino's chips. Then, turn in the casino's chips for caps. You will notice that when you turn the chips in, you don't have them removed from your inventory; however, you get the payout. You can exploit this for as long as you want.

### VATS GLITCH

Obtain the Anti-Material Rifle and equip it with incendiary rounds. With the rifle equipped, target someone in VATS and then close VATS. They should catch fire and lose health. You can also select more than one person in VATS before closing it to burn more people. You will not lose karma or reputation.

### MORE XP GLITCH

You need Speech of 30 or the perk Confirmed Bachelor. You must also be on the good side of NCR. Go to HELIOS One and the lady should automatically talk to you. Once she allows you access to HELIOS One, you should be able to start the mission "That Lucky Old Sun." Follow the mission and talk to Fantastic and Ignacio Rivas. While talking to Rivas, make sure you get him to reveal that he's a Follower of the Apocalypse by using Speech or Confirmed Bachelor and agree with his ideals about peace or just say you're neutral. Do the mission regularly until you get to the point where you activate the Mainframe Terminal. Configure the Power Grid to Full Region (Emergency Output Level). Finish the mission by hitting the Reflector Control Panel outside on top of the tower. Go back to Ignacio Rivas and choose the option "I overloaded the plant. No one . . ." The glitch is that the option never disappears, so you can choose to keep pressing it. You get 350 XP, 3 Stimpacks, and 2 Doctor's Bags.

### INFINITE XP

This glitch can be found when arriving at the strip for the first time and you are invited into the Lucky 38 casino. Talk with Mr. House and ask about his lifespan (This requires a medicine check of 35). This will award 35 XP. Asking about his age again and reselecting the option "you appear to be more computer than man" will present the medicine check again, granting 35 XP each time (this glitch works in the current patched version of the game).

## FALLOUT: NEW VEGAS (PS3)

### INFINITE XP IN VAULT 11

Reach the sacrificial chamber and eliminate the robots, then go to the computer terminal through the previously closed wall and enter it. The last option can be pressed repeatedly to gain 500 XP each time. If any of the other options are chosen or if the terminal is exited, then you cannot use this exploit.

### INFINITE CAPS

Once Primm obtains a new sheriff, The Vikki and Vance Casino will become available. If you save before each hand in blackjack, you can reload the game if you lose. You can trade in your chips for caps at the register. The NPC will give you the equivalent chips in caps, but will not take any away. This is repeatable.

### EASY KILL

Obtain and equip the Anti-Material Rifle and then equip .50MG Incendiary rounds. Target some one in VATS and then close VATS, they should catch fire and lose health. You can also select more then one person in VATS before closing it, burning more people using the right analog. You will not aggro enemies or friendlies. Also you will not lose karma or Reputation with each kill.

### INFINITE EXPERIENCE GLITCH

If you have a speech skill of 50 or higher, you can persuade Old Ben to offer his escort services to the local bar. If you succeed in the Speech Challenge, you'll gain 61 XP. If you follow him back to the bar afterwards, waiting until he sits down, you can speak to him again and redo the same Speech Challenge repeatedly for infinite XP! You can find Old Ben sitting by a fire close to The King's headquarters in Freeside.

### INFINITE XP

Obtain "Speech" 30 or the perk "Confirmed Bachelor." You must also be friendly with NCR. Go to "HELIOS One" and the lady should automatically talk to you. Once she allows you to access HELIOS One, you will now be able to start the mission "That Lucky Old Sun". Follow the mission and talk to Fantastic and Ignacio Rivas. While speaking with Rivas, make sure you get him to reveal that he's a Follower of the Apocalypse by. This is accomplished by using Speech or Confirmed Bachelor while agreeing with his ideals about peace...or just say you're neutral. Once you get to the point where you activate the Mainframe Terminal, configure the Power Grid to "5 Full Region (Emergency Output Level). Complete the mission by hitting the Reflector Control Panel outside on top of the tower. Go back to Ignacio Rivas and select "I overloaded the plant. No one....." The glitch is that the option never disappears, so you can choose to keep pressing it. You get 350XP, 3 Stimpacks, and 2 Doctor's Bag.

## FAR CRY 2   (PlayStation 3)

### CODES

In the menu, go to Additional Content, then Promotion Code, and input the code.

| EFFECT | CODE |
| --- | --- |
| Unlock all missions. | 6aPHuswe |
| Bonus Mission | tr99pUkA |
| Bonus Mission | THaCupR4 |
| Bonus Mission | tar3QuzU |
| Bonus Mission | SpujeN7x |
| Bonus Mission | sa7eSUPR |
| Bonus Mission | JeM8SpaW |
| Bonus Mission | Cr34ufrE |
| Bonus Mission | 96CesuHu |
| Bonus Mission | 2Eprunef |
| Bonus Mission | zUmU6Rup |

## FAR CRY INSTINCTS PREDATOR   (XBOX 360)

To enter these passwords, pause the game and select the Cheat menu. Note that these passwords are case sensitive.

| UNLOCKABLE | PASSWORD |
| --- | --- |
| Enable Evolutions | FeralAttack |
| Evolution Game | GiveMeltAll |
| Heal Yourself | ImJackCarver |
| Infinite Adrenaline | Bloodlust |
| Infinite Ammo | UnleashHell |
| Unlock All Maps | GiveMeTheMaps |

## FAR CRY VENGEANCE (Wii)

### PASSWORD

| PASSWORD | EFFECT |
|---|---|
| GiveMeTheMaps | Unlock All Maps |

## FATAL FURY (Wii)

### UNLOCKABLE

| UNLOCKABLE | HOW TO UNLOCK |
|---|---|
| Good Ending | Beat the game on Normal or Hard without using a continue |

## FIFA SOCCER 12 (PlayStation 3)

### TROPHY

| UNLOCKABLE | HOW TO UNLOCK |
|---|---|
| 'Big Cup' Squad (Silver) | Enter an Ultimate Team tournament and finish a match with an overall squad rating of 85 or higher |
| 10 vs 11 (Bronze) | Win from a draw or behind while down a man in a game vs the CPU |
| 3 Points (Bronze) | Win a season game in Head to Head Seasons |
| All My Own Work (Bronze) | Win a Match with Manual Controls (including Tactical Defending) |
| Being Social (Bronze) | Play an Online Friendlies Match |
| Block Party (Bronze) | Manually block 5 shots while defending in a single game |
| Campaign Complete (Silver) | Complete a Season in Head to Head Seasons |
| Century of Goals (Silver) | Score 100 goals in FIFA 12 match play |
| Challenge Accepted (Bronze) | Complete an EA SPORTS Football Club Game Scenario Challenge |
| Club Legend (Bronze) | Play 100 matches with any player in FIFA 12 Ultimate Team |
| Comeback Kid (Bronze) | Win after being down 3 goals in the 2nd half in a game vs. the CPU |
| Don't Blink (Bronze) | Score within the first 5 minutes of a game in a game vs the CPU |
| EAS FC Starting 11 (Silver) | Reach level 20 in the EA SPORTS Football Club |
| EAS FC Youth Academy (Bronze) | Reach level 5 in the EA SPORTS Football Club |
| FIFA for Life (Silver) | Spend 50 hours on the pitch |
| Football Legend (Platinum) | Unlock all other trophies (excluding additional content trophies) |
| Friendly (Bronze) | Finish a match against a Friend in FIFA 12 Ultimate Team |
| Friends now Enemies? (Bronze) | Win an Online Friendlies season |
| Fully Formed (Silver) | Have three players be in full form at the same time on your club in Career Mode |
| Growing Club (Bronze) | Achieve a club value of 85,000,000 in FIFA 12 Ultimate Team |
| Happy 20th EA SPORTS! (Bronze) | Score 20 match goals in FIFA 12 to celebrate 20 years of EA SPORTS! |
| How Great is that? (Bronze) | Find a team of the week player in an Ultimate Team pack |
| I'll have that one (Bronze) | Open your first pack in FIFA 12 Ultimate Team |
| Legendary (Silver) | Win a game vs. the CPU on legendary difficulty against a club of the same or higher star level |
| Legends start with Victories (Bronze) | Win a match with your FIFA 12 Ultimate Team club |
| Marquee Signing (Silver) | Purchase a Gold Player from the trade market for 15,000 or more coins using Buy now |

| | |
|---|---|
| **Massive Signing (Bronze)** | Sign a player better than anyone else on your club during the transfer window |
| **Megged (Silver)** | Successfully dribble the ball through a defender's legs |
| **New Club in Town (Bronze)** | Create your FIFA 12 Ultimate Team club |
| **No Draw for You! (Bronze)** | Score a 90th minute winner in a game vs. the CPU |
| **Pack King (Gold)** | Open 100 packs in FIFA 12 Ultimate Team |
| **Path to the Cup (Bronze)** | Win a cup game in Head to Head Seasons |
| **Precision Tackler (Bronze)** | Obtain a successful tackle percentage of 80% with a minimum of 5 tackles in a game |
| **Procrastinator (Bronze)** | Sign a player on Deadline Day in the transfer window in Career Mode |
| **Puppet Master (Bronze)** | Talk to the Press in Career Mode |
| **Quickly Now! (Bronze)** | Score shortly after a quick throw-in |
| **Riding Bikes (Silver)** | Score with a bicycle kick |
| **Ruud Boy (Bronze)** | Score a goal on a volley |
| **Sweet Music (Bronze)** | Set up some Custom Audio in FIFA 12 |
| **Tournament Victory (Bronze)** | Win a tournament in FIFA 12 Ultimate Team |
| **Trophy Time (Silver)** | Win the league title in any league in Career Mode |
| **Virtual Debut (Bronze)** | Play an online Pro Club or Pro Ranked match with your Virtual Pro |
| **Virtual Legend (Silver)** | Play 50 Matches with your Virtual Pro |
| **Warrior (Bronze)** | Score a goal after suffering a non-contact injury with a player |
| **We'll need a larger trophy case (Silver)** | Win your 10th trophy in FIFA 12 Ultimate Team |
| **Youth is Served (Silver)** | Sign a player to your youth squad in Career Mode |

## FIFA STREET 3 (XBOX 360, PlayStation 3)

### BONUS TEAMS

Complete the following tasks to unlock the corresponding team.

| UNLOCKABLE | HOW TO UNLOCK |
|---|---|
| Predator (Gerrard, Beckham, etc.) | Complete Adidas Challenge in FIFA Street Challenge. |
| The Blasters (Gerrard, Ballack, etc.) | Win 40 Games in FIFA Street Challenge. |
| The Champions (Baresi, Voller, etc.) | Complete Champion Challenge in FIFA Street Challenge. |
| The Classics (Cantona, Zico, etc.) | Complete Classic Challenge in FIFA Street Challenge. |
| World Stars (Ronaldinho, Eto'o, etc.) | Complete All Stars Challenge in FIFA Street Challenge. |

## FIFA WORLD CUP SOUTH AFRICA - 2010 (XBOX 360)

### CELEBRATIONS

In the Main menu, go to EA Extras and then enter the codes below.

| EFFECT | CODE |
|---|---|
| Flying Dive | ZTSMBDRGJLQBUMSA |
| African Dance | QCZCGTXKWYWBNPJK |
| Baby Cradle | VXYJZLXTRPBZUXXJ |
| Side Slide | BNDIPYYTCDZVJCCN |
| River Dance | NLGAHWCHCCUCTNUH |
| Prancing Bird | YMEOCBDOIWYUEVQN |
| Ice Skating | TLHDMYMCUITLAYJL |

## FIFA WORLD CUP SOUTH AFRICA - 2010 (Wii)

### UNLOCKABLES

| UNLOCKABLE | HOW TO UNLOCK |
| --- | --- |
| Play the World Classic XI Team | Get at least a bronze medal against every team in Zakumi's Dream Team Mode. |
| Use the World Classic XI Team | Beat the World Classic XI Team (Hit the Pitch Mode only). |

### CELEBRATION PACKS

| UNLOCKABLE | HOW TO UNLOCK |
| --- | --- |
| Goal Celebration Pack #1 | Win the Adidas Golden Boot Award by winning the FIFA World Cup and having one of the members on your team be the top scorer of the World Cup. |
| Goal Celebration Pack #2 | Take the lead by scoring within the first 5 minutes of any match. |
| Goal Celebration Pack #3 | Score within 5 minutes following a goal you just made. |
| Goal Celebration Pack #4 | Score 100 goals. |
| Goal Celebration Pack #5 | Perform a Hat Trick or score three goals with the same player in a single match. |

## FIGHT NIGHT CHAMPION (PlayStation 3)

### TROPHIES

| UNLOCKABLE | HOW TO UNLOCK |
| --- | --- |
| A Champion Emerges (Bronze) | Defeat Isaac Frost in Champion Mode |
| A Fight Amongst Friends I (Bronze) | Complete a Lightweight League Match in an Online Gym |
| A Fight Amongst Friends II (Bronze) | Complete a Middleweight League Match in an Online Gym |
| A Fight Amongst Friends III (Bronze) | Complete a Heavyweight League Match in an Online Gym |
| A Fist For Every Face (Gold) | Defeat the entire Fight Night Champion roster in Fight Now |
| A Little This, A Little That (Silver) | Knockdown an opponent with a head shot and a body shot in a Ranked Match |
| A Verdict Is In (Silver) | Win a 10-round Ranked Match |
| Alphabet Soup (Bronze) | Own all belts within one weight class at the same time in Legacy Mode |
| Bench Pressing (Bronze) | Obtain boxer level 30 in OWC |
| Bicep Curling (Bronze) | Obtain boxer level 15 in OWC |
| Breaking a Sweat (Gold) | Get a Champion rating on every Training Game |
| Can You Feel The Power? (Bronze) | Max out any skill of a Legacy Mode, OWC, or Online Gyms boxer |
| Every Second Counts (Gold) | Knockdown an opponent in a Ranked Match with less than 10 seconds left in the round |
| Everything You Got Left (Bronze) | Defeat Meldrick Johnson in Champion Mode |
| Gold Medal Performance (Bronze) | Knockout Joel Savon in Champion Mode |
| Hamstring Blasting (Silver) | Obtain boxer level 45 in OWC |
| How Poetic (Silver) | Retire as the GOAT in Legacy Mode |
| I Brought My Own Judges (Bronze) | Defeat Ricardo Alvarez in Champion Mode |
| I'm Just Doing My Jab (Silver) | Jab 10,000 times |
| Low Down Dirty Tricks (Bronze) | Defeat Kobe Nichols in Champion Mode |
| Mr. Reliable (Bronze) | Earn a Reliability Multiplier of more than 85% after playing at least 100 Ranked Matches |

| My Defense Is Impregnable (Silver) | Win a Ranked Match with your opponent's accuracy at or below 20% |
|---|---|
| No Time To Bleed (Bronze) | Knockout Dwight Cooper before the 6th round in Champion Mode |
| Numba One Stunna (Gold) | Stun your opponents 1000 times |
| Platinum Trophy (Platinum) | Unlock all other trophies |
| Represent the Crew I (Bronze) | Complete a Lightweight fight against a member of a Rival Gym |
| Represent the Crew II (Bronze) | Complete a Middleweight fight against a member of a Rival Gym |
| Represent the Crew III (Bronze) | Complete a Heavyweight fight against a member of a Rival Gym |
| Road To Glory (Bronze) | Complete 100 fights In Online World Championship |
| Squat Thrusting (Gold) | Obtain boxer level 60 in OWC |
| Survival of the Fittest (Bronze) | Defeat the prison gang leader in Champion Mode |
| The Awakening (Silver) | Knockdown Mason Brooks in under 3 minutes in Champion Mode |
| This Is Going Well (Silver) | Knockdown an opponent twice in the same round of a Ranked Match |
| THIS is Sim (Bronze) | Create and upload a Settings file to EA SPORTS World |
| Turnabout If Fair Play (Silver) | Knockdown Keyshawn Hayes with a left hook in Champion Mode |
| Welcome to the Jungle (Bronze) | Defeat the prison gang member in Champion Mode |
| Will They Believe You? (Silver) | Get up from a fourth knockdown during a Ranked Match |

## FIGHT NIGHT ROUND 4   (XBOX 360)

### UNLOCKABLES

| UNLOCKABLE | HOW TO UNLOCK |
|---|---|
| Unlock Extra Offline Accessories | In Legacy Mode, become a champion in two weight divisions then reach "G.O.A.T" status. |
| Unlock Extra Online Accessories | Win the Lightweight, Middleweight, and Heavyweight Online belts. |

## FINAL FANTASY CRYSTAL CHRONICLES: THE CRYSTAL BEARERS   (Wii)

### UNLOCKABLES

| UNLOCKABLE | HOW TO UNLOCK |
|---|---|
| Layle Moogle in Alfitaria Entrance | Start a New Game + |
| New Game + | Defeat the final boss, then save at the end. |

## FINAL FANTASY FABLES: CHOCOBO'S DUNGEON   (Wii)

### ADDITIONAL DUNGEONS

| UNLOCKABLE | HOW TO UNLOCK |
|---|---|
| Chocobo's Memories (Standard Dungeon) | Accessed through the Chocobo statue in the park |
| Croma's Future (Special Dungeon) | Accessed through Croma in Stella's House |

### JOBS

Jobs are like classes. You begin with the "Natural" job and can unlock nine others during the game.

| UNLOCKABLE | HOW TO UNLOCK |
|---|---|
| Black Mage | Make it to 10F in Guardian of the Flame. |
| Dancer | Enter "Pirouette" (capital P at the beginning, the rest lowercase, AND a musical note at the end) as a Romantic Phrase. |

| Dark Knight | Defeat Croma Shade in 30F in Guardian of the Light. |
| Dragoon | Complete Meja's Memories. |
| Knight | Complete Freja's Memories. |
| Ninja | Complete Volg's Memories. |
| Scholar | Defeat the four elements in 20F Guardian of the Water. |
| Thief | Steal the item behind Merchant Hero X in any of his dungeon shops. |
| White Mage | Complete Pastor Roche's Memories. |

## FINAL FANTASY IV: COMPLETE COLLECTION (PSP)

### UNLOCKABLE

| UNLOCKABLE | HOW TO UNLOCK |
|---|---|
| Lunar Ruins | You must beat the final boss with each character atleast once. |
| Music Player | Beating the game once unlocks the Music Player. It can be accessed under "Extra" on the title screen. |
| The Cave of Trials | Once you unlock Party Switching and head back to Mysidia, you'll be informed of a new challenge at Mt. Ordeals. A scene will occur once you get there and the Cave of Trials will be accessible. |
| Easter Egg | The Developers' room is now renamed the 1991 Dev Team Office. To get there, reach the Underworld for the first time. After gaining access to the armory (after beating Golbez in the crystal room) go down to the Weapon/Armor room and go behind the pillar between the two shop desks. From there, go up, you'll then be in the Lali Ho Pub (another secret room). Then, go right to where there's a dark marking on the floor and progress right through the wall and down a stairway. You will now be at the 1991 Dev Team Office entrance, where you can talk to the developers of the original game, complete with their rank back when they worked on the game in 1991. |
| "1991 Dev Team Office" | The Developers' room is now renamed the 1991 Dev Team Office. To get there, reach the Underworld for the first time. After gaining access to the armory (after beating Golbez in the crystal room) go down to the Weapon/Armor room and go behind the pillar between the two shop desks. From there, go up, you'll then be in the Lali Ho Pub (another secret room). Then, go right to where there's a dark marking on the floor and progress right through the wall and down a stairway. You will now be at the 1991 Dev Team Office entrance, where you can talk to the developers of the original game, complete with their rank back when they worked on the game in 1991. |

## FINAL FANTASY XIII (XBOX 360, PlayStation 3)

### GAMER PICS

| UNLOCKABLE | HOW TO UNLOCK |
|---|---|
| Fang | Obtain the Treasure Hunter (Gold) trophy. |
| Hope | Obtain the Instrument of Change (Gold) trophy. |
| Lightning | Obtain the Superstar (Gold)" trophy. |
| Sazh | Obtain the Lore Master (Gold) trophy. |
| Serah | Obtain the Ultimate Hero (Platinum) trophy. |
| Snow | Obtain the L'Cie Paragon (Gold) trophy. |
| Vanille | Obtain the Instrument of Faith (Silver) trophy. |

## FINAL FIGHT: DOUBLE IMPACT (PlayStation 3)

### STREET FIGHTER CARTOON

Earn 570,000 points in the Uptown stage and you will be able to view the episode of the "Street Fighter Cartoon" in which the Final Fight Characters have cameo roles.

## FINAL FIGHT: DOUBLE IMPACT (XBOX 360)

### STREET FIGHTER CARTOON

Earn 570,000 points in the Uptown stage and you will be able to view the episode of the "Street Fighter Cartoon" in which the Final Fight Characters have cameo roles.

## FINAL SOLDIER (Wii)

### LEVEL SELECT

| UNLOCKABLE | HOW TO UNLOCK |
|---|---|
| Level Select | Before the demo starts, press ⬆, ⬆, ①, ⬇, ⬇, ②, ⬅, ⬅, ⬅, ⬅ |

## FLATOUT: HEAD ON (PSP)

### CODES

At main screen, go to Extras, then to Enter Code.

| EFFECT | CODE |
|---|---|
| All Cars and 1 Million Credits | GIEVEPIX |
| All Tracks | GIVEALL |
| Big Rig | ELPUEBLO |
| Big Rig Truck | RAIDERS |
| Flatmobile Car | WOTKINS |
| Mob Car | BIGTRUCK |
| Pimpster Car | RUTTO |
| Rocket Car | KALJAKOPPA |
| School Bus | GIEVCARPLZ |

## FLOCK (PlayStation 3 , XBOX 360)

### UNLOCKABLES

| UNLOCKABLE | HOW TO UNLOCK |
|---|---|
| Blanka Ball | Get a perfect abduction on all single-player levels. |
| Chicken Trophy | Get at least a Bronze Medal on all single-player levels. |
| Cow Trophy | Get Gold Medals on all single-player levels. |
| Infinite Boost | Get Gold Medals on all single-player levels. |
| Pig Trophy | Get at least a Silver Medal on all single-player levels. |
| Sheep Trophy | Get a perfect abduction on all single-player levels. |

## FOLKLORE (PlayStation 3)

### SPECIAL FOLKS

| UNLOCKABLE | HOW TO UNLOCK |
|---|---|
| Ellen—Collbrande | Score 150,000 Campaign Points in Dungeon Trial mode. |
| Ellen—Duergar | Score 30,000 Campaign Points in Dungeon Trial mode. |
| Ellen—Kaladbolg | Upload a 4,500-point dungeon. |
| Keats—Alphard | Upload a 4,500-point dungeon. |
| Keats—Collbrande | Score 150,000 Campaign Points in Dungeon Trial mode. |
| Keats—Duergar | Score 30,000 Campaign Points in Dungeon Trial mode. |
| Keats—Valiant | Score 100,000 Campaign Points in Dungeon Trial mode. |

## FORZA MOTORSPORT 4 (XBOX 360)

### ACHIEVEMENT

| UNLOCKABLE | HOW TO UNLOCK |
|---|---|
| Amateur (25) | Complete the first year of Season Play. |
| Autocrosser (10) | Complete 10 Autocross events without hitting gate cones. |
| Awesome Drift (20) | Earn a perfect Drift score. |

| | |
|---|---|
| **Born Competitor (30)** | Post a time in every Rivals mode event. |
| **Bucket List (80)** | Finish 1st in every single race in the Event List in Career play mode. |
| **Car Explorer (10)** | Fully explore any car in Autovista. |
| **Champion (25)** | Complete the ninth year of Season Play. |
| **Clubbed Up (15)** | Create or join a Car Club. |
| **Clubman (25)** | Complete the second year of Season Play. |
| **Daily Rewards (5)** | Visit the Message Center on at least five unique days. |
| **Driver Level 1 (20)** | Reach Driver Level 1 in Career mode. |
| **Driver Level 10 (20)** | Reach Driver Level 10 in Career mode. |
| **Driver Level 20 (20)** | Reach Driver Level 20 in Career mode. |
| **Driver Level 30 (20)** | Reach Driver Level 30 in Career mode. |
| **Driver Level 40 (20)** | Reach Driver Level 40 in Career mode. |
| **Driver Level 50 (20)** | Reach Driver Level 50 in Career mode. |
| **Elite (25)** | Complete the eighth year of Season Play. |
| **Entrepreneur (10)** | Sell a car tuning, paint job, or vinyl group from your storefront. |
| **Exclusive Taste (50)** | Own the five most expensive cars in the game (not including DLC). |
| **Expert (25)** | Complete the fifth year of Season Play. |
| **Factory Driver (60)** | Get any Car Manufacturer to Affinity level 50. |
| **Ferrari Collector (40)** | Own every Ferrari included on Disc 1. |
| **Flat Out (5)** | Earn a perfect Speed score. |
| **Forza Faithful (15)** | Import a file from Forza Motorsport 3. |
| **Forza World Tourer (60)** | Finish a race on every race track in Forza Motorsport 4. |
| **Grease Monkey (10)** | Create a car tuning file for your car. |
| **Here's My Card (10)** | Create a custom playercard with badges and titles. |
| **Kingpin (5)** | Knock down a gold bowling pin in Car Bowling. |
| **Legend (50)** | Complete the tenth year of Season Play. |
| **Legendary Battle (15)** | Beat a Ferrari 330 P4 in any race while driving a Ford GT40 Mark II. |
| **Look Ma, No Controller! (5)** | Use Kinect to drive any car in Free Play. |
| **Masters (25)** | Complete the seventh year of Season Play. |
| **My Car is Your Car (10)** | Share a car in your garage with your Car Club. |
| **Nice Pass (15)** | Earn a perfect Pass score. |
| **On Location (20)** | Take a photo of any car in every Home Space. |
| **Outta Time (10)** | Reach 88 mph in a DeLorean. |
| **Painter (10)** | Create a paint job or vinyl group for your car. |
| **Perfect Turn (15)** | Earn a perfect Turn score. |
| **Professional (25)** | Complete the sixth year of Season Play. |
| **Rivals Shootout (10)** | Race and defeat an opponent in Rivals mode. |
| **Semi-Pro (25)** | Complete the fourth year of Season Play. |
| **Show Off (10)** | Upload a movie to Forzamotorsport.net. |
| **Slipstreamin' (5)** | Earn a perfect Draft score. |
| **Speed Demon (10)** | Reach 240 mph in any car. |
| **Sportsman (25)** | Complete the third year of Season Play. |
| **Star in a Reasonably Priced Car (10)** | Complete a lap around the TopGear Test Track while driving a KIA cee'd. |

| Unicorn Hunter (10) | Be the winning bidder on any "unicorn" car in the Auction House. |
| Welcome to Forza Motorsport (15) | Complete the very first race in the game. |

## UNLOCKABLE

| UNLOCKABLE | HOW TO UNLOCK |
|---|---|
| Autovista T-Shirt | Fully explore any car in Autovista. |
| Stopwatch Cap | Post a time in every Rivals Mode Event. |
| 1931 Bentley 8 Litre | Complete 9 Autovista Challenges. |
| Halo 3 Warthog | Complete all Autovista challenges. |

# FROGGER (XBOX 360)

## MAKE FROGGER BIGGER

| UNLOCKABLE | HOW TO UNLOCK |
|---|---|
| Make Frogger Bigger | At the screen where you are selecting to choose One or Two players, enter ⬇ ⬇ ⬆ ⬆ ⬅ ➡ ⬅ ➡ Ⓑ Ⓐ |

# FRONTLINES: FUEL OF WAR (PlayStation 3)

## MORE LEVELS

To unlock two extra single-player levels, insert the following passwords at the in-game Passwords menu.

| UNLOCKABLE | HOW TO UNLOCK |
|---|---|
| Urban Level | sp-street |
| Village Level | sp-village |

# FULL AUTO 2: BATTLELINES (PlayStation 3)

In the Option menu, select the Cheats option to enter these codes.

| UNLOCKABLE | CODE |
|---|---|
| Unlock Sceptre and Mini-Rockets | 10E6CUSTOMER |
| Unlock Vulcan and Flamethrower | 5FINGERDISCOUNT |

# FULL AUTO 2: BATTLELINES (PSP)

Enter these codes in the codes section under features.

| UNLOCKABLE | CODE |
|---|---|
| All Cars | ⬆, ⬆, ⬆, ⬆, ⬅, ⬅, ⬆, ➡, ⬇, ⬇, ⬇, ⬇ |
| All Events | START, ⬅, SELECT, ➡, ➡, ▲, ✕, ■, START, R, ⬇, SELECT |

## G.I. JOE: THE RISE OF COBRA (XBOX 360)

### CODES

Enter the following codes with the D-pad at the Main menu. A sound effect will play if you entered the code correctly.

| EFFECT | CODE |
|---|---|
| Shana "Scarlett" O'Hara Costumae | ⬅,⬆,⬇,⬇,⬇ |
| Duke Costume | ⬅,⬆,⬇,⬆,➡,⬇ |

## GAIN GROUN (Wii)

### LEVEL SELECT

| UNLOCKABLE | HOW TO UNLOCK |
|---|---|
| Level Select | On the Options screen press Ⓐ, Ⓒ, Ⓑ, Ⓒ |

## GALAGA '90 (Wii)

### UNLOCKABLES

| UNLOCKABLE | HOW TO UNLOCK |
|---|---|
| Galactic Bonus | Just stand still (don't move) and don't shoot in the bonus stage. |
| Red Capsule | Hold ⬆ and press RUN at the title screen. The capsule on the ship will turn red instead of blue to confirm code entry. Shoot the last target on the first level to capture the red capsule and power-up to a triple ship. |

## GAUNTLET (XBOX 360)

### WALLS BECOME EXITS

| UNLOCKABLE | HOW TO UNLOCK |
|---|---|
| Walls Become Exits | On any level, all players must stand still for 200 seconds. After 200 seconds, all the walls in the level will become exit doors. If players wish to, they can shoot enemies, and change the direction of their shooting, just as long as they do not move. This works on single and multiplayer. |

## GEARS OF WAR (XBOX 360)

| UNLOCKABLE | HOW TO UNLOCK |
|---|---|
| Insane Difficulty | Complete the game on either Casual or Hardcore difficulty. |
| Secret Gamer Pic | Complete the game on Insane difficulty to unlock a secret gamer picture. |
| Secret Gamer Pic #2 | Unlock the "Seriously..." achievement by getting 10,000 kills in ranked multiplayer matches to get that respective GamerPic. |

## GEARS OF WAR 2 (XBOX 360)

### SKINS

Successfully complete the following tasks to unlock the corresponding skin in multiplayer mode.

| UNLOCKABLE | HOW TO UNLOCK |
|---|---|
| Anthony Carmine | Successfully complete Act 1 in the original Gears Of War. |
| Dizzy Wallin | Successfully complete Act 1 in single-player mode. |
| Flame Grenadier | Successfully complete Act 4 in single-player mode. |
| Kantus | Successfully complete Act 2 in single-player mode. |

| Lt. Minh Young Kim | Find 10 COG tags in the original Gears Of War. |
| RAAM | Defeat RAAM in the original Gears of War on Hardcore difficulty. |
| Skorge | Successfully complete Act 5 in single-player mode. |
| Tai Kaliso | Successfully complete Act 3 in single-player mode. |

## GEARS OF WAR 3 (XBOX 360)

### ACHIEVEMENT

| UNLOCKABLE | HOW TO UNLOCK |
| --- | --- |
| Ain't My First Rodeo (50) | Complete all campaign Acts on Hardcore Difficulty (Standard or Arcade). |
| All for One, One for All (10) | Earn the Bronze "Force Multiplier" medal. |
| Anvil Gate's Last Resort (10) | Story Progression in Act 3 Chapter 1 (Standard or Arcade). |
| Award Winning Tactics (25) | Earn at least one Onyx medal. |
| Baird's Favorite Kind of Toy (10) | Story Progression in Act 4 Chapter 5 (Standard or Arcade). |
| Brothers to the End (10) | Story Progression in Act 3 Chapter 5 (Standard or Arcade). |
| Collector (5) | Recover 5 Campaign Collectibles (any difficulty, Standard or Arcade). |
| Enriched and Fortified (10) | Complete all 50 waves of Horde mode (any difficulty, any map). |
| First Among Equals (25) | Earn the Silver "Number 1" medal. |
| Hoarder (15) | Recover all 42 Campaign Collectibles (any difficulty, Standard or Arcade). |
| It's All About the Loot! (25) | Earn the Bronze "Loot Courtesan" medal. |
| Judge, Jury and Executioner (10) | Get a kill with every possible execution finishing move (any mode). |
| Lambency (50) | Execute an Epic employee, or someone who already has Lambency, in Versus multiplayer (any mode). |
| Level 10 (10) | Reach level 10. |
| Level 15 (15) | Reach level 15. |
| Level 25 (25) | Reach level 25. |
| Level 5 (5) | Reach level 5. |
| Level 50 (50) | Reach level 50. |
| Look at That, Instant Summer. (10) | Story Progression in Act 5 Chapter 2 (Standard or Arcade). |
| Lost Your Good Driver Discount (10) | Story Progression in Act 3 Chapter 3 (Standard or Arcade). |
| Marcus, It's Your Father (5) | Story Progression in Prologue (Standard or Arcade). |
| My Fellow Gears (50) | Complete all Campaign Acts in Co-op (any difficulty, Standard or Arcade). |
| My Turf! Cougars Territory! (10) | Story Progression in Act 1 Chapter 5 (Standard or Arcade). |
| Oh Yeah, It's Pirate Time (10) | Story Progression in Act 2 Chapter 5 (Standard or Arcade). |
| Ok. Faith. Yeah. Got It. (10) | Story Progression in Act 5 Chapter 5 (Standard or Arcade). |
| Okay, Now We Find Hoffman (10) | Story Progression in Act 2 Chapter 1 (Standard or Arcade). |
| Pack Rat (10) | Recover 20 Campaign Collectibles (any difficulty, Standard or Arcade). |

| | |
|---|---|
| Putting it Scientifically... (10) | Story Progression in Act 1 Chapter 6 (Standard or Arcade). |
| Ready for More (50) | Complete all campaign Acts on Casual or Normal Difficulty (Standard or Arcade). |
| Remember the Fallen (15) | Recover all 15 COG Tags during the Campaign (any difficulty, Standard or Arcade). |
| Respect for the Dead (5) | Your respect for the dead earned you access to Griffin's special weapons stash. |
| Seriously 3.0 (100) | Reach level 100 and earn every Onyx medal. |
| Socialite (70) | Earn the Onyx "War Supporter" medal. |
| Swimmin' in Glowie Gravy (10) | Story Progression in Act 1 Chapter 2 (Standard or Arcade). |
| Thanks For Flying GasBag Airways (10) | Story Progression in Act 2 Chapter 7 (Standard or Arcade). |
| That's Just Crazy (75) | Complete all campaign Acts on Insane Difficulty (Standard or Arcade). |
| The Versus Sampler Platter (10) | Complete one match of all six Versus game modes (Standard or Casual). |
| Think You Can Handle That? (10) | Story Progression in Act 4 Chapter 3 (Standard or Arcade). |
| Wait, What Time is it? (10) | Earn the maximum Consecutive Match Bonus in Versus multiplayer (Standard or Casual). |
| Was it Good For You? (10) | Story Progression in Act 3 Chapter 2 (Standard or Arcade). |
| We Few, We Happy Few... (50) | Complete all Campaign Acts in 4 player Co-op (any difficulty, Standard or Arcade). |
| We Struck Gold, Son! (10) | Story Progression in Act 1 Chapter 3 (Standard or Arcade). |
| Welcome To -redacted- (10) | Story Progression in Act 4 Chapter 6 (Standard or Arcade). |
| Welcome to Arcade Mode (10) | Complete 5 Arcade Campaign chapters in co-op (any difficulty). |
| Welcome to Beast Mode (10) | Survive all 12 waves of Beast mode (any difficulty, any map). |
| Welcome to Horde Mode (10) | Survive the first 10 waves of Horde mode (any difficulty, any map). |
| Welcome to the Big multiplayer. Leagues (0) | Demonstrate your skill in Casual Versus |
| Welcome to Versus (10) | Kill 10 enemies in Team Deathmatch (Standard or Casual). |
| Wreaking Locust mode Vengence (10) | Get a kill with every Locust monster in Beast (any difficulty). |
| You're Dead! Now Stay Dead! (10) | Story Progression in Act 5 Chapter 6 (Standard or Arcade). |

**UNLOCKABLE**

| UNLOCKABLE | HOW TO UNLOCK |
|---|---|
| Aaron Griffin | Receive the Big Money Onyx Medal or "Like" the Gears of War 3 Facebook page to get an unlock code. |
| Adam Fenix | Preorder code with purchase of the Gears of War 3 Limited or Epic Edition. |
| Anthony Carmine | Reach Level 75. |
| Benjamin Carmine | Reach Level 34. |
| Chairman Prescott | Receive the silver Allfathers medal. |
| Civilian Anya | Reach Level 45. |

| | |
|---|---|
| Classic Baird | Reach Level 30. |
| Classic Cole | Reach Level 23. |
| Classic Dom | Reach Level 17. |
| Classic Marcus | Receive the silver Veteran medal. |
| Clayton Carmine | Reach Level 14. |
| COG Gear | Reach Level 2. |
| Cole Train | Play the multiplayer beta. |
| Colonel Hoffman | Reach Level 50. |
| Commando Dom | Preorder code from GameStop. |
| Dizzy Wallin | Reach Level 7. |
| Golden Gear | Receive the bronze War Supporter medal. |
| Jace Stratton | Reach Level 10. |
| Mechanic Baird | Preorder code from Best Buy. |
| Samantha Byrne | Reach Level 4. |
| Superstar Cole | Receive the gold MVP medal. |
| Unarmored Marcus | Finish the campaign on any difficulty level. |
| Beast Rider | Reach Level 5. |
| Flame Grenadier | Reach Level 26. |
| Golden Hunter | Receive the gold Master-at-Arms medal. |
| Golden Miner | Receive the gold Rifleman medal. |
| Grenadier | Reach Level 39. |
| Hunter | Reach Level 8. |
| Hunter Elite | Reach Level 60. |
| Kantus | Receive the gold Medic medal. |
| Miner | Reach Level 3. |
| Savage Grenadier Elite | Preorder code from Walmart. |
| Savage Kantus | Preorder code from Amazon.com. |
| Savage Theron Guard | Complete Beast Mode without failing, on all difficulties. |
| Sniper | Receive the bronze Headshot medal. |
| Spotter | Reach Level 20. |
| Theron Guard | Reach Level 12. |
| Big Explosions | In any mode, unlock the Hail Mary ribbon 100 times. |
| Big Head | In Horde Mode, unlock the Gold Horder medal. |
| Comet | In Versus Mode, unlock the Gold Shock Trooper medal. |
| Enemy Regeneration | In Arcade Mode, unlock the Silver Afficianado medal. |
| Flower Blood | In Arcade Mode, unlock the Silver King of Cog medal. |
| Friendly Fire | In Co-op Campaign, complete the co-op campaign with four players. |
| Infinite Ammo | In Horde Mode, unlock the Combat Engineer ribbon 100 times. |
| Instagib Melee | In Beast Mode, play as a Wretch and score 200 kills. |
| Laugh Track | Unlock the Bronze Tour of Duty, For the Horde, I'm a Beast, and Warmonger medals. |
| Must Active Reload | Unlock the Silver Active Reloader medal. |
| Pinata | In Beast Mode, unlock the Gold Investor medal. |

NEW!

A
B
C
D
E
F
G
H
I
J
K
L
M
N
O
P
Q
R
S
T
U
V
W
X
Y
Z

| Super Reload | In Versus Mode, unlock the Bronze Master at Arms medal. |
|---|---|
| Vampire | In Versus Mode, unlock the Executioner ribbon 100 times. |
| Horde Shirt | Get the "Welcome to Horde mode" achievement for beating Horde mode. |
| Locust Drone Mask | Get the "Welcome to Beast Mode" achievement for beating Beast mode. |
| Marcus' Doo-rag | Beat the campaign on any difficulty. |

## GENPEI TOUMADEN    (Wii)

### UNLOCKABLE

| UNLOCKABLE | HOW TO UNLOCK |
|---|---|
| Options Menu | At the title screen, press ⬆, ⬆, ⬆, ⬆, ①, ② |

## GHOSTBUSTERS THE VIDEOGAME    (PlayStation 3, XBOX 360)

### NES GHOSTBUSTERS ENDING SCREEN

In the Ghostbusters headquarters, one of the monitors on the upstairs desks has the ending screen from the original Ghostbusters game on the NES. The monitor comes complete with all the spelling and punctuation errors.

## GHOULS 'N GHOSTS    (Wii)

### UNLOCKABLES

| UNLOCKABLE | HOW TO UNLOCK |
|---|---|
| Japanese Mode | Enter the Options menu. Choose "26" for the music and "56" for sound selections, then hold ⬆+ Ⓐ+Ⓑ+Ⓒ+START. |
| Slow-Mo | At the title screen, press ⬆, Ⓐ, ⬆, Ⓐ, ⬆, Ⓐ, ⬆, Ⓐ. Begin the game, press START to pause, and hold Ⓑ and unpause. |

### LEVEL SELECT

Press ⬆, ⬇, ⬅, ➡ repeatedly at the title screen. You'll hear a harp if you did it right. Enter one of the following controller actions to select the corresponding level.

| EFFECT | CODE |
|---|---|
| The Execution Place | Press START |
| The Floating Island | Press Ⓐ, START |
| The Village of Decay | Press ⬆, START |
| Town of Fire | Press ⬆+Ⓐ, START |
| Baron Rankle's Tower | Press ⬇, START |
| Horrible Faced Mountain | Press ⬇+Ⓐ, START |
| The Crystal Forest | Press ⬅, START |
| The Ice Slopes | Press ⬅+Ⓐ, START |
| Beginning of Castle | Press ➡, START |
| Middle of Castle | Press ➡+Ⓐ, START |
| Loki | Press ⬇, START |

### DEBUG MODE

While "Press Start Button" is flashing at the title screen, input Ⓐ, Ⓐ, Ⓐ, Ⓐ, ⬆, ⬇, ⬅, ➡ and you hear a chime. Start the game and you are in debug mode. Three functions can be accessed from the Pause menu now.

| CODE | EFFECT |
|---|---|
| Tap ⬇ During Pause | Frame Advance |
| Pause, Ⓐ, Pause | Invincibility Toggle (falling is still fatal) |
| Hold Ⓑ During Pause | Slow Motion |

## THE GODFATHER (XBOX 360)

### CHEAT CODES

| CODE | EFFECT |
|---|---|
| Y ◁ ○ ▷ ⊗ ○ | Full Ammo |
| ◁ ⊗ ○ Y ○ LB | Full Health |
| Y Y Y ⊗ Y LB (click) | Film Clips |

### INFINITE AMMO

| UNLOCKABLE | HOW TO UNLOCK |
|---|---|
| Infinite Ammo | Become Don of NYC |

## THE GODFATHER: BLACKHAND EDITION (Wii)

Enter these codes while the game is paused. For the film clips, enter that clip in the Film Archives screen.

| UNLOCKABLE | CODE |
|---|---|
| $5,000 | ⊝, ②, ⊝, ⊝, ②, ✛ |
| Full Ammo | ②, ✛, ②, ✛, ⊝, ✛ |
| Full Health | ✛, ⊝, ✛, ②, ✛, ✛ |
| Unlock Film Clips | ②, ⊝, ②, ⊝, ⊝, ✛ |

*THESE CODES MAY ONLY BE ENTERED ROUGHLY EVERY FIVE MINUTES. IF YOU REALLY NEED THE HEALTH OR AMMO BEFORE FIVE MINUTES, PAUSE AND WAIT A FEW MINUTES, THEN ENTER THE GAME.*

## THE GODFATHER: THE DON'S EDITION (PlayStation 3)

Enter these codes while the game is paused.

| UNLOCKABLE | CODE |
|---|---|
| $5,000 | ■, ▲, ■, ■, ▲, L2 |
| Full Ammo | ▲, ⇦, ▲, ⇨, ■, R1 |
| Full Health | ⇦, ■, ⇨, ▲, ⇨, L2 |

## GOD OF WAR III (PlayStation 3)

### BONUS PLAY ITEMS

There are several bonus play items that can be collected throughout the game. Once they have been obtained, they can be used during bonus play (after you have beaten the game once). Note: enabling any bonus play items will disable Trophies.

| UNLOCKABLE | HOW TO UNLOCK |
|---|---|
| Hades' Helm —Max health, magic, item meters | After killing Hades and jumping into the River Styx, swim down and to the right (against the current) and and locate the helm at the bottom of the river. |
| Helios' Shield —Triples combo meter | Located to the right of where you kill Helios. |
| Hera's Chalice —Slowly drains health meter | Located to the left of where Hera falls in the garden. |
| Hercules' Shoulder Guard —Decrease damage taken by a third. | After finding Hercules floating in the water, swim beneath him to find his Shoulder Guard. |
| Hermes' Coin—10x red orbs | Located behind the rubble while chasing Hermes. |
| Poseidon's Conch Shell —Infinite Magic | Located in the chamber where you rescue the Poseidon Princess. |
| Zeus' Eagle —Infinite Rage of Sparta | Climb the wall to the right of the Heart of Gaia; item is located on the ground in plain view. |

### UNLOCKABLES

| UNLOCKABLE | HOW TO UNLOCK |
|---|---|
| Challenges of Olympus | Beat the game. |
| Combat arena | Beat all challenges. |
| Chaos Difficulty | Complete any difficulty. |
| Fear Kratos Costume | Complete any difficulty. |

## GOD OF WAR: GHOST OF SPARTA (PSP)

### THE TEMPLE OF ZEUS

The Optional Bonus Temple that allows you to get the Grave Digger's Shovel relic.

| UNLOCKABLE | HOW TO UNLOCK |
| --- | --- |
| The Temple of Zeus | Complete the game on any difficulty |

### COSTUMES

| UNLOCKABLE | HOW TO UNLOCK |
| --- | --- |
| Deimos | Beat the game on Spartan mode (Hard) |
| Ghost of Sparta | Beat the game on God mode (Very Hard) |
| God Armor | Beat the game on Spartan mode (Hard) |
| Grave Digger | Beat Temple of Zeus |
| Robotos | Purchase for 250,000 in Temple of Zeus |

### MODES

| UNLOCKABLE | HOW TO UNLOCK |
| --- | --- |
| Combat Arena | Beat the game |
| God (Very Hard) | Beat the game |

### SPECIAL ITEMS

These items can be used after finding them and completing the game.

| UNLOCKABLE | HOW TO UNLOCK |
| --- | --- |
| Aphrodite's Ambrosia: Gain the Might of Sparta attack | Complete the sex minigame in Sparta 3 times. |
| Athena's Owl: Helps find treasures | After Kratos destroys the Athena statue in a cutscene, search the right side in a pile of debris. |
| Bonds of Ares: Infinite Magic | After you enter the Domain of Death through the Death Gate in Atlantis, look in the south section of the screen. |
| Callisto's Armlet: Automatically win context-sensitive minigames. | Right after you beat Callisto, search the ground by the battle. |
| Grave Digger's Shovel: Play as Zeus in Arena Combat | Unlock everything in the Temple of Zeus and follow the path created. |
| King's Ring: Collects 10 times the amount of red orbs | After King Midas turns the lava into gold, drop down by the area where he touched it. |

## GODZILLA: UNLEASHED (Wii)

### CODES

At the main menu, press Ⓐ and ✛ at the same time.

| CODE | EFFECT |
| --- | --- |
| 31406 | Add 90,000 store points. |
| 0829XX | Set day (where the "xx" equals the actual day you wish to set to). |
| 411411 | Show monster moves. |
| 787321 | Toggle version number. |
| 204935 | Unlock everything. |

## GOLDEN AXE (Wii)

### UNLOCKABLES

| UNLOCKABLE | HOW TO UNLOCK |
| --- | --- |
| 9 Continues | Hold ✛+Ⓐ+ⓒ. Release and press START. |
| Level Select | Select Arcade mode. Hold ✛+Ⓑ and press START at the Character Selection screen. A number that corresponds to the starting level appears in the screen's upper left. Use the D-pad to change it to the level you want. |

## GOLDEN AXE 2 (Wii)

### UNLOCKABLES

| UNLOCKABLE | HOW TO UNLOCK |
|---|---|
| Level Select | While the opening screen scrolls, simultaneously hold down Ⓐ+Ⓑ+Ⓒ+START. Still holding Ⓐ, release Ⓑ+Ⓒ and press them again. This brings you to the Options screen. Still holding Ⓐ, let go of the other two, pick "exit," and press Ⓑ+Ⓒ once more. You'll be back at the main menu. Still holding Ⓐ, release Ⓑ+Ⓒ and hit them again to choose the number of players. Keep all the buttons down and press START. Release only START, select your character, then still holding down Ⓐ+Ⓑ+Ⓒ, press ➕ and hit START. You can now select the level you want to play. |
| Level Select and 8 Credits (ultimate procedure) | With the cursor go to "Options" sign. Now press and hold Ⓐ+Ⓑ+Ⓒ. In the Options screen, release only Ⓑ+Ⓒ. Now configure the game if you want. Use Ⓑ to confirm successive selections, until the warrior selection. For the 8 credits, the cheat is identical, but release only Ⓐ and use START to confirm successive selections. |

## GOLDENEYE 007: RELOADED (XBOX 360)

### ACHIEVEMENT

| UNLOCKABLE | HOW TO UNLOCK |
|---|---|
| 007 (25) | Complete all objectives for every mission on 007 difficulty. |
| Agent (15) | Complete all objectives for every mission on Agent difficulty. |
| Arkhangelsk Dossier (40) | Complete all objectives in Arkhangelsk on 007 difficulty or higher. |
| Au-ned (30) | Public Match: Achieve 79 kills with the Golden Gun in Golden Gun mode. |
| Barcelona Dossier (15) | Complete all objectives in Barcelona on 007 difficulty or higher. |
| Boxing Clever (30) | Public Match: Earn all accolades specific to Black Box. |
| Boys with Toys (50) | Public Match: Kill 50 enemies with Proximity Mines. |
| Braced for Impact (15) | Public Match: As Jaws, survive a shot to the head which would otherwise have killed you. |
| Bullet Dance (20) | Get 40 kills with the Wolfe .44 in 'Nightclub'. |
| Butter Hook (15) | Public Match: As Tee Hee, get the most kills with a melee strike (min 3 melee kills). |
| Cheated (3) | Public Match: Get killed the most times by Oddjob's hat (min 3 deaths). |
| Choppers Down (15) | Shoot down 15 helicopters in 'Tank'. |
| Classic (40) | Complete all objectives for every mission on 007 Classic difficulty. |
| Clobbering (30) | Public Match: Achieve 64 melee kills with the KL-033 Mk2. |
| Console Compliancy (30) | Public Match: Capture and defend the most consoles in one match of GoldenEye mode. |
| Dance Commander (5) | Surrender to the music in 'Nightclub'. |
| Dressed to Kill (20) | Single Player: Complete any mission without collecting any body armor on 007 Classic difficulty. |
| Dubai Dossier (15) | Complete all objectives in Dubai on 007 difficulty or higher. |
| Emblem Elite (15) | Single Player: Find and destroy 50 Janus emblems. |
| Emblem Hunter (5) | Single Player: Find and destroy a Janus emblem. |
| Emblem Marksman (10) | Single Player: Find and destroy 20 Janus emblems. |
| For England, Alec (20) | Public Match: As Bond, kill 006 with an explosive device. |
| Full Deck (15) | Public Match: Play at least one complete match of Classic Conflict with every character. |
| Get to the Chopper (15) | Complete 'Carrier' in under 11:00 (007 difficulty or higher). |

| Going Dark (15) | Get to master engineering in 'Facility' without reinforcements getting called in. |
| --- | --- |
| Had Your Six (30) | Public Match: Kill six enemies with the Wolfe .44 or Gold Plated Revolver without reloading. |
| Hat Trick (20) | Public Match: In one life, make three kills with Oddjob's hat. |
| Haven't Got Nine Minutes (15) | Complete 'Airfield' in under 4:35 (007 Classic difficulty). |
| I am INVINCIBLE! (25) | Single Player: Complete any mission without taking any damage. |
| Invisible Descent (15) | Get to the server room in 'Bunker' without reinforcements getting called in. |
| Lucky Seven (40) | Public Match: Defuse a planted bomb which has exactly 0:07 seconds remaining on its fuse. |
| Made you feel it, did he? (10) | Single Player: Silently subdue 30 enemies. |
| Master at Arms (10) | Single Player: Make a kill with every weapon. |
| MI6 Ops Elite (45) | Earn 44 stars in MI6 Ops. |
| MI6 Ops Recruit (10) | Earn 10 stars in MI6 Ops. |
| MI6 Ops Specialist (25) | Earn 25 stars in MI6 Ops. |
| Nigeria Dossier (40) | Complete all objectives in Nigeria on 007 difficulty or higher. |
| Operative (10) | Complete all objectives for every mission on Operative difficulty. |
| Orbis Non Suffict (15) | Public Match: Complete a match on every map. |
| Phone a Friend (15) | Get 20 kills with hacked drone guns in 'Jungle'. |
| Rocket Man (15) | Kill an enemy with the RPG in 'Dam'. |
| Royal Flush (2) | In 'Facility', successfully kill the enemy in the toilet cubicle without any shots being fired. |
| Russian Escape (15) | Complete 'Archives' in under 15:10 (Agent difficulty or higher). |
| Secret Servers (10) | Destroy all the servers in 'Archives' within 40 secs of the first being damaged. |
| Severnaya Dossier (30) | Complete all objectives in Severnaya on 007 difficulty or higher. |
| Solar Agitated (15) | Complete 'Solar' in under 13:00 (007 Classic difficulty). |
| St. Petersburg Dossier (40) | Complete all objectives in St. Petersburg on 007 difficulty or higher. |
| The Man Who Cannot Die (15) | Public Match: As Baron Samedi, survive a bullet which would otherwise have killed you. |
| The Other Cheek (20) | Public Match: As Bond, kill Zukovsky with a melee strike. |
| Welcome to Russia (5) | Make the initial rendezvous with 006 in 'Dam'. |

## GRADIUS   (Wii)

### UNLOCKABLES

| UNLOCKABLE | HOW TO UNLOCK |
| --- | --- |
| 10,000 Bonus Points | Get 6 power-ups so that the ? box is selected, then, when the thousands digit of your score is a 5, get a 7th power-up |
| Continue | At the Game Over Screen, press ⬆, ⬆, ⬇, Ⓐ, ⬅, Ⓐ, ⬇, Ⓐ, START (once per game) |
| Full Option Command | Press START during the game, then press ⬆, ⬆, ⬇, ⬇, ⬅, ➡, ⬅, ➡, ⬇, Ⓐ, START. |
| Warp to Level 3 (after defeating Core Fighter) | In level 1, when the thousands digit of your score is even, destroy 4 hatches |
| Warp to Level 4 | Destroy Xaerous Core at end of level 2 within 2 seconds of its core turning blue |
| Warp to Level 5 (after beating level) | Destroy 10 stone heads in level 3 |

## GRADIUS 2 (Wii)

### UNLOCKABLES

| UNLOCKABLE | HOW TO UNLOCK |
|---|---|
| 30 Lives | At the title screen, press ⬆,⬆,⬇,⬇,⬅,➡,⬅,➡, Ⓑ, Ⓐ |
| Max Out Abilities | During game, press ⬆,⬆,⬇,⬇,⬅,➡,⬅,➡, Ⓑ, Ⓐ (once per level) |
| Sound Test Menu | Hold Ⓐ+Ⓑ and turn on. When the screen comes up, press START, hold Ⓐ+Ⓑ until title screen, then press START again. |

## GRADIUS 3 (Wii)

### UNLOCKABLES

| UNLOCKABLE | HOW TO UNLOCK |
|---|---|
| 30 Extra Ships | At the title screen, hold ◄Ⓒ and press ⟳, ⟳, ⟳, START |
| Arcade Mode | In the Options menu, highlight the Game Level, and rapidly tap Ⓐ until the level turns into ARCADE |
| Extra Credits | At the title screen, press ⬇ as many times as you can and then press START before the screen fades out |
| Easy Final Boss | The final boss, Bacterion, will die whether or not you attack him. Just dodge his blasts, and in 15 or so seconds, he will spontaneously die. Even cheaper, park your ship in the screen's bottom center, and you can't be hit! |
| Extended Demo Mode | Continue to hold Ⓐ through the initial demo, and you'll see the entire first stage including the boss. |
| Full Power-Up | Pause the game and press ⬆,⬆,⬇,⬇,◄Ⓒ,Ⓒ►,◄Ⓒ,Ⓒ►,Ⓧ,Ⓨ |
| Full Power-Up (without using the code) | Choose "speed down" for the "!" option in the Weapon highlight Select screen. If you can get enough power-ups to the last weapon, which will not be visible, and use it without powering up on speed up, you get all four options, missiles, and the shield. But if you have the laser already, it will be taken away. |
| Random Weapon Select | At the Weapon Select screen, press Ⓒ► to enter Edit mode, then press ⬇, Ⓒ, ⬇, ⬇, Ⓒ, Ⓒ, ⬇, Ⓒ |
| Spread the Options | Activate the R-Option and collect enough power-ups that the option selection is highlighted. Now press and hold Ⓐ. |
| Suicide | Pause the game and press ⬆, ⬆, ⬇, ⬇, ◄Ⓒ, Ⓒ►, ◄Ⓒ, Ⓒ►, Ⓧ, Ⓐ, START |

### BONUS STAGES

When you clear a bonus stage, you end up in the next level. That's right, you don't have to fight the boss of the level you were in previously. However, if you get killed in the bonus stage, you go back to the regular level, and cannot reenter the bonus stage.

| STAGE | HOW TO UNLOCK |
|---|---|
| Stage 2 | When you see a hole in the wall at the bottom of the screen, fly down there. Prerequisite: None. |
| Stage 3 | When you reach the lower level, a platform in the ceiling drops down. Fly just below the part where the platform was. Prerequisite: Destroy all of the ground targets in the stage up to that point. |

| STAGE | HOW TO UNLOCK |
|---|---|
| Stage 4 | In the last set of Moai heads (they look like Easter Island heads), one that's lying down lifts up. Fly behind it. Prerequisite: Nothing must be highlighted on your power-up bar. |
| Stage 5 | Fly just below the ceiling before the narrow corridor. Prerequisite: The hundreds digit of your score reads 5, 7, or 3. |

**Stage 7** Just after the long downward slope in the second half of the level, stay close to the ground and fly into the wall formation shaped like this:

```
......./
.......\
____*/
```

(Key: dots are empty space, lines are walls, the asterisk is where your ship should be.) Prerequisite: Unknown.

## GRADIUS COLLECTION   (PSP)

### CODES

| Unlockable | How to Unlock |
|---|---|
| All Power-ups and Weapons | Pause the game and then insert the famous "Konami Code": ↑,↑,↓,↓,←,→,←,→,←,→ |

## GRAND THEFT AUTO 4   (PlayStation 3, XBOX 360)

### CODES

During gameplay, pull out Niko's phone and dial these numbers for the corresponding effect. Cheats will affect missions and achievements.

| EFFECT | CODE |
|---|---|
| Change weather | 468-555-0100 |
| Get the Ak-47, knife, Molotov Cocktails, pistol, RPG, sniper rifle and Uzi | 486-555-0150 |
| Get the baseball bat, grenades, M4, MP5, pistol, RPG, and sniper rifle | 486-555-0100 |
| Raise wanted level | 267-555-0150 |
| Remove wanted level | 267-555-0100 |
| Restore armor | 362-555-0100 |
| Restore health | 482-555-0100 |
| Spawn a Cognoscenti | 227-555-0142 |
| Spawn a Comet | 227-555-0175 |
| Spawn a Jetmax | 938-555-0100 |
| Spawn a Sanchez | 625-555-0150 |
| Spawn a SuperGT | 227-555-0168 |
| Spawn a Turismo | 227-555-0147 |
| Spawn an Annihilator | 359-555-0100 |
| Spawn an FIB Buffalo | 227-555-0100 |
| Spawn an NRG-900 | 625-555-0100 |

### MAP LOCATIONS

Enter the password into any of the in-game computers.

| EFFECT | CODE |
|---|---|
| Weapon, health, armor, vehicle, pigeon, ramp/stunt, and entertainment locations | www.whattheydonotwantyoutoknow.com |

### UNLOCKABLES

| UNLOCKABLE | HOW TO UNLOCK |
|---|---|
| Annihilator Helicopter | Kill all 200 Flying Rats (Pigeons) |

### EASTER EGGS

| UNLOCKABLE | HOW TO UNLOCK |
|---|---|
| The Heart of Liberty City | Gain access to Happiness Island. Once you're able to go there legally, find the Helicopter Tours (which is directly east of Happiness Island) and steal a helicopter. Fly over the Statue of Liberty and jump out at the statue's feet. Land on the topmost tier of the statue, which is basically a square platform with a door in the center of each side. Look for a door with a plaque on either side of it that reads, "No Hidden Content Here." Don't try to open the door; just walk through it. Inside, you'll find an empty room with a tall ladder. Climb it, and when you reach the top, look up; there is a gigantic beating heart, held in place by chains. |

### FRIENDSHIP BONUSES

Gain the following bonuses by gaining the corresponding amount of friendship.

| UNLOCKABLE | HOW TO UNLOCK |
| --- | --- |
| Boom? (Call Packie for him to make you a car bomb) | Gain 75% friendship with Packie. |
| Chopper Ride (He will pick you up in his helicopter) | Gain 70% friendship with Brucie. |
| Discount Guns (Buy weapons at a cheaper price from Little Jacob) | Gain 60% friendship with Little Jacob. |
| Extra Help (A car of gang members will be sent to help you out) | Gain 60% friendship with Dwayne. |
| Free Ride (Call for a taxi) | Gain 60% friendship with Roman. |
| 50% Off for All Clothing Stores | Gain 80% Relationship Status with Alex. |
| Health Boost (Call Carmen and select "Health Boost") | Gain 80% Relationship Status with Carmen. |
| Remove Up to 3 Wanted Stars (Call Kiki and select "Remove Wanted") | Gain 80% Relationship Status with Kiki. |

### UNLOCKABLES

| UNLOCKABLE | HOW TO UNLOCK |
| --- | --- |
| Rastah Color Huntley SUV | Complete 10 Package Delivery missions. |
| Remove Ammo Limit | Get 100% completion. |

## GRAND THEFT AUTO 4: THE BALLAD OF GAY TONY (XBOX 360)

### CODES

| EFFECT | CODE |
| --- | --- |
| Akuma (Bike) | 625-555-0200 |
| APC(Tank) | 272-555-8265 |
| Buzzard(Helicopter) | 359-555-2899 |
| Change Weather | 468-555-0100 |
| Floater(Boat) | 938-555-0150 |
| Health & Armor | 362-555-0100 |
| Health, Armor and Advanced Weapons | 482-555-0100 |
| Parachute | 359-555-7272 |
| Raise Wanted Level | 267-555-0150 |
| Remove Wanted Level | 267-555-0100 |
| Sniper rifle bullets explode | 486-555-2526 |
| Spawn Annihilator | 359-555-0100 |
| Spawn Bullet GT | 227-555-9666 |
| Spawn Cognoscenti | 227-555-0142 |
| Spawn Comet | 227-555-0175 |
| Spawn Jetmax | 938-555-0100 |
| Spawn NRG-900 | 625-555-0100 |
| Spawn Sanchez | 625-555-0150 |
| Spawn Super GT | 227-555-0168 |
| Spawn Turismo | 227-555-0147 |
| Spawns a FIB Buffalo | 227-555-0100 |
| Super Punch (exploding punches) | 276-555-2666 |
| Vader(Bike) | 625-555-3273 |
| Weapons (Advanced) (New Weapons) | 486-555-0100 |
| Weapons (Poor) | 486-555-0150 |

## GRAND THEFT AUTO: CHINATOWN WARS (DS)

### CODES

Enter these during gameplay without pausing

| EFFECT | CODE |
|---|---|
| Armor | Ⓛ, Ⓛ, Ⓡ, Ⓑ, Ⓑ, Ⓐ, Ⓐ, Ⓡ |
| cloud | ⬆, ⬇, ⬅, ➡, Ⓧ, Ⓨ, Ⓛ, Ⓡ |
| Explosive Pistol Round | Ⓛ, Ⓡ, Ⓧ, Ⓨ, Ⓐ, ⬇, ⬅, ⬆ |
| health | Ⓛ, Ⓛ, Ⓡ, Ⓐ, Ⓐ, Ⓑ, Ⓑ, Ⓡ |
| Hurricane | ⬆, ⬇, ⬅, ➡, Ⓑ, Ⓨ, Ⓡ, Ⓛ |
| lots of rain | ⬆, ⬇, ⬅, ➡, Ⓐ, Ⓧ, Ⓡ, Ⓛ |
| rain | ⬆, ⬇, ⬅, ➡, Ⓨ, Ⓐ, Ⓛ, Ⓡ |
| sunny | ⬆, ⬇, ⬅, ➡, Ⓐ, Ⓑ, Ⓛ, Ⓡ |
| wanted level down | Ⓡ, Ⓧ, Ⓧ, Ⓨ, Ⓨ, Ⓡ, Ⓛ, Ⓛ |
| wanted level up | Ⓛ, Ⓛ, Ⓡ, Ⓨ, Ⓨ, Ⓧ, Ⓧ, Ⓡ |
| weapons 1 (grenade, nightstick, pistol, minigun, assault, micro SMG, stubby shotgun) | Ⓡ, ⬆, Ⓑ, ⬅, ➡, Ⓡ, Ⓑ, ⬇ |
| weapons 2 (molotov, taser, dual pistols, flamethrower, carbine, SMG, dual-barrel) | Ⓡ, ⬆, Ⓐ, ⬅, ➡, Ⓡ, Ⓐ, ⬇ |
| weapons 3 (mine, chainsaw, revolver, flamethrower, carbine, SMG, dual-barrel) | Ⓡ, ⬆, Ⓨ, ⬅, ➡, Ⓡ, Ⓨ, ⬇ |
| weapons 4 (flashbang, bat, pistol, RPG, carbine, micro SMG, stubby shotgun) | Ⓡ, ⬆, Ⓧ, ⬅, ➡, Ⓡ, Ⓧ, ⬇ |

## GRAND THEFT AUTO: CHINATOWN WARS (PSP)

### BONUS MISSION REWARDS

| UNLOCKABLE | HOW TO UNLOCK |
|---|---|
| Ammunition Discount | Score gold medals on all weapons at the Gun-Club. |
| Bullet Proof Taxis | Complete 15 Taxi Fares in a row (in the same taxi). |
| Immune to Fire | Complete five waves of Fire Brigade Missions. |
| increased Body Armor | Complete five waves of Vigilante Missions with a 100% kill rate. |
| infinite Sprint | Complete five Paramedic Missions. |
| Regenerating Health | Beat both Noodle Delivery Missions (with a Gold ranking). |
| Upgraded Delivery Bag | Beat both Mail Courier Missions (with a Gold ranking). |

## GRAND THEFT AUTO: LIBERTY CITY STORIES (PSP)

Enter these codes during gameplay. Do not pause the game.

| UNLOCKABLE | CODE |
|---|---|
| $250,000 | Ⓛ, Ⓡ, △, Ⓛ, Ⓡ, ●, Ⓛ, Ⓡ |
| Aggressive Drivers | ■, ■, Ⓡ, ✕, ✕, Ⓛ, ●, ● |
| All Green Lights | △, △, Ⓡ, ■, ■, Ⓛ, ✕, ✕ |
| All Vehicles Chrome Plated | △, Ⓡ, Ⓛ, ⬇, ⬇, Ⓡ, Ⓡ, △ |
| Black Cars | ●, ●, Ⓡ, △, △, Ⓛ, ■, ■ |
| Bobble Head World | ⬆, ⬇, ⬇, ●, ●, ✕, Ⓛ, Ⓡ |
| Cars Drive On Water | ●, ✕, ⬇, ●, ✕, ⬆, Ⓛ, Ⓡ |
| Change Bike Tire Size | ●, ⬅, ⬇, ➡, ✕, ⬆, Ⓛ, ■ |
| Clear Weather | ⬆, ⬇, ●, ⬆, ⬇, ■, Ⓛ, Ⓡ |
| Commit Suicide | Ⓛ, ⬇, ⬅, Ⓡ, ✕, ●, ⬆, △ |
| Destroy All Cars | Ⓛ, Ⓛ, ⬅, Ⓛ, Ⓛ, ⬇, ✕, ■ |
| Display Game Credits | Ⓛ, Ⓡ, Ⓛ, Ⓡ, ⬆, ⬇, Ⓛ, Ⓡ |
| Faster Clock | Ⓛ, Ⓛ, ⬅, Ⓛ, Ⓛ, ⬇, ●, ✕ |
| Faster Gameplay | Ⓡ, Ⓡ, Ⓛ, Ⓡ, Ⓡ, Ⓛ, ⬇, ✕ |
| Foggy Weather | ⬆, ⬇, △, ⬆, ⬇, ✕, Ⓛ, Ⓡ |

| Full Armor | L, R, ●, L, R, ✕, L, R |
| --- | --- |
| Full Health | L, R, ✕, L, R, ■, L, R |
| Have Girls Follow You | ⇩, ⇩, ⇩, ▲, ▲, ●, L, R |
| Never Wanted | L, L, ▲, R, R, ✕, ■, ● |
| Overcast Weather | ⇧, ⇩, ✕, ⇧, ⇩, ▲, L, R |
| Pedestrians Attack You | L, L, R, L, L, R, ⇧, ▲ |
| Pedestrians Have Weapons | R, R, L, R, R, L, ⇨, ● |
| Pedestrians Riot | L, L, R, L, L, R, ⇦, ■ |
| Perfect Traction | L, ⇧, ⇦, R, ▲, ●, ⇩, ✕ |
| Rainy Weather | ⇧, ⇩, ■, ⇧, ⇩, ●, L, R |
| Raise Media Attention | L, ⇧, ⇦, R, ▲, ■, ⇩, ✕ |
| Raise Wanted Level | L, R, ■, L, R, ▲, L, R |
| Random Pedestrian Outfit | L, L, ⇦, L, L, ⇨, ■, ▲ |
| Slower Gameplay | R, ▲, ✕, R, ■, ⇦, ⇦, ⇨ |
| Spawn Rhino | L, L, L, L, L, ⇦, ▲, ● |
| Spawn Trashmaster | ▲, ●, ⇩, ▲, ●, ⇧, L, L |
| Sunny Weather | L, L, ●, R, R, ■, ▲, ✕ |
| Upside Down Gameplay | ⇩, ⇩, ⇩, ✕, ✕, ■, R, L |
| Upside Up | ▲, ▲, ▲, ⇧, ⇧, ⇨, L, R |
| Weapon Set 1 | ⇧, ■, ■, ⇩, ⇦, ■, ■, ⇨ |
| Weapon Set 2 | ⇧, ●, ●, ⇩, ⇦, ●, ●, ⇨ |
| Weapon Set 3 | ⇧, ✕, ✕, ⇩, ⇦, ✕, ✕, ⇨ |
| White Cars | ✕, ✕, R, ●, ●, L, ▲, ▲ |

## GRAND THEFT AUTO: VICE CITY STORIES (PSP)

Enter any of these codes while playing.

| UNLOCKABLE | CODE |
| --- | --- |
| 25% of MP Content | ⇧, ⇧, ⇧, ■, ■, ▲, R, L |
| 50% of MP Content | ⇧, ⇧, ⇧, ●, ●, ✕, L, R |
| 75% of MP Content | ⇧, ⇧, ⇧, ⇧, ✕, ✕, ■, R, L |
| 100% of MP Content | ⇧, ⇧, ▲, ▲, ●, L, R |
| All Cars Are Black | L, R, L, R, ⇦, ●, ⇧, ✕ |
| Armor | ⇧, ⇩, ⇦, ⇨, ■, ■, L, R |
| Cars Avoid You | ⇧, ⇩, ⇨, ⇦, ▲, ●, ●, ■ |
| Chrome Cars | ⇨, ⇧, ⇩, ⇩, ▲, ▲, L, R |
| Clear Weather | ⇦, ⇩, R, L, ⇩, ⇧, ⇦, ✕ |
| Commit Suicide | ⇨, ⇩, ●, ●, L, R, ⇩, ✕ |
| Destroy All Cars | L, R, R, ⇦, ⇨, ■, ⇩, R |
| Faster Clock | R, L, L, ⇩, ⇧, ✕, ⇩, L |
| Faster Gameplay | ⇦, ⇦, R, R, ⇧, ▲, ⇩, ✕ |
| Foggy Weather | ⇦, ⇩, ▲, ✕, ⇨, ⇧, ⇦, L |
| $250,000 | ⇧, ⇧, ⇦, ⇨, ✕, ✕, L, R |
| Guys Follow You | ⇩, L, ⇩, L, ●, ⇧, L, ■ |
| Health | ⇧, ⇩, ⇦, ⇨, ●, ●, L, R |
| Lower Wanted Level | ⇧, ⇨, ▲, ▲, ⇩, ⇨, ✕, ✕ |
| Nearest Ped Gets in Your Vehicle (Must Be in a Car) | ⇩, ⇨, ⇨, L, L, ■, ⇧, L |
| Overcast Weather | ⇦, ⇩, L, R, ⇨, ⇧, ■ |
| Peds Attack You | ⇩, ▲, ⇧, ✕, L, R, L, R |
| Peds Have Weapons | ⇧, L, ⇩, R, ⇩, ●, ⇨, ▲ |
| Peds Riot | R, L, L, ⇩, ⇦, ●, ⇩, L |
| Perfect Traction | ⇩, ⇦, ⇧, L, R, ▲, ●, ✕ |
| Rainy Weather | ⇦, ⇩, L, R, ⇨, ⇧, ⇦, ▲ |

| Raise Wanted Level | ⇧, ⇨, ■, ■, ⇩, ⇦, ●, ● |
| Slower Gameplay | ⇦, ⇦, ●, ●, ⇩, ⇧, ▲, ✕ |
| Spawn Rhino | ⇧, L, ⇩, R, ⇦, L, ⇨, R |
| Spawn Trashmaster | ⇦, ⇨, ⇧, ▲, L, ▲, L, ▲ |
| Sunny Weather | ⇦, ⇩, R, L, ⇨, ⇧, ● |
| Upside Down Mode 1 | ■, ■, ■, L, L, R, ⇦, ⇨ |
| Upside Down Mode 2 | ⇦, ⇦, ⇦, R, R, L, ⇨, ⇦ |
| Weapon Set 1 | ⇦, ⇨, ✕, ⇧, ⇩, ■, ⇦, ⇨ |
| Weapon Set 2 | ⇦, ⇨, ■, ⇧, ⇩, ▲, ⇦, ⇨ |
| Weapon Set 3 | ⇦, ⇨, ▲, ⇧, ⇩, ●, ⇦, ⇨ |

# GRAN TURISMO 5 (PlayStation 3)

## LICENSE TESTS

| UNLOCKABLE | HOW TO UNLOCK |
| --- | --- |
| A License Tests | Reach Level 3 and complete the B license tests |
| B License Tests | Buy your first car |
| International A License Tests | Reach Level 12 and complete the International B license tests |
| International B License Tests | Reach Level 9 and complete the International C license tests |
| International C License Tests | Reach Level 6 and complete the A license tests |
| S License Tests | Reach Level 15 and complete the International A license tests |

# GUITAR HERO 3: LEGENDS OF ROCK (XBOX 360)

Enter the following in the Cheats menu under Options. You must strum every note/chord. The letters correspond to colored frets G=Green, R=Red, Y=Yellow, B=Blue, O=Orange

| CODE | EFFECT |
| --- | --- |
| (BY) (GY) (GY) (RB) (RB) (RY) (RY) (BY) (GY) (GY) (RB) (RB) (RY) (RY) (GY) (GY) (RY) (RY) | Air guitar |
| (GR) (GR) (GR) (GB) (GB) (GB) (RB) R R R (RB) R R R (RB) R R R | Bret Michaels singer |
| (GR) (GY) (YB) (RB) (BO) (YO) (RY) (RB) | Easy Expert |
| O, B, O, Y, O, B, O, Y | Hyperspeed |
| (GR) (B) (GR) (GY) (B) (GY) (RY) (O) (RY) (GY) (Y) (GY) (GR) | No fail (does not work in Career mode) |
| RY, RB, RO, RB, RY, GB, RY RB | Performance mode |
| GR, GR, GR, RY, RY, RB, RB, YB, YO, YO, GR, GR, GR, RY, RY, RB, RB, YB, YO, YO | Precision mode |
| YO, RB, RO, GB, RY, YO, RY, RB, GY, GY, YB, YB, YO, YO, YB, Y, R, RY, R, Y, O | Unlock all songs |
| (GR_BO) (GRYB_) (GRY_O) (G_BYO) (GRYB_) (_RYBO) (GRYB_) (G_YBO) (GRYB_) (GRY_O) (GRY_O) (GRYB_) (GRY_O) | Unlock everything (no sound plays when you enter these chords) |

| CODE | EFFECT |
| --- | --- |
| Lou | Defeat this boss and you can buy him for $15,000 |
| Slash | Defeat this boss and you can buy him for $10,000 |
| Tom Morello | Defeat this boss and you can buy him for $10,000 |

After unlocking these guitars, you can buy them in the shop.

## UNLOCKABLE GUITARS

| UNLOCKABLE | HOW TO UNLOCK |
| --- | --- |
| Assassin Bass | 5-star Co-op Expert mode. |
| Bat Guitar | 5-star all songs in Easy mode. |
| Beach Life Bass | Complete Co-Op Career Hard mode. |

| | |
|---|---|
| El Jefe Guitar | 5-star all songs in Expert mode. |
| Jolly Roger Guitar | 5-star all songs in Medium mode. |
| Moon Guitar | Complete Easy mode. |
| Pendulaxe Blade Bass | Complete Co-op Expert mode. |
| Risk Assessment Guitar | Complete Expert mode. |
| Rojimbo! Guitar | Complete Hard mode. |
| Saint George Guitar | Complete Medium mode. |
| Tiki Face Guitar | 5-star all songs in Hard mode. |
| Tiki Fortune 4 Bass | Complete Co-op Easy mode. |

## GUITAR HERO 5 (XBOX 360, PlayStation 3)

### CODES

Enter these codes to activate the following cheats. (G = Green; R = Red; Y = Yellow; B = Blue)

| EFFECT | CODE |
|---|---|
| Air Instruments | R R B Y G G G Y |
| All HOPOs | G G B G G G Y G |
| Always Slide | G G R R Y B Y B |
| AutoKick | Y G R B B B B R |
| Contest Winner 1 | G G R R Y R Y B |
| Focus Mode | Y G R G Y B G G |
| HUD-Free Mode | G R G G Y G G G |
| Invisible Characters | G R Y Y Y B B G |
| Performance Mode | Y Y B R B G R R |
| Unlock All Characters | B B G G R G R Y |

### UNLOCKABLES

| UNLOCKABLE | HOW TO UNLOCK |
|---|---|
| Character: Carlos Santana | Complete the song "No One to Depend On (Live)" on any difficulty, any instrument. |
| Character: Johnny Cash | Complete the song "Ring of Fire" on any difficulty, any instrument. |
| Character: Kurt Cobain | Complete the song "Smells Like Teen Spirit" on any difficulty, any instrument. |
| Character: Matt Bellamy | Complete the song "Plug In Baby" on any instrument on any difficulty. |
| Character: Shirley Manson | Complete the song "I'm Only Happy When It Rains" on any difficulty, any instrument. |
| Cheat: All HOPOs (Changes almost every note possible into a HOPO or Hammer-On/Pull-Off note) | As guitarist, whammy sustain notes on the song "Hurts So Good" for 25 seconds total or more (in Club Boson venue). |

| UNLOCKABLE | HOW TO UNLOCK |
|---|---|
| Cheat: All Slider Gems (All single notes are changed into slider/tap notes) | As guitarist, hit 230 tap notes on the song "Du Hast" (in Neon Oasis venue). |
| Cheat: Auto-kick (all kick bass notes are autoplayed) | As drummer, hit 200 non-cymbal notes on "Mirror People" (in Angel's Crypt venue, fills don't count). |
| Extra: Air Instruments (Instruments will be almost completely invisible, guitar strings will still be visible) | As Guitarist, strum 340 chords or more on the song "Sultans of Swing" (in O'Connel's Corner venue). |
| Extra: Focus Mode (blacks out background) | As a drummer, hit 265 tom notes on "Brianstorm" (in the Golden Gate venue). |
| Extra: HUD-Free Mode (removes rock meter, star power gauge, score display) | as a vocalist, get Excellent on 75 consecutive phrases in the rap song "Bring The Noise 20XX" (in Neon Oasis venue). |

| Extra: Performance Mode (removes track and HUD) | With two players, get a band multiplier for 42 seconds on "Bleed American" (in the Aqueduct venue). |
| Quickplay Venue "Wormhole" (required for The Grand Tour) | As guitarist, 4X multiplier for 50 seconds on "Play That Funky Music" (in Sideshow venue). |

## GUITAR HERO 5 (Wii)

### CODES

Enter these codes to activate the following cheats. (G = Green; R = Red; Y = Yellow; B = Blue)

| EFFECT | CODE |
| --- | --- |
| Air Instruments | R R B Y G G G Y |
| All HOPOs | G G B G G G Y G |
| Always Slide | G G R R Y B Y B |
| AutoKick | Y G R B B B B R |
| Contest Winner 1 | G G R R Y R Y B |
| Focus Mode | Y G R G Y B G G |
| HUD-Free Mode | G R G G Y G G G |
| Invisible Characters | G R Y Y Y B B G |
| Performance Mode | Y Y B R B G R R |
| Unlock All Characters | B B G G R G R Y |

## GUITAR HERO: AEROSMITH (XBOX 360, PlayStation 3)

### CHEAT CHORDS

Strum the following chords in the "Cheats" menu. A message should appear if you strummed them correctly. You can then turn them on or off in from the menu.

| EFFECT | CODE |
| --- | --- |
| Air Guitar (Guitarist plays without a guitar in the game) | (RY) (GR) (RY) (RY) (RB) (RB) (RB) (RB) (RB) (YB) (YB) (YO) |
| Hyperspeed (Faster Gameplay) | (YO) (YO) (YO) (YO) (YO) (RY) (RY) (RY) (RY) (RB) (RB) (RB) (RB) (RB) (YB) (YO) (YO) |
| No Fail (Makes it impossible to fail a song, doesn't work in Career mode, and disables online scores) | (GR) (B) (GR) (GY) (B) (GY) (RY) (O) (RY) (GY) (Y) (GY) (GR) |
| Performance Mode (No notes, just the song playing) | (GR) (GR) (RO) (RB) (GR) (GR) (RO) (RB) |
| Precision Mode (Makes it harder to miss notes) | (RY) (RB) (RB) (RY) (RY) (YB) (YB) (YB) (RB) (RY) (RB) (RB) (RY) (RY) (YB) (YB) (YB) (RB) |
| Unlock All Songs (except for "Pandora's Box" by Aerosmith) | (RY) (GR) (GR) (RY) (RY) (GR) (RY) (RY) (GR) GR) (RY) (RY) (GR) (RY) (RB) |

### CHARACTERS

Once unlocked, the following characters will be available for purchase in Career mode.

| UNLOCKABLE | HOW TO UNLOCK |
| --- | --- |
| DMC | Beat "King of Rock" by Run DMC. |
| Joe Perry | Defeat Joe Perry in a Guitar Battle in Career mode. |

### SONGS

Once unlocked, the following songs can be accessed by pushing the blue fret button on the main setlist.

| UNLOCKABLE | HOW TO UNLOCK |
| --- | --- |
| Aerosmith: "Kings and Queens" | Complete the Career Tour. |
| Joe Perry: "Joe Perry Guitar Battle" | Defeat Joe Perry in a Guitar Battle in Career mode. |

## GUITAR HERO: METALLICA  (XBOX 360, PlayStation 3)

### CODES

At the main menu select "Settings," "Cheats," and then "Enter New Cheat." Input the cheats below using the Green, Red, Yellow, and Blue colored fret buttons. You will receive a special message if you entered the codes correctly.

| EFFECT | CODE |
| --- | --- |
| Air Instruments | RRBYGGGY |
| Always Drum Fill | RRRBBGGY |
| Always Slide | GGRRYRYB |
| Auto Kick | YGRBBBBR |
| Black Highway | YRGRGRRB |
| Extra Line 6 Tones | GRYBRYBG |
| Flame Color | GRGBRRYB |
| Gem Color | BRRGRGRY |
| Hyperspeed Mode | GBRYYRGG |
| Invisible Characters | GRYYYBBG |
| Metallica Costumes | GRYBBYRG |
| Performance Mode | YYBRBGRR |
| Star Color | RRYRBRRB |
| Vocal Fireball | RGGYBGYG |

### UNLOCKABLES

| UNLOCKABLE | HOW TO UNLOCK |
| --- | --- |
| James Hetfield | Earn 100 stars in vocalist career. |
| James Hetfield Classic | Earn 150 stars in vocalist career. |
| James Hetfield Zombie | Earn 200 stars in vocalist career. |
| King Diamond | Beat the song "Evil" in any instrument career. |
| Kirk Hammett | Earn 100 stars in guitar career. |
| Kirk Hammett Classic | Earn 150 stars in guitar career. |
| Kirk Hammett Zombie | Earn 200 stars in guitar career. |
| Lars Ulrich | Earn 100 stars in drum career. |
| Lars Ulrich Classic | Earn 150 stars in drum career. |
| Lars Ulrich Zombie | Earn 200 stars in drum career. |
| Lemmy | Beat the song "Ace of Spades" in any instrument career mode. |
| Robert Trujillo | Earn 100 stars in bass career. |
| Robert Trujillo Classic | Earn 150 stars in bass career. |
| Robert Trujillo Zombie | Earn 200 stars in bass career. |

## GUITAR HERO: METALLICA  (Wii)

### CODES

At the main menu select "Settings," "Cheats," and then "Enter New Cheat." Input the cheats below using the Green, Red, Yellow, and Blue colored fret buttons. You will receive a special message if you entered the codes correctly.

| EFFECT | CODE |
| --- | --- |
| Air Instruments | RRBYGGGY |
| Always Drum Fill | RRRBBGGY |
| Always Slide | GGRRYRYB |
| Auto Kick | YGRBBBBR |
| Black Highway | YRGRGRRB |
| Extra Line 6 Tones | GRYBRYBG |

| Flame Color | GRGBRRYB |
|---|---|
| Gem Color | BRRGRGRY |
| Hyperspeed Mode | GBRYYRGG |
| Invisible Characters | GRYYYBBG |
| Metallica Costumes | GRYBBYRG |
| Performance Mode | YYBRBGRR |
| Star Color | RRYRBRRB |
| Vocal Fireball | RGGYBGYG |

## GUITAR HERO: VAN HALEN    (XBOX 360)

### CODES

From the Main menu go to "Settings," then "Cheats," then "Enter New Cheat."

| EFFECT | CODE |
|---|---|
| Air instruments | R,R,B,Y,G,G,G,Y |
| Always Drum Fill | R,R,R,B,B,G,G,Y |
| Always Slide | G,G,R,R,Y,R,Y,B |
| Auto Kick | Y,G,R,B,B,B,B,R |
| Black Highway | Y,R,G,R,G,R,R,B |
| Extra Line 6 Tones | G,R,Y,B,R,Y,B,G |
| Flame Color | G,R,G,B,R,R,Y,B |
| Gem Color | B,R,R,G,R,G,R,Y |
| Invisible Rocker | G,R,Y,Y,Y,B,B,G |
| Performance Mode | Y,Y,B,R,B,G,R,R |
| Star Color | R,R,Y,R,B,R,R,B |
| Vocal Fireball | R,G,G,Y,B,G,Y,G |

## GUITAR HERO: WARRIORS OF ROCK    (XBOX 360, PlayStation 3)

### CODES

Input at the "Input Cheat" menu.

| EFFECT | CODE |
|---|---|
| Absolutely nothinge | Press Green, Green, Green, Green, Green, Green, Green, Green |
| Air instruments | Press Yellow, Red, Red, Blue, Yellow, Green, Green, Green |
| Placebo | Press Green, Green, Green, Blue, Blue, Green, Green, Green |
| All taps | Press Blue, Green, Green, Red, Red, Yellow, Blue, Yellow |
| Color shuffle | Press Blue, Green, Blue, Red, Yellow, Green, Red, Yellow |
| Focus mode | Press Green, Yellow, Green, Red, Green, Yellow, Blue, Green |
| HUD Free mode | Press Green, Green, Red, Green, Green, Yellow, Green, Green |
| Invisible rocker | Press Green, Green, Red, Yellow, Yellow, Yellow, Blue, Blue |
| Note shuffle | Press Blue, Blue, Red, Blue, Green, Green, Red, Green |
| Performance mode | Press Red, Yellow, Yellow, Blue, Red, Blue, Green, Red |
| Unlock all characters | Press Blue, Green, Green, Red, Green, Red, Yellow, Blue |
| Unlock all venues | Press Red, Blue, Blue, Red, Red, Blue, Blue, Red |

## GUITAR HERO: WARRIORS OF ROCK    (Wii)

### CODES

Input at the "Input Cheat" menu.

| EFFECT | CODE |
|---|---|
| Unlock all characters | Press Blue, Green, Green, Red, Green, Red, Yellow, Blue |
| Unlock all venues | Press Red, Blue, Blue, Red, Red, Blue, Blue, Red |

## THE GUNSTRINGER (XBOX 360)

### ACHIEVEMENT

| UNLOCKABLE | HOW TO UNLOCK |
| --- | --- |
| A Fistful of Revenge (50) | Ride "Burrito" the Dog into the sunset. |
| A Long Fall to Hell (20) | Find a way to kill an undead puppet. |
| Awesomeness Detected (20) | Do something really awesome. |
| Back Seat Commentator (5) | Listen to a different kind of narrator while you play. |
| Big Spender (25) | Purchase everything in the bonus store. |
| Death Rides a Steamboat (20) | Commit mass destruction with a paddleboat. |
| For A Few Gallons More (30) | Take down Big Oil. |
| Gold Medallist (20) | Reach a Gold Medal score on a single act. |
| Great Balls of Fire (20) | Survive an epic battle against a kite. |
| Hot Lead Pusher (20) | Get a crazy high kill streak. |
| How The East Was Won (30) | Possess a lush, full beard. |
| Hundred Thousand Dollar Baby (20) | Spend a whole chunk of money in the bonus store. |
| Legend of the 8000 Samurai (20) | Find the Great Wall of China in an unexpected place. |
| Living Large in the Saddle (10) | Hoard all the tacos and hearts in an act. |
| Lonely Are The Dead (30) | Face Death and live to tell the tale. |
| Lucky Prize Winner (15) | Find an achievement hidden in a piece of concept art. |
| Money is the Best Medicine (20) | Earn cash, not health, for every heart in an act. |
| My Horse, A Gun, Your Lumberjack (20) | Find a place to saw some logs. |
| No Country for Old Barons (20) | Carjack a stagecoach. |
| No Insurance (15) | Don't scratch the paint while piloting a paddleboat. |
| Once Upon a Time in the West (20) | End an artist's career. |
| Perfect Performance (25) | Win gold medals in all acts of a single play. |
| Perfectionist (30) | Win a gold medal in every act of every play. |
| Pistol for a Hundred Skeletons (20) | Kill 18,675,309,000 Skeletons. |
| Requiem for a Gunstringer (20) | Walk amongst the dead. |
| Russian Chicken (10) | In a shootout, play chicken with a bullet before shooting it. |
| Sellout (10) | Buy an achievement from the bonus store. |
| Seven Shooter (5) | Defy laws of physics by shooting more than six enemies without reloading. |
| Stranger in New Orleans (20) | Take Andrew Jackson to the Madam's district. |
| Strings of Steel (50) | Beat every play in one session. On Hardcore Mode. Also, never die. |
| The Backwards Bandit (20) | Complete a level with "Lefty Mode" enabled. |
| The Bandit Sheriff (20) | Close your bank account. |
| The Big Easy Reckoning (30) | Get close and personal with the Madam. |
| The Brute and the Beast (20) | See things that you will never be able to unsee. |
| The Canyon Runs Red (20) | Fall thousands of feet without dying. |
| The Great Wall of Vengeance (20) | Ride a rocket over a battlefield. |
| The Gunstringer Rides Again (15) | Destroy the advertising plan of a small business. |
| The Hidden Fortress (20) | Crash into someone's house uninvited. |

| | |
|---|---|
| The Last Undead Boy Scout (20) | Collect a gold medal, hardcore award, and 2P award in a single act. |
| The Lone Star (20) | Finish an act while playing on Hardcore Mode. |
| The Red Baron (25) | Kill 100 enemies while strapped to a rocket in "The Great Wall of Vengeance". |
| Tin Marksman (5) | Shoot all the cans in the Prologue. |
| Took a Bullet for the Team (10) | Take down the developers. |
| Turbo Deflation (10) | Deflate the first boss in under 30 seconds. |
| Two Hearts to Live (20) | Complete all acts in a play without ever dropping to one heart. |
| Undead and Untouchable (20) | Reach the end of "Requiem for a Gunstringer" without losing a single heart. |
| Undead or Alive (20) | Remember the time you scorned a woman. |
| What's Next? (5) | Visit the Download Content screen to see what new content is available. |
| Why Would You Even Do This? (25) | Complete an act with every single modifier enabled. |
| With a Little Help from a Friend (15) | Complete an act with a friend. |

### UNLOCKABLE

| UNLOCKABLE | HOW TO UNLOCK |
|---|---|
| The Brim Of Justice | Take out the posse member with the biggest hat. |
| The Castolon Poncho | Take out the posse member that looks the least flattering in a poncho. |
| Vengeance Trail Walkers | Find closure on the vengeance trail. |

## GUNSTAR HEROES     (Wii)

### UNLOCKABLES

| UNLOCKABLE | HOW TO UNLOCK |
|---|---|
| Hidden Special Move | With either Gunstar Red or Gunstar Blue motion: ⬇, ◌⬇, ◌, ◌⬆, ⬆+shot button to execute a powerful standing slide. |
| Make the Logo Rotate | Hold ⬇ on controller 1 before the Gunstar Heroes logo appears on the screen in order to rotate it. |
| Timeron's Secret | During the second Timeron encounter (which is in the Space Battle stage) a timer begins ticking from 00'00"00. As the timer keeps going, the Timeron's attacks change, and every 20 minutes or so, a circular drone appears, accompanied by Smash Daisaku's laughter. Avoid this drone for about 2 minutes until it self-destructs, because a single hit will reduce your health to zero. At about 50'00"00 or so, large blue balls appear. These rebound once against the screen, and do 11 points of damage instead of the normal 10 points from the smaller ones. Once the timer gets up to 99'50"00 or so, don't destroy the Timeron yet. Instead, wait out the remaining 10 seconds while avoiding the Timeron's attacks, but don't stay too close to the Timeron, or you'll get killed by the drone. Once the timer reaches 00'00"00 again, you'll hear that nasty laughter again, but this time, "GIVE UP!!" appears in the middle of the screen, and the Timeron self-destructs, accompanied by the message, "YOU OPENED THE - SATORI MIND -." A bit more of that nasty laughter accompanies the next message, "REPROGRAMMED BY NAMI - 1993." Now, instead of getting a Timer Bonus as you usually would, a Soul Bonus of exactly 930,410 points is added to your score. |

NEW!

A
B
C
D
E
F
G
**H**
I
J
K
L
M
N
O
P
Q
R
S
T
U
V
W
X
Y
Z

## HALF-LIFE 2: THE ORANGE BOX  (XBOX 360)

### HALF-LIFE 2 *CODES*

Enter the code while playing *Half Life 2*. No specific requirements other than the game. Can be entered at any time on any level. Using cheats does not disable Achievements.

| CODE | EFFECT |
| --- | --- |
| LB, ◇, RB, ◇, LB, LB, ◇, RB, RB, ◇ | Invincibility |
| ◇, ◇, ◇, ♡, ◁, ▷, ◁, ▷, ●, ▲ | Restores health by 25 points |
| ▼, ●, ▲, ✕, RB, ▼, ▲, ●, RB | Restores ammo for current weapon |
| ◈, ◈, ◈, ◈, P, ▷, ▷, ▷, ▷, RB | Unlocks all levels, which can then be accessed from the new game window |

### PORTAL *CODES*

Enter these codes anytime during gameplay.

| CODE | EFFECT |
| --- | --- |
| ♡, ●, ▲, ●, ♡, ♡, ●, ▲, ●, ▼ | Create box |
| LB, ♡, RB, ♡, LB, LB, ◇, RB, RB, ◇ | Enables invincibility |
| ◇, ▼, ●, ▲, ◇, ◇, ▲, ●, ●, ◇ | Fire energy ball |
| ▼, ▲, ●, ▲, ●, ▼, ▼, ▲, ◁, ▷ | Portal placement anywhere |
| ✕, ●, LB, RB, ◁, ▷, LB, RB, LT, RT | Upgrade Portalgun |

## HALF-LIFE 2: THE ORANGE BOX  (PlayStation 3)

### HALF-LIFE 2 *CODES*

Enter the code while playing. Codes can be entered at any time on any level.

| EFFECT | CODE |
| --- | --- |
| Restore Ammo (for current weapon) | R1, ▲, ●, ✕, ■, R1, ▲, ■, ✕, ●, R1 |
| Restore Health by 25 Points | ↑, ↑, ↓, ↓, ←, →, ←, →, ●, ✕ |
| Unlock All Levels | ←, ←, ←, ←, L1, →, →, →, →, R1 |

### PORTAL *CODES*

Enter these codes any time during gameplay.

| EFFECT | CODE |
| --- | --- |
| Create a Cube | ↓, ●, ✕, ●, ▲, ↓, ●, ✕, ●, ▲ |
| Fire Energy Ball | ↑, ▲, ▲, ■, ■, ✕, ✕, ●, ●, ↑ |
| Unlock All Levels | ←, ←, ←, ←, L1, →, →, →, →, R1 |

## HALO 3  (XBOX 360)

### CODES

The following cheats can be performed during a local match or replay only. Press and hold the corresponding buttons for 3 SECONDS to toggle the effect on / off.

| EFFECT | CODE |
| --- | --- |
| Toggle Hide Weapon | LB, RB, L3, ▲, ♡ |
| Toggle Pan-Cam / Normal while Show Coordinates is enabled. | Hold L3 and R3 and press ◀ |
| Toggle Show Coordinates / Camera Mode | LB, +, L3, ▲, ◇ |

## ARMOR PERMUTATIONS UNLOCKABLES

Body Pieces: Spartan marked with (S) and Elite marked with (E).

| UNLOCKABLE | HOW TO UNLOCK |
| --- | --- |
| (E) Ascetic Body | Unlock "Up Close and Personal" Achievement |
| (E) Ascetic Head | Unlock "Steppin' Razor" Achievement |
| (E) Ascetic Shoulders | Unlock "Overkill" Achievement |
| (E) Commando Body | Unlock "Triple Kill" Achievement |
| (E) Commando Head | Unlock "Overkill" Achievement |
| (E) Commando Shoulders | Unlock "Killing Frenzy" Achievement |
| (E) Flight Body | Complete Tsavo Highway on Heroic or Legendary |
| (E) Flight Head | Complete Campaign mode on Heroic |
| (E) Flight Shoulders | Complete The Ark on Heroic difficulty or higher |
| (S) EOD Body | Complete Tsavo Highway on Legendary |
| (S) EOD Head | Complete Campaign mode on Legendary |
| (S) EOD Shoulders | Complete The Ark on Legendary |
| (S) EVA Body | Complete Tsavo Highway on Normal or higher |
| (S) EVA Head | Complete Campaign mode on Normal |
| (S) EVA Shoulders | Complete The Ark on Normal difficulty or higher |
| (S) Hayabusa Chest | Collect 5 hidden skulls |
| (S) Hayabusa Helmet | Collect 13 hidden skulls |
| (S) Hayabusa Shoulders | Collect 9 hidden skulls |
| (S) Mark V Head | Unlock "UNSC Spartan" Achievement |
| (S) ODST Head | Unlock "Spartan Graduate" Achievement |
| (S) Rogue Head | Unlock "Spartan Officer" Achievement |
| (S) Scout Body | Unlock "Too Close to the Sun" Achievement |
| (S) Scout Head | Unlock "Used Car Salesman" Achievement |
| (S) Scout Shoulders | Unlock "Mongoose Mowdown" Achievement |
| (S) Security Head | Earn 1,000 Gamerscore points |
| (S) Security Shoulders | Earn 850 Gamerscore points |
| Katana | Complete all Achievements (1,000/1,000) |

### BLACK-EYE SKULL

**Effect:** Melee hits instantly recharge your shield.

**Level:** Crow's Nest

**Location:** As soon as you start the level, head straight up to the higher level. Head toward the door with the red light, then turn around. Jump onto the racks, onto the red metal light holders, then onto the ventilation tube. The skull spawns at the end.

### BLIND SKULL

**Effect:** "Shoot from the hip."

**Level:** First Stage

**Location:** When you get to the area where you see the Phantom overhead (one of the marines points it out) jump over the rocks and keep following the path on the right. When you get to the cliff, there's a rock over on the side. The skull is on the end of the rock. Note: This skull has to be activated before you start a Campaign map.

### CATCH SKULL

**Effect:** all enemies have 2 grenades, throw more grenades.

**Level:** The Storm

**Location:** From the start, go through until you go outside again. Outside, look straight across to a small round building. The skull is on top. To get up there, either use a warthog as a platform or grenade-jump. DO NOT destroy the wraith near the door or the skull will disappear.

NEW!

## COWBELL SKULL

**Effect:** Explosive force increased (sputnik from H2).

**Level:** The Ark

**Location:** First pick up a grav lift from the small building near where you fight the scarab. Now proceed through the level until you reach the second sloping hallway (stairway). You should see some partitioned risers (platforms) halfway down. The skull is on the top level. Toss the grav-lift on the right side of the hall so it lands on the fourth little green dot from the door. Then run, jump, and use the grav-lift to propel you to the top. You reach a checkpoint just as you enter the room, so if you miss, just try again.

## FAMINE SKULL

**Effect:** "Trust us. Bring a magazine." Dropped weapons have very little ammo compared to normal.

**Level:** The Ark

**Location:** When you first go into the valley to the right after the wrecked phantom, look left to see a huge boulder. Use a ghost and get to the side of the boulder closest to the bridge overhead. It is easy to pilot the ghost up the side of the wall using the thrust. To get the skull, pilot 2 ghosts up the side of the bridge to the top of the bridge and stack them one on top of another next to the beam where the skull is placed. Simply jump from the top of the ghosts toward the skull and land on the beam.

## FOG SKULL

**Effect:** "You'll miss those eyes in the back of your head." Your motion sensor disappears.

**Level:** Floodgate

**Location:** As you are walking down from the anti-air gun you destroyed in the previous mission, you encounter a ramp (next to a missile launcher). Around this ramp, you hit a checkpoint. At this point, you should also hear a marine yelling, "There! Over There!" Look up and to the right, directly at the roof of the building next to the missile launcher. A single flood form (not to be mistaken for the two other flood forms jumping in front of you) holds the skull. Kill him before he jumps, and he drops the skull down to the ground where you can retrieve it. If you shoot too early, and the skull gets stuck on the roof.

## GRUNT BIRTHDAY PARTY SKULL

**Effect:** Headshots on grunts cause heads to explode with confetti.

**Level:** Crow's Nest

**Location:** Right after the first objective, while en route to the barracks, you fall onto a pipe. At the end of this pipe, look over the edge to see a small space a few feet below you. Drop over and as quickly as you can, pull back to land under the floor you were just on. The skull is at the end.

## IRON SKULL

**Effect:** When either player dies in Co-Op on any difficulty both players restart at last checkpoint. In single player, you restart the level if you die.

**Level:** Sierra 117

**Location:** In the area where you rescue Sarge, behind the prison cell is a large ledge. Go to the far right side and jump on the boxes, then onto the pipes to get up on the ledge. Go to the far end of the ledge, turn two corners, and the skull is at the far end.

## IWHBYD SKULL

**Effect:** "But the dog beat me over the fence." Unlocks bonus dialogue throughout the game. For most, this is the last skull, so this gives you the Hayabusa Helmet as well.

**Level:** The Covenant

**Location:** To get this, get to the room where you "fight" the Prophet of Truth. Let the Arbiter kill him, turn around, and kill all the flood here as well. This makes it a lot easier. Then jump through the Halo holograms in this order: 4 6 5 4 5 3 4. When you jump through the final hologram, they all light up in a sequential pattern. The skull is at the end, right before the energy bridge leading to Truth's corpse.

## MYTHIC SKULL

**Effect:** Every enemy on the field now has double the normal amount of health.

**Level:** Halo

**Location:** As soon as the mission starts, walk up the hill in front of you and into the cave. Hug the right side of the cave, and after a large boulder you see a path on your right. Take the short path and find it at the end.

A
B
C
D
E
F
G
**H**
I
J
K
L
M
N
O
P
Q
R
S
T
U
V
W
X
Y
Z

**CODES & CHEATS**

### THUNDERSTORM SKULL

**Effect:** "Field promotions for everyone!" Upgrades enemies to their stronger versions.

**Level:** The Covenant

**Location:** After you shut down tower 1 and get access to the hornet, fly to tower 2 (the one the Arbiter shut down). While walking up the stairs, go to the middle part that connects both. A stair leads up to a platform where the skull is.

### TILT SKULL

**Effect:** "What was once resistance is now immunity." Enemies have different body parts that may be resistant to certain bullet types.

**Level:** Cortana

**Location:** When in the circular type room with all the flood, look for a small structure piece next to two archways. Jump on top of it and up on the rocks to the top left, turn left and jump up again, then do a 180 and jump to the rocks across from you. Follow the rock sticking out and leading up on top of the original circular room. The skull is in a pile of blood.

### TOUGH LUCK SKULL

**Effect:** Enemies do saving throws.

**Level:** Tsavo Highway

**Location:** On Tsavo Highway, about halfway through the mission (right after you are forced to walk through a large blue barrier), you will come out of a tunnel on the highway, and see a large pipeline on your left. Drop down in between the two, and run to the wall in front of you. Follow the wall all the way to where it connects with the cliff on your right, and turn to the left. There should be a few ledges—simply crouch-jump from ledge to ledge, and the last one should have the "Tough Luck" skull on it.

### THE SEVEN TERMINALS

**The Ark:**

1. Start the mission and once you enter the first building, take a left into another door and emerge in a curved corridor. On the inside is a Terminal.

2. After activating the bridge to let your comrades across the gap, do a 180 and you should see it. (It does not open until you activate the bridge.)

3. In the third building after defeating the scarab, kill the group of sleeping covenant, then follow the corridor downward. Once you reach a door in front that is locked, immediately on the left there's an open door. Go through and walk straight, then do a 180 to find a secret room. It is in there.

**The Covenant:**

1. When in the first tower standing on the lift, face the access panel and turn left. Jump over and it's right there.

2. Land your hornet on the second tower, walk toward the entrance, but when you see the locked door, do a 180.

3. When in the third tower standing on the lift, face the access panel and turn right. Jump over.

**Halo:**

1. After reaching the end of the first cave, hug the right wall and you see a building. Jump up onto the walkway and hang a left once inside.

## HALO 3: ODST (XBOX 360)

### FIREFIGHT MISSIONS

Complete certain campaign missions to unlock new maps for the Firefight game mode.

| UNLOCKABLE | HOW TO UNLOCK |
| --- | --- |
| Alpha Site | Complete the ONI Alpha Site campaign mission on any difficulty. |
| Chasm Ten | Complete the Date Hive campaign mission on any difficulty. |
| Last Exit | Complete the Coastal Highway campaign mission on any difficulty. |
| Lost Platoon | Complete the Uplift Reserve campaign mission on any difficulty. |

## FIREFIGHT UNLOCKABLE CHARACTERS

Perform the task to unlock characters for use in Firefight mode.

| UNLOCKABLE | HOW TO UNLOCK |
| --- | --- |
| Buck Firefight Character | Complete "Tayari Plaza" on Normal or higher. |
| Dare Firefight Character | Complete the campaign on Legendary difficulty. |
| Dutch Firefight Character | Complete "Uplift Reserve" on Normal or higher. |
| Mickey Firefight Character | Complete "Kizingo Boulevard" on Normal or higher. |
| Romeo Character | Complete "NMPD HQ" on Normal or higher. |

# HALO: REACH (XBOX 360)

## AVATAR AWARDS

| UNLOCKABLE | HOW TO UNLOCK |
| --- | --- |
| Carter's Helmet | Clear a Campaign mission on Legendary without dying. |
| Emile's Helmet | Earned a Bulltrue medal in either multiplayer or Firefight Matchmaking. |
| Jorge's Helmet | Earn a Killtacular in multiplayer Matchmaking. |
| Jun's Helmet | Kill 100 enemies in a row without dying in either the Campaign or Firefight. |
| Kat's Helmet | Avenged a teammate's death in multiplayer Matchmaking. |

## MULTIPLAYER NAMEPLATES

| UNLOCKABLE | HOW TO UNLOCK |
| --- | --- |
| Assault Rifle | Played the Halo Reach Beta in May 2010. |
| Halo 2 logo | Played Halo 2 on Xbox Live before April 15, 2010. |
| Halo 3 logo | Play any Campaign level in Halo 3 while connected to Xbox Live. |
| Marathon Durandal symbol | Have Marathon Durandal in your recently played games list and log in at Bungie.net. |
| MJOLNIR Mk VI helmet logo | Unlock any 4 of the Halo PC, Halo 2, Halo 3, Halo 3: ODST, or Halo Reach Beta nameplates. |
| ODST logo | Play Halo 3:ODST while connected to Xbox Live. |
| Original Halo logo | Register your Halo PC product code at Bungie.net. |
| The Septagon (7th Column symbol) | Join Bungie.net and log in with your Gamertag's e-mail address. |

# HALO WARS (XBOX 360)

## BLACK BOXES

Black boxes in each level unlock new Halo History entries.

| UNLOCKABLE | HOW TO UNLOCK |
| --- | --- |
| All Others | Win on each Skirmish map and win Skirmish with each leader. |
| Black Box 01—Alpha Base | Under the last bridge before entering Alpha Base. |
| Black Box 02—Relic Approach | Top left of the map, behind a Covenant shield. |
| Black Box 03—Relic Interior | On the small ramp on the left side, right at the start, before going inside the Relic. |
| Black Box 04—Arcadia City | Just north of the starting point, right next to the skyscraper where you can save Adam. |
| Black Box 05—Arcadia Outskirts | Go down the first ramp as you are fleeing from the Covenant; it's behind a downed Pelican. |
| Black Box 06—Dome of Light | Far left of the map, to the left of where you transport the third Rhino tank. |
| Black Box 07—Scarab | Far right side of the map, in a small alcove with supply crates. |
| Black Box 08—Anders' Signal | Near the big brute fire line at the start, on a ridge to the right. |

| Black Box 09—The Flood | Straight out from the base ramp on the other side of the map. |
|---|---|
| Black Box 10—Shield World | Alongside Bravo platoon, which is the middle platoon you pick up. |
| Black Box 11—Cleansing | Left rear of the ship, on wings that slant down; you'll need a flying unit. |
| Black Box 12—Repairs | Left edge of Spirit of Fire, not far from the Power Core building, on the left side. |
| Black Box 13—Beachhead | On a ledge near the second set of teleporters, near the Covenant base. |
| Black Box 14—Reactor | Up and left at the top of the first ramp, on the edge of the ramp. |
| Black Box 15—Escape | Directly opposite the starting point on the north edge of the map, between the Flood and the Covenant base. |

## SKULLS LOCATIONS/REQUIREMENTS

In each mission, you must meet the requirement before heading to the skull's location.

| UNLOCKABLE | HOW TO UNLOCK |
|---|---|
| Skull Name: Boomstick (Mission 12: Repairs) | Kill 12 Spirit Transports—take a Hawk to the Lower 2 Airlocks and it's right up the little ramp in the air. |
| Skull Name: Bountiful Harvest (Mission 14: Reactor) | Kill 20 Vampires—head to the second Covenant base and it's in the far corner at the bottom of the next ramp. |
| Skull Name: Catch (Mission 10: Shield World) | Kill 350 Swarms—get at least 2 Hornets and fly east of you base past the First Tower to a Plateau covered with Flood Eggs; it is in the center. |
| Skull Name: Cowbell (Mission 3: Relic Interior) | Kill 45 Hunters—take a Grizzly, Anders, Forge and your Marines back to where they were held up on the central pad. |
| Skull Name: Emperor (Mission 15: Escape) | Kill 3 Scarabs—Head to the very north of the map and it's dead center in the flood. |
| Skull Name: Fog (Mission 5: Arcadia Outskirts) | Kill 5 Wraiths—get a Warthog and rush back up the tracks to the left of your main base and just keep going straight past the split in the tracks. |
| Skull Name: Grunt Birthday Party (Mission 2: Relic Approach) | Kill 20 Jackals—head back to Alpha base with a Warthog; it's in the south end of the base. |
| Skull Name: Look Daddy! (Mission 1: Alpha Base) | Kill 100 Grunts—get a Warthog and rush back to the front gate of Alpha base; the skull is where the Marines were held up. |
| Skull Name: Pain Train (Mission 13: Beachhead) | Kill 10 Bomber Forms—head back to the beginning of the map by the first teleporter and head down the path to a flood nest; it's right next to it. |
| Skull Name: Rebel Leader (Mission 9: The Flood) | Kill 20 Flood Stalks—just to the northeast of your main base is a downed Pelican. Just take a Warthog to claim it fast and easy. |
| Skull Name: Rebel Supporter (Mission 8: Anders' Signal) | Kill 750 Infection Forms—head to north side of the map where you got the Elephant, head east toward a cliff. But you'll see a ridge. Go into ridge. |
| Skull Name: Rebel Sympathizer (Mission 7: Scarab) | Kill 10 Locusts—get a Warthog and take it to the top-left of the map, where there were 2 Locusts and a Power Nod; it's right there. |
| Skull Name: Sickness (Mission 6: Dome of Light) | Kill 50 Banshees—take a squad of Marines to the hanger behind your base; it's right there. |

| Skull Name: Sugar Cookies (Mission 11: Cleansing) | Kill 100 Sentinels—take a Hornet to the front end of the Spirit of Fire and it is right on the nose of the ship. |
|---|---|
| Skull Name: Wuv Woo (Mission 4: Arcadia City) | Kill 50 Elites—where you set up base 2 in the streets there are some stairs next to it leading to a bronze statue. It's next to the statue. |

## HARRY POTTER AND THE DEATHLY HALLOWS, PART 1 (XBOX 360)

### CODES

| EFFECT | CODE |
|---|---|
| Elite Challenges | Y, Up, X, LT, RT, A |
| Protego Totalum | Y, B, Up, Left, RT, Right |
| Superstrength potions | X, Left, Right, A, RT, RB |

## HARRY POTTER AND THE DEATHLY HALLOWS, PART 2 (XBOX 360)

### ACHIEVEMENT

| UNLOCKABLE | HOW TO UNLOCK |
|---|---|
| A Good Offence (10) | Defeated 10 enemy wizards before they cast a spell |
| A Good Start (10) | Defeated 100 enemy wizards, in the Main Story OR Challenges |
| Accomplished Wizard (150) | Completed the game on Expert |
| Back to You ... (10) | Defeated 10 enemy wizards with Protego deflections |
| Best Friend (5) | Played as Ron |
| Blind Luck (5) | Defeated 10 enemy wizards from cover, without aiming |
| Boom! (5) | Played as Seamus |
| Burning Bridges (10) | Completed 'A Job to Do' |
| Care of the Castle (20) | Escaped Voldemort with minimal damage to Hogwart |
| Casting from Cover (5) | Defeated an enemy wizard from cover for the first time |
| Change of Plans (20) | Completed 'A Turn of Events' |
| Complete Collection (50) | Collected 100% of all items |
| Confringo! (10) | Defeated 100 enemy wizards with Confringo |
| Covert Confidence (20) | Defeated 100 enemy wizards from cover |
| Defiant Daughter (5) | Played as Ginny |
| Don't Bank on it! (10) | Completed 'Gringotts' |
| Expelliarmus! (20) | Successfully dispelled 100 Protego shields with Expelliarmus |
| Expulso! (10) | Defeated 100 enemy wizards with Expulso |
| Familiar Faces (15) | Completed 'Surrender' |
| First Rung (10) | Completed your first challenge |
| Full of Character (40) | Found all characters |
| Future Auror (50) | Got all achievements, 100% the game! |
| Getting There ... (20) | Defeated 500 enemy wizards in the Main Story OR Challenges |
| Got It Covered! (5) | Played as Neville |
| Having a Blast (5) | Triggered 5 explosive reactions |
| Hogwarts Burning (15) | Completed 'The Battle of Hogwarts' |
| Hogwarts Defender (20) | Defeated 1000 enemy wizards in the Main Story OR Challenges |
| It's All Come Down to This ... (20) | Completed 'Voldemort's Last Stand' |
| Listen Up (40) | Found all Music Tracks |
| Lost and Found (15) | Completed 'The Lost Diadem' |

| Magical McGonagall (5) | Played as McGonagall |
|---|---|
| Mastering Magic (80) | Completed the game on Advanced |
| Motherly Love (20) | Completed 'Not My Daughter' |
| Not a Scratch (5) | Completed a level without being defeated |
| Now You See Me (10) | Apparated over 100 metres |
| Petrificus Totalus! (15) | Successfully paralysed 100 enemy wizards using Petrificus Totalus |
| Protego! (20) | Used Protego against 100 spells |
| Pulling Teeth (10) | Completed 'The Basilisk Fang' |
| Shining Example (50) | Completed all challenges at Gold standard |
| Snape Sacked (10) | Completed 'A Problem of Security' |
| Stay Away from Her (5) | Played as Molly |
| Stopped in Their Tracks (10) | Defeated 5 enemy wizards with one Impedimenta cast |
| Strategic Spell-casting (10) | Defeated 50 enemy wizards using more than one spell |
| Streets of Hogsmeade (10) | Completed 'The Streets of Hogsmeade' |
| That Showed Them ... (10) | Defeated 4 enemy wizards with a Confringo cast |
| The Best Defence ... (10) | Used Protego to defeat 20 enemy wizards at close range |
| The Bigger They Are ... (15) | Completed 'A Giant Problem' |
| The Brightest Witch (5) | Played as Hermione |
| Up to the Challenge (30) | Completed all challenges |
| Wizard-in-Training (40) | Completed the game on Normal |

## HARRY POTTER AND THE HALF BLOOD PRINCE (XBOX 360)

### UNLOCKABLES

Collect the following number of crests to unlock the corresponding bonuses.

| UNLOCKABLE | HOW TO UNLOCK |
|---|---|
| Two-Player Dueling Pack 4: Paved Courtyard Dueling Arena | 113 Hogwarts Crests |
| More mini-crests with each cast | 129 Hogwarts Crests |
| Two-Player Dueling Pack 2: Training Ground Dueling Arena | 14 Hogwarts Crests |
| Dungbombs in prank boxes around Hogwarts | 21 Hogwarts Crests |
| Two-Player Dueling Pack 2: Crabbe & Goyle | 29 Hogwarts Crests |
| Two-Player Dueling Pack 1: Draco & Luna | 3 Hogwarts Crests |
| Score boost in flying events | 38 Hogwarts Crests |
| Exploding Cauldrons in prank boxes around Hogwarts | 48 Hogwarts Crests |
| Two-Player Dueling Pack 4: The Transfiguration Dueling Arena | 59 Hogwarts Crests |
| Even More health in duels | 71 Hogwarts Crests |
| More health in duels | 8 Hogwarts Crests |
| Two-Player Dueling Pack 5: Ginny & Hermione | 84 Hogwarts Crests |
| Love Potion in Potions Club | 98 Hogwarts Crests |

## HARVEST MOON: THE TALE OF TWO TOWNS (DS)

### UNLOCKABLE

| UNLOCKABLE | HOW TO UNLOCK |
|---|---|
| Alpaca | Unlocked in year 2 Fall. |
| Jersey Cow/Calf | Unlocked in Year 2. |
| Owl | Unlocked after the 1st tunnel upgrade. |
| Shetland Horse | Unlocked after you complete the three tunnel upgrades. |
| Silkie Chicken/Chick | Unlocked in year 2. |

| | |
|---|---|
| **Suffolk Sheep/Lamb** | Unlocked in year 2. |
| **Throughbred Horse** | Unlocked after the first tunnel upgrade. |
| **Alisa** | Raise Nathan's friendship to 2 White Flowers, be in Fall of year 2 or later, and then walk to the Mountain Summit between 10:00 pm-3:00 am on sunny. |
| **Dirk** | In Summer of your 1st year walk from the Konohana low-mountain area to the Konohana entrance area between 9:00am-8:00 pm on a sunny, snowy to unlocked. |
| **Mikhail** | Introduced to you by mayor in Fall 6. He will move into whichever town you are living in at the time. |
| **Nathan** | Winter 3, the mayor will introduce you to him he'll be at the church in Bluebell from now on. |
| **Oracle** | Walk from the Bluebell Low-Mountain to Bluebell Mid-Mountain area after 8:00 pm starting in year 2 to unlock her. |
| **Cardboard Cart** | Raise Oracle's friendship to 2 Flowers and have Request Level rank 4 or higher. You need 1 Mythic Ore, 5 Brown Alpaca Wool, and 30,000,000 G. |
| **Chicken Cart** | Available at either Animal shop starting in year 3. |
| **Fancy Cart** | Win any Cooking Festival in year 2. |
| **Lion Cart** | Available at either Animal shop starting in year 3. |
| **Shrine Cart** | Win any Cooking Festival in year 2. |
| **Sled** | Own the Shrine Cart and the Fancy Cart and have the tunnel between both towns reconnected, and then win a cooking festival starting in year 2. |
| **UFO Cart** | Raise Oracle's friendship to 2 Flowers and have Request Level rank 4 or higher. You need 1 Stone Tablet, 5 White Alpaca Wool, and 19,771,116 G. |
| **Axe** | Requested by Sheng in 1st year you need to raise 5,000 FP to unlocked the request needed 8000 G and 10 branches. |
| **Fishing Rod** | Given to you by mayor in Summer 1 at 1st Year. |
| **Hammer** | Requested by Sheng in Spring 12 at 1st year needed 8 stones. |
| **Master Rod** | Requested by Rutger needed 10 old boots and 10 old balls |
| **Skateboard** | Requester by Oracle in year 2 needed 10 old balls and 10 material lumber. |
| **Snowboard** | Requested by Oracle in year2 needed 10 elli leaves and 10 snow balls. |
| **Stethoscope** | Requested by Ash needed 5 milk and 5 egg plus 1,500g |

## CAPSULES

Capsules contain items that are added to the course. They have no effect on the gameplay, they are just there for show.

| UNLOCKABLE | HOW TO UNLOCK |
|---|---|
| **Armored Zombie** | Play 20 rounds at Euro Classic G.C. (Regular Tee). |
| **Bear** | Play 20 rounds at Highland C.C. (Long Tee). |
| **Blue Whale** | Play 20 rounds at The Crown Links (Long Tee). |
| **Child Witch** | Play 20 rounds at Euro Classic G.C. (Long Tee). |
| **Glider** | Play 20 rounds at The Crown Links (Regular Tee). |
| **Gnome** | Play 20 rounds at Silver Peaks G.C. (Regular Tee). |
| **Helicopter** | Play 20 rounds at Highland C.C. (Regular Tee). |
| **Jet Formation** | Play 20 rounds at Okinawa Golf Resort (Regular Tee). |
| **Lion** | Play 20 rounds at Great Safari C.C. (Long Tee). |
| **Manta** | Play 20 rounds at Okinawa Golf Resort (Long Tee). |
| **Rhino** | Play 20 rounds at Great Safari C.C. (Regular Tee). |
| **Unicorn** | Play 20 rounds at Silver Peaks G.C. (Long Tee). |

**CODES & CHEATS**

## THE HOUSE OF THE DEAD: OVERKILL (Wii)

### UNLOCKABLES

| UNLOCKABLE | HOW TO UNLOCK |
|---|---|
| Director's Cut mode | Complete Story mode to unlock Director's Cut mode. |
| Dual Wield mode | Clear Director's Cut. |
| Handcannon Weapon | Complete Story mode to unlock the handcannon. |
| Mini-Gun Weapon | Complete all levels in Director's Cut. |

## HULK HOGAN'S MAIN EVENT (XBOX 360)

### ACHIEVEMENT

| UNLOCKABLE | HOW TO UNLOCK |
|---|---|
| Armed and Dangerous (25) | Grab a chair in air, in the Chair Hit stunt. |
| Bad Altitude (25) | Successfully throw your opponent out of the ring via a Choke Slam. |
| Be Super, Man (25) | Perform a high flying splash in Aerial Assault. |
| Become Someone (25) | Create any wrestler in Create A Wrestler mode. |
| Blockbuster (25) | Complete the Ladder Bash Stunt without getting hit by your opponent. |
| Can't Touch This! (25) | Complete the Irish Whip Stunt without getting hit by your opponent. |
| Champ of the Ring (50) | Complete an entire Exhibition Mode match on Average Joe Difficulty. |
| Chiropractor Disaster (25) | Perform a piledriver in the Body Slam stunt. |
| Failure to Fail (25) | Fight your way out of the corner and knock your opponent out of the ring in the On The Ropes stunt. |
| Flippin' Perfect (25) | Flip your opponent 3 times in the Grapple stunt without ever being flipped. |
| Get in the Ring (25) | Complete any stunt in Quick Play Mode on Average Joe Difficulty. |
| Getting a Sandwich, BRB (0) | Player leaves sensor area in middle of any stunt. |
| Hulkstering Up (50) | Win a match in Trade Blows via Hulkstering Up. |
| I am Hardcore (175) | Complete the Career Mode on Hardcore Difficulty. |
| If the Boot Fits (25) | Successfully perform a Hulk Hogan "Boot" attack in The Irish Whip stunt. |
| Just the Beginning (125) | Complete the Career Mode on Average Joe Difficulty. |
| Just the Two of Us (50) | Complete an entire Head To Head match on Average Joe Difficulty. |
| Just the Two of Us, 2X (100) | Complete an entire Head To Head match on Hardcore Difficulty. |
| Listen Like the Great One (25) | Perform the Hulk Hogan Listen pose to the crowd in the Entrance stunt. |
| Perfect Punch (25) | Finish your opponent off with a punch in Trade Blows. |
| Pin and Win (25) | Successfully pin your opponent for a 3 count in the Pin To Win stunt. |
| Profit, Prophet (50) | Earn over 100,000 points in a single stunt. |
| Roger, Dodger (50) | Complete the Entrance without getting hit by any object. |

## ICE AGE 2: THE MELTDOWN (Wii)

### CODES

Pause the game and press the following codes.

| UNLOCKABLE | HOW TO UNLOCK |
|---|---|
| Unlimited Health | ⬆, ⬅, ⬇, ➡, ⬆, ⬅, ⬇, ➡ |

## IMAGE FIGHT (Wii)

### UNLOCKABLES

| UNLOCKABLE | HOW TO UNLOCK |
|---|---|
| Arcade Mode | Do a reset (START+SELECT), then immediately hold ① |
| Mr. Heli mode | Highlight song C in Sound Test mode and press ⬇, SELECT, ②+①, then press ① on Mr. Heli and then press RUN |
| Sound Test | Press SELECT on the title screen |

## INDIANA JONES AND THE STAFF OF KINGS (Wii)

### CODES

| EFFECT | CODE |
|---|---|
| Unlock Fate of Atlantis game | In the main menu, while holding down Ⓩ press: Ⓐ,⬇,⬅Ⓑ,⬇,⬆,⬇,⬅,⬇,Ⓑ |

### UNLOCKABLE SKINS

| UNLOCKABLE | HOW TO UNLOCK |
|---|---|
| Big Heads | 6 Artifacts |
| Han Solo | 36 Artifacts |
| Henry Jones | 34 Artifacts |
| Tuxedo Indy | 16 Artifacts |

### UNLOCKABLE CONCEPT ART

| UNLOCKABLE | HOW TO UNLOCK |
|---|---|
| Allies | 12 Artifacts |
| Co-op Levels(Wii Only) | 8 Artifacts |
| Cutting Room Floor | 36 Artifacts |
| Enemies | 22 Artifacts |
| Extras | 20 Artifacts |
| Istanbul | 28 Artifacts |
| Nepal | 26 Artifacts |
| Odin and Seabed | 32 Artifacts |
| UNLOCKABLE | HOW TO UNLOCK |
| Panama | 18 Artifacts |
| San Francisco | 14 Artifacts |
| Sudan | 2 Artifacts |

### UNLOCKABLE TRAILERS

| UNLOCKABLE | HOW TO UNLOCK |
|---|---|
| "Raiders of the Lost Ark" movie trailer | 3 Artifacts |
| "Temple of Doom" movie trailer | 10 Artifacts |
| "The Last Crusade movie trailer" | 24 Artifacts |
| "The Kingdom of the Crystal Skull" movie trailer | 30 Artifacts |

**CODES & CHEATS**

## INFAMOUS 2 (PlayStation 3)

### TROPHY

| UNLOCKABLE | HOW TO UNLOCK |
|---|---|
| A Streetcar Named 'Boom!' (Bronze) | Complete BOOM! |
| Am I The Daddy? (Bronze) | Complete Nix's New Family. |
| Ambulance Chaser (Bronze) | Complete Hearts and Minds Campaign. |
| Arch Villain (Silver) | Earn full negative Karma. |
| Army Of Me (Bronze) | Defeat 300 enemies. |
| Back to the Bayou (Bronze) | Return to the swamp blockade. |
| Behind the Curtain (Bronze) | Collect 50% of the available Dead Drops. |
| Closed Casket Affair (Bronze) | Give Bertrand what he wants. |
| Cole' Blooded (Bronze) | Defeat 100 civilians. |
| Dazed and Defused (Bronze) | Take down the Blast Shard Bomber. |
| Discerning Taste (Bronze) | Take down a street performer who is imitating a statue. |
| Don't Fence Me In (Bronze) | Climb a chain link fence and rejoice. |
| Exposure (Bronze) | Complete Exposing Bertrand. |
| Express Elevator (Bronze) | Ascend 50 vertical launch poles. |
| Extreme Makeover (Bronze) | Destroy 30 verandas or other large objects. |
| Fight the Good Fight (Silver) | Unlock the good ending. |
| Finish What You Started (Bronze) | Perform 100 finishers or ultra melee combos. |
| Forging Your Own Path (Silver) | Unlock the evil ending. |
| Frozen Asset (Bronze) | Complete the ice Conduit side missions. |
| Get Nix'ed (Bronze) | Choose Nix in Storm the Fort. |
| Go Long! (Bronze) | Hurl 50 objects using the Kinetic Pulse ability. |
| Head Hunter (Bronze) | Use the Precision ability to rack up three head shots in rapid succession. |
| Heavy Hitter (Bronze) | Use your Ionic Powers 30 times. |
| Hero to the People (Bronze) | Stop 80 crimes in progress. |
| I'm As Shocked As You Are (Bronze) | Defeat an enemy or civilian by stepping in water. |
| Incorruptible (Silver) | Earn full positive Karma. |
| inFAMOUS 2 Platinum Trophy (Platinum) | Collect all other inFAMOUS 2 Trophies |
| It's My Town, Now (Silver) | Take over the second island in New Marais. |
| Just One More (Gold) | Pick up all the blast shards scattered around New Marais. |
| Knockout in the Blackout (Bronze) | Defeat 50 enemies in powered down areas while no missions are active. |
| Land Lord (Silver) | Take over the first island in New Marais. |
| Level Up (Bronze) | Create a new mission using the UGC level editor. |
| Matching Set (Bronze) | Unlock and purchase a power of each type by performing stunts. |
| Mountaineer (Bronze) | Climb to the top of the 3 tallest buildings in New Marais. |
| Nothing Can Bring Me Down (Bronze) | Stay off the ground for 130 meters. |
| Pain Builds Character (Gold) | Finish the game on hard difficulty. |
| Playing Both Sides (Bronze) | Complete Fooling the Rebels. |
| Quid Pro Kuo (Bronze) | Complete Leading the Charge. |

| | |
|---|---|
| **Return to Sender (Bronze)** | Send a Helicopter's rockets back at it using any Blast ability. |
| **Shardcore (Silver)** | Pick up 50% of blast shards scattered around New Marais. |
| **Shock and Awe (Bronze)** | Thunder drop into a group of 5 or more enemies. |
| **Status Kuo (Bronze)** | Choose Kuo in Storm the Fort. |
| **Take Them For A Spin (Bronze)** | Hit at least 6 cars in a single Ionic Vortex. |
| **The Cleaner (Bronze)** | Complete the assassination side missions. |
| **Thunder Flop (Bronze)** | Thunder drop from the highest place in New Marais. |
| **Trail Blazer (Bronze)** | Play 5 user-generated missions under the Newest filter. |
| **UGC Curious (Bronze)** | Play 10 user-generated missions. |
| **UGC Veteran (Bronze)** | Play 25 user-generated missions. |
| **Vehicular Manslaughter (Bronze)** | Defeat 25 enemies by throwing cars at them. |
| **Watch That First Step (Bronze)** | Defeat an enemy by destroying the object they stand on. |
| **Well inFORMED (Silver)** | Collect all Dead drops. |
| **With Great Power Comes Greater Power (Silver)** | Unlock and purchase all powers. |

### UNLOCKABLE

Complete the story twice, once with the Hero route and once as Infamous. Once the credits end after the second playthrough, the post game is available and you have unlocked access to the opposite Karma powers of your current Cole along with the powers of the character with which you didn't transfer. You are also awarded 15,000 XP.

## INFINITE SPACE (DS)

### UNLOCKABLE

Infinite Space has two unlockable modes. New Game+ is Story Mode with additional blue prints that are not available in the first play-through. Extra Mode is a challenging mode in which the player is given limited resources to hunt down and conquer 13 systems, each with 3 out of 5 unique opponents per system.

| UNLOCKABLE | HOW TO UNLOCK |
|---|---|
| Extra Mode | Complete Story Mode once. |
| New Game+ | Complete Story Mode once. |

## JASF: JANE'S ADVANCED STRIKE FIGHTERS (XBOX 360)

### ACHIEVEMENT

| UNLOCKABLE | HOW TO UNLOCK |
|---|---|
| 5th Generation (15) | Unlock the F-22 Raptor in Campaign mode (Single-player or Co-Op). |
| Aerial Photographer (80) | Locate Jedhi Borzai (Single-player or Co-Op). |
| Air Superiority (30) | Destroy 5 enemies without dying in a single match in Multiplayer mode. |
| Be My Wingman (15) | Destroy an enemy aircraft that has a lock on a team mate in Co-Op Campaign mode. |
| Bite Marks (15) | Destroy an enemy in any match in Multiplayer mode. |
| Blitzkrieg (25) | Complete a Co-Op Campaign mission as a host with one or more team mates. |
| Bombardier (15) | Destroy a target with a bomb dropped from higher than 1000m (Single-player or Co-Op). |
| Bombs Away (15) | Successfully bomb a target in Campaign mode (Single-player or Co-Op). |
| Comrades in Arms (15) | Win a Team Dogfight match in Multiplayer mode. |
| Down the Rabbit Hole (15) | Win a Rabbit match in Multiplayer mode. |
| Easy Rider (15) | Complete Campaign mode on Easy Difficulty or higher (Single-player or Co-Op). |
| Eliminator (30) | Win 5 Base Assault matches in Multiplayer mode. |
| Flying Solo (15) | Win a Dogfight match in Multiplayer mode. |
| Grim Reaper (30) | Win 5 Dogfight matches in Multiplayer mode. |
| Hardcore (80) | Complete Campaign mode on Hard Difficulty (Single-player or Co-Op). |
| I Am Dangerous (15) | Kill 50 enemy units in Campaign mode (Single-player or Co-Op). |
| Man on a Mission (15) | Complete a Mission in Campaign mode (Single-player or Co-Op). |
| Master of Arms (30) | Destroy 3 enemy planes within 10 seconds in Campaign mode (Single-player or Co-Op). |
| Master of Evasion (15) | Evade 10 missiles with countermeasures in Campaign mode (Single-player or Co-Op). |
| Missile Jockey (15) | Destroy 250 enemies in Campaign mode (Single-player or Co-Op). |
| Normality (30) | Complete Campaign mode on Normal Difficulty or higher (Single-player or Co-Op). |
| Oscar Mike Golf (80) | Destroy 10 enemies without dying in a single match in Multiplayer mode. |
| Sharpshooter (30) | Destroy 50 enemy planes with cannons in Campaign mode (Single-player or Co-Op). |
| Stain Removal (80) | Kill General Demichvia (Single-player or Co-Op). |
| Straight Shooter (30) | Destroy an enemy plane with rockets (Single-player or Co-Op). |
| Survivor (15) | Win a Base Assault match in Multiplayer mode. |
| Team Guy (30) | Win 5 Team Dogfight matches in Multiplayer mode. |
| Teamblitz (25) | Complete a Co-Op Campaign mission as a client. |

| | |
|---|---|
| Throwback (15) | Complete a mission using only cannons in Campaign mode (Single-player or Co-Op). |
| Transmission Ends (30) | Kill Chairman Borzai (Single-player or Co-Op). |
| Underneath the Radar (15) | Destroy a Radar Station without being detected (Single-player or Co-Op). |
| Vectored Thrust (15) | Perform a thrust vector maneuver in Campaign mode (Single-player or Co-Op). |
| Weapons Hot (15) | Destroy an enemy aircraft with your cannons in Campaign mode (Single-player or Co-Op). |
| White Rabbit (30) | Win 5 Rabbit matches in Multiplayer mode. |
| Who Needs Brakes? (30) | Complete a Campaign mission while full speed for 90% of the mission (Single-player or Co-Op). |
| Without a Scratch (30) | Complete a Campaign mission without taking any damage (Single-player or Co-Op). |

## JONAH LOMU RUGBY CHALLENGE (XBOX 360)

### ACHIEVEMENT

| UNLOCKABLE | HOW TO UNLOCK |
|---|---|
| A Gentleman's Game (15) | Do not concede more than 2 penalties in a single match |
| Bank of Toulon (100) | Collect $100,000 Rugby Dollars |
| Conversion Point Pro (35) | Score a conversion on pro difficulty |
| End-To-End (40) | Make a try-scoring run which starts within your own in-goal area |
| Good Sport (40) | Complete 25 online matches |
| Hardcore Fan (100) | Complete Career Mode |
| Lack of Discipline (10) | The ref calls one red card against you |
| No School Boy Difficulty Here (30) | Get gold medals in every tutorial |
| Online Captain (125) | Complete 50 online matches |
| Played for Our Sins (35) | Win a match with 2 players sent off |
| Possessed (10) | Maintain Over 60% possession in a match |
| Super, Thanks For Asking (50) | Win the Rugby 15 Competition |
| Tall as Metcalfe (15) | Win 60% of lineouts in a match that aren't thrown by your team |
| Team Player (40) | Win 10 matches, each as a different team |
| That's No Oil Painting, But OK (10) | Create and save a custom player |
| The Catt Memorial Service (20) | Break through a full back with Jonah Lomu |
| There's No Forfeiting This One (50) | Win the Top 14 Competition |
| This is My House (10) | Maintain over 60% territory in a match |
| Where is Tim Timber? (50) | Win the ITM Cup Competition |
| Working On My Quads (50) | Win the Quad Nations Competition |
| World Champ Domination (60) | Win the World Championship Competition without losing or drawing a match |

## JUICED 2: HOT IMPORT NIGHTS (XBOX 360)

### DRIVER DNA CAR UNLOCKABLES

Enter the passwords in the DNA lab to unlock the special challenges. If you win the challenges, you unlock a custom version of the following cars.

| UNLOCKABLE | HOW TO UNLOCK |
|---|---|
| Audi TT 1.8L Quattro | YTHZ |
| BMW Z4 Roadster | GVDL |
| Frito-Lay Infiniti G35 | MNCH |

| Holden Monaro | RBSG |
|---|---|
| Hyundai Coupe 2.7L V6 | BSLU |
| Infiniti G35 | MRHC |
| Koenigsegg CCX | KDTR |
| Mitsubishi Prototype X | DOPX |
| Nissan 350Z | PRGN |
| Nissan Skyline R34 GT-R | JWRS |
| Saleen S7 | WIKF |
| Seat Leon Cupra R | FAMQ |

## JURASSIC: THE HUNTED (XBOX 360)

### UNLOCKABLE

| UNLOCKABLE | HOW TO UNLOCK |
|---|---|
| Laser Rifle | Beat the game on normal to unlock the Laser Rifle for Hard mode. |

## JUST CAUSE 2 (XBOX 360)

### UNLOCKABLES

| UNLOCKABLE | HOW TO UNLOCK |
|---|---|
| Bubble Blaster | South-Southwest of the Communication Outpost Gurun Lautan Lama Gamma in the Lautan Lama Desert Territory, there is a wide-open field full of trees with white leaves. In the northern part of this field there is a lone bell tower. If you climb to the top of this bell tower you will find a small table with a purple gun on it. You can equip this gun. It is the called the Bubble Blaster. |
| Lost Easter Egg | If you go to the top-left corner of the map you see an island shaped like a square. If you fly a plane over the island your plane will explode, causing you to parachute down to the beach (if over it). You will see a search sign on the beach with an arrow pointing to the jungle. Go into the jungle and you'll find the hatch from "Lost." It is even said by people that you actually can hear the smoke monster in the background. |

## JUST DANCE 3 (XBOX 360)

### ACHIEVEMENT

| UNLOCKABLE | HOW TO UNLOCK |
|---|---|
| Ace Pair - Bronze (5) | Finish a Duet with 2 players getting at least 3 stars on both choreographies (songs with 2 coaches) |
| Ace Pair - Gold (35) | Finish any Duet with 2 players getting 5 stars on both choreographies (songs with 2 coaches) |
| Ace Pair - Silver (25) | Finish a Duet with 2 players getting at least 4 stars on both choreographies (songs with 2 coaches) |
| Big Band Theory - Bronze (5) | Finish any Dance Crew with all 4 players getting at least 3 stars (songs with 4 coaches) |
| Big Band Theory - Gold (35) | Finish any Dance Crew with all 4 players getting 5 stars (songs with 4 coaches) |
| Big Band Theory - Silver (25) | Finish any Dance Crew with all 4 players getting at least 4 stars (songs with 4 coaches) |
| Choreographer - Bronze (5) | Create a choreography in Just Create |
| Choreographer - Gold (35) | Create 50 choreographies in Just Create |
| Choreographer - Silver (25) | Create 25 choreographies in Just Create |
| Constellation Maker - Bronze (5) | Get at least 3 stars on every choreography in the "Songs" menu |
| Constellation Maker - Gold (35) | Get 5 stars on every choreography in the "Songs" menu |
| Constellation Maker - Silver (25) | Get at least 4 stars on every choreography in the "Songs" menu |
| Dancing with The Devil (25) | Dance between Midnight and 4am |
| Eyes Closed - Bronze (5) | Get 5 stars on any song after disabling pictograms in the Settings menu (excluding Just Create) |

| | |
|---|---|
| **Eyes Closed - Gold (35)** | Get 5 stars on 10 songs in a row after disabling pictograms in Settings menu (excluding Just Create) |
| **Eyes Closed - Silver (25)** | Get 5 stars on 5 songs in a row after disabling pictograms in Settings menu (excluding Just Create) |
| **Highway to Stars - Bronze (5)** | Get 5 stars on 2 songs in a row from the "Songs" menu |
| **Highway to Stars - Gold (35)** | Get 5 stars on 10 songs in a row from the "Songs" menu |
| **Highway to Stars - Silver (25)** | Get 5 stars on 6 songs in a row from the "Songs" menu |
| **I could do this all night! (25)** | Dance every song in the "Songs" menu in a row while in the same game |
| **Just Dance Master! (15)** | Play every song in the "Songs" menu at least once |
| **Marathon (25)** | Dance for more than 1 hour in Non-Stop Shuffle |
| **Morning Exercise (15)** | Get 1000 Sweat Points between 5am and 9am with Sweat Mode activated |
| **Part of the community - Bronze (5)** | Play one of your own choreographies |
| **Part of the community - Gold (5)** | Upload one of your own choreographies |
| **Part of the community - Silver (5)** | Download one Just Create choreography |
| **Perfectionist - Bronze (5)** | Finish any song in the "Songs" menu without missing a move |
| **Perfectionist - Gold (35)** | Finish any song in the "Songs" menu with at least 90% of "Perfect" moves |
| **Perfectionist - Silver (25)** | Finish any song in the "Songs" menu, and score "Good" or better on all moves |
| **Saturday Night Fever (15)** | Play at least 3 hours Between 8pm and 3am on a Saturday |
| **Simon's Best - Bronze (5)** | Get 3 stars in Simon Says |
| **Simon's Best - Gold (35)** | Get 5 stars in Simon Says |
| **Simon's Best - Silver (25)** | Get 4 stars in Simon Says |
| **Singer - Bronze (5)** | Shout Out at least once in a song |
| **Singer - Gold (35)** | Shout Out at least once in 20 different songs |
| **Singer - Silver (25)** | Shout Out at least once in 10 different songs |
| **Stylist - Bronze (5)** | Get all Styles once (excluding Just Create) |
| **Stylist - Gold (35)** | Get all Styles with the same player during one game session! (excluding Just Create) |
| **Stylist - Silver (25)** | Get four Dance Styles at the same time! (excluding Just Create) |
| **Super Dancer - Bronze (5)** | Play 50 songs (excluding Just Create) |
| **Super Dancer - Gold (35)** | Play 200 songs (excluding Just Create) |
| **Super Dancer - Silver (25)** | Play 100 songs (excluding Just Create) |
| **Sweat & Score - Bronze (5)** | Reach 150 Sweat Points with a 3-star rating on any song with Sweat Mode activated |
| **Sweat & Score - Gold (35)** | Reach 350 Sweat Points with a 5-star rating on any song with Sweat Mode activated |
| **Sweat & Score - Silver (25)** | Reach 250 Sweat Points with a 4-star rating on any song with Sweat Mode activated |
| **Sweat Me a River - Bronze (5)** | Earn 1,000 Sweat Points with Sweat Mode activated |
| **Sweat Me a River - Gold (35)** | Earn 20,000 Sweat Points with Sweat Mode activated |
| **Sweat Me a River - Silver (25)** | Earn 10,000 Sweat Points with Sweat Mode activated |
| **That's my jam! (5)** | Play the same song five times in a row |
| **The Daltons (15)** | Get 4 Players to line up side by side from shortest to tallest while in the pre-game Lobby |

# KARAOKE REVOLUTION (XBOX 360, PlayStation 3)

## UNLOCKABLES

Meet the following conditions to unlock these items for use in Edit Venue Mode.

| UNLOCKABLE | HOW TO UNLOCK |
|---|---|
| Angel Heart Venue Item | Complete 30 gigs in Career Mode. |
| Area 51 Venue Item | Complete 55 gigs in Career Mode. |
| Cityscapes Venue Backdrops | Complete three gigs in Career Mode. |
| Flaming Biker Venue Item | Complete 90 gigs in Career Mode. |
| Giant Gorilla Venue Item | Complete 80 gigs in Career Mode. |
| Glowing Stairway and Fire Valley Backdrops | Complete 25 gigs in Career Mode. |
| Hearts Venue Item | Complete 60 gigs in Career Mode. |
| Hong Kong Venue Item | Complete seven gigs in Career Mode. |
| Leaping Tiger Venue Item | Complete 35 gigs in Career Mode. |
| Liberty Venue Item | Complete 45 gigs in Career Mode. |
| Music Genres Venue Item | Complete five gigs in Career Mode. |
| Nature Venue Backdrops | Complete 70 gigs in Career Mode. |
| Pirate Ship Venue Item | Complete 65 gigs in Career Mode. |
| Pods Venue Item | Complete 50 gigs in Career Mode. |
| Space Cruiser Venue Set | Complete 20 gigs in Career Mode. |
| Stone Heads Venue Item | Complete 15 gigs in Career Mode. |
| Urban Venue Backdrops | Complete 10 gigs in Career Mode. |
| Zombie Venue Item | Complete 40 gigs in Career Mode. |

# KILLZONE 3 (PlayStation 3)

## TROPHIES

| UNLOCKABLE | HOW TO UNLOCK |
|---|---|
| Aerial Superiority - Kill 5 Helghast while in the air (Bronze) | Killed 5 Helghast while airborne using the Jetpack |
| Bring It Down - Defeat the MAWLR (Bronze) | Defeated the MAWLR defending the Space Elevator |
| Cagefighter - Kill 10 Helghast using Brutal Melee (Bronze) | Killed 10 Helaghast using Brutal Melee |
| Close Quarters Killer - Kill 25 Helghast Brutal Melee (Silver) | Killed 25 Helghast using Brutal using Melee |
| Completist - Destroy everything on the MAWLR (Bronze) | Destroyed every destructible weapon on the MAWLR while on foot and on the Intruder |
| Double Trouble - Reach the river in Co-op (Bronze) | Made it to the Corinth River in Co-op mode |
| Eagle Eye - Every Sniper Rifle bullet is a kill (Bronze) | Shot and killed 6 Helghast using the Sniper Rifle without reloading or switching weapons |
| Evening The Odds - Kill 500 Helghast (Bronze) | Kill 500 Helghast |
| Excessive Force - Kill a lone Helghast with the WASP secondary fire (Bronze) | Used the secondary fire function of the WASP launcher to kill a single Helghast |

| | |
|---|---|
| **Fight To The Last - Kill 1500 Helghast (Silver)** | Killed 1500 Helghast |
| **Frag Out - Kill 3 Helghast with 1 Frag Grenade (Bronze)** | Killed 3 Helghast using 1 fragmentation grenade |
| **Frazzle Dazzle - Kill 3 Helghast with one) shot from the StA5X Arc Cannon (Bronze** | Used the StA5X Arc Cannon to kill 3 Helghast with one shot |
| **Go Down And Stay Down - Destroy the ATAC (Bronze)** | Defeated the ATAC outside the Stahl Arms facility |
| **Grand Slam - Win a match in 3 multiplayer (Gold)** | Won a match in Operations, **modes** Warzone & Guerrilla Warfare modes |
| **Hand To Hand Master - Kill 50 Helghast Brutal Melee (Silver)** | Killed 50 Helghast using Brutal **using** Melee |
| **Handy Man - Repair an object (Bronze)** | Repaired an object for the first time |
| **Iced - Destroy all Ice-Saws and Dropships (Bronze)** | Destroyed all 4 Helghast Ice-Saws and all 6 Dropships |
| **In Your Face - First Brutal Melee (Bronze)** | Performed first Brutal Melee move |
| **Into The Lair - Reach the cable car (Bronze)** | Reached the cable car and gained access to Stahl Arms South |
| **Iron Man - Get a kill with the Exo (Bronze)** | Killed a player using the Exo in any multiplayer mode |
| **ISA TV - Establish communications (Bronze)** | Made contact with Earth |
| **Jail Break - Liberate Narville (Bronze)** | Liberated Narville from Stahl Arms South |
| **Let's Go Home - Destroy Stahl's Cruiser (Gold)** | Destroyed Stahl's Cruiser and left the planet on any difficulty |
| **Medic! - Revive another player (Bronze)** | Revived a friendly player for the first time |
| **Minigunned - Destroy all targets (Bronze)** | Destroyed everything while using the Minigun on the Intruder |
| **Mopping Up - Kill 40 Helghast foot soldiers (Bronze)** | Killed 40 or more Helghast foot soldiers on the beach |
| **Never There - Sneak past Helghast (Bronze)** | Sneaked past all Helghast in the Jungle without alerting any of them |
| **No Witnesses - Destroy all dropships on Highway (Bronze)** | Destroy all dropships on the **the** Highway |
| **Now It's Personal - Kill 1000 Helghast (Silver)** | Killed 1000 Helghast |
| **Now You See Me - Kill using Cloak (Bronze)** | Killed another player while cloaked |
| **One Each - Kill 3 Helghast with Shotgun Pistol, no reloads (Bronze)** | Shot and killed 3 Helghast using the Shotgun Pistol without reloading or switching weapons |
| **Pilot's Wings - Mid-air kill (Bronze)** | Got a mid-air kill using the Jet Pack in any multiplayer mode |
| **Pinpoint - Kill the Heavy with an StA-14 (Bronze)** | Killed the Heavy using the StA-14 rifle |
| **Platinum (Platinum)** | Collect all Killzone 3 trophies |
| **Power Spike - Nail a Helghast to an exploding object (Bronze)** | Used the Boltgun to nail a Helghast to an exploding object |
| **Quick Exit - Escape the Oil Rig quickly (Bronze)** | Got off the 2nd rig within 2 minutes. |
| **Ready For Battle - Complete weapons training (Bronze)** | Completed weapons training in Prologue |
| **Save The Intruders - Arc APCs destroyed (Bronze)** | Successfully assisted with defeating the Arc APCs |
| **Sawn Off - Destroy all chasing APC's (Bronze)** | Destroyed all chasing SawBlade APC's in the Senlin Beach section |
| **Shattered - Destroy all glass in the Labs (Bronze)** | Destroy all glass panes in the Stahl Arms South laboratories |

| | |
|---|---|
| Smoking Wrecks - Destroy all Tanks on Senlin Beach (Bronze) | Destroyed all the Helghast Tanks in the Senlin Beach section |
| Spiky Personality - Kill a Helghast using a Burster (Bronze) | Killed a Helghast by shooting a Burster plant |
| Spread The Love - Kill 5 Helghast at once using the WASP's secondary fire (Bronze) | Killed 5 Helghast at once using the secondary fire mode of the WASP launcher |
| Spy Game - Kill using Disguise (Bronze) | Killed another player while disguised |
| Stranded Together - Reach the Extraction Point in Co-op (Bronze) | Made it to the Extraction Point in Co-op mode |
| Team Player - Play a match as part of a squad (Bronze) | Joined and completed a match as part of a squad |
| Time For A Dip - Reach the river (Bronze) | Reached the Corinth River with the convoy |
| Turf War - Capture a Tactical Spawn Point (Bronze) | Captured a Tactical Spawn Point for the first time |
| Turn The Tables - Melee Kill a Capture Trooper (Bronze) | Killed a Capture Trooper using melee |
| Up Close & Personal - Brutal Melee another player (Bronze) | Used the Brutal Melee move against another player |
| Victory - Complete Campaign on Elite (Gold) | Completed every mission on Elite difficulty |
| You Drive - Drive the Mobile Factory (Bronze) | Took over the controls of the Mobile Factory |

## KINECT SPORTS SEASON TWO (XBOX 360)

### ACHIEVEMENT

| UNLOCKABLE | HOW TO UNLOCK |
|---|---|
| 180 Star! (25) | Hit ten 180s when playing darts (cumulative) |
| Ace Pitcher (20) | Use all pitching techniques and speeds when playing baseball |
| Ace-Tastic (20) | Hit your 1st 'Ace' serve when playing tennis |
| All... The... Way (20) | Score a touchdown on a kick return when playing Football |
| Balloon Buster (25) | Score more than 25 points in Pop Darts |
| Below Par Star! (25) | Play the full nine holes of Maple Lake and finish under par |
| Big Air (20) | Perform a perfect jump on any ski run when playing Skiing |
| Birds Eye View (20) | View a golf hole using the 'hole preview' gesture when playing golf |
| Bobble and Out (20) | Catch a bobbled ball when playing baseball |
| Bull's Eye Bonanza (20) | Hit the bull's eye three times in one turn (three darts) when playing darts |
| Bunker Beater (20) | Hit the ball into the hole straight out of a sand bunker when playing golf |
| Calling the Shot (20) | Complete a pass after calling an audible when playing Football |
| Challenge Challenger (25) | Send out your first challenge in Kinect Sports: Season Two |
| Challenge Squashed (25) | Beat your first challenge in Kinect Sports: Season Two |
| Crowd Control (5) | Avateer to work the crowd up into a frenzy in any sport |
| Far Out Field Goal (20) | Score a field goal with at least 40 yards to go when playing Football |
| Game Winning Field Goal (20) | Win a game of Football on a field goal |
| Go! Go! Go! (20) | Perform a perfect start out of the starting gate when playing Skiing |
| Grand Slam (20) | Hit a home run with the bases loaded when playing baseball |

| | |
|---|---|
| **Home Runs for Fun (20)** | Score 5 home runs in a single game when playing baseball |
| **Kinect Sports-a-thon (25)** | Play Kinect Sports: Season Two for more than 2 hours (cumulative time) |
| **Let the games commence (5)** | Play any sport on Kinect Sports: Season Two for the first time |
| **Long Bomb (20)** | Score a touchdown with a 60+ yard passing play when playing football |
| **Maximum Checkout (20)** | Score 170 (triple-20, triple-20, bull's eye) to end a game of darts |
| **Maximum Velocity (20)** | Go fast by holding the tuck position for at least 10 seconds when playing Skiing |
| **Nine Darter (20)** | Complete a game of darts with a nine-dart checkout. |
| **Not so Ace! (20)** | Score a return point from an incoming perfect serve when playing tennis |
| **One and Done (20)** | Score a touchdown on your 1st down when playing football |
| **Out of the Park (25)** | Score more than 2500 points in Home Run Hero |
| **Peak Perfection (20)** | Race a perfect race on all three hills at Sunny Peaks |
| **Perfect Race (20)** | Race a perfect race (don't miss any gates) on both ski runs when playing Skiing |
| **Perfect Race Star! (25)** | Complete six perfect races when playing skiing (cumulative score) |
| **Pitching for Points (25)** | Score more than 50 points in Ocean Driver |
| **Putting Perfection (20)** | Putt the ball in from over 40 yards on Lighthouse Bay when playing golf |
| **Read the Signs (20)** | Match the catcher's signal when pitching a ball when playing baseball |
| **Return Master (20)** | Score a point using the 'power' shot technique when playing tennis |
| **Rickrolled (10)** | Have your first motivational song play when playing Kinect Sports: Season Two |
| **Running Star! (25)** | Run 1000 yards when playing Football (cumulative score) |
| **Shanghai (20)** | Hit a single, double and triple of the same number when playing darts |
| **Slugger Star! (25)** | Hit the ball 5000 feet when playing baseball (cumulative score) |
| **Smash Shot Star! (25)** | Win five points on smash shots when playing tennis (cumulative) |
| **Smashing Service (25)** | Score more than 90 points in Smash Alley |
| **Spin And In (20)** | Make the ball roll around the rim of the hole and in when playing golf |
| **Tee and in (20)** | Hit the ball in the hole from the tee off for a hole in one when playing golf |
| **Ton 80 (20)** | Score 180 (3 triple-20s) in one turn when playing darts |
| **Victory! (5)** | Win any sport on Kinect Sports: Season Two for the first time |
| **What Obstacles? (25)** | Score more than 50 points in Downhill Dodge |
| **You cannot be serious (20)** | Win your first "objection" scenario when playing tennis |
| **You did it for the Fans! (5)** | Earn your 1st group of Fans by playing Kinect Sports: Season Two |
| **You're the judge, I'm the jury (20)** | Hit a line judge with the tennis ball when playing tennis |

## UNLOCKABLE

| UNLOCKABLE | HOW TO UNLOCK |
| --- | --- |
| Kinect Sports Darts Top Hat | Stay on target throughout your career with this awesome award for reaching level 5. Woohoo! |
| Kinect Sports Football Hat | Show your love for all things football with this award for reaching fan level 2. I'm so jealous! |
| Kinect Sports Golf Green Cap | Impress everyone at the clubhouse with this award for reaching the dizzy heights of fan level 10. |

# KINGDOM HEARTS: BIRTH BY SLEEP (PSP)

## UNLOCKABLES

| UNLOCKABLE | HOW TO UNLOCK |
| --- | --- |
| Final Chapter | Acquire all Xehanort Reports |
| Lingering Spirit Vanitas boss | Clear Final Story |
| Mysterious Figure boss | Beat Lingering spirit Vanitas at Keyblade Graveyard |
| Trinity Archives | Complete the story with any character |

## SECRET MOVIE

To unlock the secret movie, you must do the following:

| UNLOCKABLE | HOW TO UNLOCK |
| --- | --- |
| On Critical mode | Complete the final episode |
| On Proud mode | Complete the final episode |
| On Standard mode | Complete 100% of the Reports Section % and complete the final episode |

# KNIGHTS IN THE NIGHTMARE (DS)

## UNLOCKABLES

| UNLOCKABLE | HOW TO UNLOCK |
| --- | --- |
| Hard Mode | Beat the game on Normal mode. |
| Play as Astart | Beat the game. |
| Nightmare mode | Beat the game on Hard mode. |

# KUNG FU PANDA (XBOX 360, PlayStation 3)

## CODES

From the main menu, select Extras and then select Cheats.

| EFFECT | CODE |
| --- | --- |
| All Multiplayer Characters | ←,↓,←,→,↓ |
| Big Head Mode (Story Mode) | ↓,↑,←,→,→ |
| Infinite Chi | ↓,→,←,↑,↓ |
| Invulnerability | ↓,↓,→,↑,← |
| Dragon Warrior Outfit (Multiplayer Mode) | ←,↓,→,←,↑ |
| 4x Damage Multiplier | ↑,↓,↑,→,← |

# KUNG FU PANDA (Wii)

## CODES

From the main menu, select Extras and then select Cheats.

| EFFECT | CODE |
| --- | --- |
| All Multiplayer Characters | ⇦,⇩,⇦,⇨,⇩ |
| Big Head Mode (Story Mode) | ⇩,⇧,⇦,⇨,⇨ |
| Infinite Chi | ⇩,⇨,⇦,⇧,⇩ |
| Invulnerability | ⇩,⇩,⇨,⇧,⇦ |
| Dragon Warrior Outfit (Multiplayer Mode) | ⇦,⇩,⇨,⇦,⇧ |
| 4x Damage Multiplier | ⇧,⇩,⇧,⇨,⇦ |

## LAIR   (PlayStation 3)

### PASSWORDS

Enter into the game's Cheat menu:

| PASSWORD | EFFECT |
|---|---|
| chicken | Chicken Curry video |
| 686F7420636F66666565 | Hot Coffee video |
| koelsch | Unlocks Stable option for all levels on the Mission Select screen |

## LEFT 4 DEAD   (XBOX 360)

| UNLOCKABLE | HOW TO UNLOCK |
|---|---|
| Rocket Launcher | Complete the game on any difficulty. |

## LEGO BATMAN   (XBOX 360), (PlayStation 3)

### CODES

Enter the codes on the second level of the Batcave at the computer above the outfit changer.

| EFFECT | XBOX 360 CODE | PLAYSTATION 3 CODE |
|---|---|---|
| Alfred | ZAQ637 | ZAQ637 |
| Bat-Tank | KNTT4B | KNTT4B |
| Batgirl | JKR331 | JKR331 |
| Bruce Wayne | BDJ327 | BDJ327 |
| Bruce Wayne's Private Jet | LEA664 | LEA664 |
| Catwoman (Classic) | M1AAWW | M1AAWW |
| Catwoman's Motorcycle | HPL826 | HPL826 |
| Clown Goon | HJK327 | HJK327 |
| Commissioner Gordon | DDP967 | DDP967 |
| Fishmonger | HGY748 | HGY748 |
| Freeze Girl | XVK541 | XVK541 |
| Garbage Truck | DUS483 | DUS483 |
| Glideslam | BBD7BY | BBD7BY |
| Goon Helicopter | GCH328 | GCH328 |
| Harbor Helicopter | CHP735 | CHP735 |
| Harley Quinn's Hammer Truck | RDT637 | RDT637 |
| Joker Goon | UTF782 | UTF782 |
| Joker Henchman | YUN924 | YUN924 |
| Mad Hatter | JCA283 | JCA283 |
| Mad Hatter's Glider | HS000W | HS000W |
| Mad Hatter's Steamboat | M4DM4N | M4DM4N |
| Man-Bat | NYU942 | NYU942 |
| Military Policeman | MKL382 | MKL382 |
| Mr. Freeze's Iceberg | ICYICE | ICYICE |
| Mr. Freeze's Kart | BCT229 | BCT229 |
| Nightwing | MVY759 | MVY759 |

**CODES & CHEATS**

| | | |
|---|---|---|
| Penguin Goon | NKA238 | NKA238 |
| Penguin Goon Submarine | BTN248 | BTN248 |
| Penguin Henchman | BJH782 | BJH782 |
| Penguin Minion | KJP748 | KJP748 |
| Poison Ivy Goon | GTB899 | GTB899 |
| Police Bike | LJP234 | LJP234 |
| Police Boat | PLC999 | PLC999 |
| Police Car | KJL832 | KJL832 |
| Police Helicopter | CWR732 | CWR732 |
| Police Marksman | HKG984 | HKG984 |
| Police Officer | JRY983 | JRY983 |
| Police Van | MAC788 | MAC788 |
| Police Watercraft | VJD328 | VJD328 |
| Riddler Goon | CRY928 | CRY928 |
| Riddler Henchman | XEU824 | XEU824 |
| Riddler's Jet | HAHAHA | HAHAHA |
| Robin's Submarine | TTF453 | TTF453 |
| S.W.A.T. | HTF114 | HTF114 |
| Sailor | NAV592 | NAV592 |
| Scientist | JFL786 | JFL786 |
| Security Guard | PLB946 | PLB946 |
| The Joker (Tropical) | CCB199 | CCB199 |
| The Joker's Van | JUK657 | JUK657 |
| Two-Face's Armored Truck | EFE933 | EFE933 |
| Yeti | NJL412 | NJL412 |
| Zoo Sweeper | DWR243 | DWR243 |

## EXTRA CODES

| EFFECT | XBOX 360 CODE | PLAYSTATION 3 CODE |
|---|---|---|
| Always Score Multiply | 9LRGNB | 9LRGNB |
| Area Effect | TL3EKT | TL3EKT |
| Armor Plating | N8JZEK | N8JZEK |
| Bats | XFP4E2 | XFP4E2 |
| Beep Beep | RAFTU8 | RAFTU8 |
| Character Studs | DY13BD | DY13BD |
| Decoy | TQ09K3 | TQ09K3 |
| Disguise | GEC3MD | GEC3MD |
| Extra Toggle | EWAW7W | EWAW7W |
| Extra Hearts | ML3KHP | ML3KHP |
| Fast Batarangs | JRBDCB | JRBDCB |
| Fast Build | GHJ2DY | GHJ2DY |
| Fast Grapple | RM4PR8 | RM4PR8 |
| Fast Walk | ZOLM6N | ZOLM6N |
| Faster Pieces | EVG26J | EVG26J |
| Flaming Batarangs (Used with heat batman) | D8NYWH | D8NYWH |
| Freeze Batarang | XPN4NG | XPN4NG |
| Ice Rink | KLKL4G | KLKL4G |
| Immune to Freeze | JXUDY6 | JXUDY6 |
| Invincible | WYD5CP | WYD5CP |

| Minikit Detector | ZXGH9J | ZXGH9J |
| --- | --- | --- |
| More Batarang Targets | XWP645 | XWP645 |
| More Detonators | TNTN6B | TNTN6B |
| Piece Detector | KHJ544 | KHJ544 |
| Power Brick Detector | MMN786 | MMN786 |
| Regenerate Hearts | HJH7HJ | HJH7HJ |
| Score x2 | N4NR3E | N4NR3E |
| Score x4 | CX9MAT | CX9MAT |
| Score x6 | MLVNF2 | MLVNF2 |
| Score x8 | WCCDB9 | WCCDB9 |
| Score x10 | 18HW07 | 18HW07 |
| Silhouettes | YK4TPH | YK4TPH |
| Slam | BBD7BY | BBD7BY |
| Sonic Pain | THTL4X | THTL4X |
| Stud Magnet | LK2DY4 | LK2DY4 |

## LEGO BATMAN (Wii)

### CODES

Enter the codes on the second level of the Batcave at the computer above the outfit changer.

| EFFECT | CODE |
| --- | --- |
| Bruce Wayne | BDJ327 |
| Commissioner Gordon | DDP967 |
| More Batarang Targets | XWP645 |
| Nightwing | MVY759 |
| Penguin Minion | KJP748 |
| Police Van | MAC788 |
| The Joker (Tropical) | CCB199 |
| Yeti | NJL412 |

### FREE PLAY CODES

| EFFECT | CODE |
| --- | --- |
| Unlocks Alfred in Free Play | ZAQ637 |
| Unlocks Commissioner Gordon in Free Play | DPP967 |
| Unlocks Free Girl in Free Play | XVK541 |
| Unlocks Harley Quinn's Hammer Truck | RDT637 |
| Unlocks More Batarang Targets | XWP645 |
| Unlocks Penguin Henchman in Free Play | BJH782 |
| Unlocks Yeti in Free Play | NJL412 |

## LEGO BATMAN (DS)

### CODES

Enter the following codes at the main menu. If you enter them correctly you will hear a sound.

| EFFECT | CODE |
| --- | --- |
| Add 1 Million Studs | Ⓧ, Ⓨ, Ⓑ, Ⓑ, Ⓨ, Ⓧ, L, L, R, R, ⬇, ⬇, ⬆, ⬆, +START, +SELECT |
| All Characters | Ⓧ, ⬇, Ⓑ, ⬆, Ⓨ, ⬅, +START, ⬆, R, R, L, R, R, ⬇, ⬆, ⬇, Ⓨ, Ⓨ, +START, +SELECT |
| All Episodes and Free Play mode | ⬇, ⬆, R, L, Ⓧ, Ⓨ, ⬆, ⬆, Ⓑ, L, R, L, ⬇, ⬇, ⬆, Ⓨ, Ⓨ, Ⓧ, Ⓑ, Ⓑ, ⬇, L, R, +START, +SELECT |
| All Extras | ⬇, ⬆, L, R, L, R, ⬇, ⬆, Ⓧ, Ⓨ, Ⓨ, Ⓑ, Ⓑ, L, ⬇, ⬆, L, R, L, R, ⬇, ⬇, +START, +SELECT |

## LEGO BATMAN (PSP)

### CODES

Enter the codes on the second level of the Batcave at the computer above the outfit changer.

| EFFECT | CODE |
| --- | --- |
| Alfred | ZAQ637 |
| Bat-Tank | KNTT4B |
| Batgirl | JKR331 |
| Bruce Wayne | BDJ327 |
| Bruce Wayne's Private Jet | LEA664 |
| Catwoman (Classic) | M1AAWW |
| Catwoman's Motorcycle | HPL826 |
| Clown Goon | HJK327 |
| Commissioner Gordon | DDP967 |
| Fishmonger | HGY748 |
| Freeze Girl | XVK541 |
| Garbage Truck | DUS483 |
| Glideslam | BBD7BY |
| Goon Helicopter | GCH328 |
| Harbor Helicopter | CHP735 |
| Harley Quinn's Hammer Truck | RDT637 |
| Joker Goon | UTF782 |
| Joker Henchman | YUN924 |
| Mad Hatter | JCA283 |
| Mad Hatter's Glider | HS000W |
| Mad Hatter's Steamboat | M4DM4N |
| Man-Bat | NYU942 |
| Military Policeman | MKL382 |
| Mr. Freeze's Iceberg | ICYICE |
| Mr. Freeze's Kart | BCT229 |
| Nightwing | MVY759 |
| Penguin Goon | NKA238 |
| Penguin Goon Submarine | BTN248 |
| Penguin Henchman | BJH782 |
| Penguin Minion | KJP748 |
| Poison Ivy Goon | GTB899 |
| Police Bike | LJP234 |
| Police Boat | PLC999 |
| Police Car | KJL832 |
| Police Helicopter | CWR732 |
| Police Marksman | HKG984 |
| Police Officer | JRY983 |
| Police Van | MAC788 |
| Police Watercraft | VJD328 |
| Riddler Goon | CRY928 |
| Riddler Henchman | XEU824 |
| Riddler's Jet | HAHAHA |
| Robin's Submarine | TTF453 |
| S.W.A.T. | HTF114 |
| Sailor | NAV592 |
| Scientist | JFL786 |

| | |
|---|---|
| Security Guard | PLB946 |
| The Joker (Tropical) | CCB199 |
| The Joker's Van | JUK657 |
| Two-Face's Armored Truck | EFE933 |
| Yeti | NJL412 |
| Zoo Sweeper | DWR243 |

## EXTRA CODES

| EFFECT | CODE |
|---|---|
| Always Score Multiply | 9LRGNB |
| Area Effect | TL3EKT |
| Armor Plating | N8JZEK |
| Bats | XFP4E2 |
| Beep Beep | RAFTU8 |
| Character Studs | DY13BD |
| Decoy | TQ09K3 |
| Disguise | GEC3MD |
| Extra Toggle | EWAW7W |
| Extra Hearts | ML3KHP |
| Fast Batarangs | JRBDCB |
| Fast Build | GHJ2DY |
| Fast Grapple | RM4PR8 |
| Fast Walk | ZOLM6N |
| Faster Pieces | EVG26J |
| Flaming Batarangs (Used with heat batman) | D8NYWH |
| Freeze Batarang | XPN4NG |
| Ice Rink | KLKL4G |
| Immune to Freeze | JXUDY6 |
| Invincible | WYD5CP |
| Minikit Detector | ZXGH9J |
| More Batarang Targets | XWP645 |
| More Detonators | TNTN6B |
| Piece Detector | KHJ544 |
| Power Brick Detector | MMN786 |
| Regenerate Hearts | HJH7HJ |
| Score x2 | N4NR3E |
| Score x4 | CX9MAT |
| Score x6 | MLVNF2 |
| Score x8 | WCCDB9 |
| Score x10 | 18HW07 |
| Silhouettes | YK4TPH |
| Slam | BBD7BY |
| Sonic Pain | THTL4X |
| Stud Magnet | LK2DY4 |

## LEGO HARRY POTTER: YEARS 1-4 (XBOX 360), (PlayStation 3), (Wii)

### GOLD BRICK CODES

Enter the codes upstairs in Wiseacres Wizarding Supplies.

| EFFECT | XBOX 360 CODE | PLAYSTATION 3 CODE | WII CODE |
|---|---|---|---|
| Gold Brick 01 | QE4VC7 | QE4VC7 | QE4VC7 |
| Gold Brick 02 | FY8H97 | FY8H97 | FY8H97 |
| Gold Brick 03 | 3MQT4P | 3MQT4P | 3MQT4P |

| Gold Brick 04 | PQPM7Z | PQPM7Z | PQPM7Z |
| Gold Brick 05 | ZY2CPA | ZY2CPA | ZY2CPA |
| Gold Brick 06 | 3GMTP6 | 3GMTP6 | 3GMTP6 |
| Gold Brick 07 | XY6VYZ | XY6VYZ | XY6VYZ |
| Gold Brick 08 | TUNC4W | TUNC4W | TUNC4W |
| Gold Brick 09 | EJ42Q6 | EJ42Q6 | EJ42Q6 |
| Gold Brick 10 | GFJCV9 | GFJCV9 | GFJCV9 |
| Gold Brick 11 | DZCY6G | DZCY6G | DZCY6G |

## MISCELLANEOUS CODES

Enter the codes upstairs in Wiseacres Wizarding Supplies.

| EFFECT | XBOX 360 CODE | PLAYSTATION 3 CODE | WII CODE |
| --- | --- | --- | --- |
| Carrot Wands | AUC8EH | AUC8EH | AUC8EH |
| Character Studs | H27KGC | H27KGC | H27KGC |
| Character Token Detector | HA79V8 | HA79V8 | HA79V8 |
| Christmas | T7PVVN | T7PVVN | T7PVVN |
| Disguise | 4DMK2R | 4DMK2R | 4DMK2R |
| Extra Hearts | J9U6Z9 | J9U6Z9 | J9U6Z9 |
| Fall Rescue | ZEX7MV | ZEX7MV | ZEX7MV |
| Fast Dig | Z9BFAD | Z9BFAD | Z9BFAD |
| Fast Magic | FA3GQA | FA3GQA | FA3GQA |
| Gold Brick Detector | 84QNQN | 84QNQN | 84QNQN |
| Hogwarts Crest Detector | TTMC6D | TTMC6D | TTMC6D |
| Ice Rink | F88VUW | F88VUW | F88VUW |
| Invincibility | QQWC6B | QQWC6B | QQWC6B |
| Red Brick Detector | 7AD7HE | 7AD7HE | 7AD7HE |
| Regenerate Hearts | 89ML2W | 89ML2W | 89ML2W |
| Score x2 | 74YKR7 | 74YKR7 | 74YKR7 |
| Score x4 | J3WHNK | J3WHNK | J3WHNK |
| Score x6 | XK9ANE | XK9ANE | XK9ANE |
| Score x8 | HUFV2H | HUFV2H | HUFV2H |
| Score x10 | H8X69Y | H8X69Y | H8X69Y |
| Silhouettes | HZBVX7 | HZBVX7 | HZBVX7 |
| Singing Mandrake | BMEU6X | BMEU6X | BMEU6X |
| Stud Magnet | 67FKWZ | 67FKWZ | 67FKWZ |

## SPELL CODES

Enter the codes upstairs in Wiseacres Wizarding Supplies.

| EFFECT | XBOX 360 CODE | PLAYSTATION 3 CODE | WII CODE |
| --- | --- | --- | --- |
| Accio | VE9VV7 | VE9VV7 | VE9VV7 |
| Anteoculatia | QFB6NR | QFB6NR | QFB6NR |
| Calvorio | 6DNR6L | 6DNR6L | 6DNR6L |
| Colovaria | 9GJ442 | 9GJ442 | 9GJ442 |
| Engorgio Skullus | CD4JLX | CD4JLX | CD4JLX |
| Entomorphis | MYN3NB | MYN3NB | MYN3NB |
| Flipendo | ND2L7W | ND2L7W | ND2L7W |
| Glacius | ERA9DR | ERA9DR | ERA9DR |
| Herbifors | H8FTHL | H8FTHL | H8FTHL |
| Incarcerous | YEB9Q9 | YEB9Q9 | YEB9Q9 |
| Locomotor Mortis | 2M2XJ6 | 2M2XJ6 | 2M2XJ6 |
| Multicorfors | JK6QRM | JK6QRM | JK6QRM |

| | | | |
|---|---|---|---|
| Redactum Skullus | UW8LRH | UW8LRH | UW8LRH |
| Rictusempra | 2UCA3M | 2UCA3M | 2UCA3M |
| Slugulus Eructo | U6EE8X | U6EE8X | U6EE8X |
| Stupefy | UWDJ4Y | UWDJ4Y | UWDJ4Y |
| Tarentallegra | KWWQ44 | KWWQ44 | KWWQ44 |
| Trip Jinx | YZNRF6 | YZNRF6 | YZNRF6 |

## LEGO HARRY POTTER: YEARS 1-4 (DS)

### GOLD BRICK CODES

Enter the codes upstairs in Wiseacres Wizarding Supplies.

| EFFECT | CODE |
|---|---|
| Gold Brick 01 | QE4VC7 |
| Gold Brick 02 | FY8H97 |
| Gold Brick 03 | 3MQT4P |
| Gold Brick 04 | PQPM7Z |
| Gold Brick 05 | ZY2CPA |
| Gold Brick 06 | 3GMTP6 |
| Gold Brick 07 | XY6VYZ |
| Gold Brick 08 | TUNC4W |
| Gold Brick 09 | EJ42Q6 |
| Gold Brick 10 | GFJCV9 |
| Gold Brick 11 | DZCY6G |

## LEGO HARRY POTTER: YEARS 5-7 (PlayStation 3)

### TROPHY

| UNLOCKABLE | HOW TO UNLOCK |
|---|---|
| 'That's Unfortunate' (Bronze) | Complete 'The Thief's Downfall' |
| 10 Points to Gryffindor (Platinum) | Collect all Trophies |
| A Dish Best Served Cold (Bronze) | Defeat Bellatrix with Neville (Waiter) in a duel |
| A Minifig's Best Friend (Silver) | Unlock every character with a pet (Single Player Only) |
| A Riddle Revealed (Bronze) | Complete 'Felix Felicis' |
| A Sirius Family Issue (Bronze) | Defeat Bellatrix as any Sirius Black character variant in a duel |
| A Wise Disguise (Bronze) | Complete 'Magic is Might' |
| Accordion to Grawp (Bronze) | Complete 'A Giant Virtuoso' |
| Albus Percival Wulfric Brian (Bronze) | Complete 'Dark Times' |
| All Was Well (Bronze) | Complete Year 8 |
| Attempt to Resist (Bronze) | Complete 'Focus!' |
| Avid Reader (Silver) | Use a Quibbler dispenser 25 times |
| But... I Am The Chosen One (Gold) | Complete the game to 100% (Single Player Only) |
| Cake or Death Eater? (Bronze) | Complete 'The Seven Harrys' |
| Chair-ismatic (Bronze) | Complete 'Out of Retirement' |
| Collector's dream (Silver) | Complete the Bonus Level |
| Dark Times Ahead (Silver) | Unlock every bad wizard (Single Player Only) |
| Did Santa Eat That Cake? (Bronze) | Complete 'Kreacher Discomforts' |
| Dumbledore's Demise (Bronze) | Complete 'Horcrux and the Hand' |

| | |
|---|---|
| **Halfway There (Silver)** | Unlocked on hitting 50% game completion (Single Player Only) |
| **He's Back! (Bronze)** | Complete 'A Veiled Threat' |
| **Here Lies a Free Elf (Bronze)** | Complete 'DOBBY!' |
| **Hogwarts has Changed (Silver)** | Visit the Hogwarts Foyer in Year 7 |
| **I am the Half-Blood Prince (Bronze)** | Complete Year 6 |
| **Idling (Bronze)** | Stand still with no controller input for 5 minutes |
| **Kick the Bucket (Bronze)** | Complete 'Snape's Tears' |
| **Knuts and Vaults (Gold)** | Collect 1 billion studs (Single Player Only) |
| **Lessons Learned (Silver)** | Complete all lessons (Single Player Only) |
| **Lighten Up (Bronze)** | Use the Deluminator |
| **Not 'Fun Guys' (Bronze)** | Defeat 30 Red Caps |
| **O Children (Bronze)** | Complete the scene where Hermione and Harry dance in the tent |
| **Off the Beaten Track (Bronze)** | Complete 'Dumbledore's Army' |
| **Phoenix Rising (Bronze)** | Complete Year 5 |
| **Pyjama Drama (Bronze)** | Unlock every pyjama character variant (Single Player Only) |
| **Sectumsempra (Bronze)** | Complete 'Love Hurts' |
| **Shedding Skin (Bronze)** | Complete 'In Grave Danger' |
| **Soul Searching (Bronze)** | Complete 'Sword and Locket' |
| **Tall Order (Silver)** | Unlock ALL of the Order of the Phoenix character variants (Single Player Only) |
| **The Slug Club (Bronze)** | Complete 'Just Desserts' |
| **The Tale of the Three Brothers (Bronze)** | Complete 'Lovegood's Lunacy' |
| **To Be Continued (Bronze)** | Complete Year 7 |
| **Undesirable No. 1 (Bronze)** | Complete 'Back to School' |
| **Voldemort's Demise (Bronze)** | Complete 'The Flaw in the Plan' |
| **We are the D.A. (Silver)** | Unlock all of the members of Dumbledore's Army (Single Player Only) |
| **Weasley Does It (Bronze)** | Use a Weasley box with every Weasley |
| **Weasleys' Wizard Woes (Bronze)** | Complete 'A Not So Merry Christmas' |
| **What if? (Silver)** | Defeat every Harry freeplay variant as Lord Voldemort |
| **Wit Beyond Measure... (Bronze)** | Complete 'Fiendfyre Frenzy' |
| **Witch! (Bronze)** | Unlock all witch characters (Single Player Only) |
| **You and Whose Army? (Bronze)** | Complete 'Burning Bridges' |

### TROPHY

Enter the following passwords in the Start Menu under Extras while in game. It's the first option of the Extras menu.

| UNLOCKABLE | CODE |
|---|---|
| **Character Studs** | H27KGC |
| **Character Token Detector** | HA79V8 |
| **Christmas (everyone wears Santa hats)** | T7PVVN |
| **Collect Ghost Studs** | 2FLY6B |
| **Extra Hearts** | J9U6Z9 |
| **Fall Rescue** | ZEX7MV |

| | |
|---|---|
| Gold Brick Detector | 84QNQN |
| Hogwarts Crest Detector | TTMC6D |
| Invincibility | QQWC6B |
| Red Brick Detector | 7AD7HE |
| Score Multiplier x10 | H8X69Y |
| Score Multiplier x2 | 74YKR7 |
| Score Multiplier x6 | XK9ANE |
| Score Multiplier x8 | HUFV2H |
| Super Strength (can pull heavy objects w/o potion) | BMEU6X |

## LEGO HARRY POTTER: YEARS 5-7 (XBOX 360)

### ACHIEVEMENT

| UNLOCKABLE | HOW TO UNLOCK |
|---|---|
| "That's Unfortunate" (10) | Complete "The Thief's Downfall" |
| A Dish Best Served Cold (20) | Defeat Bellatrix with Neville (Waiter) in a duel |
| A Minifig's Best Friend (30) | Unlock every character with a pet (Single Player Only) |
| A Riddle Revealed (10) | Complete "Felix Felicis" |
| A Sirius Family Issue (20) | Defeat Bellatrix as any Sirius Black character variant in a duel |
| A Wise Disguise (10) | Complete "Magic is Might" |
| Accordion to Grawp (10) | Complete "A Giant Virtuoso" |
| Albus Percival Wulfric Brian (10) | Complete "Dark Times" |
| All Was Well (50) | Complete Year 8 |
| Attempt to Resist (10) | Complete "Focus!" |
| Avid Reader (25) | Use a Quibbler dispenser 25 times |
| But... I Am The Chosen One (100) | Complete the game to 100% (Single Player Only) |
| Cake or Death Eater? (10) | Complete "The Seven Harrys" |
| Chair-ismatic (10) | Complete "Out of Retirement" |
| Collector's dream (25) | Complete the Bonus Level |
| Dark Times Ahead (25) | Unlock every bad wizard (Single Player Only) |
| Did Santa Eat That Cake? (10) | Complete "Kreacher Discomforts" |
| Dumbledore's Demise (10) | Complete "Horcrux and the Hand" |
| Halfway There (30) | Unlocked on hitting 50% game completion (Single Player Only) |
| He's Back! (10) | Complete "A Veiled Threat" |
| Here Lies a Free Elf (10) | Complete "DOBBY!" |
| Hogwarts has Changed (30) | Visit the Hogwarts Foyer in Year 7 |
| I am the Half-Blood Prince (25) | Complete Year 6 |
| Idling (20) | Stand still with no controller input for 5 minutes |
| Kick the Bucket (10) | Complete "Snape's Tears" |
| Knuts and Vaults (50) | Collect 1 billion studs (Single Player Only) |
| Lessons Learned (30) | Complete all lessons (Single Player Only) |
| Lighten Up (10) | Use the Deluminator |
| Not "Fun Guys" (15) | Defeat 30 Red Caps |
| O Children (20) | Complete the scene where Hermione and Harry dance in the tent |
| Off the Beaten Track (10) | Complete "Dumbledore's Army" |

| | |
|---|---|
| **Phoenix Rising (25)** | Complete Year 5 |
| **Pyjama Drama (20)** | Unlock every pyjama character variant (Single Player Only) |
| **Sectumsempra (10)** | Complete "Love Hurts" |
| **Shedding Skin (10)** | Complete "In Grave Danger" |
| **Soul Searching (10)** | Complete "Sword and Locket" |
| **Tall Order (40)** | Unlock ALL of the Order of the Phoenix character variants (Single Player Only) |
| **The Slug Club (10)** | Complete "Just Desserts" |
| **The Tale of the Three Brothers (10)** | Complete "Lovegood's Lunacy" |
| **To Be Continued (25)** | Complete Year 7 |
| **Undesirable No. 1 (10)** | Complete "Back to School" |
| **Voldemort's Demise (10)** | Complete "The Flaw in the Plan" |
| **We are the D.A. (30)** | Unlock all of the members of Dumbledore's Army (Single Player Only) |
| **Weasley Does It (25)** | Use a Weasley box with every Weasley |
| **Weasleys' Wizard Woes (10)** | Complete "A Not So Merry Christmas" |
| **What if? (20)** | Defeat every Harry freeplay variant as Lord Voldemort |
| **Wit Beyond Measure... (10)** | Complete "Fiendfyre Frenzy" |
| **Witch! (50)** | Unlock all witch characters (Single Player Only) |
| **You and Whose Army? (10)** | Complete "Burning Bridges" |

### ACHIEVEMENT

Enter the following passwords in the Start Menu under Extras while in game. It's the first option of the Extras menu.

| UNLOCKABLE | CODE |
|---|---|
| **Character Studs** | H27KGC |
| **Character Token Detector** | HA79V8 |
| **Christmas** | T7PVVN |
| **Extra Hearts** | J9U6Z9 |
| **Fall Rescue** | ZEX7MV |
| **Fall Rescue** | ZEX7MV |
| **Ghost Coins** | 2FLY6B |
| **Gold Brick Detector** | 84QNQN |
| **Hogwarts Crest Detector** | TTMC6D |
| **Invincibility** | QQWC6B |
| **Red Brick Detector** | 7AD7HE |
| **Score x10** | H8X69Y |
| **Score x2** | 74YKR7 |
| **Score x6** | XK9ANE |
| **Score x8** | HUFV2H |
| **Super Strength** | BMEU6X |

## LEGO HARRY POTTER: YEARS 5-7 (Wii)

### CODE

Enter the following passwords in the Start Menu under Extras while in game. It's the first option of the Extras menu.

| UNLOCKABLE | PASSWORD |
|---|---|
| **Carrot Wands** | AUC8EH |
| **Character Studs** | H27KGC |

| | | | | |
|---|---|---|---|---|
| **Character Token Detector** | HA79V8 | | | |
| **Collect Ghost Studs** | 2FLY6B | | | |
| **Extra Hearts** | J9U6Z9 | | | |
| **Fall Rescue** | ZEX7MV | | | |
| **Fast Dig** | Z9BFAD | | | |
| **Gold Brick Detctor** | 84QNQN | | | |
| **Hogwarts Crest Detector** | TTMC6D | | | |
| **Invinbility** | QQWC6B | | | |
| **Red Brick Detector** | 7AD7HE | | | |
| **Score x10** | H8X69Y | | | |
| **Score x2** | 74YKR7 | | | |
| **Score x6** | XK9ANE | | | |
| **Score x8** | HUFV2H | | | |

### CODE

Enter the following password in the Weasleys' Joke Shop in Diagon Alley

| UNLOCKABLE | CODE |
|---|---|
| Immobulus | AAAAAA |

## LEGO INDIANA JONES: THE ORIGINAL ADVENTURES

### (XBOX 360), (PlayStation 3), (Wii),

### CHARACTER CODES

Enter the codes on the blackboard in the math classroom of Barnett College (the 2nd door on the left in the main hallway).

| EFFECT | XBOX 360 CODE | PS3 CODE | WII CODE | PS2 CODE |
|---|---|---|---|---|
| **Bandit** | 12N68W | 12N68W | 12N68W | 12N68W |
| **Bandit Swordsman** | 1MK4RT | 1MK4RT | 1MK4RT | 1MK4RT |
| **Barranca** | 04EM94 | 04EM94 | 04EM94 | 04EM94 |
| **Bazooka Trooper (Crusade)** | MK83R7 | MK83R7 | MK83R7 | MK83R7 |
| **Bazooka Trooper (Raiders)** | S93Y5R | S93Y5R | S93Y5R | S93Y5R |
| **Belloq** | CHN3YU | CHN3YU | CHN3YU | CHN3YU |
| **Belloq (Jungle)** | TDR197 | TDR197 | TDR197 | TDR197 |
| **Belloq (Robes)** | VEO29L | VEO29L | VEO29L | VEO29L |
| **British Officer** | VJ5TI9 | VJ5TI9 | VJ5TI9 | VJ5TI9 |
| **British Troop Commander** | B73EUA | B73EUA | B73EUA | B73EUA |
| **British Troop Soldier** | DJ5I2W | DJ5I2W | DJ5I2W | DJ5I2W |
| **Captain Katanga** | VJ3TT3 | VJ3TT3 | VJ3TT3 | VJ3TT3 |
| **Chatter Lal** | ENW936 | ENW936 | ENW936 | ENW936 |
| **Chatter Lal (Thuggee)** | CNH4RY | CNH4RY | CNH4RY | CNH4RY |
| **Chen** | 3NK48T | 3NK48T | 3NK48T | 3NK48T |
| **Colonel Dietrich** | 2K9RKS | 2K9RKS | 2K9RKS | 2K9RKS |
| **Colonel Vogel** | 8EAL4H | 8EAL4H | 8EAL4H | 8EAL4H |
| **Dancing Girl** | C7EJ21 | C7EJ21 | C7EJ21 | C7EJ21 |
| **Donovan** | 3NFTU8 | 3NFTU8 | 3NFTU8 | 3NFTU8 |
| **Elsa (Desert)** | JSNRT9 | JSNRT9 | JSNRT9 | JSNRT9 |
| **Elsa (Officer)** | VMJ5US | VMJ5US | VMJ5US | VMJ5US |
| **Enemy Boxer** | 8246RB | 8246RB | 8246RB | 8246RB |
| **Enemy Butler** | VJ48W3 | VJ48W3 | VJ48W3 | VJ48W3 |

**CODES & CHEATS**

| | | | |
|---|---|---|---|
| Enemy Guard | VJ7R51 | VJ7R51 | VJ7R51 | VJ7R51 |
| Enemy Guard (Mountains) | YR47WM | YR47WM | YR47WM | YR47WM |
| Enemy Officer (Desert) | 2MK450 | 572 E61 | 572 E61 | 572 E61 |
| Enemy Officer | 572 E61 | 2MK450 | 2MK450 | 2MK450 |
| Enemy Pilot | B84ELP | B84ELP | B84ELP | B84ELP |
| Enemy Radio Operator | 1MF94R | 1MF94R | 1MF94R | 1MF94R |
| Enemy Soldier (Desert) | 4NSU7Q | 4NSU7Q | 4NSU7Q | 4NSU7Q |
| Fedora | V75YSP | V75YSP | V75YSP | V75YSP |
| First Mate | 0GIN24 | 0GIN24 | 0GIN24 | 0GIN24 |
| Grail Knight | NE6THI | NE6THI | NE6THI | NE6THI |
| Hovitos Tribesman | H0V1SS | H0V1SS | H0V1SS | H0V1SS |
| Indiana Jones (Desert Disguise) | 4J8S4M | 4J8S4M | 4J8S4M | 4J8S4M |
| Indiana Jones (Officer) | VJ850S | VJ850S | VJ850S | VJ850S |
| Jungle Guide | 24PF34 | 24PF34 | 24PF34 | 24PF34 |
| Kao Kan | WMO46L | WMO46L | WMO46L | WMO46L |
| Kazim | NRH23J | NRH23J | NRH23J | NRH23J |
| Kazim (Desert) | 3M29TJ | 3M29TJ | 3M29TJ | 3M29TJ |
| Lao Che | 2NK479 | 2NK479 | 2NK479 | 2NK479 |
| Maharaja | NFK5N2 | NFK5N2 | NFK5N2 | NFK5N2 |
| Major Toht | 13NS01 | 13NS01 | 13NS01 | 13NS01 |
| Masked Bandit | N48SF0 | N48SF0 | N48SF0 | N48SF0 |
| Mola Ram | FJUR31 | FJUR31 | FJUR31 | FJUR31 |
| Monkey Man | 3RF6YJ | 3RF6YJ | 3RF6YJ | 3RF6YJ |
| Pankot Assassin | 2NKT72 | 2NKT72 | 2NKT72 | 2NKT72 |
| Pankot Guard | VN28RH | VN28RH | VN28RH | VN28RH |
| Sherpa Brawler | VJ37WJ | VJ37WJ | VJ37WJ | VJ37WJ |
| Sherpa Gunner | ND762W | ND762W | ND762W | ND762W |
| Slave Child | 0E3ENW | 0E3ENW | 0E3ENW | 0E3ENW |
| Thuggee | VM683E | VM683E | VM683E | VM683E |
| Thuggee Acolyte | T2R3F9 | T2R3F9 | T2R3F9 | T2R3F9 |
| Thuggee Slavedriver | VBS7GW | VBS7GW | VBS7GW | VBS7GW |
| Village Dignitary | KD48TN | KD48TN | KD48TN | KD48TN |
| Village Elder | 4682 E1 | 4682 E1 | 4682 E1 | 4682 E1 |
| Willie (Dinner Suit) | VK93R7 | VK93R7 | VK93R7 | VK93R7 |
| Willie (Pajamas) | MEN4IP | MEN4IP | MEN4IP | MEN4IP |
| Wu Han | 3NSLT8 | 3NSLT8 | 3NSLT8 | 3NSLT8 |

## ITEM CODES

Enter the codes on the blackboard in the math classroom of Barnett College (the 2nd door on the left in the main hallway).

| EFFECT | XBOX 360 CODE | PS3 CODE | WII CODE | PS2 CODE |
|---|---|---|---|---|
| Artifact Detector | VIKED7 | VIKED7 | VIKED7 | VIKED7 |
| Beep Beep | VNF59Q | VNF59Q | VNF59Q | VNF59Q |
| Character Treasure | VIES2R | VIES2R | VIES2R | VIES2R |
| Disarm Enemies | VKRNS9 | VKRNS9 | VKRNS9 | VKRNS9 |
| Disguises | 4ID1N6 | 4ID1N6 | 4ID1N6 | 4ID1N6 |
| Fast Build | V83SLO | V83SLO | V83SLO | V83SLO |
| Fast Dig | 378RS6 | 378RS6 | 378RS6 | 378RS6 |
| Fast Fix | FJ59WS | FJ59WS | FJ59WS | FJ59WS |

| Fertilizer | B1GW1F | B1GW1F | B1GW1F | B1GW1F |
|---|---|---|---|---|
| Ice Rink | 33GM7J | 33GM7J | 33GM7J | 33GM7J |
| Parcel Detector | VUT673 | VUT673 | VUT673 | VUT673 |
| Poo Treasure | WWQ1SA | WWQ1SA | WWQ1SA | WWQ1SA |
| Regenerate Hearts | MDLP69 | MDLP69 | MDLP69 | MDLP69 |
| Secret Characters | 3X44AA | 3X44AA | 3X44AA | 3X44AA |
| Silhouettes | 3HE85H | 3HE85H | 3HE85H | 3HE85H |
| Super Scream | VN3R7S | VN3R7S | VN3R7S | VN3R7S |
| Super Slap | 0P1TA5 | 0P1TA5 | 0P1TA5 | 0P1TA5 |
| Treasure Magnet | H86LA2 | H86LA2 | H86LA2 | H86LA2 |
| Treasure x2 | VM4TS9 | VM4TS9 | VM4TS9 | VM4TS9 |
| Treasure x4 | VLWEN3 | VLWEN3 | VLWEN3 | VLWEN3 |
| Treasure x6 | V84RYS | V84RYS | V84RYS | V84RYS |
| Treasure x8 | A72E1M | A72E1M | A72E1M | A72E1M |
| Treasure x10 | VI3PS8 | VI3PS8 | VI3PS8 | VI3PS8 |

## LEGO INDIANA JONES: THE ORIGINAL ADVENTURES (DS)

### CODES

| EFFECT | CODE |
|---|---|
| All Characters Unlocked | (X), ⬇, (B), ⬆, (Y), ⬆, ⬇, +START, +SELECT, ⬅, (B), (B), ⬅, (B), (B), ⬇, ⬅, ⬇, (Y), (Y), +START, +SELECT |
| All Episodes Unlocked + Free Play | ⬆, ⬅, (B), ⬅, (X), (Y), ⬆, ⬆, (B), ⬅, (B), ⬅, ⬆, ⬅, ⬇, (Y), (X), (X), (B), (B), ⬆, ⬅, (L), (B), +START, +SELECT |
| All Extras Unlocked | ⬅, ⬆, ⬅, (B), ⬆, (L), (B), ⬅, ⬆, ⬅, ⬆, (X), (X), (Y), (Y), (B), (B), ⬅, ⬅, ⬆, ⬅, (L), (B), ⬅, (B), ⬇, ⬆, ⬅, ⬆, +START, +SELECT |
| Start with 1,000,000 Studs | (X), (Y), (B), (B), (Y), (X), (L), (L), (B), (B), ⬆, ⬆, ⬆, ⬆, +START, +SELECT |
| Start with 3,000,000 Studs | ⬆, ⬅, (B), ⬆, ⬅, (X), (Y), ⬆, ⬅, (Y), ⬅, (L), (B), (L), (B), (B), (Y), (X), +START, +SELECT |

## LEGO INDIANA JONES: THE ORIGINAL ADVENTURES (PSP)

### CHARACTER CODES

Enter the codes on the blackboard in the math classroom of Barnett College(the 2nd door on the left in the main hallway).

| EFFECT | CODE |
|---|---|
| Bandit | 12N68W |
| Bandit Swordsman | 1MK4RT |
| Barranca | 04EM94 |
| Bazooka Trooper (Crusade) | MK83R7 |
| Bazooka Trooper (Raiders) | S93Y5R |
| Belloq | CHN3YU |
| Belloq (Jungle) | TDR197 |
| Belloq (Robes) | VEO29L |
| British Officer | VJ5TI9 |
| British Troop Commander | B73EUA |
| British Troop Soldier | DJ5I2W |
| Captain Katanga | VJ3TT3 |
| Chatter Lal | ENW936 |
| Chatter Lal (Thuggee) | CNH4RY |
| Chen | 3NK48T |
| Colonel Dietrich | 2K9RKS |
| Colonel Vogel | 8EAL4H |
| Dancing Girl | C7EJ21 |

**CODES & CHEATS**

| | |
|---|---|
| Donovan | 3NFTU8 |
| Elsa (Desert) | JSNRT9 |
| Elsa (Officer) | VMJ5US |
| Enemy Boxer | 8246RB |
| Enemy Butler | VJ48W3 |
| Enemy Guard | VJ7R51 |
| Enemy Guard (Mountains) | YR47WM |
| Enemy Officer | 572 E61 |
| Enemy Officer (Desert) | 2MK450 |
| Enemy Pilot | B84ELP |
| Enemy Radio Operator | 1MF94R |
| Enemy Soldier (Desert) | 4NSU7Q |
| Fedora | V75YSP |
| First Mate | 0GIN24 |
| Grail Knight | NE6THI |
| Hovitos Tribesman | H0V1SS |
| Indiana Jones (Desert Disguise) | 4J8S4M |
| Indiana Jones (Officer) | VJ850S |
| Jungle Guide | 24PF34 |
| Kao Kan | WMO46L |
| Kazim | NRH23J |
| Kazim (Desert) | 3M29TJ |
| Lao Che | 2NK479 |
| Maharaja | NFK5N2 |
| Major Toht | 13NS01 |
| Masked Bandit | N48SF0 |
| Mola Ram | FJUR31 |
| Monkey Man | 3RF6YJ |
| Pankot Assassin | 2NKT72 |
| Pankot Guard | VN28RH |
| Sherpa Brawler | VJ37WJ |
| Sherpa Gunner | ND762W |
| Slave Child | 0E3ENW |
| Thuggee | VM683E |
| Thuggee Acolyte | T2R3F9 |
| Thuggee Slavedriver | VBS7GW |
| Village Dignitary | KD48TN |
| Village Elder | 4682 E1 |
| Willie (Dinner Suit) | VK93R7 |
| Willie (Pajamas) | MEN4IP |
| Wu Han | 3NSLT8 |

## ITEM CODES

Enter the codes on the blackboard in the math classroom of Barnett College(the 2nd door on the left in the main hallway).

| EFFECT | CODE |
|---|---|
| Artifact Detector | VIKED7 |
| Beep Beep | VNF59Q |
| Character Treasure | VIES2R |
| Disarm Enemies | VKRNS9 |
| Disguises | 4ID1N6 |
| Fast Build | V83SLO |

| Fast Dig | 378RS6 |
|---|---|
| Fast Fix | FJ59WS |
| Fertilizer | B1GW1F |
| Ice Rink | 33GM7J |
| Parcel Detector | VUT673 |
| Poo Treasure | WWQ1SA |
| Regenerate Hearts | MDLP69 |
| Secret Characters | 3X44AA |
| Silhouettes | 3HE85H |
| Super Scream | VN3R7S |
| Super Slap | 0P1TA5 |
| Treasure Magnet | H86LA2 |
| Treasure x2 | VM4TS9 |
| Treasure x4 | VLWEN3 |
| Treasure x6 | V84RYS |
| Treasure x8 | A72E1M |
| Treasure x10 | VI3PS8 |

### INVINCIBILITY

Enter the code on the blackboard of the math classroom.

| EFFECT | CODE |
|---|---|
| Invincibility | B83EA1 |

### SECRET LEVELS

| UNLOCKABLE | HOW TO UNLOCK |
|---|---|
| Ancient City | Collect all of the artifacts in Temple of Doom. |
| Warehouse Level | Collect all of the artifacts in The Last Crusade. |
| Young Indy level | Collect all of the artifacts in Raiders of the Lost Ark. |

## LEGO INDIANA JONES 2: THE ADVENTURE CONTINUES (XBOX 360), (Wii)

### CODES

| EFFECT | XBOX 360 CODE | WII CODE |
|---|---|---|
| Beep Beep | UU3VSC | UU3VSC |
| Disguise | Y9TE98 | Y9TE98 |
| Fast Build | SNXC2F | SNXC2F |
| Fast Dig | XYAN83 | XYAN83 |
| Fast Fix | 3Z7PJX | 3Z7PJX |
| Fearless | TUXNZF | TUXNZF |
| Hot Rod | YLG2TN | YLG2TN |
| Ice Rink | TY9P4U | TY9P4U |
| Indiana Jones: 1 | PGWSEA | PGWSEA |
| Indiana Jones: 2 | DZFY9S | DZFY9S |
| Indiana Jones: Desert | M4C34K | M4C34K |
| Indiana Jones: Disguised | 2W8QR3 | 2W8QR3 |
| Indiana Jones: Kali | J2XS97 | J2XS97 |
| Indiana Jones: Officer | 3FQFKS | 3FQFKS |
| Invincibility | 6JBB65 | 6JBB65 |
| Lao Che | 7AWX3J | 7AWX3J |
| Mola Ram | 82RMC2 | 82RMC2 |
| Mutt | 2GK562 | 2GK562 |
| Poo Money | SZFAAE | SZFAAE |

NEW!

A
B
C
D
E
F
G
H
I
J
K
**L**
M
N
O
P
Q
R
S
T
U
V
W
X
Y
Z

**CODES & CHEATS**

| | | |
|---|---|---|
| Professor Henry Jones | 4C5AKH | 4C5AKH |
| Rene Belloq | FTL48S | FTL48S |
| Sallah | E88YRP | E88YRP |
| Score x2 | U38VJP | U38VJP |
| Score x3 | PEHHPZ | PEHHPZ |
| Score x4 | UXGTB3 | UXGTB3 |
| Score x6 | XWJ5EY | XWJ5EY |
| Score x8 | S5UZCP | S5UZCP |
| Score x10 | V7JYBU | V7JYBU |
| Silhouettes | FQGPYH | FQGPYH |
| Snake Whip | 2U7YCV | 2U7YCV |
| Stud Magnet | EGSM5B | EGSM5B |
| Willie: Singer | 94RUAJ | 94RUAJ |

## LEGO PIRATES OF THE CARIBBEAN (XBOX 360), (PlayStation 3), (Wii)

### UNLOCKABLE

Enter the following codes at the Unlock section of the main menu.

| EFFECT | CODE |
|---|---|
| Ammand the Corsair | ew8t6t |
| Angelica (Disguised) | dlrr45 |
| Angry Cannibal | vgf32c |
| Blackbeard | d3dw0d |
| Clanker | zm37gt |
| Clubber | zm37gt |
| Davy Jones | 4djlkr |
| Governor Weatherby Swann | ld9454 |
| Gunner | y611wb |
| Hungry Cannibal | 64bnhg |
| Jack Sparrow (Musical) | vdjspw |
| Jimmy Legs | 13glw5 |
| King George | rked43 |
| Koehler | rt093g |
| Mistress Ching | gdetde |
| Phillip | wev040 |
| Quartermaster | rx58hu |
| The Spaniard | p861jo |
| Twigg | kdlfkd |

## LEGO PIRATES OF THE CARIBBEAN (DS), (PSP), (3DS)

### UNLOCKABLE

At the Main Menu, go to Options, then Codes. Type in the code to unlock these characters.

| EFFECT | CODE |
|---|---|
| Ammand the Corsair | ew8t6t |
| Angelica (Disguised) | dlrr45 |
| Angry Cannibal | vgf32c |
| Blackbeard | d3dw0d |
| Clanker | zm37gt |
| Clubber | zm37gt |
| Davy Jones | 4djlkr |

| | |
|---|---|
| Governor Weatherby Swann | ld9454 |
| Gunner | y611wb |
| Hungry Cannibal | 64bnhg |
| Jack Sparrow (Musical) | vdjspw |
| Jimmy Legs | 13glw5 |
| King George | rked43 |
| Koehler | rt093g |
| Mistress Ching | gdetde |
| Phillip | wev040 |
| Quartermaster | rx58hu |
| The Spaniard | p861jo |
| Twigg | kdlfkd |

## LEGO ROCK BAND (DS)

### UNLOCK GUEST ARTISTS

Complete the following songs in Tour Mode to unlock the corresponding guest artist and their parts for use in your own band.

| UNLOCKABLE | HOW TO UNLOCK |
|---|---|
| Blur | Beat "Song 2" in Tour. |
| David Bowie | Beat "Let's Dance" in Tour. |
| Iggy Pop | Beat "The Passenger" in Tour. |
| Queen | Beat "We Are The Champions" in Tour. |

## LEGO STAR WARS: THE COMPLETE SAGA (XBOX 360)

### CHARACTERS

To use the codes, enter the Cantina, go to the bar, access the codes command, and type in the codes.

| CHARACTER | XBOX 360 CODES | PS3 CODE | WII CODE |
|---|---|---|---|
| Admiral Ackbar | ACK646 | ACK646 | ACK646 |
| Battle Droid Commander | KPF958 | KPF958 | KPF958 |
| Boba Fett (Boy) | GGF539 | GGF539 | GGF539 |
| Boss Nass | HHY697 | HHY697 | HHY697 |
| Captain Tarpals | QRN714 | QRN714 | QRN714 |
| Count Dooku | DDD748 | DDD748 | DDD748 |
| Darth Maul | EUK421 | EUK421 | EUK421 |
| Ewok | EWK785 | EWK785 | EWK785 |
| General Grievous | PMN576 | PMN576 | PMN576 |
| Greedo | ZZR636 | ZZR636 | ZZR636 |
| IG-88 | GIJ989 | GIJ989 | GIJ989 |
| Imperial Guard | GUA850 | GUA850 | GUA850 |
| Indiana Jones | After you watch the trailer for the upcoming Indiana Jones game in the Bonus Room, Indy will become a playable character. | | |
| Jango Fett | KLJ897 | KLJ897 | KLJ897 |
| Ki-Adi-Mundi | MUN486 | MUN486 | MUN486 |
| Luminara | LUM521 | LUM521 | LUM521 |
| Padmé | VBJ322 | VBJ322 | VBJ322 |
| R2-Q5 | EVILR2 | EVILR2 | EVILR2 |
| Sandtrooper | CBR954 | CBR954 | CBR954 |
| Stormtrooper | NBN431 | NBN431 | NBN431 |
| Super Battle Droid | XZNR21 | XZNR21 | XZNR21 |

| | | | |
|---|---|---|---|
| Taun We | PRX482 | PRX482 | PRX482 |
| Vulture Droid | BDC866 | BDC866 | BDC866 |
| Watto | PLL967 | PLL967 | PLL967 |
| Zam Wesell | 584HJF | 584HJF | 584HJF |

### SHIPS

| UNLOCKABLE SHIPS | XBOX 360 CODES | PS3 CODE | WII CODE |
|---|---|---|---|
| Droid Trifighter | AAB123 | AAB123 | AAB123 |
| Imperial Shuttle | HUT845 | HUT845 | HUT845 |
| Slave I | Collect all 10 Minikits on each level. | | |
| TIE Fighter | DBH897 | DBH897 | DBH897 |
| UNLOCKABLE SHIPS | XBOX 360 CODES | PS3 CODE | WII CODE |
| TIE Interceptor | INT729 | INT729 | INT729 |
| Zam's Speeder | UUU875 | UUU875 | UUU875 |

### SKILLS

| UNLOCKABLE SKILLS | XBOX 360 CODES | PS3 CODE | WII CODE |
|---|---|---|---|
| Disguise | BRJ437 | BRJ437 | BRJ437 |
| Force Grapple Leap | CLZ738 | CLZ738 | CLZ738 |

## LEGO STAR WARS II: THE ORIGINAL TRILOGY (XBOX 360)

### DIFFERENT CHARACTERS

| PASSWORD | EFFECT |
|---|---|
| Beach Trooper | UCK868 |
| Ben Kenobi's Ghost | BEN917 |
| Bespin Guard | VHY832 |
| Bib Fortuna | WTY721 |
| Boba Fett | HLP221 |
| Death Star Trooper | BNC332 |
| Emperor | HHY382 |
| Ewok | TTT289 |
| Gamorean Guard | YZF999 |
| Gonk Droid | NFX582 |
| Grand Moff Tarkin | SMG219 |
| Han Solo with Hood | YWM840 |
| IG-88 | NXL973 |
| Imperial Guard | MMM111 |
| Imperial Officer | BBV889 |
| Imperial Shuttle Pilot | VAP664 |
| Imperial Spy | CVT125 |
| Lobot | UUB319 |
| Palace Guard | SGE549 |
| Rebel Pilot | CYG336 |
| Rebel Trooper from Hoth | EKU849 |
| Red Noses on All Characters | NBP398 |
| Santa Hat and Red Clothes | CL4U5H |
| Skiff Guard | GBU888 |
| Snowtrooper | NYU989 |
| Stormtrooper | PTR345 |
| TIE Fighter | HDY739 |
| TIE Fighter Pilot | NNZ316 |

| TIE Interceptor | QYA828 |
| Ugnaught | UGN694 |
| Unlock Greedo | NAH118 |
| Unlock Jawa | JAW499 |
| Unlock Sandtrooper | YDV451 |
| Unlock Tusken Raider | PEJ821 |
| White Beard Extra | TYH319 |

## LEGO STAR WARS II: THE ORIGINAL TRILOGY (DS)

Enter this password in the Cantina.

| UNLOCKABLE | PASSWORD |
| --- | --- |
| 10 extra studs | 4PR28U |

## LEGO STAR WARS II: THE ORIGINAL TRILOGY (PSP)

### PASSWORDS

Enter the following codes at the Mos Eisley Cantina to unlock the character for purchase in Free Play mode.

| UNLOCKABLE | HOW TO UNLOCK |
| --- | --- |
| Beach Trooper | UCK868 |
| Ben Kenobi's Ghost | BEN917 |
| Bespin Guard | VHY832 |
| Bib Fortuna | WTY721 |
| Boba Fett | HLP221 |
| Death Star Trooper | BNC332 |
| Emperor | HHY382 |
| Ewok | TTT289 |
| Gamorean Guard | YZF999 |
| Gonk Droid | NFX582 |
| Grand Moff Tarkin | SMG219 |
| Han Solo with Hood | YWM840 |
| IG-88 | NXL973 |
| Imperial Guard | MMM111 |
| Imperial Officer | BBV889 |
| Imperial Shuttle Pilot | VAP66 |
| Imperial Spy | CVT125 |
| Lobot | UUB319 |
| Palace Guard | SGE549 |
| Rebel Pilot | CYG336 |
| Rebel Trooper from Hoth | EKU849 |
| Red Noses on All Characters | NBP398 |
| Santa Hat and Red Clothes | CL4U5H |
| Skiff Guard | GBU888 |
| Snow Trooper | NYU989 |
| Stormtrooper | PTR345 |
| TIE Fighter | HDY739 |
| TIE Fighter Pilot | NNZ316 |
| TIE Interceptor | QYA828 |
| Ugnaught | UGN694 |
| White Beard Extra | TYH319 |

## UNLOCKABLE CHARACTERS

Complete challenge by collecting 10 Blue Minikits within the time limit allowed per level.

| UNLOCKABLE | HOW TO UNLOCK |
|---|---|
| R4-P17, PK Droid | Episode 4, Chapter 2 |
| Battle Droid, B. D. (Security), B. D. (Geonosis), B. D. (Commander) | Episode 4, Chapter 4 |
| Chancellor Palpatine, General Grievous, Grievous' Bodyguard | Episode 6, Chapter 5 |
| Clone (Episode III, Pilot) | Episode 4, Chapter 6 |
| Clone (Episode III, Swamp) | Episode 5, Chapter 4 |
| Clone, Clone (Episode III), Commander Cody, Clone (Episode III Walker) | Episode 6, Chapter 3 |
| Disguised Clone, Boba Fett (Boy) | Episode 6, Chapter 1 |
| Droideka | Episode 4, Chapter 5 |
| Geonosian | Episode 5, Chapter 3 |
| Jango Fett | Episode 6, Chapter 2 |
| Luminara, Ki-Adi-Mundi, Kit Fisto, Shaak Ti | Episode 5, Chapter 1 |
| Mace Windu, Mace Windu (Episode 3) | Episode 6, Chapter 6 |
| Padmé (Battle), Padmé (Clawed), Padmé (Geonosis) | Episode 5, Chapter 2 |
| Padmé, Anakin Skywalker (boy) | Episode 4, Chapter 3 |
| Queen Amidala, Royal Guard, Captain Panaka | Episode 5, Chapter 6 |
| Super Battle Droid | Episode 5, Chapter 5 |
| TC-14 | Episode 4, Chapter 1 |
| Wookiee, Jar Jar Binks | Episode 6, Chapter 4 |

## LEGO STAR WARS III: THE CLONE WARS (PlayStation 3, (XBOX 360)

### UNLOCKABLE

Pause game during play and go to Extras to enter these passwords.

| EFFECT | CODE |
|---|---|
| Character Studs | qd2c31 |
| Dark Side | x1v4n2 |
| Dual Wield | c4es4r |
| Fast Build | gchp7s |
| Geonosian Starfighter unlocked. | EDENEC |
| Glow in the Dark | 4gt3vq |
| Invincibility | j46p7a |
| Minikit Detector | csd5na |
| Perfect Deflect | 3F5L56 |
| Regenerate Hearts | 2d7jns |
| Score X10 | n1ckr1 |
| Score X2 | yzphuv |
| Score X4 | 43t5e5 |
| Score X6 | sebhgr |
| Score X8 | byfsaq |
| Stud Magnet | 6mz5ch |
| Super Saber Cut | bs828k |
| Super Speeders | b1d3w3 |
| Unlock Savage Oppress | MELL07 |
| Vulture Droid unlocked | 7w7k7s |

## LEGO STAR WARS III: THE CLONE WARS (Wii)

### UNLOCKABLE

At the Pause menu, select Extras and enter these passwords at "Enter Code".

| EFFECT | CODE |
|--------|------|
| Makes multiplier available - Every stud collected in game is multiplied by the number stated | Yzphuv |
| Makes Perfect Deflect available - Deflected lasers always hit a target | 3f5l56 |
| Unlock Dual Wield | c4es4r |
| Unlock Fast Build | gchp7s |
| Unlock Glow in the Dark | 4gt3vq |
| Unlock Invincibility | j46p7a |
| Unlock Regenerativ Hearts | 2d7jns |
| Unlock Super Saber Cut | bs828k |
| Unlock Super Speeders | b1d3w3 |
| Unlock the Character Studs | qd2c31 |
| Unlock the Dark Side | x1v4n2 |
| Unlock the Minikit Detector | csd5na |
| Unlock the Stud Magnet | 6mz5ch |
| Unlock X10 Score Multiplier | n1ckr1 |
| Unlock X4 Score Multiplier | 43t5e5 |
| Unlock X6 Score Multiplier | sebhgr |
| Unlock X8 Score Multiplier | byfsaw |
| Vulture Droid unlocked | 7w7k7s |

## LIMBO (XBOX 360)

### AVATAR AWARDS

| UNLOCKABLE | HOW TO UNLOCK |
|------------|---------------|
| LIMBO Pet | Beat the game. |
| LIMBO T-shirt | Get your first LIMBO achievement. |

## LITTLE BIG PLANET (PlayStation 3)

### COSTUMES

Complete the corresponding level without dying to unlock the following costumes.

| UNLOCKABLE | HOW TO UNLOCK |
|------------|---------------|
| Bunny Tail | The Collectors Lair |
| Chicken Beak | The Dancers Court |
| Chicken Gloves | Great Magicians Palace |
| Chicken Tail | Elephant Temple |
| Cowboy Boots and Leather Gloves | Boom Town |
| Cowboy Hat | Serpent Shrine |
| Dinosaur Mask | The Construction Site |
| Dinosaur Tail | Lowrider |
| Googly Eye Glasses | Sensei's Lost Castle |
| Green Sock Puppet | Subway |
| Japanese Festival Headband | The Terrible Oni's Volcano |
| Japanese Festival Robe | Endurance Dojo |
| Jeans with a Belt and Cowboy Bandana | The Mines |
| Moustache | Burning Forest |

**CODES & CHEATS**

| | |
|---|---|
| Neon Helmet | The Bunker |
| Pirate Hat | Skate to Victory |
| Pirate Hook and Pirate Eye Patch | First Steps |
| Pirate Waistcoat and Pirate Shorts | Get a Grip |
| Ringmaster Jacket | Swinging Safari |
| Ringmaster Top Hat and Gold Monocle | The Meerkat Kingdom |
| Roman Armor | The Darkness |
| Roman Helmet | Skulldozer |
| White Neon Eyes | The Frozen Tundra |
| Wooden Sword | The Wedding Reception |
| Yellow Head | The Collector |

### LEVEL COMPLETION PRIZES

Gain the following prizes by achieving 100% level completion (collect all the prize bubbles on that level).

| UNLOCKABLE | HOW TO UNLOCK |
|---|---|
| Anteater concept and Anteater concept with frame | The Mines 100% |
| Bad Witch concept, Bad Witch concept with frame | The Bunker 100% |
| Big Cat and Big Cat concept with frame | Burning Forest 100% |
| Big Sumo, The Islands concept, and The Islands concept with frame | Sensei's Lost Castle 100% |
| Boom Town concept and Boom Town concept with frame | Boom Town 100% |
| Boss concept, Boss concept with frame, and a monster truck | The Construction Site 100% |
| Bunny Tail and The Gardens | Skate to Victory 100% |
| Circus concept, Circus concept with frame | The Frozen Tundra 100% |
| Costumes concept and Costumes concept with frame | Elephant Temple 100% |
| Early Sackboy and Early Sackboy with frame | Lowrider 100% |
| Fairy Tale concept and Fairy Tale concept with frame | Get a Grip 100% |
| Grabbing Machine, Rock God, and Rock God with frame | Subway 100% |
| Graveyard concept, The Wedding concept with frame, and Skulldozer | Skulldozer 100% |
| Jumping Tank, Very First LBP concept, Very First LBP concept with frame | The Collectors Lair 100% |
| LBP concept with frame, Background Environment concept | The Dancers Court 100% |
| LBP Cosmos concept, Magicians Box, and Cosmos concept with frame | Great Magicians Palace 100% |
| Savannah concept and Savannah concept with frame | Swinging Safari 100% |
| Sheriff Zapata's Explosives Machine, The Mines concept with frame, and The Mines concept | Serpent Shrine 100% |
| Temple concept, Temple concept with frame, and a Mystical Dragon | Endurance Dojo 100% |
| Terrible Oni, Islands City concept, and Islands City concept with frame | The Terrible Volcano 100% |
| The Collector Boss, The Collector's Pod, and the Collector | The Collector 100% |
| The Gardens concept and The Gardens concept with frame | First Steps 100% |
| The Savannah and The Pink Scarf | The Meerkat Kingdom 100% |
| Theme Characters concept with frame and Theme Characters Concept | The Darkness 100% |
| Wrestling Ring with frame and Wrestling concept | The Wedding Reception 100% |

## LITTLE BIG PLANET 2 (PlayStation 3)

### SECRET PINS

These special pins do not appear normally in the pin list (and do not count toward your pin total).

| UNLOCKABLE | HOW TO UNLOCK |
|---|---|
| Amy's Birthday Pressie | Play on Amy's Birthday (July 29) |
| Festive Spirit | Wear a Christmas costume on Christmas Day |
| Halloween Hauntings | Wear the Pumpkin Head costume on Halloween |
| Mm Picked! | Have one of your levels feature in Mm Picks |
| Mm's Birthday | Play LBP2 on Media Molecule's birthday (January 4) |
| Royalty | You are awarded a Crown (LBP1 or LBP2) |
| Thanksgiving Turkey | Wear the Turkey Head costume on Thanksgiving |
| Who's Who | Watch the credits all the way through |

## LITTLEST PET SHOP: JUNGLE (DS)

### CODES

Enter the following code in the options menu under the "Enter Passwords" section.

| EFFECT | CODE |
|---|---|
| Giraffe | LPSTRU |

## LODE RUNNER (Wii)

### UNLOCKABLES

| UNLOCKABLE | HOW TO UNLOCK |
|---|---|
| Game Speed | Press SELECT to view current level. Hold SELECT and press Ⓑ to decrease game speed, or Ⓐ to increase game speed. |
| Level Select | Press select to view current level. Press SELECT then press Ⓐ to increase a level and Ⓑ to drop one. |

## LORD OF ARCANA (PSP)

### UNLOCKABLE

Unlock "Titles" by copmpleting the following tasks.

| UNLOCKABLE | HOW TO UNLOCK |
|---|---|
| Dragon Hegemony | Defeat 30 or more Bahamut-type monsters |
| Dragonier | Defeat 15 or more Bahamut-type monsters |
| Emperor | Defeat 15 or more Vermilion-type monsters |
| Fire Spinner | Defeat 30 or more Agni-type monsters |
| Giant | Defeat 30 or more Hecatoncheir-type monsters |
| Grace Under Pressure | Defeat 5 or more Hecatoncheir-type monsters |
| Gravity | Defeat 15 or more Hecatoncheir-type monsters |
| Heavenly Ruler | Defeat 5 or more Bahamut-type monsters |
| Poison-Eater | Defeat 5 or more Azdaja-type monsters |
| Scarlet King | Defeat 30 or more Vermilion-type monsters |
| Slashing Soul | Defeat 5 or more Vermilion-type monsters |
| Soul Of Fire | Defeat 5 or more Agni-type Monsters |
| Two-Headed | Defeat 30 or more Azdaja-type monsters |
| Viper | Defeat 15 or more Azdaja-type monsters |
| Volcano | Defeat 15 or more Agni-type monsters |

NEW!

A
B
C
D
E
F
G
H
I
J
K
**L**
M
N
O
P
Q
R
S
T
U
V
W
X
Y
Z

## THE LORD OF THE RINGS: WAR IN THE NORTH (XBOX 360)

### ACHIEVEMENT

| UNLOCKABLE | HOW TO UNLOCK |
|---|---|
| Against All Odds (80) | Complete a playthrough on Legendary difficulty. |
| Bane of Mordor (25) | Kill 600 enemies in a single playthrough. |
| Battle-master (20) | Unlock every active-cast ability in one character's skill tree. |
| Begone, lord of carrion! (20) | Defeat the Barrow Wight Lord. |
| Champion of the North (20) | Achieve level 20. |
| Defender of the North (10) | Achieve level 10. |
| Dragon-hoard (20) | Amass 25,000 coins. |
| Eagle Savior (20) | Defeat Agandaûr without the aid of Beleram. |
| Elf-friend (10) | Join forces with the sons of Elrond. |
| Expert Treasure-hunter. (25) | Locate 5 gilded treasure chests in a single playthrough. |
| Fell-handed (20) | Deal 1500 damage in a single melee strike. |
| Foe-hammer (10) | Kill 200 enemies in a single playthrough. |
| Friend of the Woodland Realm (10) | Free the elf from his captors in Mirkwood Marsh. |
| Friend to the Eagles (20) | Help free the Great Eagle Beleram. |
| Friend to the Ring-bearer (10) | Speak with Frodo in Rivendell. |
| Gem-studded (10) | Slot an elfstone into an item. |
| Giant-slayer (20) | Slay Bargrisar the stone giant. |
| Herb-master (10) | Create 15 potions in a single playthrough. |
| Hero of Legend (50) | Complete a playthrough on Heroic difficulty. |
| Hero of the North (80) | Defeat Sauron's Lieutenant Agandaûr. |
| In the Dragon's Den (20) | Meet a dragon and survive. |
| Keen-eyed Marksman (20) | Kill 50 enemies with headshots in a single playthrough. |
| Like a Thunderbolt (20) | Deal 3000 damage with a single ranged strike. |
| Living Shield (20) | Absorb 25,000 total damage during the course of 1 level. |
| Many deeds, great and small (20) | Complete 15 quests in a single playthrough. |
| Mountain-breaker (25) | Help destroy the citadel within Mount Gundabad. |
| Now for wrath, now for ruin! (20) | Kill 4 enemies simultaneously. |
| Relentless (20) | While in Hero Mode, perform a streak of 50 hits. |
| Seeker (20) | Discover 25 secrets in a single playthrough. |
| Siege-breaker (35) | Help weather the siege of Nordinbad. |
| Spider-slayer (25) | Slay Saenathra. |
| Strength of Our Alliance (25) | Slay one enemy together with 2 other players. |
| Sudden Fury (10) | Perform 3 critical hits within 10 seconds. |
| Swift-winged Warrior (20) | Summon Beleram 10 times in a single playthrough. |
| Tharzog's Bane (20) | Defeat Agandaûr's lieutenant Tharzog. |
| The Lidless Eye (25) | Complete the investigation of the Cult of the Lidless Eye. |
| Tracker (10) | Discover what happened to the missing Rangers. |
| Troll's Bane (10) | Slay the wild snow trolls. |
| Trusted with the Secret (10) | Learn of the Ring of Power and the plan for its destruction. |

| | |
|---|---|
| Victorious in Battle (25) | Complete a playthrough on at least Normal difficulty. |
| War-hardened (10) | Achieve at least 1 rank in a tier 3 skill. |
| War-machinist (20) | Kill 150 enemies with war machines in a single playthrough. |
| Warrior Exemplar (25) | For one character unlock every skill that provides a modification to War Cry, Sanctuary or Evasion. |
| Well-arrayed (25) | Equip a complete magical armor set. |
| Where there's life, there's hope (10) | Revive a fallen ally. |
| Wulfrun's Bane (20) | Defeat the Sorceror Wulfrun. |

## LOST PLANET 2 (XBOX 360)

### UNLOCKABLES

| UNLOCKABLE | HOW TO UNLOCK |
|---|---|
| Albert Wesker | Have a save from Resident Evil 5. |
| Devil May Cry Noms de Guerre | Have a Devil May Cry 4 save. |
| Frank West | Have a save from Dead Rising. |
| Marcus Phoenix and Dom Santiago | Finish Campaign. |
| Street Fighter Noms de Guerre | Have a save of Street Fighter IV. |

### WEAPONS

| UNLOCKABLE | HOW TO UNLOCK |
|---|---|
| Akrid Launcher | Reach level 50 with Snow Pirate Elites. |
| Energy Gun SP | Reach level 70 with Femme Fatale. |
| Fire Cracker | Reach level 30 with Femme Fatale. |
| Gun Sword SP | Reach level 70 with the Rounders. |
| Hand Cannon SP | Reach level 50 with the Rounders. |
| Machine Gun SP | Have a saved game file from the Lost Planet 2 demo. |
| Plasma Gun SP | Get NEVEC Black Ops to level 30. |
| Shotgun SP | Reach level 50 with Femme Fatale. |
| Shuriken | Reach level 30 with the Rounders. |
| V-Device SP | Achieve career level 70 with NEVEC. |

### UNLOCKABLES

| UNLOCKABLE | HOW TO UNLOCK |
|---|---|
| AI Enemy Battle | Beat all the training levels and modes for both Basic and Advanced training. |
| Extreme Difficulty | Beat Hard Difficulty. |

### CODES

From any character customization screen, press Y to bring up the slot machine, then enter the password.

| EFFECT | CODE |
|---|---|
| 4Gamer.net Shirt | 25060016 |
| Black shirt | 63152256 |
| Blue shirt | 56428338 |
| Famitsu Weekly Magazine T-Shirt | 73154986 |
| Famitsu.com Shirt | 88020223 |
| Green shirt with WCP baseball cap T-shirt | 18213092 |
| Midnight Live 360 shirt | 69088873 |
| Monthly GAMEJAPAN shirt | 52352345 |
| Pink JP Playboy shirt | 34297758 |
| Purple + tan | 65162980 |

| Purple shirt with "D" logo and Japanese characters T-shirt | 71556463 |
| Street Jack | 12887439 |
| White shirt with blue sleeves with face T-shirt | 26797358 |
| White shirt with person holding Gatling gun T-shirt | 31354816 |
| Xbox 360 shirt (male and female) | 94372143 |
| Yellow shirt | 96725729 |

## LOST PLANET 2 (PlayStation 3)

### SKINS

| UNLOCKABLE | HOW TO UNLOCK |
| --- | --- |
| Albert Wesker | Have save data of Resident Evil 5 or Resident Evil 5 Gold Edition. |
| Frank West | Have a saved game file from the original Lost Planet. |

### TITLES

| UNLOCKABLE | HOW TO UNLOCK |
| --- | --- |
| BSAA | Have a saved game file from Resident Evil 5. |
| Decorated Soldier | Have Lost Planet save data on your hard drive. |
| Devil May Cry | Have a saved game file from Devil May Cry 4. |
| I Played the Demo | Have Lost Planet 2 Multiplayer Demo save data on your hard drive. |
| Legendary Warrior | Have Lost Planet save data on your hard drive. |
| Street Fighter | Have a saved game file from Street Fighter 4. |

### WEAPONS

| UNLOCKABLE | HOW TO UNLOCK |
| --- | --- |
| Akrid Launcher | Reach level 50 with Snow Pirate Elites. |
| Energy Gun SP | Reach level 70 with Femme Fatale. |
| Fire Cracker | Reach level 30 with Femme Fatale. |
| Gun Sword SP | Reach level 70 with the Rounders. |
| Hand Cannon SP | Reach level 50 with the Rounders. |
| Machine Gun SP | Have a saved game file from the Lost Planet 2 demo. |
| Plasma Gun SP | Get NEVEC Black Ops to level 30. |
| Shotgun SP | Reach level 50 with Femme Fatale. |
| Shuriken | Reach level 30 with the Rounders. |
| V-Device SP | Achieve career level 70 with NEVEC. |

### UNLOCKABLES

| UNLOCKABLE | HOW TO UNLOCK |
| --- | --- |
| AI Enemy Battle | Beat all the training levels and modes for both Basic and Advanced training. |
| Extreme Difficulty | Beat Hard difficulty. |

### CODES

From any character customization screen, press Y to bring up the slot machine, then enter the password.

| EFFECT | CODE |
| --- | --- |
| 4Gamer.net Shirt | 25060016 |
| Black shirt | 63152256 |
| Blue shirt | 56428338 |
| Famitsu Weekly Magazine T-Shirt | 73154986 |
| Famitsu.com Shirt | 88020223 |
| Green shirt with WCP baseball cap t-shirt | 18213092 |
| Midnight Live 360 shirt | 69088873 |
| Monthly GAMEJAPAN shirt | 52352345 |

| EFFECT | CODE |
|---|---|
| Pink JP Playboy shirt | 34297758 |
| Purple + Tan | 65162980 |
| Purple shirt with "D" logo and Japanese characters T-shirt | 71556463 |
| Street Jack | 12887439 |
| White shirt with blue sleeves with face T-shirt | 26797358 |
| White shirt with person holding Gatling gun T-shirt | 31354816 |
| Xbox 360 shirt (male and female) | 94372143 |
| Yellow shirt | 96725729 |
| Man in Uniform | I LOVE A MAN IN UNIFORM |
| Play as Jack | OH MY SON, MY BLESSED SON |
| Sharp Dressed Man | DON'T YOU LOOK FINE AND DANDY |
| Spawn a horse-drawn coach. | NOW WHO PUT THAT THERE? |
| Spawn a horse | BEASTS AND MAN TOGETHER |
| Unlock all areas | YOU GOT YOURSELF A FINE PAIR OF EYES |
| Unlock all gang outfits | YOU THINK YOU TOUGH, MISTER? |

## LOST PLANET: EXTREME CONDITION (XBOX 360)

Enter these codes when the game is paused. They can be used only on Easy mode.

| UNLOCKABLE | CODE |
|---|---|
| 500 Thermal Energy | Up, Down, Left, Right, Left, Right, X, Y, RB, LB |
| Infinite Ammunition | LB, LT, RT, RB, Y, X, Right, Left, Up, Down, LB, LT, RT, LT, LB, RB |
| Infinite Health | Up, Up, Up, Up, Down, Down, Down, Down, Left, Left, Left, Up, X, Y, X, Y, X, Left, Y, Right, X, Left, Y, Up, X, RB, LB |
| Infinite Ammunition | RT, RB, Y, X, Right, Left, Up, Down, LB, LT, RT, RB, Y, X, Right, Left, LB, LT, RT, LT, LB, RB, X, Left, Up, X, RB, LB |

## MADDEN NFL 10 (Wii)

### CODES

From the "Extras" menu select "Enter Codes"

| EFFECT | CODE |
| --- | --- |
| Franchise Mode | TEAMPLAYER |
| Master Code (unlocks everything) | THEWORKS |
| Situation Mode | YOUCALLIT |
| Superstar Mode | EGOBOOST |
| Unlocks Pro Bowl Stadium | ALLSTARS |
| Unlocks Super Bowl Stadium | THEBIGSHOW |

## MADDEN NFL 12 (XBOX 360)

### ACHIEVEMENT

| UNLOCKABLE | HOW TO UNLOCK |
| --- | --- |
| Adrian Peterson Award (25) | Score on an 80+ yard TD run (No OTP or co-op) |
| Arian Foster Award (25) | Rush for 231+ yards in a game with one player (No OTP or co-op) |
| Bryan McCann Award (30) | Return an interception 100+ yards (No OTP or co-op) |
| Dan Carpenter Award (50) | Kick a 60+ yard FG (No OTP or co-op) |
| Darren McFadden Award (25) | Score 4+ rushing TDs in a single game (No OTP or co-op) |
| David Bowens Award (50) | Have 2 pick 6's in the same game (No OTP or co-op) |
| DeAngelo Hall Award (50) | Intercept 4+ passes in one game (No OTP or co-op) |
| DeSean Jackson Award (25) | Return a punt for a TD (No OTP or co-op) |
| Happy 20th EA SPORTS! (20) | Score 20 points in a game and celebrate 20 years of EA Sports! (No OTP or co-op) |
| Hey, Can I Talk to You? (10) | User complete one season's final cut day in Franchise Mode |
| Jahvid Best Award (25) | Gain 154+ yards receiving with Jahvid Best (No OTP or co-op) |
| Kenny Britt Award (25) | Gain 225+ yards receiving with one player (No OTP or co-op) |
| Leon Washington Award (50) | Return 2+ kicks for touchdowns in one game with one player (No OTP or co-op) |
| Mario Manningham Award (25) | Catch a 92+ yard TD pass (No OTP or co-op) |
| Matt Schaub Award (25) | Pass for 497+ yards in one game with one player (No OTP or co-op) |
| Michael Vick Award (30) | Rush for 130+ yards with your QB (No OTP or co-op) |
| MUT Maniac (40) | Complete 20 MUT Games |
| New York Giants Award (30) | Record 10+ sacks as a team in one game (No OTP or co-op) |
| New York Jets Award (25) | Gain over 100+ yards rushing with 2 RBs in the same game (No OTP or co-op) |
| Oakland Raiders Award (30) | Win by 45 points or more (No OTP or co-op) |
| Peyton Hillis Award (25) | Rush for 184+ yards in one game with Peyton Hillis (No OTP or co-op) |

| | |
|---|---|
| Put Da Team On My Back (50) | Catch a 99 yard TD pass with Greg Jennings (No OTP or co-op) |
| Reggie Wayne Award (25) | Catch 14+ passes in one game with one player (No OTP or co-op) |
| Rob Gronkowski Award (25) | Catch 3+ TD passes with a TE in a game (No OTP or co-op) |
| San Diego Chargers Award (30) | Hold your opponent to under 67 yds of total offense (minimum 5 min. qtr., no OTP or co-op) |
| Santonio Holmes Award (25) | Catch a game winning TD pass in OT (No OTP or co-op) |
| The Next Big Thing (5) | Create an NFL Superstar |
| This One is Easy (5) | Create a MUT team |
| This One is Hard (50) | Build an 80 rated MUT team |
| Tim Tebow Award (30) | Score a 40+ yard TD run with a QB (No OTP or co-op) |
| Tom Brady Award (25) | Have a passer rating of 149+ in a game (No OTP or co-op) |
| Ultimate Veteran (20) | Complete 10 MUT Games |
| Verizon Scoreboard Overload (40) | Score 50 points in one game (No OTP or co-op) |
| We're Talking About Practice (10) | Complete a practice in Superstar mode |
| Wheel and Deal (10) | Make a MUT Trade |
| Winning (10) | Win a FA bidding in Franchise Mode |

## MAGIC: THE GATHERING—DUELS OF THE PLANESWALKERS (XBOX 360)

### CLAWS OF VENGEANCE

Win matches using this deck to unlock cards for it.

| UNLOCKABLE | HOW TO UNLOCK |
|---|---|
| Angel's Feather | 2nd win |
| Angel's Feather | 10th win |
| Brion Stoutarm | 9th win |
| Bull Cerodon | 6th win |
| Cho Manno, Revolutionary | 15th win |
| Dragon's Claw | 7th win |
| Godsire | 14th win |
| Knight of the Skyward Eye | 11th win |
| Pariah | 4th win |
| Sangrite Surge | 8th win |
| Sigil B Blessinlessing | 3rd win |
| Sigil Blessing | 12th win |
| Woolly Thoctar | 1st win |
| Wrath of God | 13th win |
| Wurms Tooth | 5th win |

### EARS OF ELVES

Win matches using this deck to unlock cards for it.

| UNLOCKABLE | HOW TO UNLOCK |
|---|---|
| Coat of Arms | 12th win |
| Elvish Champion | 1st win |
| Elvish Champion | 6th win |
| Eyeblight's Ending | 13th win |
| mmaculate Magistrate | 3rd win |
| Imperious Perfect | 9th win |
| Jagged-Scar Archers | 8th win |

| Lys Alana Scarblade | 11th win |
| Nath of the Gilt-Leaf | 14th win |
| Rhys the Exiled | 4th win |
| Talara's Battalion | 15th win |
| Wurm's Tooth | 7th win |
| Wurm's Tooth | 5th win |
| Wurm's Tooth | 10th win |
| Wurm's Tooth | 2nd win |

## EYES OF SHADOW

Win matches using this deck to unlock cards for it.

| UNLOCKABLE | HOW TO UNLOCK |
| --- | --- |
| Ascendant Evincar | 13th win |
| Corrupt | 15th win |
| Crowd of Cinders | 8th win |
| Deathmark | 9th win |
| Deathmark | 5th win |
| Demon's Horn | 1st win |
| Demon's Horn | 6th win |
| Demon's Horn | 4th win |
| Demon's Horn | 3rd win |
| Dread | 16th win |
| Hollowborn Barghest | 17th win |
| Mind Shatter | 10th win |
| Mortivore | 11th win |
| Nekrataal | 14th win |
| Plague Wind | 2nd win |
| Royal Assassin | 12th win |
| Soot Imp | 7th win |

## HANDS OF FLAME

Win matches using this deck to unlock cards for it.

| UNLOCKABLE | HOW TO UNLOCK |
| --- | --- |
| Blaze | 7th Win |
| Bloodmark Mentor | 9th win |
| Cinder Pyromancer | 3rd win |
| Cryoclasm | 6th win |
| Cryoclasm | 10th win |
| Dragon's Claw | 5th win |
| Dragon's Claw | 2nd win |
| Dragon's Claw | 8th win |
| Dragon's Claw | 12th win |
| Furnace of Rath | 16th win |
| Hostility | 17th win |
| Incinerate | 4th win |
| Kamahl, Pit Fighter | 13th win |
| Rage Reflection | 14th win |
| Seismic Assault | 11th win |
| Shivan Dragon | 1st win |
| Shivan Hellkite | 15th win |

## SCALES OF FURY

Win matches using this deck to unlock cards for it.

| UNLOCKABLE | HOW TO UNLOCK |
|---|---|
| Blighting | 3rd win |
| Broodmate Dragon | 11th win |
| Crucible of Fire | 4th win |
| Demon's Horn | 5th win |
| Dragon Roost | 6th win |
| Dragon's Claw | 7th win |
| Fervor | 13th win |
| Flameblast Dragon | 1st win |
| Flameblast Dragon | 14th win |
| Hellkite Overlord | 15th win |
| Shivan Dragon | 9th win |
| Threaten | 8th win |
| Violent Ultimatum | 12th win |
| Wurm's Tooth | 10th win |
| Wurm's Tooth | 2nd win |

## TEETH OF THE PREDATOR

Win matches using this deck to unlock cards for it.

| UNLOCKABLE | HOW TO UNLOCK |
|---|---|
| Blanchwood Armor | 1st win |
| Blanchwood Armor | 11th win |
| Elvish Piper | 14th win |
| Howl of the Night Pack | 4th win |
| Karplusan Strider | 12th win |
| Karplusan Strider | 10th win |
| Karplusan Strider | 6th win |
| Loxodon Warhammer | 16th win |
| Molimo, Maro-Sorcerer | 3rd win |
| Roughshod Mentor | 7th win |
| Troll Ascetic | 15th win |
| Troll Ascetic | 9th win |
| Verdant Force | 13th win |
| Vigor | 17th win |
| Wurm's Tooth | 8th win |
| Wurm's Tooth | 5th win |
| Wurm's Tooth | 2nd win |

## THOUGHTS OF WIND

Win matches using this deck to unlock cards for it.

| UNLOCKABLE | HOW TO UNLOCK |
|---|---|
| Counterbore | 4th win |
| Denizen of the Deep | 16th win |
| Flashfreeze | 10th win |
| Flashfreeze | 6th win |
| Flow of Ideas | 14th win |
| Kraken's Eye | 5th win |
| Kraken's Eye | 2nd win |

NEW!

A
B
C
D
E
F
G
H
I
J
K
L
**M**
N
O
P
Q
R
S
T
U
V
W
X
Y
Z

| Kraken's Eye | 8th win |
|---|---|
| Kraken's Eye | 12th win |
| Mahamoti Djinn | 1st win |
| Mind Spring | 11th win |
| Mind Spring | 17th win |
| Put Away | 7th Win |
| Thieving Magpie | 13th win |
| Thieving Magpie | 15th win |
| Thieving Magpie | 3rd win |
| Thieving Magpie | 9th win |

### WINGS OF LIGHT

Win matches using this deck to unlock cards for it.

| UNLOCKABLE | HOW TO UNLOCK |
|---|---|
| Angel's Feather | 2nd win |
| Angel's Feather | 12th win |
| Angel's Feather | 5th win |
| Angel's Feather | 8th win |
| Angel's Feather | 13th win |
| Luminesce | 6th win |
| Mass Calcify | 15th win |
| Paladin en-Vec | 10th win |
| Purity | 17th win |
| Reya Dawnbringer | 16th win |
| Serra Angel | 1st win |
| Serra's Embrace | 3rd win |
| Skyhunter Skirmisher | 7th win |
| Soul Warden | 11th win |
| Spirit of the Hearth | 14th win |
| Voice of All | 4th win |
| Wrath of God | 9th win |

### GAMER PICTURES

| UNLOCKABLE | HOW TO UNLOCK |
|---|---|
| Jace Beleren gamer pic | Complete all Challenges in single-player campaign. |
| Chandra Nalaar gamer pic | Beat the single-player campaign on any difficulty. |

## MAGICIAN'S QUEST: MYSTERIOUS TIMES (DS)

### UNLOCKABLES

| UNLOCKABLE | HOW TO UNLOCK |
|---|---|
| Bug Wizard | Catch all bugs. |
| Evil Wizard | Cause mischief all around town. |
| Fish Wizard | Catch all fish. |
| Flower Wizard | Make 200 flowers bloom in your town. |
| Forgetful Wizard | Don't save four times and get this title. |
| Gallant Wizard | Talk to everyone for 10 consecutive days. |
| Love Wizard | Have 10 classmates confess love. |
| Skull Wizard | Kill 100 ghosts with the flatulence spell. |
| Wise Wizard | Finish all mystery cases. |
| Great Wizard | Win some tournaments during extracurricular lessons, then get evaluated by Principal Sol. |

| Righteous Wizard | Beat Captain Dot 20 Times. |
|---|---|
| Evil Wizard | Use Prank Magic on your classmates over 100 times. |
| A La Mode Wizard | Get 12 different hair styles. |
| Stylish Wizard | Change into four different sets of clothes every day for 10 days. |

## MAJOR LEAGUE BASEBALL 2K8 (XBOX 360)

### CODES

Enter the codes in the Codes menu located in the Trading Card Album.

| EFFECT | CODE |
|---|---|
| Unlocks all of the American League Central Classic Jersey Trading Cards. | ALCENTRALCLASSICTHREADS08 |
| Unlocks all of the American League East Classic Jersey Trading Cards. | ALEASTCLASSICTHREADS08 |
| Unlocks all of the American League West Classic Jersey Trading Cards. | ALWESTCLASSICTHREADS08 |
| Unlocks all of the National League Central Classic Jersey Trading Cards. | NLCENTRALCLASSICTHREADS08 |
| Unlocks all of the National League East Classic Jersey Trading Cards. | NLEASTCLASSICTHREADS08 |
| Unlocks all of the National League West Classic Jersey Trading Cards. | NLWESTCLASSICTHREADS08 |

## MAJOR LEAGUE BASEBALL 2K11 (PlayStation 3)

### TROPHIES

| UNLOCKABLE | HOW TO UNLOCK |
|---|---|
| 2-Peat (Silver) | Win Back to Back World Series? in My Player Mode. |
| A Day in the Life (Bronze) | Play a game of MLB Today. |
| A Job Well Done (Bronze) | Win 100+ games in a season in My Player Mode. |
| A Pitcher's Best Friend (Bronze) | Turn a double play in a non-simulated game. |
| A Virtue (Silver) | Face 10 pitches as the batter in a non-simulated game. |
| Back To The Cage (Bronze) | Get a Golden Sombrero (strikeout 4 times in 1 game) in My Player Mode. |
| Count It (Bronze) | Complete and win a ranked match. |
| Domination (Bronze) | Strikeout 200 batters with your user profile. |
| Don't Call it a Comeback (Bronze) | Win after being down by 4 after the 6th inning in a non-simulated game. |
| Down But Not Out (Bronze) | Get a hit with 2 strikes in a non-simulated game. |
| Dual Threat (Bronze) | Steal base with pitcher in a non-simulated game. |
| EpidemiK (Silver) | Complete an online game against a 2K developer or a player who already has this achievement. |
| Grab Some Pine (Bronze) | Get a strikeout to end the inning in a non-simulated game. |
| Hawkeye (Bronze) | Draw a walk on a full count in a non-simulated game. |
| He Taketh Away (Bronze) | Rob a Home Run in a non-simulated game. |
| I Came, I Saw... (Bronze) | Hit a Walk-off Home Run in a non-simulated game. |
| I Like to be Thorough (Bronze) | Hit for the Cycle in a non-simulated game. |
| King of the Hill (Bronze) | Get to the top of the Best of the Best ladder in Home Run Derby? Mode. |
| Learning the Ropes (Bronze) | Achieve gold in all the drills. |
| Mid-Summer Classic (Silver) | Play the All-Star game in MLB Today. |
| Mr. Consistency (Silver) | Get a hit in all 9 innings in a non-simulated game. |

**CODES & CHEATS**

| | |
|---|---|
| My Fellow Man (Bronze) | Complete and win an online league game. |
| My Main Squeeze (Bronze) | Bunt the man home in a non-simulated game. |
| No Hole too Deep (Bronze) | Battle Back: Down 0-2, get walked in a non-simulated game. |
| One Man Show (Gold) | Throw a Perfect Game or a No-Hitter on Pro or higher in a 9 inning game, in a non-simulated game. |
| Payback (Bronze) | Hit a HR off a former team in My Player Mode. |
| Power Grab (Bronze) | Hit 50 HR with your user profile. |
| Production (Bronze) | Drive in 250 RBI with your user profile. |
| Remember Me (Bronze) | Break a record in Franchise Mode. (play at least 20 games) |
| State Farm™- The Road to Victory (Bronze) | Get 3 consecutive batters on base in a non-simulated game. |
| Stooges (Bronze) | Strikeout all three hitters in the inning in a non-simulated game. |
| Take That (Bronze) | Get an RBI after being brushed back off the plate in a non-simulated game. |
| The Call (Silver) | Get called up to the Majors in My Player Mode. |
| The Champs (Silver) | Win a World Series? in Franchise Mode. (play at least 20 games) |
| The Goal (Bronze) | Accomplish a Team Season Goal in My Player Mode. |
| The Hall (Silver) | Make the Hall of Fame in My Player Mode. |
| The Road to Greatness (Bronze) | Complete and win 3 ranked matches in a row. |
| The Spice of Life (Bronze) | Play 10 ranked matches using 10 different teams. |
| The Star (Bronze) | Make the All-Star team in My Player Mode. |
| The Start of Something Special (Bronze) | Lead off an inning by hitting a triple in a non-simulated game. |
| The Team to Beat (Bronze) | Beat the San Francisco Giants in a completed online match. |
| The Top (Silver) | Become the #1 ranked player in your My Player organization. |
| This is Why I'm Here My (Bronze) | Be successful in a major league clutch moment in Player Mode. |
| Throw First and Aim Later (Bronze) | Miss your throw to first base with 2 outs in a non-simulated game. |
| To the Rescue (Bronze) | Get a save with the tying run on base in a non-simulated game. |
| Upset Alert (Bronze) | Use the Pittsburgh Pirates in a completed ranked match. |
| Walk Off (Platinum) | Unlock all Trophies |
| What's Your Ring Size? (Gold) | Win a World Series? in My Player Mode. |
| You Did What? (Bronze) | Hit a HR with a pitcher in a non-simulated game. |
| You're Special (Bronze) | Win a Season award in Franchise Mode. (play at least 20 games) |
| Your Day (Bronze) | Win player of the game in an MLB game in My Player |

## MAN VS. WILD   (XBOX 360)

### ACHIEVEMENT

| UNLOCKABLE | HOW TO UNLOCK |
|---|---|
| All God's Creatures (20) | Find all the animals of interest in the Everglades |
| Animal Kingdom (20) | Locate all Animals of Interest in the Rockies |

| | |
|---|---|
| As I Scan This Wasted Land (100) | Complete the "Sahara" campaign. |
| Bear Grylls (100) | Reach the Level "Bear Grylls" |
| Bob's Boats (20) | Find all of Bob McClure's Boats in the Everglades |
| Born Survivor (100) | Complete all episodes without passing out |
| Casted Away (20) | Find all the Man Made Items in Deserted Island |
| Climbing the Rockies (100) | Complete the "Rocky Mountains" campaign. |
| Down in the Low, Low Land (100) | Complete the "Everglades" campaign. |
| Flight 815 (20) | Find all the Plane Debris in Deserted Island |
| Hard to Pronounce, Hard to Find (20) | Find all Five Andiperla Willinkis in Patagonia |
| Horticulture Grylls (20) | Locate the Rare Plants in the Rockies |
| How about A Winter's Tale (100) | Complete the "Patagonia" campaign. |
| Nice Place You Had Here (20) | Locate all the Trash in Patagonia |
| Only Hope Can Keep Me Together (100) | Complete the "Deserted Island" campaign. |
| Osteologist Grylls (20) | Find all the Camel Bones in the Sahara |
| Pack Rat Grylls (20) | Tag all the Junk in the Everglades |
| Patton Was Here (20) | Find all the WWII Artifacts in the Sahara |
| Reminders of the Rush (20) | Locate all the Gold Rush Trash in the Rockies |
| These Belong in a Museum (20) | Find all the Ancient Artifacts in the Sahara |
| Wild, Man! (40) | Completed the Tutorial in Base Camp |

# MARVEL: ULTIMATE ALLIANCE 2 (XBOX 360)

## CODES

Enter one of the following codes at the indicated screen (saving is disabled).

| EFFECT | CODE |
|---|---|
| Fusion | ◁, ▷, △, ▽, △, △, ◁, START |
| Heroes (All Characters) | △, △, ▽, ▽, ◁, ◁, ◁, START |
| Hulk (Character) | ▽, ◁, ◁, △, ▷, ▽, ▽, ◁, START |
| Jean Grey (Character) | ◁, ◁, ▷, ▷, △, ▽, △, ▽, START |
| Money | △, △, ▽, ▽, △, △, ▽, ▽, START |
| Movies | △, ◁, ◁, △, ▷, ▷, △, ▽, START |
| Skins (Costumes) | △, ▽, ◁, ▷, ◁, ▷, START |
| Thor (Character) | △, ▷, ▷, ▽, ▷, ▽, ◁, ▷, START |

## TEAM BONUSES

Certain character combinations unlock special boosts.

| UNLOCKABLE | HOW TO UNLOCK |
|---|---|
| Agile Warriors: +2 all Attributes | Daredevil, Spider-Man, Deadpool, Iron Fist |
| Bruisers: +5 Striking | Juggernaut, Hulk, Thing, Luke Cage, Thor |
| Classic Avengers: +15% Max Stamina | Hulk, Thor, Iron Man, Captain America |
| Fantastic Four: +35% Fusion Gain | Mr. Fantastic, Human Torch, Thing, Invisible Woman |
| Femmes Fatales: +5% Damage | Jean Grey, Storm, Invisible Woman, Ms. Marvel |
| Martial Artists: +5 Striking | Daredevil, Wolverine, Iron Fist, Deadpool |
| Masters of Energy: +15% Max Health | Gambit, Iron Fist, Jean Grey, Ms. Marvel, Nick Fury, Penance |

| Natural Forces +5% Damage inflicted as Health Gain | Storm, Iceman, Thor, Human Torch |
|---|---|
| New Avengers: +10% to all resistances | Ms. Marvel, Spider-Man, Wolverine, Iron Man, Luke Cage, Iron Fist |
| Pro-Reg Heroes: +15% Max HP | Iron Man, Mr. Fantastic, Deadpool, Songbird, Ms Marvel, Spider-Man |
| Secret Avengers: +3 Teamwork | Captain America, Iron Fist, Luke Cage, Invisible Woman, Human Torch, Storm, Spider-Man |
| Shut Up Already! - 15% Extra Health | Play as a team of Spider-Man, Iceman, Deadpool, and Human Torch. |
| Think Tank: +15% Max HP | Mr. Fantastic, Iron Man, Green Goblin, Spider-Man, Hulk |
| Thunderbolts: +5% Damage | Green Goblin, Songbird, Venom, Penance |
| Weapon Specialists: +5% Criticals | Daredevil, Deadpool, Gambit, Thor, Green Goblin, Captain America |
| X-Men: +15% Max Stamina | Gambit, Jean Grey, Wolverine, Storm, Ice Man, Juggernaut (interchangeable) |

## SPECIAL CHARACTERS

Unlock the following characters by performing the actions listed.

| UNLOCKABLE | HOW TO UNLOCK |
|---|---|
| Deadpool | Beat the D.C. Level |
| Green Goblin and Venom | Beat them at the end of Wakanda Act 3. |
| Hulk | Collect all five Gamma Regulators. |
| Iron Fist | Choose the Rebel side when faced with the choice. |
| Jean Grey | Collect all five M'Kraan Shards. |
| Ms. Marvel | Beat the NYC Level. |
| Nick Fury | Beat the game. |
| Penance | Defeat him in the portal room to the negative zone. |
| Songbird | Choose the Register side when faced with the choice. |
| Thor | Collect all five Asgardian Runes. |

## MARVEL: ULTIMATE ALLIANCE 2 (PlayStation 3)

### CODES

Enter one of the following codes at the indicated screen (saving is disabled).

| EFFECT | CODE |
|---|---|
| Diaries | ⇦, ⇨, ⇨, ⇦, ⇧, ⇧, ⇨, START |
| Dossier | ⇩, ⇩, ⇦, ⇨, ⇨, ⇦, ⇩, START |
| Fusion | ⇨, ⇨, ⇨, ⇩, ⇧, ⇨, ⇦, START |
| Heroes (All Characters) | ⇧, ⇧, ⇩, ⇩, ⇦, ⇦, ⇦, START |
| Hulk (Character) | ⇩, ⇦, ⇨, ⇧, ⇨, ⇩, ⇦, START |
| Jean Grey (Character) | ⇦, ⇨, ⇦, ⇨, ⇧, ⇩, ⇧, ⇩, START |
| Money | ⇧, ⇧, ⇩, ⇩, ⇧, ⇧, ⇩, ⇩, START |
| Movies | ⇧, ⇦, ⇨, ⇧, ⇨, ⇦, ⇧, START |
| Power | ⇧, ⇧, ⇩, ⇩, ⇦, ⇨, ⇦, START |
| Skins (Costumes) | ⇧, ⇩, ⇦, ⇨, ⇦, ⇨, START |
| Thor (Character) | ⇧, ⇨, ⇩, ⇦, ⇩, ⇦, ⇨, START |

### TEAM BONUSES

Certain character combinations unlock special boosts.

| UNLOCKABLE | HOW TO UNLOCK |
|---|---|
| Agile Warriors: +2 all Attributes | Daredevil, Spider-Man, Deadpool, Iron Fist |
| Bruisers: +5 Striking | Juggernaut, Hulk, Thing, Luke Cage, Thor |

| | |
|---|---|
| **Classic Avengers:** +15% Max Stamina | Hulk, Thor, Iron Man, Captain America |
| **Fantastic Four:** +35% Fusion Gain | Mr. Fantastic, Human Torch, Thing, Invisible Woman |
| **Femmes Fatales:** +5% Damage | Jean Grey, Storm, Invisible Woman, Ms. Marvel |
| **Martial Artists:** +5 Striking | Daredevil, Wolverine, Iron Fist, Deadpool |
| **Masters of Energy:** +15% Max Health | Gambit, Iron Fist, Jean Grey, Ms. Marvel, Nick Fury, Penance |
| **Natural Forces** +5% Damage inflicted as Health Gain | Storm, Iceman, Thor, Human Torch |
| **New Avengers:** +10% to all resistances | Ms. Marvel, Spider-Man, Wolverine, Iron Man, Luke Cage, Iron Fist |
| **Pro-Reg Heroes:** +15% Max HP | Iron Man, Mr. Fantastic, Deadpool, Songbird, Ms Marvel, Spider-Man |
| **Secret Avengers:** +3 Teamwork | Captain America, Iron Fist, Luke Cage, Invisible Woman, Human Torch, Storm, Spider-Man |
| **Shut Up Already!** —15% Extra Health | Play as a team of Spider-Man, Iceman, Deadpool, and Human Torch. |
| **Think Tank:** +15% Max HP | Mr. Fantastic, Iron Man, Green Goblin, Spider-Man, Hulk |
| **Thunderbolts:** +5% Damage | Green Goblin, Songbird, Venom, Penance |
| **Weapon Specialists:** +5% Criticals | Daredevil, Deadpool, Gambit, Thor, Green Goblin, Captain America |
| **X-Men:** +15% Max Stamina | Gambit, Jean Grey, Wolverine, Storm, Ice Man, Juggernaut (interchangeable) |

## SPECIAL CHARACTERS

Unlock the following characters by performing the actions listed.

| UNLOCKABLE | HOW TO UNLOCK |
|---|---|
| **Deadpool** | Beat the D.C. Level. |
| **Green Goblin and Venom** | Beat them at the end of Wakanda Act 3. |
| **Hulk** | Collect all five Gamma Regulators. |
| **Iron Fist** | Choose the Rebel side when faced with the choice. |
| **Jean Grey** | Collect all five M'Kraan Shards. |
| **Ms. Marvel** | Beat the NYC Level. |
| **Nick Fury** | Beat the game. |
| **Penance** | Defeat him in the portal room to the negative zone. |
| **Songbird** | Choose the Register side when faced with the choice. |
| **Thor** | Collect all five Asgardian Runes. |

## MARVEL: ULTIMATE ALLIANCE 2 (Wii)

### CODES

Enter the following codes with the D-Pad

| EFFECT | CODE |
|---|---|
| **All Bonus Missions (at Bonus Missions screen)** | ⬇⬆⬇⬆⬇⬆⬇⬇ |
| **All Heroes (at Character Select screen)** | ⬇⬆⬇⬆⬇⬆⬇⬇ |
| **Characters Advance 10 Levels (at Pause menu)** | ⬇⬆⬇⬆⬇⬆⬇⬇ |
| **Fusion Power Always Four Stars** | ⬇⬆⬇⬆⬇⬆⬇⬇ |
| **God Mode (at Pause menu)** | ⬇⬇⬇⬇⬇⬇⬇⬇ |

## MASS EFFECT (XBOX 360)

### CHARACTER BENEFIT UNLOCKABLES

Attain certain achievements to gain benefits on future playthroughs.

| UNLOCKABLE | HOW TO UNLOCK |
|---|---|
| +10% Experience Bonus | Complete 75% of game. |
| +10% Hardening Bonus | Complete 75% of game with Ashley in squad. |
| +10% Health Bonus | Kill 150 organic beings. |
| +10% Shield Bonus | Kill 250 synthetics. |
| +25% Marksman Cooldown Bonus | Attain 150 kills with pistol. |
| 10% Reduced Cooldown for Barrier and Stasis | Complete 75% of game with Liara in squad. |
| 10% Reduced Cooldown for Lift and Throw | Complete 75% of game with Kaiden in squad. |
| 10% Reduced Cooldown for Overload and Damping | Complete 75% of game with Garrus in squad. |
| 10% Reduced Cooldown for Sabotage and AI Hacking | Complete 75% of game with Tali in squad. |
| 10% Shield Increase | Sustain more shield damage than health damage during one playthrough. |
| 5% Increase in Weapon Damage | Complete the game twice on any difficulty. |
| Assault Rifle Skill for New Characters | Attain 150 kills with assault rifle. |
| Barrier Skill for New Characters | Use Barrier 75 times. |
| Decryption Skill for New Characters | Use Sabotage 75 times. |
| Electronics Skill for New Characters | Use Overload 75 times. |
| First Aid Skill for New Characters | Use medi-gel 150 times. |
| Hacking Skill for New Characters | Use AI Hacking 75 times. |
| Lift Skill (for non-biotics) | Use Lift 75 times. |
| Medicine Skill for New Characters | Use Neural Hacking 75 times. |
| Regenerate 1 Health per Second | Complete 75% of game with Wrex in squad. |
| Shielding Skill for New Characters | Use Dampening 75 times. |
| Shotgun Skill for New Characters | Attain 150 kills with shotgun. |
| Sniper Rifle Skill for New Characters | Attain 150 kills with sniper rifle. |
| Spectre Grade Weapons for Purchase | Attain 1,000,000 credits in your wallet. |
| Singularity Skill for New Characters | Use Singularity 75 times. |
| Statis Skill for New Characters | Use Statis 75 times. |
| Throw Skill for New Characters | Use Throw 75 times. |
| Warp Skill for New Characters | Use Warp 75 times. |

### UNLOCKABLE GAMER PICS

Complete the game on the Hardcore and Insanity difficulties to unlock two special gamer pics for your profile.

| UNLOCKABLE | HOW TO UNLOCK |
|---|---|
| "N7" Gamer Pic | Gain the Medal of Valor achievement. |
| Saren Gamer Pic | Gain the Distinguished Combat Medal achievement. |

### UNLOCKABLES

Complete the game on Normal to unlock the secrets.

| UNLOCKABLE | HOW TO UNLOCK |
|---|---|
| Hardcore Mode | Complete the game once. |
| Increased Level Cap (51–0) | Complete the game once. |
| Insane Difficulty | Beat the game on the Hardcore difficulty without changing the difficulty. |

| New Game + | Start a New Game, then select existing Career. You'll be playing with your older character (with all items and skills intact). |
|---|---|

## MASS EFFECT 2 (XBOX 360)

### *UNLOCKABLES*

| UNLOCKABLE | HOW TO UNLOCK |
|---|---|
| Bonus 25% Experience | Beat the game on any difficulty |
| 200k Credits | Start New Game after 1 Playthrough |
| 50k of each Resource | Start New Game after 1 Playthrough |
| New Colors for Party Members | Complete a party member's loyalty mission. |
| Unlock Loyalty Skills | Complete the Loyalty missions for each of your party members to unlock their individuals skills. |

## MASS EFFECT 2 (PlayStation 3)

### *UNLOCKABLE*

After you complete a character's Loyalty Mission, the character gains their loyalty power. Research Advanced Training as Shepard at the research terminal in Mordin's lab. You can learn a single loyalty power as a "bonus power". Each time Shepard undergoes Advanced Training, the new power replaces the previous one and the skill points allotted to the old power will transfer to the new bonus power. Any bonus powers gained during previous playthroughs will be available at the start of the new game at character creation aas well as at research terminals.

| UNLOCKABLE | HOW TO UNLOCK |
|---|---|
| Armor Piercing Ammo | Complete Archangel's Loyalty Mission |
| Barrier | Complete Jacob's Loyalty Mission |
| Dominate | Side with Morinth in Samara's Loyalty Mission |
| Flashbang Grenade | Complete Kasumi's Loyalty Mission |
| Fortification | Complete Grunt's Loyalty Mission |
| Geth Shield Boost | Complete Legion's Loyalty Mission |
| Inferno Grenade | Complete Zaeed's Loyalty Mission. |
| Neural Shock | Complete Mordin's Loyalty Mission. |
| Reave | Side with Samara in Samara's Loyalty Mission. |
| Shield Drain | Complete Tali's Loyalty Mission. |
| Shredder Ammo | Complete Thane's Loyalty Mission. |
| Slam | Complete Miranda's Loyalty Mission. |
| Stasis | Complete the Lair of the Shadow Broker DLC. |
| Warp Ammo | Complete Jack's Loyalty Mission. |
| 25% Experience Boost | Start a new game after beating the game once. |
| Start with 200,000 Credits | Start a new game after beating the game once. |
| Start with 50,000 of Each Resource | Start a new game after beating the game once. |
| New Game+ | Clear Suicide Mission |

## MEDAL OF HONOR: AIRBORNE (XBOX 360)

### *CODES*

| UNLOCKABLE | HOW TO UNLOCK |
|---|---|
| Enter Cheat menu | Press ⓇⒷ+ⓁⒷ, then press ❌,Ⓑ,Ⓨ,Ⓐ,Ⓐ |
| Full Ammo | Press and hold ⓁⒷ+ⓇⒷ then press Ⓑ,Ⓑ,Ⓨ,❌,Ⓐ,Ⓨ |
| Full Health | Ⓨ,❌,❌,Ⓨ,Ⓐ,Ⓑ |

## MEDIEVIL RESURRECTION (PSP)

To enter this code, pause the game.

| UNLOCKABLE | CODE |
|---|---|
| Invincibility and All Weapons | Hold Ⓡ, then press ⬇, ⬆, ■, ▲, ▲, ●, ⬇, ⬆, ■, ▲ |

## MEGA MAN (Wii)

### UNLOCKABLES

| UNLOCKABLE | HOW TO UNLOCK |
|---|---|
| Select Trick | When using a weapon that goes through an enemy, press the SELECT button (this pauses the game without bringing up the weapon menu) when the weapon is making contact with the enemy. While the game is paused this way the enemy continues to flash. When the flashing has stopped, press the SELECT button again to un-pause the game and the weapon hits the enemy again, causing more damage. You can do this trick repeatedly with many of the bosses, making them very easy to beat. |

## MEGA MAN 10 (Wii)

### CHALLENGES

There are two challenge types. Type 1 are like mini-stages or boss battles and are accessed from the Challenge menu. Type 2 are like Xbox's Achievements and don't need to be unlocked to do them. Type 1 boss and miniboss challenges generally require reaching the corresponding boss on the corresponding difficulty mode (the challenge is unlocked when you reach the boss, not when you kill it).

| UNLOCKABLE | HOW TO UNLOCK |
|---|---|
| Easy boss challenges | Reach the boss on Easy difficulty. |
| Easy miniboss challenges | Reach the miniboss on Easy or Normal difficulty. |
| Hard boss challenges | Reach the boss on Hard difficulty. |
| Hard miniboss challenges | Reach the miniboss on Hard difficulty. |
| Normal boss challenges | Reach the boss on Normal difficulty. |
| Normal minboss challenges | Reach the miniboss on Normal difficulty. |

## MERCENARIES 2: WORLD IN FLAMES (XBOX 360)

### UNLOCKABLE COSTUMES

To unlock costumes, you must complete Level 3 of a weapon challenge, which can be done by talking to Fiona at your PMC. Each time you complete a Level 3 weapon challenge, you receive one of three costumes.

## METAL GEAR ACID (PSP)

Enter the following in the Passwords menu through the Main menu.

| CARD | PASSWORD |
|---|---|
| Gives Card No. 173 - Viper | Viper |
| Gives Card No. 178 - Mika Slayton | Mika |
| Gives Card No. 182 - Karen Houjou | Karen |
| Gives Card No. 184 - Jehuty | Jehuty |
| Gives Card No. 199 - XM8 | Xmeight |
| Gives Card No. 200 - Kosaka Yuka | Kobe |
| Gives Card No. 201 - Asaki Yoshida | umeda |
| Gives Card No. 202 - Yu Saito | YEBISU |
| Gives Card No. 203 - Shibuya Eri | Roppongi |

## METAL GEAR ACID 2 (PSP)

Enter these passwords at the password screen. You'll obtain them as you load your saved games.

| PASSWORD | EFFECT |
|---|---|
| Ronaldsiu | Banana Peel Card |
| Dcy | Card No. 203—Decoy Octopus |
| SONOFSULLY | Card No. 291—Jack |
| Vrs | Card No. 046—Strain (JP Version only) |
| Cct | Card No. 099—Gijin-san (JP Version only) |
| Konami | Card No. 119—Reaction Block |
| Viper | Card No. 161—Viper |
| Mika | Card No. 166—Mika Slayton |
| Karen | Card No. 170—Karen Houjou |
| Jehuty | Card No. 172—Jehuty |
| Xmeight | Card No. 187—XM8 |
| Signt | Card No. 188—Mr. Sigint |
| Sgnt | Card No. 188—SIGINT (JP Version only) |
| Hrrr | Card No. 197—Sea Harrier (JP Version only) |
| Dcyctps | Card No. 203—Decoy Octopus (JP Version only) |
| Rgr | Card No. 212—Roger McCoy (JP Version only) |
| Xx | Card No. 281—Hinomoto Reiko (JP Version only) |
| Kinoshitaa | Card No. 285—Kinoshita Ayumi (JP Version only) |
| Shiimeg | Card No. 286—Ishii Meguru (JP Version only) |
| Nonat | Card No. 287—Sano Natsume (JP Version only) |
| No Place | Card No. 288—MGS4 (JP Version only) |
| Snake | Card No. 294—Solid Snake (MGS4) |
| Otacon | Card No. 295—Otacon (MGS4) |
| shrrr | Card No. 197 Sea Harrier (US version ) |
| Ginormousj | Emma's Parrot Card |
| Gekko | Gekko (US Version) |
| NEXTGEN | Get MGS4 card |
| shinta | Gives you card Gijin-san |
| nojiri | Gives you card Strand |
| mgr | Ishii Meguru |
| aym | Kinoshita Ayumi |
| mk2 | Metal Gear MK. II (MGS4) Card unlocked |
| smoking | No Smoking card (US Version) |
| thespaniard | Possessed Arm card |
| gcl | Reaction Block 119 (Japanese version only) |
| tobidacid | Solid Eye card (US/UK Version) |
| ntm | Unlocks Natsume Sano Card an Solid Eye Video |
| Hnmt | Unlocks Reiko Hinomoto card |
| Mccy | Unlocks the Roger McCoy card |

### CARD PACK UPGRADES

Complete the game once. Load your finished game save and play through the game again. At the points where you received the card packs, they will be upgraded into newer versions.

| UNLOCKABLE | HOW TO UNLOCK |
|---|---|
| Chronicle Unlimited Pack | Upgrade Chronicle Pack |
| MGS1 Integral Pack | Upgrade MGS1 Pack |
| MGS2 Substance Pack | Upgrade MGS2 Pack |
| MGS3 Subsistence Pack | Upgrade MGS3 Pack |

## UNLOCKABLE CARDS

Complete the game on any difficulty and get a certain rare card.

| UNLOCKABLE | HOW TO UNLOCK |
|---|---|
| "E-Z Gun" Card | Beat 6 levels in Arena mode on Easy setting |
| "G36C" Card | Beat 6 levels in Arena mode on Extreme setting |
| "Stealth Camo" Card | Beat 6 levels in Arena mode on Normal setting |
| Metal Gear RAY | Beat Campaign mode twice |
| Metal Gear Rex | Complete game on Normal |
| MGS4 | Complete game on Easy |
| Running Man Card | Complete 6 rounds in the Arena on Hard setting |

## METAL GEAR SOLID 4: GUNS OF THE PATRIOTS (PlayStation 3)

### BONUS WEAPONS

| UNLOCKABLE | HOW TO UNLOCK |
|---|---|
| Bandanna | Complete a single-player session, on any difficulty, without killing anyone (including bosses). |
| Desert Eagle, Long Barrel | Earn the Fox emblem on a single-player session. |
| Digital Camera | In the Nomad vehicle during the mission intermission; you can unlock a special photo by picking up this item in stage 4 instead of earlier. |
| Patriot Future Assault Weapon | Earn the Big Boss emblem on a single-player session. |
| Race (Ricochet) Gun | Clear the single-player game once. |
| Scanning Plug S | Log more than 10 hours of Metal Gear Online play time on the same profile as your Metal Gear 4 game. You purchase this from Drebin. |
| Solar Gun | Collect the five statues (those of the four Battle Beauties and the Frog Soldier/Haven Troopers in stage 1) using non-lethal means on their respective idols. |
| Stealth Item | Complete a single-player session without instigating a single alert (caution is okay, but not alert). You can do this on any difficulty. |
| Thor 45-70 | Earn the Fox Hound emblem on a single-player session. |
| World War I Pistol | Earn the Hound emblem on a single-player session. |

### COMPLETION UNLOCKABLES

| UNLOCKABLE | HOW TO UNLOCK |
|---|---|
| Big Boss Extreme Difficulty | Complete the single-player mode once (and saving the cleared data). |
| New Combat Vests | Clear the single-player game once. |

### COSTUMES

| UNLOCKABLE | HOW TO UNLOCK |
|---|---|
| Altair | Obtain the Assassin emblem. |
| Civilian Disguise | Start Eastern Europe level. |
| Corpse Camo | Get 41 continues or more in a single playthrough to unlock this Octocamo. |
| Middle East Militia Disguise | Middle East in the Militia Safe House. |
| South American Rebel Disguise | South America (Cove Valley Village). |
| Suit | Clear the game once. |

### DOLLS/STATUES

| UNLOCKABLE | HOW TO UNLOCK |
|---|---|
| Crying Wolf Doll/Statue | In a side of a building just where you start after killing her beast form |
| Frog Soldier Doll/Statue | At the garage at the end of the battle |

| | |
|---|---|
| **Laughing Beast Doll/Statue** | On a bed in a little room |
| **Raging Raven Doll/Statue** | On the upper floor on a corner |
| **Screaming Mantis Doll/Statue** | On the corridor where you started |

## FACE PAINT

| UNLOCKABLE | HOW TO UNLOCK |
|---|---|
| **Big Boss's** | Earn the Big Boss emblem on a single-player session. |
| **Crying Wolf** | Defeat the Battle Beauty (human form) Crying Wolf by non-lethal means. |
| **Drebin** | Purchase and keep more than 60 different weapons. |
| **FaceCamo** | Defeat the Battle Beauty Laughing Octopus (the overall battle, no specifics involved). |
| **Laughing Octopus** | Defeat the Battle Beauty (human form) Laughing Octopus by non-lethal means. |
| **Otacon** | Shock Dr. Emmerich using the Metal Gear II during the intermission scene. |
| **Raging Raven** | Defeat the Battle Beauty (human form) Raging Raven by non-lethal means. |
| **Raiden Mask A** | Shock Sunny using the Metal Gear II during the intermission scene. |
| **Raiden Mask B** | Shock Dr. Naomi Hunter using the Metal Gear II during the intermission scene. |
| **Roy Campbell** | Shock Colonel Campbell using the Metal Gear II during the intermission scene. |
| **Screaming Mantis** | Defeat the Battle Beauty (human form) Screaming Mantis by non-lethal means. |
| **Young Snake** | Beat Act 2. |
| **Young Snake with Bandana** | Beat Act 2. |

## IPOD TUNES

Snake's iPod can download specific tunes throughout the course of the game. Some songs have an additional "secret" effect when it is played in the game.

| UNLOCKABLE | HOW TO UNLOCK |
|---|---|
| **Beyond the Bounds (increases power stun damage done by Snake from non-lethal weapons)** | Stage 4 Shadow Moses, Tank Hangar. After is restored, backtrack to the upper catwalk and explore all rooms. |
| **Big Boss (increases stun damage and increases Snake's accuracy when played)** | Earn the Big Boss emblem. |
| **Bio Hazard** | Frisk the resistance fighter in Easter Europe. |
| **Bio Hazard (cause soldiers held by Snake to scream in terror)** | Stage 3 Europe, Midtown. |
| **Boktai 2 Theme** | Act 2, Mission Briefing, upstairs in the Nomad. |
| **Bon Dance** | Act 2, Marketplace. |
| **Destiny's Call (causes soldiers held by Snake to go enraged)** | A random gift from a militia or rebel soldier if Snake gives them a healing item. |
| **Flowing Destiny (causes soldiers held by Snake to weep like a little girl)** | Stage 4 Shadow Moses, Canyon. Before leaving the canyon area, examine the rocky walls for a hole hiding this item. |
| **Fury, The (causes soldiers held by Snake to go enraged)** | Stage 2 South America, Cove Valley Village. Inside the fire ravaged house. |
| **Inorino Uta** | Act 1, Mission Briefing. |
| **Level 3 Warning** | Act 1, Advent Palace. |
| **Lunar Knights Main Theme** | Act 4, Mission Briefing, upstairs in the Nomad. |

NEW!

A
B
C
D
E
F
G
H
I
J
K
L
**M**
N
O
P
Q
R
S
T
U
V
W
X
Y
Z

**CODES & CHEATS**

| | |
|---|---|
| *Metal Gear* 20 Years History: Part 2 | Act 4, Warhead Storage Building B2. |
| *Metal Gear* 20 Years History: Part 3 | Act 2, South America Confinement Facility. In room with beds inside the house. |
| *Metal Gear Solid* Main Theme (The Document Remix) | Act 5, under hatch to the left at the beginning of area. |
| MGS 4 Love Theme / Action (causes soldiers held by Snake to weep like a little girl) | A random gift from a militia or rebel soldier if Snake gives them a healing item. |
| On Alert | Act 3, Midtown N Sector. |
| One Night in Neo Kobe City (causes soldiers held by Snake to laugh) | Act 3, Midtown, hold-up PMC. |
| Opening—Old L.A. 2040 (increases Snake's accuracy) | Stage 4 Shadow Moses, Nuclear Warhead Storage B2. Input 78925 into Otacon's lab computer. |
| Policenaughts Ending (causes soldiers held by Snake to fall asleep on touch) | Stage 4 Shadow Moses, Nuclear Warhead Storage B2. Input 13462 into Otacon's lab computer. |
| Rock Me (increases Snake's amount of life recovered from items and other means) | Stage 2 South America, Confinement Facility. Island in the southeastern quadrant. |
| Sailor (increases Snake's amount of life recovered from items and other means) | Stage 2 South America, Vista Mansion. Between the east wall and a cargo container |
| Shin Bokura no Taiyou Theme | Act 3, Mission Briefing, upstairs in the Nomad. |
| Show Time (causes soldiers held by Snake to scream in terror) | A random gift from a militia or rebel soldier if Snake gives them a healing item. |
| Snake Eater (increase the life recovery rate of Snake through items and other actions) | Unlocked by earning all 40 game clear emblems. |
| Subsistence (increase Snake's accuracy) | Play at least one game of Metal Gear Online. You must start the match with at least two players. |
| Test Subject's Duality | Act 3, Midtown S Sector. |
| The Best Is Yet To Come | Act 4, Snow Field. Just before the "Disc Change" Codec scene. |
| The Essence of Vince | Act 3, Echo's Beacon. |
| The Fury | Act 2, in the Cave Valley Village in badly burned building. |
| Theme of Solid Snake | Act 1, Millennium Park. |
| Theme of Tara | Act 1, Militia Safehouse. Just before seeing the unmanned flying-bomber on the table. |
| Warhead Storage | Act 4, Tank Hanger. Upper floor ventilation shaft. |
| Yell (Dead Cell) | Act 4, Casting Facility North. |
| Zanzibarland Breeze | Act 1, Urban Ruins before cutscene. |

### UNLOCKABLE EMBLEMS

| UNLOCKABLE | HOW TO UNLOCK |
|---|---|
| Ant Emblem | Shake 50 enemies for items. |
| Assassin's Emblem | Beat the game with 50+ knife kills, 50+ CQC holds, and 25 or less alerts. |
| Bear Emblem | Choke 100 enemies to death. |
| Bee Emblem | Use the Scanning Plug S or Syringe on 50 enemies. |
| Big Boss Emblem | Beat the game on the highest difficulty with no deaths, no alerts, no kills, no recovery items, no stealth suit, no bandana items, in under 5 hours. |

| | |
|---|---|
| Blue Bird Emblem | Give friendly soldiers 50 items. |
| Centipede | Get less than 75 alert phases, less than 250 kills, and over 25 continues. |
| Chicken | Get over 150 alert phases, over 500 kills, over 50 continues, use over 50 recovery items and finish the game in over 35 hours. |
| Cow | Activate over 100 alerts. |
| Crocodile | Have over 400 kills. |
| Eagle Emblem | Get 150 headshots. |
| Fox Emblem | Beat the game on Normal or higher with no deaths, 5 or less alerts, no kills, no recovery items, no stealth suit, no bandana items, in under 6 hours. |
| Fox Hound Emblem | Beat the game on Hard or higher with no deaths, 3 or less alerts, no kills, no recovery items, no stealth suit, no bandana items, in under 5.5 hours. |
| Frog Emblem | Dive or roll 200 times. |
| Gecko Emblem | Press against walls for a total of 1 hour. |
| Giant Panda Emblem | Complete the game after 30 cumulative hours of play. |
| Gibbon Emblem | Hold up 50 enemies. |
| Hawk Emblem | Be admired by 25 friendly soldiers. |
| Hog Emblem | Get 10 combat highs. |
| Hound Emblem | Beat the game on hard or higher with no deaths, 3 or less alerts, no kills, no recovery items, no stealth suit, no bandana items, in under 6.5 hours. |
| Hyena Emblem | Pick up 400 dropped weapons. |
| Inch Worm Emblem | Crawl on the ground for a total of 1 hour. |
| Jaguar | Get over 75 alert phases, less than 250 kills, and less than 25 continues. |
| Leopard | Get over 75 alert phases, less than 250 kills, and over 25 continues. |
| Little Gray Emblem | Collect all 69 weapons. |
| Lobster Emblem | Spend a total of 2.5 hours crouching. |
| Mantis | Finish the game with no alerts activated; no continues; no rations, noodles, or regains used; and in under 5 hours. |
| Octopus | Beat the game without activating any alert phases. |
| Panther | Get over 75 alert phases, over 250 kills, and less than 25 continues. |
| Pig | Use more than 50 recovery items. |
| Pigeon | Beat the game without killing a single person (Gekkos and Dwarf Gekkos don't count). |
| Puma | Get over 75 alert phases, over 250 kills, and over 25 continues. |
| Rabbit | Flick through 100 *Playboy* pages. |
| Rabbit Emblem | Look at 100 *Playboy* pages. |
| Raven | Beat the game in under 5 hours. |
| Scarab | Perform over 100 rolls. |
| Scorpion | Get less than 75 alert Phases, less than 250 kills, and less than 25 continues. |
| Spider | Get less than 75 alert phases, over 250 kills, and over 25 continues. |
| Tarantula | Get less than 75 alert phases, over 250 kills, and less than 25 continues. |
| Tortoise | Spend more than 60 minutes inside the drum can or cardboard box (this can be done throughout the game, not all at once), |
| Wolf | Beat the game with no continues and no rations, regains, or noodles used. |

NEW!

A
B
C
D
E
F
G
H
I
J
K
L
M
N
O
P
Q
R
S
T
U
V
W
X
Y
Z

## METAL MARINES (Wii)

### CODES

| CODE | EFFECT |
|------|--------|
| Enter CSDV as a password | Start with more Money and Energy for each level |
| HBBT | Level 02 |
| PCRC | Level 03 |
| NWTN | Level 04 |
| LSMD | Level 05 |
| CLST | Level 06 |
| JPTR | Level 07 |
| NBLR | Level 08 |
| PRSC | Level 09 |
| PHTN | Level 10 |
| TRNS | Level 11 |
| RNSN | Level 12 |
| ZDCP | Level 13 |
| FKDV | Level 14 |
| YSHM | Level 15 |
| CLPD | Level 16 |
| LNVV | Level 17 |
| JFMR | Level 18 |
| JCRY | Level 19 |
| KNLB | Level 20 |

## MICHAEL JACKSON THE EXPERIENCE (DS)

### UNLOCKABLE

Collect the required nubmer of coins to unlock a tour set list. Here are the requirements for each tour set list.

| UNLOCKABLE | HOW TO UNLOCK |
|------------|---------------|
| Tour Set List 2 (Heal The World & Bad) | Collect 6 coins in Tour Mode. |
| Tour Set List 3 (The Way You Make Me Feel, Don't Stop 'Til You Get Enough & Black or White | Collect 13 coins in Tour Mode. |
| Tour Set List 4 (Wanna Be Startin' Somethin', Streetwalker, Leave Me Alone & Smooth Criminal) | Collect 25 coins in Tour Mode. |
| Tour Set List 5 (Beat It) | Collect 41 coins in Tour Mode. |

## MICHAEL JACKSON THE EXPERIENCE (XBOX 360)

### ACHIEVEMENTS

| UNLOCKABLE | HOW TO UNLOCK |
|------------|---------------|
| A Lover Not A Fighter (20) | Achieved a 5 star rating in "The Girl is Mine" in vocal performance mode |
| A Star Is Born (20) | Achieved at least 3 stars in 5 different songs |
| And Again... (20) | Achieved a 5 star rating in "Stranger In Moscow" in performance mode |
| Annie Are You Okay? (20) | Achieved a 5 star rating in "Smooth Criminal" in performance mode |
| Be Careful Of What You Do (25) | Achieved a 5 star rating in "Billie Jean" in master performance mode |
| Because I'm Bad (20) | Achieved a 5 star rating in "Bad" in performance mode |
| But I'm Only Human (20) | Achieved a 5 star rating in "Will You Be There" in vocal performance mode |
| Call It A Night (30) | Performed 300 songs in Solo Mode |

| | |
|---|---|
| **Dance You Into Day (20)** | Achieved a 5 star rating in "Rock With You" in performance mode |
| **Dare Me (20)** | Achieved a 5 star rating in "In the Closet" in performance mode |
| **Do Or Dare (20)** | Achieved a 5 star rating in "Money" in performance mode |
| **Do You Remember The Time? (20)** | Achieved a 5 star rating in "Remember the Time" in performance mode |
| **From Sun Up To Midnight (20)** | Achieved a 5 star rating in "Workin' Day And Night" in performance mode |
| **Gravity Check (20)** | Became MJ while performing The Leaning in "Smooth Criminal" |
| **Happy Birthday (25)** | Played the game on August 29th, MJ's Birthday |
| **I Am The One (20)** | Achieved a 5 star rating in "Billie Jean" in performance mode |
| **I Feel On Fire (25)** | Achieved a 5 star rating in "Don't Stop 'Til You Get Enough" in master performance mode |
| **Just Beat It (25)** | Achieved a 5 star rating in "Beat It" in master performance mode |
| **Keep On With The Force (20)** | Achieved a 5 star rating in "Don't Stop 'Til You Get Enough" in performance mode |
| **Let Me Be! (20)** | Achieved a 5 star rating in "Dirty Diana" in performance mode |
| **Love Is The Answer (20)** | Achieved a 5 star rating in "I Just Can't Stop Loving You" in vocal performance mode |
| **Make It A Better Place (20)** | Achieved a 5 star rating in "Heal the World" in vocal performance mode |
| **Midnight Rider (20)** | Achieved a 5 star rating in "Sunset Driver" in performance mode |
| **Moonwalker (20)** | Achieved a perfect score performing The Moonwalk in "Billie Jean" |
| **No One Wants To Be Defeated (20)** | Achieved a 5 star rating in "Beat It" in performance mode |
| **Nothin' Gonna Stop Me (20)** | Achieved a 5 star rating in "Speed Demon" in performance mode |
| **Now I Believe In Miracles (20)** | Achieved a 5 star rating in "Black Or White" in performance mode |
| **Opening Night (15)** | Achieved your first star in Solo Mode |
| **Pretty Baby (20)** | Achieved a 5 star rating in "Streetwalker" in performance mode |
| **She Knows Your Game (20)** | Achieved a 5 star rating in "Blood On the Dance Floor" in performance mode |
| **Sounding Heart Beats (25)** | Achieved a 5 star rating in "Smooth Criminal" in master performance mode |
| **Super Star (30)** | Beat a 5 star #1 on a leaderboard |
| **Thanks For Playing! (15)** | Watched the credits sequence. Thank you for your support |
| **There's A Tappin' In The Floor (20)** | Achieved a 5 star rating in "Ghosts" in performance mode |
| **Those Special Times (25)** | Achieved a 5 star rating in "Remember the Time" in master performance mode |
| **Thriller Night (20)** | Achieved a 5 star rating in "Thriller" in performance mode |
| **Very Talented (20)** | Achieved an 8x multiplier in any song |
| **We Can Rock Forever (25)** | Achieved a 5 star rating in "Rock With You" in master performance mode |

| We Made Our Vows (20) | Achieved a 5 star rating in "Who Is It" in performance mode |
| What About Sunrise? (20) | Achieved a 5 star rating in "Earth Song" in vocal performance mode |
| Who's Bad? (25) | Achieved a 5 star rating in "Bad" in master performance mode |
| Who's Laughing Baby (20) | Achieved a 5 star rating in "Leave Me Alone" in performance mode |
| You Can Never Break Me (20) | Achieved a 5 star rating in "They Don't Care About Us" in performance mode |
| You Can Never Kill Me (25) | Achieved a 5 star rating in "They Don't Care About Us" in master performance mode |
| You Fight To Stay Alive (25) | Achieved a 5 star rating in "Thriller" in master performance mode |
| You Got To Be Startin' Somethin' (20) | Achieved a 5 star rating in "Wanna Be Startin' Something" in performance mode |
| You Knock Me Off Of My Feet (20) | Achieved a 5 star rating in "The Way You Make Me Feel" in performance mode |

## MILITARY MADNESS (Wii)

### UNLOCKABLES

| UNLOCKABLE | HOW TO UNLOCK |
| --- | --- |
| Alternate Colors | Power on the system, and hold SELECT to reset. While continuing to hold SELECT, choose the 1-player continue option and enter a map name. |
| Play as Axis | Select the new game or 1-player continue option on the title screen, then hold SELECT and press ①. |
| Switch Sides | Hold SELECT and press RUN before choosing the 1-player continue option. |

### PASSWORDS

| PASSWORD | EFFECT |
| --- | --- |
| REVOLT | Level 01 |
| ICARUS | Level 02 |
| CYRANO | Level 03 |
| RAMSEY | Level 04 |
| NEWTON | Level 05 |
| SENECA | Level 06 |
| SABINE | Level 07 |
| ARATUS | Level 08 |
| GALIOS | Level 09 |
| DARWIN | Level 10 |
| PASCAL | Level 11 |
| HALLEY | Level 12 |
| BORMAN | Level 13 |
| APOLLO | Level 14 |
| KAISER | Level 15 |
| NECTOR | Level 16 |
| MILTON | Level 17 |
| IRAGAN | Level 18 |
| LIPTUS | Level 19 |
| INAKKA | Level 20 |
| TETROS | Level 21 |
| ARBINE | Level 22 |

| RECTOS | Level 23 |
|--------|----------|
| YEANTA | Level 24 |
| MONOGA | Level 25 |
| ATTAYA | Level 26 |
| DESHTA | Level 27 |
| NEKOSE | Level 28 |
| ERATIN | Level 29 |
| SOLCIS | Level 30 |
| SAGINE | Level 31 |
| WINNER | Level 32 |
| ONGAKU | Sound Test |

## MILON'S SECRET CASTLE (Wii)

### UNLOCKABLES

| UNLOCKABLE | HOW TO UNLOCK |
|------------|---------------|
| Continue Game | Hold down left and press START when you die after getting the first crystal |

## MLB 11: THE SHOW (PlayStation 3)

### TROPHIES

| UNLOCKABLE | HOW TO UNLOCK |
|------------|---------------|
| 100% Clear (Platinum) | This is the platinum trophy and is unlocked automatically when all trophies have been unlocked. |
| Advanced Cooperation (Bronze) | With different users controlling the pitcher and fielders, complete a strike 'em out throw 'em out double play. |
| Batting Performance Evaluated (Silver) | As a Batter in RttS, have 3 or more 'Good' or better At Bats in a single game at the MLB Level. |
| Beat LA (Gold) | Beat the Dodgers. Must be completed vs. the CPU with both pitching and batting set to Legend. RttS excluded. |
| Challenger (Silver) | Place in the top 33% in any single week of Challenge of the Week. |
| Cooperation (Bronze) | Win a co-op game. |
| Daddy Long Legs (Bronze) | In any season mode, hit a triple on Father's Day. |
| Day at the Beach (Bronze) | Hit a Home Run into the sand at Petco Park. |
| Dig that long ball (Bronze) | In any mode (excluding HRD) hit a Home Run with a pitcher. |
| Experienced (Bronze) | Accumulate 100 XP across any online game modes. |
| Fill'er Up (Bronze) | After falling behind in the count 0-2 work back to full count. Completed vs. CPU with both pitching and batting set to All-Star or higher difficulty. |
| Have a CoW Man! (Bronze) | Compete in the Challenge of the Week in back to back weeks. |
| Ice Cold (Bronze) | Hit a Home Run to dead center in Coors Field. |
| Insider (Gold) | In any mode get an inside the park Home Run. Must be completed vs. the CPU. |
| Lean On Me (Bronze) | Pick off the CPU runner on 1st. |
| Momma's Boy (Bronze) | In any season mode, hit a Home Run on Mother's Day with a pink bat. |
| Patience... (Bronze) | Draw a 4 pitch walk in any mode. Must be completed vs. the CPU on All-Star or higher difficulty. |
| Peak Training (Gold) | In RTTS, reach level 5 in all training modes as a pitcher or a batter. |
| Pesky... (Bronze) | In any single at bat, see 10 or more pitches. Must be |

| | |
|---|---|
| | completed vs. the CPU on All-Star or higher difficulty. |
| **Pitching Performance Evaluated (Silver)** | As a Pitcher in RttS, in a single game, face 6 or more consecutive batters achieving a 'Good' or better rating at the MLB Level. |
| **Poor Billy... (Bronze)** | Win a game on an error. |
| **Psychic (Gold)** | With Guess Pitch on, in any mode, correctly guess 10 pitches in a row (Location OR Pitch) vs. the CPU on All-Star or higher difficulty. |
| **Running Down a Dream (Silver)** | In a single game, steal 3rd twice. Must be completed vs. the CPU. |
| **Salute the Troops (Bronze)** | Win a game using the Padres while wearing Camo Jerseys. |
| **Seasoned (Silver)** | Achieve an All-Star rank across all online game modes. |
| **Sell Your Body (Bronze)** | Make a diving catch in foul territory for an out. |
| **Splash Down II (Bronze)** | Hit a Home Run into the hot tub in Chase field. |
| **Stay on Target (Bronze)** | At Target Field, land your foul ball or tailing Home Run on the Target sign down the right field line. |
| **Stone Hands (Bronze)** | Make 5 or more errors in a single game. |
| **Strong Arm (Bronze)** | Throw the ball into the stands when attempting to throw out a runner at 1st. |
| **Swim With The Fishes (Bronze)** | Hit a Home Run into the Ray's aquarium. |
| **The Bacon (Bronze)** | In RttS, earn more than 20,000,000 over the course of your career. |
| **The Billy Goat (Bronze)** | In Season or Franchise mode, win World Series as the Cubs. Must be full 9 inning games, simulating of World Series games will invalidate the trophy. |
| **Today... I am the greatest (Gold)** | In any mode, with any single player, accumulate 130 or more stolen bases in a single Season. |
| **Tough Loss (Bronze)** | As the away team, take a shutout into the bottom of the 9th and lose the game. Must be completed vs. the CPU. |
| **Yankees 'Inhale Deeply Through The Mouth'! (Gold)** | Beat the Yankees. Must be completed vs. the CPU with both pitching and batting set to Legend. RttS excluded. |

## MONSTER TALE (DS)

### CODES

Enter the code at the title screen

| UNLOCKABLE | HOW TO UNLOCK |
|---|---|
| New color palette (Yellow Clothes) for Ellie and 5% off on item | Press ⬆, ⬆, ⬇, ⬇, ⬅, ➡, ⬅, ➡, +SELECT. |

## MORTAL KOMBAT (PlayStation 3)

### CODE

| UNLOCKABLE | HOW TO UNLOCK |
|---|---|
| Original / Classic Stage Music | During Player Select, go to the Arena Select Menu, and hit the Start button on the arena music you want to select. |

### CODE

At the versus screen before the match starts, Player 1 enters the first 3 digits while Player 2 enters the last 3.

| EFFECT | CODE |
|---|---|
| Armless Kombat | P1: 9-1-1 P2: 9-1-1 |
| Blocking Disabled | P1: 0-2-0 P2: 0-2-0 |
| Breakers Disabled | P1: 0-9-0 P2: 0-9-0 |
| Dark Kombat | P1: 0-2-2 P2: 0-2-2 |

| | |
|---|---|
| **Double Dash** | P1: 3-9-1 P2: 1-9-3 |
| **Dream Kombat** | P1: 2-2-2 P2: 5-5-5 |
| **Enhance Moves Disabled** | P1: 0-5-1 P2: 1-5-0 |
| **Explosive Kombat** | P1: 2-2-7 P2: 2-2-7 |
| **Foreground Objects Disabled** | P1: 0-0-1 P2: 0-0-1 |
| **Headless Kombat** | P1: 8-0-8 P2: 8-0-8 |
| **Health Recovery** | P1: 0-1-2 P2: 0-1-2 |
| **Hyper Fighting** | P1: 0-9-1 P2: 0-9-1 |
| **Invisible Kombat** | P1: 7-7-0 P2: 7-7-0 |
| **Jumping Disabled** | P1: 8-3-1 P2: 8-3-1 |
| **Kombos Disabled** | P1: 9-3-1 P2: 9-3-1 |
| **No Blood** | P1: 9-0-0 P2: 9-0-0 |
| **Player 2 Half Health** | P1: 0-0-0 P2: 1-1-0 |
| **Power Bars Disabled** | P1: 4-0-4 P2: 4-0-4 |
| **Psycho Kombat** | P1: 7-0-7 P2: 7-0-7 |
| **Quick Uppercut Recovery** | P1: 3-0-3 P2: 3-0-3 |
| **Rainbow Kombat** | P1: 2-3-4 P2: 2-3-4 |
| **Sans Power** | P1: 0-4-4 P2: 4-4-0 |
| **Silent Kombat** | P1: 3-0-0 P2: 3-0-0 |
| **Specials Disabled** | P1: 7-3-1 P2: 7-3-1 |
| **Super Recovery** | P1: 1-2-3 P2: 1-2-3 |
| **Throwing Disabled** | P1: 1-0-0 P2: 1-0-0 |
| **Throwing Encouraged** | P1: 0-1-0 P2: 0-1-0 |
| **Tournament Mode** | P1: 1-1-1 P2: 1-1-1 |
| **Unlimited Super Meter** | P1: 4-6-6 P2: 4-6-6 |
| **Vampire Kombat** | P1: 4-2-4 P2: 4-2-4 |
| **X-Rays Disabled** | P1: 2-4-2 P2: 2-4-2 |
| **Zombie Kombat** | P1: 6-6-6 P2: 6-6-6 |

## UNLOCKABLE

These secret battles can only be unlocked in Arcade Mode.

| UNLOCKABLE | HOW TO UNLOCK |
|---|---|
| Secret "Jade" Battle | Get a double flawless victory and perform a fatality on Shang Tsung when battling against him. |
| Secret "Noob Saibot" Battle | When you see Noob in "The Temple" stage's background win that battle without using the R2 (Block) button. |
| Secret "Reptile" Battle | On "The Pit 2 (Night)" stage wait until a shadowy figure flies across the moon, then get a double flawless victory and perform a stage fatality. |
| Secret "Smoke" Battle | On "The Living Forest" stage wait until Smoke appears behind one of the trees. On that moment press Down + Select repeatedly. |

## UNLOCKABLE

| UNLOCKABLE | HOW TO UNLOCK |
|---|---|
| Mileena's Fleshpit Costume (Third costume) | Complete the last level (Level 300) of the Challenge Tower. |
| Play as Cyber Sub-Zero | Complete Chapter 13 in Story Mode. From then on he will be selectable on the Character Selection screen. |
| Play as Quan Chi | Complete all chapters in Story Mode. From then on he will be selectable on the Character Selection screen. |

## SECRET

Highlight the character you want to play as and press "[START]." Press "✕" to get the original color, press "[START]" again to get the alternate color

## MORTAL KOMBAT (XBOX 360)

### CODE

After selecting a character at the Character select screen in Ladder Mode, hold down 🅠 while selecting difficulty. The game will default to include Goro, rather than Kintaro in the boss fight.

| UNLOCKABLE | HOW TO UNLOCK |
|---|---|
| Always fight Goro in Ladder Mode | Hold down 🅠 when selecting difficulty mode |

### UNLOCKABLE

These secret battles can only be unlocked in Arcade Mode.

| UNLOCKABLE | HOW TO UNLOCK |
|---|---|
| Secret "Jade" Battle | Get a double flawless victory and perform a fatality on Shang Tsung when battling against him. |
| Secret "Noob Saibot" Battle | When you see Noob in "The Temple" stage's background win that battle without using the R2 (Block) button. |
| Secret "Reptile" Battle | On "The Pit 2 (Night)" stage wait until a shadowy figure flies across the moon, then get a double flawless victory and perform a stage fatality. |
| Secret "Smoke" Battle | On "The Living Forest" stage wait until Smoke appears behind one of the trees. On that moment press 🅠 + Select repeatedly. |

### UNLOCKABLE

| UNLOCKABLE | HOW TO UNLOCK |
|---|---|
| Mileena's Fleshpit Costume (Third costume) | Complete the last level (Level 300) of the Challenge Tower. |
| Play as Cyber Sub-Zero | Complete Chapter 13 in Story Mode. From then on he will be selectable on the Character Selection screen. |
| Play as Quan Chi | Complete all chapters in Story Mode. From then on he will be selectable on the Character Selection screen. |

### CODE

At the versus screen before the match starts, Player 1 enters the first 3 digits while Player 2 enters the last 3.

| UNLOCKABLE | HOW TO UNLOCK |
|---|---|
| Armless Kombat | P1: 9-1-1 P2: 9-1-1 |
| Blocking Disabled | P1: 0-2-0 P2: 0-2-0 |
| Breakers Disabled | P1: 0-9-0 P2: 0-9-0 |
| Dark Kombat | P1: 0-2-2 P2: 0-2-2 |
| Double Dash | P1: 3-9-1 P2: 1-9-3 |
| Dream Kombat | P1: 2-2-2 P2: 5-5-5 |
| Enhance Moves Disabled | P1: 0-5-1 P2: 1-5-0 |
| Explosive Kombat | P1: 2-2-7 P2: 2-2-7 |
| Foreground Objects Disabled | P1: 0-0-1 P2: 0-0-1 |
| Headless Kombat | P1: 8-0-8 P2: 8-0-8 |
| Health Recovery | P1: 0-1-2 P2: 0-1-2 |
| Hyper Fighting | P1: 0-9-1 P2: 0-9-1 |
| Invisible Kombat | P1: 7-7-0 P2: 7-7-0 |
| Jumping Disabled | P1: 8-3-1 P2: 8-3-1 |
| Klassik Music | P1: 1-0-1 P2: 1-0-1 |
| Kombos Disabled | P1: 9-3-1 P2: 9-3-1 |

| No Blood | P1: 9-0-0 P2: 9-0-0 |
| Power Bars Disabled | P1: 4-0-4 P2: 4-0-4 |
| Psycho Kombat | P1: 7-0-7 P2: 7-0-7 |
| Quick Uppercut Recovery | P1: 3-0-3 P2: 3-0-3 |
| Rainbow Kombat | P1: 2-3-4 P2: 2-3-4 |
| Sans Power | P1: 0-4-4 P2: 4-4-0 |
| Silent Kombat | P1: 3-0-0 P2: 3-0-0 |
| Specials Disabled | P1: 7-3-1 P2: 7-3-1 |
| Super Recovery | P1: 1-2-3 P2: 1-2-3 |
| Throwing Disabled | P1: 1-0-0 P2: 1-0-0 |
| Throwing Encouraged | P1: 0-1-0 P2: 0-1-0 |
| Tournament Mode | P1: 1-1-1 P2: 1-1-1 |
| Unlimited Super Meter | P1: 4-6-6 P2: 4-6-6 |
| Vampire Kombat | P1: 4-2-4 P2: 4-2-4 |
| X-Rays Disabled | P1: 2-4-2 P2: 2-4-2 |
| Zombie Kombat | P1: 6-6-6 P2: 6-6-6 |

### SECRET

When selecting a stage in Versus Mode, press "Ⓞ" and you hear a laugh. Now the stage soundtrack will be replaced with a song from one of the previous Mortal Kombat titles.

### SECRET

To select an alternate color for your character, go to the character select screen, then select your character by pressing Ⓞ, then press Ⓞ again on either costume 1 or 2 to get the corresponding alternative color.

## MORTAL KOMBAT VS. DC UNIVERSE (XBOX 360)

### UNLOCKABLES

Both of these characters can be unlocked by beating story mode with a certain side. Hold down ⑧ on character select.

| UNLOCKABLE | HOW TO UNLOCK |
| --- | --- |
| Darkseid | Beat the DC side of story mode. |
| Shao Kahn | Beat the MK side of story mode. |

## MORTAL KOMBAT VS. DC UNIVERSE (PlayStation 3)

### UNLOCKABLES

Both of these characters can be unlocked by beating story mode with a certain side. To play as these characters, hold down Ⓡ1 on character select.

| UNLOCKABLE | HOW TO UNLOCK |
| --- | --- |
| Darkseid | Beat the DC side of story mode. |
| Shao Kahn | Beat the MK side of story mode. |

## MOTIONSPORTS ADRENALINE (PlayStation 3)

### TROPHY

| UNLOCKABLE | HOW TO UNLOCK |
| --- | --- |
| Adrenaline License (Bronze) | Complete your first race in any event |
| Arachnosapien (Bronze) | Climb up 10 handholds in 20 seconds in Mountain Climbing |
| Back in One Piece (Bronze) | Finish any Kayak track hitting no more than five rocks, banks or roll obstacles |
| Better the Devil you Know (Bronze) | Win a friend's challenge |
| Boarding Pass (Silver) | Unlock all tracks in the game |
| Build to Last (Silver) | Win 5 challenges |

| | |
|---|---|
| **Bullseye (Silver)** | Hit 8 speed rings on the Kite Surf Moonlight Bay track in one run |
| **Challenging (Bronze)** | Post a challenge |
| **Clean Slate (Silver)** | Complete all 3 Wingsuit tracks without hitting an obstacle |
| **Competitive Streak (Silver)** | Own 5 challenges |
| **Frequent Flyer (Bronze)** | Race on every track in every event |
| **Friendly Competition (Bronze)** | Own a friend's challenge |
| **Hardheaded (Bronze)** | Use Adrenaline Power to protect yourself from falling rocks in Mountain Climbing |
| **Helping Hand (Bronze)** | Play every co-op and relay event |
| **Hot Dog (Bronze)** | Perform 3 tricks in a single Kite Surf race |
| **It's Better on 'Vine'yl (Silver)** | Spend a total of 1 minute swinging from vines in Mountain Climbing |
| **Just in Time (Silver)** | Own a challenge in its final minutes |
| **Let's Have a Party (Bronze)** | Team up with 3 friends to play Adrenaline Party mode |
| **License To Spill (Bronze)** | Nail your opponent with a weapon twice in the same Kite Surf race |
| **Midas Touch (Gold)** | Earn a gold medal in all relay, coop and single player modes in all events |
| **Motion Sickness (Bronze)** | Use Adrenaline Boost 4 times in any one race |
| **Nothing Left to Prove (Platinum)** | Unlock all Trophies |
| **One-sided (Bronze)** | Play 25 competitive two player events |
| **Overachiever (Silver)** | Post 10 challenges |
| **Party's Over (Bronze)** | Complete an Adrenaline Party |
| **Poetry in Motion (Bronze)** | Finish 1 relay race without missing a single hand-off |
| **Rail to the Chief (Bronze)** | Perform 3 tricks off of rails in a single Skiing track |
| **Risky Bidness (Bronze)** | Successfully take the inside lane for all turns on a Mountain Bike track |
| **Row your Boat (Silver)** | Row constantly for 30 seconds in the Kayak event |
| **Sampler (Bronze)** | Play all game modes in one event |
| **Silver Rush (Silver)** | Earn a silver medal in all relay, coop and single player modes in all events |
| **Solid Gold (Gold)** | Earn a gold medal in every round in Adrenaline Party mode |
| **Stuck With It (Silver)** | Win a challenge |
| **Tailgater (Silver)** | Perform 10 Speed Boosts & win a two player Speed Freak Mountain Bike race |
| **The Completionist (Gold)** | Unlock everything in the game |
| **Trick Hop (Bronze)** | Score over 50,000 points from tricks in a Mountain Bike track |
| **Trickster (Bronze)** | Jump, trick & land perfectly on 5 ramps in a single Skiing track |
| **Vidi Veni Vici (Bronze)** | Own a challenge launched from the Challenge Hub |
| **Wet Behind the Ears (Bronze)** | Roll for a total of 500 meters in the Kayak event |
| **What's Mine Is Mine (Bronze)** | Take back a challenge that you posted |
| **What's Next? (Bronze)** | Earn a gold medal in all relay, coop and single player modes in one event |
| **What's Yours is Mine... (Bronze)** | Own a challenge |

| Windbreaker (Bronze) | Use an Adrenaline Boost in a wind zone in the Wingsuit Event |
| Window Cleaner (Bronze) | Wave off 20 weapon attacks in the Wingsuit event |

## MOTOGP 10/11 (XBOX 360)

### ACHIEVEMENTS

| UNLOCKABLE | HOW TO UNLOCK |
| --- | --- |
| 125cc Elite (30) | Win a 125cc class season on Insane difficulty. Not unlockable by Co-riders. |
| 125cc World Champion (15) | Win a 125cc class season. Not unlockable by Co-riders. |
| 1st Servic (30) | Ride over 1000 miles. Not unlockable by Co-riders. |
| A Class (15) | Obtain an 'A' rating in all sessions of a race weekend in Career Mode. Not unlockable by Co-riders. |
| Addicted (15) | Earn first place 20 times in any mode. Not unlockable in Splitscreen Mode or by Co-riders. |
| Admired (15) | Obtain a reputation level of 15 in Career Mode. Not unlockable by Co-riders. |
| Bedded In (15) | Ride over 400 miles. Not unlockable by Co-riders. |
| Been Practicing (30) | Win any race on Insane difficulty. Not unlockable in Splitscreen Mode or by Co-riders. |
| Big Business (15) | Hire a full complement of staff in Career Mode. Not unlockable by Co-riders. |
| Collected (15) | Obtain a full complement of sponsors. Not unlockable by Co-riders. |
| Consistency (15) | Earn first place 10 times in any mode. Not unlockable in Splitscreen Mode or by Co-riders. |
| Dedicated (15) | Use your own Career Mode motorbike and rider in a multiplayer race. |
| DING (15) | Obtain a reputation level of 1 in Career Mode. Not unlockable by Co-riders. |
| Dinner with Friends (15) | Win a race against a full grid of human riders. |
| DIY (15) | Customise every aspect of your bike and rider. Not applicable to co-riders. |
| Fixed Overheads (15) | Spend over 100,000 on staff wages in one pay day. Not unlockable by Co-riders. |
| Hardcore (90) | Complete a full Challenge Mode season without using a continue. |
| Hoarder (30) | Amount 100,000 in savings in Career Mode. Not unlockable by Co-riders. |
| Hometown Champion (15) | Win on your home circuit in Career Mode. Not unlockable by Co-riders. |
| Leader of the Pack (15) | Qualify for pole position. Not unlockable by Co-riders. |
| Methodical (15) | Get every type of time bonus within the same lap on Challenge Mode. |
| Moto2 Elite (30) | Win a Moto2 class season on Insane difficulty. Not unlockable by Co-riders. |
| New Kid on the Block (15) | Obtain a reputation level of 5 in Career Mode. Not unlockable by Co-riders. |
| Oil Change (15) | Ride over 200 miles. Not unlockable by Co-riders. |
| Online Dominator (15) | Win 21 races online. |
| Piggy Bank Full (15) | Amount 50,000 in savings in Career Mode. Not unlockable by Co-riders. |
| Professional (15) | Obtain a reputation level of 20 in Career Mode. Not unlockable by Co-riders. |

| | |
|---|---|
| **Ride your way (10)** | Host a multiplayer race. |
| **Running on economy (15)** | Spend a total of 10 minutes slipstreaming in Challenge Mode. |
| **Savvy (25)** | Spend over 100,000 on upgrades. Not unlockable by Co-riders. |
| **Self Sufficient (15)** | Obtain a reputation level of 10 in Career Mode. Not unlockable by Co-riders. |
| **Show off (15)** | Do a wheelie lasting at least 500 feet on a motorbike. Not unlockable by Co-riders. |
| **Spick and Span (15)** | Win with no penalties, all clean sections, no crashes, no collisions. Not unlockable by Co-riders. |
| **Stabilisers are off (15)** | Ride over 100 miles. Not unlockable by Co-riders. |
| **Staff Liability (30)** | Spend over 200,000 on staff wages in one pay day. Not unlockable by Co-riders. |
| **Star (30)** | Obtain a reputation level of 25 in Career Mode. Not unlockable by Co-riders. |
| **Superstar (90)** | Obtain a reputation level of 30 in Career Mode. Not unlockable by Co-riders. |
| **The G.O.A.T. (30)** | Win a MotoGP class season on Insane difficulty. Not unlockable by Co-riders. |
| **Time Hoarder (15)** | Finish a race with more time than you started with without using any continues in Challenge Mode. |
| **Untouchable (30)** | Earn first place 30 times in any mode. Not unlockable in Splitscreen Mode or by Co-riders. |
| **Victory (5)** | Your first win. Not unlockable by Co-riders. |
| **Voltaire (15)** | Successfully perform every type of dynamic objective. Not unlockable by Co-riders. |
| **World Champion (90)** | Win a MotoGP class season. Not unlockable by Co-riders. |

## MOTORSTORM (PlayStation 3)

Enter this code at the main menu.

| UNLOCKABLE | CODE |
|---|---|
| Unlock Everything | Hold L1, L2, R1, R2, R2 pushed up, L2 pushed down |

Enter this code while the game is paused.

| UNLOCKABLE | CODE |
|---|---|
| Big Head on ATVs and Bikes | Hold L1, L2, R1, R2, R2 pushed right, L1 pushed left |

## MOTORSTORM: APOCALYPSE (PlayStation 3)

### TROPHY

| UNLOCKABLE | HOW TO UNLOCK |
|---|---|
| 'And Mash wins!' (Silver) | Survive the Festival as Mash. |
| 'Any questions?' (Silver) | Complete 'Sea Spray' as Big Dog. |
| 'Eat my dust, tough guy!' (Bronze) | Complete 'Aces High' as Mash. |
| 'I guess you love trouble...' (Silver) | Complete 'Wargames' as Tyler. |
| 'I'm all in.' (Bronze) | Complete 'Suburban Shakedown' as Tyler. |
| 'I'm just waiting for a sucker to beat.' (Bronze) | Complete 'Road Warriors' as Tyler. |
| 'If you start, you got to finish...' (Bronze) | Complete 'Final Drive' as Big Dog. |
| 'It's about life and death.' (Bronze) | Complete 'End of the Line' as Tyler. |
| 'Okay, let's do this.' (Bronze) | Complete 'Credit Crunch' as Mash. |
| 'Only one of us is making it out of this city alive.' (Bronze) | Complete 'The End is Nigh' as Tyler. |
| 'Restricted my ass!' (Bronze) | Start the party as Big Dog. |
| 'Time to lose these guys...' (Bronze) | Complete 'High Way' as Big Dog. |

| | |
|---|---|
| 'Want a Magic Nut Bar?' (Silver) | Complete 'Baked' as Mash. |
| 'We're gonna race - in that?' (Bronze) | Complete 'Off the Rails' as Mash. |
| 'We're the best... it's that simple.' (Gold) | Survive the Festival as Tyler. |
| 'You wanna play?' (Bronze) | Make it to the party as Mash. |
| 'You wanna stay, shut your mouth.' (Bronze) | Make it to the party as Tyler. |
| 'You're greased.' (Gold) | End the Festival as Big Dog. |
| Air Assault (Bronze) | Punch a fellow rider off their bike or ATV while you're both in mid-air. |
| Croupier (Silver) | Reach Rank 30 in Multiplayer. |
| Decorated Stormer (Bronze) | Earn 25 Medals in Multiplayer. |
| Double or Quits? (Silver) | Win a bet while on a x2 Hot Streak. |
| Energy Efficient (Bronze) | Win a race without ever entering Critical Boost. |
| Found 'em All! (Silver) | Collect 150 of the hidden MotorStorm Cards |
| Found One! (Bronze) | Collect 1 of the hidden MotorStorm Cards. |
| FPR (Bronze) | Win a race using only the vehicle-mounted camera. |
| Gently Does it (Bronze) | Complete your first online race. |
| Grease Monkey (Bronze) | Swap out at least one vehicle part on each of the 13 vehicle classes. |
| High Five! (Bronze) | Reach Rank 5 in Multiplayer. |
| Hot Air (Bronze) | Use in-air cooling to entirely cool your full Boost gauge from Critical in a single jump. |
| I Made it Myself (Bronze) | Modify your vehicle using all the available options. |
| Jackpot (Gold) | Reach Rank 40 in Multiplayer. |
| Kudos (Bronze) | Earn 250 Chips from a single drift in Multiplayer. |
| Motion Master (Bronze) | Complete a race steering with the motion sensor function. |
| Nail'd it (Silver) | Pass 25 Special Events. |
| Now for the Main Event... (Bronze) | Pass 5 Special Events. |
| Over There! (Bronze) | 'Look At' 5 unique race incidents over 5 different races. |
| Pure as Mud (Bronze) | Successfully perform 3 stunts in a single race. |
| Rampage! (Bronze) | Use the Ram to wreck 10 opponents. |
| Stacked (Bronze) | Reach Rank 15 in Multiplayer. |
| Starter for 10 (Bronze) | Pass 10 Special Events. |
| Target Locked (Bronze) | Ram and wreck the same opponent twice during a race. |
| The Big One (Platinum) | Obtain every other trophy in the game. |
| Unlucky for Some (Bronze) | Win a race with each of the 13 vehicle classes. |
| Variety is the Spice of Life (Bronze) | Complete a race in all of the standard game modes. |
| Wheelin' an' Dealin' (Bronze) | Pull a continuous wheelie for 5 seconds. |
| Where Do You Put Them All? (Bronze) | Earn 50 Accolades in Multiplayer. |
| Where's My Money? (Bronze) | Place and win a bet in Matchmaking. |

## MVP BASEBALL   (PSP)

Under the "My MVP" menu, create a player named "Dan Carter." Once you do this, there will be a message indicating that the code was successful.

## MX VS. ATV REFLE (XBOX 360)

### CODES

Enter codes in Cheat Code screen.

| EFFECT | CODE |
|---|---|
| Unlocks KTM's and Justin Brayton | READYTORACE |
| Unlocks all AI guys | allai |
| Unlocks all ATVs | couches |
| Unlocks all boots | kicks |
| Unlocks all gear | gearedup |
| Unlocks all goggles | windows |
| Unlocks all helmets | skullcap |
| Unlocks all locations | whereto |

## MX VS. ATV UNLEASHED (PlayStation 2)

Enter in the Cheats menu.

| UNLOCKABLE | CODE |
|---|---|
| 50cc Bikes | Minimoto |
| Unlock all freestyle tracks | Huckit |
| Unlock Everything | Toolazy |

## MX VS. ATV UNTAMED (XBOX 360), (PlayStation 3), (PlayStation 2)

### UNLOCKABLES

Type in the following codes in the Cheats menu to unlock the gear.

| UNLOCKABLE | HOW TO UNLOCK |
|---|---|
| All Handlebars | NOHANDS |
| FOX Riding Gear | CRAZYLIKEA |

## MX VS. ATV UNTAMED (Wii)

### CODES

Go to the Options screen and go to the Cheat Code input screen.

| EFFECT | CODE |
|---|---|
| 1 Million Store Points | MANYZEROS |
| 50cc Bike Class | LITTLEGUY |
| All Bikes | ONRAILS |
| All Challenges | MORESTUFF |
| All Gear | WELLDRESSED |
| All Machines | MCREWHEELS |
| All Riders | WHOSTHAT |
| Freestyle Tracks | FREETICKET |
| Paralyzer Monster Truck | PWNAGE |
| Unlock Everything | YOUGOTIT |

## MYSIMS (Wii)

### CODES

While running around town, pause the game, then push the following buttons on the Wiimote to get to the hidden password system: ⓐ,ⓑ,⬆,⬇,⬅,➡,⬅,➡,⬅,➡. A keyboard appears to allow you to type in the following case-sensitive codes.

| UNLOCKABLE | HOW TO UNLOCK |
|---|---|
| Bunk Bed (Furniture) | F3nevr0 |
| Camouflage Pants | N10ng5g |
| Diamond Vest (Outfit) | Tglg0ca |
| Genie Outfit | Gvsb3k1 |

| | |
|---|---|
| Hourglass Couch | Ghtymba |
| Kimono Dress (Outfit) | l3hkdvs |
| Modern Couch | T7srhca |
| Racecar Bed (Furniture) | Ahvmrva |
| Rickshaw Bed | ltha7da |
| White Jacket | R705aan |

### TOOLS

Once you reach a certain level, you get a message saying you've earned the following new tools.

| UNLOCKABLE | HOW TO UNLOCK |
|---|---|
| Blow Torch | Have your town reach four stars. |
| Crowbar | Have your town reach one star. |
| Pickaxe | Have your town reach three stars. |
| Saw | Have your town reach two stars. |
| Town Monument Blueprint | Have a five-star town. |

### U8ER-SIMS

After getting your interest level to 100% in any of the six categories, you get a message about a special guest waiting for you in the hotel. Check the next day and find the following Sims.

| UNLOCKABLE | HOW TO UNLOCK |
|---|---|
| Amazing Daryl | 100% Fun Town |
| Chancellor Ikara | 100% Tasty Town |
| Hopper | 100% Cute Town |
| Mel | 100% Spooky Town |
| Samurai Bob | 100% Studious Town |
| Star | 100% Geeky Town |

## MYSIMS AGENTS  (Wii)

### LEVEL SELECT

Do the specified objectives to gain a new recruit for your HQ. This can involve completing a part of a game, doing dispatch missions, etc.

| UNLOCKABLE | HOW TO UNLOCK |
|---|---|
| Annie Radd | Complete dispatch mission "Roadie Despair." |
| Beebee | Complete the Snowy Mountains level. |
| Elmira Clamp | Complete dispatch mission "Assistant Librarian." |
| Gonk | Complete dispatch mission "Gonk Need Food, Badly." |
| Gordon | Complete the Boudreaux Mansion level. |
| Hopper | Complete dispatch mission "Tainted Broth." |
| King Mike | Complete the Jungle Temple level. |
| Leaf | During Evelyn's house robbery case, dig around one of the holes west of the Forest Park. If you dig in the right hole, Leaf will be found. |
| Liberty | Complete dispatch mission "Snake on the Loose!" |
| Lyndsay | Complete the Jungle Temple level. |
| Madame Zoe | Complete the Boudreaux Mansion level. |
| Magellan | Complete the Jungle Temple level. |
| Makoto | Complete dispatch missions "High School Yearbook" and "Prom Date." |
| Marlon | Complete dispatch missions "Magical Assistant" and "Magical Disaster." |
| Master Aran | Complete dispatch mission "Penguin Style." |
| Ms. Nicole Vogue | Complete the Boudreaux Mansion level. |
| Petal | Complete dispatch mission "Failing Forest." |

| | |
|---|---|
| **Pinky** | Complete dispatch mission "Blue Thing!" |
| **Preston Winthrop** | Complete the Snowy Mountains level. |
| **Professor Nova** | Complete the Snowy Mountains level. |
| **Renée** | Complete dispatch mission "Pig, Camera, Action!" |
| **Roger** | Complete the Evelyn robbery case. |
| **Rosalyn P. Marshall** | Complete the Snowy Mountains level. |
| **Sir Spencer** | Complete dispatch mission "H4XX0R3D!" |
| **Sir Vincent Skullfinder** | Complete the Jungle Temple level. |
| **Star** | Complete dispatch mission "Blade of Destiny." |
| **Travis** | Available to recruit by default once you become a special agent. |
| **Trevor Verily** | Complete the Boudreaux Mansion level. |
| **Vic Vector** | Complete the Snowy Mountains level. |
| **Violet Nightshade** | Complete the Boudreaux Mansion level. |
| **Wendalyn** | Complete dispatch mission "Reagent Run." |
| **Wolfah** | Complete the Snowy Mountains level. |
| **Zombie Carl** | Complete the Boudreaux Mansion level. |

## MYSIMS KINGDOM (Wii)

### CODES

From the Pause menu enter the following codes to get the desired effect.

| EFFECT | CODE |
|---|---|
| **Detective outfit** | ⬇,⬅,⬇,⬅,⬇,⬅ |
| **Tattoo Vest outfit** | Ⓒ,Ⓩ,Ⓒ,Ⓩ,Ⓑ,Ⓐ,Ⓑ,Ⓐ |
| **Swordsman outfit** | ⬆,⬇,⬆,⬇,⬆,⬇,⬆,⬇ |

## MYSIMS PARTY (Wii)

### UNLOCKABLES

| UNLOCKABLE | HOW TO UNLOCK |
|---|---|
| **New inhabitants** | Get at least 60 points in the minigame they're hosting. |
| **New playable characters** | Get at least 80 points in the minigame they're hosting. |

## MYSIMS RACING (Wii)

### CODES

From the main menu go to Extras, then to Cheats. After entering the code a message will appear telling you that a new car part has been unlocked. Go to "Story Mode" and enter the garage to equip your new car part.

| EFFECT | CODE |
|---|---|
| **Unlocks Butterflies (Wheels)** | z74hsv |
| **Unlocks Holstein (Hood Ornament)** | 36mj5v |
| **Unlocks Mega Spoiler (Rear Accessory)** | k4c2sn |

## N+ (DS)

### CODES

Hold Ⓛ and Ⓡ and insert the following code at the Unlockables menu.

| EFFECT | CODE |
| --- | --- |
| Unlocks Atari Bonus Levels | Ⓐ,Ⓑ,Ⓐ,Ⓑ,Ⓐ,Ⓐ,Ⓑ |

## N+ (PSP)

### CODES

Hold Ⓛ and Ⓡ and insert the following code at the Unlockables menu.

| EFFECT | CODE |
| --- | --- |
| Unlocks Atari Bonus Levels | ✕,●,✕,●,✕,✕,● |

## NAMCO MUSEUM ESSENTIALS (PlayStation 3)

### DIG DUG UNLOCKABLES

| UNLOCKABLE | HOW TO UNLOCK |
| --- | --- |
| Carrot | Grab the Carrot. |
| Complete Dig | Successfully dig the whole entire level. |
| Cucumber | Grab the Cucumber. |
| Eggplant | Grab the Eggplant. |
| Green Pepper | Grab the Green Pepper. |
| Mushroom | Grab the Mushroom. |
| No Dig | Complete the level without digging. |
| Pineapple | Grab the Pineapple. |
| Quad Squash | Successfully squash four enemies with one rock. |
| Tomato | Grab the Tomato. |
| Turnip | Grab the Turnip. |
| Watermelon | Grab the Watermelon. |

### DRAGON SPIRIT UNLOCKABLES

| UNLOCKABLE | HOW TO UNLOCK |
| --- | --- |
| Earthquake | Collect the Earthquake power-up. |
| Endurance | Successfully survive against a boss under a timed limit without killing him. |
| Fire Breath | Collect the Fire Breath power-up. |
| Homing Fire | Collect the Homing Fire power-up. |
| Incubation | Collect the Incubation power-up. |
| Maximum | Successfully get three heads and six fire power orbs without getting hit. |
| Over The Jungle | Get to the Jungle Area. |
| Power Down | Collect the Power Down power-up. |
| Power Wing | Collect the Power Wing power-up. |
| Small Dragon | Collect the Small Dragon power-up. |
| Small N Wide | Collect the Small Dragon, followed by Wide Fire without getting hit. |
| Wide Fire | Collect the Wide Fire power-up. |

## GALAGA UNLOCKABLES

| UNLOCKABLE | HOW TO UNLOCK |
|---|---|
| Blue Spaceship | Destroy the Blue Spaceship. |
| Boss Alien | Destroy the Boss Alien. |
| Destroy Fighter | Successfully destroy your captured ship. |
| Dragonfly | Destroy the Dragonfly. |
| Dual Fighter | Successfully destroy the enemy holding your ship captive. |
| Maple | Destroy the Maple. |
| Perfect | Win a perfect game in the Challenging Stage. |
| Scorpion | Destroy the Scorpion. |
| Stage 10 | Reach Stage 10. |
| Stage 20 | Reach Stage 20. |
| Stage 30 | Reach Stage 30. |
| Stingray | Destroy the Stingray. |

## NARUTO: CLASH OF NINJA REVOLUTION     (Wii)

### CHARACTERS

To unlock the following characters, beat the Mission mode at least once, then do the following:

| UNLOCKABLE | HOW TO UNLOCK |
|---|---|
| Gaara | Beat Single Player mode with Naruto and Shikamaru. |
| Guy | Clear Mission 13.5. |
| Hinata Hyuuga | Beat Single Player mode with Neji. |
| Ino Yamanaka | Beat Single Player mode with Sakura. |
| Itachi Uchiha | Beat Mission "Rematch Itachi vs. Saskue," after unlocking all other starting characters plus Guy and Kankuro. |
| Kankuro | Clear Mission mode once. |
| Kisame | Beat Single Player mode with Naruto, Sasuke, Kakashi, Guy, and Jiraiya. |
| Orochimaru | Beat Single Player mode with Naruto, Sasuke, Kakashi, and Jiraiya. |
| Shino Aburame | Beat Arcade mode with Kankuro. |
| Temari | Beat Shikamaru's Single Player mode. |
| Tenten | Clear Mission 20. |
| Tsunade | Beat Single Player mode with Jiraiya. |

## NARUTO SHIPPUDEN: SHINOBI RUMBLE     (DS)

### UNLOCKABLE

After fulfilling the requirements to unlock a character, their mark will appear in the Kuchiyose menu. Select their mark and copy it onto the grid on the bottom screen using the stylus, taking care to use the proper stroke order. Correctly drawing a character's mark will unlock them, even if their mark hasn't been acquired.

| UNLOCKABLE | HOW TO UNLOCK |
|---|---|
| Deidara | Complete Arcade Mode with Itachi |
| Fukusaku & Shima | Complete Arcade Mode with all characters |
| Itachi | Complete Story Mode |
| Jiraiya | Complete Arcade Mode with Naruto |
| Jugo | Complete Arcade Mode with Karin |
| Karin | Complete Arcade Mode with Suigetsu |
| Konan | Complete Arcade Mode with Jiraiya |
| Orochimaru | Complete Arcade Mode with Jugo |

| Pain | Complete Arcade Mode with Konan |
| Suigetsu | Complete Arcade Mode with Sasuke |

### UNLOCKABLE

You can unlock additional jutsus for each character by playing Mission Mode. As you complete missions, depending on the mission's diffculty, you will gain either 1, 2, or 3 marks on that character's Bingo Sheet. When a row, column, or diagnol is complete, a new ability will be unlocked for that character, until the entire Bingo Sheet has been completed. A character's ability set can be customized after selecting the character in Battle, Arcade, and Mission Modes.

## NARUTO SHIPPUDEN: ULTIMATE NINJA IMPACT (PSP)

### UNLOCKABLE

| UNLOCKABLE | HOW TO UNLOCK |
|---|---|
| Sakura Hauno | Beat "A Test of Strength" in Ultimate Road |

## NASCAR 09 (XBOX 360)

### CODES

| EFFECT | CODE |
|---|---|
| Unlocks All Fantasy Drivers | CHECKERED FLAG |
| Unlocks Walmart Track (Chicago Pier) and the Walmart Car | Walmart Everyday |

## NASCAR 2011: THE GAME (PlayStation 3)

### TROPHY

| UNLOCKABLE | HOW TO UNLOCK |
|---|---|
| 'Let's Go Racin Boys' (Bronze) | Take part in your first online race. |
| Any Place, Any Time (Silver) | Compete in every International Event. |
| Boy Scout (Gold) | Unlock every NASCAR Pin in the game. |
| Car Stylist (Bronze) | Create a custom Pain Scheme. |
| Celebration Shot (Bronze) | You photographed the driver celebrating on the car after a Career Mode race win. |
| Cup Contender (Silver) | Achieve a top 10 finish in every Career Mode race. |
| Decorated Driver (Silver) | Advance to Rank 20. |
| Finishing in First! (Bronze) | Win a race crossing the line in first gear. |
| Give me 4 (Bronze) | Perform your first 4-tire pit stop in any race. |
| Groovy (Bronze) | Master a track. Complete all the objectives on a Master the Track card. |
| Hotrod (Bronze) | Create a custom tuning setup. |
| Keep Diggin' (Bronze) | Drive a total of 500 miles or more. |
| Kingly (Silver) | Defeat Richard Petty's race win record of 200 wins. |
| Last Man Standing (Bronze) | Survive a 43 car eliminator race to the end. |
| MVP (Silver) | Receive full sponsorship for your driver in Career Mode. |
| Name to Remember (Silver) | Unlock every Gold Legends Coin in the game. |
| NASCAR Legend (Gold) | Advance to Rank 30. |
| Now ya Talkin' (Bronze) | Advance to Rank 10. |
| NXP Challenge (Bronze) | Achieve over 6,666 NXP in a single race. |
| One for the Road (Bronze) | Rank up for the first time. |
| Pedal to the Metal (Bronze) | Achieve the fastest lap of the race during an online race. |
| Pit Perfection (Silver) | Perform a 4-tire pit stop, and go on to win the race. (Online Only) |
| Platinum (Platinum) | Unlock every trophy in the game. |
| Race Rivalry (Silver) | Achieve 20 rival victories. (Online Only) |

| | |
|---|---|
| Race to the Chase (Silver) | Achieve enough points in Career Mode to move into The Chase, as one of the top 12 drivers. |
| Ride in Style (Silver) | Collect 88 Paint Schemes by racing in Invitational Events and reaching rank 29. |
| Rookie Mistake (Bronze) | You received a drive through or speeding penalty. |
| Rubbin is Racin! (Bronze) | Race online at every track. |
| Run the Gauntlet (Bronze) | Win a Gauntlet Invitational Event. |
| Saddle Up & Hang On (Silver) | Qualify in pole position at every circuit in the game in Career Mode. |
| Series Champion (Gold) | Finish top of Career Mode standings and become the Sprint Cup series champion. |
| Sprint to the Finish (Bronze) | Win a race in Career Mode and get the full 195 points. |
| Star of Tomorrow (Silver) | Achieve a total of 100 fastest laps. |
| Styling 'N' Profiling (Bronze) | Win a race with a personalized Paint Scheme. |
| Surfin' USA (Silver) | Master every track in the game. |
| Tailgating (Bronze) | Perform a draft of 500 yards or more. |
| The Champ is here! (Bronze) | Win the Championship Showdown Invitational Event. |
| Up on the Wheel (Bronze) | Lead 5 consecutive laps in an online race. |
| Victory Lane (Silver) | Win a race at every circuit in the game. |
| VIP (Bronze) | Complete all three objectives for a single sponsor in Career Mode. |
| Win on Sunday, Sell on Monday (Silver) | Win a race in all brands of car. |

## NASCAR KART RACING  (Wii)

### CODES

| EFFECT | CODE |
|---|---|
| Joey Logano as a driver | 426378 |

## NASCAR UNLEASHED  (XBOX 360)

### ACHIEVEMENT

| UNLOCKABLE | HOW TO UNLOCK |
|---|---|
| 2 Birds, 1 Stone (10) | Make 2 rivals at the same time. |
| Beat The Clock! (10) | Earn a trophy on any time trial track. |
| Beatdown! (10) | Make 3 rivals in a single race. |
| Crowd Pleaser (80) | Make 7 rivals in a single race. |
| Didn't See You There (10) | Bump another car into a hazard. |
| Domination! (40) | Score higher than 225,000 in a single race. |
| Drive By Healing (10) | Boost through the pit lane restore. |
| Eat My Dust (10) | Place 1st in any race against your friend. |
| Friendly Rivalry (10) | Wreck your friend making him/her a rival. |
| Good Effort! (10) | Finish a quick race season in any place but 1st. |
| Gotta Have 'em All (40) | Unlock all vehicle paint jobs. |
| Heavy Hitter (80) | Score 25 slams in a single race. |
| High Score (10) | Score higher than 175,000 in a single race. |
| Hot Shot (10) | Place 1st in any race. |
| I Meant To Do That (10) | Drive over 15 oil slicks. |
| In The Groove (80) | Avoid walls and track barriers to score 2 perfect laps in one race. |
| It Still Counts! (10) | Wreck your car across the finish line. |
| Just A Scratch (10) | Use pit lane to repair your vehicle 50 times. |

| | |
|---|---|
| **Just That Good (10)** | Finish 3 races without wrecking or using pit lane. |
| **Learning The Ropes (10)** | Complete the rookie tier in championship mode. |
| **Light Touch (10)** | Perform 125 slams. |
| **Lightning Reflexes (40)** | Drive in boost mode for 12 seconds. |
| **Look Mom! (10)** | Drive over 35 ramp jumps. |
| **Not On My Watch (10)** | Wreck a car in pit lane before the repair. |
| **Over Achiever (10)** | Complete 5 challenges in one race. |
| **Perfectionist (80)** | Earn gold trophies on all time trial tracks. |
| **Piece Of Cake (10)** | Complete 10 challenges. |
| **Revenge! (10)** | Score a payback. |
| **Rocketman (10)** | Slingshot into 25 ramp jumps. |
| **Scenic Route (10)** | Drive over oil, dirt, sand, gravel, water, and grass. |
| **Showboater! (10)** | Drift around 75 turns. |
| **Showing Promise (10)** | Complete the professional tier in championship mode. |
| **Showoff (10)** | Perform a donut and go on to win the race. |
| **So Close (40)** | Earn silver trophies on all time trial tracks. |
| **Stuntman (10)** | Perform 5 barrel rolls in mid-air. |
| **Stylin' (10)** | Customize any car with an unlocked paint job. |
| **That All You Got? (80)** | Complete the legend tier in championship mode. |
| **That'll Learn Ya! (10)** | Score 10 paybacks. |
| **The Hard Way (10)** | Finish 5 races without using pit lane. |
| **The Real Deal (10)** | Place 1st in a quick race season. |
| **The Sun Was In My Eyes (10)** | WRECK YOUR CAR 15 TIMES. |
| **Thrashing! (10)** | MAKE 5 RIVALS IN A SINGLE RACE. |
| **Time To Spare (40)** | EARN A GOLD TROPHY ON ANY TIME TRIAL TRACK. |
| **Tough Guy (10)** | MAKE 75 RIVALS. |
| **Turbo Speed! (10)** | PERFORM 50 SLINGSHOT BOOSTS. |
| **Unnecessary Roughness (10)** | PERFORM 250 SLAMS. |
| **Watch Your Step (10)** | BUMP ANOTHER CAR INTO AN OIL SLICK. |
| **Well Played (10)** | SCORE HIGHER THAN YOUR FRIEND IN A QUICK RACE SEASON. |
| **Winner! (10)** | PLACE 1ST ON THE DAYTONA OVAL. |
| **World Traveler (10)** | UNLOCK ALL RACE TRACKS. |

## NAUGHTY BEAR (XBOX 360)

### UNLOCKABLES

| UNLOCKABLE | HOW TO UNLOCK |
|---|---|
| **Cop Naughty (hat)** | Get Gold on Episode 1. |
| **Epic Naughty (hat)** | Get Gold on all Top Hat Challenges. |
| **Naughticorn** | Get a Total Score of 100,000,000. |
| **Naughty the Party Animal (hat)** | Complete Chapter 1. |

## NBA 09: THE INSIDE (PlayStation 3)

### UNLOCK NEW JERSEYS

From Main Menu choose Progression, go to Extras, then Jerseys, press left or right to get to nba.com tab and press Square to enter code.

| UNLOCKABLE | CODE |
|---|---|
| **Eastern All-Stars 09 Jersey** | SHPNV2K699 |
| **L.A. Lakers Latin Night Jersey** | NMTWCTC84S |

| Miami Heat Latin Night Jersey | WCTGSA8SPD |
| San Antonio Spurs Latin Night Jersey | JFHSY73MYD |
| Phoenix Suns Latin Night Jersey | LKUTSENFJH |
| Western All-Stars 09 Jersey | K8AV6YMLNF |

## NBA 2K10 (XBOX 360)

### CODES

Go into the Options menu and select the Codes section to enter these codes.

| EFFECT | CODE |
| --- | --- |
| 2K Sports team | 2ksports |
| ABA ball | payrespect |
| Blazers "Rip City" Jersey | ycprtii |
| Cavs, Jazz, Magic, Raptors, T'Wolves, Trail Blazers, Warriors Hardwood Classic Jerseys Unlocked | wasshcicsl |
| Grizzlies, Hawks, Mavericks, and Rockets secondary road jerseys | eydonscar |
| Unlock the 2K China team | 2kchina |
| Unlock the 2K development team | nba2k |
| Unlock visual concepts team | vcteam |

## NBA 2K10 (PlayStation 3)

### CODES

Go into the Options menu and select the Codes section to enter these codes.

| EFFECT | CODE |
| --- | --- |
| 2K Sports team | 2ksports |
| ABA ball | payrespect |
| Blazers "Rip City" Jersey | ycprtii |
| Cavs, Jazz, Magic, Raptors, T'Wolves, Trail Blazers, Warriors Hardwood Classic Jerseys Unlocked | wasshcicsl |
| Grizzlies, Hawks, Mavericks, and Rockets secondary road jerseys | eydonscar |
| Unlock the 2K China team | 2kchina |
| Unlock the 2K development team | nba2k |
| Unlock visual concepts team | vcteam |

## NBA 2K10 (Wii)

### CODES

Go into the Options menu and select the Codes section to enter these codes.

| EFFECT | CODE |
| --- | --- |
| 2K Sports team | 2ksports |
| ABA ball | payrespect |
| Blazers "Rip City" Jersey | ycprtii |
| Cavs, Jazz, Magic, Raptors, T'Wolves, Trail Blazers, Warriors Hardwood Classic Jerseys Unlocked | wasshcicsl |
| Grizzlies, Hawks, Mavericks, and Rockets secondary road jerseys | eydonscar |
| Unlock the 2K China team | 2kchina |
| Unlock the 2K development team | nba2k |
| Unlock visual concepts team | vcteam |

## NBA 2K11 (PSP)

### CODES

Accessed in the cheat menu under "features."

| EFFECT | CODE |
|--------|------|
| 2K Development Team | nba2k |
| 2K Sports China Team | 2kchina |
| 2K Sports team | 2ksports |
| ABA Ball | payrespect |
| Bobcats Nascar Racing Uniform | agsntrccai |
| Cavs Cavfanatic Uniform | aifnaatccv |
| Hardwood Classics Uniforms (7 teams only) | wasshcicsl |
| Hornets Mardi Gras Uniform | asrdirmga |
| Secondary Road Uniforms (Grizzlies, Hawks, Mavs, and Rockets) | eydonscar |
| St Patrick's Day Uniforms (Bulls, Celtics, Knicks, and Raptors) | riiasgerh |
| Trail Blazers Rip City Uniform | ycprtii |
| Visual Concepts Team | vcteam |

## NBA 2K11 (XBOX 360)

### CODES

Accessed in the cheat menu under "features."

| EFFECT | CODE |
|--------|------|
| 2k Sports team | 2Ksports |
| 2k China team | 2kchina |
| ABA Ball | payrespect |
| MJ: Creating a Legend | icanbe23 |
| NBA2k Development Team | nba2k |
| Visual Concepts Team | vcteam |

## NBA 2K11 (PlayStation 3)

### CODES

Accessed in the cheat menu under "features."

| EFFECT | CODE |
|--------|------|
| 2k Sports team | 2Ksports |
| 2k China team | 2kchina |
| ABA Ball | payrespect |
| MJ: Creating a Legend | icanbe23 |
| NBA2k Development Team | nba2k |
| Visual Concepts Team | vcteam |

## NBA 2K12 (PlayStation 3)

### TROPHY

| UNLOCKABLE | HOW TO UNLOCK |
|------------|---------------|
| 4-Point Line (Bronze) | Pull off a successful 4-point play with any player, in a non-simulated game. |
| A 2K to Call My Own (Bronze) | Create a My2K Account. |
| Another Day, Another Win (Bronze) | Win 5 NBA Today matchups. |
| Back to Back to Back (Bronze) | Win 3 Versus matches in a row. |
| Birthday (Bronze) | Create-a-Player. |
| Block Party (Bronze) | Record 10 or more blocks with any team, in a non-simulated game. |

| | |
|---|---|
| **Buzzer Beater (Bronze)** | Make a game winning shot with no time left on the clock, in a non-simulated game. |
| **Check! (Bronze)** | Complete all 3 in-game objectives in My Player mode. |
| **Come Fly with Me (Bronze)** | Purchase Michael Jordan's dunk package (His Airness) in My Player mode. |
| **Dawn of an Era (Bronze)** | Get drafted as a lottery pick in the NBA draft in My Player mode. |
| **Don't Hate the Player (Gold)** | Win the championship in an Online Association. |
| **Dub-Dub (Bronze)** | Record two double doubles with any teammates, in a non-simulated game. |
| **Five by Five (Bronze)** | Record 5 or more in 5 different stats with any player in a non-simulated game. |
| **G Performance (Bronze)** | Score at least 48 points with Kevin Durant to set a new career high, in a non-simulated game. |
| **G Prime (Silver)** | End the 1st period with a 15 point lead or greater on the Hall of Fame difficulty setting. |
| **G Recovery (Bronze)** | Play an entire game using manual substitutions, in a non-simulated game. |
| **Giveth and Taketh Away (Bronze)** | Record 10 or more rebounds and assists with any player, in a non-simulated game. |
| **Hamilton (Bronze)** | Win 10 Versus matches total. |
| **Hey Mr. DJ (Bronze)** | Create a 2K Beats Playlist. |
| **Hold the Fat Lady (Bronze)** | Start the 4th period losing by 10 or more points and win with any team, in a non-simulated game. |
| **Home Court (Silver)** | Earn the NBA's best record in The Association mode (at least 30 games played). |
| **I'm Worth It (Silver)** | Land a contract that pays at least $10M per season in My Player mode. |
| **Immortality (Gold)** | Make the Hall of Fame in My Player mode. |
| **It's Better to Give (Bronze)** | Share any file type through 2K Share. |
| **It's Raining (Bronze)** | Make 15 or more 3-pointers with any team, in a non-simulated game. |
| **Left My Mark (Bronze)** | Complete 10 of the NBA's Greatest challenges. |
| **Lincoln (Bronze)** | Win 5 Versus matches total. |
| **Made My Name (Bronze)** | Complete 5 of the NBA's Greatest challenges. |
| **Men of Steal (Bronze)** | Record 10 or more steals with any team, in a non-simulated game. |
| **Money Bags (Bronze)** | Purchase 3,000 skill points in a single transaction in My Player mode. |
| **My All-Star (Bronze)** | Be named an NBA All-Star in My Player mode. |
| **My Big Eight-O (Bronze)** | Earn an 80 overall rating in My Player mode. |
| **My Every Day Player (Bronze)** | Become a starter in the NBA in My Player Mode. |
| **My Player of the Game in My (Bronze)** | Be named Player of the Game (in an NBA game) Player mode. |
| **NBA Cares (Bronze)** | Make a donation to the NBA Cares global community outreach initiative in My Player mode. |
| **Not Your Father's Association (Bronze)** | Join an Online Association. |
| **Shooting Star (Bronze)** | Win the MVP award in NBA: Creating a Legend mode. |
| **Smothering (Bronze)** | Hold the opposing team's FG% below 40% with any team, in a non-simulated game. |
| **Sprite Slam Cam (Bronze)** | Get the Sprite Slam Cam replay after a dunk with LeBron James. |

| | |
|---|---|
| **Streaking (Silver)** | Win 5 games in a row in The Association mode (playing all 5 games). |
| **Swat and Swipe (Bronze)** | Record at least 5 blocks and 5 steals with any team, in a non-simulated game. |
| **The Closer (Bronze)** | Hold the opposing team to 0 points in the final two minutes of regulation, in a non-simulated game. |
| **The Sum of Its Parts (Bronze)** | Play a Team Up Game. |
| **The Whole Shebang (Platinum)** | Earn every trophy in NBA 2K12. |
| **This One Counts (Bronze)** | Win one online Versus match. |
| **Ticker Tape (Gold)** | Win an NBA Championship in The Association mode (playing every playoff game). |
| **Trip-Dub (Bronze)** | Record a triple double with any player, in a non-simulated game. |
| **Wire to Wire (Bronze)** | Do not allow your opponent to lead the game at any point with any team, in a non-simulated game. |
| **Wrote My Legend (Silver)** | Complete all 15 of the NBA's Greatest challenges. |
| **You're Officially Hot (Silver)** | Win 5 Versus matches in a row. |

### CODE

| UNLOCKABLE | CODE |
|---|---|
| **Unlock 2K Sports team** | 2ksports |
| **Unlock All Retro Jordan Shoes** | 23 |
| **Unlock NBA 2K Development Team** | nba2k |
| **Unlock Visual Concepts Team** | vcteam |
| **Unlocks 2K China team** | 2kchina |
| **Unlocks ABA Basketball (toggle)** | payrespect |

## NBA BALLERS: REBOUND (PSP)

Enter these passwords in the Phrase-ology under Inside Stuff.

| UNLOCKABLE | PASSWORD |
|---|---|
| **All Alternate Gear, Players, and Movies** | NBA Ballers True Playa |
| **Allen Iverson's Recording Studio** | The Answer |
| **Alonzo Mourning Alternate Gear** | Zo |
| **Ben Gordon's Yacht** | Nice Yacht |
| **Chris Weber's Alternate Gear** | 24 Seconds |
| **Clyde Drexler's Alternate Gear** | Clyde The Glide |
| **Dikembe Mutumbo's Alternate Gear** | In The Paint |
| **Emanuel Ginobli Alternate Gear** | Manu |
| **Jerry Stackhouse Alternate Gear** | Stop Drop And Roll |
| **Julius Irving Alternate Gear** | One On One |
| **Kevin McHale Alternate Gear** | Holla Back |
| **Lebron James' Alternate Gear** | King James |
| **Magic Johnson Alternate Gear** | Laker Legends |
| **Nene's Hilarios Alternate Gear** | Rags To Riches |
| **Pete Maravich's Alternate Gear** | Pistol Pete |
| **Rasheed Wallace Alternate Gear** | Bring Down The House |
| **Rick Hamilton's Alternate Gear** | Rip |
| **Stephon Marbury's Alternate Gear** | Platinum Playa |
| **Steve Francis Alternate Gear** | Ankle Breaker |
| **Steve Francis' Alternate Gear** | Rising Star |
| **Tim Duncan Alternate Gear** | Make It Take It |
| **Wilt Chamberlain's Alternate Gear** | Wilt The Stilt |

## NBA JAM (XBOX 360)

### CHARACTERS

| UNLOCKABLE | HOW TO UNLOCK |
|---|---|
| Allen Iverson | Elusive // Perform 10 successful shove counters. |
| Beastie Boys Team | 3 The Hard Way // Defeat the Beastie Boys team in Remix Tour. |
| Bill Laimbeer, Isiah Thomas | Central Division Represent // Beat the Central Division Legend Team in Classic Campaign. |
| Brad Daugherty | Double Up // Beat the CPU in a 2V2 game by doubling their score or better. |
| Bryant Reeves | 100 Club // Win 100 games. |
| Chris Mullin, Tim Hardaway | Pacific Division Represent // Beat the Pacific Division Legend Team in Classic Campaign. |
| Chuck Person | Fired Up // Get on Fire 4 times in a single game. |
| Clyde Drexler | NBA Domination // Beat Classic Campaign with a team from each division in the NBA. |
| Dan Majerle | Century Scorer // Score 100 points in one game. |
| Danny Manning | Grand Scorer // Score 1,000 points. |
| Patrick Ewing and John Starks | Beat Atlantic Legend Team in Classic Campaign |

## NBA LIVE 10 (XBOX 360, PlayStation 3)

### ALTERNATE JERSEYS

Go to the Main menu, My NBA Live 10, EA Sports Extras, NBA Codes and then input the code.

| CODE | EFFECT |
|---|---|
| ndnba1rooaesdc0 | Unlocks alternate jerseys. |

## NBA LIVE 10 (XBOX 360)

### CODES

Go to Main menu, My NBA Live 10, EA Sports Extras, NBA Codes, then type the code.

| EFFECT | CODE |
|---|---|
| Unlock the Blazers, Cavaliers, Jazz, Magic, Raptors, Timberwolves, and Warriors Hardwood Retro Jerseys. | hdogdrawhoticns |

| EFFECT | CODE |
|---|---|
| Unlock the Rockets, Mavericks, Hawks, and Grizzlies alternate jerseys | ndnba1rooaesdc0 |
| Nike Air Max LeBron VII's 1 | ere1nbvlaoeknii |
| Nike Air Max LeBron VII's 2 | 2ovnaebnkrielei |
| Nike Air Max LeBron VII's 3 | 3rioabeneikenvl |
| Nike Huarache Legion | aoieuchrahelgn |
| Nike KD 2 | kk2tesaosepinrd |
| Nike Zoom Flip'n | epfnozaeminolki |
| Nike Zoom Kobe V's 1 | ovze1bimenkoko0 |
| Nike Zoom Kobe V's 2 | m0kveokoiebozn2 |
| Nike Zoom Kobe V's 3 | eev0nbimokk3ozo |
| Nike Zoom Kobe V's 4 | bmo4inozeeo0kvk |

## NBA LIVE 10 (PlayStation 3)

### CODES

Go to Main menu, My NBA Live 10, EA Sports Extras, NBA Codes, then type the code.

| EFFECT | CODE |
|--------|------|
| Second set of secondary jerseys for Cleveland, Golden State, Minnesota, Orlando, Philadelphia, Portland, Toronto, Utah, and Washington | hdogdrawhoticns |
| Bobcats NASCAR Race Day Jersey | ceobdabacarstcy |
| Mavericks, Rockets, Grizzlies, Hawks secondary road jerseys | Ndnba1rooaesdc0 |
| Hornets Mardi Gras Jersey | nishrag1rosmad0 |
| Jordan CP3 III | iaporcdian3ejis |
| Jordan Melo M6 | emlarmeoo6ajdsn |
| Jordan Sixty Plus | aondsuilyjrspxt |
| Nike Air Max LeBron VII | ivl5brieekaeonn |
| Nike Air Max LeBron VII | n6ieirvalkeeobn |
| Nike Air Max LeBron VII | ri4boenanekilve |
| Nike Air Max LeBron VII | 3rioabeneikenvl |
| Nike Air Max LeBron VII | 2ovnaebnkrielei |
| Nike Air Max LeBron VII | ere1nbvlaoeknii |
| Nike Huarache Legion | aoieuchrahelgn |
| Nike KD 2 | kk2tesaosepinrd |
| Nike Zoom Flip | epfnozaeminolki |
| Nike Zoom Kobe V | m0kveokoiebozn2 |
| Nike Zoom Kobe V | eev0nbimokk3ozo |
| Nike Zoom Kobe V | bmo4inozeeo0kvk |
| Nike Zoom Kobe V | ovze1bimenkoko0 |

## NBA LIVE 10 (PSP)

### CODES

Go to My NBA Live, go to Options, and select Codes. Now type the codes.

| EFFECT | CODE |
|--------|------|
| Unlock additional Hardwood Classics Nights for the Cleveland Cavaliers, Golden State Warriors, Minnesota Timberwolves, Orlando Magic, Philadelphia 76e | hdogdrawhoticns |

| EFFECT | CODE |
|--------|------|
| Unlock the Adidas Equations. | adaodqauieints1 |
| Unlock the Adidas TS Creators with ankle braces. | atciadsstsdhecf |
| Unlock the Charlotte Bobcats' 2009/2010 Race Day alternate jerseys. | ceobdabacarstcy |
| Unlock the Jordan CP3 IIIs. | iaporcdian3ejis |
| Unlock the Jordan Melo M6s. | emlarmeoo6ajdsn |
| Unlock the Jordan Sixty Pluses. | aondsuilyjrspxt |
| Unlock the new alternate jerseys for the Atlanta Hawks, Dallas Mavericks, Houston Rockets and Memphis Grizzlies. | ndnba1rooaesdc0 |
| Unlock the New Orleans Hornets' 2009/2010 Mardi Gras alternate jerseys. | nishrag1rosmad0 |
| Unlock the Nike Huarache Legions. | aoieuchrahelgn |
| Unlock the Nike KD 2s. | kk2tesaosepinrd |
| Unlock the Nike Zoom Flip'Ns. | epfnozaeminolki |
| Unlock the TS Supernatural Commanders. | andsicdsmatdnsr |
| Unlock TS Supernatural Creators. | ard8siscdnatstr |

## NCAA FOOTBALL 10 (XBOX 360)

### UNLOCKABLE

| UNLOCKABLE | HOW TO UNLOCK |
|---|---|
| All 34 Championship Trophies—In 1 Dynasty! | Play Dynasty Mode through to the postseason. When you get to Week 1 of the Bowl Season, play and win each bowl game with any team. These will count on your profile, and when you finish every bowl (including the National Championship), you will get the Trophy! |

## NCAA FOOTBALL 12 (PlayStation 3)

### TROPHY

| UNLOCKABLE | HOW TO UNLOCK |
|---|---|
| 1st Option For 6 (Bronze) | Score a touchdown handing off to the fullback on a triple option play (excludes co-op) |
| A Legend is Born (Bronze) | Defeat a rival using your backup QB. Minimum 15 pass attempts (excludes co-op) |
| Balanced Attack (Bronze) | Gain 200 rushing yards and 200 passing yards in the same game (excludes co-op and Road to Glory). |
| Battle Tested (Silver) | Win a position battle in Road To Glory |
| Best Class Ever (Bronze) | Have the #1 ranked recruiting class in a season in single team Dynasty Mode. |
| Best in Class (Bronze) | Finish High School as a 5 star prospect in Road to Glory. |
| Best of All-Time (Gold) | In Road to Glory Mode, earn a spot on the NCAA All-Time leaderboard. |
| Campus Legend (Bronze) | In Road to Glory Mode, earn a spot on your team's All-Time leaderboard. |
| Changing The Landscape (Bronze) | Edit a conference's members in a Dynasty off-season |
| Check This Out (Bronze) | Upload a photo or video to EASports.com |
| Conference King (Silver) | In Road to Glory Mode, earn a spot on your conference's All-Time leaderboard. |
| Cool Off The Hot Seat (Silver) | Escape the hot seat (less than 30% security) to keep your job for next Season (Coach contracts on) |
| Dream Job (Silver) | Become the head coach of your alma mater in Dynasty (Coach Contracts on) |
| Dual Threat Coach (Gold) | Win the BCS Championship & have the #1 recruiting class in a single season as head coach in Dynasty |
| Earn My Trust (Silver) | Reach the max coach trust in Road to Glory |
| Happy 20th EA SPORTS! (Bronze) | Break off a 20 yard run to celebrate 20 years of EA SPORTS! |
| Head Of The PAC (Bronze) | Play and win the inaugural PAC-12 Championship game in Dynasty |
| High School Champ (Bronze) | Play and win the High School Championship Game in any state. |
| Hometown Hero (Silver) | Lead your alma mater to a National Championship as a head coach in Dynasty (Coach Contracts on) |
| In Your Crosshairs (Bronze) | Spotlight a receiver and get an interception on him in a Play Now or Dynasty game (excludes co-op). |
| Independence Day (Silver) | Play and win the National Championship game with BYU in the first year of Dynasty |
| Ironman Performance (Bronze) | Score an offensive and defensive touchdown in a Road to Glory high school game. |
| Leaders Of Legends (Bronze) | Play and win the inaugural Big Ten Championship game in Dynasty |
| Let's Do It Again (Silver) | As a head coach in Dynasty, sign an extension to stay at the same school (Coach Contracts on) |

| | |
|---|---|
| Living Legend (Gold) | Reach a coach prestige of A+ with a created coach in Dynasty (Coach Contracts on) |
| Lock and Load (Bronze) | With Player Lock on, return an interception for a TD (excludes co-op). |
| My Conference is Super (Bronze) | Create a 16 team super conference in Dynasty |
| My Two Cents (Bronze) | In Online Dynasty, write a comment n a Dynasty Wire story |
| On Second Thought (Bronze) | Edit a division name of a conference in Dynasty |
| One Of The Big Boys (Bronze) | Edit the BCS tie-ins to grant a BCS tie-in to a non-AQ conference |
| Platinum Trophy (Platinum) | Unlock every trophy |
| Point Some Fingers (Bronze) | In a single phone call, take 250 points away from one school by downplaying pitches. |
| Speed Reader (Bronze) | Score a touchdown on a QB Choice run play (excludes co-op). |
| Strike the Pose (Bronze) | Win the Heisman Memorial Trophy in a single team Dynasty Mode or Road to Glory Mode. |
| Take a Stab Downfield (Bronze) | Complete a pass for 50 or more yards in a Play Now or Dynasty Mode game (excludes co-op). |
| Take What You Want (Bronze) | Create a custom playbook |
| Taking the Snaps (Bronze) | Become a starter in Road to Glory Mode. |
| Tire Fire Offense (Silver) | Win a game without scoring an offensive touchdown and gaining less than 200 yards (excludes co-op) |
| Ultimate Ironman (Silver) | Finish High Chool as a 5 star prospect in Road to Glory on both offense and defense. |
| Unstoppable (Bronze) | Win a game by 35+ points on Heisman difficulty (excludes co-op). |

## NCIS (XBOX 360)

### ACHIEVEMENT

| UNLOCKABLE | HOW TO UNLOCK |
|---|---|
| Abbycadabra (15) | Complete first chemical analysis |
| Abigail Sciuto FTW (15) | Complete first fingerprint comparison |
| Atlantic City (50) | Complete first crime scene |
| Bank Heist (50) | Complete third crime scene |
| BBQ'd Apartment (50) | Complete fourth crime scene |
| Cooking up some awesome (15) | Complete first footprint comparison |
| Dirty Harry (50) | Complete second crime scene |
| Five Star Accommodations (50) | Complete seventh crime scene |
| Front Lines (50) | Complete fifth crime scene |
| Hey, I'm a hacker. (15) | Complete first database search |
| Like shooting fish in a pond (15) | Complete first safe cracking |
| McGPS (15) | Complete first satellite tracking |
| NCIS 1, Terrorists 0 (50) | Save the world from terrorists |
| NCIS Agent (100) | Complete Episode 3 |
| NCIS Investigator (100) | Complete Episode 2 |
| Nice goin' Abs. (15) | Complete first fingerprint lifting |
| Probie Wan Kenobie (100) | Complete Episode 1 |
| Rule #1 (10) | Complete first co-op activity |
| Rule #3 (15) | Complete first interrogation |
| Rule #38 (15) | Complete first deduction |
| Rule #39 (15) | Complete first ballistics test |

| | |
|---|---|
| Rule #8 (15) | Complete first interview |
| Torture Chamber (50) | Complete sixth crime scene |
| Very Special Agent (100) | Complete Episode 4 |
| Waddaya got for me, Duck (15) | Complete first autopsy |
| You know I'm awesome (10) | Collect first piece of evidence |

## NEED FOR SPEED: MOST WANTED (XBOX 360)

All codes should be entered at the Start screen.

| UNLOCKABLE | CODE |
|---|---|
| Unlocks Burger King Challenge Event (#69) | ↑, ←, ←, ←, →, →, ←, → |
| Unlocks Free Engine Upgrade Bonus Marker (Can be used in the backroom of the customization shops) | ↑, ↑, ←, ←, →, →, ↑, ← |
| Unlocks Special Edition Castrol Ford GT (Which is added to your bonus cars) | →, →, ←, →, ↑, ←, ↑, ← |

## NEED FOR SPEED: PROSTREET (PlayStation 3, XBOX 360)

### CODES

Go to the "Enter Codes" section of the Career menu and enter the following codes.

| UNLOCKABLE | HOW TO UNLOCK |
|---|---|
| Extra $2,000 | 1MA9X99 |
| Extra $4,000 | W2iOLLO1 |
| Extra $8,000 | L1iS97A1 |
| Extra $10,000 | 1Mi9K7E1 |
| Extra $10,000 | REGGAME |
| Extra $10,000 | CASHMONEY |
| Extra $10,000 and Castrol Syntec Bonus Vinyl | CASTROLSYNTEC |
| 5 Repair Tokens | SAFETYNET |
| Audi TT 3.2 Quattro (In Garage) | ITSABOUTYOU |
| Bonus Energizer Lithium Vinyl | ENERGIZERLITHIUM |
| Dodge Viper (In Garage) | WORLDSLONGESTLASTING |
| K&N Bonus Vinyl | HORSEPOWER |
| Lancer Evo (In Garage) | MITSUBISHIGOFAR |
| Pre-tuned Grip Coke Zero Golf GTI (In Garage) and Bonus Coke Zero Vinyl | ZEROZEROZERO |
| Re-Locks Everything Unlocked by "Unlockallthings" | LEIPZIG |
| Unlocks Everything (maps, cars, parts) | UNLOCKALLTHINGS |

## NEED FOR SPEED: PROSTREET (Wii)

### CODES

Go to the "Enter Codes" section of the Career menu and enter the following codes.

| UNLOCKABLE | HOW TO UNLOCK |
|---|---|
| Audi TT 3.2 Quattro (In Garage) | ITSABOUTYOU |
| Bonus Energizer Lithium Vinyl | ENERGIZERLITHIUM |
| Dodge Viper (In Garage) | WORLDSLONGESTLASTING |
| Extra $2,000 | 1MA9X99 |
| Extra $4,000 | W2iOLLO1 |
| Extra $8,000 | L1iS97A1 |
| Extra $10,000 | 1Mi9K7E1 |
| Extra $10,000 | REGGAME |
| Extra $10,000 | CASHMONEY |

| | |
|---|---|
| Extra $10,000 and Castrol Syntec Bonus Vinyl | CASTROLSYNTEC |
| Five Repair Tokens | SAFETYNET |
| K&N Bonus Vinyl | HORSEPOWER |
| Lancer Evo (In Garage) | MITSUBISHIGOFAR |
| Pre-tuned Grip Coke Zero Golf GTI (In Garage) and Bonus Coke Zero Vinyl | ZEROZEROZERO |
| Re-Locks Everything Unlocked by "Unlockallthings" | LEIPZIG |
| Unlocks Everything (maps, cars, parts) | UNLOCKALLTHINGS |

## NEED FOR SPEED: THE RUN (PlayStation 3)

### TROPHY

| UNLOCKABLE | HOW TO UNLOCK |
|---|---|
| All for one (Bronze) | Complete a Group Objective |
| Bonus Wheel (Gold) | Win this Bonus Wheel reward in Multiplayer |
| Champion (Bronze) | Reach Driver Level 20 |
| Choices... (Bronze) | Complete 15 online objectives and unlock all Playlists |
| City Gold (Silver) | Earn a gold medal or better for each event in the 'Windy City' Challenge Series |
| Coast to Coast (Gold) | Complete The Run on any difficulty |
| Cop Out (Silver) | Complete Stage 4 |
| Current Events (Bronze) | Read a News Article |
| East Coast Gold (Silver) | Earn a gold medal or better for each event in the 'East Coast Express' Challenge Series |
| Gold Rush (Silver) | Earn a gold medal or better for each event in the 'Coastal Rush' Challenge Series |
| Got to the Chopper (Silver) | Complete Stage 8 |
| Hot Pursuit (Silver) | Complete Stage 9 |
| I Heart NY (Silver) | Complete Stage 10 |
| Industrial Gold (Silver) | Earn a gold medal or better for each event in the 'Industrial Run' Challenge Series |
| Interstate Gold (Silver) | Earn a gold medal or better for each event in the 'Plains Interstate' Challenge Series |
| King for a Day (Silver) | Become a Stage Leader in The Run (fastest time posted) |
| Legendary (Silver) | Reach Driver Level 30 |
| Mr. Plow (Silver) | Complete Stage 5 |
| National Gold (Silver) | Earn a gold medal or better for each event in the 'National Park' Challenge Series |
| Nevada Gold (Silver) | Earn a gold medal or better for each event in the 'Nevada Dreams' Challenge Series |
| New Car Smell (Bronze) | Reach Driver Level 5 |
| One for all (Silver) | Complete 5 Group Objectives |
| Platinum Trophy (Platinum) | Earn all Need for Speed™ The Run Trophies |
| Professional (Bronze) | Reach Driver Level 15 |
| Rural Gold (Silver) | Earn a gold medal or better for each event in the 'Rural Track Attack' Challenge Series |
| Show Off (Bronze) | Post a photo using Photo Mode |
| Street Racer (Bronze) | Reach Driver Level 10 |
| The Windy City (Silver) | Complete Stage 7 |
| Thunder Road (Silver) | Complete Stage 6 |
| Valley Gold (Silver) | Earn a gold medal or better for each event in the 'Desert Valley' Challenge Series |

| Vegas Baby! (Silver) | Complete Stage 3 |
| Veteran (Bronze) | Reach Driver Level 25 |
| Walk in the Park (Silver) | Complete Stage 2 |
| Welcome to The Run (Silver) | Complete Stage 1 |
| What else you got? (Bronze) | Beat a Friend Recommends |
| Win at Winning (Silver) | Play through The Run on Extreme Difficulty |
| Winter Gold (Silver) | Earn a gold medal or better for each event in the 'Winter Blast' Challenge Series |

### CODE

Go to "Extras" on the main menu, then "Enter Cheat Code".

| UNLOCKABLE | CODE |
|---|---|
| Unlock the AEM Intake Challenge Series | aemintakes |

## NEED FOR SPEED: UNDERCOVER (XBOX 360, PlayStation 3)

### CODES

| EFFECT | CODE |
|---|---|
| $10,000 in-game currency | $EDSOC |
| Die-Cast Lexus IS F bonus car | 0;5M2; |
| Die-Cast Nissan 240SX (S13) bonus car | ?P:COL |
| Die-Cast Volkswagen R32 bonus car | !2ODBJ: |
| NeedforSpeed.com Lotus Elise bonus car | -KJ3=E |

## NEUTOPIA II (Wii)

### EVERYTHING COLLECTED

| PASSWORD | EFFECT |
|---|---|
| At the Password screen, enter the following passwords: IbnoBJt$ AyUkJ7Wa XACpGDjm q1j1uR1Q M8ozNOQa cPUM&XcX | Puts you in the Town of Oasis ready to tackle the last dungeon, The Atra Labyrinth |
| Music_From_Neutopia | Sound Test |
| Thats_Entertainment_Neutopia | View Enemies |

## NEW ADVENTURE ISLAND (Wii)

### UNLOCKABLES

| UNLOCKABLE | HOW TO UNLOCK |
|---|---|
| Level Select | Press ⬆, ⬆, ①, ⬇, ⬇, ②, ⬅, ⬅, ➡, ➡ |
| Level Skip | Insert a NEC Avenue 6 pad in 6-button mode into port 1 |

## NHL 10 (XBOX 360), (PlayStation 3)

### CODES

Enter the following code at the EA Extras screen

| EFFECT | CODE |
|---|---|
| Unlocks third jerseys | rwyhafwh6ekyjcmr |

## NHL 12 (PlayStation 3)

### TROPHY

| UNLOCKABLE | HOW TO UNLOCK |
|---|---|
| A Smash Hit (Bronze) | Break a pane of glass with a hit on a CPU player |
| Amateur Contender (Bronze) | Qualify for a Hockey Ultimate Team Amateur monthly playoff tournament |
| Benched! (Bronze) | Check an opposing player into the benches |
| Complete Set (Silver) | Collect all player, jersey and logo cards for any team in the Collection |
| EASHL Hero (Bronze) | Score the OT winner in an EA Sports Hockey League match |

| | |
|---|---|
| **EASHL Legend (Gold)** | Achieve Legend 1 status for your online Pro |
| **EASHL Playoffs (Bronze)** | Be a member of an EA SPORTS Hockey League team when they participate in a monthly playoff |
| **EASHL Pro (Silver)** | Achieve Pro 1 status for your online Pro |
| **EASHL Rookie (Bronze)** | Achieve Rookie 1 status for your online Pro |
| **EAUHL 24/7 Victory (Bronze)** | Win a match against a downloaded Hockey Ultimate Team |
| **Elite Contender (Silver)** | Qualify for a Hockey Ultimate Team Elite monthly playoff tournament |
| **Every Man (Bronze)** | Play as every skater position while completing EA SPORTS Hockey League matches |
| **From the Office (Bronze)** | Have 7 assists in a single NHL Be A Pro game with a created Pro on Pro difficulty or higher |
| **Happy 20th EA SPORTS! (Bronze)** | Play & get 20 goals in a Be A Pro CHL season with a created Pro to celebrate 20 years of EA SPORTS |
| **Hats Off To You (Bronze)** | Be the player that scores 3 goals consecutively in an EA SPORTS Hockey League match |
| **High Flying (Bronze)** | Score a goal after completing a jump deke in a Ranked Online Shootout match |
| **HUT Playoff Winner (Silver)** | Win any Hockey Ultimate Team monthly playoff tournament |
| **King of the Crease (Bronze)** | Win a goalie versus goalie fight |
| **Le Magnifique (Bronze)** | Earn 8 points in a single NHL Be A Pro playoff game with a created Pro on Pro difficulty or higher |
| **Legend GM (Silver)** | Achieve Legendary GM Status |
| **Legend Player (Silver)** | Play and win any NHL player trophy in Be A Pro with a created Pro |
| **Lost His Lid (Bronze)** | Knock the helmet off an opposing player's head |
| **Magnificent Mario (Bronze)** | Score goals 5 different ways in a NHL Be A Pro game with a created Pro on Pro difficulty or higher |
| **Magnificently Great (Bronze)** | Score 4 goals in one period of a NHL Be A Pro game as a created Pro on Pro difficulty or higher |
| **Memorial Cup (Bronze)** | Play and win the Memorial Cup in Be A Pro with a created Pro |
| **Mr. Hockey (Bronze)** | Complete a Gordie Howe Hat Trick (Goal/Assist/Fight) in a Be A Pro NHL game with a created Pro |
| **On Bended Knee (Bronze)** | Score with a one knee one timer |
| **One Great Career (Gold)** | Earn 2,858 NHL career points in Be A Pro with a created Pro on Pro difficulty or higher |
| **One Great Season (Silver)** | Earn 216 NHL career points in a single Be A Pro season with a created Pro on at least Pro difficulty |
| **Past Their Potential (Bronze)** | Train a player past their potential |
| **PP Powerhouse (Silver)** | Have 30 PP goals in 2 different NHL Be A Pro seasons with a created Pro on Pro difficulty or higher |
| **Pro Contender (Silver)** | Qualify for a Hockey Ultimate Team Pro monthly playoff tournament |
| **Raise the Cup (Silver)** | Play and win the Stanley Cup in Be A Pro with a created Pro |
| **Raise Your Banner '12 (Platinum)** | Acquire all of the Bronze, Silver and Gold trophies |
| **Russian Rocket (Bronze)** | Score a goal after completing a skate-to-stick deke in a Ranked Online Shootout match |

| Superstar (Bronze) | Have 4 five goal games in a NHL Be A Pro career with a created Pro on Pro difficulty or higher |
| Taking Shots (Bronze) | Play as the goalie while completing an EA SPORTS Hockey League match |
| Team Doctor (Bronze) | Use a Healing card to heal an injured player in Hockey Ultimate Team |
| The Comeback Kid (Bronze) | Have three 8 point games in a NHL Be A Pro career with a created Pro on Pro difficulty or higher |
| The Great One (Silver) | Score 93 goals in a single NHL Be A Pro season with a created Pro on Pro difficulty or higher |
| Top Prospect (Bronze) | Qualify for and complete the CHL Top Prospects game in Be A Pro with a created Pro |
| Unlucky for Some (Silver) | Score 14 shorthanded goals in a NHL Be A Pro season with a created Pro on Pro difficulty or higher |
| Versus Legend (Silver) | Reach level 25 of online Versus |
| Versus Pro (Silver) | Reach level 10 of online Versus |
| Versus Rookie (Bronze) | Reach level 5 of online Versus |
| Winter Classic (Bronze) WSH | Complete a NHL Winter Classic Match with PIT versus |

## NHL 2K6  (XBOX 360)

Enter this as a profile name. Case Sensitive.

| UNLOCKABLE | PASSWORD |
| --- | --- |
| Unlock everything | Turco813 |

## NHL 2K9  (XBOX 360), (PlayStation 3)

### UNLOCKABLES

Go to Features, and enter the code into the Code menu.
The code is case sensitive.

| EFFECT | CODE |
| --- | --- |
| Unlocks the third jerseys | R6y34bsH52 |

## NHL 2K10  (XBOX 360), (Wii)

### CODES

In the cheats/password option located in the extras menu enter the following codes.

| EFFECT | CODE |
| --- | --- |
| 2K/Visual Concepts developer teams | vcteam |
| The five alternates for this season | G8r23Bty56 |

## NINJA GAIDEN  (Wii)

### UNLOCKABLES

| UNLOCKABLE | HOW TO UNLOCK |
| --- | --- |
| Sound Test | When the screen says Techmo Presents 1989: Hold Ⓐ+Ⓑ+⬅+➡+SELECT, and press START |
| Extra Lives | In Area 5-3, there's a 1UP on the third floor of the tower. Go back down the ladder to the second floor, and then back up to the third floor. The 1UP has returned. You can do this as many times as you want. |

## NINJA GAIDEN II  (XBOX 360)

### UNLOCKABLES

| UNLOCKABLE | HOW TO UNLOCK |
| --- | --- |
| Black Jaguar Costume | Complete Path of Mentor. |
| Camouflage Ninja Outfit | Complete the game on Warrior. |
| Gamerpic of Ryu | Complete the game on Path of the Master Ninja. |

| Gamerpic | Collect all 30 crystal skulls. |
|---|---|
| Golden Ninja Costume | Complete the game on Path of The Master Ninja. |
| Music Test | Clear the game on any difficulty. |
| New Game + | Complete the game and save after Credit Scroll. |
| Old Film Filter | Beat the game. |
| Path of the Master Ninja | Beat Path of the Mentor. |
| Path of the Mentor | Beat Path of the Warrior. |
| Red Ninja Outfit | Complete the game on Acolyte. |

### EASTER EGGS: HIDDEN SILVER XBOX

At the bottom of the Statue of Liberty diagonally across from where the save point there is a false wall. Inside of the breakable wall is a silver Xbox that will regenerate Ryu's health.

## NO MORE HEROES 2: DESPERATE STRUGGLE    (Wii)

### UNLOCKABLES

| UNLOCKABLE | HOW TO UNLOCK |
|---|---|
| Bitter Mode | Complete the game on Mild. |
| BJ5 Video | Beat BJ5 game, then select from TV menu. |
| Deathmatch (Boss Rush) | Beat the game, then select from Main menu. |
| E3 Trailer | Beat the game, then select from TV menu. |
| No Jacket | Complete all the "Revenge" missions. |
| New Game + | Beat the game and save your data. When you start No More Heroes 2 again you will be brought to the intro fight where you have all of your old equipment and items from the previous game. |

## OKAMIDEN (DS)

### UNLOCKABLE

Your final end-of-game evaluation based on what you did in the game will determine what you get once you beat the game.

| UNLOCKABLE | HOW TO UNLOCK |
|---|---|
| Dark Sun (Dark Chibi) | Beat the game |
| First Sunrise (Chibi Shiranui) | Complete everything |
| Karmic Returner (Original Amaterasu) | Beat the game |
| Moon's Legacy (Made of Ice) | Complete the Treasure Tome |
| Painter's Legend (Ishaku's armor) | Complete the Bestiary |

### UNLOCKABLE

Complete the story, save your game when prompted, and select Continue on the title screen to begin a new game with all the health and ink pots earned in the previous save, as well as bonus items you might have earned.

## ONSLAUGHT (Wii)

### STAGES

In addition to the three difficulty settings available from the start, there are two unlockable difficulty settings.

| UNLOCKABLE | HOW TO UNLOCK |
|---|---|
| Expert difficulty | Finish the game on Hard difficulty. |
| Ultra difficulty | Finish the game on Expert difficulty. |

### UPGRADE LOCATIONS

Each weapon has 2 upgrades that count as additional weapons.

| UNLOCKABLE | HOW TO UNLOCK |
|---|---|
| 2nd level Assault Rifle | Box in Mission 5. |
| 2nd level Grenades | Clear Missions 1, 2, and 3 in Normal difficulty (S rank). |
| 2nd level Rocket Launcher | Clear Missions 9, 10, and 11 in Normal difficulty (S rank). |
| 2nd level Shotgun | Box in Mission 11. |
| 2nd level SMG | Box in Mission 3. |
| 2nd level Whip | Clear Missions 5, 6, and 7 in Normal difficulty (S rank). |
| 3rd level Assault Rifle | Beat the game in Ultra difficulty. |
| 3rd level Grenades | Clear Missions 1 to 8 in Hard difficulty (S rank). |
| 3rd level Rocket Launcher | Clear Missions 1 to 12 in Ultra difficulty (S rank). |
| 3rd level Shotgun | Beat the game in Expert difficulty. |
| 3rd level SMG | Beat the game in Hard difficulty. |
| 3rd level Whip | Clear Missions 1 to 8 in Expert difficulty (S rank). |

## OPEN SEASON (Wii)

### UNLOCKABLE MINIGAMES

| UNLOCKABLE | HOW TO UNLOCK |
|---|---|
| Duck Chorus | Complete "Crazy Quackers" |
| Flowers for My Deer | Complete "Meet the Skunks" |
| Rise, Rise to the Top! | Complete "Beaver Damage" |

| Shake That Butt! | Complete "Hunted" |
| Wild Memory | Complete "Shaw's Shack" |

## OPERATION FLASHPOINT: DRAGON RISING (XBOX 360)

### CODES

| EFFECT | CODE |
|---|---|
| Unlocks "Ambush" mission | AmbushU454 |
| Unlocks "Close Quarters" mission | CloseQ8M3 |
| Unlocks "Coastal Stronghold" mission | StrongM577 |
| Unlocks "F.T.E." mission | BLEEDINGBADLY |
| Unlocks "Night Raid" mission | RaidT18Z |
| Unlocks "Debris Field" mission | OFPWEB2 |
| Unlocks "Encampment" mission | OFPWEB1 |

## OPERATION FLASHPOINT: RED RIVER (XBOX 360)

### ACHIEVEMENT

| UNLOCKABLE | HOW TO UNLOCK |
|---|---|
| Buzz Kill (5) | You destroyed an enemy aircraft with an anti aircraft weapon |
| Catch This! (5) | You destroyed an enemy vehicle with the FGM-148 Anti Tank Weapon |
| Danger Close (5) | You called in Combat Support within 300m of your location |
| Defender (10) | You completed one of the Last Stand FTE maps |
| Devils At The Crossroad (20) | You completed Careful What You Wish For... |
| Doing It The Hard Way (20) | You completed Almost Too Easy |
| Driver's Ed (5) | You drove a humvee |
| Florence Nightingale Award 2.0 (20) | You healed a development team member or someone who already has this achievement |
| Freeing The Eagles (20) | You completed Vantage Point |
| Get To The Chopper! (20) | You completed a Last Stand mission to stage 4, wave 4 and escaped alive |
| Hardened (10) | You maxed out one core soldier skill |
| Keeping It Simple (20) | You completed 1st & 10, Let's Do It Again |
| Lifer (30) | You maxed out all core soldier skills |
| Of The People, For The People (5) | You picked up an enemy AK |
| Old Enemies Die Hard (5) | You killed your first PLA soldier in Red River campaign |
| Operation Dragon Slayer (100) | You completed Act 3 of the campaign |
| Operation Enduring Shield (50) | You completed Act 1 of the campaign |
| Operation Unbroken Resistance (75) | You completed Act 2 of the campaign |
| Outlaw 2's Brave (10) | You obtained the highest level for one character class |
| Outlaw 2's Finest (30) | You obtained the highest level for two character classes |
| Outlaw 2's Hero (50) | You obtained the highest level for all character classes |
| Package Delivered (20) | You completed and survived a CSAR mission, rescuing both pilots |
| Peacekeeper (20) | You completed and survived a Combat Sweep mission having killed all enemies and destroyed all caches |
| Pride Of Balletto (10) | You completed a mission as the Auto Rifleman |

| Pride Of Kirby (10) | You completed a mission as the Rifleman |
|---|---|
| Pride Of Soto (10) | You completed a mission as the Scout |
| Pride Of Taylor (10) | You completed a mission as the Grenadier |
| Protection Detail (20) | You completed Meet The Neighbors |
| Protector (10) | You completed one of the Rolling Thunder FTE maps |
| Rescuer (10) | You completed one of the CSAR FTE maps |
| Rule #1 (20) | Don't get shot |
| Rule #10 (20) | Beware of confined spaces |
| Rule #2 (20) | Short, controlled bursts |
| Rule #3 (20) | You discovered what Knox's Rule #3 is |
| Rule #4 (20) | Watch your bullet drop |
| Rule #5 (20) | Patch your wounds |
| Rule #6 (20) | Keep a full mag |
| Rule #7 (20) | If in doubt, fall back |
| Rule #8 (20) | Keep the enemy suppressed |
| Rule #9 (20) | Orders |
| Shock And Ore (20) | You completed End Of The Beginning |
| Sweeper (10) | You completed one of the Combat Sweep FTE maps |
| The Alamo, Vahdat (20) | You completed Line In The Sand |
| Thunder Run (20) | You completed and survived a Rolling Thunder mission with the entire convoy surviving |
| Venomous Bite (20) | You completed The Human Terrain |
| Veteran (20) | You maxed out three core soldier skills |
| Weaponsmith (5) | You customized a weapon |
| Welcome To Gissar (20) | You completed Welcome To Tajikistan |
| With A Little Help (10) | You played Red River with three other friends |
| Work Your Bolt (20) | You completed The Wrong Way |

## OPOONA (Wii)

### UNLOCKABLES

| UNLOCKABLE | HOW TO UNLOCK |
|---|---|
| Fifth Citizen Ranking Star | Acquire the Five-Star Landroll Ranger License. Must be done before talking to woman for Sixth Star. |
| Five-Star Landroll Ranger License | Win 100 battles in the Intelligent Sea server room. |
| Sixth Citizen Ranking Star | Talk to a woman on the bottom floor of the Moon Forest Tokione Hotel after spending the night. |

## ORDYNE (Wii)

### UNLOCKABLES

| UNLOCKABLE | HOW TO UNLOCK |
|---|---|
| Continue Game | While falling, hold ① and press RUN |
| Princess Mode | At the title screen, hold ① for about 10 seconds |
| Secret Test Mode | At the title screen, hold down RUN while pressing SELECT, SELECT, SELECT, SELECT, SELECT, SELECT, then release. Hold down ①+②+⬆+➡, then press RUN. Press SELECT and RUN simultaneously to reach each part of the Secret Test mode. You can access a Sound Test, select your starting stage and your starting number of ships, among other things. |

## PAC-MAN WORLD 3 (PSP)

Enter this code at the main menu.

| UNLOCKABLE | CODE |
| --- | --- |
| Unlock levels and mazes | ⇦, ⇨, ⇦, ⇨, ●, ⇧ |

## PATAPON 2 (PSP)

### UNLOCKABLES

Complete the following tasks to gain the corresponding miracles.

| UNLOCKABLE | HOW TO UNLOCK |
| --- | --- |
| Attack Miracle | Beat invincible Dragon Majidonga Level 3 |
| Blizzard Miracle | Finish Watchtower and Two Karmen Mission. |
| Defense Miracle | Beat Fearful Tentacle Monster Darachura Level 3. |
| Earthquake Miracle | Beat Living Fortress Cannodears Level 3. |
| Rain Miracle | Finish Mushroom shroom shroom Nyokiri Swamp Mission in the Second Time. |
| Storm Miracle | Beat God General of Staff Hookmen. |
| Tailwind Miracle | Finish Mystery of the Desert's Sandstorm Mission in the Second Time. |

## PATAPON 3 (PSP)

### UNLOCKABLE

Complete the following requirements to unlock these shops.

| UNLOCKABLE | HOW TO UNLOCK |
| --- | --- |
| Hoshipon Shop | Achieve a team goal. |
| Meden Mart | Complete the Cave of Valour. |

## PINBALL HALL OF FAME (PSP)

Enter these passwords on the Password screen.

| UNLOCKABLE | PASSWORD |
| --- | --- |
| 999 Credits | JAT |
| Freeplay on Big Shot | UJP |
| Freeplay on Black Hole | LIS |
| Freeplay on Goin' Nuts | PHF |
| Freeplay on Love Meter | HOT |

Enter these passwords on the Password screen.

| UNLOCKABLE | PASSWORD |
| --- | --- |
| Freeplay on Tee'd Off | PGA |
| Freeplay on Xolten | BIG |
| Unlocks Payout mode | WGR |
| Unlocks Aces High for freeplay | UNO |
| Unlocks Central Park for freeplay | NYC |
| Unlocks custom balls in Options | CKF |
| Unlocks freeplay on Strikes 'N Spares | PBA |
| Unlocks optional tilt in Options | BZZ |
| Unlocks Play Boy table for freeplay | HEF |

## PIRATES OF THE CARIBBEAN: AT WORLD'S END (DS)

### UNLOCKABLES

| UNLOCKABLE | HOW TO UNLOCK |
|---|---|
| Secret Cove | Collect all 7 Secret Map Fragments in Shipwreck Cove. |

## PIRATES PLUNDARRR (Wii)

### UNLOCKABLE CHARACTERS

| UNLOCKABLE | HOW TO UNLOCK |
|---|---|
| Amazon | Defeat Tecciztecatl, Witch Doctor. |
| Spectral | Defeat Nanauatl, Hero of the Sun. |

## PIXELJUNK EDEN (PlayStation 3)

### CUSTOM SOUNDTRACK

Find all 50 spectra to unlock in-game custom soundtrack.

## PLANTS VS. ZOMBIES (XBOX 360)

### CODES

To enter a cheat code, press LB, RB, LT, RT in game; some codes require a tall enough tree of wisdom.u.

| EFFECT | CODE |
|---|---|
| A shower of candy when a zombie dies | pinata |
| Alternate lawn mower appearance | trickedout |
| Gives zombies futuristic shades | future |
| Mustaches for zombie | mustache |
| Once zombies are killed, they leave small daisies behind | daisies |
| Toggles the zombie's call for brains sound | sukhbir |
| Zombies dance | dance |

## POKÉMON BLACK (DS)

### UNLOCKABLE

| UNLOCKABLE | HOW TO UNLOCK |
|---|---|
| National Dex | Beat the Elite Four once and upon leaving your house after the credits Professor Juniper's Dad will reward you with a National Dex. |

### UNLOCKABLE

Get new wallpapers for beating the elite four for the first time, then some more when you beat them the second time.

| UNLOCKABLE | HOW TO UNLOCK |
|---|---|
| Wallpapers | Beat the Elite Four twice. |

### UNLOCKABLE

The color of your Trainer Card changes as you complete certain objectives.

| UNLOCKABLE | HOW TO UNLOCK |
|---|---|
| Color Change | Complete the National Pokedex |
| Color Change | Obtain all Entralink Powers |
| Color Change | Obtain all Pokemon Musical Items |
| Color Change | Get a 49 Streak in both Super Single and Super Double Subway lines in the Battle Subway (Good Luck) |
| Color Change | Deafeat the Elite 4 |

## POKÉMON HEARTGOLD (DS)

### UNLOCKABLES

| UNLOCKABLE | HOW TO UNLOCK |
|---|---|
| National Dex | Beat the Elite Four once and go to the S.S Aqua ship in Olivine City to get the National Dex. |
| Beautiful Beach | Obtain 200 Watts. |
| Beyond the Sea | Obtain a foreign Pokémon via use of the GTS. |
| Big Forest | Obtain 40,000 Watts and own the National Dex. |
| Blue Lake | Obtain 2,000 Watts. |
| Dim Cave | Obtain 1,000 Watts. |
| Hoenn Field | Obtain 5,000 Watts and own the National Dex. |
| Icy Mountain Rd. | Obtain 30,000 Watts and own the National Dex. |
| Night Sky's Edge | Trade a fateful-encounter Jirachi onto your HG or SS. |
| Noisy Forest | Available from the start. |
| Quiet Cave | Obtain 100,000 Watts and own the National Dex. |
| Refreshing Field | Available from the start. |
| Resort | Obtain 80,000 Watts and own the National Dex. |
| Rugged Road | Obtain 50 Watts. |
| Scary Cave | Obtain 20,000 Watts and own the National Dex. |
| Sinnoh Field | Obtain 25,000 Watts and own the National Dex. |
| Stormy Beach | Obtain 65,000 Watts and own the National Dex. |
| Suburban Area | Obtain 500 Watts. |
| Town Outskirts | Obtain 3,000 Watts. |
| Tree House | Obtain 15,000 Watts and own the National Dex. |
| Volcano Path | Obtain 10,000 Watts and own the National Dex. |
| Warm Beach | Obtain 7,500 Watts and own the National Dex. |
| White Lake | Obtain 50,000 Watts and own the National Dex. |

## POKÉMON RUMBLE BLAST (3DS)

### CODE

Use these codes to unlock special Pokémon in the specified levels. Speak to Munna in Easterly Town to enter a code. You must defeat them to add them to your collection.

| UNLOCKABLE | HOW TO UNLOCK |
|---|---|
| Gallade (in 4-2 Everspring Valley) 3535-6928 | |
| Gliscor (in 4-3 Sunny Seashore) 9625-7845 | |
| Heat Stamp Emboar (in 1-3 Echo Valley) 8902-7356 | |
| Oshawott (in 2-4 Shimmering Lake) 7403-2240 | |
| Pikachu (in 3-2 Volcanic Slope) 7746-3878 | |
| Tornadus (in 3-2 Volcanic Slope) 0250-7321 | |

### UNLOCKABLE

As you meet people with the game on Street Pass, you'll be able to find new Legendary Pokemon on different areas.

| UNLOCKABLE | HOW TO UNLOCK |
|---|---|
| Azelf [Shimmering Lake: Lake Area] | Meet 10 People |
| Celebi [Everspring Valley: Forest Area] | Meet 60 People |
| Jirachi [Firebreathing Mountain: Tower Area] | Meet 40 People |
| Manaphy [Rugged Flats: Beach Area] | Meet 20 People |
| Mesprit [Soothing Shore: Lake Area] | Meet 5 People |
| Mew [Sunny Seashore: Factory Area] | Meet 80 People |

| Phione [Rugged Flats: Beach Area] | Meet 20 People |
|---|---|
| Shaymin (Land Forme) [World Axle Underground 2F: Ice Area] | Meet 100 People |
| Shaymin (Sky Forme) [World Axle Underground 1F: Forest Area] | Meet 120 People |
| Uxie [Sun-Dappled Bank: Lake Area] | Meet 2 People |
| Victini [World Axle Underground 2F: Tower Area] | Meet 150 People |

## POKÉMON SOULSILVER (DS)

### UNLOCKABLES

| UNLOCKABLE | HOW TO UNLOCK |
|---|---|
| National Dex | Beat the Elite Four once and go to the S.S. Aqua ship in Olivine City to get the National Dex. |
| Amity Meadow | Unreleased to all versions. |
| Beautiful Beach | Collect 200 Watts. |
| Beyond the Sea | Trade for an International Pokémon in the GTS in Goldenrod City. |
| Big Forest | Collect 40,000 Watts + National Dex. |
| Blue Lake | Collect 2,000 Watts. |
| Dim Cave | Collect 1,000 Watts. |
| Hoenn Field | Collect 5,000 Watts + National Dex. |
| Icy Mountain Road | Collect 30,000 Watts + National Dex. |
| Night Sky's Edge | Obtain the PokéDex Data for Jirachi. |
| Quiet Cave | Collect 100,000 Watts + National Dex. |
| Rally | Unreleased to U.S. versions. |
| Rugged Road | Collect 50 Watts. |
| Scary Cave | Collect 20,000 Watts + National Dex. |
| Sightseeing | Unreleased to U.S. versions. |
| Sinnoh Field | Collect 25,000 Watts + National Dex. |
| Stormy Beach | Collect 65,000 Watts + National Dex. |
| Suburban Area | Collect 500 Watts. |
| The Resort | Collect 80,000 Watts + National Dex. |
| Town Outskirts | Collect 3,000 Watts. |
| Treehouse | Collect 15,000 Watts + National Dex. |
| Volcano Path | Collect 10,000 Watts + National Dex. |
| Warm Beach | Collect 7,500 Watts + National Dex. |
| White Lake | Collect 50,000 Watts + National Dex. |

## POKEMON WHITE (DS)

### UNLOCKABLE

After beating the game, leave your house and Professor Juniper's Father will upgrade your Pokedex to National Mode.

### UNLOCKABLE

Get new wallpapers for beating the elite four for the first time, then some more when you beat them the second time.

| UNLOCKABLE | HOW TO UNLOCK |
|---|---|
| Wallpapers | Beat the Elite Four twice. |

## PORTAL: STILL ALIVE (XBOX 360)

### UNLOCKABLES

| UNLOCKABLE | HOW TO UNLOCK |
| --- | --- |
| Portal Gamer picture | In test chamber 17, incinerate the companion cube. |
| Portal Gamer picture (2) | Defeat GLaDOS and escape |

## PORTAL 2 (XBOX 360)

### UNLOCKABLE

| UNLOCKABLE | HOW TO UNLOCK |
| --- | --- |
| Alternate Title Screen | Beat the game to get a different title screen |

### UNLOCKABLE

Complete the task to earn an item for your avatar.

| UNLOCKABLE | HOW TO UNLOCK |
| --- | --- |
| Companion Cube | Complete Portal 2 Single Player. |
| Love Shirt | Hug 3 friends in Portal 2 Coop. |
| Portal 2 Hat | Survive the manual override. |
| Portal 2 Shirt | Complete Portal 2 Coop |
| Turret Shirt | Complete Test Chamber 10 in under 70 seconds. |

### EASTER EGG

| UNLOCKABLE | HOW TO UNLOCK |
| --- | --- |
| Singing Turrets | Look for a turret in a ventilation shaft in one of the test chambers at the very beginning. Use the laser and reflector cube to destroy it, then go through the new opening to find singing turrets. |

### ACHIEVEMENT

| UNLOCKABLE | HOW TO UNLOCK |
| --- | --- |
| Air Show (20) | Perform 2 aerial gestures before touching the ground in co-op |
| Asking for Trouble (10) | Taunt GLaDOS in front of a camera in each of the five co-op courses |
| Bridge Building (15) | Complete all test chambers in the Hard-Light Surfaces co-op course |
| Bridge Over Troubling Water (10) | Complete the first Hard Light Bridge test |
| Can't Touch This (10) | Dance in front of a turret blocked by a hard light bridge in co-op |
| Confidence Building (10) | Complete all test chambers in the Mass and Velocity co-op course |
| Door Prize (20) | Examine all the vitrified test chamber doors |
| Drop Box (20) | Place a cube on a button without touching the cube |
| Dual Pit Experiment (15) | Do the same test twice |
| Empty Gesture (25) | Drop your co-op partner in goo while they are gesturing by removing the bridge under them |
| Final Transmission (20) | Find the hidden signal in one of the Rat Man's dens |
| Four Ring Circus (25) | Enter 4 different portals without touching the ground in co-op |
| Friends List With Benefits (50) | While playing co-op, hug 3 different people on your friends list |
| Gesticul-8 (15) | Perform all 8 gestures of your own volition in co-op |
| Good Listener (5) | Take GLaDOS' escape advice |
| High Five (5) | Celebrate your cooperative calibration success |
| Iron Grip (20) | Never lose a cube in Chamber 6 of the Mass and Velocity co-op course |
| Lunacy (20) | That just happened |

A B C D E F G H I J K L M N O P Q R S T U V W X Y Z

| | |
|---|---|
| **Narbacular Drop (25)** | Place a portal under your co-op partner while they are gesturing |
| **No Hard Feelings (10)** | Save a turret from redemption |
| **Obstacle Building (15)** | Complete all test chambers in the Excursion Funnels co-op course |
| **Overclocker (30)** | Complete Test Chamber 10 in 70 seconds |
| **Party of Three (25)** | Find the hidden companion cube in co-op test chamber |
| **Pit Boss (30)** | Show that pit who's boss |
| **Portal Conservation Society (20)** | Complete Chamber 3 in the Hard-Light Surfaces co-op course using only 5 total portal placements |
| **Portrait of a Lady (10)** | Find a hidden portrait |
| **Preservation of Mass (20)** | Break the rules in Test Chamber 07 |
| **Professor Portal (75)** | After completing co-op, complete Calibration Course online with a friend who hasn't played before |
| **Pturretdactyl (5)** | Use an Aerial Faith Plate to launch a turret |
| **Rock Portal Scissors (20)** | Win 3 co-op games of rock-paper-scissors in a row |
| **SaBOTour (10)** | Make a break for it |
| **Scanned Alone (5)** | Stand in a defective turret detector |
| **Schrodinger's Catch (20)** | Catch a blue-painted box before it touches the ground |
| **Ship Overboard (10)** | Discover the missing experiment |
| **Smash TV (75)** | Break 11 test chamber monitors |
| **Stalemate Associate (15)** | Press the button! |
| **Still Alive (15)** | Complete Course 4 with neither you nor your co-op partner dying |
| **Stranger Than Friction (15)** | Master the Propulsion Gel |
| **Tater Tote (15)** | Carry science forward |
| **Team Building (10)** | Complete all test chambers in the Team Building co-op course |
| **The Part Where He Kills You (20)** | This is that part |
| **Triple Crown (15)** | Solve 3 co-op chambers in the Mass and Velocity course in under 60 seconds each |
| **Tunnel of Funnel (15)** | Master the Excursion Funnel |
| **Undiscouraged (10)** | Complete the first Thermal Discouragement Beam test |
| **Vertically Unchallenged (15)** | Master the Repulsion Gel |
| **Wake Up Call (5)** | Survive the manual override |
| **White Out (15)** | Complete the first Conversion Gel test |
| **You Made Your Point (10)** | Refuse to solve the first test in Chapter 8 |
| **You Monster (5)** | Reunite with GLaDOS |
| **You Saved Science (100)** | Complete all test chambers in all courses of co-op |

## POWERUP HEROES (XBOX 360)

### ACHIEVEMENT

| UNLOCKABLE | HOW TO UNLOCK |
|---|---|
| **Best of the Best (50)** | Won a Tournament |
| **Chain (5)** | Chained two Super Attacks |
| **Fearless fighter (50)** | Won a match without dodging |
| **Here I am (25)** | Won a Ranked match |
| **Modernist (200)** | Unlocked all PowerUps |
| **No more secrets (100)** | All Super Attacks have been performed |
| **Super Chain (20)** | Chained two Super Attacks by changing Suit |

| The untouchable (75) | Won a fight without being hit |
|---|---|
| This is just the beginning (25) | Won your first fight in Campaign Mode |
| Ultimate Chain (100) | Chained three Super Attacks by changing Suit twice |
| Ultra Chain (50) | Chained three Super Attacks by changing Suit once |
| You've beaten the world (200) | Completed the Campaign Mode |
| You've made it halfway (100) | Won against Malignance |

## PRINCE OF PERSIA: CLASSIC   (XBOX 360)

### PASSWORDS

| PASSWORD | EFFECT |
|---|---|
| 73232535 | Level 2 |
| 96479232 | Level 3 |
| 53049212 | Level 4 |
| 51144526 | Level 5 |
| 18736748 | Level 6 |
| 42085223 | Level 7 |
| 98564243 | Level 8 |
| 51139315 | Level 9 |
| 53246739 | Level 10 |
| 32015527 | Level 11 |
| 44153123 | Level 12 |
| 96635134 | Level 13 |
| 75423134 | Level 14 |
| 89012414 | End |

## PRO EVOLUTION SOCCER 09   (XBOX 360)

### UNLOCKABLES

| UNLOCKABLE | HOW TO UNLOCK |
|---|---|
| Classic Argentina | Win the international cup with Argentina. |
| Classic Brazil | Win the international cup with Brazil. |
| Classic England | Win the international cup with England. |
| Classic France | Win the international cup with France. |
| Classic Germany | Win the international cup with Germany. |
| Classic Italy | Win the international cup with Italy. |
| Classic Netherlands | Win the international cup with the Netherlands. |

## PRO EVOLUTION SOCCER 2010   (XBOX 360)

### UNLOCKABLES

Unlock by winning the International Cup with the respective team

| UNLOCKABLE | HOW TO UNLOCK |
|---|---|
| Classic Argentina | Win International Cup with Argentina. |
| Classic Brazil | Win International Cup with Brazil. |
| Classic England | Win International Cup with England. |
| Classic France | Win International Cup with France. |
| Classic Germany | Win International Cup with Germany. |
| Classic Italy | Win International Cup with Italy. |

## PRO EVOLUTION SOCCER 2010 (PlayStation 3)

### UNLOCKABLES

Unlock by winning the International Cup with the respective team.

| UNLOCKABLE | HOW TO UNLOCK |
|---|---|
| Classic Argentina | Win International Cup with Argentina. |
| Classic Brazil | Win International Cup with Brazil. |
| Classic England | Win International Cup with England. |
| Classic France | Win International Cup with France. |
| Classic Germany | Win International Cup with Germany. |
| Classic Italy | Win International Cup with Italy. |

## PRO EVOLUTION SOCCER 2012 (PlayStation 3)

### TROPHY

| UNLOCKABLE | HOW TO UNLOCK |
|---|---|
| Champion Chairman (Silver) | Awarded for winning a Top Flight League Title in [Club Boss]. |
| Champion Manager (Silver) | Awarded for winning the League Title in any of the Top Leagues featured in [Master League]. |
| Copa Santander Libertadores King (Silver) | Awarded for becoming a [Copa Santander Libertadores] Winner. |
| Copa Santander Libertadores R16 (Bronze) | Awarded for making it through the Group stage in [Copa Santander Libertadores]. |
| Copa Santander Libertadores Win (Bronze) | Awarded for defeating the COM for the first time in [Copa Santander Libertadores]. |
| European Elite 16 (Bronze) | Awarded for making it through the Group stage of the UEFA Champions League in [Master League]. |
| First Glory: Club Boss (Bronze) | Awarded for your first win as a Club Owner in [Club Boss]. |
| First Glory: Competition (Bronze) | Awarded for your first win in an [Online Competition]. |
| First Glory: Exhibition (Bronze) | Awarded for defeating the COM for the first time in [Exhibition]. |
| First Glory: Master League (Bronze) | Awarded for your first win in [Master League]. |
| First Glory: Quick Match (Bronze) | Awarded for winning your first [Quick Match]. No disconnections permitted. |
| First Win: UEFA Champions League (Bronze) | Awarded for defeating the COM for the first time in [UEFA Champions League]. |
| International Champion (Silver) | Awarded for winning a National Team Competition in [League/Cup]. |
| Kings of Europe (Silver) | Awarded for becoming a UEFA Champions League Winner in [Master League]. |
| League Best Eleven (Silver) | Awarded for being picked for the Team of the Season in [Become a Legend]. |
| League Champion (Silver) | Awarded for single-handedly winning a League Title in [League/Cup]. |
| League Champions (Silver) | Awarded for winning the League Title in [Become a Legend]. |
| Mr. Versatility (Bronze) | Awarded for learning to play in another position in [Become a Legend]. |
| No.1 Club (Gold) | Awarded for being named the No.1 Club in the [Master League] Club Rankings. |
| No.1 Owner (Gold) | Awarded for being the Greatest Owner within the Beautiful Game in [Club Boss]. |
| Online Debutant (Bronze) | Awarded for completing your debut match in [Online]. No disconnections permitted. |

| | |
|---|---|
| **Pride of a Nation (Silver)** | Awarded for playing in the International Cup in [Become a Legend]. |
| **Promoted (Bronze)** | Awarded for Winning Promotion to a Top League in [Master League]. |
| **Proud Skipper (Bronze)** | Awarded for being named Club Captain in [Become a Legend]. |
| **Super Star (Gold)** | Awarded for winning the UEFA Club Footballer of the Year Award [Become a Legend]. |
| **The Community Associate (Silver)** | Awarded for joining your first [Online Community]. |
| **The Debutant (Bronze)** | Awarded for making a professional debut in [Become a Legend]. |
| **The Highlight Show (Bronze)** | Awarded for watching Highlight Footage in [Final Highlights]. |
| **The Multi-Talented (Bronze)** | Awarded for acquiring a New Skill in [Become a Legend]. |
| **The Treble Winner (Silver)** | Awarded for winning the League, UEFA Champions League and League Cup in a [Master League] season. |
| **Theatre Connoisseur (Bronze)** | Awarded for watching a Highlight Reel uploaded by another user in the [Theatre of Legends]. |
| **UEFA Champions League Debut (Silver)** | Awarded for making your UEFA Champions League debut in [Become a Legend]. |
| **UEFA Champions League Elite 16 (Bronze)** | Awarded for making it through the Group stage in [UEFA Champions League]. |
| **UEFA Champions League Winner (Silver)** | Awarded for becoming a [UEFA Champions League] Winner. |
| **Ultimate Player (Platinum)** | Perfect Collection |
| **Wheeler and Dealer (Bronze)** | Awarded for making your first ever signing in [Master League Online]. |
| **World Footballer of the Year (Gold)** | Awarded for being named World Footballer of the Year in [Become a Legend]. |

## PRO WRESTLING   (Wii)

### UNLOCKABLES

| UNLOCKABLE | HOW TO UNLOCK |
|---|---|
| **Battle the Great Puma** | Once you are VWA Champion, defend your title for 10 matches. Then you will have a match with the Great uma. |

## PROFESSOR LAYTON AND THE DIABOLICAL BOX   (DS)

### UNLOCKABLES

After beating the game, go to the Top Secret section of the Bonuses menu to access the following unlockables.

| UNLOCKABLE | HOW TO UNLOCK |
|---|---|
| **Art Gallery** | Beat the game. |
| **Character Profiles List** | Beat the game. |
| **Layton's Challenges: The Sweetheart's House** | Beat the game. |

## PROTOTYPE   (XBOX 360)

### CODES

Select "Extras" from the Main menu and go to "Cheats."

| EFFECT | CODE |
|---|---|
| **Unlock Body Surf Ability** | ➡,➡,➡,⬇,♀,⬆,⬆,⬇,♀ |

## PROTOTYPE (PlayStation 3)

### CODES

Select "Extras" from the Main Menu and go to "Cheats."

| EFFECT | CODE |
|---|---|
| Unlock Body Surf Ability | →,→,←,↓,↑,↑,↑,↓ |

## PULSEMAN (Wii)

### UNLOCKABLES

| UNLOCKABLE | HOW TO UNLOCK |
|---|---|
| Level SELECT | At the Sega logo, press (in joystick 2): Ⓐ, Ⓑ, Ⓒ, Ⓒ, Ⓑ, Ⓐ. After this, go to Options and use the Map option. |

## PUSS IN BOOTS (XBOX 360)

### ACHIEVEMENT

| UNLOCKABLE | HOW TO UNLOCK |
|---|---|
| Adios, Amigo (10) | Boot an enemy into a trap |
| All I need are the boots, baby! (100) | Complete the game |
| Always Land on my Feet (15) | Complete a best of three team challenge |
| Born with Cat-like Moves (15) | Complete The Chase |
| Care to Dance-Fight? (20) | Perform a perfect dance in the Cantina |
| Check me Out (15) | Complete The Hotel |
| Conquistador of the clouds (15) | Complete The Beanstalk |
| Copycat (20) | Perform a perfect shape match |
| Danger is my Game (15) | Complete The Great Terror |
| Don't Desert Me (20) | Get a perfect time in the Canyon |
| En Garde (15) | Defeat the cat lover |
| Feisty Feline (20) | Get a high score in Market Mayhem |
| Hero (25) | Silver medal on every level |
| Holy Frijoles (20) | Defeat 20 enemies using the guitar |
| I Flirt with Danger (15) | Rock a pig back to sleep |
| I Thirst for Leche (15) | Complete The Thieves' Bar |
| Legendary (50) | Gold medal on every level |
| Light on my Feet (20) | Perform a perfect sneak |
| Looking Sharp (20) | Defeat 10 enemies using Claw Frenzy |
| Me-ow! (15) | Serenade a senorita |
| Nice moves, Senor (15) | Complete The Cantina |
| Ole! (10) | Block an enemy attack |
| Over Easy (50) | Collect all nine golden egg pieces |
| Pet Peeved (10) | Defeat 3 enemies with one guitar attack |
| Pray For Mercy (50) | Collect all nine wanted posters |
| Purrfecto (20) | Get a high score in Barrel Barrage |
| Purrrrrfect Score (20) | Serenade three different senoritas with a perfect score |
| Real Cats Wear Boots (20) | Get a high score in Bandit Boot |
| Scratch That (10) | Perform a Claw Frenzy |
| Stage Complete (15) | Complete The Stagecoach Robbery |
| Such Moves, Such Handsomeness (20) | Get a perfect time in the Beanstalk |
| Swashbuckler (10) | Bronze medal on every level |

| The Cat's Whiskers (100) | Complete the game with 100% progress |
| --- | --- |
| These Eyes Tell No Lies (100) | Discover every type of trap |
| This Cat is En Fuego (15) | Complete The Mine |
| Touche! (10) | Perform a deflect |
| Virtuoso (10) | Play every guitar tune |
| Viva Gato! (20) | Get a high score in Shape It Up! |
| Well Balanced (20) | Perform a perfect balance |
| Wild Goose Chased (15) | Complete The Giant's Castle |

## PUYO POP FEVER  (DS)

To enter this code, go into Options, then Gallery, then highlight Cutscene Viewer.

| UNLOCKABLE | CODE |
| --- | --- |
| Unlock all characters and cutscenes | Hold ⊗ and press ↑, ↓, ←, → |

## QUAKE 4  (XBOX 360)

To enter these codes, press the Back button while playing.

| UNLOCKABLE | CODE |
| --- | --- |
| Ammo Refill for All Weapons | ⓑ, Ⓐ, ⊗, Ⓨ, ⬅, ➡, ⬅ |
| Full Health Refill | ⓑ, Ⓐ, ⓑ, Ⓐ, ⬆, ⬆, ⬇, ⊗ |

## QUANTUM REDSHIFT  (XBOX)

Enter Cheat as your name, then in the Options menu, select the Cheats menu to enter these codes. Codes are case sensitive.

| UNLOCKABLE | CODE |
| --- | --- |
| All Characters | Nematode |
| All Speeds | zoomZOOM |
| Infinite Turbo | FishFace |
| Infinite Shields | ThinkBat |
| Upgrade All Characters | RICEitup |

## R-TYPE (Wii)

### UNLOCKABLES

| UNLOCKABLE | HOW TO UNLOCK |
|---|---|
| Extra Credits | Set the turbo switch for I to full. Then, hold SELECT+① and press RUN on the title screen. |

### PASSWORDS

| PASSWORD | EFFECT |
|---|---|
| CPL-3590-CM | Hard mode |

## R-TYPE 2 (Wii)

### PASSWORDS

| PASSWORD | EFFECT |
|---|---|
| JJL-6589-MB | All items and 99 lives |

## R-TYPE 3 (Wii)

### UNLOCKABLES

| UNLOCKABLE | HOW TO UNLOCK |
|---|---|
| Level Select | At the continue screen, press ⬆, ⬆, ⬆, ⬆, ⬆, ⬆, ⬆, ⬆, ⬆, ⬆ then press ⬇ one or more times, then press START (the number of times L is pressed dictates the level you skip to) |

## RAGE (XBOX 360)

### ACHIEVEMENT

| UNLOCKABLE | HOW TO UNLOCK |
|---|---|
| A True Legend (25) | Complete a Legend of the Wasteland on Nightmare difficulty |
| Anthology (20) | Complete all Legends of the Wasteland |
| Arts and Crafts (10) | Construct 10 Engineering Items |
| Bringin' Home the Bacon (20) | Earn 750 Dollars in one episode of Bash TV in the Campaign |
| Debunked (10) | Complete Shrouded Bunker in the Campaign |
| Decapathon (15) | Get 10 Headshot kills with the Wingstick |
| Decrypted (10) | Complete Jackal Canyon in the Campaign |
| Deliverance (15) | Complete the final round of Strum |
| Demolition Man (20) | Destroy 100 Enemy Cars |
| Dev Graffiti (15) | Find the secret Developer Graffiti Room |
| Fresh Meat (10) | Complete a public Road RAGE match |
| Ghost Buster (10) | Complete Ghost Hideout in the Campaign |
| Gladiator (10) | Complete Mutant Bash TV in the Campaign |
| Gotta Have 'Em All (20) | Collect all Playing Cards on one play-through |
| Hardest Deck (25) | Beat Teague's hardest Deck |
| Hat Trick (15) | Kill at least 3 Enemies with a single Mind Controlled Enemy |
| Hey, not too rough (50) | Finish the Campaign on any difficulty |
| Hurt me plenty (25) | Finish the Campaign on at least Normal difficulty |

| It's Alive! (10) | Complete Dead City in the Campaign |
|---|---|
| It's Good! (15) | Score each of the 3 Field Goals from the ATV |
| JACKPOT! (15) | Roll 4 Targets in the first round of Tombstones |
| Jail Break (10) | Complete Authority Prison in the Campaign |
| Jetpacker (20) | Kill an Authority Enforcer during Jetpack descent |
| Jumper (20) | Perform all 18 Vehicle Jumps |
| Just a Flesh Wound (15) | Complete the final round of 5 Finger Filet |
| Keep 'Em Coming (30) | Get 5 kills with one deployed Sentry Turret |
| Lead Foot (10) | Win a Race in the Campaign |
| Master Chef (20) | Collect all Recipes and Schematics in one play-through |
| Mechanocide (50) | Kill 100 Enemies with Sentry Bots, Sentry Turrets, or RC Bomb Cars |
| Minigamer (15) | Win all Minigames |
| Mr. Oddjob (40) | Complete 5 Job Board Quests in one play-through |
| Mutie Blues (10) | Complete Blue Line Station in the Campaign |
| MVP (20) | Get first place in a public Road RAGE match |
| No Room for Sidekicks (15) | Complete a Legend of the Wasteland without any player(s) becoming incapacitated |
| Obsessive Compulsive (75) | Reach 100% Completion in the Campaign |
| Open Minded (15) | Get 10 Headshot kills with the Sniper Rifle |
| Passive Aggressive (30) | Get 3 kills with a single Sentry Bot |
| Power Struggle (10) | Complete Power Plant in the Campaign |
| Rage Cup (50) | Win all Races in the Campaign |
| RAGE Nightmare (25) | Finish the Campaign on Nightmare difficulty |
| Roadkill (15) | Run over 10 Mutants |
| Silent But Deadly (15) | Stealth kill 10 Enemies with the Striker Crossbow |
| The Legend Begins... (10) | Complete a Legend of the Wasteland |
| Three Birds, One Bomb Car (30) | Kill 3 Enemies with one RC Bomb Car |
| Tinkerer (20) | Construct 50 Engineering Items |
| Ultra-violence (25) | Finish the Campaign on at least Hard difficulty |
| Vault Assault (10) | Complete Gearhead Vault in the Campaign |
| Waste Management (10) | Complete Wasted Garage in the Campaign |
| Wellness Plan (10) | Complete The Well in the Campaign |
| ytiC daeD (10) | Complete Dead City Reverse in the Campaign |

## RAGNAROK DS   (DS)

### MIRAGE TOWER

Mirage Tower consists of 50 floors with random monsters. This dungeon allows you to play online with other Ragnarok Online DS players. This dungeon is found at the lower-right portal of the North Sograt Desert

| UNLOCKABLE | HOW TO UNLOCK |
|---|---|
| Mirage Tower | Complete the main quest till quest 25. |

## RAIDEN FIGHTERS JET   (XBOX 360)

### SECRET PLANES

| UNLOCKABLE | HOW TO UNLOCK |
|---|---|
| Fairy | On the ship select screen hold B on Miclus and then press A (B must still be held down). |
| Slave | On the ship select screen Hold B on any ship except Miclus and then press A (while B is still held down). |

## RAMPAGE: TOTAL DESTRUCTION (Wii)

At the main menu, press the ⊖+⊕ to open the Password screen.

| UNLOCKABLE | PASSWORD |
|---|---|
| All Monsters Unlocked | 141421 |
| Demo Mode with Two Random Monsters | 082864 |
| Disable All Active Codes | 000000 |
| Display Game Version | 314159 |
| Instant Demo Mode with Two Random Monsters | 874098 |
| Invincible to Military Attacks, Bombers, Infantry, Tanks, Etc. | 986960 |
| Obtain All Ability Upgrades | 011235 |
| One Hit Destroys a Building | 071767 |
| Unlock All Cities | 271828 |
| View Credits | 667302 |
| View Ending Theme | 667301 |
| View Opening Theme | 667300 |

## RAVING RABBIDS: ALIVE & KICKING (XBOX 360)

### ACHIEVEMENT

| UNLOCKABLE | HOW TO UNLOCK |
|---|---|
| 1 Kilo-rab-Bit (10) | Hit, flatten or make 1,024 Rabbids explode in the various games. |
| 10 Kilo-rab-Bits (50) | Hit, flatten or make 10,240 Rabbids explode in the various games. |
| 5 Kilo-rab-Bits (30) | Hit, flatten or make 5,120 Rabbids explode in the various games. |
| Babysitter (30) | In My Raving Rabbid, find 7 different ways to interact with the Rabbid without using an object. |
| Big party (10) | Start a game mode for 16 players. |
| Break the piggy bank (10) | Buy something in My Raving Rabbid. |
| Cinderella (10) | In the Sauce Wars game, mop up the floor with your hands. |
| Close-up (20) | In My Raving Rabbid, take a photo of the Rabbid that crashes into your screen. |
| Colonel Major (50) | Get 1 star in all games. |
| Copycow (20) | Get 100 moves right in Udder Nonsense. |
| First Party (10) | Start a game mode for several players. |
| Flaming friends (15) | In the Flaming balls of fire game, earn 180 points during a rally against another player. |
| Harakiri (10) | In Forfeits!, get 100% negative opinions for a forfeit. |
| Hop you can do it (20) | Play an entire game of Tenderfoot Dance on just one foot. |
| Ibiza (10) | Make the Rabbids dance in Life's a Beach. |
| Insomniac (10) | The name says it all. |
| Jackpot (20) | In The Kitty game mode, bank the highest possible amount. |
| King of TP (20) | Accumulate 20,000 TP DollarZ in your kitty. |
| Lumberjack (20) | Saw through 90 blocks in Hacked Off! |
| Major-General (100) | Get 3 stars in all games. |
| Marathon (30) | Play for 2 hours, 3 minutes and 59 seconds in one session. |
| Minor squaddie (10) | Get 1 star in a game. |

| Missing (10) | In My Raving Rabbid, stay out of the sensor's line of sight for 30 seconds. |
|---|---|
| Monkey! (10) | In My Raving Rabbid, take a photo while doing a pose. |
| No mean feet! (10) | In Rabbids-in-the-Hole, play using your feet. |
| Olé! (10) | In Hot Dogs in Danger, let all the Rabbids through without leaving the play space. |
| Pacifist (10) | In My Raving Rabbid, don't hit the Rabbid for 2 minutes. |
| Psycho (20) | Successfully make 90 shapes in Silhou-wet. |
| Pump 'n' Pose (20) | Do 200 successful poses in Pumped Up. |
| Rock Star (15) | Finish Guitar Zero with 35 correctly played notes in a row. |
| Round the clock (30) | Clock up 24 hours of total play time. |
| Sergeant Major (20) | Get 3 stars in a game. |
| Show-off (20) | Do 100 headbutts in Rabbzilla. |
| Showbiz star (10) | Let all the spotlights hit you in Now You See Me... |
| Six machine (10) | In the Big Brother game, play as a team of 6 players. |
| Slashed prices (15) | In the Crazy Sales game, fire at all the special offer signs on the sides. |
| Snotput slinger (10) | During Snot Funny, steal the snot from the other player. |
| Social netnerd (20) | Upload a photo to the Rabbids site. |
| Spendthrift (50) | Buy everything in My Raving Rabbid. |
| Still at it? (30) | Play 6 months after your first game. |
| Super Suppository (10) | In Inner Journey, maintain maximum speed for 20 seconds. |
| Super sushi (20) | Jump 120 times in Salmon Rush Day. |
| Talk to the hand (10) | In the Whack a Rabbid game, smash a Rabbid with your hand. |
| Thank you, friend! (15) | In the Rabbid-o-matic game, get the Rabbid to the end without it falling into a trap. |
| They help you see in the dark (20) | In Carrot Juice, drink 10 glasses in infinite mode. |
| TP Emperor (50) | Accumulate 50,000 TP DollarZ for your kitty. |
| Udder slapper (15) | In the Slapping Station game, slap 4 cows during a game. |
| Welcome to HQ (5) | Launch the game for the first time. |
| You should take a break (10) | Chalk up 100 failures in the cartoon games. |
| You're completely Uplay (10) | Launch Uplay and sign up. |

### UNLOCKABLE

| UNLOCKABLE | HOW TO UNLOCK |
|---|---|
| 1 Kilo-rab-Bit (10) | Hit, flatten or |
| Rabbid Helmet | A Rabbid helmet to stay incognito. |
| Rabbids A&K T-Shirt | The official T-Shirt supporting ravingness around the world. |
| T.V. Helmet | A TV set that acts a stunning piece of headgear. |

## RAYMAN ORIGINS (XBOX 360)

### ACHIEVEMENT

| UNLOCKABLE | HOW TO UNLOCK |
|---|---|
| B Side! (15) | Played an Unlocked Character in any map. |
| Back At You! (15) | You Bubblized a Hunter with his own live missile! |

| Beautiful Beats! (15) | Holly Luya, the Music Nymph is Free! |
|---|---|
| Betilla's Back! (15) | Head Nymph Betilla is Free! |
| Blue Baron! (35) | Beat the Giant Eel within 60 Seconds in "Aim for the Eel." |
| Boing! Boing! Boing! (15) | Bounce-Bubblized 11 Enemies without landing in "Polar Pursuit!" |
| Crush Combo! (15) | Simultaneously crushed 4 enemies. |
| Crusher! (15) | Crushed 50 Enemies. |
| Dr. Lividstone, I presume? (80) | You found ALL hidden cages. |
| Electoon Friend (15) | Completed 10 Medallions. |
| Electoon Hero (35) | Completed 25 Medallions. |
| Electoon Legend (80) | Completed ALL Medallions. |
| Explorer (35) | You found 25 hidden cages. |
| Feed the Fairy! (15) | Edith Up, the Gourmet Fairy is Free! |
| Fisher King! (20) | Swam a Marathon! |
| Full Mouth (35) | Earned 5 Skull Teeth. |
| Hover Happy! (20) | One hour of flight time! |
| Hyperspeed! (35) | Sprinted for an Entire Level! |
| I'm Back! (15) | Replayed any completed map. |
| Kung Fu Combo! (15) | Perform a swipe-to-air Kick Combo! |
| Merm-Aid! (15) | Annetta Fish, the Ocean Nymph is Free! |
| Milk Tooth (15) | Earned 1 Skull Tooth. |
| Nitro! (80) | Earned ALL speed trophies! |
| No Panic! (15) | Saved ALL Darktooned Wizards in "Port 'O Panic". |
| Nothing Lasts Forever... (80) | Ding, Dong, the Livid Boss is Dead! |
| Nymphs Rock! (15) | Helena Handbasket, the Mountain Nymph is Free! |
| Painless! (15) | Completed a level without taking a hit! |
| Pop! Pop! BOOM! (15) | Popped 50 Enemy Bubbles. |
| Scout (15) | You found 10 hidden cages. |
| Speedy! (15) | Earned 5 speed trophies! |
| Sprinter! (20) | Sprinted a Marathon! |
| Survivor! (15) | Survived a Piranha Pond without a scratch! |
| The Bubblizer! (15) | Chain-Bubblized 4 Enemies. |
| The Jaw! (80) | Earned ALL Skull Teeth. |
| Turbo! (35) | Earned 15 speed trophies! |
| Vacuum Snack! (15) | Inhaled 50 things on Moskito-back. |

**UNLOCKABLE**

| UNLOCKABLE | HOW TO UNLOCK |
|---|---|
| Land of the Livid Dead | Collect all ten Skull Teeth. |

## RED DEAD REDEMPTION (PS3)

### CODES

Enabling a code will permanently prevent the game from being saved and trophies from being earned.

| EFFECT | CODE |
|---|---|
| Become a nobody | HUMILITY BEFORE THE LORD |
| Decrease Bounty | THEY SELL SOULS CHEAP HERE |
| Diplomatic Immunity | I WISH I WORKED FOR UNCLE SAM |

| Enable the Sepia filter | THE OLD WAYS IS THE BEST WAYS |
|---|---|
| Fame | I AM ONE OF THEM FAMOUS FELLAS |
| Get $500 | THE ROOT OF ALL EVIL, WE THANK YOU! |
| Good Guy | IT AINT PRIDE. IT'S HONOR |
| Gun Set 1 | IT'S MY CONSTITUTIONAL RIGHT |
| Gun Set 2 | I'M AN AMERICAN. I NEED GUNS |
| Infinite ammo | ABUNDANCE IS EVERYWHERE |
| Infinite Dead Eye | I DON'T UNDERSTAND IMNFINITY |
| Infinite Horse Stamina | MAKE HAY WHILE THE SUN SHINES |
| Invincibility | HE GIVES STRENGTH TO THE WEAK |
| Man in Uniform | I LOVE A MAN IN UNIFORM |
| Play as Jack | OH MY SON, MY BLESSED SON |
| Sharp Dressed Man | DON'T YOU LOOK FINE AND DANDY |
| Spawn a horse-drawn coach | NOW WHO PUT THAT THERE? |
| Spawn a horse | BEASTS AND MAN TOGETHER |
| Unlock all areas | YOU GOT YOURSELF A FINE PAIR OF EYES |
| Unlock all gang outfits | YOU THINK YOU TOUGH, MISTER? |

## RED DEAD REDEMPTION  (XBOX 360)

### CODES

Enabling a code will permanently prevent the game from being saved and achievements from being earned.

| EFFECT | CODE |
|---|---|
| Become a nobody | HUMILITY BEFORE THE LORD |
| Decrease Bounty | THEY SELL SOULS CHEAP HERE |
| Diplomatic Immunity | I WISH I WORKED FOR UNCLE SAM |
| Enable the Sepia filter | THE OLD WAYS IS THE BEST WAYS |
| Fame | I AM ONE OF THEM FAMOUS FELLAS |
| Get $500 | THE ROOT OF ALL EVIL, WE THANK YOU! |
| Good Guy | IT AINT PRIDE. IT'S HONOR |
| Gun Set 1 | IT'S MY CONSTITUTIONAL RIGHT |
| Gun Set 2 | I'M AN AMERICAN. I NEED GUNS |
| Infinite ammo | ABUNDANCE IS EVERYWHERE |
| Infinite Dead Eye | I DON'T UNDERSTAND IMNFINITY |
| Infinite Horse Stamina | MAKE HAY WHILE THE SUN SHINES |
| Invincibility | HE GIVES STRENGTH TO THE WEAK |

## RED FACTION: ARMAGEDDON  (XBOX 360)

### ACHIEVEMENT

| UNLOCKABLE | HOW TO UNLOCK |
|---|---|
| All For One, One For All (25) | Finish a 4 player Infestation game beyond wave 9 without anyone bleeding out. |
| Back At Ya! (20) | Make an enemy kill themselves while shooting at your Shell. |
| Boom Goes The Dynamite (10) | Kill 2 other enemies with a single exploding Berserker. |
| Breathe Easy (30) | Put an end to the threat, once and for all. |
| Bug Hunt (20) | Finish at least one wave on each map in Infestation. |
| Catch! (30) | Use the Magnet Gun to fling debris BACK at a Tentacle. |
| Cheater! (20) | Buy a Cheat. |
| Chronicler (25) | Listen to 40 Audio Logs. |

| | |
|---|---|
| **Commando (50)** | Finish waves 1 through 20 on any map in Infestation. |
| **Crack Shot (10)** | Kill a Wraith before it re-stealths. |
| **Crusader (15)** | Kill 175 enemies while in the L.E.O. exoskeleton. |
| **Exterminator (15)** | Destroy 100 Pods while piloting the Mantis. |
| **Family Business (20)** | Defeat the Mantis. |
| **Field Surgeon (15)** | Perform Revival 25 times in Infestation. |
| **Haymaker (10)** | Kill 5 enemies in one shot with Impact. |
| **Hit 'N Run (15)** | Kill an enemy by ramming them with the Inferno GX. |
| **Hold Still (10)** | Kill 6 enemies in one use of Shockwave. |
| **Honorary Mason (75)** | Finish waves 1 through 30 on any map in Infestation. |
| **I Need A Nap (75)** | Finish the Single Player game on Insane Difficulty. |
| **I'm All You've Got (15)** | Defend the Red Faction. |
| **In. The. Face! (25)** | Kill one of each enemy type with the Maul. |
| **It's All In The Wrist (15)** | Send an enemy at least 30 meters with Impact. |
| **Knock, Knock (15)** | Open up the secret entrance. |
| **Liftoff (10)** | Send an enemy at least 50 meters with the Magnet Gun. |
| **Lock And Load (20)** | Keep Berserk active for at least 21 seconds in one use. |
| **Losses (15)** | Make it through to the lair. |
| **Martian Can Opener (40)** | Buy every Upgrade. |
| **Martian Drive-By (15)** | Kill 100 enemies while in the Marauder Scout Walker. |
| **Martian Matchmaker (10)** | Fire an enemy into another enemy with the Magnet Gun. |
| **Money Well Spent (15)** | Buy out any one Upgrade ring. |
| **Must Go Faster (15)** | Travel to the Marauder homelands. |
| **Nanergy! (30)** | Gather 25,000 total salvage. |
| **Old Friends, Older Enemies (15)** | Safely escort Winters through the depths. |
| **One Big, Ugly Motha... (20)** | Defeat the source of it all. |
| **Ooooh Yeah! (10)** | Kill 5 enemies with one L.E.O. shoulder bash. |
| **Plan B (15)** | Find out how to reach the lair. |
| **Salvager (20)** | Find 200 piles of salvage. |
| **Secrets Long Buried (10)** | Remove the Seal. |
| **Soldier (25)** | Finish waves 1 through 10 on any map in Infestation. |
| **Survival Of The Fittest (15)** | Make it to the surface. |
| **That Coulda Gone Better (30)** | Finish the Single Player game on Hard Difficulty. |
| **Things Fall Apart (20)** | Destroy the Water Filtration Plant. |
| **Unto The Breach (15)** | Gain entry into the Terraformer. |
| **Vanguard (15)** | Escort the convoy. |
| **We're Not Alone (10)** | Make it back to civilization. |
| **Weather The Storm (15)** | Destroy the Jamming Devices. |
| **What Is Best In Life? (15)** | Perform melee finishers on 25 Creepers (single player only). |
| **Zero G War (20)** | Kill 50 Shockwaved enemies before they hit the ground. |

### UNLOCKABLE

| UNLOCKABLE | HOW TO UNLOCK |
|---|---|
| **Cheats** | Beat the Game |
| **Mr.Toots** | Beat the Game |
| **New Game +** | Beat the Game |

## RED FACTION: GUERRILLA (XBOX 360)

### CODES

Fom the main menu select "Options," then "Extras," then enter code.

| EFFECT | CODE |
| --- | --- |
| Bonus multiplayer map pack featuring four maps | MAPMAYHEM |
| Unlocks golden sledgehammer for single-player use | HARDHITTER |

## RED FACTION: GUERRILLA (PlayStation 3)

### CODES

Fom the main menu select "Options," then "Extras," then enter code.

| EFFECT | CODE |
| --- | --- |
| Bonus multiplayer map pack featuring four maps | MAPMAYHEM |
| Unlocks golden sledgehammer for single-player use | HARDHITTER |

## RED STEEL 2 (Wii)

### CODES

Go to the Extras menu then to "Preorder" and enter the codes.

| EFFECT | CODE |
| --- | --- |
| Barracuda | 3582880 |
| Nihonto Hana Sword (alternate code) | 58855558 |
| Sora Katana of the Katakara Clan | 360152 |
| Tataro Magnum | 357370402 |
| The Lost Blade of the Kusagari Clan | 360378 |

## RESIDENT EVIL 5 (PlayStation 3)

### REGENERATE ITEMS

In Chapter 2-1, take all the items at the beginning and then quit the game. Resume the game by pressing "Continue" to start Chapter 2-1 again. This time you will have items you got before you quit the game in your inventory, however, new sets of the items are there for you to collect. Repeat the process to get as many as you like. This glitch is also available in Chapter 3-1.

## RESIDENT EVIL 5: LOST IN NIGHTMARES (XBOX 360)

### UNLOCKABLES

| UNLOCKABLE | HOW TO UNLOCK |
| --- | --- |
| Jill Valentine playable character | Complete Lost in Nightmares |
| Figures | Beat the game to unlock figurines. Viewable in the Bonus Gallery. |
| Old-School Resident Evil Camera Mode: | When the chapter starts, turn around and try to open the front door. Do this three times and a "?" will appear. Click to activate classic camera! |

## RESIDENT EVIL: THE MERCENARIES 3D (3DS)

### UNLOCKABLE

| UNLOCKABLE | HOW TO UNLOCK |
| --- | --- |
| Barry (American) | Get 20 Medals |
| Chris (Pilot) | Mission Level 1-3 get an SS-rank, or get 10 Medals |
| Claire (Suit) | Get 25 Medals |
| HUNK (Reaper) | Get all A-rank on all Mission Level (except Level Ex) |
| Jill (RE3) | Get an S-rank on Mission Level 3-5 |
| Krauser (Exoskaleton) | Get S-rank on Mission Level 5-5 |
| Rebacca (Nurse) | Get all S-rank on all Mission Level (except Level Ex) |
| Wesker (Uroboros) | Get a B-rank or above for all Mission |

### UNLOCKABLE

| UNLOCKABLE | HOW TO UNLOCK |
|---|---|
| Albert Wesker's loadout | Get rank A or higher on all missions up to 5-5 with Wesker. |
| Barry Barton's loadout | Get rank A or higher on all missions up to 5-5 with Barry. |
| Chris Redfield's loadout | Get rank A or higher on all missions up to 5-5 with Chris. |
| Claire Redfield's loadout | Get rank A or higher on all missions up to 5-5 with Claire. |
| Extra loadout | Unlock all character loadout. |
| Hunk's loadout | Get rank A or higher on all missions up to 5-5 with Hunk. |
| Jack Krauser's loadout | Get rank A or higher on all missions up to 5-5 with Krauser. |
| Jill Valentine's loadout | Get rank A or higher on all missions up to 5-5 with Jill. |
| Rebecca Chambers's loadout | Get rank A or higher on all missions up to 5-5 with Rebecca. |

### UNLOCKABLE

To make a particular character's weapons accessible to all other characters, score S rank using the character on every Missions up to Mission 5-5. You can also spend 10 Nintendo 3DS Play Coins to unlock the character's weapons.

### UNLOCKABLE

| UNLOCKABLE | HOW TO UNLOCK |
|---|---|
| Barry | Clear Mission 4-5 with a B rank |
| Claire | Clear Mission 1-3 with a B rank |
| Krauser | Clear Mission 3-5 with a B rank |
| Rebecca | Clear Mission 2-3 with a B rank |
| Wesker | Clear Mission 5-5 with a B rank |

### UNLOCKABLE

Clear mission 5-5 with at least B rank. After watching the credits the EX Missions are available.

### UNLOCKABLE

| UNLOCKABLE | HOW TO UNLOCK |
|---|---|
| Adrenaline | Clear Mission 5-4 with a B rank |
| Bomber | Clear Mission 5-2 with a B rank |
| Close Range | Clear Mission Level 4-3 with an S rank |
| Combat | Clear Mission 4-2 with a S rank |
| Extension | Clear Mission 4-1 with a S rank |
| Friendship | Obtain "Social Butterfly" Medal |
| Full Burst | Clear Mission EX-6 with a B rank |
| Giant Killing | Clear Mission 4-5 with a S rank |
| Handgun Custom | Clear Mission EX-1 with a B rank |
| Handgun Technique | Clear Mission 4-1 with a B rank |
| Infinity 7 | Collect 30 Medals |
| Lucky 7 | Clear Mission 5-3 with a B rank |
| Machine Gun Custom | Clear Mission EX-2 with a B rank |
| Machine Gun Technique | Clear Mission 4-3 with a B rank |
| Magnum Technique | Clear Mission 5-2 with a S rank |
| Maximizer | Clear Mission 4-4 with a B rank |
| Medic | Clear Mission 1-3 with a B rank |
| Revenge | Clear Mission 4-2 with a B rank |
| Reversal | Clear Mission 5-4 with a S rank |
| Rifle Technique | Clear Mission 5-1 with a B rank |
| Shotgun Custom | Clear Mission EX-5 with a B rank |

| Shotgun Technique | Clear Mission 5-1 with a S rank |
|---|---|
| Smart Reload | Clear Mission EX-4 with a B rank |
| Technician | Clear Mission 5-3 with a S rank |
| Thunderbolt | Clear Mission EX-7 with a B rank |
| Toughness | Earn the Like a Phoenix medal |
| Weapon Master | Clear Mission EX-8 with a B rank |

## RESISTANCE 2 (PlayStation 3)

### COOPERATIVE MEDIC UNLOCKABLES

Reach the corresponding level to unlock.

| UNLOCKABLE | HOW TO UNLOCK |
|---|---|
| Phoenix (Weapon) | Level 1 |
| Ring of Life (Berserk) | Level 1 |
| Rossmore 238 (Weapon) | Level 10 |
| Phoenix Ash (Berserk) | Level 12 |
| Air Fuel Grenades | Level 12 Medic |
| Bioplasm Tracking Tech | Level 14 |
| Assault Pack | Level 16 |
| HE .44 Magnum (Weapon) | Level 18 |
| M5A2 Carbine (Weapon) | Level 2 |
| Bio-amp Scope | Level 22 |
| Voltaic Body Armor | Level 24 |
| Leech Barrel | Level 26 |
| V7 Splicer (Weapon) | Level 28 |
| Psychokinetic Helmet | Level 30 |
| Chloroform (Berserk) | Level 4 |
| Kinetic Gloves | Level 6 |
| High Density Bioplasm Chamber | Level 8 |

### COOPERATIVE SOLDIER UNLOCKABLES

Reach the corresponding level to unlock.

| UNLOCKABLE | HOW TO UNLOCK |
|---|---|
| HVAP Wraith (Weapon) | Level 1 |
| Ironheart (Berserk) | Level 1 |
| Auger (Weapon) | Level 10 |
| Air Fuel Grenades (Weapon: Grenades) | Level 12 |
| Backlash (Berserk) | Level 12 |
| Advanced Timing Motor | Level 14 |
| Assault Pack | Level 16 |
| Bullseye (Weapon) | Level 18 |
| Rossmore 238 (Weapon) | Level 2 |
| Voltaic Body Armor | Level 24 |
| Precision Scope | Level 26 |
| Laark (Weapon) | Level 28 |
| Psychokinetic Helmet | Level 30 |
| Overload (Berserk) | Level 4 |
| Kinetic Gloves | Level 6 |
| High Capacity Ammo Belt | Level 8 |
| Titanium Barrels | Level 22 |

NEW!

A
B
C
D
E
F
G
H
I
J
K
L
M
N
O
P
Q
**R**
S
T
U
V
W
X
Y
Z

## COOPERATIVE SPEC. OPS. UNLOCKABLES

Reach the corresponding level to unlock.

| UNLOCKABLE | HOW TO UNLOCK |
| --- | --- |
| Marksmen (Weapon) | Level 1 |
| Prototype Ammo (Berserk) | Level 1 |
| Proximity Mines (Weapon: Alternate to Ammo) | Level 10 |
| Snake Eyes (Berserk) | Level 12 |
| L23 Fareye (Weapon) | Level 12 |
| Shock Suppressor | Level 14 |
| Assault Pack | Level 16 |
| Auger (Weapon) | Level 18 |
| Bullseye (Weapon) | Level 2 |
| Hawkeye Scope | Level 22 |
| Voltaic Body Armor | Level 24 |
| Mag-Propulsion Barrel | Level 26 |
| Bellock (Weapon) | Level 28 |
| Psychokinetic Helmet | Level 30 |
| Invisibility (Berserk) | Level 4 |
| Kinetic Gloves | Level 6 |
| High Density Ammo Chamber | Level 8 |

## RESISTANCE 3 (PlayStation 3)

### TROPHY

| UNLOCKABLE | HOW TO UNLOCK |
| --- | --- |
| Access Denied (Bronze) | Absorb 1000 damage with Auger Shields |
| Archivalist (Silver) | Collect all journals |
| Backstabber (Bronze) | Kill 20 enemies with melee while they are idle |
| BARF! (Bronze) | Make 6 Wardens puke at the same time in the prison |
| Bloodborne (Bronze) | Kill 3 enemies simultaneously using a single mutated body |
| Body Count (Bronze) | Kill 1000 enemies |
| Bookworm (Bronze) | Collect 50% of the journals |
| Boomstick (Bronze) | Use the upgraded Rossmore secondary fire to set 6 enemies on fire at once |
| Bouncer (Bronze) | Keep Chimeran forces from entering the Brewpub |
| Brutal (Gold) | Complete Campaign Mode on Superhuman |
| Buckshot (Bronze) | Kill 2+ enemies with one Rossmore blast |
| Bull in a China Shop (Bronze) | Freeze and melee kill 3 Ravagers |
| Calm Under Pressure (Bronze) | Defeat the Brawler in the Post Office in under 2 minutes |
| Chamber Full of Death (Bronze) | Kill 5+ Hybrids at once by using the HE .44 Magnum secondary fire |
| Cheap Shots (Bronze) | Kill 25 enemies firing the Auger through an object |
| Collector (Bronze) | Collect 10 journals |
| Corpse Wagon (Bronze) | Detonate fallen Leeches to kill 25 enemies |
| Counter-Sniper (Bronze) | Use the Deadeye to kill 20 snipers |
| Electric Avenue (Bronze) | Use the EMP to take down 25 drones |
| Expert Sniper (Bronze) | Get 50 headshot kills in Campaign Mode |

| | |
|---|---|
| **Feeling Lucky, Punk (Bronze)** | Detonate multiple Magnum rounds to kill 2+ enemies at once, 5 times |
| **Fireworks (Bronze)** | Use the Wildfire secondary fire to kill 6 enemies in one shot |
| **Frickin' Laser Beams (Bronze)** | Get to the first mineshaft without being hit by sniper fire in Mt. Pleasant, PA |
| **From the Hip (Bronze)** | Kill 50 enemies with the Bullseye or Marksman while moving, without using zoom |
| **Gardener (Bronze)** | Destroy 100 blast roots |
| **Good Fences (Bronze)** | Don't allow any counter-attackers into the Washington Square base |
| **Grasshopper Unit (Bronze)** | Kill 5 Longlegs in mid-jump |
| **Grenadier (Bronze)** | Kill 3 or more Military Chimera with a single Grenade |
| **Hello Driver (Bronze)** | Kill 5 drivers without destroying their vehicle |
| **Helping Hands (Bronze)** | Revive a Co-op partner 20 times |
| **In This Together (Bronze)** | Defeat the Widowmaker in Times Square without killing a single Hybrid |
| **Irresistible Force (Silver)** | Complete Campaign Mode on any difficulty |
| **Juggler (Bronze)** | Simultaneously burn, freeze and poison 4 separate enemies |
| **Land, Sea, and Air (Bronze)** | Travel in 3 different vehicles on your journey |
| **Master Mechanic (Silver)** | Fully upgrade all weapons in Campaign Mode |
| **Medusa (Bronze)** | Freeze 5 enemies at once and destroy them with a blast of the Cryogun's secondary fire |
| **No Escape (Bronze)** | Destroy all Warden vehicles in the Motorpool |
| **Nothing But Net (Bronze)** | Score a basket by lobbing a grenade through a basketball hoop |
| **One Eyed Jack (Bronze)** | Find and kill 'Jack' in Graterford Prison |
| **Opportunity Knocks (Bronze)** | Kill 20 enemies with environmental objects |
| **Overload (Bronze)** | Use the EMP to take down 10 Steelhead Auger shields |
| **Platinum Trophy (Platinum)** | Obtain all Gold, Silver, and Bronze Trophies for Resistance 3 |
| **Raining Limbs (Bronze)** | Kill 25 Grims using only grenades |
| **Roops! (Bronze)** | Knock a Hybrid off the cliffs in Mt. Pleasant, PA |
| **Sandman (Bronze)** | Kill 5 Grims in a row using only headshots |
| **Shoe Leather (Bronze)** | Travel 30 km on foot |
| **Short Out (Bronze)** | Defeat the Stalker in under 60 seconds |
| **Silent Partner (Silver)** | Damage the same enemy in Cooperative Mode for 100 kills |
| **Slaybells (Bronze)** | Make Santa and his reindeer fly |
| **Snipe Hunt (Bronze)** | Collect all Deadeye rifles without dying while fighting the Widowmaker in St. Louis |
| **Tag, You're It (Bronze)** | Kill 40 Bullseye tagged enemies |
| **This is my Rifle (Bronze)** | Fully upgrade one weapon in Campaign Mode |
| **Toast (Bronze)** | Use the upgraded Deadeye secondary fire to kill 2+ enemies, 5 times |
| **Up Your Arsenal (Bronze)** | Get a kill with every weapon in your arsenal |
| **Vehicular Manslaughter (Bronze)** | Destroy 10 Warden vehicles while on the train |
| **Warp Speed (Bronze)** | Use the Atomizer secondary fire to kill 30 enemies |

| Waste Not (Bronze) | Get 5 headshot kills with one Deadeye clip |
| Weaponsmith (Bronze) | Upgrade 5 weapons in Campaign Mode |
| Zookeeper (Silver) | Kill the Brawler in Haven without taking any damage |

## RIDGE RACER 3D (3DS)

### UNLOCKABLE

Complete the following events in Grand Prix mode to unlock these.

| UNLOCKABLE | HOW TO UNLOCK |
| --- | --- |
| Age Solo Petit500 (Special Cat. 1 Machine) | Finish Expert Grand Prix Event No. 44 |
| Catagory 1 Machines | Finish Advanced Grand Prix Event No. 26 |
| Catagory 2 Machines & Advanced Grand Prix | Finish Beginner Grand Prix Event No. 18 |
| Catagory 3 Machines | Finish Beginner Grand Prix Event No. 08 |
| Expert Grand Prix | Finish Advanced Grand Prix Event No. 36 |
| Kamata ANGL Concept (Special Cat. 1 Machine) | Finish Expert Grand Prix Event No. 42 |
| Lucky & Wild Madbull (Special Cat. 1 Machine) | Finish Expert Grand Prix Event No. 45 |
| Mirrored & Mirrored Reverse Courses | Finish Expert Grand Prix Event No. 48 |
| Namco New Rally-X (Special Cat. 1 Machine) | Finish Expert Grand Prix Event No. 47 |
| Namco Pacman (Special Cat. 1 Machine) & Pacman Music CD | Finish Expert Grand Prix Event No. 46 |
| Soldat Crinale (Special Cat. 1 Machine) | Finish Expert Grand Prix Event No. 43 |

## RISEN (XBOX 360)

### GLITCH

Seek out Rhobart in the Bandit Camp and then go and collect the 10 reeds of Brugleweed he asks for. When you return to him with the reeds, he will give you 70 gold and 50 XP. Attack him until he is unconscious but do not kill him. Loot his body and retrieve the Brugleweed you just gave him. When he gets up, give him the pilfered Brugleweed for additional gold and XP. Repeat as often as you like (will go faster with higher amounts of Brugleweed).

## RISTAR (Wii)

### PASSWORDS

| PASSWORD | EFFECT |
| --- | --- |
| STAR | A shooting star goes across the background (JP) |
| MUSEUM | Boss Rush mode |
| XXXXXX | Clears/Deactivates the current password |
| AGES | Copyright info is displayed |
| MIEMIE | Hidden items' grab points are shown with a blue star |
| FEEL | ILOVEU, MIEMIE, CANDY active all at once (JP) |
| CANDY | Invincibility (JP) |
| MACCHA | Mentions Miyake color (JP) |
| MASTER | Mentions next game (JP) |
| AAAAAA | No Continue limit (JP) |
| MAGURO | Onchi Music mode and credits music in sound test |
| HETAP | Reverses the high score in Demo mode (JP) |
| VALDI | Shows the solar system (JP) |

| ILOVEU | Stage select |
|--------|--------------|
| SUPERB | Super Difficulty mode |
| SUPER | Super Hard mode |
| DOFEEL | Time Attack mode |

## RIVER CITY RANSOM (Wii)

### PASSWORDS

| PASSWORD | EFFECT |
|----------|--------|
| XfMdZTHwiR3 jaj6jfRUDEt tilm2tWRo8b | Final Boss, with Max Stats, Dragon Feet, Stone Hands, GrandSlam, and Texas Boots |
| XfMdZTHUPR3 rztzPeQUCTt 61IxhtWRo2b | Final Boss, with Max Stats, Stone Hands, Dragon Feet, Acro Circus, Grand SlaM, 4 Karma Jolts, and $999.99 cash |
| t1izvpdOZnZ JxNkJp7Cpub XMPQgXErSMF | Ivan Beaten, High School Open |
| w412ysgtMqc MUSjKm2PqtE UJMNdUTGOQC | Power Up |
| jrYplfTgbdj nOorLTIYXwR SjTuqpilUHP | Start with all abilities and $500 in cash |
| fHUFBbvcnpa MS8iPpICZJP VKNOeVRQPDD | Strange item in inventory that gives stat increases |

### UNLOCKABLES

| UNLOCKABLE | HOW TO UNLOCK |
|------------|---------------|
| Change Character Names | On the Character Select screen, press SELECT on the controller to go to a screen where you can change Alex and Ryan's names to whatever you want. |
| Merlin's Mystery Shop | To find Merlin's Mystery Shop go to the Armstrong Thru-Way. Once inside, press up at the top wall and the wall opens. Inside you can buy the best items in the game. |

## ROCK BAND (XBOX 360)

### UNLOCK ALL

Enter quickly at the "Rock Band" title screen (disables saving).

| CODE | EFFECT |
|------|--------|
| Red, Yellow, Blue, Red, Red, Blue, Blue, Red, Yellow, Blue | Unlock All Songs |

## ROCK BAND (Wii)

### CODES

Using the colored fret buttons on the guitar, enter these codes QUICKLY on the title screen.

| EFFECT | CODE |
|--------|------|
| Unlock All Songs (Disable Saving) | R, Y, B, R, R, B, B, R, Y, B |

## ROCK BAND 2 (XBOX 360)

### CODES

Go to the "Extras" option in the main menu. Choose "Modify Game," then input the following codes. All codes disable saving.

| EFFECT | CODE |
|--------|------|
| Awesome Detection | Yellow, Blue, Orange, Yellow, Blue, Orange, Yellow, Blue, Orange |
| Stage Mode | Blue, Yellow, Red, Blue, Yellow, Red, Blue, Yellow, Red |

| EFFECT | CODE |
|--------|------|
| Unlock All Songs | Red, Yellow, Blue, Red, Red, Blue, Blue, Red, Yellow, Blue |
| Venue Select: Unlock All Venues | Blue, Orange, Orange, Blue, Yellow, Blue, Orange, Orange, Blue, Yellow |

## ROCK BAND 3 (XBOX 360)

### CODES

Enter the following codes at the Main menu of the game.

| EFFECT | CODE |
|---|---|
| Ovation D-2010 Guitar | Orange, Blue, Orange, Orange, Blue, Blue, Orange, Blue |
| Stop! Guitar unlocked | Orange, Orange, Blue, Blue, Orange, Blue, Blue, Orange |
| Unlocks Guild X-79 Guitar in Customization Options | Blue, Orange, Orange, Blue, Orange, Orange, Blue, Blue |

### SECRET INSTRUMENTS

| UNLOCKABLE | HOW TO UNLOCK |
|---|---|
| Baroque Stage Kit | Expert Hall of Fame induction in Pro Drums: Expert Song Progress |
| Clear Microphone Song | Expert Hall of Fame induction in Vocal Harmony: Expert Progress |
| Cthulhu's Revenge | Expert Hall of Fame induction in Pro Guitar: Expert Song Progress |
| DKS-5910 Pro-Tech High Performance Kit | Expert Hall of Fame Induction in Drums: Expert Song Progress |
| Gold Microphone | Expert Hall of Fame induction in Vocals: Expert Song Progress |
| Gretsch Bo-Diddley | Expert Hall of Fame induction in Guitar: Expert Song Progress |
| Gretsch White Falcon | Expert Hall of Fame induction in Bass: Expert Song Progress |
| The Goat Head | Expert Hall of Fame induction in Pro Bass: Expert Song Progress |
| The Green Day Guitar | Welcome to Paradise in Guitar: Green Day: Rock Band |
| VOX Continental | Expert Hall of Fame induction in Keys: Expert Song Progress |
| Yamaha CS-50 | Expert Hall of Fame induction in Pro Keys: Expert Song Progress |

## ROCK BAND 3 (PS3)

### CODES

Enter the following codes at the Main menu of the game.

| EFFECT | CODE |
|---|---|
| Ovation D-2010 Guitar | Orange, Blue, Orange, Orange, Blue, Blue, Orange, Blue |
| Unlocks Guild X-79 Guitar n Customization Options | Blue, Orange, Orange, Blue, Orange, Orange, Blue, Blue |

### UNLOCKABLE

| UNLOCKABLE | HOW TO UNLOCK |
|---|---|
| Play Keys on Guitar | Achieve the Guitar Immortal goal 5* 50 Medium Rock Band 3 Songs (or 3* on a higher difficulty) |

## ROCK BAND 3 (Wii)

### CODES

Enter the following codes at the Main menu of the game.

| EFFECT | CODE |
|---|---|
| Ovation D-2010 Guitar | Orange, Blue, Orange, Orange, Blue, Blue, Orange, Blue |
| Unlocks Guild X-79 Guitar in Customization Options | Blue, Orange, Orange, Blue, Orange, Orange, Blue, Blue |

## THE BEATLES: ROCK BAND (XBOX 360)

### CODES

Enter quickly at the "The Beatles Rock Band" title screen.

| EFFECT | CODE |
|---|---|
| Unlocks set of bonus photos | Blue, Yellow, Orange, Orange, Orange, Blue, Blue, Blue, Yellow, Orange |

## UNLOCKABLES

| UNLOCKABLE | HOW TO UNLOCK |
| --- | --- |
| Ringo Starr Gamer Picture | Earn Achievement: "And the Band Begins to Play." |
| John Lennon Gamer Picture | Earn Achievement: "Better Free Your Mind Instead." |
| George Harrison Gamer Picture | Earn Achievement: "No One's Frightened of Playing." |
| Paul McCartney Gamer Picture | Earn Achievement: "Things That Money Just Can't Buy." |
| Gold Plate (for your instruments) | Earn 30 Achievements. |
| Platinum Plate (for your instruments) | Earn 50 Achievements. |
| Silver Plate (for your instruments) | Earn 15 Achievements. |

## THE BEATLES: ROCK BAND (Wii)

### CODES

Enter quickly at The Beatles Rock Band title screen

| EFFECT | CODE |
| --- | --- |
| Unlocks set of bonus photos | Blue, Yellow, Orange, Orange, Orange, Blue, Blue, Blue, Yellow, Orange |

## ROCKSMITH (XBOX 360)

### ACHIEVEMENT

| UNLOCKABLE | HOW TO UNLOCK |
| --- | --- |
| All Rounder (20) | Beat 100,000 points in a Combo Arrangement |
| Art + Functionality (30) | Collect all guitars |
| Batter Up (5) | Play the Guitarcade game: Big Swing Baseball |
| Beat Harmonics (20) | Beat 1,000,000 points in the Guitarcade game: Harmonically Challenged |
| Beneficial Friends (20) | Play multiplayer with 2 guitars |
| Better Than An Encore? (20) | Qualify for a Double Encore |
| Cente-beater (10) | Beat a 100 Note Streak |
| Challenge Harmonics (5) | Play the Guitarcade game: Harmonically Challenged |
| Chordinated (20) | Beat 100,000 points in a Chord Arrangement |
| D-licious (10) | Use the Tuner to tune to Drop-D |
| Duck Hunter (5) | Play the Guitarcade game: Ducks |
| Ducks x 6 (5) | Play the Guitarcade game: Super Ducks |
| Elite Guitarist (60) | Reach Rank 9 |
| Fret Fast (20) | Beat 10,000,000 points in the Guitarcade game: Ducks |
| Furious Plucker (20) | Beat 5,000,000 points in the Guitarcade game: Quick Pick Dash |
| Giant! (20) | Beat 2,000,000 points in the Guitarcade game: Big Swing Baseball |
| Guitardead (20) | Beat 1,000,000 points in the Guitarcade game: Dawn of the Chordead |
| Half-K (25) | Beat a 500 Note Streak |
| Happy Shopper (5) | Visit the shop |
| Hear Me Now (10) | Use the Amp |
| International Headliner (40) | Reach Rank 8 |
| International Support Act (40) | Reach Rank 7 |
| Just Awesome (40) | Beat a 750 Note Streak |

| Just Singing? (10) | Using a mic, sing along and achieve Nice Singing |
| Just Super! (20) | Beat 150,000,000 points in the Guitarcade game: Super Ducks |
| Local Headliner (10) | Reach Rank 4 |
| Local Support Act (10) | Reach Rank 3 |
| My 1st Encore (10) | Qualify for an Encore |
| My 1st Gig (5) | Play an Event |
| National Headliner (20) | Reach Rank 6 |
| National Support Act (20) | Reach Rank 5 |
| New Act (5) | Reach Rank 2 |
| No Dischord (20) | Beat a 25 Chord Streak |
| OK, I Learned (20) | Beat 200,000 points in Master Mode |
| Rocksmith (100) | Reach Rank 11 |
| Scales Owned (20) | Beat 50,000,000 points in the Guitarcade game: Scale Runner |
| Singles Rock (20) | Beat 100,000 points in a Single Note Arrangement |
| Slide Puzzle (5) | Play the Guitarcade game: Super Slider |
| Slide to Victory (20) | Beat 15,000,000 points in the Guitarcade game: Super Slider |
| Solo Foundations (5) | Play the Guitarcade game: Scale Runner |
| Stage Ready (40) | Complete a Master Event |
| Strummer (5) | Beat a 5 Chord Streak |
| Super Elite Guitarist (60) | Reach Rank 10 |
| The Basics (5) | Complete Soundcheck (Reach Rank 1) |
| The One With Zombies (5) | Play the Guitarcade game: Dawn of the Chordead |
| The Rocksmith Method (20) | Earn all Bronze Technique Medals |
| Tone is My Avatar (10) | Create and save a custom tone |
| Tone Peddler (30) | Collect 50 effects pedals |
| Tutorials My Axe (30) | Earn all Gold Technique Medals |
| Where Rainbows Come From (5) | Play the Guitarcade game: Quick Pick Dash |

## ROCKSTAR GAMES PRESENTS TABLE TENNIS    (Wii)

### UNLOCKABLE SHIRTS

| UNLOCKABLE | HOW TO UNLOCK |
| --- | --- |
| Carmen's blue/green/gray Shirt | Win a match using a heavy leftspin shot. |
| Carmen's dark blue shirt | Win a match using a heavy topspin shot. |
| Carmen's grey shirt | Shut out the CPU in at least one game in the match. |
| Cassidy's brown shirt | Win a match using a heavy backspin shot. |
| Cassidy's dark blue shirt | Win a match using a heavy rightspin shot. |
| Cassidy's yellow/white shirt | Win a match by making the ball bounce 2or more times on the CPU's side of the table. |
| Liu Ping's green shirt | Win a match using a late swing. |
| Liu Ping's red/white shirt | Win a match by returning a shot from the CPU that dropped short. |
| Liu Ping's yellow shirt | Win a match using a forehand shot. |
| Solayman's dark blue shirt | Win a match with a 4-point deficit comeback. |
| Solayman's green shirt | Win a match using a backhand shot. |
| Solayman's gray shirt | Win a match using a smash shot. |

## RUGBY WORLD CUP 2011 (PlayStation 3)

### TROPHY

| UNLOCKABLE | HOW TO UNLOCK |
|---|---|
| At The Death (Bronze) | Score to win a match with no time left in the 2nd half against CPU (Medium or higher) |
| Between The Sticks (Bronze) | Score a drop goal, penalty goal or a conversion |
| Big Guy's Glory (Bronze) | Score a try with a player currently playing in a Prop position |
| Booming Punt (Bronze) | Punt into touch from behind your team's 22 metre line for a territorial gain of 50+ metres |
| Brick Wall (Silver) | Do not concede any points in a match against CPU (Hard) |
| Catch The Bomb (Bronze) | Score try directly after recovering an Up and Under Kick against CPU (Medium or higher) |
| Cheers Mate! (Bronze) | Win a match with 2 or more human-controlled players on your team |
| Chip And Score (Bronze) | Score a try directly after recovering a Scrum Half Kick against CPU (Medium or higher) |
| Don't Even Try (Bronze) | Win a match where your team doesn't score a try against CPU (Medium or higher) |
| Down South (Silver) | Win every match of every Southern Hemisphere tour playing against CPU (Hard) |
| Early Shower (Bronze) | Be awarded a red card |
| End To End (Silver) | Score a try by running with the ball directly from one goal line to the other |
| Epic Try-pocalypse (Silver) | Score 15 tries in a match (5 or 10 min halves) |
| Experimentor (Bronze) | Attempt all four of your team's assigned set plays in a match |
| First Try (Bronze) | Score a try |
| Hammer And Tongs (Silver) | Score 50+ unanswered points against CPU (Medium or higher, 5 or 10 min halves) |
| Hardcore Rugger (Gold) | Beat New Zealand with a team rated less than 80 against CPU (Hard, 20 min halves) |
| Hat Trick Hero (Bronze) | Score 3 tries with the same player in a match against CPU (Medium or higher) |
| Hey This Ain't Soccer! (Bronze) | Perform a soccer kick |
| Hit The Sticks (Bronze) | Score a penalty goal or conversion off the post or crossbar |
| Just Like Pudding (Bronze) | Score a drop goal with a player currently playing in a Prop position |
| Kick With The Wind (Bronze) | Score a penalty goal or conversion from 55+ metres |
| King Of Crunch (Bronze) | Successfully complete 20 dive tackles in a match |
| Minnow No More (Silver) | Win the Rugby World Cup 2011 Final with a team rated less than 60 against CPU (Hard) |
| Multi-Union (Silver) | Win a match with every International team |
| Nice Pickup! (Bronze) | Perform a Quick Pickup from a tackled player then directly run and score a try |
| One Of Each (Bronze) | Score a try, conversion, penalty goal and drop goal all in the same match |
| Online Rugger (Bronze) | Play a match Online |
| Picked Off (Bronze) | Intercept an opposition team's line-out throw |
| Quick Turnaround (Bronze) | Score a try in one phase or less of possession against CPU (Medium or higher) |

| Rage Against The Head (Bronze) | Gain possession of the ball at a scrum when playing as the defensive team |
|---|---|
| Rugby Purist (Platinum) | Acquire all Bronze, Silver, and Gold trophies |
| Rule The Pool (Gold) | Earn 20 pool stage points in Rugby World Cup 2011 playing against CPU (Hard) |
| Sel The Dummy (Bronze) | Perform a dummy pass and fool a defending player |
| Setpiece Setup (Bronze) | Execute a set play from a ruck, scrum or mail and score a try on the same phase of possession |
| Shades Of Jonny (Silver) | Score a decisive winning drop goal during an Extra Time or Sudden Death period |
| Showboat I (Bronze) | Throw the ball down to score a try without diving and without being tackled |
| Showboat II (Bronze) | Stay in the offensive in-goal area for at least 5 seconds directly before scoring a try |
| Sin Bin (Bronze) | Be awarded a yellow card |
| Talent From The Tee (Bronze) | Win a match in the Place-Kick Shootout mode against CPU (Hard) |
| That's Commitment! (Gold) | Play 100 matches in total (including matches played in any mode) |
| Tough It Out (Bronze) | Beat an 85+ rated team with a team rated less than 70 against CPU (Hard) |
| Trytime In Quicktime (Bronze) | Score a try directly from a kick-off, or restart kick, which occurred on the 50 metre line |
| Up North (Silver) | Win every match of eery Northern Hemisphere tour playing against CPU (Hard) |
| World Champions (Silver) | Win the Rugby World Cup 2011 Final |
| Worm Burner (Bronze) | Score a try directly after recovering a Grubber Kick against CPU (Medium or higher) |

## RUNE FACTORY 2: A FANTASY HARVEST MOON (DS)

### UNLOCKABLES

These are only accessible in the Second Generation, from the dresser on the left side of the second floor of the house.

| UNLOCKABLE | HOW TO UNLOCK |
|---|---|
| Handsome Armor | Win the Adventure Contest. |
| Monster Costume | Win the Monster Taming Contest. |

## RUNE FACTORY: TIDES OF DESTINY (PlayStation 3)

### TROPHY

| UNLOCKABLE | HOW TO UNLOCK |
|---|---|
| Angler (Bronze) | Successfully land a fish. |
| Behind the Mask (Gold) | See the true face of the man in the mask. |
| Crafter (Bronze) | Successfully craft an item. |
| Earth Temple Cleared (Bronze) | With the help of Lili, lift the curse of stone from the Earth Temple. |
| Failed Chef (Bronze) | Fail at cooking one time. |
| Fire Temple Cleared (Bronze) | With the help of Odette, lift the curse of stone from the Fire Temple. |
| Giant Destroyer (Bronze) | Defeat 20 giant monsters. |
| Giant Executioner (Silver) | Defeat 30 giant monsters. |
| Giant Slayer (Bronze) | Defeat 10 giant monsters. |
| Immortal (Gold) | Achieve repeat victories in the colloseum. |
| Insomniac (Bronze) | Stay awake until you collapse at 5AM and have to be carried home. |

| | |
|---|---|
| **Island Raiser (Bronze)** | Use the Plant Golem to raise an island out of the sea. |
| **Island Savior (Silver)** | Raise all of the islands out of the sea. |
| **Jump Master (Bronze)** | Perform a double-jump 500 times. |
| **Master Angler (Gold)** | Successfully land 2000 fish. |
| **Master Crafter (Gold)** | Successfully craft 1500 items. |
| **Master Salvager (Bronze)** | Successfully salvage 30 times. |
| **Monster Destroyer (Bronze)** | Defeat 500 monsters. |
| **Monster Executioner (Bronze)** | Defeat 1500 monsters. |
| **Monster Slayer (Bronze)** | Defeat 100 monsters. |
| **Most Popular (Silver)** | Draw the good will of many residents in the village. |
| **Native Giant Defeated (Silver)** | Defeat the Native Giant. |
| **Overmedicated (Silver)** | Consume 100 recovery drinks. |
| **Plant Golem Repairman (Silver)** | Find out what's wrong with the Plant Golem and get it working again. |
| **Professional Angler (Silver)** | Successfully land 1000 fish. |
| **Professional Crafter (Silver)** | Successfully craft 800 items. |
| **Rock Hard Riddle (Bronze)** | Get to the bottom of why Sprout Island turned to stone. |
| **Rune Factory Master (Platinum)** | Earned all trophies. |
| **Salvager (Bronze)** | Successfully salvage 10 times. |
| **That Which Monsters Fear (Silver)** | Defeat 3000 monsters. |
| **That Which Monsters Flee (Silver)** | Defeat 5000 monsters. |
| **Trophies 101 (Bronze)** | Listen to Marpudding's explanation about Trophies. |
| **True Hero (Silver)** | Win a battle in the colloseum. |
| **Undermedicated (Silver)** | Catch a cold 100 times. |
| **Veteran Angler (Bronze)** | Successfully land 300 fish. |
| **Veteran Crafter (Bronze)** | Successfully craft 300 items. |
| **Veteran Salvager (Bronze)** | Successfully salvage 20 times. |
| **Water Temple Cleared (Bronze)** | With the help of Iris, lift the curse of stone from the Water Temple. |

## RUSH 'N ATTACK  (XBOX 360)

### CODES

A meow confirms that the code was entered correctly.

| CODE | EFFECT |
|---|---|
| At the main menu, using the D-pad, press ⬆/⬆/⬇/⬇/⬅/➡/⬅/➡/Ⓑ/Ⓐ | Alternate Sound FX |

## 'SPLOSION MAN (XBOX 360)

### UNLOCKABLES

| UNLOCKABLE | HOW TO UNLOCK |
|---|---|
| 'Splosion Man Gamer Pic | Beat Single Level 1–4 |
| 'Splosion Man Premium Theme | Beat Single Level 3–18 |
| Scientist Gamer Pic | Beat Multiplayer Level 1–4 |
| Cowards' Way Out (Level skip feature) | Kill yourself repeatedly by holding right trigger until it unlocks. |

## SAINTS ROW (XBOX 360, PlayStation 3)

### CODES

Dial the following phone numbers in the phone book to get the corresponding effects.

| EFFECT | XBOX 360 CODE | PLAYSTATION 3 CODE |
|---|---|---|
| 12 Gauge | #cashmoneyz | #2274666399 |
| 1,000 dollars | #920 | #920 |
| .44 Cal | #921 | #921 |
| Add Gang Notoriety | #35 | #35 |
| Add Police Notoriety | #4 | #4 |
| Annihilator RPG | #947 | #947 |
| AR-200 | #922 | #922 |
| AR-50 | #923 | #923 |
| AR-50 with Grenade launcher | #924 | #924 |
| AS14 Hammer | #925 | #925 |
| Baseball Bat | #926 | #926 |
| Car Mass Increased | #2 | #2 |
| Chainsaw | #927 | #927 |
| Clear Sky | #sunny | — |
| Crowbar | #955 | #955 |
| Drunk Pedestrians | #15 | #15 |
| Everybody Is Shrunk | #202 | #202 |
| Evil Cars | #16 | #16 |
| Fire Extinguisher | #928 | #928 |
| Flame Thrower | #929 | #929 |
| Flashbang | #930 | #930 |
| Full Health | #1 | #1 |
| GAL 43 | #931 | #931 |
| GDHC | #932 | #932 |
| Get Horizon | #711 | #711 |
| Get Snipes 57 | #712 | #712 |
| Get Tornado | #713 | #713 |
| Get Wolverine | #714 | #714 |
| Giant | #200 | #200 |

| | | |
|---|---|---|
| Grenade | #933 | #933 |
| Gyro Daddy Added to Garage | #4976 | #4976 |
| Heaven Bound | #12 | #12 |
| Itty Bitty | #201 | #201 |
| K6 | #935 | #935 |
| Knife | #936 | #936 |
| Kobra | #934 | #934 |
| Lighting Strikes | #666 | #666 |
| Low Gravity | #18 | #18 |
| Machete | #937 | #937 |
| McManus 2010 | #938 | #938 |
| Milk Bones | #3 | #3 |
| Mini-Gun | #939 | #939 |
| Molotov | #940 | #940 |
| Never Die | #36 | #36 |
| Nightstick | #941 | #941 |
| No Cop Notoriety | #50 | #50 |
| No Gang Notoriety | #51 | #51 |
| NR4 | #942 | #942 |
| Pedestrian Wars | #19 | #19 |
| Pepper Spray | #943 | #943 |
| Pimp Slap | #969 | #969 |
| Pimpcane | #944 | #944 |
| Pipe Bomb | #945 | #945 |
| Player Pratfalls | #5 | #5 |
| Raining Pedestrians | #20 | #20 |
| RPG | #946 | #946 |
| Samurai Sword | #948 | #948 |
| Satchel Charge | #949 | #949 |
| Shock Paddles | #950 | #950 |
| SKR-9 | #951 | #951 |
| Sledge Hammer | #952 | #952 |
| Stun Gun | #953 | #953 |
| Super Explosions | #7 | #7 |
| Super Saints | #8 | #8 |
| TK3 | #954 | #954 |
| Tombstone | #956 | #956 |
| Unlimited Ammo | #11 | #11 |
| Unlimited Clip | #9 | #9 |
| Unlimited Sprint | #6 | #6 |
| Unlock D-STROY UFO | #728237 | #728237 |
| Unlock Peewee Mini Bike | #7266837 | #7266837 |
| Vice 9 | #957 | #957 |
| XS-2 Ultimax | #958 | #958 |

## UNLOCKABLES

| UNLOCKABLE | HOW TO UNLOCK |
|---|---|
| 75% Mechanic Discount | Complete all 5 Chop Shop lists |
| Bodyguards and Ninjas | Game Progression |

NEW!

A
B
C
D
E
F
G
H
I
J
K
L
M
N
O
P
Q
R
S
T
U
V
W
X
Y
Z

| | |
|---|---|
| **Brotherhood Gang Cars** | Complete Last Mission for the Brotherhood |
| **Brotherhood Melee** | Complete Brotherhood Mission 6 |
| **Buggy** | Complete Truck Yard Chop Shop list |
| **Chainsaw in Weapon Cache** | Complete Crowd Control (Marina) Level 6 |
| **Clothing Store Discount** | Crowd Control Level 3 (Suburbs) |
| **Crib Customization Discount** | Mayhem Level 3 (Red Light) |
| **Demo Derby Vehicles** | Complete Demo Derby Level 6 |
| **Donnie's Vehicle** | Complete Brotherhood Mission 2 |
| **Explosion Damage -5%** | Level 3, Trail Blazing (Downtown) |
| **Gang Customization Cars** | 15% hoods conquered |
| **Gang Customization Cars** | 45% hoods conquered |
| **Health Regeneration 2x** | Snatch Level 3 (Chinatown) |
| **Health Regeneration 3x** | Snatch Level 6 (Chinatown) |
| **Infinite Respect** | Raise your respect past level 99 |
| **Infinite SMG Ammo** | Successfully complete Snatch Level 6 Downtown |
| **Kobra (Pistol)** | Fuzz Level 3 (Projects) |
| **Legal Lee** | Beat Stilwater Prison Fight Club Level 3 |
| **Mechanic Discount** | Complete Demo Derby Level 3 |
| **One Follower** | Complete Prologue Mission 4 |
| **Pepper Spray in Weapon Cache** | Complete Crowd Control (Marina) Level 3 |
| **Police Notoriety Reduced** | Complete FUZZ Level 3, Suburbs |
| **Police Notoriety Reduced 2** | Complete FUZZ Level 6, Suburbs |
| **Pumped Up** | Fight Club Level 6 (Arena) |
| **Pumped Up** | Fight Club Level 3 (Arena) |
| **Red Light Apartment Crib** | Complete Prologue Mission 2 |
| **Reduced Bullet Damage** | Heli assault Level 3 (Bario) |
| **Ronin Gang Cars** | Complete Last Mission for the Ronin |
| **Ronin Melee** | Complete Ronin Mission 6 |
| **Ronin Notoriety Reduced** | Drug Trafficking Level 3 (Hotel and Marina) |
| **Saints Hideout** | Complete Prologue Mission 3 |
| **Sons of Samedi Gang Cars** | Complete Last Mission for Sons of Samedi |
| **Sons of Samedi Melee** | Complete Mission "Bad Trip" |
| **Sons of Samedi Notoriety Reduced** | Complete Escort Level 3, University |
| **Sprint Increased** | Insurance Fraud level 3 (Factories) |
| **Sprint Increased (Unlimited)** | Insurance Fraud Level 6 (Factories) |
| **The News Helicopter** | Complete Sons of Samedi Mission 3 |
| **Three Followers** | 50% hoods conquered |
| **Tobias** | Complete Sons of Samedi Mission 3 |
| **Troy** | Beat Stilwater Prison Fight Club Level 6 |
| **Two Followers** | 25% hoods conquered |
| **Unlimited Pistol Ammo** | Fuzz Level 6 (Projects) |
| **Vehicle Delivery** | Escort Level 3 (Red Light) |
| **X2 Ultimax (Shotgun)** | Drug Trafficking Level 3 (Airport) |
| **Zombie Carlos** | Call eye for an eye after you complete the brother hood story |

## SAINTS ROW: THE THIRD  (PlayStation 3)

### TROPHY

| UNLOCKABLE | HOW TO UNLOCK |
|---|---|
| **A Better Person (Bronze)** | Buy your first Upgrade from the Upgrade Store. |
| **And Boom Goes the Dynamite (Bronze)** | Complete all instances of Heli Assault. |

| | |
|---|---|
| **Bo-Duke-En (Bronze)** | Hijack 50 vehicles - Dukes style. |
| **Bright Lights, Big City (Gold)** | Complete all City Takeover gameplay in the entire city of Steelport. |
| **Cowboy Up (Bronze)** | Fully upgrade one Weapon in each slot. |
| **Dead Presidents (Bronze)** | Complete 'When Good Heists...'. |
| **Double Dose of Pimping (Bronze)** | Complete all instances of Snatch. |
| **Everything is Permitted (Bronze)** | Kill all of the hitman Assassination targets. |
| **Fence Killa 2011 (Bronze)** | Complete all instances of Mayhem. |
| **Flash the Pan (Bronze)** | Destroy all Gang Operations in Steelport. |
| **Gangstas... In Space! (Silver)** | Complete Act 3 in another way. |
| **Gellin' Like Magellan (Silver)** | Explore every hood in Steelport. |
| **Gender Equality (Bronze)** | Play for at least 2 hours as a male character AND 2 hours as a female character. |
| **Getting the Goods (Bronze)** | Find 25% of all Collectibles. |
| **Go Into the Light (Bronze)** | Complete all instances of Guardian Angel. |
| **Gotta Break Em In (Bronze)** | Complete 'The Ho Boat'. |
| **Hack the Planet (Silver)** | Complete all City Takeover gameplay in the Stanfield district. |
| **Hanging With Mr. Pierce (Silver)** | Complete all City Takeover gameplay in the Downtown district. |
| **Haters Gonna Hate (Bronze)** | Kill 1000 Gang Members. |
| **Have A Reality Climax (Bronze)** | Complete all instances of Professor Genki's Super Ethical Reality Climax. |
| **Hi-Jack It (Bronze)** | Steal and deliver all Vehicle Theft targets. |
| **I Heart Nyte Blayde (Bronze)** | Complete 'STAG Party'. |
| **Jumped In (Bronze)** | Create and share a character online. |
| **kill-deckers.exe (Bronze)** | Complete 'http://deckers.die'. |
| **Kingpin (Platinum)** | Unlock all Trophies in Saints Row: The Third. |
| **Kuh, Boom. (Bronze)** | Complete Act 1 in another way. |
| **Life of the Party (Silver)** | Find 100% of all Collectibles. |
| **Love/Hate Relationship (Bronze)** | Taunt AND/OR Compliment 50 gang members. |
| **Mourning Stars (Silver)** | Complete all City Takeover gameplay in the New Colvin district. |
| **Mr. Fury Would Be Proud (Silver)** | Complete Act 3 in one way. |
| **Murderbrawl 31 (Bronze)** | Complete 'Murderbrawl XXXI'. |
| **Once Bitten... Braaaaaaains (Bronze)** | Complete 'Zombie Attack'. |
| **Opulence, You Has It (Bronze)** | Complete 'Party Time'. |
| **Ouch. (Bronze)** | Complete all instances of Insurance Fraud. |
| **Ow My Balls! (Bronze)** | Do your first nutshot AND testicle assault. |
| **Pimped Out Pad (Bronze)** | Upgrade one Stronghold to its full glory. |
| **Porkchop Sandwiches (Bronze)** | Complete all instances of Trail Blazing. |
| **Shake and Bake (Bronze)** | Complete your first Challenge. |
| **Stay Classy Steelport (Bronze)** | Kill 25 Gang Members each with 'the Penetrator' AND the Fart in a Jar. |
| **Tank You Very Much (Bronze)** | Complete all instances of Tank Mayhem. |
| **The American Dream (Bronze)** | Customize 10 vehicles. |

NEW!

A
B
C
D
E
F
G
H
I
J
K
L
M
N
O
P
Q
R
S
T
U
V
W
X
Y
Z

| | |
|---|---|
| The Welcome Wagon (Bronze) | Complete 'I'm Free - Free Falling'. |
| Third and 30 (Gold) | Spend over 30 hours in Steelport. |
| Titanic Effort (Silver) | Complete Act 2. |
| Tower Defense (Bronze) | Complete Act 1 in one way. |
| Tune In, Drop Off (Bronze) | Complete all instances of Trafficking. |
| We're Takin' Over (Bronze) | Complete 'We've Only Just Begun'. |
| Who Loves Ya Baby (Bronze) | Kill 50 brutes. |
| You're My Hero! (Silver) | Complete ALL Challenges. |
| You're the Best... (Silver) | Complete all City Takeover gameplay in the Carver Island district. |
| Your Backseat Smells Funny (Bronze) | Complete all instances of Escort. |

## CODE

Enter one of the following codes in your phone (press select -> Extras -> Cheats) to activate the corresponding cheat function.

| UNLOCKABLE | CODE |
|---|---|
| Add Gang Notoriety | lolz |
| Add police notoriety | pissoffpigs |
| Bloody Mess | notrated |
| Cloudy Weather | overcast |
| Give D4TH Blossom (SMG) | giveblossom |
| Give GL G20 (grenade launcher) | givelauncher |
| Gives $100,000 in cash | cheese |
| Gives a full suite of weapons | letsrock |
| Gives Flamethrower | giveflamethrower |
| Gives respect | whatitmeanstome |
| Heaven Bound | fryhole |
| Infinite Sprint | runfast |
| No Gang Notoriety | oops |
| No police notoriety | goodygoody |
| One hit kill | goldengun |
| Pedestrians Are Drunk | dui |
| Pedestrians Are Mascots | mascot |
| Pedestrians are Pimps & Prostitutes | hohoho |
| Pedestrians are Zombies | brains |
| Rainy Weather | lightrain |
| Repair damage to your vehicle | repaircar |
| Spawn Air Strike | giveairstrike |
| Spawn Ambulance | giveembulance |
| Spawn Anchor | giveanchor |
| Spawn Apocafists | giveapoca |
| Spawn AS3 Ultimax | giveultimax |
| Spawn Attrazione | giveattrazione |
| Spawn Bootlegger | givebootlegger |
| Spawn Chainsaw | givechainsaw |
| Spawn Challenger | givechallenger |
| Spawn Commander | givecommander |
| Spawn Condor | givecondor |
| Spawn Cyber Blaster | givecybersmg |
| Spawn Cyber Buster | givecyber |

| | |
|---|---|
| Spawn Drone | givedrone |
| Spawn Eagle | giveeagle |
| Spawn Electric Grenade | giveelectric |
| Spawn Estrada | giveestrada |
| Spawn F69 VTol | givevtol |
| Spawn Gatmobile | givegatmobile |
| Spawn Grenade | givegrenade |
| Spawn Hammer | givehammer |
| Spawn K-8 Krukov | givekrukov |
| Spawn Kanada | givekanada |
| Spawn Kenshin | givekenshin |
| Spawn Knoxville | giveknoxville |
| Spawn Kobra KA-1 | givekobra |
| Spawn Krukov | givekrukov |
| Spawn McManus 2015 | givesniper |
| Spawn Miami | givemiami |
| Spawn Minigun | giveminigun |
| Spawn Molotov | givemolotov |
| Spawn Municipal | givemunicipal |
| Spawn Nforcer | givenforcer |
| Spawn Nocturne | givesword |
| Spawn Peacemaker | givepeacemaker |
| Spawn Phoenix | givephoenix |
| Spawn Quasar | givequasar |
| Spawn Reaper | givereaper |
| Spawn RPG | giverpg |
| Spawn Sandstorm | givesandstorm |
| Spawn Satchel Charge | givesatchel |
| Spawn Shark | giveshark |
| Spawn Sheperd | givesheperd |
| Spawn Shock Hammer | giverocket |
| Spawn Specter | givespecter |
| Spawn Status Quo | givestatusquo |
| Spawn Taxi | givetaxi |
| Spawn Tek Z-10 | givetek |
| Spawn The Penetrator | givedildo |
| Spawn Titan | givetitan |
| Spawn Toad | givetoad |
| Spawn Tornado | givetornado |
| Spawn Viper Laser Rifle | giveslm8 |
| Spawn Vortex | givevortex |
| Spawn Vulture | givevulture |
| Spawn Widowmaker | givewidowmaker |
| Spawn Woodpecker | givewoodpecker |
| Sunny Weather | clearskies |
| Vehicle Smash | isquishyou |
| Very Rainy Weather | heavyrain |
| Your vehicle is immune to damage | vroom |

NEW!
A
B
C
D
E
F
G
H
I
J
K
L
M
N
O
P
Q
R
S
T
U
V
W
X
Y
Z

## UNLOCKABLE

Alternate gang styles can be unlocked by completing certain in-game tasks. Gang styles can be changed at cribs or strongholds.

| UNLOCKABLE | HOW TO UNLOCK |
| --- | --- |
| Cops / SWAT | complete all instances of SNATCH for Kinzie |
| Deckers | complete mission 37 |
| Hos | complete all instances of SNATCH for Zimos |
| Luchadores | complete mission 43 |
| Mascots | complete all instances of Prof. Genki S.E.R.C. |
| Morningstar | complete mission 29 |
| National Guard | complete all instances of TANK MAYHEM |
| Space Saints | complete mission 47 |
| Strippers | complete all instances of ESCORT for Zimos |
| Wrestlers | complete all instances of TIGER ESCORT |
| Wraith and X2 Phantom (Tron Bike) | Complete the hard level of Trail Blazing in Deckers territory. |

## SAINTS ROW: THE THIRD (XBOX 360)

### ACHIEVEMENT

| UNLOCKABLE | HOW TO UNLOCK |
| --- | --- |
| A Better Person (15) | Buy your first Upgrade from the Upgrade Store. |
| And Boom Goes the Dynamite (20) | Complete all instances of Heli Assault. |
| Bo-Duke-En (10) | Hijack 50 vehicles - Dukes style. |
| Bright Lights, Big City (80) | Complete all City Takeover gameplay in the entire city of Steelport. |
| Cowboy Up (10) | Fully upgrade one Weapon in each slot. |
| Dead Presidents (10) | Complete 'When Good Heists...'. |
| Double Dose of Pimping (20) | Complete all instances of Snatch. |
| Everything is Permitted (10) | Kill all of the hitman Assassination targets. |
| Fence Killa 2011 (20) | Complete all instances of Mayhem. |
| Flash the Pan (10) | Destroy all Gang Operations in Steelport. |
| Gangstas... In Space! (30) | Complete Act 3 in another way. |
| Gellin' Like Magellan (20) | Explore every hood in Steelport. |
| Gender Equality (10) | Play for at least 2 hours as a male character AND 2 hours as a female character. |
| Getting the Goods (10) | Find 25% of all Collectibles. |
| Go Into the Light (20) | Complete all instances of Guardian Angel. |
| Gotta Break Em In (25) | Complete 'The Ho Boat'. |
| Hack the Planet (25) | Complete all City Takeover gameplay in the Stanfield district. |
| Hanging With Mr. Pierce (25) | Complete all City Takeover gameplay in the Downtown district. |
| Haters Gonna Hate (15) | Kill 1000 Gang Members. |
| Have A Reality Climax (20) | Complete all instances of Professor Genki's Super Ethical Reality Climax. |
| Hi-Jack It (10) | Steal and deliver all Vehicle Theft targets. |
| I Heart Nyte Blayde (25) | Complete 'STAG Party'. |
| Jumped In (10) | Create and share a character online. |
| kill-deckers.exe (25) | Complete 'http://deckers.die'. |
| Kuh, Boom. (20) | Complete Act 1 in another way. |
| Life of the Party (20) | Find 100% of all Collectibles. |

| | |
|---|---|
| **Love/Hate Relationship (10)** | Taunt AND/OR Compliment 50 gang members. |
| **Mourning Stars (25)** | Complete all City Takeover gameplay in the New Colvin district. |
| **Mr. Fury Would Be Proud (30)** | Complete Act 3 in one way. |
| **Murderbrawl 31 (25)** | Complete 'Murderbrawl XXXI'. |
| **Once Bitten... Braaaaaaains (25)** | Complete 'Zombie Attack'. |
| **Opulence, You Has It (20)** | Complete 'Party Time'. |
| **Ouch. (20)** | Complete all instances of Insurance Fraud. |
| **Ow My Balls! (10)** | Do your first nutshot AND testicle assault. |
| **Pimped Out Pad (10)** | Upgrade one Stronghold to its full glory. |
| **Porkchop Sandwiches (20)** | Complete all instances of Trail Blazing. |
| **Shake and Bake (10)** | Complete your first Challenge. |
| **Stay Classy Steelport (10)** | Kill 25 Gang Members each with 'the Penetrator' AND the Fart in a Jar. |
| **Tank You Very Much (20)** | Complete all instances of Tank Mayhem. |
| **The American Dream (10)** | Customize 10 vehicles. |
| **The Welcome Wagon (15)** | Complete 'I'm Free - Free Falling'. |
| **Third and 30 (40)** | Spend over 30 hours in Steelport. |
| **Titanic Effort (40)** | Complete Act 2. |
| **Tower Defense (20)** | Complete Act 1 in one way. |
| **Tune In, Drop Off (20)** | Complete all instances of Trafficking. |
| **We're Takin' Over (20)** | Complete 'We've Only Just Begun'. |
| **Who Loves Ya Baby (10)** | Kill 50 brutes. |
| **You're My Hero! (30)** | Complete ALL Challenges. |
| **You're the Best... (25)** | Complete all City Takeover gameplay in the Carver Island district. |
| **Your Backseat Smells Funny (20)** | Complete all instances of Escort. |

### CODE

Enter one of the following codes in your phone (press select -> Extras -> Cheats) to activate the corresponding cheat function.

| UNLOCKABLE | CODE |
|---|---|
| **Add Gang Notoriety (+1 star)** | lolz |
| **Add Police Notoriety (+1 shield)** | pissoffpigs |
| **Bloody Mess (everyone killed explodes into blood)** | notrated |
| **Clear Skies (change weather)** | clearskies |
| **Drunk Pedestrians** | dui |
| **Give 45 Sheperd** | givesheperd |
| **Give Apoca-Fists** | giveapoca |
| **Give AR 55** | givear55 |
| **Give AS3 Ultimax** | giveultimax |
| **Give Baseball Bat** | givebaseball |
| **Give Cash ($100,000)** | cheese |
| **Give Chainsaw** | givechainsaw |
| **Give Cyber Blaster** | givecybersmg |
| **Give Cyber Buster** | givecyber |
| **Give D4TH Blossom** | giveblossom |
| **Give Electric Grenade** | giveelectric |
| **Give Flamethrower** | giveflamethrower |

| | |
|---|---|
| Give Flashbang | giveflashbang |
| Give GL G20 | givelauncher |
| Give Grave Digger | givedigger |
| Give Grenade | givegrenade |
| Give K-8 Krukov | givekrukov |
| Give KA-1 Kobra | givekobra |
| Give McManus 2015 | givesniper |
| Give Mini-Gun | giveminigun |
| Give Molotov | givemolotov |
| Give Nocturne | givesword |
| Give RC Possesor | givercgun |
| Give Reaper Drone | givedrone |
| Give Respect | whatitmeanstome |
| Give Riot Shield | giveshield |
| Give S3X Hammer | givehammer |
| Give SA-3 Airstrike | giveairstrike |
| Give Satchel Charges | givesatchel |
| Give Shock Hammer | giverocket |
| Give Sonic Boom | givesonic |
| Give Stun Gun | givestungun |
| Give TEK Z-10 | givetek |
| Give The Penetrator | givedildo |
| Give Viper Laser Rifle | giveslm8 |
| Golden Gun (one-shot gun kills) | goldengun |
| Heaven Bound (dead bodies float into the air) | fryhole |
| Heavy Rain (changes weather) | heavyrain |
| Infinite Sprint | runfast |
| Light Rain (changes weather) | lightrain |
| Mascots (all pedestrians are mascots) | mascot |
| No Cop Notoriety | goodygoody |
| No Gang Notoriety | oops |
| Overcast (changes weather) | overcast |
| Pimps and Hos (all pedestrians are pimps and hos) | hohoho |
| Repair Car (fully repairs vehicle) | repaircar |
| Spawns Ambulance | giveambulance |
| Spawns Anchor | giveanchor |
| Spawns Attrazione | giveattrazione |
| Spawns Bootlegger | givebootlegger |
| Spawns Challenger | givechallenger |
| Spawns Commander | givecommander |
| Spawns Condor | givecondor |
| Spawns Eagle | giveeagle |
| Spawns Estrada | giveestrada |
| Spawns Gat Mobile | givegatmobile |
| Spawns Kaneda | givekaneda |
| Spawns Kenshin | givekenshin |
| Spawns Knoxville | giveknoxville |

| Spawns Miami | givemiami |
| Spawns Municipal | givemunicipal |
| Spawns NForcer | givenforcer |
| Spawns Peacemaker | givepeacemaker |
| Spawns Phoenix | givephoenix |
| Spawns Quasar | givequasar |
| Spawns Reaper | givereaper |
| Spawns Sandstorm | givesandstorm |
| Spawns Shark | giveshark |
| Spawns Specter | givespecter |
| Spawns Status Quo | givestatusquo |
| Spawns Taxi | givetaxi |
| Spawns Titan | givetitan |
| Spawns Toad | givetoad |
| Spawns Tornado | givetornado |
| Spawns Vortex | givevortex |
| Spawns VTOL | givevtol |
| Spawns Vulture | givevulture |
| Spawns Widowmaker | givewidowmaker |
| Spawns Woodpecker | givewoodpecker |
| Vehicles No Damage (your vehicle is immune to damage) | vroom |
| Vehicles Smash (your vehicle crushes other vehicles) | isquishyou |
| Weapons (gives a full compliment of weapons) | letsrock |
| Zombies (all pedestrians become zombies) | brains |

### UNLOCKABLE

| UNLOCKABLE | HOW TO UNLOCK |
| --- | --- |
| Oversized Gat Mask? | Completed the mission "When Good Heists…" |
| Saints Logo Shirt | Earned the "Flash the Pan" Achievement. |
| SR:TT Logo Shirt | Created and uploaded your first character to the community site! |
| Decker outfit | Assassinate Lucas by putting on the outfit kinze gives you |

## SAMURAI WARRIORS: KATANA (Wii)

### CHAOS DIFFICULTY

| UNLOCKABLE | HOW TO UNLOCK |
| --- | --- |
| Chaos Difficulty | Complete all missions with an S rank. |

## SCHIZOID (XBOX 360)

### ACHIEVEMENTS

| UNLOCKABLE | HOW TO UNLOCK |
| --- | --- |
| 21st Century Schizoid Man (15) | Complete level 21 ("Tyger Tyger") either in Local Co-Op, Xbox LIVE, or Uberschizoid. |
| Barber of Schizzville (20) | Shave the Orbiddles from 8 Astramoebas on a level, without destroying Astramoebas or losing a life. |
| Corpus Callosum Severed (20) | Complete level 119 ("Ragnarok") in Uberschizoid mode. |
| Flitt Breeder (10) | Get a gold medal on level 5 ("My Man Flitt") without destroying any Flitts. |

Side tab: NEW! A B C D E F G H I J K L M N O P Q R **S** T U V W X Y Z

**CODES & CHEATS**

| Huevos Done Naked (20) | Gold level 47 ("Los Huevos") without activating any power-ups. |
|---|---|
| One Mind, Two Goals (20) | Earn 20 silver or gold medals in Uberschizoid mode. |
| Playing the Field (15) | Play a game in each mode: Xbox LIVE, Local Co-Op, Wingman Bot Training, and Uberschizoid. |
| Schiz Hunter (20) | Destroy 30 Schizzes on a single level, using power-ups and without losing any lives. |
| Schizoid Sensei (20) | Earn 10 medals (any combination of gold, silver, and bronze) over Xbox LIVE. |
| Seafood Buffet (20) | Destroy 2,500 Scorpios. |
| Sploderific (10) | Destroy all enemies on level 12 ("Smartbomb") with a single smartbomb. |
| Wired (10) | Destroy an enemy with a razorwire. |

## SCOTT PILGRIM VS. THE WORLD    (PlayStation 3))

### UNLOCKABLES

| UNLOCKABLE | HOW TO UNLOCK |
|---|---|
| Nega-Scott | Beat the game using Kim, Stills, Ramona, and Scott. |

## SCRAP METAL    (XBOX 360)

### UNLOCKABLES

| UNLOCKABLE | HOW TO UNLOCK |
|---|---|
| Scrap Metal RC car | Complete all missions in the single-player game. |
| Scrap Metal T-Shirt | Complete first race. |

## SCRIBBLENAUTS    (DS)

### GOLD STAR RANKING

After you've completed a given puzzle, you'll be awarded a Silver Star on the puzzle selection screen to indicate your success. However, you can get a higher ranking. Retrying the same puzzle activates Advance Mode, which is a bonus challenge. You have to beat the same level three times in a row, and with different objects each time. If you restart, you'll have to begin the challenge from the beginning. If you successfully complete the Advance Mode version of a puzzle, you'll be awarded a Gold Star on the selection screen.

### MERITS

Merits are awards/achievements you can earn by doing different things in a given level. However, you need to complete the level to get them.

| UNLOCKABLE | HOW TO UNLOCK |
|---|---|
| 5th Cell | Spawn a 5th Cell employee. |
| All New | Complete a level with objects you've never used before. |
| Architect | Write two buildings. |
| Arrrrrr | Attach the Jolly Roger to a flagpole. |
| Audiophile | Write two or more instruments or audio objects. |
| Bioterrorist | Introduce the plague and infect two or more people. |
| Botanist | Write two or more plants. |
| Chauffeur | Drive a vehicle with more than one passenger. |
| Chef | Write two or more foods. |
| Closet | Write two or more clothes. |
| Combo | Combine any two objects together. |
| Cupid | Shoot a humanoid with Cupid's arrow. |
| Decorator | Write two furniture objects. |
| Electrolysis | Shock someone with electricity. |
| Elemental | Write more than one element. |
| Entertainer | Write two or more entertainment objects. |

| | |
|---|---|
| **Entomologist** | Spawn two or more insects. |
| **Environmentalist** | Write two or more environmental objects. |
| **Explosive** | Spawn two or more objects that explode. |
| **Exterminator** | Two or more humanoids or animals start a level and are destroyed. |
| **Fantasynovel** | Write two fantasy objects. |
| **Fashion Designer** | Clothe Maxwell's head, body, legs, feet and give him an accessory. |
| **Firefighter** | Put out at least two fires. |
| **Genius** | Complete a level twice in a row. |
| **Glutton** | Feed someone or something three times in a row. |
| **Gold Digger** | Spawn three or more precious stones. |
| **Grab and Go** | Write two or more grabbing tool objects. |
| **Haxxor** | Write five or more developers. |
| **Healer** | Spawn two or more medical objects. |
| **Herpetologist** | Write two or more reptiles. |
| **Humanitarian** | Write two or more humans. |
| **Infected** | Spawn a zombie and make it infect at least two humanoids. |
| **Janitor** | Spawn two or more cleaning objects. |
| **Jockey** | Use an animal as a vehicle. |
| **Joust** | Defeat a knight while Maxwell is mounted. |
| **Knight School** | Kill a dragon using a melee weapon. |
| **Luddite** | Short out three or more objects. |
| **Lumberjack** | Cut down three or more trees. |
| **Mad Hatter** | Place a hat on four or more humanoids or animals. |
| **Magician** | Use the magic wand to turn something into a toad. |
| **Marine Biologist** | Write two or more fish. |
| **Mechanic** | Jump-start a vehicle. |
| **Messiah** | Turn a humanoid into a deity. |
| **Militant** | Use two weapons and one weaponized vehicle. |
| **Miner 49er** | Dig a massive hole. |
| **Miser** | Obtain a total of 300,000 or more Ollars. |
| **New Object** | Write a completely new item. |
| **No Weapons** | Don't write a weapon to complete a level. |
| **Novice Angler** | Catch a fish with a fishing pole. |
| **Old School** | Write two or more classic video game objects. |
| **Organ Donor** | Spawn two or more organs. |
| **Ornithologist** | Write two or more birds. |
| **Paleontologist** | Spawn two ore more dinosaurs. |
| **Pariah** | Make three humanoids or animals flee. |
| **Pi** | Earn exactly 314 Ollars in a level. |
| **Picasso** | Write two or more drawing object tools. |
| **Pilot** | Spawn two or more aircraft. |
| **Prodigy** | Complete a level three times in a row. |
| **Pyromaniac** | Set at least four objects on fire in a level. |
| **Reanimator** | Bring a corpse back to life. |
| **Roped In** | Write two or more rope objects. |
| **Russian Doll** | Place an object inside another object, and then place that object into a third object. |
| **Savior** | Two or more humanoids or animals start and finish a level alive. |
| **Sea Two** | Write two or more sea vehicles. |
| **Series of Tubes** | Spawn "tube" five times. |
| **Shoveler** | Spawn two or more digging objects. |

| Smasher | Write two or more melee weapons. |
| Smuggler | Hide an item in a container. |
| Split Personality | Write two or more cutting or splitting tool objects. |
| Stealth | Destroy a security camera. |
| Sweet Tooth | Write two or more junk foods. |
| Tooling Around | Write two or more tool objects. |
| Washington | Chop down a cherry tree. |
| Water Jockey | Use a sea animal as a vehicle. |
| Whisperer | Ride a hostile animal. |
| Zookeeper | Write two or more animals. |

### HIDDEN LEVELS

If you spawn a teleporter and use it, it takes you to one of three secret levels.

### GLITCH

Challenge Mode encourages you to get creative by not allowing you to use the same words in three separate trials. If you are feeling uncreative, you can take advantage of The Great Adjective Exploit to bypass this entirely: just add an adjective (or gibberish) in front of a word and the game will give you a free pass to use it again. You can clear a stage three times by typing "Wings" the first time, "Big Wings" the second time and "Small Wings" the third time; you'll simply get the Wings all three times, but the game will register three different words and will allow it.

### BACKGROUND SCREEN

When you're at the title screen (Sandbox Mode), you can unlock 14 more backgrounds by typing words that fall into certain categories. These are some words that unlock the backgrounds.

| UNLOCKABLE | HOW TO UNLOCK |
| --- | --- |
| Background 02 | Type "cat." |
| Background 03 | Type "car." |
| Background 04 | Type "bee." |
| Background 05 | Type "tree." |
| Background 06 | Type "woman." |
| Background 07 | Type "coffin." |
| Background 08 | Type "vibes." |
| Background 09 | Type "coin." |
| Background 10 | Type "chair." |
| Background 11 | Type "zombie." |
| Background 12 | Type "court." |
| Background 13 | Type "rain" and select "rain(water)." |
| Background 14 | Type "it." |
| Background 15 | Type "pc." |

## SECTION 8 (XBOX 360)

### CODES

At the main menu go to dropship and enter the following codes. Entering the Captain's Armor code twice disables the code.

| EFFECT | CODE |
| --- | --- |
| Chrome Assault Rifle | 68432181 |
| Unlock Black Widow auto-pistol | 13374877 |
| Unlock Captain's Armor | 17013214 |

## SHADOW LAND (Wii)

### SECRET PASSWORD SCREEN

| UNLOCKABLE | HOW TO UNLOCK |
| --- | --- |
| Password Screen | At the title screen hold ①+②+SELECT and press RUN |

## PASSWORDS

| PASSWORD | EFFECT |
| --- | --- |
| PC-ENGINE | (message) |
| NAMCO | (message) |
| NAMCOT | (message) |
| 6502 | (message) |
| 6809 | (message) |
| 68000 | (message) |
| 756-2311 | (message) |
| YAMASHITA | (message) |
| AKIRA | (message) |
| KOMAI | (message) |
| KAZUHIKO | (message) |
| KAWADA | (message) |
| SPEED-UP (4 way split screen) | Reset after entering the password |
| S.62.08.22 (Start from level 5) | Reset after entering the password |

## SHADOWS OF THE DAMNED (XBOX 360)

### ACHIEVEMENT

| UNLOCKABLE | HOW TO UNLOCK |
| --- | --- |
| A Hole in your Head (20) | Perform 5 headshots in a row with the BIG BONER |
| Adios George (Beast form) (20) | Defeat George Beast Boss |
| Adios George (Human form) (20) | Defeat George Human Boss |
| An Ordinary Life (15) | Story Progression in Act 1 - Chapter 1 (any difficulty setting) |
| Annoying Mosquito (20) | Defeat Elliot Beast Boss |
| As Evil As Dead (15) | Story Progression in Act 3 - Chapter 3 (any difficulty setting) |
| Blood On The Dance Floor (15) | Defeat 10 enemies with the Stomp Attack |
| Cannibal Carnival (15) | Story Progression in Act 2 - Chapter 2 (any difficulty setting) |
| Demon Hunter (50) | Complete all chapters on Medium difficulty setting |
| Different Perspectives (15) | Story Progression in Act 5 - Chapter 2 (any difficulty setting) |
| Don't Fear the Reaper 1 (20) | Defeat Maras Grim (Sister Grim) Boss |
| Don't Fear the Reaper 2 (20) | Defeat Kauline Grim (Sister Grim) Boss |
| Don't Fear the Reaper 3 (20) | Defeat Giltine Grim (Sister Grim) Boss |
| Drunk in Public (10) | Knock back 3 drinks in a row |
| Fiesta Caliente! (30) | Defeat 5 enemies at once using the Hot Boner |
| Fire in the Hole! (15) | Defeat 3 enemies at once using the Barrels of Light |
| Flat Lust (20) | Defeat Justine Boss |
| Ghost Hunter (15) | Story Progression in Act 4 - Chapter 3 (any difficulty setting) |
| Great Demon World Forest (15) | Story Progression in Act 4 - Chapter 4 (any difficulty setting) |
| Great Demon World Village (15) | Story Progression in Act 4 - Chapter 2 (any difficulty setting) |
| High in Las Vegas (75) | Recover all available Red Gems in the game. |
| I Defeated the Last Big Boss! (20) | Defeat Fleming Boss |

CODES & CHEATS

| It's a Bughunt (15) | Story Progression in Act 3 - Chapter 1 (any difficulty setting) |
|---|---|
| Justine For All (15) | Story Progression in Act 4 - Chapter 6 (any difficulty setting) |
| Legion Hunter (100) | Complete all chapters on Hard difficulty setting |
| Lemon Hunter (20) | Complete all chapters on Easy difficulty setting |
| Love Suicide (20) | Defeat Paula Boss |
| Meatballs Lover (15) | Defeat 30 enemies with the SKULLCUSSIONER |
| My Dying Concubine (15) | Story Progression in Act 3 - Chapter 2 (any difficulty setting) |
| Nasty Headache (20) | Perform 5 Head Shots in a row with any weapon except Big Boner |
| Now That's a Big Fuckin' Gun (15) | Defeat 40 enemies with the SKULLFEST 9000 |
| Orthodontic Pleasures (15) | Defeat 50 enemies with THE DENTIST |
| Riders of the Lost Heart (15) | Story Progression in Act 2 - Chapter 4 (any difficulty setting) |
| Skullblaster Master (15) | Defeat 50 enemies with the SKULLBLASTER |
| Stingy Bastard (10) | Save more than 300 White Gems in your inventory |
| Suburban Nightmares (15) | Story Progression in Act 4 - Chapter 5 (any difficulty setting) |
| Take Me To Hell (15) | Story Progression in Act 2 - Chapter 1 (any difficulty setting) |
| That's So Hot! (15) | Defeat 20 enemies with the HOTBONER |
| The Big Boner (15) | Story Progression in Act 4 - Chapter 1 (any difficulty setting) |
| The Bird's Nest (15) | Story Progression in Act 3 - Chapter 4 (any difficulty setting) |
| The Castle of Hassle (15) | Story Progression in Act 5 - Chapter 3 (any difficulty setting) |
| The Final Chapter (15) | Story Progression in Act 5 - Chapter 4 (any difficulty setting) |
| The Orthodontist (15) | Defeat 30 enemies with the TEETHGRINDER |
| The Puppeteer (30) | Perform a Head Shot right after a Leg Mutilation when the enemy is flying back in the air |
| The Talkative One (15) | Defeat 20 enemies with the TEETHER |
| Til Death Do Us Part (15) | Story Progression in Act 5 - Chapter 5 (any difficulty setting) |
| Trash'em while they're out! (15) | Perform all 5 brutal kills on Normal Demons frozen by the Light Shot |
| Twelve Feet Under (15) | Story Progression in Act 5 - Chapter 1 (any difficulty setting) |
| What a Wonderful World (15) | Story Progression in Act 2 - Chapter 3 (any difficulty setting) |
| You Go To Hell (5) | Start a new game for the first time. (any difficulty setting) |

## SHIFT 2 UNLEASHED: NEED FOR SPEED (XBOX 360)

### ACHIEVEMENT

| UNLOCKABLE | HOW TO UNLOCK |
|---|---|
| Amateur (5) | Reached Driver Level 5 |
| Badge Collector (50) | Earned 100 Badges |
| Badge Earner (5) | Earned 10 Badges |
| Badge Hunter (10) | Earned 50 Badges |
| Bounty Hunter (20) | Earned $10,000,000 total during your career |

| | |
|---|---|
| **Competition License (10)** | Won 50 Career events on Medium difficulty or higher |
| **Cub Scout (10)** | Won your first Event Set badge |
| **Day Walker (50)** | Mastered every location in day or dusk |
| **Dialled In (10)** | Used On-Track Tuning to save a Tuning Setup for a car |
| **Dominator (100)** | Beaten all the Rivals |
| **Elitist (10)** | Placed 1st in an event using Elite handling model |
| **Globetrotter (20)** | Competed at every location in the game |
| **Going the extra mile (25)** | Completed 250 Event Objectives |
| **Grass Roots (10)** | Completed JR's Grass Roots event |
| **GT1 Champion (100)** | Beat Jamie Campbell-Walter and won the FIA GT1 World Championship |
| **GT3 Champion (50)** | Beat Patrick Soderlund and won the FIA GT3 European Championship |
| **I'm Going To Hollywood! (10)** | Got through the Qualifying round in the Driver Duel Championship |
| **I. Am. Iron Man. (10)** | Placed 1st in 5 consecutive Online events |
| **In The Zone (10)** | Won an Online event from helmet cam |
| **Intercept & Pursue (10)** | Completed an Online Catchup Pack and Online Catchup Duel event |
| **King of the Hill (10)** | Won your first Driver Duel Championship crown |
| **Leno would be proud (10)** | Have at least one car from each manufacturer in your garage |
| **Nailed It (10)** | Track Mastered your first location |
| **Night Rider (100)** | Mastered every location at night |
| **Notorious (25)** | Played Online for over 10 hours total |
| **Paparazzi (5)** | Shared a photo or replay with others |
| **Pro (50)** | Reached Driver Level (15) |
| **Proving Grounds (10)** | Won JR's GTR Challenge |
| **Race License (50)** | Won 75 Career events on Hard difficulty |
| **Recommended (5)** | Completed an event recommended by a friend |
| **Road to Glory (10)** | Beaten your first Rival |
| **Semi-Pro (10)** | Reached Driver Level 10 |
| **Sizzlin' (10)** | Beaten the 1st Target Time in a Hot Lap event |
| **Sports License (10)** | Won 25 Career events on Easy difficulty or higher |
| **The Driver's battle (5)** | Completed an event purely from helmet cam |
| **The World is my Oyster (10)** | Unlocked the FIA GT1 Branch |
| **Tic Tac Toe (10)** | Own a Modern, Retro, and Muscle car |
| **Veteran (75)** | Reached Driver Level 20 |
| **Workaholic (10)** | Upgraded 3 vehicles to Works spec |
| **Works Champion (50)** | Beat Mad Mike Whiddett and won the Works Championship |

## SHINING FORCE (Wii)

### UNLOCKABLES

| UNLOCKABLE | HOW TO UNLOCK |
|---|---|
| **Control All Opponents (JP Version Only)** | When the battle begins, quickly tap Ⓐ, Ⓑ, Ⓒ, ✛, Ⓐ, Ⓒ, Ⓐ, Ⓑ, Ⓐ |
| **Fight Any Battle (JP Version Only)** | Hold START on controller 2 then reset the system. Let go of START and hold Ⓐ+Ⓑ on controller 2. Select continue and wait until the girl says good luck. At that instant hold Ⓐ on controller 1 while continuing to hold Ⓐ+Ⓑ on controller 2. |

| Name Characters | Start a new game (must have completed game first) and go to the Name Your Character screen. Put the cursor on end and hold START+Ⓐ+Ⓑ+Ⓒ on controller 2 while holding: START+Ⓐ+Ⓒ on controller 1. You will see another character. Continue this to name all characters. |

### OTHER UNLOCKABLES

| UNLOCKABLE | HOW TO UNLOCK |
| --- | --- |
| 2 Jogurts | If you put jogurt in your army and kill an enemy with him, you get a jogurt ring item. Use this in battle on any character to make that character look like a jogurt! Repeat as many times as you want, but you will have to get another ring when it breaks. |
| Anri's Alternate Costume | During the Laser Eye battle in Chapter 3, search to the left of the three dark elves. You'll receive a hidden item called Kitui Huku ("tight clothes" in Japanese). Give it to Anri and she'll have a new outfit. |
| Tao's Alternate Costume | In Chapter 3, after fighting the first battle to get the Moon Stone, go inside the cave and search the walls for a secret item called the Sugoi Mizugi. Give it to Tao and she will have an alternate costume. |

## SILENT HILL: SHATTERED MEMORIES (Wii)

### UFO ENDING

| UNLOCKABLE | HOW TO UNLOCK |
| --- | --- |
| UFO ending | Photograph 13 hidden UFOs. |

### EASTER EGG

Press 1 on the Wii Remote, go to "Hints," click on "Cell Phone Calls," on the picture of Harry's phone with a number. Dial the number on your phone to call Konami Customer Service. Unfortunately, they are unable to help you due to the fact you're in Silent Hill.

## SIMCITY DS (DS)

### PASSWORDS

At the main menu, go to "Museum" then select "Landmark Collection," and finally "Password," then enter the following codes.

| UNLOCKABLE | CODE |
| --- | --- |
| Anglican Cathedral (UK) | kipling |
| Arc de Triomphe (France) | gaugin |
| Atomic Dome (Japan) | kawabata |
| Big Ben (UK) | orwell |
| Bowser Castle (Nintendo) | hanafuda |
| Brandenburg Gate (Germany) | gropius |
| Coit Tower (USA) | kerouac |
| Conciergerie (France) | rodin |
| Daibutsu (Japan) | mishima |
| Edo Castle (Japan) | shonagon |
| Eiffel Tower (France) | camus |
| Gateway Arch (USA) | twain |
| Grand Central Station (USA) | f.scott |
| Great Pyramids (Egypt) | mahfouz |
| Hagia Sofia (Turkey) | ataturk |
| Helsinki Cathedral (Finland) | kivi |
| Himeji Castle (Japan) | hokusai |
| Holstentor (Germany) | durer |
| Independence Hall (USA) | mlkingjr |
| Jefferson Memorial (USA) | thompson |
| Kokkai (Japan) | soseki |
| LA Landmark (USA) | hemingway |

| | |
|---|---|
| Lincoln Memorial (USA) | melville |
| Liver Building (UK) | dickens |
| Melbourne Cricket Ground (Australia) | damemelba |
| Metropolitan Cathedral (UK) | austen |
| Moai (Chile) | allende |
| Mt. Fuji (Japan) | hiroshige |
| National Museum (Taiwan) | yuantlee |
| Neuschwanstein Castle (Germany) | beethoven |
| Notre Dame (France) | hugo |
| Palace of Fine Arts (USA) | bunche |
| Palacio Real (Spain) | cervantes |
| Paris Opera (France) | daumier |
| Parthenon (Greece) | callas |
| Pharos of Alexandria (Egypt) | zewail |
| Rama IX Royal Park (Thailand) | phu |
| Reichstag (Germany) | goethe |
| Sagrada Famillia (Spain) | dali |
| Shuri Castle (Japan) | basho |
| Smithsonian Castle (USA) | pauling |
| Sphinx (Egypt) | haykal |
| St. Paul's Cathedral (UK) | defoe |
| St. Basil's Cathedral (Russia) | tolstoy |
| St. Stephen's Cathedral (Austria) | mozart |
| Statue of Liberty (USA) | pollack |
| Stockholm Palace (Sweden) | bergman |
| Sydney Opera House Landmark # 12 (Australia) | bradman |
| Taj Mahal (India) | tagore |
| Tower of London (UK) | maugham |
| Trafalgar Square (UK) | joyce |
| United Nations (USA) | amnesty |
| United States Capitol (USA) | poe |
| Washington Monument (USA) | capote |
| Westminster Abbey (UK) | greene |
| White House (USA) | steinbeck |

## UNLOCKABLE BUILDINGS FROM POPULATION GROWTH

When your city reaches a certain number of people, Dr. Simtown unlocks buildings that help your city.

| UNLOCKABLE | HOW TO UNLOCK |
|---|---|
| Center for the Arts | Reach a population of 100,000. |
| Court House | Reach a population of 25,000. |
| Mayor's House | Reach a population of 5,000. |
| Medical Research Lab | Have a population of 80,000 when you reach year 1999. |
| Museum | Reach a population of 3,000. |
| Post Office | Reach a population of 100. |

## THE SIMS 2 (DS)

### MUSIC STUFF

| UNLOCKABLE | HOW TO UNLOCK |
|---|---|
| Custom Music in Music Panels and Radios | Record music in one of the lounges and save it. It will now be available in music panels and radios. |
| Tunes from Music Mixer in Music Panels and Radios | Mix up music in the music mixer (in one of the lounges) and save it. |

### NEW SONGS

| UNLOCKABLE | HOW TO UNLOCK |
|---|---|
| "Combat Mode" | Collect 12 license plates. |
| "Credits Theme" | Beat the game. |
| "Razor Burn" | Collect 24 license plates. |

## THE SIMS 3 (DS)

### KARMA POWERS

Karma Powers can be unlocked after you have accumulated enough Lifetime Happiness for each one. To trigger Karma Powers, go to the locations that follow and click on the object described.

| UNLOCKABLE | HOW TO UNLOCK |
|---|---|
| Bless This Mess | Garden Gnome outside Landgraab house |
| Casanova | Dance Club, near the restrooms |
| Cosmic Curse | Graveyard at night only |
| Epic Fail | Statue at Goth's house |
| Giant Jackpot | Bench near the Lighthouse |
| Muse | Painting in the Art Museum |
| Super Satisfy | Wrought Iron Trellis off path near Lighthouse |
| The Riddler | Jet statue near Military Base |
| Winter Wonderland | Alcove near the Stadium |
| Wormhole | Potted flower outside Poet's Abode |

## THE SIMS 2: PETS (Wii)

### UNLOCKABLES

| UNLOCKABLE | HOW TO UNLOCK |
|---|---|
| 10,000 Simoleons | Hold ⓑ, press ⬆, ⬅, ⬇, ➡ |
| Advance 6 Hours | ⬅, ⬅, ⬅, ⬅, ⬅, ➡ |
| Change Skills | ➡, ➡, ➡, ⬆, ⬆, ⬆ |

## SKATE 2 (XBOX 360)

### CODES

Enter the code in the code entry screen in the "Extras" menu. The code for 3-D requires that you have 3-D glasses.

| EFFECT | CODE |
|---|---|
| Turns the Game 3-D | Strangeloops |
| Unlocks Big Black as a playable character | letsdowork |

### UNLOCKABLES

| UNLOCKABLE | HOW TO UNLOCK |
|---|---|
| GvR Plaza | Complete all Street Challenges to unlock the Etnies GvR Plaza. |
| King of the Mountain Crown | Beat all of the Races in Career mode (not the bonus races, though). |
| Legend Crown | Reach Legend level online. |
| Monster Skate Park | Get Sponsored and complete Team Film Challenges until you get a demo session with Rob Drydek; after completing this earn $200,000 to buy the park. |
| S.V. Dam | Complete all the Thrasher Mag challenges to drain the dam. |
| S.V. Stadium | Complete all Tranny Contests to unlock the S.V. Mega-Ramp Stadium. |
| S.V. Summit | Complete all the Death Races to unlock the peak of Cougar Mountain. |
| Training Park | Complete all Team Film Challenges to unlock the Training Park. |

## SKATE 2 (PlayStation 3)

### CODES

Enter the code in the code entry screen in the "Extras" menu. The code for 3-D requires that you have 3-D glasses.

| EFFECT | CODE |
| --- | --- |
| Turns The Game 3-D | Strangeloops |
| Unlocks Big Black as a playable character | letsdowork |

## SKATE 3 (XBOX 360)

### CODES

Activate the codes by pressing Start, Options, then Extras, and then entering them.

| EFFECT | CODE |
| --- | --- |
| Enables Mini-Skater Mode | miniskaters |
| Enables Zombie Mode Pedestrians chase you; screen goes yellowish | zombie |
| Hoverboard Mode Trucks and wheels disappear from your deck | mcfly |
| Resets all objects in every area back to their original positions | streetsweeper |
| Unlocks Isaac from Dead Space as a playable skater | deadspacetoo |

## SKATE 3 (PlayStation 3)

### CODES

Pause the game, go to Options, Extras, and then enter the following codes.

| EFFECT | CODE |
| --- | --- |
| Enables Mini-Skater Mode | miniskaters |
| Enables Zombie Mode | zombie |
| Hoverboard Mode | mcfly |
| Resets all objects in every area back to their original positions | streetsweeper |
| Unlocks Isaac from Dead Space as a playable skater | deadspacetoo |

## SMALL ARMS (XBOX 360)

### UNLOCKABLES

| UNLOCKABLE | HOW TO UNLOCK |
| --- | --- |
| Shooting Range Practice | Beat Mission mode |
| Billy Ray Logg | Beat him in Mission mode with any character |
| ISO-7982 | Complete Mission mode |
| Mousey McNuts | Beat him in Mission mode with any character |
| Professor Von Brown | Beat him in Mission mode with any character |

## SMASH T (XBOX 360)

### INVINCIBILITY

| CODE | EFFECT |
| --- | --- |
| Press ✪+✪ | Become invincible. This code must be entered in every room. You can move around and change the angle of your shooting. If you stop shooting, the code deactivates. Don't stop shooting unless you want to pick up a new weapon or prize. |

## SNOOPY FLYING ACE (XBOX 360)

### UNLOCKABLES

Use the Avatar Costumes/Shirts by downloading them from the "Download Avatar Awards" option in the Help & Options menu after completing the requirements below.

| UNLOCKABLE | HOW TO UNLOCK |
| --- | --- |
| Snoopy Gamer Pic | Obtain 5,000 Online Points. |
| Woodstock Gamer Pic | Reach level 20. |

| Red Baron Avatar Costume | Reach the rank of Flying Ace. |
| Snoopy Avatar Shirt | Receive at least one medal on all missions. |

## SOCOM 4: U.S. NAVY SEALS (PlayStation 3)

### TROPHY

| UNLOCKABLE | HOW TO UNLOCK |
|---|---|
| 10-Piece Meal (Bronze) | Eliminate a total of 10 chickens during your career. |
| Above and Beyond (Gold) | Complete a total of 100 objectives during your career. |
| All is Said, All is Done SOCOM (Platinum) | Obtain all Bronze, Silver, and Gold Trophies in 4: U.S. Navy SEALs. |
| Allegiance Exposed (Bronze) | 'Revelation' - Expose Gorman's treachery and determine his true allegiance. |
| Armed to the Teeth (Bronze) | Unlock all weapons for use in Campaign mode. |
| Beowulf (Bronze) | 'Leviathan' - Destroy the enemy stealth frigate to ensure the safety of the remaining NATO fleet. |
| Best of the Best (Gold) | Complete the Story Campaign on Elite difficulty. |
| Century Slayer (Bronze) | Eliminate a total of 100 enemies during your career. |
| Combat Medic (Bronze) | Execute a total of 25 teammate revives during your career. |
| Combined Assault (Bronze) | Complete a Custom Campaign mission in Co-Op. |
| Covert Ops (Bronze) | As Forty-Five, successfully maintain stealth in a Story Campaign mission. |
| Crowd Control (Bronze) | Eliminate 3 enemies with a single explosive. |
| Death From Above (Bronze) | Eliminate 5 enemies with a single Strike. |
| Destroy Gorman's Car (Bronze) | Destroy Gorman's Car. |
| Destroy Razad's Car (Bronze) | Destroy Razad's Car. |
| Double Down (Bronze) | Eliminate 2 chickens with a single explosive. |
| Elite Ops (Bronze) | Complete a Story Campaign mission on Elite difficulty. |
| Executioner (Bronze) | 'Animus' - Complete the Story Campaign by choosing to take Gorman's life. |
| Expert Tactician (Bronze) | Complete a Story Campaign mission using only teammates to eliminate enemies. |
| Extra Credit (Bronze) | Complete a Custom Campaign mission in Single Player. |
| Eye in the Sky (Bronze) | 'Uninvited Guest' - Secure the intel that reveals ClawHammer's true objective in the region. |
| Field Promotion (Bronze) | 'First Strike' - Complete your first mission as Ops Commander. |
| Good Game (Bronze) | Complete a Competitive Multiplayer game of every gametype. |
| Government Spending (Bronze) | Call in a total of 10 Strikes during your career. |
| Grenadier (Bronze) | Eliminate a total of 25 enemies with explosives during your career. |
| Hat Trick (Bronze) | Eliminate 3 enemies in a row with headshots. |
| I Call Her Vera (Bronze) | Master a weapon in any mode. |
| Information Warfare (Bronze) | Collect all Intel in the Story Campaign |
| Melon Hunter (Bronze) | Eliminate a total of 100 enemies with a headshot during your career. |
| Millennial Slayer (Bronze) | Eliminate a total of 1000 enemies during your career. |
| N00b (Bronze) | Complete a Competitive Multiplayer game. |

| Oracle (Bronze) | Collect an intel item in a Story Campaign mission. |
| --- | --- |
| Over-Achiever (Bronze) | Complete a Custom Campaign mission on every map in either Single Player or Co-Op. |
| Passing the Torch (Bronze) | 'Countdown' - Stop ClawHammer's missile launch and promote Forty-Five to Ops Commander. |
| Peace Keeper (Bronze) | 'Animus' - Complete the Story Campaign by choosing to bring Gorman to justice. |
| Rendezvous (Bronze) | 'Rendezvous' - Rescue the surviving allies at the NATO rally point. |
| Repo Man (Bronze) | Destroy a total of 50 vehicles during your career. |
| Shiny! (Gold) | Master a weapon of each class in any mode. |
| The Blood Orange (Bronze) | Find and collect a Tarocco. |
| The Elite 45th (Gold) | As Forty-Five, stealth kill a total of 45 enemies in the Story Campaign |
| The Sweetest, Darkest Juice is at its Core (Silver) | Find and collect the Tarocco in each Story Campaign mission. |
| Trial by Fire (Bronze) | 'Means to an End' - Confront Razad and expose Naga's partnership with ClawHammer. |
| Unseen Strike (Bronze) | Stealth kill a total of 10 enemies in a single mission. |
| Vorpal (Bronze) | Eliminate a total of 25 enemies with melee attacks during your career. |
| Whatever it Takes (Bronze) | 'Fluid Dynamics' - Stop the Naga forces from reaching the capital by whatever means necessary. |

## SOLDIER BLADE (Wii)

### CODES

| EFFECT | CODE |
| --- | --- |
| Level Select | Hold ⬆, press SELECT, hold ⬆, press SELECT, hold ⬅, press SELECT, hold ⬆, press SELECT |

## SOLDNER-X 2: FINAL PROTOTYPE (PlayStation 3)

### UNLOCKABLES

| UNLOCKABLE | HOW TO UNLOCK |
| --- | --- |
| Stage 5 | Collect at least 4 keys from any stage |
| Stage 6 | Collect at least 4 keys from any 3 stages |
| Stage 7 | Collect at least 4 keys from stages 1–6 |
| Final Ship | Complete the Challenge "Assassin" |
| Extra Hard difficulty | Complete the game on Hard difficulty |
| Hard difficulty | Complete the game on Normal difficulty |

## SOLOMON'S KEY (Wii)

### UNLOCKABLES

| UNLOCKABLE | HOW TO UNLOCK |
| --- | --- |
| Continue Game | At the "Game Deviation Value" screen, hold ⬆+Ⓐ+Ⓑ |

## SONIC 3D BLAST (Wii)

### UNLOCKABLES

| UNLOCKABLE | HOW TO UNLOCK |
| --- | --- |
| Level Select | Go to the Press Start screen and enter Ⓑ, Ⓐ, ⬆, Ⓐ, Ⓒ, ⬆, ⬆, Ⓐ (or baracuda). You're taken to the main screen. Press the Start option and the level select appears. |
| Quick Emerald Gain | Enter the Level Select code twice, and go to a level/act with Knuckles or Tails in it. Enter one of their bonus levels by collecting 50 rings. When the bonus level begins, press Ⓐ+ START and you will receive the emerald for the bonus level. |

| Skip Levels | Do the Level Select code and start the game in any level. To skip levels, pause the game and press Ⓐ. |
| --- | --- |
| Stage Select (Alternative) | Beat the entire game with all the Chaos Emeralds. After the credits, the stage select is on. |

## SONIC GENERATIONS (XBOX 360)

### ACHIEVEMENT

| UNLOCKABLE | HOW TO UNLOCK |
| --- | --- |
| (Hedge)Hogging It All Up! (50) | Get all collectibles. |
| A 30-Second Test (20) | Participate in a 30 Second Trial. |
| A Quick Breather (10) | Got the Red Star Ring atop the highest spot in ROOFTOP RUN Act 2 and reached the goal. |
| Action Hero (10) | Perform all of Sonic's moves in Act 2. |
| All Stages Cleared! (50) | Clear Sonic Generations. |
| Big Bang (50) | Get Rank S in all Acts. |
| Blazing Meteor (30) | Get Rank S in seven Acts. |
| Blue Comet (40) | Get Rank S in twelve Acts. |
| Bonds of Friendship (10) | Complete all Challenge Acts featuring Sonic's friends. |
| Boom Boom Dragoon (30) | Defeated Egg Dragoon. |
| Bright Star (15) | Get Rank S in an Act. |
| Can't Touch This (30) | Took no damage from the final boss and cleared the stage. |
| CHEMICAL PLANT Restored! (15) | Restored the CHEMICAL PLANT Stage Gate. |
| CITY ESCAPE Restored! (15) | Restored the CITY ESCAPE Stage Gate. |
| Color Power! (10) | Got the Red Star Ring by using an Orange Wisp in PLANET WISP Act 2 and reached the goal. |
| CRISIS CITY Restored! (15) | Restored the CRISIS CITY Stage Gate. |
| Demolition Derby (10) | Wrecked 30 or more cars in CITY ESCAPE Act 2. |
| Eradicator (15) | Defeat 100 enemies. |
| Greased Lightning (10) | Clear GREEN HILL Act 1 within one minute. |
| GREEN HILL Restored! (15) | Restored the GREEN HILL Stage Gate. |
| Halfway Point (30) | Clear half the Challenge Acts. |
| Join the Ranks (20) | Join the rankings. |
| Jump for Joy! (10) | Found the spring hidden in GREEN HILL Act 1 and reached the goal with a Red Star Ring. |
| Look Both Ways (10) | Reached the goal in CRISIS CITY Act 2 without being hit by a tornado-carried cars or rocks. |
| Mad Skillz (30) | Get all Skills. |
| Mission Accomplished! (30) | Clear all the Challenge Acts. |
| Perfect Punisher (25) | Defeated Perfect Chaos. |
| PLANET WISP Restored! (15) | Restored the PLANET WISP Stage Gate. |
| Red Ring Collector (30) | Get all Red Star Rings. |
| Ring King (15) | Reach the goal without dropping any of the rings you collected in GREEN HILL Act 1. |
| ROOFTOP RUN Restored! (15) | Restored the ROOFTOP RUN Stage Gate. |
| Scrap Metal (20) | Defeated Metal Sonic. |
| SEASIDE HILL Restored! (15) | Restored the SEASIDE HILL Stage Gate. |
| Secret Sleuth (10) | Got the Red Star Ring located in the hidden room in SEASIDE HILL Act 1 and reached the goal. |
| Shadow Boxing (25) | Defeated Shadow. |
| Shooting Star (20) | Get Rank S in three Acts. |

| | |
|---|---|
| Silver Got Served (30) | Defeated Silver. |
| SKY SANCTUARY Restored! (15) | Restored the SKY SANCTUARY Stage Gate. |
| SPEED HIGHWAY Restored! (15) | Restored the SPEED HIGHWAY Stage Gate. |
| Sunny Side Up (20) | Defeated Death Egg Robot. |
| Supersonic! (20) | Cleared a regular stage as Super Sonic. |
| The Byway or the route in Highway (20) | Got the Red Star Ring located on the shortcut SPEED HIGHWAY Act 2 and reached the goal. |
| The Opening Act (10) | Race through the first stage. |
| Time Attacker (30) | Play Ranking Attack on all stages. |
| Treasure Hunter (20) | Collected all the Chaos Emeralds. |
| Trickstar (10) | Pull off a seven or more trick combo or six trick combo ending in a finishing trick. |
| Walk on Air (20) | Cleared SKY SANCTUARY Act 1 without falling and losing a life. |
| Walk on Water (10) | Cleared CHEMICAL PLANT Act 2 without entering the water. |
| Walkie Talkie (10) | Chat with each of Sonic's friends you have saved. |

## CODE

When in the Collection Room, hold down the Back button until Sonic jumps down through a black hole. This lets you access the Secret Statue Room. Input the following codes to unlock different character statues.

| UNLOCKABLE | CODE |
|---|---|
| Aero-Cannon | 329 494 |
| Amy Rose | 863 358 |
| Big The Cat | 353 012 |
| Blaze The Cat | 544 873 |
| Booster | 495 497 |
| Buzz Bomber | 852 363 |
| Capsule | 777 921 |
| Chao | 629 893 |
| Chaos Emeralds | 008 140 |
| Charmy Bee | 226 454 |
| Chip | 309 511 |
| Chopper | 639 402 |
| Classic Dr. Robotnik | 103 729 |
| Classic Sonic The Hedgehog | 171 045 |
| Classic Tails | 359 236 |
| Cop Speeder | 640 456 |
| Crab Meat | 363 911 |
| Cream The Rabbit | 332 955 |
| Dark Chao | 869 292 |
| E-123 Omega | 601 409 |
| Egg Chaser | 200 078 |
| Egg Fighter | 851 426 |
| Egg Launcher | 973 433 |
| Egg Pawn | 125 817 |
| Egg Robo | 360 031 |
| Espio The Chameleon | 894 526 |

NEW!

A
B
C
D
E
F
G
H
I
J
K
L
M
N
O
P
Q
R
S
T
U
V
W
X
Y
Z

| | |
|---|---|
| Flickies | 249 651 |
| Goal Plate | 933 391 |
| Goal Ring | 283 015 |
| Grabber | 275 843 |
| GUN Beetle | 975 073 |
| GUN Hunter | 668 250 |
| Hero Chao | 507 376 |
| Iblis Biter | 872 910 |
| Iblis Taker | 513 929 |
| Iblis Worm | 711 268 |
| Item Box | 209 005 |
| Jet The Hawk | 383 870 |
| Knuckles The Echidna | 679 417 |
| Metal Sonic | 277 087 |
| Modern Dr. Eggman | 613 482 |
| Modern Sonic The Hedgehog | 204 390 |
| Modern Tails | 632 951 |
| Moto Bug | 483 990 |
| Omochao | 870 580 |
| Ring | 390 884 |
| Rouge The Bat | 888 200 |
| Sand Worm | 548 986 |
| Shadow The Hedgehog | 262 416 |
| Silver The Hedgehog | 688 187 |
| Spinner | 530 741 |
| Spiny | 466 913 |
| Spring | 070 178 |
| Spring 2 | 537 070 |
| Vector The Crocodile | 868 377 |

### UNLOCKABLE

| UNLOCKABLE | HOW TO UNLOCK |
|---|---|
| Classic Eggman Suit (Bottoms) | Defeat all rivals on Hard Mode. |
| Classic Eggman Suit (Head) | Defeat the final boss on Hard Mode. |
| Classic Eggman Suit (Tops) | Defeat all bosses on Hard Mode. |
| Super Sonic | Defeat the Final Boss |

## SONIC GENERATIONS (PlayStation 3)

### TROPHY

| UNLOCKABLE | HOW TO UNLOCK |
|---|---|
| (Hedge)Hogging It All Up! (Gold) | Get all collectibles. |
| A 30-Second Test (Bronze) | Participate in a 30 Second Trial. |
| A Quick Breather (Bronze) | Get the Red Star Ring atop the highest spot ROOFTOP RUN Act 2 and reach the goal. |
| Action Hero (Bronze) | Perform all of Sonic's moves in Act 2. |
| All Stages Cleared! (Silver) | Clear Sonic Generations. |
| All Trophies Collected! (Platinum) | Collect all Trophies. |
| Big Bang (Gold) | Get Rank S in all Acts. |
| Blazing Meteor (Silver) | Get Rank S in seven Acts. |

| | |
|---|---|
| **Blue Comet (Silver)** | Get Rank S in twelve Acts. |
| **Bonds of Friendship (Bronze)** | Complete all Challenge Acts featuring Sonic's friends. |
| **Boom Boom Dragoon (Bronze)** | Defeat Egg Dragoon |
| **Bright Star (Bronze)** | Get Rank S in an Act. |
| **CHEMICAL PLANT Restored! (Bronze)** | Restore the CHEMICAL PLANT Stage Gate. |
| **CITY ESCAPE Restored! (Bronze)** | Restore the CITY ESCAPE Stage Gate. |
| **CRISIS CITY Restored! (Bronze)** | Restore the CRISIS CITY Stage Gate. |
| **Demolition Derby (Bronze)** | Wreck 30 or more cars in CITY ESCAPE Act 2. |
| **Eradicator (Bronze)** | Defeat 100 enemies. |
| **Greased Lightning (Bronze)** | Clear GREEN HILL Act 1 within one minute. |
| **GREEN HILL Restored! (Bronze)** | Restore the GREEN HILL Stage Gate. |
| **Halfway Point (Silver)** | Clear half the Challenge Acts. |
| **Join the Ranks (Bronze)** | Join the rankings. |
| **Look Both Ways (Bronze)** | Reach the goal in CRISIS CITY Act 2 without being hit by a tornado-carried cars or rocks. |
| **Mission Accomplished! (Silver)** | Clear all the Challenge Acts. |
| **Perfect Punisher (Bronze)** | Defeat Perfect Chaos. |
| **PLANET WISP Restored! (Bronze)** | Restore the PLANET WISP Stage Gate. |
| **Red Ring Collector (Silver)** | Get all Red Star Rings. |
| **Ring King (Bronze)** | Reach the goal without dropping any of the rings you collected in GREEN HILL Act 1. |
| **ROOFTOP RUN Restored! (Bronze)** | Restore the ROOFTOP RUN Stage Gate. |
| **Scrap Metal (Bronze)** | Defeat Metal Sonic. |
| **SEASIDE HILL Restored! (Bronze)** | Restore the SEASIDE HILL Stage Gate. |
| **Secret Sleuth (Bronze)** | Get the Red Star Ring located in the hidden room in SEASIDE HILL Act 1 and reach the goal. |
| **Shadow Boxing (Bronze)** | Defeat Shadow. |
| **Shooting Star (Bronze)** | Get Rank S in three Acts. |
| **Silver got Served (Bronze)** | Defeat Silver. |
| **SKY SANCTUARY Restored! (Bronze)** | Restore the SKY SANCTUARY Stage Gate. |
| **SPEED HIGHWAY Restored! (Bronze)** | Restore the SPEED HIGHWAY Stage Gate. |
| **Sunny Side Up (Bronze)** | Defeat Death Egg Robot. |
| **The Opening Act (Bronze)** | Race through the first stage. |
| **Time Attacker (Silver)** | Play Ranking Attack on all stages. |
| **Treasure Hunter (Bronze)** | Collect all the Chaos Emeralds. |
| **Trickstar (Bronze)** | Pull off a seven or more trick combo or six trick combo ending in a finishing trick. |
| **Walk on Air (Bronze)** | Clear SKY SANCTUARY Act 1 without falling and losing a life. |
| **Walk on Water (Bronze)** | Clear CHEMICAL PLANT Act 2 without entering the water. |
| **Walkie Talkie (Bronze)** | Chat with each of Sonic's friends you have saved. |

### CODE

In the Collection room position Sonic to the right of the Movie Chair located to the left of the Art painting, Hold down Select to enter a hole which takes you to the Statue Room. Once there, press Select to bring up a code screen. Enter these codes to unlock statues.

| UNLOCKABLE | CODE |
| --- | --- |
| 008 140 | Chaos Emerald |
| 070 178 | Spring (Yellow) |
| 103 729 | Classic Eggman |
| 125 817 | Egg Pawn |
| 171 045 | Classic Sonic |
| 200 078 | Egg Chaser |
| 204 390 | Sonic the Hedgehog |
| 209 005 | Item Box |
| 226 454 | Charmy Bee |
| 249 651 | Cucky/Picky/Flicky/Pecky |
| 262 416 | Shadow the Hedgehog |
| 275 843 | Grabber |
| 277 087 | Metal Sonic |
| 283 015 | Goal Ring |
| 309 511 | Chip |
| 329 494 | Aero-Cannon |
| 332 955 | Cream the Rabbit |
| 353 012 | Big the Cat |
| 359 236 | Classic Tails |
| 360 031 | Eggrobo |
| 363 911 | Crabmeat |
| 383 870 | Jet the Hawk |
| 390 884 | Ring |
| 466 913 | Spiny |
| 483 990 | Moto Bug |
| 495 497 | Booster |
| 507 376 | Hero Chao |
| 513 929 | Iblis Taker |
| 530 741 | Spinner |
| 537 070 | Spring (Red) |
| 544 873 | Blaze the Cat |
| 548 986 | Sandworm |
| 601 409 | E-123 Omega |
| 613 482 | Dr. Eggman |
| 629 893 | Chao |
| 632 951 | Miles "Tails" Prower |
| 639 402 | Chopper |
| 640 456 | Cop Speeder |
| 668 250 | Gun Hunter |
| 679 417 | Knuckles the Echidna |
| 688 187 | Silver the Hedgehog |
| 711 268 | Iblis Worm |
| 777 921 | Capsule |

| | |
|---|---|
| 851 426 | Egg Fighter |
| 852 363 | Buzz Bomber |
| 863 358 | Amy Rose |
| 868 377 | Vector the Crocodile |
| 869 292 | Dark Chao |
| 870 580 | Omochao |
| 872 910 | Iblis Biter |
| 888 200 | Rouge the Bat |
| 894 526 | Espio the Chameleon |
| 933 391 | Goal Plate |
| 973 433 | Egg Launcher |
| 975 073 | Gun Beetle |

### UNLOCKABLE

After unlocking the classic Sonic the Hedgehog game, load the game.
After Sonic appears on the title screen press these buttons in order to
select your level.

| UNLOCKABLE | HOW TO UNLOCK |
|---|---|
| Level Select | ↑, ↓, ←, →, ✕ |

### UNLOCKABLE

At the shop to the left of the Green Hill Zone, buy the Sega controller, then
take it to the Sega console at the top left section of the Green Hill Zone.

| UNLOCKABLE | HOW TO UNLOCK |
|---|---|
| Original Sonic the Hedgehog | |

## SONIC RUSH ADVENTURE (DS)

### UNLOCKABLES

| UNLOCKABLE | HOW TO UNLOCK |
|---|---|
| Blaze the Cat | Defeat the Kraken boss in Coral Cave to unlock Blaze as a playable character. |
| Deep Core: Final extra boss stage | Collect all Sol Emeralds and Chaos Emeralds. |

## SONIC SPINBALL (Wii)

### UNLOCKABLES

| UNLOCKABLE | HOW TO UNLOCK |
|---|---|
| Level Select | Access the Options from the title screen, take controller 1, and press: Ⓐ, ➕, Ⓑ, ➕, Ⓒ, ➕, Ⓐ, Ⓑ, ➕, Ⓐ, Ⓒ, ➕, Ⓑ, Ⓒ, ➕. If you did it correctly, you hear a special sound. Go back to the title screen and hold Ⓐ and press START to begin on Level 2, Ⓑ and press START for Level 3, and ➕ and press START for level 4. |
| Multi-Ball Stage | Collect every ring in any stage. |
| Stop the Platform in The Machine | In Level 3, The Machine, a moving platform takes you to either side of the area. Stand on the platform and press up or down to make the platform stop, allowing you to get a good look around or plan your jump carefully. |

## SONIC THE HEDGEHOG (PlayStation 3)

| UNLOCKABLE | HOW TO UNLOCK |
|---|---|
| Last Episode | Beat Sonic's Episode, Shadow's Episode, and Silver's Episode |
| Audio Room | Complete Sonic, Shadow, or Silver's story 100% |
| Theater Room | Complete Sonic, Shadow, or Silver's story 100% |
| Shadow the Hedgehog | Complete "Crisis City" with Sonic |
| Silver the Hedgehog | Complete "Silver the Hedgehog" boss battle with Sonic |

## SONIC THE HEDGEHOG (Wii)

### UNLOCKABLES

| UNLOCKABLE | HOW TO UNLOCK |
|---|---|
| Config Mode | There is a code called Control mode, which is required before activating this code. To activate Control mode, press ⬆, ©, ⬇, ©, ◀, ©, ▶, ◀ at the title screen, but before pressing START to begin the game, hold Ⓐ as you hit START. Now, rather than just being in Control mode, you can enable Config mode by pressing Ⓑ. Sonic will morph into a ring, and the arrows can move him anywhere, even in the air, or through obstacles such as walls, floors, or even ceilings. You can change the item Sonic appears as by hitting Ⓐ while in Config mode. Ⓑ makes Sonic normal again, and ⬆ will place the sprite that you have selected for Sonic to appear as. For example, you press Ⓑ, and Sonic becomes a ring, press ⬆ to make a ring appear exactly where the ring icon is. WARNING!: This distorts several different things, such as the score, time, and other various icons throughout the game such as the finish signs at the end of the first two acts of each zone that spin when Sonic shoots past them, and the small score icons that appear whenever Sonic jumps high enough after finishing a level. |
| Drunk Sonic | During the demo, hold ⬆. Sonic will crash into walls and get hit by enemies. |
| Level Select | At the title screen, press ⬆, ⬇, ◀, ▶. You should hear a noise like a ring being collected. Then, hold Ⓐ and press START for a level select! |
| Secret Game Message | At the title screen, press ©, ©, ©, ©, ©, ©, ⬆, ⬆, ◀, ◀. When the demo starts, hold Ⓐ+Ⓑ+©+⬆ then press START. Instead of the Sonic Team logo, you will see a list of the game's evelopers in Japanese. When the title screen appears, a flashing "Press Start Button" will be there under Sonic's head. |
| Different Ending | Beat game with all Chaos Emeralds. |

## SONIC THE HEDGEHOG 2 (XBOX 360)

| CODE | EFFECT |
|---|---|
| 17 | Play Invincibility Music |
| 65 | Plays a Shifting Sound |
| 09 | Plays Casino Night Zone 1-Player Music |
| 19 | Plays Sonic 2 Theme |

## SONIC THE HEDGEHOG 2 (Wii)

### UNLOCKABLES

| UNLOCKABLE | HOW TO UNLOCK |
|---|---|
| Level Select | Some other cheats require you to enable this one first. Go to the Options menu from the main screen. From there, head to the Sound Select menu and play the following sounds: 19, 65, 09, 17. Once you have played each (1 time only), press ⬆ and then press START to be brought back to the title screen. Now, when you see Sonic and Tails (Miles) appear on screen, hold Ⓐ and press START to finish off the code. You're brought to a menu where you have access to any level in the game, whether you've completed the level or not. |
| 14 Continues | Go to the sound test (not the one on the level select) and put in 19, 65, 09, 17, 01, 01, 02, 04 (press Ⓐ after each one). There won't be a confirmation sound. Start the game by pressing START on the first option (character select) and you have 14 continues. |
| All 7 Chaos Emeralds | This code only works for Sonic. First, do the Level Select cheat. In the Level Select menu, go to Sound Test and play the sounds 04, 01, 02, 06. If done correctly, you'll hear a Chaos Emerald sound effect. Now, select any stage from this menu and you can turn into Super Sonic with 50 rings plus you'll get Sonic's second ending after beating Death Egg Zone. |

| | |
|---|---|
| **Change Tails' Name to Miles** | Press ⬆, ⬆, ⬇, ⬇, ⬅, ➡, ⬇ at the title screen. |
| **Debug Mode** | First enter the Level Select code. Now, go to Sound Test option, and play the following tunes: 01, 09, 09, 02, 01, 01, 02, 04. It should make a ring sound when track 4 is played to signify you've entered it correctly. Now select the stage you want to go to, and press START while holding Ⓐ until the stage starts, and you'll have debug activated. Press Ⓑ to turn Debug on/off, Ⓐ to switch object, and ⬇ to put down object selected. Pressing Ⓐ while the game is paused will cause the game to reset. |
| **Debug Mode (Alternate)** | At Sound Test, enter: 19, 65, 09, 17, then press Ⓐ+START, then when Sonic and Tails pop up, press Ⓐ+START to go to the Level Select screen. On the Sound Test area, enter 01, 09, 09, 02, 01, 01, 02, 04, and then press Ⓐ+START. |
| **Debug Mode and All Emeralds (when locked-on to Sonic and Knuckles)** | First activate and go to the Stage Select. Play the following tracks in Sound Test with Ⓑ: 01, 09, 09, 04, 01, 00, 01, 08. This enables the Debug code, and you should hear a ring chime if the code is entered correctly. Start the selected level with Ⓐ+START. To get all 7 Chaos Emeralds, input this code the same way: 01, 06, 07, 07, 07, 02, 01, 06. You should hear the Emerald chime. Note: this code may not work without the Debug code. |
| **Enable Super Sonic** | First, head to the Options menu from the title screen, and then into the Sound Select menu from there. Play the following sounds in this order: 19, 65, 09, 17. After that, press ⬇, START. You will be taken back to the title screen. Now, when you see Sonic and Tails (Miles) appear on the screen, press and hold Ⓐ and press START to be taken to the Level Select menu. From this menu, enter the Sound Test feature, and play the following sounds: 04, 01, 02, 06. If done correctly, a familiar tune plays. Exit this menu and start the game as normal. Once you collect a minimum of 50 coins in any level, Jump (Press Ⓐ) to activate the Super Sonic code. |
| **Get Super Sonic on Emerald Hill** | First, enter the Stage Select code, shown above. Then you go into the Special Stage in the Stage Select menu. Every time you finish the special stage, press reset and go back to the special stage. Keep doing this until you get the sixth emerald. Then don't press reset. It zaps you with your 6 emeralds into Emerald Hill. Get the last emerald on Emerald Hill, get 50 rings, and jump to be Super Sonic. Don't run out of rings or you will change into Sonic again. The rings start disappearing when you are Super Sonic. |
| **Infinite Lives** | First, enable the Level Select cheat and the Debug mode. Choose Sonic and Tails as the players. After entering the codes, choose any stage from the Level Select menu (preferably stage 1). As soon as you can move Sonic, hold ⬇ and press Ⓐ (don't let go of down on the D-pad). This activates Sonic's spin; Tails will copy the Sonic spin also. Press Ⓑ and Sonic will become the Debug cursor. (Tails will be locked in the Sonic spin move.) Press Ⓐ until the debug cursor displays an enemy sprite, like the monkey or that bee robot. Now that the debug cursor displays an enemy sprite, move the debug cursor to where Tails is, and repeatedly tap ⬇. This produces enemies where Tails is, and because Tails is locked in the Sonic spin move, he destroys the enemies. As Tails destroys enemies in this position, press ⬇ more until the score for destroying an enemy increases from 100 to 8,000 to a 1Up. Once you have enough 1Ups, press Ⓑ again to revert to Sonic. |
| **Level Select (When Locked-On to Sonic and Knuckles)** | At the title screen, press ⬇, ⬇, ⬇, ⬇, ⬇, ⬇, ⬅, ⬇, ⬅, ⬇. Then, hold Ⓐ and press START to be taken to the Level Select menu. |
| **Night Mode** | Activate level select and hold ⬇ while selecting a stage to darken the level. The effect wears off when you die or when you beat the level. |

A
B
C
D
E
F
G
H
I
J
K
L
M
N
O
P
Q
R
S
T
U
V
W
X
Y
Z

| Level Select Screen | At the title screen, select Options. Highlight Sound Test then play the following music and sounds: 19, 65, 09, and 17. You hear a ring-collecting sound for correct code entry. Then press START to return to the title screen. Highlight 1-Player, hold Ⓐ, and press START. You are directed to Level Select screen. Choose a level then press START to begin. |
|---|---|
| Slow Motion | First, enter the Level Select code. Then start your game in any level. When you start, press pause. Then hold Ⓑ and try to do anything with Sonic. The game plays in slow motion as long as you hold down Ⓑ. |
| Oil Ocean Music Forever | Go to the Sound Test in the Options menu and put in the sounds, 02, 01, 02, 04, and hold Ⓐ and press START. The Oil Ocean music will now be playing constantly, no matter what stage. |
| Pseudo Super Sonic | In Oil Ocean Zone, if you manage to take a hit and end up landing in one of those green-and-gold checkered cannons, you'll fall right out, but you'll be moving at twice your normal speed as well as jumping twice your normal height (with twice as much gravity). A good place for doing this would be in Oil Ocean Zone, Act 2, near the first set of pop-tops and cannons. Just jump into the semi-hidden bed of spikes on the right and land in the cannon. Note: Moving at twice normal velocity can often get you stuck in a wall. Also, this wears off if you Super Spin Dash or Spin Dash. It also only lasts for that act. |
| Super Tails | Normally, when you turn into Super Sonic you lose Tails behind you all the time. Well, after you put in the debug cheat and have started a level (preferably Emerald Hill), turn yourself into a box and place it somewhere on the floor while you are Super Sonic. It should be a switch places box. Hit it and Tails has a permanent invincible circle around him. He stays like this through the whole level. |
| Unlimited Speed Shoes in 2-Player vs. Mode | In 2-Player vs. mode, get speed shoes and die (while you still have them) and you get to keep your speed shoes until the end of the level. |

## CODES

| CODE | EFFECT |
|---|---|
| 17 | Play Invincibility Music |
| 65 | Plays a Shifting Sound |
| 09 | Plays Casino Night Zone 1-Player Music |
| 19 | Plays Sonic 2 Theme |

## SONIC THE HEDGEHOG 3 (Wii)

### UNLOCKABLES

| UNLOCKABLE | HOW TO UNLOCK |
|---|---|
| All 7 Chaos Emeralds and Super Sonic | To get all 7 Chaos Emeralds without having to complete their Special Stages, first enter the Level Select and Sound Test codes. Go to the Sound Test and play the following tunes in order: 02, 04, 05, 06. You will hear an emerald sound if the code is entered correctly. To get Super Sonic after entering the previous code, just select any level from the level select and start it. Once you acquire 50 Rings, do a double-jump to become Super Sonic. |
| Control Tails in a 1-Player Game | Start a 1-player game with Sonic and Tails as the characters. With controller 2, you can take control of Tails while also using Sonic. |
| Hidden Special Stage | On the Level Select menu, play sounds 01, 03, 05, 07. Highlight Special Stage 2 and press Ⓐ+START. |
| Infinite Lives | Get up to Launch Base Zone. Sound any of the alarms, so that the Kamikaze birds come after you. Charge up a Super Sonic Dash in between the alarm, but do not let go of the button. The birds continually crash into you. After about 30 seconds, you have gained enough points to get an extra life. Continue the process for as many lives as you want. |

| Level Select (When Locked-On to Sonic and Knuckles) | Start a game and go to Angel Island Zone, Act 1. Go to one of the swings that you hang from and grab on. While Sonic is swinging, press ⬆, ⬆, ⬆, ⬆, ⬆, ⬆, ⬆, ⬆, ⬆. You will hear a ring if you entered the code correctly. Pause the game and press Ⓐ to take you back to the title screen. Press ⬆, ⬆ to find the newly unlocked Sound Test menu. Enter it, where you can play all of the sounds/music in the game and warp to any level. |
| --- | --- |
| Turn into Super Sonic | After entering the Level Select and Debug code, you can use the debug to turn yourself into Super Sonic without getting all of the Chaos Emeralds. With the debug on, go into any level and press Ⓐ to turn yourself into a ring. Then press Ⓐ to turn yourself into a monitor. Now, press ⬆ to duplicate the monitor, and then Ⓑ again to change back into Sonic. Jump on the monitor and you will become Super Sonic. |
| Level Select | When the "SEGA" screen fades, quickly press ⬆, ⬆, ⬆, ⬆, ⬆, ⬆, ⬆, ⬆. If you have done this right, you should be able to scroll down to "Sound Test" below "Competition." |
| Sonic and Knuckles Mini-Boss Music | Get to the end of Act 1 of Hydrocity Zone (Zone 2). When facing the mini-boss, keep yourself underwater until the water warning music plays. Then jump out of the water. The game should now be playing the mini-boss music from Sonic and Knuckles, which wasn't out at the time (the music was evidently included in *Sonic 3* to make the backward compatibility feature easier). |
| Walk Thru Walls | In the Icecap Zone, Act 1, when you come to a wall that only Knuckles can bust through, hold ⬆ until Sonic or Tails looks down, and the screen pans all the way down. Then press ⬆ and jump at the same time. The screen starts to rotate. Walk in the direction of the wall and you will walk right through it. |
| 100,000 Points | Beat a stage at with your time at exactly 9:59. |
| Frame by Frame | When playing a level after enabling the Level Select cheat, pause the game, then press ⬆ to advance the game by one frame. |
| Slow Motion Mode | When playing any level that you have accessed using the Cheat menu, pause the game and hold Ⓑ. While Ⓑ is held down, the game plays in Slow Motion mode. |

## CODES

| CODE | EFFECT |
| --- | --- |
| Hold Ⓑ and press ⬆ | Your character shows all of his sprite animations |
| Hold Ⓑ and press ⬆ again | Your character stops the sprite show if it is activated |

## SONIC THE HEDGEHOG 4: EPISODE I (PlayStation 3)

### SUPER SONIC

Complete all 7 special stages by collecting the Chaos Emerald at the end. Then enter any level, collect 50 rings, and press the Square button or Triangle button to transform into Super Sonic.

## SONIC THE HEDGEHOG 4: EPISODE I (XBOX 360)

### AVATAR AWARDS

| UNLOCKABLE | HOW TO UNLOCK |
| --- | --- |
| Sonic Costume (Body) | After collecting the 7 Chaos Emeralds, defeat the final boss one more time. |
| Sonic Costume (Head) | Collect all rings during the ending of the final stage. |

## SOULCALIBUR IV (XBOX 360)

### ITEMS/WEAPONS

| UNLOCKABLE | HOW TO UNLOCK |
| --- | --- |
| Advanced Equipment | Achieve 20 achievements. |
| All Weapons for a Character | Clear Story mode with that character. |
| Animal Head Equipment | Achieve 25 achievements. |
| Basic Equipment | Achieve 5 achievements. |

| Intermediate Equipment | Achieve 15 achievements. |
| Leviathan and Voodoo Equipment | Achieve 30 achievements. |
| More Equipment | Achieve 10 achievements. |

## CHARACTERS

| UNLOCKABLE | HOW TO UNLOCK |
| --- | --- |
| Algol | Beat Story mode with a character that faces him as the last boss (Mitsurugi, Taki, etc.). |
| Amy | Purchase her in the Character Creation for 4,000 gold. |
| Angol Fear | Defeat her in Story mode. |
| Ashlotte | Defeat her in Story mode. |
| Cervantes | Purchase him in the Character Creation for 4,000 gold. |
| Hong Yun-seong | Purchase him in the Character Creation for 4,000 gold. |
| Kamikirimusi | Defeat her in Story mode. |
| Lizardman | Buy for 4,000 gold. |
| Rock | Purchase him in the Character Creation for 4,000 gold. |
| Scheherazade | Defeat her in Story mode. |
| Seong Mi Na | Highlight and purchase for 4,000 gold. |
| Setsuka | Highlight and purchase for 4,000 gold. |
| Shura | Defeat her in Story mode. |
| Sophitia | Purchase her in the Create a Soul mode for 4,000 Gold. |
| Talim | Buy her for 4,000 gold in Character Creation mode. |
| The Apprentice | Beat Arcade mode with Yoda. |
| Yoshimitsu | Highlight and purchase for 4000 gold. |
| Zasalamel | Buy him for 4,000 gold in Character Creation mode. |

## TOWER OF LOST SOULS HIDDEN ITEMS (ASCENDING)

| UNLOCKABLE | HOW TO UNLOCK |
| --- | --- |
| 01f Soldier's Hat | Clear stage while taking no damage. |
| 02f Warrior Trousers | Clear stage with no ring outs from either side. |
| 03f Pauldron | Switch with ally more than 2 times. |
| 04f Warlord's Belt | Perform 3 attack throws. |
| 05f Clergy Clothes | Defeat an enemy with a ring out. |
| 06f Wonder Jacket | Throw an opponent. |
| 07f Warrior Trousers | Clear the stage without missing any attacks. |
| 08f Armor Ring: Ice Mirror | Switch characters twice. |
| 09f Scarlett Blossoms | Guard against the opponent's attack 3 times in a row. |
| 10f Silver Boots | Guard the opponent's attack 10 times in a row. |
| 11f Grim Horn | Defeat all enemies with a critical finish. |
| 12f Magus Cloth | Defeat all enemies with ring outs. |
| 13f Pegasus Sallet | Destroy all the walls. |
| 14f Stage: Phantom Pavilion Seesaw | Perform guard impact more than 3 times. |
| 15f Submissions Belt | Clear the stage using only the A and G buttons. |
| 16f Warlord's Belt | Clear the stage with 0 time remaining. |
| 17f Arm Bandages | Execute a 5+ combo. |
| 18f Kouchu Kabuto | Stand on all corners of the stage. |
| 19f Longhua Qippo | Switch with ally more than 5 times. |
| 20f Life Gem: Sun | Clear the stage with a critical finish. |
| 21f Longhua Qippo | Voluntarily ring yourself out. |

| | |
|---|---|
| 22f Honor Boots | Perform more than 4 counter hits. |
| 23F Frilled Skirt | Guard more than 3 times in a row. |
| 24f Protect Gem: Cardinal Directions | Perform a combo with more than 240 damage. |
| 25f Zhuque Changpao | Throw more than 5 times. |
| 26f Warthog Cuirass | Execute a 10+ combo. |
| 27f Iron Gauntlets | Clear the stage with no damage taken. |
| 28F Aculeus Suit | Opponent guards a guard break attack at least twice. |
| 29f Menghu Boots | Switch with ally 5+ times. |
| 30f Spirit Gem: Noniple Heads | Clear stage without guarding. |
| 31f Longming Qippo | Perform 5+ Just Inputs. |
| 32f Vane Mask | Perform a low throw. |
| 33f Battle Dress | Perform 3 attack throws. |
| 34f Power Gem: Warrior Princess | Perform guard impact 3+ times. |
| 35f Warthog Pauldrons | Clear without switching. |
| 36f Parlor Blouse | Clear stage with 0 time remaining. |
| 37f Siren's Helm | Defeat all enemies with critical finishes. |
| 38f Gorgon Fauld | Defeat all enemies with ring out. |
| 39f Kingfisher Greaves | Clear the stage without changing position. |
| 40f Deer Head | Execute a 5+ combo. |
| 41f Minotaur | Perform 5+ Just Inputs. |
| 42f Demonic Gloves | Clear the stage without letting opponents invoke a skill. |
| 43f Repel Gem: Iron Shell | Perform an over the back throw. |
| 44f War Cloak | No ring outs either side. |
| 45f Tiger Lily Kabuto | Defeat enemies without using any skills. |
| 46f Butterfly Salet | Defeat enemies without using any skills. |
| 47f Succubus Boots | Throw 5 times. |
| 48f Life Dem: Jade | Clear stage with a character equipped with the "invisible" skill. |
| 49f Horns of Calamity | Clear stage with no attacks missing. |
| 50f Tiger Lily Breastplates | Execute a 10+ combo. |
| 51f Tiger Lily Fauld | Perform more than 4 counter hits. |
| 52f Feathered Wings | Clear stage with a critical finish. |
| 53f Blade Ring: Demon Lord | Defeat all enemies with a ring out. |
| 54f Leviathan Pauldron | Destroy all the walls. |
| 55f Priestess Kimono | Perform 3 attack throws. |
| 56f Leviathan Burgonet | Perform a combo with more than 240 damage. |
| 57f Voodoo Armlets | Voluntarily perform a ring out. |
| 58f Tiger Pauldrons | Defeat all enemies without any skills equipped. |
| 59f Voodoo Greaves | Guard an enemy's attack 10 times in a row. |
| 60f Voodoo Breastplate | Clear the stage without switching character. |

## TOWER OF LOST SOULS REWARD ITEMS (DESCENDING)

| UNLOCKABLE | HOW TO UNLOCK |
|---|---|
| B05 | Dark Knight's Cloak |
| B10 | Blade Ring: Raging Thunder |
| B15 | Lapin Chapeau |
| B20 | Repel Gem: Fox Demon |
| B25 | Succubus Gauntlets |
| B30 | Demonic Armor |

| B35 | Demonic Pauldrons |
|-----|-------------------|
| B40 | Voodoo Crown |

## CREATE-A-SOUL ITEMS/WEAPONS

| UNLOCKABLE | HOW TO UNLOCK |
|------------|---------------|
| Advanced Equipment | Achieve 20 achievements. |
| All Weapons for a Character | Clear Story mode with that Character. |
| Animal Head Equipment | Achieve 25 achievements. |
| Basic Equipment | Achieve 5 achievements. |
| Intermediate Equipment | Achieve 15 achievements. |
| Leviathan and Voodoo Equipment | Achieve 30 achievements. |
| More Equipment | Achieve 10 achievements. |

## EASTER EGGS

| UNLOCKABLE | HOW TO UNLOCK |
|------------|---------------|
| Metallic Characters | At the Character Select screen, hold down ⑪ and choose a character by pressing ⓐ. When the battle begins, your character is metallic. |

## SPACE MARINE (XBOX 360)

### ACHIEVEMENT

| UNLOCKABLE | HOW TO UNLOCK |
|------------|---------------|
| Angel of Death (20) | Kill 500 enemies using Ranged weapons. |
| Armored in Glory (15) | Complete 10 armor challenges. |
| Battle Brother (10) | Get a Multiplayer character to Lvl 10. |
| Blast Radius (5) | Multi-kill -- 5 enemies with 1 Frag grenade. |
| Brute Force...Unleashed (5) | Complete a Chapter of the single-player game using only the Vengeance Launcher and Power Axe. |
| Burn Them All (5) | Complete a Chapter of the single-player campaign using only Plasma weapons. |
| But I Am Finished With You (10) | Kill Warboss Grimskull once and for all. |
| Captain (20) | Get a Multiplayer character to Lvl 30. |
| Chain of Death (10) | Multi-kill -- Detonate a chain of 5 consecutive Vengeance Launcher rounds, killing 10 enemies. |
| Chapter Master (30) | Get a Multiplayer character to Lvl 40. |
| Command Squad (10) | Reunite with your Space Marine brothers. |
| Death from Above (15) | Kill 25 enemies with Ground Pound. |
| Defender (10) | Kill 25 opponents who are capturing your Control Point in Seize Ground. |
| Devastation! (25) | Have 10 times more kills than deaths in a single game of Annihilation. |
| Die, Heretics (20) | Kill 50 Chaos Space Marines. |
| Down to Earth (30) | Kill 50 Assault Marines/Raptors in mid-air. |
| Feel My Wrath (30) | Kill 250 enemies using Melee Fury attacks. |
| Finesse and Fury (5) | Complete a Chapter of the single-player game using only Stalker-Pattern Bolter and Chainsword. |
| Firepower (10) | Kill 250 enemies using Exotic weapons. |
| Glorious Slaughter (10) | Kill 75 enemies using Executions. |
| Hammer of the Imperium (10) | Use the Invictus to destroy the Orbital Spire. |
| Here, At the End of All Things (20) | Kill Daemon Prince Nemeroth. |

| | |
|---|---|
| **Into the Breach (10)** | Fight your way to the crashed Rok. |
| **Jack of All Trades (25)** | Play 10 Multiplayer games using each class. |
| **Keeper of the Armory (30)** | Complete all the weapon challenges. |
| **Lexicanum (10)** | Collect 10 Servo Skulls. |
| **Librarian of Macragge (75)** | Collect all Servo Skulls. |
| **Master Crafted (10)** | Fully customize a Space Marine and a Chaos Space Marine character. |
| **Master of Arms (20)** | Complete 5 weapon challenges. |
| **Master of Sword and Gun (5)** | Complete a Chapter of the single-player campaign using only the Bolt Pistol and Chainsword. |
| **Master of the Clean Kill (30)** | Get 250 Headshots. |
| **Nob Down (20)** | Win 10 struggles against the Ork Nob. |
| **None Can Stand Before You (125)** | Complete the entire game on Hard difficulty. |
| **Not So Tough (20)** | Kill 10 'Ard Boyz. |
| **Precision Killer (5)** | Multi-kill -- 2 enemies with 1 Stalker-Pattern bolter shot. |
| **Put Them Down (10)** | Get 100 Headshots. |
| **Shapeshifter (10)** | Play each class in Multiplayer. |
| **Shock & Awe (20)** | Kill 150 enemies using the Charge attack. |
| **Silence the Cannon (10)** | Destroy the Orbital Gun. |
| **Success is Measured in Blood (20)** | Kill 500 enemies using Melee weapons. |
| **The Bigger They Are... (20)** | Kill 25 Ork Nobs. |
| **The Emperor Protects (25)** | Complete Part 1 of the game on Hard difficulty in a single session without dying or restarting. |
| **The Emperor's Marksman (20)** | Kill 10 enemies in a row in a single Ranged Fury activation. |
| **The Might of the Righteous (5)** | Kill 100 enemies. |
| **True Son of the Emperor (75)** | Kill 40,000 enemies in the game (all game modes combined). |
| **Veteran (15)** | Get a Multiplayer character to Lvl 20. |
| **Visible, Violent Death (30)** | Kill 2500 enemies. |
| **Warrior of Darkness 10 and Light (15)** | Play 10 Multiplayer games as Space Marine and Multiplayer games as Chaos Marine. |
| **We Take Our Chances (10)** | Fire the Psychic Scourge. |
| **You Must Carry It (5)** | Retrieve the Power Source. |

## SPEED RACER (Wii)

### CODES

Enter the following codes in the "Enter Code" section of the "Options" menu. Enter the codes again to disable them.

| EFFECT | CODE |
|---|---|
| **Aggressive Opponents** | ⊕⬆⊕⬆⊕⬆⊕⬆ |
| **Granite Car** | ⑬⬆⊖⊕①⬆⊕ |
| **Helium** | ⊖⬆⊖②⊖⬆⊖ |
| **Invulnerability** | Ⓐ⬅Ⓑ⬆⬆⬆⬆ |
| **Monster Truck** | ⑬⬆⊖②⬆⬆⬆ |
| **Moon Gravity** | ⬆⊕⬆⬅⊖⬆⊖ |
| **Overkill** | Ⓐ⊖⊕⬆⬆⊕① |
| **Pacifist Opponents (other racers don't attack you)** | ⬆⬆⬆⬅⬆⬆⬆ |

| Psychedelic | ⬅,Ⓐ,⬅,⬆,Ⓑ,⬆,⊖ |
| Tiny Opponents | Ⓑ,Ⓐ,⬅,⬆,⊖,⬆,⊖ |
| Unlimited Boost | Ⓑ,Ⓐ,⬆,⬆,Ⓑ,Ⓐ,⬆ |
| Unlock the Last 3 Cars | ①,②,①,②,Ⓑ,Ⓐ,⊕ |

## UNLOCKABLES

Complete the championships with a ranking of 3rd or higher to unlock the corresponding racer.

| UNLOCKABLE | HOW TO UNLOCK |
|---|---|
| Booster Mbube | Complete Class 2, Championship 6. |
| Colonel Colon | Complete Class 3, Championship 4. |
| Delila | Complete Class 3, Championship 3. |
| Denise Mobile | Complete Class 3, Championship 6. |
| Esther "Rev" Reddy | Complete Class 3, Championship 7. |
| Gothorm Danneskjblo | Complete Class 3, Championship 2. |
| Grey Ghost | Complete Class 1, Championship 3. |
| Kellie "Gearbox" Kalinkov | Complete Class 2, Championship 4. |
| Mariana Zanja | Complete Class 3, Championship 5. |
| Nitro Venderhoss | Complete Class 2, Championship 5. |
| Pitter Pat | Complete Class 3, Championship 1. |
| Prince Kabala | Complete Class 2, Championship 3. |
| Rosey Blaze | Complete Class 1, Championship 1. |
| Snake Oiler | Complete Class 1, Championship 2. |
| Sonic "Boom Boom" Renaldi | Complete Class 2, Championship 2. |
| Taejo Togokahn | Complete Class 2, Championship 1. |

## SPIDER-MAN: EDGE OF TIME (XBOX 360)

### ACHIEVEMENT

| UNLOCKABLE | HOW TO UNLOCK |
|---|---|
| Airborne Assailer (25) | Perform 3 of each Air Attack on enemies |
| Alchemaxed Out! (50) | Buy all Combat Upgrades |
| Ambitious Arachnid Acquirer (10) | Obtain 1/4 of the Golden Spiders |
| Anti-Venom Vanquisher (10) | Defeated Anti-Venom on any difficulty level |
| Astounding Archives Achiever (10) | Gained access to the Restricted Archives Computer |
| Awesome Atomic Acquirer (10) | Collected all three Atomic Fuses |
| Boss Of Bosses (25) | Defeated the CEO on any difficulty level |
| Bot Hotshot (10) | Erased the Prototype Combat Robot from existence |
| Collector Detector (50) | Collect 2000 Orb Fragments |
| Complete Data Diviner (10) | Analyzed all Data Modules |
| Consumate Completist (50) | Web of Challenges - Obtain all Gold Medals |
| Dangerous Destination Decider (10) | Floor 66 Reached |
| Daringly Determined Dodger (10) | Evaded 100 attacks with Hyper-Sense |
| Defeated Atrocity on any difficulty level | Defeated Atrocity on any difficulty level |
| Determined Do-gooder (25) | Complete Act 2 on any difficulty level |
| Dread Destiny Determiner (10) | Foreseen the death of Spider-Man |
| Excellent Emblem Enthusiast (25) | Collect 1000 Orb Fragments |

| | |
|---|---|
| Fabulous Feline Fury (10) | Defeated Black Cat on any difficulty level |
| Fantastic Five Hundred (10) | Collect 500 Orb Fragments |
| Fearless Front-Facer (25) | Complete all levels on Normal |
| Furious Fist Fighter (10) | Execute a 50-hit combo |
| Ghost With The Most (10) | Avoided 100 attacks with Accelerated Decoy |
| Gold Standard (50) | Buy all Character Upgrades |
| Gorgeous Gold Grabber (10) | Web of Challenges - Obtain all Gold Medals for a Chapter |
| Hammer Slammer (25) | Damage enemies with Roundhouse Spin and Web Hammer 10 times each |
| Hundred Hit Hero (25) | Execute a 100-hit combo |
| Incinerator Rex! (10) | Brought the Incinerator to Maximum Power |
| Infinite Slugger (50) | Execute a 200-hit combo |
| Intrepid Adventurer (50) | Complete Act 3 on any difficulty level |
| Jack Of All Attacks (25) | Perform 3 of each type of Grab Attacks on enemies |
| Jackpot, Tiger! (10) | Saved Mary Jane |
| Larrupin' Locksmith (10) | Teleported back to Alchemax with the Key |
| Master of All You Survey (50) | Complete all levels on Hard |
| Mighty Marvel Booster (10) | Completed a Freefall section by boosting the entire time |
| Mighty Medal Master (25) | Web of Challenges - Obtain all Gold Medals for an Act |
| Mighty Meltdown Misser (10) | Stopped the future from becoming a radioactive wasteland |
| Mighty Monster Master (10) | Retrieved all three DNA Samples from the knocked-out Atrocity |
| Read All About It! (25) | Obtained all Newspapers |
| Restricted Room Rogue (10) | Gained access to the Future Restricted Area |
| Sizzling Century Mark (10) | Defeat 100 enemies |
| Spider Slugger Supreme (25) | Defeat 500 enemies |
| Spider Snagger Supreme (50) | Obtain all Golden Spiders |
| Super Trooper (10) | Complete Act 1 on any difficulty level |
| Super-Suited Swinger (25) | Obtain all Alternate Suits |
| Superb Spider Searcher (25) | Obtain 1/2 of the Golden Spiders |
| Survivor Supreme (10) | Complete Session 3 or later without dying |
| That's The Parker Luck, Chuck (10) | Spider-Man was down and out |

## CODE

At the main menu, use the D-pad to enter the code. Select the new costume from the bonus gallery.

| UNLOCKABLE | CODE |
|---|---|
| Big Time Costume is unlocked | ⬦⬦♀♀⬦⬦♀♀⬦ |

## CODE

Select a saved game, then enter this code. Select the costume at the bonus gallery.

| UNLOCKABLE | CODE |
|---|---|
| Unlock Future Foundation Costume | ⬦♀⬦♀♀⬦⬦⬦ |

## SPIDER-MAN: EDGE OF TIME (Wii)

### CODE

Select a save game and then enter the code at the main menu using the D-pad.

| UNLOCKABLE | CODE |
| --- | --- |
| Big Time Costume | right down down up left down down right |

### CODE

Start a new game with Spider-Man: Shattered Dimension data, the find new outfits in the "Alternate Suits Menu."

| UNLOCKABLE | CODE |
| --- | --- |
| 8 Spiderman Outfits | Spider-Man: Shattered Dimension data |

## SPIDER-MAN: FRIEND OR FOE (XBOX 360)

### CODES

Venom and new Green Goblin (from the movie) can be unlocked by entering the following codes using the d-pad when standing in the Helicarrier in between levels. You hear a tone if you entered the code correctly, and they are then be selectable from the sidekick select console.

| CODE | EFFECT |
| --- | --- |
| ↑, ↑, ↓, ↓, ←, → | Gain 5,000 upgrade points |
| ←, ↓, →, →, ↓, ← | New Green Goblin |
| →, ←, →, ↓, ↓, ↑ | Venom |

## SPIDER-MAN: FRIEND OR FOE (Wii)

### CODES

| CODE | EFFECT |
| --- | --- |
| 5,000 Tech Tokens, One Time Only | ⇧, ⇧, ⇧, ⇧, ⇧, ⇧ |
| Unlock New Goblin | ⇧, ⇧, ⇦, ⇦, ⇦, ⇦ |
| Unlock Sandman | ⇩, ⇩, ⇩, ⇨, ⇨, ⇨ |
| Unlock Venom | ⇧, ⇧, ⇦, ⇧, ⇧, ⇧ |

## SPIDER-MAN 2 (PSP)

Go to Options, Special, and Cheats on the Main menu, and then type in the following passwords.

| UNLOCKABLE | PASSWORD |
| --- | --- |
| All Levels Unlocked | WARPULON |
| All Moves Purchased | MYHERO |
| All Movies Unlocked | POPPYCORN |
| Enemies Have Big Heads and Feet | BAHLOONIE |
| Infinite Health | NERGETS |
| Infinite Webbing | FILLMEUP |
| Spidey Has Big Head and Feet | HEAVYHEAD |
| Tiny Spider-Man | SPIDEYMAN |
| Unlock All Production Art | SHUTT |
| Unlock Storyboard Viewer | FRZFRAME |

## SPIDER-MAN 3 (Wii)

### UNLOCKABLES

| UNLOCKABLE | HOW TO UNLOCK |
| --- | --- |
| Collect all 50 Spider Emblems | Unlock black suit Spider-man after you destroy the suit |

## SPLATTERHOUSE (Wii)

### UNLOCKABLES

| UNLOCKABLE | HOW TO UNLOCK |
| --- | --- |
| Hard Mode | At the title screen, hold SELECT until "HARD" appears on the screen |

| Sound Test | First enter the code to access the Stage Select option. When the screen comes up and asks you to select what stage you want to start on, press and hold the select button. After a second or two, the Stage Select option becomes a Sound Test menu, allowing you to listen to various "songs" and sound effects. Hold select again to change it back to the Stage Select menu. |
| --- | --- |
| Stage Select | When the prologue starts up and there's a house in the rain, press SELECT, SELECT, SELECT, hold ⬇ and then press ① or ②. It brings up the option to select a level. |

## SPLATTERHOUSE (Xbox 360)

### UNLOCKABLE CLASSIC SPLATTERHOUSE GAMES

| UNLOCKABLE | HOW TO UNLOCK |
| --- | --- |
| Splatterhouse | Finish Phase 2: "The Doll That Bled" |
| Splatterhouse 2 | Finish Phase 4: "The Meat Factory" |
| Splatterhouse 3 | Finish Phase 8: "Reflections in Blood" |

## SPLATTERHOUSE (PS3)

### UNLOCKABLES

| UNLOCKABLE | HOW TO UNLOCK |
| --- | --- |
| Splatterhouse | Finish Phase 2: "The Doll That Bled" |
| Splatterhouse 2 | Finish Phase 4: "The Meat Factory" |
| Splatterhouse 3 | Finish Phase 8: "Reflections in Blood" |
| Unlock PS3 Exclusive Mask | Complete the Splatterhouse Story mode |

## SPONGEBOB SQUAREPANTS: CREATURE FROM THE KRUSTY KRAB (Wii)

### PASSWORDS

| PASSWORD | EFFECT |
| --- | --- |
| ROCFISH | 30,000 Z-Coins |
| HOVER | Alternate Plankton hovercraft |
| ROBOT | Astronaut suit for Plankton in Revenge of the Giant Plankton |
| LASER | Extra laser color in Revenge of the Giant Plankton level |
| ROCKET | Extra rocket for Patrick in Hypnotic Highway level |
| PILOT | Get Aviator SpongeBob costume |
| BRAIN | Get Exposed-Brain SpongeBob costume |
| INVENT | Get Inventor Plankton costume |
| SPIN | Get Patrick's different POW! effect |
| BUNRUN | Get Patrick's purple rocket |
| SAFARI | Get Safari Patrick costume |
| BONES | Get Skeleton Patrick costume |
| KRABBY | Get Skeleton SpongeBob costume |
| FLAMES | Get SpongeBob's flame effect color |
| HYPCAR | Get SpongeBob's Hypnotic car skin |
| DUCKGUN | Get SpongeBob's Squeaky Duck Gun |
| GASSY | Infinite Fuel (in Flying levels) |
| VIGOR | Infinite Health (in platforming levels) |
| SCOOTLES | Obtain all sleepy seeds |
| TISSUE | Obtain Sleepy Seed Detector |
| PIRATE | Play as Pirate Patrick in Rooftop Rumble level |
| SPONGE | Play as Punk SpongeBob in Diesel Dreaming level |
| PANTS | Play as SpongeBob Plankton in Super-Size Patty level |
| HOTROD | Unlock a bonus vehicle in the Diesel Dreaming level |
| PORKPIE | Unlock all bonus games |

| GUDGEON | Unlock all levels |
| SPACE | Unlock bonus ship in the Rocket Rodeo level |
| PATRICK | Unlock tuxedo for Patrick in Starfishman to the Rescue |

## SPYBORGS (Wii)

### UNLOCKABLES

| UNLOCKABLE | HOW TO UNLOCK |
| --- | --- |
| Infinite Arena | Complete the game on any difficulty level. |

## SSX BLUR (Wii)

In the Options menu, select Cheat to enter this code.

| UNLOCKABLE | CODE |
| --- | --- |
| All Characters Unlocked | NoHolds |

## STAR OCEAN: THE LAST HOPE INTERNATIONAL (PlayStation 3)

### UNLOCKABLES

| UNLOCKABLE | HOW TO UNLOCK |
| --- | --- |
| Chaos difficulty | Beat the game on Universe Mode. |
| Universe difficulty | Beat the game on Galaxy Mode. |
| Additional Battle Voices, Set 1 | Obtain 30% of the character's Battle Trophies. |
| Additional Battle Voices, Set 2 | Obtain 75% of the character's Battle Trophies. |
| Level cap increase | Obtain 50% of the character's Battle Trophies. |
| More CP | Obtain 100% of the character's Battle Trophies. |

## STAR SOLDIER (Wii)

### UNLOCKABLES

| UNLOCKABLE | HOW TO UNLOCK |
| --- | --- |
| Powered Up Ship | At the title screen, press SELECT 10 times on controller 1. Then, hold ⬇+⬇ on controller 2. Then, hold ⬇+⬇+Ⓐ+Ⓑ on controller 1, finally press START, START on controller 1. |

## STAR TREK: LEGACY (XBOX 360)

| UNLOCKABLE | HOW TO UNLOCK |
| --- | --- |
| Unlock the U.S.S. Legacy | To unlock the secret ship (and receive the achievement), beat the game once on any difficulty, then load your game. When you do, you should be on the ship buying screen right before the final mission. From there; sell and/or buy ships to make sure you have 3 Sovereign-class ships. The final ship you buy will be the U.S.S. Legacy. |

## STAR WARS BATTLEFRONT II (PSP)

Pause the game and enter this code.

| UNLOCKABLE | CODE |
| --- | --- |
| Invincibility | ⬆, ⬆, ⬆, ⬅, ⬇, ⬇, ⬇, ⬅, ⬆, ⬆, ⬆, ⬅, ➡ |

## STAR WARS: THE CLONE WARS—REPUBLIC HEROES (XBOX 360)

### ULTIMATE LIGHTSABER

| EFFECT | CODE |
| --- | --- |
| Unlock Ultimate Lightsaber | ➡,⬇,⬇,◇,⬅,◇,◇,◇,⬇ |

## STAR WARS: THE CLONE WARS—REPUBLIC HEROES (Wii)

### CONCEPT ART

| UNLOCKABLE | HOW TO UNLOCK |
| --- | --- |
| Character Costumes | Beat 27 Challenges. |
| Early Work | Beat nine Challenges. |

| Evolution of the EG-5 Jedi Hunter Droid | Beat 40 Challenges. |
|---|---|
| Level Design | Beat 18 Challenges. |

## COSTUMES

| UNLOCKABLE | HOW TO UNLOCK |
|---|---|
| Ahsoka Tano: Ilum Battle Gear | Beat 32 Challenges. |
| Ahsoka Tano: Padawan Robes | Beat Challenge Mode as Ahsoka. |
| Ahsoka Tano: Training Gear | Beat Battle Mode as Ahsoka. |

| UNLOCKABLE | HOW TO UNLOCK |
|---|---|
| Anakin Skywalker: ARC Battle Gear | Beat 32 Challenges. |
| Anakin Skywalker: Jedi Knight Robes | Beat Challenge Mode as Anakin. |
| Anakin Skywalker: Tatooine Battle Gear | Beat Battle Mode as Anakin. |
| Asajj Ventress: Acolyte Robes | Beat Challenge Mode as Ventress. |
| Asajj Ventress: Assassin Battle Gear | Beat Battle Mode as Ventress. |
| Asajj Ventress: Gladiatorial Outfit | Beat 36 Challenges. |
| Count Dooku: Confederacy Battle Gear | Beat Battle Mode as Dooku. |
| Count Dooku: Separatist Uniform | Beat 36 Challenges. |
| Count Dooku: Sith Robes | Beat Challenge Mode as Dooku. |
| EG-1 Jedi Hunter Droid | Beat 36 Challenges. |
| EG-3 Jedi Hunter Droid | Beat Battle Mode as EG-5 Droid. |
| EG-4 Jedi Hunter Droid | Beat Challenge Mode as EG-5 Droid. |
| General Grievous: Kaleesh Markings | Beat 36 Challenges. |
| General Grievous: Sith Markings | Beat Challenge Mode as Grievous. |
| General Grievous: Supreme General Battle Gear | Beat Battle Mode as Grievous. |
| Kit Fisto: High General Robes | Beat Battle Mode as Kit. |
| Kit Fisto: Jedi Council Robes | Beat Challenge Mode as Kit. |
| Kit Fisto: Jedi Taskforce Robes | Beat 40 Challenges. |
| Mace Windu: Jedi Council Robes | Beat Challenge Mode as Mace. |
| Mace Windu: Jedi Master Robes | Beat Battle Mode as Mace. |
| Mace Windu: Jedi Taskforce Robes | Beat 40 Challenges. |
| Obi-Wan Kenobi: ARC Battle Gear | Beat 32 Challenges. |
| Obi-Wan Kenobi: Kashyyyk Battle Gear | Beat Challenge Mode as Obi-Wan. |
| Obi-Wan Kenobi: Tatooine Battle Gear | Beat Battle Mode as Obi-Wan. |
| Plo Koon: Jedi Council Robes | Beat Challenge Mode as Plo. |
| Plo Koon: Jedi Master Robes | Beat Battle Mode as Plo. |
| Plo Koon: Kel Dorian Robes | Beat 40 Challenges. |

## MISCELLANEOUS

| UNLOCKABLE | HOW TO UNLOCK |
|---|---|
| Ahsoka Tano for Challenge | Clear the Campaign |
| Count Dooku for Challenge | Clear the Campaign |
| Credits | Clear Campaign |
| EG-5 Jedi Hunter Droid for Challenge | Clear the Campaign |
| General Grievous for Challenge | Clear the Campaign |
| Kit Fisto for Challenge | Unlock Kit Fisto. |
| Mace Windu for Challenge | Unlock Mace Windu. |
| Movies | Clear the Campaign. |
| Obi-Wan Kenobi for Challenge | Clear the Campaign. |
| Plo Koon for Challenge | Unlock Plo Koon. |

**CODES & CHEATS**

## SECRET CHARACTERS

| UNLOCKABLE | HOW TO UNLOCK |
|---|---|
| Count Dooku | Clear the Campaign. |
| EG-5 Jedi Hunter Droid | Clear the Campaign. |
| General Grievous | Clear the Campaign. |
| Kit Fisto | Beat nine Challenges. |
| Mace Windu | Beat 18 Challenges. |
| Plo Koon | Beat 27 Challenges. |

## STAGES

| UNLOCKABLE | HOW TO UNLOCK |
|---|---|
| Mustafar | Beat 32 Challenges |
| Raxus Prime | Beat 13 Challenges. |
| Sarlacc Pit | Beat 22 Challenges. |
| Separatist Droid Factory | Beat 4 Challenges. |
| Separatist Droid Factory | Beat 4 Challenges. |
| Separatist Listening Post | Clear the Campaign. |
| Tatooine Dune Sea | Clear the Campaign. |
| Teth Castle Ramparts | Clear the Campaign. |
| The Malevolence | Clear the Campaign. |
| The Negotiator | Clear the Campaign. |
| The Tranquility | Clear the Campaign. |

## STAR WARS: THE FORCE UNLEASHED (XBOX 360), (PlayStation 3)

### CODES

Input the following codes at the "Input Code" screen.

| EFFECT | CODE |
|---|---|
| All Databank Entries Unlocked | OSSUS |
| All Force Push Ranks Unlocked | EXARKUN |
| All Saber Throw Ranks Unlocked | ADEGAN |
| All Talents Unlocked | JOCASTA |
| Combo Unlock | RAGNOS |
| Incinerator Trooper | PHOENIX |
| Makes Levels Mirrored | MINDTRICK |
| New Combo | FREEDON |
| New Combo | LUMIYA |
| New Combo | MARAJADE |
| New Combo | MASSASSI |
| New Combo | SAZEN |
| New Combo | YADDLE |
| Proxy Skin Code | PROTOTYPE |
| Shadowtrooper Costume | BLACKHOLE |
| Snowtrooper | SNOWMAN |
| Stormtrooper Commander Costume | TK421BLUE |
| Unlock All Lightsaber Crystals | HURRIKANE |
| Unlock Emperor Costume | MASTERMIND |
| Unlocks All 32 Costumes | SOHNDANN |
| Unlocks All Force Combos | MOLDYCROW |
| Unlocks Bail Organa Costume | VICEROY |
| Unlocks Deadly Saber | LIGHTSABER |

| Unlocks Kashyyyk Trooper Costume | TK421GREEN |
|---|---|
| Unlocks Maximum Force Powers | KATARN |
| Unlocks Maximum Force Repulse Ranks | DATHOMIR |
| Unlocks Scout Trooper Costume | FERRAL |
| Unlocks Sith Master difficulty | SITHSPAWN |
| Unlocks Stormtrooper Costume | TK421WHITE |
| Unlocks the Aerial Ambush Combo | VENTRESS |
| Unlocks the Aerial Assault Combo | EETHKOTH |
| Unlocks the Ceremonial Jedi Robes | DANTOOINE |
| Unlocks the Devastating Lightsaber Impale | BRUTALSTAB |
| Unlocks the Drunken Kota Costume | HARDBOILED |
| Unlocks the Jedi Adventure Robes | HOLOCRON |
| Unlocks the Master Kento Costume "The Apprentice's Father" | WOOKIEE |
| Unlocks the Rahm Kota Costume | MANDALORE |
| Unlocks the Saber Slam Combo | PLOKOON |
| Unlocks the Saber Sling Combo | KITFISTO |
| Unlocks the Sith Slash Combo | DARAGON |
| Unlocks the Sith Stalker Armor | KORRIBAN |

## STAR WARS: THE FORCE UNLEASHED (Wii)

### CODES

From the "Extras" menu inside the Rogue Shadow, select "Cheat Codes" and enter the following codes.

| EFFECT | CODE |
|---|---|
| 1,000,000 Force Points | SPEEDER |
| God Mode | CORTOSIS |
| Max All Force Powers | KATARN |
| Max Combos | COUNTDOOKU |
| Unlimited Force Power | VERGENCE |
| Unlock All Force Powers | TYRANUS |
| Your Lightsaber One Hit Kills All Normal Enemies | LIGHTSABER |

### SKIN CODES

| EFFECT | CODE |
|---|---|
| Aayla Secura | AAYLA |
| Admiral Ackbar | ITSATWAP |
| Anakin Skywalker | CHOSENONE |
| Asajj Ventress | ACOLYTE |
| Chop'aa Notimo | NOTIMO |
| Classic Stormtrooper | TK421 |
| Clone Trooper | LEGION |
| Count Dooku | SERENNO |
| Darth Desolus | PAUAN |
| Darth Maul | ZABRAK |
| Darth Phobos | HIDDENFEAR |
| Darth Vader | SITHLORD |
| Drexl Roosh | DREXLROOSH |
| Emperor Palpatine | PALPATINE |
| Episode IV Luke Skywalker | YELLOWJCKT |
| Episode VI Luke Skywalker | T16WOMPRAT |

NEW!

A
B
C
D
E
F
G
H
I
J
K
L
M
N
O
P
Q
R
**S**
T
U
V
W
X
Y
Z

| Imperial Shadow Guard | INTHEDARK |
| Juno Eclipse | ECLIPSE |
| Kleef | KLEEF |
| Lando Calrissian | SCOUNDREL |
| Mace Windu | JEDIMASTER |
| Mara Jade | MARAJADE |
| Maris Brood | MARISBROOD |
| Navy Commando | STORMTROOP |
| Obi-Wan Kenobi | BENKENOBI |
| PROXY | HOLOGRAM |
| Qui-Gon Jinn | MAVERICK |
| Rahm Kota | MANDALORE |
| Shaak Ti | TOGRUTA |

### EXTRA COSTUMES

| EFFECT | CODE |
| --- | --- |
| Ceremonial Jedi Robes | DANTOOINE |
| Kento Marek's Robes | WOOKIEE |
| Sith Stalker Armor | KORRIBAN |
| Unlocks All Costumes | GRANDMOFF |

## STAR WARS: THE FORCE UNLEASHED (DS)

### CODES

From the main menu select "Extras," then "Unleashed Codes," and then enter the codes.

| EFFECT | CODE |
| --- | --- |
| Uber Lightsaber | lightsaber |
| Rahm Kota's costume | mandalore |
| Sith Robes | holocron |
| Starkiller's Father's Robes | wookiee |

## STAR WARS: THE FORCE UNLEASHED (PSP)

### CODES

From the "Extras" menu inside the Rogue Shadow, select "Cheat Codes" and enter the following codes. Specific skin codes are not necessary after you enter the "Unlock All Costumes" code.

| EFFECT | CODE |
| --- | --- |
| 1,000,000 Force Points | SPEEDER |
| All Combos at Maximum Level | COUNTDOOKU |
| All Force Powers | TYRANUS |
| All Force Powers at Maximum Level | KATARN |
| Amplified Lightsaber Damage | LIGHTSABER |
| Immunity to All Damage | CORTOSIS |
| Unlimited Force Power | VERGENCE |
| Unlock All Costumes | GRANDMOFF |

### SKIN CODES

| EFFECT | CODE |
| --- | --- |
| 501st Legion | LEGION |
| Aayla Secura | AAYLA |
| Admiral Ackbar | ITSATWAP |
| Anakin Skywalker | CHOSENONE |
| Asajj Ventress | ACOLYTE |

| | |
|---|---|
| Ceremonial Jedi Robes | DANTOOINE |
| Chop'aa Notimo | NOTIMO |
| Classic Stormtrooper | TK421 |
| Count Dooku | SERENNO |
| Darth Desolous | PAUAN |
| Darth Maul | ZABRAK |
| Darth Phobos | HIDDENFEAR |
| Darth Vader | SITHLORD |
| Drexl Roosh | DREXLROOSH |
| Emperor Palpatine | PALPATINE |
| General Rahm Kota | MANDALORE |
| Han Solo | NERFHERDER |
| Heavy Trooper | SHOCKTROOP |
| Juno Eclipse | ECLIPSE |
| Kento's Robe | WOOKIEE |
| Kleef | KLEEF |
| Lando Calrissian | SCOUNDREL |
| Luke Skywalker | T16WOMPRAT |
| Mace Windu | JEDIMASTER |
| Mara Jade | MARAJADE |
| Maris Brood | MARISBROOD |
| Navy Commando | STORMTROOP |
| Obi-Wan Kenobi | BENKENOBI |
| PROXY | HOLOGRAM |
| Qui-Gon Jinn | MAVERICK |
| Shaak Ti | TOGRUTA |
| Shadowtrooper | INTHEDARK |
| Sith Robes | HOLOCRON |
| Sith Stalker Armor | KORRIBAN |
| Twi'lek | SECURA |
| Yavin Luke | YELLOWJCKT |

## STAR WARS: THE FORCE UNLEASHED II  (Wii)

### CODES

Enter Story mode and go to the corresponding menu for the code you intend to input. Hold Z until you hear a sound, then press buttons on your Wii Remote:

| EFFECT | CODE |
|---|---|
| Unlocks all costumes (Costume menu) | Hold down Z (until you hear a sound) then press LEFT, RIGHT, C, LEFT, RIGHT, C, UP, DOWN |

### UNLOCKABLE

| UNLOCKABLE | HOW TO UNLOCK |
|---|---|
| Unlimited Force Energy | Upgrade all force powers to max level |
| Unlimited Health | Find all of the holocrons |

## STAR WARS: THE FORCE UNLEASHED II  (XBOX 360)

### CODES

In the "Options" selection of the Pause Game menu, select the "Cheat Codes" option, then enter the following codes.

| EFFECT | CODE |
|---|---|
| Dark Green Lightsaber Crystal (healing) | LIBO |
| Experimental Jedi Armor | NOMI |
| Jedi Mind Trick | YARAEL |
| Jumptrooper Costume | AJP400 |

| | |
|---|---|
| Lightsaber Throw | TRAYA |
| Play as a Neimoidian | GUNRAY |
| Play as Boba Fett | Mandalore |
| Stormtrooper character skin | TK421 |
| Force Repulse | MAREK |
| Dark Apprentice costume | VENTRESS |
| Saber guard outfit | MORGUKAI |
| Sith acolyte costume | HAAZEN |
| General Kota costume | RAHM |
| Rebel trooper costume | REBELSCUM |
| Terror trooper costume | SHADOW |
| Wisdom Lightsaber crystals | SOLARI |

### UNLOCKABLE

| UNLOCKABLE | HOW TO UNLOCK |
|---|---|
| General Kota costume | Achieve Silver medal in "Deadly Path Trial" Challenge |
| Saber guard costume | Achieve Silver medal in "Cloning Spire Trial" Challenge |
| Terror trooper costume | Achieve Silver Medal in "Terror Trial" Challenge |
| Ceremonial Jedi robes | Have a Force Unleashed save file with the Light Side ending unlocked |
| Sith stalker armor | Have a Force Unleashed save file with the Dark Side ending unlocked |
| Sith training gear | Have a Force Unleashed save file in your hard drive |
| Guybrush Threepkiller Costume | On the second level after the casino type rooms, you'll come to a room with a Jabba the Hutt hologram and some golden Guybrush Threepwood statues. Unlock the costume by destroying the three machines in the room. |

## STRANGLEHOLD   (PlayStation 3)

### DIFFICULTIES

| UNLOCKABLE | HOW TO UNLOCK |
|---|---|
| Hard Boiled Difficulty | Complete the game on Casual mode once to unlock this difficulty. |

### EASTER EGGS

| UNLOCKABLE | HOW TO UNLOCK |
|---|---|
| Movie Theater Trailers | In the first chapter in the Hong Kong Marketplace, go into the Ambushed section. When you finish killing everyone, go into the building. Break the door, and follow the corridor until you reach a movie theater. The screen is showing trailers for *Wheelman* and *Blacksite*. |

## STREET FIGHTER 4   (XBOX 360)

### CHARACTERS

| UNLOCKABLE | HOW TO UNLOCK |
|---|---|
| Akuma | After unlocking Sakura, Dan, Cammy, Fei Long, Gen, and Rose, fight him on arcade mode; to do that, get at least 2 perfects and 2 Ultra Finishes. |
| Cammy | End the arcade mode with Crimson Viper. |
| Dan | End the arcade mode with Sakura. |
| Fei Long | End the arcade mode with Abel. |
| Gen | End the arcade mode with Chun-Li. |
| Gouken | After unlocking Akuma, Sakura, Dan, Cammy, Fei Long, Gen, and Rose, fight him on arcade mode; to do that, get at least 2 perfects and 3 Ultra Finishes. |
| Rose | End the arcade mode with M. Bison. |

| Sakura | End the arcade mode with Ryu. |
| Seth | End the game with all the other characters. |

## COLORS

To unlock every color in the game you have to play the Time Trial and Survival modes in order. Don't skip to the challenges where the colors are. Once completed you gain the colors for every fighter on the roster.

| UNLOCKABLE | HOW TO UNLOCK |
| --- | --- |
| Color 10 | Survival Normal 16 |
| Color 3 | Time Attack Normal 1 |
| Color 4 | Survival Normal 1 |
| Color 5 | Time Attack Normal 6 |
| Color 6 | Survival Normal 6 |
| Color 7 | Time Attack Normal 11 |
| Color 8 | Survival Normal 11 |
| Color 9 | Time Attack Normal 16 |

## PERSONAL ACTIONS

| UNLOCKABLE | HOW TO UNLOCK |
| --- | --- |
| Personal Action 2 | Beat Time Attack Normal level 2 |
| Personal Action 3 | Beat Survival Normal level 2 |
| Personal Action 4 | Beat Time Attack Normal level 7 |
| Personal Action 5 | Beat Survival Normal level 7 |
| Personal Action 6 | Beat Time Attack Normal level 12 |
| Personal Action 7 | Beat Survival Normal level 12 |
| Personal Action 8 | Beat Time Attack Normal level 17 |
| Personal Action 9 | Beat Survival Normal level 17 |
| Personal Action 10 | Beat Time Attack Normal level 20 |

## SPECIAL VIDEOS

You must complete arcade mode with the two characters that are in each special video.

| UNLOCKABLE | HOW TO UNLOCK |
| --- | --- |
| Seth Vs. M. Bison video | Beat the game with M. Bison and Seth. |
| The Chun Li Vs. Crimson Viper video | Beat arcade mode with Chun Li and Crimson Viper. |
| The Gouken Vs. Akuma video | Beat Arcade mode with Gouken and Akuma. |
| The Guile Vs. Abel video | Beat arcade mode with Guile and Abel. |
| The Ryu Vs. Ken video | Beat arcade mode with Ryu and Ken. |

## CHARACTER ARTWORK

Complete each character's Trials in Challenge mode to unlock their respective artwork in the gallery option.

## CHARACTER SPECIFIC TITLES

In Challenge mode, each time you beat a challenge you get a character-specific title. Challenges must be played in order.

| UNLOCKABLE | HOW TO UNLOCK |
| --- | --- |
| Amigo | Beat El Fuerte's 1st Hard challenge. |
| Anti ShoRyuKen | Beat Sagat's 1st Hard challenge. |
| Bath Time | Beat E. Honda's 1st Hard challenge. |
| Blonde Arrow | Beat Cammy's 5th Hard challenge. |
| Delta Red | Beat Cammy's 1st Hard challenge. |
| Doofus | Complete Rufus's 3rd Hard challenge. |
| Family Man | Beat Guile's 5th Hard challenge. |

**CODES & CHEATS**

| | |
|---|---|
| Fists of Fire | Beat Ken's 5th Hard challenge. |
| Fists of Wind | Beat Ryu's 5th Hard challenge. |
| Flashy Fighter | Beat Fei Long's 5th Hard challenge. |
| Heavenly Sky | Beat Akuma's 5th Hard challenge. |
| High School Girl | Beat Sakura's 5th Hard challenge. |
| Hitenryu Kung fu | Beat Fei Long's 1st Hard challenge. |
| Hope You're Ready! | Beat Chun Li's 1st Hard challenge |
| I love Candy | Complete Rufus's 2nd Hard challenge. |
| I wish I had a family | Beat Abel's 5th Hard challenge. |
| I'm Number One | Complete Rufus's 5th Hard challenge. |
| I'm Ready For Ya! | Beat Ken's 1st Hard challenge. |
| Invincible Tiger | Beat Sagat's 5th Hard challenge. |
| Jimmy | Beat Blanka's 5th Hard challenge. |
| Jungle Boy | Beat Blanka's 1st Hard challenge. |
| Kung Food | Complete Rufus's 4th Hard Trial. |
| Legs of Legend | Beat Chun Li's 5th Hard challenge. |
| MESSATSU!! | Beat Akuma's 1st Hard challenge. |
| Red Cyclone | Beat Zangief's 5th Hard challenge. |
| Rice For The Win | Beat Sakura's 1st Hard challenge. |
| Righteous Avenger | Beat Guile's 1st Hard challenge. |
| Ruler Of Darkness | Beat M. Bison's 5th Hard challenge. |
| Samurai Fighter | Beat Ryu's 1st Hard challenge. |
| Seriously Emo | Beat Abel's 1st Hard challenge. |
| Spin It again | Beat Zangief's 1st Hard challenge. |
| Sumo Slammer | Beat E. Honda's 5th Hard challenge. |
| Viva Mexico | Beat El Fuerte's 5th Hard challenge. |
| Working up a Sweat | Complete Rufus's 1st Hard Trial. |
| You Are Beneath Me | Beat M. Bison's 1st Hard challenge. |

## STREET FIGHTER 4  (PlayStation 3)

### CHARACTERS

| UNLOCKABLE | HOW TO UNLOCK |
|---|---|
| Akuma | After unlocking Sakura, Dan, Cammy, Fei Long, Gen and Rose, fight him on Arcade mode. To do that, get at least 2 perfects and 2 Ultra Finishes. |
| Cammy | End the Arcade mode with Crimson Viper. |
| Dan | End the Arcade mode with Sakura. |
| Fei Long | End the Arcade mode with Abel. |
| Gen | End the Arcade mode with Chun-Li. |
| Gouken | After unlocking Akuma, Sakura, Dan, Cammy, Fei Long, Gen and Rose, fight him on Arcade mode. To do that, get at least 2 perfects and 3 Ultra Finishes. |
| Rose | End the Arcade mode with M. Bison. |
| Sakura | End the Arcade mode with Ryu. |
| Seth | End the game with all the other characters. |

### PERSONAL ACTIONS

| UNLOCKABLE | HOW TO UNLOCK |
|---|---|
| Personal Action 10 | Beat Time Attack Normal Level 20. |
| Personal Action 2 | Beat Time Attack Normal Level 2. |
| Personal Action 3 | Beat Survival Normal level 2 |

| Personal Action 4 | Beat Time Attack Normal level 7 |
| Personal Action 5 | Beat Survival Normal level 7 |
| Personal Action 6 | Beat Time Attack Normal level 12 |
| Personal Action 7 | Beat Survival Normal level 12 |
| Personal Action 8 | Beat Time Attack Normal level 17 |
| Personal Action 9 | Beat Survival Normal level 17 |

## COLORS

To unlock every color in the game you have to play the Time Trial and Survival modes in order. Don't skip to the challenges where the colors are. Once completed you gain the colors for every fighter on the roster.

| UNLOCKABLE | HOW TO UNLOCK |
| --- | --- |
| Color 10 | Survival Normal 16 |
| Color 3 | Time Attack Normal 1 |
| Color 4 | Survival Normal 1 |
| Color 5 | Time Attack Normal 6 |
| Color 6 | Survival Normal 6 |
| Color 7 | Time Attack Normal 11 |
| Color 8 | Survival Normal 11 |
| Color 9 | Time Attack Normal 16 |

## STREETS OF RAGE (Wii)

### UNLOCKABLES

| UNLOCKABLE | HOW TO UNLOCK |
| --- | --- |
| Bad Ending | Choose to be Mr. X's righthand man the first time you meet him. Then complete the game. |
| Extra Continues | Press ⬆, ⬆, ⓑ, ⓑ, ⓑ, ©, ©, ©, START at the title screen. |
| Final Boss Duel | When you get to the final boss in 2-player mode, have one player choose "yes" and the other choose "no." You duel against each other. |
| Level and Lives Select | Go to the main menu. Hold Ⓐ+Ⓑ+©+⬆ on controller 2 while selecting Options on controller 1 (best if done with two people). You can now select how many lives you start with and which stage to start on. |

## STREETS OF RAGE 2 (Wii)

### UNLOCKABLES

| UNLOCKABLE | HOW TO UNLOCK |
| --- | --- |
| Level and Lives Select | Go to the main menu. Hold Ⓐ+Ⓑ on controller 2 while selecting Options. Now select how many lives you start with (up to 9), choose your starting stage, and play at the Very Easy and Mania difficulty levels. |
| Same Character in 2 Player | At the title screen, hold ⬆+Ⓑ on controller 1 and hold ⬆+Ⓐ on controller 2. Press ⬆ on controller 2 with everything else still held down. Now both players can be the same person in 2 Player! |

## STREETS OF RAGE 3 (Wii)

### UNLOCKABLES

| UNLOCKABLE | HOW TO UNLOCK |
| --- | --- |
| Ending 1 | Rescue the Chief in Stage 6 before his health runs out. Then, at the end of Stage 7, defeat Robot Y before the time limit runs out. |
| Ending 2 | Rescue the Chief before his health runs out in Stage 6. Then, in Stage 7, defeat Robot Y but let the time limit run out. |
| Ending 3 | Let the Chief's health run out in Stage 6. When you go to Stage 7, you will see that it is changed. Make it to the last boss and defeat him. |
| Ending 4 | Set the difficulty to Easy and beat Robot X in Stage 5. |

| | |
|---|---|
| **Extra Lives Select** | Go to the Options screen and select the "Lives" option. Press and hold ✚+Ⓐ+Ⓑ+Ⓒ on controller 2, and press ✚ or ✚ on controller 1 to select the number of lives you can start the game with. You can now select 9 lives, instead of the default max of 5. |
| **Play as Ash** | To select Ash, defeat him, then hold Ⓐ on controller 1. After losing all of your lives, continue, and you can choose Ash as your character. |
| **Play as Roo** | When you fight the clown and Roo, defeat the clown first and Roo should hop away off the screen. When you lose all your lives and continue, cycle through the characters and Roo is now available. |
| **Play as Roo** | At the title screen, hold ✚+Ⓑ, then press START. A kangaroo named Roo is now available at the Character Select screen. |
| **Play as Shiva** | After beating Shiva in the first stage when you get the last hit, hold Ⓑ+START. When the continue screen comes up, you can play as Shiva. (He is weaker than his *Streets of Rage 2* character). |
| **Play as Super Axel** | Press ✚ to select a player, then quickly hold Ⓐ and sweep the D-pad in a clockwise circle until Axel appears. Then press Ⓐ. |
| ***THIS CHEAT IS VERY HARD TO GET WORKING.*** | |
| **Play as Super Skate** | Pick Skate. As the first level starts, lose your first life having 0 points. You will now be Super Skate, with a much more powerful combo. |
| **Play as the Same Character** | Hold ✚+Ⓒ on controller 2 as you enter 2-player mode with controller 1. |
| **Secret Items** | In Stage 1, at the Warehouse area, go to the bottom-left region blocked by the crates in the background and press Ⓑ. You get 5,000 points and a 1-UP. Stage 7, (City Hall) also contains lots of hidden items. Search in areas blocked off by the background such as lampposts, flower pots, etc. |
| **Secret Passageways** | On Stage 5, in the first room with all the ninjas, there are three secret routes that you can access by killing all enemies here. These rooms have more items than the normal rooms. Route 1: Above the door where you follow your normal route, notice a white wall with cracks near the top. Punch it to access Secret Route 1. Route 2: Go to the bottom center of this room and punch it a few times. You eventually bust a hole in the floor leading you to the basement of Stage 5 and also Secret Route 2. Route 3: Go to the top of the screen and go up to the red walls. A certain red wall has a few cracks in it. Punch it to access Secret Route 3. There are a lot of enemies here, so be careful. |
| **Stage Select** | Hold Ⓑ+✚, then press START. Stage Select appears on the Options screen. |

## SUPER C  (Wii)

### UNLOCKABLES

| UNLOCKABLE | HOW TO UNLOCK |
|---|---|
| **10 Lives (Player 1)** | On the title screen, press ✚, ✚, ✚, ✚, Ⓐ, Ⓑ, then START |
| **10 Lives (Player 2)** | On the title screen, press ✚, ✚, ✚, ✚, Ⓐ, Ⓑ, SELECT, then START |
| **Access Sound Test** | On the title screen, hold down Ⓐ+Ⓑ then press START |
| **Retain Old Score and # of Lives on New Game** | On the title screen, after you've beaten the game, press Ⓐ, and then START |
| **Retain Old Score on New Game** | On the title screen, after you've beaten the game, press Ⓐ, Ⓑ, then START |

## SUPER CASTLEVANIA IV  (Wii)

### UNLOCKABLES

| UNLOCKABLE | HOW TO UNLOCK |
|---|---|
| **Higher Difficulty** | Heart, Axe, Space, Water. Axe, Space, Space, Heart. Space, Axe, Space, Space. Space, Heart, Space, Space. |

## DIFFICULT LEVEL PASSWORDS

Use these passwords to get to stages on the Difficult setting. You need to use a blank name.

| PASSWORD | EFFECT |
|---|---|
| Space, Axe, Space, Space. Water, Water, Space, Space. Space, Heart, Space, Axe. Water, Axe, Space, Space. | Difficult mode Stage 6 level 1 |
| Space, Axe, Space, Heart. Water, Heart, Space, Space. Space, Space, Space, Water. Space, Axe, Space, Space. | Difficult mode Stage 7 level 1 |
| Space, Axe, Space, Space. Water, Water, Space, Space. Space, Heart, Space, Water. Water, Water, Space, Space. | Difficult mode Stage 8 level 1 |

## STAGE PASSWORDS

*WHEN YOU COME TO "ENTER YOUR NAME," LEAVE THE SPACE BLANK OR THESE PASSWORDS WON'T WORK.*

| PASSWORD | EFFECT |
|---|---|
| Space, Space, Space, Space. Firebombs, Space, Space, Space. Space, Space, Space, Space. Firebombs, Space, Space, Space | Level 2 |

| PASSWORD | EFFECT |
|---|---|
| Space, Space, Space, Heart. Firebombs, Space, Space, Space. Space, Space, Space, Space. Heart, Space, Space, Space | Level 3 |
| Space, Space, Space, Firebombs. Firebombs, Firebombs, Space, Space, Space. Firebombs, Space, Axe. Space, Space, Space, Space | Level 4 |
| Space, Space, Space, Space. Firebombs, Space, Space, Space. Space, Space, Space, Axe. Firebombs, Axe, Space, Space | Level 5 |
| Space, Space, Space, Space. Firebombs, Firebombs, Space, Space. Space, Firebombs, Space, Axe. Firebombs, Axe, Space, Space | Level 6 |
| Space, Space, Space, Firebombs. Firebombs, Hart, Space, Space. Space, Heart, Space, Firebombs. Space, Heart, Space, Space | Level 7 |
| Space, Space, Space, Space. Firebombs, Firebombs, Space, Space. Space, Firebombs, Space, Firebombs. Firebombs, Firebombs, Space, Space | Level 8 |
| Space, Space, Space, Heart. Firebombs, Firebombs, Space, Space. Space, Firebombs, Space, Firebombs. Heart, Firebombs, Space, Space | Level 9 |
| Space, Space, Space, Axe. Firebombs, Space, Space, Space. Space, Space, Space, Heart. Heart, Heart, Space, Space | Level B |
| Space, Space, Space, Firebombs. Firebombs, Firebombs, Space, Space. Space, Firebombs, Space, Space. Space, Heart, Axe, Space | Level B (Dracula) |

## UNLOCKABLES

| UNLOCKABLE | HOW TO UNLOCK |
|---|---|
| Full Arsenal | In the last stage, before you climb the stairs to Dracula, jump down to the left. You land on an invisible platform. Move all the way left and you will get full health, 99 hearts, a cross, a fully upgraded whip, and a III stone. |

## HIDDEN ROUTES

There are three hidden branches from the main path.

| UNLOCKABLE | HOW TO UNLOCK |
|---|---|
| Hidden Route 1 | In stage 3-1, when you must descend a short vertical shaft, halfway down here is a wall of pillars to the left. Demolish these, and you find a small side room containing hearts, cash bags, and some Roast. |

A B C D E F G H I J K L M N O P Q R S T U V W X Y Z

| Hidden Route 2 | The second secret, which is an actual hidden Block, is in stage 6-2. At the very beginning you pass a hallway with Axe Knights and falling chandeliers. The third archway has a chandelier but no guard. Hit the floor a couple of times and it'll crumble, revealing a stairwell into a secret area. |
|---|---|
| Hidden Route 3 | The last one is in Block 9-2. You jump across a bed of spikes at the beginning. After this you see several whirlwind tunnels and some coffins. The last upper platform on the right has a coffin and a tunnel. Let the tunnel suck you in and you'll find a hidden area full of bonuses. |

## SUPER CONTRA (XBOX 360)

| UNLOCKABLE | HOW TO UNLOCK |
|---|---|
| Unlimited Lives and Super Machine Gun | On the main menu, select Arcade Game, and then enter the following code: (using the D-Pad) ⬆, ⬆, ⬇, ⬇, ⬅, ➡, ⬅, ➡, Ⓑ, Ⓐ. If done correctly, the game will start up instead of backing out to the main menu. You will begin with 5 lives that never decrease when killed, and you will have a super machine gun weapon equipped at all times! Using this code disables all Achievements and you cannot upload scores to Xbox Live Leaderboards. The code remain active until you exit the game using the Exit Game option in the Pause menu. |

## SUPER GHOULS 'N GHOSTS (Wii)

### UNLOCKABLES

| UNLOCKABLE | HOW TO UNLOCK |
|---|---|
| Level Select | Highlight "Exit" on the Option screen with controller 1. Hold L + START on controller 2 and press START on controller 1. |
| Professional Mode | Beat the game on Normal mode. |

## SUPER SCRIBBLENAUTS (DS)

### MERITS

| UNLOCKABLE | HOW TO UNLOCK |
|---|---|
| Astronomer | Decorate the sky with every planet in the solar system. |
| Avatar Maniac | Purchase all avatars. |
| Behind the Scenes | Create three 5th Cell developers. |
| Brand New Pencil | Use 10 unique adjectives. |
| Break Time | Use the arcade machine. |
| Broken Pencil | Use 300 unique adjectives. |
| Clever Creation | Attach any three objects together. |
| Coloring Book | Create 10 objects with altered colors. |
| Colossal Contraption | Attach any 10 objects together. |
| Connect the Dots | Complete any constellation. |
| Cracked Pencil | Use 200 unique adjectives. |
| Creative Concoction | Attach any six objects together. |
| Cthulhu Fhtagn | Create a mythos monster. |
| Daily Horoscope | Decorate the sky with the 12 zodiac symbols. |
| Dedicated Collector | Purchase 25 avatars. |
| Easter Egg | Create 5 hidden historical figures. |
| English Eagle | Create 10 unique objects. |
| Fantasy Fulfillment | Create 5 fantasy objects or use 5 fantasy adjectives. |
| Fatality! | Destroy the world. |
| Forbidden Fruit | Use Maxwell's notebook. |
| Full Replay | Complete all advanced mode levels. |
| Ginormous | Create the largest possible object. |
| Grammar General | Create 200 unique objects. |

| | |
|---|---|
| **History Lesson** | Use the time machine. |
| **Home Grown** | Complete a custom level. |
| **Hypnotized** | Hypnotize another character. |
| **It's Alive!** | Grant life to an inanimate object. |
| **Kiss Me** | Transform a creature into a frog. |
| **Language Lion** | Create 100 unique objects. |
| **Letter Lieutenant** | Create 25 unique objects. |
| **Lion Tamer** | Ride a creature that's normally hostile. |
| **Looking Ahead** | Create 5 science-fiction objects or use 5 science-fiction adjectives. |
| **Master Morpher** | Apply 5 adjectives to an object. |
| **Maxwell in Disguise** | Play as a different avatar. |
| **Mega Mutator** | Apply 8 adjectives to an object. |
| **Micronized** | Create the smallest possible object. |
| **Money Vault** | Hold $10,000 in your bank. |
| **Nice Wallet** | Hold $5,000 in your bank. |
| **Over Budget** | Completely fill the budget meter. |
| **Piggy Bank** | Hold $1,000 in your bank. |
| **Rad Recombiner** | Apply 3 adjectives to an object. |
| **Really Big Lizards** | Create 5 dinosaurs. |
| **Replay** | Complete a level in Advanced mode. |
| **Russian Doll** | Put an object inside an object inside an object. |
| **Sharpened Pencil** | Use 25 unique adjectives. |
| **Skin of Your Teeth** | Catch a Starite while Maxwell is being defeated. |
| **Starite Apprentice** | Catch 10 Starites. |
| **Starite King** | Catch 121 Starites. |
| **Starite Master** | Catch 60 Starites. |
| **Suit Up** | Fully equip Maxwell. |
| **Syllable Savant** | Create 50 unique objects. |
| **Teleported** | Use the teleporter. |
| **Texture Artist** | Create 5 objects made out of altered materials. |
| **The Fourth Wall** | Apply the secret Super Scribblenauts adjective. |
| **Welcome Mat** | Set a custom level as your playground. |
| **Well Used Pencil** | Use 50 unique adjectives. |
| **Window Shopper** | Purchase 10 avatars. |
| **Word Warrior** | Create 300 unique objects. |
| **Worn Down Pencil** | Use 100 unique adjectives. |
| **You Can Fly** | Equip any flying gear or mount. |

### 121ST STARITE

To find the missing 121st star, create a time machine and use it repeatedly until you are taken to a stage with another Maxwell and a Starite in a tree. This Starite is the last one you need to complete the game.

## SUPER STAR SOLDIER (Wii)

### CHEAT MENU

Following code unlocks a Cheat menu where you can mess with all the options for the game such as level selection and enemy difficulty. Input at the title screen.

| UNLOCKABLE | HOW TO UNLOCK |
|---|---|
| Unlock Cheat Menu | Press ⬆, ②, ⬇, ②, ⬅, ②, ➡②, ⬆, ①, ⬇, ①, ⬅, ①, ⬇, ①, ①+② x8, ①+SELECT x8 |

## SUPER STREET FIGHTER IV (XBOX 360), (PLAYSTATION 3)

### CHARACTER ICONS AND TITLES

There are a number of character specific icons and titles that are unlocked by clearing Arcade Mode and through each character's unique set of trials.

| UNLOCKABLE | HOW TO UNLOCK |
| --- | --- |
| **Blue Character Title** | Clear Arcade with the character on any difficulty. |
| **Character Icon #1** | Complete any trial with the character. |
| **Character Icon #2** | Complete eight different trials with the character. |
| **Character Icon #3** | Complete 16 different trials with the character. |
| **Character Icon #4** | Complete all trials with the character. |
| **Gold Character Title #1** | Complete 12 different trials with the character. |
| **Gold Character Title #2** | Complete 14 different trials with the character. |
| **Gold Character Title #3** | Complete 18 different trials with the character. |
| **Gold Character Title #4** | Complete 20 different trials with the character. |
| **Gold Character Title #5** | Complete 22 different trials with the character. |
| **Red Character Title** | Clear Arcade with the character on the hardest difficulty. |
| **Silver Character Title #1** | Complete two different trials with the character. |
| **Silver Character Title #2** | Complete three different trials with the character. |
| **Silver Character Title #3** | Complete four different trials with the character. |
| **Silver Character Title #4** | Complete six different trials with the character. |
| **Silver Character Title #5** | Complete 10 different trials with the character. |

### ADDITIONAL COLORS AND TAUNTS (PERSONAL ACTIONS)

For each match you use a character on, you will unlock a new color and Personal Action or Taunt.

| UNLOCKABLE | HOW TO UNLOCK |
| --- | --- |
| **Color #10** | Play 16 matches with the character. |
| **Color #11** | Start a game with a Street Fighter IV save file. |
| **Color #12** | Start a game with a Street Fighter IV save file. |
| **Color #3** | Play two matches with the character. |
| **Color #4** | Play four matches with the character. |
| **Color #5** | Play six matches with the character. |
| **Color #6** | Play eight matches with the character. |
| **Color #7** | Play 10 matches with the character. |
| **Color #8** | Play 12 matches with the character. |
| **Color #9** | Play 14 matches with the character. |
| **Taunt #10** | Play 16 matches with the character. |
| **Taunt #2** | Play one match with the character. |
| **Taunt #3** | Play three matches with the character. |
| **Taunt #4** | Play five matches with the character. |
| **Taunt #5** | Play seven matches with the character. |
| **Taunt #6** | Play nine matches with the character. |
| **Taunt #7** | Play 11 matches with the character. |
| **Taunt #8** | Play 13 matches with the character. |
| **Taunt #9** | Play 15 matches with the character. |

### UNLOCKABLES

| UNLOCKABLE | HOW TO UNLOCK |
| --- | --- |
| **Barrel Buster Bonus Stage** | Beat Arcade Mode in any difficulty. |
| **Car Crusher Bonus Stage** | Beat Arcade Mode in any difficulty. |

| Color 11 | Have saved data from Street Fighter IV. |
| Color 12 | Have saved data carry over from the original Street Fighter IV. |
| Japanese Voices | Beat Arcade Mode in any difficulty. |
| Remixed Character BGM for Use in Battles | Earn "It Begins" achievement. |

### FIGHT GOUKEN IN ARCADE MODE

The following requirements must be met while playing Arcade Mode to fight Gouken, who will appear after the battle with Seth (in default settings, i.e., three rounds):

* Do not lose a single round.

* Perform five Super or Ultra Combo Finishes.

* Score two Perfect Rounds (not get hit a single time during a round)

* Connect 10 "First Hits" (when you're the first to connect a strike during a round).

## SUPER STREET FIGHTER IV: 3D EDITION (3DS)

### CODE

Codes must be entered case-sensitve in the Figure Collection Menu

| EFFECT | CODE |
| --- | --- |
| Bronze Lv6 Adon | jeNbhRXbFR |
| Golden Abel Figurine | wRqsWklbxT |
| Golden Blanka Figurine | DmdkeRvbxc |
| Golden Chun-Li Figurine | zAAkcHVbHk |
| Golden Guile Figurine | qeJkznDbKE |
| Golden Lv. 7 Seth | PkwkDjqbja |
| Golden M.Bison Figurine | CgIsQNWbHu (I = uppercase i) |
| Golden Rufus Figurine | nnhksyvbZy |
| Golden Ryu Figurine | KjckTnSbwK |
| Golden Zangief Figurine | hinsVnebTu |
| Level 7 Silver Sagat | QWzkDXWbeH |
| Obtain a Platinum Level 7 Chun-Li Figurine | hjekwnEbxG |
| Platinum C. Viper | xopknDzbqS |
| Platinum Cammy Figurine | dfukkvGbdt |
| Platinum Dee Jay | DaRkBPubLf |
| Platinum El Fuerte Figurine | mhikghwbsf |
| Platinum Fei Long Figurine | MzisXzabBF |
| Platinum Guy | AjtsAbWbBD |
| Platinum Level 7 Ryu | DPrkMnybCd |
| Platinum M.Bison | EebkxqWbYJ |
| Silver Akuma Figurine | RYSsPxSbTh |
| Silver Balrog Figurine | PqUswOobWG |
| Silver Chun-Li Figurine | tLWkWvrblz |
| Silver Cody Figurine | naMkEQgbQG |
| Silver Dan Figurine | rDRkkSIbqS (I = uppercase i) |
| Silver E. Honda Figurine | uUDsTlmbUN |
| Silver Ibuki Figurine | ilMsRBabpB |
| Silver Juri Figurine | OfQkARpbJR |
| Silver Ken Figurine | NyosHgybuW |
| Silver Lv. 6 Dudley | ZRhsNTMblA (upper case i) |
| Silver Lv. 6 Hakan | rLPbyLgbUy |
| Silver LV. 7 T. Hawk Figurine | tWEsvzubiz |

| Silver Makoto Figurine | GHakWCTbsl |
| Silver Rose Figurine | GKkkXXtbSe |
| Silver Sakura Figurine | uzTsXzlbKn (I = uppercase i) |
| Special Akuma Figurine | uQHkWgYbJC |
| Unlock Silver Lv. 5 Dhalsim | JKbsOVHbVC |

## UNLOCKABLE

Clear Arcade mode and complete each unique character's set of trials.

| UNLOCKABLE | HOW TO UNLOCK |
|---|---|
| Blue Character Title | Clear Arcade with the character on any difficulty. |
| Character Icon #1 | Complete any trial with the character. |
| Character Icon #2 | Complete 8 different trials with the character. |
| Character Icon #3 | Complete 16 different trials with the character. |
| Character Icon #4 | Complete all trials with the character. |
| Gold Character Title #1 | Complete 12 different trials with the character. |
| Gold Character Title #2 | Complete 14 different trials with the character. |
| Gold Character Title #3 | Complete 18 different trials with the character. |
| Gold Character Title #4 | Complete 20 different trials with the character. |
| Gold Character Title #5 | Complete 22 different trials with the character. |
| Red Character Title | Clear Arcade with the character on the hardest difficulty. |
| Silver Character Title #1 | Complete 2 different trials with the character. |
| Silver Character Title #2 | Complete 3 different trials with the character. |
| Silver Character Title #3 | Complete 4 different trials with the character. |
| Silver Character Title #4 | Complete 6 different trials with the character. |
| Silver Character Title #5 | Complete 10 different trials with the character. |

### SECRETS

| UNLOCKABLE | HOW TO UNLOCK |
|---|---|
| Fight Akuma | Beat arcade mode without continuing and recieve at least one perfect. After defeating Seth, Akuma appears to challenge you. Defeat him to recieve the "Akuma Killer" title. |
| Fight Gouken in Arcade mode | Aafter the battle with Seth, Gouken appears. You can't lose a single round. Perform 5 Super or Ultra Combo Finishes, Score 2 Perfect Rounds, and Connect 10 First Hits. |
| Fight Your 2nd Rival (Arcade Mode) | During Arcade Mode, when "Fight Your Rival" flashes on the screen, hold the R button. |

## SUPER THUNDER BLADE (Wii)

### LEVEL SELECT

Press these controller actions at the title screen to begin at the desired level.

| CODE | EFFECT |
|---|---|
| Press Ⓐ, ⬇, ⬇, ⬇, ⬇, ⬇, ⬇, ⬇, START | Level 2 |
| Press Ⓐ, Ⓐ, ⬇, ⬇, ⬇, ⬇, ⬇, ⬇, ⬇, START | Level 3 |
| Press Ⓐ, Ⓐ, Ⓐ, ⬇, ⬇, ⬇, ⬇, ⬇, ⬇, ⬇, START | Level 4 |
| Press Ⓐ, Ⓐ, Ⓐ, Ⓐ, ⬇, ⬇, ⬇, ⬇, ⬇, ⬇, ⬇, START | Level 5 |

### UNLOCKABLES

| UNLOCKABLE | HOW TO UNLOCK |
|---|---|
| Avoid Enemy Fire | Begin the game with Hard difficulty. Stay in the upper right or left corners and fire your weapon continuously in levels 1 through 3. |
| Extra Lives | Enable the Level Select code and get a continue. Highlight "Option" and hold Ⓐ+Ⓑ+Ⓒ and press START. A picture of a panda appears on the "Player" selection to confirm the code. |

## SUPERMAN RETURNS (XBOX 360)

### CHEAT CODES

Anytime during gameplay after the Gladiator Battle first set, pause the game. Enter the following buttons to unlock the cheats. A chime confirms that the code has been entered correctly.

| UNLOCKABLE | HOW TO UNLOCK |
|---|---|
| Infinite Health (Metropolis) | ↑, ▷, ↓, ▷, ◇, ◁, ▷ |
| Infinite Stamina | ◇, ◇, ♀, ♀, ◁, ▷, ◁, ▷, ▽, ⊗ |
| Unlock All Costumes, Trophies, and Theater Items Unlock All Moves | ◁, ◇, ◁, ♀, ▽, ⊗, ◇, ◇, ▷, ⊗ ◁, ▽, ▷, ⊗, ♀, ▽, ◇, ♀, ⊗, ⊗ |

### UNLOCKABLES

| UNLOCKABLE | HOW TO UNLOCK |
|---|---|
| Bizarro | ◇, ▷, ♀, ▷, ◇, ◁, ♀, ▷, ◇ (Enter it when you load your game, at the menu that lets you choose Metropolis or Fortress of Solitude before you start the game you loaded.) |
| Golden Age Superman Suit | Save Metropolis from the tornadoes |
| Pod Suit | Beat Bizarro |

## SURF'S UP (PlayStation 3)

### PASSWORDS

| PASSWORD | EFFECT |
|---|---|
| MYPRECIOUS | All Boards |
| FREEVISIT | All championship locations |
| GOINGDOWN | All leaf sliding locations |
| MULTIPASS | All multiplayer levels |
| NICEPLACE | Art gallery |
| ASTRAL | Astral board |
| TOPFASHION | Customizations for all characters |
| MONSOON | Monsoon board |
| IMTHEBEST | Plan as Tank Evans |
| TINYBUTSTRONG | Play as Arnold |
| SURPRISEGUEST | Play as Elliot |
| SLOWANDSTEADY | Play as Geek |
| KOBAYASHI | Play as Tatsuhi Kobayashi |
| THELEGEND | Play as Zeke Topanga |
| TINYSHOCKWAVE | Tine shockwave board |
| WATCHAMOVIE | Video Gallery |

## SURF'S UP (Wii)

### PASSWORDS

| PASSWORD | EFFECT |
|---|---|
| NICEPLACE | Unlocks all art galleries |
| MYPRECIOUS | Unlocks all boards |
| GOINGDOWN | Unlocks all leaf-sliding locations |
| MULTIPASS | Unlocks all multiplayer levels |
| FREEVISIT | Unlocks all the locales |
| WATCHAMOVIE | Unlocks all video Galleries |
| TINYBUTSTRONG | Unlocks Arnold |
| ASTRAL | Unlocks Astral's board |
| DONTFALL | Unlocks bonus missions |
| TOPFASHION | Unlocks character customization |

**CODES & CHEATS**

| SURPRISEGUEST | Unlocks Elliot |
| SLOWANDSTEADY | Unlocks Geek |
| MONSOON | Unlocks Monsoon Board |
| IMTHEBEST | Unlocks Tank Evans |
| KOBAYASHI | Unlocks Tatsuhi Kobayashi |
| TINYSHOCKWAVE | Unlocks Tiny Shockwave board |
| THELEGEND | Unlocks Zeke Topanga |

### UNLOCKABLES

| UNLOCKABLE | HOW TO UNLOCK |
| --- | --- |
| Arnold | Obtain 30,000 points in Shiverpool 2 |
| Big Z | Obtain 100,000 points in Legendary Wave |
| Elliot | Obtain 40,000 points in Pen Gu North 3 |
| Geek | Obtain 60,000 points in Pen Gu South 4 |
| Tank | Obtain 40,000 points in the Boneyards |
| Tatsuhi | Obtain 15,000 points in Pen Gu South 2 |

## SWORD OF VERMILION (Wii)

### UNLOCKABLES
UNLOCKABLE HOW TO UNLOCK

| Quick Cash | In Keltwick, when Bearwulf gives you the dungeon key to get to Malaga, sell it. It's worth 1,000 kims and Bearwulf has an unlimited number of them. Just go back, talk to him, and he'll say "Did you lose the key? I have another one." He'll give it to you, and you can repeat the process as much as you want. |
| --- | --- |
| Test Menu | Any time during the game, hold Ⓐ+Ⓑ+Ⓒ and press START on controller 2. A test menu appears with Input, Sound, and C.R.T. tests. And when you exit, it sends you back to the SEGA logo screen. |

## TATSUNOKO VS. CAPCOM: ULTIMATE ALL STARS (Wii)

### UNLOCKABLES

| UNLOCKABLE | HOW TO UNLOCK |
|---|---|
| Hold the partner button during the character introduction sequence prior to the start of a match to start the match with your second character. | |
| Frank West | Get three different Capcom characters' Arcade endings. |
| Joe the Condor | Get six different Tatsunoko characters' Arcade endings. |
| Tekkaman Blade | Get three different Tatsunoko characters' Arcade endings. |
| Yatterman-2 | Get Frank West, Zero, Tekkaman Blade, and Joe the Condor's Arcade endings. |
| Zero | Get six different Capcom characters' Arcade endings. |
| Special Illustration #2 | Beat Survival Mode and buy it from shop. |
| Fourth Color | Clear stage 8 (final boss) of Arcade Mode. |
| Third Color | Clear stage 4 (giant opponent) of Arcade Mode. |
| Opening Movie 2 | Unlock Yatterman-2 |
| Secret Movie | Beat the game with Frank West, Zero, Tekkaman Blade, Joe the Condor, and Yatterman-2. |

## TEENAGE MUTANT NINJA TURTLES (Wii)

### UNLOCKABLES

| UNLOCKABLE | HOW TO UNLOCK |
|---|---|
| Restore Power | Find a doorway that has a pizza slice or full pizza right at the beginning. Enter, grab the pizza, and exit. The pizza regenerates when you reenter. Use this to restore power to all your turtles. |
| Remove Crushers in Level 3 | Hop in the Party Wagon. Whenever you see a pesky Crusher, press SELECT. You exit the car, and the Crusher vanishes. |
| Share Boomerangs | When you get the boomerangs, throw up to 3 of them in the air, then switch turtles, and have the new turtle catch them. The new turtle can use those boomerangs without having picked up a boomerang icon. |

## TEENAGE MUTANT NINJA TURTLES (PSP)

### CODES

Enter this in the Mission Briefing screens.

| CODE | EFFECT |
|---|---|
| ⬦, ⬦, ⬦, ⬦, ⬦, ⬦, ⬦, ⬦, ✕ | Unlocks a Fantasy Costume |

## TEENAGE MUTANT NINJA TURTLES 2: THE ARCADE GAME (Wii)

### UNLOCKABLES

| UNLOCKABLE | HOW TO UNLOCK |
|---|---|
| Extra Lives and Stage Select | At the title screen, press Ⓑ, Ⓐ, Ⓑ, Ⓐ, ⬆, ⬆, Ⓑ, Ⓐ, ⬆, ⬆, Ⓑ, Ⓐ, START |
| Extra Lives Without Stage Select | On the title screen, press ⬆, ⬆, ⬆, ⬆, ⬆, ⬆, ⬆, ⬆, ⬆, ⬆, Ⓑ, Ⓐ, START |
| Stage Select | On the title screen, press ⬆, ⬆, ⬆, ⬆, ⬆, ⬆, ⬆, ⬆, ⬆, ⬆, ⬆, ⬆, Ⓑ, Ⓐ, START |

| Easier Battle with Shredder | During the final battle against Shredder, Shredder splits up into two forms. They're identical in appearance, but only one is real and the other is fake. However, both forms use the lightning attack that instantly kills you by turning you into a normal turtle. However, when either form is weakened to near death, his helmet flies off. As you're beating up on the two forms of Shredder, one of them loses his helmet very quickly. When this happens, leave him alone. This Shredder is the fake, and he cannot use the lightning attack without his helmet on. Only the real Shredder can use the attack, but because it's only him using it, you can avoid it and slowly beat him down with ease. For the rest of the fight, ignore the fake. If you kill him, the real Shredder releases another fake. |
| --- | --- |

## TEKKEN 6 (XBOX 360)

### UNLOCKABLES

| UNLOCKABLE | HOW TO UNLOCK |
| --- | --- |
| Arena | Clear Southern Woodlands |
| Kigan Island stage | Go to Abyss Gate on Hard difficulty and defeat a man with straw hat and grab his loot. Then exit to world map. |
| Medium and Hard difficulty | Clear Azazel's Temple, Central Corridor. |
| Mishima Industries, Biotech Research Station Ruins stage | Go right at the first junction in Seahorse Grand Hotel, defeat the kangaroo and clear the stage. |
| Nightmare Train stage | Clear Azazel's Temple, Central Corridor. |
| Play as Anna in Arena | Defeat her in G Corporation, Millennium Tower. |
| Play as Armour King in Arena | Defeat him in Lost Cemetery. |
| Play as Asuka in Arena | Defeat her in Kazama-Style Traditional Martial Arts Dojo. |
| Play as Baek in Arena | Defeat him in West Coast Canal Industrial Complex. |
| Play as Bob in Arena | Defeat him in Central District, 11th Avenue. |
| Play as Bruce in Arena | Defeat him in G Security Service, Operations Headquarters. |
| Play as Bryan in Arena | Defeat him in Southern Woodlands. |
| Play as Christie in Arena | Defeat her in Seahorse Grand Hotel. |
| Play as Devil Jin | Defeat him in Nightmare Train. |
| Play as Dragunov in Arena | Defeat him in container Terminal 7. |
| Play as Eddy in Arena | Defeat him in Tekken Force 4th Special Forces Operation Group Compound. |
| Play as Feng in Arena | Defeat him in Deserted Temple. |
| Play as Ganryu in Arena | Defeat him in Aranami Stable. |
| Play as Hwoarang in Arena | Defeat him in Industrial Highway 357. |
| Play as in Heihachi Arena | Defeat him in Mshima Estate. |
| Play as Jack-6 in Arena | Defeat him in Container Terminal 3. |
| Play as Jin | Defeat him in Azazel's Temple, Central Corridor. |
| Play as Julia in Arena | Defeat all enemies in G Science and Technology, Research Building 3. |
| Play as Kazuya in Arena | Defeat him in G Corporation, Millennium Tower Heliport. |
| Play as King in Arena | Defeat him with Marduk in Mixed Martial Arts Gym "Wild Kingdom." |
| Play as Kuma or Panda in Arena | Defeat Kuma in North Nature Park. |
| Play as Law in Arena | Defeat him in West District, Chinatown. |
| Play as Lee in Arena | Defeat him in Violet Systems. |

| | |
|---|---|
| Play as Lei in Arena | Defeat all enemies in ICPO Branch Office. |
| Play as Leo in Arena | Defeat it in 16th Archaeological Expedition's Excavation Site. |
| Play as Lili in Arena | Defeat her in Queen's Harbour. |
| Play as Marduk in Arena | Defeat him with King in Mixed Martial Arts Gym "Wild Kingdom." |
| Play as Miguel in Arena | Defeat him in South Bay Warehouse Area. |
| Play as Mokujin | Defeat it in Subterranean Pavilion. |
| Play as Nina in Arena | Defeat her in Mishima Zaibatsu, Central Subway Line. |
| Play as Paul in Arena | Defeat him in West District, 13th Avenue. |
| Play as Raven in Arena | Defeat him in Secret Underground Passage. |
| Play as Roger Jr. in Arena | Defeat it in Mishima Industries, Biotech Research Station Ruins. |
| Play as Steve in Arena | Defeat him in Abyss Gate. |
| Play as Wang in Arena | Defeat him in Fujian Tulou. |
| Play as Xiaoyu in Arena | Defeat her in Mishima Polytechnic. |
| Play as Yoshimitsu | Defeat him in Kigan Island. |
| Play as Zafina | Defeat all enemies in Mystic's Village. |
| Subterranean Pavilion stage | Clear 16th Archaeological Expedition's Excavation Site on Hard difficulty. |

### WIN POSE

Just before the win sequence plays at the end of a match, hold left punch, right punch, left kick, or right kick to select your win pose. Some characters may have more win poses than others.

While the game is paused, enter code on the second controller.

| UNLOCKABLE | CODE |
|---|---|
| View Score Status | ■,■,⇩,⇧,⇧,⇧ |

## THE 3RD BIRTHDAY (PSP)

### UNLOCKABLE

Complete the tasks to unlock the following.

| UNLOCKABLE | HOW TO UNLOCK |
|---|---|
| Countless Ammo | Beat the game ten times in any mode |
| Free Cross Fire | Beat the game in any mode |
| High Regen | Beat the game in any mode |
| Extra Ending Scene after Credits | Clear the game twice |
| Deadly Mode | Beat the game in Hard Mode |
| Genocide Mode | Beat the game in Deadly Mode |
| Music files | Successfully complete the game twice in any mode. |
| Blaze Edge | Complete the game once in any mode and have at least 7 Stamps on Square-Enix Member Site. |
| M240B | Beat the game twice in Hard Mode |
| M249 | Beat the game in any mode |
| Mk.46 Mod0 | Beat the game in Normal Mode |
| Pile Bunker | Unlock and purchase all weapons and weapon parts in the game. |
| Apron Dress Costume | Complete the game on Easy Mode. |
| Business Suit Costume | Complete the game once on any mode. The Costume is found in the CTI Building in the left hand locker room. |
| China Dress Costume | Complete the game on Normal Mode. |
| Knight Armor Costume | Complete the game on Deadly Mode. |

NEW!

A
B
C
D
E
F
G
H
I
J
K
L
M
N
O
P
Q
R
S
**T**
U
V
W
X
Y
Z

CODES & CHEATS

| | |
|---|---|
| Lightning Custom Costume | Complete the game once on any mode and have at least 7 Stamp on Square-Enix Member Site |
| OD Suit Costume | Complete the game once on any Mode and have at least 1 Stamp on Square-Enix Member Site. |
| Santa Soldier Costume | Complete the game once on any Mode. You'll find it in Maeda's Base, down the stairs to the lockers, check the left one for the Costume. |
| Swim Wear Costume | Complete the game on Hard Mode. |
| Titanium Bunny Costume | Complete the game on Genocide Mode. |

## THE ADVENTURES OF TINTIN: THE GAME (PlayStation 3)

### TROPHY

| UNLOCKABLE | HOW TO UNLOCK |
|---|---|
| Acrobat reporter (Bronze) | Move along the length of the Karaboudjan using the grappling hook! |
| Acrobatic duo (Bronze) | Give your partner 5 leg-ups in 'Tintin and Haddock' mode! |
| Armor expert! (Bronze) | Sir Francis: use the armor to knock out 20 enemies! |
| Art collector (Bronze) | Knock out 10 enemies with a painting of Sir Francis! |
| Aviation ace (Bronze) | Finish every level of the three types of PLANE challenges! |
| Bagghar (Bronze) | Finish chapter 22! |
| Banana king (Bronze) | Make 15 enemies slip on a banana skin! |
| Brittany (Bronze) | Finish chapter 28! |
| Cane and able (Bronze) | Thom(p)sons: get rid of 22 enemies with your stick! |
| Cane juggler (Bronze) | Bounce 10 objects off Thom(p)son's cane! |
| Castafiore unlocked (Bronze) | Unlock the Castafiore! |
| Champion catcher (Silver) | Catch an object in full flight with the grappling hook! |
| Complete artist (Bronze) | Finish a Tintin & Haddock mode level without losing any coins! (Apart from the side-car levels). |
| Crab collector (Gold) | Collect all the crabs with golden claws! |
| Easy Rider (Bronze) | Finish all the SIDECAR challenges! |
| Ever-dry (Bronze) | In the PLANE challenges, stay near the water for 7 seconds! |
| Experienced pilot (Bronze) | Get through the storm safely and reach the desert! |
| Five go bang (Bronze) | Get rid of 2 enemies at the same time with an exploding object! |
| Football champ (Bronze) | Knock out 2 enemies in a single throw of a ball using a rebound! |
| Giant Rackham: Take 1 (Bronze) | Beat Giant Rackham a first time! |
| Giant Rackham: Take 2 (Bronze) | Destroy the galleon! |
| Giant Rackham: Take 3 (Bronze) | Beat Giant Rackham again! |
| Giant Rackham: Take 4 (Bronze) | Destroy Giant Rackham and the galleon! |
| International reporter (Bronze) | Get to Bagghar! |
| Karaboudjan (Bronze) | Finish chapter 16! |
| Lights out (Bronze) | Knock out 5 enemies with a chandelier! |

| | |
|---|---|
| **Look out below! (Bronze)** | Pull five enemies off a ledge you're hanging onto! |
| **Marlinspike (Bronze)** | Finish chapter 10! |
| **Marlinspike's heir (Platinum)** | Unlock all the game's trophies! |
| **Master rat exterminator (Bronze)** | Exterminate 20 rats! |
| **Master treasure hunter (Gold)** | Find all the TREASURES in 'Tintin and Haddock' mode! |
| **Metalhead (Bronze)** | Throw a pot at an enemy's head! |
| **Motorcycle ace (Bronze)** | Finish a SIDECAR challenge without crashing into a wall or obstacle! |
| **Passenger in transit (Bronze)** | Change characters in flight with the parrot! |
| **Pilot gold medal (Bronze)** | Get gold in all three types of PLANE challenges! |
| **Showered with platinum (Gold)** | Finish all the platinum challenges! |
| **Sidecar gold medal (Bronze)** | Get gold in all the SIDECAR challenges! |
| **Sir Francis unlocked (Bronze)** | Unlock Sir Francis! |
| **Stronger than Diego (Bronze)** | Beat Diego the Dreadful! |
| **Stronger than Red Rackham (Silver)** | Beat Red Rackham in a sword fight! |
| **Stronger than William (Bronze)** | Beat William the Pirate! |
| **Super-sleuth (Silver)** | With Snowy, find all the buried objects in 'Tintin and Haddock' mode! |
| **Supersonic parrot (Silver)** | Finish 'The mystery of the talking bird' in less than 3 minutes 30 seconds! |
| **Swashbuckler (Bronze)** | Finish all the SWORD challenges! |
| **Sword gold medal (Bronze)** | Get gold in all the SWORD challenges! |
| **The Castafiore does her turn (Bronze)** | Castafiore: do 45 spinning attacks! |
| **The flea market (Bronze)** | Finish chapter 4! |
| **Thom(p)sons unlocked (Bronze)** | Unlock the Thom(p)sons! |
| **Treasure hunter (Silver)** | Find Red Rackham's treasure! |
| **Untouchable (Bronze)** | Finish a SWORD challenge without getting a scratch! |
| **Wardrobe full (Bronze)** | Buy 30 costumes! |

## THE ELDER SCROLLS V: SKYRIM (XBOX 360)

### ACHIEVEMENT

| UNLOCKABLE | HOW TO UNLOCK |
|---|---|
| **Adept (10)** | Reach Level 10 |
| **Alduin's Wall (20)** | Complete "Alduin's Wall" |
| **Apprentice (5)** | Reach Level 5 |
| **Artificer (10)** | Make a smithed item, an enchanted item, and a potion |
| **Bleak Falls Barrow (10)** | Complete "Bleak Falls Barrow" |
| **Blessed (10)** | Select a Standing Stone blessing |
| **Blood Oath (10)** | Become a member of the Circle |
| **Bound Until Death (10)** | Complete "Bound Until Death" |
| **Citizen (10)** | Buy a house |
| **Daedric Influence (10)** | Acquire a Daedric Artifact |
| **Darkness Returns (10)** | Complete "Darkness Returns" |
| **Delver (40)** | Clear 50 dungeons |

| Diplomatic Immunity (20) | Complete "Diplomatic Immunity" |
|---|---|
| Dragon Hunter (20) | Absorb 20 dragon souls |
| Dragon Soul (10) | Absorb a dragon soul |
| Dragonslayer (50) | Complete "Dragonslayer" |
| Elder Knowledge (20) | Complete "Elder Knowledge" |
| Expert (25) | Reach Level 25 |
| Explorer (40) | Discover 100 Locations |
| Gatekeeper (10) | Join the College of Winterhold |
| Glory of the Dead (30) | Complete "Glory of the Dead" |
| Golden Touch (30) | Have 100,000 gold |
| Hail Sithis! (30) | Complete "Hail Sithis!" |
| Hard Worker (10) | Chop wood, mine ore, and cook food |
| Hero of Skyrim (30) | Capture Solitude or Windhelm |
| Hero of the People (30) | Complete 50 Misc Objectives |
| Married (10) | Get married |
| Master (50) | Reach Level 50 |
| Master Criminal (20) | Bounty of 1000 gold in all nine holds |
| Oblivion Walker (30) | Collect 15 Daedric Artifacts |
| One with the Shadows (30) | Returned the Thieves Guild to its former glory |
| Reader (20) | Read 50 Skill Books |
| Revealing the Unseen (10) | Complete "Revealing the Unseen" |
| Sideways (20) | Complete 10 side quests |
| Skill Master (40) | Get a skill to 100 |
| Snake Tongue (10) | Successfully persuade, bribe, and intimidate |
| Standing Stones (30) | Find 13 Standing Stones |
| Take Up Arms (10) | Join the Companions |
| Taking Care of Business (10) | Join the Thieves Guild |
| Taking Sides (10) | Join the Stormcloaks or the Imperial Army |
| The Eye of Magnus (30) | Complete "The Eye of Magnus" |
| The Fallen (20) | Complete "The Fallen" |
| The Way of the Voice (20) | Complete "The Way of the Voice" |
| Thief (30) | Pick 50 locks and 50 pockets |
| Thu'um Master (40) | Learn 20 shouts |
| Unbound (10) | Complete "Unbound" |
| Wanted (10) | Escape from jail |
| War Hero (10) | Capture Fort Sungard or Fort Greenwall |
| With Friends Like These... (10) | Join the Dark Brotherhood |
| Words of Power (10) | Learn all three words of a shout |

## THE KING OF FIGHTERS XIII (PlayStation 3)

### TROPHY

| UNLOCKABLE | HOW TO UNLOCK |
|---|---|
| After all, you're just trash. (Bronze) | Get an SS at the victory screen |
| And the final blow...! (Bronze) | Get 50 NEO MAX Super Special Moves Finishes (Arcade, Versus) |
| Come back later! (Bronze) | Perform 50 Drive Cancels (Arcade, Versus) |
| Do you understand now? (Silver) | Complete STORY. |
| Doesn't it feel good? (Bronze) | Win 25 [ranked matches / player matches] |

| | |
|---|---|
| Excellent! (Gold) | Win 100 [ranked matches / player matches] |
| Go easy on me! (Bronze) | Play your first [ranked match / player match] |
| Good! (Bronze) | Play 50 [ranked matches / player matches] |
| Great (Bronze) | Be challenged by "Saiki" and win in ARCADE |
| Hehe... hot, wasn't it? (Silver) | Play 100 [ranked matches / player matches] |
| Heheh. Not bad. (Bronze) | Perform 50 MAX Cancels (Arcade, Versus) |
| Here I come, buddy! (Bronze) | Create 10 characters in Customize |
| Hey! (Bronze) | Hit 100 times using NEO MAX Super Special Moves (Arcade, Versus) |
| Hey, hey, hey! (Bronze) | Be challenged by "Billy" and win in ARCADE |
| Hmph... this is only natural. (Bronze) | Get 10 straight wins (Arcade, Versus) |
| How was it? (Silver) | Clear ARCADE MODE without continuing |
| I shall not waver! (Silver) | Play 300 [ranked matches / player matches] |
| I will execute my mission! (Bronze) | Defeat 3 characters in Survival mode |
| I'm enough for this job! (Silver) | Defeat 35 characters in Survival mode |
| Isn't this fun, eh? (Silver) | Win 50 [ranked matches / player matches] |
| It's about time to start! (Bronze) | Register an icon, team and message in Customize |
| Let's play warrior! (Bronze) | Create 10 rooms |
| Let's see what you've got... (Bronze) | Clear STORY. |
| Looks like I was just on time. (Bronze) | Clear Time Attack mode for the first time |
| Mission Complete! (Bronze) | Perform 50 Super Cancels (Arcade, Versus) |
| Number 1! (Bronze) | Get 5 consecutive wins in a ranked match |
| Okay! (Bronze) | Get 2 consecutive wins in a ranked match |
| Piece of cake! (Bronze) | Perform 50 HD Cancels (Arcade, Versus) |
| Play time is over! (Bronze) | Perform 50 Super Special Moves Finishes (Arcade, Versus) |
| Show me what humans are made of... (Bronze) | Perform 10 Target Actions (Arcade) |
| Spinning! (Bronze) | Hit 100 times using EX Special Moves (Arcade, Versus) |
| Strength! (Bronze) | Hit 100 times using Special Moves (Arcade, Versus) |
| That should do it! (Silver) | Complete all trials for 1 character in Trial mode |
| THE KING OF FIGHTERS (Platinum) | Unlock all trophies. |
| This is... my victory! (Silver) | Clear ARCADE MODE on VERY HARD |
| This was just a greeting! (Bronze) | Win 5 [ranked matches / player matches] |
| Time will soon turn to ashes... (Bronze) | Get an S at the victory screen |
| What's wrong? (Silver) | Perform 300 Target Actions (Arcade) |
| Yahoooo! (Bronze) | Hit 100 times using Super Special Moves (Arcade, Versus) |
| Yay! Perfect! (Bronze) | Perform 10 Perfect Victories (Arcade, Versus) |
| Yeah! (Bronze) | Win your first [ranked match / player match] |
| Yeah! I did it! (Silver) | Get 10 consecutive wins in a ranked match |
| Yeeeeaaah! (Bronze) | Hit 100 times using EX Super Special Moves (Arcade, Versus) |

NEW!

A
B
C
D
E
F
G
H
I
J
K
L
M
N
O
P
Q
R
S
T
U
V
W
X
Y
Z

**CODES & CHEATS**

| Yes! I'm the best! (Gold) | Clear 200 trials in Trial mode |
|---|---|
| You can't compare to me. (Silver) | Clear Time Attack mode with 30 characters |
| You can't win against me! (Bronze) | Be challenged by "Ash" and win in ARCADE |
| You're not so bad! (Bronze) | Complete the tutorial |

### CODE

After selecting certain characters, pressing "select" before selecting a color can yield either an alternate costume or a separate color palette.

| UNLOCKABLE | CODE |
|---|---|
| Andy - Ninja Mask | Press "select" before selecting his color. |
| Elisabeth - KOF XI Outfit | Press "select" before selecting her color. |
| Joe - Tiger-Striped Boxers | Press "select" before selecting his color. |
| K' - Dual-Colored Outfit | Press "select" before selecting his color. |
| Kyo - Orochi Saga Outfit | Press "select" before selecting his color. |
| Raiden - Big Bear Outfit | Press "select" before selecting his color. |
| Ralf - Camouflage | Press "select" before selecting his color. |
| Takuma - Mr. Karate Outfit | Press "select" before selecting his color. |
| Yuri - Braided Ponytail | Press "select" before selecting her color. |

### UNLOCKABLE

| UNLOCKABLE | HOW TO UNLOCK |
|---|---|
| Battle Againts Ash | Get 4,000,000 Points before the 6th Stage. |
| Battle Against Dark Ash (Final Stage) | Defeat True Saiki in stage 6. |
| Battle Againts True Saiki (stage 7) | Get 2,500,000 after by the end of stage 6 |
| Billy Kane | Perform at least 2 target actions per match in arcade mode. He should then appear as a challenger, defeating him will unlock him |
| Saiki | Perform at least 5 target actions per match in arcade mode. Saiki should then appear as a challenger, defeating him will unlock him |

## THE KING OF FIGHTERS XIII (XBOX 360)

### ACHIEVEMENT

| UNLOCKABLE | HOW TO UNLOCK |
|---|---|
| After all, you're just trash. (30) | Get an SS at the victory screen |
| And the final blow...! (20) | Get 50 NEO MAX Super Special Moves Finishes (Arcade, Versus) |
| Come back later! (20) | Perform 50 Drive Cancels (Arcade, Versus) |
| Do you understand now? (40) | Complete STORY. |
| Doesn't it feel good? (20) | Win 25 [ranked matches / player matches] |
| Excellent! (50) | Win 100 [ranked matches / player matches] |
| Go easy on me! (10) | Play your first [ranked match / player match] |
| Good! (20) | Play 50 [ranked matches / player matches] |
| Great (20) | Be challenged by "Saiki" and win in ARCADE |
| Hehe... hot, wasn't it? (30) | Play 100 [ranked matches / player matches] |
| Heheh. Not bad. (10) | Perform 50 MAX Cancels (Arcade, Versus) |
| Here I come, buddy! (20) | Create 10 characters in Customize |
| Hey! (10) | Hit 100 times using NEO MAX Super Special Moves (Arcade, Versus) |
| Hey, hey, hey! (20) | Be challenged by "Billy" and win in ARCADE |
| Hmph... this is only natural. (10) | Get 10 straight wins (Arcade, Versus) |

| | |
|---|---|
| **How was it? (30)** | Clear ARCADE MODE without continuing |
| **I shall not waver! (40)** | Play 300 [ranked matches / player matches] |
| **I will execute my mission! (10)** | Defeat 3 characters in Survival mode |
| **I'm enough for this job! (30)** | Defeat 35 characters in Survival mode |
| **Isn't this fun, eh? (30)** | Win 50 [ranked matches / player matches] |
| **It's about time to start! (10)** | Register an icon, team and message in Customize |
| **Let's play warrior! (10)** | Create 10 rooms |
| **Let's see what you've got... (30)** | Clear STORY. |
| **Looks like I was just on time. (10)** | Clear Time Attack mode for the first time |
| **Mission Complete! (20)** | Perform 50 Super Cancels (Arcade, Versus) |
| **Number 1! (30)** | Get 5 consecutive wins in a ranked match |
| **Okay! (20)** | Get 2 consecutive wins in a ranked match |
| **Piece of cake! (20)** | Perform 50 HD Cancels (Arcade, Versus) |
| **Play time is over! (10)** | Perform 50 Super Special Moves Finishes (Arcade, Versus) |
| **Show me what humans are made of (20)** | Perform 10 Target Actions (Arcade) |
| **Spinning! (10)** | Hit 100 times using EX Special Moves (Arcade, Versus) |
| **Strength! (10)** | Hit 100 times using Special Moves (Arcade, Versus) |
| **That should do it! (30)** | Complete all trials for 1 character in Trial mode |
| **This is... my victory! (40)** | Clear ARCADE MODE on VERY HARD |
| **This was just a greeting! (10)** | Win 5 [ranked matches / player matches] |
| **Time will soon turn to ashes... (20)** | Get an S at the victory screen |
| **What's wrong? (30)** | Perform 300 Target Actions (Arcade) |
| **Yahoooo! (10)** | Hit 100 times using Super Special Moves (Arcade, Versus) |
| **Yay! Perfect! (10)** | Perform 10 Perfect Victories (Arcade, Versus) |
| **Yeah! (10)** | Win your first [ranked match / player match] |
| **Yeah! I did it! (40)** | Get 10 consecutive wins in a ranked match |
| **Yeeeeaaah! (10)** | Hit 100 times using EX Super Special Moves (Arcade, Versus) |
| **Yes! I'm the best! (50)** | Clear 200 trials in Trial mode |
| **You can't compare to me. (40)** | Clear Time Attack mode with 30 characters |
| **You can't win against me! (20)** | Be challenged by "Ash" and win in ARCADE |
| **You're not so bad! (10)** | Complete the tutorial |

### *UNLOCKABLE*

| UNLOCKABLE | HOW TO UNLOCK |
|---|---|
| Billy Kane | You must do 2+ TAs during each match (At average 6 TAs per stage.) before Stage 4. Defeat him when he challenges you. |
| Human Saiki | You must do 5+ TAs during each match (At average 15 TAs per stage.) before Stage 4. Defeat him when he challenges you. |

## THRILLVILLE (PSP)

### CODES

Enter these while in a park. You hear a chime if it worked.

| UNLOCKABLE | HOW TO UNLOCK |
|---|---|
| Add $50,000 | ■, ●, ▲, ■, ●, ▲, ✕ |
| Mission Complete | ■, ●, ▲, ■, ●, ▲, ● |
| Unlock All Parks | ■, ●, ▲, ■, ●, ▲, ■ |
| Unlock All Rides in Park | ■, ●, ▲, ■, ●, ▲, ▲ |

## TIGER WOODS PGA TOUR '10 (XBOX 360)

### UNLOCKABLES

| UNLOCKABLE | HOW TO UNLOCK |
|---|---|
| Bonus Challenge 1 | Complete all Tournament Challenges. |
| Bonus Challenge 2 | Complete Bonus Challenge 1. |
| Bonus Challenge 3 | Complete Bonus Challenge 2. |
| Bonus Challenge 4 | Complete Bonus Challenge 3. |

## TIGER WOODS PGA TOUR '10 (PlayStation 3)

### UNLOCKABLES

| UNLOCKABLE | HOW TO UNLOCK |
|---|---|
| Doral | Beat the first Tournament Challenge on this course or buy the course pass. |
| East Lake | Beat the first Tournament Challenge on this course or buy the course pass. |
| Harbor Town | Beat the first Tournament Challenge on this course or buy the course pass. |
| Hazeltine | Beat the first Tournament Challenge on this course or buy the course pass. |
| Oakmont | Beat the first Tournament Challenge on this course or buy the course pass. |
| Pebble Beach | Beat the first Tournament Challenge on this course or buy the course pass. |
| Pinehurst no.2 | Beat the first Tournament Challenge on this course or buy the course pass. |
| Torrey Pines | Beat the first Tournament Challenge on this course or buy the course pass. |
| Tpc Boston | Beat the first Tournament Challenge on this course or buy the course pass. |
| Wentworth | Beat the first Tournament Challenge on this course or buy the course pass. |

## TIGER WOODS PGA TOUR 12: THE MASTERS (XBOX 360)

### ACHIEVEMENT

| UNLOCKABLE | HOW TO UNLOCK |
|---|---|
| 1 Is The Loneliest Number (10) | Be the #1 Ranked Golfer for 10 consecutive weeks. |
| 2005 Masters Champion (25) | Win the 2005 Historic Masters Event (Tiger at the Masters) |
| A New Generation (25) | Break the top 10 in the EA SPORTS Golf Rankings |
| Ad Wizard (25) | Play in a Major with Callaway Golf® Level 4 Sponsorship equipped |
| Aspiring Amateur (10) | Complete the EA SPORTS™ AM TOUR |
| Bling my Tag (15) | Apply 3 pins to your Bag Tag |
| Born with Skillz (25) | Master 8 courses |
| Broken Record (40) | Hold down the #1 spot on the EA SPORTS Golf Rankings for more than 281 weeks |

| | |
|---|---|
| Caddie with a Master's Degree (50) | Master 16 Courses |
| Choke Artist (15) | Land within 1 yard of the flagstick using a choked approach shot from at least 50 yards out. |
| Commercial Icon (35) | Play in a Major with Nike Level 4 Sponsorship equipped |
| Course Master (10) | Master 1 course |
| Drop and give me 15 (25) | Earn 15 pins |
| Earned my Card! (20) | Complete Q-School |
| Egg on the Dance Floor (10) | Sink a 30ft putt without boosting the green read |
| FIR (5) | Land the ball on the Fairway after your tee shot. FIR = Fairway in Regulation |
| First Time EVER! (35) | Win both the Par 3 and the Masters on the same week in the Road to the Masters mode. |
| Flowering Crab Apple in 1! (10) | Hole in one on Hole 4 of Augusta (only one hole in one has ever been recorded on this hole) |
| GamerNet Tourist (10) | Earn 2,500 Player Points in EA SPORTS™ GamerNet |
| GIR (5) | Land the ball on the Green with at least 2 fewer strokes than par. GIR = Green in Regulation |
| Give me the Goodies! (10) | Win a Sponsored Challenge Event in the Road to the Masters mode. |
| Great Suggestion (15) | Sink a Hole in One using a Caddie Recommendation |
| HAMMERhead Swag (65) | Equip a HAMMERhead Prototype Outfit |
| History is Yours (15) | Compete in a Historic Masters Event (Tiger at the Masters) |
| Hold my bag as I post my clip (5) | Post an EA SPORTS™ GamerNet Challenge |
| I AM CADDIE! (15) | Accept and follow thru on 25 Caddie Suggestions in an 18 hole round of golf |
| I Got This (15) | From the Fairway, land within 1 yard of the flagstick from 100 yards out using a Custom shot. |
| Masters Legend (75) | Win the Green Jacket for a Record 7 times in the Road to the Masters mode. |
| Masters Master (15) | Master Augusta National & Augusta Par 3 (Gold Course Mastery) |
| New Record Holder! (15) | Beat the course record of 63 at the Masters (In Road to the Masters) |
| On the Radar (10) | Break the top 50 in the EA SPORTS Golf Rankings |
| On top of the World (50) | Become #1 in the EA SPORTS Golf Rankings |
| Online Participation (10) | Play a Live Tournament |
| Pin Collector (50) | Earn All Pins |
| Ping Pitchman (15) | Play in a Major with PING® Level 4 Sponsorship equipped |
| Road to the Masters (35) | Win the Green Jacket in the Road to the Masters mode. |
| Shark Attack! (65) | Equip a HAMMERhead Prototype Club |
| Short But Sweet (15) | Beat the course record of 20 at Augusta Par 3 |
| Sponsorship is Calling (10) | Play in a Major with Cleveland Golf Level 4 Sponsorship equipped |
| The Presidents Cup Champion (15) | Win The Presidents Cup |
| Tiger Quickness (10) | Use the new Speed Play option in game |
| Tournament Pro (10) | Complete an 18 hole round under par with Tournament Difficulty turned ON |

NEW!

A
B
C
D
E
F
G
H
I
J
K
L
M
N
O
P
Q
R
S
T
U
V
W
X
Y
Z

**CODES & CHEATS**

| | |
|---|---|
| Training Wheels (10) | Win a training event in the Road to the Masters mode. |
| We've Only Just Begun (15) | Compete in a Nationwide Tour event |
| Who's your Caddie?! (5) | Complete the Prologue |
| Winner! And Still... (25) | Defend your title in any Major |

## TIME CRISIS 2 (PlayStation 2)

| UNLOCKABLE | OBJECTIVE |
|---|---|
| Auto Bullets | Clear the Story mode twice at any difficulty level to be able to fire 20 bullets in one trigger. |
| Auto Reload | Clear the Story mode at any difficulty level using Auto Bullets to earn unlimited firepower with your gun. |
| Increase Your Credits in Arcade Mode | Receive extra credits if you clear the Story mode at any difficulty level. (See below for more info) |
| Mirror Mode | To activate the Mirror mode, clear the Story mode without using the "Continue" function. |
| Music Player | To access the Music Player, clear the final mission of the "Crisis" Mission. |
| Shoot Away 2 Arrange Mode | To access Arrange mode, score very high points in the Arcade Original mode (Retro). Hit two clay pigeons with one bullet to double your points for that shot. |
| Shoot Away 2 Extra Mode | To access Extra mode, score good points in the Arcade Original mode (Retro). |
| Stage Trial 2 | To reach Stage Trial 2, clear Stage 1 of the Story mode at any difficulty level. |
| Stage Trial 3 | To reach Stage Trial 3, clear Stage 2 of the Story mode at any difficulty level. |
| Wide Shots | Clear the Story mode at any difficulty level with the Auto Reload function to enable your firearm to shoot wide shots (shotgun type with nine bullets per reload). |

*FOR THE "INCREASE YOUR CREDITS IN ARCADE MODE" CODE, ONCE YOU'VE CLEARED THE MODE SEVERAL TIMES, YOU ARE EVENTUALLY ENTITLED TO "FREE PLAY" AND A MAXIMUM OF NINE LIVES THAT YOU CAN SET IN THE "GAME" OPTIONS.*

## TMNT (XBOX 360)

### CODES

At the main menu screen, hold ⓛ and enter the code, then release ⓛ. You should hear a sound to confirm you entered the code right.

| CODE | EFFECT |
|---|---|
| AABA | Unlocks challenge map 2 |
| BYAX | Unlocks Don's big head goodie |

## TMNT (Wii)

### UNLOCKABLES

At the main menu, hold ⓩ on the Nunchuk and enter the following codes. Release ⓩ after each code to hear a confirmation sound.

| UNLOCKABLE | CODE |
|---|---|
| Unlock Don's Big Head Goodie | ①, Ⓐ, Ⓒ, ② |
| Unlock Challenge Map 2 | Ⓐ, Ⓐ, Ⓐ, ①, Ⓐ |

## TOEJAM AND EARL (Wii)

### UNLOCKABLES

| UNLOCKABLE | HOW TO UNLOCK |
|---|---|
| Free Presents | Sneak up on Santa Claus before he takes off and he gives you a few presents. |
| Level 0 | On Level 1, on the bottom left side, a small hole leads to level 0, which has hula dancers in a tub and a lemonade man who gives you another life. |

| Present Island | At the top right of the map on level 1, there is a hidden island with a load of presents for the taking. You need rocket skates, an inner-tube, or icarus wings to get there. |
|---|---|
| Ultimate Cheat | Pause the game, then press the following button combinations: ✛+Ⓐ+Ⓑ+Ⓒ, ✛+Ⓐ, ✛+Ⓑ, ✛+Ⓠ. You hear a sound if you entered the code correctly. Unpause the game, and you have all but one of the ship pieces collected. The last piece will always be located on the next level. |

## TOEJAM AND EARL IN PANIC ON FUNKOTRON   (Wii)

### PASSWORDS

| PASSWORD | EFFECT |
|---|---|
| R-F411W9Q986 | Level 3 |

| PASSWORD | EFFECT |
|---|---|
| PJ04EK-5WT82 | Level 5 |
| MW0WEE6JRVF7 | Level 7 |
| VANDNEHF9807L | Level 9 |
| MWAAK!8MDT76 | Level 11 |
| F!!NEHNW0Q73 | Level 15 |
| T0EJAMTEARL! | View Credits |

### HIGH FUNK PASSWORDS

Enter these passwords at the password screen to go to your desired level with lots of Funk.

| PASSWORD | EFFECT |
|---|---|
| RWJ21EW1R80X | Level 03 with 37 Funk |
| VJW6EK21-J07 | Level 05 with 80 Funk |
| P0W09KAN-VQ | Level 07 with 95 Funk |
| VDJF7M2DyT6L | Level 09 with 99 Funk |
| VYJF73TH1PQQ | Level 11 with 99 Funk |
| DKYQHX4!EV!7 | Level 13 with 89 Funk |
| J11L3R4C13H7 | Level 15 with 49 Funk |

## TOM CLANCY'S ENDWAR   (XBOX 360)

### CODES

Under Community and Extras, press "Y" on Downloadable Content. Battalions can be used in Theater of War mode.

| EFFECT | CODE |
|---|---|
| Unlock upgraded European Federation (EFEC) Battalion | EUCA20 |
| Unlock upgraded Joint Strike Force (JSF) Battalion | JSFA35 |
| Unlock upgraded Spetznaz (Russian) Battalion | SPZT17 |
| Unlock upgraded Spetznaz (Russian) Battalion | SPZA39 |

## TOM CLANCY'S ENDWAR   (PlayStation 3)

### CODES

Go to the Community & Extras screen on the Main Menu, highlight the VIP option and press the Triangle button to input the special codes.

| EFFECT | CODE |
|---|---|
| European Enforcer Corps | EUCA20 |
| Russian Spetsnaz Guard Brigade | SPZA39 |
| U.S. Joint Strike Force | JSFA35 |
| Unlocks the special Spetsnaz Battalion | SPZT17 |

NEW!
A
B
C
D
E
F
G
H
I
J
K
L
M
N
O
P
Q
R
S
**T**
U
V
W
X
Y
Z

**CODES & CHEATS**

### TOM CLANCY'S GHOST RECON: ADVANCED WARFIGHTER (XBOX 360)

When the game is paused, enter these codes while holding ⚪, ⓛⓣ, ⓡⓣ.

| UNLOCKABLE | CODE |
|---|---|
| Full Life | ⓛ③, ⓛ③, ⓡⒷ, ✕, ⓡⒷ, ⓨ |
| Scott Mitchell Invincible | ⓨ, ⓨ, ✕, ⓡⒷ, ✕, ⓛ③ |
| Team Invincible | ✕, ✕, ⓨ, ⓡⒷ, ⓨ, ⓛ③ |
| Unlimited Ammo | ⓡⒷ, ⓡⒷ, ⓛ③, ✕, ⓛ③, ⓨ |

Enter this code on the Mission Select screen while holding ⚪, ⓛⓣ, ⓡⓣ.

| UNLOCKABLE | CODE |
|---|---|
| All Levels | ⓨ, ⓡⒷ, ⓨ, ⓡⒷ, ✕ |

### TOM CLANCY'S GHOST RECON: ADVANCED WARFIGHTER 2 (XBOX 360)

Enter this password as a name.

| UNLOCKABLE | CODE |
|---|---|
| FAMAS in Quick Missions Only (works in Australian version only) | GRAW2QUICKFAMAS |

### TOM CLANCY'S HAWX (XBOX 360)

#### CODES

Go to the hangar screen, then enter the codes to unlock the corresponding aircraft.

| | |
|---|---|
| Unlocks A-12 Avenger II | Hold ⓛⓣ and enter ✕, ⓛⒷ, ✕, ⓡⒷ, ⓨ, ✕ |
| Unlocks F-18 HARV | Hold ⓛⓣ and enter ⓛⒷ, ⓨ, ⓛⒷ, ⓨ, ⓛⒷ, ✕ |
| Unlocks FB-22 | Hold ⓛⓣ and enter ⓡⒷ, ✕, ⓡⒷ, ✕, ⓡⒷ, ⓨ |

### TOM CLANCY'S HAWX (PlayStation 3)

#### CODES

Go to the hangar screen, then enter the codes to unlock the corresponding aircraft.

| EFFECT | CODE |
|---|---|
| Unlocks A-12 Avenger II | Hold ⓛ② and press ■, ⓛ①, ■, ⓡ①, ▲, ■ |
| Unlocks F-18 HARV | Hold ⓛ② and press ⓛ①, ▲, ⓛ①, ▲, ⓛ①, ■ |
| Unlocks FB-22 | Hold ⓛ② and press ⓡ①, ■, ⓡ①, ■, ⓡ①, ▲ |

### TOM CLANCY'S RAINBOW SIX VEGAS 2 (XBOX 360)

#### CODES

During gameplay, pause the game, hold the right shoulder button, and enter the following codes.

| UNLOCKABLE | HOW TO UNLOCK |
|---|---|
| GI John Doe Mode | ⓛ③, ⓛ③, Ⓐ, ⓡⒷ, ⓡⒷ, Ⓑ, ⓛ③, ⓛ③, ✕, ⓡⒷ, ⓡⒷ, ⓨ |
| Super Ragdoll | Ⓐ, Ⓐ, Ⓑ, Ⓑ, ✕, ✕, ⓨ, ⓨ, Ⓐ, Ⓑ, ⓨ |
| Third Person Mode | ✕, Ⓑ, ✕, Ⓑ, ⓛ③, ⓛ③, ⓨ, Ⓐ, ⓨ, Ⓐ, ⓡⒷ, ⓡⒷ |

#### WEAPONS

When you are customizing your character, hold down the right bumper and insert the following code.

| UNLOCKABLE | HOW TO UNLOCK |
|---|---|
| AR-21 Assault Rifle | ↓, ↓, ↑, ↑, ✕, Ⓑ, Ⓑ, ✕, ⓨ, ↑, ↑, ⓨ |

#### COMCAST MULTIPLAYER MAP

At the main menu, go to the Extras menu, select Comcast Gift, then enter the following password.

| PASSWORD | EFFECT |
|---|---|
| Comcast faster | Comcast multiplayer map |

## TOM CLANCY'S RAINBOW SIX VEGAS 2 (PlayStation 3)

### CODES

At the Title screen, hold R1 and press the following.

| UNLOCKABLE | HOW TO UNLOCK |
| --- | --- |
| M468 Assault Rifle | ↑,▲,↓,×,←,■,→,●,←,←,→,■ |
| MTAR-21 Assault Rifle | ↓,↓,↑,↑,■,●,■,●,▲,↑,↑,▲ |

### SINGLE PLAYER CODES

During gameplay, pause the game, hold R1, and insert the following codes.

| UNLOCKABLE | HOW TO UNLOCK |
| --- | --- |
| Red and Blue Tracers (also works online, host must enter code) | L3, L3, ×, R3, R3, ●, L3, L3, ■, R3, R3, ▲ |
| Third-Person View | ■, ●, ■, ●, L3, L3, ▲, ×, ▲, ×, R3, R3 |
| Super Ragdoll Mode | ×, ×, ●, ●, ■, ■, ▲, ▲, ×, ●, ■, ▲ |

### COMCAST MULTIPLAYER MAP

At the game's main menu, go to the Extras menu, select Comcast Gift, then enter the following password.

| PASSWORD | EFFECT |
| --- | --- |
| Comcast faster | Comcast multiplayer map |

## TOM CLANCY'S SPLINTER CELL: CHAOS THEORY (DS)

### UNLOCKABLES

| UNLOCKABLE | HOW TO UNLOCK |
| --- | --- |
| Argus Mercenary Costume | In Machi Akko, go to the bar and use the microphone. Look behind you for a keycard. Go back to the hallway with three doors, and use it on the closet. |
| Camouflage Sam Costume | In the Lighthouse level, snipe the man on the roof, but don't rappel down. On the high right corner is the costume. |
| Displace Mercenary Costume in Display Level | Go to floor three. Use the optic cable to see which room has the green package. Enter the room, and use keypad code 5800. |
| Displace Suit | Room next to the room where you have a last chance to save, code is 5800. |
| Masked Sam Costume | In the Penthouse level, go to Zherkezhi's apartment, and go to the first room on the top floor. Go down the long, dark hall and type 5698 in the pad. |
| National Guard Costume | In the Manhattan Streets level, go to the open area before the penthouse. Climb the pipe, jump left, and go down to the next platform, in the corner. |
| Shadownet Agent Costume | In Kokubo Sosho, go down the elevator, where lasers are at the bottom. Find a ladder to climb back up. The room will have lasers and the costume. |
| Short Sleeved Sam Costume in Bank Level | Go to the small vault left of the computer and use the lockpick. |
| Snow Guard Costume in Battery Level | Get the wrench, and go to the U-shaped room. Enter the keycard room, take out the guard, climb on the crate, and bash next crate. |
| Thermal Suit Costume in Hokkaido Level | Find the wrench, and find the man who is shooting on the roof, get to him and fall through the vent, exiting the room, and bash the door. |
| Full Equipment Mode (infinite ammo etc.) | Beat the game at least once. |

NEW!

A
B
C
D
E
F
G
H
I
J
K
L
M
N
O
P
Q
R
S
**T**
U
V
W
X
Y
Z

**CODES & CHEATS**

## TOM CLANCY'S SPLINTER CELL: ESSENTIALS (PSP)

### BONUS MISSION CODES

Enter the following at the bonus mission screen (you have to enter the code each time you want to play the mission).

| UNLOCKABLE | HOW TO UNLOCK |
|---|---|
| Unlock the Heroin Refinery Mission | Hold Select and press ⬜+Ⓡ three more times |
| Unlock the Paris-Nice Mission | Hold Select and press ⬜+Ⓡ 12 more times |
| Unlock the Television Free Indonesia Mission | Hold Select and press ⬜+Ⓡ three times |

## TOMB RAIDER LEGENDS (XBOX 360)

Enter these codes in game. Codes can not be used until they are unlocked.

| UNLOCKABLE | CODE |
|---|---|
| Bulletproof | Hold ⓛⓣ press Ⓐ, ⓡⓣ, Ⓨ, ⓡⓣ, Ⓧ, ⓛⓑ |
| Draw enemies' health | Hold ⓛⓣ press Ⓧ, Ⓑ, Ⓐ, ⓛⓑ, ⓡⓣ, Ⓨ |
| Excalibur | Hold ⓛⓑ press Ⓨ, Ⓐ, Ⓑ, ⓡⓣ, Ⓨ, ⓛⓣ |
| Infinite Assault Ammo | Hold ⓛⓑ press Ⓐ, Ⓑ, Ⓐ, ⓛⓣ, Ⓧ, Ⓨ |
| Infinite Grenade Launcher Ammo | Hold ⓛⓑ press ⓛⓣ, Ⓨ, ⓡⓣ, Ⓑ, ⓛⓣ, Ⓧ |
| Infinite Shotgun Ammo | Hold ⓛⓑ press ⓡⓣ, Ⓑ, Ⓧ, ⓛⓣ, Ⓧ, Ⓐ |
| Infinite SMG Ammo | Hold ⓛⓑ press Ⓑ, Ⓨ, ⓛⓣ, ⓡⓣ, Ⓐ, Ⓑ |
| One Shot Kills | Hold ⓛⓣ press Ⓨ, Ⓐ, Ⓨ, Ⓧ, ⓛⓑ, Ⓑ |
| Soul Reaver | Hold ⓛⓑ press Ⓐ, ⓡⓣ, Ⓑ, ⓡⓣ, ⓛⓣ, Ⓧ |
| Textureless Mode | Hold ⓛⓣ press ⓛⓑ, Ⓐ, Ⓑ, Ⓐ, Ⓨ, ⓡⓣ |

## TOMB RAIDER: LEGENDS (PSP)

### CODES

Enter these codes while playing a level, but they only work once you have unlocked them.

| CODE | EFFECT |
|---|---|
| Bulletproof | Hold ⬜, then: ✕, Ⓡ, ▲, Ⓡ, ■, Ⓡ |
| Draw Enemy Health | Hold ⬜, then: ■, ●, ✕, Ⓡ, Ⓡ, ▲ |
| Infinite Assault Rifle Ammo | Hold ⬜, then: ✕, ●, ✕, Ⓡ, ■, ▲ |
| Infinite Grenade Launcher | Hold ⬜, then: Ⓡ, ▲, Ⓡ, ●, Ⓡ, ■ |
| Infinite Shotgun Ammo | Hold ⬜, then: Ⓡ, ●, ■, Ⓡ, ■, ✕ |
| Infinite SMG Ammo | Hold ⬜, then: ●, ▲, Ⓡ, Ⓡ, ✕, ● |
| One Shot Kill | Hold ⬜, then: ▲, ✕, ▲, ■, Ⓡ, ● |
| Wield Excalibur | Hold ⬜, then: ▲, ✕, ●, Ⓡ, ▲, Ⓡ |
| Wield Soul Reaver | Hold ⬜, then: ✕, Ⓡ, ●, Ⓡ, Ⓡ, ■ |
| Zip | Collect 20% of all bronze rewards |

## TOMB RAIDER: UNDERWORLD (XBOX 360)

### UNLOCKABLES

| UNLOCKABLE | HOW TO UNLOCK |
|---|---|
| Lara's bathing suit | Complete the game on any difficulty setting and this becomes unlocked in Treasure Hunt mode when you revisit the Mediterranean Sea Expedition. |
| Treasure Hunt mode | Complete the game on any difficulty to unlock Treasure Hunt mode, which allows you to revisit all levels to claim Treasures/Relics missed through storm. |

## TOMB RAIDER: UNDERWORLD (PlayStation 3)

### UNLOCKABLES

All items can be found under the Extras section once the following conditions are met.

| UNLOCKABLE | HOW TO UNLOCK |
|---|---|
| **All environment concept art for Arctic Sea and Amelia concepts** | Complete Arctic Sea Expedition. |
| **All environment concept art for Coastal Thailand and Alister concepts** | Complete Coastal Thailand Expedition. |
| **All environment concept art for Croft Manor and Doppelganger concepts** | Complete Croft Manor Expedition. |
| **All environment concept art for Jan Mayen Island and Gear and Artifacts concepts** | Complete Jan Mayen Island Expedition. |
| **All environment concept art for Mediterranean Sea and Amanda concepts** | Complete Mediterranean Sea Expedition. |
| **All environment concept art for Mexico and All Men concepts** | Complete Southern Mexico Expedition. |
| **All environment concept art for Ship and Natla concepts** | Complete Andaman Sea Expedition. |
| **Creature concepts** | Collect every single Treasure. |
| **Game flow storyboards** | Complete the entire game on the Master Survivalist difficulty level. |
| **Lara concepts** | Collect all six Relics. |
| **Zip and Winston concepts** | Complete Prologue. |

## TONY HAWK'S AMERICAN WASTELAND (XBOX 360)

In the Options menu, select the Cheats menu and enter these passwords. (Note: case sensitive)

| UNLOCKABLE | PASSWORD |
|---|---|
| **Matt Hoffman** | the_condor |
| **Perfect Grinds** | grindXpert |
| **Perfect Manuals** | 2wheels! |

### CODES

Enter codes in the Options menu under "codes."

| EFFECT | CODE |
|---|---|
| **Helps you keep balance when grinding** | grindXpert |

| EFFECT | CODE |
|---|---|
| **Hitch a ride on the back of cars** | h!tchar!de |
| **Lil John** | hip2DHop |
| **Moon Gravity** | 2them00n |
| **Perfect manuals** | 2wheels! |
| **Play as Jason Ellis** | sirius-DJ |
| **Play as Mindy** | help1nghand |
| **Unlock legendary skater Matt Hoffman** | the_condor |

## TONY HAWK'S DOWNHILL JAM (Wii)

Enter these passwords in the Cheats menu.

| UNLOCKABLE | PASSWORD |
|---|---|
| **Always Special** | PointHogger |
| **Chipmunk Voices** | HelloHelium |
| **Demon Skater** | EvilChimneySweep |
| **Display Coordinates** | DisplayCoordinates |
| **Enables Manuals** | IMISSMANUALS |
| **Extreme Car Crashes** | WatchForDoors |
| **First Person Skater** | FirstPersonJam |

**CODES & CHEATS**

| | |
|---|---|
| Free Boost | OotbaghForever |
| Giganto-Skater | IWannaBeTallTall |
| Invisible Skater | NowYouSeeMe |
| Large Birds | BirdBirdBirdBird |
| Mini Skater | DownTheRabbitHole |
| Perfect Manual | TightRopeWalker |
| Perfect Rail | LikeTiltingAPlate |
| Perfect Stats | IAmBob |
| Picasso Skater | FourLights |
| Power of the Fish! | TonyFishDownhillJam |
| Shadow Skater | ChimneySweep |
| Tiny People | ShrinkThePeople |
| Unlock All Boards and Outfits | RaidTheWoodshed |
| Unlock All Events | AdventuresOfKwang |
| Unlock All Movies | FreeBozzler |
| Unlock All Skaters | ImInterfacing |

## TONY HAWK'S PROJECT 8 (XBOX 360)

Enter these passwords in the Cheats menu.

| UNLOCKABLE | PASSWORD |
|---|---|
| All decks unlocked and free except for inkblot deck and Gamestop deck | needaride |
| All specials in shop | yougotitall |
| Travis Barker | plus44 |
| Grim Reaper (Freeskate) | enterandwin |
| Jason Lee | notmono |
| Anchor Man | newshound |
| Big Realtor | shescaresme |
| Christian Hosoi | hohohosoi |
| Colonel and Security Guard | militarymen |
| Inkblot Deck | birdhouse |
| Kevin Staab | mixitup |
| Nerd | wearelosers |
| Photographer Girl and Filmer | themedia |
| Zombie | suckstobedead |
| Dad and Skater Jam Kid | strangefellows |

## TONY HAWK'S PROJECT 8 (PlayStation 3)

In the Options menu, select Cheats to enter these passwords.

| UNLOCKABLE | PASSWORD |
|---|---|
| Big Realtor | shescaresme |
| Christian Hosoi | hohohosoi |
| Colonel and Security Guard | militarymen |
| Dad and Skater Jam Kid | strangefellows |
| Full Air Stats | drinkup |
| Grim Reaper | enterandwin |
| Inkblot Deck | birdhouse |
| Jason Lee | notmono |
| Kevin Staab | mixitup |
| Mascot | manineedadate |
| Most Decks | needaride |

| Nerd | wearelosers |
|------|-------------|
| Photographer and Cameraman | themedia |
| Travis Barker | plus44 |
| Unlock Specials in Skate Shop | yougotitall |

## TONY HAWK'S PROVING GROUND (PlayStation 3)

### CHEATS
Enter the codes in the options menu of the main menu

| UNLOCKABLE | HOW TO UNLOCK |
|------------|---------------|
| 100% Branch Completion (NTT) | FOREVERNAILED |
| Invisible Man | THEMISSING |
| Mini Skater | TINYTATER |
| No Bails | ANDAINTFALLIN |
| No Board | MAGICMAN |
| Perfect Manual | STILLAINTFALLIN |
| Perfect Rail | AINTFALLIN |
| Super Check | BOOYAH |
| Unlimited Focus | MYOPIC |
| Unlimited Slash Grind | SUPERSLASHIN |
| Unlock Judy Nails | LOVEROCKNROLL |

### ITEMS

| UNLOCKABLE | HOW TO UNLOCK |
|------------|---------------|
| 50 Extra Skill Points | NEEDSHELP |
| All CAS Items | GIVEMESTUFF |
| All Decks | LETSGOSKATE |
| All Fun Items | OVERTHETOP |
| All Game Movies | WATCHTHIS |
| All Lounge Bling Items | SWEETSTUFF |
| All Lounge Themes | LAIDBACKLOUNGE |
| All Rigger Pieces | IMGONNABUILD |
| All Special Tricks Available | LOTSOFTRICKS |
| All Video Editor Effects | TRIPPY |
| All Video Editor Overlays | PUTEMONTOP |
| Full Stats | BEEFEDUP |

### LEVELS

| UNLOCKABLE | HOW TO UNLOCK |
|------------|---------------|
| Unlock Air & Space Museum | THEINDOORPARK |
| Unlock FDR | THEPREZPARK |
| Unlock Lansdowne | THELOCALPARK |

### SKATERS

| UNLOCKABLE | HOW TO UNLOCK |
|------------|---------------|
| Boneman | CRAZYBONEMAN |
| Bosco | MOREMILK |
| Cam | NOTACAMERA |
| Cooper | THECOOP |
| Eddie X | SKETCHY |
| El Patinador | PILEDRIVER |
| Eric | FLYAWAY |
| Mad Dog | RABBIES |
| MCA | INTERGALACTIC |

NEW!

A
B
C
D
E
F
G
H
I
J
K
L
M
N
O
P
Q
R
S
T
U
V
W
X
Y
Z

| Mel | NOTADUDE |
|-----|----------|
| Rube | LOOKSSMELLY |
| Shayne | MOVERS |
| Spence | DAPPER |
| TV Producer | SHAKER |

## TONY HAWK'S PROVING GROUND (Wii)

### ITEMS

| UNLOCKABLE | HOW TO UNLOCK |
|------------|---------------|
| 50 Extra Skill Points | NEEDSHELP |
| All CAS Items | GIVEMESTUFF |
| All Decks | LETSGOSKATE |
| All Fun Items | OVERTHETOP |
| All Game Movies | WATCHTHIS |
| All Rigger Pieces | IMGONNABUILD |
| All Special Tricks Available | LOTSOFTRICKS |
| Full Stats | BEEFEDUP |

### LEVELS

| UNLOCKABLE | HOW TO UNLOCK |
|------------|---------------|
| Unlock Air and Space Museum | THEINDOORPARK |
| Unlock FDR | THEPREZPARK |
| Unlock Lansdowne | THELOCALPARK |

### SKATERS

| UNLOCKABLE | HOW TO UNLOCK |
|------------|---------------|
| Boneman | CRAZYBONEMAN |
| Bosco | MOREMILK |
| Cam | NOTACAMERA |
| Cooper | THECOOP |
| Eddie X | SKETCHY |
| El Patinador | PILEDRIVER |
| Eric | FLYAWAY |
| Mad Dog | RABBIES |
| MCA | INTERGALACTIC |
| Mel | NOTADUDE |
| Rube | LOOKSSMELLY |
| Shayne | MOVERS |
| Spence | DAPPER |
| TV Producer | SHAKER |

## TONY HAWK'S PROVING GROUND (DS)

### CHEATS

Enter the codes in the Options menu of the main menu.

| UNLOCKABLE | HOW TO UNLOCK |
|------------|---------------|
| 100% Branch Completion (NTT) | FOREVERNAILED |
| Invisible Man | THEMISSING |
| Mini Skater | TINYTATER |
| No Bails | ANDAINTFALLIN |
| No Board | MAGICMAN |
| Perfect Manual | STILLAINTFALLIN |
| Perfect Rail | AINTFALLIN |
| Super Check | BOOYAH |
| Unlimited Focus | MYOPIC |

| Unlimited Slash Grind | SUPERSLASHIN |
|---|---|
| Unlock Judy Nails | LOVEROCKNROLL |

### ITEMS

| UNLOCKABLE | HOW TO UNLOCK |
|---|---|
| 50 Extra Skill Points | NEEDSHELP |
| All CAS Items | GIVEMESTUFF |
| All Decks | LETSGOSKATE |
| All Fun Items | OVERTHETOP |
| All Game Movies | WATCHTHIS |
| All Lounge Bling Items | SWEETSTUFF |
| All Lounge Themes | LAIDBACKLOUNGE |
| All Rigger Pieces | IMGONNABUILD |
| All Special Tricks Available | LOTSOFTRICKS |
| All Video Editor Effects | TRIPPY |
| All Video Editor Overlays | PUTEMONTOP |
| Full Stats | BEEFEDUP |

### LEVELS

| UNLOCKABLE | HOW TO UNLOCK |
|---|---|
| Unlock Air & Space Museum | THEINDOORPARK |
| Unlock FDR | THEPREZPARK |
| Unlock Lansdowne | THELOCALPARK |

### SKATERS

| UNLOCKABLE | HOW TO UNLOCK |
|---|---|
| Boneman | CRAZYBONEMAN |
| Bosco | MOREMILK |
| Cam | NOTACAMERA |
| Cooper | THECOOP |
| Eddie X | SKETCHY |
| El Patinador | PILEDRIVER |
| Eric | FLYAWAY |
| Mad Dog | RABBIES |
| MCA | INTERGALACTIC |
| Mel | NOTADUDE |
| Rube | LOOKSSMELLY |
| Shayne | MOVERS |
| Spence | DAPPER |
| TV Producer | SHAKER |

## TONY HAWK'S UNDERGROUND 2 REMIX    (PSP)

Go to Game Options, then Cheat Codes and enter the following codes.

| UNLOCKABLE | CODE |
|---|---|
| Perfect Rail Balance | Tightrope |
| Unlock Tony Hawk from Tony Hawk Pro Skater 1 | Birdman |

## TOSHINDEN    (Wii)

### UNLOCKABLE CHARACTERS

| UNLOCKABLE | HOW TO UNLOCK |
|---|---|
| Dan | Beat Story Mode on hard difficulty |
| Lilith | Beat Story Mode on any difficulty. |
| Moritz | Beat Story Mode on any difficulty. |
| Shouki | Beat Story Mode on hard difficulty. |

**CODES & CHEATS**

## TOUCH THE DEAD  (DS)

### CODES

Enter the following code at the main menu. A zombie will moan if you enter the code successfully and the Logo Screen will turn red. After that you will have access to all missions, all modes, and all bonuses. You will also be able to use the L and R shoulder buttons to switch to the next/previous camera.

| EFFECT | CODE |
| --- | --- |
| Unlocks everything, allows camera switching | Ⓧ,Ⓨ,⇩,⇧,Ⓧ |

## TOWER OF DRUAGA  (Wii)

### CODES

Enter this code at the title screen. If entered properly, the word "DRUA-GA" will turn green. The game is now harder and the levels require different solutions.

| CODE | EFFECT |
| --- | --- |
| ⇧, ⇧, ⇧, ⇧, ⇧, ⇧, ⇩, ⇩, ⇩, ⇩, ⇩, ⇩, ⇩ | Another Druaga (Second Quest) |

## TOY SOLDIERS  (XBOX 360)

### UNLOCKABLES

| UNLOCKABLE | HOW TO UNLOCK |
| --- | --- |
| Gas Mask (Avatar Item) | Buy the game and play the first level on campaign. |
| Allied Toy Soldier Gamerpic | Play the first level after buying the game. |
| Central Toy Soldier Gamerpic | Destroy all 24 golden cubes. |

## TRANSFORMERS: REVENGE OF THE FALLEN  (XBOX 360)

### CODES

Enter with the D-Pad in the "Cheat Codes" option in the Main menu. Note: These characters will only be playable in multiplayer.

| EFFECT | CODE |
| --- | --- |
| Always in Overdrive Mode | LB, B, LB, A, X, R3 |
| Extra Energon (ex: 4x from defeated enemies) | Y, X, B, R3, A, Y |
| Golden Megatron | ⇩, ⇧, ⇨, ⇨, ⇦, ⇧ |
| Golden Optimus Prime | ⇧, ⇩, ⇨, ⇦, ⇨, ⇩ |
| Increased Enemy Accuracy | Y, Y, B, A, X, LB |
| Increased Enemy Damage | LB, Y, A, Y, R3, R3 |
| Increased Enemy Health | B, X, LB, B, R3, Y |
| Increased Weapon Damage in Root Form | Y, Y, R3, A, LB, Y |
| Increased Weapon Damage in Vehicle Form | Y, B, R3, X, R3, L3 |
| Invincibility | R3, A, X, L3, X, X |
| Lower Enemy Accuracy | X, L3, R3, L3, R3, RB |
| Melee Instant Kills | R3, A, X, B, R3, LB |
| No Special Cool Down Time | R3, X, R3, B, X, A |
| No Weapon Overheat | L3, X, A, L3, Y, LB |
| Play as Autobot Protectobot Scout MP in Autobot-based Single-player (only when mission begins, not in character select) Does not work in Deep 6. | R3, LB, LB, Y, X, A |
| Plays as Decepticon Seeker Warrior MP in Decepticon-based Single-player (only when mission begins, not in character select) | X, X, X, LB, A, LB |
| Special Kills Only Mode (Cannot kill enemies except with special kills) | B, B, RB, B, A, L3 |
| Unlimited Turbo | B, L3, X, B, A, Y |
| Unlock all Cairo Missions and Zones | R3, Y, A, Y, L3, LB |

| Unlock All Deep Six Missions and Zones | Ⓧ, (RB), Ⓨ, Ⓑ, Ⓐ, (LB) |
|---|---|
| Unlock All East Coast Missions and Zones | (R3), (L3), (RB), Ⓐ, Ⓑ, Ⓧ |
| Unlock All Shanghai Missions and Zones | Ⓨ, (L3), (R3), (LB), Ⓨ, Ⓐ |
| Unlock All West Coast Missions and Zones | (LB), (RB), (R3), Ⓨ, (R3), Ⓑ |
| Unlock and activate ALL Upgrades | (LB), Ⓨ, (LB), Ⓑ, Ⓧ, Ⓧ |
| Unlocks Generation 1 Starscream | Ⓑ, Ⓐ, Ⓑ, (RB), Ⓨ, (RB) |

## TRANSFORMERS: REVENGE OF THE FALLEN    (PlayStation 3)

### CODES

From the Main Menu go to Cheat Codes and enter the codes there.

| EFFECT | CODE |
|---|---|
| Always in Overdrive Mode | (L1), ●, (L1), ✕, ■, (R3) |
| Extra Energon (ex: 4x from defeated enemies) | ▲, ■, ●, (R3), ✕, ▲ |
| G1 Colors Ironhide (single-player only) | (L1), (R1), (R1), ✕, ●, ▲ |
| G1 Starscream | ●, ✕, ●, (R1), ▲, (R1) |
| Gold Megatron | ↓, ↑, →, →, ←, ↑ |
| Gold Optimus Prime | ↑, ↓, ←, ←, →, ↓ |
| Increased Enemy Accuracy | ▲, ▲, ●, ✕, ■, (L1) |
| Increased Enemy Damage | (L1), ▲, ✕, ▲, (R3), (R3) |
| Increased Enemy Health | ●, ■, (L1), ●, (R3), ▲ |
| Increased Weapon Damage in Robot Form | ▲, ▲, (R3), ✕, (L1), ▲ |
| Increased Weapon Damage in Vehicle Form | ▲, ●, (R1), ■, (R3), (L3) |
| Invincibility | (R3), ✕, ■, (L3), ■, ■ |
| Lower Enemy Accuracy | ■, (L3), (R3), (L3), (R3), (R1) |
| Melee Instant Kills | (R3), ✕, (L1), ●, B, (L1) |
| No Special Cooldown Time | (R3), ■, (R1), (R3), ■, ✕ |
| No Weapon Overheat | (L3), ■, ✕, (L3), ▲, (L3) |
| Play as Autobot Protectobot Scout MP in Autobot-based single-player (only when mission begins, not in character select) Does not work in Deep 6. | (R3), (L1), (L1), ▲, ■, ✕ |
| Plays as Decepticon Seeker Warrior MP in Decepticon-Based single-player (only when mission begins, not in character select) | ■, ▲, ■, (L1), ✕, (L1) |
| Special Kills Only Mode (Cannot kill enemies except with special kills) | ●, ●, (R1), ●, ✕, (L3) |
| Unlimited Turbo | ●, (L3), ■, ✕, ▲ |
| Unlock all Cairo Missions and Zones | (R3), ▲, ✕, ▲, (L3), (L1) |
| Unlock All Deep Six Missions and Zones | ■, (R1), ▲, ●, ✕, (L1) |
| Unlock All East Coast Missions and Zones | (R3), (L3), (R1), ●, ■ |
| Unlock All Shanghai Missions and Zones | ▲, (L3), (R3), (L3), ▲, ✕ |
| Unlock All West Coast Missions and Zones | (L1), (R1), (R3), ▲, (R3), ● |
| Unlock and activate ALL Upgrades | (L1), ▲, (L1), ●, ■, ■ |

## TRANSFORMERS: THE GAME    (XBOX 360)

### CODES

Enter codes at the "Campaign/Bonus Features" main menu. Enter codes for each character during one of their missions. This changes the character's appearance to their Generation 1 skin. Note: Using these cheats prevents you from achieving gamerscore!

| CODE | EFFECT |
|---|---|
| ◊, ○, ○, ◊, ○, ○, ◊ | Generation 1 Skin Megatron |
| ◊, ○, ○, ◊, ◊, ◊, ○ | Generation 1 Skin Prime |

| | |
|---|---|
| ◇,◇,♀,♀,◇,◇,◇ | Generation 1 Skin Jazz |
| ♀,♀,◇,◇,◇,◇,◇ | Generation 1 Skin Optimus Prime |
| ◇,♀,◇,◇,♀,◇,◇ | Generation 1 Skin Starscream |
| ◇,◇,◇,◇,◇,♀,◇ | Infinite Health—Invincible |
| ◇,♀,◇,◇,◇,◇,♀ | No Ammo Reload |
| ◇,◇,◇,◇,◇,◇,◇ | No Military or Police |
| ♀,◇,◇,◇,◇,◇,◇,♀ | Unlock All mission including 2 special mission |
| ◇,◇,◇,♀,◇,◇,◇ | Unlocks the two Cybertron missions. |

### UNLOCKABLES

| UNLOCKABLE | HOW TO UNLOCK |
|---|---|
| G1 Megatron | Collect all the Transformer Shields in the Decepticons Story mode |
| G1 Optimus Prime (Cartoon Model) | Find all the Autobot faction symbols during the Autobot campaign. |
| G1 Robo-vision Optimus | Finish the Autobot campaign. |
| Jazz G1 Repaint | Complete all of the "challenge" sub-missions in both Autobot and Decepticon campaigns. |
| Starscream G1 repaint | Complete Decepticon Story mode. |

## TRANSFORMERS: THE GAME   (Wii)

### CODES

Enter the following codes at the Campaign/Bonus Features/Credits menu.

| CODE | EFFECT |
|---|---|
| ⇧,⇧,⇩,⇩,⇦,⇨,⇧,⇩ | Unlock all missions |
| ⇧,⇧,⇩,⇩,⇦,⇨,⇩ | Infinite health—invincible |
| ⇩,⇩,⇩,⇧,⇧,⇧,⇩ | No vehicles running on the street and no tanks/cops attack |
| ⇩,⇧,⇩,⇧,⇩,⇧,⇩ | Unlock Cybertron missions |

| CODE | EFFECT |
|---|---|
| ⇩,⇩,⇧,⇩,⇩,⇩,⇩ | Unlock G1 Optimus Prime |
| ⇧,⇩,⇩,⇩,⇧,⇩,⇩ | Unlock Generation 1 Jazz Repaint |
| ⇩,⇧,⇩,⇩,⇩,⇩,⇩ | Unlock Generation 1 Starscream Repaint |
| ⇩,⇧,⇩,⇩,⇩,⇩,⇩ | Unlock Robovision Optimus Prime |
| ⇧,⇩,⇩,⇩,⇩,⇩,⇩ | Unlock G1 Megatron |

### UNLOCKABLES

| UNLOCKABLE | HOW TO UNLOCK |
|---|---|
| G1 Jazz Repaint | Clear all sub-missions in Autobot and Decepticon Story modes |
| G1 Megatron | Collect all of the Decepticon icons on all of the maps |
| G1 Optimus Prime | Collect all of the Autobot Icons on all of the maps |
| G1 Starscream Repaint | Beat the Decepticon's Story mode |
| Robovision Optimus Prime | Beat the Autobot's Story mode |

## TRINITY UNIVERSE   (Wii)

### UNLOCKABLES

| UNLOCKABLE | HOW TO UNLOCK |
|---|---|
| Unlock EX form characters | Get 10 or more wins in Survival mode in Single Battle. To use a of character's EX form, press left or right on the Character Select screen. |
| Unlock images from Gallery mode | Beat Story mode using two characters from the same franchise to unlock the first three rows of images. To obtain the other images, beat Story mode using the same method but in their EX form. |

| Unlockable narrators (system voices) | Beat All Battle mode with any character to unlock their voice in the System Voice option in the Sound Settings. |
|---|---|

## TRON EVOLUTION (PSP)

### CODES

Enter the codes on the Code menu. These codes are case sensitive.

| EFFECT | CODE |
|---|---|
| Unlock Rectifier Disc Battle Arena for Quickplay | Endofline |

## TRON EVOLUTION: BATTLE GRIDS (Wii)

### CODES

These are typed in the Cheat Code menu.

| EFFECT | CODE |
|---|---|
| Makes your lightcycle trails taller | lctalltrails |
| Sharp sliding turns for light cycle arena | lcsupersharpslide |

## TROPICO 4 (XBOX 360)

### ACHIEVEMENT

| UNLOCKABLE | HOW TO UNLOCK |
|---|---|
| Building Blues (20) | Unlock 20 Blueprints in a single mission |
| Competent (15) | Have Character Trait at level 5 |
| Coup de Grace (10) | Suppress a Military Coup |
| Curse of the Llama (10) | Survive 10 disasters |
| Dictatorship for Dummies (10) | Finish all tutorial missions |
| Domestic Agenda (20) | Complete 10 Faction tasks in a single mission |
| Elitist (30) | Construct 1337 buildings |
| Expert (30) | Have all Character Traits at level 5 |
| Filthy Rich (20) | Make $100 000 for your Swiss Bank account in a mission |
| Foreign Agenda (20) | Complete 10 Foreign tasks in a single mission |
| Foreign Cuisine (20) | Import 2 000 food |
| God Complex (10) | Finish a Sandbox game in God mode |
| Head for High Ground (20) | Survive a Tsunami with no human casualties |
| Heavy Traffic (15) | Construct at least 1000 meters of roads and 4 Garages |
| Homes for Everyone (20) | Have population of over 300 and no Shacks |
| IMPORTant business (30) | Import 10 000 resources |
| Instant Construction (10) | Issue the Quick-build command on 10 constructions |
| Iron Fist (15) | Suppress an uprising |
| It's a Trap! (30) | Kill 5 rebels at once with a trap in your Mausoleum |
| Kill Juanito (15) | Issue an Execution order on a citizen called Juanito |
| Made In China (30) | Distribute more than 1 000 Luxury Goods from a Shopping mall |
| Metropolis (20) | Construct 200 buildings on one island |
| Militarist (15) | Have more than 20 soldiers and generals in one game |
| Modern Agriculture (20) | Have no dry fields at the end of a Drought |
| Mona Llama (15) | Earn more than $30 000 from selling Tropican art in a Museum of Modern Art |

| | |
|---|---|
| **National Agenda (10)** | Complete 20 agenda tasks in a single mission |
| **Nuclear Future (30)** | Have a Nuclear Power Plant and a Nuclear Program built on your island |
| **Old Faithful (20)** | Survive 3 Volcanic eruptions in a single mission |
| **Paradise Island (20)** | Earn $1 000 000 from tourism profits in a single game |
| **Past and Present (15)** | Have both a Dungeon and a Colonial Museum in the same mission |
| **Prepared For Everything (15)** | Buy all upgrades for a Weather Station |
| **Smells Like Chemistry (10)** | Buy all upgrades for a Chemical Plant |
| **Special Taxes (15)** | Gain $15 000 for your Swiss account from a Customs Office |
| **Specialist (25)** | Have 3 Character Traits at level 5 |
| **The Full Monty (10)** | Have a full Ministry cabinet |
| **The Golf Balls Solution (20)** | Clean an Oil Spill in less than 4 months |
| **The Power of the Atom (30)** | Generate 1 000 MW of electricity in a Nuclear Power Plant |
| **The Rumors of my Death... (20)** | Have one of your clones die instead of you during an assassination attempt |
| **Theme Park (10)** | Have a Roller Coaster near a Ferris Wheel and an Aqua park |
| **Top Exporter (20)** | Earn $1 000 000 from industry in a single game |
| **Tornado Valley (20)** | Survive a Tornado Outbreak with no human casualties |
| **Tropican Fiesta (50)** | Finish a game with overall Happines of your citizens above 70% |
| **War on Crime (10)** | Arrest 10 Criminals in a single mission |
| **Year Of the Dragon (20)** | Put out 10 buildings on fire in a single mission |
| **You are Fired! (10)** | Fire a Minister because of his gaffe |
| **Your Lucky Day (30)** | Hire an unemployed citizen as a Minister |

## TWISTED METAL HEAD ON (PSP)

Input these codes during gameplay.

| UNLOCKABLE | CODE |
|---|---|
| **Invulnerability** | →, ←, ↓, ↑ and finally press L1 + R1 |
| **Infinite Weapons** | ▲, ▲, ↓, ↓, L1 + R1 |

## TWO WORLDS II (XBOX 360)

### CODES

Hold down LB + RB, then while still holding it, press and release buttons in the following order: Y -> A -> Y -> B. The console box appears. Press X to bring up an in-game keyboard and type in the following codes. Using these cheats will disable Achievements on this game save permanently. If you want to earn achievements later, you must restart the game from the dashboard and use a non-cheated game save.

| EFFECT | CODE |
|---|---|
| **Add Auras (Currency)** | addgold # (Replace # with any positive number) |
| **Add skill points** | AddSkillPoints # |
| **Adds parameter points to spend (Strength, Accuracy etc.)** | AddParamPoints # (replace # with any positive number) |
| **Enables console cheats** | TWOWORLDSCHEATS |

| Gain Experience Points | AddExperiencePoints # (# is any positive number) |
|---|---|
| God mode off | GOD 0 |
| God Mode on (Maxes all stats and abilities) | GOD 1 |
| Invisible To Enemies | Player.InvisibleForEnemies 1 |
| Jump Height/Gravity (use a negative number) | ms.Grav # |
| Run Speed | Hero.Move.FastRunSpeed # |
| Set time of day (0-255, with 0=midnight, 40=dawn, 20=sunset, 255=just before midnight) | Time # |
| Sets player level | ec.dbg levels # (replace # with any positive number) |
| Turns off immortality | IMMORTAL 0 |
| Turns on immortality (Unkillable) | IMMORTAL 1 |
| Walk Up Any Rock or Mountain (use a big negative number) | Physx.Char.SlopeLimit.Rock # |
| Walk Up Any Slope (use a big negative number) | Physx.Char.SlopeLimit # |
| With equipped weapon, kill selected enemy | KILL |

### UNLOCKABLE

Pause the game and enter the code at "Enter Bonus Code".

| EFFECT | CODE |
|---|---|
| Anathros Sword | 6770-8976-1634-9490 |
| Axe | 1775-3623-3298-1928 |
| Black Legion Ax | 4802-6468-2848-6286 |
| Dragon Armor | 4149-3083-9823-6545 |
| Dragon Scale Armor | 9199-0035-9610-2338 |
| Dusty Scroll | 8233-3296-3311-2976 |
| Elexorie | 3542-3274-8350-6064 |
| Elexorien Sword | 4677-1553-6730-1272 |
| Hammer | 6231-1890-4345-5988 |
| Lucienda Sword | 9122-5287-3591-0927 |
| Scroll | 6972-5760-7685-8477 |

## TWO WORLDS II (PlayStation 3)

### CODES

During the game, hold L1 + R1 and press START, ✥, START, ✥. You should see the debug menu appear. Enter the following codes for the desired effect. This will disable Trophies.

| EFFECT | CODE |
|---|---|
| Activation Code | TWOWORLDSCHEATS |
| Add Experience Points | AddExperiencePoints X - Experience points, where X is a number between 0 and 255 |
| Add Gold | Addgold X - Gold, where X is a number between 0 and 255 |
| Add Skill Points | AddSkillPoints X - Skill points, where X is a number between 0 and 255 |
| God Mode | GOD X - Toggle God Mode, , where X is a number is 0 or 1 |
| Set attributes to 1000 | ec.dbg iamcheater |
| Unlock all Skills | ec.dbg skills |

**CODES & CHEATS**

### UNLOCKABLE

Select the "Bonus Code" option, then enter one of the following codes to get the corresponding item

| EFFECT | CODE |
| --- | --- |
| **Anathros sword** | 6770-8976-1634-9490 |
| **Axe** | 1775-3623-3298-1928 |
| **Dragon scale armor** | 4149-3083-9823-6545 |
| **Elexorien two-handed sword** | 3542-3274-8350-6064 |
| **Hammer** | 6231-1890-4345-5988 |
| **Labyrinth Level** | 1797-3432-7753-9254 |
| **Lucienda sword** | 9122-5287-3591-0927 |
| **Luciendar Sword** | 6624-0989-0879-6383 |
| **Scroll bonus map** | 6972-5760-7685-8477 |
| **Two-handed hammer** | 3654-0091-3399-0994 |

NEW!
A
B
C
D
E
F
G
H
I
J
K
L
M
N
O
P
Q
R
S
T
U
V
W
X
Y
Z

## UFC 2009 UNDISPUTED (XBOX 360, PlayStation 3)

### UNLOCKABLE

| UNLOCKABLE | HOW TO UNLOCK |
|---|---|
| Unlock Punkass | To unlock the TapOut crew member Punkass as a fighter, obtain a Sponsorship from TapOut during Career mode. |
| Unlock Mask | In Career mode, get 3 consecutive wins by tapout/submission. He will then be selectable in exhibition matches in the light heavyweight weight class. |

## UFC PERSONAL TRAINER: THE ULTIMATE FITNESS SYSTEM (XBOX 360)

### ACHIEVEMENT

| UNLOCKABLE | HOW TO UNLOCK |
|---|---|
| "Thunder" Kickboxer (10) | Successfully complete all 12 Javier Mendez-specific exercises. |
| 1 Hour Photo Finish (5) | Work out in the game for an hour. |
| 10 Hour Power (15) | Work out in the game for 10 hours. |
| 5 Hours of Energy (10) | Work out in the game for 5 hours. |
| All Business (30) | Complete one 60-day program of any goal type. |
| As Real As It Gets (50) | Successfully complete 500 exercises or activities. |
| Average Joe (5) | Perform a workout at least 3 times in a week. |
| Bronze Bomber (15) | Earn a Bronze Medal in every exercise. |
| Century Mark (20) | Successfully complete 100 exercises or activities. |
| Crowd Pleaser (50) | Perform 1000 gesture streaks in the game. |
| Dialed In (20) | Perform a workout every day for 30 days. |
| Epic Milestone (30) | Work out in the game for 30 hours. |
| Experienced Competitor (30) | Complete 6 Hit the Mitts routines without missing any strikes. |
| Expert Warrior (40) | Complete 10 Hit the Mitts routines without missing any strikes. |
| Film Study (10) | Unlock all Videos. |
| Fitness Guru (10) | Successfully complete all Standard exercises. |
| Flawless Fighter (10) | Complete 1 Hit the Mitts routine without missing any strikes. |
| Flipped Out (5) | Get 3 wins in the Side by Side Multiplayer Tire Flip activity. |
| Full Plate (20) | Create and successfully complete a custom workout with the maximum number of exercise slots filled. |
| Fully Pledged (20) | Complete all three 60-day programs. |
| Gym Rat (10) | Perform a workout every day in the week. |
| Head of the Class (50) | Get a score of A or higher in all Standard exercises. |
| Heating Up (15) | Successfully complete 5 Hot Seat Multiplayer Challenges. |
| Heavy Medal (30) | Earn 60 medals in the game. |
| Hit the Mitts Machine (50) | Complete all Hit the Mitts routines without missing any strikes. |
| Let's Get It Started (5) | Complete the Fitness Test. |

**CODES & CHEATS**

| | |
|---|---|
| Medal Detector (10) | Earn 20 medals in the game. |
| Medal of the Road (20) | Earn 40 medals in the game. |
| Motivated (25) | Complete one 30-day program of any goal type. |
| No Nonsense (50) | Complete all three 30-day programs. |
| Opening Bell (10) | Successfully complete 1 exercise at all three fitness levels. |
| Quite Accomplished (30) | Successfully complete all the Accomplishments. |
| Rare Intensity (20) | Complete all exercises at all three fitness levels. |
| Shaping Up (30) | Successfully complete 300 exercises or activities. |
| Silver Star (25) | Earn a Silver Medal in every exercise. |
| Sityodtong Disciple (10) | Successfully complete all 12 Mark DellaGrotte-specific exercises. |
| Speed Bag Pro (5) | Get 3 wins in the Side by Side Multiplayer Speed Bag activity. |
| Streaky (20) | Perform 100 gesture streaks in the game. |
| Submission Fighter (10) | Successfully complete all 12 Greg Jackson-specific exercises. |
| The Gold Standard (30) | Earn a Gold Medal in every exercise. |
| Training Devotee (50) | Perform a workout every day for 100 days. |
| Unequaled Brawler (20) | Complete 3 Hit the Mitts routines without missing any strikes. |
| Unstoppable (20) | Work out in the game for 15 hours. |
| Up the Challenge (10) | Successfully complete any Xbox LIVE Challenge. |
| Versatile Combatant (20) | Complete a Pre-made Workout with each trainer. |
| Won't Back Down (20) | Successfully complete 10 Xbox LIVE Challenges. |

### UNLOCKABLE

To unlock these Avatar Awards, earn the required number of medals.

| UNLOCKABLE | HOW TO UNLOCK |
|---|---|
| UFC Trainer Gloves | Earn 10 Medals. |
| UFC Trainer Shirt | Earn 150 Medals. |
| UFC Trainer Shorts | Earn 50 Medals. |

## ULTIMATE MARVEL VS. CAPCOM 3 (PlayStation 3)

### TROPHY

| UNLOCKABLE | HOW TO UNLOCK |
|---|---|
| A Friend in Need (Bronze) | Perform 100 Crossover Assists. (Arcade/Online only) |
| A Warrior Born (Bronze) | Earn 5,000 Player Points (PP). |
| Above Average Joe (Bronze) | Land a Viewtiful Combo. (Arcade/online only) |
| Advancing Guardian (Bronze) | Perform 100 Advancing Guards. (Arcade/Online only) |
| Assemble! (Bronze) | Participate in an 8 player Lobby online. |
| Big Bang Theory (Bronze) | Perform 30 Hyper Combo Finishes. (Arcade/online only) |
| Brave New World (Bronze) | Participate in any mode online. |
| Comic Collector (Gold) | Unlock all items in the Gallery. |
| Crazy Good (Bronze) | Surpass the rank of Fighter. |
| Defender (Bronze) | Block 100 times. (Arcade/Online only) |
| Devil with a Blue Coat (Bronze) | Earn 30,000 Player Points (PP). |
| Divine Brawler (Silver) | Earn 100,000 Player Points (PP). |
| Dominator (Silver) | Collect 100 titles. |

| | |
|---|---|
| **Dreaded Opponent (Bronze)** | Participate in 200 matches online. |
| **Fighting Machine (Silver)** | Win 100 battles in Ranked Match. |
| **First Strike (Bronze)** | Land 50 First Attacks. (Arcade/Online only) |
| **Forged From Steel (Silver)** | Participate in 300 matches online. |
| **Full Roster (Silver)** | Battle against all characters online. |
| **Gravity? Please... (Bronze)** | Land 50 Team Aerial Combos. (Arcade/Online only) |
| **Hard Corps (Bronze)** | Perform 30 Crossover Combination Finishes. (Arcade/online only) |
| **Hellbent (Bronze)** | Participate in 100 matches online. |
| **High-Score Hero (Silver)** | Earn 500,000 points in Arcade mode. |
| **Hotshot (Bronze)** | Win 10 battles in Ranked Match. |
| **Incredible (Bronze)** | Win without calling your partners or switching out in an online match. |
| **Master of Tasks (Silver)** | Clear 480 missions in Mission mode. |
| **Mega Buster (Bronze)** | Use 1,000 Hyper Combo Gauge bars. (Arcade/online only) |
| **Mega Good (Silver)** | Surpass the 6th rank of any class. |
| **Mighty Teamwork (Bronze)** | Land 30 Team Aerial Counters. (Arcade/Online only) |
| **Missions? Possible. (Bronze)** | Clear 120 missions in Mission mode. |
| **Mutant Master (Bronze)** | Land an Uncanny Combo. (Arcade/online only) |
| **Need a Healing Factor (Bronze)** | Win without blocking in an online match. |
| **Noble Effort (Bronze)** | Get a 5-game win streak in Ranked Match. |
| **Passport to Beatdown Country (Bronze)** | Fight in all of the stages. |
| **Perfect X-ample (Bronze)** | Use X-Factor 50 times. (Arcade/Online only) |
| **Quick Change-Up (Bronze)** | Perform 50 Crossover Counters. (Arcade/Online only) |
| **Rivals Welcome (Silver)** | Play in Online Mode for over 30 hours. |
| **Savage Playing (Bronze)** | Perform 50 Snap Backs. (Arcade/Online only) |
| **Saving My Quarters (Bronze)** | Beat Arcade mode without using any continues. |
| **Seductive Embrace (Bronze)** | Play in Online Mode for over 5 hours. |
| **Slam Master (Bronze)** | Win 50 battles in Ranked Match. |
| **The Best There Is (Bronze)** | Beat Arcade mode on the hardest difficulty. |
| **The Points Do Matter (Bronze)** | Earn 400,000 points in Arcade mode. |
| **The Ultimate (Platinum)** | Obtain all Trophies. |
| **Training in Isolation (Silver)** | Play in Offline Mode for over 30 hours. |
| **Training Montage (Bronze)** | Play in Offline Mode for over 5 hours. |
| **Up To The Challenge (Silver)** | Clear 240 missions in Mission mode. |
| **Waiting for the Trade (Gold)** | View all endings in Arcade mode. |

*CODE*

| UNLOCKABLE | CODE |
|---|---|
| **Play as Galactus** | L1+Select+X while highlighting arcade mode |
| **Galactus** | Earn 30,000 points on your player card. |

**CODES & CHEATS**

## ULTIMATE MARVEL VS. CAPCOM 3 (XBOX 360)

### ACHIEVEMENT

| UNLOCKABLE | HOW TO UNLOCK |
|---|---|
| A Friend in Need (20) | Perform 100 Crossover Assists. (Arcade/Xbox LIVE) |
| A Warrior Born (10) | Earn 5,000 Player Points (PP). |
| Above Average Joe (10) | Land a Viewtiful Combo. (Arcade/Xbox LIVE) |
| Advancing Guardian (10) | Perform 100 Advancing Guards. (Arcade/Xbox LIVE) |
| Assemble! (15) | Participate in an 8 player Lobby over Xbox LIVE. |
| Big Bang Theory (15) | Perform 30 Hyper Combo Finishes. (Arcade/Xbox LIVE) |
| Brave New World (10) | Participate in any mode over Xbox LIVE. |
| Comic Collector (50) | Unlock all items in the Gallery. |
| Crazy Good (10) | Surpass the rank of Fighter. |
| Defender (10) | Block 100 times. (Arcade/Xbox LIVE) |
| Devil with a Blue Coat (15) | Earn 30,000 Player Points (PP). |
| Divine Brawler (50) | Earn 100,000 Player Points (PP). |
| Dominator (30) | Collect 100 titles. |
| Dreaded Opponent (20) | Participate in 200 matches in Xbox LIVE. |
| Fighting Machine (40) | Win 100 battles in Ranked Match. |
| First Strike (10) | Land 50 First Attacks. (Arcade/Xbox LIVE) |
| Forged From Steel (30) | Participate in 300 matches in Xbox LIVE. |
| Full Roster (30) | Battle against all characters over Xbox LIVE. |
| Gravity? Please... (10) | Land 50 Team Aerial Combos. (Arcade/Xbox LIVE) |
| Hard Corps (15) | Perform 30 Crossover Combination Finishes. (Arcade/Xbox LIVE) |
| Hellbent (20) | Participate in 100 matches in Xbox LIVE. |
| High-Score Hero (30) | Earn 500,000 points in Arcade mode. |
| Hotshot (15) | Win 10 battles in Ranked Match. |
| Incredible (20) | Win without calling your partners or switching out in a Xbox LIVE match. |
| Master of Tasks (40) | Clear 480 missions in Mission mode. |
| Mega Buster (20) | Use 1,000 Hyper Combo Gauge bars. (Arcade/Xbox LIVE) |
| Mega Good (40) | Surpass the 6th rank of any class. |
| Mighty Teamwork (10) | Land 30 Team Aerial Counters. (Arcade/Xbox LIVE) |
| Missions? Possible. (20) | Clear 120 missions in Mission mode. |
| Mutant Master (10) | Land an Uncanny Combo. (Arcade/Xbox LIVE) |
| Need a Healing Factor (20) | Win without blocking in an Xbox LIVE match. |
| Noble Effort (15) | Get a 5-game win streak in Ranked Match. |
| Passport to Beatdown Country (10) | Fight in all of the stages. |
| Perfect X-ample (10) | Use X-Factor 50 times. (Arcade/Xbox LIVE) |
| Quick Change-Up (10) | Perform 50 Crossover Counters. (Arcade/Xbox LIVE) |
| Rivals Welcome (30) | Play on Xbox LIVE for over 30 hours. |
| Savage Playing (10) | Perform 50 Snap Backs. (Arcade/Xbox LIVE) |
| Saving My Quarters (10) | Beat Arcade mode without using any continues. |

| Seductive Embrace (20) | Play on Xbox LIVE for over 5 hours. |
|---|---|
| Slam Master (20) | Win 50 battles in Ranked Match. |
| The Best There Is (10) | Beat Arcade mode on the hardest difficulty. |
| The Points Do Matter (20) | Earn 400,000 points in Arcade mode. |
| The Ultimate (50) | Unlock all achievements. |
| Training in Isolation (30) | Play in Offline Mode for over 30 hours. |
| Training Montage (20) | Play in Offline Mode for over 5 hours. |
| Up To The Challenge (30) | Clear 240 missions in Mission mode. |
| Waiting for the Trade (50) | View all endings in Arcade mode. |

### CODE

| UNLOCKABLE | CODE |
|---|---|
| Galactus | Earn 30,000 points on your player card. |

## ULTIMATE MORTAL KOMBAT 3 (XBOX 360)

### CODES

Enter codes at the VS screen.

| CODE | EFFECT |
|---|---|
| Player 1: LPx9, BLx8, LKx7; Player 2: LPx6, BLx6, LKx6 | "Hold Flippers During Casino Run" Message |
| Player 1: LPx7, BLx1, LKx1; Player 2: LPx3, BLx1, LKx3 | "Rain Can Be Found in the Graveyard" Message |
| Player 1: LPx1, BLx2, LKx3; Player 2: LPx9, BLx2, LKx6 | "There Is No Knowledge That Is Not Power" Message |
| Player 1: LKx4; Player 2: LPx4 | "Whatcha Gun Do?" Message |
| Player 1: BLx2; Player 2: BLx2 | Blocking Disabled |
| Player 1: LPx6, BLx8, LKx8; Player 2: LPx6, BLx8, LKx8 | Dark Kombat |
| Player 1: LPx1, BLx2, LKx2; Player 2: LPx2, BLx2, LKx1 | Display "Skunky !!" Message |
| Player 1: LPx4, BLx4, LKx8; Player 2: LPx8, BLx4, LKx4 | Don't Jump at Me |
| Player 1: LPx2, BLx2, LKx7; Player 2: LPx2, BLx2, LKx7 | Explosive Combat (2 on 2 only) |
| Player 1: LPx6, BLx8, LKx8; Player 2: LPx4, BLx2, LKx2 | Fast Uppercut Recovery Enabled |
| Player 1: BLx9, BLx1; Player 2: LPx1, BLx9 | Kombat Zone: Bell Tower |
| Player 1: LPx3, BLx3; Player 2: BLx3, LKx3 | Kombat Zone: Jade's Desert |
| Player 1: LKx4; Player 2: BLx7 | Kombat Zone: Kahn's Kave |
| Player 1: LPx8, BLx8; Player 2: LPx2, BLx2 | Kombat Zone: Kahn's Tower |
| Player 1: LPx6; Player 2: BLx4 | Kombat Zone: Kombat Temple |
| Player 1: BLx5; Player 2: BLx5 | Kombat Zone: Noob Saibot Dorfen |
| Player 1: LKx2; Player 2: LKx3 | Kombat Zone: River Kombat |
| Player 1: LPx3, BLx4, LKx3; Player 2: LPx3, BLx4, LKx3 | Kombat Zone: Rooftop |
| Player 1: LPx9, BLx3, LKx3 | Kombat Zone: Scislac Busorez |
| Player 1: LPx6, BLx6, LKx6; Player 2: LPx4, BLx4, LKx4 | Kombat Zone: Scorpion's Lair |
| Player 1: LPx1, BLx2, LKx3; Player 2: LPx9, LKx1 | Kombat Zone: Soul Chamber |
| Player 1: BLx7, LKx9; Player 2: BLx3, LKx5 | Kombat Zone: Street |
| Player 1: LPx8, BLx8; Player 2: BLx8, LKx8 | Kombat Zone: Subway |
| Player 1: BLx7, LKx7; Player 2: BLx2, LKx2 | Kombat Zone: The Bridge |

NEW!

A
B
C
D
E
F
G
H
I
J
K
L
M
N
O
P
Q
R
S
T
U
V
W
X
Y
Z

**CODES & CHEATS**

| Player 1: LPx6, BLx6, LKx6; Player 2: LPx3, BLx3, LKx3 | Kombat Zone: The Graveyard |
| Player 1: LPx8, BLx2; Player 2: BLx2, LKx8 | Kombat Zone: The Pit 3 |
| Player 1: LPx2, BLx8, LKx2; Player 2: LPx2, BLx8, LKx2 | No Fear = EB Button, Skydive, Max Countdown |
| Player 1: LPx9, BLx8, LKx7; Player 2: LPx1, BLx2, LKx3 | No Powerbars |
| Player 1: BLx3, LKx3 | Player 1 Half Power |
| Player 1: LPx7, LKx7 | Player 1 Quarter Power |
| Player 2: BLx3, LKx3 | Player 2 Half Power |
| Player 2: LPx7, LKx7 | Player 2 Quarter Power |
| Player 1: LPx4, BLx4, LKx4; Player 2: LPx4, BLx4, LKx4 | RandPer Kombat (Method 1) |
| Player 1: LPx4, BLx6; Player 2: LPx4, BLx6 | RandPer Kombat (Method 2) |
| Player 1: LPx9, BLx9, LKx9; Player 2: LPx9, BLx9, LKx9 | Revision |
| Player 1: LPx5, BLx5; Player 2: LPx5, BLx5 | See the Mortal Kombat LiveTour !! |
| Player 1: LPx3; Player 2: LPx3 | Silent Kombat |
| Player 1: LPx1; Player 2: LPx1 | Throwing Disabled |
| Player 1: LPx6, BLx4, LKx2; Player 2: LPx4, BLx6, LKx8 | Two-Player Minigame of Galaga |
| Player 1: BLx4, LKx4; Player 2: LPx4, BLx4 | Unikoriv Referri: Sans Power |
| Player 1: LPx4, BLx6, LKx6; Player 2: LPx4, BLx6, LKx6 | Unlimited Run |
| Player 1: LPx9, BLx6, LKx9; Player 2: LPx1, BLx4, LKx1 | Winner of this round battles Motaro |
| Player 1: BLx3, LKx3; Player 2: LPx5, BLx6, LKx4 | Winner of this round battles Shao Kahn |
| Player 1: LPx2, LKx5; Player 2: LPx2, LKx5 | Winner of this round battles Smoke |
| Player 1: LPx7, BLx6, LKx9; Player 2: LPx3, BLx4, LKx2 | Winner of this round battles Noob Saibot |

### UNLOCK AND SAVE HIDDEN CHARACTERS

Choose Arcade mode, lose a match. Then let the timer run out. You have 10 seconds to enter the ultimate kombat code for the character, one at a time. After unlocking them in Arcade mode, get to the Character Select screen. Pause, then exit the game. You'll have them for the rest of that play session. Now, very important, when you start the game up the next time around, you need to first go to the Arcade mode. This loads the characters you unlocked. Just wait and get to the Character Select screen, then exit. Now you can play with the characters online. If you do not go to the Arcade mode first, you will erase the characters. Just load and exit, then play online

## UNCHARTED: DRAKE'S FORTUNE  (PlayStation 3)

### DRAKE'S JERSEY

To unlock a baseball jersey for Drake, go to the Costume section of the game, and input the following code.

| UNLOCKABLE | HOW TO UNLOCK |
| Baseball Jersey | ←,→,↓,↑,▲,R1,L1,■ |

### SECRET VIDEOS

To unlock secret videos in the Making a Cutscene section of the game, input the following codes.

| UNLOCKABLE | HOW TO UNLOCK |
| Video for Grave Robbing | ←,R2,→,↑,L2,▲,■,↓ |
| Video for Time's Up | L1,→,■,↓,←,▲,R1,↑ |

### CONCEPT ART

Go to the Rewards section of the game, and insert the following codes.

| UNLOCKABLE | HOW TO UNLOCK |
|---|---|
| More Art | ■, L1, →, ←, ↓, R2, ▲, ↑ |
| Video | L2, →, ↑, ■, ←, ▲, R1, ↓ |

## UNCHARTED 2: AMONG THIEVES   (PlayStation 3)

### UNLOCKABLES

| UNLOCKABLE | HOW TO UNLOCK |
|---|---|
| Crushing Difficulty | Beat the game on Hard difficulty to unlock. |
| Genghis Khan Villain Skin | Beat Crushing difficulty. Cost: 1,500,000 |
| Marco Polo Hero Skin | Get the Platinum trophy. Cost: Free. |

### FREE IN-GAME MONEY

In Uncharted 2: Among Thieves, you'll have the option to hit the Square button when in the store to check for Uncharted: Drake's Fortune save data. If you have any save data you get cash! The cash can be used in both single-player, and multiplayer stores.

| | |
|---|---|
| **$20,000 In-Game Cash** | Have a saved game of Uncharted: Drake's Fortune. |
| **$80,000 In-Game Cash** | Have a saved game of Uncharted: Drake's Fortune with the story completed at least once. |

### MULTIPLAYER BOOSTERS

Boosters give your character more tools to use in multiplayer. Unlock them by reaching certain levels (for the most part you unlock a booster every two levels), then purchase them from the multiplayer store. There are two different booster slots you can use.

| UNLOCKABLE | HOW TO UNLOCK |
|---|---|
| Bandoleer (Booster Slot 2) | Reach Level 4; Costs $2,000 |
| Break Up (Booster Slot 1) | Reach Level 10; Costs $11,250 |
| Come Get Some (Booster Slot 2) | Reach Level 58; Costs $2,000,000 |
| Deposit (Booster Slot 2) | Reach Level 40; Costs $98,250 |
| Down the Irons (Booster Slot 1) | Reach Level 14; Costs $18,750 |
| Evasion (Booster Slot 1) | Reach Level 50; Costs $210,000 |
| Explosive Expert (Booster Slot 2) | Reach Level 20; Costs $32,250 |
| Fleet Foot (Booster Slot 2) | Reach Level 16; Costs $23,250 |
| From the Hip (Booster Slot 1) | Reach Level 6; Costs $5,000 |
| Glass Jaw (Booster Slot 1) | Reach Level 56; Costs $1,500,000 |
| Half Loaded (Booster Slot 2) | Reach Level 54; Costs $400,000 |
| Hell Blazer (Booster Slot 1) | Reach Level 18; Costs $27,750 |
| Invalid (Booster Slot 1) | Reach Level 52; Costs $350,000 |
| Juggler (Booster Slot 1) | Reach Level 38; Costs $94,500 |
| Keep Firing (Booster Slot 2) | Reach Level 12; Costs $14,250 |
| Launch Man (Booster Slot 2) | Reach Level 28; Costs $58,500 |
| Monkey Man (Booster Slot 2) | Reach Level 32; Costs $72,000 |
| Point and Shoot (Booster Slot 1) | Reach Level 2; Costs $2,000 |
| Rapid Hands (Booster Slot 1) | Reach Level 42; Costs $111,000 |
| Revenge (Booster Slot 2) | Reach Level 48; Costs $134,250 |
| Rocket Man (Booster Slot 2) | Reach Level 44; Costs $120,000 |
| Scavenger (Booster Slot 2) | Reach Level 8; Costs $8,250 |
| Scoped In (Booster Slot 2) | Reach Level 36; Costs $87,000 |
| Situational Awareness (Booster Slot 1) | Reach Level 46; Costs $129,000 |
| Sure Foot (Booster Slot 2) | Reach Level 26; Costs $52,500 |

**CODES & CHEATS**

| | |
|---|---|
| Sure Shot (Booster Slot 1) | Reach Level 30; Costs $64,500 |
| Treasure Bearer (Booster Slot 2) | Reach Level 24; Costs $43,500 |
| Turtle (Booster Slot 1) | Reach Level 22; Costs $40,500 |
| Veiled (Booster Slot 1) | Reach Level 51; Costs $300,000 |
| Walk Softly (Booster Slot 1) | Reach Level 34; Costs $79,500 |

## MULTIPLAYER SKINS

These skins that can be purchased in the multiplayer store after you reach certain levels.

| UNLOCKABLE | HOW TO UNLOCK |
|---|---|
| Cameraman Jeff | Reach Level 30; Costs $100,000 |
| Doughnut Drake | Reach Level 60; Costs $2,000,000 |
| Genghis Khan Villain Skin | Beat Crushing Difficulty. Cost: 1,500,000 |
| Harry Flynn | Reach Level 20; Costs $50,000 |
| Heist Drake | Reach Level 10; Costs $20,000 |
| Heist Flynn | Reach Level 20; Costs $50,000 |
| Karl Schafer | Reach Level 50; Costs $1,000,000 |
| Lieutenant Draza | Reach Level 50; Costs $1,000,000 |
| Marco Polo Hero Skin | Get the Platinum trophy. Cost: Free. |
| Skelzor | Reach Level 60; Costs $2,000,000 |
| Winter Chloe | Reach Level 20; Costs $50,000 |
| Winter Drake | Reach Level 40; Costs $250,000 |
| Winter Elena | Reach Level 30; Costs $100,000 |
| Winter Flynn | Reach Level 30; Costs $100,000 |
| Zoran Lazarevic | Reach Level 40; Costs $250,000 |
| Zorskel | Reach Level 10; Costs $20,000 |

## MULTIPLAYER TAUNTS

| UNLOCKABLE | HOW TO UNLOCK |
|---|---|
| Flex Taunt | Reach Level 20; Costs $50,000 |
| Flurry Taunt | Reach Level 30; Costs $100,000 |
| Kiss Taunt | Reach Level 10; Costs $10,000 |
| Pump Taunt | Reach Level 53; Costs $500,000 |
| Yes Taunt | Reach Level 40; Costs $250,000 |

## GLITCH

This glitch is to enable "tweaks" on difficulties that have not been completed. First, start a game on a difficulty you haven't finished and play through until you have a real gun. Next, go to in-game options and set the difficulty where you have unlocked the tweaks. Enable your tweaks, then select "Save and quit". Finally, go to main menu and set the difficulty back to the one you where you just got a real gun. Start the game on that difficulty and enjoy.

## UNCHARTED 3: DRAKE'S DECEPTION (PlayStation 3)

### TROPHY

| UNLOCKABLE | HOW TO UNLOCK |
|---|---|
| 100 Headshots (Silver) | Defeat 100 enemies with headshots |
| 20 Headshots (Bronze) | Defeat 20 enemies with headshots |
| 30 Kills: Arm Micro (Bronze) | Defeat 30 enemies with the Arm Micro |
| 30 Kills: Dragon Sniper (Bronze) | Defeat 30 enemies with the Dragon Sniper |
| 30 Kills: G-MAL (Bronze) | Defeat 30 enemies with the G-MAL |
| 30 Kills: KAL 7 (Bronze) | Defeat 30 enemies with the KAL 7 |

| 30 Kills: M9 (Bronze) | Defeat 30 enemies with the M9 |
| 30 Kills: Mag 5 (Bronze) | Defeat 30 enemies with the Mag 5 |
| 30 Kills: Mk-NDI (Bronze) | Defeat 30 enemies with the Mk-NDI |
| 30 Kills: PAK-80 (Bronze) | Defeat 30 enemies with the PAK-80 |
| 30 Kills: RPG7 (Bronze) | Defeat 30 enemies with the RPG-7 |
| 30 Kills: SAS-12 (Bronze) | Defeat 30 enemies with the SAS-12 |
| 30 Kills: T-Bolt Sniper (Bronze) | Defeat 30 enemies with the T-Bolt Sniper |
| 30 Kills: TAU Sniper (Bronze) | Defeat 30 enemies with the Tau Sniper |
| Adept Fortune Hunter (Bronze) | Find 60 treasures |
| Apprentice Fortune Hunter (Bronze) | Find 10 treasures |
| Bare-knuckle Brawler (Bronze) | Defeat 20 enemies with hand-to-hand combat |
| Bare-knuckle Slugger (Bronze) | Defeat 50 enemies with hand to hand combat |
| Blindfire Marksman (Bronze) | Defeat 20 enemies by blind-firing while in cover (without aiming with L1) |
| Brute Beater (Bronze) | Successfully counter all of a Brute's damage-giving attacks |
| Buddy System (Bronze) | Complete one Cooperative Multiplayer game |
| Charted! - Crushing (Gold) | Finish the game in Crushing Mode |
| Charted! - Easy (Bronze) | Finish the game in Easy Mode |
| Charted! - Hard (Silver) | Finish the game in Hard Mode |
| Charted! - Normal (Silver) | Finish the game in Normal Mode |
| Combat Leapfrog (Silver) | Defeat 10 enemies in a row, alternating hand-to-hand combat and gunplay |
| Drop the Bomb Headshot (Bronze) | Make 5 enemies drop their grenades by shooting them |
| Dyno-Might Master (Silver) | Defeat four enemies with one explosion |
| Expert Fortune Hunter (Bronze) | Find 80 treasures |
| Expert Ninja (Silver) | Defeat 5 enemies in a row using stealth attacks |
| First Treasure (Bronze) | Find one treasure |
| Grenade Hangman (Bronze) | Defeat 10 enemies with grenades while hanging |
| Hangman (Bronze) | Defeat 20 enemies with gunfire by aiming while hanging |
| He's Gonna Need a Sturgeon (Bronze) | Hit three enemies with fish in the market |
| Headshot Expert (Bronze) | Defeat 5 enemies in a row with headshots |
| Land Shark (Bronze) | Defeat 20 enemies while swimming |
| Marco Solo (Bronze) | Play in the swimming pool on the Cruise Ship |
| Master Fortune Hunter (Silver) | Find 100 treasures |
| Master Ninja (Bronze) | Defeat 50 enemies with stealth attacks |
| Pro-Pain (Bronze) | Defeat 10 enemies with propane of acetylene tank explosions |
| Quick Study (Bronze) | Inspect every display case in the Cartagena Museum |
| Relic Finder (Bronze) | Find the Strange Relic |
| Reload Master (Silver) | Defeat 50 enemies in a row without auto-reloading |
| Ride the Crocodile (Bronze) | Stand on the crocodile in the Secret Library |
| Riot Rocker (Bronze) | Defeat 5 Riot Shield enemies by running over their shield |

NEW!

A
B
C
D
E
F
G
H
I
J
K
L
M
N
O
P
Q
R
S
T
U
V
W
X
Y
Z

**CODES & CHEATS**

| | |
|---|---|
| **Rolling Ammo Master (Silver)** | 20 times in a row, pick up ammo while rolling |
| **Run-and-Gunner (Bronze)** | Defeat 20 enemies by shooting from the hip (without aiming with L1) |
| **Side Arm Master (Bronze)** | Defeat 30 enemies in a row with your side arm |
| **Skilled Fortune Hunter (Bronze)** | Find 40 treasures |
| **Survivor (Silver)** | Defeat 75 enemies in a row without dying |
| **Thrillseeker (Bronze)** | Complete one Competitive Multiplayer game |
| **Throwback (Bronze)** | Kill 10 enemies with thrown-back grenades |
| **Throwback Master (Bronze)** | Throw back a grenade and defeat two enemies at once |
| **Truck Brawler (Bronze)** | Defeat 10 enemies using hand-to-hand combat on the back of the convoy trucks |

### UNLOCKABLE

| UNLOCKABLE | HOW TO UNLOCK |
|---|---|
| Crushing Mode | Beat the game on any difficulty. |

A
B
C
D
E
F
G
H
I
J
K
L
M
N
O
P
Q
R
S
T
U
V
W
X
Y
Z

## VALKYRIA CHRONICLES (PlayStation 3)

### GAME COMPLETION BENEFITS

After you complete the game you are given the opportunity to save the game. This is the New Game + data, and when you load it, you're given a couple of benefits that are listed below:

| UNLOCKABLE | HOW TO UNLOCK |
|---|---|
| Character Stats | You retain the EXP, Money, Weapons and Levels that you've gained on your previous excursions. |
| Hard Mode | You unlock Hard Mode which can be selected ONLY for Skirmishes. |
| Mission Replayability | You can now play all of the storyline missions as many times as you'd like. (You will need to go through chapter by chapter clearing the missions first). |
| Music Tab | You can now listen to the various musical pieces from the game. |
| Statistics Tab | You can now see the statistics of the missions. (The rank you gained for the particular mission, and the number of turns it took you to complete.) |

### HIDDEN RECRUITS

Unlock the following hidden characters for each class by doing specific in-game tasks.

| UNLOCKABLE | HOW TO UNLOCK |
|---|---|
| Audrey (Lancer) | Earn 10 or more medals. |
| Emile (Sniper) | Unlock Oscar's hidden potential, the let him die in battle. |
| Knute (Engineer) | Enter the Command Room with 1,000,000 DCT. |
| Musaad (Scout) | Beat the game. |

## VALKYRIA CHRONICLES: BEHIND HER BLUE FLAME DLC (PlayStation 3)

### UNLOCKABLES

| UNLOCKABLE | HOW TO UNLOCK |
|---|---|
| Mission 2a | Finish the first mission without defeating the "Boss" tank in the southwest part of the map. |
| Mission 2b | Defeat the "Boss" tank in the southwest part of the map and finish the first mission. |
| Mission 3 | To unlock the last mission you have to get an A rank in all the previous missions (the first, and both 2a and 2b). |
| Ruhm | Complete two missions (the first and either 2a or 2b) to unlock this weapon in the main game. |

## VANDAL HEARTS: FLAMES OF JUDGMENT (PlayStation 3)

### UNLOCKABLES

Optional battle map stages. In case you miss any, all stages can be returned to once you reach Act 4. You can go back to get any of the optional maps up until you board the ship to the research facility.

| UNLOCKABLE | HOW TO UNLOCK |
|---|---|
| Avery Fields | Examine the well at the top of the Church of Restoration on your second visit. |
| Foreign Quarter | Examine the barrel at the beginning of the Biruni University stage to your left. |
| Four Swordsman Spring | Examine the hollowed out tree at the dry riverbed. |

| Gillbari's Gardens | Examine the skeleton on the side of the central tree opposite from the chest in Timion Vale. |
| Halls of Atonement | Examine the king's throne in the Royal Courtyard. |
| Keliask's Tomb | Examine the glimmering tablet on the ground in the ancient ruins. |
| Ragnar's Gorge | Examine one of the crates during the mission in Tolby. |
| Trivishim's Corridor | Use the second mine cart in Dread to open up a cave entrance. |

## VANQUISH   (XBOX 360)

### UNLOCKABLES

| UNLOCKABLE | HOW TO UNLOCK |
| --- | --- |
| Unlock God Hard Difficulty | Rotate right analog stick clockwise 20 times at the title screen. |

## VECTORMAN   (Wii)

### UNLOCKABLES

| UNLOCKABLE | HOW TO UNLOCK |
| --- | --- |
| Blow Up SEGA Logo | At the SEGA screen, move Vectorman slightly to the right of the logo. Aim upward and shoot. There is a hidden TV monitor there. Once it is broken, grab and use an orb power-up. The SEGA logo goes dark and the background stops moving. |
| Debug Mode | On the Options screen press Ⓐ, Ⓑ, Ⓑ, Ⓐ, ✛, Ⓐ, Ⓑ, Ⓑ, Ⓐ. A menu then offers health, lives, level select, and weapon options. |
| Full Health | Pause the game and press Ⓐ, Ⓑ, ✛, Ⓐ, Ⓒ, Ⓐ, ✛, Ⓐ, Ⓑ, ✛, Ⓐ. |
| Invisibility and Invincibility | First grab a bomb morph, and detonate Vectorman. Pause the game while Vectorman is still exploding and enter CALLACAB (Ⓒ, Ⓐ, ✛, ✛, Ⓐ, Ⓒ, Ⓐ, Ⓑ). Unpause the game. Pause again and enter the CALLACAB code. Unpause it, and Vectorman is invisible and invincible. Reenter the CALLACAB code to turn it off. No bomb morph is needed to disable it. |
| Level Warp | When you turn on the game, you can move Vectorman around on the SEGA screen. Shoot the SEGA logo 24 times, jump and hit the SEGA logo with Vectorman's head 12 times, and the letters S, E, G, and A start falling. Catch 90 to 110 letters to start on Stage 5, catch more than 110 letters to start on Day 10. |
| Light Bulbs | During gameplay, pause and enter Ⓐ, Ⓑ, Ⓐ, Ⓒ, Ⓐ, Ⓑ and press pause. A group of lights should be around you. The four lights that surround Vectorman indicate the field of collision detection. The light at the bottom indicates the collision detection of Vectorman's jets. |
| Slow Motion | This code slows down the game whenever you're hit. While playing, pause and press ✛, ✛, Ⓐ, Ⓒ, ✛, ✛, Ⓐ. Turn it off by entering the code again. |
| Stage Select | Ⓑ, Ⓐ, Ⓐ, Ⓑ, ✛, Ⓑ, Ⓐ, Ⓐ, Ⓑ |
| Taxi Mode | Pause and press Ⓒ, Ⓐ, ✛, ✛, Ⓐ, Ⓒ, Ⓐ, Ⓑ (Call a Cab). You turn into a small cursor/arrow and can travel anywhere in the level. Enemies can also be killed by coming in contact with them. Bosses cannot be killed this way. To return to normal, pause and enter the code again. |

## VIRTUA FIGHTER 2   (Wii)

### UNLOCKABLES

| UNLOCKABLE | HOW TO UNLOCK |
| --- | --- |
| Different Costumes | To play in a character's different costumes, Hold ✛ and then select your character with Ⓐ or ✛. Or hold ✛ and select your character with Ⓐ, ✛, or START. |
| Extra Character Selection Time | Press ✛, ✛, ✛, Ⓐ+✛ at the Character Selection Screen for 99 seconds of extra time. |
| Hidden Options | Enter the Options screen, highlight the "Exit" selection, and tap ✛ until the hidden options are displayed. |

| No Damage | Hold ⑧ while highlighting player 1's life selection at the Options screen, until the message "No Damage" appears. Then press START. |
| Play as Dural | Highlight Akira using controller 1 or Jacky using controller 2. Then press ⇦, ⇧. Repeat this a few times and Dural appears as a selectable character. |

## VIRTUA FIGHTER 5 (PlayStation 3)

| UNLOCKABLE | CODE |
| --- | --- |
| DOJO training stages | Complete the Time Attack mode |
| Costume C | Reach the rank of 1st Dan |
| Costume D | Complete the first orb disc |

## VIRTUA TENNIS 3 (XBOX 360)

Enter these codes at the main menu.

| UNLOCKABLE | CODE |
| --- | --- |
| Unlock All Courts | ⇧, ⇧, ⇩, ⇩, ⇦, ⇨, ⇦, ⇨ |
| Unlock King & Duke | ⇧, ⇧, ⇩, ⇩, ⇦, ⇨, ⇦, ⇨ |
| Unlock All Gear | ⇦, ⇨, ⇩, ⇦, ⇨, ⇩, ⇧, ⇩ |
| Test End Sequence (win one match to win tournament) | ⇩, ⇦, ⇨, ⇩, ⇦, ⇧, ⇩, ⇩ |

## VIRTUA TENNIS WORLD TOUR (PSP)

Enter these codes at the Main menu while holding R3.

| UNLOCKABLE | CODE |
| --- | --- |
| All Racquets and Clothing Available in the Home Screen | ⇨, ⇦, ⇨, ⇨, ⇧, ⇧, ⇧ |
| Begin World Tour mode with $1,000,000 | ⇧, ⇩, ⇦, ⇩, ▲, ▲, ▲ |
| Earn $2000 Every Week in World Tour mode | ⇧, ⇩, ⇨, ⇩, ▲, ■, ▲ |
| Unlock All Stadiums | ⇧, ⇩, ⇦, ⇩, ■, ■, ■ |
| Unlock the players King & Queen | ⇧, ⇩, ⇧, ⇩, ■, ▲, ■ |

## VIVA PIÑATA (XBOX 360)

Enter these passwords as names for your garden.

| UNLOCKABLE | PASSWORD |
| --- | --- |
| Five Extra Accessories at the Pet Shop | chewnicorn |
| Items for Your Piñatas to Wear | goobaa nlock |
| Items for Your Piñatas to Wear | Bullseye |
| YMCA Gear | Kittyfloss |

NEW!

A
B
C
D
E
F
G
H
I
J
K
L
M
N
O
P
Q
R
S
T
U
V
W
X
Y
Z

# W

## WALL-E    (XBOX 360)

### CHEATS

Enter the following codes in the cheat section of the Bonus Features menu.

| EFFECT | CODE |
| --- | --- |
| All Bonus Features Unlocked | WALL-E, Auto, EVE, ZPM |
| All Game Contents Unlocked | M-O, Auto, ZPM, EVE |
| Costumes | ZPM, WALL-E, M-O, Auto |
| Gives WALL-E Super Laser Blaster | WALL-E, Auto, EVE, Mo |
| Invincibility | WALL-E, M-O, Auto, M-O |
| Make Any Cube Any Time | Auto, M-O, Auto, M-O |

## WALL-E    (Wii)

### CHEATS

In the password screen enter the codes for the following effects. ZPM = Zero Point Mover.

| EFFECT | CODE |
| --- | --- |
| All Bonus Features Unlocked | WALL-E, Auto, EVE, ZPM |
| All Game Content Unlocked | M-O, Auto, ZPM, EVE |
| All Holiday Costumes Unlocked | Auto, Auto, ZPM, ZPM |
| All Multiplayer Costumes Unlocked | ZPM, WALL-E, M-O, Auto |
| All Multiplayer Maps Unlocked | EVE, M-O, WALL-E, Auto |
| All Single Player Levels Unlocked | Auto, ZPM, M-O, WALL-E |
| EVE Permanent Super Laser Upgrade | EVE, WALL-E, WALL-E, Auto |
| Infinite Health | WALL-E, M-O, Auto, M-O |
| WALL-E & EVE Laser Gun Any Time | ZPM, EVE, M-O, WALL-E |
| WALL-E & EVE Make Any Cube Any Time | M-O, ZPM, EVE, EVE |
| WALL-E Always Has Super Laser | WALL-E, Auto, EVE, M-O |
| WALL-E Makes Any Cube Any Time | Auto, M-O, Auto, M-O |
| WALL-E with Laser Gun Any Time | WALL-E, EVE, EVE, WALL-E |

## WALL-E    (PSP)

### CHEATS

Enter the following codes in the Cheats menu in the corresponding code slot.

| EFFECT | CODE |
| --- | --- |
| Code 1: Kills or Stuns Everything within Range | BOTOFWAR |
| Code 2: Can Move Undetected by any Enemy | STEALTHARMOR |
| Code 3: Laser Switches Color Continuously | RAINBOWLASER |
| Code 4: Every Cube Is a Explosive Cube | EXPLOSIVEWORLD |
| Code 5: Lights Dark Areas | GLOWINTHEDARK |
| Code 6: Wears Ski Goggles | BOTOFMYSTERY |
| Code 7: WALL-E has Golden Tracks | GOLDENTRACKS |

## WANTED: WEAPONS OF FATE (XBOX 360)

### CODES

Enter these at the "Secret Codes" screen in the Main menu.

| EFFECT | CODE |
| --- | --- |
| Unlocks Airplane Bodyguard | 01010111 |
| Unlocks Cinematic Mode | 01110100 |
| Unlocks Close Combat Mode | 01100101 |
| Unlocks Cross | 01010100 |
| Unlocks Health Improvement | 01001100 |
| Unlocks Infinite Adrenaline | 01101101 |
| Unlocks Infinite Ammo | 01101111 |
| Unlocks Janice | 01000100 |
| Unlocks One Shot One Kill | 01110010 |
| Unlocks Special Suit | 01100001 |
| Unlocks Super Weapons | 01001111 |
| Unlocks Wesley | 01000011 |

## WANTED: WEAPONS OF FATE (PlayStation 3)

### CODES

Enter these at the "Secret Codes" screen in the "Main Menu."

| EFFECT | CODE |
| --- | --- |
| Unlocks Airplane Bodyguard | 01010111 |
| Unlocks Cinematic Mode | 01110100 |
| Unlocks Close-Combat Mode | 01100101 |
| Unlocks Cross | 01010100 |
| Unlocks Health Improvement | 01001100 |
| Unlocks Infinite Adrenaline | 01101101 |
| Unlocks Infinite Ammo | 01101111 |
| Unlocks Janice | 01000100 |
| Unlocks One Shot One Kill | 01110010 |
| Unlocks Special Suit | 01100001 |
| Unlocks Super Weapons | 01001111 |
| Unlocks Wesley | 01000011 |

## WATER WARFARE (Wii)

### UNLOCKABLES

By clearing single player mission mode you can unlock new characters to play as.

| UNLOCKABLE | HOW TO UNLOCK |
| --- | --- |
| Biker Ben | Beat Biker Ben on the Training Level 6. |
| Cavegirl Carmen | Beat Cavegirl Carmen on Mission 8 of the Nature Park. |
| Rabid Rabbit | Beat Rabid Rabbit on Mission 8 of the Playground. |
| Snorkel Jane | Beat Snorkel Jane on Mission 8 of the Beach. |
| Trooper Tim | Beat Trooper Tim on Mission 8 of the Plaza. |

## WET (XBOX 360)

### UNLOCKABLE

Beat the game on any difficulty. After the credits roll Challenge Modes are unlocked.

| UNLOCKABLE | HOW TO UNLOCK |
| --- | --- |
| Boneyard Challenges | Beat the game. |
| Points Count | Beat the game. |

## WHERE THE WILD THINGS ARE (XBOX 360)

### UNLOCKABLES

These are unlockable cheats that can be activated once you have completed the requirements.

| UNLOCKABLE | HOW TO UNLOCK |
| --- | --- |
| Infinite Health | Collect all skulls (60). |
| Kill enemies in one hit | Collect all turtles (60). |
| The Wild Things won't eat you | Collect all beehives (60). |
| Treasures show up when holding the back button | collect all geodes (60). |
| Your ship doesn't take damage | Collect all seeds (60). |

## WHITE KNIGHT CHRONICLES II (PlayStation 3)

### TROPHY

| UNLOCKABLE | HOW TO UNLOCK |
| --- | --- |
| Anura's Ruby (Silver) | Complete 300 binds |
| Bronze Medal (Silver) | Reached Guildrank 2 |
| Bronze Plaque (Bronze) | Proof of completing 1 monster-slaying quest |
| Bronze Satchel (Bronze) | Spend a total of 100,000 G |
| Bronze Star (Bronze) | Learn 1 entire set of skills |
| Gold Medal (Gold) | Reacged Guildrank 30 |
| Gold Plaque (Gold) | Proof of completing 40 monster-slaying quests |
| Gold Satchel (Silver) | Spend a total of 10,00,000 G |
| Gold Star (Gold) | Learn 8 entire sets of skills |
| Hikari to Yami no Kakusei (Bronze) | Finish the main story White Knight Chronicles 2 |
| Inishie no Kodou (Bronze) | Finish the main story White Knight Chronicles 1 |
| Letter of Thanks (Bronze) | Rid 1 person of their worries |
| Mercenary's Badge (Bronze) | Complete 1 quest with an S rank |
| Perfectionist's Badge (Gold) | Complete 100 quests with an S rank |
| Phibianacci's Diamond (Gold) | Complete 800 binds |
| Platinum (Platinum) | Got all trophies |
| Professional's Badge (Silver) | Complete 50 quests with an S rank |
| Rare Collector (Silver) | Collect 20 rare pieces of GR26 equipment |
| Rare Dabbler (Bronze) | Collect 1 rare piece of GR26 equipment |
| Rare Maniac (Gold) | Collect 50 rare pieces of GR26 equipment |
| Royal Certificate of Apprecation (Gold) | Rid 150 people of their worries |
| Silver Medal (Silver) | Reached Guildrank 17 |
| Silver Plaque (Silver) | Proof of completing 20 monster-slaying quests |
| Soul of Evil (Gold) | Finish upper floor boss of Veruganda |
| Toadstone (Bronze) | Complete 1 bind |

## UNLOCKABLE

Connect ar PSP to the PS3 and at the start screen, select Data Import and import your Origins save data. You can then buy these in Adventure Store's Dahlia Exchange

| UNLOCKABLE | HOW TO UNLOCK |
|---|---|
| Balandor Knight Set, Def 5 Res 5 Vit 5 | 500 Dahlia Points |
| Black Hero II Set - Male Only, Def 5 Res 5 Spr 5 MP 10 | 900 Dahlia Points |
| Black Hero Set - Male Only, Def 5 Res 5 Spr 5 | 700 Dahlia Points |
| Blue Hero II Set, Def 5 Res 5 Vit 5 MP 10 | 900 Dahlia Points |
| Blue Hero Set, Def 5 Res 5 Vit 5 | 700 Dahlia Points |
| Cook Set, Def 5 Res 5 Spr 5 | 500 Dahlia Points |
| Green Hero II Set, Def 5 Res 5 Str 5 MP 10 | 900 Dahlia Points |
| Green Hero Set, Def 5 Res 5 Str 5 | 700 Dahlia Points |
| Honey Set - Female Only, Def 5 Res 5 Dex 5 | 500 Dahlia Points |
| Hunter Set - Male Only, Def 5 Res 5 Str 5 | 500 Dahlia Points |
| Lily Set - Female Only, Def 5 Res 5 Int 5 | 500 Dahlia Points |
| Magi Soldier Set, Def 5 Res 5 Vit 5 | 500 Dahlia Points |
| Mine Set, Def 5 Res 5 Vit 5 | 500 Dahlia Points |
| Misty Set - Female Only, Def 5 Res 5 Str 5 | 500 Dahlia Points |
| Noble Set - Male Only, Def 5 Res 5 Agi 5 | 500 Dahlia Points |
| Pink Hero II Set - Female Only, Def 5 Res 5 Int 5 MP 10 | 900 Dahlia Points |
| Pink Hero Set - Female Only, Def 5 Res 5 Int 5 | 700 Dahlia Points |
| Purple Hero II Set - Male Only, Def 5 Res 5 Int 5 MP 10 | 900 Dahlia Points |
| Purple Hero Set - Male Only, Def 5 Res 5 Int 5 | 700 Dahlia Points |
| Quester Set - Male Only, Def 5 Res 5 Dex 5 | 500 Dahlia Points |
| Red Hero II Set, Def 5 Res 5 Dex 5 MP 10 | 900 Dahlia Points |
| Red Hero Set, Def 5 Res 5 Dex 5 | 700 Dahlia Points |
| Ruler Set - Male Only, Def 5 Res 5 Int 5 | 500 Dahlia Points |
| Sylpheed Set - Female Only, Def 5 Res 5 Agi 5 | 500 Dahlia Points |
| White Hero II Set - Female Only, Def 5 Res 5 Spr 6 MP 10 | 900 Dahlia Points |
| White Hero Set - Female Only, Def 5 Res 5 Spr 6 | 700 Dahlia Points |
| Yellow Hero II Set, Def 5 Res 5 Agi 5 MP 10 | 900 Dahlia Points |
| Yellow Hero Set, Def 5 Res 5 Agi 5 | 700 Dahlia Points |

## WIPEOUT IN THE ZONE     (XBOX 360)

### ACHIEVEMENT

| UNLOCKABLE | HOW TO UNLOCK |
| --- | --- |
| Ahead of the Curve (40) | Finished the game with an average time of 5:00.000 per episode or better. Nice job! |
| Ain't Got That Swing (25) | Swung from Rope to Rope 5 times without falling. |
| Boys Smell (20) | Trudged through mud as a male character for 10 seconds. |
| Cardio Workout (25) | Ran on a Treadmill for 45 seconds. |
| Epic Fail (5) | Wiped out on every obstacle of a Wipeout Zone. |
| Epic Win (55) | Finished a Hard Wipeout Zone without wiping out once. |
| Episode 1 Gold (15) | Finished Episode 1 with a time of 4:30.000 or better. |
| Episode 2 Gold (15) | Finished Episode 2 with a time of 4:30.000 or better. |
| Episode 3 Gold (15) | Finished Episode 3 with a time of 4:00.000 or better. |
| Episode 4 Gold (20) | Finished Episode 4 with a time of 4:00.000 or better. |
| Episode 5 Gold (20) | Finished Episode 5 with a time of 4:00.000 or better. |
| Episode 6 Gold (20) | Finished Episode 6 with a time of 3:30.000 or better. |
| Episode 7 Gold (25) | Finished Episode 7 with a time of 3:30.000 or better. |
| Episode 8 Gold (25) | Finished Episode 8 with a time of 3:30.000 or better. |
| Episode 9 Gold (25) | Finished Episode 9 with a time of 3:30.000 or better. |
| Firing Squad (15) | Got hit by 3 blaster shots simultaneously. |
| Fun for the Whole Family (20) | Each player was blasted at least once in a 4-player game. |
| Girl Power (15) | Won a 4-player multiplayer episode as the only female character. |
| Home Run (30) | Finished Bruiseball without touching any mud or water. |
| Hopscotch (30) | Earned a bonus of 30 seconds or more on the Sweeper. |
| I Like Big Balls (25) | Bounced between the Mega Big Balls 10 times and loved it. |
| Karmic Justice (5) | Got flung into the background as Matt Kunitz. |
| Making Fun of Myself (20) | Finished Episode 5 as John Henson or John Anderson. |
| Model Behaviour (15) | Completed a Mimic Board as Jill Wagner. |
| Nemeses (25) | Beaten John Anderson as John Henson in 2-player multiplayer, or vice versa. |
| Now Just Sign the Waiver (5) | Passed the Tryouts. |
| Practice Makes Better (15) | Finished Bruiseball or Medieval Wipealot 4 times in a Practice session. |
| Practice Makes Good (14) | Finished any Qualifier 3 times in a Practice session. |
| Practice Makes Perfect (16) | Finished any Wipeout Zone 5 times in a Practice session. |
| Primetime Special (55) | Finished every Hard episode. We knew you had it in you! |
| Pump You Up (25) | Pumped a Pump 20 times in 10 seconds. Whew! |
| Sack of Potatoes (15) | Got Motivated and survived. |
| Shafted (15) | Got hit by the Crankshaft and survived. |
| So Close (30) | Suffered just one wipeout on the last obstacle of a course. |
| Summer Hit (55) | Finished all the Medium episodes. |
| Syndication (40) | Finished all the Easy episodes. |
| That Wasn't an Obstacle (5) | Wiped out within the first 5 seconds. |
| That's Gotta Hurt (15) | Got flung forward by a Hammer. |
| The Moonwalk (15) | Backpedaled for 15 seconds. |

| Way Ahead of the Curve (55) | Finished the game with an average time of 4:00.000 per episode or better. Way to go! |
| --- | --- |
| Where's the Pole? (30) | Crossed the Big Balls without wiping out. |
| Yoga Master (25) | Balanced for 15 seconds. |
| You Da Man (15) | Won a 4-player multiplayer episode as the only male character. |
| You Hit a Girl?!? (5) | Was blasted as a female character. |

## WOLFENSTEIN (XBOX 360)

### UNLOCKABLES

| UNLOCKABLE | HOW TO UNLOCK |
| --- | --- |
| Cheats | Beat the game on any difficulty. Activating cheats will disable achievements. |

## WONDER BOY IN MONSTER WORLD (Wii)

### UNLOCKABLES

| UNLOCKABLE | HOW TO UNLOCK |
| --- | --- |
| Stay at the Inn for Free | Any Inn throughout the game will let you spend the night, even if you don't have enough gold. They just take whatever You have, even if you don't have any gold at all. |

## WORLD SERIES OF POKER: TOURNAMENT OF CHAMPIONS (Wii)

### UNLOCKABLES

| UNLOCKABLE | HOW TO UNLOCK |
| --- | --- |
| All Locations | Input ⬇, ⬆, ⬇, ⬆, ⬇ at the main menu |

## WRC: FIA WORLD RALLY CHAMPIONSHIP (PSP)

Enter these passwords as Profile names.

| UNLOCKABLE | PASSWORD |
| --- | --- |
| Bird camera | dovecam |
| Enables Supercharger cheat | MAXPOWER |
| Extra avatars | UGLYMUGS |
| Ghost car | SPOOKY |
| Reverses controls | REVERSE |
| Time trial ghost cars | AITRIAL |
| Unlock everything | PADLOCK |

## WRECKING CREW (Wii)

### UNLOCKABLES

| UNLOCKABLE | HOW TO UNLOCK |
| --- | --- |
| Gold Hammer | In Phase 6, there are five bombs, 2 on the bottom, 2 in the middle of the level, and 1 on the top. Hit the 2 bombs on the bottom and then hit the middle left bomb. In a few seconds, a hammer appears. Hit it to obtain it. You now have the gold hammer. The music changes and you can hit enemies. You have the hammer until you die. |

## WWE '12 (XBOX 360)

### ACHIEVEMENT

| UNLOCKABLE | HOW TO UNLOCK |
| --- | --- |
| A Creator is Born (15) Creations | Upload one creation to the WWE Community |
| A Man Destined to Be a WrestleMania Champion (15) | Win the final match at WWE UNIVERSE PPV (Single Player) |
| A Successful Cash In (15) | Cash In Money In The Bank in WWE UNIVERSE and win using a Custom Superstar (Single Player) |

A
B
C
D
E
F
G
H
I
J
K
L
M
N
O
P
Q
R
S
T
U
V
**W**
X
Y
Z

**CODES & CHEATS**

| | |
|---|---|
| Against the Odds (15) | Win a ONE ON THREE FREE BRAWL (Single Player) |
| Arena Designer (15) | Create one arena in Create-An-Arena. |
| Berserker (30) | Break 50 tables, ladders, or chairs in one session (Single Player) |
| Challenger (20) | Win at least once on Hard difficulty or higher (Single Player) |
| COMEBACK!!! (15) | Use COMEBACK ability to increase momentum to MAX (Single Player) |
| Creative With The Moves (15) | Create a front, top rope and corner finishing move in Custom Finisher Move |
| Critic (15) | Review 5 or more items on Community Creations |
| Custom Logo Wizard (15) | Apply a Custom Logo to a Custom Superstar, Video, or Arena |
| Declaration of War (15) | Interfere in an AI vs AI WWE UNIVERSE fight and beat one opponent (Single Player) |
| Destroyer (15) | Inflict heavy damage to opponent's head, arms, and legs (Single Player) |
| Finished HERO Episode!!! (50) | Complete HERO episode in ROAD TO WrestleMania (Single Player) |
| Finished OUTSIDER Episode!! (30) | Complete OUTSIDER episode in ROAD TO WrestleMania (Single Player) |
| Finished VILLAIN Episode! (30) | Complete VILLAIN episode in ROAD TO WrestleMania (Single Player) |
| First Step of a Glorious Career (20) | Win one Championship title in WWE UNIVERSE using a Custom Superstar (Single Player) |
| For Whom the Bell Tolls (15) | Pin or submit Undertaker in the WrestleMania arena on Legend difficulty (Single Player) |
| Grand Slam Champion (50) | Win 5 championship titles in WWE UNIVERSE using a Custom Superstar (Single Player) |
| Holla! (15) | Create your own show in WWE Universe |
| I Ain't Losing to Anyone! (15) | Build momentum up to 100% in WWE UNIVERSE using a Custom Superstar (Single Player) |
| I Like Titles (30) | Win 3 championship titles in WWE UNIVERSE using a Custom Superstar (Single Player) |
| I'm Gonna be Champion (15) | Become #1 Contender for a Championship in WWE UNIVERSE using a Custom Superstar (Single Player) |
| Legend Status Accomplishments (50) | Win 50 times on Hard difficulty or higher in one session (Single Player) |
| Look! Look at my Titantron! (15) | Use a movie created in Custom Entrance Video in an entrance scene (Single Player) |
| Master of the Brawl (30) | Continue playing to unlock this secret achievement. |
| Merciless Attack (15) | Injure an opponent in WWE UNIVERSE (Single Player) |
| Mr. Money in the Bank (15) | Win the Money In The Bank match in WWE UNIVERSE using a Custom Superstar (Single Player) |
| My target at WrestleMania is...! (15) | As WWE UNIVERSE Royal Rumble winner, participate in the Royal Rumble Winner's Event |
| Pandemonium (15) | Interfere in an AI vs AI WWE UNIVERSE fight and beat all opponents (Single Player) |
| Professional Material (30) | Win 20 times on Hard difficulty or higher in one session (Single Player) |
| Reach the Ropes! (15) | Crawl to the ropes during a submission (Single Player) |

| | |
|---|---|
| **Rolling Now! (15)** | Build momentum up to 75% in WWE UNIVERSE using a Custom Superstar (Single Player) |
| **Start as a Pro (15)** | Win using a Custom Superstar in WWE UNIVERSE (Single Player) |
| **Start Xbox LIVE NXT! (15)** | Play in an Xbox LIVE match (Player match/Ranked match) |
| **Submission Specialist (30)** | Win 20 times with submissions in one session (Single Player) |
| **Superstar Contender (15)** | Win a Superstar match at the WWE UNIVERSE Draft Event (Single Player) |
| **Thank You Edge (15)** | Win 37 times with Edge in one session (Single Player) |
| **That's gotta hurt! (15)** | Win a FREE BRAWL by throwing your opponent through the window (Single Player) |
| **The Art of Submission (15)** | Win by applying a submission to a heavily damaged body part (Single Player) |
| **The Birth of a Historic Tag Team (15)** | Win or defend one Tag Team Championship in WWE UNIVERSE using a Custom Superstar (Single Player) |
| **The WWE Arrives at a New Arena! (15)** | Hold an Exhibition at a Custom Arena (Single) Player |
| **This Combo is Lethal! (30)** | Perform a Wake-Up taunt, hit your finisher, and then win via pinfall (Single Player) |
| **Unique Original Story (15)** | Create a story that includes a Custom Superstar or Custom Arena |
| **Well Scouted (15)** | Reverse an opponent's finishing move (Single Player) |
| **Wildman of the Ring (15)** | Break 20 tables, ladders, or chairs in one session (Single Player) |
| **Worked the Limb (15)** | Use the limb targeting system to attack the same part 10 times in one match (Single Player) |
| **WrestleMania's My Destiny! (30)** | Win a Royal Rumble match at Royal Rumble PPV in WWE UNIVERSE (Single Player) |
| **You've Got Fans! (30)** | Content you uploaded to Community Creations is downloaded 5 or more times by other players |

### CODE

At the main menu, select "My WWE", "Options", then "Cheat Codes".

| UNLOCKABLE | CODE |
|---|---|
| **Unlock the WWE Attitude Era Heavyweight Championship.** | OhHellYeah! |

### UNLOCKABLE

Unlock these in g Road to Wrestlemania or Universe Mode

| UNLOCKABLE | HOW TO UNLOCK |
|---|---|
| **Arn Anderson's Civilian Attire** | Hero Story Scene 5-1 |
| **Dashing Cody Rhodes** | Villain Story Scene 4-1 |
| **Drew McIntyre Suit Attire** | Villain Story Scene 13-2 |
| **Edge Entrance Attire** | Villain Story 15-2 |
| **HHH Street Attire** | Outsider Story Cutscene |
| **John Cena Entrance Attire** | Villain Story 1-4 |
| **John Cena Purple Attire & John Cena with T-Shirt** | Play two different Wrestlemania Matches featuring Cena in Universe |
| **Kevin Nash Suit Attire** | Hero Story 14-1 |
| **Mr.McMahon Suit Attire** | Hero Story Cutscene |
| **Randy Orton without Beard** | Go into a Wretlemania Match with Randy in Universe |

NEW!

A
B
C
D
E
F
G
H
I
J
K
L
M
N
O
P
Q
R
S
T
U
V
**W**
X
Y
Z

**CODES & CHEATS**

| | |
|---|---|
| **Sheamus Suit Attire** | Villain Story 18-1 |
| **Sheamus T-Shirt Attire** | Villain Story 5-4 |
| **Undertaker Hooded Attire** | Go into a Wretlemania Match with Undertaker in Universe |
| **Wade Barrett Suit Attire** | Villain Story 19-2 |
| **William Regal Suit Attire** | Villain Story 8-5 |
| **Bragging Rights** | Win a match in this ppv in Universe |
| **Clash of Champions** | Hero Story Cutscene at PPV |
| **Extreme Rules** | Win a match in this ppv in Universe |
| **Fatal 4-Way** | Win a match in this ppv in Universe |
| **Hell in a Cell** | Win a match in this ppv in Universe |
| **Money in the Bank** | Win a match in this ppv in Universe |
| **Night of Champions** | Win a match in this ppv in Universe |
| **NXT Arena** | Hero Story Cutscene |
| **Over the Limit** | Win a match in this ppv in Universe |
| **Starrcade** | Hero Story Cutscene |
| **Survivor Series** | Win a match in this ppv in Universe |
| **TLC** | Win a match in this ppv in Universe |
| **Tribute to the Troops** | Finish a year of Universe |
| **WCW Monday Nitro** | Hero Story 21-1 |
| **Jacob Cass Entrance** | Hero Story Cutscene 2-1 |
| **King of Kings Theme** | Outsider Story Cutscene |
| **Mr. McMahon Entrance** | Hero Story Cutscene |
| **Undertaker Entrance** | Win with Undertaker at Wrestlemania in Universe |
| **United Kingdom Entrance** | Villain Story Cutscene |
| **Champion of Champions Title** | Win a title at Night of Champions |
| **Classic Intercontinental Title** | Win the Intercontinental Title |
| **ECW Title** | Win a title at Extreme Rules |
| **European Title** | Villain Story 10-1 |
| **Hardcore Title** | Win a title in a falls count anywhere match |
| **Light Heavyweight Title** | Win a title with Mysterio |
| **Million Dollar Title** | With a title with Ted DiBiase |
| **WCW Spray Painted World Heavyweight Title** | Hero Story Cutscene 13-1 |
| **WCW Spray Painted WWE Title** | Hero Story Cutscene |
| **WCW Title** | Hero Story Cutscene |
| **World Tag Team Title** | With the titles on SmackDown |
| **WWE Attitude Era Title** | Win the WWE title with Stone Cold |
| **WWE Tag Team Title** | Win the titles on Raw |
| **WWE Undisputed Title** | Win the WWE title with HHH at a PPV |
| **Arn Anderson** | Viillain Story Cutscene |
| **Booker T** | Hero Story Cutscene 8-1 |
| **Brock Lesnar** | Win a singles match in Universe |
| **Demolition** | Win the Undisputed Tag Titles in Universe |
| **Eddie Guerrero** | Hero Story 7-1 |
| **Edge** | Villain Cutscene |
| **Goldust** | Win the Intercontinental Championship as Cody Rhodes in WWE Universe |

| Kevin Nash | Outsider Story Cutscene 5-2 |
| Michelle McCool | Win Divas Title in Universe |
| Ricky Steamboat | Hero Story Cutscene |
| Road Warriors | Hero Story Cutscene 10-1 |
| Stone Cold | Complete Villain Story or Defend WWE Title in Universe Mode |
| Vader | Hero Story Cutscene 6-2 |
| Vince McMahon | Hero Story Cutscene |

## WWE '12 (Wii)

### CODE

At Options, Unlockables, Cheat Codes--enter these this code

| UNLOCKABLE | CODE |
| --- | --- |
| "Attitude Era" WWE Championship belt | OhHellYeah! |

### UNLOCKABLE

Unlock these in WWE Universe Mode

| UNLOCKABLE | HOW TO UNLOCK |
| --- | --- |
| ECW Championship (Classic) | Win any title in an Extreme Rules match. |
| Hardcore Championship | Win any title in a Falls Count Anywhere match |
| Intercontinental Championship (Classic) | Win the Intercontinental title |
| The Champion of Champions | Win any title at the Clash of the Champions arena |
| The Million Dollar Championship | Win any title with Ted DiBiase |
| The Undisputed WWE Championship | Win the WWE Championship with Triple H at a PPV |
| WCW Championship (Classic) | Complete Hero Story |
| World Heavyweight Championship (Spray-painted) | Complete Hero Story match in Royal Rumble, after Big Show spray paints the belt |
| World Tag Team Championship | Unlock Demolition |
| WWE Championship (Attitude Era) | Win the WWE Championship with Stone Cold Steve Austin |
| WWE Championship (Spray-painted) | Complete Hero Story match in Elimination Chamber |
| WWE European Championship | Win the United States title in Villain Story |
| WWE Light Heavyweight Championship | Win any title with Rey Mysterio |
| WWE Tag Team Championship (Classic) | Unlock the Road Warriors |
| Arn Anderson | Complete Royal Rumble match in Villain Story |
| Booker T | Complete Hero Story match, when Booker T appears, during your match with Husky Harris |
| Brock Lesnar | Win the first one-on-one match in WWE Universe |
| Demolition | Win the WWE Tag Team Championship in WWE Universe |
| Eddie Guerrero | Complete Hero Story match as Eddie, defeating Rey Mysterio |
| Edge | Complete the battle royal in Villain Story |
| Goldust | Complete a singles match with Cody Rhodes in WWE Universe |
| Kevin Nash | Complete Outsider Story match, after meeting him in the locker room |
| Michelle McCool | Win Divas Championship in WWE Universe |

NEW!

A
B
C
D
E
F
G
H
I
J
K
L
M
N
O
P
Q
R
S
T
U
V
W
X
Y
Z

| | |
|---|---|
| Mr. McMahon | Complete Hero Story |
| Ricky "The Dragon" Steamboat | Complete Royal Rumble match in Hero Story |
| Stone Cold Steve Austin | Start in Outsider Story |
| The Road Warriors | Complete Hero Story match, as Animal appears during your match with Kofi Kingston |
| The Rock | Complete Outsider Story |
| Vader | Defeat Vader, following your match with Tyson Kidd in Hero Story |
| "DASHING" Cody Rhodes | Villain Story scene 4-1 after you match with Rhodes as Sheamus |
| Arn Anderson civilian attire | Hero Story scene 5-1 after Kevin Nash introduces Arn Anderson |
| Drew McIntyre with Suit | Villain Story 13-2 after you weaken John Cena in the ring as Sheamus |
| Edge Entrance Attire | Villain Story 15-2 after you defeat Arn Anderson in the ring. |
| HHH Street Attire | Outsider Story cutscene WrestleMania |
| Hooded Undertaker Entrance Attire | Go into a WrestleMania match featuring Undertaker as one of the competitors. It should be his entrance attire. |
| John Cena Entrance Attire | Villain Story scene 1-4 after you defeat Cena on the stage as Sheamus |
| John Cena Purple Attire & John Cena with T Shirt | Go into a WrestleMania match featuring John Cena as one of the competitors. It should be his entrance attire. |
| Kevin Nash with suit | Hero story cutscene 14-1 after Nash slams Jacob Cass and Rey Mysterio after their tag team match with Big Show and Cody Rhodes |
| Mr. McMahon with Suit | Hero cutscene Steel Cage 1 |
| Randy Orton without Beard | Go into a WrestleMania match featuring Randy Orton as one of the competitors. It should be his model during his entrance AND his match |
| Sheamus with Suit | Villain Story 18-1 after you finish off HHH in the ring as Sheamus |
| Sheamus with T-Shirt | Villain Story scene 5-4 after your tag team match as William Regal, Drew McIntyre, and Sheamus |
| The Miz Entrance Attire | Villain Story Scene 2-1 after The Miz comes out on stage with Wade Barrett |
| The Miz with Suit | Outsider story scene 10-1 after the Miz announces he is the new General Manager |
| Wade Barrett with Suit | Villain Story 19-2 after your backstage brawl with Wade Barrett |
| William Regal with Suit | Villain Story 8-5 after United Kingdom wins Survivor Series |
| Bragging Rights | Win a match in the Bragging Rights arena in WWE Universe mode. |
| Extreme Rules | Win a match in the Extreme Rules arena in WWE Universe mode. |
| Fatal 4-Way | Win a match in Fatal-4-Way arena in WWE Universe. |
| Hell In A Cell | Win a match in Hell in a Cell arena in WWE Universe. |
| Money In The Bank | Win a match in Money In The Bank arena in WWE Universe. |
| Night of Champions | Win a match in Night of Champions arena in WWE Universe. |

| | |
|---|---|
| Nitro | Reach cutscene 21-1 after the Monday Night Nitro match in the Hero storyline in RTWM mode. |
| Over The Limit | Win a match in the Over The Limit arena in WWE Universe mode. |
| Starrcade | Reach the Steel Cage match 2 cutscene in the Hero storyline in RTWM mode. |
| Survivor Series | Win a match in the Survivor Series arena in WWE Universe mode. |
| TLC | Win a match in the TLC arena in WWE Universe mode. |
| Tribute To The Troops | Successfully complete first year in WWE Universe mode. |

## WWE ALL STARS (PlayStation 3)

### UNLOCKABLE

Input the following codess during the Main Menu to unlock features

| EFFECT | CODE |
|---|---|
| All Wrestlers, Arenas, Attires | ←, ▲, ↓, ←, ▲, ■, ←, ■, ▲, ↓, →, ■, ←, ↑, ■, → |
| Austin & Punk Attires | ←, ←, →, →, ↑, ↓, ↑, ↓ |
| Roberts & Orton Attires | ↑, ↓, ←, →, ↑, ↑, ↓, ↓ |
| Savage & Morrison Attires | ↓, ←, ↑, →, →, ↑, ←, ↓ |

### UNLOCKABLE

Complete the tasks to unlock.

| UNLOCKABLE | HOW TO UNLOCK |
|---|---|
| Classic Smackdown Arena | Complete a Path Of Champions With Your Created Superstar |
| Summerslam Arena | Win 10 Matches With Yor Created Superstar |
| WWE All-Stars Arena | Create a WWE Superstar |

### UNLOCKABLE

Complete the tasks to unlock

| UNLOCKABLE | HOW TO UNLOCK |
|---|---|
| Drew McIntyre | Win the Fantasy Warfare Match with him against Roddy Piper |
| Eddie Guerrero | Win the Fantasy Warfare Match with him against Rey Mysterio Jr. |
| Edge | Win the Fantasy Warfare Match with him against Bret Hart |
| Jack Swagger | Win the Fantasy Warfare Match with him against Sgt. Slaughter |
| Jimmy Snuka | Win the Fantasy Warfare Match with him against Kane |
| Kane | Win the Fantasy Warfare Match with him against Jimmy Snuka |
| Mr. Perfect | Win the Fantasy Warfare Match with him against The Miz |
| Sgt. Slaughter | Win the Fantasy Warfare Match with him against Jack Swagger |
| Shawn Micheals | Win the Fantasy Warfare Match with him against The Undertaker |
| The Miz | Win the Fantasy Warfare Match with him against Mr. Perfect |

## WWE ALL STARS (XBOX 360)

### UNLOCKABLE

Input the following codess during the Main Menu to unlock features

| UNLOCKABLE | HOW TO UNLOCK |
|---|---|
| All Wrestlers, Arenas, Attires | ←, ⓨ, ↓, ←, ⓨ, ⓧ, ←, ⓧ, ⓨ, ↓, →, ⓧ, ←, ↑, ⓧ, → |
| Austin & Punk Attires | ←, ←, →, →, ↑, ↓, ↑, ↓ |
| Roberts & Orton Attires | ↑, ↓, ←, →, ↑, ↑, ↓, ↓ |
| Savage & Morrison Attires | ↓, ←, ↑, →, →, ↑, ←, ↓ |

### UNLOCKABLE

Complete the tasks to unlock

| UNLOCKABLE | HOW TO UNLOCK |
|---|---|
| Classic Smackdown Arena | Complete a Path Of Champions With Your Created Superstar |
| Summerslam Arena | Win 10 Matches With Yor Created Superstar |
| WWE All-Stars Arena | Create a WWE Superstar |

### UNLOCKABLE

Complete the tasks to unlock

| UNLOCKABLE | HOW TO UNLOCK |
|---|---|
| Drew McIntyre | Win the Fantasy Warfare Match with him against Roddy Piper |
| Eddie Guerrero | Win the Fantasy Warfare Match with him against Rey Mysterio Jr. |
| Edge | Win the Fantasy Warfare Match with him against Bret Hart |
| Jack Swagger | Win the Fantasy Warfare Match with him against Sgt. Slaughter |
| Jimmy Snuka | Win the Fantasy Warfare Match with him against Kane |
| Kane | Win the Fantasy Warfare Match with him against Jimmy Snuka |
| Mr. Perfect | Win the Fantasy Warfare Match with him against The Miz |
| Sgt. Slaughter | Win the Fantasy Warfare Match with him against Jack Swagger |
| Shawn Micheals | Win the Fantasy Warfare Match with him against The Undertaker |
| The Miz | Win the Fantasy Warfare Match with him against Mr. Perfect |

## WWE ALL STARS   (Wii)

### UNLOCKABLE

Complete any Path of Superstars with each WWE Legend or Superstar to unlock their 2nd attire. Complete another path again with Andre the Giant, Hulk Hogan, John Cena, Rey Mysterio, and Randy Savage to unlock their 3rd attire

### UNLOCKABLE

Complete the tasks to unlock

| UNLOCKABLE | HOW TO UNLOCK |
|---|---|
| Drew McIntyre | Win the Fantasy Warfare Match with him against Roddy Piper |
| Eddie Guerrero | Win the Fantasy Warfare Match with him against Rey Mysterio Jr. |
| Edge | Win the Fantasy Warfare Match with him against Bret Hart |
| Jack Swagger | Win the Fantasy Warfare Match with him against Sgt. Slaughter |
| Jimmy Snuka | Win the Fantasy Warfare Match with him against Kane |
| Kane | Win the Fantasy Warfare Match with him against Jimmy Snuka |
| Mr. Perfect | Win the Fantasy Warfare Match with him against The Miz |
| Sgt. Slaughter | Win the Fantasy Warfare Match with him against Jack Swagger |
| Shawn Micheals | Win the Fantasy Warfare Match with him against The Undertaker |
| The Miz | Win the Fantasy Warfare Match with him against Mr. Perfect |

## WWE SMACKDOWN VS. RAW 2010   (XBOX 360)

### CODES

Go to "options" then "cheat codes"; the codes are case-sensitive.

| EFFECT | CODE |
|---|---|
| Unlock Dirt Sheet Set and Mr. McMahon's Office backstage areas. | BonusBrawl |
| Unlock The Rock | The Great One |

## ROAD TO WRESTLEMANIA UNLOCKABLES

| UNLOCKABLE | HOW TO UNLOCK |
|---|---|
| **The Million Dollar Man Ted DiBiase** | In "Randy Orton's RTWM," beat Ted DiBiase Jr. at Wrestlemania and KO "The Million Dollar Man" after the match. |
| **Alternate Attire for Chris Jericho** | Week 6 of "HBK's RTWM," Make Jericho bleed. |
| **Alternate Attire for Edge** | Week 6 of "Edge's RTWM," Win in under 3 minutes. |
| **Alternate Attire for JBL** | Week 8 of "HBK's RTWM," win the match in under 4 minutes. |
| **Alternate Attire for Mickie James** | Week 6 of "Mickie James' RTWM," beat Michelle McCool in under 3 minutes. |
| **Alternate Attire for Mr. Kennedy** | In "Edge's RTWM," eliminate Mr. Kennedy from the Royal Rumble Match. |
| **Alternate attire for Mr. McMahon (suit)** | Week 5 of "Create-A-Superstar's RTWM," spend at least one minute of the match outside the ring. |
| **Alternate Attire for Natalya** | Week 9 of "Mickie James' RTWM," choose Kendrick over Natalya. Then at week 10, win the match suffering minimal damage. |
| **Alternate Attire for Santino Marella (Street clothes)** | Week 12 of "Create-A-Superstar's RTWM," make a successful diving attack from the top of the ladder. |
| **Alternate Attire for Shawn Michaels** | Week 4 of "HBK's RTWM," hit both opponents with Sweet CHIN Music. |
| **Alternate Attire for Shawn Michaels (DX) (Option 1)** | Week 10 of "HBK's RTWM," accept the Retirement Match. Then at Week 11, have your partner be the legal man longer. |
| **Alternate Attire for Shawn Michaels (DX) (Option 2)** | Week 10 of "HBK's RTWM," decline the Retirement Match, then at Week 11, execute three Double Team attacks. |
| **Alternate Attire for The Brian Kendrick** | Week 9 of 'Mickie James' RTWM," choose Natalya over Kendrick. Then at week 12, win the match without using a signature move or finisher. |
| **Alternate Attire for Vince McMahon (Chicken Head)** | Win the WrestleMania Match in "Create-A-Superstar's RTWM." |
| **Alternate Attires for Miz and Morrison (Street clothes) & Dirt Sheet area for Backstage Brawl** | Week 11 of "Brand Warfare's RTWM," win the handicap match as either Triple H or John Cena. |
| **Champion of Champions title belt** | Win at Wrestlemania in "Brand Warfare's RTWM." |
| **Cowboy Bob Orton** | Week 9 of "Randy Orton's RTWM," don't use any strikes in your match. |
| **Dusty Rhodes** | In "Randy Orton's RTWM," beat Cody Rhodes at WrestleMania and KO Dusty after the match. |
| **Eve** | Week 2 of "Mickie James' RTWM," pin or submit Maryse |
| **Ezekiel Jackson** | Week 3 of "Create-A-Superstar's RTWM," throw each opponent out of the ring at least once. |
| **Green and Red Dummies as Playable Characters** | Week 3 of "Randy Orton's RTWM," refuse Cody's help and then reverse three of Batista's attacks. |
| **Interview Room for Backstage** | Complete Shawn Michaels RTW. |
| **Jesse** | Week 2 of "Edge's RTWM," hit every opponent with a finisher. |
| **John Cena Alternate Attire (Street Clothes)** | Week 4 of "Brand Warfare's RTWM," you must put Kane through a table in less than 2:30 as John Cena. |
| **Locker Room Backstage area** | In "Edge's RTWM," at No Way Out, drag Mr. Kennedy on top of the Big Show and count the pinfall. |

| | |
|---|---|
| Mr. McMahon (Playable Character) | Week 11 of "Edge's RTWM," Put Triple H through an announcer table. |
| Randy Orton's Alternate Attire | In "Randy Orton's RTWM," at No Way Out, RKO Dusty Rhodes. |
| Road to Wrestlemania Event Skip Feature | Week 12 of "Randy Orton's RTWM," spend less than 2 minutes in the ring as the legal superstar. |
| Santino Marella Story Designer story | Week 11 of "Create-A-Superstar's RTWM," reach 500 degrees at least four times. |
| The Hardys, DX, & Morrison and The Miz Tag Entrances | Week 2 of "Brand Warfare's RTWM," you must win the battle royal as either Triple H or John Cena. |
| The Rock | Complete Edge's Road to Wrestlemania. |
| Triple H Alternate Attire (DX) | Week 6 of "Brand Warfare's RTWM," win your match in under 3 minutes as Triple H. |
| Trish Stratus | Complete Mickie's Road to Wrestlemania |
| Vince's Office in Backstage Brawl | Week 6 of "Create-A-Superstar's RTWM," win your match. |

## UNLOCKABLE ABILITIES

| UNLOCKABLE | HOW TO UNLOCK |
|---|---|
| Durability | Must get Durability Attribute score of 85. |
| Exploder Turnbuckle Attack | Must get your speed attribute score of 75. |
| Fan Favorite | Must get charisma score of 80. |
| Fired Up | Must get an overall rating of 90. |
| Hardcore Resurrection | Must get hardcore score of 90. |
| Kip Up | Must get a technical score of 85. |
| Lock Pick | Must get a submission score of 80. |
| Object Specialist | Must get a hardcore score of 70. |
| Resiliency | Must get an overall rating of 92. |
| Strong Strike | Must get a strike score of 75. |

# WWE SMACKDOWN VS. RAW 2010 (PlayStation 3)

## CODES

Go to "options" then "cheat codes"; the codes are case-sensitive.

| EFFECT | CODE |
|---|---|
| Unlock Dirt Sheet Set and Mr. McMahon's Office backstage areas. | BonusBrawl |
| Unlock The Rock | The Great One |

## ROAD TO WRESTLEMANIA UNLOCKABLES

| UNLOCKABLE | HOW TO UNLOCK |
|---|---|
| The Million Dollar Man Ted DiBiase | In "Randy Orton's RTWM," beat Ted DiBiase Jr. at Wrestlemania and KO "The Million Dollar Man" after the match. |
| Alternate Attire for Chris Jericho | Week 6 of "HBK's RTWM," make Jericho bleed. |
| Alternate Attire for Edge | Week 6 of "Edge's RTWM," win in under 3 minutes. |
| Alternate Attire for JBL | Week 8 of "HBK's RTWM," win the match in under 4 minutes. |
| Alternate Attire for Mickie James | Week 6 of "Mickie James' RTWM," beat Michelle McCool in under 3 minutes. |
| Alternate Attire for Mr. Kennedy | In "Edge's RTWM," eliminate Mr. Kennedy from the Royal Rumble Match. |
| Alternate attire for Mr. McMahon (suit) | Week 5 of "Create-A-Superstar's RTWM," spend at least one minute of the match outside the ring. |

| | |
|---|---|
| **Alternate Attire for Natalya** | Week 9 of "Mickie James' RTWM," choose Kendrick over Natalya. Then at week 10, win the match suffering minimal damage. |
| **Alternate Attire for Santino Marella (Street clothes)** | Week 12 of "Create-A-Superstar's RTWM," make a successful diving attack from the top of the ladder. |
| **Alternate Attire for Shawn Michaels** | Week 4 of "HBK's RTWM," hit both opponents with Sweet CHIN Music. |
| **Alternate Attire for Shawn Michaels (DX) (Option 1)** | Week 10 of "HBK's RTWM," accept the Retirement Match. Then at Week 11, have your partner be the legal man longer. |
| **Alternate Attire for Shawn Michaels (DX) (Option 2)** | Week 10 of "HBK's RTWM," decline the Retirement Match. Then at Week 11, execute three Double Team attacks. |
| **Alternate Attire for The Brian Kendrick** | Week 9 of 'Mickie James' RTWM," choose Natalya over Kendrick. Then at week 12, win the match without using a signature move or finisher. |
| **Alternate Attire for Vince McMahon (Chicken Head)** | Win the WrestleMania Match in "Create-A-Superstar's RTWM." |
| **Alternate Attires for Miz and Morrison (Street clothes) & Dirt Sheet area for Backstage Brawl** | Week 11 of "Brand Warfare's RTWM," win the handicap match as either Triple H or John Cena |
| **Champion of Champions title belt** | Win at Wrestlemania in "Brand Warfare's RTWM." |
| **Cowboy Bob Orton** | Week 9 of "Randy Orton's RTWM," don't use any strikes in your match. |
| **Dusty Rhodes** | In "Randy Orton's RTWM," beat Cody Rhodes at WrestleMania and KO Dusty after the match. |
| **Eve** | Week 2 of "Mickie James' RTWM", pin or submit Maryse. |
| **Ezekiel Jackson** | Week 3 of "Create-A-Superstar's RTWM," throw each opponent out of the ring at least once. |
| **Green and Red Dummies as Playable Characters** | Week 3 of "Randy Orton's RTWM," refuse Cody's help and then reverse three of Batista's attacks. |
| **Interview Room for Backstage** | Complete Shawn Michaels RTW |
| **Jesse** | Week 2 of "Edge's RTWM," hit every opponent with a finisher. |
| **John Cena Alternate Attire (Street Clothes)** | Week 4 of "Brand Warfare's RTWM," you must put Kane through a table in less than 2:30 as John Cena. |
| **Locker Room Backstage area** | In "Edge's RTWM," at No Way Out, drag Mr. Kennedy on top of the Big Show and count the pinfall. |
| **Mr. McMahon (Playable Character)** | Week 11 of "Edge's RTWM," put Triple H through an announcer table. |
| **Randy Orton's Alternate Attire** | In "Randy Orton's RTWM," at No Way Out, RKO Dusty Rhodes. |
| **Road to Wrestlemania Event Skip Feature** | Week 12 of "Randy Orton's RTWM," spend less than 2 minutes in the ring as the legal superstar. |
| **Santino Marella Story Designer story** | Week 11 of "Create-A-Superstar's RTWM," reach 500 degrees at least four times. |
| **The Hardys, DX, & Morrison and The Miz Tag Entrances** | Week 2 of "Brand Warfare's RTWM," you must win the battle royal as either Triple H or John Cena. |
| **The Rock** | Complete Edge's Road to Wrestlemania. |
| **Triple H Alternate Attire (DX)** | Week 6 of "Brand Warfare's RTWM," win your match in under 3 minutes as Triple H. |

**NEW!**

A
B
C
D
E
F
G
H
I
J
K
L
M
N
O
P
Q
R
S
T
U
V
**W**
X
Y
Z

**CODES & CHEATS**

| Trish Stratus | Complete Mickie's Road to Wrestlemania. |
|---|---|
| Vince's Office in Backstage Brawl | Week 6 of "Create-A-Superstar's RTWM," win your match. |

### UNLOCKABLE ABILITIES

| UNLOCKABLE | HOW TO UNLOCK |
|---|---|
| Durability | Must get Durability Attribute score of 85. |
| Exploder Turnbuckle Attack | Must get your speed attribute score of 75. |
| Fan Favorite | Must get charisma score of 80. |
| Fired Up | Must get your overall rating of a 90. |
| Hardcore Resurrection | Must get hardcore score of 90. |
| Kip Up | Must get a technical score of 85. |
| Lock Pick | Must get a submission score of 80. |
| Object Specialist | Must get a hardcore score of 70. |
| Resiliency | Must get an overall rating of 92. |
| Strong Strike | Must get a strike score of 75. |

## WWE SMACKDOWN VS. RAW 2010 (PSP)

### CODES

Go to "options" then "cheat codes," the codes are case-sensitive.

| EFFECT | CODE |
|---|---|
| Unlock Dirt Sheet Set and Mr. McMahon's Office backstage areas. | BonusBrawl |
| Unlock The Rock | The Great One |

## WWE SMACKDOWN VS. RAW 2011 (Wii)

### CODES

You can access the cheat code menu by going to "My WWE," then "Options," then "Cheat Codes."

| EFFECT | CODE |
|---|---|
| John Cena Street Fight gear and Avatar T-Shirt | SLURPEE |
| Randy Orton Alternate Attire | apexpredator |
| "Tribute to the Troops" arena | 8thannualtribute |

## WWE SMACKDOWN VS. RAW 2011 (XBOX360)

### CODES

You can access the cheat code menu by going to "My WWE," then "Options," then "Cheat Codes."

| EFFECT | CODE |
|---|---|
| John Cena Street Fight gear and Avatar T-Shirt | SLURPEE |
| Randy Orton Alternate Attire | apexpredator |
| "Tribute to the Troops" arena | 8thannualtribute |

### UNLOCKABLES

| UNLOCKABLE | HOW TO UNLOCK |
|---|---|
| ECW Create Modes Content | Hold 10 matches in Exhibition Mode |
| Edge/Christian custom entrance (as seen in Christian's RTWM) | In Christian's RTWM, between Weeks 10 and 12, cash in the money in the bank against Edge and win |
| Backlash | Win once at Backlash with any superstar (WWE Universe, select match, not custom) |
| Bragging Rights | Win once at Bragging Rights with any superstar (WWE Universe, select match, not custom) |
| Breaking Point | Win once at Breaking Point with any superstar (WWE Universe, select match, not custom) |

| | |
|---|---|
| **Druid Arena** | Complete all 5 RTWMs |
| **ECW** | Win once at SummerSlam with any superstar (WWE Universe, select match, not custom) |
| **Extreme Rules** | Win once at Extreme Rules with any superstar (WWE Universe, select match, not custom) |
| **Hell In A Cell** | Win once at Hell In A Cell with any superstar (WWE Universe, select match, not custom) |
| **Judgment Day** | Win once at Royal Rumble with any superstar (WWE Universe, select match, not custom) |
| **Night of Champions** | Win once at Night of Champions with any superstar (WWE Universe, select match, not custom) |
| **Survivor Series** | Win once at Survivor Series with any superstar (WWE Universe, select match, not custom) |
| **The Bash** | Win once at the Bash with any superstar (WWE Universe, select match, not custom) |
| **TLC** | Win once at TLC with any superstar (WWE Universe, select match, not custom) |
| **Tribute to the Troops** | Win once at WrestleMania XXVI with any superstar (WWE Universe, select match, not custom) |
| **Batista (Civilian)** | In Jericho's RTWM, win against Kofi, Henry, and Batista in Week 8 |
| **Edge (Civilian)** | In Christian's RTWM, defeat Big Show in a locker room area during Elimination Chamber |
| **Jake the Snake Roberts** | In week 9 of the vs Undertaker RTWM, win your match with minimal damage taken |
| **Masked Kane Attire** | In week 11 of the vs Undertaker RTWM, win your match |
| **Mickie James** | When Vince McMahon says you have to wrestle Mickie James after you've won a match, defeat Mickie James and she'll be unlocked for play. |
| **MVP (Civilian)** | In Cena's RTWM, win both Week 5 and Week 7 Tag Team Challenge Match against R-Truth and Mike Knox. |
| **Paul Bearer** | In week 12 of the vs Undertaker RTWM, knock him out backstage in less than 90 seconds. |
| **Play as Finlay** | When Vince McMahon says you have to wrestle Finlay after you've won a match, defeat Finlay and he'll be unlocked for play. |
| **Play as Vladimir Kozlov** | When Vince McMahon says you have to wrestle Kozlov after you've won a match, defeat Kozlov and he'll be unlocked for play. |
| **Ricky "The Dragon" Steambot** | In week 12 of Jericho's RTWM, defeat him in a singles match. |
| **Rob Van Dam** | Complete Rey Mysterio's RTWM |
| **Superfly Jimmy Snuka** | In week 10 of the vs Undertaker RTWM, win your match in less than 3 minutes. |
| **Ted DiBiase (T-Shirt)** | In Cena's RTWM, defeat Ted DiBiase to win the Week 11 Tag Team Challenge against Ted DiBiase and Cody Rhodes. |
| **Terry Funk** | Defeat him at Wrestlemania in Rey Mysterio's RTWM. |
| **The Rock** | In week 12 of the vs Undertaker RTWM, you can find the Rock in the food room, and you have to win the match against him to get him. |
| **Todo Americano attire for Jack Swagger** | Perform your finisher against him in Rey Mysterio's RTWM |
| **Triple H (Civilian)** | In Jericho's RTWM, during Week 6, escape to the parking lot without losing to Triple H. |
| **Zack Ryder** | Win a Falls Count Anywhere Match in WWE Universe. |

**NEW!**

A
B
C
D
E
F
G
H
I
J
K
L
M
N
O
P
Q
R
S
T
U
V
W
X
Y
Z

## X-BLADES (XBOX 360)

### UNLOCKABLES

| UNLOCKABLE | HOW TO UNLOCK |
|---|---|
| New Costumes | Beat the game once to unlock two new costumes: A health Regeneration outfit, and an Armored outfit. |
| Pro Mode | You can unlock the Pro difficulty by completing the game. |

## X-BLADES (PlayStation 3)

### NEW COSTUMES

Complete the game on HARD difficulty to unlock both secret costumes at once.

| UNLOCKABLE | HOW TO UNLOCK |
|---|---|
| Armored Costume | Beat game on Hard mode. |
| Regeneration Costume | Beat game on Hard mode. |

## X-MEN: DESTINY (PlayStation 3)

### TROPHY

| UNLOCKABLE | HOW TO UNLOCK |
|---|---|
| Ace In The Hole (Bronze) | Defeat Gambit. |
| Alpha Level Mutant (Gold) | Finish the game on X-Man difficulty. |
| An Unstoppable Force (Bronze) | Defeat Magneto and Juggernaut. |
| Another Shrimp on the Barbie (Bronze) | Stop Pyro from being mind-controlled. |
| Archivist (Silver) | Collect 15 dossiers. |
| At Least It's Aerodynamic... (Bronze) | Equip your first suit. |
| Beginner's Luck (Bronze) | Complete your first Great combo. |
| Beta Level Mutant (Gold) | Finish the game on New Mutant difficulty. |
| Better than the Best (Bronze) | Defeat more enemies than Wolverine in the Prime Enforcer factory. |
| Broken Glass, Everywhere... (Bronze) | Break 30 Combat Text Pop Ups. |
| Choose Wisely (Bronze) | Make second power destiny choice. |
| Cleaned up the City (Silver) | Destroy 25 pieces of propaganda. |
| Completionist (Silver) | Complete all 15 unique challenge missions. |
| David Beats Goliath (Bronze) | Defeat Sublime. |
| Destiny Begins (Bronze) | Select a Power. |
| Diamond in the Rough (Bronze) | Help Emma Frost defend mutant civilians from Purifier attacks. |
| Fight Terror with Terror (Bronze) | Defeat 10 enemies with one Ultra power. |
| Fist of the... (Bronze) | Stop Northstar from being mind-controlled. |
| Flash Fire (Bronze) | Help Pyro, Juggernaut and Quicksilver defeat the Purifiers. |
| Four of a Kind (Bronze) | Equip a complete X-Gene set and suit. |
| Fully Evolved (Silver) | Fully level up all powers. |

| | |
|---|---|
| **Garbage Collection (Bronze)** | Destroy your first piece of propaganda. |
| **Got My Eye on You (Silver)** | Join Cyclops and the X-Men. |
| **Homo Superior (Platinum)** | Collect all other trophies. |
| **How Strong Could It Be? (Bronze)** | Trigger X-Mode. |
| **I've Got the Power (Bronze)** | Fully level up a power. |
| **It's a Secret to Everybody (Bronze)** | Find the U-Men secret lab. |
| **Logan's Run (Bronze)** | Help Emma Frost turn Wolverine back to normal. |
| **Magneto Is Right (Silver)** | Join Magneto and the Brotherhood. |
| **Mechageddon (Bronze)** | Defeat 20 Purifier Stalker Mechs. |
| **Mutant Tracker (Bronze)** | Rescue Caliban. |
| **Omega Level Mutant (Gold)** | Finish the game on X-treme difficulty. |
| **Profiler (Bronze)** | Collect your first dossier. |
| **Purify the Purifiers (Bronze)** | Defeat 2000 Purifiers. |
| **Reinforced (Bronze)** | Defeat 20 Prime Enforcers. |
| **Satellite Interference (Bronze)** | Interrupt the transmission. |
| **Shock and Awe (Bronze)** | Defeat Cameron Hodge. |
| **Side-tracked (Bronze)** | Complete your first challenge mission. |
| **Splicer (Bronze)** | Equip your first X-Gene. |
| **Stay Frosty (Bronze)** | Help Iceman, Cyclops and Emma Frost defeat the Purifiers. |
| **Taking Every Opportunity (Bronze)** | Complete 10 unique challenge missions. |
| **Teleport This! (Bronze)** | Help Nightcrawler rescue mutants. |
| **The Choice Is Made (Bronze)** | Make third power destiny choice. |
| **The Goon Squad (Bronze)** | Defeat 500 MRD Troops. |
| **The Roof, the Roof... (Bronze)** | Help Pyro set the roof on fire. |
| **Things Look So Bad Everywhere... (Bronze)** | Survive Magneto's attack on the Purifiers. |
| **Think About It... (Bronze)** | Make first power destiny choice. |
| **This can't be happening! (Bronze)** | Complete your first Insane combo. |
| **U Mad, Bro? (Bronze)** | Defeat 30 U-Men in the Secret Lab. |
| **Why Do They Keep Coming? (Bronze)** | Help Forge's hacked Purifier Stalker Mech defeat the MRD Troops. |

## CODE

Enter the code at the "X START" screen on the menu.

| UNLOCKABLE | CODE |
|---|---|
| **Juggernaut Suits** | Hold ⎣L1⎦+⎣R1⎦, press ↓, →, ↑, ←, ▲, ● |
| **Unlocks Emma Frost's costume** | Hold (⎣R1⎦+ ⎣L1⎦) and press ↑, ↓, →, ←, ●, ▲ |

## X-MEN: DESTINY (XBOX 360)

### ACHIEVEMENT

| UNLOCKABLE | HOW TO UNLOCK |
|---|---|
| **Ace In The Hole (15)** | Defeat Gambit. |
| **Alpha Level Mutant (50)** | Finish the game on X-Man difficulty. |
| **An Unstoppable Force (15)** | Defeat Magneto and Juggernaut. |
| **Another Shrimp on the Barbie (15)** | Stop Pyro from being mind-controlled. |
| **Archivist (30)** | Collect 15 dossiers. |

| | |
|---|---|
| At Least It's Aerodynamic... (10) | Equip your first suit. |
| Beginner's Luck (10) | Complete your first Great combo. |
| Beta Level Mutant (50) | Finish the game on New Mutant difficulty. |
| Better than the Best (15) | Defeat more enemies than Wolverine in the Prime Enforcer factory. |
| Broken Glass, Everywhere... (20) | Break 30 Combat Text Pop Ups. |
| Can I Get A Valkyrie? (0) | You were defeated 100 times. |
| Choose Wisely (20) | Make second power destiny choice. |
| Cleaned up the City (30) | Destroy 25 pieces of propaganda. |
| Completionist (50) | Complete all 15 unique challenge missions. |
| David Beats Goliath (15) | Defeat Sublime. |
| Destiny Begins (15) | Select a Power. |
| Diamond in the Rough (15) | Help Emma Frost defend mutant civilians from Purifier attacks. |
| Fight Terror with Terror (20) | Defeat 10 enemies with one Ultra power. |
| Fist of the... (15) | Stop Northstar from being mind-controlled. |
| Flash Fire (15) | Help Pyro, Juggernaut and Quicksilver defeat the Purifiers. |
| Four of a Kind (20) | Equip a complete X-Gene set and suit. |
| Fully Evolved (30) | Fully level up all powers. |
| Garbage Collection (10) | Destroy your first piece of propaganda. |
| Got My Eye on You (30) | Join Cyclops and the X-Men. |
| How Strong Could It Be? (20) | Trigger X-Mode. |
| I've Got the Power (20) | Fully level up a power. |
| It's a Secret to Everybody (15) | Find the U-Men secret lab. |
| Logan's Run (15) | Help Emma Frost turn Wolverine back to normal. |
| Magneto Is Right (30) | Join Magneto and the Brotherhood. |
| Mechageddon (20) | Defeat 20 Purifier Stalker Mechs. |
| Mutant Tracker (15) | Rescue Caliban. |
| Omega Level Mutant (50) | Finish the game on X-treme difficulty. |
| Profiler (10) | Collect your first dossier. |
| Purify the Purifiers (20) | Defeat 2000 Purifiers. |
| Reinforced (20) | Defeat 20 Prime Enforcers. |
| Satellite Interference (15) | Interrupt the transmission. |
| Shock and Awe (15) | Defeat Cameron Hodge. |
| Side-tracked (10) | Complete your first challenge mission. |
| Splicer (10) | Equip your first X-Gene. |
| Stay Frosty (15) | Help Iceman, Cyclops and Emma Frost defeat the Purifiers. |
| Taking Every Opportunity (25) | Complete 10 unique challenge missions. |
| Teleport This! (15) | Help Nightcrawler rescue mutants. |
| The Choice Is Made (20) | Make third power destiny choice. |
| The Goon Squad (20) | Defeat 500 MRD Troops. |
| The Roof, the Roof... (15) | Help Pyro set the roof on fire. |
| Things Look So Bad Everywhere... (15) | Survive Magneto's attack on the Purifiers. |
| Think About It... (20) | Make first power destiny choice. |
| This can't be happening! (20) | Complete your first Insane combo. |

| U Mad, Bro? (20) | Defeat 30 U-Men in the Secret Lab. |
| Why Do They Keep Coming? (15) | |

### CODE

Enter the code at the "X START" screen on the menu.

| UNLOCKABLE | CODE |
| --- | --- |
| Emma Frost's costume | Hold (LB+RB) and press ↑, ↓, →, ←, Ⓑ, Ⓨ |
| Juggernaut Suits | Hold LB+RB, press ↓, →, ↑, ←, Ⓨ, Ⓑ |

## X-MEN LEGENDS (PlayStation 3)

### COSTUMES

| UNLOCKABLE | HOW TO UNLOCK |
| --- | --- |
| Bobby Drake, Original Iceman | Beat the game |
| Colossus Without Metal, Colossus 90's | Beat the game |
| Gambit's Animated Series Outfit | Beat the game |
| Original Beast | Beat the game |
| Original Cyclops, Cyclops 80's | Beat the game |
| Original Jean Grey, Phoenix | Beat the game |
| Original Nightcrawler | Beat the game |
| Street Clothes Magma | Beat the game |
| Wolverine 90's, Weapon X | Beat the game |

### CHARACTERS

| | |
| --- | --- |
| Colossus | Beat Nuclear Facility level |
| Cyclops | Beat Mystique |
| Emma Frost | Beat Nuclear Facility level (meet in X-mansion) |
| Gambit | Finish Third Level |
| Ice Man, Jean Grey, Beast, Rogue, and Storm | Finish first level |
| Jubilee and Nightcrawler | Finish second level |
| Magma (on field missions) | Beat Blob in Magma/Cyclops mission |
| Psylocke | Beast NYC Riot, Morlock Rescue, and Muir Isle fight levels |

## X-MEN LEGENDS 2: RISE OF APOCALYPSE (PSP)

These codes must be entered on the pause screen.

| UNLOCKABLE | CODE |
| --- | --- |
| 1-Hit Kills with Punches | ⇦, ⇦, ⇨, ⇨, ⇦, ⇨, ⇧, START |
| God Mode | ⇩, ⇧, ⇩, ⇧, ⇩, ⇩, ⇨, ⇦, |
| Super Speed | ⇧, ⇧, ⇧, ⇩, ⇩, ⇩, START |
| Unlimited XTreme Power | ⇦, ⇩, ⇨, ⇩, ⇩, ⇧, ⇩, ⇧, START |

Enter these at Forge or Beast's equipment screen.

| UNLOCKABLE | CODE |
| --- | --- |
| 100,000 techbits | ⇧, ⇧, ⇧, ⇩, ⇨, ⇨, START |

Enter these codes at the team management screen.

| UNLOCKABLE | CODE |
| --- | --- |
| All Characters | ⇨, ⇦, ⇦, ⇨, ⇧, ⇧, ⇧, START |
| All Character Skins | ⇩, ⇧, ⇦, ⇨, ⇧, ⇧, START |
| All Skills | ⇦, ⇨, ⇦, ⇨, ⇩, ⇧, START |
| Level 99 Characters | ⇧, ⇦, ⇧, ⇩, ⇨, ⇦, ⇨, ⇩, START |

Enter these in the Review menu.

| UNLOCKABLE | CODE |
| --- | --- |
| All Comic Books | ⇨, ⇦, ⇦, ⇨, ⇧, ⇧, ⇩, START |
| All Concept Art | ⇦, ⇩, ⇦, ⇨, ⇧, ⇩, ⇩, START |
| All Game Cinematic | ⇦, ⇧, ⇨, ⇦, ⇩, ⇩, ⇦, START |

NEW!

A
B
C
D
E
F
G
H
I
J
K
L
M
N
O
P
Q
R
S
T
U
V
W
X
**Y**
Z

**CODES & CHEATS**

Enter this in the Danger Room.

| UNLOCKABLE | CODE |
|---|---|
| All Danger Room Courses | ⇩, ⇨, ⇦, ⇨, ⇧, ⇩, ⇧, ⇧, START |

## X-MEN ORIGINS: WOLVERINE (XBOX 360)

### CODES

Enter the following codes during gameplay. Activating the cheats disables Achievements. The costume will be available from the Main menu.

| EFFECT | CODE |
|---|---|
| Unlock classic Wolverine costume | Ⓐ, Ⓧ, Ⓑ, Ⓧ, Ⓐ, Ⓨ, Ⓐ, Ⓨ, Ⓐ, Ⓨ, Ⓐ, Ⓑ, Ⓑ, Ⓧ, R3 |
| Faster Enemy Reflex (Every kill you'll gain double reflex) | Ⓐ, Ⓐ, Ⓧ, Ⓧ, Ⓧ, Ⓨ, Ⓨ, Ⓑ, Ⓑ, Ⓨ, Ⓨ, Ⓧ, Ⓧ, Ⓐ, Ⓐ, R3 |
| Infinite Rage | Ⓨ, Ⓧ, Ⓧ, Ⓨ, Ⓑ, Ⓑ, Ⓨ, Ⓐ, Ⓐ, Ⓨ, R3 |
| Undying (You will lose health but you'll never die) | Ⓧ, Ⓐ, Ⓐ, Ⓧ, Ⓨ, Ⓨ, Ⓧ, Ⓑ, Ⓑ, Ⓧ, R3 |

## X-MEN ORIGINS: WOLVERINE (PlayStation 3)

### CODES

Enter the following codes during gameplay. Activating the cheats disables Trophies. The costume will be available from the main menu.

| EFFECT | CODE |
|---|---|
| Unlocks classic Wolverine costume | ×, ■, ●, ×, ▲, ×, ▲, ×, ■, ●, ●, ■, R3 |
| Doubles enemy reflex points | ×, ×, ■, ■, ▲, ▲, ●, ●, ▲, ▲, ■, ■, ×, ×, R3, |
| Infinite rage | ▲, ■, ■, ▲, ●, ●, ▲, ×, ×, ▲, R3, |
| Undying (health goes down but you never die) | ■, ×, ×, ■, ▲, ▲, ■, ●, ●, ■, R3, |

## YAKUZA 4 (PlayStation 3)

### UNLOCKABLES

Complete the tasks to unlock these

| UNLOCKABLE | HOW TO UNLOCK |
|---|---|
| 1000000 yen bonus | Clear Easy mode |
| 2000000 yen bonus | Clear Normal mode |
| 3000000 yen bonus | Clear Hard mode |
| 5000000 yen bonus | Clear EX-Hard mode |
| Asagao Special Torso Wrap | Have an existing Ryuu ga Gotoku 3 system file |
| Bell of Gion | Have an existing Ryuu ga Gotoku Kenzan! save file |
| EX-Hard Mode | Clear Hard mode |
| Premium Adventure | Clear the game on any difficulty |
| Premium New Game | Clear the game on any difficulty |
| Reminiscence (Kaisou) | Clear the game on any difficulty |
| Ultimate Competition (Kyuukyoku Tougi) | Clear the game on any difficulty |
| Underground SP Championship | Clear the game on any difficulty. Enter Naomi no Yakata located on Tenkaichi Street. Talk to Utsunomiya Bob A. |

## YOU DON'T KNOW JACK (XBOX 360)

### UNLOCKABLE

Complete the following to unlock these awards

| UNLOCKABLE | HOW TO UNLOCK |
|---|---|
| A Bald-Headed Ski Mask | Play episode 58 score over $0. |
| A Beautiful Ladies' Pant (Female) | Play episode 9 and score over $0. |
| A Classy Men's T-Shirt (Male) | Play any episode and score over $0. |
| A Fashionable Men's Pant (Male) | Play episode 9 and score over $0. |
| A Trenty Ladies' T-Shirt (Female) | Play any episode and score over $0. |
| Billy O'Brien Replica Dummy | Find the episode 73 wrong answer of the game. |

## YU-GI-OH! 5D'S WORLD CHAMPIONSHIP 2010 REVERSE OF ARCADIA (DS)

### CLOTHES AND DUEL DISKS

| UNLOCKABLE | HOW TO UNLOCK |
|---|---|
| Academia Disk (Blue) | Buy for five star chips from Chihiro. |
| Academia Disk (Red) | Buy for five star chips from Chihiro. |
| Academia Disk (Yellow) | Buy for five star chips from Chihiro. |
| Black Bird Disk | Beat Crow 10 times in Turbo Duels. |
| Black Chain Disk | Defeat each level of the single tournament once. |
| Black Jail Disk | Win all levels of Tournament Mode. |
| Career Suit | Box item found in the southwest room of the Securities building. |
| Dark magician outfit | Defeat the duel runner owners 10 times. |

**CODES & CHEATS**

| Dark Singer | Buy for 15 star chips from Chihiro after beating the main story. |
| Dark Singer Disk | Buy for 10 star chips from Chihiro after beating the main story. |
| Denim Jacket | Buy for five Star Chips from Chihiro if male. |
| K.C. Mass Production Disk | Buy for five star chips from Chihiro. |
| King Replica Model | Beat Jack 10 times in both duels and Turbo Duels. |
| Leo's Custom Disk | Beat Leo and Luna in 10 Tag Duels. |
| Luna's Custom Disk | End three duels in a draw. |
| One-piece | Buy for five star chips from Chihiro if female. |
| Race Queen | Buy for five star chips from Chihiro if female. |
| Rock N' Roller | Box item found inside the third duel gang's hideout if male. |
| Rose Disk | Box item found in the southwest room of the Securities building. |
| Rough Style | Box item found in the basement of the first duel gang's hideout. |
| Sailor Uniform | Box item found inside Zeman's castle if female. |
| Security Disk | Securities' building, northeast room |
| Security Helmet | 60% card completion |
| Security Uniform | Given to you by Crow during Chapter 2. |
| Stuffed Collar Uniform | Box item found inside Zeman's castle if male. |
| Tag Force Set | 100% card completion |
| The Enforcers | Unlocked automatically at the start of Chapter 2. |
| Wheel of Fortune (Disk) | Beat Jack 10 times in both duels and Turbo Duels. |
| Wild Style | Buy for five Star Chips from Chihiro if male. |
| Witch's dress | Defeat Akiza 10 times in a Turbo Duel. |

| UNLOCKABLE | HOW TO UNLOCK |
| --- | --- |
| Worn-out Clothes | Box item found inside the third duel gang's hideout if female. |
| Yusei Jacket | Beat Yusei 10 times in Turbo Duels. |
| Yusei's Hybrid Disk | Beat Yusei 10 times. |

## CPU OPPONENTS

Fulfill the following conditions to unlock CPU opponents for World Championship Mode. Teams not listed are either unlocked from the start, or unlocked by progressing through Story Mode.

| UNLOCKABLE | HOW TO UNLOCK |
| --- | --- |
| Ancient Gear Gadjiltron Dragon | Summon Ancient Gear Gadjiltron Dragon. |
| Archlord Kristya | Beat "Green Baboon, Defender of the Forest" three times. |
| Blackwing-Vayu the Emblem of Honor | Summon Blackwing-Silverwind the Ascendant. |
| Blue-Eyes White Dragon | Beat "Darklord Desire" three times. |
| Chaos Sorcerer | Beat "Solar Flare Dragon" three times. |
| Crusader of Endymion | Activate Mega Ton Magical Cannon. |
| Cyber Eltanin | Beat "B.E.S. Big Core MK-2" three times. |
| Dark Simorgh | Beat "Great Shogun Shien" three times. |
| Darkness Neosphere | Play for 100 hours. |
| Destiny End Dragoon | Beat "Underground Arachnid" three times. |
| Dragunity Knight-Gadearg | Beat "Ancient Fairy Dragon" three times. |

| Earthbound Immortal Wiraqocha Rasca | Win with by using the effect of Final Countdown. |
|---|---|
| Elemental Hero Absolute Zero | Beat "Fabled Leviathan" three times. |
| Elemental Hero Neos | Beat "Ancient Sacred Wyvern" three times. |
| Explosive Magician | Beat "Ally of Justice Decisive Armor" three times. |
| Fabled Ragin | Beat "Evil Hero Dark Gaia" three times. |
| Fossil Dyna Pachycephalo | Have 666 or more Summons. |
| Garlandolf, King of Destruction | Play for 50 hours. |
| Gigaplant | Summon Perfectly Ultimate Great Moth. |
| Gladiator Beast Gyzarus | Summon Gladiator Beast Heraklinos. |
| Gravekeeper's Visionary | Beat "Jurrac Meteor" three times. |
| Green Gadget | Beat "Power Tool Dragon" three times. |
| Harpie Queen | Win by using the effect of Vennominaga the Deity of Poisonous Snakes. |
| Hundred Eyes Dragon | Beat "Ojama Yellow" three times. |
| Judgment Dragon | Summon Judgment Dragon. |
| Locomotion R-Genex | Summon Flying Fortress Sky Fire. |
| Lonefire Blossom | Beat "Gungnir, Dragon of the Ice Barrier" three times. |
| Majestic Red Dragon | Summon Majestic Red Dragon. |
| Naturia Beast | Beat "Reptilianne Vaskii" three times. |
| Raiza the Storm Monarch | Beat "Lava Golem" three times. |
| Stardust Dragon /Assault Mode | Unlock 50% or more Duel Bonuses. |
| Supersonic Skull Flame | Beat "Mist Valley Apex Avian" three times. |
| Swap Frog | Beat "The Dark Creator" three times. |

| UNLOCKABLE | HOW TO UNLOCK |
|---|---|
| The Immortal Bushi | Beat "Naturia Landoise" three times |
| Worm Zero | Highest damage is 10,000 or more. |
| XX-Saber Hyunlei | Win 10 duels in a row. |

## TAG TEAMS

Fulfill the following conditions to unlock CPU Teams for Tag Duel in World Championship Mode. Teams not listed are either unlocked from the start, or unlocked automatically as you progress through Story Mode.

| UNLOCKABLE | HOW TO UNLOCK |
|---|---|
| Child of Chaos | Beat Team "Water & Fire" three times. |
| Cyber Regeneration | Beat Team "Angels & The Fallen" three times. |
| Dragon & Dragon | Summon Five-Headed Dragon. |
| Dual Duel | Beat Team "Removal Guys" three times. |
| Duel Ritual | Complete 300 Single Duels. |
| E & D Impact | Beat Team "Darkness + Fiends" three times. |
| Earthbound Crystal | Summon Rainbow Dragon. |
| Fish-the-World | Have 200 Spells and Traps activated. |
| Gadget Emperor | Complete 150 Tag Duels. |
| Grinder Summoning | Beat Team "Explosive Tag" three times. |
| Legend's Anniversary | Beat Team "Love Reptiles " three times. |
| Lo and Behold | Beat Team "Protect & Burn" three times. |
| Mausoleum's Legend | Beat Team "Order in Chaos" three times. |
| Simochi Study | Beat Team "Cyber Dragunity" three times. |

NEW!

A
B
C
D
E
F
G
H
I
J
K
L
M
N
O
P
Q
R
S
T
U
V
W
X
Y
Z

**CODES & CHEATS**

| Storm of Darkness | Beat Team "Fusion & Synchro" three times. |
| To the Graveyard | Complete 75 Turbo Duels. |
| Trago Genex | Summon VWXYZ-Dragon Catapult Cannon. |
| Zombie Path | Win by attacking with Skull Servant. |

### DUEL RUNNERS

| UNLOCKABLE | HOW TO UNLOCK |
|---|---|
| Blackbird (crow's d-wheel) | Unlock every other frame. |
| Chariot Frame | Beat the headless ghost in a duel (speak to Trudge after completing Story Mode). |
| Giganto L (Kalins duel runner) | Buy for 40 star chips from Chihiro after beating the main story. |
| Wheel of Fortune D-Wheel Frame | Clear all Duel Runner Race battles courses with S Rank. |
| Yusei D-Wheel Frame | Clear all Duel Runner Race Time courses with S Rank. |

## YU-GI-OH! 5D'S WORLD CHAMPIONSHIP 2011: OVER THE NEXUS (DS)

### UNLOCKABLE

Fulfill the following conditions to unlock different booster packs in the game.

| UNLOCKABLE | HOW TO UNLOCK |
|---|---|
| Absolute Powerforce | Win 3 consecutive Rental Duels in the Daimon Area |
| Acceleration Finish | Start the final chapter |
| Acceleration Next | Start Chapter VI |
| Acceleration Start | Turbo Duel with Toru in Chapter IV |
| All Cards at Random | Collect 95% of all available cards |
| Ancient Prophecy | Defeat Torunka and Regulus 3 times each |
| Champion of Chaos!! | Defeat Heitmann, Hans, and Nicholas 3 times each in single and Tag Duels |
| Charge of Genex!! | Defeat Chief, Syd, Lawton, Ramon, and Malcolm 3 times each |
| Crimson Crisis | Start the final chapter |
| Crossroads of Chaos | Start Chapter V |
| Cyberdark Impact | 200 single duels |
| Cybernetic Revolution | Duel Jack in Chapter II |
| Dragunity Hurricane!! | Defeat Trudge, Akiza, Leo, and Luna 3 times each in single, Tag, and Tag Turbo Duels |
| Duelist Revolution | Defeat Andre in the final chapter |
| Elemental Energy | 100 single duels |
| Enemy of Justice | Defeat Reimi, Lillie, Hayakawa, Masaki, Gordon, and Kuroe 3 times each |
| Extra Pack | Clear the side event in your apartment building in the Daimon Area |
| Extra Pack 2 | Clear Toru's side event |
| Extra Pack 3 | Clear Misaki's side event |
| Fabled Revival!! | Defeat Carly, Mina, and Stephanie 3 times each in single duels and Tag Duels |
| Flaming Eternity | Get the parts for Toru in Chapter II |
| Force of the Breaker | Defeat Rossi, Kazuhiro, Honda, Yanagigaura, Helio, Angie, Nelson, Figaro, and Corse 3 times each |
| Gladiator's Assault | Defeat Lenny, Hunter Pace, Lug, Larry and Randsborg 3 times each |
| Invasion of Worms!! | Available from the start |

| | |
|---|---|
| **Judgment of Omega!!** | Defeat Toru and Misaki 3 times each in single, Tag, Turbo, and Tag Turbo duels |
| **Justice Strikes Back!!** | Available from the start |
| **Light of Destruction** | Defeat Lazar, Sherry, and Elsworth 3 times each |
| **Power of the Duelist** | Start Chapter III |
| **Pulse of Trishula!!** | Duel all of the shop workers |
| **Raging Battle** | Clear the side event where you defeat Team Satisfaction (the Enforcers) in a race |
| **Rise of Destiny** | 50 single duels |
| **Shadow of Infinity** | Start Chapter III |
| **Soul of the Duelist** | Start Chapter II |
| **Stardust Overdrive** | Clear a side event in which you duel 3 members of Team 5Ds in Rental Duels |
| **Starstrike Blast** | Defeat Yusei, Jack, and Crow, 3 times each in single duels, Tag Duels, and Tag Turbo Duels |
| **Steelswarm Invasion!!** | Complete all of Nico and the Bootleg owner's puzzles |
| **Storm of Ragnarok** | Defeat Team Ragnarok 3 times each in single duels, Tag Duels, and Tag Turbo Duels |
| **Strike of Neos** | Duel Virgil in Chapter III |
| **Synchro, Awaken!!** | Available from the start |
| **Tactical Evolution** | Start Chapter IV |
| **The Duelist Genesis** | Start Chapter VI |
| **The Lost Millenium** | Defeat Bronson, Minegishi, Gemma, Virgil, Zeruga, Scotch, and Clint 3 times each |
| **The Shining Darkness** | Defeat Nico, West, Sergio, Barbara, and Kalin 3 times each |
| **Vylon Descends!!** | Defeat all single duelists 3 times each |
| **WC Edition 1** | Defeat the 6 CPU Duel opponents available at the start 3 times each |
| **WC Edition 10** | Unlock 8 CPU Tag Turbo Duel opponents |
| **WC Edition 11** | Unlock 9 CPU Tag Turbo Duel opponents |
| **WC Edition 2** | Unlock 36 CPU Duel opponents |
| **WC Edition 3** | Unlock 48 CPU Duel opponents |
| **WC Edition 4** | Unlock 7 CPU Tag Duel opponents |
| **WC Edition 5** | Unlock 12 CPU Tag Duel opponents |
| **WC Edition 6** | Unlock 16 CPU Tag Duel opponents |
| **WC Edition 7** | Unlock 12 CPU Turbo Duel opponents |
| **WC Edition 8** | Unlock 16 CPU Turbo Duel opponents |
| **WC Edition 9** | Unlock 7 CPU Tag Turbo Duel opponents |

## UNLOCKABLE

Fulfill the following conditions to unlock CPU opponents.

| UNLOCKABLE | HOW TO UNLOCK |
|---|---|
| **Archlord Kristya** | Beat [Guardian Eatos] 3 times |
| **Blackwing- Zephyrus the Elite** | Summon [Blackwing - Silverwind the Ascendant] |
| **Bountiful Artemis** | Beat [Deep Sea Diva] 3 times |
| **Dark Simorgh** | Beat [Vylon Omega] 3 times |
| **Dragunity Arma Leyvaten** | Have 666 Total Summons |
| **Ehren, Lightsworn Monk** | Summon [Judgment Dragon] |
| **Elemental Hero The Shining** | Summon [Vylon Omega] |
| **Evil Hero Dark Gaia** | 50 Hours Total Play Time |
| **Gladiator Beast Gyzarus** | Have 10 Consecutive Wins |

**CODES & CHEATS**

| | |
|---|---|
| Guardian Eatos | 100 Hours Total Play Time |
| Infernity Doom Dragon | Win with [Final Countdown]'s effect |
| Junk Destroyer | Summon [Shooting Star Dragon] |
| Legendary Six Samurai - Shi En | Summon [Gladiator Beast Heraklinos] |
| Machina Fortress | Summon [Odin, Father of the Aesir] |
| Malefic Paradox Dragon | Summon [Malefic Paradox Dragon] |
| Master Hyperion | Beat [Tiki Curse] 3 times |
| Meklord Emperor Granel Infinity | Beat [Earthbound Immortal Ccapac Apu] 3 times |
| Power Tool Dragon | Beat [Wynnda, Priestess of Gusto] 3 times |
| Queen Angel of Roses | Beat [Flamvell Baby] 3 times |
| Red-Eyes Darkness Metal Dragon | Summon [Red Nova Dragon] |
| Stardust Dragon/Assault Mode | Beat [Great Maju Garzett] 3 times |
| Thestalos the Firestorm Monarch | Have 50% of all Bonuses |
| Thunder King Rai-Oh | Beat [Gravekeeper's Visionary] 3 times |
| X-Saber Souza | Have 10000 Max Damage |

### UNLOCKABLE

Fullfill the following requirements to get these items

| UNLOCKABLE | HOW TO UNLOCK |
|---|---|
| 5D's Standard Disk | Complete the Game |
| Blackbird | S Rank on all Battle Royale |
| Different Facial Expressions | Duel Torunka and Win |
| Duel Phantom (Duel Runner Frame) | Talk to the broken Ghost with Misaki as your partner |
| DWE-CG | Talk to Klaus post-game |
| DWE-X | Talk to Jack and complete his event |
| Golden Shield Disk | Talk to Ransborg post-game, and complete his event |
| King Replica Model | Talk to Jack Post-game |
| KPC-000 | 4th Floor of Apartment, must have Lucky Key |
| Lambda Frame | Talk to Mina with Misaki as your partner and complete her event postgame |
| Leather Top and Bottom Set (Yusei's Outfit) | Found behind Team 5D's Garage |
| Leo's Custom Disk | Outside of Sector Security |
| Lucky Key | Talk to the guy behind Team 5D's garage and choose the right box |
| Luna's Custom Disk | Outside Securities building (Female only) |
| Missing Ring | See Spirit World |
| Speed Spell - Deceased Synchron | Can be found as a Blue card on Battle Royal Race |
| Stuffy Collar Shirt | See Spirit World |
| Suit Style | 4th Floor of Apartment, must have Lucky Key |
| The Spirit World | To Access the Spirit World, Duel all 3 Computer Ghosts |
| Waiter Outfit | Talk to Stephanie and complete her event |
| Wheel of Fortune | S Rank on all Battle Races |
| Yusei-Go | S Rank on all Time Races |

### UNLOCKABLE

Fulfill the following conditions to unlock different structure decks in the game.

| UNLOCKABLE | HOW TO UNLOCK |
|---|---|
| **Curse of Darkness** | Duel Gordon in Chapter II |
| **Dinosaur's Rage** | Start Chapter II |
| **Dragunity Legion** | Start Chapter VI |
| **Fury From The Deep** | Play in the Rental Deck Tournament in Chapter I |
| **Invincible Fortress** | Play in the Rental Deck Tournament in Chapter I |
| **Lord of the Storm** | Start Chapter II |
| **Lost Sanctuary** | Start Chapter VI |
| **Machina Mayhem** | Start Chapter V |
| **Machine Re-Volt** | Start Chapter II |
| **Rise of the Dragon Lords** | Start Chapter III |
| **Spellcaster's Command** | Start Chapter V |
| **Spellcaster's Judgment** | Play in the Rental Deck Tournament in Chapter I |
| **Surge of Radiance** | Duel Gordon in Chapter II |
| **The Dark Emperor** | Start Chapter III |
| **Warrior's Strike** | Start Chapter IV |
| **Warrior's Triumph** | Play in the Rental Deck Tournament in Chapter I |
| **Zombie World** | Start Chapter IV |

## ZOMBIE APOCALYPSE (XBOX 360)

### UNLOCKABLE

| UNLOCKABLE | HOW TO UNLOCK |
|---|---|
| Chainsaw Only Mode | Complete a day with only a chainsaw. |
| Hardcore Mode | Survive for seven consecutive days. |
| Turbo Mode | Achieve a multiplier over 100. |

## ZOMBIE APOCALYPSE (PlayStation 3)

### UNLOCKABLE

| UNLOCKABLE | HOW TO UNLOCK |
|---|---|
| Chainsaw Only Mode | Complete a day with only a chainsaw. |
| Hardcore Mode | Survive for seven consecutive days. |
| Turbo Mode | Achieve a multiplier over 100. |

## ZOMBIE PANIC IN WONDERLAND (Wii)

### UNLOCKABLE

| UNLOCKABLE | HOW TO UNLOCK |
|---|---|
| Alice | Beat Story Mode twice |
| Bunny Girl Snow White | Beat Story Mode three times. |
| Dorothy | Reach Stage 2-1 in Story Mode. |
| Little Red Riding Hood | Beat Story Mode four times. |
| Snow White | Reach Stage 3-2 in Story Mode. |
| Survival Stage in Arcade Mode (Pirate Ship) | Beat Story Mode once. |